W9-ABZ-337

THE PERSUASION HANDBOOK

The study of persuasion has engaged scholars for many generations, and we believe that it will for many more. To honor that tradition, we dedicate this book to our academic family—those who came before us and those who came after, people with whom we have worked closely and who share our passion for the field of persuasion:

To our mentor, Michael Burgoon, University of Arizona and Michigan State University

To his mentor, Gerald R. Miller (deceased)

To the following students who we have mentored during their doctoral studies at the University of Wisconsin–Madison:

James Brentar, Cleveland, Ohio

Janie Harden Fritz, Duquesne University

John Gastil, University of Washington

Linda Godbold, East Carolina University

R. Lance Holbert, University of Missouri

Terry Kinney, University of Minnesota

Wei-Peng Lee, Nanyang Technological University

Wei-Kuo Lin, Chinese Culture University

Linda Penaloza, Real World Research

Chris Segrin, University of Arizona

Pradeep Sopory, University of Memphis

Erin Allison Szabo, St. John's University

Kyle Tusing, University of Arizona

Hua-Hsin Wan, State University of New York at Oswego

THE PERSUASION HANDBOOK

Developments in Theory and Practice

James Price Dillard ■
University of Wisconsin-Madison

■ Michael Pfau
University of Wisconsin-Madison

SAGE Publications
International Educational and Professional Publisher
Thousand Oaks ■ London ■ New Delhi

For information:

Sage Publications, Inc.
2455 Teller Road
Thousand Oaks, California 91320
E-mail: order@sagepub.com

Sage Publications Ltd.
6 Bonhill Street
London EC2A 4PU
United Kingdom

Sage Publications India Pvt. Ltd.
M-32 Market
Greater Kailash I
New Delhi 110 048 India

Printed in the United States of America

Library of Congress Cataloging-in-Publication Data

The persuasion handbook: developments in theory and practice / James
Price Dillard and Michael Pfau, editors.
      p. cm.
Includes bibliographical references and index.
      ISBN 0-7619-2006-4 (c)
      1. Persuasion (Psychology)—Social aspects. 2. Persuasion (Rhetoric)
I. Dillard, James Price. II. Pfau, Michael.
      HM1196 .P47 2002
      303.3'42—dc21   2001007175

02 03 04 05 10 9 8 7 6 5 4 3 2 1

Acquiring Editor:	Margaret H. Seawell
Editorial Assistant:	Alicia Carter
Copy Editor:	D. J. Peck
Production Editor:	Claudia A. Hoffman
Typesetter:	Tina Hill
Indexer:	Molly Hall
Cover Designer:	Michelle Lee

Contents

Introduction

JAMES PRICE DILLARD
MICHAEL PFAU

How individuals exercise influence via communication is a question so basic and so important that it has challenged scholars for centuries. The first period of sustained attention to it began in Greece during the 5th century B.C. (but see McCroskey, 1997, pp. 4-5). During this period, Corax and Tisias "composed some of the first known scholarly essays on rhetorical communication" (Perloff, 1993, p. 37). A Sophist named Gorgias devised a perspective on public speaking based principally on style and emotional appeals. His approach was scathingly rejected by Plato, who held that the only moral means of persuasion was grounded in logic (Katula & Murphy, 1995). It was Plato's student, Aristotle, who provided the first comprehensive theory of rhetorical discourse. He defined rhetoric in terms of "observing in a given case the available means of persuasion" (Solmsen, 1954, pp. 24-25), instructing that the "available means" encompassed a range of appeals, some grounded in logic (logos), others in emotion (pathos), and still others in the communicator (ethos). In what can be described as a receiver-oriented view of persuasion, Aristotle urged communi-cators to base judgments about the most appropriate means of persuasion on the nature of the audience. His views had long-lasting impact: "Aristotle's theory of rhetorical discourse has withstood the test of time, furnishing axioms that guide today's practitioners of persuasion and campaigns" (Pfau & Parrott, 1993, p. 25).

Of course, the study of rhetoric continued after the Greeks. Other waves of interest occurred in Rome during the 1st century B.C. and throughout Europe during both the Renaissance and the Colonial Period (McCroskey, 1997). However, by the middle of the 20th century, social scientific methods, employing a blend of logically grounded theory plus systematic observation, had grown increasingly prevalent. This development prompted the late Gerald R. Miller to declare that, despite its origins in ancient Greece, the "systematic empirical study of persuasion is . . . relatively recent . . . , its roots extending less than 50 years deep" (Miller, 1987, p. 448).

While acknowledging the enormous debt that contemporary persuasion research owes to the 2,000-plus-year history of rhetoric, this handbook embraces the younger communication science perspective to which Miller alluded (cf. Berger & Chaffee, 1987). The contributions contained herein share two noteworthy features that flow directly from that perspective. For one, they are uniformly grounded in theories whose purpose is to organize and explain patterns of facts. Some chapters take, as their central thrust, the exposition and evaluation of particular theories (Section II: Theories of Persuasion). For other chapters, their relationship to theory is less explicitly developed, although it is present to no lesser degree (but see Zhao's chapter [Chapter 25]). Second, as dictated by the scientific model, explanations are pitted against the facts as we understand them. The chapter authors sift and winnow the shards of empirical findings in their efforts to advance broad and generalizable knowledge claims about fundamental persuasive processes.

There are also a number of themes, not a part of the scientific model, that deserve to be stated unambiguously. In large measure, these themes arise from editorial decisions that reflect our conception of persuasion and how it might be studied most profitably at this moment in history. They include the appropriate boundaries for persuasion research, the impact of persuasive practices, and the dynamic nature of persuasion inquiry. Each requires elaboration.

1. *The appropriate boundaries for persuasion inquiry include and extend beyond the effects of message features.* In our judgment, one of the most intellectually exciting areas of the persuasion literature examines the impact of message style, structure, and content. Indeed, the chapters that appear in Section IV (Message Features) make a convincing case for the centrality of this area to the study of persuasion. Focused as they are on language, outcome framing, metaphor, evidence, and nonverbal behavior, Chapters 19 through 21 show

that research on message features is vibrant, active, and essential. Yet messages do not exist in a vacuum; meaning is always drawn from the interplay between message and context. Hence, it is incumbent on us to conceive of persuasion broadly enough to include not only the elements of suasory discourse but also all of those social and institutional factors that contribute to the creation of persuasive context.

To render an accurate portrayal of the phenomenon, the scope of persuasion research must be more expansive than a focus on message features alone. Accordingly, we have cast the net widely. In addition to sections on basic conceptual concerns (Section I: Basic Issues) and fundamental processes (Section II: Theories of Persuasion), we have included contributions on some of the contexts in which persuasion occurs (Section V: Contexts); large-scale, highly planful persuasive attempts (Section VI: Persuasion Campaigns); and the media (Section VII: Media). In our view, this approach is required for understanding the multifaceted phenomenon that is persuasion.

2. *The practice of persuasion is of immense social consequence.* It has been said that communication is a practical discipline (Craig, 1999). There can be no question that Craig's assertion applies to persuasion. Consideration of even a few of the venues in which persuasive discourse occurs is sufficient to illustrate its enormous pragmatic impact. One such venue is, of course, politics. Mutz, Sniderman, and Brody (1996) maintained, "Persuasion is ubiquitous in the political process; it is also the central aim of political interaction. It is literally the stuff of politics" (p. 1). Here the stakes are high. Suasory discourse in the political realm is responsible for the outcome of campaigns at all levels of government, for the passage of legislation in the House and Senate, and for the formation of citizen opinion in churches, taverns, and other public meeting

places. In fact, the concept of civic deliberation, thought by many to be a defining feature of effective democracy (Cohen, 1989; Fishkin, 1992), resides beneath the broad umbrella of persuasion.

The legal setting too is shot through with persuasive interaction. In civil and criminal actions, judges and juries serving as processors of persuasive appeals must weigh the evidence and render verdicts of consequence. It is no understatement to claim that persuasion can be a matter of life and death. So long as the death penalty remains legal, the relative suasory skill of prosecuting and defense attorneys will play an important role in determining whether or not defendants in murder trials receive the ultimate sanction. Persuasion is also implicated in many more common matters such as child custody arrangements, the settlement of contracts, and the resolution of property disputes.

In addition, the engines that power economic expansion are fueled by consumer spending that is, in turn, at least partially a product of the advertising and marketing industries. Information regarding the price of goods and services is vital to market efficiency. But just as in the political and legal arenas, the role of persuasion in commerce is not all to the good. Members of the persuasion industries strive to sell particular products through mind-numbing, repetitive exhortation. At both a more subtle and a more powerful level, it has been argued that the persuasion profession "serves not so much to advertise products as to promote consumption as a way of life" (Lasch, 1978, p. 72). But many of these same marketing techniques are also used to help solve pressing social problems such as improvement of the nation's health (U.S. Department of Health and Human Services, 2000).

These examples illustrate, but hardly exhaust, the venues in which persuasion has an impact on contemporary society. Individually, many of the chapters contained herein address themselves to persuasion as it occurs in various content areas: politics, legal settings, the environment, advertising, and health. Collectively, these examples strike a broader theme that resonates throughout the book: Persuasive discourse matters.

3. *The practice and the study of persuasion are dynamic endeavors.* As noted earlier, interest in the study of rhetoric/persuasion has waxed and waned several times over the past two millennia. Within each period of heightened activity, the scholarly community's ideas of how rhetoric should be conceptualized and which aspects of it were worthy of study varied a great deal. In every instance, those ideas were molded by the events and problems of the day. Thus, Aristotle identified three sorts of public speaking—deliberative, forensic, and epideictic—because, given the culture of Greece at the time he penned the *Rhetoric,* only these forums were considered worthy of study. And during the Renaissance, rhetoric was viewed primarily as the study of style and delivery, a perspective subsequently taken to excess by members of the elocutionary movement during the 1700s. The lesson here, of course, is that the current study of persuasion is similarly constituted from the complex interactions among culture, history, and research findings. In structuring the handbook, we attempted to strike a balance between issues of enduring interest and those that are currently flourishing. Accordingly, the largest single segment of the book (Section II: Theories of Persuasion) is devoted to theory. Although none of the frameworks examined in that section has yet demonstrated the staying power of Aristotle's thinking, most are mature and durable theories when measured against the relatively brief history of persuasion as a science.

Our efforts to highlight contemporary issues also necessitated some difficult decisions regarding coverage. For example, we elected to include an entire section on pathos (Section III: Affect and Persuasion), largely at the expense of logos and ethos. The book contains only one contribution focused on logical reasoning (Reynolds and Reynolds' chapter [Chapter 22]) and not a single entry devoted entirely to source judgments. Where we must count the chapters on message features (Section IV) as grounded in issues that span the centuries, much of the material on properties of attitudes (Section I), campaigns (Section VI), and media (Section VII) could not have been considered 25 years ago. Suffice it to say that even in a volume of this size, coverage of a topic as large as persuasion is still necessarily selective.

Before turning to an examination of individual contributions, we wish to make one final point regarding the dynamics of persuasion inquiry and the Janus-like quality of the contents of this volume. All of the chapters have a substantial backward-looking component. Authors were charged with the task of reviewing and synthesizing research in their respective areas. We also asked that the contributors cast their eyes roughly a decade into the future—not to predict what the field of persuasion *will* look like but instead to set an agenda concerning the directions that research *should* take. Thus, to varying degrees, all of the chapters are a combination of prior research and future promise.

OVERVIEW OF THE CHAPTERS

There are seven sections to the handbook, and they are ordered, roughly, on a micro-macro continuum. The earlier chapters emphasize issues that are at once more rapid and more individualistic. Although there are exceptions, later contributions show a greater appreciation for social factors and tend to highlight phenomena that are, relatively speaking, slower to unfold.

Section I (Basic Issues) includes work on basic conceptual issues and cognitive processes that underlie persuasion. Section II (Theories of Persuasion) consists of nine contributions that review and evaluate full-blown theoretical frameworks. Section III (Affect and Persuasion) focuses more narrowly on developments in understanding the impact of mood and emotion on persuasion. Contributors to Section IV (Message Features) offer an array of work on aspects of persuasive appeals themselves, whereas Section V (Contexts) moves to an examination of persuasion as it occurs in four specific settings. Subsequently, developments in the study of large-scale, organized persuasive efforts are addressed in Section VI (Persuasion Campaigns). Finally, Section VII (Media) is comprised of four chapters that jointly examine micro- and macroprocesses by which media create and delimit the boundaries of persuasion.

Section I: Basic Issues

We have taken the unusual step of opening this section with a previously published chapter. Miller's (Chapter 1) analysis of what it means to be persuaded is as fresh, as insightful, and (most important) as *useful* as it was when it first appeared two decades ago in Roloff and Miller's (1980) edited volume. While the chapter was prescient in its emphasis on the conceptual difference between attitude extremity and attitude intensity, perhaps its greater contribution derives from the distinctions Miller draws among three types of persuasion. *Response shaping* is roughly the acquisition of an attitude, whereas *response reinforcement* can be equated with strengthening a preexisting attitude. By contrast, *response changing* references movement across the midpoint of an attitude scale. An appreciation of these three distinct forms of persuasion provides a foundation for the analysis of applied and theoretical problems.

In contrast to much work on persuasion, Fink, Kaplowitz, and Hubbard (Chapter 2) remind us that beliefs and attitudes are dynamic entities. Both during and after message exposure, these cognitive entities oscillate around the point at which they finally settle. The authors present a spatial spring model of beliefs that predicts variation in the frequency and amplitude of oscillation as a function of classic persuasion variables: source credibility, argument strength, discrepancy from initial opinion, and type of decision (dichotomous vs. discrete). In addition to the exciting theoretical questions that the chapter raises, the authors note an important methodological implication: Research designs that measure attitude only once after message exposure may suffer from what appears to be unreliability because the attitudes and beliefs under study have not yet reached equilibrium.

Attitude accessibility refers to the speed and ease with which an evaluation is retrieved from memory. As Roskos-Ewoldsen, Arpan-Ralstin, and St. Pierre (Chapter 3) make clear, accessibility is conceptually independent of evaluative extremity. The authors describe how accessibility shapes the persuasion process in a variety of ways, including the attention granted to a message and the degree to which the message is elaborated. Accessibility can also bias processing and influence the attitude-behavior correlation. In light of such effects, it is important to understand what factors determine accessibility, and consequently, the authors take up exactly this issue. They consider the effects of expectations and cognitive elaboration in addition to recency and frequency of activation.

Like Roskos-Ewoldsen and colleagues' contribution, Kosicki's (Chapter 4) contribution assumes that concepts in a cognitive system can be fruitfully modeled as an associative network. But whereas Chapter 3 unpacks this point with regard to attitudes, Chapter 4 endeavors to show how media act to prime various concepts that become the basis for attitude formation and change. Although this is not persuasion in the usual sense of the word, priming processes are certainly responsive to the manner in which an issue is framed. Thus, Kosicki's work helps to explain how various characterizations of an event activate particular concepts that, in turn, shape persuasive discourse on that topic.

The tendency for negative information to be weighted more heavily than positive information in the formation of social judgments is known as the negativity effect. Allen and Burrell (Chapter 5) present a review and quantitative synthesis of research bearing on the negativity effect in political judgments. In brief, they find evidence of a negativity effect with regard to both issues and candidates. Importantly, their summary also reveals that the use of negative information in political campaigns erodes the desire to participate in the political process. Because most of these effects are rather small (r's = .05 to .08), we might be tempted to dismiss them as interesting but hardly powerful enough to matter in the rough-and-tumble of real-world politics. However, even a moment's reflection on the 2000 presidential election quickly brings one to the recognition that seemingly minute effects can produce dramatic differences, especially when decision outcomes are dichotomous.

Section II: Theories of Persuasion

Even a cursory survey of the history of persuasion research would show that dissonance theory ranks as one of the most provocative perspectives ever to emerge from social science. No doubt, its capacity to inspire controversy accounts, in part, for its longevity. For nearly half a decade, it has inspired criticism, extension, and reinterpretation. Harmon-Jones (Chapter 6) offers a review and critique of dissonance theory that includes a close look at the experimental paradigms used to test it as well as the numerous revisions and modifications of the theory itself. Then he presents his own rewriting of dissonance theory based on the premise that the motivation to reduce dissonance derives from the need for effective behavior. A series of empirical studies lend considerable support to his revision.

Similar to dissonance theory, research on language expectancy theory has a lengthy history that shows no signs of abating. As Burgoon, Denning, and Roberts (Chapter 7) discuss, the theory itself is grounded in the assumption that individuals possess expectations about the communication behavior of others. When a speaker behaves in such a way as to exceed expectations positively, message recipients tend to overestimate the degree of positivity of those unanticipated actions. The inverse occurs in situations where the message source violates expectations negatively. This simple, but powerful, principle forms the bedrock of a theory that is formalized in a network of interrelated propositions and applied to an assortment of persuasive contexts.

The matching hypothesis, derived from functional theories of attitude, asserts that persuasion will be maximized when message content is matched to the functional basis of the attitude. Shavitt and Nelson (Chapter 8) review the impressive empirical support for the matching hypothesis before they go on to detail important newfound qualifications to that simple formulation. Their chapter succinctly describes the implications of contemporary functional theory for persuasive outcomes, message processing, and (most notably) person perception. This latter area moves functional theory into previously uncharted territory and demonstrates the continuing vitality of the perspective.

Since the early 1980s, the dual-process models of persuasion have dominated the persuasion landscape. Booth-Butterfield and Welbourne (Chapter 9) provide a review of one of those theories, specifically the Elaboration Likelihood Model (ELM). After a detailed illustration of the workings of the ELM, the authors summarize the criticisms of the model that have accumulated over the years and present their own evaluation of the merits of those criticisms.

Slater (Chapter 10) explicates a theoretical stance that he labels the Extended ELM. Although his points of extension are many, the most important departure from the existing ELM is with regard to the dimensionality of involvement. Whereas the progenitors of the model hew to a unified conception of involvement as personal importance (Petty & Cacioppo, 1990), Slater contends that a more differentiated approach is required. He parses involvement according to six distinct message processing goals and reviews evidence that distinguishes among them.

Todorov, Chaiken, and Henderson (Chapter 11) conclude the tour of dual-process models with their chapter on the Heuristic-Systematic Model (HSM). The authors provide a compact overview of wide-ranging research generated by the HSM while simultaneously showing us how the theory has evolved since its inception. As is typical of social scientific theories in the growth phase of their life cycle, the HSM has expanded from its original tight focus on persuasion to a broader theory of social perception (although still retaining important implications for the study of persuasion).

Burgoon, Alvaro, Grandpre, and Voulodakis (Chapter 12) argue that much of value in persuasion research has been forgotten. Specifically, they contend that Brehm's reactance theory deserves to be returned to a place of greater prominence in current theoretical and applied research. Such a thorough review of the reactance literature and the multitudinous applications of the theory leaves little doubt as to the veracity of their claims.

Most persuasion research focuses on how attitudes and beliefs are often changed by contrasting the effects of some message variable against a no-message control group. Research on inoculation turns this experimental approach on its head by taking as its focus the degree to which attitudes or beliefs remain unchanged in the face of persuasive attack. Szabo and Pfau (Chapter 13) examine the principles that underlie inoculation before providing a thorough update on more nuanced aspects of that effect and the mechanisms that underlie it. And with an eye toward applied concerns, they also explore how inoculation functions in a variety of contexts ranging from politics to health.

The section concludes with Hale, Greene, Householder, and Greene's (Chapter 14) comprehensive summary of the theories of reasoned action and planned behavior. Because the theories have stimulated so much research, they have also been the focus of many reviews and several meta-analyses. The authors were in the enviable position of synthesizing this rich literature of prior work. They present a thorough evaluation and critique of the theories and their scope conditions.

Section III: Affect and Persuasion

Persuasion is sometimes characterized as opinion change that follows from consideration of reasoned discourse. Yet even in this highly cognitive view, affect is waiting in the wings. Often it is cast as an irrational force insofar as affect is expected to bias an otherwise evenhanded process of evaluating evidence (e.g., James, 1894). But writers such as Aristotle understand affect to be an essential element of life that is, in some cases, a necessary condition for creating suasory impact

(Solmsen, 1954). Nabi (Chapter 15) leans rather more in the direction of Aristotle than of James. She adopts a functional perspective on emotion, a position that assumes emotion's adaptive information processing programs resulting from lengthy evolutionary processes. Through the lens of that perspective, she carefully surveys a series of discrete emotions (e.g., sadness, happiness, envy), analyzing in each case its role in persuasion.

Dillard and Meijnders (Chapter 16) begin their contribution by noting the existence of several apparently competing views of the structure of affect. These views range from the very simple positive versus negative model to the more elaborate discrete emotions position that is the mainstay of Chapter 15. Rather than attempt to resolve the rivalry in favor of one structure or another, the authors contend that all of the structures may have merit in circumscribed domains.

O'Keefe's (Chapter 17) contribution is tightly focused on a single emotion: guilt. This focus is justified not only by the fairly sizable literature on the topic of guilt and persuasion but also by the fact that "the reactions characteristically associated with guilt make it especially well-suited to exploitation for purposes of social influence." In fact, as O'Keefe details, guilt does produce substantial persuasive impact whether it arises from some transgression that occurs prior to the message, from the message itself, or in reaction to the belief that one may fail *in the future* to behave in accordance with some personal or social standard.

In a volume as large at this one, it would be reasonable to expect a chapter on fear appeals. Yet for several reasons, we elected not to include such a chapter. For one, Nabi's Chapter 15 provides a brief but accurate summary of what is known about fear appeals. Another reason is that several narrative (Dillard, 1994) and quantitative (Floyd, Prentice-Dunn, & Rogers, 2000; Mongeau, 2000; Witte & Allen, 2000) reviews have recently appeared in print. We wished to avoid redundancy with those pieces. Finally, we believed that much was to be gained from an analysis of that same problem (i.e., How can risks be conveyed?) from the perspective of an often overlooked literature. Thus, deTurck (Chapter 18) offers a comprehensive synthesis of work on warning labels that includes an explicit comparison of that literature with research on fear appeals. He notes, for example, that warning labels possess four content components—signal word, hazard statement, hazard avoidance statement, and consequences statement— some of which have direct correlates with prescriptions for the structure of fear appeals.

Section IV: Message Features

Questions concerning how messages might be designed to produce the greatest suasory impact lie at the very center of persuasion research. This section addresses an important subset of the huge range of possibilities. Hosman's (Chapter 19) contribution, which opens the section, provides a mountaintop view of research on language and persuasion. Although an analysis of language could be undertaken from a virtually limitless number of perspectives, Hosman neatly subdivides his review in terms of phonology, syntax, lexicon, and text/narrative before turning to an examination of the effects of each on judgments of the message source, recall, and attitude change.

The three chapters that follow take up much more specific topics. Salovey, Schneider, and Apanovitch (Chapter 20) report on research in the message framing tradition. Persuasive appeals that use gain-framed language emphasize the benefits that result from compliance. By contrast, loss-framed messages highlight the disadvantages of failure to comply. Working in the context of health commu-

nication, the authors show that the question of which is the more powerful persuasive tool is too simple a question. Rather, issues of effectiveness must be couched within a framework that addresses whether the sought-after behavior is designed to prevent or to detect a health problem. And in a nod to the centrality of affect in persuasion, the authors speculate that anticipated affect mediates message framing effects.

Scholarly thought regarding figurative language stretches back in time at least as far as Aristotle, who believed that the function of metaphor was primarily ornamental. He argued that one must be wary of the ambiguity and obscurity inherent in metaphor. By contrast, Sopory and Dillard (Chapter 21) contend that metaphoric language produces reasonably consistent suasory impact, which can be substantial if the proper moderating conditions are present. They summarize the meta-analytic findings prior to reviewing a set of theories that predict and purport to explain the role of metaphor in persuasion.

Reynolds and Reynolds (Chapter 22) turn away from the use of language and toward message content, specifically the use of evidence. The short version of their story is that, relative to simple assertions or the absence of evidence, citing support for an argument enhances the persuasive weight of the message. But this general proposition is qualified by several necessary side conditions. To wit: "Receivers must be aware that evidence is being presented, they must cognitively process the evidence, and they must evaluate the evidence as legitimate." The side conditions themselves require additional specification, a task that the authors use as an opportunity to integrate a diverse set of research findings.

In closing the section on message features, Burgoon, Dunbar, and Segrin (Chapter 23) return us to the mountaintop, in this case to survey the literature on nonverbal influence. Their chapter is structured around three classic topics: attraction/similarity, power/dominance displays, and the role of expectations. Each of these literatures is substantial in its own right. The authors compactly summarize existing research in all three areas and provide an overview of the competing theoretical views that currently are in play.

Section V: Contexts

The notion of context is as important as it is ubiquitous. The significance of this often nebulous concept arises from the fact that it is context that defines the opportunities and obstacles faced by anyone who seeks to influence another (Dillard & Solomon, 2000). In fact, it might by noted that context both enables and delimits "the available means of persuasion" (cf. Solmsen, 1954). Hence, there is much to be gained from a consideration of the contexts in which persuasion actually takes place. The chapters in this section examine four such contexts.

The essential condition underlying the idea of a group is that some set of persons comprise the group, while others must remain outside of those selective confines. It is precisely this observation that Boster and Cruz (Chapter 24) exploit to constitute their chapter on persuasion in small groups. Hence, they ask the following questions. Do group members persuade one another? Can out-group individuals persuade in-group members? And do groups persuade persons who are not members of their group? As they studiously address each question, the authors demonstrate that much depends on the perceived value of the utterances exchanged during discussion, the relative frequency of those utterances, and the degree to which individuals are viewed as individuals or as in-group/out-group social actors.

Although it may be the case that all advertising is persuasion, it is readily apparent that not all persuasion is advertising. Zhao (Chapter 25) argues that the more narrow, necessarily prosaic concerns of advertising demand that we privilege variables and channels over theory. Accordingly, he organizes his review of current literature in terms of a two-dimensional matrix consisting of communication media on one axis and the manipulability of independent variables on the other. Within the various cells of the matrix, he summarizes advertising research with a particular emphasis on recognition, recall, and liking for the advertisement.

Rhoads and Cialdini (Chapter 26) take up the topic of influence and persuasion in business and commercial contexts. The approach they offer is unique in this volume in that they derive their material from an evolutionary analogy that is itself predicated on the notion that some members of society occupy the role of compliance professionals. Because their livelihoods depend on it, these generations of salespeople, advertisers, and lobbyists are quite attentive to the means by which they create behavioral change in others. Over time, successful techniques remain in the influence "gene pool," while others that fail to replicate fade away. By this logic, the place to look for principles of influence is among the professionals practice influence, that is, those persons who create the selection pressures that screen out weak members of the influence species and allow the strong to thrive and reproduce. Coupling this evolutionary logic with participant observation yields six principles of compliance that the authors argue are fundamental and transcontextual.

By contrast, Reinard's (Chapter 27) contribution on persuasion in the legal setting is baldly contextual. Reinard offers a detailed commentary on research conducted within the highly structured confines of the judicial process. Although classic communication concepts such as credibility, message-sidedness, and attitude have clear application, they assume narrower meaning in the legal arena. Credibility, for example, references juror perceptions of particular players such as attorneys and witnesses. Message-sidedness becomes a property not just of persuasive messages generally but also of opening and closing arguments. And pre-message attitude is transformed into a highly specialized concept that asks whether or not a juror is "death qualified," that is, willing to impose the death penalty in principle. But perhaps what is most intriguing about Reinard's chapter is his consideration of issues of external validity. One provocative issue is the use of students versus nonstudents in mock juries. Although one might suspect that a broader nonstudent approach would be inherently superior, there appears to be little, if any, difference in the way in which students and nonstudents respond to message variations. They do differ, apparently, in their reaction to various person variables such as sex and victim status.

Section VI: Persuasion Campaigns

In their frequently cited definition, Rogers and Storey (1987) asserted that persuasion campaigns are intended to "generate specific outcomes or effects in relatively large numbers of individuals, usually within a specified period of time and through an organized set of communication activities" (p. 821). Certainly, the trio of chapters in this section of the handbook highlight persuasion's role in producing outcomes and effects of enormous social significance. Furthermore, as suggested by the Rogers and Storey quote, each of the chapters considers the organization of communication activities over time.

Participants in the political process have an array of communicative options that include

deceit, puffery, coercion, and espionage. Persuasion also must be included in that array, although it surely differs from the other methods in terms of both ethics and its capacity to create lasting change. Perloff (Chapter 28) examines the role of persuasion in political campaigns, with a special emphasis on American presidential campaigns. After providing a solid historical grounding, he turns his attention to the elements of a political campaign: advertising, presidential debates, opinion leaders, talk radio, and news. For each of these elements, Perloff presents a cogent synthesis of the research findings as well as a critique of the literature as a whole.

Parrott, Egbert, Anderton, and Sefcovic (Chapter 29) make the case for expanding attention to the environment as a means of producing more effective health campaigns. In particular, they suggest consideration of both the social and structural aspects of the environment. Of course, persuasive campaigns are inherently social. Campaign designers create appeals in hopes that they will influence the target audience. Audience members receive and collectively digest those appeals. And the relative success of the suasory attempt depends largely on the interplay between the message and the socially constructed meaning of "health" in that target audience. Operating in parallel with the social environment is that array of factors that comprise the structural environment. Attention to the structural environment means considering the physical resources (or lack thereof) that enable access to health practice information as well as consumption of tangible aspects of health care. Clearly, greater consideration of both aspects of the environment is needed.

O'Keefe and Shepard (Chapter 30) also address the environment in the subsequent chapter, but these authors use the term in a "greener" sense. They take a look at persuasive campaigns that focus on maintaining air and water quality, the use of pesticides, global warming, recycling, and so on. They maintain that environmental campaigns face several unique and difficult challenges. One of them is issue complexity. By definition, ecological systems are comprised of intricate reciprocal interactions among a variety of entities. Although many individuals may have expertise in one aspect of a system, efforts to view it as a whole can be daunting. This problem is compounded by the presence of conflicting scientific evidence and the delay in visible consequences (assuming that a remedy has been put in place). And of course, the various social actors who are stakeholders in the problem are often at odds with one another. Given this set of challenges, it would be easy to view the likelihood of success as bordering on hopeless. But the authors provide a solid set of recommendations for overcoming the challenges to environmental campaigns before they go on to illustrate many of them using the topic of watershed conservation.

Section VII: Media

Individuals' attitudes and actions are often swayed by what they believe about their neighbors, members of their communities, and their countrymen. And as Eveland (Chapter 31) tells us, these perceptions of social reality are influenced to no small degree by the consumption of news and entertainment media. Unfortunately for those who see inherent virtue in accuracy, "One common finding of the research on social reality perceptions is simply put as follows: They are often wrong—very wrong." The causes and effects of such discrepancies have occupied the attention of researchers in several distinct traditions that Eveland brings together in this wide-ranging synthesis.

In a complementary vein, Newhagen (Chapter 32) examines how meaning is constructed from television images. Adopting an informa-

tion processing perspective, he concentrates initially on cognitive processes such as attention and memory before shifting to a focus on emotion-evoking stimuli and questioning the traditional conception of cognition and emotion as oppositional. Newhagen also implores us to attend to the persuasive power of narrative, especially as it pertains to the impending convergence between television and the Internet.

Of course, there is more to persuasion than the message itself. Holbert (Chapter 33) addresses "form effects," that is, the notion that media have a pronounced impact on persuasion that occurs apart from style, structure, or content. Grounding his exposition in the prior efforts of McLuhan, Glenberg, Piaget, and Salomon, Holbert examines the constraints and affordances that follow from the interaction between a medium and what a person can do within the constraints afforded by that medium. In line with some of these earlier authors, he posits the existence of sensorimotor schemata that are medium specific. All of these ideas then play out in Holbert's reassessment of several traditional lines of persuasion research.

Fogg, Lee, and Marshall (Chapter 34) make it clear that interactive technology simultaneously permits and prohibits the available means of persuasion. Most intriguing, however, is the authors' contention that it does so in three distinctly different ways. Computers function as *tools* and, in so doing, may enhance self-efficacy and provide information tailored to the needs of the user. In addition, technology can operate as a *persuasive medium* by simulating objects and environments as well as the causal relations among elements of the environment. Finally, computers persuade as *social actors* when they adopt animate characteristics (e.g., voices) or roles (e.g., coach) or when they display knowledge of social rules (e.g., expressing greetings).

REFERENCES

Berger, C. R., & Chaffee, S. H. (Eds.). (1987). *The handbook of communication science.* Newbury Park, CA: Sage.

Cohen, J. (1989). Deliberation and democratic legitimacy. In A. Hamlin & P. Pettit (Eds.), *The good polity* (pp. 17-34). New York: Basil Blackwell.

Craig, R. T. (1999). Communication theory as a field. *Communication Theory, 9,* 119-161.

Dillard, J. P. (1994). Rethinking the study of fear appeals: An emotional perspective. *Communication Theory, 4,* 295-323.

Dillard, J. P., & Solomon, D. H. (2000). Conceptualizing context in message-production research. *Communication Theory, 10,* 167-175.

Fishkin, J. (1992). *Democracy and deliberation.* New Haven, CT: Yale University Press.

Floyd, D. L., Prentice-Dunn, S., & Rogers, R. W. (2000). A meta-analysis of research on protection motivation theory. *Journal of Applied Social Psychology, 30,* 408-429.

James, W. (1894). The physical basis for emotion. *Psychological Review, 1,* 516-529.

Katula, R. A., & Murphy, J. J. (1995). The Sophists and rhetorical consciousness. In J. J. Murphy, R. A. Katula, F. I. Hill, D. C. Ochs, & P. A. Meador (Eds.), *The synoptic history of classical rhetoric* (2nd ed., pp. 17-50). Davis, CA: Hermagoras Press.

Lasch, C. (1978). *The culture of narcissism.* New York: Norton.

McCroskey, J. C. (1997). *An introduction to rhetorical communication.* Boston: Allyn & Bacon.

Miller, G. R. (1987). Persuasion. In C. R. Berger & C. H. Chaffee (Eds.), *Handbook of communica-* *tion science* (pp. 446-483). Newbury Park, CA: Sage.

Mongeau, P. A. (2000). Another look at fear-arousing persuasive appeals. In M. Allen & R. W. Preiss (Eds.), *Persuasion: Advances through meta-analysis* (pp. 53-68). Cresskill, NJ: Hampton.

Mutz, D. C., Sniderman, P. M., & Brody, R. A. (1996). Political persuasion: The birth of a field of study. In D. C. Mutz, P. M. Sniderman, & R. A. Brody (Eds.), *Political persuasion and attitude change* (pp. 1-14). Ann Arbor: University of Michigan.

Perloff, R. M. (1993). *The dynamics of persuasion.* Hillsdale, NJ: Lawrence Erlbaum.

Petty, R., & Cacioppo, J. (1990). Involvement and persuasion: Tradition versus integration. *Psychological Bulletin, 107,* 367-374.

Pfau, M., & Parrott, R. (1993). *Persuasive communication campaigns.* Boston: Allyn & Bacon.

Rogers, E. M., & Storey, J. D. (1987). Communication campaigns. In C. R. Berger & S. H. Chaffee (Eds.), *Handbook of communication science* (pp. 817-846). Newbury Park, CA: Sage.

Roloff, M., & Miller, G. R. (Eds.). (1980). *Persuasion: New directions in theory and research.* Beverly Hills, CA: Sage.

Solmsen, F. (Ed.). (1954). *The rhetoric and poetics of Aristotle.* New York: Random House.

U.S. Department of Health and Human Services. (2000). *Healthy people.* [Online]. Available: www.health.gov/healthypeople/

Witte, K., & Allen, M. (2000). A meta-analysis of fear appeals: Implications for effective public health campaigns. *Health Education and Behavior, 27,* 591-615.

PART I

BASIC ISSUES

1

On Being Persuaded
Some Basic Distinctions

THE LATE GERALD R. MILLER

A volume dealing with the process of persuasion should profit from a tentative answer to the question: What does it mean to be *persuaded*? The well-advised qualifier "tentative" underscores two limitations of the analysis offered in this chapter. First, as with most complex definitional issues, the author has no illusions that his answer will satisfy every reader—or, for that matter, any reader. After all, a lively debate has raged for centuries over the defining characteristics of the term *persuasion,* and it would be the height of naïveté or arrogance to assume that this brief analysis will lay to rest all outstanding definitional controversies. Second, at a more modest level, this chapter certainly does not address all of the questions raised in succeeding chapters of this

volume. The authors of these chapters have attacked numerous theoretical and applied issues of persuasion from various vantage points; to subsume all the nuances of their remarks about the persuasive process is a formidable, if not impossible, task far exceeding the capabilities of this writer.

Notwithstanding these disclaimers, this chapter can assist readers in making sense out of many of the issues explored later by providing a general frame of reference for viewing the process of persuasion. Stated differently, the chapter seeks to establish broad definitional boundaries for the phase "being persuaded." Furthermore, in the process of staking out these boundaries, certain persistent issues will inevitably be identified, issues that heavily influence some of the positions taken in other chapters. Thus, this chapter anticipates rather than resolves subsequent scholarly debates.

BEING PERSUADED: THE CENTRAL ELEMENTS

Persuasive attempts fall short of blatant coercion; persuasion, as typically conceived of, is not *directly* coercive. Coercion takes the form of guns or economic sanctions, while persuasion relies on the power of verbal and nonverbal symbols. Frequently, of course, coercive acts are preceded by persuasive messages; seldom is a child's allowance suspended or an armed attack launched on a neighboring state without a period of message exchanges. These messages are aimed at persuading the child to study harder at school or at persuading the neighboring state to relinquish claim to a parcel of disputed territory. If persuasion proves inadequate to the task at hand, economic or military force may be employed to achieve the desired compliance.

From these examples, it follows that much persuasive discourse is *indirectly* coercive; that is, the persuasive effectiveness of messages often depends heavily on the credibility of threats and promises proffered by the communicator. If the child perceives that the threatening parent is, for some reason or another, unlikely to suspend the child's allowance, the parent's persuasive messages will have minimum impact on the child's study habits. Similarly, threats of armed attacks by nations with powerful defense establishments usually cause potential adversaries to take persuasive appeals quite seriously, while the same threats uttered by countries of limited military might are likely to be greeted with scorn or amusement. One can only speculate how the ensuing 1962 scenario might have differed had the government of Haiti, rather than that of the United States, called on the Soviet Union to dismantle its missiles in Cuba under threat of naval blockade and possible attack on the missile sites themselves.

Some students of persuasion have found it distasteful to ponder the indirectly coercive dimension of many persuasive exchanges, perhaps because the notion of *means control*—Kelman's (1961) term for describing a situation where the influence agent, or persuader, is successful because of his or her ability to dispense rewards or punishments—conflicts with the way persuasion ought to function in a democratic society. Simons (1974) captured the crux of this ideological opposition well:

> Although persuasion is often characterized as a weak sister in relation to its relatives within the influence family—note such expressions as "talk is cheap," "talk rather than substance," and "mere rhetoric"—it is nevertheless regarded by many as a more ethical method of influencing others. One generally shuns the coercive label like the plague, takes pains to deny that he is bribing others when he offers them inducements, and represents himself as a persuader—if possible, as someone using "rational persuasion." Persuasion is especially valued as an instrument of democracy. . . . Officials of government proudly proclaim that ours is indeed a system run by persuasion. . . . Inducements and constraints are said to have no place in ideally democratic forms of government; they are the coinage of the realm of corrupt governments or of totalitarian regimes. (pp. 174-175)

Simon went on to argue convincingly that in the rough-and-tumble world of everyday social conflict, as distinct from the polite confines of drawing room controversy, coercive potential determines the relative impact of most persuasive messages.

The prevalence of indirectly coercive elements in many persuasive transactions can also be detected by examining the symbolic weapons readily available to would-be persuaders. Marwell and Schmitt (1967) have generated a list of 16 strategies that can be used to gain compliance from others. Several of these strategies—among them *promise, threat,* and *aversive stimulation*—clearly derive their effectiveness from the persuader's ability to dispense rewards or mete out punishments to the intended persuadee(s). More subtlety dependent on coercive pressure are strategies stressing the harmful social consequences of failure to comply with message recommendations as well as strategies underscoring the social rewards resulting from compliance—such as *moral appeal, altruism, esteem position,* and *esteem negative.* To be sure, many people would hesitate to equate blackballing with blackjacking. Nevertheless, in a society where the pervasive importance of "being respected," "being popular," and "being 'in' " extends to matters so trivial as the name tag one sports on a pair of denim jeans, it would be a mistake to underestimate the coercive potential of social approval and disapproval, a fact readily grasped by those who create the country's daily diet of media advertisements and commercials.

The preceding discussion has alluded to a second defining characteristic of the phrase "being persuaded": Persuasion relies on symbolic transactions. Although a Mafia hireling in a Hollywood production may remark menacingly, "It looks like you need a little persuading," as he starts to work over a stubborn merchant who has refused to purchase mob protection, the scholarly endeavors of persuasion researchers—and, for that matter, the ordinary language uses of the term *persuasion*—have consistently centered on the manipulation of symbols. In the domain of verbal utterances, this distinction fosters little ambiguity because language is inherently symbolic. When Chairman Brezhnev recently appealed for Senate ratification of the SALT II treaty by linking its adoption with "divine"

approval, most observers probably would have agreed that he was embarked on a persuasive campaign, albeit one employing symbolic weapons not usually found in Communist arsenals. In the nonverbal realm, however, the distinction does not emerge as crisply, and there is often room for disagreement as to whether a particular nonverbal act is or is not symbolic. When Chairman Khruschev banged his shoe on a United Nations table during his 1959 visit to the United States, some observers might have interpreted his behavior as symbolic and reflecting persuasive intent, but others might have interpreted it as nothing more than a manifestation of poor manners by an uncouth visitor. Granted, the latter interpretation also involved a symbolic inference, but not one directly linked to conscious persuasive intent.

In view of the ambiguous status of some nonverbal behaviors, the utility of restricting the term *persuasion* to symbolic transactions may seem questionable. Unfortunately, the conceptual alternative is even more troublesome, for it would permit any act that sought to modify another's behavior to qualify as an instance of persuasion. Rather than falling prey to the unmanageable generality fostered by such definitional permissiveness and allowing the persuasive process to be conceived of so broadly that it embraces nearly every instance of social behavior, it seems wiser to struggle with occasional uncertainty. In most instances, language is an integral aspect of the persuasive transaction, with nonverbal behavior coming into play as an instrument for reinforcing the meaning and/or credibility of verbal messages. Because the goal of this chapter is to identify the central definitional elements of the phrase "being persuaded" rather than to fix its precise outer boundaries, imposition of a symbolic criterion is consistent with the prevailing theoretical and empirical concerns of persuasion scholars.

On agreeing that individuals are persuaded by symbolic means, the question can be raised as to whether certain types of symbolic strategies should be viewed as typifying the persuasion process, with others being exempted. More specifically, some writers (such as Rowell, 1932a, 1932b; Woolbert, 1917) have explored the wisdom of distinguishing between convincing and persuading—the so-called *conviction/persuasion duality*. This duality holds that persuasion relies primarily on symbolic strategies that trigger the emotions of intended persuadees, while conviction is accomplished primarily by using strategies rooted in logical proof and that appeal to persuadees' reason and intellect. Stated in evaluative terms, conviction derives its force from people's rationality, while persuasion caters to their irrationality.

While this distinction has unquestionably influenced some of the research carried out by contemporary persuasion researchers—for example, studies comparing the relative persuasiveness of logical and emotional appeals such as those conducted by Hartmann (1936), Matthews (1947), and Weiss (1960)—its utility seems dubious at best. Attempts to crisply conceptualize and operationalize distinctions between logical and emotional appeals have been fraught with difficulty (Becker, 1963). As a result of prior learning, nearly all ordinary language is laden with emotional overtones. Even the appeal to "be logical" itself carries strong normative force; indeed, Bettinghaus (1973, pp. 157-158) found that messages containing cues stressing the importance of logical thought were highly persuasive, even though the arguments presented were themselves illogical. Faced with these considerations, it seems more useful to conceive of persuasive discourse as an amalgam of logic and emotion while at the same time granting that particular messages may differ in the relative amount of each element. Furthermore, the motivation for distinguishing between con-

viction and persuasion rests largely on value concerns for the way influence ought to be accomplished; influence resulting from rational reasoned messages is ethically preferable to influence resulting from appeals to the emotions—appeals that, in the eyes of some writers (e.g., Diggs, 1964; Nilsen, 1966), "short-circuit" the reasoning processes. Although questions regarding the relative moral acceptability of various means and ends of persuasion are of vital import to all citizens of the democratic society (including persuasion researchers), conceptual distinctions that make for sound ethical analysis may sometimes make for unsound scientific practice. The conviction/persuasion duality strikes the author as such a conceptual animal. People are seldom, if ever, persuaded by "pure" logic or "pure" emotion; indeed, as the previous comments suggest, it is doubtful that these "pure" cases exist in humanity's workaday persuasive commerce.

Thus, the phrase "being persuaded" applies to *situations where behavior has been modified by symbolic transactions (messages) that are sometimes, but not always, linked with coercive force (indirectly coercive) and that appeal to the reason and emotions of the person(s) being persuaded*. This definition still suffers from lack of specificity concerning the kinds of behavioral modification that can result from persuasive communication. Let us next turn our attention to this problem.

BEING PERSUADED: THREE BEHAVIORAL OUTCOMES

In popular parlance, "being persuaded" is equated with instances of behavioral conversion; that is, individuals are persuaded when they have been induced to abandon one set of behaviors and to adopt another. Thus, the assertion, "I am going to try to persuade Gerry to quit smoking," translates into the following situation: (1) Gerry is presently engaged in smoking behaviors, and (2) I want to induce him to stop these behaviors and begin to perform nonsmoking behaviors. On the surface, the phrase "nonsmoking behaviors" may seem nonsensical, but as any reformed smoker will attest, the transition from smoking to not smoking involves acquisition of a whole new set of behavioral alternatives ranging from substituting gum or mints for cigarettes to sitting in the nonsmoking rather than the smoking sections of restaurants. Indeed, the success of attempts to persuade people to stop smoking may often hinge on inducing them to adopt certain of these new behaviors.

Despite the tendency to equate persuasion with behavioral conversion, it seems useful to distinguish among three different behavioral outcomes commonly served by the persuasion process. Although some overlapping must be granted (the three outcomes are not always mutually exclusive), the utility of the distinction rests on the fact that the outcome sought sometimes affects the relative importance of variables contained in the persuasive equation as well as the probable ease or difficulty with which persuaders may hope to accomplish their goals.

Being Persuaded as a Response-Shaping Process

Frequently, individuals possess no clearly established pattern of responses to specific environmental stimuli. In such instances, persuasion takes the form of shaping and conditioning particular response patterns to these stimuli. Such persuasive undertakings are particularly relevant when dealing with persons who have limited prior learning histories or with situations where radically new and novel stimuli have been introduced into the environment.

Although it may be fallacious to assert that the mind of a small child is a tabula rasa, it is indisputable that children initially lack a response repertory for dealing with most social, political, economic, and ethical matters. Much of what is commonly referred to as *socialization* consists of persuading the child to respond consistently (shaping responses) to stimuli associated with these matters. Thus, at a relatively early age, the child can be observed responding as a "good" Catholic (Lutheran, Presbyterian, Unitarian-Universalist, atheist, etc.) should respond, expressing rudimentary opinions about political candidates or programs, and manifesting a relatively consistent code of conduct and ethics in dealing with others. In these instances, parents, teachers, ministers, peers, and others collectively shape and condition the responses the child performs.

It should be emphasized that all instances of response-shaping are not commonly thought of as instances of being persuaded. This distinction, while admittedly nebulous and slippery, implies that persuasion is a species of the genus commonly labeled *learning*. For instance, it would sound strange to speak of children "being persuaded." It would sound strange to speak of children *being persuaded* to tie their shoes correctly; typically, we assert that they have *learned* to tie their shoes. On the other hand, should children refuse to attempt shoe-tieing behaviors, rebel against feeding themselves, and neglect to pick up clothing or toys, they are likely to be bombarded with messages by parents and teachers aimed at shaping these behaviors. If such messages produce the desired effect, the communicators are likely to claim they have persuaded the children to become more self-reliant or independent; if not, they will probably lament the failure of their persuasive mission and devise other strategies for coping with the problem. In short, the behaviors associated with "being persuaded" are usually directly linked with more abstract attitudes and values that are prized by society or some significant segment of it—or, as Doob (1947) phrased it, responses considered socially significant by the individual's society.

As indicated earlier, response-shaping is not limited to small children. When the first nuclear device exploded over Hiroshima, Japan, in 1945, humanity witnessed the advent of a radically new energy source whose effects were so awesome they could scarcely be compared with anything preceding them. Before that August day, no one, save perhaps a few sophisticated physicists and technologists, had acquired patterns of responding to concepts such as *nuclear warfare* and *nuclear power* because these concepts were literally unheard of by most persons. That considerable response-shaping has occurred during the interim from 1945 to 1980 is attested to by the currently raging controversy regarding the wisdom of developing nuclear power sources; members of the Clamshell Alliance have been persuaded that the dangers of nuclear power far outweigh its potential benefits, while officials of the Nuclear Regulatory Agency have been convinced that the contributions of nuclear energy can be realized without serious attendant risks for humankind.

It must be granted, of course, that such instances of response-shaping are often confounded by elements of people's prior learning histories. While citizens of 1945 had acquired no established patterns of responding to the concept of *nuclear warfare*, most of them had developed response repertoires vis-à-vis the concept of *warfare*. For those who already viewed warfare as ethically and politically irresponsible, nuclear weapons were yet a further argument for the abolition of armed conflict, a powerful new persuasive weapon in their pacific arsenal. Conversely, those who sought to defend the continued utility of war as an instrument of national policy were forced to reevaluate their strategic doctrines;

post-World War II Realpolitik, as embodied in the messages of spokespersons like Henry Kissinger, spawned doctrinal concepts such as *limited war* and *strategic deterrence*. (As an aside, these concepts have not seemed to carry the same persuasive force as earlier ones; people who were motivated to enthusiastic efforts by the battle cry for "unconditional surrender" in World War II grew quickly disenchanted with the "limited war/limited objectives" rhetoric of the Korean and Vietnam conflicts.)

In the case of the concept *nuclear power*, the confounding influences of prior learning, while more subtle, are nevertheless present. Arguing for greater concern with values than with attitudes in studying persuasion, Rokeach (1973) has contended that

> a person has as many values as he has learned beliefs concerning desirable modes of conduct and end-states of existence, and as many attitudes as direct or indirect encounters he has had with specific objects and situations. It is thus estimated that values number in the dozens, whereas attitudes number in the thousands. (p. 18; see also Rokeach, 1968)

Applying Rokeach's contention to this example, it follows that while individuals may have no established response patterns for the stimulus "nuclear power"—to use his terminology, they may have no present attitude about the issue—they are likely to have well-developed response repertoires for terminal values (Rokeach, 1973) such as *family security* and *a comfortable life*. Inevitably, messages seeking to persuade these persons to adopt a particular response stance regarding nuclear power will be linked to these values. Thus, an anti-nuclear power spokesperson may assert, "The existence of nuclear power plants, such as Three Mile Island, poses a threat to the safety of your family," while an advocate of increased development of nuclear power facilities may contend, "Only by expanded use of nuclear power can you hope to retain the many comforts and conveniences you now enjoy." In both cases, success in shaping the responses of the intended persuadee hinges on the linkage of these responses to strongly held values; that is, the public will be persuaded to the extent it perceives that maintenance of an important value, or values, mandates adoption of a particular set of responses regarding the issue of nuclear power.

In spite of the limitations and complications just outlined, it remains useful to conceive of response-shaping and conditioning as one behavioral manifestation of "being persuaded." Traditionally, the persuasion literature has characterized this process as "attitude formation," reserving the term "attitude change" for attempts to replace one set of established behaviors with another. From a pragmatic vantage point, messages seeking to shape and condition responses may have a higher likelihood of success than do communications aiming to convert established behavioral patterns; in addition, the two goals may imply the use of differing persuasive strategies. Moreover, from a scientific perspective, the two outcomes may suggest different theoretical and empirical literatures; for example, learning theories thus far have been most frequently and profitably employed in the arena of response-shaping and conditioning. Thus, for persuasive practitioners and researchers alike, the distinction possesses potential utility.

Being Persuaded as a Response-Reinforcing Process

> Rather than aiming at changes in attitudes and behaviors, much persuasive communication seeks to reinforce currently held convictions and to make them more resistant to change. Most Sunday sermons serve this function, as do key-

note speeches at political conventions and presidential addresses at meetings of scholarly societies. In such cases, emphasis is on making the persuadees more devout Methodists, more active Democrats, or more committed psychologists, not on converting them to Unitarianism, the Socialist Workers Party, or romance languages. (Miller & Burgoon, 1973, p. 5)

The position espoused in the preceding quotation is certainly not earth-shaking, even though the popular tendency to view persuasion as a tool for bringing about conversion may cause people to overlook, or shortchange, this important behavioral outcome. The response-reinforcing function underscores the fact that "being persuaded" is seldom, if ever, a one-message proposition; instead, people are constantly *in the process of* being persuaded. If an individual clings to an attitude (and the behaviors associated with it) more strongly after exposure to a communication, then persuasion has occurred as surely as if the individual had shifted from one set of responses to another. Moreover, those beliefs and behaviors most resistant to change are likely to be grounded in a long history of confirming messages along with other positive reinforcers. One current theory of attitude formation and change holds that the strength of people's attitudes depends entirely on the number of incoming messages about the attitude issue they have processed (Saltiel & Woelfel, 1975).

There are strong grounds for believing that much persuasive communication in our society serves a response-reinforcing function. Although students of persuasion disagree about the extent to which the selective exposure principle (Festinger, 1957) dictates message choices (Freedman & Sears, 1965; Sears & Freedman, 1967), few, if any, would question people's affinity for supportive information (McGuire, 1969). Such an affinity, in turn, suggests that under conditions of voluntary exposure, the majority of individuals' persuasive transactions will involve messages that reinforce their existing response repertories. This possibility is further supported by early mass media research documenting the reinforcement function served by the media (e.g., Katz & Lazarsfeld, 1955).

If people do, in fact, relish hearing what they already believe, it may seem that the response-reinforcing function of persuasion is so simple as to require little concern. Distortion of information is not as likely to occur, and the initial credibility of the communicator should have less impact than in cases where persuasive intent centers on response-shaping or behavioral change—although even in the case of response reinforcement, the work of Osgood and his associates (Osgood, Suci, & Tannenbaum, 1957; Osgood & Tannenbaum, 1955) indicates that extremely low credibility may inhibit persuasive impact. Logical fallacies and evidential shortcomings are likely to be overlooked, while phenomena such as counterarguing (Brandt, 1976; Festinger & Maccoby, 1964; Osterhouse & Brock, 1970) will be largely absent. Unquestionably, message recipients are set to be persuaded; hence, would-be persuaders are assured of optimal conditions for plying their communicative wares.

Nevertheless, there are at least three good reasons for not losing sight of the response-reinforcing dimension of "being persuaded." For the practicing communicator, this dimension underscores the importance of keeping old persuasive friends as well as making new ones. In the heat of a political campaign or a fund-raising drive, it may be tempting to center efforts on potential converts at the expense of ignoring those whose prevailing response tendencies already coincide with the intent of the political candidate or the fund-raiser. Such a mistake can easily yield low vote counts or depleted treasuries. Turning to the interper-

sonal sphere, close relationships may be damaged, or even terminated, because the parties take each other for granted—in the terminology employed here, fail to send persuasive messages aimed at reinforcing mutually held positive attitudes and mutually performed positive behaviors. In short, failure to recognize that being persuaded is an ongoing process requiring periodic message attention can harm one's political aspirations, pocketbook, or romantic relationship.

The need for continued reinforcement of acquired responses also constitutes one possible explanation for the ephemerality of many persuasion research outcomes. The typical persuasion study involves a single message, presented to recipients under controlled laboratory conditions, with a measure of attitude or behavior change taken immediately afterward. On numerous occasions, researchers have observed immediate changes, only to discover that they have vanished when later follow-up measures were taken. Although a number of substantive and procedural reasons can be offered for the fleeting impact of the persuasive stimulus, one obvious explanation rests in the likelihood that the behaviors engendered by the message received no further reinforcement after the recipients departed from the research setting. Thus, the response-reinforcing dimension of being persuaded has implications for the way persuasion researchers design and interpret their studies.

Perhaps most important, however, is the fact that all response-reinforcing strategies and schedules are not destined to be equally effective. Research using cultural truisms (McGuire, 1964, 1969) has demonstrated the low resistance to change that results when behaviors and attitudes rest on a history of nearly 100% positive reinforcement; apparently, too much exclusively behavior-congruent information is not a good thing. Although studies such as those of McGuire and of

Burgoon and his associates (Burgoon & Chase, 1973; Burgoon & King, 1974) have been characterized as dealing with the problem of *inducing resistance to persuasion*, the conceptualization that has been offered here views this label as a misnomer. Research dealing with the response-reinforcing function of persuasion is research on *how* to persuade, albeit in a different sense from what the popular use implies, a position that has also recently been espoused by other writers (Burgoon, Cohen, Miller, & Montgomery, 1978). Including response reinforcement as one of the three behavioral outcomes subsumed under the phrase "being persuaded" not only calls attention to the continued need for research concerning the workings of the reinforcing process but also results in a tidier conceptualization than has previously existed.

Being Persuaded as a Response-Changing Process

As has been repeatedly noted, "being persuaded" is most typically thought of as a response-changing process; smokers are persuaded to become nonsmokers, automobile drivers are persuaded to walk or use public transportation, Christians are persuaded to become Moslems, and so on. Popular use equates "being persuaded" with "being changed." Moreover, definitions of persuasions found in most texts emphasize the notion of changing responses (Bettinghaus, 1973; Cronkhite, 1969), and even when other terms such as *modify* (Brembeck & Howell, 1952) and *influence* (Scheidel, 1967) are used, the lion's share of the text is devoted to analysis of persuasion as a response-changing process.

This view of persuasion is, of course, consistent with the ideological tenets of democratic societies. Problems of social and political change are problems of persuasion; the public must be induced to change current attitudes and behaviors to comport with the realities of new situations. The current energy crisis provides a convenient illustration of the process at work. Eschewing more coercive steps such as rationing, those charged with managing America's energy resources have bombarded the public with messages urging behavioral changes calculated to conserve these resources: dialing down thermostats, driving at slower speeds (a message buttressed by the coercive power of speeding laws), and voluntarily sharing rides—to mention but a few. Naturally, patience and faith in persuasion are not boundless; nevertheless, the democratic ethic strongly mandates that attempts to change behavior symbolically should precede more coercive remedies.

If one departs from the realm of public policy issues to conceive also of persuasion as a process involving modification of people's relational behaviors, a step recently urged by this writer (Miller, 1978), the same change-centered orientation is readily apparent. For instance, the continuing popularity of Dale Carnegie-type courses rests primarily on the following claim: Our instruction will motivate you to change your manner of self-presentation (i.e., to alter established patterns of social behavior); this change, in turn, will cause others to change dramatically their patterns of responding to you (i.e., others will be persuaded by your changed behavior to relate to you in different ways). Similarly, the popularity of Zimbardo's (1977) shyness volume and the spate of books and courses that deal with assertiveness training attest to the pervasiveness of people's attempts to alter their ongoing social behaviors and, concomitantly, to persuade others to respond differently to them. Although these processes are typically treated under rubrics such as *interpersonal communication* and *interpersonal relations*, the conceptualization outlined here argues that they should be counted as instances of the response-changing dimension of "being persuaded."

The largely unchallenged hegemony of the response-changing conception of persuasion obviates the need for further discussion. Most prior research in persuasion deals with behavioral change; at best, it treats response-shaping and response reinforcement indirectly. What remains in order to complete this analysis of the phrase "being persuaded" is a brief consideration of the way persuasive effects have typically been characterized.

Although terms such as *response* and *behavior* have been employed herein to refer to the effects of persuasive communications, the concept of *attitude* has also been mentioned on several occasions. Its emergence is not surprising, for concern with attitude formation and change has consistently guided the efforts of persuasion researchers ever since Allport (1935) confidently proclaimed *attitude* to be the single most important concept in social psychology. Notwithstanding widespread faith in the utility of the attitude construct, certain of its conceptual aspects pose knotty problems for students of persuasion. If "being persuaded" is to be considered synonymous with "shaping, reinforcing, and changing attitudes," these problems eventually must be resolved.

In persuasion research, an attitude is an *intervening variable*; that is, it is an internal mediator that intrudes between presentation of a particular overt stimulus and observation of a particular overt response (Fishbein & Ajzen, 1975; Triandis, 1971). Oskamp (1977) captured the crux of the matter, stating, "In social science, the term [attitude] has come to mean 'a posture of the mind' rather than of the body" (p. 7).

Given its conceptual status, all statements about the construct of *attitude* (or *attitude for-*

mation or *attitude change*) are, of necessity, inferential; no means exist for directly observing or measuring an attitude. If someone asserts, "Roloff has a positive attitude about research," it means that the speaker has probably observed one or more of the following behaviors: Roloff proclaiming the importance of research, Roloff gathering data, Roloff writing research reports, Roloff forgoing a recreational outing to analyze data at the computer center, Roloff investing substantial sums of money in journals containing research reports, and so on. What the person has *not* observed is Roloff's *attitude* toward research; instead, his "positive attitude" is an inference (in the terminology of one currently popular theoretical position, an *attribution*) based on observation of Roloff's research-related behaviors.

Although this point is patently obvious, its implications have often escaped persuasion researchers. Nowhere has the mischief perpetrated by this oversight been more evident than in the countless pages written about the misleadingly labeled *attitude-behavior* problem (Liska, 1975). The crux of this problem lies in the minimal relationship often observed between verbal indicators of an attitude (i.e., paper-and-pencil "attitude" scales) and other attitudinally related behaviors. While the issue centers on lack of correlation between two behavioral measures, persuasion researchers have fallen into the trap of reifying the paper-and-pencil verbal reports traditionally used as inferential measures of the attitude construct.

Despite any rational justification for doing so, persuasion researchers have continued to equate responses to these scales with the intervening variable of attitude and to speak of other responses as behavior—hence, the roots of the so-called *attitude-behavior* problem. (Miller, 1980, p. 322)

Pointing out this basic conceptual confusion in no way suggests that the minimal relationships observed between verbal attitude reports and other attitudinally related behaviors are unimportant to persuasion researchers. Because they are convenient to administer and lend themselves to a variety of statistical operations, paper-and-pencil verbal reports have been, and are likely to continue to be, widely used to measure persuasive effects. Any useful, reasonably fully developed theory of persuasion must seek to identify the conditions that determine when verbal reports will be correlated with other types of attitudinal behavior. Still, the continuing emphasis on attitude as the primary dependent variable, along with the prevailing tendency to view verbal reports as attitudes, may have done more to hinder this search than to help it.

Most writers also posit that attitudes are motivational or drive producing (Allport, 1935; Doob, 1947; Oskamp, 1977). Whether current methods of attitude measurement tap this drive-producing dimension is open to serious question. The motivational force of an attitude stems from the strength or intensity with which it is held. Most widely used attitude scales measure only the magnitude of the attitude's deviation from zero, in other words, the degree of positiveness or negativeness respondents assign to their positions. If pressed, many persuasion researchers would probably argue that extremely deviating responses—for example, *plus three* or *minus three* responses on a seven-interval, semantic differential-type scale—reflect more strongly held attitudes than do responses falling closer to the scale's midpoint. *There is no necessary relationship between the position of one's attitude about an issue and the strength with which the attitude is held; position and intensity may be viewed usefully as two relatively independent dimensions.* Undoubtedly, people frequently have middling plus three or minus three attitudes;

they may, for example, say that killing harp seals is *very good* or *very bad* yet not feel strongly about the issue. Conversely, less sharply polarized viewpoints sometimes may be held with great intensity; after weighing the matter thoroughly, an individual may conclude that killing harp seals is *slightly good* or *slightly bad* and at the same time feel quite strongly about the issue. It should be noted that the drive-producing potential of the attitude is one potentially important determinant of the extent to which verbal responses will correlate with other attitudinally consistent behaviors; if a respondent consistently says that killing harp seals is *very bad* but the issue is relatively uninvolving, that person will be unlikely to engage in more demanding, higher threshold responses (Campbell, 1963) such as giving money to naturalist organizations that oppose harp seal harvests, circulating anti-harp seal harvest petitions, and journeying to the scene of the harvest to demonstrate against it. On the other hand, if the issue is very involving and the drive-producing potential of the attitude is therefore high, these related behaviors are more likely to occur.

In some preliminary work, several of us (Miller, 1967; Peretz, 1974) have sought to index the drive-producing potential of attitudinal stimuli by measuring the vigor of the respondent's behavior (Brown, 1961). Rather than marking responses to attitudinal stimuli on paper, respondents press the appropriate button and the vigor of the button press is recorded. Because respondents experiencing high drive states are expected to behave more vigorously, the magnitude of the button press is assumed to be directly related to the attitude's intensity. Although findings have been mixed as well as confounded with numerous technical problems encountered in developing the instrumentation, some encouraging results have been obtained. In one study, Michigan State University football players responded quite vigorously to highly involving items dealing with the abolition of football scholarships and the presumed academic inferiority of athletes while at the same time responding less vigorously (yet positively or negatively) to items judged on an a priori basis to be less involving.

If using attitude as a primary behavioral indicant of "being persuaded" poses perplexing problems, what can be done to remedy the situation? One approach lies in retaining the construct while at the same time seeking to refine it and add to its utility by building more comprehensive models of attitude change (Fishbein & Ajzen, 1975). A second possibility involves replacing attitude with some other intervening construct such as value (Rokeach, 1968, 1973). Finally, persuasion researchers can abandon their reliance on mediating processes and focus exclusively on behavioristic analyses of persuasive effects. Although this latter possibility has received limited attention, a recent controversial paper (Larson & Sanders, 1975) has questioned the utility of predispositional mediating constructs and suggested that the function of persuasion might be viewed more fruitfully as the appropriate alignment of *behavior* in various social situations.

Regardless of the direction in which a researcher's preferences may point, it remains clear that "being persuaded" is a process grounded in behavioral data. No matter whether the goal is shaping, reinforcing, or changing responses, both practical and scientific successes hinge on careful observation and measurement of persuasive impact. Perhaps inferences to intervening variables, such as attitudes and values, will eventually prove indispensable to theoretical success, but these constructs are not essential ingredients of the conceptual analysis of "being persuaded" that has been offered in this chapter.

REFERENCES

Allport, G. W. (1935). Attitudes. In C. M. Murchison (Ed.), *Handbook of social psychology* (pp. 798-844). Worcester, MA: Clark University Press.

Becker, S. L. (1963). Research on logical and emotional proof. *Southern Speech Journal, 28,* 198-207.

Bettinghaus, E. P. (1973). *Persuasive communication.* New York: Holt, Rinehart & Winston.

Brandt, D. R. (1976, May). Listener propensity to counterargue, distraction, and resistance to persuasion. Paper presented at the convention of the International Communication Association, Portland, OR.

Brembeck, W. L., & Howell, W. A. (1952). *Persuasion.* Englewood Cliffs, NJ: Prentice Hall.

Brown, J.S. (1961). *The motivation of behavior.* New York: McGraw-Hill.

Burgoon, M., & Chase, L. J. (1973). The effects of differential linguistic patterns in messages attempting to induce resistance to persuasion. *Speech Monographs, 40,* 1-7.

Burgoon, M., & King, L. B. (1974). The mediation of resistance to persuasion strategies by language variables and active-passive participation. *Human Communication Research, 1,* 30-41.

Burgoon, M., Cohen, M., Miller, M. D., & Montgomery, C. L. (1978). An empirical test of a model of resistance to persuasion. *Human Communication Research, 5,* 27-39.

Campbell, D. T. (1963). Social attitudes and other acquired behavioral dispositions. In S. Koch (Ed.), *Psychology: A study of a science* (Vol. 6, pp. 94-172). New York: McGraw-Hill.

Cronkhite, G. L. (1969). *Persuasion: Speech and behavioral change.* Indianapolis, IN: Bobbs-Merrill.

Diggs, B. J. (1964). Persuasion and ethics. *Quarterly Journal of Speech, 50,* 359-373.

Doob, L. W. (1947). The behavior of attitudes. *Psychological Review, 54,* 135-156.

Festinger, L. (1957). *A theory of cognitive dissonance.* Evanston, IL: Row, Peterson.

Festinger, L., & Maccoby, N. (1964). On resistance to persuasive communications. *Journal of Abnormal and Social Psychology, 68,* 359-366.

Fishbein, M., & Ajzen, I. (1975). *Belief, attitude, intention, and behavior: An introduction to theory and research*. Reading, MA: Addison-Wesley.

Freedman, J. L., & Sears, D. O. (1965). Selective exposure. In L. Berkowitz (Ed.), *Advances in experimental social psychology* (Vol. 2, pp. 57-97). New York: Academic Press.

Hartmann, G. W. (1936). A field experiment on the comparative effectiveness of "emotional" and "rational" political leaflets in determining election results. *Journal of Abnormal and Social Psychology, 31*, 99-114.

Katz, E., & Lazarsfeld, P. F. (1955). *Personal influence*. New York: Free Press.

Kelman, H. C. (1961). Processes of opinion change. *Public Opinion Quarterly, 25*, 57-78.

Larson, C., & Sanders, R. (1975). Faith, mystery, and data: An analysis of "scientific" studies of persuasion. *Quarterly Journal of Speech, 61*, 178-194.

Liska, A. E. (1975). *The consistency controversy: Readings on the impact of attitude on behavior*. Cambridge, MA: Schenkman.

Marwell, G., & Schmitt, D. R. (1967). Dimensions of compliance-gaining behavior: An empirical analysis. *Sociometry, 30*, 350-364.

Matthews, J. (1947). The effect of loaded language on audience comprehension of speeches. *Speech Monographs, 14*, 176-187.

McGuire, W. J. (1964). Inducing resistance to persuasion: Some contemporary approaches. In L. Berkowitz (Ed.), *Advances in experimental social psychology* (Vol. 1, pp. 191-229). New York: Academic Press.

McGuire, W. J. (1969). The nature of attitudes and attitude change. In G. Lindzey & E. Aronson (Eds.), *Handbook of social psychology* (Vol. 3, pp. 136-314). Reading, MA: Addison-Wesley.

Miller, G. R. (1967). A crucial problem in attitude research. *Quarterly Journal of Speech, 53*, 235-240.

Miller, G. R. (1980). Afterword. In D. P. Cushman & R. McPhee (Eds.), *Message-attitude-behavior relationship: Theory, methodology, and application* (pp. 319-327). New York: Academic Press.

Miller, G. R., & Burgoon, M. (1973). *New techniques of persuasion*. New York: Harper & Row.

Miller, G. R. (1978). Persuasion research: Review and commentary. In B. D. Ruben (Ed.), *Communication yearbook 2* (pp. 29-47). New Brunswick, NJ: Transaction Books.

Nilsen, T.R. (1966). *Ethics of speech communication*. Indianapolis, IN: Bobbs-Merrill.

Osgood, C. E., Suci, G. J., & Tannenbaum, P. H. (1957). *The measurement of meaning*. Urbana: University of Illinois Press.

Osgood, C. E., & Tannenbaum, P. H. (1955). The principle of congruity in the prediction of attitude change. *Psychological Review, 62*, 42-55.

Oskamp, S. (1977). *Attitudes and opinions*. Englewood Cliffs, NJ: Prentice Hall.

Osterhouse, R. A., & Brock, T. C. (1970). Distraction increases yielding to propaganda by inhibiting counter-arguing. *Journal of Personality and Social Psychology, 15*, 344-358.

Peretz, M. D. (1974). *Studies on the measurement of attitude intensity*. Unpublished master's thesis, Michigan State University.

Rokeach, M. (1968). *Beliefs, attitudes, and values*. San Francisco: Jossey-Bass.

Rokeach, M. (1973). *The nature of human values*. New York: Free Press.

Rowell, E. Z. (1932a). Prolegomena to argumentation: Part I. *Quarterly Journal of Speech, 18*, 1-13.

Rowell, E. Z. (1932b). Prolegomena to argumentation: Part II. *Quarterly Journal of Speech, 18*, 224-248.

Saltiel, J., & Woelfel, J. (1975). Inertia in cognitive processes: The role of accumulated information in attitude change. *Human Communication Research, 1*, 333-344.

Scheidel, T. M. (1967). *Persuasive speaking*. Glencoe, IL: Scott, Foresman.

Sears, D. O., & Freedman, J. L. (1967). Selective exposure to information: A critical review. *Public Opinion Quarterly, 31*, 194-213.

Simons, H. W. (1974). The carrot and stick as handmaidens of persuasion in conflict situations. In G. R. Miller & H. W. Simons (Eds.), *Perspectives on communication in social conflict*. Englewood Cliffs, NJ: Prentice Hall.

Triandis, H. C. (1971). *Attitude and attitude change*. New York: John Wiley.

Weiss, W. (1960). Emotional arousal and attitude change. *Psychological Reports, 6,* 267-280.

Woolbert, C. H. (1917). Conviction and persuasion: Some considerations of theory. *Quarterly Journal of Speech, 3,* 249-264.

Zimbardo, P. G. (1977). *Shyness: What it is and what to do about it.* Reading, MA: Addison-Wesley.

2

Oscillation in Beliefs and Decisions

EDWARD L. FINK
STAN A. KAPLOWITZ
SUSAN McGREEVY HUBBARD

John Dewey, in his classic *How We Think,* stated that thinking "involves a jump, a leap, a going beyond what is surely known to something else accepted on its warrant. . . . The very inevitableness of the jump, the leap, to something unknown only emphasizes the necessity of attention to the conditions under which it occurs" (Dewey, 1991, p. 26). Our research on attitude and belief change and decision making has attempted to explicate the cognitive forces at work as individuals think, consider alternatives, and resolve issues.

All of us can recall when our decisions have come about after vacillation, wavering, or oscillation. We believe that such oscillation is an important phenomenon. This chapter reviews our most recent research about oscillation of beliefs. It also suggests a possible new direction for research by examining chaos-based measures to understand these oscillations.

Lorenz (1977) posited that "any self-regulating process in whose mechanisms inertia plays a role tends toward oscillation" (p. 237). Because there is evidence that cognition has such an inertial principle (see, e.g., Saltiel & Woelfel, 1975), it is reasonable to expect oscillatory dynamics for cognition.

With a few exceptions (e.g., Lewin, 1951), until the late 1970s, the theory and research on attitudes and decisions focused on the outcome of the process rather than on its dynamics. For example, a review of the decision-making literature (Abelson & Levi, 1985) focused on models predicting decisions based on the probability of and utility of various outcomes. In attitude research, the major emphasis during this time has been on how

AUTHORS' NOTE: Portions of this chapter are based on Kaplowitz, S. A., & Fink, E. L. (1996). Cybernetics of attitudes and decisions. In J. H. Watt & C. A. VanLear (Eds.), *Dynamic patterns in communication processes* (pp. 277-300). Thousand Oaks, CA: Sage.

source, message, and receiver characteristics influence an attitude, typically measured only once after an experimental treatment. Thus, those investigating decision making and attitude change have generally failed to measure the time course of variables associated with the underlying psychological dynamics.

However, understanding dynamics in general and cognitive oscillations in particular is critically important. First, understanding the time course of attitude and belief change may add considerably to our understanding of the forces causing this change, thereby allowing the creation of a model that governs the process.

Second, because beliefs are typically measured at one point in time, the existence of oscillations can introduce what appears to be unreliability into the measurement of beliefs. In other words, *systematic* change, in the form of oscillation, can be mistaken for the *random* disturbances in a measurement, which we usually think of as unreliability. Determining the time parameters of such oscillations may allow us to separate unreliability from instability in the measurement of an attitude or a belief (see, e.g., Heise, 1969). It also may tell us how long we need to wait for the attitude to reach equilibrium or "settle down."

Both attitude and decision researchers have recently begun paying more attention to process and dynamics. In the attitude area, not only have thoughts been considered an important intervening variable (see, e.g., Chaiken, Liberman, & Eagly, 1989; Petty & Cacioppo, 1986), but a number of studies (Liberman & Chaiken, 1991; Millar & Tesser, 1986) suggest that thinking is sufficient to bring about attitude change. Thus, McGuire (1989) stated that those who study attitudes increasingly view them as an interacting dynamic system. The decision-making literature has also shown increasing concern with the dynamics of the process (see, e.g., Janis & Mann, 1977; Tversky & Shafir, 1992).

COGNITIVE OSCILLATION: INDIRECT EVIDENCE

From studying post-decisional attitudes, Walster (1964) and Brehm and Brehm (1981) have found that people often initially regret a choice that they have just made. Only later do they reduce their post-decisional dissonance with that choice (see also Landman, 1993). The regret-dissonance reduction process may, in fact, be one cycle of oscillation in beliefs; dissonance researchers did not measure attitudes with sufficient frequency in any experiment to know whether attitudinal oscillation might continue.

Gilbert, Krull, and Malone (1990) showed that an idea must first be entertained as true before it can be rejected as false. If correct, this idea suggests that an individual's beliefs must change at least once in the process of rejecting a proposition. Moreover, Latané and Darley (1970) stated that bystanders experiencing the stress of an emergency can "cycle back and forth" between beliefs such as "the building's on fire—I should do something" and "I wonder if the building's really on fire" (p. 122). For other evidence relevant to the possibility of cognitive oscillations, see Poole and Hunter (1979, 1980) and Wegner (1989, pp. 34, 113).

How have cognitive oscillations been explained? Lewin (1951) posited that as we approach a goal, both the attractive and repulsive forces associated with the goal get stronger, but the repulsive forces increase more rapidly than the attracting ones. Thus, whereas at great distances the net force is attractive, as the goal is approached, the net force becomes repulsive (see Lewin, 1951, p. 264). Similarly, in Brehm and Brehm's (1981) analysis of reactance, moving toward one choice alternative threatens the freedom to choose another choice alternative. This process causes the previously rejected alternative to become more attractive. Both of these approaches suggest an oscillatory decision trajectory.

A SPATIAL-SPRING MODEL OF COGNITIVE FORCES

A spatial-spring model of attitude change and decision making has two basic components. First is a *geometry* of cognition in which similarity in the meaning of concepts is indicated by their distance from each other (see Woelfel & Fink, 1980) and in which the degree to which a concept is positively evaluated is indicated by how close it is to some other concept (e.g., "things I like") indicating positive evaluation (see Neuendorf, Kaplowitz, Fink, & Armstrong, 1986).

Second, cognitive oscillation suggests the existence of restoring (negative feedback) *forces*. Such restoring forces are built into this model by assuming that there are associative linkages between concepts and that these linkages are spring-like (see Fink & Kaplowitz, 1993; Fink, Monahan, & Kaplowitz, 1989; Kaplowitz & Fink, 1982, 1988, 1992, 1996; Kaplowitz, Fink, & Bauer, 1983; for earlier treatments, see Barnett & Kincaid, 1983; Kincaid, Yum, Woelfel, & Barnett, 1983; Woelfel & Fink, 1980, esp. pp. 158-159). Consistent with the operation of a mechanical spring, we assume that the forces attracting one *toward* an alternative increase in strength as the individual cognitively moves *away* from that alternative.

We found the spring imagery especially attractive for two reasons. First, a spring system fits our geometric model in making the forces dependent on the instantaneous distances among concepts. Second, as discussed more fully in what follows, a spring analogy helps to make sense of the tension people feel when experiencing opposing forces.

A model incorporating spring-like forces assumes that a linkage between two concepts,

A and *B*, creates a force satisfying the following equation:

$$F_{A,B} = K_{A,B}[d_{Eq}(A,B) - d(A,B)], \qquad (1)$$

where $F_{A,B}$ is the force between the concepts, $d_{Eq}(A,B)$ is the equilibrium distance of the linkage, $d(A,B)$ is the distance between those concepts in the receiver's cognitive space, and $K_{A,B}$ is the restoring coefficient of the linkage. This model posits that on either side of the equilibrium location, the net force is directed toward the equilibrium location.

People often see a choice alternative as consisting of both attractive and unattractive features (cf. value conflict as discussed in Liberman & Chaiken, 1991). In this choice situation, there should be spring-like linkages pulling in opposite directions. The equilibrium of the system is that point at which the opposing forces balance; the relevant restoring coefficient is the sum of the effects of all the individual linkages.

We now consider the motion of a system consistent with Equation (1). From Newton's laws of force and motion, acceleration is proportional to the product of the distance of a concept from its equilibrium location and *K*, the net restoring coefficient computed from all linkages on a concept. If *K* is constant over time, then this equation leads to a sinusoidal trajectory of *undamped oscillations* (i.e., with a constant amplitude and a constant period of oscillation). Moreover, the period of oscillation is a decreasing function of the restoring coefficient.

Sometimes people manifest no perceptible cognitive oscillation. Furthermore, even when they do oscillate, it appears that such oscillations usually die out. Just as mechanical systems have friction, which serves to damp oscillations, we assume a *cognitive damping* process whose force is proportional to, and in the opposite direction from, the velocity of the concept in motion. Whether the system exhibits oscillation depends on the size of the damping coefficient as compared to the restoring coefficient.

Like Lewin (1951), we see the forces on a person's decision as depending on the cognitive distance from an alternative. The spatial-spring model, however, explains Lewin's ad hoc assumption that as one approaches a goal, the repulsive force increases more rapidly than the attractive force. In addition, the spatial-spring model's explicit equations of force and motion enable us to predict the time course of change more precisely.

THE PSYCHOLOGICAL MEANING OF THE MODEL

Equilibrium Length

The equilibrium length of a linkage is the distance between concepts that the linkage implies when one ignores the effect of other linkages. The equilibrium length of the linkage between an attribute and an evaluative concept represents the evaluation of the attribute, again ignoring the effect of other linkages. Thus, for most people the linkage between *good pay* and *jobs I want* has a small equilibrium length, whereas the linkage between *long hours* and *jobs I want* has a large equilibrium length.

We extend the model to persuasion by assuming that a message linking concepts A and B establishes a linkage between them, whose equilibrium length, $d_{Eq}(A,B)$, is the dissimilarity between A and B specified in the message. Thus, the equilibrium length is the position advocated by the message.

Restoring Coefficient

The restoring coefficient reflects the importance of the attribute in the decision calcu-

lus. Attributes that are more important have greater restoring coefficients. The cognition and memory literature (e.g., Anderson, 1983) suggests that more frequent associations between concepts cause stronger linkages and that the lack of recent co-occurrence causes these linkages to weaken. Thus, we see the restoring coefficient as related to co-occurrence (for exceptions, see, e.g., Bornstein & Pittman, 1992).

Although messages are assumed to establish spring-like linkages between concepts, they do not fully determine the receiver's new view. The force created by a new message linkage is opposed by and ultimately in balance with the preexisting forces from the network of other linkages in the receiver's cognitive system. These *anchoring* linkages represent the strength of the receiver's initial view and are the result of prior messages.

Thus, our model posits two distinct spring-like linkages. One is called the *message* linkage and is represented by the symbol $K_{A,B}$. The other is called the *anchoring* linkage[1] and is represented by K_R. Given Equation (1), we find that when the system is in equilibrium, attitude change can be predicted by the following equation:

$$\Delta P = \frac{K_{A,B} Dp}{K_R + K_{A,B}} \qquad (2)$$

where Dp is the discrepancy (between the position advocated by the message and the initial position of the receiver.

$K_{A,B}$ should be an increasing function of factors that enhance attitude change such as source credibility and argument strength. However, various studies (e.g., Aronson, Turner, & Carlsmith, 1963) have shown that as discrepancy increases, attitude change becomes a smaller proportion of the discrepancy. Therefore, $K_{A,B}$ should be a decreasing function of message discrepancy.

The strength of the anchoring linkage K_R is expected to be an increasing function of pre-message factors that inhibit attitude change such as the strength of the initial attitude (or value-relevant involvement [see Johnson & Eagly, 1990]).

We have stated that all linkages are assumed to decay over time (see Ebbinghaus, 1964); however, new messages or self-generated thoughts may have the effect of strengthening these linkages.

Frequency and Amplitude of Oscillation

The frequency of oscillation of a spring is an increasing function of its restoring coefficient. Because the total restoring coefficient is the sum of the coefficients of the message linkage and the anchoring linkages, we can derive some interesting hypotheses based on the preceding discussion of these factors:

Hypothesis 1: Other things being equal, the frequency of oscillation is an increasing function of (a) source credibility, (b) argument strength, and (c) strength of initial opinion.

Hypothesis 2: Other things being equal, the frequency of oscillation is a decreasing function of message discrepancy.

We now examine determinants of the amplitude of oscillation. The spatial-linkage model predicts sinusoidal trajectories that are symmetric about the equilibrium location and that have amplitudes that are greatest at the start of the cognitive trajectory. Thus, the maximum possible amplitude is the distance between (a) the equilibrium location of a concept after persuasion and (b) the concept's original location. By definition, this distance is the final attitude change. Thus, we have the following hypothesis:

Hypothesis 3: The greater the attitude change, the greater the amplitude of oscillation (cf. Kaplowitz & Fink, 1982).

As indicated previously, attitude change is predicted to be an increasing function of source credibility and argument strength and (usually) of discrepancy, and it is predicted to be a decreasing function of the strength of the receiver's initial belief. Combining these with Hypothesis 3 leads us to the following hypothesis:

Hypothesis 4: The amplitude of oscillation is an *increasing* function of (a) source credibility, (b) argument strength, and (usually) (c) discrepancy, and it is a *decreasing* function of (d) the strength of the receiver's initial belief.

TESTING THE PREDICTIONS OF THIS MODEL

To summarize, the spatial-linkage model has very elegant and clear predictions. It predicts oscillatory trajectories with constant frequencies, which are either damped (getting steadily smaller in amplitude) or totally undamped (staying the same in amplitude). Moreover, the amplitude and frequency should be functions of the persuasion variables discussed previously.

Our first study to examine oscillations (Kaplowitz et al., 1983) used more than 1,000 participants, each of whose attitude was measured only once. However, their attitudes were measured at different times from the receipt of the persuasive message. We then treated the mean response of all participants who received the same experimental treatment and who responded at the same time after the message as if it were a point on the trajectory of a single individual. We treated the within-cell variance as measurement error.

We found modest but significant support for the existence of oscillations; however, there was no evidence of damping.

Aside from time until measurement, our other independent variable in that study was message discrepancy. Consistent with Hypothesis 4, the message with the greatest discrepancy not only induced the most attitude change but also induced the trajectory with the greatest amplitude. But inconsistent with Hypothesis 2, no relationship between discrepancy and the frequency of oscillation was found.

Obviously, the technique used in the Kaplowitz et al. (1983) study has serious drawbacks, and we have since developed better ways to measure oscillation. The technique we have used most often requires participants to think about an issue and use a computer mouse to indicate their instantaneous opinions about the issue. Mouse position is recorded at least every 18 milliseconds, thereby giving us trajectories of individual attitudes or decisions. When participants determine that they have made a final decision, they press the mouse button, and this signal indicates the end of the trajectory.

We tested Hypotheses 1 through 4 with a study that had 99 participants. We provided a message that manipulated discrepancy and source credibility and then had the participants use the mouse while thinking about the issue. We measured attitude trajectories for two separate issues. One issue was the appropriate sentence for a convicted armed robber (a scenario used in Kaplowitz & Fink, 1991). The other issue was the appropriate increase in tuition at the students' university (a scenario used in Fink, Kaplowitz, & Bauer, 1983).

There were some very striking qualitative findings that came from examining the nearly 200 trajectories generated by this study. The first is that oscillatory trajectories, in which participants' mouse motion reverses direction, are quite common. In both scenarios, more than half of the participants changed direction at least once. This finding has been confirmed with other decision problems as well (see Table 2.1).

However, the oscillatory trajectories do not look like the trajectories predicted by the simple version of the spatial-spring model discussed earlier. That model predicted constant periods and amplitudes that either remained constant or got steadily smaller (i.e., were damped). None of the oscillatory trajectories found showed constant periods. Moreover, some amplitudes suddenly got larger, and oscillations abruptly ended with no gradual damping (see Figure 2.1).

Because we did not have regular trajectories, we could not measure frequency and amplitude in the usual way. Our analogue to amplitude became the *pseudo-amplitude* (half of the difference between the maximum and minimum values of the decision trajectory). We created two analogues to the frequency. One was the *total number of changes of direction* the participant made. The other was the *pseudo-frequency* (the number of changes of direction divided by the decision time).

In determining the number of changes of direction, we wanted to distinguish mouse motion that reflected attitude change from unintentional motion. Thus, any change had to be at least 4% of the range of the scale for us to consider it a true change of direction. In addition, spike-like changes, in which the participant, on reaching a position, *immediately* moved in the opposite direction, were also interpreted as unreliable motion. Here, we assumed that the participant, having overshot a "true" position, was hastening to correct it.

Although credibility was successfully manipulated, contrary to Hypothesis 1a, it had virtually no effect on number of changes of direction. For both scenarios, the Pearson correlation between credibility and number of changes was less than .08. Contrary to Hy-

TABLE 2.1 Statistics From Online Oscillation Studies

		Criminal Sentencing	*Tuition*	*College Admission (Wang Experiment 2)*[a]		*College Admission (McGreevy)*[b]	
		Continuous Discreteness	*Continuous Discreteness*	*Dichotomous Discreteness*		*Dichotomous Discreteness*	
				Easy	*Difficult*	*Easy*	*Difficult*
Sample size		99	91	31	36	50-51	47-51
Percentage changing direction at least once		72.7	59.3	77.4	97.2	64.7	76.5
Number of changes of direction	Adjusted geometric mean[c]	1.33	0.91	1.66	5.04	0.89	1.60
	25th percentile	0	0	1	3	0	1
	Median	1	1	2	5.5	1	2
	75th percentile	2	2	3	9	3	4
	Maximum[d]	7	11	14	14	12	18
Decision time (seconds)	Adjusted geometric mean[c]	26.59	26.60	17.20	38.81	6.38	45.05
	25th percentile	15.60	15.93	8.01	23.96	1.00	4.00
	Median	27.67	26.85	18.02	40.98	6.50	58.00
	75th percentile	42.40	45.37	35.98	57.75	40.50	103.00
	Minimum	4.84	4.89	3.00	9.00	0.00	0.00
	Maximum	95.18	100.46	84.00	130.00	121.0	217

a. Wang Experiment 2 is the experiment described in this chapter.

b. For McGreevy, the results reported in the table are only from the post-message phase.

c. Let $\log(x + c)$ be the transformation used to create a functional form whose skew was approximately zero, where x is the variable of interest and c is a constant. Adjusted geometric mean = (antilog of the mean of transformed variable) – c. If c were zero, the adjusted geometric mean would equal the geometric mean.

d. For this variable, the *minimum* was zero in all experiments.

pothesis 2, for both scenarios, the Pearson correlation between discrepancy and number of changes was slightly positive, but it was not significantly different from zero in either scenario. We also found our independent variables to have no significant effect on pseudo-frequency.

Hypothesis 3a predicts that the greater the attitude change, the greater the amplitude. Using the pseudo-amplitude (and counting the

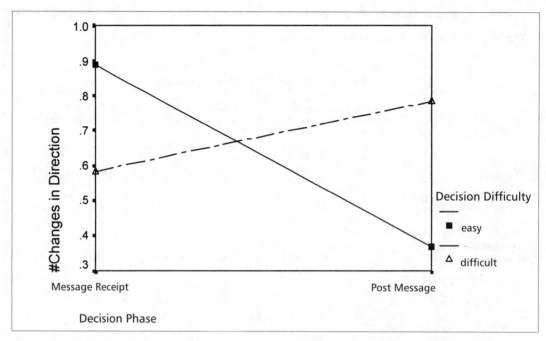

Figure 2.1. Mean Number of Changes in Direction, by Phase and by Object Similarity

amplitude as missing when there were no changes in direction), strong support for this hypothesis was found, but only for the sentencing scenario.[2] For the criminal sentencing scenario, the Pearson correlation between amplitude and final attitude change was .45 ($p < .01$). However, for the tuition scenario, the Pearson correlation between these variables was only .08 (*ns*).

Although several of our findings disconfirmed our hypotheses, other evidence by Vallacher, Nowak, and Kaufman (1994) was consistent with the spatial-spring model. In that study, participants evaluated a stimulus person as they thought about that person and used a computer mouse to record their instantaneous judgments. Consistent with our spring model, they found in their Experiment 1 that the further someone's attitude is from its equilibrium position, the greater the acceleration.

To summarize, we have some support for the idea that people oscillate, but not for the

more specific predictions of the spatial-spring model. One obvious explanation of this outcome comes from the logic of the model itself. We have assumed that every message a participant receives creates a new linkage. But as is well-known, as people process an external message, they often send themselves messages (i.e., cognitive responses) (see, e.g., Petty & Cacioppo, 1986; Petty, Ostrom, & Brock, 1981). If these self-generated messages create new linkages and affect the receiver's attitude, they will lead to trajectories that are far more complex and chaotic than those implied by the simple model. We now consider other variables that may affect the trajectories.

AMBIVALENCE, ELABORATION, DISTRACTION, AND NEED FOR COGNITION

Janis and Mann (1977) predicted that "vacillation" occurs when the conflict felt by the decision maker involves a "serious risk from the current course of action" or a "serious risk from a new course of action" and when "a better solution may be found" (p. 78). Similarly, Bruss (1975) attributed "a wavering in the process of deliberation" to

> an unclear ranking of preferences or incommensurable preferences, vague or uncertain beliefs about how well an object or act will satisfy a preference, what the available alternatives are and the relative probabilities of attaining each, and unresolved notions of the risk that is warranted or tolerable if a chosen alternative fails. (pp. 557-558)

Katz (1981) also argued that ambivalent attitudes tend to be unstable—a finding supported by Bargh, Chaiken, Govender, and Pratto (1992).

Situations in which people are ambivalent tend to be experienced as situations involving a great deal of tension. In these situations, people often are said to feel torn, pulled apart, or strained by conflicting demands of competing roles (see, e.g., Goode, 1960) as well as by the difficulty of making some decisions (see, e.g., Festinger, 1957; Heider, 1958). Such situations are clearly ones of great tension or stress. Thus, we predict the following:

> *Hypothesis 5:* Oscillation is more likely for issues on which the respondent is ambivalent (i.e., most likely to have conflicting feelings) and for which a decision is difficult.

Those studying cognitive responses to persuasion (see, e.g., Petty & Cacioppo, 1986; Petty et al., 1981) have shown that such cognitive responses have a strong relationship to attitude change. This idea suggests the following:

> *Hypothesis 6:* The number of cognitive responses should be positively correlated with the number of changes of direction.

If oscillation requires cognitive elaboration, it is more likely when people have the ability and motivation to elaborate (see Petty & Cacioppo, 1986). The *ability* to elaborate should be related to the availability and accessibility of the decider's thoughts (see Fazio, 1989; on the availability heuristic, see also Tversky & Kahneman, 1974) and should be more likely when the decider has a detailed or complex schema for understanding the issue (see, e.g., Tetlock, 1983a, 1983b). It should also be more likely when the decider is not distracted from concentration (see, e.g., Petty, Wells, & Brock, 1976).

Based on the Elaboration Likelihood Model, the motivation to elaborate should also be a function of the individual's need for cognition and of the importance of the issue to the decider. If thoughts have the effects we expect, then the number of changes of direction will be related to the number of cognitive responses. Thus, we have the following hypotheses:

> *Hypothesis 7:* Oscillation is more likely for issues the respondent considers important.

> *Hypothesis 8:* Oscillation is more likely for those who are high in need for cognition.

> *Hypothesis 9:* Distraction will cause fewer oscillations.

Our study, employing criminal sentencing and tuition increases as the topics for consideration by the participants, provides some evidence in support of Hypothesis 5. Respondents clearly regarded the tuition issue as more important to themselves, and a significantly greater percentage (47%) showed oscillation in this scenario than in the sentencing scenario (35%).

The results dealing with ambivalence are more extensive. We did a self-report study (see Fink & Kaplowitz, 1993, p. 261) in which participants were given a set of hypothetical decision problems (scenarios) and asked for paper-and-pencil responses to them. Consistent with Hypothesis 5, those who reported the decision to be difficult were more likely to also report having oscillated.

Similarly, Vallacher et al. (1994) provided other evidence that ambivalence contributes to oscillations. In their studies, participants received information about a stimulus person that was either positive, negative, or mixed (ambivalent) and then indicated how their instantaneous evaluations of the stimulus changed. Although participants in all conditions were likely to oscillate initially, the amplitude and frequency of oscillation of those receiving the positive or negative information declined, whereas the oscillations of the ambivalent participants did not.

Several of our online studies (i.e., those in which the participant employs a computer mouse to encode the trajectory of thoughts while thinking) have also examined the effect of ambivalence on oscillation. In the criminal sentencing and tuition attitude study, we measured ambivalence in two ways. One was by asking participants to list their thoughts about the sentence and the tuition. The other was by a set of closed-ended questions asking the participants' views on these issues.

Ambivalent participants were those who agreed with the arguments on both sides of the issue. For example, the following statement indicates a belief system that might oppose severe punishment for criminals: "Two wrongs do not make a right. Even though the criminal has behaved badly, this does not justify society violating the criminal's human rights." By contrast, the statement, " 'An eye for an eye' is an appropriate principle of justice," indicates a belief system that might favor severe punish-ment. Ambivalent participants were those who might agree with both of these positions.

In the study described previously, ambivalence had no significant relationship with the number of changes of direction in the attitude trajectory. Moreover, contrary to Hypothesis 6, the Pearson correlation between number of thoughts and number of changes of direction was less than .10 (*ns*) in each scenario.

We have also experimentally manipulated ambivalence by varying the difficulty of the decision the respondents are asked to make. In these studies, participants were asked to choose which of two fictitious candidates should be admitted to their university. In one case, the information was designed so that participants would find it to be a difficult decision. In the other case, the information was designed to make it likely that the participants would see one candidate as more suitable. As participants thought about the admissions decision, they used a computer mouse to indicate their instantaneous opinions as to which applicant should be admitted. At one end of the scale (from 0 to 100) was *definitely admit* [*Candidate A*]; the other end was *definitely admit* [*Candidate B*]. At intermediate points on the scale, the respondents could indicate leaning toward one candidate without total certainty.

In the first of these studies (Wang, 1993), one of the candidates for admission was Black and the other was White. To vary the decision difficulty, the hypothetical Black applicant was described either in an *individuated* way (i.e., in ways that the participants considered atypical of Black applicants) or in a *stereotypical* way. Note that in neither condition were evaluatively negative terms or beliefs used to describe either applicant. From the literature on racial attitudes (e.g., Bobo & Kluegel, 1991; Jackman & Senter, 1983), and on individuation (see, e.g., Wilder, 1978, 1981), we expected White participants to have a more positive attitude toward the Black applicant when the Black applicant was individuated than when he was stereotypical. Consequently, we expected participants to find the admissions decision to be more difficult (i.e., more ambivalent) when the Black applicant was individuated than when he was stereotypical. Thus, we expected a greater amplitude and a greater number of changes in direction in the decision trajectory of the individuated than in the stereotype-consistent condition.

In this study, we also manipulated distraction. In the *high distraction* condition, there was distracting noise on the tape-recorded instructions, and the experimenter rustled papers and snacked on crunchy foods. In the *no distraction* condition, neither of these things happened. Manipulation checks showed that both independent variables were manipulated successfully. We also measured need for cognition using Petty and Cacioppo's (1986) scale.

Of the 67 participants, 59 (88%) had at least one change of direction. Moreover, the individuation manipulation created significantly greater self-reported decision difficulty. Individuation also had positive and significant (at $p < .01$) linear correlations with (a) the number of direction changes in the participant's decision trajectory ($r = .541$), (b) decision time ($r = .460$), and (c) pseudo-amplitude ($r = .401$). The linear correlations with self-reported decision difficulty were less strong (perhaps because of unreliability of the manipulation check of decision difficulty). Although individuation and decision difficulty were significantly correlated with each other ($r = .372, p < .01$), neither individuation nor decision difficulty was significantly correlated with pseudo-frequency (for individuation, $r = .003$; for decision difficulty, $r = .086$). In short, the more difficult decision involved more changes of direction, but these changes had the same frequency in both the easy and hard decisions. Thus, whether decision diffi-

culty increases oscillation depends on whether one is using the total number of changes or their rate as the dependent measure.

Consistent with Hypotheses 5 and 6, individuation produced more thoughts ($r = .368$, $p < .01$), and the number of thoughts was positively correlated with the number of changes of direction ($r = .411, p < .01$). Consistent with Hypothesis 8, the need for cognition scale had a positive correlation with the number of changes of direction ($r = .262, p < .05$). However, these results also contained some surprises. The need for cognition scale had a near zero correlation with the number of thoughts. Moreover, distraction had a positive correlation ($r = .221$, *ns*) with the number of thoughts and contrary to Hypothesis 9, a significant and positive correlation ($r = .420, p < .01$) with the number of changes in direction.

Thus, decisional conflict increases the tendency to change one's mind, which apparently made the decision process take longer. This conflict did not, however, increase the rate of the oscillation. Contrary to the findings of previous studies (e.g., Petty et al., 1976), distraction did not reduce thought production. Rather, it made the thinking process take longer.[3]

McGreevy's (1996) study ($N = 102$) used a similar methodology to Wang's (1993) study and examined the effect of both decision difficulty and distraction. In the *difficult* decision, both college applicants were *similar* in that both were appropriate for admission into college. In the *easy* decision, only one candidate was appropriate for admission into college. The difficulty manipulation in this study was successful.

The results generally replicated those just reported. For cognitive processing *after reading the message*, participants again showed significantly more oscillation for the difficult decision than for the easy one. They also took significantly more time in the condition in which they were distracted. (As explained later, McGreevy, 1996, also measured the trajectory as the participants read the message.)

NEED FOR CLOSURE
AND DECISION PHASE

Kruglanski's (1989, 1990) theory of lay epistemics suggests that people differ in their *need for closure*. Need for closure is defined as "the desire for a definite answer on some topic, any answer as opposed to confusion and ambiguity" (Kruglanski, 1989, p. 14). On the other hand, *need to avoid closure* occurs in situations "where judgmental non-commitment is valued or desired" (p. 18). Kruglanski (1989, 1990) claimed that need for closure can result in an "epistemic freezing" (Kruglanski, 1989, p. 14), in which participants are not motivated to process information and have a strong desire to come to a quick conclusion. We hypothesize that individuals who experience a *high need for closure* are unwilling to expend the cognitive effort required to make a decision. Therefore, we have the following hypothesis:

> *Hypothesis 10:* Need for closure correlates negatively with (a) the time to make a decision and (b) the number of changes of direction.

There is evidence that different kinds of cognitive processing may occur during different phases of the decision-making process (see Bassili, 1989; Hastie & Park, 1986; Hastie & Pennington, 1989). Hastie and Pennington (1989) have found differences in cognitive processing between social inference tasks that were made online ("during the process of perception, when the other person is present to the senses") and social inference tasks that were memory based ("when we think about a person in their absence") (p. 1).

Research on online cognition suggests that a great deal of cognitive processing can occur

while an individual receives a message. This cognitive processing may be different from the type of processing that occurs once the message has been received and while an individual thinks about the information contained in the message in order to make a decision. To explore this possibility, we divided the attitude trajectory into two phases: (a) the *message receipt phase*, which occurs as an individual is receiving the attitude message; and (b) the *post-message phase*, which occurs after the message has been received and while the individual is considering the information in the message.

In addition to examining the effect of decision difficulty and distraction, McGreevy's (1996) study examined the effect of need for closure and decision phase on the attitude trajectory. Need for closure was manipulated by varying environmental noise (Kruglanski & Webster, 1994). In the *high need for closure* condition, a loud humming noise was piped into the experimental room. In the *low need for closure* condition, participants were warned that the noise might occur; however, no noise was actually used. There was also one individual difference variable, *trait* need for closure, which was measured by Webster and Kruglanski's (1994) need for closure scale.

Manipulation checks showed that individuals who heard the noise reported the environment to be significantly more distracting and also reported a significantly greater motivation to complete the task quickly than did those who did not hear the noise. Thus, this manipulation both increased the participants' need for closure and made them feel more distracted. They did not, however, report that their cognitive capacity was affected by the noise.

This study measured the attitude trajectory using the same computer mouse technique described earlier, with one important change. The previous studies had participants use the mouse only after reading the message. In this study, participants started indicating their instantaneous preferences with the mouse *while they read the information about the candidates.* Participants were further instructed to push the left mouse button when they finished reading the information. Then, as in previous studies, they were to continue to move the mouse as they thought about the issue until they made a final choice as to whom they preferred. At this point, they were to push the left mouse button a second time. This procedure allowed each participant's decision trajectory to be divided into two parts: (a) the *message receipt phase* (i.e., while the participant was receiving the message) and (b) the *post-message phase* (i.e., while the participant was thinking about the message and deciding between the candidates).

Overall Trajectory

Those with a high need for closure were expected to take less time on the decision-making process (Hypothesis 10a) and have decision trajectories that exhibit fewer oscillations (i.e., fewer changes in direction) (Hypothesis 10b) than those with low need for closure. We first examine these results for the overall trajectory over two decision-making phases and then examine the phases separately.

As expected, participants with a difficult decision took significantly more time to decide between the candidates ($p = .001$) than did those with an easy decision (see Table 2.1). But contrary to Hypothesis 5, the number of changes of direction exhibited by the mouse had no significant relation to the difficulty of the decision. However, a *self-report* measure of changes in cognitive direction produced results consistent with Hypothesis 5. In what follows, we examine this finding.

A statistically significant interaction between manipulated need for closure and the

candidates' similarity (decision difficulty) on decision time was also found. Consistent with Hypothesis 10a, when participants faced the more difficult decision, the higher the need for closure, the less time participants took to make their decision. But when participants dealt with the easy decision, contrary to Hypothesis 10a, the greater the manipulated need for closure, the more time the participants took.

We found a somewhat similar interaction effect when the number of changes of direction was our dependent variable. Consistent with Hypothesis 10b, when the decision was rated as difficult by the participants, those in the high need for closure condition had fewer changes in direction than did those in the low need for closure condition. However, when the decision was rated as less difficult, those in the high need for closure condition exhibited more changes in direction than those in the low need for closure condition.

The results that are contrary to Hypothesis 10a or 10b can be better understood when we remember that the need for closure manipulation was a distraction. Wang (1993) found that those who experienced a distraction took longer to come to a final decision than did those who did not experience a distraction. And it is also possible that the distraction not only increased the time spent but also caused people to reconsider their decision, resulting in additional oscillations. However, the reason that this effect was found only in the easy decision scenario is not clear.

Separate Decision Phases

In the post-message phase, we found mixed results for both hypotheses. Consistent with Hypothesis 10b, the need for closure scale had a significantly negative linear correlation with the number of changes in direction. But contrary to Hypothesis 10a, it had a near zero

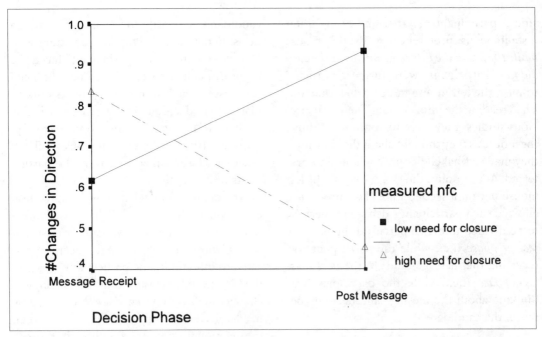

Figure 2.2. Mean Number of Changes in Direction, by Phase and by Measured Need for Closure

linear correlation with the decision time. Consistent with Hypothesis 10a, manipulated need for closure had a negative (but nonsignificant) linear correlation with decision time. But contrary to Hypothesis 10b, it had a near zero linear correlation with number of changes in direction.[4]

Examination of trajectories showed that the independent variables had different relations to the trajectories in the two different phases. As indicated previously, for the post-message phase, those with a difficult decision showed more changes in direction than did those asked to choose between different candidates. For the message receipt phase, however, the results were in the opposite direction and the interaction was significant (see Figure 2.1).

We also found a significant interaction between decision phase and measured (trait) need for closure (see Figure 2.2). As indicated previously, the post-message phase shows the expected results. Those measuring high in need for closure exhibited fewer oscillations

than did those measuring low in need for closure. For the message receipt phase, however, the results were in the opposite direction.

These results suggest that different kinds of cognitive processing occur at different points in the attitude change process. Those with a high need for closure do most of their oscillating (and perhaps most of their cognitive processing) while receiving the message. Evidence of oscillation while receiving a message is consistent with current research about online cognition (Bassili, 1989). But consistent with Kruglanski (1989), those with low need for closure are more likely to oscillate after the message has been received.

Let us now return to the findings relating number of changes of direction to difficulty of decision (similarity of candidates). We have found that (a) the overall trajectory shows no significant effect of difficulty, (b) there is a significant effect of difficulty on the self-reported oscillations, and (c) the effect of decision difficulty on the number of observed changes is as predicted in the post-message phase but is in the opposite direction in the message receipt phase.

Taken together, these findings may suggest that the observed trajectory is a more accurate reflection of the cognitive process in the post-message phase than in the message receipt phase. In the message receipt phase, participants were asked to read the message and record their preferences as they were having them. In this phase, it is possible that when they were asked to choose between two similar candidates, they were concentrating so hard that they forgot to move the cursor in conjunction with their thoughts. When asked to recall the number of times they changed their minds between candidates, however, they were able to recall changing their minds more often for the difficult decision scenarios. Further research is needed to clarify this issue.

DEGREE OF RANDOMNESS AND CHAOS

As indicated previously, we started with a model that predicted periodic trajectories. We found this prediction to be disconfirmed. Furthermore, we proposed that cognitive responses create trajectories that are chaotic. Indeed, such chaos is suggested by the Dewey quote that begins this chapter.

The (most positive) Lyapunov exponent is a statistic that permits us to examine the degree of pattern in a trajectory. This statistic is "a measure of the rate at which nearby trajectories in a phase space diverge" (Sprott & Rowlands, 1992, p. 19; see also Casti & Karlqvist, 1991). Periodic orbits have Lyapunov exponents that are near zero, chaotic orbits have at least one positive Lyapunov exponent, and random orbits have still larger Lyapunov exponents. In other words, the higher the Lyapunov exponent, the more unpredictable the future trajectory is based on its past values.

We find that in McGreevy's (1996) study, out of 102 trajectories, only 1 has a negative Lyapunov exponent and 1 more has a value less than 0.10. Fully 75% of the trajectories have Lyapunov exponents that are 0.24 or greater. The median value for the Lyapunov exponents of these trajectories is 0.30 (range: −0.10 to 1.66). This result suggests that the trajectories are chaotic.

A reexamination of the attitude trajectories in Wang's experiment (see Fink, Kaplowitz, & Wang, 1994) showed that whereas greater oscillation occurred when the decision was difficult than when the decision was easy, those in the difficult decision conditions exhibited attitude trajectories that were less patterned (having higher Lyapunov exponents) than the attitude trajectories of those in the easy decision conditions.

The results from the McGreevy (1996) experiment were different. These results showed no significant effects of any of our independent variables on the Lyapunov exponents of the attitude trajectories. However, when we enter the participants' assessments of how careful they were as a covariate and also have it interact with our independent variables, several highly significant ($p < .01$) effects are found. The trajectories of those with high manipulated need for closure have higher Lyapunov exponents than do those with low manipulated need for closure. There is a significant interaction between decision difficulty and manipulated need for closure, such that the trajectories of those with an easy decision but low manipulated need for closure have relatively low Lyapunov exponents, whereas those with an easy decision but high manipulated need for closure have relatively high Lyapunov exponents. There are also several significant interactions that are not easily interpreted.

CONTINUOUS VERSUS DICHOTOMOUS DECISIONS

Some decisions require a choice between two opposing alternatives (e.g., which of two candidates to choose), whereas others allow for the possibility of a compromise between them. Some decisions, in fact, allow for a nearly continuous range of possible outcomes (e.g., the amount of money to contribute to an organization). This distinction, the *discreteness* of the decision outcome, may affect oscillations.

Suppose that the balance of attitudinal forces causes the decider to be uncomfortable with either end point of the set of decisional choice alternatives and to prefer some compromise. If the decision is continuous, this equilibrium location is a viable decision. However, if the decision is dichotomous, any such compromise is an impossibility. Thus, with dichotomous decisions, for oscillations to die down, it is not sufficient that the individual settle down at the position where the cognitive forces balance. It may also be necessary that the strength of these forces be *altered* so that one decisional end point can become the equilibrium location. The preceding discussion suggests the following hypothesis:

> *Hypothesis 11:* Difficult dichotomous decisions are likely to sustain more oscillations and take longer than are continuous decisions.

This prediction may be investigated by employing the data summarized in Table 2.1. We have identified two independent variables that should affect oscillation. One is the importance of the decision to the respondent; the other is the difficulty of the decision. Among all of the oscillation studies, the one in which the decision is probably most important to the respondents is the tuition study. This issue affects the respondents in a way that none of the others affects them. On the other hand, the most difficult decisions were probably those admissions decisions that were designed to be difficult. In these decisions, the respondents truly were pulled in both directions. The tuition study allows a continuous outcome, whereas the admission decisions requires a dichotomous choice.

In Table 2.1, we see that the continuous decisions have a smaller mean time of decision and fewer changes than do the difficult dichotomous ones. But we also see that the continuous decisions and the easy dichotomous ones do not differ in the number of oscillations. The two easy dichotomous decisions, however, took less time than the continuous ones. Moreover, because the discreteness of the decisions is confounded with decision difficulty, we cannot reach any conclusions about whether continuous decisions produce fewer oscillations than dichotomous ones.

LENGTH OF DECISION AND RELIABILITY

At the beginning of this chapter, we said that studying oscillations might tell us how long we need to wait for the attitude to reach equilibrium. At equilibrium, an attitude should be stable and its measurement should be reliable. Table 2.1 provides some useful information on this issue. Looking at decision time, across all studies it seems that even in the easiest decision, if we want at least 75% of the respondents to reach a decision that they consider complete, we need to wait at least 36 seconds. This time period is a slight overestimate of how long the participants oscillate because participants usually waited several seconds after reaching their final position before declaring themselves done. However, it indicates that when people are creating an attitude response online (rather than retrieving a rating stored in memory), it takes more time to do so than an attitude survey typically allows.

CONCLUSION AND FUTURE RESEARCH

Clearly, oscillation occurs (especially for difficult decisions) and exhibits a systematic relation to theoretically relevant independent and dependent variables. Evidence indicates that attitude trajectories are not simple sinusoids. This finding suggests that we need to supplement our oscillation model with theory based on consideration of conscious cognition. Results also suggest that the attitude change process is more complex than current models imply.

Conclusions from our online investigations are based on two assumptions. First, the motion of the computer mouse represents true cognitive motion (i.e., attitude or belief change). Second, the attitudinal position indicated by the mouse is the position the respondent would take if required to make a final decision at that moment.

We have seen evidence that the first assumption is not always met. Trajectories sometimes contain vibrations and spikes that look like random motion. However, we have corrected for this apparent noise by not counting these motions as true change. We also have seen that our independent variables have a different effect on the trajectories created while people are reading a message as compared to their post-reading trajectories. We suggest that people may sometimes forget to move the mouse while they are reading. If so, the trajectory of mouse movement that is created while reading does not fully reflect the cognitive changes. This point merits further research.

At first glance, it might appear that if the first assumption (i.e., that the recorded motion of the mouse is true change) is valid, then the second one (i.e., that the position at any instant represents the decision at that instant) must also be valid. However, rather than being what the participant would choose if forced to decide, the mouse motion may be the cognitive equivalent of "trying on" a position or decision to see whether it "fits."

To resolve this question, we propose the following experiment. One could, at a predetermined time, interrupt the participants while they are thinking and moving the mouse. (Participants would be randomly assigned to different interruption times.) One could then ask for a paper-and-pencil response, allowing the participants different amounts of time to think before responding. A finding that the correlation between the final mouse position and the paper-and-pencil rating is much higher when participants are required to respond immediately than when they are given more time to think would support our assumption that the mouse position is, in fact, the choice the participant would make at that point.

Future research should also focus on a deeper understanding of the relationship among the many variables responsible for oscillation in attitudes and beliefs. In addition, we want to resolve some confusing findings regarding distraction. Distraction sometimes slows cognitive processing, and at other times it apparently creates a need to finish more quickly, speeding up the decision process and reducing oscillation. Future research should further examine the relationship among variables such as decision time, the number of thoughts, the number of changes in direction, and the amplitude of the oscillation. Results from our research provide exciting evidence regarding differences in the types of cognitive processing that occur (a) while individuals receive a message and (b) while individuals consider the information contained in the message. A closer examination of these subprocesses, including how the different types of processing affect the outcome of persuasive messages, will lead to a clearer understanding of the entire attitude change process.

A second set of issues relates to interactions involving the message receipt phase of cognitive processing. McGreevy (1996) found that in the post-message phase, those faced with a difficult decision oscillated more than did those faced with an easy decision. She also found that those with a low need for closure oscillated more than did those with a high need for closure. Neither of those findings was surprising. What was surprising, however, was that while reading the message, both of these findings were reversed. We have suggested that perhaps those dealing with the difficult decision were so absorbed in reading that they forgot to move the mouse. But why did they show this effect only in the message-reading phase and not in the post-message phase? Research and theory are needed to investigate this question.

Furthermore, why does need for closure play such a different role in the two phases? Recall that during the message receipt phase, individuals with a high need for closure have greater oscillation. What is the link between need for closure, speed of message processing, and oscillation? Do those with a high need for closure process messages more thoroughly? What are the characteristics of the message on which oscillation and speed of processing depend?

The Lyapunov exponent indicates that attitude trajectories that we observed are rather chaotic, suggesting that Dewey (1991) may be correct. We found some very interesting interactions involving the Lyapunov exponents. But although several experimental variables clearly have a substantial effect on these exponents, we currently lack a theory that can make sense of these results.

We should be engaged in theory building from several directions. First, it appears that the process of decision making and attitude change may be best described by the mathe-matics of nonlinear dynamics and chaos. Understanding this mathematics offers the possibility of making explicit the links between the psychological forces and the attitudinal trajectory.

Second, we should improve our understanding of how various features of the trajectory lead to higher versus lower Lyapunov exponents. Does the total number of changes of directions have an effect? Does the speed at which the changes in direction take place make a difference? How do changes in the amplitude and frequency affect the Lyapunov exponent?

Once we investigate these issues, we may be better able to understand how various psychological and communication variables influence the decision trajectory. If we can use this information to predict the effects of certain theoretically relevant independent variables, we will be better able to understand and explain the cognitive processes at work.

NOTES

1. The equilibrium predictions of this model are isomorphic with those of an information integration model we have used (see Fink, Kaplowitz, & Bauer, 1983; Kaplowitz, Fink, Armstrong, & Bauer, 1986; Kaplowitz & Fink, 1991). These models, in turn, have been based on earlier ones proposed by Anderson (1981), Anderson and Hovland (1957), and Saltiel and Woelfel (1975). In the Information Integration Model, the weight of the initial attitude is analogous to the anchoring linkage, and the weight of the message position is analogous to the message linkage. Equation (2) is actually a special case of a more general equation proposed by Kaplowitz and Fink (1992, p. 353).

2. An alternative would be to consider the amplitude to be zero in those cases without any changes in direction. However, if this were done, the Pearson correlation between amplitude and the number of changes would exceed .80, and it would

then not be possible to disentangle the effects of our predictors on amplitude and frequency.

3. Subsequent analysis of the data suggests that distraction led to thoughts that were more concrete and sequential.

4. Statistical analysis within the linear model requires that residuals be normal and homoscedastic. Although these methods are robust with respect to modest violations of these assumptions, in many cases our data indicated gross violations (e.g., large positive skews). Where this was the case, the dependent variable was logarithmically transformed prior to analysis.

REFERENCES

Abelson, R. P., & Levi, A. (1985). Decision making and decision theory. In G. Lindzey & E. Aronson (Eds.), *The handbook of social psychology* (3rd ed., Vol. 1, pp. 231-309). New York: Random House.

Anderson, J. R. (1983). *The architecture of cognition*. Cambridge, MA: Harvard University Press.

Anderson, N. H. (1981). Integration theory applied to cognitive responses and attitudes. In R. E. Petty, T. M. Ostrom, & T. C. Brock (Eds.), *Cognitive responses in persuasion* (pp. 361-397). Hillsdale, NJ: Lawrence Erlbaum.

Anderson, N. H., & Hovland, C. (1957). The representation of order effects in communication research. In C. Hovland (Ed.), *The order of presentation in persuasion* (pp. 158-169). New Haven, CT: Yale University Press.

Aronson, E., Turner, J. A., & Carlsmith, J. M. (1963). Communicator credibility and communication discrepancy as determinants of opinion change. *Journal of Abnormal and Social Psychology, 67,* 31-36.

Bargh, J. A., Chaiken, S., Govender, R., & Pratto, F. (1992). The generality of the automatic attitude-activation effect. *Journal of Personality and Social Psychology, 62,* 892-912.

Barnett, G. A., & Kincaid, D. L. (1983). A mathematical theory of convergence. In W. B. Gudykunst (Ed.), *Intercultural communication theory: Current perspectives* (pp. 171-194). Beverly Hills, CA: Sage.

Bassili, J. N. (1989). *On-line cognition in person perception.* Hillsdale, NJ: Lawrence Erlbaum.

Bobo, L., & Kluegel, J. R. (1991, August). *Modern American prejudice: Stereotypes, social distance, and perceptions of discrimination towards Blacks, Hispanics, and Asians.* Paper presented at the meeting of the American Sociological Association, Cincinnati, OH.

Bornstein, R. F., & Pittman, T. S. (Eds.). (1992). *Perception without awareness: Cognitive, clinical, and social perspectives.* New York: Guilford.

Brehm, S. S., & Brehm, J. W. (1981). *Psychological reactance: A theory of freedom and control.* New York: Academic Press.

Bruss, E. (1975). Beggars can't be choosers: The case of the indecisive woman. In M. Black (Ed.), *Problems of choice and decision* (pp. 550-577). Ithaca, NY: Cornell University Program on Science, Technology, and Society.

Casti, J. L., & Karlqvist, A. (Eds.). (1991). *Beyond belief: Randomness, prediction, and explanation in science.* Boca Raton, FL: CRC.

Chaiken, S., Liberman, A., & Eagly, A. H. (1989). Heuristic and systematic information processing within and beyond the persuasion context. In J. S. Uleman & J. A. Bargh (Eds.), *Unintended thought* (pp. 212-253). New York: Guilford.

Dewey, J. (1991). *How we think.* Lexington, MA: D. C. Heath.

Ebbinghaus, H. E. (1964). *Memory: A contribution to experimental psychology.* New York: Dover.

Fazio, R. H. (1989). On the power and functionality of attitudes: The role of accessibility. In A. R. Pratkanis, S. J. Breckler, & A. G. Greenwald (Eds.), *Attitude structure and function* (pp. 153-179). Hillsdale, NJ: Lawrence Erlbaum.

Festinger, L. (1957). *A theory of cognitive dissonance.* Stanford, CA: Stanford University Press.

Fink, E. L., & Kaplowitz, S. A. (1993). Oscillation in beliefs and cognitive networks. In G. A. Barnett & W. Richards (Eds.), *Progress in communication sciences* (Vol. 12, pp. 247-272). Norwood, NJ: Ablex.

Fink, E. L., Kaplowitz, S. A., & Bauer, C. L. (1983). Positional discrepancy, psychological discrepancy, and attitude change: Experimental tests of some mathematical models. *Communication Monographs, 50,* 413-430.

Fink, E. L., Kaplowitz, S. A., & Wang, M-L. (1994, August). *The cognitive effects of stereotype modification.* Paper presented at the meeting of the Association for Education in Journalism and Mass Communication, Atlanta, GA.

Fink, E. L., Monahan, J. L., & Kaplowitz, S. A. (1989). A spatial model of the mere exposure effect. *Communication Research, 16,* 746-769.

Gilbert, D. T., Krull, D. S., & Malone, P. S. (1990). Unbelieving the unbelievable: Some problems with the rejection of false information. *Journal of Personality and Social Psychology, 59,* 601-613.

Goode, W. J. (1960). A theory of role strain. *American Sociological Review, 25,* 483-496.

Hastie, R., & Park, B. (1986). The relationship between memory and judgement depends on whether the judgement task is memory-based or on-line. *Psychological Review, 93,* 258-268.

Hastie, R., & Pennington, N. (1989). Notes on the distinction between memory-based versus on-line judgements. In J. N. Bassili (Ed.), *On-line cognition in person perception* (pp. 1-17). Hillsdale, NJ: Lawrence Erlbaum.

Heider, F. (1958). *The psychology of interpersonal relations.* New York: John Wiley.

Heise, D. R. (1969). Separating reliability and stability in test-retest correlation. *American Sociological Review, 34,* 93-101.

Jackman, M. R., & Senter, M. S. (1983). Different, therefore unequal: Beliefs about trait differences between groups of unequal status. In D. J. Treiman & R. V. Robinson (Eds.), *Research in social stratification and mobility* (Vol. 2, pp. 309-335). Greenwich, CT: JAI.

Janis, I. L., & Mann, L. (1977). *Decision making: A psychological analysis of conflict, choice, and commitment.* New York: Free Press.

Johnson, B. T., & Eagly, A. H. (1990). The effects of involvement on persuasion: A meta-analysis. *Psychological Bulletin, 106,* 290-314.

Kaplowitz, S. A., & Fink, E. L. (1982). Attitude change and attitudinal trajectories: A dynamic multidimensional theory. In M. Burgoon (Ed.), *Communication yearbook 6* (pp. 364-394). Beverly Hills, CA: Sage.

Kaplowitz, S. A., & Fink, E. L. (1988). A spatial-linkage model of cognitive dynamics. In G. A. Barnett & J. Woelfel (Eds.), *Readings in the Galileo system: Theory, methods, and applications* (pp. 117-146). Dubuque, IA: Kendall/Hunt.

Kaplowitz, S. A., & Fink, E. L., with Mulcrone, J., Atkin, D., & Dabil, S. (1991). Disentangling the effects of discrepant and disconfirming information. *Social Psychology Quarterly, 54,* 191-207.

Kaplowitz, S. A., & Fink, E. L. (1992). Dynamics of attitude change. In R. L. Levine & H. E. Fitzgerald (Eds.), *Analysis of dynamic psychological systems,* Vol. 2: *Methods and applications* (pp. 341-369). New York: Plenum.

Kaplowitz, S. A., & Fink, E. L. (1996). Cybernetics of attitudes and decisions. In J. H. Watt & C. A. VanLear (Eds.), *Dynamic patterns in communication processes* (pp. 277-300). Thousand Oaks, CA: Sage.

Kaplowitz, S. A., Fink, E. L., Armstrong, G. B., & Bauer, C. L. (1986). Message discrepancy and the persistence of attitude change: Implications of an Information Integration Model. *Journal of Experimental Social Psychology, 22,* 507-530.

Kaplowitz, S. A., Fink, E. L., & Bauer, C. L. (1983). A dynamic model of the effect of discrepant information on unidimensional attitude change. *Behavioral Science, 28,* 233-250.

Katz, I. (1981). *Stigma: A social psychological analysis.* Hillsdale, NJ: Lawrence Erlbaum.

Kincaid, D. L., Yum, J. O., Woelfel, J., & Barnett, G. A. (1983). The cultural convergence of Korean immigrants in Hawaii: An empirical test of a mathematical theory. *Quality and Quantity, 18,* 59-78.

Kruglanski, A. W. (1989). *Lay epistemics and human knowledge.* New York: Plenum.

Kruglanski, A. W. (1990). Lay epistemic theory in social psychology. *Psychological Inquiry, 1,* 181-197.

Kruglanski, A. W., & Webster, D. M. (1994). *Motivated closing of the mind: Its cognitive and social effects.* Unpublished manuscript, University of Maryland.

Landman, J. (1993). *Regret: The persistence of the possible.* New York: Oxford University Press.

Latané, B., & Darley, J. M. (1970). *The unresponsive bystander: Why doesn't he help?* New York: Appleton-Century-Crofts.

Lewin, K. (1951). *Field theory in social science.* New York: Harper & Brothers.

Liberman, A., & Chaiken, S. (1991). Value conflict and thought-induced attitude change. *Journal of Experimental Social Psychology, 27,* 203-216.

Lorenz, K. (1977). *Behind the mirror.* New York: Harcourt Brace Jovanovich.

McGreevy, S. E. (1996). *Cognitive oscillations, need for closure, and the social inference process: The roles of cognition and motivation during decision making.* Unpublished doctoral dissertation, University of Maryland.

McGuire, W. J. (1989). Individual attitudes and attitude systems. In A. R. Pratkanis, S. J. Breckler, & A. G. Greenwald (Eds.), *Attitude structure and function* (pp. 37-69). Hillsdale, NJ: Lawrence Erlbaum.

Millar, M. G., & Tesser, A. (1986). Thought induced attitude change: The effects of schema structure and commitment. *Journal of Personality and Social Psychology, 51,* 259-269.

Neuendorf, K. S., Kaplowitz, S. A., Fink, E. L., & Armstrong, G. B. (1986). Assessment of the use of self-referential concepts for the measurement of cognition and affect. In M. McLaughlin (Ed.), *Communication Yearbook 10* (pp. 183-199). Beverly Hills, CA: Sage.

Petty, R. E., & Cacioppo, J. T. (1986). *Communication and persuasion: Central and peripheral routes to attitude change.* New York: Springer-Verlag.

Petty, R. E., Ostrom, T. M., & Brock, T. C. (Eds.). (1981). *Cognitive responses in persuasion.* Hillsdale, NJ: Lawrence Erlbaum.

Petty, R. E., Wells, G. L., & Brock, T. C. (1976). Distraction can enhance or reduce yielding to propaganda: Thought disruption vs. effort justification. *Journal of Personality and Social Psychology, 34,* 874-884.

Poole, M. S., & Hunter, J. E. (1979). Change in hierarchical systems of attitudes. In D. Nimmo (Ed.), *Communication Yearbook 3* (pp. 157-176). New Brunswick, NJ: Transaction Books.

Poole, M. S., & Hunter, J. E. (1980). Behavior and hierarchies of attitudes: A deterministic model. In D. P. Cushman & R. D. McPhee (Eds.), *Message-attitude-behavior relationships: Theory, methodology, and application* (pp. 245-271). New York: Academic Press.

Saltiel, J., & Woelfel, J. (1975). Inertia in cognitive processes: The role of accumulated information in attitude change. *Human Communication Research, 1,* 333-344.

Sprott, J. C., & Rowlands, G. (1992). *Physics academic software user's manual: Chaos data analyzer.* New York: American Institute of Physics.

Tetlock. P. E. (1983a). Accountability and complexity of thought. *Journal of Personality and Social Psychology, 45,* 74-83.

Tetlock. P. E. (1983b). Cognitive style and political ideology. *Journal of Personality and Social Psychology, 45,* 118-126.

Tversky, A., & Kahneman, D. (1974). Judgment under uncertainty: Heuristics and biases. *Science, 185,* 1124-1131.

Tversky, A., & Shafir, E. (1992). Choice under conflict: The dynamics of deferred decision. *Psychological Science, 3,* 358-361.

Vallacher, R. R., Nowak, A., & Kaufman, J. (1994). Intrinsic dynamics of social judgment. *Journal of Personality and Social Psychology, 67,* 20-34.

Walster, E. (1964). The temporal sequence of postdecision processes. In L. Festinger (Ed.), *Conflict, decision, and dissonance* (pp. 112-128). Stanford, CA: Stanford University Press.

Wang, M-L. T. (1993). *The cognitive effects of stereotype modification.* Unpublished doctoral dissertation, University of Maryland.

Webster, D. M., & Kruglanski, A. W. (1994). Individual differences in need for cognitive closure. *Journal of Personality and Social Psychology, 67,* 1049-1062.

Wegner, D. M. (1989). *White bears and other unwanted thoughts.* New York: Penguin.

Wilder, D. A. (1978). Reduction of intergroup discrimination through individuation of the outgroup. *Journal of Personality and Social Psychology, 36,* 1361-1374.

Wilder, D. A. (1981). Perceiving persons as a group: Categorization and intergroup relations. In D. L. Hamilton (Ed.), *Cognitive processes in stereotyping and intergroup behavior* (pp. 213-253). Hillsdale, NJ: Lawrence Erlbaum.

Woelfel, J., & Fink, E. L. (1980). *The measurement of communication processes: Galileo theory and method.* New York: Academic Press.

3

Attitude Accessibility and Persuasion
The Quick and the Strong

DAVID R. ROSKOS-EWOLDSEN
LAURA ARPAN-RALSTIN
JAMES ST. PIERRE

The study of attitudes has one of the longest and richest traditions in the social sciences. Attitudes have been a focus of study within psychology beginning during the 1920s (Eagly & Chaiken, 1993). Since that time, many disciplines have joined in the study of attitudes and persuasion, including political science, marketing, communication studies, and advertising. Interestingly, the concept of "attitude" has undergone little revision since the advent of this area of study. Research on attitudes continues to focus on evaluative responses directed toward some object or idea.

Traditionally, research on social influence has focused either on attitude formation or on changing the extremity of people's attitudes. The assumption is that extreme attitudes are stronger in the sense that they are more persistent and will be more predictive of future behavior. Of course, refinements in our understanding of attitudes continue to occur, and these refinements should influence how we theorize about social influence. For example,

recent research on attitude accessibility is advancing our understanding of how attitudes function (Fazio, 1989; Roskos-Ewoldsen, 1997). This research demonstrates that accessible attitudes play a central role in how social influence messages are processed and the likely impact of these messages (Roskos-Ewoldsen, 1997). The research on attitude accessibility suggests that if communication scholars are interested in more than changing the evaluative reaction to an object, we need to begin to understand not only how persuasion influences attitude extremity but also how persuasion influences attitude accessibility. In terms of pragmatic outcomes (e.g., changing behaviors, creating resistant attitudes), increasing attitude accessibility is probably more important than changing someone's evaluative response to an object (Dillard, 1993).

In this chapter, we discuss the implications of research on attitude accessibility for our understanding of persuasion. First, the model of attitudes on which this research is based is presented. The second section considers the impact of accessible attitudes on the processing of persuasive messages. The third section addresses mechanisms by which persuasive messages might affect attitude accessibility. The fourth section focuses on belief accessibility and attitude formation. Finally, we provide some speculations concerning the future direction of research on attitude accessibility and persuasion.

ATTITUDE ACCESSIBILITY

Simply put, when a person has an accessible attitude, that attitude is quickly and relatively effortlessly retrieved from memory when the person is exposed to the corresponding attitude object. Attitudes can range from being automatically accessible from memory to being extremely low in accessibility. Typically, attitude accessibility is measured by the length of time it takes someone to evaluate an attitude object on its presentation (Fazio, 1990b). The faster someone can indicate that he or she likes or dislikes the attitude object, the more accessible the attitude is from memory.

To understand attitude accessibility, it is first necessary to think of human memory as a highly integrated network of concepts, attributes, and beliefs. In a network model of memory (see Anderson, 1990; Greene, 1984; Smith, 1994),[1] each piece of acquired information is represented in memory as a node. Nodes that are similar in some way are connected by associative pathways. Inactive nodes can be activated by exposure to information in the environment or by thoughts about associated pieces of information. The associative pathways are what allow the activation of a concept to spread to other nodes. Within a network model, attitudes can be viewed as associations in memory between the attitude object and one's evaluation of the object.

In addition, network models assume that the strength of the connection between nodes can vary such that certain nodes are connected by stronger pathways (Anderson, 1990). The strength of the association between an object and the attitude toward that object determines the accessibility of the attitude toward that object, with stronger associations resulting in higher levels of attitude accessibility. As stated earlier, attitudes that are quickly retrieved from memory are said to be highly accessible, whereas attitudes that are difficult to retrieve are low in accessibility.

THE INFLUENCE OF ATTITUDE ACCESSIBILITY ON THE PERSUASION PROCESS

Attitude accessibility can influence several steps within the persuasion process, most notably the orienting of attention to a message, how extensively a message is processed, whether the message is processed in a biased manner, and the resulting behavior (which can be either deliberative or spontaneous). Figure 3.1 focuses on the consequences of accessible attitudes. Once an accessible attitude is developed, the attitude influences how attention is allocated, how information is interpreted, how extensively people process information, and how people act (Fazio, 1986; Roskos-Ewoldsen, 1997).

Influence of Attitude Accessibility on Attention

As we move through the world, there are countless items in the environment competing for our attention. What influences which of the boundless number of social stimuli attracts

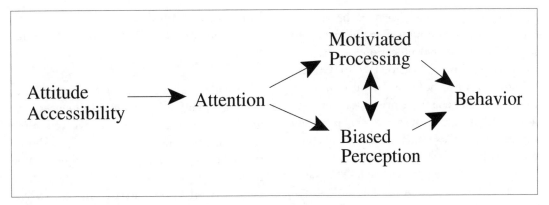

Figure 3.1. A Model of the Influences of Accessible Attitudes

our attention? Obviously, numerous factors influence what we attend to in the environment. Basic considerations such as whether the stimuli is vivid or moving influence whether our attention is drawn to the stimuli. Likewise, what attracts our attention depends on our current goals. In addition, recent research suggests that our attitudes can influence what we attend to in the environment (Fazio, Roskos-Ewoldsen, & Powell, 1994; Roskos-Ewoldsen & Fazio, 1992b).

A functional system should, through some mechanism, direct its attention to stimuli that it likes or dislikes (Roskos-Ewoldsen & Fazio, 1992b). Thus, attitudes could serve an orienting function because they direct attention to attitude-evoking objects. An important question concerns whether *all* attitudes serve an orienting function. Recent models of affect propose that affective responses may precede cognitive responses (e.g., Kitayama & Howard, 1994; Zajonc, 1980), in which case the attitude toward an object may be activated from memory at a very early stage in the processing of the visual field. Once the attitude is elicited, attention may be oriented to the attitude-eliciting object so that ultimately the stimulus receives sufficient processing for the individual to report having noticed the presence of the object. Thus, attitudes that are acti-

vated from memory could play a role in the allocation of attention, thus serving the orienting function. Research has found that accessible attitudes do, in fact, serve an orienting function. In a series of four experiments, Roskos-Ewoldsen and Fazio (1992b) demonstrated that people are more likely to orient their attention to an object if they have an accessible attitude toward that object.

The finding that objects toward which an individual has accessible attitudes attract that individual's attention has important implications for persuasion research. We are constantly bombarded by numerous persuasive messages. Obviously, if a persuasive message is going to influence our attitudes, we must attend to that message at some level. Little research has been conducted on why our attention is attracted to certain messages and not to others. The Roskos-Ewoldsen and Fazio (1992b) research on the orienting function of attitudes indicates that as the accessibility of an individual's attitude toward the topic of a message increases, there should be a corresponding increase in the likelihood that the person's attention will be attracted to the message.

An interesting ramification of the finding that accessible attitudes serve an orienting function is that attitudes have to be activated, at some level, extremely early in the processing of incoming stimuli if attitudes are going to influence the allocation of attention (Roskos-Ewoldsen & Fazio, 1992b). One implication of this finding is that attitudes may influence other cognitive processes that occur at the early stages of the processing of incoming stimuli. For example, accessible attitudes could influence basic processes such as how incoming stimuli are categorized. One characteristic of social situations is that most stimuli are open to a multitude of classifications. When interacting with a person, do we pay attention to that person's race, gender, age, physical characteristics, and so forth? Smith, Fazio, and Cejka (1996) established that the accessibility of our attitudes toward the various possible categorizations of an object ultimately influence how the object is categorized and perceived. Likewise, Fazio and Dunton (1997) found that as the accessibility of participants' attitudes toward race increased, the more likely they were to categorize novel people in terms of race (see also Fazio, 2000; Fazio & Towles-Schwen, 1999).

At one level, the research on the influence of attitude accessibility on categorization seems far removed from the interests of most persuasion scholars. But we believe that this finding does have important implications for persuasion scholars. To illustrate, accessible attitudes bias how information is processed, and the finding that accessible attitudes influence how information is categorized provides an explanatory mechanism for *how* accessible attitudes influence the interpretation of information. Accessible attitudes influence how the ambiguous stimuli are categorized and what they come to mean. Furthermore, the influence of accessible attitudes on categorization provides a mechanism for explaining how high fear-arousing messages can result in defensive avoidance of information relating to the fear-arousing topic.

Influence of Attitude Accessibility on the Elaborative Processing of Persuasive Messages

Attitude accessibility not only influences the orienting of attention but also influences how much attention and effort are involved in the processing of a message. Research has shown that when a person has an accessible attitude toward an issue, he or she will expend more cognitive effort in interpreting a message about that issue (Fabrigar, Priester, Petty, & Wegener, 1998; Wu & Shaffer, 1987). For example, individuals with accessible attitudes toward vegetarianism were more sensitive to variations in the strength of the arguments in a pro-vegetarian message (Fabrigar et al., 1998). Sensitivity to the strength of the arguments that appear in a message has been interpreted as indicative of elaborative message processing (Petty & Cacioppo, 1986; Petty & Wegener, 1998).

The accessibility of attitudes toward the source of a message has also been shown to affect message elaboration. A series of experiments demonstrated that message recipients with more accessible attitudes toward the *source* of a message were more persuaded by a message attributed to the source than were participants with less accessible evaluations of the source (Roskos-Ewoldsen & Fazio, 1992a). Several explanations were proposed for the finding that increases in the accessibility of a person's attitude toward the source of a message could influence persuasion. For example, it is possible that as the accessibility of the attitude toward the source increased, there was a corresponding increase in the likelihood that a likeability heuristic was used when judging the message (Eagly & Chaiken, 1993). A second possibility is that the accessibility of the attitude toward the source resulted in biased processing of a message attributed to that source. A final possibility is that the activation of the attitude toward the source of the message resulted in an attitudinal reaction that acted as a marker that this is an important topic (Krosnick, 1989; Lavine, Sullivan, Borgida, & Thomsen, 1996; Roese & Olson, 1994) that motivated the person to centrally process the message. Recently, Roskos-Ewoldsen, Bichsel, and Hoffman (2002) found support for the third explanation: People with more accessible attitudes toward the source of a message were more likely to systematically process a message attributed to that source. Hence, an affective reaction to the topic of the message, or any significant feature of that message, should lead to a judgment that this is an important message and motivate systematic processing of the message content.

Traditionally, theorizing on the effect of attitudes on the processing of persuasive messages has focused on how attitudes influence perceptions of persuasive messages (Chaiken, Liberman, & Eagly, 1989; Eagly & Chaiken, 1993; Fazio & Williams, 1986; Houston & Fazio, 1989; Lord, Ross, & Lepper, 1979; Petty & Cacioppo, 1986; Sherif & Sherif, 1967). Within this line of theorizing, attitudes are hypothesized to bias how messages are perceived. Critically, according to these traditional approaches, the attitude serves as a lens that biases how the message is perceived. However, the research by Roskos-Ewoldsen et al. (2002) suggests that attitudes can also influence the processing of persuasive messages by operating as *information* that these are important messages. In the Roskos-Ewoldsen et al. research, the attitude toward the source did not result in biased processing of the message. Rather, the accessible attitude toward the source of the message acted as a piece of information that this is an important message (see also Fabrigar et al., 1998; Roese & Olson, 1994). This *attitude-as-information* explanation is similar to recent research and theorizing on the effects of mood on judgment

that has found that mood can both act as information that influences people's judgments and bias how information is interpreted (Clore, 1992).

The results of the experiments on the effects of the accessibility of attitudes toward the topic or source of the message are important because they highlight additional ways in which people can be motivated to centrally process a message. The majority of earlier research conducted within dual process frameworks such as the Elaboration Likelihood Model and the Heuristic-Systematic Model (Chaiken et al., 1989; Eagly & Chaiken, 1993; Petty & Cacioppo, 1986; Petty & Wegener, 1998) has manipulated motivation to process a message by presenting a message that was personally relevant to the message recipients. The personal relevance of the topic should result in judgments by message recipients that this is an important issue toward which they need to hold a correct attitude. However, the research on attitude accessibility and elaborative message processing provides evidence that attitude accessibility has an important influence on the processing of persuasive messages. Individuals will allocate more attention to the processing of the persuasive message when the activation of an accessible attitude acts as a marker that this is an important message.

The Influence of Accessible Attitudes on the Biased Perception of Persuasive Messages

Early attitude scholars hypothesized that attitudes can guide how we understand our social world (Allport, 1935; Katz, 1960; Smith, Bruner, & White, 1956). In a classic illustration of the influence of attitudes on perception, Lord et al. (1979) demonstrated that as attitude extremity increased, so did the magnitude of biased interpretations of attitudinally relevant information. Given the influence of accessible attitudes on how information is categorized (Fazio & Dunton, 1997; Smith et al., 1996), it makes sense that attitudes that are more accessible from memory would influence how information is interpreted and could lead to more biased processing of information. Initial support for the accessibility hypothesis was found in a study focusing on people's attitudes toward the two presidential candidates (Ronald Reagan and Walter Mondale) in the 1984 election (Fazio & Williams, 1986). Of concern was whether people's attitudes influenced their perception of who won the first presidential and vice-presidential (George Bush vs. Geraldine Ferraro) debates. As one might expect, people who liked Reagan perceived Reagan and Bush as winning their respective debates, and people who liked Mondale perceived Mondale and Ferraro as winning their respective debates. More important, the study found that as attitude accessibility increased, individuals' perception of who won the debates was increasingly biased by their attitudes. Interestingly, when it was more difficult to determine a clear winner for the debate (as it was for the vice-presidential debate), attitude accessibility had a significantly greater biasing effect on perceptions of the messages (see also Fazio et al., 1994; Houston & Fazio, 1989).

At this point in time, the research on attitude accessibility suggests two conclusions about the effects of accessible attitudes on information processing. First, accessible attitudes bias information processing. Second, accessible attitudes motivate critical processing of information. More recent research has also suggested that when people are motivated, they can, but do not necessarily, override the biasing effects of accessible attitudes (Schuette & Fazio, 1995). The question is how accessible attitudes can bias information processing if activation of attitudes motivates critical processing and critical processing can overcome the effects of accessible attitudes. One possibility is that the nature of the motivation that is evoked by the activation of an accessible attitude is different from the motivation that overrides the biasing effects of accessible attitudes. The activation of an accessible attitude probably affects motivation to process a message because the activation of the attitude indicates that this topic is important to the individual. However, Schuette and Fazio (1995) created a motivation for research participants *to be accurate* that created a strong impression management component that is probably not involved when people are motivated to process a message because of personal topic importance.

Recent research has identified one important caveat to the research on the biasing effects of accessible attitudes on the processing of messages. DeBono, Green, Shair, and Benson (1995) found that accessible attitudes of low self-monitors biased how they processed a message. However, no relationship was found between attitude accessibility and biased information processing in high self-monitors. This finding suggests that not only must the attitude be accessible from memory, but the person must feel that the attitude is relevant to processing the message (see also DeBono & Snyder, 1995). Low self-monitors are more likely to feel that their attitudes are relevant when making decisions (Snyder & Kendzierski, 1982). However, high self-monitors are less likely to rely on their attitudes and are more likely to use situational cues in making decisions.

The research on self-monitoring and attitude accessibility provides a hint at how to get around one problem that accessible attitudes pose to potential persuaders. Highly accessible attitudes may put severe constraints on the effectiveness of counterattitudinal persuasive campaigns (Sherman, 1987) because individuals with highly accessible attitudes are likely to process information in a biased manner. However, attempting to change highly accessible attitudes might not be as hopeless as the studies on attitude accessibility and biased information processing suggest. First, accessible attitudes are more likely to result in biased processing when the information is ambiguous and open to multiple interpretations. When information is less ambiguous, accessible attitudes exert proportionately less influence on how the information is interpreted. In addition, when people are highly motivated and given sufficient opportunity, they can "override" the effects of highly accessible attitudes and consider information in a less theory-driven manner (Fazio, 1990a; Sanbonmatsu & Fazio, 1990; Schuette & Fazio, 1995). Third, the finding that high self-monitors are not biased by accessible attitudes suggests that if the attitude is deemed not to be relevant to the current judgments, then the accessible attitude should not result in biased information processing.

Attitude Accessibility and the Consequences of Persuasive Messages: The Attitude-Behavior Relationship

Perhaps the most exciting aspect of research on attitude accessibility is the part this research played in the renewed examination of the attitude-behavior relationship. A major impetus for the study of attitudes was the axiomatic assumption that attitudes predicted behavior (see most notably Allport, 1935; Doob, 1947). However, the apparent inability to find a strong relationship between attitudes and behavior almost led to the demise of attitude research during the early 1970s (Larson & Sanders, 1975; Wicker, 1969). Fortunately, the resurgence of attitude-behavior research

during the 1970s and 1980s turned from examining whether attitudes always predict behavior to examining the factors, such as accessibility, that influence *when* and *how* attitudes predict behavior (Fazio & Roskos-Ewoldsen, 1994; Zanna & Fazio, 1982). Indeed, a number of studies have found that highly accessible attitudes are more likely to predict behavior than are less accessible attitudes (for general reviews, see Fazio, 1986; Fazio & Roskos-Ewoldsen, 1994; Roskos-Ewoldsen, 1997). The basic idea is that an attitude can affect behavior only if the attitude has been activated from memory. Hence, attitudes that are more accessible from memory are more likely to be activated and influence the behavioral process.

Accessibility is a particularly important consideration when examining behavior in social situations. Typically, a social situation is characterized by ambiguity because there are many potential interpretations of the situation (Smith et al., 1996). How the situation is perceived plays an integral role in how people respond to that situation (Latane & Darley, 1970). Consequently, any factor biasing how the situation is interpreted should influence how the individual responds to the situation. As discussed earlier, attitudes influence the categorization and interpretation of ambiguous information (Fazio et al., 1994; Fazio & Towles-Schwen, 1999; Fazio & Williams, 1986; Houston & Fazio, 1989; Smith et al., 1996). This biased interpretation allows attitudes to affect how persons respond to situational cues. Once the interpretation of the situation is colored by attitudes, the behavior within the situation is likely to be consistent with the attitude(s) that influenced the interpretation of that situation. However, in those situations where the individual does not have an accessible attitude from memory, salient features of the situations are more likely to influence behavior (Fazio, Powell, & Williams, 1989).

This basic idea underlies the process model of the attitude-behavior relationship (Fazio, 1986). When an attitude toward some object is activated from memory, that object attracts attention. Once attention is attracted to that object, the attitude influences the perceptions of the attitude object. Thus, attitudes influence behavior because attitudes have the potential to bias how a situation is perceived. Of course, other factors influence both how the situation is defined and behavior within that situation.

To fully understand how attitudes and behavior are related, it is important to note that human behavior is influenced by both reflective introspection and more spontaneous cognitive processes (e.g., heuristic or theory-driven processing). To reflect the different antecedents of spontaneous and reflective social behavior, the MODE (Motivation and Opportunity as DEterminants of processing) model of attitudes was developed (Fazio, 1990a; Sanbonmatsu & Fazio, 1990). The MODE model maintains that whether an individual's social behavior is deliberative or spontaneous depends on whether that person is motivated and has the opportunity to deliberate before acting. When people are highly motivated and are given sufficient opportunity to consider the relevant information, their behavior is more likely to be deliberative. When behavior is deliberative, the MODE model hypothesizes that attitudes are likely to influence behavior through the processes outlined by models such as Fishbein and Ajzen's (1975) theory of reasoned action or Ajzen's (1988) theory of planned behavior. However, when people have low motivation and/or do not have sufficient opportunity to consider the relevant information, their behavior is more likely to be spontaneous and their attitudes should influence their behavior through

the processes outlined by the Fazio (1986) process model.

Interestingly, the attitude-as-information hypothesis suggests that accessible attitudes may influence both spontaneous and deliberative behavior through the two distinct processes outlined by the MODE model. When accessible attitudes result in biased perception, they can influence behavior because the attitude influences the interpretation of the situation as outlined in the Fazio (1986, 1990a) process model. However, when accessible attitudes result in motivated processing, they can influence behavior through more introspective processes, as outlined in Fishbein and Ajzen's (1975) theory of reasoned action. In this manner, accessible attitudes might influence both spontaneous and deliberative behaviors.

FACTORS THAT AFFECT THE ACCESSIBILITY OF ATTITUDES

Changing the accessibility of an attitude can be just as important as, or more important than, changing the actual attitude. This notion is a departure from the traditional emphasis on changing attitude extremity or valence (Dillard, 1993). Unfortunately, despite the large number of studies documenting the functions that accessible attitudes perform, relatively little research has been conducted on ways to increase attitude accessibility (Roskos-Ewoldsen, 1997). Based on the research and theorizing within social and cognitive psychology, Roskos-Ewoldsen (1997) developed a transactive model of attitude accessibility. This model proposes four basic mechanisms by which attitudes become more accessible (see Figure 3.2): expectations, elaboration, recency of attitude activation, and frequency of attitude activation. The following sections review each of these mechanisms for increasing attitude accessibility and dis-

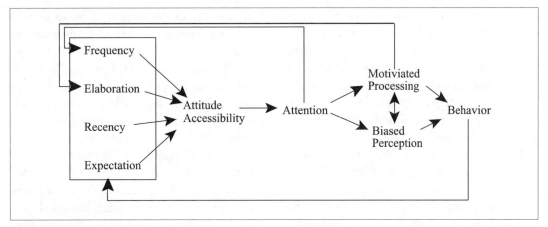

Figure 3.2. The Transactive Model of Attitude Accessibility
SOURCE: Roskos-Ewoldsen (1997).

cuss recent research suggesting that persuasive messages can increase attitude accessibility through these mechanisms.

Expectations

When an individual anticipates the need to evaluate an object in the future, the individual should consolidate or develop an attitude toward that object. Indeed, research has demonstrated that research participants expecting to make attitudinal judgments about a novel object in the future spontaneously formed an attitude toward that object (Fazio, Lenn, & Effrein, 1984). In addition, the attitudes of those students who spontaneously formed attitudes were more accessible than the attitudes of students who had the same experience with the novel object but who did not anticipate a future need for the attitude. Thus, the expectation that one would later "need" an attitude resulted in the spontaneous formation of an attitude, and this attitude will be relatively more accessible from memory.

There has been little research focusing on expectation-based attitude formation and attitude accessibility within a persuasion context.

However, research on comparative advertising suggests at least one situation where expectation-based attitude formation may occur and lead to more accessible attitudes. Comparative advertising involves explicit comparisons of a product to a competitor's product. Yi, Phelps, and Roskos-Ewoldsen (1998) found that comparative advertising increases the accessibility of attitudes toward the target brand of the commercial. In that original study, we speculated that comparative advertising may motivate people to spontaneously form attitudes because of the explicit evaluative comparison of one brand with a successful (and hence probably liked) brand. A follow-up experiment replicated the finding that comparative advertising did increase the accessibility of participants' attitudes toward a novel brand for direct comparative advertisements (e.g., there is an explicit comparison with the market leader) (Motherbaugh, Viosca, Phelps, & Roskos-Ewoldsen, 1999). However, indirect comparative advertisements (e.g., there is a generic comparison with "leading brands") did not increase the accessibility of participants' attitudes toward the novel brand. In addition, the follow-up experiment used a manipulation designed to get participants to consolidate or initially form and store their attitudes in memory (see Fazio et al., 1984). The results of this experiment demonstrate that comparative advertisements do increase attitude accessibility, at least in part, because the expectation of needing the attitude in the future resulted in spontaneous attitude formation.

There is a final point we would like to make about expectation-based accessible attitudes and spontaneous attitude formation. Persuasion research has been criticized because the standard paper-and-pencil attitude measures are insensitive to whether the measured attitude is "real" or simply expressed as a response to an attitude query (Larson & Sanders, 1975). For example, when listening to low involvement persuasive messages, research participants might not form attitudes toward the topic of the message until explicitly asked for attitudinal responses. Understanding when attitudes are spontaneously formed would aid in our understanding of when attitudes are actually consolidated and stored in memory versus when they are responses to a measurement scale. The best technique available to determining whether somebody has already formed an attitude or is reporting a response to an attitude query is to use reaction time measures (see Fazio, 1990b).

Cognitive Elaboration

According to network models of memory discussed earlier, related pieces of information (nodes) in memory are linked by associative pathways. The more nodes to which a given node is connected, the greater the likelihood that node will be activated repeatedly as activation of the related concepts spreads across the associative network of nodes. In addition, the more frequently a node is activated, the more accessible that piece of information becomes.

Systematic or elaborative processing of a message's content has been hypothesized to result in more accessible attitudes from memory (Chaiken et al., 1989; Petty & Cacioppo, 1986; Sherman, 1987) due to the greater amount of cognitive "work" involved in such processing, with the result being better integrated attitudes that are more accessible from memory. In short, elaboration of the message's content paves more associative pathways for the given attitude and makes those pathways linked to the attitude stronger. Kardes (1988) found that when research participants were highly involved *and* the conclusion of advertisement was *implicit,* the resulting attitude was more accessible than in the low involvement conditions or when involvement was high but the conclusion was explicitly provided by the message (see also Stayman & Kardes, 1992). Interestingly, the conclusion of the advertisement was equally accessible from memory in the explicit conclusion conditions and the high involvement/implicit conclusion condition. Thus, it was not the accessibility of knowledge per se that resulted in more accessible attitudes. Rather, the elaborative processing that was required to ascertain the conclusion in the implicit conclusion condition increased the accessibility of the attitude from memory. Consistent with Kardes's (1988) research, Mothersbaugh et al.'s (1999) study of comparative advertising found that participants developed more accessible attitudes toward the novel brand in conditions of high involvement.

In addition, other research has found that attitudes that individuals consider important tend to be more accessible from memory (Krosnick, 1989). This heightened accessibility is probably due to elaboration because, as Krosnick speculated, important attitudes are likely linked to a number of beliefs and attitudes. As a result, the attitudes can be activated via the spread of activation from a number of different associative links. Furthermore, consistent with the attitudes-as-information hypothesis, attitudes can be judged as important *because* they are accessible from memory (Roese & Olson, 1994).

Fear appeals have long been used in persuasive messages in an attempt to scare people into performing adaptive behaviors. Fear appeals is one domain of persuasive appeals where elaborative message processing should increase attitude accessibility (Roskos-Ewoldsen, 1997; Yu & Roskos-Ewoldsen, 1997). Our discussion of fear appeals and attitude accessibility focuses on Witte's (1992, 1994, 1995) Extended Parallel Process Model (EPPM) of fear appeals.

The EPPM maintains that when people receive a fear appeal, they engage in perceived threat appraisal and perceived efficacy appraisal. Perceived threat appraisal involves judging the severity of the danger and one's susceptibility to the danger. Perceived efficacy appraisal incorporates judgments of the efficacy of the proposed response and self-efficacy judgments. If the perceived threat judgment results in an at-risk judgment and the efficacy judgment suggests that the individual can respond to the threat, the individual should be motivated to engage in *danger control processes* that will lead to acceptance and performance of the adaptive behavior to decrease the danger to the self. However, if the person judges the threat as real but does not feel that the proposed action can be effectively carried out, *fear control processes* will result and the individual will be motivated to undertake defensive processes such as avoiding future information on the topic and derogating the source of the information (see the top panel of Figure 3.3 for a simplified version of the EPPM).

We feel that the EPPM could be strengthened by incorporating attitude accessibility into the model. First, like earlier models of fear appeals, the EPPM does not detail the processes by which successful fear appeal messages influence subsequent behavior. Rather, the model simply states that people will be motivated to perform the adaptive behavior. Second, while the EPPM predicts that under certain circumstances avoidance and defensive processing are the likely results of fear appeal messages, the model does not explain the mechanisms by which these defensive processes occur. Basically, the fear response to the message is temporally bounded (e.g., the fear dissipates with time), and the EPPM does not explain future defensive processing after the fear reaction to the original message has faded. Focusing on the impact of fear appeal messages on the accessibility of people's attitudes toward the proposed adaptive behavior and the threat provides the mechanisms by which fear appeal messages influence adaptive behavior and defensive processing.

Incorporating attitude accessibility into the EPPM would provide a mechanism for how fear appeals result in long-term behavior change. First, fear appeal messages may successfully influence behavior because they enhance the accessibility of the receiver's attitude toward the adaptive behavior (see the middle panel of Figure 3.3). Successful threat appeals incorporate both the danger of the threat as well as the individual's susceptibility to the threat (Rogers, 1983; Witte, 1993; Witte, Stokols, Ituarte, & Schneider, 1993). These two components of the threat appeal should motivate the individual to critically elaborate the message's content (Chaiken et al., 1989; Petty & Cacioppo, 1986; Roser & Thompson, 1995). In addition, threat appeals tend to rely on the use of highly personalized language (Witte, 1992, 1993), and research has demonstrated that the use of personalized language increases the motivation for individuals to elaboratively process persuasive messages (Burnkrant & Unnava, 1989).

The EPPM also predicts that when perceived efficacy is low, fear control processes

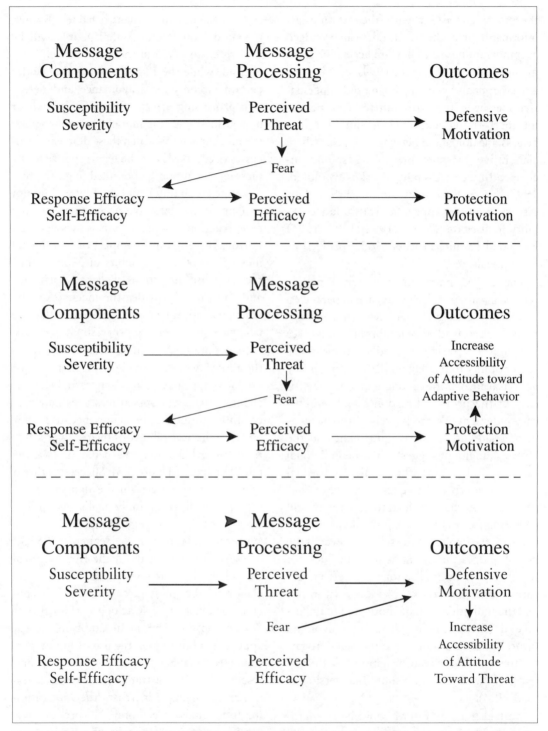

Figure 3.3. **A** Simplified Version of Witte's Extended Parallel Process Model (top panel) of Fear Appeals and Proposed Modifications to the Model, Including How Fear Appeals Increase the Accessibility of Attitudes Toward the Adaptive Behavior (middle panel) and the Threat (bottom panel)

will dominate and people may subsequently show defensive processing by avoiding information concerning the threat or disparaging information about the threat. What we propose occurs is that when fear control processes predominate, the consequent fear will lead to attempts to suppress thinking about the threatening event (Hovland, Janis, & Kelley, 1953). However, attempts to suppress unwanted thoughts tend to backfire and actually result in more thinking about the threatening event (Wegner, Schneider, Carter, & White, 1987; Wenzlaff, Wegner, & Roper, 1988). This rumination should increase the accessibility of people's attitudes toward the threat (see bottom panel of Figure 3.3). The increase in the accessibility of the attitudes toward the threat may lead to subsequent avoidance of information relevant to the threat or defensive disparagement of information relevant to the threat. If accessible attitudes influence how ambiguous stimuli are categorized and whether attention is allocated to that stimuli, then highly accessible negative attitudes toward a threat could operate to bring about attentional avoidance.

However, one difficulty we faced with this explanation is how to operationalize the prediction that fear control processes should result in more accessible attitudes toward the threat. The standard technique for measuring attitude accessibility is through a reaction time procedure. Faster reaction times on this task are indicative of more accessible attitudes from memory (Fazio, 1990b). However, recent research suggests that very extreme attitudes, such as attitudes toward threats, may result in slower reaction times because of an initial startle reaction to the threatening stimuli (Glaser & Banaji, 1999). Thus, the possibility exists that reaction times will be slower to the threatening stimuli because the accessible attitude will influence processes such as the allocation of attention that presumably

precedes that expression of an accessible attitude.

Roskos-Ewoldsen and Yu (1999) found support for these hypothesis in a study of fear appeal messages concerning breast cancer and breast self-exams. The results of this study are straightforward. First, when the efficacy of breast self-exams was stressed, participants' attitudes toward performing breast self-exams were more accessible. Second, as predicted, when the message was high in fear, the participants took longer to express their attitudes toward breast cancer than when the message was low in fear. We interpret this finding as evidence that the message increased the accessibility of their attitudes toward breast cancer but that the reaction times were slower because of defensive processing that occurred prior to their expression of their attitudes in the reaction time task. Further evidence for this interpretation comes from the finding that the effect of high fear messages on the accessibility of participants' attitudes toward breast cancer disappeared when we controlled for effect of defensive reactions to the message.

Recency of Activation

Concepts that have been recently activated will temporarily be more accessible from memory (Anderson, 1990). However, this activation dissipates relatively quickly unless the concept is reactivated (Higgins, Bargh, & Lombardi, 1985). Studies on attitude priming provide evidence that recently activated attitudes can be made temporarily more accessible from memory and can influence the processing of subsequently presented information (Bargh, Chaiken, Govender, & Pratto, 1992; Fazio, 1993; Fazio, Sanbonmatsu, Powell, & Kardes, 1986). Within the paradigms used by these researchers, recent presentation of an attitude-evoking prime resulted in the brief activation of an attitude, perhaps for only 550 to 600 milliseconds (Franks, Roskos-Ewoldsen, Bilbrey, & Roskos-Ewoldsen, 1999). Thus, priming effects appear to dissipate too quickly to affect the persuasion process. However, these studies dealt with priming using a very specific task, and research procedures that more closely approach a persuasive context have shown priming effects on the *judgment* of ambiguous information after a much longer delay (Fazio, Powell, & Herr, 1983).

Evidence that persuasive messages may act as a prime that influences later judgments of ambiguous information comes from the research on media priming. Media priming refers to the potential for the media to influence later judgments and behavior. For example, research on the effects of media violence has found that watching a violent program increases the likelihood that people interpret later ambiguous information in a hostile manner and are more likely to act aggressively as a consequence (Josephson, 1987; Roskos-Ewoldsen, Klinger, & Roskos-Ewoldsen, in press).

Frequency of Activation

A common finding is that the more frequently a concept is activated, the more accessible that concept will be from memory (Higgins et al., 1985). In addition, asking respondents to make repeated attitude judgments about an object increases accessibility of that attitude toward that object (Downing, Judd, & Brauer, 1992; Fazio et al., 1986; Houston & Fazio, 1989; Roskos-Ewoldsen & Fazio, 1992a, 1992b). Support for the generality of these findings is provided by Berger and Mitchell's (1989) study, in which participants' repeated viewing of a commercial about a candy bar resulted in more accessible attitudes toward that candy bar. In addition, the accessible attitudes that resulted from re-

peated viewings of the commercial were more predictive of subsequent behavior (see also Weiss, 1967; Weiss, Chalupa, Gorman, & Goodman, 1968; Weiss & Pasamanick, 1964). Likewise, having research participants make short speeches about their feelings on a topic increases the accessibility of their attitudes (Downing et al., 1992).[2] The effect of such repeated expression of attitudes has been found to have an impact on accessibility 4 months after the experimental manipulation (Zanna, Fazio, & Ross, 1994).

Full Model of Attitude Accessibility

At this point, the model of attitude accessibility we have been discussing includes both the consequences of attitude accessibility and the hypothesized antecedents of attitude accessibility. A final point we would like to make is that accessible attitudes operate like a homeostatic system; accessible attitudes operate to maintain their accessibility. The activation level of chronically accessible constructs do fade with time unless the accessibility of the construct is reinforced (Grant & Logan, 1993). Interestingly, there are several mechanisms by which accessible attitudes can operate to maintain the accessibility of the attitude. When the activation of an accessible attitude influences the allocation of attention, attitudinal processing occurs that should help to maintain the accessibility of the attitude through frequent and recent activation (Roskos-Ewoldsen, 1997). Also, when the activation of an accessible attitude motivates elaborative processing, the motivated processing should result in a more elaborative memory trace, which will maintain or enhance the accessibility of the attitude. Finally, an attitude based on direct experience with the attitude object is more accessible from memory than an attitude based on indirect experience

(Fazio & Zanna, 1981).[3] Recent research supports the homeostatic nature of accessible attitudes. DeBono and Snyder (1995) replicated the finding that direct experience increases the accessibility of an attitude from memory. Furthermore, they found that people with accessible attitudes were more likely to participate in situations that required them to perform behaviors related to the accessible attitudes.

ATTITUDE FORMATION AND BELIEF ACCESSIBILITY

A final question we address concerns the role of belief accessibility in the persuasion process. A number of theories within the information integration framework are concerned with the representation of beliefs in memory and how these beliefs influence people's attitudes. However, one troublesome question arises for these models. Which beliefs, given the overwhelming number of beliefs potentially related to any object, influence the attitude that is formed toward an object?

By far the most developed model of the relationship between beliefs and attitudes is Fishbein's *Summation Model* (for general reviews, see Eagly & Chaiken, 1993; Fishbein & Ajzen, 1975). Fishbein hypothesized that the beliefs about the attitude object are brought into short-term memory and that the evaluations of the beliefs are combined to form the attitude. The Summation Model assumes that associated with each belief is an evaluation of that belief. In addition, each belief varies in how likely it is true of the attitude object. Finally, when the attitude object is considered, the beliefs toward the attitude object are summed to form the attitude. The general formula is: $A_o = \sum b_i e_i$, where A_o is the attitude toward object o, b_i is the likelihood that belief i is true of o, and e_i is the evaluation of belief i. A number of empirical tests have

supported the Summation Model of attitudes (Fishbein, 1963; Fishbein & Raven, 1962; Kaplan & Fishbein, 1969; Smith & Clark, 1973).

The Summation Model maintains that the *salient* beliefs about the object influence the attitude that is formed (Fishbein, 1969; Fishbein & Ajzen, 1975). Unfortunately, belief salience is an ambiguous concept. If the Summation Model is going to inform our understanding of persuasion, it is critical to understand what makes a belief salient. Within the theory, the relevance of belief salience to an individual's cognitive processes during attitude formation is not obvious. Based on these developments in cognitive psychology, Roskos-Ewoldsen and Fazio (1997) proposed that it is the *accessibility* of a belief that determines its role in attitude formation. Specifically, beliefs that are more accessible are more likely to be considered when thinking about or confronting the attitude object. Given the limitations of working memory, it is more likely that highly accessible beliefs will be activated and brought into working memory.

The findings of studies involving both attitude formation (Roskos-Ewoldsen & Fazio, 1997) and existing attitudes (Ajzen, Nichols, & Driver, 1995) demonstrated that accessible beliefs do play a greater role in determining the attitude toward the given object. For example, in Roskos-Ewoldsen and Fazio's (1997) experimental study of attitude formation, a simple model capturing the accessibility of beliefs toward the attitude object accounted for more of the variance than did Fishbein's (1963; see also Fishbein & Raven, 1962; Kaplan & Fishbein, 1969) Summation Model ($r^2 = .36$ vs. $.13$, respectively). As the results of this experiment indicate, the Fishbein strength of relation measure does not capture accessibility. Apparently, when participants were unexpectedly asked to evaluate an attitude object, they considered their beliefs regarding that object. However, those beliefs that are more accessible from memory are more likely to be recalled and to influence attitudinal evaluation.

An important question concerns the role of belief accessibility in persuasion. Assume that two friends are discussing the relative merits of the restaurants in town. According to Fishbein's model, the first friend needs to focus on convincing the second friend to accept beliefs that have positive implications for the particular restaurant he or she likes best and/or change the likelihood that certain beliefs are true. However, based on the research on belief accessibility, the second strategy of focusing on the likelihood that beliefs are true will be ineffectual. Instead, the first friend needs to focus on making those positive beliefs more accessible from memory so that these beliefs are more likely to influence the second friend's attitude toward the restaurant.

FUTURE RESEARCH ON ATTITUDE ACCESSIBILITY AND PERSUASION

As is evident from the discussion of how to increase attitude accessibility, research on how social influence strategies can influence attitude accessibility is in its infancy. Clearly, given the persistence of accessible attitudes (Roskos-Ewoldsen, 1997; Sherman, 1987; Zanna et al., 1994) and their influence on information processing (Fazio et al., 1994; Fazio & Williams, 1986; Roskos-Ewoldsen, 1997) and behavior (Fazio, 1986; Fazio & Roskos-Ewoldsen, 1994; Roskos-Ewoldsen, 1997), understanding how social influence strategies can be used to increase attitude accessibility has important practical implications. We would argue that social influence should be more concerned with changes in attitude accessibility than with changes in the extremity of attitudes. Indeed, it is possible to

increase the accessibility of a person's attitude without changing the extremity of the person's attitude (Roskos-Ewoldsen & Yu, 1999; Yi et al., 1998).

The influence of elaborative message processing on attitude accessibility is probably the best understood of the four mechanisms that Roskos-Ewoldsen (1997) proposed for increasing attitude accessibility. However, even in this area, extensive research still needs to be conducted before we have a good understanding of how and when elaborative message processing influences attitude accessibility. For example, two persuasive strategies that should enhance attitude accessibility via elaborative message processing are inoculation and two-sided arguments. Inoculation (McGuire, 1964) involves exposing audience members to weak attacks on their existing attitudes or beliefs, which causes them to develop resistance to stronger future attacks on those attitudes or beliefs. The initial weak attacks (inoculation) and the (sometimes) concurrent provision of arguments against the position favored by the upcoming attacks are thought to strengthen message recipients' elaborative network of supportive beliefs. Such elaboration should increase the accessibility of beliefs and related attitudes. A number of studies have demonstrated that inoculation increases the resistance of attitudes to counterattitudinal attacks (Benoit, 1991; Burgoon, Pfau, & Birk, 1995; Pfau, 1992; Pfau & Burgoon, 1989; Pfau, Kenski, Nitz, & Sorenson, 1990; Pfau et al., 1997). The strategy of presenting audience members with a two-sided, as opposed to a one-sided, argument related to a given issue is posited to increase accessibility and resistance to attitude change in much the same manner as inoculation. Likewise, two-sided messages are more persuasive than one-sided messages (Burgoon, 1989). In addition, two-sided refutational messages appear to be moderately more persuasive than two-sided nonrefutational messages (Allen, 1991, 1993,

1998; Hale, Mongeau, & Thomas, 1991; O'Keefe, 1993). Support for the idea that two-sided messages result in greater elaboration was found by Hale et al. (1991).

Emotional appeals should also increase attitude accessibility. Several studies have found that attitudes that are primarily affectively based are more accessible from memory (Fazio, 1995; Verplanken, Hofstee, & Janssen, 1998). One explanation for this finding is the affect-as-primary hypothesis that was originally proposed by Zajonc (1980). This explanation maintains that the affective system is separate from the cognitive system and often operates prior to the cognitive system. However, a second explanation for the finding that affectively based attitudes are more accessible from memory is that affectively based attitudes are more likely to be spontaneously formed based on the expectation that the attitudes toward the object will be functional in the future. Recall the attitude-as-information hypothesis proposed earlier, where attitudes act as information that an object is important. Based on this hypothesis, we would expect that the affective reactions that people have to an object operate as a piece of information that this object is important and that they will need an attitude toward this object in the future. As a consequence, based on this attitudinal information, people will spontaneously form an accessible attitude.

CONCLUSIONS

Despite more than 60 years of study, our understanding of the interrelationship between attitudes and persuasion has flourished and is still growing. While attitude accessibility has been a concern for attitude scholars for close to 20 years, research on increasing attitude accessibility via persuasion is virtually nonexistent. Instead, persuasion research has focused almost exclusively on attitude formation and change. Yet in terms of practical outcomes, increasing the accessibility of an attitude is probably more important (Dillard, 1993). Accessible attitudes are more resistant to attempts at counterpersuasion, longer lasting, better at predicting behavior, and more likely to bias how future information is interpreted.

While there has been extensive research on attitude accessibility, this research has tended to focus on the consequences of accessible attitudes—the consequences of accessible attitudes on the orienting of attention, the processing of messages, and future behavior. However, our understanding of the development of accessible attitudes is still in its infancy. Importantly, the research on attitude accessibility suggests that attitude accessibility should be one of the dependent *and independent* variables of choice for persuasion scholars. Future research needs to focus both on how messages influence attitudes (i.e., attitude accessibility as dependent variable) and on how attitudes influence attention to, and processing of, persuasive messages (i.e., attitude accessibility as independent variable).

NOTES

1. This discussion draws heavily from Anderson's (1990) ACTr network model of memory. However, given the level of discussion in this chapter, most network models would make the same predictions. In fact, Smith (1994) has argued that attitude accessibility could be handled within a production system framework. Likewise, connectionist models of attitude accessibility have been proposed (Franks, Roskos-Ewoldsen, Bilbrey, & Roskos-Ewoldsen, 1999; Smith, 1997).

2. Downing, Judd, and Brauer (1992) argued that repeated attitude expression results in more extreme attitudes that are also more accessible from memory. If this is the case, there is a potential confounding of attitude accessibility and attitude extremity. A number of studies have found a mod-

erate correlation between attitude accessibility and attitude extremity (Bargh, Chaiken, Govender, & Pratto, 1992; Fazio & Williams, 1986; Houston & Fazio, 1989; Judd, Drake, Downing, & Krosnick, 1991). However, a number of other studies have found no effect of repeated expression on attitude extremity (Fazio, 1995; Houston & Fazio, 1989; Powell & Fazio, 1984; Roskos-Ewoldsen & Fazio, 1992a, 1992b). In addition, all of these studies found that attitude accessibility and attitude extremity have independent effects on behavior, perception, and attention.

3. However, how behavior influences the accessibility of an attitude from memory is unclear. Behavior could create an expectation that the attitude will be functional in the future, causing the attitude to be spontaneously developed. On the other hand, behavior could result in a more elaborative memory trace because the behavioral information will be stored in memory as episodic memory traces. Because it is unclear how behavior influences attitude accessibility, this feedback loop is left unspecified.

REFERENCES

Ajzen, I. (1988). *Attitudes, personality, and behavior.* Chicago: Dorsey.

Ajzen, I., Nichols, A. J., & Driver, B. L. (1995). Identifying salient beliefs about leisure activities: Frequency of elicitation versus response latency. *Journal of Applied Social Psychology, 25,* 1391-1410.

Allen, M. (1991). Meta-analysis comparing the persuasiveness of one-sided and two-sided messages. *Western Journal of Speech Communication, 55,* 390-404.

Allen, M. (1993). Determining the persuasiveness of message sidedness: A prudent note about utilizing research summaries. *Western Journal of Speech Communication, 57,* 98-103.

Allen, M. (1998). Comparing the effectiveness of one- and two-sided messages. In M. Allen & R. W. Preiss (Eds.), *Persuasion: Advances through meta-analysis* (pp. 87-98). Cresskill, NJ: Hampton.

Allport, G. W. (1935). Attitudes. In C. A. Murchison (Ed.), *Handbook of social psychology* (Vol. 2, pp. 798-844). Worchester, MA: Clark University Press.

Anderson, J. R. (1990). *The adaptive character of thought.* Hillsdale, NJ: Lawrence Erlbaum.

Bargh, J. A., Chaiken, S., Govender, R., & Pratto, F. (1992). The generality of the automatic attitude activation effect. *Journal of Personality and Social Psychology, 62,* 893-912.

Benoit, W. L. (1991). Two tests of the mechanisms of inoculation theory. *Southern Communication Journal, 56,* 219-229.

Berger, I. E., & Mitchell, A. A. (1989). The effect of advertising on attitude accessibility, attitude confidence, and the attitude-behavior relationship. *Journal of Consumer Research, 16,* 269-279.

Burgoon, M. (1989). Messages and persuasive effects. In J. J. Bradac (Ed.), *Message effects in communication science* (pp. 129-164). Newbury Park, CA: Sage.

Burgoon, M., Pfau, M., & Birk, T. S. (1995). An inoculation theory explanation of the effects of corporate issue/advocacy advertising campaigns. *Communication Research, 22,* 485-505.

Burnkrant, R. E., & Unnava, H. R. (1989). Self-referencing: A strategy for increasing processing of message content. *Personality and Social Psychology Bulletin, 15,* 628-638.

Chaiken, S., Liberman, A., & Eagly, A. H. (1989). Heuristic and systematic information processing within and beyond the persuasion context. In J. S. Uleman & J. A. Bargh (Eds.), *Unintended thought* (pp. 212-252). New York: Guilford.

Clore, G. L. (1992). Cognitive phenomenology: Feelings and the construction of judgment. In L. L. Martin & A. Tesser (Eds.), *The construction of social judgments* (pp. 133-163). Hillsdale, NJ: Lawrence Erlbaum.

DeBono, K. G., Green, S., Shair, J., & Benson, M. (1995). Attitude accessibility and biased information processing: The moderating role of self-monitoring. *Motivation and Emotion, 19,* 269-277.

DeBono, K. G., & Snyder, M. (1995). Acting on one's attitudes: The role of a history of choosing situations. *Personality and Social Psychology Bulletin, 21,* 629-636.

Dillard, J. P. (1993). Persuasion past and present: Attitudes aren't what they used to be. *Communication Monographs, 60,* 90-97.

Doob, L. W. (1947). The behavior of attitudes. *Psychological Review, 54,* 135-156.

Downing, J. W., Judd, C. M., & Brauer, M. (1992). Effects of repeated expressions on attitude extremity. *Journal of Personality and Social Psychology, 63,* 17-29.

Eagly, A. H., & Chaiken, S. (1993). *The psychology of attitudes.* Fort Worth, TX: Harcourt Brace Jovanovich.

Fabrigar, L. R., Priester, J. R., Petty, R. E., & Wegener, D. T. (1998). The impact of attitude accessibility on elaboration of persuasive messages. *Personality and Social Psychology Bulletin, 24,* 339-352.

Fazio, R. H. (1986). How do attitudes guide behavior? In R. H. Sorrentino & E. T. Higgins (Eds.), *The handbook of motivation and cognition: Foundations of social behavior* (pp. 204-243). New York: Guilford.

Fazio, R. H. (1989). On the power and functionality of attitudes: The role of attitude accessibility. In A. R. Pratkanis, S. J. Breckler, & A. G. Greenwald (Eds.), *Attitude structure and function* (pp. 153-179). Hillsdale, NJ: Lawrence Erlbaum.

Fazio, R. H. (1990a). Multiple processes by which attitudes guide behavior: The MODE model as an integrative framework. In M. Zanna (Ed.), *Advances in experimental social psychology* (Vol. 23, pp. 75-109). Orlando, FL: Academic Press.

Fazio, R. H. (1990b). A practical guide to the use of response latency in social psychological research. In C. Hendrick & M. S. Clark (Eds.), *Research methods in personalty and social psychology* (Vol. 11, pp. 74-97). Newbury Park, CA: Sage.

Fazio, R. H. (1993). Variability in the likelihood of automatic attitude activation: Data re-analysis and commentary on the paper by Bargh, Chaiken, Govender, and Pratto. *Journal of Personality and Social Psychology, 64,* 753-758.

Fazio, R. H. (1995). Attitudes as object-evaluation associations: Determinants, consequences, and correlates of attitude accessibility. In R. E. Petty & J. A. Krosnick (Eds.), *Attitude strength: Antecedents and consequences* (pp. 247-282). Mahwah, NJ: Lawrence Erlbaum.

Fazio, R. H. (2000). Accessible attitudes as tools for object appraisal: Their costs and benefits. In G. Maio & J. Olson (Eds.), *Why we evaluate: Functions of attitudes* (pp. 1-36). Mahwah, NJ: Lawrence Erlbaum.

Fazio, R. H., & Dunton, B. C. (1997). Categorization by race: The impact of automatic and controlled components of racial prejudice. *Journal of Experimental Social Psychology, 69,* 1013-1027.

Fazio, R. H., Lenn, T. M., & Effrein, E. A. (1984). Spontaneous attitude formation. *Social Cognition, 2,* 217-234.

Fazio, R. H., Powell, M. C., & Herr, P. M. (1983). Toward a process model of the attitude-behavior relation: Accessing one's attitude upon mere observation of the attitude object. *Journal of Personality and Social Psychology, 44,* 723-735.

Fazio, R. H., Powell, M. C., & Williams, C. J. (1989). The role of attitude accessibility in the attitude-to-behavior process. *Journal of Consumer Research, 16,* 280-288.

Fazio, R. H., & Roskos-Ewoldsen, D. R. (1994). Acting as we feel: When and how attitudes guide behavior. In T. C. Brock & S. Shavitt (Eds.), *Psychology of persuasion* (pp. 71-94). Boston: Allyn & Bacon.

Fazio, R. H., Roskos-Ewoldsen, D. R., & Powell, M. C. (1994). Attitudes, perception, and attention. In P. M. Niedenthal & S. Kitayama (Eds.), *The heart's eye: Emotional influences in perception and attention* (pp. 197-216). Orlando, FL: Academic Press.

Fazio, R. H., Sanbonmatsu, D. M., Powell, M. C., & Kardes, F. F. (1986). On the automatic activation of attitudes. *Journal of Personality and Social Psychology, 50,* 229-238.

Fazio, R. H., & Towles-Schwen, T. (1999). The MODE model of attitude-behavior processes. In S. Chaiken & Y. Trope (Eds.), *Dual-process theories in social psychology* (pp. 97-116). New York: Guilford.

Fazio, R. H., & Williams, C. J. (1986). Attitude accessibility as a moderator of the attitude-perception and attitude-behavior relations: An investigation of the 1984 presidential election. *Journal of Personality and Social Psychology, 51,* 505-514.

Fazio, R. H., & Zanna, M. P. (1981). Direct experience and attitude-behavior consistency. In L. Berkowitz (Ed.), *Advances in experimental social psychology* (Vol. 14, pp. 161-202). Orlando, FL: Academic Press.

Fishbein, M. (1963). An investigation of the relationships between belief about an object and the attitude toward the object. *Human Relations, 16*, 233-239.

Fishbein, M. (1969). A behavior theory approach to the relations between beliefs about an object and the attitude toward the object. In M. Fishbein (Ed.), *Readings in attitude theory and measurement* (pp. 389-400). New York: John Wiley.

Fishbein, M., & Ajzen, I. (1975). *Belief, attitude, intention, and behavior.* Reading, MA: Addison-Wesley.

Fishbein, M., & Raven, B. H. (1962). The AB scales: An operational definition of belief and attitude. *Human Relations, 15*, 35-44.

Franks, J. J., Roskos-Ewoldsen, D. R., Bilbrey, C. W., & Roskos-Ewoldsen, B. (1999). *Is attitude priming an artifact?* Unpublished manuscript, Vanderbilt University.

Glaser, J., & Banaji, M. R. (1999). When fair is foul and foul is fair: Reverse priming in automatic evaluation. *Journal of Personality and Social Psychology, 77*, 669-687.

Grant, S. C., & Logan, G. D. (1993). The loss of repetition priming and automaticity over time as a function of degree of initial learning. *Memory & Cognition, 21*, 611-618.

Greene, J. O. (1984). A cognitive approach to human communication: An action assembly theory. *Communication Monographs, 51*, 289-306.

Hale, J. L., Mongeau, P. A., & Thomas, R. M. (1991). Cognitive processing of one- and two-sided persuasive messages. *Western Journal of Speech Communication, 55*, 380-389.

Higgins, E. T., Bargh, J. A., & Lombardi, W. (1985). Nature of priming effects on categorizing. *Journal of Experimental Psychology: Learning, Memory, and Cognition, 11*, 59-69.

Houston, D. A., & Fazio, R. H. (1989). Biased processing as a function of attitude accessibility: Making objective judgments subjectively. *Social Cognition, 7*, 51-66.

Hovland, C. I., Janis, I. L., & Kelley, H. H. (1953). *Communication and persuasion: Psychological studies of opinion change.* New Haven, CT: Yale University Press.

Josephson, W. L. (1987). Television violence and children's aggression: Testing the priming, social script, and disinhibition predictions. *Journal of Personality and Social Psychology, 53*, 882-890.

Judd, C. M., Drake, R. A., Downing, J. W., & Krosnick, J. A. (1991). Some dynamic properties of attitude structures: Context-induced response facilitation and polarization. *Journal of Personality and Social Psychology, 60*, 193-202.

Kaplan, K. J., & Fishbein, M. (1969). The source of beliefs, their salience, and prediction of attitude. *Journal of Social Psychology, 78*, 63-74.

Kardes, F. R. (1988). Spontaneous inference processes in advertising: The effects of conclusion omission and involvement on persuasion. *Journal of Consumer Research, 15*, 225-233.

Katz, D. (1960). The functional approach to the study of attitudes. *Public Opinion Quarterly, 24*, 163-204.

Kitayama, S., & Howard, S. (1994). Affective regulation of perception and comprehension: Amplification and semantic priming. In P. M. Niedenthal & S. Kitayama (Eds.), *The heart's eye: Emotional influences in perception and attention* (pp. 41-65). San Diego: Academic Press.

Krosnick, J. A. (1989). Attitude importance and attitude accessibility. *Personality and Social Psychology Bulletin, 15*, 297-308.

Larson, C., & Sanders, R. (1975). Faith, mystery, and data: An analysis of "scientific" studies of persuasion. *Quarterly Journal of Speech, 61*, 178-194.

Latane, B., & Darley, J. M. (1970). *The unresponsive bystander: Why doesn't he help?* New York: Appleton-Century-Crofts.

Lavine, H., Sullivan, J. L., Borgida, E., & Thomsen, C. J. (1996). The relationship of national and personal issue salience to attitude accessibility on foreign and domestic policy issues. *Political Psychology, 17*, 293-316.

Lord, C. G., Ross, L., & Lepper, M. R. (1979). Biased assimilation and attitude polarization: The effects of prior theories on subsequently considered information. *Journal of Personality and Social Psychology, 37,* 2098-2109.

McGuire, W. J. (1964). Inducing resistance to persuasion: Some contemporary approaches. In L. Berkowitz (Ed.), *Advances in experimental social psychology* (Vol. 1, pp. 191-229). Orlando, FL: Academic Press.

Mothersbaugh, D. L., Viosca, R. C., Phelps, J. E., & Roskos-Ewoldsen, D. R. (1999). *Comparative advertising effects on attitude accessibility and valence: The role of elaboration, consolidation, and comparison-brand usage.* Unpublished manuscript, University of Alabama.

O'Keefe, D. J. (1993). The persuasive effects of message sidedness variations: A cautionary note concerning Allen's (1991) meta-analysis. *Western Journal of Communication, 57,* 87-97.

Petty, R. E., & Cacioppo, J. T. (1986). *Communication and persuasion: Central and peripheral routes to attitude change.* New York: Springer-Verlag.

Petty, R. E., & Wegener, D. T. (1998). Attitude change: Multiple roles for persuasion variables. In D. T. Gilbert, S. T. Fiske, & G. Lindzen (Eds.), *Handbook of social psychology* (5th ed., Vol. 1, pp. 323-390). New York: McGraw-Hill.

Pfau, M. (1992). The potential of inoculation in promoting resistance to the effectiveness of comparative advertising messages. *Communication Quarterly, 40,* 26-44.

Pfau, M., & Burgoon, M. (1989). Inoculation in political campaign communication. *Human Communication Research, 15,* 91-111.

Pfau, M., Kenski, H. C., Nitz, M., & Sorenson, J. (1990). Efficacy of inoculation strategies in promoting resistance to political attack messages: Application to direct mail. *Communication Monographs, 57,* 25-43.

Pfau, M., Tusing, K. J., Koerner, A. F., Lee, W., Godbold, L. C., Penaloza, L. J., Yang, V. S., & Hong, Y. (1997). Enriching the inoculation construct: The role of critical components in the process of resistance. *Human Communication Research, 24,* 187-215.

Powell, M. C., & Fazio, R. H. (1984). Attitude accessibility as a function of repeated attitude expression. *Personality and Social Psychology Bulletin, 10,* 139-148.

Roese, N. J., & Olson, J. M. (1994). Attitude importance as a function of repeated attitude expression. *Journal of Experimental Social Psychology, 30,* 39-51.

Rogers, R. W. (1983). Cognitive and physiological processes in fear appeals and attitude change: A revised theory of protection motivation. In J. T. Cacioppo & R. E. Petty (Eds.), *Social psychophysiology: A sourcebook* (pp. 153-176). New York: Guilford.

Roser, C., & Thompson, M. (1995). Fear appeals and the formation of active publics. *Journal of Communication, 45,* 103-121.

Roskos-Ewoldsen, D. R. (1997). Attitude accessibility and persuasion: Review and a transactive model. In B. Burleson (Ed.), *Communication Yearbook 20* (pp. 185-225). Thousand Oaks, CA: Sage.

Roskos-Ewoldsen, D. R., Bichsel, J., & Hoffman, K. (2002). The influence of accessibility of source likability on persuasion. *Journal of Experimental Social Psychology, 38,* 137-143.

Roskos-Ewoldsen, D. R., & Fazio, R. H. (1992a). The accessibility of source likability as a determinant of persuasion. *Personality and Social Psychology Bulletin, 18,* 19-25.

Roskos-Ewoldsen, D. R., & Fazio, R. H. (1992b). On the orienting value of attitudes: Attitude accessibility as a determinant of an object's attraction of visual attention. *Journal of Personality and Social Psychology, 63,* 198-211.

Roskos-Ewoldsen, D. R., & Fazio, R. H. (1997). The role of belief accessibility in attitude formation. *Southern Communication Journal, 62,* 107-116.

Roskos-Ewoldsen, D. R., Klinger, M., & Roskos-Ewoldsen, B. (in press). Media priming. In J. B. Bryant & R. A. Carveth (Eds.), *Meta-analysis of media effects.* Mahwah, NJ: Lawrence Erlbaum.

Roskos-Ewoldsen, D. R., & Yu, J. (1999). *The influence of fear appeal messages on attitude accessibility.* Unpublished manuscript, University of Alabama.

Sanbonmatsu, D. M., & Fazio, R. H. (1990). The role of attitudes in memory-based decision making. *Journal of Personality and Social Psychology, 59,* 614-622.

Schuette, R. A., & Fazio, R. H. (1995). Attitude accessibility and motivation as determinants of biased processing: A test of the MODE model. *Personality and Social Psychology Bulletin, 21,* 704-710.

Sherif, M., & Sherif, C. W. (1967). Attitude as the individual's own categories: The social judgment-involvement approach to attitude and attitude change. In C. W. Sherif & M. Sherif (Eds.), *Attitude, ego-involvement, and change* (pp. 105-139). New York: John Wiley.

Sherman, S. J. (1987). Cognitive processes in the formation, change, and expression of attitudes. In M. P. Zanna, J. M. Olson, & C. P. Herman (Eds.), *Social influence: The Ontario Symposium* (Vol. 5, pp. 75-106). Hillsdale, NJ: Lawrence Erlbaum.

Smith, A. J., & Clark, R. D. (1973). The relationship between attitudes and beliefs. *Journal of Personality and Social Psychology, 26,* 231-326.

Smith, E. R. (1994). Procedural knowledge and processing strategies in social cognition. In R. S. Wyer, Jr., & T. K. Srull (Eds.), *Handbook of social cognition,* Vol. 1: *Basic processes* (pp. 99-151). Hillsdale, NJ: Lawrence Erlbaum.

Smith, E. R. (1997). Preconscious automaticity in a modular connectionist system. In R. S. Wyer, Jr. (Ed.), *The automaticity of everyday life* (pp. 187-202). Mahwah, NJ: Lawrence Erlbaum.

Smith, E. R., Fazio, R. H., & Cejka, M. A. (1996). Accessible attitudes influence categorization of multiply categorizable objects. *Journal of Personality and Social Psychology, 71,* 888-898.

Smith, M. B., Bruner, J. S., & White, R. W. (1956). *Opinions and personality.* New York: John Wiley.

Snyder, M., & Kendzierski, D. (1982). Acting on one's attitudes: Procedures for linking attitude and behavior. *Journal of Experimental Social Psychology, 18,* 165-183.

Stayman, D. M., & Kardes, F. R. (1992). Spontaneous inference processes in advertising: Effects of need for cognition and self-monitoring on inference generation and utilization. *Journal of Consumer Psychology, 1,* 125-142.

Verplanken, B., Hofstee, G., & Janssen, H. J. (1998). Accessibility of affective versus cognitive components of attitudes. *European Journal of Social Psychology, 28,* 22-35.

Wegner, D. M., Schneider, D. J., Carter, S. R., III, & White, T. L. (1987). Paradoxical effects of thought suppression. *Journal of Personality and Social Psychology, 53,* 5-13.

Weiss, R. F. (1967). A delay of argument gradient in the instrumental conditioning of attitudes. *Psychonomic Science, 8,* 457-458.

Weiss, R. F., Chalupa, L. M., Gorman, B. S., & Goodman, N. H. (1968). Classical conditioning of attitudes as a function of number of persuasion trials and argument (UCS) strength. *Psychonomic Science, 11,* 59-60.

Weiss, R. F., & Pasamanick, B. (1964). Number of exposures to persuasive communication in the instrumental conditioning of attitudes. *Journal of Social Psychology, 63,* 373-382.

Wenzlaff, R. M., Wegner, D. M., & Roper, D. W. (1988). Depression and mental control: The resurgence of unwanted negative thoughts. *Journal of Personality and Social Psychology, 55,* 862-892.

Wicker, A. W. (1969). Attitudes versus actions: The relationship of verbal and overt behavioral responses to attitude objects. *Journal of Social Issues, 25,* 41-78.

Witte, K. (1992). Putting the fear back into fear appeals: The Extended Parallel Process Model. *Communication Monographs, 59,* 329-349.

Witte, K. (1993). Message and conceptual confounds in fear appeals: The role of threat, fear, and efficacy. *Southern Communication Journal, 58,* 147-155.

Witte, K. (1994). Fear control and danger control: A test of the Extended Parallel Process Model (EPPM). *Communication Monographs, 61,* 113-134.

Witte, K. (1995). Generating effective risk messages: How scary should your risk communication be? In B. R. Burleson (Ed.), *Communication Yearbook 18* (pp. 229-254). Thousand Oaks, CA: Sage.

Witte, K., Stokols, D., Ituarte, P., & Schneider, M. (1993). Testing the Health Belief Model in a field study to promote bicycle safety helmets. *Communication Research, 20,* 564-586.

Wu, C., & Shaffer, D. R. (1987). Susceptibility to persuasive appeals as a function of source credibility and prior experience with the attitude object. *Journal of Personality and Social Psychology, 52,* 677-688.

Yi, H., Phelps, J. E., & Roskos-Ewoldsen, D. R. (1998). Examining the effectiveness of comparative advertising: The role of attitude accessibility. *Journal of Current Issues and Research in Advertising, 20,* 61-74.

Yu, H. J., & Roskos-Ewoldsen, D. R. (1997, April). *Fear appeals, behavior, and defensive processing: The role of attitude accessibility.* Paper presented at the annual meeting of the Southern States Communication Association, Savannah, GA.

Zajonc (1980). Feeling and thinking: Preferences need no inferences. *American Psychologist, 35,* 151-175.

Zanna, M. P., & Fazio, R. H. (1982). The attitude-behavior relation: Moving toward a third generation of research. In M. P. Zanna, E. T. Higgins, & C. P. Herman (Eds.), *Consistency in social behavior: The Ontario Symposium* (Vol. 2, pp. 283-301). Hillsdale, NJ: Lawrence Erlbaum.

Zanna, M. P., Fazio, R. H., & Ross, M. (1994). The persistence of persuasion. In R. C. Schank & E. Langer (Eds.), *Beliefs, reasoning, and decision making: Psycho-logic in honor of Bob Abelson* (pp. 347-362). Hillsdale, NJ: Lawrence Erlbaum.

4

The Media Priming Effect

News Media and Considerations Affecting Political Judgments

GERALD M. KOSICKI

Public officials, lobbyists, professional communicators, public interest group leaders, social activists, and corporate officials work tirelessly to bring their side of political and social controversies to the public. Through a variety of venues including television interviews, press releases, news conferences, photo opportunities, and paid advertising, potential news sources with a point of view to explain or promote hope to make themselves visible to the public (Pan & Kosicki, 1993; Price & Tewksbury, 1997). Sources and items selected for inclusion in the news are chosen for their news values (Gans, 1979; Manning, 2001; Pan & Kosicki, 2001), a practice that gives the news a certain set of themes or perspectives (Turow, 1992, p. 108). Other values, such as quality, accuracy, completeness, and diversity, can promote effective public discourse, understanding, and judgment or can hinder it.

When considering the impact of news reports on public opinion about political issues, agenda-setting has been a dominant model guiding research (McCombs, Shaw, & Weaver, 1997). In fact, the agenda-setting perspective has become so common that many use the phrase *agenda-setting* to refer to nearly any type of research question involving public issues and media. Scholars working in this framework have become adept at expanding it in many directions, incorporating new dimensions as part of the expanding area of agenda-setting. However, agenda-setting is more properly viewed as a single type of media effects hypothesis that concerns the connection between the news media and public issues (Kosicki, 1993).

Agenda-setting was arguably a leading edge of the new look in mass communication research of the late 1960s that rejected simple models of persuasion as they were understood at that time and embraced "cognitive effects" that concentrated more on what people learned, how they thought, or what they thought about (Becker, McCombs, & McLeod, 1975; McLeod & Reeves, 1980;

Reeves, Chaffee, & Tims, 1982). This cognitive perspective has tended to focus on indirect effects (Becker & Kosicki, 1995). Work in persuasion was redirected by information processing models, which led to an expansion of media effects studies in both persuasion and other aspects of public affairs media effects.

Agenda-setting research concerns itself with establishing links between what broad topical areas the media consider important by the amount and prominence of their coverage and public acceptance of this list of concerns. Agenda-setting research typically defines public issues as rather broad, topical, and abstract areas such as "trust in government," "the economy" "environment," and "crime." This innovation makes it possible to track the media agenda in a general way over long periods of time and to use a wide variety of survey data to assess the public agenda. Correlations between the rank orders of aggregated media and public agendas are taken as evidence of an agenda-setting effect (McCombs & Shaw, 1972). Survey-based studies continue in this line to the present day, albeit with many refinements, distinctions, and caveats (Kosicki, 1993). Research that was explicitly cognitive began appearing during the 1980s. Most such research used experimental methods to examine media influence on public agendas (Iyengar & Kinder, 1987; Iyengar, Peters, & Kinder, 1982). Agenda-setting remains a model with tremendous heuristic value to many scholars of political communication, and the literature continues to build in the area despite certain theoretical and methodological flaws (Kosicki, 1993).

Iyengar et al. (1982) developed the media priming hypothesis as an outgrowth of some experiments on agenda-setting as a way of showing how people's views of public issues might have real-world political consequences. One way to do this was to attempt to show what processes guide the formation and expression of views about public policies and political figures. In other words, what are the ingredients of public affairs judgments?

Media priming is a media effects hypothesis that suggests that the news media influence the standards by which political figures or public policies are judged by calling attention to some matters and ignoring others (Iyengar & Kinder, 1987, p. 63). As noted by Price and Tewksbury (1997), media priming refers to the tendency of audience members to evaluate their political leaders according to the particular events and issues that have been highlighted in news reports. This approach to persuasive communication, by focusing on the standards of political judgment and how they are formed, represents a particularly widespread and important phenomenon in political life because it provides the basis for matters such as voting for candidates and issues. It is also a principal mechanism for explaining mass media effects in many political contexts. Media priming is a general type of effect and thus can be applied across many types of persuasive communication and in many types of contexts, from election campaigns to routine news coverage between election periods.

Price and Tewksbury (1997, p. 198) argued that agenda-setting is, in theoretical terms, a special case of media priming. This is so, they argued, because media priming is a temporary accessibility effect. Media messages make a particular construct applicable and activate it. After activation, the construct remains temporarily accessible. When an individual needs to evaluate the performance of a public official, this concept is likely to be summoned to mind. Unless deemed inapplicable to the evaluation, it will be used for making a judgment about that official's performance. Price and Tewksbury argued that one such judgment could be issue importance, in other words, agenda-setting. This argument makes sense logically but does not account for the historical development of either perspective given that agenda-setting grew out of a very different intellectual tradition from the media priming literature. This theoretical convergence highlights one powerful advantage of the cognitive approach: a comprehensive, flexible set of theory-building tools that can be applied in many settings (Price & Tewksbury, 1997). One of the many strengths of the cognitive approach is that it begins with a series of realistic assessments of human thinking powers. Basic to this approach is the notion that people are faced with many complex mental tasks and that these tasks, if approached with an equal degree of diligence, would be overwhelming. Accordingly, for many matters, individuals do not attempt to make the best possible decisions. Instead, especially for routine matters or relatively unimportant concerns, they employ series of mental shortcuts that are expected to yield decisions that are good enough. Simon (1957) has called this decision-making strategy "satisficing." It assumes that people do not have the ability, time, or interest to make the best possible decision in every case, so they satisfice rather than optimize.

Cognitive theory suggests that satisficing strategies are typical for most matters most of the time unless the issue is particularly important or salient to the individual. The more important a problem, the more likely individuals are to expend cognitive effort. This also suggests that for most issues, most of the time, people engage in satisficing. This is particularly so when people do not see their stake in an issue as being very great. Lacking reasons for taking more time or energy with a particular decision, people are thought to rely not on an exhaustive search of all their stored information but instead on a subset of information that comes to mind (e.g., Taylor & Fiske, 1978). For many people, media may be the principal source of this information.

The priming hypothesis provides a theoretically driven perspective from which to consider the question of media influence in the world of public affairs and politics. It has been most heavily used to date in studying the criteria that people use to evaluate the president, and that emphasis is reflected in this chapter. Satisficing is important to understanding political judgments because for most people, most of the time, political matters are not of intense interest. In fact, politics often gets slight attention. Media cues are often the main ones that people turn to when asked to make political judgments. Furthermore, few people would feel the need to optimize on formulating their answers to political questions.

This chapter discusses media and their connection to an effect of media called media priming. Media are seen as industrialized processes for the creation and distribution of messages that have certain properties that are influential in the priming process. These properties include systematic problems that may make priming more powerful in certain areas of political life, depending on media performance. Media treatments of public policy issues and candidates suggest that the media will present certain considerations such as facts, emotional appeals, exemplars, and framing. Media priming is thus seen to be a "subtle mechanism by which the media alter the conduct of public policy-making" (Miller & Krosnick, 1996, p. 80). The chapter continues with a discussion of media production factors and content. It moves from content to audience factors in priming and then to public policy considerations.

DEFINING MASS COMMUNICATION

While there are many ways to define mass communication, a particularly useful one is provided by Turow (1992): "Mass communication is the industrialized [mass] production, reproduction, and multiple distribution of messages through technological devices" (p. 107). In this definition, "messages" can be any linguistic or pictorial representations that appear purposeful. The word "industrialized" indicates that the process is carried out by mass media firms, that is, by "conglomerations of organizations that interact regularly in the process of producing and distributing messages" (p. 107).

The definition means that industrial application of technology is a key defining feature of mass communication, and this is crucial in separating mass communication from other forms of communication. The industrial process suggests that large numbers of messages and audience members are involved. The definition calls special attention to the industrial nature of message creation, particularly the relationships between media and other sources of social, political, and economic power.

A key element of this perspective is that in stressing attention to the production and distribution processes, along with the considerations that shape news, information, and entertainment, there is a recognition that these cultural patterns lead to similar cultural models across individual stories. As Turow (1992) noted,

> Even when the specific subjects that media carry are not the same, the similarity with which creators approach the world can still yield similar perspectives. When local TV [television] stations across the country daily fill their 7:25 a.m. newscasts with tales of overnight murders, robberies, and accidents, the general knowledge and worldview gleaned from those patterns might be the same, even though individual stories might not be. (p. 108)

Although journalists like to say that they simply cover the news and reflect reality, it is commonly recognized in the literature of the field that things are more complex than that. If news simply reflected the world of official announcements and the activities of business and political elites, there would be few reasons to make news treatment of topics a subject of study.

FRAMING NEWS AND PUBLIC AFFAIRS

Public deliberation is the process of collective and open reasoning and discussion about the merits of public policy (Page, 1996), and it is fundamental to the health of democratic societies (Kinder & Herzog, 1993). Framing is one perspective from which to approach the study of public deliberation, which includes "the discursive process of strategic actors utilizing symbolic resources to participate in collective sense-making about public issues" (Pan & Kosicki, 2001, p. 36). Framing analysis is an analytical approach connecting normative propositions from "deliberative democracy" and the empirical questions of collective decision making to understand political participation and experiences in democratic society (Baumgartner & Jones, 1993; Kingdon, 1984).

Goffman (1974) defined frames as "schemata of interpretation" that enable individuals to locate, perceive, identify, and label occurrences in everyday life. Framing analysis deals with how various social actors act and interact to produce organized ways of making sense of the world. Frames are "central organizing ideas to understand and organize political reality" (Gamson & Modigliani, 1987, p. 143).

Framing owes much to its roots in cognitive science. Price and Tewksbury (1997) reviewed this literature well, and it is not repeated here. Others such as Iyengar (1991), Cappella and Jamieson (1997), and Scheufele (1999) made this case well in the area of media effects. But the effects tradition does not exhaust what framing brings to the study of public opinion and communication.

Frames define the boundaries of discourse surrounding an issue and categorize each political actor involved in the issue in a particular way. Heated political contestation surrounds these boundaries as well as what is an acceptable definition of a given issue. Pan and Kosicki (2001) argued that framing analysis needs to place political and social actors in the center of the process. The framing potency of any actor comes from the resources one can bring to bear on a framing situation, one's strategic alliances, and one's stock of skills and knowledge in the arts of frame sponsorship and management. Through such resources, they argued, political actors weave "webs of subsidies" to privilege the dissemination and packaging of information in the most advantageous directions.

The combination of a frame and its symbolic devices or "packages" functions as a narrative that may resonate in the minds of other actors under certain conditions, which include credibility and other shared experiences (which form the basis for "frame alignment" [Snow & Benford, 1988]). This alignment is enhanced to the extent that an actor can link his or her frame to some enduring values in the society and thus subsidize other actors in processing and packaging information concerning a given issue. Framing potency is also determined by certain sociological factors such as the size and depth of an actor's web of subsidies and the framing actor's ability to mobilize such subsidies with strategic targeting (Pan & Kosicki, 2001). In general, the broader a discursive community becomes and the more clear its identity becomes, the greater the likelihood of achieving its goals.

The type of framing analysis discussed here requires the use of tools and strategies for analysis quite different from those in public opinion analysis, although public opinion analysis might be one part of the total picture. Developing an understanding and empirical verification of such framing efforts requires data about the various framing actors and groups, their communication and other organizing strategies, and their messages to other groups and the public. Although many types of data in various combinations may prove useful in understanding these processes, the richness and interconnected nature of the activities and actors implies that case history approaches may be favored for this part of the story (e.g., Gamson & Modigliani, 1987; Gitlin, 1980).

Pan and Kosicki (1997) have also introduced the notion of "issue regime" to denote "periods in which a news story is so big that it dominates the amount of total media attention available" (p. 4). Examples include the Clinton-Lewinsky scandal during the late 1990s and the saturation coverage of the Gulf War. These giant stories occupy so much time and space, and consume so many media resources, that they tend to crowd out other news items and thus have a profound impact on public discourse and public attention. Following the work of Hilgartner and Bosk (1988), they rely on the notion of public arena, that is, the totality of channels, forums, and means of public deliberation about public policy and the relevant venues in which such matters are discussed. This is based on the insight, among others, that there is only so much channel capacity in the public arena, and so issues compete for resources. The issue regime concept has proven useful in the analysis of public opinion during and after the Gulf War, in which President Bush went from the most popular American president to one of the least popular, in part because of declining media attention to the war and the increasing attention to the economy, which was in recession. Issue regime as a concept allowed the researchers to document the public opinion effects of media switching between the Gulf War and the economy and the consequences of this for Bush's approval rating.

Similar systematic media coverage or biases in media coverage have been documented over far longer periods of time. For example, Gilens (1996, 1999) used a variety of data in innovative ways to carefully describe media emphasis on social welfare as an issue, particularly the shift in media focus over the years from whites to blacks and the growing use of black examples in news coverage. This leads to a picture of the world in news that is, in certain ways, the opposite of real-world indicators; for example, only about 29% of poor Americans are black, but 62% of poor people portrayed in major newsmagazines between 1988 and 1992 were black (Gilens, 1996). This kind of systematic misrepresentation can be expected to influence people's judgments about social welfare policies.

Of course, framing of public issues is an inevitable process because all news is necessarily told from some point of view, even as journalists struggle to be objective or fair. Consensus values of the larger society are always present, a phenomenon that Gans (1979) called "enduring values in the news." Beyond this, however, media cover public policy issues and events in ways that may provide clear signals to audience members about the ways in which the issue is to be understood and processed.

Fundamentally, news reporters tell stories about things that happen in the world that they think are important for people to know or contain elements that people will find interesting. In so doing, journalists provide a steady flow of information to the public about current affairs and politics. While telling their stories, journalists make active choices about what information to select, what issues to stress, and how to present this information. In the political sphere, media might be said to present at least four types of information that are highly relevant to people's understanding of public issues.

First, the news media provide factual information about conditions in the world. Such reports provide individuals, communities, and nations with a shared information base that people use in forming their basic understanding of the world. Much of this information closely tracks the pronouncements of officials and reports of conditions as provided by official government agencies, corporations, academics, and other types of qualified experts (e.g., Ericson, Baranek, & Chan, 1989; Gans, 1979). If we accept this characterization of journalism as a type of activity relying primarily on human sources, it becomes a major concern as to how these sources are selected and used (e.g., Gans, 1979). Mainstream media make attempts to screen sources carefully, often to the point where they are vulnerable to criticism for sampling experts too narrowly to provide truly diverse discourse and perspectives about issues of the day.

Second, the news media also provide images, examples, and episodes that function as exemplars or explications of more abstract ideas and principles of public policy matters. Stories of the "deserving poor," or of individuals struggling against racial animosity and inequality, may help to explicate the principle of equal opportunity and what it means or does not mean in contemporary American life. News filled with images of single mothers on social welfare, crack addicts, prostitution, and alcoholic homeless people, without discussion of the social conditions that tend to foster or exacerbate such problems, will encourage the view that affirmative action, social welfare, and related policies tend to give unearned advantages (Pan & Kosicki, 1996; see also Gilens, 1999; Iyengar, 1991; Sniderman, Brody, & Tetlock, 1991).

Third, the vividness and immediacy of news media reports help to arouse, sustain, and renew various affective and emotional experiences about an issue. Television coverage of the Gulf War fostered patriotic emotions and pride that contributed to the rally effect, in which the public supported the country's leader during difficult times. In this case, that meant contributing increased support to the president's policies once the war started (Pan & Kosicki, 1994, 1996). In terms of domestic public policy issues such as affirmative action, the media may renew aversive feelings toward blacks with stories that associate blacks with crime, militancy, welfare, and so on (Entman, 1992; Pan & Kosicki, 1996; van Dijk, 1991). Television may be more effective than print media in helping people to activate their emotional responses due to the unique combination of visual and sound stimuli.

Fourth, the news media, through the use of exemplars, emotional appeals, metaphors, visual images, sound bites, and other symbolic devices, frame public policy issues in unique ways (Gamson, 1988; Gamson & Modigliani, 1987). Framing suggests an interpretation of issues or events in the news (Pan & Kosicki, 1993). Framing effects tend to limit the scope of discussion among members of the public, but they also supply the vocabulary for public discussion (Gamson, 1992; Iyengar, 1991). For example, framing policies about race as either "affirmative action" or "reverse discrimination" brings different considerations to the public's mind and may consequently lead to different opinion responses (Kinder & Sanders, 1990). Chong (1996) discussed the need to create common frames of reference or considerations between elites and public when thinking of public policy.

Question wording experiments that vary these types of word choices in the context of surveys, growing out of a concern about the robustness of the method, are now motivated by concerns arising from cognitive psychology (e.g., Feldman, 1995; Schwarz & Sudman, 1996; Sirken et al., 1999). Although primarily methodological in character, they may be seen as examples of such framing effects and even

given substantive interpretations under certain circumstances (Kinder & Sanders, 1996).

This discussion of framing has been intended to describe in a theoretical way variations in news media content as it relates to public issues. In the next section, the priming hypothesis helps to connect these issues illuminated in media content to the study of variations in public opinion in the evaluations of presidents and public policies.

PRIMING

As has been discussed, the media priming hypothesis suggests that the news media stress certain considerations, and not others, in their news materials about public policies or candidates for office. In so doing, media alter the standards by which these policies or candidates for office are evaluated. Of course, it is well-known that media content alone does not produce effects (McLeod & Reeves, 1980). In other words, learning and many other effects of media messages are subject to the usual limits of physical exposure, attention, and other information processing strategies, in which the audience member may reject or accept the basic premise of the information (e.g., Cappella & Jamieson, 1997; see also Austin & Pinkleton, 1999; Kosicki & McLeod, 1989; Zaller, 1992).

Priming Versus Agenda-Setting and Framing

The agenda-setting model has been so pervasive in the field that virtually any reference to the topic of media and public issues will be said by some to be a case of agenda-setting.[1] Yet we have seen that framing and priming have their places as well; therefore, it is useful to offer a comparison among the various concepts so that each will be understood with minimal ambiguity in the discussion that follows.

Agenda-setting is commonly understood as a model that links the salience or priority of issues in the media with the priorities of the public (Kosicki, 1993). A key to understanding agenda-setting is the typical conceptualization of public issues as relatively broad, abstract categories such as environment, trust in government, and poverty. Mutz (1998, p.70) called agenda-setting a "nondirectional" effect, by which she meant the effect is supposed to result from the amount of salience of the coverage of a particular issue and does not matter whether the coverage is favorable or unfavorable. There are both strengths and weaknesses of this approach. On the one hand, the use of abstract issues makes it possible to study the rise and fall of salience of a slate of issues over many decades. On the other hand, the abstract nature of what is studied is quite removed from the details of the issue. This suggests that often we are left with the feeling that agenda-setting studies do not tell very much about the nature of news discourse or the audience effects that they purport to study. As Kosicki (1993) has described this, issues are, or ought to be, a type of contested discourse, yet "the agenda-setting framework strips away almost everything worth knowing about how the media cover an issue and leaves only the shell of the topic" (p. 112). Cappella and Jamieson (1997) made a similar point concerning media priming:

> Media priming, like agenda setting, is not concerned with how issues are treated in news coverage, only with their relative frequency. Priming would treat a story about President Clinton's decision to send troops to Haiti described as a ploy to drum up support prior to fall elections as equivalent to a story about sending troops to Haiti to ensure the return of democracy. These two stories are framed very differ-

> ently, but they are equivalent from the viewpoint of media priming. (p. 52)

Despite these reservations about priming research, in contrast to agenda-setting, it is often more complex and detailed. Priming relies on a series of evaluative criteria that vary in detail and relates these to both media and their effects on overall evaluations of issues or political figures. The dependent variables are often evaluations of policies or political figures, not the mere salience of an issue.

Framing, by contrast, is a conceptual framework for examining the details of how issues are conceptualized in public discourse as highly contested matters over which there is often considerable disagreement. Framing takes as a starting point the idea that language matters in the study of media and issues and makes the analysis of metaphor and other lexical choices very prominent (Pan & Kosicki, 1993, 2001). Framing as explained by Iyengar (1991) is a particular type of context effect. News stories are either told as event-driven stories, which he called "episodic," or reported with some larger background material, which he referred to as "thematic." In Iyengar's framing effects work, it does not matter whether the actual context is positive or negative. For this notion of framing effects, Iyengar drew on the work of Kahneman and Tversky (1987), who showed in experiments that equivalent choices could be presented to participants in such a way that their choices would be systematically altered depending on the mode of presentation.

Unpacking the Expectations of Priming

The priming perspective suggests that when people are asked to give an evaluation of a public policy or public figure, they do not evaluate all of the information they have or can find about that topic, weight it according to some priorities, and then calculate a logical response. Instead, people use only a sample of readily available information. This sample of information that is stimulated by priming has nothing to do with motivation. The sample is small and biased because of the limited nature of the cognitive system. Furthermore, this sample is not a random sample of all information but instead a specific subset of what is cognitively accessible (e.g., Feldman, 1995; Higgins, 1996; Higgins & King, 1981; Zaller, 1992). Accessible information for most people is what is presented by news media. Issues that have been portrayed in the news repeatedly are most likely to be evoked in people's mental calculations at a given time by media. This is the basis of the priming hypothesis.

Media coverage of an issue is an indication of the salience of the issue in media content. This may affect the cognitive processes that audience members use to make sense of a given issue. Pan and Kosicki (1997, p. 10) noted that the process may happen in at least three ways: (a) by increasing the ease with which the related thought elements or considerations are activated, (b) by increasing the breadth of the accessible thought elements related to a given topic or issue, or (c) by tightening the links of the various thought elements. This means that individuals will be more likely to use the aspects of issues activated by media in their calculations for evaluating a given policy or policy actor such as the president.

Note that priming is thus very different from traditional persuasion research, as explained by Miller and Krosnick (1996):

> Whereas persuasion focuses on media messages advocating particular positions, priming can be invoked simply by a news story devoting attention to an issue without advocating a position. And whereas persuasion is thought to result from effortful decision making about a message's likely veracity, priming presumably occurs

as a result of automatic and effortless processes of spreading activation in people's minds. (p. 81)

A key point in any type of determination of media effects is to specify precisely what is the proposed effect (McLeod & Reeves, 1980). Building on these insights, Miller and Krosnick (1996) posed several subhypotheses, which they claimed form the core of the concept of priming. The first of these is known as the *target gradient hypothesis*. This suggests that priming effects will decrease in strength as attitudes become more remote from those being directly activated by a news story. Miller and Krosnick (1996, p. 83) asserted that this gradient hypothesis actually has two parts. The first part relates to the target and addresses which attitudes have their accessibility altered by priming and by how much. In other words, priming induced by a news story should occur mostly for attitudes directly related to the content of the story. News stories about the president's economic policies should presumably mainly affect attitudes about the president's economic policy performance, and these effects should be strongest. The effects might spread to judgments about the president's health policies because of their possible economic implications (p. 82).

The second part, known as the *consequence gradient hypothesis*, concerns which overall presidential evaluations are altered and to what extent. The argument here is that the relevance of a given attitude will, in part, determine the extent to which the accessible attitudes make a difference to the judgment being made. Scandal information might not be seen as relevant to economic or international relations performance (Miller & Krosnick, 1996, p. 82).

These hypotheses are best explained by noting that political attitudes are structured in memory as part of an associative network (e.g., Collins & Loftus, 1975; Higgins, 1996). This network is made up of nodes (i.e., political attitudes) and strong links to other sets of related attitudes. Nodes that are less logically related or not related at all will have weaker links or perhaps no links at all. When circumstances are such that a particular node is activated, related nodes are also pulled into short-term memory. This spreading activation is what gives priming its power to connect various thought elements. The extent to which concepts are activated in this type of network depends on many things that are beyond the scope of this chapter.

In the case of candidates, it has become customary to conceptualize evaluations in terms of competence, leadership, integrity, and empathy (Kinder, 1986). Because individuals do not have the motivation or ability to simultaneously think about all considerations, we are likely to see patterns in which those closer to the topic at hand are considered more, whereas others that are more remote are relied on less. Media, as noted earlier, are also limited in terms of the comprehensiveness of their reports and in any case tend to stress certain aspects of stories that are thought to be especially newsworthy. For example, a personal scandal can be expected to have greater effects on integrity than on competence or leadership. Similarly, information made accessible by news coverage that is highly relevant for one of these dimensions may be irrelevant for another. For example, information from the news that activates integrity might not also activate competence.

The *dosage hypothesis* refers to the amount of media coverage on an issue that enters a person's consciousness (Miller & Krosnick, 1996, p. 83). In general, the expectation is that the greater one's use of media content and the more attention that is paid to it, the more one should be influenced by it.

Miller and Krosnick (1996) also discussed the *resistance hypothesis,* by which they meant that "holding dosage constant, the more knowledge of politics one has, the more resis-

tant one should be" to priming effects.[2] This suggests that more knowledgeable individuals have greater cognitive experiences, which helps them to resist fluctuations in the accessibility of information. On the other hand, those with little knowledge are more likely to be responsive to media primes.

Empirical Tests of the Priming Hypothesis

The basic priming hypothesis has been tested using survey and experimental methods. The results are generally confirming for studies of both types. A typical experiment might manipulate aspects of stories relating to a single theme in the context of a newscast or series of newscasts viewed over time. For example, Iyengar and Kinder (1987) developed early studies in which experimental participants viewed newscasts that emphasized inadequacies in defense preparedness or not. They were testing participants to see whether the treatment would influence the standards that viewers applied to evaluating the president's overall performance. A day after the final newscast was shown to participants, they were asked to rate the president's performance on matters such as defense and overall performance. The expectation is that people who saw stories about defense inadequacies should give more weight to the president's performance on that problem when evaluating his overall performance. In the experiment, for people who saw multiple stories about defense (i.e., those who were primed on that theme), the impact of ratings on the president's performance on defense was more than twice as great as that for people who were not so primed.

Priming studies using survey research typically attempt to measure various aspects of people's constructions of the issues and relate these to exposure to aspects of news content.

Iyengar and Kinder (1987) reported some priming results using data from the National Election Studies (NES, 1980 major panel, $N = 1,008$), with data gathered at four points during the election year. A series of standard items were asked to measure concepts of "competence" and "integrity" of President Carter. The raw items were factor-analyzed separately for Carter, and then overall evaluation was estimated by regression analysis with predictors including inflation performance, energy policy performance, unemployment performance, hostage crisis performance, and Afghanistan performance. The expectations were that the evaluations on specific topics that had been in the news—inflation, energy crisis, and Iranian hostage crisis—would predict Carter's general evaluation but not judgments of his competence and integrity. Results confirmed these expectations, with the strongest relations shown between inflation and Carter's general performance, less with judgments of his competence, and only small effects with judgments of his integrity.

Experimental data are generally confirming of the priming gradient and general priming hypothesis but not the dosage hypothesis. It was found that even moderate exposure triggered priming responses (Iyengar, Kinder, Peters, & Krosnick, 1984). Participants viewed one of three 40-minute sets of network news coverage with varied levels of exposure to energy stories. Priming effects were measured by unstandardized regression coefficients on evaluations of general performance, competence, and integrity under experimental conditions of "some coverage." Effects of energy performance on overall performance ratings were larger in the coverage conditions than in the no coverage conditions. This confirms the general priming hypothesis but not the dosage hypothesis given that there were no differences between the high and moderate exposure conditions. The consequence gradient

hypothesis was supported given that priming of energy performance ratings showed greater influence on evaluations of overall job performance than on judgments of competence and integrity (Iyengar et al., 1984). These results were replicated in a second study, but with added qualification. The second study of general attitudes toward Carter's performance also confirmed that knowledge does help to resist priming, as more knowledgeable individuals are less likely to be primed, and the less knowledgeable consistently are more influenced by their exposure to the experimental media primes. In this case, regression coefficients predicting overall performance ratings from ratings of energy, inflation, and defense performance were considerably lower for the high knowledge group than for the low knowledge group.

Krosnick and Brannon (1993), in their Gulf War study, found that knowledge, exposure, and interest all had the same effect on priming; that is, higher involvement was associated with reduced priming. This finding is quite common in the literature (e.g., Iyengar et al., 1984; Krosnick & Kinder, 1990). But when knowledge, exposure, and interest are studied simultaneously, their effect turned around; that is, high levels of knowledge increased priming, and high levels of exposure and interest reduced priming.

In explaining these results, Krosnick and Brannon (1993) noted that while a traditional view of political involvement suggests that greater exposure and interest would indicate a stronger dose of media content, and that greater knowledge suggests resistance to new information, such results might not be found in practice. They interpreted knowledge as providing individuals with a greater ability to interpret, store, and retrieve new information, while media exposure and interest are associated with a higher probability of online processing and decision making. If this is true, then one should expect weakened priming effects due to exposure because it opens the individual to a wider range of stimuli that can be activated by media. Krosnick and Brannon concluded that the assumptions of the dosage and resistance models are likely correct due to available evidence from various areas of psychology. However, they noted that the real question relates to their application in priming research (p. 972). More work is clearly needed in this area to understand the roles of these concepts in priming and the possible effect of issue or setting on the results.

Survey data reinforce the basic priming, gradient, and target gradient hypotheses. In a study of the Iran-Contra affair, attitudes toward President Reagan's performance were better predicted by attitudes toward aid to the Contras and aid to Central America than were items such as general isolationism, U.S. military strength in general, health of the national economy, and federal aid to blacks (Krosnick & Kinder, 1990). Using data from the NES, the authors took advantage of a natural experiment by dividing the sample into "prerevelation" and "postrevelation" groups depending on their date of interview in relation to the national television announcement by Attorney General Meese that money from the secret sale of weapons to Iran had been diverted to the Nicaraguan Contras. Regressions predicting Reagan's overall performance rating were predicted by variables such as aid to Contras, isolationism, U.S. strength, economic assessments, and aid to blacks. As examined in the postrevelation sample, the basic priming hypothesis was supported in that aid to Contras was the most important predictor of overall evaluations. The target gradient hypothesis was supported because a slightly smaller priming effect occurred for views about isolationism, which is related to Contra-Central America support. Priming was not seen for the more distant predictors of economic assessments and aid to blacks.

In the same study, the consequence gradient hypothesis was also supported. However, the effect of Contra-Central America support extended not just to judgments of overall competence but to integrity as well. Miller and Krosnick (1996, p. 88) noted that this is appropriate given that the Iran-Contra affair raised questions that were widely debated about Reagan's competence and integrity.

In a survey study of priming during the Gulf War, Krosnick and Brannon (1993) found additional support for priming in general and the target gradient hypothesis in that the impact of foreign policy performance and domestic economic policy performance did not change much. However, Pan and Kosicki (1997), using additional data from the NES, were able to show how a change in media emphasis on the war after the gulf crisis to the economy shifted public opinion focus from one issue to the other. These results were shown through a more complete data set that encompassed a longer time frame than that employed by Krosnick and Brannon (1993). In addition, Pan and Kosicki augmented the NES data with a detailed month-by-month content analysis. This was effective in showing the shift in media emphasis from the Gulf War issue regime to the presidential campaign regime in which then Democratic challenger, Bill Clinton, effectively kept the focus on the economy, to the severe disadvantage of President Bush. This study effectively documents the fall of Bush from the most favorable presidential ratings in history to one of the lowest in the space of several months, and it clearly shows the shift in media and public opinion emphasis from Gulf War to the economy.

Conceptualizing the media's role in the priming process, Pan and Kosicki (1997) employed the notion of "issue regime," which is a period in which one issue dominates the public arena or "an overall consonance of all the channels and apparatuses of public deliberation concerning public issues during the period" (p. 10). A greater reliance on this dominant issue in evaluating a political figure such as the president results from and indicates the dominance of the issue in the public arena, which includes media coverage, real-world cues, and interpersonal communication. As successful as this strategy is, it still leaves us with the need to demonstrate the direct priming effect of media.

Krosnick and Brannon (1993) linked their analysis to media exposure and argued that people with lower levels of exposure are more affected by priming because these people will absorb the "big message" from media, but without details. This study suggests that people form their judgments by retrieving information only when needed by a task such as retrieving a memory-based judgment. They are, in effect, arguing that media exposure is only a contingent condition for the priming effect, in other words, necessary but not sufficient.

Pan and Kosicki (1997) considered media a priming agent and estimated priming effects directly from media exposure variables. In this formulation, heavy exposure to media coverage of a dominant issue leads to stronger or more frequent activation of thought elements related to that issue. Thus, increased media exposure is related to increased activation. They added the notion of affective valence, that is, the negative or positive tone associated with each issue. In their example, media coverage of the Gulf War carried a positive "big message" for President Bush because he was getting credit for the military victory. Coverage of the economic recession in the United States was negative for Bush.

Pan and Kosicki (1997), using panel data from the NES covering the period from late 1990 to 1992, showed that priming is temporary and situational. Media changed their dominant issue focus, and President Bush's approval ratings changed together with shifting issue dominance. Pan and Kosicki noted

that the timing of data gathering in the context of such fluid political reality is an issue that deserves more consideration by scholars, in terms of the pragmatic issues of when to gather data but also in theoretical terms. If priming activation and decay are to be studied as dynamic concepts, then the current commonly used methods of pre- and posttest studies might not be optimal. More theoretical work is needed in the temporal aspects of priming.

A few other variables have also been investigated in terms of their mediation role in priming with mixed results. Krosnick and Brannon (1993) found greater knowledge related to priming in the context of the Gulf War, although in other settings, Krosnick and Kinder (1990) found the opposite—that priming was limited to those who know the least. Although the analysis in the former study is more detailed, the relationship of priming to knowledge is clearly an area that needs additional attention due to its importance.

In a study of President Clinton's performance evaluation, Miller and Krosnick (1997) found significant positive results in their examination of the relationship between trust in media and priming. In this case, using a mix of media trust measures that included credibility and respondents' sense that the media were appropriately focusing on important news, they found that people who were high on trust of media were more likely than others to be primed by issues that the media raised. In a subsequent study, Miller and Krosnick (2000) produced additional support for the effects of media credibility on priming.

Cappella and Jamieson (1997) noted that "framing effects are more subtle than media priming and agenda setting" (p. 83). By this, they meant to draw attention not just to the presence of certain topics in the news but also to how topics are treated, similar to the valence issues discussed previously but extending beyond this into framing effects. Their study, of media and their role in fostering cynicism, employed an explicitly cognitive model incorporating elements of spreading activation with particular journalistic details to suggest that people can be primed in ways that priming theory suggests. However, Cappella and Jamieson studied far more subtle journalistic details than have been proposed to date in the mainstream priming studies. This suggests a major avenue for future studies in the area.

Price, Tewksbury, and Powers (1997, p. 403) reported a pair of experimental studies developed as a clear extension of priming research into more subtle terrain akin to some of the experiments on value framing of Ball-Rokeach, Power, Guthrie, and Waring (1990) and Shah, Domke, and Wackman (1996). Price et al. (1997) studied a process where "by activating some ideas, feelings, and values rather than others, the news can encourage particular trains of thought about political phenomena and lead audience members to arrive at more or less predictable conclusions" (p. 404).

Priming research over the next few years should develop in several directions. First, we can expect more detailed studies to understand the mechanisms of priming. In one of the early reported studies of priming, Iyengar and Kinder (1986, pp. 148-150) discussed the need to demonstrate that the effects they were calling priming were not, in fact, effects of projection. Projection, defined as the opposite of priming, would be present if news coverage of a particular problem caused people to adjust their rating of the political figure on that problem to match their overall rating of the political figure. Iyengar and Kinder (1987) pointed out that this could occur in a situation where supporters of the president might interpret unfavorable economic news as not caused by the president's policies. At the same time, the president's opponents see the bad news as a good opportunity to hold him accountable for what they already see are his failed policies

(p. 72). It is important to note that this occurs not because the economic news dominates their overall impression but because they interpret the economic news according to their view of the president. Controlling this requires an "over time" design and an analysis strategy in which reciprocal causal effects can be eliminated. Iyengar and Kinder examined the impact of problem performance ratings on the overall performance ratings after adjusting for the impact of overall performance ratings on the problem performance ratings. They conducted their experiment in two waves 6 weeks apart and asked for evaluations of President Reagan at both time points: before and after television news containing priming stimuli. Their results indicate that after projection was eliminated, priming effects were clarified. In fact, they concluded that "if anything, our earlier estimates of priming actually understated the impact of television news" (p. 150). The various priming hypotheses such as gradient, target gradient, resistance, and projection will likely be the focus of considerable additional work during the years ahead.

Another question about priming has been raised by Miller and Krosnick (1996). They noted that an important issue to consider in future research relates to the role of accessibility, which is normally considered the key mechanism in priming research (e.g., Wyer & Srull, 1981). Miller and Krosnick (1996) argued that the mediational role of accessibility has never been fully documented, and they provided a few suggestions for attempting to do so. Although they cast doubt on both accessibility and agenda-setting as mediational processes for priming, they did not provide a clear alternative explanation. Additional research is warranted to identify the mechanisms that account for the effects.

Mutz (1998, p. 72) raised an additional concern about accessibility and its possible confound with negativity. She noted that although the priming effect is often explained in terms of simple accessibility and thus is supposed to be, like agenda-setting, a nondirectional effect, this nondirectional aspect has not been adequately demonstrated. She correctly noted that most of the stimuli used in experiments have been of bad news, not good news, and that positive news has not resulted in significant effects. This suggests that while there may be nondirectional effects (as priming theorists argue), there may also (or instead) be directional effects of negative information. This also suggests avenues for additional studies. Because much news is indeed negative, this is a significant issue for scholars to consider carefully in the design of future work. More work is certainly indicated in each of these areas, particularly in terms of making sure that priming and negativity effects are not confounded.

Another area of importance involves judgments of information quality as important mediating factors in priming. Miller and Krosnick (2000) examined cognitive mediators of news media priming, namely trust in media. Because this has proven to be a useful concept, as it has to some extent in agenda-setting, further exploration is certainly warranted here. In addition to trust in the media in general, it is natural to explore the various individual media. This might also be done by issue regime or story given that people may very well have reactions to a whole stream of news such as the media's coverage of the Clinton-Lewinsky scandal or the Gulf War. It is also important to note that trust and credibility do not exhaust the possible responses that media engender in their viewers. Indeed, people bring a wide range of views about various aspects of media performance to their encounters with media, and many of these have been shown to be influential in shaping the effects of media (Kosicki & McLeod, 1989).

Priming effects research has mainly focused on evaluations of the president, although in principle the theoretical apparatus is such that it can readily be extended to evaluations of other political figures, office holders, candidates for office, and issues. Accessibility effects of the type discussed in priming can certainly be studied in many different venues. It is likely that in future years, priming research will spread out quite far from its current base in evaluations of presidents. As research spreads to other contexts such as other political leaders (e.g., governors, senators), one can expect increased importance of media treatment of the issues and thus greater attention to the total context of the studies. Once such studies appear in large numbers, it will be possible to employ meta-analysis techniques to provide empirical summaries that will highlight the importance of such contexts in public opinion. As priming studies spread to public evaluations of issues such as abortion and trade policy, still other contingencies, such as the way the issues are described by media, are likely to become very important.

CONCLUSION

Media priming studies have been carried on in many contexts, using many types of research designs and measures of priming effects as well as a wide range of participants. We have also seen some studies incorporate both experimental and survey evidence, whereas others rely on surveys alone. This is important not so much for theoretical reasons as for matters of external validity, although the survey studies have often dealt with an interesting mix of real-world issues and media content and with unique periods in our political history such as the Iran-Contra affair, the Gulf War, and the 1992 presidential election. There would seem to be considerable scalability in priming studies, however, to the extent that despite certain ambiguities in the results, the perspective has, for the most part, been a useful addition to the wide-ranging literature on persuasion. The future is very promising in that political figures and issues besides the president can be examined in detail. In other words, priming seems to represent a good, dependable, theoretically motivated type of media effect that can be detected in many types of political and social contexts. The future research agendas of scholars will determine whether this assessment is correct.

In addition, other recent work, such as that of Price and Tewksbury (1997), Price et al. (1997), Cappella and Jamieson (1997), Nelson and Kinder (1996), Nelson, Clawson, and Oxley (1997), and Nelson, Oxley, and Clawson (1997), suggests that exciting new work will emerge, perhaps blending priming with more subtle cues propagated by the emerging framing research. This emerging literature will likely go well beyond simple dichotomies of episodic versus thematic in describing and studying frames and framing effects. Furthermore, the empirical literature will be developed using both laboratory and real-world contexts. The future of this area of research seems bright.

NOTES

1. Various individuals (e.g., McCombs & Bell, 1996) have attempted to stretch the meaning of agenda-setting to the limits and beyond by discussing agenda-setting as referring to the transfer of salience not only from media content to audiences but also from media sources to journalists (agenda-building). Some authors (e.g., Ghanem, 1997) working in this tradition have also referred to second-level agenda-setting, in which the attributes of the issue were also studied in relation to media content.

2. For more on resistance, see McGuire (1968). For a discussion of various conceptualizations of resistance, see Zaller (1992, pp. 121-122).

REFERENCES

Austin, E. W., & Pinkleton, B. E. (1999). The relation between media content evaluations and political disaffection. *Mass Communication & Society, 2,* 105-122.

Ball-Rokeach, S. J., Power, G. J., Guthrie, K. K., & Waring, H. R. (1990). Value-framing abortion in the United States: An application of media system dependency theory. *International Journal of Public Opinion Research, 2,* 249-273.

Baumgartner, F. R., & Jones, B. D. (1993). *Agendas and instability in American politics.* Chicago: University of Chicago Press.

Becker, L. B., & Kosicki, G. M. (1995). Understanding the message-producer/message-receiver transaction. *Research in Political Sociology, 7,* 33-62.

Becker, L. B., McCombs, M. E., & McLeod, J. M. (1975). The development of political cognitions. In S. H. Chaffee (Ed.), *Political communication: Issues and strategies for research* (pp. 21-63). Beverly Hills, CA: Sage.

Cappella, J. N., & Jamieson, K. H. (1997). *Spiral of cynicism.* New York: Oxford University Press.

Chong, D. (1996). Creating common frames of reference on political issues. In D. C. Mutz, P. M. Sniderman, & R. A. Brody (Eds.), *Political persuasion and attitude change* (pp. 195-224). Ann Arbor: University of Michigan Press.

Collins, A., & Loftus, E. (1975). A spreading activation theory of semantic memory. *Psychological Review, 82,* 407-428.

Entman, R. M. (1992). Blacks in the news: Television, modern racism, and cultural change. *Journalism Quarterly, 69,* 341-361.

Ericson, R. V., Baranek, P. M., & Chan, J. B. L. (1989). *Negotiating control: A study of news sources.* Toronto: University of Toronto Press.

Feldman, S. (1995). Answering survey questions: The measurement and meaning of public opinion. In M. Lodge & K. McGraw (Eds.), *Political judgment* (pp. 249-270). Ann Arbor: University of Michigan Press.

Gamson, W. A. (1988). A constructionist approach to mass media and public opinion. *Symbolic Interaction, 11,* 161-174.

Gamson, W. A. (1992). *Talking politics*. Cambridge, UK: Cambridge University Press.

Gamson, W. A., & Modigliani, A. (1987). The changing culture of affirmative action. *Research in Political Sociology, 3*, 137-177.

Gans, H. J. (1979). *Deciding what's news*. New York: Vintage.

Ghanem, S. (1997). Filling in the tapestry: The second level of agenda-setting. In M. E. McCombs, D. L. Shaw, & D. Weaver (Eds.), *Communication and democracy* (pp. 3-14). Mahwah, NJ: Lawrence Erlbaum.

Gilens, M. (1996). Race and poverty in America. *Public Opinion Quarterly, 60*, 515-541.

Gilens, M. (1999). *Why Americans hate welfare*. Chicago: University of Chicago Press.

Gitlin, T. (1980). *The whole world is watching*. Berkeley: University of California Press.

Goffman, E. (1974). *Frame analysis*. New York: Harper & Row.

Higgins, E. T. (1996). Knowledge activation: Accessibility, applicability, and salience. In E. T. Higgins & A. W. Kruglanski (Eds.), *Social psychology: Handbook of basic principles* (pp. 133-168). New York: Guilford.

Higgins, E. T., & King, G. (1981). Accessibility of social constructs: Information processing consequences of individual and contextual variability. In N. Cantor & J. F. Kihlstrom (Eds.), *Personality, cognition, and social interaction* (pp. 69-121). Hillsdale, NJ: Lawrence Erlbaum.

Hilgartner, S., & Bosk, C. L. (1988). The rise and fall of social problems: A public arenas model. *American Journal of Sociology, 94*, 53-78.

Iyengar, S. (1991). *Is anyone responsible?* Chicago: University of Chicago Press.

Iyengar, S., & Kinder, D. R. (1986). More than meets the eye: Priming and public evaluations of the president. *Public Communication and Behavior, 1*, 135-171.

Iyengar, S., & Kinder, D. R. (1987). *News that matters: Television and American public opinion*. Chicago: University of Chicago Press.

Iyengar, S., Kinder, D. R., Peters, M. D., & Krosnick, J. A. (1984). The evening news and presidential evaluations. *Journal of Personality and Social Psychology, 46*, 778-787.

Iyengar, S., Peters, M. D., & Kinder, D. R. (1982). Experimental demonstrations of the "not-so-minimal" consequences of television news programs. *American Political Science Review, 76*, 848-858.

Kahneman, D., & Tversky, A. (1987). Rational choice and the framing of decisions. In R. M. Hogarth & M. W. Reder (Eds.), *Rational choice: The contrast between economics and psychology* (pp. 67-94). Chicago: University of Chicago Press.

Kinder, D. R. (1986). Presidential character revisited. In R. R. Lau & D. O. Sears (Eds.), *Political cognition* (pp. 233-256). Hillsdale, NJ: Lawrence Erlbaum.

Kinder, D. R., & Herzog, D. (1993). Democratic discussion. In G. E. Marcus & R. L. Hanson (Eds.), *Reconsidering the democratic public* (pp. 347-377). University Park: Pennsylvania State University Press.

Kinder, D. R., & Sanders, L. M. (1990). Mimicking political debate with survey questions. The case of white opinion on affirmative action for blacks. *Social Cognition, 8*, 73-103.

Kinder, D. R., & Sanders, L. M. (1996). *Divided by color: Racial politics and democratic ideals*. Chicago: University of Chicago Press.

Kingdon, J. (1984). *Agendas, alternatives, and public policies*. New York: HarperCollins.

Kosicki, G. M. (1993). Problems and opportunities in agenda-setting research. *Journal of Communication, 43*, 2: 100-127.

Kosicki, G. M., & McLeod, J. M. (1989). Learning from political news: Effects of media images and information processing strategies. In S. Kraus, (Ed.), *Mass communication and political information processing* (pp. 69-83). Hillsdale, NJ: Lawrence Erlbaum.

Krosnick, J. A., & Brannon, L. A. (1993). The impact of the Gulf War on the ingredients of presidential evaluations: Multidimensional effects of political involvement. *American Political Science Review, 87*, 963-975.

Krosnick, J. A., & Kinder, D. R. (1990). Altering the foundations of support for the president through priming. *American Political Science Review, 84*, 497-512.

Manning, P. (2001). *News and news sources: A critical introduction*. London: Sage.

McCombs, M. E., & Bell, T. (1996). The agenda-setting role of mass communication. In M. B.

Salwen & D. W. Stacks (Eds.), *An integrated approach to communication theory and research* (pp. 93-110). Mahwah, NJ: Lawrence Erlbaum.

McCombs, M. E., & Shaw, D. L. (1972). The agenda-setting function of the mass media. *Public Opinion Quarterly, 36,* 176-187.

McCombs, M. E., Shaw, D. L., & Weaver, D. (1997). *Communication and democracy: Exploring the intellectual frontiers in agenda-setting theory.* Mahwah, NJ: Lawrence Erlbaum.

McGuire, W. J. (1968). Personality and susceptibility to social influence. In E. F. Borgatta & W. W. Lambert (Eds.), *Handbook of personality theory and research* (pp. 1130-1187). Chicago: Rand McNally.

McLeod, J. M., & Reeves, B. (1980). On the nature of mass media effects. In S. B. Withey & R. P. Abeles (Eds.), *Television and social behavior* (pp. 17-54). Hillsdale, NJ: Lawrence Erlbaum.

Miller, J., & Krosnick, J. A. (1996). News media impact on the ingredients of presidential evaluations: A program of research on the priming hypothesis. In D. M. Mutz, P. M. Sniderman, & R. A. Brody (Eds.), *Political persuasion and attitude change* (pp. 79-99). Ann Arbor: University of Michigan Press.

Miller, J., & Krosnick, J. A. (1997). Anatomy of news media priming. In S. Iyengar & R. Reeves (Eds.), *Do the media govern?* (pp. 258-275). Thousand Oaks, CA: Sage.

Miller, J., & Krosnick, J. A. (2000). News media impact on the ingredients of presidential evaluations: Politically knowledgeable citizens are guided by a trusted source. *American Journal of Political Science, 44,* 301-315.

Mutz, D. C. (1998). *Impersonal influence.* Cambridge, UK: Cambridge University Press.

Nelson, T. E., Clawson, R. A., & Oxley, Z. M. (1997). Media framing of a civil liberties conflict and its effect on tolerance. *American Political Science Review, 91,* 567-583.

Nelson, T. E., & Kinder, D. R. (1996). Issue frames and group-centrism in American public opinion. *Journal of Politics, 58,* 1055-1078.

Nelson, T. E., Oxley, Z. M., & Clawson, R. A. (1997). Toward a psychology of framing effects. *Political Behavior, 19,* 221-246.

Page, B. I. (1996). *Who deliberates? Mass media in modern democracy.* Chicago: University of Chicago Press.

Pan, Z., & Kosicki, G. M. (1993). Framing analysis: An approach to news discourse. *Political Communication, 10,* 55-75.

Pan, Z., & Kosicki, G. M. (1994). Voters' reasoning processes and media influences during the Persian Gulf War. *Political Behavior, 16,* 117-156.

Pan, Z., & Kosicki, G. M. (1996). Assessing news media influences on the formation of whites' racial policy preferences. *Communication Research, 23,* 147-178.

Pan, Z., & Kosicki, G. M. (1997). Priming and media impact on the evaluations of the president's performance. *Communication Research, 24,* 3-30.

Pan, Z., & Kosicki, G. M. (2001). Framing as strategic action in public deliberation. In S. D. Reese, O. H. Gandy, & A. E. Grant (Eds.), *Framing public life: Perspectives on media and our understanding of the social world* (pp. 35-65). Mahwah, NJ: Lawrence Erlbaum.

Price, V., & Tewksbury, D. (1997). News values and public opinion: A theoretical account of media priming and framing. In G. Barnett & F. J. Boster (Eds.), *Progress in communication sciences* (pp. 173-212). Norwood, NJ: Ablex.

Price, V., Tewksbury, D., & Powers, E. (1997). Switching trains of thought: The impact of news frames on readers' cognitive responses. *Communication Research, 24,* 481-506.

Reeves, B., Chaffee, S. H., & Tims, A. (1982). Social cognition and mass communication research. In M. E. Roloff & C. R. Berger (Eds.), *Social cognition and communication* (pp. 287-326). Beverly Hills, CA: Sage.

Scheufele, D. A. (1999). Framing as a theory of media effects. *Journal of Communication, 49,* 103-122.

Schwarz, N., & Sudman, S. (Eds.). (1996). *Answering questions: Methodology for determining cognitive and communicative processes in survey research.* San Francisco: Jossey-Bass.

Shah, D. V., Domke, D., & Wackman, D. B. (1996). "To thine own self be true": Values, framing, and voter decision-making strategies. *Communication Research, 23,* 509-560.

Simon, H. A. (1957). *Models of man.* New York: John Wiley.

Sirken, M. G., Herrmann, D. J., Schechter, S., Schwarz, N., Tanur, J. M., & Tourangeau, R. (1999). *Cognition and survey research.* New York: John Wiley.

Sniderman, P. M., Brody, R. A., & Tetlock, P. E. (1991). *Reasoning and choice: Explorations in political psychology.* Cambridge, UK: Cambridge University Press.

Snow, D-A., & Benford, R. D. (1988). Ideology, frame resonance, and participant mobilization. In B. Klandermans et al. (Eds.), *From structure to action: Comparing social movement research across countries* (pp. 197-217). Greenwich, CT: JAI.

Taylor, S. E., & Fiske, S. T. (1978). Salience, attention, and attribution: Top of the head phenomena. *Advances in Experimental Social Psychology, 11,* 249-288.

Turow, J. (1992). On reconceptualizing "mass communication." *Journal of Broadcasting and Electronic Media, 36,* 105-110.

van Dijk, T. A. (1991). *Racism and the press.* London: Routledge.

Wyer, R. S., & Srull, T. K. (1981). Category accessibility: Some theoretical and empirical issues concerns in the processing of social stimulus information. In E. T. Higgins, C. P. Herman, & M. P. Zanna (Eds.), *Social cognition: The Ontario Symposium* (Vol. 1, pp. 161-197). Hillsdale, NJ: Lawrence Erlbaum.

Zaller, J. R. (1992). *The nature and origins of mass opinion.* New York: Cambridge University Press.

5

The Negativity Effect in Political Advertising

A Meta-analysis

MIKE ALLEN
NANCY BURRELL

Imagine that a person receives a message containing equivalent quantities of positive and negative information. One might suppose that the two sets of information would cancel each other out and that the resulting attitude toward the topic would be zero. However, a good deal of research on the "negativity effect" suggests that such will not be the case (Fiske, 1980; Kanouse & Hanson, 1972; Kellermann, 1984). The negativity effect occurs when negative information is disproportionately weighted relative to positive information (Kellermann, 1984, 1989). Knowledge of the existence of this effect among designers of political campaigns may account for the growing frequency of negative political advertising. Whereas most research on the negativity effect has been conducted in the interpersonal context, this chapter considers the negativity effect when applied to persuasion involving politics. The chapter first defines the negativity effect in persuasion and then considers some theoretical

explanations for this effect. The next section presents the results of a meta-analysis that examines the available literature on this issue. The final section presents a discussion of the findings and identifies some unresolved issues and directions for future research.

DEFINING THE NEGATIVITY EFFECT IN PERSUASION

The negativity effect describes an outcome where negative information contributes more to the formation or change of an opinion than does positive information. Essentially, if the negativity effect exists, then a person receiving two messages with information equivalent in extremity but opposite in value should be more persuaded by the negative information than by the positive information. The key is that the information must be considered equivalent; the only distinction is the valence (positive vs. negative) of the information. For example, a person may find out that a 60-year-old presidential candidate consistently attends religious services (the person considers this positive information) but also discovers that the candidate smoked marijuana while attending high school at 17 years of age (the person considers this negative information). The negativity effect predicts that the ultimate evaluation becomes negative (assuming that these two facts are all that is known about the candidate). The negative information is given disproportionate importance relative to the positive information. The negative information (smoking marijuana while in high school) carries more importance in determining a person's evaluation than does the positive information (regular attendance at religious services).

Mass media information about candidates is contained in new reports and advertisements, and it often focuses on character issues. The negativity effect in persuasion is most often applied to political communication, particularly candidates vying for public office. Typically, the voter does not personally know a candidate. The impression of the candidate comes from mass mediated experience rather than from direct experience. Presidential political information often focuses on the past of the candidate; in addition to the legislative history or other public records or positions on specific issues, it includes scrutiny of the private life of the candidate. The issue for some candidates becomes a discussion, in response to probing questions by reporters, of the sexual practices, use or nonuse of drugs, or family experiences that candidates had during their youth. The awareness of negative information can generate a less desirable image of the candidate. Another source of negative information about the candidate is the opposition, who will point out the negative information.

This negative information coming from the opposition can be responded to as unfair and a violation of the sense of decency or honesty about campaign conduct. Such information can be "cloaked" as the need to address an issue. "My opponent, if elected, will raise taxes" provides an example of how a candidate may offer inferences about the opposing candidate; "of course he did not tell you that" indicates a lack of honesty. A candidate may point to an action or a statement by the opposing candidate (e.g., "the failure to support the legislation effecting X") and issue an explanation casting doubt on the integrity of the opponent (e.g., "such a vote is probably motivated by the campaign contributions of Company Y, which is hurt by this move," indicating that the candidate has been bought and paid for).

In some cases, the existence of negative information about the candidate (e.g., "I overcame an alcoholic father," "I suffered a childhood disease," "I suffered as a result of my military service") becomes evidence of suitability for the office. The negative information about the past and the story of how the candidate overcame that challenge provide evidence of the determination and ability of the candidate to succeed. The spin or interpretation of the negative information becomes an important aspect of the political process, and the candidate makes the questions an issue (e.g., a smear campaign, the stories are planted, a right- or left-wing conspiracy). The result is that the ability to simply classify in an objective sense any particular piece of information as positive or negative becomes extremely difficult. The issue is how individuals evaluating the information view that information in terms of the value in deciding how to cast a ballot.

Candidates understandably seek to avoid negative press and information that would hurt their images created by exposure in the media. For unknown or little known candidates, an early negative bit of information can prove disastrous to their chances in an election. Gary Hart's potential bid for the White House unraveled when he told the media that he was faithful to his wife and challenged the media to "follow him around." They did, and pictures of his extramarital affair created a kind of backlash that ruined his chances for a run at the presidency. In short, Hart represented himself as victimized by an overzealous media, who were only reporting the facts of his involvement in an extramarital affair. This negative piece of information affected Hart's perceived integrity at a time when the issue was crucial to an evaluation of his suitability for office. The key for candidates is to generate a great deal of positive information that will promote the public's perception of the candidate to win votes. Probably every major political candidate has some aspect of her or his life (current or past) that can be viewed negatively by some portion of the electorate.

The use of attack advertisements in political campaigns has become an argument for why voters abandon the political system. Ansolabehere and Iyengar (1995) estimated that in their experiments, "the effect of seeing a negative as opposed to a positive advertisement is to drop intentions to vote by nearly 5 percentage points" (p. 112). The continuous barrage of negative information disheartens the voters and convinces them that the entire process of politics and campaigning is something to be avoided rather than viewed as an opportunity to change the course of our country by voting for the "best" candidate. Johnson-Cartee and Copeland (1991) contended that the most likely effect of negative political advertising is voter alienation.

Another possibility exists that the votes cast are not really votes for a candidate and that, instead, there is a sense of voting to avoid the negative outcome that one side convinces the voters will happen if an opposing candidate wins the election. A negative view of a particular candidate may increase the level of involvement by voters opposed to the candidate. Voters may feel that they have to become involved to "stop that candidate" as a result of information provided to them. The impact of negative information may be to increase involvement as well as to polarize the electorate. Negativity effects do occur in other means of persuasion, sometimes unintentionally. An established corporation (e.g., Exxon, Tylenol) with a positive brand recognition may lose a lawsuit, be declared in violation of an environmental regulation or worker safety, be accused of cheating on tax regulations, or be found to violate some part of the equal employment law and, ultimately, is perceived as exploitative, profit hungry, and/or morally corrupt. Corporations in a competitive environment seek to avoid the problems associated with developing a negative image that consumers may develop toward specific products or brands. The idea that the brand name of a product carries some value that deserves protection provides a basis to avoid the introduction of negative information. For example, Exxon may consider the need to send out messages to reestablish a good relationship with consumers after an oil spill. The construction of an advertising campaign emphasizing the sensitivity of the corporation to environmental issues becomes a necessity. Exxon produced commercials that provided evidence of a corporation committed to cleaning up the oil spill as a means of image restoration. Even a corporation with years of positive consumer image and little concern may find the results of a single incident a threat to its corporate identity. The impact of a single serious incident may cause significant damage to a reputation that was generally perceived as positive.

THEORETICAL APPROACHES TO THE NEGATIVITY EFFECT

Attribution of Figure Ground Explanation

Attribution theorists suggest that learning about some aspect of a person creates the basis for inference into other personality characteristics. Kanouse and Hanson (1977) suggested that it is the existence of a positivity bias that ironically creates the effect. People generally perceive individuals, including public figures, in a positive light and therefore expect that those persons will behave accordingly. When the undesirable actions of a public official become known, this information stands out against a backdrop of generally positive information. The allegations concerning President Clinton's behavior with Monica Lewinsky are juxtaposed against the prior image of a chief executive conducting the national business. The negative evaluation of Clinton as a president on this single incident against the positive background provides an example of how the act must be viewed against the foreground or backdrop of other information.

The introduction of negative information about an individual increases the attribution of responsibility for that person. Kanouse and Hanson (1977) stated, "By standing in contrast to the norm, the insincere individual invites attributions of responsibility for this trait" (p. 57). The very process of making the attribution creates an aura of importance and centrality for the trait (or, in this case, the information) when evaluating the individual. What happens is that the negative information creates a kind of snowball effect by making the information important and then causing a reevaluation of the individual against the view of a general positive view of other persons. The person is viewed as responsible for this negative act, and the assignment of responsibility creates the need to explain the basis of why the person would commit this act. The process of explaining the responsibility creates negative aspects of the persona, and those negative attributes can be used to predict the possibility of additional negative actions. In the case of President Clinton, we could suggest that if he lied about his relationship with Lewinsky, then he would probably lie about matters of state.

Establishing one fact serves as the basis for the evaluation of similar characteristics about the individual. The assumption that most people would make in the absence of evidence is that public officials are assumed to be honest and not having sex with employees or interns. However, once that perception is disrupted and an individual is not considered part of the general set of assumptions because of some identifiable view, the attribution process highlights the negative information.

Consider, however, that as information surfaced about the Clinton-Lewinsky affair, numerous public officials were also said to have had affairs or some type of inappropriate sexual relations. As sources of information provided examples of alternative persons (several leading Republicans) with similar stories, the uniqueness of the information faded. Clinton had been accused of this action a number of times in the past, so both the motives of the accuser and the uniqueness of the information as applied to Clinton did not exist. In other words, the existence of the foreground changed; Clinton's previous "alleged behaviors" and the existence of other allegations reduced the uniqueness and the impact of the information.

What happens is that as the foreground of comparison changes, public officials are not assumed to be positive. The ability to change this context provides an interesting perspective on "spinning" a story about events. The question of the foreground by which a story is compared provides the basis of whether the information should be considered negative. Hillary Rodham Clinton, the wife of the president, argued on NBC's *Today* that the real story was the right-wing conspiracy against the president. Such statements are efforts to change the context in which the negative information is evaluated.

An assumption of attribution theory is that the disposition of the person is one of positivity toward the subject/target that information surrounds. If a person already believed that President Clinton was disreputable, then the negative information only confirmed the prior existing opinion. Amabile and Glazebrook (1981) argued that the foundation of the bias derives from personality characteristics of the message receiver. Simply put, some people are more distrusting and suspicious than are other people and, as a result, are more likely to seize on negative information as true and to dismiss individuals more readily than are others. The effect of the negative information becomes an "I told you so" attitude, and the negative information has little impact.

The question of attribution and comparison to figure ground provides an informational basis for examination and explanation of the negativity effect. The negativity effect exists because the informational environment for public officials is positive and the report of negative information is viewed in the context of an anomaly. The implication is that changing the environment to include a large amount of negative information would reduce or eliminate this effect by making the negative information no longer unique.

Cost Orientation Hypothesis

Lau (1979) argued that an extension of the Kanouse and Hanson (1977) position is that the motivation exists for a person to view negative information as more persuasive. If negativity is viewed as a cost for the acceptance of the position, then negative information increases the cost of acceptance of the position criticized. Unlike the attribution model, which focuses on the impact of information and the implications or attributions, the cost orientation hypothesis provides a motivational explanation based on risk. In short, if the negative information is correct, then the risk of accepting the positive information is unacceptable.

The more important the position or the issue, the more likely a person may be to sensitive information and view negative information as risk. A person sensitive to risk may very rationally act or react more strongly to negative information than to positive information. Consider that investment strategies may offer potentially lucrative outcomes but that if the risk involves the potential loss of all capital, then the risk may be small but unacceptable. The potential consequences of a negative outcome make the action unacceptable regardless of the arguments about the potential positive outcome, and to some extent, even the probability of the positive outcome may become less salient.

The application of the cost orientation hypothesis to President Clinton and Lewinsky is simply one of motivation. In other words, does the negative information put anything at risk from the standpoint of the voter? The person must determine the degree of risk that the information, if true, would provide for the interests of the person. The lack of motivation on the part of the public to change an opinion stems from the assumption that the allegations

TABLE 5.1 Studies Included in the Meta-analysis

Study[a]	Date	N	Effect of Message on Attitude Toward:[b]			
			Position	Person	Voting	Sponsor
Amabile (Study I)	1981	44	+.295			
Amabile (Study II)	1981	104		+.194		
Ansolabehere	1995	2,216			−.025	−.020
Cohen	1991	95		+.101		
Garramone	1984	211		+.218		−.548
Garramone	1985	112		+.224	+.172	
Garramone	1990	372		+.052	−.052	
Hill	1989	120		−.063		−.305
Hitchon	1995	75				−.398
Hitchon	1997	72				−.392
Kahn	1994	209				−.483
Kaid	1992	283			−.673	−.597
Kaid	1997	116		+.313		+.138
Lodge	1989	322		+.148		
Mathews	1998	125		+.235		−.247
Roddy	1988	274		−.104	−.077	−.020
Shapiro	1992	106	−.153	−.761	+.448	−.211
Thorson	1991	627			.000	
Wadsworth	1987	44				+.150
Weinberger (Study I)	1992	300	+.115			
Weinberger (Study II)	1992	280	+.119			

a. Only the first authors are listed. See references for complete citations.
b. A positive correlation indicates support for the negativity effect (negative information more persuasive or increased willingness to vote), while a negative correlation indicates that the positive information was more effective.

about Clinton's sexual relations, even if true, put nothing at risk in the voter's mind. In other words, the focus becomes one of what potential cost existed as a result of the allegations. Without a specified cost or something that the voter could find at risk, the reaction to the information, even if perceived as negative, lacks motivational value. The cost orientation hypothesis points to a potential additional issue not addressed in the attribution explanation's focus on information, that is, the motivational aspects of the negative information.

This theoretical discussion provides the reasons (informational or motivational) why a negativity effect would occur. The next section involves a statistical summary, or meta-analysis, of existing data. The intent of the meta-analysis is simply to establish whether or not a negativity effect exists rather than to provide a detailed comparison of which account is more accurate. What follows is a discussion about meta-analysis, its utility, and its application to the negativity effect.

META-ANALYSIS

Literature Search Procedure

Appropriate computer and published indexes as well as published reviews of the literature (Ansolabehere & Iyengar, 1995; Basil, Schooler, & Reeves, 1991; Johnson-Cartee & Copeland, 1991; Lau, 1986; Pfau & Kenski, 1990; Sears & Whitney, 1973) were consulted for information relevant to this review of the negativity effect. Special attention was given to the Lau, Sigelman, Heldman, and Babbitt (in press) meta-analysis of the effects of negative political advertisements because of the shared issues.[1] This analysis could not obtain three of the articles cited by the authors that the authors indicated contain potentially relevant data. The pool of studies in this analysis contains six studies with relevant estimates *not* included in the Lau et al. analysis. A comparison of effect estimates demonstrates a high degree of agreement between the two analyses with respect to both estimation of the effect and designation of coded outcomes. Table 5.1 provides a list and description of the studies incorporated into this analysis. For inclusion in this meta-analysis, a manuscript/article had to use some form of media to provide negative information to form an impression that could be compared to the use of positive information. The designs had to

incorporate some type of public policy or election issue that involved political contexts where the evaluations involved the use of real or fictional candidates.[2]

Several articles were deleted because the design did not fit the requirements for this analysis. Investigations considering the influence of inconsistent, unfavorable, or contradictory information or the impact of personality characteristics on the interpretation of negative information were not included (Bear & Hodun, 1975; Beigel, 1973; Erber & Lau, 1990). Some articles lacked sufficient statistical information to permit the calculation of an effect size (Finkel & Geer, 1998; Hibbing & Theiss-Morse, 1998; Kinder, 1978; Lau, 1982, 1985). All four just-cited articles (the Lau data set was published twice) were generated in the area of political science, where often the results are represented in the form of a multiple regression equation. These studies were not included in the Lau et al. (in press) meta-analysis for these reasons. Without the inclusion of a zero-order correlation matrix, it is impossible to estimate the effects from the multiple regression equation.[3]

Comparing Various Outcomes of Such Messages

Studies were coded for four possible dependent attitude and/or behavioral intentions in this examination: (a) attitude toward a position, (b) attitude toward the target of the information, (c) attitude toward and intention about voting, and (d) attitude toward the sponsor of the negative information. The first dependent variable had four studies providing data on how the combination of positive and negative information affected the attitude toward a proposition or policy. The second dependent variable cluster centered on how the target of the messages (a political candidate) was affected by the combination of positive and negative information. The third dependent variable was how the combination of positive and negative information affected the desire to vote. This variable is the assessment of how the process affects the willingness of a person to continue to participate in the political process. The final variable considers how the use of negative advertising affects the sponsor of such information in an environment where the opposition is providing supportive messages.

Statistical Analysis

The technique used for this meta-analysis was the variance-centered method of analysis developed by Hunter and Schmidt (1990). The technique consists of three parts: (a) conversion to a common statistical metric, (b) averaging the various effects, and (c) examination of variability in the original data. The conversion to a common metric represents the process of taking the raw statistical information in the article and converting it to some metric for comparison. This study uses the correlation coefficient as the metric for analysis due to the ease of calculation and interpretation.

The second step of the analysis involves taking the converted effects and averaging the coefficients, weighting on the basis of sample size. The weighting by sample size reflects the statistical assumption that studies with larger samples have less sampling error than do effects with smaller samples.

The final step provides an examination of the variability in the sample of correlations. Theoretically, a homogeneous solution is one where the differences between the individually observed effects are the result of random sampling error. The test for this possibility is a chi-square test that compares the observed variability existing in the actual data to the predicted variability that exists if the differ-

ences between the studies were the result of random sampling error. A significant chi-square indicates that the distribution of effects is heterogeneous. A nonsignificant chi-square indicates that the variability in the effects could be the result of sampling error, and the differences are considered to be homogeneous with no evidence of a potential moderator variable.

RESULTS

The first analysis considers the impact of a combination of negative and positive messages on attitudes toward a proposition. The four studies (Amabile & Glazebrook, 1981, Study I; Shapiro & Rieger, 1992; Weinberger, Allen, & Dillon, 1992, Studies I and II) demonstrate an average positive effect (average $r = .088$, $k = 4$, $N = 730$, variance of average $r = .0117$), and the distribution of observed effects is heterogeneous, χ^2 (3, $N = 730$) = 8.65, $p < .05$. This indicates support for the negativity effect. However, the average effect should be interpreted cautiously due to the presence of a possible moderator variable (as indicated by the significant χ^2).

The second cluster of effects examined the impact on the target of the information. The average positive effect indicates some support for a negativity effect (average $r = .058$, $k = 10$, $N = 1,862$, variance of average $r = .0561$). However, this conclusion is qualified because the sample of estimates exhibits significant departure from a normal distribution, χ^2 (9, $N = 1,862$) = 105.24, $p < .05$. It is likely that one or more moderator variable influences the relationship between negative information and the target of that information.

The third set of variables considers the impact of issues surrounding voting or participation in the process. The question is whether the impact of the introduction of negative information diminishes the desire to participate in the process. The average effect was small and negative, indicating that negative advertising *decreased* the desire or intention to vote (average $r = -.051, k = 8, N = 4,085$, variance of average $r = .0359$), and the distribution was heterogeneous, $\chi^2 (8, N = 4,085) = 147.39, p < .05$.

The final set of outcomes examines whether the sponsor of negative information suffers when positive information also exists. Only one study demonstrated a positive effect on the view of the sponsor (Kaid, 1997; see also Wadsworth et al., 1987), all other effects indicate that the view held of the sponsor was worse after the use of a negative advertisement. The average effect demonstrates a relatively large negative average correlation (average $r = -.146, k = 12, N = 3,851$, variance of average $r = .0473$). However, as with the previous examples, the distribution of observed effects was heterogeneous, $\chi^2 (11, N = 3,851) = 189.98, p < .05$.

DISCUSSION AND FUTURE DIRECTIONS

The accumulated evidence provides limited support for the existence of the negativity effect in the context of political advertising. The summary of the existing data does indicate that negative information produces a larger effect on opinion formation when compared to positive information, whether for a position ($r = .088$) or a candidate ($r = .058$). The additional impacts of negative information is that negative information is more likely to diminish the desire to vote ($r = -.051$) and create an unfavorable impression of the sponsor of the information ($r = -.146$). However, the effects should be interpreted cautiously because every average estimate was generated from a heterogeneous set of effects. No adequate explanation is offered to account for this particular heterogeneity; with relatively

few effects, there is little ability to systematically examine the potential sources of variability. This is consistent with the finding of Lau et al. (in press), who after an extensive search for moderator variables concluded that although "some critical factor must be present for the expected effects of negative advertising to emerge, we have not been able to identify it."

No attempt was made to examine the veracity of the two theoretical positions regarding the negativity effect (attribution and cost orientation) because the data were not the result of designs that permitted us to systematically examine the outcomes that would separate the two explanations. Future research might examine the explanations to determine which of the theoretical accounts provides the best account of the observed negativity effect. The current examinations do not consider how the particular information is incorporated or evaluated by the message receiver in terms of decision making.

The net benefit of making accusations in an ongoing political campaign is probably not high and certainly not guaranteed. This lack of a demonstrable positive outcome creates a need for persuasive campaign designers to reconsider the use of such strategies. Two parties exist in political negative advertising: the target of the message and the source of the message. Any political attack advertisement can produce effects on both parties. The current data indicate that the sponsor of such an advertisement probably generates no relative advantage by the use of such advertising. Any reduction in support for the target of the advertisement is compensated by an equal reduction in support for the sponsor of the commercial. This conclusion must be considered limited by the design of the current investigations, which typically use a fictitious candidate as opposed to a real election. In an election, there are (at least) two sides issuing positive and negative messages. The voter is choosing between or among the candidates rather than evaluating a single candidate. Many of the designs do not consider the dynamic process of a campaign involving at least two sides. In addition, the media and other agencies make comments about the candidates as well as about the tenor, tone, and accuracy of the information supplied. Although it may be impossible to include all of these agents in well-controlled research, it is surely the case that designs that include more rather than fewer sources of information would better simulate information flow in a political campaign.

"Going negative" has become a term applied to the decision of a political candidate to use negative information in an effort to improve the chances of winning an election. Such an advantage appears at best temporary and at worst illusionary. The problem is that the impact of the messages sponsored by an opponent typically does not provide much, if any, of a comparative advantage for the candidate using the strategy. The results indicate little advantage for the person relying on negative advertisement to promote the absolute or relative advantage of the candidate.

Ansolabehere and Iyengar (1995) pointed out that so long as the negative trend continues,

> the trajectory is downward. By all accounts, campaigns will only continue to become more negative and nasty. Many political consultants have come to believe that all Americans are cynical about their government and that the electorate responds only to negatives and thus that they must go negative. (p. 114)

The implications of the continued large-scale use of negative political advertising, as well as the escalation of such efforts, would be to continue to see the erosion of participation in the political system. The effect on participation was relatively small ($r = -.051$), but this effect was demonstrated on a relatively small set of exposures. The cumulative effect of a series of negative campaigns may be more substantial.

The fundamental problem becomes the belief that such advertising efforts are successful and improve the chances of winning an election. The evidence supported by the outcome of this meta-analysis is that negative political advertising fails to improve the position of the candidate. However, the desire to gain retribution creates a form of mutually assured destruction. As would result from a nuclear war, negative advertising may produce fallout that destroys the political environment.

Pfau and Kenski (1990) documented a rapid growth of attack politics during the 1980s. The election campaigns saw a growth in the use of negative information that sought to undermine the candidacy of opponents. The response was the attempt to inoculate the population against the expectation of attacks in the media (by opponents or by members of the media). The inoculation metaphor is used to describe the practice of exposing a person to a weakened form of the argument and thereby gaining some protection by strengthening a psychological immune system to subsequent attacks with that information. Referring to their own investigation, Pfau and Kenski (1990; see also Pfau & Burgoon, 1988, 1989) concluded, "The two investigations, taken together, offer a solid foundation for findings concerning the effectiveness of inoculation in political campaign advertising" (p. 99). The analysis of elections indicates the possibility that a candidate may work to inoculate voters by providing the potential accusation and the response prior to the attack. The historical evidence indicates that inoculation may reduce the impact of political attack advertising. Research on the effectiveness of inoculation demonstrates the potential to blunt the impact of various image problems (Pfau, 1992; Pfau, Kenski, Nitz, & Sorenson, 1990; Pfau et al., 1997). An understanding of the ability to counter negative attack ads before the process starts may offer a potential solution to the problem of negative political advertising from the standpoint of the candidate.

Another research agenda should be the examination of what happens after the release of negative information and the impact of subsequent communication to rehabilitate the image of the person or corporation. The process in rhetoric is called apologia, where one purpose of the discourse is the restoration of membership in the community after a known transgression. Corporate apologia occurs when something happens and a corporation seeks to restore the value of the brand or avoid the impact of developing a negative image from information provided to the public. President Clinton offered a variety of messages to provide an account for his negative behavior (the Lewinsky episodes). This process points to the problem of understanding the negativity effect as simply a snapshot in what is often a dynamic process of attitude formation and evaluation. Often the negative information is just one set of information in a changing and dynamic informational environment where many messages on various topics are constantly disseminated.

Future research should examine the impact of a candidate refusing to respond with negative information about an opponent once attacked. The use of negative information is often seen as a tactic to recover momentum or to slow an opponent who is starting to pull ahead. The impact of negative information needs to be set in a context. This means that future research may have to be more longitudinal and ongoing during actual campaigns rather than with experimental captive audiences. The movement to "field" research will result in a certain lack of control, but when combined with experimental findings, it will provide a more complete picture.

The largest consideration should be given to the calibration or measurement of the extent to which information is considered positive or negative to the message receiver. If the valence of the message was treated as a covariate and then compared to the attitude of the receiver toward the candidate, then the understanding should improve. The tendency to treat message content as an independent variable rather than as a constructed perception makes the designs not reflect the persuasive reality of the situation. This treatment of message valence would help to understand how audience members may be responding fundamentally differently to the same attack message. Designs need to reflect the ability of audience members to react and evaluate differently because it is the differences in evaluation, as well as the differences in messages, that should be predictive.

This chapter has pointed to an important and continuing issue in the practical art of persuasion. The links between the theoretical issues in persuasion are those most important when they consider the current practice of those engaged in the art of persuasion in the community. Given the high level of use of negative political advertising, the need exists to explore the various implications of continued use of this approach to persuasion. The current data are very sparse but indicate that such advertising, while effective in reducing the desirability of the target, has no net effect because of the reduction in desirability of the sponsor. In other words, the research provides no support for the view of a general benefit to the sponsor of political attack advertising. Continued use of negative political advertising may only further alienate the voting populace. The need to conduct additional research on this outcome is apparent.

NOTES

1. There is considerable overlap between this investigation and the Lau et al. (in press) meta-analysis. However, differences in the sample (this meta-analysis includes eight investigations not

included in that report), in the assumptions (e.g., studies in this investigation had to have both positive and negative information present), and in a number of technical statistical procedures make the analyses not identical.

2. Studies designed to examine the impact of inoculation were not included in this analysis. Inoculation studies are intended to examine the impact of prior information on subsequent exposure to contrary information rather than to compare the relative impact of positive and negative information. In a sense, this meta-analysis, when combined with one examining inoculation and the existing analyses on message sidedness, would provide a more complete understanding of the impact of information valence.

3. The coefficients in a multiple regression equation are the result of an analysis that considers the interrelationship among variables to provide the contribution of another variable after removing the influence of all other variables in the equation. An infinite number of potential correlation matrices exist that will generate any given multiple regression solution. Therefore, it is impossible to go backward from the multiple regression equation to the particular set of correlations that generated that equation. It should be noted that the Lau et al. (in press) meta-analysis does use such data and provides a justification for that procedure with which these authors disagree.

REFERENCES

*Amabile, T., & Glazebrook, A. (1981). A negativity bias in interpersonal evaluation. *Journal of Experimental Social Psychology, 18*, 1-22.

*Ansolabehere, S., & Iyengar, S. (1995). *Going negative: How attack ads shrink and polarize the electorate*. New York: Free Press.

Basil, M., Schooler, C., & Reeves, B. (1991). Positive and negative political advertising: Effectiveness of ads and perceptions of candidates. In F. Biocca (Ed.), *Television and political advertising*, Vol. 1: *Psychological processes* (pp. 245-262). Hillsdale, NJ: Lawrence Erlbaum.

Bear, G., & Hodun, A. (1975). Implicational principles and the cognition of confirmatory, contra-

dictory, incomplete, and irrelevant information. *Journal of Personality and Social Psychology, 32*, 594-604.

Beigel, A. (1973). Resistance to change: Differential effects of favorable and unfavorable initial communications. *British Journal of Social and Clinical Psychology, 12*, 153-158.

*Cohen, J., & Davis, R. (1991). Third-person effects and the differential impact in negative political advertising. *Journalism Quarterly, 68*, 680-688.

Erber, R., & Lau, R. (1990). Political cynicism revisited: An information-processing reconciliation of policy-based and incumbency-based interpretations of change in trust in government. *American Journal of Political Science, 34*, 236-253.

Finkel, S., & Geer, J. (1998). A spot check: Casting doubt on the demobilizing effect of attack advertising. *American Journal of Political Science, 42*, 573-595.

Fiske, S. (1980). Attention and weight in person perception: The impact of negative and extreme behavior. *Journal of Personality and Social Psychology, 38*, 889-908.

*Garramone, G. (1984). Voter responses to negative political ads. *Journalism Quarterly, 61*, 250-259.

*Garramone, G. (1985). Effects of negative political advertising: The roles of sponsor and rebuttal. *Journal of Broadcasting and Electronic Media, 29*, 147-159.

*Garramone, G., Atkin, C., Pinkleton, B., & Cole, R. (1990). Effects of negative political advertising on the political process. *Journal of Broadcasting and Electronic Media, 34*, 229-311.

Hibbing, J., & Theiss-Morse, E. (1998). The media's role in public negativity toward Congress: Distinguishing emotional reactions and cognitive evaluations. *American Journal of Political Science, 42*, 475-498.

*Hill, R. (1989). An exploration of voter responses to political advertisements. *Journal of Advertising, 18*, 14-22.

*Hitchon, J., & Chang, C. (1995). Effects of gender schematic processing on the reception of political commercials for men and women candidates. *Communication Research, 22*, 430-458.

*Hitchon, J., Chang, C., & Harris, R. (1997). Should women emote? Perceptual bias and opinion change in response to political ads for candidates of different genders. *Political Communication, 14,* 49-69.

Hunter, J., & Schmidt, F. (1990). *Methods of meta-analysis: Correcting for error and bias in research findings.* Newbury Park, CA: Sage.

Johnson-Cartee, K., & Copeland, G. (1991). *Negative political advertising: Coming of age.* Hillsdale, NJ: Lawrence Erlbaum.

*Kahn, K., & Geer, J. (1994). Creating impressions: An experimental investigation of political advertising on television. *Political Behavior, 16,* 93-116.

*Kaid, L. (1997). Effects of television spots on images of Dole and Clinton. *American Behavioral Scientist, 40,* 1085-1094.

*Kaid, L., Chanslor, M., & Hovind, M. (1992). The influence of program and commercial type on political advertising effectiveness. *Journal of Broadcasting and Electronic Media, 36,* 303-320.

Kanouse, D., & Hanson, L. (1972). Negativity in evaluations. In E. Jones, D. Kanouse, H. Kelly, R. Nisbett, S. Valins, & B. Weiner (Eds.), *Attribution: Perceiving the causes of behavior* (pp. 121-135). Morristown, NJ: General Learning Press.

Kanouse, D., & Hanson, L. (1977). Negativity in evaluations. In E. Jones, D. Kanouse, H. Kelly, R. Nisbett, S. Valins, & B. Weiner (Eds.), *Attribution: Perceiving the causes of behavior* (pp. 47-62). Morristown, NJ: General Learning Press.

Kellermann, K. (1984). The negativity effect and its implications for initial interaction. *Communication Monographs, 51,* 37-55.

Kellermann, K. (1989). The negativity effect in interaction: It's all in your point of view. *Human Communication Research, 16,* 147-183.

Kinder, D. (1978). Political person perception: The asymmetrical influences of sentiment and choice on perceptions of presidential candidates. *Journal of Personality and Social Psychology, 36,* 859-871.

Lau, R. (1979). *Negativity in person perception with applications to political behavior.* Unpublished doctoral dissertation, University of California, Los Angeles.

Lau, R. (1982). Negativity in political perception. *Political Behavior, 4,* 353-377.

Lau, R. (1985). Two explanations for negativity effects in political behavior. *American Journal of Political Science, 29,* 119-138.

Lau, R. (1986). Political motivation and political cognition. In E. Higgins & R. Sorrentino (Eds.), *Handbook of motivation and cognition* (Vol. 2, pp. 297-327). New York: Guilford.

*Lodge, M., McGraw, K., & Stroh, P. (1989). An impression-driven model of candidate evaluation. *American Political Science Review, 83,* 399-419.

Lau, R., Sigelman, L., Heldman, C., & Babbitt, R. (in press). The effects of negative political advertisements: A meta-analytic assessment. *American Political Science Review.*

*Mathews, D., & Dietz-Uhler, B. (1998). The black-sheep effect: How positive and negative advertisements affect voters' perceptions of the sponsor of the advertisement. *Journal of Applied Social Psychology, 28,* 1903-1915.

Pfau, M. (1992). The potential of inoculation in promoting resistance to the effectiveness of comparative advertising messages. *Communication Quarterly, 40,* 26-44.

Pfau, M., & Burgoon, M. (1988). Inoculation in political campaign communication. *Human Communication Research, 15,* 91-111.

Pfau, M., & Burgoon, M. (1989). The efficacy of issue and character attack message strategies in political campaign communication. *Communication Reports, 2,* 53-61.

Pfau, M., & Kenski, H. (1990). *Attack politics: Strategy and defense.* New York: Praeger.

Pfau, M., Kenski, H., Nitz, M., & Sorenson, J. (1990). Efficacy of inoculation strategies in promoting resistance to political attack messages: Application to direct mail. *Communication Monographs, 57,* 25-43.

Pfau, M., Tusing, K., Koerner, A., Lee, W., Godbold, L., Penaloza, L., Yang, V., & Hong, Y. (1997). Enriching the inoculation construct: The role of critical components in the process of resistance. *Human Communication Research, 24,* 187-215.

*Roddy, B., & Garramone, G. (1988). Appeals and strategies of negative political advertising. *Jour-*

nal of Broadcasting and Electronic Media, 32,
415-427.

Sears, D., & Whitney, R. (1973). Political persuasion. In I. Pool, S. Frey, W. Schramm, N. Maccoby, & E. Parker (Eds.), *Handbook of communication* (pp. 253-289). Chicago: Rand McNally.

*Shapiro, M., & Rieger, R. (1992). Comparing positive and negative political advertising on radio. *Journalism Quarterly, 69,* 135-145.

*Thorson, E., Christ, W., & Caywood, C. (1991). Selling candidates like tubes of toothpaste: Is the comparison apt? In F. Biocca (Ed.), *Television and political advertising* (Vol. 1, pp. 163-175). Hillsdale, NJ: Lawrence Erlbaum.

*Wadsworth, A., Patterson, P., Kaid, L., Cullers, G., Malcomb, D., & Lamirand, L. (1987). "Masculine" vs. "feminine" strategies in political ads: Implications for female candidates. *Journal of Applied Communication Research, 15,* 77-94.

*Weinberger, M., Allen, C., & Dillon, W. (1992). The impact of negative network news. *Journalism Quarterly, 69,* 287-294.

Asterisk (*) indicates study included in the meta-analysis.

PART II

THEORIES OF PERSUASION

6

A Cognitive Dissonance
Theory Perspective on Persuasion

EDDIE HARMON-JONES

Research and conceptual development on the theory of cognitive dissonance continues in full force more than 40 years after the theory's conception. Part of the reason for the theory's longevity may be that it was stated abstractly; could be applied to a wide array of issues; dealt with the interaction of cognition, motivation, and affect; and generated research that suggested ways of inducing lasting attitude, belief, and behavior change. For example, dissonance research has demonstrated that dissonance processes can reduce prejudice (Leippe & Eisenstadt, 1994), increase water conservation (Dickerson, Thibodeau, Aronson, & Miller, 1992), increase the purchasing of condoms (Stone, Aronson, Crain, Winslow, & Fried, 1994), reduce hunger and thirst (Brehm, 1962), and reduce pain (Zimbardo, Cohen, Weisenberg, Dworkin, & Firestone, 1969). In addition, dissonance processes can lead to changes in attitudes toward a variety of objects and issues, such as boring tasks (Festinger & Carlsmith, 1959), boring reading passages (Harmon-Jones, Brehm, Greenberg, Simon, & Nelson, 1996), delicious chocolate (Harmon-Jones, 2000a), eating grasshoppers (Zimbardo, Weisenberg, Firestone, & Levy, 1965), sour beverages made with vinegar (Harmon-Jones et al., 1996), increasing tuition at one's university (Elliot & Devine, 1994), and mandatory comprehensive final exams (Simon, Greenberg, & Brehm, 1995).

Currently, researchers are approaching issues related to cognitive dissonance processes with a level of intensity that typically occurs at the birth of a theory. Several generative revisions to the original theory have been

AUTHOR'S NOTE: This chapter and portions of the research described herein were supported by funds from the University of Wisconsin Graduate School, the Wisconsin Alumni Research Foundation, a Wisconsin/Hilldale Undergraduate/Faculty Research Fellowship, and the National Science Foundation (BCS-9910702). Thanks go to Jim Dillard, Cindy Harmon-Jones, and Michael Pfau for providing useful comments on a draft of this chapter.

proposed, and there is much controversy regarding the processes by which the cognitive and behavioral changes occur. In this chapter, I provide a brief review of original theory of cognitive dissonance and revisions of the original theory. Then, I critically evaluate the revisions of the theory by discussing recent research that has challenged each of these revisions. Finally, I present a recently proposed revision and preliminary tests of this revision.

ORIGINAL VERSION OF COGNITIVE DISSONANCE THEORY

According to the original version of the theory (Festinger, 1957), the presence of a cognitive inconsistency of sufficient magnitude will evoke an aversive motivational state—dissonance—that drives cognitive work aimed at reducing the cognitive inconsistency. The magnitude of dissonance aroused in regard to a particular cognition is a function of the number and psychological importance of cognitions dissonant (inconsistent) and consonant (consistent) with this cognition. Thus, dissonance will increase as the number and importance of dissonant cognitions relative to consonant cognitions increase. From the ratio used to compute the magnitude of dissonance (dissonant cognitions / dissonant + consonant cognitions, with each weighted by its importance), the routes of dissonance reduction are as follows: subtracting dissonant cognitions, adding consonant cognitions, decreasing the importance of dissonant cognitions, and increasing the importance of consonant cognitions. These modes of dissonance reduction may manifest themselves in attitude, belief, value, or behavior maintenance or change. Dissonance reduction will be aimed at altering the cognition least resistant to change.

The term *dissonance* has been used to refer to both the cognitive inconsistency and the aversive motivational state the inconsistency produces. However, it is important to distinguish the affective-motivational state of dissonance from the cognitive inconsistency and the cognitive and behavioral changes that result from the affective-motivational state of dissonance. I refer to the affective-motivational state as dissonance, to the cognitive inconsistency as cognitive discrepancy, and to cognitive and behavioral changes as cognitive discrepancy reduction.

MAJOR PARADIGMS USED IN DISSONANCE RESEARCH

Four research paradigms have been used extensively in the investigation of dissonance processes. To facilitate the presentation of experiments within this chapter, I briefly review these paradigms.

Free Choice Paradigm. In the free choice paradigm, developed by Brehm (1956), it is assumed that once a decision is made, dissonance may be aroused. After the person makes a decision, each of the negative aspects of the chosen alternative and the positive aspects of the rejected alternative is dissonant with the decision. By contrast, each of the positive aspects of the chosen alternative and the negative aspects of the rejected alternative is consonant with the decision. Difficult decisions arouse more dissonance than do easy decisions because there is a greater proportion of dissonant cognitions after a difficult decision than after an easy one. Post-decision dissonance can be reduced by subtracting negative aspects of the chosen alternative or positive aspects of the rejected alternative, or it can be reduced by adding positive aspects to the chosen alternative or negative aspects to the rejected alternative. Thus, dissonance may be reduced by viewing the chosen alternative as more desirable and the rejected alternative as less desirable. This effect has been termed *spreading of the alternatives.*

Induced Compliance Paradigm. In the induced compliance paradigm, which was used by Festinger and Carlsmith (1959), it is assumed that dissonance is aroused when a person does or says something that is contrary to a prior belief or attitude. From the cognition of the prior belief or attitude, it follows that one would not engage in such behavior. On the other hand, inducements to engage in such behavior—promises of reward or threats of punishment—provide cognitions that are consonant with the behavior. That is, these cognitions provide external justifications for the behavior. The greater the number and importance of these cognitions (justifications), the less the dissonance aroused. The amount of justification for engaging in the action has been manipulated using different amounts of money or different amounts of social influence that give persons the perception of having little choice or much choice over engaging in the action. When persons engage in the counterattitudinal action and believe they have little justification for doing so because they were paid a relatively small amount or because they were left with the perception that they chose to engage in the action, they will experience dissonance and reduce it by changing the belief or attitude to correspond more closely to what was said or done (see reviews by Beauvois & Joule, 1996; Brehm & Cohen, 1962; Harmon-Jones & Mills, 1999a; Wicklund & Brehm, 1976).

Belief Disconfirmation Paradigm. A third paradigm used in the investigation of dissonance theory is the belief disconfirmation paradigm, first used by Festinger, Riecken, and Schachter (1956). In this paradigm, it is assumed that dissonance is aroused when persons are exposed to information inconsistent with their beliefs. If the dissonance is not reduced by changing one's belief, the dissonance can lead to misperception or misinterpretation of the information, rejection or refutation of the information, seeking support from those who agree with the belief, and attempts to persuade others to accept the belief.

Hypocrisy Paradigm. Aronson, Fried, Stone, and colleagues developed another paradigm to test the theory—the hypocrisy paradigm (Aronson, Fried, & Stone, 1991). In this paradigm, persons are induced to make a public attitudinally consistent statement, and then they are reminded of times when they did not act in accord with their statement. In other words, participants are induced to say one thing and then are reminded of times when they did not practice what they "preached." Research using this paradigm has demonstrated that individuals will reduce the dissonance by being more likely to act in accord with their pro-attitudinal statement (Stone et al., 1994) or by changing their attitudes to be more consistent with their past behavior, depending on whether the recent speech or past behavior was more resistant to change (Fried, 1998).

REVISIONS OF THE ORIGINAL THEORY

What is the psychological mechanism that is responsible for these persuasion effects? Festinger (1957) proposed that cognitive inconsistency evoked motivation to reduce inconsistency. In an effort to increase the predictive power of the theory, other theorists have suggested that different motivations underlie the persuasion effects observed in dissonance settings. Currently, this is the source of serious inquiry by dissonance theorists (see Harmon-Jones & Mills, 1999a). In what follows, I review these alternative motivational explanations.[1]

Self-Consistency

One of the first motivational alternative explanations for dissonance theory was proposed as a refinement of Festinger's original statement. In this self-consistency theory, Aronson (1968) proposed that dissonance theory made its most precise predictions when "a firm expectancy was involved as one of the cognitions in question" (p. 23). He further proposed that the theory is

> clearer still when that firm expectancy involves the individual's self-concept, for—almost by definition—our expectancies about our own behavior are firmer than our expectancies about the behavior of another person. Thus, at the very heart of dissonance theory, where it makes its clearest and neatest prediction, we are not dealing with just any two cognitions; rather, we are usually dealing with the self-concept and cognitions about some behavior. If dissonance exists, it is because the individual's behavior is inconsistent with his self-concept. (p. 23)

Aronson (1968, 1969, 1992, 1999) thus proposed that a violation of a self-concept was necessary to create dissonance. According to this theory, the self-concepts of morality, competence, and consistency are the self-concepts that serve as the standards against which behavior is compared. These self-concepts are standards for behavior that are often in "accord with the conventional morals and prevailing values of society" (Thibodeau & Aronson, 1992, p. 592). However, Aronson noted that persons with negative self-concepts would expect to behave immorally and incompetently and hence would experience disso-

nance when they behave in contrary ways, that is, morally or competently.

Evaluation of Self-Consistency Explanation

The self-consistency revision retains inconsistency as the motivating force behind dissonance and its effects. Although the self-consistency revision is quite similar to the original theory, it limits dissonance theory to a self theory and thus restricts dissonance processes to organisms with self-concepts, thereby excluding most nonhuman animals and humans under 3 years of age. However, experiments demonstrating that dissonance effects occur in white rats, which presumably lack self-concepts (Lawrence & Festinger, 1962), contradict this revision. In addition, the self-consistency revision restricts dissonance processes to organisms whose self-concepts become accessible as a standard for comparison whenever cognitive discrepancies are encountered. This restriction would probably omit several situations because it does not seem plausible that a self-concept would become accessible every time a cognitive discrepancy is encountered (for further criticisms of this theory, see Brehm, 1992, and the discussion below).

Self-Affirmation

A second motivational explanation of dissonance effects is self-affirmation theory (Steele, 1988; Steele & Liu, 1983; Steele, Spencer, & Lynch, 1993). This revision proposes that the effects observed in dissonance situations are not the result of cognitive inconsistency or self inconsistency. In fact, Steele et al. (1993) suggested that "not only is a motive for self-consistency absent from dissonance processes, but it is absent from mental life altogether" (p. 894). The self-affirmation revision posits that situations that create dissonance exert their effects because of the threat to the individual's need to perceive oneself as having global integrity, that is, being morally and adaptive adequate in general.

Research on self-affirmation theory has suggested that providing persons with an opportunity to affirm their self-integrity reduces the attitude change that typically occurs in the induced compliance paradigm (Steele & Liu, 1983). Steele has argued that these effects result because acting counterattitudinally threatens self-integrity, and the attitude change that is typically observed occurs to reduce this threat to self-integrity. Having persons affirm their self-worth will thus reduce the need to change attitudes.

In contrast to E. Aronson's self-consistency model, the self-affirmation model asserts that the motivating force in producing dissonance effects is not inconsistency but rather the need for self-integrity. Thus, for self-affirmation theory, the need for a positive self-concept is a condition necessary for dissonance.

Evaluation of Self-Affirmation Explanation

Relevance of the Affirmation. Recent research suggests that the self-affirmation manipulations prevent attitude change only when the affirmation is irrelevant to the counterattitudinal action. When the affirmation is relevant to the counterattitudinal action, attitude change may actually increase because it enhances the accessibility of a personal standard. Blanton, Cooper, Skurnik, and Aronson (1997) conducted an experiment in which persons reflected on a positive aspect of the self that was either relevant or irrelevant to the counterattitudinal action. They found that when persons had freely chosen to write essays arguing against funding for handicapped services at their university and then had received personality feedback indicating

that they were high in the trait of compassion (relevant affirmation), they changed their attitudes even more in the direction of their behavior. By contrast, when persons had freely chosen to write essays on the same issue and then received personality feedback indicating that they were high in the trait of creativity (irrelevant affirmation), they did not change their attitudes. Blanton et al. interpreted these effects to indicate that dissonance reduction is not the result of a motive for self-affirmation.

These effects could be reinterpreted in original dissonance theory terms. Accordingly, the counterattitudinal behavior is the cognition most resistant to change, the conception of oneself as compassionate is dissonant with the counterattitudinal behavior, and thus the magnitude of dissonance is increased relative to a situation in which the conception of oneself as compassionate is not made more accessible. Thus, this increased dissonance caused more attitude change. By contrast, the conception of oneself as creative is a cognition that is not relevant to the cognitions involved in the dissonant relationship. Hence, it should have no effect on the magnitude of dissonance. However, affirming aspects of the self that are not relevant to the discrepancy may alter the amount of dissonance aroused because this cognition distracts one from the dissonance (McGregor, Newby-Clark, & Zanna, 1999), reduces the importance of the relevant cognitions (Simon et al., 1995), or decreases the negative affect associated with the dissonance (Harmon-Jones, 2000b).

Importance of Cognitions. Research by Simon et al. (1995) has shown that a typical self-affirmation manipulation (i.e., participants complete a scale on which they report their important values) causes persons to perceive their counterattitudinal behavior and preexisting attitudes as less important, which reduces the likelihood of observing dissonance-related attitude change. In one experiment, Simon et al. found that making an important but non-self-affirming issue salient (i.e., world hunger) caused reductions in the perceived importance of the counterattitudinal behavior and preexisting attitude rather than attitude change following freely choosing to write a counterattitudinal statement. Taken together, these results show that self-affirmation may exert its effects on the dissonance process by reducing persons' perception of the importance of the cognitions associated with the preexisting attitude and counterattitudinal behavior. Thus, the original theory of dissonance can explain the effects generated by self-affirmation theory.

Pitting Consistency Against Self-Affirmation. Stone, Wiegand, Cooper, and Aronson (1997) provided further evidence suggesting that the primary motive underlying discrepancy reduction is not the restoration of the global moral and adaptive integrity of the entire self-system, as self-affirmation theory predicts; rather, the primary motive is the resolution of the specific discrepancy, as the original theory and self-consistency theory predict. Using a hypocrisy paradigm in which participants delivered a public speech advocating using condoms to prevent AIDS and were then reminded of their failures to use condoms, Stone et al. (1997) found that when given a choice between purchasing condoms (which would reduce the specific discrepancy) and donating to a homeless project (which would restore global self-worth), more participants chose to purchase condoms. In a second experiment using a hypocrisy paradigm in which participants delivered a public speech advocating the importance of volunteering to help the homeless and were then reminded of their failures to volunteer, Stone et al. found that more participants chose to donate to the homeless than to purchase condoms, even when participants had rated using condoms to prevent AIDS as more important to their global self-worth than

donating to feed the homeless. Results from the experiments also indicated that persons were more likely to choose an option that would restore global self-worth in conditions where a sufficient discrepancy was aroused (hypocrisy) than in comparison conditions. These results suggest that persons will choose to restore global self-worth following a discrepant action if it is the only available option. However, if given a choice, persons opt for direct discrepancy reduction, suggesting that avoiding discrepancy rather than restoring global self-worth is a more prominent concern of persons in dissonance situations. Thus, the results from these experiments cast doubt on the self-affirmation explanation of dissonance effects.

In sum, recent research from several different perspectives has challenged the self-affirmation interpretation of dissonance effects. However, the research on self-affirmation has identified important ways of reducing dissonance, has contributed to a more thorough understanding of dissonance processes, and has been useful in other arenas examining self-protective motivations (Aronson, Cohen, & Nail, 1999).

Aversive Consequences

In another motivational explanation for dissonance theory, Cooper and Fazio (1984) posited that cognitive inconsistency was neither necessary nor sufficient for dissonance to occur. They proposed that for dissonance to occur, individuals must engage in behavior that has the perceived potential to cause an irrevocable unwanted consequence. That is, Cooper and Fazio asserted that a sense of personal responsibility for producing foreseeable aversive consequences is necessary for dissonance to be aroused.

Cooper and Fazio (1984) reviewed evidence suggesting that when persons engaged in a counterattitudinal action but did not produce aversive consequences, they did not change their attitudes to be consistent with their behavior. For instance, Cooper and Worchel (1970) suggested that participants in the low-justification condition of Festinger and Carlsmith (1959) changed their attitudes not because of cognitive inconsistency but rather because they felt personally responsible for producing the aversive consequence of convincing another person to believe that boring tasks were interesting. To test this explanation, Cooper and Worchel replicated and extended the design of the Festinger and Carlsmith (1959) experiment. They found that when low-justification participants were led to believe that they did not convince another person that a boring task was interesting, they subsequently did not rate the task as more interesting. Other experiments have replicated these results by finding that when participants believe that their counterattitudinal statements do not persuade others, they do not change their attitudes (e.g., Cooper, Zanna, & Goethals, 1974; Goethals & Cooper, 1972; Hoyt, Henley, & Collins, 1972; Nel, Helmreich, & Aronson, 1969).

Evaluation of Aversive Consequences Explanation

It is important to note that the evidentiary basis for the aversive consequences model relies solely on the production of no attitude change in conditions where aversive consequences are not produced. Because this is a null effect, several alternative explanations can be offered. For example, in these past experiments, participants were encouraged to produce lengthy counterattitudinal statements. These statements may have reduced the likelihood of detecting dissonance-related attitude change, as research has demonstrated that length of statement is inversely related to amount of dissonance-related attitude change

(Beauvois & Joule, 1996, 1999; Rabbie, Brehm, & Cohen, 1959). This inverse relation may result because longer statements allow for more consonant cognitions that support the counterattitudinal behavior and hence reduce the dissonance. Thus, the overall level of dissonance in these experiments may have been rather low, and the addition of the production of aversive consequences was necessary to produce sufficient dissonance to cause attitude change. Another explanation for the past failures to find attitude change in nonaversive consequences experiments is that dissonance was aroused but reduced in a manner other than attitude change in the no aversive consequences conditions. Other alternative explanations have been presented (Harmon-Jones, 1999).

My colleagues and I were not convinced by the past evidence regarding the necessity of aversive consequences. To test whether cognitive discrepancy in the absence of aversive consequences can produce dissonance, we conducted induced compliance experiments in which participants behaved counterattitudinally but did not produce aversive consequences (Harmon-Jones, 1999, 2000a; Harmon-Jones et al., 1996). We designed these experiments so that factors that may have inhibited attitude change in the past experiments were omitted in our experiments. In these experiments, which were presented as studies on how writing different types of statements affects memory, participants were exposed to a simple stimulus about which they held a positive or negative attitude (e.g., boring passage, delicious chocolate) and then were given low or high choice to write sentences in privacy and with anonymity that were inconsistent with their attitudes. Participants were told to discard their counterattitudinal statements once they finished writing them. Then, they expressed their attitudes toward the stimulus in privacy and with anonymity. Results have indicated that participants given high choice to write the counter-attitudinal statements shifted their attitudes to align them with their behavior, whereas participants given low choice did not. Moreover, results have indicated that participants given high choice, as compared to low choice, to write the statements evidence increased electrodermal activity (Harmon-Jones et al., 1996, Experiment 3) and report more discomfort (Harmon-Jones, 2000a, Experiments 1 and 2) during the period of time between the writing of the statement and the assessment of the attitude, suggesting that this manipulation produced dissonance. In addition, following the attitude change opportunity, persons report less discomfort, suggesting that the attitude change reduced the dissonance (Harmon-Jones, 2000a, Experiment 2).

Evidence from belief disconfirmation studies also suggests that the production of aversive consequences is not necessary to create dissonance. In these studies (e.g., Batson, 1975; Brock & Balloun, 1967; Burris, Harmon-Jones, & Tarpley, 1997; Russell & Jones, 1980), persons are exposed to information inconsistent with a highly important and highly resistant to change belief, and they show dissonance effects (e.g., negative affect, belief intensification, selective avoidance of inconsistent information, transcendence) as a result of this exposure. In the belief disconfirmation paradigm, persons have not produced aversive consequences and thus cannot feel responsible for having done so. Persons are simply exposed to information from an external source; they have not done anything for which to feel responsible.

Aronson (1992, 1999; see also Thibodeau & Aronson, 1992) and Stone and colleagues (e.g., Stone et al., 1994) also questioned whether the production of aversive consequences is necessary to create dissonance effects. In their program of research on hypocrisy, they have found that when persons give a public speech advocating a prosocial policy

that will produce positive consequences and then are reminded of times when they have not behaved in accord with the position advocated in their speech, they experience dissonance and engage in cognitive and behavioral changes to reduce the dissonance.

McGregor et al. (1999) further pointed out that recent attitudinal ambivalence research has provided evidence of dissonance-related negative affect in the absence of feeling personally responsible for producing negative consequences.

ASSESSMENT OF THE CURRENT STATUS OF THE THEORY

Recent research has strongly supported the idea that dissonance is a motivational theory and that dissonance produces genuine and lasting attitude, belief, and behavior changes. Festinger proposed that cognitive discrepancy was inherently aversive. Other theorists have proposed alternate motivations that underlie the motivating effects putatively due to cognitive discrepancy (Aronson, 1968; Cooper & Fazio, 1984; Steele, 1988). Much debate centers around determining the underlying motivation (Harmon-Jones & Mills, 1999a). Most of the revisions concur with the original theory and postulate that the situations that create a discrepancy evoke negative affect and that this negative affect motivates the cognitive and behavioral adjustments found. However, these revisions differ in their explanations of why these situations evoke negative affect and why individuals engage in the cognitive and behavioral adjustments. That is, each of the revisions implicitly views negative affect as a *proximal* motivation for the cognitive changes observed in dissonance settings, and each revision proposes a different *distal* motivation underlying the arousal of the negative affect. Although each of these revisions has yielded important data, recent research has been presented that challenges each of these revisions and supports the original version of the theory (e.g., Beauvois & Joule, 1996, 1999; Harmon-Jones, 1999; Harmon-Jones et al., 1996; McGregor et al., 1999; Simon et al., 1995).

AN ACTION-BASED MODEL OF COGNITIVE DISSONANCE

Thus, the evidence supports the idea that a cognitive inconsistency of sufficient magnitude evokes an aversive motivational state that causes cognitive and behavioral changes, in accord with the original version of the theory. However, the understanding of dissonance processes could be improved and extended with an explanation of *why* cognitive inconsistency arouses an aversive motivational state and *why* this state causes the cognitive and behavioral adjustments.

The action-based model of cognitive dissonance has recently been proposed to address these questions. The model begins with the assumption that cognitions, broadly defined, can serve as action tendencies, an idea endorsed by several scholars (Cacioppo & Berntson, 1994; James, 1890/1950). For the model, the cognitions that are of primary concern are those that provide useful information, and usefulness of information is defined by its relevance to actions and goals. When information inconsistent with cognitions that guide action is encountered, an aversive motivational state—dissonance—is aroused because the dissonant information has the potential to interfere with effective and unconflicted action.

Thus, cognitive discrepancy may create dissonance because discrepancy among cognitions undermines the potential for effective and unconflicted action (Beckmann & Irle, 1985; Harmon-Jones, 1999; Jones & Gerard,

1967). Previous dissonance scientists viewed commitment as occurring when an individual freely chose to engage in a behavior of which they knew or could know the consequences (Beauvois & Joule, 1996; Brehm & Cohen, 1962; Festinger, 1964). However, it is also possible that commitment or attachment to a cognition or perception can occur without an obvious behavioral commitment and that individuals would experience dissonance if information contradicted this commitment. Consider the law of gravity. Most persons would probably experience considerable dissonance if, while they were walking through a calm forest, a tree suddenly flew into the atmosphere. Thus, regarding a cognition or perception as true or as reality established a commitment in the perceivers' minds. This commitment to a reality then serves the function of guiding information processing, which then serves the ultimate function of activating and directing behavior.

When dissonant information is encountered, dissonance may result in motivating the individual to engage in information processing that would support the commitment. With further increases in dissonant information, the dissonance may increase to the point where the individual is motivated to accept the information and reject the commitment. Which cognition is supported or accepted depends on the resistance to change of each cognition.

As an example, consider a situation where a hiker is lost deep in the woods. Based on her calculations, she is in the middle of the woods, has just enough time and resources to cover 15 miles, and knows that an exit (and thus safety) is 15 miles to the east or west. She perceives that she has two options: She can begin walking either to the west or to the east. Each option has advantages (she is very familiar with the east route, while she has heard that the west route requires less effort) and disadvantages (the east route will require crossing a river, while the west route will require climbing a mountain). Once the hiker makes a decision to walk east, the disadvantages of walking east and the advantages of walking west become discrepant cognitions. If she continues to weigh the relative merits of the options, vacillating between them, beginning to walk one way and then turning around and walking the other, action will be impeded and she might never arrive to safety. She must reduce the discrepancy and follow through with the option she has chosen. Even if the route she chooses is not the best, she will be better off persisting in one course of action than going halfway only to turn back.

From the current perspective, the *proximal* motivation to reduce cognitive discrepancy stems from the need to reduce the aversive state of dissonance, while the *distal* motivation to reduce cognitive discrepancy stems from the requirement for effective action. When the potential for effective action is threatened by information that is sufficiently discrepant from the psychological commitment, dissonance results, which prompts attempts at the restoration of cognitions supportive of the commitment (i.e., discrepancy reduction). It is important to note that while the proximal and distal motivations are often linearly related—that is, an increase in the need to produce effective behavior will be related to an increase in negative affect—the two motivations may operate independently in some circumstances.

The current model is consistent with views that have been presented previously but have not been given due consideration (e.g., Beckmann & Irle, 1985; Gollwitzer, 1990; Heckhausen, 1986; Jones & Gerard, 1967; Kuhl, 1984; Lewin, 1951). One reason for the lack of consideration of the these conceptual ideas may be due to the difficulty of understanding how the effects observed in the laboratory experiments would be produced by a concern over effective action. For example, why would women in Brehm's (1956) experi-

ment rate a toaster more positively after choosing it? At least two arguments can be advanced to address this question. First, it would be beneficial to value the objects that one owns to maintain their quality and get use out of them. Second, the current model can be applied to results obtained in dissonance experiments by assuming that a mechanism that survived because of its adaptive value is able to produce effects in conceptually similar situations that do not have obvious adaptive significance.

Experimental Results Consistent With the Action-Based Model

We have recently completed experiments that test predictions derived from the action-based model. In two experiments, we have tested the hypothesis that processes that facilitate an action-orientation will increase cognitive discrepancy reduction (Harmon-Jones & Harmon-Jones, in press). The action-oriented mind-set is posited to prime one toward being more able to enact decisions and hence bring cognitions in line with the decision. In other words, the action-oriented mind-set will facilitate the ease with which one can reduce cognitive discrepancy without actually increasing the amount of negative affect. Such a finding would support the theoretically derived hypothesis that the distal motivation (effective behavior) can be activated independently of the proximal motivation (negative affect).

Action-Oriented Mind-Set Experiment

In the first experiment, university students evaluated how desirable they found seven physical exercises that were described in writing to them. They then decided to participate in one of two of the exercises. Either the two used in the decision were rated equally (difficult decision) or one was rated highly and the other lowly (easy decision). After the decision, the participants completed one of two questionnaires; they either provided demographic information (control condition) or described their implemental intentions for the upcoming exercise (action-oriented mind-set). Then, the experimenter asked the participants to re-rate the desirability of the seven exercises. The change in rating of the chosen exercise minus the change in rating of the rejected exercise was used as the dependent variable. As predicted, a significant 2 (Decision Difficulty) × 2 (Mind-Set) interaction emerged. Follow-up tests revealed that spreading of alternatives was greatest in the action-oriented/difficult decision condition.

Action-Oriented Mind-Set and Prefrontal Cortical Activation Experiment

We conducted a second experiment to further test the hypothesis that an action-oriented mind-set would facilitate the justification of a decision. Recent research (Gollwitzer & Kinney, 1989; Taylor & Gollwitzer, 1995) has found that after making a decision and thinking about steps needed to implement it (action-oriented mind-set), persons are more likely to have positive illusions and more of an illusion of control. In other words, thinking about implementing one decision has effects on actions and cognitions that are unrelated to the decision. That is, the effects of the action-oriented mind-set can transfer to unrelated actions and cognitions. Therefore, in the second experiment, we tested whether having persons think about implementing one decision would affect the spreading of alternatives for a different decision.

We also tested the effects of implemental intentions on prefrontal cortical activity. Specifically, we predicted that the activation of an approach-related, action-oriented mind-set will increase left prefrontal cortical activity.

The left frontal cortical region has been described as an important center for intention, self-regulation, and planning (Kosslyn & Koenig, 1995; Petrides & Milner, 1982; Tomarken & Keener, 1998). These functions have often been described as properties of the will, a hypothetical construct important in guiding approach-related behavior. Damage to the left frontal region results in behavior and experience that may be described as involving a deficit in approach. Persons with damage to this region are apathetic, experience less interest and pleasure, and have difficulty in initiating actions (e.g., Robinson & Downhill, 1995).

Research using measures of electroencephalographic (EEG) activity has found that decreased left frontal activity relates to depression (Henriques & Davidson, 1990, 1991) and that increased left frontal cortical activation relates to trait and state measures of approach motivation (Harmon-Jones & Allen, 1997, 1998; Sobotka, Davidson, & Senulis, 1992; Sutton & Davidson, 1997) and trait repression (Tomarken & Davidson, 1994). It is interesting to note that repression has been linked to an increased likelihood of reducing dissonance via attitude change (Olson & Zanna, 1979; Zanna & Aziza, 1976). Thus, as approach-related, action-oriented thinking increases, greater left frontal activation may occur.

In the second experiment, participants evaluated how desirable they found eight experiments that were described to them in writing. Then, they decided to participate in one of two of them that would supposedly occur within a few minutes after the decision. In this experiment, the decision was always difficult, that is, between two equally and highly valued alternatives. After the decision, they completed "personality questionnaires." The personality questionnaires contained the manipulation of mind-set. Participants were randomly assigned to complete either (a) a questionnaire that asked them to write about a project they had decided to do and to describe the steps they would need to implement to accomplish the project (action-oriented mind-set), (b) a questionnaire that asked them to write about a decision in their lives that they were currently deliberating and had not yet decided on how to act (deliberative mind-set), or (c)a questionnaire that asked them to write about a typical day in their lives (control mind-set). After completing the questionnaire, they were asked to think about the information they provided in the questionnaire for 2 minutes while their brain activity was recorded. Then, they re-rated the decision alternatives. As predicted, participants in the action-oriented mind-set condition evidenced more spreading of alternatives than did participants in the other two conditions. Moreover, participants in the action-oriented mind-set condition evidenced greater left prefrontal cortical activity after the mind-set manipulation than did participants in the other two conditions. However, this latter effect resulted only for women and not for men. A similar Sex of Participant × Mind-Set condition interaction did not emerge for spreading of alternatives. In addition, relative left frontal activity mediated the effect of mind-set on spreading of alternatives for women. The sex effect was not expected, and we are currently conducting an experiment to assess its replicability.[2]

Emotion as Action Tendency Experiment

An experiment has also been conducted to test the hypothesis that dissonance should be increased as the salience of the action implications of cognitions that are involved in a dissonant relationship are increased. Several perspectives consider emotion to involve action tendencies (Frijda, 1986; Lang, 1995). To the extent that an emotion generates an action tendency, as the intensity of one's current emotion is increased and is involved in a dissonant relationship with other information, dissonance should be increased.

Much research has demonstrated that the emotion of sympathy (empathy) increases helping behavior because it evokes altruistic motivation, that is, motivation to relieve the distress of the person in need of help (for a review, see Batson, 1991). We have conducted one experiment that tested whether an inconsistency between the emotion of sympathy and knowledge about past behavior evoked motivation to reduce this inconsistency (Harmon-Jones, Peterson, & Vaughn, in press).

In the experiment, we tested the hypothesis that, after experiencing sympathy for a target person in need of help, individuals will be more motivated to help that person when they are reminded of times when they failed to help similar persons (for evidence that feeling sympathy for one target person can transfer to the target person's group and cause attitude change toward the group, see Batson et al., 1997). Participants were informed that they would be listening to a pilot broadcast for a local radio station and that the researchers would like students' reactions to the tape. Participants then listened to a tape-recorded message that was supposedly from a person in need of help (an adolescent with cancer). Before listening to the tape, participants were assigned to one of two conditions: one in which they tried to imagine how the person must feel (high-empathy set) or one in which they tried to remain objective as they listened to the tape (low-empathy set). Then, they listened to the tape-recorded message and afterward completed questionnaires assessing self-reported emotional responses and evaluations of the tape-recorded message. Then, either participants were asked to list times when they failed to help other persons who were in need of help or they completed a demographic survey. Finally, participants were given an opportunity to help by volunteering time to assist the person with addressing letters that would request money from possible donors or by donating money to the person's family. The design was a 2 (Empathy: low vs. high) × 2 (Times When Did Not Help: reminded vs. not reminded) between-subjects factorial. Results indicated that more helping occurred in the high-empathy/reminded of past failures condition than in other conditions.

FUTURE DIRECTIONS

Serious challenges to each of the revisions of the original theory have been offered, thus questioning the necessity of the motivations for dissonance processes proposed by these revisions. The action-based model offers a new motivational explanation of the dissonance process, and its motivation—the need for effective and unconflicted action—may be superordinate to the motivations offered by other models. However, the challenges to the revisions have not cogently demonstrated the insufficiency of these motivations for dissonance processes, and it is thus possible that these alternative motivations can influence dissonance processes, perhaps depending on the context. Thus, each of the proposed motivations may independently influence dissonance processes. Future research will need to address whether these motivations are sufficient to independently alter dissonance processes or whether they are perhaps subordinate to and part of another motivation such as the need for effective action.

To more thoroughly understand the motivation(s) underlying the dissonance process, future research will need to focus on the mediators of the process. In our recent research derived from the action-based model, we have examined neural mechanisms involved in the dissonance process, and we plan to continue this line of research. In addition to investigations of the neural mechanisms, future research will need to examine experiential mediators of the process, perhaps in conjunction with the neural mechanisms.

Another suggestion for future research is the investigation of the role of individual differences in the dissonance process, an area that has been relatively neglected in past research. We have recently obtained evidence that trait action-orientation for decision-related contexts relates to spreading of alternatives. Not only will investigations of individual differences contribute to a more thorough understanding of dissonance motivation, but the examination of individual differences will provide suggestions for effectively implementing dissonance-related techniques for inducing persuasion outside the laboratory with different groups of individuals. Investigations of the role of individual differences in the dissonance process, however, need to carefully consider the various places in the process at which the individual difference could play a role in affecting outcome variables.

The precise prediction of the manner in which dissonance will be reduced depends on a specification of the cognition that is most resistant to change. Thus, when a person is exposed to a counterattitudinal communication, the person will experience dissonance and the dissonance could lead to different outcomes, such as either rejection or acceptance of the communication. Which outcome will occur should depend on the resistance to change of the involved cognitions (Harmon-Jones, 2000b). In laboratory settings, the experimenter has control over which cognition is more resistant to change and thus can predict how dissonance will be reduced. But as dissonance research is used outside the laboratory and to test the moderating role of individual differences, the specification of the determinants of resistance to change and the measurement of resistance to change will become necessary. Future research is needed to address these issues.

An understanding of these basic mechanisms involved in the dissonance process will ultimately lead to more precise specifications of conditions necessary to produce persuasion in naturally occurring circumstances.

CONCLUSION

The original theory proposed that cognitive inconsistency generated an aversive state that motivated cognitive and behavioral changes, which often result in persuasion. Several revisions to the theory have proposed alternative motivations presumably responsible for the persuasion effects observed in dissonance experiments. Challenges to each of these revisions have been offered, and recent research supports the original version over these revisions. However, the original theory never clearly specified *why* cognitive inconsistency generated an aversive motivational response. An action-based model of dissonance theory has been proposed that extends the original theory by specifying why cognitive inconsistency evokes an aversive motivational state. In addition to linking the study of dissonance to models of self-regulation, the action-based model suggests important lines of inquiry into understanding how affect and motivation influence the cognitive and behavioral changes that lead to persuasion.

NOTES

1. Two other prevalent accounts for dissonance effects were self-perception theory (Bem, 1972) and impression management theory (Tedeschi, Schlenker, & Bonoma, 1971). Because both of these revisions have been discussed extensively elsewhere, and because the extant evidence supports a dissonance theory interpretation over these interpretations, they are not discussed in this chapter (see Cooper & Fazio, 1984; Fazio, Zanna, & Cooper, 1977; Harmon-Jones & Mills, 1999b; Kiesler & Pallak, 1976; Wicklund & Brehm, 1976).

2. The Harmon-Jones and Harmon-Jones (in press) article does not report the EEG results. We are currently attempting to replicate the EEG findings.

REFERENCES

Aronson, E. (1968). Dissonance theory: Progress and problems. In R. P. Abelson, E. Aronson, W. J. McGuire, T. M. Newcomb, M. J. Rosenberg, & P. H. Tannenbaum (Eds.), *Theories of cognitive consistency: A sourcebook* (pp. 5-27). Chicago: Rand McNally.

Aronson, E. (1969). The theory of cognitive dissonance: A current perspective. In L. Berkowitz (Ed.), *Advances in experimental social psychology* (Vol. 4, pp. 1-34). New York: Academic Press.

Aronson, E. (1992). The return of the repressed: Dissonance theory makes a comeback. *Psychological Inquiry, 3,* 303-311.

Aronson, E. (1999). Dissonance, hypocrisy, and the self concept. In E. Harmon-Jones & J. Mills (Eds.), *Cognitive dissonance: Progress on a pivotal theory in social psychology* (pp. 103-126). Washington, DC: American Psychological Association.

Aronson, E., Fried, C., & Stone, J. (1991). Overcoming denial and increasing the intention to use condoms through the induction of hypocrisy. *American Journal of Public Health, 81,* 1636-1638.

Aronson, J., Cohen, G., & Nail, P. R (1999). Self-affirmation theory: An update and appraisal. In E. Harmon-Jones & J. Mills (Eds.), *Cognitive dissonance: Progress on a pivotal theory in social psychology* (pp. 127-147). Washington, DC: American Psychological Association.

Batson, C. D. (1975). Rational processing or rationalization? The effect of disconfirming information on a stated religious belief. *Journal of Personality and Social Psychology, 32,* 176-184.

Batson, C. D. (1991). *The altruism question: Toward a social-psychological answer.* Hillsdale, NJ: Lawrence Erlbaum.

Batson, C. D., Polycarpou, M. P., Harmon-Jones, E., Imhoff, H. J., Mitchener, E. C., Bednar, L. L., Klein, T. R., & Highberger, L. (1997). Empathy and attitudes: Can feeling for a member of a stigmatized outgroup improve attitudes toward the group? *Journal of Personality and Social Psychology, 72,* 105-118.

Beauvois, J. L., & Joule, R. V. (1996). *A radical dissonance theory.* London: Taylor & Francis.

Beauvois, J. L., & Joule, R. V. (1999). A radical point of view on dissonance theory. In E. Harmon-Jones & J. Mills (Eds.), *Cognitive dissonance: Progress on a pivotal theory in social psychology* (pp. 43-70). Washington, DC: American Psychological Association.

Beckmann, J., & Irle, M. (1985). Dissonance and action control. In J. Kuhl & J. Beckmann (Eds.), *Action control: From cognition to behavior* (pp. 129-150). Berlin: Springer-Verlag.

Bem, D. J. (1972). Self-perception theory. In L. Berkowitz (Ed.), *Advances in experimental social psychology* (Vol. 6, pp. 1-62). New York: Academic Press.

Blanton, H., Cooper, J., Skurnik, I., & Aronson, J. (1997). When bad things happen to good feedback: Exacerbating the need for self-justification with self-affirmations. *Personality and Social Psychology Bulletin, 23,* 684-692.

Brehm, J. W. (1956). Postdecision changes in the desirability of alternatives. *Journal of Abnormal and Social Psychology, 52,* 384-389.

Brehm, J. W. (1962). Motivational effects of cognitive dissonance. In M. R. Jones (Ed.), *Nebraska Symposium on Motivation* (pp. 51-77). Lincoln: University of Nebraska Press.

Brehm, J. W. (1992). An unidentified theoretical object. *Psychological Inquiry, 3,* 314-315.

Brehm, J. W., & Cohen, A. R. (1962). *Explorations in cognitive dissonance.* New York: John Wiley.

Brock, T. C., & Balloun, J. C. (1967). Behavioral receptivity to dissonant information. *Journal of Personality and Social Psychology, 6,* 413-428.

Burris, C. T., Harmon-Jones, E., & Tarpley, W. R. (1997). "By faith alone": Religious agitation and cognitive dissonance. *Basic and Applied Social Psychology, 19,* 17-31.

Cacioppo, J. T., & Berntson, G. G. (1994). Relationship between attitudes and evaluative space: A critical review, with emphasis on the separability of positive and negative substrates. *Psychological Bulletin, 115,* 401-423.

Cooper, J., & Fazio, R. H. (1984). A new look at dissonance theory. In L. Berkowitz (Ed.), *Advances in experimental social psychology* (Vol. 17, pp. 229-264). Orlando, FL: Academic Press.

Cooper, J., & Worchel, S. (1970). Role of undesired consequences in arousing cognitive dissonance. *Journal of Personality and Social Psychology, 16,* 199-206.

Cooper, J., Zanna, M. P., & Goethals, G. R. (1974). Mistreatment of an esteemed other as a consequence affecting dissonance reduction. *Journal of Experimental Social Psychology, 10,* 224-233.

Dickerson, C. A., Thibodeau, R., Aronson, E., & Miller, D. (1992). Using cognitive dissonance to encourage water conservation. *Journal of Applied Social Psychology, 22,* 841-854.

Elliot, A. J., & Devine, P. G. (1994). On the motivation nature of cognitive dissonance: Dissonance as psychological discomfort. *Journal of Personality and Social Psychology, 67,* 382-394.

Fazio, R. H., Zanna, M. P., & Cooper, J. (1977). Dissonance and self-perception: An integrative view of each theory's proper domain of application. *Journal of Experimental Social Psychology, 13,* 464-479.

Festinger, L. (1957). *A theory of cognitive dissonance.* Stanford, CA: Stanford University Press.

Festinger, L. (1964). *Conflict, decision, and dissonance.* Stanford, CA: Stanford University Press.

Festinger, L., & Carlsmith, J. M. (1959). Cognitive consequences of forced compliance. *Journal of Abnormal and Social Psychology, 58,* 203-210.

Festinger, L., Riecken, H. W., & Schachter, S. (1956). *When prophecy fails.* Minneapolis: University of Minnesota Press.

Fried, C. B. (1998). Hypocrisy and identification with transgressions: A case of undetected dissonance. *Basic and Applied Social Psychology, 20,* 145-154.

Frijda, N. H. (1986). *The emotions.* Cambridge, UK: Cambridge University Press.

Goethals, G. R., & Cooper, J. (1972). Role of intention and postbehavioral consequence in the arousal of cognitive dissonance. *Journal of Personality and Social Psychology, 23*, 293-301.

Gollwitzer, P. M. (1990). Action phases and mind-sets. In E. T. Higgins & R. M. Sorrentino (Eds.), *Handbook of motivation and cognition: Foundations of social behavior* (Vol. 2, pp. 53-92). New York: Guilford.

Gollwitzer, P. M., & Kinney, R. F. (1989). Effects of deliberative and implemental mind-sets on illusion of control. *Journal of Personality and Social Psychology, 56*, 531-542.

Harmon-Jones, E. (1999). Toward an understanding of the motivation underlying dissonance effects: Is the production of aversive consequences necessary to cause dissonance? In E. Harmon-Jones & J. Mills (Eds.), *Cognitive dissonance: Progress on a pivotal theory in social psychology* (pp. 71-99). Washington, DC: American Psychological Association.

Harmon-Jones, E. (2000a). Cognitive dissonance and experienced negative affect: Evidence that dissonance increases experienced negative affect even in the absence of aversive consequences. *Personality and Social Psychology Bulletin, 26*, 1490-1501.

Harmon-Jones, E. (2000b). A cognitive dissonance theory perspective on the role of emotion in the maintenance and change of beliefs and attitudes. In N. H. Frijda, A. R. S. Manstead, & S. Bem (Eds.), *Emotions and beliefs* (pp. 185-211). Cambridge, UK: Cambridge University Press.

Harmon-Jones, E., & Allen, J. J. B. (1997). Behavioral activation sensitivity and resting frontal EEG asymmetry: Covariation of putative indicators related to risk for mood disorders. *Journal of Abnormal Psychology, 106*, 159-163.

Harmon-Jones, E., & Allen, J. J. B. (1998). Anger and prefrontal brain activity: EEG asymmetry consistent with approach motivation despite negative affective valence. *Journal of Personality and Social Psychology, 74*, 1310-1316.

Harmon-Jones, E., Brehm, J. W., Greenberg, J., Simon, L., & Nelson, D. E. (1996). Evidence that the production of aversive consequences is not necessary to create cognitive dissonance. *Journal of Personality and Social Psychology, 70*, 5-16.

Harmon-Jones, E., & Harmon-Jones, C. (in press). Testing the action-based model of cognitive dissonance: The effect of action-orientation on post-decisional attitudes. *Personality and Social Psychology Bulletin*.

Harmon-Jones, E., & Mills, J. (1999a). *Cognitive dissonance: Progress on a pivotal theory in social psychology*. Washington, DC: American Psychological Association.

Harmon-Jones, E., & Mills, J. (1999b). An introduction to cognitive dissonance theory and an overview of current perspectives on the theory. In E. Harmon-Jones & J. Mills (Eds.), *Cognitive dissonance: Progress on a pivotal theory in social psychology* (pp. 3-21). Washington, DC: American Psychological Association.

Harmon-Jones, E., Peterson, H., & Vaughn, K. (in press). Sympathy and dissonance: A test of the action-based model of cognitive dissonance. *Basic and Applied Social Psychology*.

Heckhausen, H. (1986). Why some time out might benefit achievement motivation research. In J. H. L. van den Bercken, E. E. J. De Bruyn, & T. C. M. Bergen (Eds.), *Achievement and task motivation* (pp. 7-39). Lisse, Netherlands: Swets & Zeitlinger.

Henriques, J. B., & Davidson, R. J. (1990). Regional brain electrical asymmetries discriminate between previously depressed and healthy control subjects. *Journal of Abnormal Psychology, 99*, 22-31.

Henriques, J. B., & Davidson, R. J. (1991). Left frontal hypoactivation in depression. *Journal of Abnormal Psychology, 100*, 535-545.

Hoyt, M. F., Henley, M. D., & Collins, B. E. (1972). Studies in forced compliance: Confluence of choice and consequence on attitude change. *Journal of Personality and Social Psychology, 23*, 205-210.

James, W. (1950). *The principles of psychology.* New York: Dover. (Original work published 1890)

Jones, E. E., & Gerard, H. B. (1967). *Foundations of social psychology.* New York: John Wiley.

Kiesler, C. A., & Pallak, M. S. (1976). Arousal properties of dissonance manipulations. *Psychological Bulletin, 83*, 1014-1025.

Kosslyn, S. M., & Koenig, O. (1995). *Wet mind: The new cognitive neuroscience.* New York: Free Press.

Kuhl, J. (1984). Volitional aspects of achievement motivation and learned helplessness: Toward a comprehensive theory of action-control. In B. A. Maher (Ed.), *Progress in experimental personality research* (Vol. 13, pp. 99-171). New York: Academic Press.

Lang, P. J. (1995). The emotion probe. *American Psychologist, 50,* 372-385.

Lawrence, D. H., & Festinger, L. (1962). *Deterrents and reinforcement.* Stanford, CA: Stanford University Press.

Leippe, M. R., & Eisenstadt, D. (1994). The generalization of dissonance reduction: Decreasing prejudice through induced compliance. *Journal of Personality and Social Psychology, 67,* 395-413.

Lewin, K. (1951). *Field theory in social science.* New York: Harper.

McGregor, I., Newby-Clark, I. R., & Zanna, M. P. (1999). Epistemic discomfort is moderated by simultaneous accessibility of inconsistent elements. In E. Harmon-Jones & J. Mills (Eds.), *Cognitive dissonance: Progress on a pivotal theory in social psychology* (pp. 325-353). Washington, DC: American Psychological Association.

Nel, E., Helmreich, R., & Aronson, E. (1969). Opinion change in the advocate as a function of the persuasibility of his audience: A clarification of the meaning of dissonance. *Journal of Personality and Social Psychology, 12,* 117-124.

Olson, J. M., & Zanna, M. P. (1979). A new look at selective exposure. *Journal of Experimental Social Psychology, 15,* 1-15.

Petrides, M., & Milner, B. (1982). Deficits on subject-ordered tasks after frontal- and temporal-lobe lesions in man. *Neuropsychologia, 20,* 249-262.

Rabbie, J. M., Brehm, J. W., & Cohen, A. R. (1959). Verbalization and reactions to cognitive dissonance. *Journal of Personality, 27,* 407-417.

Robinson, R. G., & Downhill, J. E. (1995). Lateralization of psychopathology in response to focal brain injury. In R. J. Davidson & K. Hugdahl (Eds.), *Brain asymmetry* (pp. 693-711). Cambridge, MA: MIT Press.

Russell, D., & Jones, W. H. (1980). When superstition fails: Reactions to disconfirmation of paranormal beliefs. *Personality and Social Psychology Bulletin, 6,* 83-88.

Simon, L., Greenberg, J., & Brehm, J. W. (1995). Trivialization: The forgotten mode of dissonance reduction. *Journal of Personality and Social Psychology, 68,* 247-260.

Sobotka, S. S., Davidson, R. J., & Senulis, J. A. (1992). Anterior brain electrical asymmetries in response to reward and punishment. *Electroencephalography and Clinical Neurophysiology, 83,* 236-247.

Steele, C. M. (1988). The psychology of self-affirmation: Sustaining the integrity of the self. In L. Berkowitz (Ed.), *Advances in experimental social psychology* (Vol. 21, pp. 261-302). San Diego: Academic Press.

Steele, C. M., & Liu, T. J. (1983). Dissonance processes as self-affirmation. *Journal of Personality and Social Psychology, 45,* 5-19.

Steele, C. M., Spencer, S. J., & Lynch, M. (1993). Self-image resilience and dissonance: The role of affirmational resources. *Journal of Personality and Social Psychology, 64,* 885-896.

Stone, J., Aronson, E., Crain, A. L., Winslow, M. P., & Fried, C. B. (1994). Inducing hypocrisy as a means for encouraging young adults to use condoms. *Personality and Social Psychology Bulletin, 20,* 116-128.

Stone, J., Wiegand, A. W., Cooper, J., & Aronson, E. (1997). When exemplification fails: Hypocrisy and the motive for self-integrity. *Journal of Personality and Social Psychology, 72,* 54-65.

Sutton, S. K., & Davidson, R. J. (1997). Prefrontal brain asymmetry: A biological substrate of the behavioral approach and inhibition systems. *Psychological Science, 8,* 204-210.

Taylor, S. E., & Gollwitzer, P. M. (1995). Effects of mindset on positive illusions. *Journal of Personality and Social Psychology, 69,* 213-226.

Tedeschi, J. T., Schlenker, B. R., & Bonoma, T. V. (1971). Cognitive dissonance: Private ratiocination or public spectacle? *American Psychologist, 26,* 685-695.

Thibodeau, R., & Aronson, E. (1992). Taking a closer look: Reasserting the role of the self-concept in dissonance theory. *Personality and Social Psychology Bulletin, 18,* 591-602.

Tomarken, A. J., & Davidson, R. J. (1994). Frontal brain activation in repressors and nonrepressors. *Journal of Abnormal Psychology, 103,* 339-349.

Tomarken, A. J., & Keener, A. D. (1998). Frontal brain asymmetry and depression: A self-regulatory perspective. *Cognition and Emotion, 12,* 387-420.

Wicklund, R. A., & Brehm, J. W. (1976). *Perspectives on cognitive dissonance.* Hillsdale, NJ: Lawrence Erlbaum.

Zanna, M. P., & Aziza, C. (1976). On the interaction of repression-sensitization and attention in resolving cognitive dissonance. *Journal of Personality, 44,* 577-593.

Zimbardo, P. G., Cohen, A., Weisenberg, M., Dworkin, L., & Firestone, I. (1969). The control of experimental pain. In P. G. Zimbardo (Ed.), *The cognitive control of motivation: The consequences of choice and dissonance* (pp. 100-122). Glenview, IL: Scott, Foresman.

Zimbardo, P. G., Weisenberg, M., Firestone, I., & Levy, B. (1965). Changing appetites for eating fried grasshoppers with cognitive dissonance. *Journal of Personality, 33,* 233-255.

7

Language Expectancy Theory

MICHAEL BURGOON
VICKIE PAULS DENNING
LAURA ROBERTS

It appears that at least once every decade or so, there appears a renewed interest, as evidenced by public discussion and publication activity, in two recurring issues in the discipline of communication. The first focuses on the general health, or even the viability, of the study of persuasion. Nearly a quarter of a century ago, Miller and M. Burgoon (1978) asked the question of whether or not a case could be made for persuasion research. They claimed that while it would be hyperbolic to state that the guns are silent on the persuasive battleground, the roar of these guns has been sporadic and muted. They further added that traditional persuasion research had been swimming against the ideological and scholarly currents of the past decade. They were writing at a time when persuasion research, not only in the discipline of communication but also in allied

social science disciplines, no longer was front and center stage but rather had been displaced by other concerns such as interpersonal communication and social cognition.

A dozen years later, M. Burgoon and Miller (1990) followed up on their earlier essay commenting on whether the former article's suggestions, injunctions, and conclusions about the directions of persuasion research had much, if any, influence on the extant state of research in the area of social influence. They speculated that there would be a "rebirth" of interest in persuasion research during the final decade of the final century of the then current millennium. Specifically, Burgoon and Miller predicted more concern for macro-social concerns with an interest in the role of massive social change. They also suggested a greater emphasis on natural

AUTHORS' NOTE: Support for this research was provided by grants from the Arizona Disease Control Research Commission (Contracts 9804 and 9805), RO1HD31360 (National Institute for Child Health and Development), RO1DA12578 (National Institute on Drug Abuse), and 5POCA77502 (National Cancer Institute) to the senior author. The opinions expressed are those of the authors and not of the various funding agencies.

setting research that would allow researchers to scrutinize cultural and sociological patterns of communication so that persuasion researchers could participate in socially important, tangible goals such as reducing the incidence of cancer by 50% by the year 2000.

Perhaps most interesting—and not all of the current chapter authors are unbiased observers of their musings—was the following commentary by M. Burgoon and Miller (1990):

> If the course of communication inquiry follows the course of normal science (and we suspect it will), then attention to macro-level and micro-level issues in natural settings will trigger a pendulum-like action. A concern for greater ecological validity (our reading of the present intellectual atmosphere) is almost inevitably followed by demands for more control and precision in explanation and prediction. Thus, it would not be surprising if a future call for vigilant experimental control rejuvenates present-day "mechanistic empiricist" defectors and recruits new hands to laboratory research efforts reminiscent of the work being done several decades ago. (p. 158)

Most of the observations turned out to be relatively accurate harbingers of what the decade would bring in terms of the study of persuasion. Moreover, that the study of social influence is relatively healthy and concerned with a number of areas of social import is not at issue, as it has been in the past, and is attested to by the existence of the current handbook, replete with examples of lively theoretical debate and interesting empirical data.

A second recurring issue is the claim that the discipline of communication is bereft of rigorous formalized theories. Berger (1991) relegated theories to the status of "curios" in one such reprise of the issue. M. Burgoon (1994) joined the chorus by claiming that there was some consensus that the discipline of communication had been somewhat bradytelic in

developing rigorous content-specific theories. He further added that theoretical precision was going to be difficult to obtain. Such lamentations about the state of theory development across the full spectrum of communication studies might be warranted. It might be less warranted for Burgoon to cast the critical net so widely as to encompass the study of social influence processes. Again, the current handbook highlights the extent to which theoretical development, debate, and perhaps debunking are part of the universe of discourse of persuasion scholars.

While the question of *"whether"* theory development might not be as relevant in the social influence area as in the rest of the discipline, there are certainly issues about *"which"* of the many extant theories merit attention. The composition of this handbook probably speaks as well as anything I might write in this prolegomenon to the somewhat ephemeral nature of our peripatetic fascination with certain theories and, perhaps, premature dismissal of others. If theories were to be judged scientifically useful by referendum, then the dual-processing models (Chaiken, 1980, 1987; Petty & Cacioppo, 1981, 1986) would win in a walk. However, there is little reason to accept current popularity as any kind of indicator of scientific value for any theoretical position. What is not currently in vogue in communication, at least as evidenced by this handbook, is much of a recognition of the lively interest (evident in the allied social science disciplines) in the reconstruction of the theory of cognitive dissonance (Festinger, 1957) or the refinement and advancement of the theory of reasoned action (Fishbein & Ajzen, 1975) in applied areas such as public health and mass media effects. One could also argue that persuasion scholars, in general, tend to be less attuned to theoretical formulations emanating from the discipline of communication than is warranted. However, the argument that is advanced in this chapter is that there is at least one theory that merits serious consideration and research attention.

Language expectancy theory (LET) has been refined, refurbished, and remodeled over the past quarter of a century. First, it advances a relatively formalized propositional framework focusing directly on how message features positively or negatively violate (or conform to) macro-level expectations about what constitutes *appropriate* suasory communication attempts. Those propositions have been refined and extended at various times throughout the development of LET.

Second, the boundary conditions not only are specified but also are, in reality, quite broad compared to extant theories of social influence. This particular theoretical formulation includes propositions about (a) the traditional passive message reception situation, in which a persuader presents a message to a target or target audience with a desire to change attitudes and/or behaviors; (b) the active participation paradigm, in which individuals are "self-persuaded" by actually producing messages, usually at odds with their own privately held attitudes, resulting in changing their private attitudes to more closely conform to their public communication behavior; and (c) how language and expectancy violations operate in tandem in the resistance to persuasion paradigm. Obviously, attempting to cross three distinct persuasive situations, each with its own voluminous wealth of research findings and collection of sometimes confounded and contradictory results, is an ambitious undertaking.

Third, LET has been able to advance a number of hypotheses in a series of research efforts to provide empirical evidence of the explanatory and predictive power of the propositional formulation. In study after study, there has been a confirmation of hypotheses that are not easily interpretable without reference to the theory from which they were derived.

While LET appears to have a considerable amount to add to the study of persuasion, there are future actions that must be taken to provide additional validation of the explanatory calculus in natural settings in which socially important issues are the focus of suasory attempts. Also, even though one can claim that the current boundary conditions are quite broad, attempts to directly test the persistence of expectancy violations effects in more interpersonal or face-to-face attempts is overdue. Questions about how expectancies are developed and exactly what expectations are held about specific persuasion tactics must also be the focus of future research efforts. In addition, questions that plague most experimental research in persuasion remain a problem for this particular theory. For example, research needs to determine the persistence of the effects of expectancy over time. Sequential messages, not one message delivered in experimental isolation, need to be examined to determine how expectancies change and how violations either enhance or inhibit persuasion in ongoing persuasion attempts. These and other issues are addressed after presenting an overview of LET.

AN OVERVIEW OF LANGUAGE EXPECTANCY THEORY

Origins and Assumptions of LET

Brooks (1970) published research that sparked interest in the role that expectations about what a source might or might not say in persuasive discourse plays in attitude and/or behavior change. Brooks was interested in "reversals of previously held attitudes" and specifically stereotypes. He concluded his brief research report with an insightful comment that provided the spark to begin to formally develop LET:

The possibility of contrast effects should be considered. This principle assumes that we carry stereotypes into such social situations as the public speech. There, the speaker's behavior may be discrepant with stereotyped expectations. If the discrepant stimuli cannot be assimilated or ignored, they are likely to be exaggerated in a listener's perceptions. . . . One explanation . . . is this: unfavorable (or favorable) speakers may be perceived more (or less) favorably not because their behavior is intrinsically persuasive (or dissuasive) but because it contrasts with stereotyped expectations which audiences hold. (p. 155)

These comments prompted questions about the nature of what Brooks called stereotypes and about what determines what would later be called expectations. First, to what degree could the individual, as a unit of analysis, be jettisoned in favor of a more aggregate look at shared expectations of groups and even societies? Second, would it be fruitful to pursue research to determine whether there are indeed cultural and sociological forces that shape patterns of ordinary language and determine normative and non-normative usage? There was ample evidence to assume that as communicators mature, they learn not only the mechanics of language but also what to say and when to say it. Finally, the question of whether such normative expectations were limited to notorious (or popular) public figures, as used in previous research, or were applied to all communicators of a given type, group, class, or even all societal members was intriguing.

Prior research (McPeek & Edwards, 1975) bolstered the contention that receivers do have shared expectations about the behaviors a communicator *should* exhibit. When these expectations are violated, receivers overreact to the behaviors *actually* exhibited. If a communicator is initially perceived negatively and then demonstrates more positive behaviors

than anticipated, receivers overestimate the positiveness of the unanticipated behaviors. The reverse also holds; when an initially positively valenced communicator exhibits unexpectedly negative communication behaviors, receivers tend to exaggerate their negative evaluation of the communicator and/or the message (Brooks, 1970; McPeek & Edwards, 1975).

One of the first tests of what was to become LET began with a fascination and curiosity with the impact of different linguistic strategies on securing persuasive outcomes (M. Burgoon, Jones, & Stewart, 1975). This three-part seminal article provided evidence that strategic linguistic choices can be significant predictors of persuasive success. Following the success of this novel approach to influence inquiry, programmatic research began examining *passive reactions* to persuasive messages and evolved into inquiry into *active participation* (or self-persuasion) (M. Burgoon & Miller, 1971) and *resistance to persuasion* (M. Burgoon, Cohen, Miller, & Montgomery, 1978; Miller & M. Burgoon, 1979), placing the three paradigms under the expectancy umbrella.

Language expectancy theory assumes that language is a rule-governed system and that people develop macro-sociological expectations and preferences concerning the language or message strategies employed by others in persuasive attempts. These expectations are primarily a function of cultural and sociological norms. Preferences, according to this sociological perspective, are usually a function of cultural values and societal standards or ideals for what is competent communication performance.

M. Burgoon and Miller (1985) published a detailed propositional logic outlining the formative explanatory calculus of LET, which is explicated in some detail later in this chapter. M. Burgoon (1989, 1990) later presented a major refinement of the model and discussed the effects of both positive and negative violations of expectations in persuasive attempts. In summary form, LET posits that changes in the direction desired by an actor occur when positive violations of expectations occur. Positive violations occur (a) when the enacted behavior is better or more preferred than that which was expected in the situation and (b) when negatively evaluated sources conform more closely than expected to cultural values, societal norms, or situational exigencies. Change occurs in the first case because enacted behavior is outside the normative bandwidth in a positive direction, and such behavior prompts attitude and/or behavioral changes. In the second condition, a person who is expected to behave incompetently or inappropriately conforms to cultural norms and/or expected social roles, resulting in an overly positive evaluation of the source and subsequently change advocated by that actor. Negative violations of expectations result from language choices or the selection of message strategies that lie outside the bandwidth of socially acceptable behavior in a negative direction. Negative violations result in no attitude and/or behavioral changes or in changes in the opposite direction intended by the actor.

M. Burgoon (1995) provided a detailed etiology of the formulation of LET in a *festschrift* for his collaborator, the late Gerry Miller. The review provides a bit of sociology of knowledge as it describes how this theoretical formulation has taken a few steps forward and some steps backward over the years in attempting to develop a sound basis for understanding how expectations and a host of message variables interact to enhance or inhibit persuasion effects. That historical perspective is available elsewhere and might be of interest to researchers experiencing difficulty in devel-

oping and refining a theory over the course of a programmatic research effort.

The Propositional Framework of LET

Passive Message Reception Paradigm. Language expectancy theory is an axiomatic theory that, as discussed previously, expounds on the effects of linguistic variations on message persuasiveness. It is a message-centered theory of persuasion (M. Burgoon, 1995) that explains why certain linguistic formats in persuasive messages influence persuasive outcomes. The theory makes assumptions about human nature that, in turn, explain the effects of using unconventional language styles on message persuasiveness.

Certain basic assumptions have guided the development of LET and have influenced all of the research completed under the umbrella of this theoretical formulation. Language is viewed as a rule-governed system (M. Burgoon & Miller, 1985) in which people develop norms and expectations concerning appropriate language use in given situations. Cultural and sociological forces shape our patterns of ordinary language and determine normative and non-normative use. Based on these assumptions, the following propositions have been developed and refined (M. Burgoon, 1989, 1990, 1995; M. Burgoon & Miller, 1985):

> *Proposition 1:* People develop cultural and sociological expectations about language behaviors that subsequently affect their acceptance or rejection of persuasive messages.

As corollaries, LET advances two propositions delineating the impact on persuasive outcomes that result from conformance or nonconformance to expectations:

> *Proposition 2:* Use of language that negatively violates societal expectations about appropriate persuasive communication behavior inhibits persuasive behavior and results either in no attitude change or in changes in position opposite to that advocated by the communicator.

> *Proposition 3:* Use of language that positively violates societal expectations about appropriate persuasive communication behavior facilitates persuasive effectiveness.

Original research projects examined the effects of varying language intensity in some manner in persuasive message (M. Burgoon, 1970a, 1970b). In a series of empirical studies investigating the effects of the use of highly intense language, M. Burgoon et al. (1975) provided experimental tests of the combined effects of source characteristics and language intensity. They identified types of individuals (e.g., females, low-credible communicators) who were presumed to be expected to use less aggressive language choices (low-intensity language) in their persuasive messages. When these individuals used more instrumental verbal aggression (a term coined much later), they were seen as negatively violating expectations, and thus attitude change was inhibited. Furthermore, the studies revealed that males and highly credible sources could use either aggressive or unaggressive verbal strategies and be persuasive. However, it seemed that more aggressive behavior was the expected and/or preferred mode of argument only for highly credible male advocates. The results of these empirical tests of expectancy-based predictions were accompanied by a discussion of what was then called a message-centered theory of persuasion.

What the discussion of the empirical studies of language intensity and source characteristics actually provided was perhaps a skeletal formulation of what would later be developed as LET. Arguments that were advanced in the interpretation of this experimental research were markedly different from prevailing theories of social influence of the day. First, the focus was distinctly macro-social in orientation. It was argued that entire social categories (e.g., females, members of different ethnic groups) were bound by relatively rigid normative expectations of what was "appropriate" or expected communication behaviors. Such expectations were not unique to specific communicators but were unique to aggregates of like individuals in this society. Second, the previously discussed concept of normative bandwidths varying in size for different social groups for expected language behaviors was empirically demonstrated. People of high credibility and male speakers in general appeared to have linguistic freedom (wide bandwidths) and could select from a number of persuasive strategies (low- or high-intense language) without violating preset expectations. On the other hand, large numbers of the population had constricted bandwidths of expected communication behaviors and concomitantly very constrained choices in how they could argue if they wished to be successful at persuasion. Finally, this elementary theoretical formulation provided a plausible explanation for "boomerang" effects—change opposite to the position advocated by the communicator—that had proven enigmatic to persuasion researchers at the time. People negatively violating expectations by using intense language in a perceived extremely inappropriate manner produced such a contrast effect that people moved to opposing attitudinal positions to distance themselves from advocacy of such communicators.

Later, attention shifted from a focus solely on one message variable, language intensity, to a host of message variables (discussed in more detail later in this chapter) that were of interest to persuasion researchers. Detailed reviews of research on fear appeals, opinionatedness, and language intensity are readily available in published social influence literature (e.g., M. Burgoon & Miller, 1985). M. Burgoon (1989) extended that review to include a number of micro-level message variables as special cases of what has been called a type of instrumental verbal aggression (which includes, but is not limited to, fear appeals, opinionated language, language intensity, and aggressive compliance-gaining strategies) and placed them under the theoretical umbrella of LET. M. Burgoon (1990) also explained the results of more macro-level persuasion strategies (e.g., sequential message strategies such as foot-in-the-door [Dillard, Hunter, & M. Burgoon, 1984] and door-in-the-face [Cann, Sherman, & Elkes, 1975] techniques), as well as the compliance-gaining message strategy research (e.g., Marwell & Schmitt, 1967a, 1967b; Miller, Boster, Roloff, & Seibold, 1977, 1987), from an expectancy theory perspective.

Language expectancy theory, as suggested previously, has been used as a theoretical framework to explain the effects of several source, message, and receiver variables on message persuasiveness. Each of those research foci merits some detailed attention in that different propositions are advanced from these three somewhat distinct domains of published literature. The research that focused on just source variables has included gender (M. Burgoon, Dillard, & Doran, 1983; M. Burgoon, Dillard, Koper, & Doran, 1984), physician gender (M. Burgoon, Birk, & Hall, 1991; Klingle, 1993), credibility (M. Burgoon et al., 1975), and trustworthiness (Miller & Baseheart, 1969). All of this source-oriented research indicates that highly credible communicators are privileged, with a greater degree of freedom to use a range of

language appeals and remain persuasive. However, individuals who are perceived as low-credible sources have a more limited bandwidth of messages they may use to be effective (Hamilton, Hunter, & M. Burgoon, 1990).

Derived from the fundamental propositions and supported by copious empirical findings, the following propositions are proffered:

Proposition 4: Highly credible communicators have the freedom (wide bandwidth) to select varied language strategies and compliance-gaining techniques in developing persuasive messages, while low-credible communicators must conform to more limited language options if they wish to be effective.

Proposition 5: Because of normative impact of source credibility, highly credible sources can be more successful using low-intensity appeals and more aggressive compliance-gaining messages than can low-credible communicators using either strong or mild language or more prosocial compliance-gaining strategies.

Proposition 6: Communicators perceived as low credible or those unsure of their perceived credibility will usually be more persuasive if they employ appeals low in instrumental verbal aggression or elect to use more prosocial compliance-gaining message strategies.

In addition to general source credibility differences, there are also gender-specific expectations about appropriate communication behavior. LET posits that males and females have differing bandwidths in terms of persuasive message choices. Fairly rigid norms develop about what is and what is not acceptable use of language by males and females. Subsequently, enactment of compliant behaviors reinforces these norms. M. Burgoon et al.

(1975) found support for the relationship between gender and variations in language intensity such that males could use more intense language and maintain their persuasiveness, whereas females were not persuasive using intense language.

Gender-specific expectations also exist about the appropriate use of more general compliance-gaining strategy use. The early research examining Marwell and Schmitt's (1967a) compliance strategy checklist did not deal with the various strategies in any conceptually oriented manner. Hunter and Boster (1978, 1979) were the first to suggest that compliance-gaining strategies were a unidimensional continuum ranging from high to low on empathy. M. Burgoon et al. (1983) disagreed with this conceptualization and argued that the continuum was best viewed as variations in instrumental verbal aggression, not empathy.

M. Burgoon et al. (1983) then tested hypotheses derived from LET about gender and the use of compliance-gaining strategies, conceptualized as a continuum of instrumental verbal aggression. They reasoned that because male sources are more persuasive using intense language, male sources should also be expected to use more antisocial and verbally aggressive compliance-gaining strategies. As anticipated, they found that males were expected to use more threat and aversive stimulation (verbally aggressive) strategies, while females were expected to use positive moral appeal and altruism (less verbally aggressive) strategies. Supported by research, LET posits the following:

Proposition 7: People in this society have normative expectations about appropriate persuasive communication behavior that are gender specific such that (a) males are usually more persuasive using highly intense persuasive appeals and compliance-gaining message attempts, while (b) females

are usually more persuasive using low-intensity appeals and unaggressive compliance-gaining messages.

In addition to the vast amount of research on source characteristics, message variables have received considerable research attention under the LET framework. Those message features include language intensity (Buller, Borland, & M. Burgoon, 1998), opinionatedness (Miller & Lobe, 1967), fear appeals (Miller & Hewgill, 1966), verbal aggression (M. Burgoon, 1989, 1990), and sequential message strategies such as foot-in-the-door (Dillard et al., 1984), and door-in-the-face (Cann et al., 1975).

One example from the research on such message variables is the interpretation of the fear appeal literature from this particular perspective. Language expectancy theory is able to serve as an explanatory mechanism for existing—and sometimes contradictory—findings from various research efforts on fear-arousing messages. Extant research findings on fear appeals have shown that in some cases high fear appeals were more effective, while other studies have produced results suggesting the relative efficacy of appeals low in fear. Yet other studies have found no consistent effects based on intensity. Similar findings have been reported by researchers for opinionated language, profanity, and instrumental verbal aggression. M. Burgoon (1989, 1990) conceptualized fear appeals, opinionated language, profanity, and instrumental verbal aggression as special cases of language intensity that could be incorporated under the general framework of LET. The following proposition was then added to the original LET formulation:

Proposition 8: People in this society have normative expectations about the level of fear-arousing appeals, opinionated language, language intensity, sequential message techniques, and compliance-gaining attempts varying in instrumental verbal aggression appropriate to persuasive discourse.

In extensive literature reviews, M. Burgoon (1989, 1990) suggested that highly fear-arousing messages, instrumentally verbally aggressive message strategies, profanity, and so on are negative violations of expectations for low-credible sources and other groups such as women and minorities. The use of such strategies should result in the same inhibition or enhancement of persuasion as outlined in the earlier propositions about the effects of intensive language.

There has been very little research on receiver variables conducted directly from an expectancy perspective. While the message variable research literature has looked at some individual difference variables, such as open- versus closed-minded individuals (Miller & Lobe, 1967) and receiver's need for approval (Baseheart, 1971) in the fear appeals arena, such attention to receiver characteristics has not yielded much of interest.

However, one interesting line of inquiry suggests that the amount of anxiety experienced by the receiver will influence evaluations of a persuasive message. M. Burgoon et al. (1975) tested whether people experiencing irrelevant fear (arousal) would respond differently from individuals in a low- or no-fear condition. They found that messages that were intense or verbally aggressive were generally ineffective with people already in state of high arousal such as that produced by the induction of irrelevant fear (anxiety unrelated to the persuasive message itself). This is consistent with previous research that individuals who are highly aroused will resist experiencing additional arousing stimuli (Carmichael & Cronkhite, 1965) and suggests that bombarding aroused people with highly intense language or verbally aggressive message strate-

gies would negatively violate expectations and inhibit persuasion. More recently, Hamilton et al. (1990) examined the relationship between receiver anxiety and language intensity. Results indicated that when the receivers of the message were experiencing high anxiety, male sources were more persuasive using low-intensity language. On the other hand, receivers not experiencing irrelevant fear were more persuaded by male sources using highly intense language. Overall, the state of mind that the receiver is experiencing at the time of receiving a persuasive message will significantly affect the evaluation and outcome of the persuasive attempt:

Proposition 9: Fear arousal that is irrelevant to the content of the message of the harmful consequences of failure to comply with the advocated position mediates receptivity to different levels of language intensity and compliance-gaining strategies varying in instrumental verbal aggression. Receivers aroused by the induction of irrelevant fear or suffering from specific anxiety are most receptive to persuasive messages using low-intensity and verbally unaggressive compliance-gaining attempts but are unreceptive to intense appeals or verbally aggressive suasory strategies.

Active participation paradigm. This persuasive situation involves an exchange in roles taken by the persuader and the persuadee (target). Within the active participation paradigm, the target prepares a counterattitudinal message for public display. By developing and presenting a belief-incongruent message, the persuadee is considered actively involved in the persuasion process. It is argued that the act of preparing counterattitudinal messages increases arousal in the persuadee in the form of cognitive stress. The level of cognitive stress, in turn, affects the production of the counterattitudinal message. People experiencing high levels of cognitive stress do not want to increase their arousal level and, thereby, will produce less intense and more ambivalent messages and will elect to use less verbally aggressive messages (M. Burgoon & Miller, 1971). Under circumstances of increased cognitive stress, self-persuasion is induced as people change their private attitudes to conform to public communication behavior. M. Burgoon and Miller (1985) translated these findings into an expectancy framework claiming that the act of producing messages that are not privately accepted induces a violation of expectations about one's own norms and expectations about appropriate communication behavior. They offered the following propositions:

Proposition 10: Communicators experiencing cognitive stress produce less intense, more ambivalent messages and elect to use less aggressive compliance-gaining message strategies.

Proposition 11: When forced to violate their own norms about appropriate communication behavior by encoding highly intense messages or using aggressive compliance-gaining message strategies, communicators experience increased cognitive stress, which facilitates attitude change toward the belief-discrepant position being advocated.

Proposition 12: There is a direct linear relationship between level of language intensity used in counterattitudinal advocacy and concomitant attitude change.

Resistance to Persuasion Paradigm. Language expectancy theory was extended into the context of resistance to persuasion as an extension and a refinement of McGuire's (1964) inoculation theory. The concern was with how to make receivers more resistant to future persuasive messages. A program of research looking at sequential message strategies

in which pretreatment messages were viewed as developing expectancies and attack messages as either positively or negatively violating those induced expectations yielded some interesting and often counterintuitive findings (M. Burgoon & Chase, 1973; M. Burgoon et al., 1978; M. Burgoon & King, 1974; Miller & M. Burgoon, 1979). It was determined that inducing resistance to persuasion is a two-step process: forewarning the target about the forthcoming message (pretreatment) followed by delivering the actual persuasive message. Language expectancy theory posits that the pretreatment message provides the receiver with expectations about the subsequent persuasive message. Whether the persuasive message confirms or disconfirms the expectations afforded by the pretreatment message affects the persuasive outcome. M. Burgoon and Miller (1985) translated this empirical research from the *inducing resistance* paradigm into a propositional framework consistent with their theorizing about the role of expectancies in the *attitude change* process:

Proposition 13: When supportive pretreatment strategies are used, attitude change following a subsequent persuasive attack varies inversely with the linguistic intensity of the supportive pretreatment strategy.

Proposition 14: Refutational pretreatments create expectations by forewarning receivers about the nature of the forthcoming attacks such that (a) when persuasive attack messages do not violate the linguistic expectations created by refutational pretreatments, maximum resistance to persuasion is conferred, but (b) when the linguistic properties of attack messages violate the expectations created by refutational pretreatments either positively or negatively, receivers are less resistant to persuasion.

According to LET, refutational messages create expectations about future attack messages simply by virtue of the language used in the pretreatment message. When highly intense pretreatment messages are delivered, expectations are induced for highly intense subsequent attack messages. If those expectations are violated, the receiver will be less resistant to the attack messages and persuasion may occur. Thus, a receiver expecting a high-intensity attack message but receiving a more moderate one (a positive violation) may be persuaded by the *reasonableness* of the moderate message (M. Burgoon & Miller, 1985). On the other hand, a receiver expecting a low-intensity attack message but receiving an intense one might not have felt threatened enough to prepare for the unexpectedly persuasive attack (M. Burgoon & Chase, 1973). In this resistance to persuasion model, the objective is to minimize violating expectations induced by pretreatment messages. However, in general, high-intensity encoding tends to be less persuasive, especially when used in an attack message following any type of pretreatment effect (M. Burgoon & King, 1974).

Proposition 15: Given passive message reception, low-intensity attack messages are generally more effective than highly intense messages in overcoming resistance to persuasion conferred by supportive, refutational, or combination pretreatments.

Proposition 16: When the persuasive attack relies on an active participation strategy, a direct relationship exists between language intensity in the actively created attack and overcoming resistance conferred by any kind of pretreatment message strategy (supportive, refutational, or combination) such that matching intensity in the pretreatment and attack messages confers the most resistance to persuasion.

Proposition 17: When receivers are exposed to more than one message arguing the same position, the confirmation or disconfirmation of linguistic expectancies in the first message systematically affects the acceptance of the second message such that (a) when linguistic expectations are positively violated in an initial message, the initial message is persuasive, but a reversal of attitudes to the original position occurs after exposure to a subsequent message advocating the same counterattitudinal position, and (b) when linguistic expectations are negatively violated in an initial message, the initial message is not persuasive, but receivers are more vulnerable to the arguments of a subsequent message advocating the same counterattitudinal position.

FUTURE DIRECTIONS OF LANGUAGE EXPECTANCY THEORY

Attention to the Theoretical Formulation and Generalizability of LET

Research emanating from LET has been claimed by its own primary formulator to being subject to criticism for possibly being teleological in nature (M. Burgoon, 1995). Because normative sociological or expected communication behaviors have not routinely been specified on an a priori basis in many empirical tests of this theory, it can be difficult—if not impossible—in some situations to determine when a positive or negative violation of expectations has actually occurred. Some investigators have concluded that when attitude/behavior change occurs, a positive violation of expectations must have occurred. Similarly, when no attitude/behavior change occurs or there is a boomerang effect, the conclusions drawn are that a negative violation must have occurred. Such interpretations of the empirical data make the theoretical model unfalsifiable. While such a criticism should be directed more at the way experimental social science is sometimes conducted than at the theoretical model per se, a priori specification of expectations in experimental situations and, certainly, naturally occurring research settings makes for much stronger scientific claims.

While attention to specification of exactly what expectations people have about appropriate communication behavior requires additional scrutiny, there is also an attendant need to specify even more clearly exactly what is meant by "expectations." A pivotal definitional distinction that needs to be made regarding expectancies is whether they are regarded as predictive or prescriptive. Predictive expectancies pertain only to the typicality of behavior—to its central tendency or regularity of occurrence (as might be measured by the mean, median, or mode). Prescriptive expectancies pertain to idealized standards for conduct. They capture evaluative connotations of behavior such as appropriateness and desirability; in other words, they carry an associated *valence* ranging from negative to positive (J. Burgoon & M. Burgoon, 2001). Recent work (e.g., J. Burgoon & White, 1997; Floyd & J. Burgoon, 1999) has attempted to create a crisper distinction by reserving the term *expected* for the predictive variety and using the term *desired* for that which is valenced. Language expectancy theory has avoided dealing almost entirely with such definitional issues, and by default it has accepted predictive expectancies and not really idealized behavior as earlier formulations might have implied. The working definition of *appropriate* persuasion behavior was clearly about predicted future behavior. It is not entirely clear what might be gained by refining the predictions to incorporate distinctions between violations of preferences and predic-

tions, but it is of sufficient theoretical import to warrant serious consideration.

J. Burgoon and M. Burgoon (2001) pointed out that the ubiquity of expectancies in guiding human conduct is so widely conceded that it is perhaps unsurprising that expectancy-related concepts populate, under one guise or another, so many theories of human communication and psychology. They dealt in detail only with LET, Berger and colleagues' (Berger, Fisek, Norman, & Zelditch, 1977; Ridgeway & Berger, 1986; Ridgeway & Walker, 1995; Shelly, 1998) expectation states theory, and J. Burgoon's expectancy violations theory (J. Burgoon 1992, 1993, 1995; J. Burgoon & Hale, 1988). In addition to having generated a substantial body of research, these theories were highlighted because they represent a good sampling of perspectives on expectancies and their violations emanating from the fields and foci of social psychology, sociology, and communication. Even though expectancies are central to many research efforts, there have been very limited attempts to incorporate theorizing and compare empirical findings across what are now quite separate lines of inquiry. That remains a challenge for people interested in better explaining the role of expectations in social influence processes.

Obviously, the empirical evidence supporting LET is the product of research conducted in but one culture, namely North America. However, it should be noted that if the theory is robust, the effects of *violations of expectations, whether positive or negative,* should be culturally invariant. That is certainly not to say that expectations about what is *appropriate* or even desired persuasive communication behavior will be the same in different cultural contexts. Obviously, no one would expect this to be the case. Not only would it be valuable to know the extent to which expectations are different or similar across cultures, but it would also be enlightening to determine whether the seeming magnitude of effects of expectancy violations on attitude and/or behavior change are as dramatic in other cultures as the research evidence suggests they are in this culture.

Testing LET in Natural Settings

The bulk of the research supporting LET has been conducted in laboratory-like research settings. Data in support of the theoretical formulation provide considerable encouragement for proponents of this perspective. Clearly, testing in natural settings with a variety of methods and media being used to change socially important attitudes and behaviors is the long-term goal. That testing is now in its first stage. Because of funding opportunities, a step has been taken in testing a small part of LET in a longitudinal field study concerning skin cancer prevention.

Based on LET, Buller et al. (2000) predicted that members of credible institutions, such as school administrators, health care professionals, and physicians, would have a wider bandwidth of language choices and would be able to use high-intensity, graphic messages aimed at parents and children, encouraging family sun safety. Furthermore, the researchers proposed that pediatricians and other medical doctors would be most successful at gaining compliance when they used more intense, verbally aggressive messages as opposed to low-intensity messages. It was further hypothesized that, overall, highly intense (instrumentally verbally aggressive) prevention messages would be more effective than messages lacking in instrumental verbal aggression (low-intensity messages). Moreover, as derived directly from LET, an interaction between instrumental verbal aggression and organizational structure of persuasive messages was hypothesized such that (a) highly verbally aggressive messages organized in a deductive format would be the most effective strategy to produce

change, and (b) low-intensity (low instrumental verbal aggression) messages organized in an inductive pattern of reasoning would be superior to high-intensity, inductive messages. The results of this 4-year longitudinal study, in which each family received multiple messages across time, were supportive of the LET predictions.

Buller et al. (1998) examined data from the same field study to test the prediction that the effects of message intensity may vary as a function of the stage of behavior change of individual participants. The concept of stage changes claims that behavior change is a process whereby people progress through phases from some form of contemplation to changes in beliefs, thoughts, and receptivity until at some point the desired behavior change is enacted. They found that highly graphic and intense messages were effective with people who were already receptive to taking sun safety measures. Such messages from highly credible sources were both expected and effective. However, for the subset of the population who had already decided not to comply with the desired changes, highly intense messages were seen as inappropriate and were not persuasive.

Data from the family sun safety project also provided valuable information about the persistence of change when highly intense, graphic messages initially induced attitude and behavioral changes. While most sun safety campaigns concentrate their persuasive activities during peak sun periods, this study looked at on-peak and off-peak seasonal differences in message effects. It was encouraging to find that when people were exposed to highly intense, deductively constructed messages, their sun safety behavior remained at very high levels 6 months later when the risk of sun damage was at its lowest point.

This campaign is an exemplar of the kind of research that needs to be done in further testing the LET framework. It tested but a very small part of the entire formulation. However, it did provide support in a natural setting for some very fundamental elements of the theory. It also allowed the use of multiple messages delivered by different sources in various media over time. This demonstration of the predictive power of the theory (or at least a small number of hypotheses derived from the more complete formulation), coupled with data on the persistence of behavior changes, is at least a small step toward establishing claims of ecological validity for a theory mostly borne of laboratory research with too many convenience samples as the basis for inference to some larger population. This is the kind of natural setting research that needs to be conducted in arenas such as anti-tobacco campaigns, drug abuse reduction efforts, elimination of risky behavior, and a variety of other arenas ripe for research attention by persuasion scholars.

Extending LET to Interpersonal Influence Situations

As with most extant theories of persuasion, there is more evidence on suasory communication in one-to-many contexts than in face-to-face influence attempts. It has already been suggested that much would be gained by incorporating the thinking of other theories with a more interpersonal orientation. It is also the case that future research needs to extend LET to better focus on interpersonal influence attempts.

While any number of interpersonal contexts are replete with social influence attempts, the clinical practice of medicine is one worthy of study, if only because it is an exemplar of face-to-face persuasion with outcome measures of extreme import. One relatively recent research project built directly on the earlier LET propositions (a) to provide more precision in specifying what communication

behaviors are expected of physicians by their patients, (b) to incorporate additional variables to directly test the effects of verbal aggression on satisfaction and compliance, and (c) to determine whether LET could be used to generate hypotheses and provide results that would be parsimonious explanations and potent predictors of the outcome variables of concern in the medical context. This research effort, in line with earlier comments about needed theoretical precision, eliminates the possibility of a teleological interpretation of results in that differences in enacted and expected behaviors are clearly specified in advance. Moreover, given such precision in specifying expected behaviors in advance and measuring the valence of such communication styles, clear distinctions can be made among the expected, enacted, and preferred communication behaviors of physicians. Such a procedure allows an unequivocal specification of what sets of behaviors should be considered as positive or negative violations of expectations and what behaviors merely conform to societal norms about communication in the medical context.

M. Burgoon et al. (1991) applied the general expectancy model to the medical context. As indicated previously, early research (M. Burgoon & Miller, 1985) clearly demonstrated that the bandwidth of normatively expected behaviors is not invariant for individuals or groups of people. For example, it has been clearly demonstrated that females have a much narrower bandwidth of socially acceptable behavior than do males in this society. In other words, females are limited in their choice of strategies if they wish to avoid negatively violating expectations and being ineffective in compliance-gaining attempts. It is very difficult for a female to positively violate expectations. Yet it is quite likely that any deviations—even relatively trivial changes—from the expected roles of females will result in negative violations of expectations and increase the probability of noncompliance. A significant problem in studying physicians' enacted and expected behavior is that any resulting conclusions may generalize only to male physicians. Little research has addressed the influence of gender on the physician-patient interaction and subsequent outcomes. The lack of research in this area is due, in part, to the fact that, until recently, few women have entered those medical specialties most responsible for adult health care, namely family practice and internal medicine. Thus, generalizations advanced about expectations in clinical medicine (M. Burgoon & J. Burgoon, 1990) may be applicable only to male physicians.

While there has been little research on the effects of gender differences in the medical context, there is a wealth of research to suggest that females are more nurturing, more likely to express caring and concern, more empathic in their enacted communication behaviors, and less verbally aggressive (e.g., M. Burgoon et al., 1983; Eakins & Eakins, 1978; Infante & Wigley, 1986). To the extent that such behaviors are products of early sex role socialization, they are most resistant to change (Scanzoni, 1975). It is therefore unlikely that professional socialization would completely counteract sex role differences among physicians. This is supported by the finding that female medical students tend to elicit more psychosocial issues from patients, while males tend to see themselves in control of communication with patients and give directions and make demands (Rosenberg, 1979). If female physicians have indeed been socialized to the traditional female sex role, they will be more nurturing and expressive and will have stronger interpersonal communication orientations than male physicians.

Another line of reasoning, based on notions of credibility, suggests that female physicians have a high probability of negatively violating expectations if they do not use verbally un-

aggressive message strategies in compliance-gaining attempts. While physicians, both male and female, have relatively high normative status in this society, there are differences in the perceptions of credibility of males and females in the health care professions. For example, Engleman (1974) found that a majority of both men (84%) and women (75%) preferred a male for their regular physician. A limited amount of research attests to the fact that while female physicians are held in somewhat high esteem by most people in this society, they are still seen as less credible than their male counterparts. Therefore, according to the tenets of LET, female physicians should have less freedom to use aggressive strategies. This credibility differential, coupled with socialization processes, results in the enactment of unaggressive strategies because part of the female role suggests that any deviation from such verbally unaggressive compliance-gaining strategies will increase noncompliance.

It is clear that male physicians have a great deal of freedom to select compliance-gaining strategies. First, they have high normative status, and the socialization process provides them with an extremely wide bandwidth of acceptable behaviors. Second, much research demonstrates that socialization makes aggressive behavior not only acceptable but also preferred for highly credible male communicators in this society. Yet the expected communication behaviors for male physicians, as evidenced by the generalizations put forth by M. Burgoon and J.Burgoon (1990), are to be affectively neutral, give directions, and use negative expertise. All of these strategies fall near the center of the instrumental verbal aggression continuum. However, there is considerable evidence to suggest that high levels of verbal aggression on the part of male physicians are often perceived by patients as expressions of personal concern and considered a positive violation of expectations, increasing levels of compliance. Moreover, because male physicians are expected to be affectively neutral in treatment and prevention situations, affiliative strategies such as the expression of caring and concern can also be a positive violation of expectations for male physicians. Such personalization of the clinical visit is preferred by most people but rarely experienced in visits to male physicians. Thus, the only strategies that seem to be ineffective for male physicians are the ones currently used most often: a combination of simple direction giving and expertise. M. Burgoon et al. (1991) found convincing support for these expectancy-based hypotheses in this applied context.

Obviously, this kind of research needs to be replicated and extended to other face-to-face influence attempts to determine whether LET has the same predictive power in other situations. Again, this one study is offered only as an example of how LET should be tested in different contexts.

Reinforcement Expectancy Theory: Future Developments

What is needed is not only to follow the above injunctions to extend the boundary conditions of LET by dealing with multiple messages and face-to-face interactions but also to resurrect some important theoretical legacies that have been prematurely dismissed by persuasion researchers. Klingle (1993) developed a theoretical perspective that extends LET in these important ways. She was interested in methods for improving both initial and long-term medical adherence and for examining physician-patient communication over the course of several different clinical interventions. Again, while the medical context was selected for this particular study, the important point is to urge the extension of this theory to explain situations in which sequen-

tial messages violate or conform to established expectations.

There is a lack of research assessing how physicians should communicate to assist people in dealing with problems that occur over time. Using the recently developed reinforcement expectancy theory (Klingle, 1993), a two-part study was undertaken (Klingle & M. Burgoon, 1995) to assess the effectiveness of communication strategies designed to improve *both* initial and long-term medical adherence. The first study analyzed patients' evaluations of communication regard strategies and the effectiveness of these strategies in *initial* encounters. As predicted, negative regard strategies used by male physicians were perceived as more appropriate than negative regard strategies used by female physicians. In addition, physician gender interacted with strategy effectiveness such that male physicians were persuasive if they used either positive or negative regard strategies, whereas female physicians were limited to using only positive regard strategies. The results also indicated that the use of negative regard strategies by male physicians did not hinder patient satisfaction or physician perceptions, whereas the use of negative regard strategies by female physicians was negatively related to these outcome measures. This provided a relatively complete replicate of the earlier research conducted from a LET perspective that dealt with one-time medical encounters (M. Burgoon et al., 1991).

The reinforcement expectancy framework tested in the second study argued that occasional use of nonrewarding communication would facilitate communication effectiveness for both male and female physicians in ongoing physician-patient relationships. A very complex design was used to test the effects of neutral, negative, and positive reward strategies over five different clinical visits. As predicted, mixed types of strategies over time were generally superior to either all negative or all positive strategies over time with the same patient.

The investigation proved successful on several fronts. The fact that previous research on strategy effectiveness in initial encounters could be replicated using a different influence categorization scheme with a different population of individuals over a variety of consultation sessions suggests that the findings are probably quite robust. This investigation extends previous research by offering tentative support for the claim that health care providers who have repeated exposure to a patient can strategically use nonaffiliative communication to improve adherence rates while maintaining satisfaction and person perception. Specifically, it was argued that strategies involving a combination of reinforcing and nonreinforcing communication (i.e., reinforcement violations) are more persuasive than continual reinforcement or continual nonreinforcement.

While many psychologists and communication scholars have recently been less concerned with reinforcement/learning models, perhaps O'Keefe (1990) was premature in his unsubstantiated claim that for "good conceptual and empirical reasons," such reinforcement-based inquiries "are poor prospects" for people interested in the efficacy of persuasive messages (p. 7). Steps are being taken to determine whether out-of-favor positions, such as learning models and the theory of psychological reactance, can indeed inform and be informed by LET. This is at least one journey worth taking as we ponder future efforts to extend the predictive and explanatory power of what has proved to be an intriguing explanation of social influence processes.

REFERENCES

Baseheart, J. (1971). Message opinionation and approval-dependence as determinants of receiver attitude change and recall. *Speech Monographs, 38,* 302-310.

Berger, C. R. (1991). Communication theories and other curios. *Communication Monographs, 58,* 101-113.

Berger, J., Fisek, M. H., Norman, R. Z., & Zelditch, M., Jr. (1977). *Status characteristics in social interaction: An expectation states approach.* New York: Elsevier-North Holland.

Brooks, R. D. (1970). The generalizability of early reversals of attitudes toward communication sources. *Speech Monographs, 37,* 152-155.

Buller, D. B., Borland, R., & Burgoon, M. (1998). Impact of behavioral intention on effectiveness of message features: Evidence from the Family Sun Safety Project. *Human Communication Research, 24,* 433-453.

Buller, D. B., Burgoon, M., Hall, J. R., Levine, N., Beach, B., Buller, M. K., & Melcher, C. (2000). Long-term effects of language intensity in preventive messages on planned family solar protection. *Health Communication, 12,* 261-275.

Burgoon, J. K. (1992). Applying a comparative approach to nonverbal expectancy violations theory. In J. Blumler, K. E. Rosengren, & J. M. McLeod (Eds.), *Comparatively speaking: Communication and culture across space and time* (pp. 53-69). Newbury Park, CA: Sage.

Burgoon, J. K. (1993). Interpersonal expectations, expectancy violations, and emotional communication. *Journal of Language and Social Psychology, 12,* 13-21.

Burgoon, J. K. (1995). Cross-cultural and intercultural applications of expectancy violations theory. In R. L. Wiseman (Ed.), *Intercultural communication theory: International and intercultural communication annual* (Vol. 19, pp. 194-214). Thousand Oaks, CA: Sage.

Burgoon, J. K., & Burgoon, M. (2001). Expectancy theories. In W. P. Robinson & H. Giles (Eds.), *The new handbook of language and social psychology* (2nd ed., pp. 79-102). Sussex, UK: Wiley.

Burgoon, J. K., & Hale, J. L. (1988). Nonverbal expectancy violations: Model elaboration and application to immediacy behaviors. *Communication Monographs, 55,* 58-79.

Burgoon, J. K., & White, C. A. (1997). Researching nonverbal message production: A view from interaction adaptation theory. In J. O. Greene (Ed.), *Message production: Advances in communication theory* (pp. 279-312). Mahwah, NJ: Lawrence Erlbaum.

Burgoon, M. (1970a). The effects of response set and race on message interpretation. *Speech Monographs, 37,* 264-268.

Burgoon, M. (1970b). *Prior attitude and language intensity as predictors of message style and attitude change following counterattitudinal communication behavior.* Unpublished doctoral dissertation, Michigan State University.

Burgoon, M. (1989). Messages and persuasive effects. In J. Bradac (Ed.), *Message effects in communication science* (pp. 129-164). Newbury Park, CA: Sage.

Burgoon, M. (1990). Language and social influence. In H. Giles & P. Robinson (Eds.), *Handbook of language and social psychology* (pp. 51-72). London: Wiley.

Burgoon, M. (1994). PATHS II: The garden variety. *Communication Theory, 20,* 431-436.

Burgoon, M. (1995). Language expectancy theory: Elaboration, explication, and extension. In C. R. Berger & M. Burgoon (Eds.), *Communication and social influence processes* (pp. 29-52). East Lansing: Michigan State University Press.

Burgoon, M., Birk, T. S., & Hall, J. R. (1991). Compliance and satisfaction with physician-patient communication: An expectancy theory interpretation of gender differences. *Human Communication Research, 18,* 177-208.

Burgoon, M., & Burgoon, J. K. (1990). Compliance-gaining and health care. In J. P. Dillard (Ed.), *Seeking compliance: The production of interpersonal influence messages* (pp. 161-188). Scottsdale, AZ: Gorsuch Scarisbrick.

Burgoon, M., & Chase, L. J. (1973). The effects of differential linguistic patterns in messages attempting to induce resistance to persuasion. *Speech Monographs, 40,* 1-7.

Burgoon, M., Cohen, M., Miller, M. D., & Montgomery, C. L. (1978). An empirical test of a model of resistance to persuasion. *Human Communication Research, 5,* 27-39.

Burgoon, M., Dillard, J. P., & Doran, N. (1983). Friendly or unfriendly persuasion: The effects of violations of expectations by males and females. *Human Communication Research, 10,* 283-294.

Burgoon, M., Dillard, J. P., Koper, R., & Doran, N. (1984). The impact of communication context and persuader gender on persuasive message selection. *Women's Studies in Communication, 7,* 1-12.

Burgoon, M., Jones, S. B., & Stewart, D. (1975). Toward a message-centered theory of persuasion: Three empirical investigations of language intensity. *Human Communication Research, 1,* 240-256.

Burgoon, M., & King, L. B. (1974). The mediation of resistance to persuasion strategies by language variables and active-passive participation. *Human Communication Research, 1,* 30-41.

Burgoon, M., & Miller, G. R. (1971). Prior attitude and language intensity as predictors of message style and attitude change following counterattitudinal advocacy. *Journal of Personality and Social Psychology, 20,* 246-253.

Burgoon, M., & Miller, G. R. (1985). An expectancy interpretation of language and persuasion. In H. Giles & R. N. St. Clair (Eds.), *Recent advances in language communication and social psychology* (pp. 199-229). London: Lawrence Erlbaum.

Burgoon, M., & Miller, G. R. (1990). PATHS. *Communication Monographs, 57,* 152-160.

Cann, A., Sherman, S. J., & Elkes, R. (1975). Effects of initial request size and timing of the second request on compliance: The foot-in-the-door and the door-in-the-face. *Journal of Personality and Social Psychology, 32,* 774-782.

Carmichael, C. W., & Cronkhite, G. (1965). Frustration and language intensity. *Speech Monographs, 32,* 107-111.

Chaiken, S. (1980). Heuristic versus systematic information processing and the use of source versus message cues in persuasion. *Journal of Personality and Social Psychology, 39,* 752-766.

Chaiken, S. (1987). The Heuristic Model of persuasion. In M. P. Zanna, J. M. Olson, & C. P. Herman (Eds.), *Social influence: The Ontario Symposium* (Vol. 5, pp. 3-39). Hillsdale, NJ: Lawrence Erlbaum.

Dillard, J. P., Hunter, J. E., & Burgoon, M. (1984). A meta-analysis of two sequential request strategies for gaining compliance: Foot-in-the-door and door-in-the-face. *Human Communication Research, 10,* 461-488.

Eakins, B. W., & Eakins, R. G. (1978). *Sex differences in human communication.* Boston: Houghton Mifflin.

Engleman, E. G. (1974). Attitudes toward women physicians: A study of 500 clinic patients. *Western Journal of Medicine, 120,* 95.

Festinger, L. (1957). *A theory of cognitive dissonance.* Evanston, IL: Row, Peterson.

Fishbein, M., & Ajzen, I. (1975). *Belief, attitude, intention, and behavior: An introduction to theory and research.* Reading, MA: Addison-Wesley.

Floyd, K., & Burgoon, J. K. (1999). Reacting to nonverbal expressions of liking: A test of interaction adaptation theory. *Communication Monographs, 66,* 219-239.

Hamilton, M. A., Hunter, J. E., & Burgoon, M. (1990). An empirical test of an axiomatic model of the relationship between language intensity and persuasion. *Journal of Language and Social Psychology, 9,* 235-255.

Hunter, J. E., & Boster, F. J. (1978, November). *An empathy model of compliance-gaining message strategy selection.* Paper presented at the annual meeting of the Speech Communication Association, Minneapolis, MN.

Hunter, J. E., & Boster, F. J. (1979, November). *Situational differences in the selection of compliance-gaining messages.* Paper presented at the annual meeting of the Speech Communication Association, San Antonio, TX.

Infante, D. A., & Wigley, C. J. (1986). Verbal aggressiveness: An interpersonal model and measure. *Communication Monographs, 53,* 61-69.

Klingle, R. S. (1993). Bringing time into physician compliance gaining research: Toward a reinforcement expectancy theory of strategy effectiveness. *Health Communication, 5,* 283-308.

Klingle, R. S., & Burgoon, M. (1995). Patient compliance and satisfaction with physician influence attempts: A reinforcement expectancy approach to compliance-gaining over time. *Communication Research, 22,* 148-187.

Marwell, G., & Schmitt, D. R. (1967a). Compliance-gaining behavior: A synthesis and model. *Sociological Quarterly, 8,* 317-328.

Marwell, G., & Schmitt, D. R. (1967b). Dimensions of compliance-gaining behavior: An empirical analysis. *Sociometry, 30,* 350-364.

McGuire, W. (1964). Inducing resistance to persuasion. In L. Berkowitz (Ed.), *Advances in experimental social psychology I* (pp. 191-229). New York: Academic Press.

McPeek, R. W., & Edwards, J. D. (1975). Expectancy disconfirmation and attitude change. *Journal of Social Psychology, 96,* 193-208.

Miller, G. R., & Baseheart, J. (1969). Source trustworthiness, opinionated statements, and response to persuasive communication. *Speech Monographs, 36,* 1-7.

Miller, G. R., Boster, F., Roloff, M., & Seibold, D. (1977). Compliance-gaining message strategies: A typology and some findings concerning effects of situational differences. *Communication Monographs, 44,* 37-51.

Miller, G. R., Boster, F., Roloff, M., & Seibold, D. (1987). MBRS rekindled: Some thoughts on compliance gaining in interpersonal settings. In M. E. Roloff & G. R. Miller (Eds.), *Interpersonal processes: New directions in communication research* (pp. 89-116). Newbury Park, CA: Sage.

Miller, G. R., & Burgoon, M. (1978). Persuasion research: Review and commentary. In B. D. Ruben (Ed.), *Communication Yearbook II* (pp. 29-47). New Brunswick, NJ: Transaction Books.

Miller, G. R., & Hewgill, M. (1966). Some recent research on fear-arousing message appeals. *Speech Monographs, 33,* 377-391.

Miller, G. R., & Lobe, J. (1967). Opinionated language, open- and closed-mindedness, and response to persuasive communications. *Journal of Communication, 17,* 333-341.

Miller, M. D, & Burgoon, M. (1979). The relationship between violations of expectations and the induction of resistance to persuasion. *Human Communication Research, 5,* 301-313.

O'Keefe, D. (1990). *Persuasion: Theory and research.* Newbury Park, CA: Sage.

Petty, R. E., & Cacioppo, J. T. (1981). *Attitudes and persuasion: Classic and contemporary approaches.* Dubuque, IA: William C. Brown.

Petty, R. E., & Cacioppo, J. T. (1986). *Communication and persuasion: Central and peripheral routes to attitude change.* New York: Springer-Verlag.

Ridgeway, C. L., & Berger, J. (1986). Expectations, legitimation, and dominance behavior in task groups. *American Sociological Review, 62,* 218-235.

Ridgeway, C. L., & Walker, H. A. (1995). Status structures. In K. S. Cook, G. A. Fine, & J. S. House (Eds.), *Sociological perspectives on social psychology* (pp. 281-310). Boston: Allyn & Bacon.

Rosenberg, P. R. (1979). Catch-22: The medical model. In E. C. Shapiro & L. M. Lowenstein (Eds.), *Becoming a physician: Development of values and attitudes in medicine* (pp. 81-92). Cambridge, MA: Ballinger.

Scanzoni, J. H. (1975). *Sex roles, lifestyles, and childbearing.* New York: Free Press.

Shelly, R. K. (1998). Some developments in expectation states theory: Graduated expectations? In E. J. Lawler, J. Skvoretz, & J. Szmatka (Eds.), *Advances in group processes* (pp. 41-57). Greenwich, CT: JAI.

8

The Role of Attitude Functions in Persuasion and Social Judgment

SHARON SHAVITT
MICHELLE R. NELSON

During the 1950s and 1960s, a class of theories was proposed that was the first to focus attention on the motives or functions that attitudes serve for the individual. These functional theories of attitude held that attitudes serve a variety of purposes important to psychological functioning (Katz, 1960; Katz & Stotland, 1959; Kelman, 1958, 1961; Smith, Bruner, & White, 1956). Functional theories were the first to recognize attitudes as instrumental constructs designed to serve individuals' physical, social, and emotional needs.

THE FUNCTIONS OF ATTITUDES

Although different functional labels were used within each theory, the functions that were proposed can be grouped into similar categories (Insko, 1967). Katz (1960) proposed that attitudes serve a knowledge function, helping to organize and structure one's environment and to provide consistency in one's frame of reference (see also Smith et al., 1956). All attitudes likely serve this basic function to some extent.

In addition, attitudes likely serve any of a number of other motives. Many attitudes serve a utilitarian function (Katz, 1960; see also Smith et al., 1956), helping to maximize the rewards and minimize the punishments obtained from objects in the environment. Such utilitarian attitudes serve to summarize the outcomes intrinsically associated with objects and to guide behavioral responses that maximize one's interests. For example, one's attitude toward ice cream may serve a utilitarian function because it is likely to be based on the rewards (e.g., enjoyable taste) and punishments (e.g., weight gain) associated with ice cream and to guide behavior that maximizes benefits while minimizing costs (e.g., eating low-fat ice cream).

Attitudes also serve an important social role, aiding in one's self-expression and social interaction. Holding particular attitudes can serve to foster identification with important reference groups (Kelman, 1958, 1961), to express one's central values, and to establish one's identity (Katz, 1960). Moreover, Smith et al. (1956) noted that attitudes mediate our relations with other people through the judicious expression of those attitudes (see also Kelman, 1958, 1961). For instance, one's attitude toward the death penalty may mediate one's relations with others because it is likely to be based on what the issue symbolizes and on what the attitude is perceived to express about the self (Tyler & Weber, 1982). This social role of attitudes has been referred to as the social identity function (Shavitt, 1989) and comprises both public identity and private identity motives.

Finally, attitudes can serve to build and maintain self-esteem in a variety of ways. The original functional theories focused on psychodynamic mechanisms by which attitudes support self-esteem, suggesting that attitudes can serve as defense mechanisms for coping with intrapsychic conflict (Katz, 1960; Smith et al., 1956). The assumption was that attitudes distance the self from threatening out-groups or objects by projecting one's unacceptable impulses onto them. This analysis was particularly pertinent to the conceptualization of prejudiced attitudes and resulted in important contributions in this domain (e.g., Adorno, Frenkel-Brunswik, Levinson, & Sanford, 1950; Katz, Sarnoff, & McClintock, 1956; McClintock, 1958; for a review and critique, see Shavitt, 1989).

Attitudes serve a self-esteem maintenance function in other ways as well. Indeed, recent research has shown that attitudes toward a variety of targets are motivated by their implications for self-assessment (Dunning, 1999; Klein & Kunda, 1993, 1994). For instance, attitudes toward people with whom we affiliate are based in part on their implications for self-enhancing social comparison (Tesser & Campbell, 1983). Attitudes that associate the self with successful groups (e.g., winning sports teams) may be based on their implications for boosting self-esteem through a process of "basking in reflected glory" (Cialdini et al., 1976).

Functional theories have been influential and widely cited in the domain of attitudes and persuasion. In particular, they have offered critical insights into persuasion processes. Functional theories held that in order to change an attitude, it is necessary to know the motivational basis for that attitude. The central principle of these theories is that attitudes that serve different functions will change in response to different types of appeals.

Despite the fundamental importance of this insight, however, this and other functional predictions went largely untested for several years, in part because the theories did not frame these hypotheses in readily testable terms. The lack of an accepted methodology for identifying or manipulating attitude functions meant that these provocative theories lay dormant for a quarter century or more.

Recent Approaches to the Study of Attitude Functions

During recent years, the growing interest in the motivational underpinnings of cognitive and judgment processes has led to a strong resurgence of interest in testing functional predictions. The resulting studies have filled multiple volumes and articles (see Maio & Olson, 2000; Pratkanis, Breckler, & Greenwald, 1989) and greatly expanded our knowledge of both the antecedents and consequences of attitude functions.

As noted earlier, one of the main stumbling blocks to empirical progress in this area had been the lack of methods for operationalizing attitude functions. It is in this area in particular that important advances have been made.

Researchers have employed and validated a variety of approaches to establishing the functions of an attitude. These include assessment of functions through the classification of open-ended responses (e.g., Herek, 1987; Prentice, 1987; Shavitt, 1990), as well as direct assessment of functions through structured questionnaires (e.g., Herek, 1987; see also Lutz, 1981).

Other research has capitalized on personality assessments to operationalize attitude functions, identifying individuals for whom attitudes are typically likely to serve a particular function. Most of these studies have employed the self-monitoring construct (Snyder, 1974) to identify the social functions that individuals' attitudes are assumed to serve (e.g., DeBono, 1987; DeBono & Harnish, 1988; Lavine & Snyder, 1996; Petty & Wegener, 1998; Snyder & DeBono, 1985). The focus of this research is on the contrasting aspects of the social identity function. Snyder and DeBono (1985) suggested that high self-monitoring individuals, who strive to fit into various social situations, should tend to form attitudes that guide behavior appropriate to the relevant reference groups in each situation. This, they argued, implies that high self-monitors' attitudes generally serve to establish their public identity (what Smith et al., 1956, labeled the *social adjustment function*). By contrast, low self-monitoring individuals, who strive to remain true to their inner values and preferences, should tend to form attitudes that reflect and express their true selves and establish their private identities (what Katz, 1960, labeled the *value-expressive function*). Research has generally supported these assumptions, suggesting that personality differences tend to predict differences in the functions that one's attitudes tend to serve.

Direct manipulations of attitude functions have also been developed and validated, involving manipulations of the judgment context. For instance, heightening the salience of function-relevant dimensions prior to an evaluative judgment appears to induce or prime different functional underpinnings for the same attitude (e.g., Maio & Olson, 1995; Shavitt & Fazio, 1991). Indeed, utilitarian, social identity, and self-esteem goals all could underlie attitudes toward social groups, political issues, and many consumer products.

However, not all attitude objects are necessarily multifunctional. Some may be more limited in their functions, and this point has operational implications. Shavitt (1989, 1990) proposed that the purposes or functions that an object can serve should influence the functions that attitudes toward that object will serve, with some objects serving primarily a single type of purpose. For instance, aspirin serves primarily a utilitarian purpose due to the outcomes intrinsically associated with it. Thus, attitudes toward aspirin will typically serve a utilitarian function, guiding behaviors that maximize the rewards and minimize the punishments associated with this product. By contrast, flags primarily serve the social identity purpose of communicating one's identities and loyalties to others. Thus, attitudes toward flags will primarily serve this same function, guiding behavior designed to express or display this attitude to particular audiences.

By presenting participants with different types of single-function attitude objects to respond to, the functions of their attitudes can be varied experimentally. Such object-based manipulations of attitude functions have been validated in several studies using multiple objects and products (e.g., Nelson, Shavitt, Schennum, & Barkmeier, 1997; Shavitt, 1990; Shavitt & Fazio, 1991; Shavitt, Lowrey, & Han, 1992).

In sum, a variety of methods have been developed recently for operationalizing functional theories. Direct measures, individual differences, situational variations, and object variations all have proven useful in testing functional predictions.

CONSEQUENCES OF ATTITUDE FUNCTIONS

Persuasion Consequences

As mentioned earlier, one of the key predictions of functional theory is that messages will be persuasive to the extent that they match the functional underpinnings of the attitude they target. This *matching hypothesis,* as it has come to be known, has received extensive empirical support across studies using a variety of functional operations and outcome measures (e.g., DeBono, 1987; Prentice, 1987; Shavitt, 1990; Shavitt et al., 1992; Snyder & DeBono, 1985, 1987; Spivey, Munson, & Locander, 1983).

For instance, DeBono (1997) showed that persuasive appeals are accepted by high self-monitors to the extent that the appeals address the social adjustive function (e.g., messages about the consensus of their peers). By contrast, appeals are accepted by low self-monitors to the extent that the appeals address the value-expressive function (e.g., messages about the values reflected by the advocated attitude). In the context of advertising, Snyder and DeBono (1985, 1987) showed that high self-monitors respond more favorably to image-oriented ads (social adjustive appeals), whereas low self-monitors respond more favorably to ads about product quality (what Snyder & DeBono called value-expressive appeals).

Shavitt (1990) provided evidence for the matching effect using an object-based method. Participants read advertising appeals about products that were expected primarily to engage either a utilitarian function (e.g., air conditioners, coffees) or a social identity function (e.g., perfumes, greeting cards). For each product, participants read an appeal for a brand advertised with utilitarian arguments stressing product benefits and attributes (e.g., "The delicious, hearty flavor and aroma of Sterling Blend coffee come from a blend of the freshest coffee beans") and an appeal for a brand advertised with social identity arguments stressing what the product conveys to others (e.g., "The coffee you drink says something about the type of person you are. It can reveal your rare discriminating taste"). Functionally matched ads elicited more favorable attitudes, cognitive responses, and purchase intentions than did mismatching ads. Subsequent research yielded a functional matching effect when participants were asked to write their own ads for utilitarian and social identity products (Shavitt et al., 1992).

Information Processing Consequences

What processes underlie this matching effect? A variety of answers to this question have been offered. Lavine and Snyder (1996) showed that the effect can be mediated by the perception that functionally matched messages are higher in quality. In other words, matched messages may induce favorably biased processing of their content. By contrast, DeBono (1987) suggested that the effect is largely a peripheral process that does not require the processing (or even the presence) of substantive message arguments.

However, several studies (including DeBono, 1987, Study 1) have indicated that functionally matched messages can trigger elaborated processing of message elements. Indeed, this processing can be relatively objective, resulting in counterarguments as well as supportive responses (DeBono & Harnish, 1988; Petty & Wegener, 1998; Shavitt, Swan, Lowrey, & Wänke, 1994). For instance, DeBono and Harnish (1988) demonstrated that an attractive source can stimulate elaborated processing of message arguments among high self-monitoring persons, whereas an expert source can stimulate such processing among low self-monitors. Therefore, high self-monitors agreed with an expert source regardless of the quality of the arguments that he presented (i.e., expertise served as a peripheral cue regarding the merits of the message) but agreed with an attractive source only when he presented strong arguments. By contrast, low self-monitors agreed with an attractive source regardless of argument strength but agreed with an expert source only when he presented strong arguments.

Similarly, Petty and Wegener (1998) showed that matching the substantive content of a message to the attitude function influences the degree of scrutiny that the message receives. Specifically, the attitudes of high and low self-monitors were strongly affected by the strength of message arguments when those arguments matched rather than mismatched the functional basis of their attitudes.

Finally, Shavitt et al. (1994) demonstrated that the attractiveness of endorsers in an ad, a message element that is particularly relevant to social identity goals, is used as a shortcut or cue to product evaluation when utilitarian goals are made salient (and involvement is low), whereas it is scrutinized as relevant information about the image of the product when social identity goals are made salient (and involvement is high). In other words, the attractiveness or unattractiveness of endorsers elicits greater scrutiny and elaboration when their presence is relevant to the functional basis of the attitude. When recipients are involved in evaluating the focal product with social identity goals in mind, the presence of endorsers who are less than attractive may be worse than no endorser at all.

Thus, the goal-relevant elements of a message can affect the nature of the processing in which message recipients engage (for consideration of this issue, see also Slater's chapter in this volume [Chapter 10]). Moreover, as these studies make clear, functional matching may have more than a simple effect on persuasion. By examining the cognitive processes that can account for the functional matching effect, researchers have identified some of its boundary conditions. In some cases, function-relevant material appears to be processed more systematically than function-irrelevant material. This means that functionally matching messages are not necessarily more persuasive than mismatching ones. Instead, the effect of functional matching on the persuasiveness of a message can depend on the cogency of the arguments presented (for a detailed consideration of these processes, see Petty & Wegener, 1998).

Implications for Predicting Long-Term Message Effectiveness

If function-relevant material in a message can elicit increased scrutiny, then one might expect thoughts that reflect the by-products of such scrutiny to be more important to persuasion than other thoughts. This would be expected both because such thoughts may reflect more systematic processing and because such thoughts are relevant to the goals associated with one's attitude. Thus, to the extent that cognitive responses to a message are functionally relevant, those thoughts should also link more closely to one's attitudes.

Will function-relevant thoughts be more important in predicting attitudes than thoughts that reflect other functional goals? This issue was investigated in the context of a study on long-term advertising effectiveness (Nelson et al., 1997). Long-term effects of a message are particularly important in consumer contexts, where delayed thoughts and attitudes about brands can be critical to the decision-making process. For example, one's first exposure to an advertisement for a new product may trigger cognitive responding but may or may not trigger formation of an attitude toward the brand. Evaluating the brand might not become relevant until, say, one is at the grocery store a week later. At that point, the cognitive responses that one remembers may help to determine one's judgment.

In a two-session study of advertising effects, Nelson et al. (1997) investigated the role of functionally relevant cognitive responding to an ad in predicting ad persuasiveness, focusing on the functions associated with product categories and personality categories. For instance, it was expected that the relevance of listed thoughts to the function associated with the advertised product would influence the predictiveness of those listed thoughts—perhaps because functionally relevant thoughts reflect more systematic processing than do functionally irrelevant thoughts.

In the first session, participants were shown print advertisements for a number of products varying in the functions they were expected to engage (e.g., utilitarian products such as a toothbrush, social identity products such as flowers, multiple-function products such as mineral water). The product functions were determined by pretesting. The ads employed were for fictitious brands but were designed to appear realistic. Utilitarian and social identity claims were balanced within each ad. Therefore, there was consistency in the type of advertising content used across products and function categories, and participants could focus on any combination of utilitarian claims or social identity claims for any product. After looking at each ad, participants listed their thoughts. A week later, participants returned and reported their attitudes toward the advertised brands and then attempted to recall the thoughts that they had listed during the first session. Finally, participants completed several other measures, including the 25-item Self-Monitoring Scale (Snyder, 1974).

The results indicated that the types of thoughts that tended to be more predictive of attitudes at a 1-week delay were those that were more relevant to the functional basis of the attitude. Specifically, there was a consistent trend for the predictive value of each thought type to vary with the type of product (see Table 8.1). For utilitarian products, the utilitarian thoughts that one recalled at a delay were significantly more consistent with attitude than were the social identity thoughts that one recalled. The opposite was the case, although not significantly, for social identity products. These findings are consistent with assumptions about the functions associated with these product categories, as the types of thoughts that were predictive corresponded with the ascribed functions of the products.

In addition, interactive effects were found for product and personality, which might be explained in terms of how well the functions of the product correspond to the goals of the individual. In general, the thoughts that low self-monitors listed initially, as well as the thoughts that they recalled (see Table 8.1), were more consistent with their attitudes than were those of high self-monitors. More important, for low self-monitors, recalled utilitarian thoughts were significantly more consistent with attitudes for utilitarian products than with those for social identity products. The reverse was true for high self-monitors, for whom recalled social identity thoughts were significantly more consistent with attitudes for social identity products than with those for utilitarian products. Thus, the responses that participants recalled to an advertisement correlated with persuasion to the extent that the function associated with the responses and with the target product matched the goals of the individual.

These findings suggest that cognitive responses that "match" the functional basis of one's attitudes may play a more important

TABLE 8.1   Correlations Between Favorability of Thoughts Recalled at a Delay (Time 2) and Attitude Toward the Brand (Time 2) as a Function of Thought Type, Product Type, and Level of Self-Monitoring

	Recalled Utilitarian Thoughts	Recalled Social Identity Thoughts
Utilitarian product		
Low self-monitoring	.74 (n = 16)**	.50 (n = 14)**
High self-monitoring	.33 (n = 16)**	−.30 (n = 17)**
Overall[a]	.54 (n = 32)	.14 (n = 31)
Multiple-function product		
Low self-monitoring	.58 (n = 16)*	.73 (n = 19)**
High self-monitoring	.18 (n = 19)*	.15 (n = 17)**
Overall	.41 (n = 35)	.46 (n = 36)
Social identity product		
Low self-monitoring	.28 (n = 18)	.58 (n = 14)
High self-monitoring	.38 (n = 12)	.28 (n = 15)
Overall	.35 (n = 30)	.43 (n = 29)

SOURCE: Nelson, Shavitt, Schennum, and Barkmeier (1997). © 1997 by Lawrence Erlbaum. Used by permission.

NOTE: Participants who did not provide any thoughts for a given thought type were not included in the relevant thought index analyses.

a.   Within participants for this product category, correlations for recalled utilitarian thoughts and recalled social identity thoughts differed at $p < .05$.

 *For this thought type, within this product category, correlations for low and high self-monitors differed at $p < .10$.

**For this thought type, within this product category, correlations for low and high self-monitors differed at $p < .05$.

role in persuasion than do other cognitive responses. This makes sense from the functional theory perspective of attitudes as goal-relevant constructs; that is, thoughts that reflect one's goals matter more than thoughts that do not. It also fits well with research described earlier that showed enhanced processing of function-relevant material. Apparently, the by-products of such processing continue to be important in long-term persuasion.

Implications of Functional Theory for Person Perception

The previous section outlined ways in which the social identity function of attitudes has been investigated from the perspective of the attitude holder—in terms of persuasiveness of appeals and the processing of function-relevant versus function-irrelevant information. However, functional theory also posits that people often hold or express their attitudes and preferences to communicate something about themselves to other people (Katz, 1960; Smith et al., 1956). That is, our attitudes toward specific issues, products, or ideas can serve to convey broader information about us to interested parties. To the extent that an attitude serves this social identity function, one would expect it to affect the judgments that observers make about the attitude holder based on their knowledge of that person's attitude. For example, attitudes about political issues are often communicated to others via badges or bumper stickers—not only conveying information about an individual's political attitudes but also likely triggering inferences about personality and preferences more generally. Similarly, the type of car one admires might be seen as offering clues to others about one's personality. These examples demonstrate how the social identity function may implicate person perception processes.

This notion shifts the focus of attention from the attitude holder to the observer and the judgments made by that observer on the basis of attitudinal information. Prior research using conceptual frameworks other than functional theory has demonstrated that observers do make judgments about targets based on knowledge of their attitudes. This is true for attitudes regarding social issues as well as attitudes toward a variety of consumer products, from clothing to supermarket goods (for a review, see Shavitt & Nelson, 2000). Our object-based approach to functional theory makes specific predictions about *when* person impressions are likely to be informed by targets' attitudes. We would expect person impressions to be based on attitudes to the extent that the attitude object engages a social identity function. Shavitt and Nelson (2000) tested this hypothesis in a series of studies in the context of attitudes toward a variety of consumer products.

In initial studies, participants were randomly assigned a product in one of three function categories—utilitarian (e.g., aspirin), social identity (e.g., team banner), and multiple function (e.g., sweatshirt)—and were instructed to list words that described the type of person who uses the target product. We expected that, to the extent products engaged attitudes that served a social identity function, they would elicit individuating descriptors of their users, with social identity products eliciting the greatest number of such descriptors and utilitarian products eliciting the least. The words listed by respondents were coded into three categories: (a) personality traits/individuating descriptors (e.g., "flashy"), (b) demographic characteristics (e.g., "old"), and (c) "other" words that did not necessarily describe anything enduring about the target person but tended instead to focus on product-related needs (e.g., "has a headache").

No differences were observed between product categories in the total number of descriptors listed. However, several differences emerged in the types of descriptors listed (see Figure 8.1). As expected, participants used significantly more personality/individuating descriptors to describe users of social identity or multiple-function products than to describe users of utilitarian products. Conversely, "other" words appeared more often for users of utilitarian products than for users of multiple-function products, and they appeared more often for users of multiple-function products than for users of social identity products. That is, users of social identity products were described primarily in terms of their traits, interests, and activities. By contrast, users of utilitarian products were more likely to be described in terms of their product-related needs. Overall, these results confirmed that product attitudes are likely to elicit individuating person descriptions to the extent that those product attitudes tend to serve a social identity function. In other

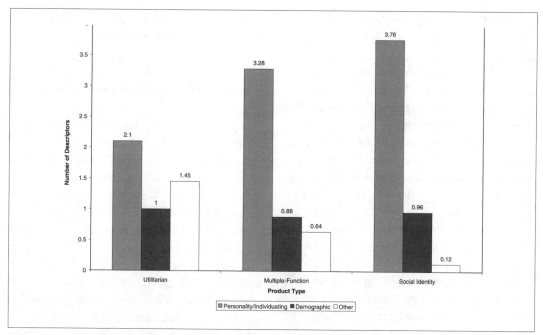

Figure 8.1. Mean Number of Descriptors as a Function of Product Type
SOURCE: Shavitt and Nelson (2000).

words, the attitudes reflected by product use clearly did communicate information about the product users, but some attitudes appeared to communicate substantially more individuating information than did others.

In another study, we examined the influence of product purchase information on judgment of an individual target person (rather than a "type of person"). Respondents were shown a scenario in which they incidentally encountered product purchase information embedded within other information about the person. Participants' involvement or motivation to form a careful evaluation of the target person was manipulated, as was the functional category of the product the target was purchasing.

In addition, the favorability of the product purchase information in the scenario was manipulated so that the effects of that information would be reflected in differences in the favorability of person judgments. The prod-

ucts employed were (a) utilitarian (fresh-squeezed orange juice [favorable], instant orange drink [unfavorable]) and (b) social identity (fresh flowers [favorable], plastic flowers [unfavorable]). Participants read a scenario in which they imagined themselves encountering the target person in a grocery store and, in the context of conversation, learning that the target intended to purchase one of these items. Similar to the previous studies, after reading the scenario, respondents listed as many words as they could think of to describe the target person. These descriptors were subsequently coded for their favorability.

Results indicated that product purchase information did influence descriptions of a specific target person even though that information was acquired incidentally in the context of other information about the person. Moreover, as in the initial studies, the function associated with the product affected the impact of the product purchase information. Specifically, as the motivation to form a careful evaluation of the target increased, evaluations of the person became more consistent with the favorability of her social identity purchases and less consistent with the favorability of her utilitarian purchases (see Figure 8.2). This pattern of results suggests that, when seeking to form a careful evaluation of a target person, social identity attitudes are seen as more informative for that evaluation than are utilitarian attitudes.

In summary, perceivers can and will infer individuating information about a person from his or her attitudes. However, the degree to which a given attitude is seen as informative about dispositional characteristics of a target person depends on the functions engaged by the attitude object. Social identity attitudes appear to be perceived as a better, more informative basis for making person judgments than are utilitarian attitudes. These studies suggest that the social identity function has broader implications than considered previously. Indeed, functional theory may offer a useful framework for examining person perception processes.

ADDITIONAL CONSIDERATIONS AND FUTURE DIRECTIONS

As reviewed above, functional theories have important implications for the understanding of persuasion, message processing, and person perception. Nevertheless, one should keep in mind some limitations on the perspective that these theories afford. For instance, functional theories rarely address the diverse and cluttered contexts in which attitudes are often formed. Addressing these limitations can help point the way to a productive agenda for future functional theorizing and research. Below, some future directions are proposed that consider the roles of competitive com-

munication contexts and differing cultural contexts in attitude functions.

The Role of Choice and Competition

Functional theories have tended to focus on absolute judgments and the factors that influence them. It is important, however, not to overlook a key aspect of most mass communication situations. Virtually every mass communication context is characterized by a choice of available messages in a competitive environment.

Slater's chapter in this volume (Chapter 10) addresses this aspect of the communication environment in a broader context, noting that persuasion researchers often overlook the goal-directed choices that people make pertaining to message exposure. Indeed, intense competition for the audience's attention is a standard feature of mass communication domains, including advertising. Consider that studies have suggested that message factors, such as sexual content, that increase attention may do so at the cost of subsequent comprehension and/or elaboration (e.g., Severn, Belch, & Belch, 1990). One may be tempted to conclude that those attention-getting factors interfere with effective persuasion. However, in a highly competitive and message-dense environment, such as exists for many consumer product categories, attracting attention to one's advertising is crucial. Indeed, the task of "breaking through the clutter" of other ads is often a more difficult challenge than eliciting favorable responses once attention is paid.

Wells (1993) noted that laboratory research on advertising, in which consistent levels of attention to stimuli are generally assured, has led to a neglect of the factors that drive attention and sometimes to erroneous conclusions. For instance, although highly absorbing television programs have been found to interfere

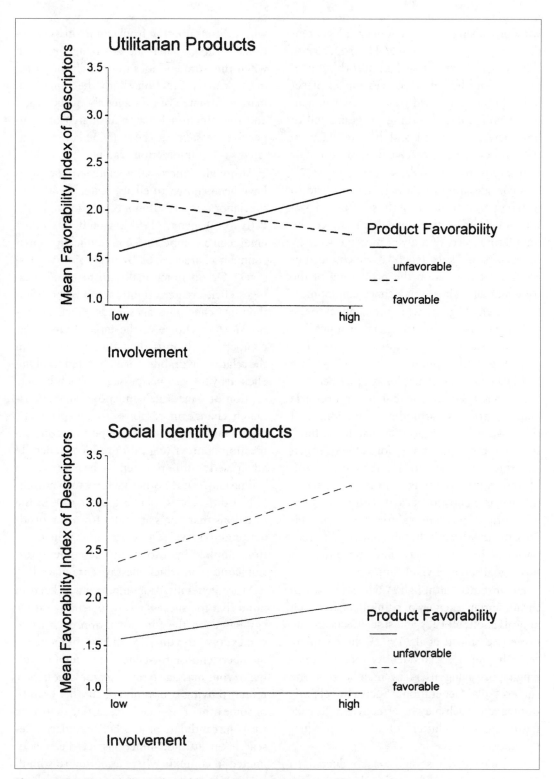

Figure 8.2. Favorability Index of Descriptions of the Target Person
SOURCE: Shavitt and Nelson (2000).

with processing of the commercial content they carry (e.g., Schumann & Thorson, 1990), this does not mean that less absorbing programs would be better choices for ad placement. In the real-world viewing environment of the home, less absorbing programs fail to hold viewers' attention, and thus ads placed in those programs may receive little attention or even exposure (see Wells, 1993).

A consideration of these issues can lead to different predictions from those afforded by a functional perspective alone. For instance, the long-term effects of a given message strategy on persuasion likely depend as much on competitors' actions as on the processing of the focal message. The result is that a communication strategy (e.g., matching the appeal to the functional basis of the attitude) that appears to work in an absolute sense might not work in a competitive atmosphere.

To take just one example, as described earlier, it has been shown that many products engage particular attitudinal functions and that advertising appeals that match the function(s) of the product are more effective than advertisements that do not (Shavitt, 1990). However, in a competitive situation, marketing managers are concerned with finding the appropriate "positioning" for their brand relative to other brands. In this context, differentiation is the key concern, and appealing to a novel goal can be a viable approach.

For instance, although Advil competes in the utilitarian category of painkillers, in which appeals about efficacy and side effects are the norm (see Shavitt et al., 1992), the company recently ran a social identity-focused campaign portraying users as members of the can do "Advil Generation." Such a novel positioning approach may be effective in "breaking through the clutter" of ads in a product category.

Future research should be conducted to address the impact of functional matching in real-world communication environments, where differentiation from competitors' functional strategies may be advantageous even when this strategy does not match the product's primary function. Both the functional match/mismatch of messages about the target and the functional match/mismatch of competitive messages can be examined or manipulated so that interactions can be observed.

Although functionally matched messages have been shown to elicit greater scrutiny in the laboratory (DeBono & Harnish, 1988; Petty & Wegener, 1998), would this effect emerge in a competitive communication environment characterized by many similar messages? Or do functionally *mis*matched messages elicit greater attention and elaboration than matched messages under such conditions? Does choice of the target brand over competitors' brands then simply depend on the relative favorability of elaborated thinking elicited by the various messages? Does the perception of a message's functional match/mismatch change in response to the product's dominant framing in the competitive communication context (e.g., do products generally advertised as utilitarian tend to be perceived as utilitarian)? Or do other factors, such as individual differences, play a greater role in the functions that one's attitudes toward a product tend to serve? These are among the questions implied by a focus on the communication context in which messages are placed.

More generally, it is important to keep in mind that the success of any persuasive strategy based on the functional approach often comes down to a question of how the audience members choose to spend their time (attending to your message or another message), their money (buying your brand or another brand), or some other resource (e.g., casting their vote for your candidate or another candidate). Research on attitude functions has been conducted in contexts where attention to stimuli is virtually ensured and information about alternatives is typically omitted. This highlights the need for greater attention to the links between attitude functions, absolute judgments, and selections among available alternatives.

The Role of Cultural Differences

Although functional theory offers considerable value for understanding persuasion and behavior in Western cultures, its relevance cross-culturally has not yet been tested. A number of caveats relevant to its cross-cultural application are outlined next, with a view toward identifying productive directions for future research.

The emic approach, which examines culture-specific characteristics from within a single cultural system (Berry, 1969), would argue against the theory's universal application. First, from a strictly economic view, the categorization of products into social identity and utilitarian functions may assume a certain level of economic development not appropriate everywhere. For example, the social identity function refers to the goal of conveying a particular social image or identity, expressing one's values, or gaining social approval. The luxury of obtaining goods to communicate aspects of one's identity might not apply in less developed countries where people are primarily interested in satisfying their basic physiological needs (Samli, 1995). In impoverished nations, consumer needs may be related to food, shelter, or basic clothing and therefore may best be considered utilitarian.

On the other hand, some research suggests that attitudes toward Western brands of various products serve a social identity function in less developed nations (Batra, Ramaswamy, Alden, Steenkamp, & Ramachander, 2000). Future studies should therefore examine the strengths and limitations of basing functional assumptions on economic development status. More generally, additional research is needed on attitudes, persuasion, and consumer behavior in developing countries because these countries have been largely overlooked in cultural consumer research (Maheswaran & Shavitt, 2000).

An additional emic argument might question the validity of using an individual's attitudes and perceptions as explanatory constructs in every culture. In individualist societies such as the United States, personal goals take precedence over the goals of one's group, and attitudes and perceptions link rather closely to behavior. However, in collectivist societies such as those of the Far East, the group is of greater importance than the individual, and consequently personal goals are secondary to group goals (Triandis, 1995). This means that one's self-concept and social perceptions are also focused on the group and not on the individual (e.g., Markus & Kitayama, 1991; Trafimow, Triandis, & Goto, 1991).

Because the cognitive approach focuses on individuals' perceptual processes and on attempts by individuals to actively seek information, it has been suggested that cognitive approaches in general may be somewhat more relevant in individualist or industrialized societies (Ozanne, Brucks, & Grewal, 1992). It has also been suggested that attitudes themselves are more functional in individualist societies than in collectivist societies (see Bagozzi, Wong, & Yi, 1999). In collectivist cultures, people do not "need" attitudes to guide behavior. It is often norms rather than attitudes that drive behaviors in these societies (Bontempo & Rivero, 1992; Ybarra & Trafimow, 1998). Thus, whereas accessible attitudes have been shown to have functional benefits for easing decision making among U.S. participants (Fazio, Blascovich, & Driscoll, 1992), future research could examine whether accessible attitudes confer similar benefits in collectivist societies.

Indeed, in collectivist cultures, information incongruity (inconsistency in the valence of information presented about a target of judgment) and ambivalence (co-occurring negative and positive emotions or attitudes) appear to be readily tolerated and accepted without a need for resolution (Aaker & Sengupta, 2000; Bagozzi et al., 1999). Moreover, expectations about attitude-behavior consistency are lower in collectivist cultures than in individualist cultures (Kashima, Siegel, Tanaka, & Kashima, 1992). These findings are consistent with the notion that collectivist cultures place less importance on the opinions and preferences of the individual. Thus, personal attitudes may have less functional value in these societies than in individualist cultures.

On the other hand, the etic approach, which examines culturally general dimensions by comparing attitudes or behaviors across cultures (Berry, 1969), might offer a different view. Those espousing an etic approach might argue that the functional theory of attitudes is applicable across cultures but that the meaning and importance of the functional categories or of the products within them may vary cross-culturally. For example, as discussed earlier, the social identity function has been studied in the United States in terms of how one's product attitudes may convey individuating information to others about one's identity or image. However, in collectivist cultures, where the group is the relevant unit of identity, the product attitude may instead convey information about group identity or image. Do social identity appeals in collectivist cultures tend to use group identity rather than individual identity themes? If so, to what degree are such culturally relevant appeals effective? Future research could be profitably directed toward such questions.

Similarly, the utilitarian benefits that matter in collectivist societies may be those that accrue to the collectivity and not necessarily to the individual. Indeed, studies of the advertisements that are used or that are persuasive in collectivist societies show that ads stressing in-group and family benefits are typically preferred over those stressing benefits to the individual (Han & Shavitt, 1994; Zhang & Gelb, 1996).

In addition, the implications of products for achieving a given functional goal might vary by culture. For example, in horizontally based ("same self") individualist cultures such as Scandinavia and Australia, it is important not to be conspicuous among other people (Triandis, 1995). Therefore, the public display of wealth or status so useful for achieving social identity goals in the United States is frowned on. For example, in Denmark and Norway, there is an ingrained social modesty clause that reminds individuals not to think they are better than anyone else. In such societies, products may help to establish a desired social identity to the extent that they reflect such values. In a study of values and consumer behavior in Denmark (Nelson, 1997), one informant said that when rich people buy nice cars as a way to display their success, "people don't like it and you don't have friends" (p. 179). This is not the same admiration most Americans feel when they see a BMW.

Finally, how products are functionally categorized is likely dependent on historical, economic, and social values within a culture. Studies could be conducted to determine whether the nature of products preferred for their social identity benefits differs across cultures. For example, a refrigerator might be considered a utilitarian good in Western developed cultures but may be regarded as a sign of wealth or status (and thus a social identity product) in less developed cultures. Also, individuals in collectivist cultures may assign greater social identity significance to products that are effective in conveying a desired group or relational identity (e.g., team banners, wedding rings) as opposed to products that convey a desired personal identity (e.g., fountain pens). Future research on such questions could shed important light on the link between cultural values and attitudinal goals or functions.

CONCLUSIONS

The recent resurgence of interest in functional theories of attitude has opened new theoretical avenues and suggested new applications as well. In this chapter, we have illustrated some of the ways in which a functional approach offers considerable heuristic value. It should be recognized that functional theory offers implications not only for the study of persuasion but also for the understanding of other social processes, including person perception.

It is recommended that future research on the role of attitude functions in message processing reexamine functional predictions in light of the realities associated with competitive media environments. A systematic approach to the role of culture in the application of the theory would also be very useful. Research in these areas would substantially expand the value of functional theory for understanding the motivational underpinnings of social judgments.

REFERENCES

Aaker, J. L., & Sengupta, J. (2000). Averaging versus attention: The role of culture in the resolution of information incongruity. *Journal of Consumer Psychology, 9*(2), 67-82.

Adorno, T. W., Frenkel-Brunswik, E., Levinson, D. J., & Sanford, R. N. (1950). *The authoritarian personality.* New York: Harper & Row.

Bagozzi, R. P., Wong, N., & Yi, Y. (1999). The role of culture and gender in the relationship between positive and negative affect. *Cognition & Emotion, 13*, 641-672.

Batra, R., Ramaswamy, V., Alden, D. L., Steenkamp, J-B. E. M., & Ramachander, S. (2000). Effects of brand local/non-local origin on consumer attitudes in developing countries. *Journal of Consumer Psychology, 9*(2), 83-95.

Berry, J.W. (1969). On cross-cultural comparability. *International Journal of Psychology, 1*, 207-229.

Bontempo, R., & Rivero, J. C. (1992, August). *Cultural variation in cognition: The role of self-concept in the attitude behavior link.* Paper presented at the meeting of the American Academy of Management, Las Vegas, NV.

Cialdini, R. B., Borden, R. J., Thorne, A., Walker, M. R., Freeman, S., & Sloan, I. R. (1976). Basking in reflected glory: Three (football) field studies. *Journal of Personality and Social Psychology, 34*, 366-375.

DeBono, K. G. (1987). Investigating the social-adjustive and value-expressive functions of attitudes: Implications for persuasion processes. *Journal of Personality and Social Psychology, 52*, 279-287.

DeBono, K. G., & Harnish, R. (1988). Source expertise, source attractiveness, and the processing of persuasive information: A functional approach. *Journal of Personality and Social Psychology, 55*, 541-546.

Dunning, D. (1999). A newer look: Motivated social cognition and the schematic representation of social concepts. *Psychological Inquiry, 10*, 1-11.

Fazio, R. H., Blascovich, J., & Driscoll, D. M. (1992). On the functional value of attitudes: The influence of accessible attitudes on the ease and quality of decision making. *Personality and Social Psychology Bulletin, 18*, 388-401.

Han, S., & Shavitt, S. (1994). Persuasion and culture: Advertising appeals in individualistic and collectivistic societies. *Journal of Experimental Social Psychology, 30*, 326-350.

Herek, G. M. (1987). Can functions be measured? A new perspective on the functional approach to attitudes. *Social Psychology Quarterly, 50*, 285-303.

Insko, C. A. (1967). *Theories of attitude change.* New York: Appleton-Century-Crofts.

Kashima, Y., Siegel, M., Tanaka, K., & Kashima, E. S. (1992). Do people believe behaviors are consistent with attitudes? Toward a cultural psychology of attribution processes. *British Journal of Social Psychology, 331,* 111-124.

Katz, D. (1960). The functional approach to the study of attitudes. *Public Opinion Quarterly, 24,* 163-204.

Katz, D., Sarnoff, I., & McClintock, C. (1956). Ego-defense and attitude change. *Human Relations, 9,* 27-46.

Katz, D., & Stotland, E. (1959). A preliminary statement to a theory of attitude structure and change. In S. Koch (Ed.), *Psychology: A study of a science* (Vol. 3, pp. 423-475). New York: McGraw-Hill.

Kelman, H. C. (1958). Compliance, identification, and internalization: Three processes of attitude change. *Journal of Conflict Resolution, 2,* 51-60.

Kelman, H. C. (1961). Processes of opinion change. *Public Opinion Quarterly, 25,* 57-78.

Klein, W. M., & Kunda, Z. (1993). Maintaining self-serving social comparisons: Biased reconstruction of one's past behaviors. *Personality and Social Psychology Bulletin, 19,* 732-739.

Klein, W. M., & Kunda, Z. (1994). Exaggerated self-assessments and the preference for controllable risks. *Organizational Behavior and Human Decision Processes, 59,* 410-427.

Lavine, H., & Snyder, M. (1996). Cognitive processing and the functional matching effect in persuasion: The mediating role of subjective perceptions of message quality. *Journal of Experimental Social Psychology, 32,* 580-604.

Lutz, R. J. (1981). A reconceptualization of the functional approach to attitudes. *Research in Marketing, 5,* 165-210.

Maheswaran, D., & Shavitt, S. (2000). Issues and new directions in global consumer psychology. *Journal of Consumer Psychology, 9*(2), 59-66.

Maio, G. R., & Olson, J. M. (1995). Relations between values, attitudes, and behavioral intentions: The moderating role of attitude function. *Journal of Experimental Social Psychology, 31,* 266-285.

Maio, G. R., & Olson, J. M. (2000). *Why we evaluate: Functions of attitudes.* Mahwah, NJ: Lawrence Erlbaum.

Markus, H. R., & Kitayama, S. (1991). Culture and self: Implications for cognition, emotion, and motivation. *Psychological Review, 98,* 224-253.

McClintock, C. (1958). Personality syndromes and attitude change. *Journal of Personality, 26,* 479-493.

Nelson, M. R. (1997). *Examining the horizontal and vertical dimensions of individualism within the United States and Denmark: How culture affects values, moral orientations, and advertising persuasion.* Unpublished dissertation, University of Illinois at Urbana-Champaign.

Nelson, M. R., Shavitt, S., Schennum, A., & Barkmeier, J. (1997). Prediction of long-term advertising effectiveness: New cognitive response approaches. In W. Wells (Ed.), *Measuring advertising effectiveness* (pp. 133-155). Mahwah, NJ: Lawrence Erlbaum.

Ozanne, J. L., Brucks, M., & Grewal, D. (1992). A study of information search behavior during the categorization of new products. *Journal of Consumer Research, 18,* 452-463.

Petty, R. E., & Wegener, D. T. (1998). Matching versus mismatching attitude functions: Implications for scrutiny of persuasive messages. *Personality and Social Psychology Bulletin, 24,* 227-240.

Pratkanis, A. R., Breckler, S. J., & Greenwald, A. G. (1989). *Attitude structure and function.* Hillsdale, NJ: Lawrence Erlbaum.

Prentice, D. A. (1987). Psychological correspondence of possessions, attitudes, and values. *Journal of Personality and Social Psychology, 53,* 993-1003.

Samli, A. C. (1995). *International consumer behavior.* Westport, CT: Quorum Books.

Schumann, D. W., & Thorson, E. (1990). The influence of viewing context on commercial effectiveness: A selection processing model. In J. H. Leigh & C. R. Martin, Jr. (Eds.), *Current issues and research in advertising* (Vol. 12, pp. 1-24). Ann Arbor: University of Michigan.

Severn, J., Belch, G. E., & Belch, M. A. (1990). The effects of sexual and non-sexual advertising appeals and information level on cognitive processing and communication effectiveness. *Journal of Advertising, 19,* 14-22.

Shavitt, S. (1989). Operationalizing functional theories of attitude. In A. R. Pratkanis, S. J. Breckler, & A. G. Greenwald (Eds.), *Attitude structure and function* (pp. 311-337). Hillsdale, NJ: Lawrence Erlbaum.

Shavitt, S. (1990). The role of attitude objects in attitude functions. *Journal of Experimental Social Psychology, 26,* 124-148.

Shavitt, S., & Fazio, R. H. (1991). Effects of attribute salience of the consistency between attitudes and behavior predictions. *Personality and Social Psychology Bulletin, 17,* 507-516.

Shavitt, S., Lowrey, T. M., & Han, S. (1992). Attitude functions in advertising: The interactive role of products and self-monitoring. *Journal of Consumer Psychology, 1,* 337-364.

Shavitt, S., & Nelson, M. R. (2000). The social identity function in person perception: Communicated meanings of product preferences. In G. R. Maio & J. M. Olson (Eds.), *Why we evaluate: Function of attitudes* (pp. 37-58). Mahwah, NJ: Lawrence Erlbaum.

Shavitt, S., Swan, S., Lowrey, T. M., & Wänke, M. (1994). The interaction of endorser attractiveness and involvement in persuasion depends on the goal that guides message processing. *Journal of Consumer Psychology, 3*(2), 137-162.

Smith, M. B., Bruner, J. S., & White, R. W. (1956). *Opinions and personality.* New York: John Wiley.

Snyder, M. (1974). Self-monitoring of expressive behavior. *Journal of Personality and Social Psychology, 30,* 526-537.

Snyder, M., & DeBono, K. G. (1985). Appeals to image and claims about quality: Understanding the psychology of advertising. *Journal of Personality and Social Psychology, 49,* 586-597.

Snyder, M., & DeBono, K. G. (1987). A functional approach to attitudes and persuasion. In M. P.

Zanna, J. M. Olson, & C. P. Herman (Eds.), *Social influence: The Ontario Symposium* (Vol. 5, pp. 107-125). Hillsdale, NJ: Lawrence Erlbaum.

Spivey, A. W., Munson, M. J., & Locander, W. B. (1983). Improving the effectiveness of persuasive communications: Matching message with functional profile. *Journal of Business Research, 11,* 257-269.

Tesser, A., & Campbell, J. (1983). Self-definition and self-evaluation maintenance. In J. Suls & A. G. Greenwald (Eds.), *Psychological perspectives on the self* (Vol. 2, pp. 1-31). Hillsdale, NJ: Lawrence Erlbaum.

Trafimow, D., Triandis, H. C., & Goto, S. (1991). Some tests of the distinction between private self and collective self. *Journal of Personality and Social Psychology, 60,* 649-655.

Triandis, H. C. (1995). *Individualism and collectivism.* Boulder, CO: Westview.

Tyler, T. R., & Weber, R. (1982). Support for the death penalty: Instrumental response to crime, or symbolic attitude? *Law & Society Review, 17,* 21-45.

Wells, W. D. (1993). Discovery-oriented consumer research. *Journal of Consumer Research, 19,* 489-504.

Ybarra, O., & Trafimow, D. (1998). How priming the private self or collective self affects the relative weights of attitudes and subjective norms. *Personality and Social Psychology Bulletin, 24,* 362-370.

Zhang, Y., & Gelb, B. D. (1996). Matching advertising appeals to culture: The influence of products' use conditions. *Journal of Advertising, 25,* 29-46.

9

The Elaboration Likelihood Model

Its Impact on Persuasion Theory and Research

STEVE BOOTH-BUTTERFIELD
JENNIFER WELBOURNE

Over the past two decades, the Elaboration Likelihood Model (ELM) has been instrumental in integrating the literature on source, message, receiver, and context effects in persuasion and has also been a springboard for new research in this domain. Prior to the development of the ELM (and the conceptually similar Heuristic-Systematic Model [Chaiken, 1978, 1987]), this domain of research was in a state of disarray characterized by an abundance of seemingly inconsistent and contradictory findings. For example, some studies had demonstrated that credible sources increased the persuasive impact of a message (Hovland & Weiss, 1951; Kelman & Hovland, 1953); however, other studies showed the reverse effect or no effect of source credibility on persuasion (Norman, 1976; Rhine & Severance, 1970; Sternthal, Dholakia, & Leavitt, 1978). The same type of conflicting evidence also appeared in other research investigating message, receiver, and context effects on persuasion (see Eagly & Himmelfarb, 1978;

Himmelfarb & Eagly, 1974; Sherif, 1977). The ELM, with its capacity to theoretically predict how, and under what circumstances, these different types of variables will affect the impact of a persuasive message, provided a much-needed coherence for the empirical work in this domain.

In this chapter, we demonstrate how the ELM has significantly advanced knowledge in the field of persuasion through its ability to integrate and stimulate research over these past decades. Although the ELM has garnered considerable praise for its achievements, it has also sparked some controversy and criticism among both communication researchers (Allen & Reynolds, 1993; Hamilton, Hunter, & Boster, 1993; Mongeau & Stiff, 1993; Stiff, 1986) and social psychologists (Johnson & Eagly, 1989). Therefore, we also provide a review of these criticisms and discuss how they have been refuted and/or resolved. Finally, in light of the considerable amount of research that has already stemmed from the

ELM during the past two decades, we believe that the framework of the ELM holds great promise for generating future lines of research for decades to come. We discuss several directions for ELM research that we envision for the coming years.

To address these issues, this chapter is composed of four sections. First, we briefly characterize the ELM. Second, we explore research lines on the basic principles of the model. Third, we discuss the communication and social psychology criticisms of the ELM. Fourth, we present new directions and extensions for future research. We then conclude with a consideration of the scientific utility of the ELM.

THE ELM: AN OVERVIEW

The integrative power of the ELM comes from its divergence from the previous "variable-oriented" approaches to persuasion to embrace a more "process-oriented" approach. Rather than focusing on source, message, or receiver variables in and of themselves, the ELM focuses on the *processes* by which these aspects of a message influence people to change their attitudes. Specifically, the ELM posits that attitude change may occur through one of two different processing routes: the central route or the peripheral route (Petty & Cacioppo, 1986a, 1986b; Petty & Wegener, 1999). Central route processing produces attitude change based on careful evaluation of the arguments contained within a message, whereas persuasion via the peripheral route is associated with less thoughtful processing, such as a reliance on cues or heuristics that are unrelated to the actual merits of the message (e.g., the message is associated with an attractive source).

A person's motivation and ability to elaborate on a message should determine whether he or she will engage in central or peripheral processing. The ELM assumes that people are bombarded with so many different persuasive communications that it is nonadaptive, if not impossible, to carefully evaluate the merits of each and every one of these attempts at persuasion. Therefore, people are likely to exert considerable elaborative effort in some situations, and much less effort in others, depending on their levels of motivation and ability. If motivation and ability to elaborate is high, central processing of the message will occur; a person will carefully scrutinize the merits of the message. If motivation and/or ability to elaborate on the merits of the message is low, a person will be less likely to engage in thoughtful evaluation of the message; instead, his or her attitude toward the message will be based on less thoughtful, peripheral route processes. Although a person might reach the same attitude through either the peripheral or the central route to persuasion, the ELM posits that the path (or process) that is taken has important implications for the resulting attitude (Petty & Cacioppo, 1986a, 1986b; Petty & Wegener, 1999).

CENTRAL ROUTE PROCESSES

The central route to persuasion involves effortful processing of attitude-relevant information to determine the merits of a persuasive communication. Thus, a person who processes a persuasive message via the central route is likely to evaluate and think critically about the arguments contained in the message. It is important to clarify the nature of this elaborative processing. Elaboration goes beyond simply paying attention to or comprehending the arguments contained in the message; elaboration involves generating one's own thoughts in response to the information to which one is exposed. In particular, central route processing focuses on elaboration that is issue relevant, in other words, additional message-relevant or issue-relevant thoughts generated by a person that go beyond what was provided in the message itself (Petty & Wegener, 1999). Therefore, a person processing a persuasive communication through the central route would generate many of his or her own thoughts in response to the arguments contained in the communication.

Attitude change resulting from central route processing should be based on careful evaluation of the merits of the arguments and should reflect the content of the thoughts that were generated by the person during exposure to the communication (Chaiken, 1980; Harkins & Petty, 1981; Petty & Cacioppo, 1979). If arguments are perceived as strong, a person should generate many positive thoughts regarding the message/issue, and greater persuasion should occur. If, on careful scrutiny, the arguments are perceived as weak, issue- and message-relevant thoughts should be less positive (or even negative), and consequently less persuasion (or attitude change in the opposite direction) should occur. This has been demonstrated in numerous studies that examined the impact of argument quality on persuasion when people are induced to engage in central route processing (Cacioppo & Petty, 1989; Harkins & Petty, 1981; Petty, Cacioppo, & Goldman, 1981; Petty, Cacioppo, & Heesacker, 1981; Smith & Shaffer, 1991; Wood, Kallgren, & Preisler, 1985).

Although central processing is characterized by careful scrutiny of the message, this does not imply that attitude change through the central route is always based on objective reasoning. The authors of the ELM suggest that the central route can be characterized by either objective or biased elaborative processing (Petty & Cacioppo, 1986b; Petty & Wegener, 1998). Biased processing should be most likely to occur when a person has a vested interest or an unbalanced amount of information about the message topic (Petty & Wegener, 1999). For instance, if a person is motivated to form an unfavorable attitude toward a communication (due to vested interest), elaborative thought might take the form of effortful counterarguing against the arguments contained in the communication rather than an objective evaluation of the merits of the communication. A similar bias in elaboration can occur if a person simply has more information for one side of an issue than for the opposing stance. Research has produced empirical evidence for this proposition that biased processing can occur at high levels of elaboration. For instance, Chen, Reardon, Rea, and Moore (1992) found that forewarning participants that researchers were going to try to change their attitudes produced biased elaborative processing of the message under high-elaboration conditions. In addition, work by Petty and colleagues (Petty, Shumann, Richman, & Strathman, 1993) has demonstrated the biasing effects of mood on processing at high levels of elaboration.

Regardless of whether elaborative processing is objective or biased, attitudes formed through the central route should be distinguished from those formed through the peripheral route by their strength. The ELM proposes that central route persuasion results in attitudes that are more resistant to counterpersuasion, persistent over time, and predictive of future behavior than are those formed through peripheral processes (Petty & Cacioppo, 1986b; Petty, Haugtvedt, & Smith, 1995). Evidence for this postulate of the ELM was provided by Haugtvedt and Petty (1992), who demonstrated that following initial attitude change, persons who formed their attitudes through the central route were more resistant against a new counterattitudinal message than were those who formed their attitudes peripherally. It is suggested that these effects are due to mediating factors such as increased accessibility of attitudes, heightened confidence in attitudes, and increased memory for issue-relevant information that may result from elaborative processing (Chaiken, Pomerantz, & Giner-Sorolla, 1995; Petty et al., 1995).

PERIPHERAL PROCESSES

Attitude change through the peripheral route results from less thoughtful processing of the communication (Petty & Cacioppo, 1986a, 1986b). Processing through the peripheral route can be distinguished from central route processing of persuasive messages in two ways. First, the peripheral route differs quantitatively from the central route such that elaborative, thoughtful consideration of message arguments occurs to a lesser extent in the peripheral route than in the central route (Petty & Wegener, 1999). For example, if a persuasive message contains six arguments in favor of participating in an exercise program, a person processing this message through the peripheral route might thoughtfully consider one or two of these arguments, whereas a person processing through the central route might elaborate on all six of the arguments; a person processing the message peripherally might spend only a brief amount of time elaborating on each of the arguments, whereas a person processing the message centrally might spend a great deal of time thinking about each argument. Because the person processing the message through the peripheral route is engaging in less elaborative thought, the resulting attitude change is less likely to be based on the merit of the arguments than for the person engaging in central route processing.

Peripheral processing can differ from central route processing of a persuasive message not only quantitatively but also qualitatively. In other words, not only do the peripheral and central routes differ in the amount of processing that takes place, but they may also be characterized by qualitatively different types of processing (Petty & Wegener, 1999). For instance, whereas attitudes changed through the central route are based on thoughtful evaluation of the arguments, attitudes changed through the peripheral route are often not based on any evaluation of the arguments but instead are based on heuristics or "rules of thumb." For instance, rather than evaluating *any* of the arguments in the pro-exercise message, a person who is processing the message peripherally may simply use the rule of thumb that "more is better" and be persuaded because of the sheer number of arguments that are provided in the message (regardless of the actual quality of the arguments). Similarly, attitudes formed through the peripheral route may be based on a cue that is irrelevant to the content or merit of the communication. For instance, if a message is processed through the peripheral route, a person may be persuaded to adopt the message simply because it was presented by an attractive source, a factor completely unrelated to the merits of the message itself.

In addition to the use of heuristics or cues during peripheral processing, the authors of the ELM identified other processes that could potentially occur as part of the peripheral route to persuasion. For instance, classical conditioning, or learning to associate affect with previously neutral objects (Cacioppo, Marshall-Goodell, Tassinary, & Petty, 1992; Cacioppo, Priester, & Berntson, 1993; Staats & Staats, 1958) is a relatively effortless process that may occur during peripheral processing of a message. Similarly, self-perception, or inferring one's attitudes from one's behavior (Bem, 1965), and mere exposure (Zajonc & Markus, 1982), or forming more positive attitudes due to repeated exposure to the attitude object, both are processes that require little elaborative effort and are therefore likely to occur via the peripheral route to persuasion. In all of these cases, attitudes in response to a persuasive communication are based on something other than a careful evaluation of the merits of the message.

Attitudes that are formed through this less thoughtful route should not be as strong as attitudes formed through the central route (Petty & Cacioppo, 1984; Petty & Wegener, 1998). Specifically, peripheral route attitudes should not be as resistant to counterattempts at persuasion, should be less predictive of behavior, and should persist for shorter periods of time. However, some research suggests that if peripheral processes influence the variables (e.g., accessibility) that mediate the attitude strength effects found for the central route, persistent attitudes may also be formed through these less thoughtful processes (Zanna, Fazio, & Ross, 1994).

THE ELABORATION LIKELIHOOD CONTINUUM

To summarize the previous sections, the ELM proposes a dual-process model of persuasion. Persuasion through the central route is associated with thoughtful evaluation of the merits of a message, whereas peripheral route persuasion is associated with less thoughtful processing and a reliance on issue-irrelevant cues or heuristics. Due to cognitive constraints that prevent people from thoughtfully processing *all* of the messages to which they are exposed, in some instances persuasion will occur through the central route, and in other instances it will occur through the peripheral route. Importantly, the ELM provides a coherent framework for understanding when people will engage in each type of processing. This framework is structured around the concept of an "elaboration likelihood continuum." Specifically, the ELM posits that elaboration likelihood is the determinant of whether attitude change in a given instance occurs through the central or peripheral route. When elaboration likelihood is high,

people will be more likely to engage in central route processing, whereas when elaboration likelihood is low, peripheral processing is more likely (Petty & Cacioppo, 1986a, 1986b; Petty & Wegener, 1998, 1999).

Motivational and Ability Factors

Elaboration likelihood can be influenced by both motivation and ability. For instance, if an individual is highly involved in an issue, motivation to elaborate on the merits of the message should be quite high, leading to central route processing. On the other hand, if an individual is not particularly involved in an issue (for instance, if the person is reading about an issue that is not personally or immediately relevant to him or her), the individual should be less motivated to elaborate on the message and consequently more likely to rely on peripheral cues or heuristics.

Ability can also influence elaboration likelihood. For instance, even if individuals are highly involved in the attitude issue and therefore very motivated to elaborate, if they are distracted by loud noises while they are reading the message, they will not have the ability to elaborate or scrutinize the merits of the message. Similarly, factors such as the level of knowledge needed to evaluate a particular message may constrain the degree to which participants are able to elaborate.

Considerable research has accumulated to demonstrate that motivational factors (e.g., personal relevance: Petty, Cacioppo, & Goldman, 1981; accountability: Harkins & Petty, 1981; Tetlock, 1983; anticipated interaction regarding the issue: Chaiken, 1980), as well as ability factors (e.g., distraction: Petty, Wells, & Brock, 1976; message repetition: Cacioppo & Petty, 1989; time pressures: Kruglanski & Freund, 1983; message complexity: Hafer, Reynolds, & Obertynski, 1996), determine (through their influence on elaboration likelihood) whether persuasion will be based on message scrutiny or peripheral cues.

Situational and Personal Factors

According to the ELM (Petty & Cacioppo, 1986a; Petty & Wegener, 1999), factors that influence elaboration likelihood may be either situationally induced or internal to the person processing the communication. For instance, the previously discussed motivation and ability variables were situationally manipulated (e.g., involvement, distraction, message repetition); however, it has been empirically demonstrated that individual differences that occur between people may also lead to varying levels of elaboration likelihood. For instance, research suggests that one individual difference that influences motivation to elaborate is the need for cognition. People who score high on the "need for cognition" scale (which assesses the degree to which people enjoy thinking and exerting cognitive effort) are more likely to engage in higher levels of elaboration when processing a persuasive communication (Cacioppo & Petty, 1982; Cacioppo, Petty, & Morris, 1983). Similarly, individual differences can also influence one's ability to elaborate on a message. For instance, it has been demonstrated that high levels of knowledge about a topic encourage greater elaboration on a persuasive message pertaining to that topic (Wood, Rhodes, & Biek, 1995). Conversely, if a person has very little knowledge about a topic, thoughtful scrutiny of the arguments in a message might not be possible, leading to a reliance on peripheral cues (Wood & Kallgren, 1988).

The Peripheral/Central Trade-Off

The ELM postulates that at high levels of elaboration likelihood, central route processes (e.g., careful argument scrutiny) will have a heightened impact on resulting attitudes compared to peripheral processes (e.g., use of heuristics, peripheral cues). However, at low levels of elaboration likelihood, peripheral processes (e.g., use of heuristics, peripheral cues) will have a heightened impact of attitudes, whereas central route processes should have less impact. In other words, as one moves up the elaboration likelihood continuum, there is a trade-off between central and peripheral processes in their impact on attitudes.

MULTIPLE ROLES FOR PERSUASION VARIABLES

One of the most common misperceptions of the ELM is that it limits variables to playing certain specified roles in the persuasion process. For instance, some researchers have interpreted the ELM as claiming that source variables are always peripheral cues, and message variables are invariably linked to central processing, or that separate lists of central and peripheral variables should be compiled (see Allen & Reynolds, 1993; McGarty, Haslam, Hutchinson, & Turner, 1994; Stiff, 1986). However, these perceptions are misplaced. The ELM proposes that a single persuasion variable (e.g., source attractiveness) can take on multiple roles. A given variable may serve as a peripheral cue, an argument, or an elaboration moderator, or it can produce bias in elaboration, depending on the specific circumstance in which the variable is encountered (Petty & Cacioppo, 1984; Petty, Kasmer, Haugtvedt, & Cacioppo, 1987; Petty & Wegener, 1999). For instance, source attractiveness has influenced attitudes as a peripheral cue in some studies (Chaiken, 1987; Cialdini, 1987). This variable has also been shown to moderate elaboration likelihood (Puckett, Petty, Cacioppo, & Fisher, 1983). In addition, Shavitt and colleagues found that when source attractiveness was related to the central merits of a product being promoted, this variable was capable of influencing attitudes through the central, as well as the peripheral, route (Shavitt, Swan, Lowery, & Wänke, 1994). Finally, using the multiple roles concept, Booth-Butterfield and Gutowski (1994) found that source credibility interacted with message modality (print, audio, and video channels) as either a cue or an elaboration moderator.

The role that a variable takes in a given context is contingent on the level of elaboration likelihood that occurs in that context. Under low-elaboration likelihood, source attractiveness should serve as a peripheral cue. For instance, an association between the attractive source and the attitude object itself can occur with fairly effortless processing, resulting in a positive attitude. Under high-elaboration likelihood, the attractive source might actually serve as a persuasive argument for the merit of the message. For instance, if a person reads a message advocating a beauty product, the attractiveness of the source (obviously a product user) is relevant to the merit of the advertised product. If elaboration likelihood is moderate, seeing an attractive source might stimulate interest in the message; thus, the source is serving as an elaboration moderator here. Finally, seeing an attractive source for a product might put one in a good mood, biasing elaboration such that more favorable thoughts are generated to maintain one's good mood.

In short, rather than trying to pin down the effects of each individual variable or to categorize variables as exclusively peripheral or central, the ELM provides a framework for understanding the different processes by which these variables will influence attitudes. Specifically, when elaboration likelihood is low, variables can influence attitudes by acting as cues; when elaboration likelihood is moder- ate, variables can influence attitudes by increasing or decreasing the level of elaboration likelihood; and finally, when elaboration likelihood is high, variables can influence attitudes by serving as arguments or biasing the nature of the elaboration.

CRITICS OF THE ELM

Although the ELM has made strides in advancing knowledge in the domain of persuasion, there have also been criticisms of the ELM, particularly within the fields of communication and social psychology. In this section, we gather these criticisms and provide a rebuttal of the main points of these critiques. We also discuss the impact of these criticisms on the theory and research.

The Role of Involvement in the ELM

Psychology Critics. Controversy arose briefly regarding the effects of involvement on elaboration likelihood and consequent attitude change (Johnson & Eagly, 1989; Petty & Cacioppo, 1990). A distinction between two types of involvement was proposed by Johnson and Eagly (1989): outcome-relevant involvement (when a message is linked to a person's current goals and outcomes) and value-relevant involvement (when a message is linked to a person's important values). It was suggested that the involvement manipulations used in a typical ELM study focus on outcome involvement rather than on value involvement. Based on a meta-analysis that they conducted, Johnson and Eagly concluded that outcome involvement and value involvement affect the persuasion process in different ways and, furthermore, that the pattern of outcome involvement effects (which are consistent with predictions obtained from the

ELM) was obtained only by researchers associated with the Ohio State University.

In response, Petty and Cacioppo (1990) suggested that a distinction between the two types of involvement was unnecessary. Specifically, they proposed that although a focus on outcomes versus goals may differ in the way involvement is conceptualized between researchers, "personal importance" is the critical dimension that underlies both types of involvement. In addition, they proposed that the different effects for value involvement and outcome involvement that appeared in the meta-analysis could be accounted for by confounding factors (e.g., level of knowledge, confidence in attitudes) that may have accompanied the value involvement manipulations. Furthermore, they used data from Johnson and Eagly's (1989) meta-analysis to demonstrate that for *both* types of involvement, argument quality has a greater influence on attitudes at higher levels of involvement (contrary to Johnson and Eagly's proposal that this effect occurs only for outcome-relevant involvement). Finally, Petty and Cacioppo were able to counter Johnson and Eagly's claim that effects of involvement on elaboration likelihood and attitude change were confined to researchers who received training at Ohio State by producing evidence of outcome relevance effects on persuasion from researchers at other universities, including data from Johnson and Eagly themselves.

Communication Critics. A separate critique of the ELM with regard to the role of involvement in persuasion processes was provided by Stiff (1986), also using a meta-analysis procedure. Specifically, Stiff conducted a meta-analysis to examine the effects of argument quality and source credibility on attitude change at different levels of involvement. Variables from 19 studies were classified as "central" or "peripheral" variables and were included in the meta-analysis. From the results

of the meta-analysis, Stiff claimed that involvement has a positive linear relationship with argument quality and a curvilinear relationship with source credibility. Stiff suggested that this combination of findings provides better support for the Elastic Capacity Model (Kahneman, 1973) than for the ELM. Although the Elastic Capacity Model is a model of general information processing, the author suggested that this model can also be applied to the domain of persuasive cue processing. In light of these claims, Stiff proposed that the Elastic Capacity Model of information processing be adopted as a more comprehensive alternative to the ELM in the domain of persuasive cue processing.

Petty and colleagues (1987) proposed that Stiff's (1986) claims were based on misperceptions of the ELM and methodologically flawed meta-analysis procedures. First, Stiff's claim that the Elastic Capacity Model is a more comprehensive model of persuasive processes than the ELM was based solely on an examination of predictions related to involvement. It is important to note that the ELM predicts that several other variables—not only involvement—will influence elaboration likelihood and consequent attitude change. Stiff's analysis focused on involvement and did not address how the Elastic Capacity Model would account for other variables, such as ability, knowledge, need for cognition, accountability, and distraction, that have also been demonstrated to influence persuasive processes within the ELM framework.

In addition, there are several methodological aspects that call the results of Stiff's (1986) meta-analysis into question. First, variables from the studies that were included in the meta-analysis were classified as either "central" or "peripheral" variables. However, as discussed previously, an important feature of the ELM is that a single variable is able to take on multiple roles (argument, cue, or elaboration moderator), depending on the condition.

Whether a variable takes on a central or peripheral function depends on whether elaboration likelihood is high or low. The fact that a single variable can take on multiple roles has serious implications for the results of the current meta-analysis. Specifically, in the studies included in the meta-analysis, variables were classified as either central or peripheral, even though several of these variables could have taken on multiple functions, depending on the level of elaboration in a given study. To give an example, the number of arguments contained in the message was always classified as a message characteristic for the purposes of the meta-analysis, even though it has been demonstrated that this variable can serve as a peripheral cue under low-elaboration conditions. Based on this reasoning, Petty and colleagues (1987) argued that the results of the current meta-analysis are invalid because they are based on a miscategorization of variables.

Petty and colleagues (1987) called several other aspects of the meta-analysis into question. Specifically, Stiff's (1986) meta-analysis was characterized by a small sample size (19 studies were included in the meta-analysis, with some comparisons containing only two or three data points). In addition, tests of statistical significance were not reported for the linear argument quality and curvilinear source credibility effects (when Petty and colleagues computed a statistical test for the curvilinear contrast, the contrast was not statistically significant).

Does the ELM preclude multi-channel processing? The ELM proposes a trade-off in the degree to which peripheral and central aspects of the message influence attitudes at different levels of elaboration likelihood. This notion of a "central-peripheral trade-off" has sometimes led researchers to interpret the ELM as implying that individuals attend only to peripheral cues of the message if elaboration likelihood is low and only to central aspects if

elaboration likelihood is high. On these grounds, the ELM has been criticized as precluding multi-channel information processing (Stiff, 1986). However, a closer examination of the ELM's postulates reveals that the ELM does not rule out the possibility of multi-channel processing. First, to clarify a common misperception, the trade-off postulated by the ELM does not refer to whether central and peripheral aspects of the message are processed; rather, it refers to the impact that these features of the communication will have on resulting attitudes. In other words, at high levels of elaboration, a person may still notice and have a positive reaction toward the beautiful person advertising a household appliance on television; however, this peripheral cue should have less impact on the person's attitude toward the appliance than it would at lower levels of elaboration. Furthermore, the conceptualization of elaboration likelihood as a *continuum* precludes a static demarcation between peripheral and central routes. In fact, it is suggested that at most points of the continuum, central and peripheral processes both will have an influence on attitudes (Petty et al., 1987). Importantly, the trade-off between central and peripheral processes posited in the ELM simply proposes that as the impact of central processes on attitudes increases (along with elaboration likelihood), the impact of peripheral processes on attitudes will decrease.

Can the ELM account for the empirical evidence on boomerang effects? Hamilton and colleagues (1993) criticized the ELM on the grounds that it makes incorrect predictions with regard to boomerang effects in persuasion. First, these researchers interpreted the ELM as suggesting that boomerang effects (negative attitude change in response to a persuasive message) occur in all cases in which more negative than positive thoughts are generated in response to a persuasive message. They suggested that there are cases where negative thoughts dominate yet boom-erang effects do not occur. In response, Petty and colleagues (Petty, Wegener, Fabrigar, Priester, & Cacioppo, 1993) explained that the ELM does not make such an extreme claim regarding boomerang effects; rather, it is pro-posed that when thoughts toward a message are primarily negative, less positive attitude change will occur relative to when thoughts are primarily positive, and in *some* cases a boomerang effect may even occur. Hamilton and colleagues further suggested that there is a lack of empirical evidence for boomerang ef-fects in the persuasion literature. However, contrary to this claim, empirical evidence for boomerang effects has been found by sev-eral researchers (Abelson & Miller, 1967; Berscheid, 1966; Gruenfeld & Wyer, 1992), demonstrating that this phenomenon does, in fact, exist.

Does the ELM lack theoretical specificity? The ELM has been critiqued as having a lack of theoretical specificity regarding the causal relationships between variables (Mongeau & Stiff, 1993). In addition, Mongeau and Stiff (1993) faulted the ELM for relying primarily on analysis of variance (ANOVA) rather than using other statistical tests (specifically, causal structure modeling) to test causal relation-ships between variables. It is surprising that these authors would claim that the ELM lacks theoretical specificity when, in fact, the ELM outlines the specific conditions under which variables take on peripheral, central, or elabo-ration moderator functions and also makes specific predictions for interactions among argument quality, peripheral cues, and moder-ating variables such as involvement. For in-stance, the ELM makes the specific prediction that involvement will interact with argument quality and peripheral cues in the following manner: When involvement is high, attitudes will be influenced primarily by argument qual-ity and less by peripheral cues; when involve-

ment is low, attitudes will be influenced pri-marily by peripheral cues and less by argument quality. Mongeau and Stiff also argued that mediation processes are not clearly spelled out within the ELM. In a response to this criti-cism, Petty, Wegener, Fabrigar, Priester, and Cacioppo (1993) pointed out that a universal mediation process is not specified in the ELM because it is proposed that mediation pro-cesses will vary depending on the particular moderating variable that is being examined; therefore, specific mediating variables are spelled out for each particular moderating variable (e.g., involvement, expertise) rather than for the model as a whole. In response to the claim that tests of the ELM have relied too much on ANOVA statistical tests, Fabrigar and colleagues, while acknowledging that ANOVA has been the primary means of testing the ELM, pointed out instances in which other statistical tests (e.g., ANCOVA, correlation, path analysis) have been used to successfully test ELM postulates (Cacioppo & Petty, 1979; Mackie & Worth, 1989; Petty & Cacioppo, 1977; Petty, Gleicher, & Baker, 1991).

Can the central and peripheral routes be methodologically and theoretically distin-guished? It has been suggested that it is not possible for the central and peripheral routes of the ELM to be methodologically and theo-retically distinguished (Allen & Reynolds, 1993). Specifically, Allen and Reynolds (1993) claimed that empirical evidence of dif-ferences in persistence between peripheral and centrally formed attitudes has not been demonstrated, and they suggested that this finding must be established to methodo-logically distinguish between these two routes to persuasion. Petty and colleagues (Petty, Wegener, Fabrigar, Priester, & Cacioppo, 1993) suggested that this criticism is un-founded. First, this type of empirical evidence has already been demonstrated in ELM re-search. Evidence for this postulate of the ELM was provided by Chaiken (1980), Haugtvedt and Petty (1992), and Petty and Cacioppo (1986b). Second, although measures of temporal stability are surely one way to methodologically distinguish between the two paths to persuasion, it is not the only method for doing so. Specifically, process measures, such as thought listings and self-reported elaboration, can be (and have been) used to methodologically disentangle these two routes (Cacioppo & Petty, 1979; Cacioppo et al., 1983; Petty, Harkins, & Williams, 1980).

On a related note, Allen and Reynolds (1993) proposed that the temporal predictions for attitudes made by the ELM are not compatible with the empirical literature on "sleeper effects." A sleeper effect occurs when a persuasive message has a delayed effect on attitudes due to the dissociation between the message and a low-credibility source over time. The ELM makes the prediction that sleeper effects should be more likely to occur when the low-credibility source is provided after (rather than before) the persuasive message. Allen and Reynolds claimed that such a pattern of findings is not demonstrated in the empirical evidence. To refute this claim, Petty and colleagues (Petty, Wegener, Fabrigar, Priester, & Cacioppo, 1993) redid a meta-analysis conducted by Allen and Stiff (1989), including the variable of whether the low-credibility source came before or after the message (a variable that was not included in the original analysis). Interestingly, the results of a contrast test conducted by Petty and colleagues on this data indicated a significant effect for the placement of the source such that the amount of attitude change over time differed depending on whether the source came before or after the message. In addition to this data, other reviews of the sleeper effect literature have concluded that sleeper effects are most likely to occur when the source follows the message (Pratkanis, Greenwald, Leippe, & Baumgardner, 1988), a conclusion

that is consistent with the predictions of the ELM.

Criticisms of the Peripheral Route

A number of criticisms have been made with regard to the peripheral route to persuasion postulated in the ELM. First, it has been suggested that the processes and theories described within the peripheral route are contradictory (Hamilton et al., 1993). Specifically, these researchers suggest that peripheral processes such as reinforcement, balance, and social judgment cannot all occur simultaneously and that the ELM is faulty in its claim that all of the processes can occur at once. However, as pointed out by Petty and colleagues (Petty, Wegener, Fabrigar, Priester, & Cacioppo, 1993), the ELM does *not* make the claim that all of these processes take place simultaneously but instead suggests that any given one of these processes is more likely to occur under low-elaboration conditions than under high-elaboration conditions. The ELM does not propose that reinforcement, balance, and social judgment (as well as others) are processes that are universally correct or are engaged in simultaneously; it simply argues that these are types of processes that are more likely to occur under low-elaboration conditions than under high-elaboration conditions. Therefore, it appears that this criticism of the ELM was based on a simple misunderstanding of the processes by which peripheral attitude change occurs and that the postulates of the ELM are actually in accordance with this issue that Hamilton and colleagues (1993) belabored in their critique.

A second criticism of the peripheral persuasion processes postulated in the ELM is that these processes characterize attitude formation but not attitude change (Hamilton et al., 1993). However, a number of empirical studies indicate that peripheral processes can influence attitudes on issues for which prior knowledge and attitudes are held. For instance, it has been demonstrated that peripheral processes influenced attitudes toward gun control (Mackie & Worth, 1989), environmental preservation (Chaiken & Baldwin, 1981; Wood & Kallgren, 1988) and various other social issues (Wood et al., 1985). This empirical work indicates that peripheral processes not only operate in the attitude formation process but also are influential during attitude change.

Does the ELM make significant advancements in the field of persuasion? Finally, a few critics have faulted the ELM for failing to make a significant advancement beyond traditional attitude and information processing theories. Specifically, Hamilton and colleagues (1993) suggested that the ELM is simply a restatement of traditional information processing theory. Although the ELM originally stemmed from these theories, we believe that it has taken attitudes research in new directions not previously conceptualized by these earlier theories. Here we state three major ways in which the ELM has advanced prior attitude theories and research. First, the ELM suggests that there are multiple ways in which perceivers may process and evaluate a message: by expending much cognitive effort (central route) or by expending less effort or relying on cues (peripheral route). In addition, the ELM goes beyond earlier attitude theories to predict the exact conditions under which specific processes of attitude change will occur. The ELM not only specifies the specific determinants of elaboration likelihood but also predicts under what circumstances a variable will serve as a central characteristic, a peripheral cue, or an elaboration moderator. Finally, the ELM advances prior theories of persuasion and information processing in that it predicts different consequences for attitudes formed through these different processes.

Specifically, their model describes differences in strength, persistence, resistance to counterarguments, and behavioral consistency that should occur for attitudes formed through central and peripheral routes.

Impact of ELM Critiques

We judge the scientific impact of these exchanges to be at best neutral. To our knowledge, these exchanges have produced no new lines of published research or theory. Much of the material from these exchanges seems to stem from misperceptions and misinterpretations regarding postulates of the ELM. Importantly, no one has proposed any compelling data that the ELM requires modification as a result. More properly stated, the ELM has not been modified in ways consistent with these lines of criticism. In fact, these exchanges appear to be useful primarily as a ceremonial citation in various review chapters (Eagly & Chaiken, 1993; Petty & Wegener, 1998, 1999).

These observations are not meant as a flippant dismissal of the participants or the ideas at issue. Rather it is an honest evaluation of what has followed and the impact of the consequent. None of the communication criticisms has led to permanent changes in the ELM. None of the communication criticisms has spawned an additional line of research or theory that has gained anything remotely approaching widespread support and application when compared to the ELM.

This does not deny the value of sharp exchange. If anything, the controversies that the ELM generated are probably better seen as evidence of its significance to the field than as failings of the model. It is commonplace to observe that people do not argue over silly issues. The ELM is a monster of a model because of its powerful abstraction quality whereby one construct—elaboration likelihood—consumes many other major ideas (involvement, responsibility, distraction, motor behavior, head nodding and shaking, etc.). Given the large scope of the model and its wide range of applicability, it is hard to imagine that the ELM would not have generated significant comment.

FUTURE DIRECTIONS FOR THE ELM

In the preceding sections, we outlined the past achievements of the ELM in a review of the literature with commentary. But what of the future? In this section, we sketch out interesting lines of theory and research development that flow out of the lessons learned. Rather than generate a list of possible hypotheses, we attempt to push the ELM into larger domains that are themselves composed of many related hypotheses.

Argument Quality

The ELM, along with nearly every theory of persuasion ever developed, does not provide significant conceptual understanding of a most basic construct—argument. An ELM argument is defined as information that bears on the central merits of the attitude object. While this looks like a reasonable definition, it cannot be used to construct arguments a priori that will reliably produce attitude change in a high-elaboration likelihood receiver.

Instead, ELM research with arguments advances through a frank and unabashed empirical process (Petty & Cacioppo, 1986a, 1986b). Researchers think about the attitude object and generate their own potential arguments. These claims are then given to a small group of targeted receivers usually drawn of convenience rather than random sampling. The receivers are instructed to observe the attributes and then provide self-reported ratings of argument quality or self-reported listings of thoughts that are then coded for relevance and direction. Claims receiving the highest or lowest ratings, or the greatest number of positive or negative relevant thoughts, are then selected. This is how we do science in persuasion, and it is not much different from how promoters have been developing marketing campaigns since P. T. Barnum. There is method but no science here.

While we could tag this observation on virtually every modern persuasion theory, the ELM offers an important potential solution to our problem of truly understanding what an argument is. Because we are dealing with the central route process, we know by theory and result that (a) strong arguments produce (b) favorable thoughts, which lead to (c) central route attitude change. We also have reasonably good manipulations of argument quality and reasonably good measures of thought production and attitude change. Across the series of ELM (and other dual-process) studies, we have learned that under conditions of high-elaboration likelihood, we will find moderate to large correlations between the number of object relevant thoughts and attitude, with the direction of the relationship determined by argument valence. As importantly, we have learned that under conditions of low-elaboration likelihood, these correlations will range nonsignificantly around zero. Finally, we have learned that we can triangulate this correlation created from self-report measures with physiological measures of facial muscle activity and brain wave function (Cacioppo, Crites, & Gardner, 1996; Cacioppo, Crites, Gardner, & Berntson, 1994; Cacioppo, Petty, Losch, & Kim, 1986; Crites, Cacioppo, Gardner, & Berntson, 1995). Thus, we have one of the most strongly verified and reproduced effects in persuasion research: Arguments produce thought profiles that produce attitude change, but only under conditions of high-elaboration likelihood.

This effect now becomes one of our strongest tools for cracking open the nut of argument development. We should be able to work backward from downstream effects (start at the terminus of attitude change and then retreat one step to elaboration activity) to find empirically verified arguments. These things are now like fossils found in old African hills and proven to be hominid bone. We are in a position to identify species. It is our conceptual technology for looking into an idea and finding its meaning. Consider the application of this strategy to an interesting and little noted persuasion study of argument quality.

Morley has proposed that the three dimensions of significance, plausibility, and novelty drive "argument quality" (Morley, 1987; Morley & Walker, 1987). He provided experimental evidence in support of these dimensions and the requirement that all three must be present in an argument for it to be found persuasive (i.e., to produce the desired attitude change). To our knowledge, no further work has been published using this "subjective message constructs" theory in persuasion.

Consider, now, running these three dimensions through a standard ELM experiment that manipulates elaboration likelihood and each of the three dimensions in "strong" and "weak" forms. Participants would be randomly assigned to conditions in a four-way design with two levels of "high" and "low" cells in the following: involvement (or any other elaboration moderator), argument significance, argument plausibility, and argument novelty. After exposure to messages, participants would then provide manipulation checks, thought listings, and attitude. We would make two major predictions.

First, under conditions of high involvement, we would expect attitudes to be most favorable when all three argument variables are in the high levels and attitudes to be least favorable when all three argument variables are in the low levels, with attitude scores for the mixed-argument conditions falling between the two extremes. Under conditions of low involvement, we would expect no substantive differences among the argument variables (because low-elaboration likelihood participants would not be processing arguments).

Second, under conditions of high involvement, we would predict that the correlation between attitudes and topic-relevant thoughts should be strongest when all three argument variables are set in either their high or their low levels. The correlations for the other mixed conditions should be weaker than either of the two extremes (all argument variables set to high or low levels). Finally, under conditions of low involvement, there would be no substantial correlations between cognitive response and attitude for any argument conditions (again because low-elaboration likelihood participants would not be processing arguments).

Essentially, we are claiming that argument strength is composed of Morley's three dimensions. Thus, strong arguments have higher levels of significance, plausibility, and novelty, while weak arguments must have correspondingly lower levels of these attributes. Given that these empirical outcomes are obtained, we have provided a stronger refinement of the base construct—argument quality. Instead of knowing that a strong argument is something that elicits positive issue-relevant thoughts, we would know that strong arguments require information that is significant, plausible, and new. While it would always be necessary to engage in some manner of pretesting to determine argument quality, this new line of research we propose (based clearly on knowledge gained through the ELM) would provide us with a more fully articulated construct that would itself stimulate more testing (what makes a claim "significant"?).

Parameters of Persuasion

The physical sciences are noted for their parameters—the constants of nature. Absolute zero. Planck's constant. The speed of light in a vacuum. The periodic chart of elements. The double helix of DNA. It is reasonable for us to ask the question: Are there parameters of persuasion?

Those with a constructivist bent would find the question absurd, but the question is not directed to that philosophy. Rather, if persuasion can be studied as a science, then we should be looking for constants. We would also argue that these parameters or constants make sense only within a complex model such as the ELM. Consider Kuhn's (1977) perspective here: "The road from scientific law to scientific measurement can rarely be traveled in the reverse direction" (p. 219). What Kuhn was suggesting is that high-quality measurement flows from law or, in this case, theory. We would argue that, by extension, persuasion researchers should expect to profit from the ELM structure and reasonably anticipate finding or creating basic measurements of persuasion components.

We think that a main finding driven by the ELM is beyond reasonable argument and must be accepted as a scientific fact. Elaboration likelihood interacts with argument quality (and/or cue strength) to affect cognitive response and following attitude change. If this is true, then it becomes entirely reasonable to search for strong and constant measurements of these qualities followed by a detailed examination of their quantitative relationship. Stated more baldly, we should search for the bounded absolute scale of elaboration likelihood, argument quality, and cue strength. We should then manipulate these three variables and plot their relationships to determine the parameters of persuasion.

Consider a specific examination of elaboration likelihood. Currently, there is no agreed-on measurement of this crucial variable. (Need for cognition is a measure of an elaboration moderator, but it does not assess "here-and-now" elaboration likelihood.) Elaboration likelihood is typically assessed with a manipulation check on an experimental variable such as involvement, but the psychological construct itself has no scale. Given the weight of the empirical evidence supporting the theory, it is more than reasonable to believe that this construct should be measurable. But this is still not our main point.

Not only should elaboration likelihood be measurable, it should also be bounded. That is, we should reasonably be able to scale this construct from "end to end," whether those ends are infinite plus and infinite minus or perhaps begin at zero and functionally terminate at some real empirical end point. In other words, the ELM puts us in a position to start looking for an empirical measure of elaboration likelihood that has real sensible properties that go beyond a well-constructed scale.

REFERENCES

Abelson, R., & Miller, J. (1967). Negative persuasion via personal insult. *Journal of Experimental Social Psychology, 3,* 321-333.

Allen, M., & Reynolds, R. (1993). The Elaboration Likelihood Model and the sleeper effect: An assessment of attitude change over time. *Communication Theory, 3,* 73-82.

Allen, M., & Stiff, J. (1989). Testing three models for the sleeper effect. *Western Journal of Speech Communication, 53,* 411-426.

Bem, D. (1965). An experimental analysis of self-persuasion. *Journal of Experimental Social Psychology, 1,* 199-218.

Berscheid, E. (1966). Opinion change and communicator-communicatee similarity and dissimilarity. *Journal of Personality and Social Psychology, 4,* 670-680.

Booth-Butterfield, S., & Gutowski, C. (1994). Message modality and source credibility can interact to affect argument processing. *Communication Quarterly, 41,* 77-90.

Cacioppo, J., Crites, S., & Gardner, W. (1996). Attitudes to the right: Evaluative processing is associated with lateralized late positive event-related brain potentials. *Personality and Social Psychology Bulletin, 22,* 1205-1219.

Cacioppo, J., Crites, S., Gardner, W., & Berntson, G. (1994). Bioelectrical echoes from evaluative categorizations: I. A late positive brain potential that varies as a function of trait negativity and extremity. *Journal of Personality and Social Psychology, 67,* 115-125.

Cacioppo, J., Marshall-Goodell, B., Tassinary, L., & Petty, R. (1992). Rudimentary determinants of attitudes: Classical conditioning is more effective when prior knowledge about the attitude stimulus is low than high. *Journal of Experimental Social Psychology, 28,* 207-233.

Cacioppo, J., & Petty, R. (1979). Effects of message repetition and position on cognitive responses, recall, and persuasion. *Journal of Personality and Social Psychology, 37,* 97-109.

Cacioppo, J., & Petty, R. (1982). The need for cognition. *Journal of Personality and Social Psychology, 42,* 116-131.

Cacioppo, J., & Petty, R. (1989). Effects of message repetition on argument processing, recall, and persuasion. *Basic and Applied Social Psychology, 10,* 3-12.

Cacioppo, J., Petty, R., Losch, M., & Kim, H. (1986). Electromyographic activity over facial muscle regions can differentiate the valence and intensity of affective reactions. *Journal of Personality and Social Psychology, 50,* 260-268.

Cacioppo, J., Petty, R., & Morris, K. (1983). Effects of need for cognition on message evaluation, recall, and persuasion. *Journal of Personality and Social Psychology, 45,* 805-818.

Cacioppo, J., Priester, J., & Berntson, G. (1993). Rudimentary determinants of attitudes: II. Arm flexion and extension have differential effects on attitudes. *Journal of Personality and Social Psychology, 65,* 5-17.

Chaiken, S. (1978). *The use of source versus message cues in persuasion: An information processing analysis.* Unpublished doctoral dissertation. University of Massachusetts at Amherst.

Chaiken, S. (1980). Heuristic versus systematic information processing in the use of source versus message cues in persuasion. *Journal of Personality and Social Psychology, 39,* 752-766.

Chaiken, S. (1987). The Heuristic Model of persuasion. In M. P. Zanna, J. M. Olson, & C. P. Herman (Eds.), *Social influence: The Ontario Symposium* (Vol. 5, pp. 3-39). Hillsdale, NJ: Lawrence Erlbaum.

Chaiken, S., & Baldwin, M. (1981). Affective-cognitive consistency and the effect of salient behavioral information on the self-perception of attitudes. *Journal of Personality and Social Psychology, 41,* 1-12.

Chaiken, S., Pomerantz, E., & Giner-Sorolla, R. (1995). *Structural consistency and attitude strength.* In R. Petty & J. Krosnick (Eds.), *Attitude strength: Antecedents and consequences* (pp. 387-412). Hillsdale, NJ: Lawrence Erlbaum.

Chen, H., Reardon, R., Rea, C., & Moore, D. (1992). Forewarning of content and involvement: Consequences for persuasion and resistance to persuasion. *Journal of Experimental Social Psychology, 28,* 523-541.

Cialdini, R. (1987). Compliance principles of compliance professionals: Psychologists of necessity. In M. Zanna, J. Olson, & C. Herman (Eds.), *Social influence: The Ontario Symposium* (Vol. 5, pp. 165-184). Hillsdale, NJ: Lawrence Erlbaum.

Crites, S., Cacioppo, J., Gardner, W., & Berntson, G. (1995). Bioelectrical echoes from evaluative categorization: II. A late positive brain potential that varies as a function of attitude registration rather than attitude report. *Journal of Personality and Social Psychology, 68,* 997-1013.

Eagly, A., & Chaiken, S. (1993). *The psychology of attitudes.* Fort Worth, TX: Harcourt Brace Jovanovich.

Eagly, A., & Himmelfarb, S. (1978). Attitudes and opinions. *Annual Review of Psychology, 29,* 517-554.

Gruenfeld, D., & Wyer, R. (1992). Semantics and pragmatics of social influence: How affirmations and denials affect beliefs in referent propositions. *Journal of Personality and Social Psychology, 62,* 38-49.

Hafer, C., Reynolds, K., & Obertynski, M. (1996). Message comprehensibility and persuasion: Effects of complex language in counter attitudinal appeals to laypeople. *Social Cognition, 14,* 317-337.

Hamilton, M., Hunter, J., & Boster, F. (1993). The Elaboration Likelihood Model as a theory of attitude formation: A mathematical analysis. *Communication Theory, 3,* 50-66.

Harkins, S., & Petty, R. (1981). Effects of source magnification of cognitive effort on attitudes: An information processing view. *Journal of Personality and Social Psychology, 40,* 401-413.

Haugtvedt, C., & Petty, R. (1992). Personality and persuasion: Need for cognition moderates the persistence and resistance of attitude changes. *Journal of Personality and Social Psychology, 63,* 308-319.

Himmelfarb, S., & Eagly, A. (1974). Orientations to the study of attitudes and their change. In S. Himmelfarb & A. Eagly (Eds.), *Readings in attitude change.* New York: John Wiley.

Hovland, C., & Weiss, W. (1951). The influence of source credibility on communication effectiveness. *Public Opinion Quarterly, 15,* 635-650.

Johnson, B., & Eagly, A. (1989). Effects of involvement on persuasion: A meta-analysis. *Psychological Bulletin, 106,* 290-314.

Kahneman, D. (1973). *Attention and effort.* Englewood Cliffs, NJ: Prentice Hall.

Kelman, H., & Hovland, C. (1953). "Reinstatement" of the communicator in delayed measurement of opinion change. *Journal of Abnormal and Social Psychology, 48,* 327-335.

Kruglanski, A., & Freund, T. (1983). The freezing and unfreezing of lay-inferences: Effects of impression primacy, ethnic stereotyping, and numerical anchoring. *Journal of Experimental Social Psychology, 19,* 448-468.

Kuhn, T. (1977). *The essential tension.* Chicago: University of Chicago Press.

Mackie, D., & Worth, L. (1989). Processing deficits and the mediation of positive affect in persuasion. *Journal of Personality and Social Psychology, 57,* 27-40.

McGarty, C., Haslam, S., Hutchinson, K., & Turner, J. (1994). The effects of salient group memberships on persuasion. *Small Group Research, 25,* 267-293.

Mongeau, P., & Stiff, J. (1993). Specifying causal relationships in the Elaboration Likelihood Model. *Communication Theory, 3,* 67-72.

Morley, D. (1987). Subjective message constructs: A theory of persuasion. *Communication Monographs, 54,* 183-203.

Morley, D., & Walker, K. (1987). The role of importance, novelty, and plausibility in producing belief change. *Communication Monographs, 54,* 436-442.

Norman, E. (1976). When what is said is important: A comparison of expert and attractive sources. *Journal of Experimental Social Psychology, 12,* 294-300.

Petty, R., & Cacioppo, J. (1977). Forewarning, cognitive responding, and resistance to persuasion. *Journal of Personality and Social Psychology, 35,* 645-655.

Petty, R., & Cacioppo, J. (1979). Issue-involvement can increase or decrease persuasion by enhancing message-relevant cognitive responses. *Journal of Personality and Social Psychology, 37,* 1915-1926.

Petty, R., & Cacioppo, J. (1984). Source factors and the Elaboration Likelihood Model of persuasion. *Advances in Consumer Research, 11,* 668-672.

Petty, R., & Cacioppo, J. (1986a). *Communication and persuasion: The central and peripheral routes to attitude change.* New York: Springer-Verlag.

Petty, R., & Cacioppo, J. (1986b). The Elaboration Likelihood Model of persuasion. In L. Berkowitz (Ed.), *Advances in experimental social psychology* (Vol. 19, pp. 123-205). San Diego: Academic Press.

Petty, R., & Cacioppo, J. (1990). Involvement and persuasion: Tradition versus integration. *Psychological Bulletin, 107,* 367-374.

Petty, R., Cacioppo, J., & Goldman, R. (1981). Personal involvement as a determinant of argument-based persuasion. *Journal of Personality and Social Psychology, 41,* 847-855.

Petty, R., Cacioppo, J., & Heesacker, M. (1981). The effects of rhetorical questions on persuasion: A cognitive response analysis. *Journal of Personality and Social Psychology, 40,* 432-440.

Petty, R., Gleicher, F., & Baker, S. (1991). Multiple roles for affect in persuasion. In J. Forgas (Ed.), *Emotion and social judgments* (pp. 181-200). New York: Pergamon.

Petty, R., Harkins, S., & Williams, K. (1980). The effects of group diffusion of cognitive effort on attitudes: An information processing view. *Journal of Personality and Social Psychology, 38,* 81-92.

Petty, R., Haugtvedt, C., & Smith, S. (1995). *Elaboration as a determinant of attitude strength.* In R. Petty & J. Krosnick (Eds.), *Attitude strength: Antecedents and consequences* (pp. 93-130). Hillsdale, NJ: Lawrence Erlbaum.

Petty, R., Kasmer, J., Haugtvedt, C., & Cacioppo, J. (1987). Source and message factors in persuasion: A reply to Stiff's critique of the Elaboration Likelihood Model. *Communication Monographs, 54,* 233-249.

Petty, R., Shumann, D., Richman, S., & Strathman, A. (1993). Positive mood and persuasion: Different roles for affect under high- and low-elaboration conditions. *Journal of Personality and Social Psychology, 64,* 5-20.

Petty, R., & Wegener, D. (1998). Attitude change: Multiple roles for persuasion variables. In D. Gilbert, S. Fiske, & G. Lindzey (Eds.), *The handbook of social psychology* (Vol. 1, pp. 323-390). Boston: McGraw-Hill.

Petty, R., & Wegener, D. (1999). The Elaboration Likelihood Model: Current status and controversies. In S. Chaiken & Y. Trope (Eds.), *Dual process theories in social psychology* (pp. 37-72). New York: Guilford.

Petty, R., Wegener, D., Fabrigar, L., Priester, J., & Cacioppo, J. (1993). Conceptual and methodological issues in the Elaboration Likelihood Model of persuasion: A reply to the Michigan State critics. *Communication Theory, 3,* 336-363.

Petty, R., Wells, G., & Brock, T. (1976). Distraction can enhance or reduce yielding to propaganda: Thought disruption versus effort justification. *Journal of Personality and Social Psychology, 34,* 874-884.

Pratkanis, A., Greenwald, A., Leippe, M., & Baumgardner, M. (1988). In search of reliable persuasion effects: III. The sleeper effect is dead—Long live the sleeper effect. *Journal of Personality and Social Psychology, 54,* 203-218.

Puckett, J., Petty, R., Cacioppo, J., & Fisher, D. (1983). The relative impact of age and attractiveness stereotypes on persuasion. *Journal of Gerontology, 38,* 340-343.

Rhine, R., & Severance, L. (1970). Ego-involvement, discrepancy, source credibility, and attitude change. *Journal of Personality and Social Psychology, 16,* 175-90.

Shavitt, S., Swan, S., Lowery, T., & Wänke, M. (1994). The interaction of endorser attractiveness and involvement in persuasion depends on the goal that guides message processing. *Journal of Consumer Psychology, 3,* 137-162.

Sherif, M. (1977). Crisis in social psychology: Some remarks towards breaking through the crisis. *Personality and Social Psychology Bulletin, 3,* 368-382.

Smith, S., & Shaffer, D. (1991). Celerity and cajolery: Rapid speech may promote or inhibit persuasion through its impact on message elaboration. *Personality and Social Psychology Bulletin, 17,* 663-669.

Staats, A., & Staats, C. (1958). Attitudes established by classical conditioning. *Journal of Abnormal and Social Psychology, 57,* 37-40.

Sternthal, B., Dholakia, R., & Leavitt, C. (1978). The persuasive effect of source credibility: A test of cognitive response analysis. *Journal of Consumer Research, 4,* 252-260.

Stiff, J. (1986). Cognitive processing of persuasive message cues: A meta-analytic review of the effects of supporting information on attitudes. *Communication Monographs, 53,* 75-89.

Tetlock, P. (1983). Accountability and the complexity of thought. *Journal of Personality and Social Psychology, 45,* 74-83.

Wood, W., & Kallgren, C. (1988). Communicator attributes and persuasion: Recipients access to attitude-relevant information in memory. *Personality and Social Psychology Bulletin, 14,* 172-182.

Wood, W., Kallgren, C., & Preisler, R. (1985). Access to attitude-relevant information in memory as a determinant of persuasion: The role of message attributes. *Journal of Experimental Social Psychology, 21,* 73-85.

Wood, W., Rhodes, N., & Biek, M. (1995). Working knowledge and attitude strength: An information processing analysis. In R. Petty & J. Krosnick (Eds.), *Attitude strength: Antecedents and consequences* (pp. 283-313). Hillsdale, NJ: Lawrence Erlbaum.

Zanna, M., Fazio, R., & Ross, M. (1994). *The persistence of persuasion*. In R. C. Schank & E. Langer (Eds.), *Beliefs, reasoning, and decision-making: Psychologic in honor of Bob Abelson* (pp. 347-362). Hillsdale, NJ: Lawrence Erlbaum.

Zajonc, R., & Markus, H. (1982). Affective and cognitive factors in preferences. *Journal of Consumer Research, 9,* 123-131.

10

Involvement as Goal-Directed Strategic Processing

Extending the Elaboration Likelihood Model

MICHAEL D. SLATER

Researchers are unusually unanimous in agreeing about the central role of involvement in understanding persuasive processes (Chaiken, 1987; Grunig, 1989; Krugman, 1965; Petty & Cacioppo, 1986). Few concepts in the persuasion field have more intuitive appeal than that of involvement or are more central to theoretical explanation in the field. For example, a typical undergraduate persuasion textbook has more pages addressing involvement than addressing any other concept save attitudes (Perloff, 1993). Even those undergraduates who struggle with many abstract ideas seem comfortable when involvement is introduced and discussed. Involvement, after all, is introspectively familiar. We all know what it feels like to be engrossed in a novel or film, to pore over a text before an exam, or (conversely) to skim a newspaper or glance briefly at a television advertisement.

In teaching and explaining involvement, the fundamental proposition is that the nature of the processing of a message and its resulting impact depends on the recipient's involvement with the message. If a message supports a housing project that will affect one's property values, or advocates comprehensive examinations that will make one's graduation from college more difficult to achieve, obviously the message will be read with much more attention to the arguments presented than if the message addresses issues with no personal impact (Petty & Cacioppo, 1986).

However, as is so often the case, the contribution of social science is to analyze and describe the complexity that underlies what appears to be a simple and intuitive notion. Few concepts in the communication field have been approached and defined in so

AUTHOR'S NOTE: Research on which this chapter is based was supported in part by Grant AA10377 from the National Institute on Alcohol Abuse and Alcoholism.

175

many different ways. As Salmon (1986) commented, "Involvement has become a vague metaconcept that subsumes a class of related concepts that have both affective and cognitive derivations" (p. 244). Coming to terms with this complexity and arriving at a functional understanding of the involvement phenomenon is essential if we are to successfully characterize the persuasion process.

In this chapter, I present the case that involvement, as it has been used in the literature, not only subsumes various related concepts, as Salmon states, but also at times obscures our understanding of the persuasion process. For example, involvement is typically described as arising in response to the relevance of message content. Such a perspective indeed makes sense in the context of experimental research in persuasion. In the typical persuasion experiment, individuals are obliged to attend to messages constructed by a researcher in order to receive their research participation credit or incentive payment. However, in the social world, people typically choose whether or not to expose themselves to, or pay attention to, a message. People make such a choice based on their needs and desires for information and entertainment (Kim & Rubin, 1997; Olson & Zanna, 1979; Palmgreen, 1984). Therefore, understanding involvement as a response to content is at best only partially accurate.

Research—as well as personal experience—suggests that people are "cognitive misers" (e.g., Stroh, 1995). That is, people do not tend to exert more mental effort than is necessary to achieve a task. Humans might not be rational in many respects. However, we, as message processors, may be quite sensible when it comes to accomplishing processing tasks. What we attend to in a message, and the kind of attention we bring to bear, depends on why we are processing the message in the first place. A droning speaker will elicit only passing attention from a visitor who steps into a

room to see whether the presentation is worthwhile. On the other hand, students concerned about their grades may do their best to attend closely if they are to be graded on material from the presentation—pinching themselves to stay awake if need be. In turn, colleagues who are in close professional agreement or disagreement with the speaker's position will be listening carefully for comments that support or denigrate their position, perhaps rehearsing their responses (and their penetrating questions) as the speaker continues. Similarly, a person may watch a "true crime" show to relax after a hard day, to confirm one's fears about urban life, to pass time with a friend who insists on watching the program, or to learn about police procedures in anticipation of a law enforcement career.

The examples just provided include messages that are not typically considered to be overtly persuasive. Academic presentations, television crime shows, and novels are hardly the stimuli typically used in persuasion experiments or addressed in persuasion theory. The choice of examples here is deliberate. The perspective discussed here, what I call the Extended Elaboration Likelihood Model (or Extended ELM), permits consideration of persuasion processes across multiple message genres. After all, overtly persuasive messages represent only a small proportion of the messages to which people are continually exposed. Considerable research attention has been paid to the impact of entertainment and other non-overtly persuasive messages on attitudes and beliefs, with cultivation theory being perhaps the best known example (Gerbner, Gross, Morgan, & Signorielli, 1994). If we as researchers can bring the methodological and theoretical rigor of the persuasion research field to bear on a broad array of messages, we can both extend the range of our theories and increase understanding of the intended and unintended social impact of messages and the media. In addition, as I attempt to demonstrate, we can understand the processing and impact of overtly persuasive messages in a richer and more complete way as well.

Before elaborating on this theoretical perspective (and, more important, before reviewing recent empirical evidence in support of this theory), it is useful to place it in the context of existing theoretical excursions into explicating the involvement concept. Such a review illustrates the many issues that need to be incorporated into a model of involvement processes and also acknowledges key theoretical and empirical insights that helped to inform and guide the current framework.

SOME PRIOR THEORETICAL PERSPECTIVES ON INVOLVEMENT

Involvement in the Persuasion Literature

Involvement has been defined in operational terms as thoughts relating personal experience and message content (Krugman, 1965) or as links between information presented and central values (Sherif & Hovland, 1961). These approaches are invaluable as a starting point by focusing research attention on the recipients' existing beliefs, values, and priorities as a filter through which message content is processed.

Subsequent theorists developed this perspective in a manner akin in spirit to the current effort; they defined involvement in terms of the motivation to process information (Burnkrant & Sawyer, 1983; Mitchell, 1979). However, the implications of such a perspective were not developed in detail in these initial efforts. An article developing this argument included a key point (expanded on in this chapter): Motivational differences (i.e., cognitive vs. affective) are likely to lead to different types or amounts of arousal or attention (Park & Mittal, 1985), although the nature of

motivational differences and processing consequences were left largely unspecified.

Other researchers have taken a more cognitive approach, defining involvement as increased attentional capacity (Greenwald & Leavitt, 1984) or as increased cognitive activation (Cameron, 1993). The Cameron (1993) study is particularly useful in that it demonstrated what was an implicit or explicit assumption of most theoretical work in involvement. That is, Cameron found greater cognitive activation associated with cognitive arousal triggered by self-relevant message content. The Greenwald and Leavitt (1984) article is interesting in that it proposed that increased engagement of attentional capacity leads to four types of involvement, which were described as increasingly intensive message processing strategies. Again, this effort was pointing in the right direction. What remains lacking is the recognition that different motivations engage different aspects of attention, or attention to different aspects of a message, and that these differences can lead to specifying alternative processing strategies.

The recognition that different contexts lead to different types of involvement and associated processing differences was approached empirically in an important meta-analysis (Johnson & Eagly, 1989). Based on their review of experimental research in persuasion, Johnson and Eagly (1989) identified three types of involvement: *outcome relevant,* or involvement due to personal consequences related to the topic (also called *issue involvement* [see Petty & Cacioppo, 1986]); *value relevant,* or involvement arising from message context that impinges on personal value systems; and *impression relevant,* or involvement resulting from the possibility of social interaction related to message content. While they did not systematically derive differences in processing models based on these different types of involvement, they did identify some differences in processing of persuasive information in the course of their meta-analysis. In particular, they found that in value-relevant involvement conditions, unlike in more conventional outcome-relevant conditions, involvement did not predict greater attention to message argument strength—a point that I return to, and elaborate in some detail, later.

One is left, in reviewing such a plethora of definitions and conceptual approaches, with the impression of blindfolded social scientists feeling the proverbial elephant. All are providing useful observations regarding the legs, tusks, torso, and trunk; some aspects of their observations are consistent, and some are inconsistent; none has the full picture. The most plausible reason is that the intuitive concept of involvement cannot be explicated as a single construct because it is in fact not a single construct but rather represents a complex and multidimensional process (Andrews, Durvasala, & Akhter, 1990; Slater, 1997).

The work by Andrews et al. (1990) offers important insights into this process. They argued that antecedents predicting involvement (instrumental utility, value-relevance, etc.), consequences of involvement (differences in cognitive search-and-retrieval), and involvement itself (intensity, direction, and persistence of arousal or activation) should be distinguished from one another. However, all three elements must be considered together to understand the phenomenon commonly referred to as involvement. In pointing this out, they made important progress in integrating disparate observations concerning the involvement construct.

Involvement and the Volitional Audience Member

It is not enough, however, to simply point out that involvement must be understood in terms of antecedents, intensity, and resulting differences in processing strategy. To make further progress in understanding involvement in processing communication, one must articulate specific theoretical models for how various antecedents influence attention and message processing in distinctive ways—models that are applicable to specific social phenomena of interest. I have proposed (for a full discussion, see Slater, 1997) that one can do so by analyzing typical motivations—that is, the goals and purposes—of the reader or viewer, who typically chooses exposure to a message for some discernible end, whether it be to gain information or to be entertained (Blumler & Katz, 1974; Kim & Rubin, 1997; Palmgreen, 1984). Such an approach has several benefits. From a conceptual point of view, it acknowledges the active, volitional message recipient who chooses message exposure. In terms of theory development, it provides a strategy for identifying explicit models of persuasive processing applicable to genres other than conventional explicitly persuasive messages.

INVOLVEMENT AS MOTIVATED STRATEGIC PROCESSING

Elsewhere, I have described in some detail what I am here calling the Extended ELM (see Slater, 1997). I refer to this model as the Extended ELM to acknowledge its foundation in Petty and Cacioppo's work in conceptualizing persuasion in terms of recipient message processing and response patterns. It is extended in that in the Extended ELM, the traditional ELM is conceptualized as one important but special case for processing persuasive content. The traditional ELM, as Johnson and Eagly (1989) pointed out, describes responses to overtly persuasive messages addressing issue- or outcome-relevant topics. Other models, incorporating other variables and other patterns of relationships, can be discerned for other genres of overtly and implicitly persuasive messages. These models are briefly summarized here.

Involvement as Processing Goals and Processing Intensity Determinants

Before reviewing specific suggestions of the Extended ELM, however, it may be useful to overview some key features of the model. In particular, it may be helpful to identify how features of the model correspond to the concept of involvement as it is typically and intuitively used.

For example, one may think of the recipient's *processing goals*—purposes or motivations-to-process—as determining the *type* of involvement that will be engaged. By type of involvement, I refer to the variables and variable relationships that will be found in a model describing a processing strategy that serves the recipient's goals. On the other hand, *processing intensity determinants,* as that term implies, determine the *degree* of engagement within each processing type or model. These processing intensity determinants, of course, differ according to recipient goal and consequent processing strategy.

Therefore, processing determinants correspond most closely to the intuitive use of involvement, as referring to variation in engagement with a message as a function of how the recipient responds to particulars of message content. However, we know little about such variation unless we know, in each processing situation, what message variables and dimensions of response are likely to be relevant and predictive of persuasive effects. To identify these variables and dimensions, we must begin with involvement type or the goals and associated strategic models.

These rather abstract concepts become much more intuitive when put into practice. A first case to address is one that appears to cause some particular problems in persuasion

research exploring the traditional ELM: messages relevant to one's personal values.

Johnson and Eagly's (1989) meta-analysis demonstrated that value-relevant involvement was not associated with greater impact of argument quality, as is found in the ELM. As I have argued elsewhere (Slater, 1997; Slater & Rouner, 1996b), simply distinguishing value-relevant involvement from the issue- or outcome-relevant involvement manipulated in ELM research does not go far enough. The assumption that processing is goal driven and strategic forces us to ask about what message recipients would be trying to accomplish in reading, listening to, or viewing a message that either attacked beliefs that they hold dear or reinforced those same beliefs.

Value-Protective Processing

There are in fact good reasons to process a message that attacks our beliefs, even if the experience is somewhat aversive. The most logical purpose is to rehearse our defense of our beliefs, perhaps against a newly formulated argument against our point of view. After all, our beliefs are often assaulted by mediated and interpersonal communication. A second reason might be an emotional satisfaction that we may derive by belittling the persons who disagree with us or at least mocking their arguments. This, of course, might help to reinforce our sense of personal identity insofar as this is defined by our values and by a sense of belonging to a community of people who we believe share our values (and the corresponding social distance from those who oppose them).

If this analysis is at least in part accurate, elements of a distinctive persuasion processing model can be derived. Counterarguments and source derogation should dominate thought elaboration as a function of the intensity of the opposing values held and the intensity with which contrary values are espoused in the message (the processing intensity determinants in this case). Increased argument strength should also tend to increase counterarguing; the greater the processing intensity, the less effect of the message on beliefs. Central routes to belief change are unlikely if values are held with any real commitment. A single message would be unlikely to do more than perhaps reduce confidence in beliefs (Price & Allen, 1990; Slater & Rouner, 1992). However, indirect paths to belief change may exist, perhaps through messages that are personally engaging and generate positive affective evaluations of source or content (Slater & Rouner, 1996b). Messages with narrative content may also circumvent the counterarguing tendency.

Value-Affirmative Processing

On the other hand, if message content reflects one's beliefs and values, the primary purposes for processing it would be to reinforce one's belief system. I have referred to this as value-affirmative processing (Slater, 1997; Slater & Rouner, 1996b). Consistent arguments should be rehearsed and elaborated in a classic central processing (Petty & Cacioppo, 1986) framework. In such cases, argument quality may well matter, contrary to Johnson and Eagly's (1989) meta-analytic findings, which did not distinguish between value-affirmative and value-protective conditions. Also, the more extreme the value position, the less important source credentials should be and the more intensive the processing should be (Harmon & Coney, 1982). Shared ideology may be the most important credential to the true believer—especially if that source also provides what appear to be high-quality arguments (Slater & Rouner, 1996a).

Outcome-Based Processing

As Johnson and Eagly (1989) pointed out, ELM research has primarily manipulated involvement in terms of message arguments that have direct implications for the life of the message recipient (e.g., tuition increases or comprehensive exams for college students). This, of course, is an important real-world class of messages; policy debates are often framed in these terms (although in practice, of course, they are often reframed in terms of values—perhaps, as in the preceding analysis, to minimize impact of argument strength and thus short-circuit intelligent debate). Because the traditional ELM describes processing of such messages in considerable and well-researched detail (Petty & Cacioppo, 1986), I do not discuss this further here.[1]

Didactic Processing

The previous three processing strategies all exist within the domain of overtly persuasive messages. Central to the Extended ELM perspective is the assertion that we can use substantially modified ELMs to better understand the impact of other genres of messages on our beliefs and attitudes. These genres include educational materials, news coverage, and entertainment messages such as films, novels, and television programs.

Much of the mediated message content encountered by a person, especially while growing up, is intended to impart knowledge or skills. There are two motivations for processing such messages: the perceived importance of mastering content (due to one's own instrumental needs or concerns with rewards and sanctions such as grades and job evaluations) or intrinsic interest in the subject matter. The extent of perceived importance or intrinsic interest serves as the determinant of processing intensity in this context, much as value extremity did for value-based processing strategies and issue involvement did for outcome-based processing strategies.

Processing intensity should have persuasive implications in didactic processing. To comprehend a message, one must assimilate its content (Craik & Lockhart, 1972). Such assimilation should make it more difficult to counterargue and reject message content. The more important the task or the greater the intrinsic interest, the greater the effort to assimilate and the more difficult it would be to counterargue. Follow-up tasks such as examinations also require cognitive rehearsal that might operate, in some respects, similarly to elaboration of content-related arguments to influence beliefs. Increased recall should then be associated with such processing, especially as task importance or interest increases (see also Wyer, Srull, Gordon, & Hartwick, 1982). Attitude formation effects should be especially strong because recall and comprehension requires that new information be integrated into existing knowledge structures in memory (Potts, St. John, & Kirson, 1989). The extent to which didactically presented information will influence existing beliefs and values is less certain. However, the intensive processing required for assimilation should increase salience and availability (Fazio, Powell, & Williams, 1989). Because counterarguing is minimized, persuasive effects are not unlikely, especially if additional tasks such as examinations and work requirements interfere with retrospectively discounting the information received (see Gilbert, 1991).

Information Scanning

A great deal of real-world message processing is really message browsing (Bogart, 1984; Eastman & Newton, 1995). Such browsing is the principal real-world counterpart of what Petty and Cacioppo (1986) referred to as low-involvement processing. After all, low-involvement processing otherwise is an artifact of the laboratory experiment in which participants are required to read or view messages that are of no relevance or interest. The purpose for such browsing can be regarded as surveillance of the information environment (Lasswell, 1948). In this sense, information scanning serves functionally as a predecessor to other processing strategies. A newspaper reader may flip the pages, scanning articles and stopping occasionally to chuckle at a humor column (hedonic processing), to scornfully read a letter to the editor from someone whose views oppose his or her own (value-protective processing), and to study an article concerning the proposed location of a superstore near his or her home (outcome-based processing). The articles that are merely scanned do receive some processing, however, which deserves attention.

Petty and Cacioppo's (1986) characterization of peripheral processing and Chaiken's (1987) characterization of heuristic processing probably describe scanning adequately. Peripheral cues concerning the source or stylistic aspects of the message should be attended to more than substantive message content, with relatively low recall resulting. Attitude change should be rather slight and short-lived if any such change takes place at all (Petty & Cacioppo, 1986). It should be noted, however, that larger effects in terms of attitude formation are likely when prior knowledge is low (Hamilton, Hunter, & Boster, 1993). Such attitude formation effects are probably commonplace given that mediated messages provide the bulk of information regarding topics outside of our direct experience (Ball-Rokeach & DeFleur, 1982) and that such unfamiliar topics are relatively unlikely to evoke more intensive processing. The primary contributions of the Extended ELM here, then, are simply to point out that scanning is a motivated activity and is a real-world counterpart of low-involvement processing, that extent of effects should vary depending on the intensity or attention with which scanning is done, and that attitude formation effects (and effects on perceptions regarding the public agenda [McCombs & Shaw, 1972]), of scanning activities are probably nontrivial.

Hedonic Processing

In many ways, the most interesting processing problems, from the persuasion viewpoint, occur in entertainment contexts. Reading a novel, watching a television drama or sitcom, or viewing a movie can be engrossing to an extent only dreamed of by a speechwriter, a reporter, or an advertiser (Graesser, 1981; Mandler & Johnson, 1980). Yet the processing of viewpoints that may be implicitly expressed in the narrative will hardly follow a classic persuasion processing pattern.

The Extended ELM predicts, first, that counterarguing will be severely inhibited. The suspension of disbelief that appears to be a necessary component to experiencing a narrative is simply incompatible with thought elaborations questioning or debating content in that narrative (Slater, 1997, in press). Traditional persuasion variables such as source credibility and argument strength should become irrelevant. Instead, involvement in the message, and thus the impact of persuasive messages woven into the story, should be a function of identification with characters portrayed, the narrative interest of the story, and the seamlessness with which persuasive content is incorporated into the narrative. The higher the values of these variables, the less counterarguing there should be and the greater the persuasive impact should be.

The potential for persuasive impact of narratives is considerable indeed given people's inclination to engage with a compelling narrative regardless of topic and the likelihood that counterarguing will be inhibited. Moreover, a persuasive case can be made not by verbal argument but by modeling expressed attitudes and behaviors, their consequences, and the reactions of others in a way that closely mimics social reality. In this way, social learning mechanisms can be enlisted in the persuasive process as well (Bandura, 1986). Entertainment-education programming for family planning and health behavior change enlisting these principles have shown exceptionally large attitude and behavior change effects (Kincaid, 1993; Piotrow, Kincaid, Rimon, & Rinehart, 1997; Singhal & Rogers, 1999). In addition, because fictional narratives often depict unfamiliar peoples, places, and times, attitude formation effects should be substantial as well (Slater, 1990; for a more complete discussion, see also Slater, 1997, in press). Table 10.1 illustrates some of the main features of the Extended ELM.

EVIDENCE FOR AN EXTENDED ELABORATION LIKELIHOOD MODEL

Value-Affirmative Processing Versus Value-Protective Processing

Coincident with and subsequent to the initial publication of this theoretical framework (Slater, 1997), several studies have been conducted that both support the Extended ELM framework and further extend it. The first study was a test of the proposition that value-affirmative processing (processing of a message that reinforces one's value system) and value-protective processing (processing of a message that attacks one's values) consist of distinct and separate processing models.

Johnson and Eagly's (1989) meta-analysis suggested that value-relevant involvement (involvement based on message content rele-

TABLE 10.1 The Relationship of Receiver Goals, Message Genres, Processing Determinants, and Associated Message Processing Strategies

Receiver Goals	Associated Media Genres	Relevant Processing Determinants	Modal Processing Strategy
Entertainment	Novels, films, television, docudrama, historical fiction	Identification, narrative interest	Hedonic
Information/skill acquisition	Documentary, biography, history, texts, instructional media, manuals, specialized publications	Task importance, intrinsic interest	Didactic
Surveillance	Online services, advertising, general-interest periodicals, newspapers, broadcast news	Information-seeking intensity	Information scanning
Self-interest assessment	Same as surveillance	Outcome relevance	Outcome based
Value defense	Same as surveillance	Value extremity, value centrality	Value protective
Value reinforcement	Same as surveillance	Same as value defense	Value affirmative

SOURCE: Slater, M. D. (1997). Persuasion processes across receiver goals and message centers. *Communication Theory, 7*, 125-148. Copyright © Oxford University Press. Used by permission.

NOTE: As discussed in the text, multiple goals can be engaged, resulting in multiple-involvement determinant variables becoming important and perhaps resulting in hybrid processing strategies. Relations illustrated, then, are typical or modal.

vant to one's personal value system) was operationally distinct from the issue involvement typically manipulated by Petty and Cacioppo (1986). The primary distinction found in the meta-analysis was that value involvement, unlike issue involvement, was not associated with increased impact of argument strength.

My colleague Donna Rouner and I further explored the issue of value involvement by examining value-affirmative and value-protective contexts as distinct conditions. We wanted to examine, among other issues, whether or not we could find differences in the role of argument strength for value-affirmative processing versus value-protective processing. We also wanted to manipulate argument strength in a conceptually more rigorous way than was done by Petty and Cacioppo

(1986). Petty and Cacioppo's approach has been criticized as tautological (Mongeau & Stiff, 1993), a problem that they themselves acknowledged (Petty & Cacioppo, 1986, pp. 31-32). They empirically identified arguments that research participants considered to be strong or weak and used those as their manipulations. Instead, we tapped the existing communication literature on argument evidence and identified two major types of evidence that we could use to manipulate argument strength: statistical quantitative evidence and anecdotal evidence (Baesler & Burgoon, 1994; Kazoleas, 1993; Reinard, 1988). We created three different template messages—short essays, ostensibly by a college student, that attacked the social acceptability of alcohol use. The messages were buttressed by either statistical evidence, a brief anecdote describing the negative impact of alcohol use on the life of a fellow college student, neither, or both in a crossed design. We used an index of value involvement with alcohol that we developed and split the study population on the neutral point of the index (alcohol use was so normative in the study population that values proved to be more useful than alcohol consumption to identify personal investment in alcohol use). We were careful to write the essays so that alcohol use was criticized only from a value perspective. At no point were restrictive policies or interventions advocated.

Our results were strongly supportive of the proposition that value-affirmative and value-protective processing should be modeled differently. When the value-affirmative and value-protective participants were combined, we had no effect for evidence type, consistent with Johnson and Eagly's (1989) meta-analysis. However, when they were included as a factor in the analysis of variance model, we found significant interactions with evidence type: Value-affirmative participants showed more positive argument-relevant responses in the presence of statistical evidence, and value-protective participants showed more negative argument-relevant responses in this condition. In other words, statistical evidence served to encourage counterarguing among the value-protective participants. Anecdote had no impact on argument-relevant responses for either value-protective or value-affirmative study participants. However, for the value-protective participants, the presence of anecdote turned overall negative responses to the presentation of the message to a positive assessment (for means, see Table 10.2). Similarly, we tested effects of statistical and anecdotal evidence on subjective assessments of message persuasiveness, believability, and overall quality. For value-affirmative participants, statistical evidence was significantly related to persuasiveness and believability judgments, and anecdote had no effect on any of these judg-

ments. For value-protective participants, anecdotal evidence was significantly related to persuasiveness and believability judgments, and statistical evidence showed no such relationship. This evidence was clearly consistent with the findings for cognitive responses (Slater & Rouner, 1996b).

Mongeau and Stiff (1993) made a convincing case that the ELM posits mediating effects of cognitive responses on beliefs and that these relationships should be tested causally. Accordingly, we also ran path models incorporating beliefs about alcohol use at pre- and posttest, with cognitive responses and message evaluation judgments (Slater & Rouner, 1996b) as the mediating variables. Separate models were run for value-protective and value-affirmative participants to examine whether, as proposed in the Extended ELM, distinctive processing models could be clearly discerned, as illustrated in Figures 10.1 and 10.2.

As Figures 10.1 and 10.2 indicate, value-affirmative message recipients showed significant paths from statistical evidence to more positive issue-relevant responses and from there to belief change—a classic example of central processing from the ELM perspective (Petty & Cacioppo, 1986). No path from anecdotal evidence to belief change is in evidence for these value-affirmative recipients. By contrast, running the model for the value-protective message recipient subgroup resulted in significant paths from anecdotal evidence to believability and from there to belief change. In other words, anecdote influenced belief change using a peripheral route for the value-protective recipients. The most important peripheral route here, via subjective evaluations of message quality, is not one discussed by Petty and Cacioppo (1986), although we have previously found other evidence for the importance of subjective message evaluations as peripheral cues (Slater & Rouner, 1996a).

TABLE 10.2 Net Polarity of Cognitive Responses: Subgroup Analyses

	Statistical Evidence			
	Value-Affirmative Subgroup Analysis		Value-Protective Subgroup Analysis	
	Present	Absent	Present	Absent
Net polarity of argument-relevant responses	2.33	1.34*	0.35	1.54†
Net polarity of presentation-relevant responses	−0.26	−0.48	−0.27	−0.12
	Anecdote			
	Value-Affirmative	Subgroup Analysis	Value-Protective	Subgroup Analysis
	Present	Absent	Present	Absent
Net polarity of argument-relevant responses	1.80	1.88	1.00	0.88
Net polarity of presentation-relevant responses	−0.35	−0.38	0.30	−0.72**

SOURCE: Slater and Rouner (1996b), by permission of publisher.

NOTE: Net polarity is number of positive responses minus number of negative responses of each type. Significance tests are for comparison between presence and absence of the treatment within each subgroup (value affirmative or value protective) only. Subgroups are placed in the same table for ease of comparison.

†p < .10.

*p < .05.

**p < .01.

Comparable supportive findings have emerged from a recent study of anti-drug public service announcements (PSAs) (Stephenson, 1999). Stephenson (1999, in press) found that such PSAs influenced anti-drug attitudes in high sensation seekers, who also tended to be high in drug use and more resistant to such messages, in part via processing of the narrative content of the PSAs. The narrative route for the low sensation seekers, who tended to have substantially lower levels of drug use, had little effect on attitudes and may have even interfered with central processing among these message recipients.

The relevance of such findings for applied work in persuasion is obvious: These results clearly suggest that statistical evidence is superior for reinforcing beliefs of those already inclined to believe the message, and anecdotal evidence is superior for influencing a much more difficult audience—those who disagree with the message. More relevant in the current

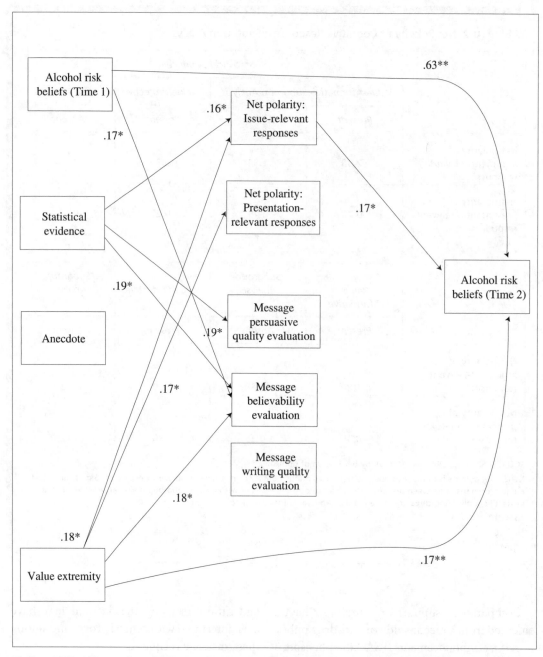

Figure 10.1. Effects of Variables Predicting Change in Personal and Social Beliefs About Alcohol for Value-Affirmative Message Recipients (*n* = 154)

SOURCE: Adapted from Slater and Rouner (1996b), by permission of publisher.

*p < .05.

**p < .01.

***p < .001.

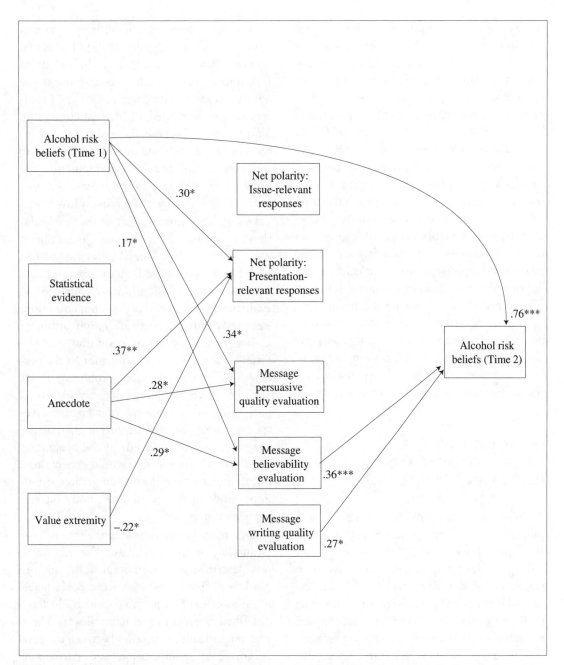

Figure 10.2. Effects of Variables Predicting Change in Personal and Social Beliefs About Alcohol for Value-Protective Message Recipients (n = 52)

SOURCE: Adapted from Slater and Rouner (1996b), by permission of publisher.

*p < .05.

**p < .01.

***p < .001.

context are the implications for theory. Johnson and Eagly (1989) were correct in asserting that value-relevant processing contexts are different from outcome-relevant (issue involvement) contexts. However, value-protective and value-affirmative processing in turn are distinct, and if combined they obscure our understanding of the persuasive processing of value-relevant message content. The findings are quite consistent with the portrait limned earlier of value-protective and value-affirmative processing. That is, value-affirmative processors presumably used statistics to buttress their beliefs, and value-protective processors used statistics as an opportunity to rehearse counterarguments. The surprise was the impact of anecdote on the value-protective processors—although perhaps it should not have been a surprise given the discussion earlier of how narrative (and anecdotes are very brief narratives) should tend to circumvent counterarguing.

DIDACTIC AND INFORMATION SCANNING PROCESSING STRATEGIES

An important study provides a comparison of didactic and information scanning processing strategies (Tewksbury, 1999). In this study, college student respondents were asked to watch a television news profile of a political candidate, with the purpose of either forming their own evaluations of the candidate (which would be assessed later in the study) or simply passing a few minutes watching television; these latter study participants were told that the television excerpt might be entertainment, sports, or news. In addition, students were identified as relative experts or novices with respect to politics. In other words, the participants in effect were instructed to engage in a didactic or information scanning processing strategy (D. Tewksbury, personal communication, February 1999). The study, however, did not manipulate the extent of task importance, which of course limits the ability to extrapolate from Tewksbury's findings to the Extended ELM predictions (see Slater, 1997). Because there were no incentives or sanctions based on task performance, one can assume that this manipulation for didactic processing was a conservative one, with task importance at a relatively low level.

Despite the conservatism of the manipulation of task importance, many of the differences expected based on the Extended ELM predictions were found. Recall of candidate issue positions was significantly higher in the evaluation (or didactic processing) condition. Recall of candidate party affiliation, although higher for the evaluation condition, was not different at statistically significant levels, perhaps due to ceiling effect problems; about 80% of all respondents correctly identified party affiliation. Issue-relevant cognitive responses were also significantly higher, as the Extended ELM predicted, in the evaluation condition. Of course, one would expect these differences to have been even greater if task importance in the evaluation condition had been greater as well.

Even more interesting were the findings for evaluation of the candidate. The candidate was described as a Democrat, although the candidate's issue positions were constructed to be as centrist as possible (and could have described a progressive Republican). There was a significant interaction between the processing goal manipulation and participant political affiliation, in which affiliation better predicted candidate evaluation in the information scanning (passing time) condition than in the didactic processing (evaluation) condition. In other words, as one would expect from the Extended ELM perspective, the low-involvement scanning condition resulted in peripheral processing and greater attention to peripheral cues such as the candidate's party, and the more cognitively demanding didactic processing condition resulted in greater attention to and influence of substantive information about the candidate—central processing, in Petty and Cacioppo's (1986) terminology.

Tewksbury also divided his research participants by political expertise, as measured by a political knowledge test. This expert/novice distinction can be considered as an approximation of the intrinsic interest variable in the didactic processing model; college students with greater political knowledge can reasonably be assumed to be more interested in information about political candidates. As predicted by the Extended ELM, the more interested the participant, the greater the recall of issue positions presented and the greater the number of political party-related thoughts; the number of issue-related thoughts was higher as well, but not at statistically significant levels.

Again, results for candidate evaluation were especially interesting from the Extended ELM perspective. In this case, the relevant analysis looked at the relationship of participant party affiliation and political knowledge in predicting candidate evaluation. The Extended ELM would suggest that this might elicit value-protective processing among Republicans and value-affirmative processing among Democrats. Such an effect should be a relatively weak one in this case given that the issues advocated were as much Republican as they were Democratic in sentiment; only the party label was available to cue value allegiance. However, this might be sufficient for those who are more politically knowledgeable and presumably more politically engaged—those with greater value extremity, using Extended ELM terminology. As a result, particularly for value-protective processors, there should be less impact of issue-relevant information.

In fact, that is what apparently took place. The more politically engaged "experts" had significantly more polarized evaluations of the candidate, consistent with their party allegiance, despite the candidate's centrist views. The findings noted earlier—that greater political engagement was associated at significant levels with the number of political party-related thoughts but showed a weaker and statistically nonsignificant effect with respect to issue-related thoughts—is also largely consistent with the value-affirmative versus value-protective processing perspective: "A source's main credential . . . may be ideological agreement with the receiver" (Slater, 1997, p. 141).

It also should be noted that these findings, while consistent with the Extended ELM, are not consistent with conventional ELM predictions if the ELM is (inappropriately, in my view) extrapolated to value-relevant involvement contexts such as this. Increased political engagement, which represents increased involvement in the message, is more associated with increases in responses regarding what Petty and Cacioppo would regard as a peripheral cue (i.e., source credentials, affiliation) and less with the substantive issue information in the message. Again, this is only an inadequacy if the ELM is incorrectly extrapolated beyond what Johnson and Eagly (1989) called outcome-relevant involvement or involvement based on a personal stake in the message topic. These findings also underscore the importance of extending the ELM to take into account a much larger range of processing contexts and message genres.

HEDONIC PROCESSING: PERSUASIVE CONTENT IN NARRATIVE MESSAGES

Rouner and I have explored some of the predictions of the Extended ELM in the context of narrative fictional messages. The approach we took was to use excerpts of short stories in which a subplot illustrates misuse of alcohol by underage drinkers and then exemplifies negative or positive outcomes associated with that misuse. The approach is conservative in that brief and rather unexceptional prose fictions are used instead of much more absorbing and dramatic film or television drama. The advantages, of course, include relative ease of manipulation and control over the ways in which implicitly persuasive content is incorporated. These studies, in particular, incorporated cognitive response measurement in response to such narrative entertainment messages—the first time, so far as we have been able to determine, that such an effort has been made.

In our studies, we examined several key components of the Extended ELM in the context of entertainment messages. First, we examined the pattern of counterarguments in response to the negative portrayals of alcohol misuse. Such counterarguments were virtually nonexistent, amounting to only 2.3% of total comments, despite a probe encouraging comments about alcohol-related issues. This stands in contrast to findings in our other studies (e.g., Slater & Rouner, 1996b), in which college student participants were quite ready to generate counterarguments concerning negative discussion of alcohol use. The relative absence of counterarguments, of course, is consistent with the Extended ELM proposition that counterarguing is not compatible with the suspension of disbelief necessary to process narrative.

Another point of contrast between the ELM and the Extended ELM concerned the variables that would predict the amount of central processing. In the ELM, of course, central processing (operationalized as the predominance of thought elaborations concerning substantive message content) is predicted by issue involvement. The Extended ELM, by contrast, argues that in the context of entertainment or narrative messages, such processing will be predicted by narrative interest and identification with protagonists, not by issue-related involvement. Results indicated that the relative proportion of persuasive content-related comments to total comments was in fact predicted by narrative interest and identification (although identification proved to be a more complex and multidimensional construct than anticipated), not by involvement with the topic (Slater & Rouner, 1997).

More recently, Green and Brock (2000) demonstrated how persuasive influence as the result of reading fictional passages was a function of what they called *transportation*, conceptually equivalent to extent of engagement with a narrative. In particular, they succeeded (after several abortive attempts) in the difficult task of experimentally manipulating hedonic versus didactic processing of a fictional narrative, and they demonstrated greater persuasive effects in the hedonic case. Further analyses distinguished effects of transportation from effects of value-relevant or outcome-relevant involvement. These results, of course, are consistent with the predictions of the Extended ELM as outlined in Slater (1997).

DIRECTIONS FOR FUTURE RESEARCH INTO THE EXTENDED ELABORATION LIKELIHOOD MODEL

The studies just described are, of course, only first steps in building on the Extended ELM framework. They illustrate the distinctive opportunities and methodological challenges of such research. I discuss the methodological challenges and associated research strategies before expanding on the opportunities.

Propositions of the Extended ELM can be most cleanly tested by comparing alternative processing strategies. However, it is not easy to do so experimentally. It is hard to imagine a clean experimental manipulation in which the same template message appears as a narrative and as a didactic or conventionally persuasive message. There are simply too many confounding differences that can be introduced when constructing these very different kinds of messages (Jackson, O'Keefe, & Jacobs, 1988; Slater, 1991).

The studies reviewed in this chapter provide several alternative strategies for coping with this difficulty. The simplest strategy is to avoid direct comparisons of the very different processing strategies altogether and instead to elaborate the mediating and moderating variables that may characterize each processing context separately. The Slater and Rouner (1997) and Stephenson (1999, in press) studies take this approach.

However, from the theory-testing perspective, direct comparative tests of processing contexts and models are desirable. In the case of value-affirmative versus value-protective processing, one can elicit comparisons simply by exposing people with different initial value stances to the same message, thereby creating a quasi-experimental but attractively valid and naturalistic comparison, as was done in Slater and Rouner (1996b). A classic manipulation technique is to attempt to cue different processing strategies through task instructions. From the Extended ELM perspective, such an approach might prove unsatisfactory. The experimenter can only hope that his or her task instructions succeed in motivating processing in a manner sufficiently similar to the motivations that arise when receivers encounter a given message genre and topic. However, Tewksbury's (1999) and Green and Brock's (2000) effective use of such task instruction manipulations to elicit distinctive processing strategies is encouraging in this regard.

Perhaps the most telling lesson from the studies reviewed, however, pertains to opportunities for expanding our knowledge of how people's beliefs may be influenced by many types and genres of messages typically unexamined by persuasion researchers. Each study described, while generally supporting key propositions of the Extended ELM, also introduces additional mediating and contingency variables that serve to further the understanding of each persuasive processing context. Examples include evidence type in Slater and Rouner (1996b), expertise and political stance in Tewksbury (1999), sensation seeking in Stephenson (1999), and types of identification in Slater and Rouner (1997). A very extensive literature has developed over two decades examining many issues regarding processing of outcome- or issue-relevant messages in the traditional ELM. It is likely that studies of persuasion processes in all processing contexts, such as entertainment, education, and news, have the potential to evolve a similarly elaborated knowledge base. The Extended ELM framework described here and in Slater (1997) is intended as a starting point or a skeleton on which such a body of knowledge can be fleshed out.

From this perspective, the persuasion research field has only begun to explore its potential to address central theoretical and applied research problems in social influence and media effects. The conceptual and methodological strengths of research in persuasion processes, most notably those developed in the ELM, can be applied to understanding intended or unintended message effects on beliefs, attitudes, and behavior across a variety of media genres. This provides a means of better understanding media effects due to news coverage, entertainment programming, and educational materials as well as due to traditional persuasive genres such as political discourse and consumer advertising. The future domain of persuasion research should prove much larger in the future than should the study of overtly persuasive messages alone.

NOTE

1. Petty and Cacioppo (1986) discuss the biased processing of counterattitudinal messages. This discussion is conceptually less developed, however, than their treatment of standard issue-relevant processing. The Heuristic-Systematic Model (Chaiken, 1987) also addresses processing of issue-relevant messages from a more explicitly motivational perspective.

REFERENCES

Andrews, C. J., Durvasala, S., & Akhter, S. H. (1990). A framework for conceptualizing and measuring the involvement construct in advertising research. *Journal of Advertising, 19,* 27-40.

Baesler, E. J., & Burgoon, J. K. (1994). The temporal effects of story and statistical evidence on belief change. *Communication Research, 21,* 582-602.

Ball-Rokeach, S., & DeFleur, M. (1982). *Theories of mass communication.* New York: Longman.

Bandura, A. (1986). *Social foundations of thought and action.* Englewood Cliffs, NJ: Prentice Hall.

Blumler, J., & Katz, E. (1974). *The uses of mass communication.* Beverly Hills, CA: Sage.

Bogart, L. (1984). The public's use and perception of newspapers. *Public Opinion Quarterly, 48,* 709-719.

Burnkrant, R. E., & Sawyer, A. G. (1983). Effects of involvement and message content on information-processing intensity. In R. J. Harris (Ed.), *Information processing research in advertising* (pp. 43-64). Hillsdale, NJ: Lawrence Erlbaum.

Cameron, G. T. (1993). Spreading activation and involvement: An experimental test of a cognitive model of involvement. *Journalism and Mass Communication Quarterly, 70,* 854-867.

Chaiken, S. (1987). The Heuristic Model of persuasion. In M. P. Zanna, J. M. Olson, & C. P. Herman (Eds.), *Social influence: The Ontario Symposium* (Vol. 5, pp. 3-39). Hillsdale, NJ: Lawrence Erlbaum.

Craik, F. I. M., & Lockhart, R. S. (1972). Levels of processing: A framework for memory research. *Journal of Learning and Verbal Behavior, 11,* 671-684.

Eastman, S. T., & Newton, G. D. (1995). Delineating grazing: Observations of remote control use. *Journal of Communication, 45,* 77-95.

Fazio, R. H., Powell, M. C., & Williams, C. J. (1989). The role of attitude accessibility in the attitude-to-behavior process. *Journal of Consumer Research, 16,* 280-288.

Gerbner, G., Gross, L., Morgan, M., & Signorielli, N. (1994). Growing up with television: The cultivation perspective. In J. Bryant & D. Zillmann (Eds.), *Media effects: Advances in theory and research* (pp. 17-42). Hillsdale, NJ: Lawrence Erlbaum.

Gilbert, D. S. (1991). How mental systems believe. *American Psychologist, 46,* 107-119.

Graesser, A. C. (1981). *Prose comprehension beyond the word.* New York: Springer-Verlag.

Green, M. C., & Brock, T. C. (2000). The role of transportation in the persuasiveness of public narratives. *Journal of Personality and Social Psychology, 79,* 701-721.

Greenwald, A. G., & Leavitt, C. (1984). Audience involvement in advertising: Four levels. *Journal of Consumer Research, 11,* 581-592.

Grunig, J. (1989). Sierra Club study shows who become activists. *Public Relations Review, 15*(8), 3-24.

Hamilton, M. A., Hunter, J. E., & Boster, F. J. (1993). The Elaboration Likelihood Model as a theory of attitude formation: A mathematical analysis. *Communication Theory, 3,* 50-65.

Harmon, R. R., & Coney, K. A. (1982). The persuasive effects of source credibility in buy and lease situations. *Journal of Marketing Research, 19,* 225-260.

Jackson, S., O'Keefe, D. J., & Jacobs, S. (1988). The search for reliable generalization about messages: A comparison of research strategies. *Human Communication Research, 15,* 127-142.

Johnson, B. T., & Eagly, A. H. (1989). Effects of involvement on persuasion: A meta-analysis. *Psychological Bulletin, 106,* 290-314.

Kazoleas, D. C. (1993). A comparison of the effects of qualitative versus quantitative evidence: A test of explanatory hypotheses. *Communication Quarterly, 41,* 40-50.

Kim, J., & Rubin, A. M. (1997). The variable influence of audience activity on media effects. *Communication Research, 24,* 107-135.

Kincaid, D. L. (1993, May). *Using television dramas to accelerate social change.* Paper presented at the annual conference of the International Communication Association, Health Communication Division. Washington, DC.

Krugman, H. E. (1965). The impact of television advertising: Learning without involvement. *Public Opinion Quarterly, 29,* 349-356.

Lasswell, H. D. (1948). The structure and function of communication in society. In L. Bryson (Ed.), *The communication of ideas* (pp. 32-51). New York: Institute for Religious and Social Studies.

Mandler, J. M., & Johnson, N. S. (1980). Remembrance of things parsed: Story structure and recall. *Cognitive Psychology, 9,* 111-151.

McCombs, M. E., & Shaw, D. L. (1972). The agenda-setting function of the mass media. *Public Opinion Quarterly, 36,* 176-188.

Mitchell, A. A. (1979). Involvement: A potentially important mediator of consumer behavior. In W. Wilkie (Ed.), *Advances in consumer research* (Vol. 6, pp. 191-196). Ann Arbor, MI: Association for Consumer Research.

Mongeau, P. A., & Stiff, J. B. (1993). Specifying causal relationships in the Elaboration Likelihood Model. *Communication Theory, 3,* 65-72.

Olson, J. M., & Zanna, M. P. (1979). A new look at selective exposure. *Journal of Experimental Social Psychology, 15,* 1-15.

Palmgreen, P. (1984). Uses and gratifications: A theoretical perspective. In R. N. Bostrom (Ed.), *Communication Yearbook 8* (pp. 20-55). Beverly Hills, CA: Sage.

Park, C. W., & Mittal, B. (1985). A theory of involvement in consumer behavior: Problems and issues. In J. N. Sheth (Ed.), *Research in consumer behavior* (pp. 201-231). Greenwich, CT: JAI.

Perloff, R. M. (1993). *The dynamics of persuasion.* Hillsdale, NJ: Lawrence Erlbaum.

Petty, R. E., & Cacioppo, J. T. (1986). *Communication and persuasion: Central and peripheral routes to attitude change.* New York: Springer-Verlag.

Piotrow, P. T., Kincaid, D. L., Rimon, J. G., & Rinehart, W. (1997). *Health communication: Lessons from family planning and reproductive health.* Westport, CT: Praeger.

Potts, G. R., St. John, M. F., & Kirson, D. (1989). Incorporating new information into existing world knowledge. *Cognitive Psychology, 21,* 303-333.

Price, V., & Allen, S. (1990). Opinion spirals, silent and otherwise: Applying small-group research to public opinion phenomena. *Communication Research, 17,* 369-392.

Reinard, J. C. (1988). The empirical study of the persuasive effects of evidence: The status after fifty years of research. *Human Communication Research, 15,* 3-59.

Salmon, C. T. (1986). Perspectives on involvement in consumer and communication research. In B. Dervin & M. J. Voigt (Eds.), *Progress in communication sciences* (Vol. 7, pp. 243-269). Norwood, NJ: Ablex.

Sherif, M., & Hovland, C. I. (1961). *Social judgment: Assimilation and contrast effects in communication and attitude change.* New Haven, CT: Yale University Press.

Singhal, A., & Rogers, E. M. (1999). *Entertainment-education: A communication strategy for social change.* Mahwah, NJ: Lawrence Erlbaum.

Slater, M. D. (1990). Processing social information in messages: Social group familiarity, fiction vs. non-fiction, and subsequent beliefs. *Communication Research, 17,* 327-343.

Slater, M. D. (1991). Use of message stimuli in mass communication experimentation: A methodological assessment and discussion. *Journalism Quarterly, 68,* 412-421.

Slater, M. D. (1997). Persuasion processes across receiver goals and message genres. *Communication Theory, 7,* 125-148.

Slater, M. D. (in press). The persuasive impact of entertainment narratives: Examples and theoretical explanations. In T. Brock, J. J. Strange, & M. C. Green (Eds.), *Narrative impact: Social and cognitive foundations.* Mahwah, NJ: Erlbaum.

Slater, M. D., & Rouner, D. (1992). Confidence in beliefs about social groups as an outcome of message exposure and its role in belief change persistence. *Communication Research, 19,* 597-617.

Slater, M. D., & Rouner, D. (1996a). How message evaluation and source attributes may influence credibility assessment and belief change. *Journalism and Mass Communication Quarterly, 73,* 974-991.

Slater, M. D., & Rouner, D. (1996b). Value affirmative and value protective processing of alcohol education messages that include statistics or anecdotes. *Communication Research, 23,* 210-235.

Slater, M. D., & Rouner, D. (1997, May). *The processing of narrative fiction containing persuasive content about alcohol use: Effects of gender and outcome.* Paper presented at the meeting of the International Communication Association, Information Systems Division. Montreal.

Stephenson, M. T. (1999). *Message sensation value and sensation seeking as determinants of message processing.* Unpublished dissertation, University of Kentucky.

Stephenson, M. T. (in press). Sensation seeking as a moderator of the processing of anti-heroin PSAs. *Communication Studies, 53*(3).

Stroh, P. K. (1995). Voters as pragmatic cognitive misers: The accuracy-effort trade-off in the candidate evaluation process. In M. Lodge & K. McGraw (Eds.), *Political judgment: Structure and process* (pp. 207-228). Ann Arbor: University of Michigan Press.

Tewksbury, D. (1999). Differences in how we watch the news: The impact of processing goals and expertise on evaluations of political actors. *Communication Research, 26*(1), 4-29.

Wyer, R. S., Srull, T. K., Gordon, S. E., & Hartwick, J. (1982). Effects of processing objectives on the recall of prose material. *Journal of Personality and Social Psychology, 43,* 674-688.

11

The Heuristic-Systematic
Model of Social Information Processing

ALEXANDER TODOROV
SHELLY CHAIKEN
MARLONE D. HENDERSON

Persuasion has been a major topic of study for scholars interested in attitude change (Eagly & Chaiken, 1993). Earlier cognitive theories focused on how people process the quality of persuasion messages (Greenwald, 1968; McGuire, 1968). For example, persuasion effects were conceptualized in terms of the attention allocated to the message, the comprehension of the message content, and the acceptance of the message conclusions (Hovland, Janis, & Kelley, 1953). Unlike these message-based theories of persuasion, the Heuristic-Systematic Model (HSM) (Chaiken, 1980, 1987), together with the Elaboration Likelihood Model (ELM) (Petty & Cacioppo, 1981, 1986b), recognized a host of variables conceptually independent of message quality that influence people. Most important, according to both the HSM and the ELM, these variables can trigger qualitatively different information processing.

Although people can carefully attend to and elaborate on the content of a persuasion message, they can also process the message quite superficially, attending only to cues peripheral to its content such as the length of the message and the source of the message. The HSM attempts to characterize these two modes of processing—systematic and heuristic—and to specify the conditions that trigger and govern a specific mode of processing. We hasten to add that the two modes of information processing (systematic vs. heuristic) are not linked in one-to-one fashion with the types of informational cues (message content vs. other cues), as suggested by some researchers (Kruglanski & Thompson, 1999). The critical assumption of the HSM is that people can engage in systematic or heuristic processing. People can scrutinize cues peripheral to the message content, or they can process the message content heuristically. The

HSM is a dual-process model (Chaiken & Trope, 1999) positing two concurrent modes of qualitatively different social information processing.

The HSM has undergone several major developments. Initially, the model specified the two modes of heuristic and systematic processing (Chaiken, 1980, 1987). Then, the model was extended to specify the psychological conditions for triggering the modes of processing in terms of the discrepancy between actual and desired subjective confidence (Chaiken, Liberman, & Eagly, 1989). Finally, in addition to the accuracy motivation assumed to be present in most persuasion situations, the HSM was extended to include two other types of underlying motivations: defensive and impression motivation (Chaiken, Giner-Sorolla, & Chen, 1996). As a general model of social information processing, the HSM has been applied to a wide range of phenomena (e.g., Bohner, Moskowitz, & Chaiken, 1995; Chen & Chaiken, 1999).

In the first part of this chapter, we outline the main assumptions of the HSM and review research supporting the model's assumptions. In the second part, we lay out directions for future research.

ASSUMPTIONS ABOUT THE NATURE OF INFORMATION PROCESSING

People rarely process information in perfect conditions. There are both environmental and cognitive constraints on information processing. These constraints have given rise to the metaphor of the cognitive miser (Fiske & Taylor, 1991). In this metaphor, people are economy-minded, investing cognitive effort in a task only when given sufficient motivation and cognitive resources. Consistent with this assumption, the HSM posits that people engage in systematic processing of persuasive

information only when they are sufficiently motivated. In a systematic mode, people consider all relevant pieces of information, elaborate on these pieces of information, and form a judgment based on these elaborations.

However, if people are not sufficiently motivated or do not have sufficient cognitive resources, they can engage in superficial or heuristic processing of available information. In a heuristic mode, people consider a few informational cues—or even a single informational cue—and form a judgment based on these cues. For instance, such cues may be the source of the message or the length of the message. That is, people use a simple decision rule such as "Experts can be trusted" to arrive at a conclusion instead of scrutinizing the quality of persuasive arguments.

The signature finding of dual-process models of persuasion is the dissociation between the effects of relatively important message content variables and the effects of relatively unimportant message variables on persuasion (Chaiken, 1980, 1987; Petty & Cacioppo, 1981, 1986a, 1986b). People induced to process persuasion information systematically differentiate between strong and weak arguments and are unaffected by variables irrelevant to substantive message content such as the length of the message. People induced to process information heuristically do not differentiate between strong and weak messages and instead are affected by ostensibly less important informational cues such as the attractiveness of the message source. For example, participants who expected to discuss a persuasion message later were affected by the number of persuasive arguments but were not affected by the attractiveness of the communicator. Presumably, the importance of the message induced systematic processing. By contrast, participants who did not expect to discuss the message were affected by the attractiveness of the communicator but were not affected by the number of persuasive arguments (Chaiken, 1980). The message was not important for the latter group of participants, and they processed it heuristically.

To obtain dissociations in effects of persuasion variables on attitudes, one needs to manipulate either the motivation of the participants or their cognitive resources and/or ability to process information. Motivational variables that have been shown to affect the mode of processing include the personal relevance of the persuasion message (Chaiken, 1980; Johnson & Eagly, 1989; Petty & Cacioppo, 1979, 1986b, 1990), the need for cognition (Cacioppo, Petty, Kao, & Rodriguez, 1986), task importance (Maheswaran & Chaiken, 1991), accountability for one's attitudes (Tetlock, 1983), and exposure to unexpected message content (Maheswaran & Chaiken, 1991). Cognitive resource variables that affect the mode of processing include distraction (Festinger & Maccoby, 1964; Osterhouse & Brock, 1970; Petty, Wells, & Brock, 1976), message repetition (Cacioppo & Petty, 1979, 1985), time pressure (Moore, Hausknecht, & Thamodaran, 1986; Ratneshwar & Chaiken, 1991), communication modality (Eagly & Chaiken, 1993), and knowledge and expertise (Alba & Marmorstein, 1987; Wood, 1982).

We should note that to find evidence for different modes of processing, it is not sufficient to demonstrate dissociation effects of persuasion variables on attitudes at the level of the group means. In addition, one should show that in a systematic mode, issue-related thoughts mediate the effect of persuasion variables on attitudes. Similarly in a heuristic mode, heuristic cues should have direct effects on attitudes.

Characteristics of Systematic and Heuristic Processing

Systematic processing is a comprehensive analytic orientation to information processing. In a systematic mode, people scrutinize available persuasion information for its relevance to their task. They evaluate the validity of the advocated position by scrutinizing the persuasive information and relating this information to their previous knowledge of the persuasion issue. Persuasion in a systematic mode is mediated by the person's understanding and cognitive elaboration of the persuasion message. By definition, systematic processing consists of extensive processing of persuasion arguments and therefore is constrained by the person's cognitive resources and motivation. Although people might not be aware of the exact nature of their systematic processing, they are aware of the contents of their message-related thoughts, and in fact such thoughts should mediate the persuasion effects in a systematic mode (e.g., Chaiken & Maheswaran, 1994).

Heuristic processing is a nonanalytic orientation to information processing. In a heuristic mode, people focus on that subset of information that enables them to use simple decision rules or heuristics (cf. Tversky & Kahneman, 1974) to form a judgment. Persuasion effects are mediated by simple rules, schemata, or heuristics that associate heuristic cues with a probability that the advocated position is valid. Such heuristics are derived from experience and have some empirical validity. For instance, some persuasion heuristics are "Experts can be trusted" and "Consensus implies correctness." Heuristics are triggered by the presence of relevant heuristic cues. For instance, the presentation of the results of an opinion poll in which the majority of respondents agree with the advocated position can trigger the "Consensus implies correctness" heuristic. In this case, the heuristic cue (the majority of respondents agree) is associated with a high probability that the advocated persuasive position is valid. Because heuristic processing uses a subset of available information, it is constrained by the person's cognitive resources and motivation to a lesser extent than is systematic processing. Furthermore, people may be completely unaware of their heuristic processing. In fact, they may deny that they were influenced by peripheral informational cues that seem irrelevant to the advocated position (Chen & Chaiken, 1999).

Conditions of Heuristic Use

The schemata or heuristics used in heuristic processing are stored in memory as are other knowledge structures. As such, heuristics are governed by principles of knowledge activation and use (Higgins, 1996). Three general principles of knowledge use are availability, accessibility, and applicability. *Availability* refers to the storage of a knowledge structure in memory (Tulving & Pearlstone, 1966). In research on heuristic processing, it has been assumed that the studied heuristics were in fact stored in the participant's memory. This assumption is plausible because most of the studied heuristics are socially shared. Note that this does not imply that most people endorse these heuristics. In short, a heuristic is available if there is a stored heuristic representation in one's memory.

Although availability is a necessary condition for heuristic use, it is not a sufficient condition. According to the *accessibility* principle, a knowledge representation should be activated or accessible in memory in order to be used (Higgins, 1996; Sedikides & Skowronski, 1991). The triggering of heuristics from heuristic cues is related to the accessibility principle. Highly salient persuasion cues associated with decision heuristics make these heuristics more accessible in memory, increasing the likelihood of their use. In addition to these factors external to the person, heuristics can be chronically accessible if the heuristics are frequently used (Higgins, King, & Mavin, 1982). The accessibility of heuris-

tics can be linked not only to the likelihood of their use but also to the confidence conferred by a judgment based on a heuristic. As suggested by Chen and Chaiken (1999), the degree of accessibility of a heuristic can translate into judgmental confidence. In turn, confidence has specific implications about heuristic and systematic processing.

Even if a knowledge structure is accessible in memory, it may not be used if the accessible knowledge is not applicable to the informational task (Todorov, 2000). *Applicability* refers to the degree of appropriateness of the activated knowledge to the judgmental task. For nonconscious forms of processing, applicability refers to the degree of match or the overlap of features of the accessible knowledge and the judgmental stimulus (Higgins, 1989, 1996). The higher the match, the stronger the effect of the accessible knowledge on the judgment. For more complex judgmental situations such as persuasion, applicability refers to the perceived relevance of the accessible knowledge. For example, even if a heuristic comes readily to mind, it will be used only if the person believes that the heuristic is relevant to the specific persuasion task.

Chaiken, Axsom, Liberman, and Wilson (1992) studied the role of accessibility and applicability for a specific persuasion heuristic: "Length implies strength." This heuristic was primed or made accessible for all participants. Participants who perceived this heuristic as reliable used the heuristic in evaluating short versus long persuasion arguments. However, the priming did not affect participants who did not perceive the heuristic as reliable. This study shows that applicability constrains accessibility effects.

Whether a heuristic is judged as relevant to the task at hand may change as a function of the person's motivation. For instance, Darke et al. (1998) presented participants with results of an opinion poll in which the majority agreed with the advocated position. The critical manipulation was the sample size of the poll. Participants were told that the poll was based on either the responses of 10 persons or the responses of 1,000 persons. Participants low in accuracy motivation were influenced by consensus opinion independent of sample size, whereas participants high in accuracy motivation used the "Consensus implies correctness" heuristic only when the poll was based on the large sample.

Interactions of Systematic and Heuristic Processing

A major issue for any dual-process model is how the two processes interact (Gilbert, 1999). For example, one can posit that the two processes are mutually exclusive. If the one is operating, then the other one is turned off. Or one may posit that the two processes are in competition. Alternatively, the two processes may act in concert. Additional issues involve the temporal characteristics of the processes. Do the processes operate in a sequential fashion or in parallel?

Unlike dual-process models assuming that central/systematic processes exclude peripheral/heuristic processes (Petty & Cacioppo, 1986b), the HSM posits that systematic and heuristic processes can act simultaneously. Furthermore, the HSM specifies the nature of the interaction of these processes. How the modes of processing interact depends on the implications of the information brought to mind by heuristic and systematic processing and on the ambiguity of the persuasion message. The HSM has outlined and provided evidence for three hypotheses concerning the interplay of systematic and heuristic processing: the additivity, attenuation, and bias hypotheses.

When the judgmental implications of heuristic cues and arguments are consistent, heuristic and systematic processing can have inde-

pendent and additive effects on persuasion. This is the *additivity* hypothesis of the model. For example, in one study participants were asked to evaluate a consumer product. When a "brand name" heuristic was consistent with the evaluative implications of the information about the product's attributes, participants who believed that their decisions were important based their product evaluations on the implications derived from both heuristic and systematic processing (Maheswaran, Mackie, & Chaiken, 1992; see also Chaiken & Maheswaran, 1994; Darke et al., 1998; Maheswaran & Chaiken, 1991).

Most of the evidence for dual-process models comes from pitting the judgmental implications of heuristic and systematic processing. For instance, an expert source delivers a message that consists of weak arguments. This is the situation where one can clearly see the contributions of systematic and heuristic processing under different levels of motivation. The *attenuation* hypothesis of the HSM states that in a situation where the implications of heuristic and systematic processing are in opposition, the implications derived from systematic processing can overwrite or attenuate the impact of heuristics given that people are sufficiently motivated. For example, highly motivated participants who were presented with consensus cue information inconsistent with the attributes of a consumer product based their judgments solely on their cognitions about the product's attributes (Maheswaran & Chaiken, 1991).

The additivity and attenuation hypotheses do not exhaust the possibilities of interplay between systematic and heuristic processing. Most persuasion experiments use unambiguous information. That is, the persuasion arguments are either strong or weak. However, in many everyday influence situations, the persuasive message may consist of strong arguments mixed with weak arguments. The *bias* hypothesis of the HSM was designed to account for such situations. The bias hypothesis states that an ambiguous persuasion message can be interpreted in line with a preceding heuristic cue even if people are highly accuracy motivated. For example, the same ambiguous message can be interpreted differently if the person believes that the message source is reliable than if the person believes that the source is unreliable. Chaiken and Maheswaran (1994) conducted such a study. In this study, participants were asked to evaluate a consumer product. They believed that the description of the product appeared either in *Consumer Reports* (a reliable source) or in a promotional pamphlet of Kmart (an unreliable source). When the description of the product was unambiguous, the study replicated the basic dissociation finding characteristic for dual-process models. Participants high in motivation were influenced by the strength of the product attributes, whereas participants low in motivation were influenced by source credibility. However, the pattern of findings for the ambiguous product description looked the same for participants both low and high in motivation. Participants were influenced more by the reliable source. Although the mean effects looked identical, mediational analyses showed that the processes for participants low and high in motivation differed. Participants low in motivation processed the product description heuristically and were thus affected by source reliability only. Participants high in motivation processed the description systematically, but their cognitions were colored by the credibility of the source. When the source was reliable, these participants generated more favorable thoughts about the product.

The bias hypothesis has also received considerable support outside the field of persuasion research. For example, Trope and Gaunt (1999) showed that contextual cues can affect person perception when information about the person is ambiguous. More important, this research has demonstrated that the effect of contextual cues on perception is implicit. That is, people are not aware of the biasing effect of context, believing that their perceptions are a veridical reading of reality. Similarly, in persuasion contexts, people might not recognize the biasing nature of heuristic cues even when they are highly motivated to be accurate.

Motivational Assumptions

We have described the systematic and heuristic modes of processing and how they interact. However, we have not discussed in detail one of the most important questions for any dual-process model. This question is about the triggering conditions for a processing mode. We noted that heuristic processing is less dependent on the availability of cognitive resources and, as such, can be triggered by external factors that constrain cognitive capacity. Such external conditions include time pressure and distraction (Moore et al., 1986; Petty et al., 1976; Ratneshwar & Chaiken, 1991). More important, we noted that people need to be sufficiently motivated to process information systematically. What is the meaning of sufficiently motivated?

The HSM makes two motivational assumptions. The first specifies the internal conditions for triggering systematic processing; in other words, it defines sufficient motivation. The second assumption specifies qualitatively different types of motivation that can be present in a persuasion situation. These two assumptions are about the quantitative and qualitative nature of motivation.

The quantitative assumption is expressed in the model's sufficiency principle (Chaiken et al., 1989, 1996). The sufficiency principle conceptualizes motivation to engage in information processing as a function of the discrepancy between the person's actual confidence and the person's desired confidence for a specific judgment task. The bigger the (negative) discrepancy between actual and desired confidence, the more likely the person is to engage in systematic processing. The sufficiency principle tries to strike a balance between the principle of least effort (people prefer less effortful information processing) and the person's accuracy concerns (people desire to make accurate judgments).

The sufficiency principle is directly linked to the selection of a mode of processing. This principle specifies that people will engage in systematic processing only if their actual confidence is lower than their desired confidence. Thus, desired confidence serves as a sufficiency threshold for triggering systematic processing. In fact, people should increase their processing effort as a function of the discrepancy between actual and desired confidence. In situations where actual confidence is higher than the desired confidence, people would not engage in systematic processing. Processing effort can be increased either by increasing the person's desired confidence, by decreasing the person's actual confidence, or by both mechanisms.

We noted earlier that a number of motivational variables such as personal relevance of the persuasion issue, task importance, accountability, and need for cognition induce systematic processing. According to the sufficiency principle, these variables induce systematic processing because they increase the person's desired judgmental confidence. For instance, participants who are presented with a personally relevant message should desire higher confidence in assessing the validity of the message than should participants presented with a personally irrelevant message. If, as assumed by the HSM, people believe that systematic processing of persuasion information can increase their judgmental confidence, they should increase their processing effort when the message is personally relevant.

The likelihood of systematic processing can be enhanced not only by increasing the person's desired confidence but also by reducing the person's actual confidence. Maheswaran and Chaiken (1991) presented participants with consensus information that was either congruent or incongruent with the valence of a persuasion message. The incongruence condition was designed to undermine the participants' actual confidence. In line with the hypothesis, participants who were not highly motivated but who received incongruent information showed substantial systematic processing.

What happens if people are sufficiently motivated but lack the ability or resources to engage in systematic processing? The HSM predicts that in such conditions, people should scrutinize the persuasion setting for relevant heuristic cues (Chaiken et al., 1989). That is, this enhancement hypothesis states that motivational variables such as personal relevance should increase heuristic processing under conditions of limited cognitive resources.

Types of Motivation in the HSM

Research on persuasion generally assumes that people are accuracy motivated. Indeed, in its early development, the HSM was based on this assumption (Chaiken, 1980, 1987). Recognizing that in many situations motives other than accuracy exist, the HSM has been extended to include two new broad types of motivation: defense motivation and impression motivation (Chaiken et al., 1989, 1996).

Accuracy-motivated people strive to achieve valid attitudes that are consistent with reality. Accuracy-motivated processing can be characterized as an open-minded processing in which persuasion information is treated evenhandedly. The most important objective for an accuracy-motivated person is to make judgments that square with the relevant objective facts. Two things should be noted about accuracy motivation. First, accuracy motivation does not exclude biased processing. For example, systematic processing can be biased by prior knowledge or by prior heuristic cues (Chaiken & Maheswaran, 1994). Nevertheless, accuracy-motivated people strive to be objective even if the processing is biased. Second, accuracy can be achieved either by systematic processing, heuristic processing, or both. Although heuristic processing can lead to less accurate judgments than systematic processing, heuristics are grounded in experience and under certain conditions can be accurate.

In contrast to accuracy motivation, defense motivation can be characterized as a closed-minded form of processing. The concept of defense motivation is related to concepts such as position involvement (Chaiken & Stangor, 1987), self-evaluation maintenance (Tesser, 1988), value-relevant involvement (Johnson & Eagly, 1989), and motivated reasoning (Kunda, 1990). In the framework of the HSM, defense-motivated people strive to defend beliefs and attitudes that are consistent with the person's vested interest or self-definitional attitudes and beliefs (Chaiken et al., 1996). Self-definitional attitudes and beliefs are closely tied to the self. For instance, these can include values and personal attributes. The defense-motivated person tries to preserve one's self-concept and associated worldviews. The processing objective in defense motivation is to confirm the validity of preferred attitudinal positions and to disconfirm the validity of nonpreferred attitudinal positions.

As in the case of accuracy motivation, defense-motivated processing can be either systematic, heuristic, or both. In fact, the HSM posits that defense-motivated people use the same heuristics that accuracy-motivated people use but use them in a selective fashion. That is, heuristics that are congruent with the attitudes of the defense-motivated person are likely to be used, whereas heuristics incongruent with these attitudes are likely to be ignored. To demonstrate this effect, Giner-Sorolla and Chaiken (1997) presented participants who had vested interests in the persuasion issue with a consensus cue heuristic in the form of poll results. When the poll results supported the participants' vested interests, they rated the poll as more reliable and criticized it less. In fact, the attitudes of these participants were primarily based on their heuristic processing of the congruent consensus cue information.

The HSM predicts that when defense motivation is high and people have sufficient cognitive resources, they will engage in systematic but biased processing of the information. Information congruent with the preexisting attitudes will be rated favorably, and information incongruent with these attitudes will be scrutinized to be disconfirmed. This has been confirmed by a number of studies (Ditto & Lopez, 1992; Liberman & Chaiken, 1992; Lord, Ross, & Lepper, 1979; Pomerantz, Chaiken, & Tordesillas, 1995; Pyszczynski & Greenberg, 1987).

Like accuracy-motivated processing, the processing in the case of defense motivation follows the sufficiency principle. However, unlike in the case of accuracy motivation, the sufficiency threshold in defense motivation is determined by the degree to which processing reinforces self-definitional attitudes and not by the degree to which processing yields an accurate judgment. The mode of processing triggered in defense motivation will depend on the discrepancy between actual and desired confidence. For example, heuristic cues incongruent with the person's preferred position would reduce the person's actual confidence, thereby extending the confidence gap. Thus, the person should engage in biased systematic processing to reduce this gap. Alternatively, heuristic cues congruent with the person's position can increase the person's actual confidence so that little confidence gap exists, and thus the person may engage in little (if any) systematic processing.

Recognizing the role of interpersonal factors in persuasion, the extended HSM also includes a third broad type of motivation: impression motivation. The concept of impression motivation is related to concepts such as impression-relevant involvement (Johnson & Eagly, 1989), impression management (Schlenker, 1980), and response involvement (Leippe & Elkin, 1987; Zimbardo, 1960). Impression motivation refers to the desire to express socially acceptable attitudes or attitudes and beliefs that satisfy the person's immediate social goals. The processing objective of impression motivation is to assess the social acceptability of alternative positions. Impression-motivated people are mainly concerned with the interpersonal consequences of expressing an attitude in the specific persuasion setting (Chaiken et al., 1996).

As in the case of defense motivation, impression-motivated persons use heuristics selectively. Furthermore, there are specific heuristics related to impression motivation situations. For example, people may use the heuristic "Moderate opinions minimize disagreements" if they expect to interact with a person with unknown views. Alternatively, if the expected interaction partner has known views, people may use the heuristic "Go along to get along." In fact, previous research has shown that impression-motivated participants express views that mirror the views of an expected audience or express moderate views when the audience position is unknown (Cialdini, Levy, Herman, & Evenbeck, 1973; McFarland, Ross, & Conway, 1984; Tetlock, 1983).

Similar to accuracy and defense motivations, processing predictions in the case of impression motivation follow the sufficiency principle. The sufficiency threshold in the lat-

ter case corresponds to the desired confidence that the person's judgments will satisfy the person's immediate interpersonal concerns. If the sufficiency threshold is high and heuristic processing does not close the gap between actual and desired confidence, people may engage in systematic processing that is biased toward achieving their social goals.

To obtain evidence for biased systematic processing, Chen, Schecter, and Chaiken (1996, Experiment 2) primed participants either with accuracy motivation or with impression motivation (in an ostensibly unrelated first task). All participants expected a discussion about a social issue with a person who held either a favorable or an unfavorable attitude toward the issue. Prior to this discussion (which in fact did not take place), participants were presented with an essay on the issue and asked to list their thoughts and indicate their attitudes. As expected, accuracy-motivated participants based their attitudes on their evenhanded systematic processing of the essay arguments, and their attitudes were not affected by their communication partner's attitude. By contrast, the attitudes of impression-motivated participants were in line with their partner's attitude. The heuristic "Go along to get along" biased the more effortful systematic processing of the essay arguments by these participants.

Summary

The HSM posits two qualitatively different modes of information processing. People can either process information systematically (attending to all relevant pieces of information) or process heuristically (focusing only on a subset of informational cues). More important, these modes can act simultaneously. If the implications of the processing modes are congruent, they have additive effects on persuasion. If the implications are incongruent, systematic processing attenuates the impact of heuristic processing. Finally, when persuasion arguments are ambiguous, heuristic cues can bias their interpretation independent of the person's motivation. The selection of mode of processing depends on both external and internal factors. External factors that reduce cognitive capacity are likely to lead to heuristic processing. Factors that increase motivation can lead to systematic processing. This motivational principle is captured by the sufficiency principle, which posits that processing effort is a function of the discrepancy between the person's actual and desired confidence. The HSM also recognizes three underlying motivations. People can be accuracy motivated, trying to achieve valid judgments. People can be defense motivated, trying to preserve valued attitudes. People can also be impression motivated, trying to satisfy interpersonal goals. It is important to emphasize that the type of motivation is conceptually independent of mode of processing. Systematic and heuristic processing can serve any of the three types of motivation. Similarly, processing across motivations follows the predictions of the sufficiency principle.

NEW DIRECTIONS FOR RESEARCH

Taking into account mode of information processing and underlying motivations, the HSM has established itself as a general model of social information processing and has been applied to a number of domains outside persuasion research (e.g., Bohner et al., 1995; Chaiken & Trope, 1999). In the final part of this chapter, we outline new directions for research within the HSM framework. We consider research further clarifying the nature of modes of processing as well as research extending the applications of the model.

Research on the Model's Assumptions

In most of the research we have cited, heuristic processing was closely associated with cues peripheral to the message content. By definition, heuristics are triggered by simple cues. On the other hand, in most research, systematic processing has been closely associated with message content. For instance, systematic processing is often measured in terms of the person's elaboration of persuasive arguments. Because of this seeming confounding of mode of processing and persuasion variables, the HSM has been criticized as confusing persuasion variables with modes of processing (Kruglanski & Thompson, 1999). Presumably, once such confounds are controlled for, a more parsimonious model positing only one type of processing could account for persuasion data. It is true that mode of processing is often empirically correlated with type of persuasion cues. And more often than not, peripheral cues will trigger heuristic rather than systematic processing. However, the nature of mode of processing is conceptually independent of the triggering informational input. The same information can be processed either heuristically or systematically (Chaiken, Duckworth, & Darke, 1999; Chen & Chaiken, 1999).

In fact, a number of studies have demonstrated systematic processing of cues unrelated to message content and heuristic processing of message-related cues. For example, Petty and Cacioppo (1984) showed that unmotivated participants were influenced by the sheer number of arguments in a persuasive message rather than by the semantic content of the arguments (see also Chaiken, 1987; Chaiken et al., 1989; Petty, 1994; Wood, Kallgren, & Preisler, 1985). Similarly, peripheral cues can be processed systematically. As described in the section on conditions of heuristic use, Darke et al. (1998) showed that accuracy-motivated participants processed a heuristic consensus cue systematically. In addition, Shavitt, Swan, Lowrey, and Waenke (1994) found that endorser attractiveness, a peripheral cue, was processed systematically by highly motivated participants when a commercial appealed to public image. This same cue was processed heuristically when the commercial appealed to sensory gratification.

These studies show that one can obtain evidence for systematic and heuristic modes of processing when these modes are not confounded with message cues. However, the Kruglanski and Thompson (1999) criticism helps point to a fruitful and relatively unexplored line of research. Such research would focus on providing *direct* evidence for the qualitatively different nature of systematic and heuristic processing. Direct evidence of this type requires the use of online measures that are independent of informational cues. Online measures assess processing at the time of its occurrence, as opposed to offline measures, which measure the outcome of processing. We sketch a few possible experiments illustrating the utility of such measures.

Because systematic processing is a comprehensive analytic orientation to information processing, systematic processors should be more attentive to new information. To study online inferences during exposure to persuasion arguments, one can present high- and low-motivated participants with a sequence of persuasion arguments on a computer screen. Participants would also perform a secondary lexical decision task in which a string of letters is presented and the participants' task would be to identify whether the letter string is a word or a nonword (Neely, 1977). Response times to lexical decisions are a good indicator of online access to word meaning. Faster response times to the word concept imply faster automatic access to its semantic meaning. In this hypothetical experiment, after each persuasive argument is presented to participants,

they would be presented with a probe word that would summarize the main idea of the argument. The HSM predicts that if highly motivated participants process information systematically, they should be faster to respond to the probe word than should low-motivated participants. This would constitute online evidence for different inferential processes in the systematic versus heuristic modes. Alternatively, one can measure the impact of heuristics by providing probe words related to the heuristic cue (e.g., majority or consensus for the heuristic "Consensus implies correctness").

The experiment described is just one example of a theory-based approach to providing direct evidence for the nature of systematic and heuristic processing. In this approach, one can manipulate variables traditionally used to induce systematic and heuristic processing such as personal involvement and time pressure. What is new in the approach is the focus on online measures of processing. Lexical decision is just one such online measure. Others could include attention span tasks, word fragment completion, reading speed, and false recognition. In all cases, one starts with a specific proposition about the nature of processing and designs an experiment to test this proposition. For example, heuristic processing is defined as focused on a narrow set of cues. In a persuasion situation where heuristic cues are not provided, people who process heuristically could focus on a single argument and ignore the rest of the arguments. One can test this hypothesis by manipulating the salience of arguments relative to the persuasion issue and by including online measures of the speed of inferences. The HSM predicts that the inference speed advantage for participants who process the arguments systematically relative to participants who process them heuristically should disappear for the most salient arguments.

Modes of Processing and Implicit and Explicit Processes

The traditional procedure for assessing systematic processing has been to ask people to list their thoughts during exposure to a message. Although this procedure has been useful, it may overestimate the use of systematic processing. Reporting one's thoughts on a persuasion issue is an explicit measure, which makes one's thoughts a salient basis for making a judgment. The procedure makes people highly aware of their thoughts and may create a consistency demand for providing a judgment congruent with these thoughts. Another problem with this procedure is that it can capture only explicit mental processes.

Two distinctions in the field of social cognition have been increasingly popular and have generated a substantial amount of research: the distinction between automatic and controlled processes (Bargh, 1989, 1994, 1999) and the distinction between implicit and explicit processes (Greenwald & Banaji, 1995). A common idea behind these distinctions is that many mental processes run outside of one's awareness (Uleman & Bargh, 1989). Implicit processes map into those processes. By contrast, explicit processes are intentional and controllable, and people are aware of them.

By definition, systematic processing requires cognitive effort and implies explicit processes (Chen & Chaiken, 1999). However, this definition does not mean that all processes involved in systematic processing are explicit. Most of the inferential work can be completely implicit in the sense that people are not aware of the nature of these inferences. Most likely, both systematic and heuristic processing will turn out to consist of sets of interacting implicit and explicit processes. In other words, the question is not whether systematic processing is explicit and whether heuristic processing is implicit; rather, the question is to

what extent the two modes of processing are linked to implicit processes.

Implicit processes can be captured with online implicit measures. What makes an implicit measure implicit is the fact that the person is not aware of the objective of the measurement (Greenwald & Banaji, 1995). For example, in the hypothetical lexical decision experiment we described, the lexical decision task can be considered an implicit measure. Whereas the person thinks that this task is secondary to the main task (and measures word knowledge), the real objective of the task is to measure inferences related to the presented persuasion arguments. Implicit measures are obviously less reactive than explicit measures. At the same time, they can be used in mediational analyses in the same way explicit measures are used. For instance, a finding that an implicit measure of argument-related inferences mediates the effect of high motivation on judgments would nicely dovetail with the traditional finding that explicit measures, such as thought listing, mediate such motivational effects.

The Bias Hypothesis of the HSM

The purpose of the proposed research we have described is to provide more direct tests of the assumptions of the HSM. However, this research also has practical implications. Implicit processes are generally inaccessible to one's consciousness. Consciousness is a prerequisite for controlled processes. Thus, implicit processes that affect systematic processing can bias people's judgments without their being able to control for this bias. The bias hypothesis of the HSM is a good example of such processes.

As described earlier in this chapter, the HSM's bias hypothesis states that preceding heuristic cues can bias interpretation of an ambiguous persuasion message (Chaiken &

Maheswaran, 1994). More important, the bias is independent of the person's motivation. It is generally assumed that systematic processing leads to better outcomes than does heuristic processing (although caveats do exist). According to the sufficiency principle, one can induce systematic processing either by undermining the actual confidence of the person or by increasing the person's desired confidence. However, this strategy might not work when persuasive arguments are ambiguous.

It is likely that ambiguous persuasion messages are more frequent in real life than in laboratory persuasion research, the latter of which has generally used unambiguous messages. A number of studies have shown that the disambiguation of social information can be an implicit process (Higgins, 1996; Trope, 1986; Trope & Gaunt, 1999). In fact, even contextual cues that are presented subliminally affect interpretation of ambiguous information (Bargh & Pietromonaco, 1982; Erdley & D'Agostino, 1988). Based on this research, there are good reasons to assume that heuristic cues can implicitly bias the interpretation of ambiguous persuasion messages. This can have important practical implications. For instance, persuasion campaigns that cannot be based on unequivocally strong arguments can use mixed strong and weak arguments preceded by positive heuristic cues such as an expert or an attractive source.

Judgmental Accuracy and Mode of Processing

It is widely believed that systematic processing can lead to more accurate judgments than can heuristic processing. This assumption fits a long and honorable tradition of research on biases and heuristics in decision making (Kahneman, Slovic, & Tversky, 1982). This research has shown that judgmental heuristics

can lead to suboptimal decisions. However, in such work, the suboptimality of judgments has always been assessed against some normative statistical standard (Todorov, 1997). Normative standards are not constrained by time and limited resources.

The main reason for the appeal of heuristic reasoning is its efficiency. Such "if-then" reasoning provides shortcuts for making judgments in a changing uncertain environment under limited cognitive and computational resources. Presumably, one has to pay with occasional inaccuracy for this efficiency. But to show that heuristics lead to inaccurate decisions, one needs to look at natural task domains and to compare heuristic decisions to actual outcomes. Comparing heuristic performance to some more sophisticated strategy is not sufficient to conclude that heuristic reasoning is inaccurate. In fact, research using objective measures of accuracy has been accumulating, and surprisingly, heuristics in the form of simple decision algorithms may be as accurate as complicated rational algorithms (Gigerenzer & Todd, 1999).

The HSM has always considered the question of judgmental accuracy as conceptually independent of the question of the mode of processing. Heuristic processing does not mean inaccurate judgmental outcomes. However, the HSM has not empirically addressed the question of the actual accuracy of heuristic strategies. This research question is well worth addressing. Indeed, one can make the counterintuitive prediction that heuristic processing can lead to more accurate judgments than can systematic processing under some conditions. Heuristic processing is characterized as focusing on a narrow set of informational cues as opposed to systematic processing, which is characterized as scrutinizing all potentially relevant cues. Under conditions of limited cognitive resources, focusing on a single subset of relevant cues may lead to more efficient and more accurate judgments than using a strategy that integrates relevant and (often times) irrelevant cues (see Chen & Chaiken, 1999; Tordesillas & Chaiken, 1999).

CONCLUSION

The HSM has undergone several theoretical developments. In its current form, the HSM specifies two modes of concurrent information processing, three broad motivational orientations, and a motivational principle (sufficiency) that makes specific predictions about the investment of processing effort in a judgmental task. The HSM was conceived as a specific persuasion model but has evolved into a general model of social information processing. In fact, the HSM is related to a number of current social judgment models (Chaiken & Trope, 1999; Chen & Chaiken, 1999). As a general judgment model, the HSM has been applied to a number of areas outside of persuasion research (e.g., Bohner et al., 1995; Chaiken, Gruenfeld, & Judd, 2000). However, the HSM can be even better specified, and here we have attempted to outline a program of research with respect to this endeavor.

REFERENCES

Alba, J. W., & Marmorstein, H. (1987). The effects of frequency knowledge on consumer decision making. *Journal of Consumer Research, 14,* 14-25.

Bargh, J. A. (1989). Conditional automaticity: Varieties of automatic influence in social perception and cognition. In J. S. Uleman & J. A. Bargh (Eds.), *Unintended thought* (pp. 3-51). New York: Guilford.

Bargh, J. A. (1994). The four horsemen of automaticity: Awareness, intention, efficiency, and control in social cognition. In R. S. Wyer & T. K. Srull (Eds.), *Handbook of social cognition* (2nd ed., pp. 1-40). Hillsdale, NJ: Lawrence Erlbaum.

Bargh, J. A. (1999). The cognitive monster: The case against the controllability of automatic stereotype effects. In S. Chaiken & Y. Trope (Eds.), *Dual-process theories in social psychology* (pp. 361-382). New York: Guilford.

Bargh, J. A., & Pietromonaco, P. (1982). Automatic information processing and social perception: The influence of trait information presented outside of conscious awareness on impression formation. *Journal of Personality and Social Psychology, 43,* 437-449.

Bohner, G., Moskowitz, G. B., & Chaiken, S. (1995). The interplay of heuristic and systematic processing of social information. *European Review of Social Psychology* (Vol. 6, pp. 33-68). New York: John Wiley.

Cacioppo, J. T., & Petty, R. E. (1979). Effects of message repetition and position on cognitive response, recall, and persuasion. *Journal of Personality and Social Psychology, 37,* 97-109.

Cacioppo, J. T., & Petty, R. E. (1985). Central and peripheral routes to persuasion: The role of message repetition. In L. F. Alwitt & A. A. Mitchell (Eds.), *Psychological processes and advertising effects* (pp. 91-111). Hillsdale, NJ: Lawrence Erlbaum.

Cacioppo, J. T., Petty, R. E., Kao, C. F., & Rodriguez, R. (1986). Central and peripheral routes to persuasion: An individual difference perspective. *Journal of Personality and Social Psychology, 51,* 1032-1043.

Chaiken, S. (1980). Heuristic versus systematic information processing and the use of source versus message cues in persuasion. *Journal of Personality and Social Psychology, 39,* 752-766.

Chaiken, S. (1987). The Heuristic Model of persuasion. In M. P. Zanna, J. M. Olson, & C. P. Herman (Eds.), *Social influence: The Ontario Symposium* (Vol. 5, pp. 3-39). Hillsdale, NJ: Lawrence Erlbaum.

Chaiken, S., Axsom, D., Liberman, A., & Wilson, D. (1992). *Heuristic processing of persuasive messages: Chronic and temporary sources of rule accessibility.* Unpublished manuscript, New York University.

Chaiken, S., Duckworth, K., & Darke, P. (1999). When parsimony fails. *Psychological Inquiry, 10,* 118-123.

Chaiken, S., Giner-Sorolla, R., & Chen, S. (1996). Beyond accuracy: Defense and impression motives in heuristic and systematic information processing. In P. M. Gollwitzer & J. A. Bargh (Eds.), *The psychology of action: Linking cognition and motivation to behavior* (pp. 553-578). New York: Guilford.

Chaiken, S., Gruenfeld, D. H., & Judd, C. M. (2000). Persuasion in negotiations and conflict situations. In M. Deutsch & P. T. Coleman (Eds.), *The handbook of conflict resolution: Theory and practice* (pp. 144-165). San Francisco: Jossey-Bass.

Chaiken, S., Liberman, A., & Eagly, A. H. (1989). Heuristic and systematic processing within and beyond the persuasion context. In J. S. Uleman & J. A. Bargh (Eds.), *Unintended thought* (pp. 212-252). New York: Guilford.

Chaiken, S., & Maheswaran, D. (1994). Heuristic processing can bias systematic processing: Effects of source credibility, argument ambiguity, and task importance on attitude judgment. *Journal of Personality and Social Psychology, 66,* 460-473.

Chaiken, S., & Stangor, C. (1987). Attitudes and attitude change. *Annual Review of Psychology, 38,* 575-630.

Chaiken, S., & Trope, Y. (Eds.). (1999). *Dual-process theories in social psychology.* New York: Guilford.

Chen, S., & Chaiken, S. (1999). The Heuristic-Systematic Model in its broader context. In S. Chaiken & Y. Trope (Eds.), *Dual-process theories in social psychology* (pp. 73-96). New York: Guilford.

Chen, S., Shechter, D., & Chaiken, S. (1996). Getting at the truth or getting along: Accuracy-vs. impression-motivated heuristic and systematic information processing. *Journal of Personality and Social Psychology, 71,* 262-275.

Cialdini, R. B., Levy, A., Herman, C. P., & Evenbeck, S. (1973). Attitudinal politics: The strategy of moderation. *Journal of Personality and Social Psychology, 25,* 100-108.

Darke, P. R., Chaiken, S., Bohner, G., Einwiller, S., Erb, H. P., & Hazlewood, J. D. (1998). Accuracy motivation, consensus information, and the law of large numbers: Effects on attitude judgment in the absence of argumentation. *Personality and Social Psychology Bulletin, 24,* 1205-1215.

Ditto, P. H., & Lopez, D. F. (1992). Motivated skepticism: Use of differential decision criteria for preferred and nonpreferred conclusions. *Journal of Personality and Social Psychology, 63,* 568-584.

Eagly, A. H., & Chaiken, S. (1993). *The psychology of attitudes.* Fort Worth, TX: Harcourt Brace Jovanovich.

Erdley, C. A., & D'Agostino, P. R. (1988). Cognitive and affective components of automatic priming effects. *Journal of Personality and Social Psychology, 54,* 741-747.

Festinger, L., & Maccoby, N. (1964). On resistance to persuasive communications. *Journal of Abnormal and Social Psychology, 68,* 359-366.

Fiske, S. T., & Taylor, S. E. (1991). *Social cognition* (2nd ed.). New York: McGraw-Hill.

Gigerenzer, G., & Todd, P. M. (Eds.). (1999). *Simple heuristics that make us smart.* New York: Oxford University Press.

Gilbert, D. T. (1999). What the mind's not? In S. Chaiken & Y. Trope (Eds.), *Dual-process theories in social psychology* (pp. 3-11). New York: Guilford.

Giner-Sorolla, R., & Chaiken, S. (1997). Selective use of heuristic and systematic processing under defense motivation. *Personality and Social Psychology Bulletin, 23,* 84-97.

Greenwald, A. G. (1968). Cognitive learning, cognitive response to persuasion, and attitude change. In A. G. Greenwald, T. C. Brock, & T. M. Ostrom (Eds.), *Psychological foundations of attitudes* (pp. 147-170). San Diego: Academic Press.

Greenwald, A. G., & Banaji, M. R. (1995). Implicit social cognition: Attitudes, self-esteem, and stereotypes. *Psychological Review, 102,* 4-27.

Higgins, E. T. (1989). Knowledge accessibility and activation: Subjectivity and suffering from unconscious sources. In J. S. Uleman & J. A. Bargh (Eds.), *Unintended thought* (pp. 75-123). New York: Guilford.

Higgins, E. T. (1996). Knowledge activation: Accessibility, applicability, and salience. In E. T. Higgins & A. W. Kruglanski (Eds.), *Social psychology: Handbook of basic principles* (pp. 133-168). New York: Guilford.

Higgins, E. T., King, G. A., & Mavin, G. H. (1982). Individual construct accessibility and subjective impressions and recall. *Journal of Personality and Social Psychology, 43,* 35-47.

Hovland, C. I., Janis, I. L., & Kelley, H. H. (1953). *Communication and persuasion: Psychological studies of opinion change.* New Haven, CT: Yale University Press.

Johnson, B. T., & Eagly, A. H. (1989). The effects of involvement on persuasion: A meta-analysis. *Psychological Bulletin, 106,* 290-314.

Kahneman, D., Slovic, P., & Tversky, A. (Eds.) (1982), *Judgment under uncertainty: Heuristics and biases.* Cambridge, UK: Cambridge University Press.

Kruglanski, A. W., & Thompson, E. P. (1999). Persuasion by a single route: A view from the unimodel. *Psychological Inquiry, 10,* 83-109.

Kunda, Z. (1990). The case for motivated reasoning. *Psychological Bulletin, 108,* 480-498.

Leippe, M. R., & Elkin, R. A. (1987). When motives clash: Issue involvement and response involvement as determinants of persuasion. *Journal of Personality and Social Psychology, 52,* 269-278.

Liberman, A., & Chaiken, S. (1992). Defensive processing of personally relevant health messages. *Personality and Social Psychology Bulletin, 18,* 669-679.

Lord, C. G., Ross, L., & Lepper, M. R. (1979). Biased assimilation and attitude polarization: The effects of prior theories on subsequently considered evidence. *Journal of Personality and Social Psychology, 37,* 2098-2109.

Maheswaran, D., & Chaiken, S. (1991). Promoting systematic processing in low-motivation settings: Effect of incongruent information on processing and judgment. *Journal of Personality and Social Psychology, 61,* 13-25.

Maheswaran, D., Mackie, D. M., & Chaiken, S. (1992). Brand name as a heuristic cue: The effects of task importance and expectancy confirmation on consumer judgments. *Journal of Consumer Psychology, 1,* 317-336.

McFarland, C., Ross, M., & Conway, M. (1984). Self-persuasion and self-presentation as mediators of anticipatory attitude change. *Journal of Personality and Social Psychology, 46,* 529-540.

McGuire, W. J. (1968). Personality and attitude change: An information-processing theory. In A. G. Greenwald, T. C. Brock, & T. M. Ostrom (Eds.), *Psychological foundations of attitudes* (pp. 171-196). San Diego: Academic Press.

Moore, D. L., Hausknecht, D., & Thamodaran, K. (1986). Time compression, response opportunity, and persuasion. *Journal of Consumer Research, 13,* 85-99.

Neely, J. H. (1977). The effects of visual and verbal satiation on a lexical decision task. *American Journal of Psychology, 90,* 447-459.

Osterhouse, R. A., & Brock, T. C. (1970). Distraction increases yielding to propaganda by inhibiting counterarguing. *Journal of Personality and Social Psychology, 15,* 344-358.

Petty, R. E. (1994). Two routes to persuasion: State of the art. In G. d'Ydewalle, P. Eelen, & P. Bertelson (Eds.), *International perspectives on psychological science,* Vol. 2: *The state of the art* (pp. 229-247). Hillsdale, NJ: Lawrence Erlbaum.

Petty, R. E., & Cacioppo, J. T. (1979). Issue involvement can increase or decrease persuasion by enhancing message-relevant cognitive responses. *Journal of Personality and Social Psychology, 37,* 1915-1926.

Petty, R. E., & Cacioppo, J. T. (1981). *Attitudes and persuasion: Classic and contemporary approaches.* Dubuque, IA: William C. Brown.

Petty, R. E., & Cacioppo, J. T. (1984). The effects of involvement on responses to argument quantity and quality: Central and peripheral routes to persuasion. *Journal of Personality and Social Psychology, 46,* 69-81.

Petty, R. E., & Cacioppo, J. T. (1986a). *Communication and persuasion: Central and peripheral routes to attitude change.* New York: Springer-Verlag.

Petty, R. E., & Cacioppo, J. T. (1986b). The Elaboration Likelihood Model of persuasion. In L. Berkowitz (Ed.), *Advances in experimental social psychology* (Vol. 19, pp. 123-205). San Diego: Academic Press.

Petty, R. E., & Cacioppo, J. T. (1990). Involvement and persuasion: Tradition versus integration. *Psychological Bulletin, 107,* 367-374.

Petty, R. E., Wells, G. L., & Brock, T. C. (1976). Distraction can enhance or reduce yielding to propaganda: Thought disruption versus effort justification. *Journal of Personality and Social Psychology, 34,* 874-884.

Pomerantz, E. M., Chaiken, S., & Tordesillas, R. S. (1995). Attitude strength and resistance processes. *Journal of Personality and Social Psychology, 69,* 408-419.

Pyszczynski, T., & Greenberg, J. (1987). Toward an integration of cognitive and motivational perspectives on social inference: A biased hypothesis-testing model. In L. Berkowitz (Ed.), *Advances in experimental social psychology* (Vol. 20, pp. 297-340). New York: Academic Press.

Ratneshwar, S., & Chaiken, S. (1991). Comprehension's role in persuasion: The case of its moderating effect on the persuasive impact of source cues. *Journal of Consumer Research, 18,* 52-62.

Schlenker, B. R. (1980). *Impression management: The self-concept, social identity, and interpersonal relations.* Pacific Grove, CA: Brooks/Cole.

Sedikides, C., & Skowronski, J. J. (1991). The law of cognitive structure activation. *Psychological Inquiry, 2,* 169-184.

Shavitt, S., Swan, S., Lowrey, T. M., & Waenke, M. (1994). The interaction of endorser attractiveness and involvement in persuasion depends on the goal that guides message processing. *Journal of Consumer Psychology, 3,* 137-162.

Tesser, A. (1988). Toward a self-evaluation maintenance model of social behavior. In L. Berkowitz (Ed.), *Advances in experimental social psychology* (Vol. 21, pp. 181-227). San Diego: Academic Press.

Tetlock, P. E. (1983). Accountability and complexity of thought. *Journal of Personality and Social Psychology, 45,* 74-83.

Todorov, A. (1997). Another look at reasoning experiments: Rationality, normative models, and conversational factors. *Journal for the Theory of Social Behaviour, 27,* 387-417.

Todorov, A. (2000). The accessibility and applicability of knowledge: Predicting context effects in national surveys. *Public Opinion Quarterly, 64,* 429-451.

Tordesillas, R. S., & Chaiken, S. (1999). Thinking too much of too little? The effects of introspection on the decision-making process. *Personality and Social Psychology Bulletin, 25,* 623-629.

Trope, Y. (1986). Identification and inferential processes in dispositional attribution. *Psychological Review, 93,* 239-257.

Trope, Y., & Gaunt, R. (1999). A dual-process model of overconfident attributional inferences. In S. Chaiken & Y. Trope (Eds.), *Dual-process theories in social psychology* (pp. 161-178). New York: Guilford.

Tulving, E., & Pearlstone, Z. (1966). Availability versus accessibility of information in memory for words. *Journal of Verbal Learning and Verbal Behavior, 5,* 381-391.

Tversky, A., & Kahneman, D. (1974). Judgment under uncertainty: Heuristics and biases. *Science, 185,* 1124-1131.

Uleman, J. S., & Bargh, J. A. (1989). *Unintended thought.* New York: Guilford.

Wood, W. (1982). Retrieval of attitude-relevant information from memory: Effects on susceptibility to persuasion and on intrinsic motivation. *Journal of Personality and Social Psychology, 42,* 798-810.

Wood, W., Kallgren, C. A., & Preisler, R. M. (1985). Access to attitude-relevant information in memory as a determinant of persuasion: The role of message attributes. *Journal of Experimental Social Psychology, 21,* 73-85.

Zimbardo, P. G. (1960). Involvement and communication discrepancy as determinants of opinion conformity. *Journal of Abnormal and Social Psychology, 60,* 86-94.

12

Revisiting the Theory of Psychological Reactance
Communicating Threats to Attitudinal Freedom

MICHAEL BURGOON
EUSEBIO ALVARO
JOSEPH GRANDPRE
MICHAEL VOULODAKIS

In the discipline of communication and among other scholars interested in dealing with important social issues, it is apparent that the study of persuasion is in a period of transition. That is true not only in terms of the theoretical perspectives being employed but also in the focus of the social phenomenon of concern, the research questions being posed, and the kinds of empirical data being collected. Persuasion, now often discussed under the more general rubric of some appellation such as social influence, has become less dependent on laboratory environments, tightly designed experiments with suspect ecological validity, and the controlling (albeit often invisible) hands of social psychologists. This transition period is marked by a focus on problems of real social import (e.g., tobacco uptake and use, alcohol abuse, use of illegal and often dangerous substances, engaging in high-risk behaviors of various and sundry kinds). Increasingly, the study of persuasion is taking an applied turn toward attempting to change attitudes and behaviors in real time and among large segments of the population.

Unfortunately, this applied turn appears doomed to repeat history, possibly because of the academic world's own ignorance of its own recent history of failed generalization of research findings. Specifically, one can enu-

AUTHORS' NOTE: Support for this research was provided by grants from the Arizona Disease Control Research Commission (Contracts 9804 and 9805), RO1HD31360 (National Institute for Child Health and Development), RO1DA12578 (National Institute on Drug Abuse), and 5POCA77502 (National Cancer Institute) to the senior author. The opinions expressed are those of the authors and not of the various funding agencies.

merate any number of failed attempts to export atheoretical, variable analytic-type prescriptions from laboratory research to actual situations in which demonstrable attitude change and behavior modification are the desired outcomes. For example, while millions of dollars from special taxes and court settlements have been spent to target young people who are most susceptible to tobacco uptake and use, there is little evidence to suggest that any of these campaigns have been successful at even decreasing smoking incidence rates (or even the rate of increase) among the most heavily targeted groups.

In campaign after campaign, there appears to be a general lack of impact of a saturation of messages using multiple channels to change attitudes and/or alter behaviors. In fact, it is often the case that such campaigns are accompanied by concomitant changes in behaviors that are in the *opposite* direction to that advocated by the designers of such social influence campaigns. This appears to be true whether the social influence attempt is aimed at change to avoid immediate dire consequences (e.g., drunk driving death rates, risky sexual behavior and HIV/AIDs infection, drug overdoses) or long-term aversive consequences such as increased rates of cardiovascular disease, cancer, and diabetes. It is also the case that such campaigns are no more effective at inhibiting potentially harmful behaviors (e.g., smoking) than they are at promoting more positive prosocial, self-benefit behaviors (e.g., exercise, diet, wellness).

Feeding at the trough of various funding agencies to conduct such atheoretical persuasion research has probably not yet run its course. However, it is only a matter of time until more measures of accountability are instituted by funding agencies, governments, and the population at large. This will force more focus on theory-driven research to explain (a) how and when attitudes and behaviors can be successfully changed, (b) why certain groups of people and behaviors remain resistant to change, and (c) when and why people may actually engage in behaviors that are in direct opposition to those being advocated—the so-called *boomerang effect* that is often witnessed.

However, incorporating theory-driven research into efforts aimed at dealing with real-time social problems is not without its challenges. On the one hand, the present fascination with cognitive theories of social influence (Chaiken, 1980, 1987; Petty & Cacioppo, 1981, 1986) has done little to enhance understanding of social influence processes with behaviors that have any applied social import. The notion that cognitive processes will be the defining characteristic of any explanation of attitude and/or behavior change has resulted in some relatively uninteresting research results and explanations that are simply not subject to falsification. There has been a nearly total lack of attention to message features, structure, and content from those embracing these intrapsychic models of information processing as explanations of persuasion. From the perspective of anyone interested in the impacts of real-world social influence attempts, this has probably done as much to *inhibit* scientific progress in understanding the phenomena of concern as has anything that one might point to in the recent history of *any* social science discipline.

On the other hand, people interested in persuasive communication have not attended to critical concerns that theories focus on message characteristics to explain change, lack of change, and change in directions opposite to those being advocated. This lack of attention has resulted in ignoring potentially enlightened theoretical expositions that do focus on explanations of the effects of communication (message structure, features, and content) on various target groups. One such body of knowledge is the theory of psychological reactance developed nearly three decades ago by

Brehm (1966; Brehm & Brehm, 1981; Jones & Brehm, 1970). While this theory developed a wealth of research for a decade or more, it has been largely moribund for a very long time.

Brehm's theory was among the first to suggest that *any message* aimed at changing one's current attitudes and behaviors might, in fact, be perceived as a threat to freedom, whether in the best interest of the intended persuadee or not. When people perceive that freedoms are being threatened, psychological reactance is claimed to result. This reactance can result in a variety of responses including simply ignoring the persuasive attempt, derogating the source, and even producing even *more* of the undesired behaviors as a means of demonstrating choice or restoring attitudinal freedom.

That such a theoretical position has not been embraced with more enthusiasm by contemporary social influence researchers is enigmatic, at best, and probably unenlightened, at worst. There is probably no other extant theoretical position that is more intuitively sensible than that outlined in the theory of psychological reactance. People do not appreciate being told how they should behave, especially in areas where they feel it is simply no one else's business. People at different developmental stages value independence and freedom and tend to reject many, if not most, authority-based appeals. Members of specific groups can be resistant to any appeal that they consider to be even remotely controlling. That people value freedom and their right to consider and make choices, and that they react negatively to attitudinal and behavioral constraints with some regularity, seems so obvious as to not require further elaboration.

While a theory's intuitive appeal is neither necessary nor sufficient to warrant the attention of the scholarly community, that is not all that the theory of psychological reactance has to offer to the study of social influence pro-

cesses. Clearly, while Brehm could have been less obtuse in outlining the basic propositions of this theory, it is the case that reactance theory does possess many of the properties of good scientific theory (which is too often claimed not to exist in the social sciences). In this chapter, several arguments are advanced that the theory of psychological reactance ought to be a mainstay of the armamentarium of anyone attempting to do battle in the social influence arena. Among these are that the structure of this theory of psychological reactance contains a series of elegantly and logically subordinated propositions that do lead to derived hypotheses important to the study of social influence and potentially useful in campaigns aimed at socially important issues. The empirical data in support of this theory are both voluminous and impressive, although not without some inconsistencies and misinterpretations in need of remediation. Also, this theoretical position has the heuristic force to suggest new research approaches that might explain why some very large campaigns fail to produce desired changes and, in effect, promote the very behaviors they attempt to extinguish.

THEORY OF PSYCHOLOGICAL REACTANCE

Psychological reactance theory (Brehm, 1966) emanated from the basic premise that humans must fulfill basic needs of survival and that "given some minimal level of valid knowledge about oneself and the environment, freedom to choose among different behavioral possibilities will generally help one to survive and thrive" (p. 2). It is a theory of social influence that focuses on how individuals act when their realm of free behavior is limited. A form of psychological arousal, reactance is considered a motivational state directed toward the reestablishment of free behaviors that have been eliminated or threatened with elimination.

According to psychological reactance theory (Brehm, 1966; Brehm & Brehm, 1981; Jones & Brehm, 1970), persuasive communication poses a potential threat to freedom. Essentially, reactance is motivated by the individual's basic need for self-determination in effecting his or her own environment. This need for *effectance* and *autonomy* is predicated on the basic assumption that, in regard to certain limited and specifiable areas of behavior, people have a distinct and strong preference to perceive themselves as masters of their own fate. The theory predicts that when an individual's perceived freedom is threatened by a proscribed attitude or behavior, the individual will experience a motivating pressure toward reestablishing the threatened freedom (Heilman & Toffler, 1976). One way to restore the freedom is to engage in the forbidden behavior or to embrace the attitude threatened by the proscription (Brehm, 1966). Research supporting this type of restoration has demonstrated a phenomenon known as the *boomerang effect*—a condition producing the opposite effect to that desired—in response to certain persuasive messages (Worchel & Brehm, 1970).

It was posited (Brehm, 1966; Brehm & Brehm, 1981) that people have a set of actions or free behaviors that they are aware of and feel they have the ability to perform and can engage in at the current moment or some time in the future. Furthermore, these free behaviors can, according to their ability to satisfy certain needs, vary in prominence and importance. Brehm (1966) hypothesized that the strength of psychological reactance is manifested in the positive relationship between the degree of threat to a behavior and the importance of that behavior.

Various responses to the arousal of reactance have been demonstrated conclusively. One response of primary import for the source of any persuasive message, or for the designers of any persuasive message campaign, is the target's attempt to reestablish a freedom by performing the threatened behavior, as mentioned previously. Such a response is termed "restoration" because it satisfies or restores the target's need for self-determination and control. A second response involves a threatened freedom increasing in attractiveness (Brehm & Sensenig, 1966; Worchel, 1972) even if the threat results from the introduction of a new, more attractive alternative or reward as a choice option or incentive. In such an event, the threatened behavior's increased attraction may stimulate information seeking to confirm or gauge the level of attraction. In addition, reactance may often be followed by aggression or hostility aimed at the threatening agent (Wicklund, 1974). In this instance, the response would also be expected to include the concomitant negative message evaluation related to source derogation as a potent form of restoration.

Free Behaviors

Within the framework of reactance theory, individuals hold "free behaviors" or a set of realistic behaviors that may be enacted at any given time, either at the moment or in the future (Brehm, 1966). It naturally follows that the impression of having such freedoms may be seen as varying from strong doubt to total conviction (Brehm & Brehm, 1981). Given such a set of free behaviors, reactance will be experienced when the freedom to enact these behaviors is either threatened or eliminated. Additional research (Brehm & Sensenig, 1966; Mazis, 1975; Worchel & Brehm, 1970; Wright, 1986) shows that when an individual must decide between two or more choices and is pressured to make a specific choice, reactance will result (Heilman & Toffler, 1976). Furthermore, if the individual has decided on one choice and is then told to make the same choice, he or she will be more inclined to change the decision in order to assert the freedom to choose. Due to the variety of situations that may induce psychological reactance, it is often experienced at different levels of intensity.

Magnitude of Reactance

Psychological reactance is experienced along a continuum of magnitude. Magnitude of reactance can be determined by the threat or elimination of perceived free behaviors through three variables: (a) the perceived importance of the free behaviors to the individual, denoting that the more important a freedom is to the individual, the greater the magnitude of reactance will be after either threat or elimination; (b) the proportion of free behaviors threatened, denoting that the magnitude of reactance also increases as the proportion of behaviors eliminated or threatened increases; and (c) the magnitude of the threat where there is only threat of elimination, denoting that the greater the magnitude, the more the individual will attempt to restore freedoms.

As perceived threats to free behaviors increase, the individual experiences higher levels of reactance. The individual's perceived free behaviors might even be threatened by the free behavior of others being threatened or eliminated. Levels of experienced reactance are, in turn, dependent on how threats increase the perceived difficulty of exercising freedoms (Brehm & Brehm, 1981). Threats of small magnitude might not by themselves even create a perceived threat. For example, if a secretary is told not to chew gum at his or her desk (and does not normally do this), the desire to chew gum will likely be minimal. A combination of such threats, however, may create and compound the magnitude of any

given threat or change attempt. Such a result depends on temporal proximity of the threats and occurs only when reactance from the initial threat has not been reduced prior to the occurrence of subsequent threats (Brehm & Brehm, 1981). With threats of moderate magnitude, the effects of reactance are dependent on the importance of the freedom to the individual (Brehm & Brehm, 1981).

Threats of great magnitude often create so much difficulty in exercising a freedom that it is effectively eliminated. With such events, the freedom is given up and reactance within the individual dissipates (Brehm & Brehm, 1981). If someone is asked at gunpoint to give his or her wallet to a total stranger, the individual will not likely be greatly motivated to restore his or her freedom to keep the wallet. Although the importance of the freedom to keep one's wallet may be great, the threat of bodily harm will most likely overcome any psychological reactance that might result from the threat. Thus, low levels of situational reactance occur when individuals experience threats of small magnitude, little importance, or extremely large magnitude. Moderate levels of reactance occur when threats to freedoms are important to the individual and realistically alleviated or when a moderate number of small-magnitude threats are made. High levels of reactance occur with multiple small-magnitude threats, threats to freedoms that are very important to the individual, and threats of a moderate to large magnitude.

Restoration of Freedoms

Psychological reactance may be reduced or alleviated by restoration of threatened or eliminated behaviors (Brehm, 1966; Worchel & Brehm, 1971). Direct restoration can be achieved by exercising a threatened freedom or by having an external agent act directly on behalf of the individual who has been threatened. An example of an external agent could be a passing police officer who restores one's freedom to keep a wallet (after being asked at gunpoint to give it up). In addition, indirect restoration can be achieved through an external agent who, by restoring his or her own freedom, restores the threatened individual's freedom by implication. An alternative method of indirect restoration is for an individual to assert a threatened freedom indirectly. In doing this, the threatened freedom is not directly enacted, but a *different* freedom is exercised.

Reactance as a Personality Trait

Although Brehm did not originally discuss reactance as a personality trait, he has acknowledged that the same situation may elicit different levels of reactance across individuals. This has resulted in recent examination of reactance as an individual difference (Dowd, Milne, & Wise, 1991; Hong & Page, 1989; Merz, 1983). Although two scales have been developed to specifically assess reactance as an individual difference variable—the Therapeutic Reactance Scale (Dowd et al., 1991) and the Hong Reactance Scale (Hong, 1990, 1992; Hong & Faedda, 1996; Hong & Giannakopoulos, 1994; Hong, Giannakopoulos, Laing, & Williams, 1994; Hong & Langovski, 1994; Hong & Page, 1989)—little empirical research has been conducted to examine the relationship between reactance as an individual difference and its impact on outcomes such as persuasion. Some exceptions include a study finding that people scoring high in reactance were less compliant to physician requests (Greybar, Antonuccio, Boutilier, & Varble, 1989) and self-reported intent to compliance with therapeutic regimens (Voloudakis & Ramirez, 1999).

In the end, efforts at construing reactance as an individual difference variable might make their most valuable contribution by providing reliable and valid measurement instruments by which this somewhat malleable construct may be empirically assessed and by which experimental manipulations may be verified.

OVERVIEW OF REACTANCE RESEARCH

Research involving psychological reactance examines how individuals respond when their behavioral freedoms are restricted in a variety of situations. The theory also suggests that the presence of reactance may mediate the persuasiveness of messages (Brehm, 1966; Brehm & Brehm, 1981). Reactance has been examined steadily since its inception and has recently received additional attention due to personality-based measures.

The rationale for examining psychological reactance theory is strongly justified. Brehm and Brehm (1981) cataloged a plethora of empirical findings during the first wave of reactance research spanning from 1966 through 1981. They discussed the foundations of the theory not only in terms of freedoms, magnitude, and effects but also in regard to topics and applications of the theory. During its first 15 years, reactance theory generated considerable research both in the laboratory and in the field. Laboratory research examined persuasion and attitude change, social relationships, the decision-making process, individual differences, impression management, and human development, while field research focused on clinical settings, social problems, consumer behavior, and power relations.

Laboratory Research

Laboratory research on reactance has explored the effects of discrepancy (Karpf, 1978;

Lenehan & O'Neill, 1981; Wicklund, 1974; Worchel & Brehm, 1970), commitment (Pallak & Sullivan, 1979; Schwarz, Frey, & Kumpf, 1980; Sullivan & Pallak, 1976), the sleeper effect (Brehm & Mann, 1975; Gruder et al., 1978), threat (Carver, 1977; Feldman-Summers, 1977; Grabitz-Gniech, 1971; Smith, 1977; Snyder & Wicklund, 1976), censorship (Worchel & Arnold, 1973; Worchel, Arnold, & Baker, 1975), and counterattitudinal messages (Karpf, 1978; Kohn & Barnes, 1977). Research on reactance and social relationships has been approached in terms of power (Dickenberger & Grabitz-Gniech, 1972; Grabitz-Gniech, 1971; Heilman, 1976; Long, 1978; Organ, 1974; Pennebaker & Sanders, 1976), interpersonal relationships (Dickenberger & Grabitz-Gniech, 1972; Pallak & Heller, 1971; Wicklund, 1974), and helping behavior (Goodstadt, 1971; Jones, 1970; Morse, Gergen, Peele, & van Ryneveld, 1977; Willis & Goethals, 1973).

Reactance and the decision-making process has been examined in terms of magnitude of threat (Hannah, Hannah, & Wattie, 1975; Linder, Wortman, & Brehm, 1971), importance of freedom (Wicklund, 1970), and certainty theory (Brounstein, Ostrove, & Mills, 1979; Mills, 1968). Researchers interested in the relationship between reactance and individual differences have conducted studies addressing locus of control (Brehm, Stires, Sensenig, & Shaban, 1966; Cherulnik & Citrin, 1974; Moyer, 1978), Type A coronary-prone behavior pattern (Carver, 1980), self-consciousness (Carver & Scheier, 1981; Swart, Ickes, & Morgenthaler, 1978), cognitive processing (Linder & Crane, 1970), and learned helplessness (Baum & Gatchel, 1981; Jardine & Winefield, 1981; Tennen & Eller, 1977).

From more of a functional approach, substantial research has been conducted on reactance and impression management formulations. This research has looked at traditional impression management (Brehm & Mann, 1975; Heilman & Garner, 1975; Heilman & Toffler, 1976) as well as impression management as a prior exercise of freedom (Baer, Hinkle, Smith, & Fenton, 1980; Snyder & Wicklund, 1976).

A body of early research also focused on reactance and human development over the life span. This research investigated the general importance of freedoms (Worchel, 1972), proportion of freedoms (Brehm, 1966), threats to freedoms (Brehm, 1966), elimination of freedoms (Hammock & Brehm, 1966), barriers (Brehm & Weinraub, 1977), and compliance with adult social influence (Brehm, 1977; Miller et al., 1975).

More recently, reactance has expanded on some of the traditional areas and has added new directions. Persuasion research examines prevention and intervention strategies (Bensley & Wu, 1991; Dowd, Hughs, Brockbank, & Halpain, 1988), television violence (Bushman & Stack, 1996), athletic performance (Carter & Kelly, 1997), freedom restoration (Schwarz, 1984), paradoxical directives (Seltzer, 1983), relinquishing control (Strube & Werner, 1984), risk taking (Truscott & Fehr, 1986), and threat (Wright, 1986). Recent research on social relationships has focused on helping behavior (Goldman, Pulcher, & Mendez, 1983), dating relationships (Hockenberry & Billingham, 1993), gift giving (Manikowske & Winakor, 1994), marital satisfaction (Oliver, Mattson, & Moore, 1993), perceived control (Propst & Kurtzz, 1989), interpersonal appeal (Wright, Wadley, Danner, & Phillips, 1992), and impression management (Wright & Brehm, 1982).

Finally, individual differences have been studied in terms of sex (Joseph, Joseph, Barto, & McKay, 1982), age (Frank et al., 1998), learned helplessness (Gannon, Heiser, & Knight, 1985; Mikulincer, Kedem, & Zilkha-Segal, 1989), self-esteem and narcissism (Hellman & McMillin, 1997; Joubert, 1990,

1992, 1995), self-consciousness (Carver & Scheier, 1981), cognitive processing (Kelly & Nauta, 1997), procrastination (Mulry, Fleming, & Gottschalk, 1994), and Type A coronary prone behavior (Rhodewalt & Comer, 1982; Rhodewalt & Davison, 1983; Rhodewalt & Fairfield, 1990; Rhodewalt & Marcroft, 1988; Rhodewalt & Strube, 1985).

Applied Research

Applied research has been conducted in clinical settings and has looked at reactance in terms of an undesirable correlate of therapy (Beutler, 1979; Brehm, 1976; Gordon, 1976; Hughes & Falk, 1981; Kanfer & Grimm, 1978; Tennen, Press, Rohrbaugh, & White, 1981) and as a treatment strategy (Tennen et al., 1981; Varela, 1978). Researchers have also looked at reactance and social problems in terms of overpopulation (Cooper, 1974), politics (Berkowitz, 1974; Samuel, 1972), public safety campaigns (Elman & Kellebrew, 1978), enactment of new laws (Mazis, 1975; Mazis, Settle, & Leslie, 1973), television viewing patterns (Herman & Leyens, 1977), and anti-littering campaigns (Reich & Robertson, 1979). Other applied contexts include consumer behavior (Clee & Wicklund, 1980; Regan & Brehm, 1972), power relations in terms of superior-subordinate relationships (Rosen & Jerdee, 1975; Tjosvold, 1978), and courtroom settings (Broeder, 1959; Wolf & Montgomery, 1977).

Recent field research has examined social problems such as sexism (Vrugt, 1992), mental health (Prandoni & Wall, 1990), alcohol consumption (Allen, Sprenkel, & Vitale, 1994; Engs & Hanson, 1989), unemployment (Baum, Fleming, & Reddy, 1986), and probation recidivism (Minor, 1987). Recent consumer behavior research has focused on product withdrawal (Ringold, 1988). New research in the health domain has been con-

ducted in terms of physician-patient relationships (Fogarty, 1997; Greybar et al., 1989; Redman, Dickinson, Cockburn, & Hennrikus, 1989) and biofeedback (Carlson, 1982). Finally, research on reactance and the therapeutic process has focused on diagnosis (Dowd et al., 1991; Dowd & Seibel, 1990; Swoboda, Dowd, & Wise, 1990), treatment (Dowd & Sanders, 1994; Dowd, Trutt, & Watkins, 1992; Hunsley, 1997), motivation (Dowd, Wallbrown, Sanders, & Yesenosky, 1994), and the relationship between therapy and personality variables (Dowd & Wallbrown, 1993).

Theoretical and Applied Concerns

Although reactance theory has received considerable consistent attention in published research efforts, notable problems with the original formulation of the theory exist. There is difficulty in operationalizing concepts in the theory, limited success of many reactance experiments, and a lack of information regarding how humans respond to threats to freedom. Also there are problems with the transformation of measurement of the psychological reactance in specific persuasion attempts to treatment of the concept as some sort of stable personality trait.

Reliance on the Boomerang Effect. One plausible explanation for the relatively early abandonment of potentially fruitful research on reactance theory is that many studies failed to provide empirical evidence of the theoretically postulated boomerang effect. Given that so much emphasis had been placed on the existence of this effect, it is quite understandable that, over time and after less than perfect studies, researchers abandoned the theory to pursue seemingly more beneficial avenues of inquiry. However, reactance theory could have benefited greatly if researchers had abandoned their efforts to carefully delineate ever more constrained conditions under which a boomerang effect should be obtained and, instead, focused on other paths also congruent with its theoretical postulates. While a relatively small subset of message receivers may indeed react to reactance-arousing messages by engaging in even more of the proscribed behaviors, it is much more likely, and potentially more valuable, to acknowledge the simple finding that reactance-arousing messages will not be successful with most people at furthering persuasion goals or altering attitudes and/or behaviors.

Focus on Intrapsychic Components. Much of the laboratory-based experimental research on reactance theory has focused on delineating the specific components of reactance and on examining how intrapsychic variables either moderate or mediate reactance effects. This kind of micro-level focus ignores the valuable contributions to be made by reactance theory at the behavioral level. Communication researchers in particular can contribute much to reactance research by moving away from questions such as "What is reactance?" and asking instead "What message factors facilitate or inhibit reactance?" Moreover, given such an approach, reactance theory may serve as a sound theoretical basis by which to explain similar outcomes obtained through the use of seemingly divergent message types.

Boundary Conditions. Reactance might not be a general phenomenon observed in the population at large in response to persuasion attempts. It is important to acknowledge that, first of all, only certain types of persuasive messages arouse reactance and, equally important, reactance effects may be most prevalent in certain sub-populations. Much of the guidance needed to delineate the boundary conditions of reactance theory may already be present in the original theoretical formula-

tion. For example, it is apparent that reactance may be quite prevalent among subgroups whose members (a) hold self-determination to be very important, (b) see that target behaviors are being chosen for attack, and (c) feel confident that they have sufficient knowledge on which to base decisions.

Freedom Acquisition and Development. It is difficult to quantify what freedoms are considered within the conceivable repertoire of any given individual. Although reactance theory does not make the acquisition of freedom a formal part of its structure, there is an obvious relationship between *how* a freedom is established and the strength of the freedom. Currently, reactance theorists suggest that information relevant to the pursuit of these issues can best be found elsewhere. It is suggested that literature that examines acquisition of beliefs should be sought, and then a special analysis concerning beliefs about behavioral freedoms could be made. An approach of this kind would presumably lead to hypotheses about the strength with which a freedom would be held and would go hand in hand with investigation of the interactive effects of strength of freedom and strength of threat.

Strength of Freedom. Although the concept of having free behaviors is a fundamental theoretical proposition, researchers have conceded a lack of knowledge regarding how the strength of freedoms is established. Because freedoms are considered beliefs, they may vary in the strength to which they are held. It is also expected that the strength of a freedom will be positively correlated with its importance to the individual (Brehm & Brehm, 1981). The interesting aspect of freedom strength is that it may limit the amount of reactance that can be aroused by any given threat.

Magnitude and Freedom Sets. A third aspect of freedoms that remains poorly understood is how they may be perceived as "sets." It is argued that although people have a large repertoire of freedoms to engage in at any given time, they are generally conscious of one or a few sets of behaviors guided by their immediate surroundings. If the theoretical proposition addressing the relationship between proportion of freedoms threatened and obtained reactance is to have some general utility in the understanding of behavior, sets of freedoms need to be further understood. In addition, because magnitude of reactance is a direct function of freedoms threatened, one part of understanding magnitude relies on an understanding of what freedoms are available and how many of these are threatened at any given time.

Reactance and Physiology. Reactance presumably includes urges (varying in strength) to respond in a manner that results in restoration of a freedom. It has been suggested that psychological reactance may even be accompanied by feelings of hostility (Brehm & Brehm, 1981). However, there has yet to be a concerted effort to measure physiological arousal concurrently with predicted reactance. The study of such physiological effects could serve to further validate the theory and open up further avenues of inquiry.

Threats to Freedom. Any event that makes it more difficult for a person to exercise a freedom constitutes a threat to that freedom. Generally, strong threats produce stronger reactance effects than do weak threats. Theoretically, one might expect that when two or more threats are applied to the same freedom, stronger reactance effects would occur than when these same threats are applied singly. This expectation has received mixed support in the literature (Brehm & Brehm, 1981). The

variation in patterns of reactance effects to multiple threats to the same freedom raises a number of theoretical issues about how threats work.

One issue concerns the possibility that as the perceived difficulty of exercising a freedom increases, there is a threshold at which the perception of threat occurs. Thus, it is possible that two or more independent events that increase the perceived difficulty of exercising a freedom (each of which is sub-threshold) can combine to form an actual perceived threat to freedom.

A related concern is the possibility that an initial threat may sensitize a person to subsequent threats to freedom. If sensitization occurs, it could magnify the amount of reactance that would occur in response to a particular threat. The notion that people may be hypersensitive to threats to their freedoms when reactance exists has important implications for understanding persuasion attempts in real-world contexts characterized by multiple messages delivered over time addressing the same issue and/or calling for the same attitudinal and/or behavioral modification.

Loss of Freedom. While the loss of a freedom should arouse some reactance, the current view of the theory emphasizes that a person will give up a freedom when it is clear there is no way to recover it. Presumably, then, the reactance that occurs from the loss dissipates once the freedom in reality is abandoned. An interesting question is whether the elimination of a freedom will lead to the freedom being given up. On the one hand, if the freedom has not been given up, then there should be a continued state of reactance with one of two possible outcomes: Either compliance will be less than complete, or the desire to engage in the proscribed behavior will intensify.

However, people may respond to elimination of freedom in a different way. It is conceivable that after the initial arousal of re-actance due to the elimination, a person can temporarily relinquish a freedom. Reactance might then dissipate, resulting in total com-pliance. In summary, there is incomplete understanding of how people respond to elim-ination of freedoms. Although research on learned helplessness indicates that feelings of anxiousness, anger, and (possibly) depression may result, it is not known how long these effects last or the duration of impact on per-suasion attempts.

FUTURE DIRECTIONS AND EXTENSIONS OF REACTANCE THEORY

Research efforts are currently under way to extend the scope and applicability of re-actance theory to varying contexts and popu-lations. It should be noted that the previous review of the research literature clearly indi-cates that the impact of psychological re-actance has been studied in a number of con-texts with concern for a variety of outcomes. However, it is fair to conclude that the lion's share of the research attention has focused on situations in which face-to-face communica-tion to restrict alternatives or force choices was the primary modality. Those interested in the social effects of the mass media and new information technologies have paid very little attention to reactance formulations. While there has been a geometric increase in the use of mediated communication to change atti-tudes and/or alter behaviors, there has not been much (if any) recognition of the poten-tial for public service announcements, paid advertisements, media advocacy, and Web sites to be seen as communications that en-hance reactance. Certainly, there are ques-tions as to whether mediated communication, in which messages can be simply ignored or discounted, might have the same potency in

arousing psychological reactance as would a face-to-face encounter in which more surveil-lance, actual means to control or restrict free-dom, and an enhanced sense of immediacy between persuader and target exist. Even though such questions currently remain un-answered, it appears that the failure of a number of media campaigns aimed at specific target audiences argues for looking at psycho-logical reactance as a potential explanation for reaction to all kinds of mediated suasory attempts.

One such target population of concern, es-pecially in the public health arena, is that of adolescents. This population is of special interest because of adolescents' propensity to engage in risky and undesirable behaviors. During the past few years, numerous health-related media campaigns attempting to re-strain undesirable behaviors (e.g., smoking, underage drinking, illicit drug use) in adoles-cents have been successful at times and inef-fective in other situations. These campaigns have been produced and disseminated with lit-tle thought as to whether the messages used might actually be contributing to the uptake of deleterious behaviors in subgroups by produc-ing varying levels reactance in this population. Therefore, research concerning those factors that may exacerbate or eliminate reactance in adolescent populations is necessary to better understand this population's acceptance or re-jection of health-related campaign messages.

Adolescence and Reactance

Prior to adolescence, children tend to believe that adults are very knowledgeable, and most children accept what adult authority figures tell them without question (Caissy, 1994). Children's beliefs, attitudes, and be-haviors are strongly shaped by their familial and social environment. For example child-rearing style and family practices influence children's health attitudes and behaviors. Children whose parents use an authoritative approach may be less likely to engage in the risky behaviors suggested by their peers at an early age. In addition, children raised to assume responsibility for their activities are more likely to engage in positive health behaviors (Tinsley, 1992). However, as children approach adolescence, their peers become much more important forces in influencing attitude development than are their parents or other authority figures (Caissy, 1994; Tinsley, 1992).

Once children enter puberty, they take the liberty of forming their own judgments and begin to observe the world more critically. They tend to question everything their parents or other authorities say, and their receptivity to messages from adults decreases drastically. Furthermore, a number of cognitive and psychosocial risk factors, which are prevalent among early adolescents, may lead to the onset of engaging in risky behaviors (Caissy, 1994). Such factors include (a) social comparison with peer groups, (b) sensitivity to peer pressure, (c) tendency to overestimate the prevalence of cigarette smoking or drug use among peers, (d) tendency to engage in shallow and oversimplified thinking, (e) emulation of adult behavior combined with a lack of understanding of the responsibilities and consequences of such behavior, (f) feelings of invincibility, and (g) rebellion against authority and adult control (Caissy, 1994; Ruble, 1983; Tinsley, 1992).

These factors indicate that children, as they enter puberty, perceive themselves as more capable of realizing and making choices, while perhaps becoming relatively unaware and/or accepting of certain choice limits. Both processes increase the likelihood that adolescents will experience reactance when they perceive a threat to their freedom, while pre-adolescents are less likely to experience such reactance. Reactance researchers most often use

adolescents as the youngest participants in their samples, yet it is likely that reactance peaks at adolescence because of this desire for independence and individuality and this disavowal of authority.

Reactance theory, then, can explain how children's reactions to health-related messages become more negative as they become adolescents. First, reactance is a function of the importance of threatened freedoms; as children age, there is a concomitant increase in the need for self-determination, the need for self-definition, and the assertion of individuality. Thus, freedom in general becomes more important with age. Second, reactance is a function of the number of freedoms threatened; as children age, a number of cognitive/developmental factors may be conducive to constructing links between threats to specific freedoms and a more general perceived threat to *all* freedoms. Third, for reactance to occur, individuals must be aware that freedoms exist and must have the competence to pursue those freedoms. By adolescence, children have developed a healthy appreciation for individual liberty and have begun to build confidence in their ability to decide for themselves. Moreover, by the time they enter middle school, children have been provided with a substantial amount of information regarding both the "pros" and "cons" of numerous health behaviors and suggested prohibitions from school curricula, family, friends, and the media. They likely feel that they are competent to make such behavior choices.

Message Features

Research strongly indicates that a participant's awareness of the intent to persuade on the part of the influencing agent will result in less message acceptance (McGrane, Toth, & Alley, 1990). Conversely, the less explicit the intent, the more receptive the participant will be to the influence (Weinstein, Grubb, & Vautier, 1986). Thus, perceived persuasive intent along with explicitly persuasive messages may result in powerful threats to freedom (White, 1959). This effect is most likely to emerge first during adolescence in that, prior to this age, children are often confused by the persuasive intent of adults or the mass media. For example, it has been demonstrated that young children are unable to correctly use a variety of attribution principles when making judgments about causality and motivation (Sedlack & Kurtz, 1981). During adolescence, enhanced needs for independence and the expression of individuality (Botvin & Eng, 1980) may contribute to both the salience of "controlling" cues and the concomitant attribution of manipulation to message sources using such cues. Therefore, messages using explicit threat in advocating a position will elicit greater reactance than will those leaving the threat implicit.

In addition, because peers play an important role in the (non)initiation of risky behaviors (Botvin & Botvin, 1992), it has often been suggested that peer support for resisting things such as illicit drug, tobacco, or alcohol use may have a significant impact on initiation and cessation (Carlson, 1994; Ellickson, Bell, & Harrison, 1993; Gorman, 1996; Logan, 1991). The general peer group model that drives many community- and school-based interventions (Jansen, Glynn, & Howard, 1996; Logan, 1991) focuses on using peers as sources of information and as positive models that aid in resisting pressure to engage in risky behaviors.

Given the reported success of community and school-based anti-drug interventions using peer leaders, it seems reasonable to propose that the use of peers in campaigns aimed at restricting the behaviors of adolescents may prove efficacious in delaying the uptake of such behaviors. Moreover, in that attributions of authoritative control and manipulation

may be less likely when peers are identified as information sources, it is likely that these messages may be attended to and not so easily dismissed by invocation of the potentially available and salient heuristic of "Reject/Avoid all authoritative adults."

Applying the previous research on message implicitness and message source (peer vs. authority) to the context of public health has produced several testable predictions concerning the response of adolescents to different health-related campaign techniques. Note that reactance, at least in the current research effort, has been operationalized as including source and message derogation, the active seeking of counterattitudinal information, and behavioral intent to engage in behaviors counter to those advocated. Accordingly, it is predicted that implicit messages delivered by peers will produce less message and source derogation, less seeking of counterattitudinal information, and less intent to engage in counteradvocated behaviors in adolescents than will explicit messages delivered by authority figures. It should be noted that the latter technique (explicit messages delivered by authority figures) is the status quo of multimillion-dollar health campaigns across the country.

SUMMARY AND CONCLUSION

The prognosis for reactance theory is quite positive. However, continued research on why and how reactance affects message acceptance in specific populations is necessary to fully resuscitate this theory and restore it to the company of more accepted persuasion theories. The application of reactance theory to adolescent populations and public health contexts is a step in the right direction. Members of any population who feel reluctant or hesitant to accept messages produced and presented by those in authority are at some risk of experiencing reactance. Minorities and underserved populations are prime examples of populations whose members may well perceive messages from the government or other authority figures as real and substantial threats to their freedoms. Explicit messages from these authority figures may produce powerful and unintended effects because people are experiencing reactance. In addition, other source and message factors such as credibility, message sidedness, and total number of messages received may influence the amount of reactance experienced by any one individual.

While it is true that reactance theory has had its share of problems, refusing to acknowledge this theory's practical import to the field of persuasion is imprudent and will only serve to return reactance theory to the conceptual junk heap. Reactance theory provides us with an excellent opportunity to examine a profusion of source and message factors within a strong theoretical framework and then to apply our results to real-world situations and problems. Given the cacophony of calls for more attention to the development of theoretical explanations of social influence phenomena, it is unclear why revisiting this manifestly message-centered theory is not long overdue. It is also not evident on what criteria (if any), of theoretical utility and scientific validity of which we are aware, are not met by the reactance formulation.

REFERENCES

Allen, D. N., Sprenkel, D. G., & Vitale, P. A. (1994). Reactance theory and alcohol consumption laws: Further confirmation among collegiate alcohol consumers. *Journal of Studies on Alcohol, 55,* 34-40.

Baer, R., Hinkle, S., Smith, K., & Fenton, M. (1980). Reactance as a function of actual versus projected autonomy. *Journal of Personality and Social Psychology, 38,* 416-422.

Baum, A., Fleming, R., & Reddy, D. M. (1986). Unemployment stress: Loss of control, reactance, and learned helplessness. *Social Science and Medicine, 22,* 509-516.

Baum, A., & Gatchel, R. J. (1981). Cognitive determinants of reaction to uncontrollable events: Development of reactance and learned helplessness. *Journal of Personality and Social Psychology, 40,* 1078-1089.

Bensley, L. S., & Wu, R. (1991). The role of psychological reactance in drinking following alcohol prevention messages. *Journal of Applied Social Psychology, 21,* 1111-1124.

Berkowitz, W. R. (1974). The impact of protest: Willingness of passersby to make anti-war commitments at anti-Vietnam demonstrations. *Journal of Social Psychology, 93,* 31-42.

Beutler, L. E. (1979). Toward specific psychological therapies for specific conditions. *Journal of Consulting and Clinical Psychology, 47,* 882-897.

Botvin, G. J., & Botvin, E. M. (1992). Adolescent tobacco, alcohol, and drug abuse: Prevention strategies, empirical findings, and assessment issues. *Developmental and Behavioral Pediatrics, 13,* 290-301.

Botvin, G. J., & Eng, A. (1980). A comprehensive school-based smoking prevention program. *Journal of School Health, 50,* 209-213.

Brehm, J. W. (1966). *A theory of psychological reactance.* New York: Academic Press.

Brehm, J. W., & Mann, M. (1975). Effect of importance of freedom and attraction to group members on influence produced by group pressure. *Journal of Personality and Social Psychology, 31,* 816-824.

Brehm, J. W., & Sensenig, J. (1966). Social influence as a function of attempted and implied usurpation of choice. *Journal of Personality and Social Psychology, 4,* 703-707.

Brehm, J. W., Stires, L. K., Sensenig, J., & Shaban, J. (1966). The attractiveness of an eliminated choice alternative. *Journal of Experimental Social Psychology, 2,* 301-313.

Brehm, S. S. (1976). *The application of social psychology to clinical practice.* Washington, DC: Hemisphere.

Brehm, S. S. (1977). The effect of adult influence on children's preference: Compliance vs. opposition. *Journal of Abnormal Child Psychology, 5,* 31-41.

Brehm, S. S., & Brehm, J. W. (1981). *Psychological reactance: A theory of freedom and control.* New York: Academic Press.

Brehm, S. S., & Weinraub, M. (1977). Physical barriers and psychological reactance: 2-year-olds' responses to threats to freedom. *Journal of Personality and Social Psychology, 35,* 830-836.

Broeder, D. (1959). The University of Chicago jury project. *Nebraska Law Review, 38,* 744-760.

Brounstein, P., Ostrove, N., & Mills, J. (1979). Divergence of private evaluations of alternatives prior to a choice. *Journal of Personality and Social Psychology, 37,* 1957-1965.

Bushman, B. J., & Stack, A. D. (1996). Forbidden fruit versus tainted fruit: Effects of warning labels on attraction to television violence. *Journal of Experimental Psychology: Applied, 2,* 207-226.

Caissy, G. A. (1994). *Early adolescence.* New York: Plenum.

Carlson, J. G. (1982). Some concepts of perceived control and their relationship to bodily self-control. *Biofeedback and Self-Regulation, 7,* 341-375.

Carlson, K. A. (1994). Prevention in its social context: Student views. *Journal of Alcohol and Drug Education, 40,* 26-35.

Carter, J. E., & Kelly, A. E. (1997). Using traditional and paradoxical imagery interventions with reactant intramural athletes. *Sport Psychologist, 11,* 175-189.

Carver, C. S. (1977). Self-awareness, perception of threat, and the expression of reactance through attitude change. *Journal of Personality, 45,* 501-512.

Carver, C. S. (1980). Perceived coercion, resistance to persuasion, and the Type A behavior pattern. *Journal of Research in Personality, 14,* 467-481.

Carver, C. S., & Scheier, M. F. (1981). Self-consciousness and reactance. *Journal of Research in Personality, 15,* 16-29.

Chaiken, S. (1980). Heuristic versus systematic information processing and the use of source versus message cues in persuasion. *Journal of Personality and Social Psychology, 39,* 752-766.

Chaiken, S. (1987). The Heuristic Model of persuasion. In M. P. Zanna, J. M. Olson, & C. P.

Herman (Eds.), *Social influence: The Ontario Symposium* (Vol. 5, pp. 3-39). Hillsdale, NJ: Lawrence Erlbaum.

Cherulnik, P. D., & Citrin, M. M. (1974). Individual difference in psychological reactance: The interaction between locus of control and mode of elimination of freedom. *Journal of Personality and Social Psychology, 29,* 398-404.

Clee, M. A., & Wicklund, R. A. (1980). Consumer behavior and psychological reactance. *Journal of Consumer Research, 6,* 389-405.

Cooper, J. (1974). Population control and the psychology of forced compliance. *Journal of Social Issues, 30,* 265-277.

Dickenberger, D., & Grabitz-Gniech, G. (1972). Restrictive conditions for the occurrence of psychological reactance: Interpersonal attraction, need for social approval, and a delay factor. *European Journal of Social Psychology, 2,* 177-198.

Dowd, E. T., Hughs, S. L., Brockbank, L., & Halpain, D. (1988). Compliance-based and defiance-based intervention strategies and psychological reactance in the treatment of free and unfree behavior. *Journal of Counseling Psychology, 35,* 370-376.

Dowd, E. T., Milne, C. R., & Wise, S. L. (1991). The Therapeutic Reactance Scale: A measure of psychological reactance. *Journal of Counseling and Development, 69,* 541-545.

Dowd, E. T., & Sanders, D. (1994). Resistance, reactance, and the difficult client. *Canadian Journal of Counselling, 28,* 13-24.

Dowd, E. T., & Seibel, C. A. (1990). A cognitive theory of resistance and reactance: Implications for treatment. *Journal of Mental Health Counseling, 12,* 458-469.

Dowd, E. T., Trutt, S. D., & Watkins, C. E. (1992). Interpretation style and reactance in counselor's social influence. *Psychological Reports, 70,* 247-254.

Dowd, E. T., & Wallbrown, F. (1993). Motivational components of client reactance. *Journal of Counseling and Development, 71,* 533-538.

Dowd, E. T., Wallbrown, F., Sanders, D., & Yesenosky, J. M. (1994). Psychological reactance and its relationship to normal personality variables. *Cognitive Therapy and Research, 18,* 601-612.

Ellickson, P. L., Bell, R. M., & Harrison, E. R. (1993). Changing adolescent propensities to use drugs: Results from Project ALERT. *Health Education Quarterly, 20,* 227-242.

Elman, D., & Kellebrew, T. J. (1978). Incentives and seat belts: Changing a resistant behavior through extrinsic motivation. *Journal of Applied Social Psychology, 8,* 72-83.

Engs, R., & Hanson, D. J. (1989). Reactance theory: A test with collegiate drinking. *Psychological Reports, 64,* 1083-1086.

Feldman-Summers, S. (1977). Implications of the buck-passing phenomenon for reactance theory. *Journal of Personality, 45,* 543-553.

Fogarty, J. S. (1997). Reactance theory and patient noncompliance. *Social Science and Medicine, 45,* 1277-1288.

Frank, S. J., Jackson-Walker, S., Marks, M., Van Egeren, L. A., Loop, K., & Olson, K. (1998). From the laboratory to the hospital, adults to adolescents, and disorders to personality: The case of psychological reactance. *Journal of Clinical Psychology, 54,* 361-381.

Gannon, L., Heiser, P., & Knight, S. (1985). Learned helplessness versus reactance: The effects of sex-role stereotypy. *Sex Roles, 12,* 791-806.

Goldman, M., Pulcher, D., & Mendez, T. (1983). Appeals for help, prosocial behavior, and psychological reactance. *Journal of Psychology, 113,* 265-269.

Goodstadt, M. S. (1971). Helping and refusal to help: A test of balance and reactance theories. *Journal of Experimental Social Psychology, 7,* 610-622.

Gordon, R. M. (1976). Effects of volunteering and responsibility on perceived value and effectiveness of a clinical treatment. *Journal of Consulting and Clinical Psychology, 44,* 799-801.

Gorman, D. M. (1996). Etiological theories and the primary prevention of drug use. *Journal of Drug Issues, 26,* 505-520.

Grabitz-Gniech, G. (1971). Some restrictive conditions for the occurrence of psychological reactance. *Journal of Personality and Social Psychology, 19,* 188-196.

Greybar, S. R., Antonuccio, D. O., Boutilier, L. R., & Varble, D. L. (1989). Psychological reactance as a factor affecting patient compliance to physi-

cian advice. *Scandinavian Journal of Behavior Therapy, 18,* 43-51.

Gruder, C. L., Cook, T. D., Hennigan, K. M., Flay, B. R., Alessis, C., & Halamaj, J. (1978). Empirical tests of the absolute sleeper effect predicted from the discounting cue hypothesis. *Journal of Personality and Social Psychology, 36,* 1061-1075.

Hammock, T., & Brehm, J. W. (1966). The attractiveness of choice alternatives when freedom to choose is eliminated by a social agent. *Journal of Personality, 34,* 546-554.

Hannah, T. E., Hannah, E. R., & Wattie, B. (1975). Arousal of psychological reactance as a consequence of predicting an individual's behavior. *Psychological Reports, 37,* 411-420.

Heilman, M. D. (1976). Oppositional behavior as a function of influence attempt intensity and retaliation threat. *Journal of Personality and Social Psychology, 33,* 574-578.

Heilman, M. D., & Garner, K. A. (1975). Counteracting the boomerang: The effects of choice on compliance to threats and promises. *Journal of Personality and Social Psychology, 31,* 911-917.

Heilman, M. D., & Toffler, B. L. (1976). Reacting to reactance: An interpersonal interpretation of the need for freedom. *Journal of Experimental Social Psychology, 12,* 519-529.

Hellman, C. M., & McMillin, W. L. (1997). The relationship between psychological reactance and self-esteem. *Journal of Social Psychology, 137,* 135-138.

Herman, G., & Leyens, J. P. (1977). Rating films on T.V. *Journal of Communication, 27,* 48-53.

Hockenberry, S. L., & Billingham, R. E. (1993). Psychological reactance and violence within dating relationships. *Psychological Reports, 73,* 1203-1208.

Hong, S. M. (1990). Effects of sex and church attendance on psychological reactance. *Psychological Reports, 66,* 494.

Hong, S. M. (1992). Hong's Psychological Reactance Scale: A further factor analytic validation. *Psychological Reports, 70,* 512-514.

Hong, S. M., & Faedda, S. (1996). Refinement of the Hong Psychological Reactance Scale. *Educational and Psychological Measurement, 56,* 173-182.

Hong, S. M., & Giannakopoulos, E. (1994). The relationship of satisfaction with life to personality characteristics. *Journal of Psychology, 128,* 547-558.

Hong, S. M., Giannakopoulos, E., Laing, D., & Williams, N. A. (1994). Psychological reactance: Effects of age and gender. *Journal of Social Psychology, 134,* 223-228.

Hong, S. M., & Langovski, N. (1994). Sex differences in psychological reactance amongst Korean residents in Australia. *Psychological Reports, 75,* 578.

Hong, S. M., & Page, S. (1989). A psychological reactance scale: Development, factor structure, and reliability. *Psychological Reports, 64,* 1323-1326.

Hughes, J. N., & Falk, R. S. (1981). Resistance, reactance, and consultation. *Journal of School Psychology, 19,* 134-142.

Hunsley, J. (1997). Defiance-based symptom prescription and psychological reactance: A critical evaluation. *Professional Psychology Research and Practice, 28,* 36-43.

Jansen, M. A., Glynn, T., & Howard, J. (1996). Prevention of alcohol, tobacco, and other drug abuse. *American Behavioral Scientist, 39,* 790-807.

Jardine, E., & Winefield, A. H. (1981). Achievement motivation, psychological reactance, and learned helplessness. *Motivation & Emotion, 5,* 99-113.

Jones, R. A. (1970). Volunteering to help: The effects of choice, dependence, and anticipated dependence. *Journal of Personality and Social Psychology, 14,* 121-129.

Jones, R. A., & Brehm, J. W. (1970). Persuasiveness of one- and two-sided communications as a function of awareness there are two sides. *Journal of Experimental Social Psychology, 6,* 47-56.

Joseph, C. A., Joseph, C. R., Barto, J., & McKay, T. D. (1982). Effects of sex of subject and emotional role-playing on reactance. *Perceptual and Motor Skills, 54,* 1282.

Joubert, C. E. (1990). Relationship among self-esteem, psychological reactance, and other personality variables. *Psychological Reports, 66,* 1147-1151.

Joubert, C. E. (1992). Antecedents of narcissism and psychological reactance as indicated by college students' retrospective reports of their parents' behaviors. *Psychological Reports, 70,* 1111-1115.

Joubert, C. E. (1995). Associations of social personality factors with personal habits. *Psychological Reports, 76,* 1315-1321.

Kanfer, F. H., & Grimm, L. G. (1978). Freedom of choice and behavioral change. *Journal of Consulting and Clinical Psychology, 46,* 673-686.

Karpf, R. J. (1978). Altering values via psychological reactance and reversal effects. *Journal of Social Psychology, 106,* 131-132.

Kelly, A. E., & Nauta, M. M. (1997). Reactance and thought suppression. *Personality and Social Psychology Bulletin, 23,* 1123-1132.

Kohn, P. M., & Barnes, G. E. (1977). Subject variables and reactance to persuasive communications about drugs. *European Journal of Social Psychology, 7,* 97-109.

Lenehan, G. E., & O'Neill, P. (1981). Reactance and conflict as determinants of judgment in a mock jury experiment. *Journal of Applied Social Psychology, 11,* 231-239.

Linder, D. E., & Crane, K. A. (1970). Reactance theory analysis of predecisional cognitive processes. *Journal of Personality and Social Psychology, 15,* 258-264.

Linder, D. E., Wortman, C. B., & Brehm, J. W. (1971). Temporal changes in predecision preference among choice alternatives. *Journal of Personality and Social Psychology, 19,* 282-284.

Logan, B. N. (1991). Adolescent substance abuse prevention: An overview of the literature. *Family Community Health, 13,* 25-36.

Long, S. (1978). Political alienation: Reality and reactance. *Journal of Social Psychology, 104,* 115-121.

Manikowske, L., & Winakor, G. (1994). Equity, attribution, and reactance in giving and receiving gifts of clothing. *Clothing and Textiles Research Journal, 12,* 22-30.

Mazis, M. B. (1975). Antipollution measures and psychological reactance theory: A field experiment. *Journal of Personality and Social Psychology, 31,* 654-660.

Mazis, M. B., Settle, R. B., & Leslie, D. C. (1973). Elimination of phosphate detergents and psychological reactance. *Journal of Marketing Research, 10,* 390-395.

McGrane, W. L., Toth, F. J., & Alley, E. B. (1990). The use of interactive media for HIV/AIDS prevention in the military community. *Military Medicine, 155*, 235-240.

Merz, J. (1983). A questionnaire for the measurement of psychological reactance. *Diagnostica, 29*, 75-82. (In German)

Mikulincer, M., Kedem, P., & Zilkha-Segal, H. (1989). Learned helplessness, reactance, and cue utilization. *Journal of Research in Personality, 23*, 235-247.

Miller, R. L., Brickman, P., & Bolen, D. (1975). Attribution versus persuasion as a means for modifying behavior. *Journal of Personality and Social Psychology, 31*, 430-441.

Mills, J. (1968). Interest in supporting and discrepant information. In R. P. Abelson, E. Aronson, W. J. McQuire, T. M. Newcomb, M. J. Rosenberg, & P. H. Tannenbaum (Eds.), *Theories of cognitive consistency: A sourcebook* (pp. 771-776). Chicago: Rand McNally.

Minor, K. I. (1987). Reactance and recidivism: Implications for probation policy and research. *Perceptual and Motor Skills, 64*, 1047-1050.

Morse, S. J., Gergen, K. J., Peele, S., & van Ryneveld, J. (1977). Reactions to receiving expected and unexpected help from a person who violates or does not violate a norm. *Journal of Experimental Social Psychology, 13*, 397-402.

Moyer, W. W. (1978). Effects of loss of freedom on subjects with internal or external locus of control. *Journal of Research in Personality, 12*, 253-261.

Mulry, G., Fleming, R., & Gottschalk, A. C. (1994). Psychological reactance and brief treatment of academic procrastination. *Journal of College Student Psychotherapy, 9*, 41-56.

Oliver, R., Mattson, D. L., & Moore, J. (1993). Psychological reactance in marital enrichment training. *TCA Journal, 22*, 3-10.

Organ, D. W. (1974). Social exchange and psychological reactance in a simulated superior-subordinate relationship. *Organizational Behavior and Human Decision Processes, 12*, 132-142.

Pallak, M. S., & Heller, J. F. (1971). Interactive effects of commitment to future interaction and threat to attitudinal freedom. *Journal of Personality and Social Psychology, 17*, 325-331.

Pallak, M. S., & Sullivan, J. J. (1979). The effect of commitment, threat, and restoration of freedom on attitude-change and action-taking. *Personality and Social Psychology Bulletin, 5*, 307-310.

Pennebaker, J. W., & Sanders, D. Y. (1976). American graffiti: Effects of authority and reactance arousal. *Personality and Social Psychology Bulletin, 2*, 264-267.

Petty, R. E., & Cacioppo, J. T. (1981). *Attitudes and persuasion: Classic and contemporary approaches*. Dubuque, IA: William C. Brown.

Petty, R. E., & Cacioppo, J. T. (1986). The Elaboration Likelihood Model of persuasion. In L. Berkowitz (Ed.), *Advances in experimental social psychology* (Vol. 19, pp. 123-205). Orlando, FL: Academic Press.

Prandoni, J. R., & Wall, S. M. (1990). Effects of mental health and reactance-reducing information on offenders' compliance with court-mandated psychiatric evaluations. *Professional Psychology Research and Practice, 21*, 204-209.

Propst, D. B., & Kurtzz, M. E. (1989). Perceived control/reactance: A framework for understanding leisure behaviour in natural settings. *Leisure Studies, 8*, 241-248.

Redman, S., Dickinson, J. A., Cockburn, J., & Hennrikus, D. (1989). The assessment of reactivity in direct observation studies of doctor-patient interactions. *Psychology & Health, 3*, 17-28.

Regan, J. W., & Brehm, J. W. (1972). Compliance in buying as a function of inducements that threaten freedom. In L. Bickman & T. Henchy (Eds.), *Beyond the laboratory: Field research in social psychology* (pp. 269-274). New York: McGraw-Hill.

Reich, J. W., & Robertson, J. L. (1979). Reactance and norm appeal in anti-littering messages. *Journal of Applied Social Psychology, 9*, 91-101.

Rhodewalt, F., & Comer, R. (1982). Coronary-prone behavior and reactance: The attractiveness of an eliminated choice. *Personality and Social Psychology Bulletin, 8*, 152-158.

Rhodewalt, F., & Davison, J. (1983). Reactance and the coronary-prone behavior pattern: The role of self-attribution in responses to reduced behavioral freedom. *Journal of Personality and Social Psychology, 44*, 220-228.

Rhodewalt, F., & Fairfield, M. (1990). An alternative approach to Type A behavior and health: Psychological reactance and medical noncompliance. *Journal of Social Behavior and Personality, 5,* 323-342.

Rhodewalt, F., & Marcroft, M. (1988). Type A behavior and diabetic control: Implications of psychological reactance for health outcomes. *Journal of Applied Social Psychology, 18,* 139-159.

Rhodewalt, F., & Strube, M. J. (1985). A self-attribution-reactance model of recovery from injury in Type A individuals. *Journal of Applied Social Psychology, 15,* 330-344.

Ringold, D. J. (1988). Consumer response to product withdrawal: The reformulation of Coca-Cola. *Psychology & Marketing, 5,* 189-210.

Rosen, B., & Jerdee, T. H. (1975). Effects of employee's sex and threatening versus pleading appeals on managerial evaluations of grievances. *Journal of Applied Psychology, 60,* 442-445.

Ruble, D. N. (1983). The development of social-comparison processes and their role in achievement-related self-socialization. In E. T. Higgins, D. Ruble, & W. W. Hartup (Eds.), *Social cognition and social development: A sociocultural perspective* (pp. 134-157). Cambridge, UK: Cambridge University Press.

Samuel, W. (1972). Response to Bill of Rights paraphrases as influenced by the hip or straight attire of the opinion solicitor. *Journal of Applied Social Psychology, 2,* 47-62.

Schwarz, N. (1984). When reactance effects persist despite restoration of freedom: Investigations of time delay and vicarious control. *European Journal of Social Psychology, 14,* 405-419.

Schwarz, N., Frey, D., & Kumpf, M. (1980). Interactive effects of writing and reading a persuasive essay on attitude change and selective exposure. *Journal of Experimental Social Psychology, 16,* 1-17.

Sedlack, A. J., & Kurtz, S. T. (1981). A review of children's use of causal inference principles. *Child Development, 52,* 759-784.

Seltzer, L. F. (1983). Influencing the "shape" of resistance: An experimental exploration of paradoxical directives and psychological reactance. *Basic and Applied Social Psychology, 4,* 47-71.

Smith, M. J. (1977). The effects of threats to attitudinal freedom as a function of message quality and initial receiver attitude. *Communication Monographs, 44,* 196-206.

Snyder, M. L., & Wicklund, R. A. (1976). Prior exercise of freedom and reactance. *Journal of Experimental Social Psychology, 12,* 120-130.

Strube, M. J., & Werner, C. (1984). Psychological reactance and the relinquishment of control. *Personality and Social Psychology Bulletin, 10,* 225-234.

Sullivan, J. J., & Pallak, M. S. (1976). The effect of commitment and reactance on action-taking. *Personality and Social Psychology Bulletin, 2,* 179-182.

Swart, C., Ickes, W., & Morgenthaler, E. S. (1978). The effect of objective self-awareness on compliance in a reactance situation. *Social Behavior and Personality, 6,* 135-139.

Swoboda, J. S., Dowd, E. T., & Wise, S. L. (1990). Reframing and restraining directives in the treatment of clinical depression. *Journal of Counseling Psychology, 37,* 254-260.

Tennen, H., & Eller, S. J. (1977). Attributional components of learned helplessness and facilitation. *Journal of Personality and Social Psychology, 35,* 265-271.

Tennen, H., Press, S., Rohrbaugh, M., & White, L. (1981). Reactance theory and therapeutic paradox: A compliance-defiance model. *Psychotherapy: Theory, Research, and Practice, 18,* 14-22.

Tinsley, B. J. (1992). Multiple influences on the acquisition and socialization of children's health attitudes and behavior: An integrative review. *Child Development, 63,* 1043-1069.

Tjosvold, D. (1978). Cooperation and conflict between administrators and teachers. *Journal of Research and Development in Education, 12,* 138-148.

Truscott, D., & Fehr, R. C. (1986). Perceptual reactance and criminal risk-taking. *Personality and Individual Differences, 7,* 373-377.

Varela, J. A. (1978). Solving human problems with human science. *Human Nature, 1,* 84-90.

Voloudakis, M., & Ramirez, A. (1999). *Predicting compliance and satisfaction in a health context? The value of measuring psychological reactance as a personality variable.* Unpublished manuscript, University of Arizona.

Vrugt, A. (1992). Preferential treatment of women and psychological reactance theory: An experiment. *European Journal of Social Psychology, 22,* 303-307.

Weinstein, N. D., Grubb, P. D., & Vautier, J. S. (1986). Increasing automobile seat belt use: An intervention emphasizing risk susceptibility. *Journal of Applied Psychology, 71,* 285-290.

White, R. W. (1959). Motivation reconsidered: The concept of competence. *Psychological Review, 66,* 297-333.

Wicklund, R. A. (1970). Prechoice preference reversal as a result of threat to decision freedom. *Journal of Personality and Social Psychology, 14,* 8-17.

Wicklund, R. A. (1974). *Freedom and reactance.* Potomac, MD: Lawrence Erlbaum.

Willis, J. A., & Goethals, G. R. (1973). Social responsibility and threat to behavioral freedom as determinants of altruistic behavior. *Journal of Personality, 41,* 376-384.

Wolf, S., & Montgomery, D. A. (1977). Effects of inadmissible evidence and level of judicial admonishment to disregard on the judgments of mock jurors. *Journal of Applied Social Psychology, 7,* 205-219.

Worchel, S. (1972). The effects of films on the importance of behavioral freedom. *Journal of Personality, 40,* 417-435.

Worchel, S., & Arnold, S. E. (1973). The effects of censorship and attractiveness of the censor on attitude change. *Journal of Experimental Social Psychology, 9,* 365-377.

Worchel, S., Arnold, S. E., & Baker, M. (1975). The effect of censorship on attitude change: The influence of censor and communication characteristics. *Journal of Applied Social Psychology, 5,* 222-239.

Worchel, S., & Brehm, J. W. (1970). Effect of threats to attitudinal freedom as a function of agreement with the communicator. *Journal of Personality and Social Psychology, 14,* 18-22.

Worchel, S., & Brehm, J. W. (1971). Direct and implied social restoration of freedom. *Journal of Personality and Social Psychology, 18,* 294-304.

Wright, R. A. (1986). Attitude change as a function of threat to attitudinal freedom and extent of agreement with a communicator. *European Journal of Social Psychology, 16,* 43-50.

Wright, R. A., & Brehm, S. S. (1982). Reactance as impression management: A critical review. *Journal of Personality and Social Psychology, 42,* 608-618.

Wright, R. A., Wadley, V. G., Danner, M., & Phillips, P. N. (1992). Persuasion, reactance, and judgments of interpersonal appeal. *European Journal of Social Psychology, 22,* 85-91.

13

Nuances in Inoculation
Theory and Applications

ERIN ALISON SZABO
MICHAEL PFAU

McGuire's inoculation theory about conferring resistance to persuasion has received renewed practical application during recent years. Jamieson (1992) argued that in contexts where challenges to existing attitudes can be foreseen, the challenge can be preempted by way of inoculation. Contemporary research alludes to inoculation's efficacy in protecting attitudes in a variety of applied settings.

Despite its demonstrated effectiveness and potential, however, much is still unknown about the process of inoculation. Pfau (1997) observed, "Despite the potential of the inoculation model, further work needs to be done to enrich the construct, providing greater precision in its use" (p. 134). Eagly and Chaiken (1993) also called for research that attempts to explicate the core processes at work in inoculation.

Existing research on inoculation demonstrates irrefutably that it is an effective technique in promoting resistance to persuasion

(McGuire, 1961a, 1961b, 1962, 1964, 1966; McGuire & Papageorgis, 1961, 1962; Papageorgis & McGuire, 1961; Pfau, Tusing, Koerner, et al., 1997; Pfau, Tusing, Lee, et al., 1997). However, while researchers know how to construct inoculation messages and how to measure resistance outcomes, they do not yet fully understand the process triggered by inoculative messages. Nonetheless, there has been progress on this front. Recent research has provided insights about the processes at work in inoculation, while ongoing research promises further understanding.

In this chapter, the inoculation approach of resistance to influence is described, both through reviewing early research on the construct and through examining contemporary applications of the approach. Research occurring since the Pfau (1997) review of inoculation is discussed with regard to how it provides a clearer picture of the nuances of inoculation. Also, applications of inoculation are explored, including research in progress. Finally, directions for future inoculation research are explored, with particular emphasis on further refinement of the inoculation model.

THE INOCULATION CONSTRUCT

Origins of the Theory

Perhaps Eagly and Chaiken (1993) best described inoculation when they termed it "the grandparent theory of resistance to attitude change" (p. 561). Inoculation was an outgrowth of Hovland, Janis, and Kelley's (1953) research on the relative comparativeness of one-sided versus two-sided messages in producing influence. Lumsdaine and Janis (1953) found that two-sided messages were more effective than one-sided messages in producing "sustained opinion change" in receivers who subsequently encountered counterarguments. They speculated that two-sided messages "inoculated" against attitude change.

While McGuire acknowledged that research on one-sided versus two-sided messages was largely the impetus for his theorizing and testing of the inoculation construct, the early 1960s were also an opportune time for research concerned with resistance to persuasion. During the Korean War, a surprising number of American prisoners of war cooperated with the enemy, not so much as a result of physical coercion but rather due to "indoctrination"—long and systematic proselytizing by the enemy about prisoners' beliefs about democracy, freedom, and capitalism (U.S. Senate, 1956). Some American prisoners found it difficult to defend these basic values when challenged. Why was this the case? Perhaps because democracy, freedom, and capitalism constituted "cultural truisms." They were accepted without question—literally,

taken for granted. As a result, they were vulnerable when subjected to a systematic attack. Another reason for McGuire's interest in inoculation concerned the emphasis since the 1920s on new, more effective methods of persuasion and the dearth of attention about methods of protecting against persuasion (Miller & Burgoon, 1973).

McGuire's original formulation of the inoculation construct "relied on a biological analogy to explain how pretreatment messages might confer resistance" (Pfau, 1997, p. 135). The guiding idea of inoculation theory is taken from the health practice of administering a weakened form of a virus to activate the body's immune system against the virus. Based on this analogy, McGuire (1964) reasoned that people can be stimulated to build up resistance to attacks on attitudes by being exposed to weakened attitude-threatening messages.

McGuire posited that people have many "overprotected" attitudes. His early research (McGuire, 1961a, 1961b; Papageorgis & McGuire, 1961) was founded on the notion of selective exposure (McGuire, 1961a). The selective exposure argument was based on two assumptions: that people are attracted to information that supports existing attitudes and that people purposely avoid information that disagrees with their attitudes. McGuire thought that selective exposure rendered most attitudes overprotected and, thus, candidates for inoculation. However, research findings cast doubt on the validity of the selective avoidance assumption of selective exposure (Brehm & Cohen, 1962), and as a result, McGuire confined the boundaries of inoculation to cultural truisms: attitudes virtually "uncontaminated by counterarguments" (Pfau, 1997, p. 135; see also Anderson & McGuire, 1965). McGuire (1970) described cultural truisms as "so generally accepted that most individuals are unaware of attacking arguments" (p. 37). McGuire focused on a limited number of truisms in his research: the benefit of a yearly physical exam, the importance of chest X-rays in detecting and preventing tuberculosis, the virtues of penicillin, and the worth of daily tooth brushing (McGuire, 1970).

Inoculation Explained

The inoculation approach is based on the assumption that *refutational pretreatments,* which consist of counterarguments challenging a person's attitude and responses to those counterarguments, threaten people. Due to the production of threat, refutational pretreatments motivate people to protect their attitudes, which elicits resistance (Papageorgis & McGuire, 1961). Refutational pretreatments consist of *threat* and *refutational preemption,* which are the two indispensable components of inoculation.

"The threat component is the most distinguishing feature of inoculation" (Pfau, 1997, p. 137). Threat motivates receivers to recognize the vulnerability of their attitudes to conceivable challenges and unleashes an "internal process" (p. 137). Threat is operationalized as a warning of possible future attacks on attitudes and the recognition of attitude vulnerability to change (Pfau, Tusing, Koerner, et al., 1997). Threat elicits the motivation to protect attitudes and, thus, cultivates resistance to counterpersuasion (Pfau & Kenski, 1990).

Refutational preemption, which is the process of replying to counterarguments before they occur, provides receivers with specific arguments they can use to strengthen their attitudes against subsequent influence (Pfau, Tusing, Koerner, et al., 1997). Refutational preemption consists of advancing, and answering, specific assaults on attitudes.

"The two components, threat and refutational preemption, work in tandem: first threat and then refutational preemption" (Pfau, 1997, p. 137). Refutational preemp-

tion provides scripts; threat provides motivation (McGuire, 1964). The inoculative pretreatment identifies attitudinal counterarguments, supplies refutations of these counterarguments, and provides an operational model of attitude defense. The success of inoculation depends on being motivated and capable of defending an attitude. Once receivers are motivated, they attempt to protect their attitudes by using "scripts" provided in the refutational preemption in addition to other applicable material.

It is the motivational component of threat that renders inoculation such a useful approach to attitude resistance. "If the construct were limited to preemptive refutation, it would afford limited utility because communicators would need to prepare specific preemptive messages corresponding to each and every anticipated attack" (Pfau & Kenski, 1990, p. 75). Rather, inoculation spreads a "broad blanket of protection against specific counterarguments raised in refutational preemption and against those counterarguments not raised" (Pfau, 1997, pp. 137-138).

In the original formulation of inoculation, McGuire handled threat as a primitive term, failing to directly measure it (Pfau, Tusing, Koerner, et al., 1997). Instead, McGuire and other researchers "relied on the inference of threat, derived from the comparable effectiveness of same and different refutational pretreatments in promoting resistance to influence" (Pfau, 1997, p. 138). As a result, Kiesler, Collins, and Miller (1969) argued that the "evidence" of threat in McGuire's studies was circumstantial, and Farkas and Anderson (1976) lamented that "there is no direct evidence for their [inoculation messages'] presumed difference in threatening power" (p. 264). McGuire and other researchers argued, however, that because threat motivates receivers to bolster their attitudes, refutational pretreatments can be formulated either as *refutational same,* preempting the specific counterarguments raised in an attack, or *refutational different,* preempting altogether different counterarguments than those raised in a subsequent attack. They reasoned that if inoculation's efficacy stems solely from providing specific counterarguments to subsequent attacks, then its effectiveness should be limited to only inoculation-same messages. However, if inoculation's power comes from threat, which motivates receivers to protect attitudes, then inoculation-same and -different pretreatments should prove to be equally effective. Since then, research has established that inoculation-different messages are as effective as inoculation-same messages and, therefore, that inoculation's strength must be interpreted in terms of the motivational boost stemming from the threat mechanism (McGuire, 1961a, 1961b, 1962, 1966, 1970; Papageorgis & McGuire, 1961; Pfau & Burgoon, 1988; Pfau, Kenski, Nitz, & Sorenson, 1990; Pfau et al., 2001; Pfau, Tusing, Koerner, et al., 1997).

As discussed previously, early inoculation research either assumed (but did not confirm) the presence of threat (McGuire, 1961b, 1966; Papageorgis & McGuire, 1961) or simply confirmed the presence of threat via manipulation checks (McGuire, 1962, 1964; McGuire & Papageorgis, 1961, 1962). However, subsequent studies measured threat level (Pfau & Burgoon, 1988; Pfau et al., 1990; Pfau et al., 2001; Pfau, Tusing, Koerner, et al., 1997; Pfau, Van Bockern, & Kang, 1992) and demonstrated that threat is positively related to increased attitude resistance. Unfortunately, *how* threat confers resistance has only recently been analyzed, as is discussed later.

Boundary Conditions

As indicated previously, McGuire's early inoculation research was limited to "cultural truisms"—uncontaminated "germ-free

beliefs" (Pfau, 1997, p. 140). This suggested boundary conditions for inoculation theory based on the nature of the issues confronted: that inoculation is restricted to noncontroversial issues. This question was addressed by several researchers during the late 1960s through the 1970s. These researchers demonstrated convincingly that refutational pretreatments effectively conferred attitude resistance on various controversial topics (Adams & Beatty, 1977; Anatol & Mandel, 1972; Burgoon et al., 1976; Burgoon & Chase, 1973; Burgoon, Cohen, Miller, & Montgomery, 1978; Burgoon & King, 1974; Crane, 1962; Cronen & LeFleur, 1977; Hunt, 1973; McCroskey, 1970; McCroskey, Young, & Scott, 1972; Miller & Burgoon, 1979; Sawyer, 1973; Szybillo & Heslin, 1973; Ullman & Bodaken, 1975). Results of these studies demonstrated that "the logic of the refutational approach applies irrespective of whether the content domain is noncontroversial or controversial" (Pfau, 1997, p. 141).

EXAMINING THE PROCESS

Enriching the Model

Threat and refutational preemption are the essential elements of inoculation. The process induced by these two components is "part motivational and part cognitive, but more needs to be learned about it" (Pfau, 1997, p. 152; see also Eagly & Chaiken, 1993). However, we maintain that threat is the most integral of the two.

What determines whether a message produces sufficient threat? A variety of components are responsible for producing threat, such as receiver sociodemographics and individual differences, content domain, message design and features, and topic involvement and context. In his review of inoculation theory, Pfau (1997) posed two questions about threat: First, "Is threat alone sufficient to confer resistance?" Second, "Precisely what cognitive processes does threat trigger?" (pp. 152-153). It is this second question that researchers have been exploring in recent research.

Pfau (1997) claimed that threat requires optimal receiver involvement levels. If receiver involvement levels are too low or too high, the threat component of an inoculation treatment might not be capable of eliciting the *additional* motivation required to *further* protect attitudes. Therefore, he maintained that involvement dictates boundary conditions for inoculation theory. Involvement, as it is conceptualized in inoculation research, is the perceived importance of an attitude object to a receiver, or what Eagly and Chaiken (1993) characterized as "outcome-relevant involvement." An important focus in recent research concerns the relationship among receiver involvement, elicited threat, and resistance to influence. Is it possible to elicit sufficient threat, and thus to inoculate, if receivers do not perceive the attitude object as sufficiently involving? Research in commercial advertising suggests that a minimal level of involvement may be a prerequisite for inoculation (Kamins & Asseal, 1987; Pfau, 1992). Conversely, is it possible to elicit further threat, and thus promote additional resistance to influence, if receivers already perceive an attitude object as high involving? It may be that involvement also provides a ceiling effect, beyond which inoculation yields diminishing returns.

Receiver involvement may be the definitive factor determining inoculation's boundaries. If threat limits the applicability of inoculation to the broad range of moderately involving issues, then it may "hold the key to the boundary conditions of the theory" (Pfau, 1997, p. 154). The inoculation approach might not be useful in situations where the topic or receiver characteristics either thwart sufficient

personal involvement or fuel particularly high personal involvement. In addition, receiver involvement may carry important implications concerning the nature of the internal processes elicited in inoculation and, therefore, the type of inoculation message that is most effective in conferring resistance.

These and other nuances in inoculation have been explored recently. Although many questions are still unanswered, patterns are beginning to surface, hinting at the processes at work in resistance.

Recent Research:
The Robustness of Inoculation

In 1996, Pfau and colleagues launched an extensive investigation aimed at uncovering subtle "nuances in inoculation" (Pfau, Tusing, Koerner, et al., 1997; Pfau, Tusing, Lee, et al., 1997). Rather than attempting to apply the theory to a specific context, this investigation sought to determine the processes triggered by threat and receiver involvement. The investigation also explored the effectiveness of central and peripheral inoculation treatments in conferring resistance to persuasion while considering the role of ego involvement, receiver need for cognition, and receiver gender. Finally, this study tested the hypothesis that social judgment theory's assimilation and contrast mechanism could explain the cognitive processes at work in inoculation.

The investigation featured three issues (determined from pretesting) of varying issue involvement. The researchers (Pfau, Tusing, Lee, et al., 1997) argued that the message processing literature provides a rationale for exploring message processing disposition in conjunction with treatment approach. Because inoculation is assumed to be an active process, it presupposes mindful elaboration of message arguments. This type of processing corresponds to the processing of the Elaboration

Likelihood Model's central route (Petty & Cacioppo, 1986) and the Heuristic-Systematic Model's systematic route (Chaiken, 1980). Therefore, the researchers argued that central or systematic message treatments should be more effective than peripheral message treatments in inoculation. In addition, they reasoned that receiver need for cognition and involvement would be positively related to resistance because both facilitate the receiver's cognitive effort. Pfau, Tusing, Lee, and colleagues (1997) designed central/ systematic (cognitive) messages such that they contained arguments backed up by statistics and research findings. Their peripheral messages contained affective and source appeals, with arguments backed by anecdotes and source expertise.

Pfau, Tusing, Lee, and colleagues' (1997) findings suggest that resistance is a complicated process that is full of nuances. In terms of message type, the results indicated that central and peripheral inoculation treatments are equally effective in conferring resistance. Results, however, did reveal differences in the relative effectiveness of inoculation treatments depending on issue involvement and need for cognition. The influence of need for cognition varied across topics of differing levels of involvement. Receiver need for cognition was positively related to resistance, but only for the high-involving topic, in which need for cognition was associated positively with experienced threat. For the low-involving topic, high need for cognition was negatively related to resistance, resulting in more positive attitudes toward the attack message and source. Pfau and colleagues reasoned that the effect of need for cognition on a high-involving issue makes theoretical sense because both issue involvement and need for cognition enhance message processing and, therefore, should increase the effectiveness of inoculation for high-involving issues. However, they lamented the lack of theoretical

explanation for the findings of the low-involvement condition.

The effects of ego involvement on inoculation's effectiveness suggest boundary conditions of inoculation, as discussed earlier. Pfau, Tusing, Lee, and colleagues (1997) proposed that experienced threat would be greatest for more ego-involved participants. With moderate- and high-involving topics, this prediction was supported. They reasoned that the more ego-involved a receiver is, "the more likely he/ she can access relevant attitudes (Fazio, 1989), thereby facilitating threat, which requires that receivers perceive the potential vulnerability of attitudes" (Pfau, Tusing, Lee, et al., 1997, p. 475). In addition, the results supported the prediction that the efficacy of inoculation is greater with more ego-involved receivers. The results indicated that greater ego involvement increases resistance, "independent of the other processes in social judgment theory, namely assimilation and contrast" (p. 465). Finally, Pfau, Tusing, Lee, and colleagues (1997) posited that the cognitive process triggered by threat was assimilation and contrast. However, the results revealed no evidence of an assimilation effect, prompting the conclusion that a "suitable rationale for the cognitive process triggered via inoculation must lie elsewhere" (p. 475).

The other facet of this investigation attempted to uncover the role of key components in the process of resistance (Pfau, Tusing, Koerner, et al., 1997)—specifically, the relationship between threat and involvement. Furthermore, it examined the role and effects of involvement, threat, counterarguments, and responses to counterarguments in resistance.

Results indicated that both inoculation-same and -different messages confer resistance to persuasion. Furthermore, the results revealed that threat and issue involvement are not related to each other but that they play similar roles in the process of resistance—in essence, paralleling each other. Threat *directly* rendered Phase 2 attitudes more resistant, but only for the low- and moderate-involving topics. This suggests that for the low- and moderate-involving topics, threat is the fundamental variable, acting as a "motivational catalyst" in causing receivers to strengthen initial attitudes.

Involvement, on the other hand, both directly and indirectly contributed to resistance to influence through a variety of paths. The pattern of results revealed that involvement was positively related to resistance and to number of responses to counterarguments, but only with moderate- and high-involving topics. Inoculation was the least effective for the low-involving condition, suggesting again that there is a floor for involvement and threat. Furthermore, the researchers (Pfau, Tusing, Koerner, et al., 1997) found consistent main effect findings for involvement on most indicators of resistance for both the moderate- and high-involving topics. Involvement seemed to play two main roles in the process of resistance. First, it directly made final attitudes more resistant to attacks for all topics. Second, it was positively related to Phase 2 attitudes and negatively related to Phase 3 attitudes. Pfau and colleagues explained this outcome by positing that delay is needed to provide time for receivers to generate counterarguments and, subsequently, "bolster attitudes against change" (p. 210). Past research supports the position that delay is needed to allow time for resistance to set in (McGuire, 1970).

Pfau, Tusing, Koerner, and colleagues (1997) also examined the potential of counterarguing to explain the process triggered via inoculation. Based on suggestions provided by Benoit (1991) on measuring counterarguing in the context of resistance, Pfau et al.'s measure of counterarguing moved beyond listing thoughts contrary to one's positions to providing specific responses to counterarguments

listed. However, Pfau and colleagues' results suggested only partial support for counterarguing as the process triggered via inoculation. Results for the moderate-involving topic revealed that inoculation messages produce threat, which triggers counterarguing. Furthermore, results revealed that involved receivers produce more responses to counterarguments.

Pfau, Tusing, Koerner, and colleagues (1997) argued that the main finding of this study is that involvement, more than any other component, reveals inoculation's terrain. With low and high involvement, inoculation treatments are unable to generate sufficient threat, which thwarts resistance—at low involvement because receivers are unmotivated and treatments are unable to raise motivational levels, at high involvement because receivers are already motivated and treatments are unable to contribute much further to motivational levels. In addition, although both threat and involvement enhanced resistance, only involvement affected counterarguing. Therefore, the models produced from these data do not suggest a "clear pattern for what are theorized to be the central variables in inoculation: threat and counterarguing" (p. 212). The evidence provided here suggests that these two elements are not enough to fully account for the process of inoculation. Inoculation promotes resistance above and beyond the contributions of threat and counterarguing, thus suggesting that the refutational preemption component of an inoculation treatment triggers (as yet unidentified) cognitive processes, which contribute to resistance.

Until recently, all research on inoculation had assumed that the process of resistance is cognitive. However, recent studies have introduced affect to inoculation in an effort to further understand the process of resistance. In the first of these investigations, Lee and Pfau (1997) compared the effectiveness of cognitive, affective-positive, and affective-negative inoculation messages in conferring resistance to cognitive and affective attacks. Cognitive messages were designed so that they were rational, objective, and factual, whereas affective messages were written to be more suggestive and consisted of metaphors, anecdotes, and stereotyping designed to elicit either positive or negative feelings. Lee and Pfau (1997) predicted that cognitive appeals would be the most effective because they consist of strong arguments and because inoculation is assumed to be an active cognitive process. They hypothesized that negative-affective messages also would be effective in conferring resistance, based on research suggesting that negative affect results in careful cognitive processing (Bless, Bohner, Schwarz, & Strack, 1990; Schwarz, Bless, & Bohner, 1991). They posited that affective-positive inoculation messages would be the least effective in conferring resistance because of research indicating that positive moods lead to peripheral processing (Bohner, Crow, Erb, & Schwarz, 1991; Schwarz et al., 1991).

The results indicated that affective and cognitive appeals confer resistance to persuasion. However, the findings pointed to greater nuance in the efficacy of various inoculation appeals when considered in light of attack type. Lee and Pfau (1997) found that cognitive inoculation treatments were effective in conferring resistance against both cognitive and affective-positive attacks but not against affective-negative attacks. Furthermore, they confirmed that, as predicted, cognitive inoculation treatments produced the most resistance. Finally, their results indicated that both affective-positive and affective-negative inoculation produced resistance, but only against cognitive attacks.

Lee and Pfau's (1997) results on affective appeals should be accepted cautiously, however, because both affect messages fell just short of eliciting significantly more affect than the cognitive messages. This suggests that the affect manipulations were only partially successful. The failure to find any significant differences between the effectiveness of the various inoculation conditions could, in fact, be due to this weak manipulation.

Pfau et al. (2001) followed up on the Lee and Pfau (1997) study with a more comprehensive investigation of inoculation that focused on cognitive and affective inoculation appeals in addition to the role of experienced affect in the process of resistance. The latter focus was motivated by the fact that threat acts as the motivational catalyst in inoculation (Pfau, 1997; Pfau, Tusing, Koerner, et al., 1997) and that motivation intrinsically is more affective than cognitive (Izard, 1993). This study examined comparative efficacy of cognitive, affective-anger, and affective-happiness inoculation messages at low, moderate, and high levels of self-efficacy while taking into account receiver involvement and prior attitude. In short, this investigation explored the role of affect in inoculation, both as a message strategy and in terms of how affect functions in the psychological processes producing resistance.

The cognitive inoculation messages featured verifiable material, such as statistics and research findings, carefully avoiding any affect-laden words or opinions. Affective inoculation messages were created to elicit the appropriate emotion—either anger or happiness. The strategy employed to construct these messages was based on Lazarus's (1991) appraisal theory. Lazarus argued that a person's appraisal of his or her environment can be negative or positive, depending on whether the person perceives the environment as enhancing or inhibiting goal attainment. Based on Lazarus's (1994) reasoning, affective-anger messages were constructed so as to suggest that "arguments contrary to the individual's attitude thwart goal attainment" (p. 213), and affective-happiness messages were constructed to imply that "the individual's present attitude facilitates goal attainment" (p. 213). The affective messages did not use verifiable facts but employed opinionated statements, anecdotes, and affect-laden words.

Because appraisal theory alone cannot explain why some people respond to threat with anger while others respond to the same threat with happiness, appraisal theorists have tried to uncover situational and personal factors affecting appraisals. Whether anger is produced from threat appraisal depends largely on an individual's perceived power over the stimulus (Dillard, Plotnick, Godbold, Freimuth, & Edgar, 1996). Self-efficacy is a measure of one's perceived power over, or confidence in, dealing with an environmental obstacle, and it is a likely predictor of how a person will perceive a threat message (Bandura, 1983). Bandura (1983) argued that anger experiences are a function of the strength of perceived self-efficacy in coping with different threats (p. 465). Therefore, Pfau and colleagues (2001) predicted that with inoculation, anger should stem from high self-efficacy.

Once again conferring the robustness of inoculation, the results of the Pfau et al. (2001) study revealed that all inoculation message approaches conferred resistance and that, contrary to prediction, all messages stimulated equal amounts of counterarguing. Also contrary to prediction, the affective-happiness messages were superior to the other approaches in conferring resistance to attacks but not through eliciting threat or counterarguing, and only at levels of low self-efficacy. At moderate and high levels of self-efficacy, cognitive messages were superior in promoting resistance. In addition, the results indicated that self-efficacy moderated emotional response, reducing threat and counterarguing (because people are more confident in their ability to defend their attitudes) but eliciting

anger and, as result, contributing to resistance.

This study produced other interesting findings about the nuances of inoculation as well. Receiver involvement once again contributed to resistance through its positive association with counterarguing. Results of structural equation analyses indicated that inoculation treatments both directly and indirectly enhance resistance. Inoculation treatments produced a direct impact on attitude resistance, independent of psychological processes. In addition, with both cognitive and affective-anger treatments, inoculation elicited threat, which, along with involvement, enhanced counterarguing and also triggered anger, indirectly promoting resistance. In fact, anger messages elicited the most threat. This study was the second one to suggest both a direct and an indirect path through threat and counterarguing as "dual routes" to resistance (Pfau et al., 2001, p. 243). This finding suggests that threat and counterarguing are necessary, but not sufficient, to fully account for inoculation's impact.

As a result of these findings, Pfau and colleagues (2001) argued that the direct path from inoculation to resistance suggests two possibilities: one, that the refutational component directly contributes to resistance; or two, that there are still untested variables in the inoculation process that help to explain resistance. Insko (1967) may have been right when he claimed, "Inoculation theory may prove to be part of a larger and more complex picture" (p. 319). Nonetheless, the most important results of this study concern the role of emotion in inoculation. The researchers proposed that anger would play an integral role in the inoculation process, and these hypotheses were confirmed and were consistent with the logic of appraisal theory. Mainly, it was found that threat is positively related to anger and that anger is positively related to counterarguing and resistance.

As a part of the same omnibus investigation, Pfau, Holbert, Zubric, Pasha, and Lin (2000) conducted a study that focused on the relative efficacy of print and video inoculation messages. This study is important because no prior research has addressed the role and influence of communication modality in resistance. Rather, inoculation researchers have tended to treat message modality as a "neutral conduit of message content" (Pfau, 1990, p. 195). However, extant research suggests that it is important to consider the medium of the message because each medium possesses a unique symbol system that shapes "what is communicated and how it is received" (Pfau, Holbert, Zubric, Pasha, & Lin, 2000, p. 2). Therefore, this study explored the success of print and video messages in conferring resistance while questioning their unique influences on the process of resistance.

Pfau, Holbert, and colleagues (2000) posited that the nature of inoculation implies that print treatments should be superior to video due to the unique nature of the two message forms. In contrast to print, video is an inherently passive medium (Chesebro, 1984; Graber, 1987), and therefore, video should be less effective in promoting careful message elaboration. However, as McGuire (1962) reasoned, inoculation triggers an intrinsically active process of counterarguing. Therefore, inoculation messages employed in research are typically cognitive in nature.

Because print is more likely to elicit active message processing (Chaiken & Eagly, 1976, 1983; Petty & Cacioppo, 1986), Pfau, Holbert, and colleagues (2000) predicted that, compared to video, print inoculation messages would elicit more counterarguing and be more effective in conferring resistance to influence. In addition, they hypothesized that video treatments confer resistance uniquely because video enhances "the primacy of the visual over the audio channel" (Paletz & Guthrie, 1987, p. 20) and because it

is assumed to be less involving (Chesebro, 1984). Therefore, video should be more likely to result in reliance on source cues. Finally, Pfau, Holbert, and colleagues (2000) questioned whether the conferral of resistance occurs at different points in time for print and video inoculation treatments.

The results once again revealed the robustness of inoculation. Mainly, print and video messages did not significantly vary in their ability to confer resistance. However, as predicted, print and video messages did differ in *how* they produced resistance. The video messages produced resistance based more on source considerations. Videos immediately generated positive relational perceptions about the source of the inoculation messages in terms of perceptions of similarity and depth, causing receivers to immediately bolster their attitudes. These positive relational thoughts about the source were then associated with more negative perceptions of the source of the attack and, as a result, with resistance to the attacks. The video messages elicited much more negative perceptions about the competence and character of the source of the attacks than did print messages.

These findings also point to a difference in the timing of resistance. Immediately following the inoculation message, the video treatments fostered more resistance than did the print messages. However, following exposure to the persuasive attacks, this difference disappeared, with both the print and video messages being equally effective in producing resistance. Overall, this study indicates that video inoculation messages confer resistance to influence uniquely through a process that relies heavily on source factors. These results suggest, as was proposed, that print emphasizes message content, while video emphasizes source factors. Furthermore, it was found that video treatments conferred immediate resistance, whereas print treatments required time to induce resistance.

The previously reviewed contemporary studies suggest much nuance in the process of resistance, pointing especially to the strong robustness of inoculation. The pattern of results of existing research reveals that, whether inoculation treatments are constructed as the same or different (McGuire, 1961b, 1962, 1966; McGuire & Papageorgis, 1961; Papageorgis & McGuire, 1961; Pfau, 1992; Pfau & Burgoon, 1988; Pfau et al., 1990, Pfau, Tusing, Koerner, et al., 1997), central or peripheral (Pfau, Tusing, Lee, et al., 1997), as content or source oriented (Freedman & Sears, 1965; Stone, 1969), or as cognitive or affective (Lee & Pfau, 1997; Pfau et al., 2001), or whether treatments are administered by video or print (Pfau, Holbert, et al., 2000), they enhance resistance to persuasion.

APPLICATIONS

Inoculation appears to be a promising strategy to foster resistance to influence in any number of contexts where people possess attitudes that are likely to be challenged. Thus, as scholars and practitioners have become aware of its usefulness, inoculation is receiving growing attention as an applied resistance strategy (Eagly & Chaiken, 1993). In this section, applications of inoculation are examined, with particular emphasis on commercial advertising, political campaigns, smoking prevention, and adolescent drinking prevention.

Commercial Advertising

Necessity was the impetus for applying the inoculation approach to attitude resistance in commercial advertising. During the late 1980s, comparative advertising, which explicitly compares a target brand to one or more competing brands, was rising in popularity (Levy, 1987). Recent research has demon-

strated impressive persuasiveness of comparative advertisements for certain items in certain conditions (Atkin, 1984; Droge, 1989; Pfau, 1994). Therefore, it is important to ask whether a company can do anything to preclude efficacy of a competitor's comparative ad.

Five studies provided the foundation for the application of inoculation to commercial advertising. Two of these early studies dealt with social marketing and were the first to attempt to apply inoculation to a marketing context. Bither, Dolich, and Nell (1971) concluded that "two-sided immunization appeals" were effective in reinforcing belief levels against messages that advocated movie censorship (p. 60). Szybillo and Heslin (1973), in addressing the question as to whether air bags should be mandated in new automobiles, found that refutational messages were more effective than supportive messages in producing attitude resistance.

Two other commercial advertising studies explored the efficacy of refutational versus supportive messages in producing resistance to Federal Trade Commission attacks. Findings here were mixed. Hunt (1973) found that refutational messages were superior to supportive messages, while Gardner, Mitchell, and Staelin (1977) found no differences between the two approaches. Another study by Sawyer (1973) looked at the relative efficacy of refutational and supportive print ads for five different products. He found that refutational ads outperformed the supportive ads, effects that were more pronounced for nonusers of products and when following a series of ads.

These initial studies suggest that the refutational two-sided approach is superior to the one-sided supportive approach in producing attitude resistance. This claim is backed further by recent commercial advertising and persuasion research. A meta-analysis of message sidedness research (Jackson & Allen,

1987) and three replications of the meta-analysis (Allen et al., 1990) suggest that two-sided messages are preferred over one-sided messages because mentioning the competing position "subsequently builds up the psychological defenses of the message recipient and makes the refutation effective" (Allen et al., 1990, p. 286). In fact, Swinyard (1981) and Kamins and Asseal (1987) provided evidence from the context of commercial advertising that two-sided messages actually suppress a receiver's counterarguments, which results in greater resistance to persuasion.

Pfau's (1992) study of inoculation in a comparative advertising context indicated that the effectiveness of inoculation as a resistance strategy depends largely on other variables at work in the environment. Pfau manipulated two variables: receiver product involvement and message format. Receiver product involvement concerned the "relevance or salience of the product class for receivers" (Pfau, 1997, p. 144), and comparative message format involved the "style and directionality of the comparative" (p. 144).

Pfau found that both inoculation-same and -different messages were effective in conferring resistance to a competitor's claims. The most intriguing finding, however, is that inoculation was more effective in producing resistance to a competitor's comparative advertisements, mainly for high-involving products (Pfau, 1992). Pfau reasoned that inoculation pretreatments may produce higher threat in high-involved receivers and, therefore, prove to be more effective.

Political Campaigns

As with commercial advertising, necessity was also the stimulus for applying inoculation to the political campaigns arena. Today, nearly half of all political ads use an attack approach, which posits a negative picture of

an opponent's record, character, or positions (Johnson-Cartee & Copeland, 1997). In contemporary campaigns for high-visibility offices in the United States, attack ads play a prominent role (Jamieson, 1992; Johnson-Cartee & Copeland, 1997; Kendall, 1991; Kern, 1989; Pfau & Kenski, 1990). The prevalence of attack ads is compounded by the fact that they are often more effective than positive advertisements due to the fact that they capture attention, penetrate and persist in memory, and in time become dissociated from the source of the attack (Lau, 1982, 1985; Shapiro & Rieger, 1989).

The questions of importance in the political arena are much the same as those in the commercial advertising arena. Mainly, what can political campaigners do to avert an opponent's attack advertisements? Campaigners can employ the post hoc strategies of responding to the ads, initiate their own counterattacks, or hope that the news media critique an opponent's ads. Because these methods all are post hoc, however, they might not "repair" the damage already done by an opponent's attack (Pfau et al., 1990).

Inoculation theory may provide an alternative preemptive response for dealing with an opponent's attacks. Inoculation theory suggests that one can design messages that make voters resistant to the influence of attack ads. Pfau and colleagues (Pfau & Burgoon, 1988; Pfau et al., 1990) explored the potential of inoculation in two large field studies: one that focused on the 1986 South Dakota campaign for U.S. Senate and one that dealt with the 1988 presidential election.

The initial study featured an intense campaign for the U.S. Senate in South Dakota. The results indicated that inoculation-same and -different strategies both work in making potential voters resistant to the influence of subsequent attack messages (Pfau & Burgoon, 1988). Voters receiving inoculation treatments were less supportive of candidates sponsoring attack ads, were less likely to change their attitudes according to the attack ad content, and were less likely to vote for the candidates sponsoring the attack ads than were control group participants. Furthermore, inoculation was effective on behalf of both candidates and for both issue and character attacks (Pfau & Burgoon, 1988). Interestingly, Pfau and Burgoon (1988) found that while inoculation decayed over time in terms of its impact on receivers' attitudes, it revealed considerable persistence in its impact on behavioral intention of voting for the candidate sponsoring the ad. Pfau and Burgoon also found that inoculation was more useful for strong party identifiers than for weak party identifiers, crossovers, or nonidentifiers. Moreover, an interaction effect suggested that inoculation-same messages produce more resistance among strong party identifiers, whereas inoculation-different messages produce more resistance for weak party identifiers.

A subsequent investigation was conducted during the 1988 presidential campaign. The study featured direct mail as the medium for inoculation pretreatments because direct mail was becoming a common medium for political communication (Armstrong, 1988), and it explored the efficacy of inoculation pretreatments versus post hoc refutation. To this point, Tannenbaum and colleagues had conducted the only test comparing inoculation and post hoc refutation. Their findings implied that inoculation was slightly more effective (Tannenbaum, Macaulay, & Norris, 1966; Tannenbaum & Norris, 1965).

Pfau and colleagues' results demonstrated that inoculation is a practical approach. Once again, both inoculation-same and -different messages made potential voters more resistant to attacks on their preferred candidate. The direct mail messages produced significant variance in all resistance variables, and the results suggest that participating voters "read and internalized the inoculative material"

(Pfau et al., 1990, p. 38). However, the researchers failed to find evidence that booster sessions enhanced inoculation's effectiveness, possibly due to a combination of strong persistence of inoculation along with premature administration of the booster sessions (Pfau et al., 1990). Finally, the results supported the hypotheses that the preemptive inoculation approach is more efficacious than the post hoc refutation approach in protecting people from changing their attitudes about their preferred candidate. Again, this effect was most pronounced for strong party identifiers. For weak party identifiers, inoculation proved to be more effective than the post hoc approach, but only for character attacks (Pfau et al., 1990).

The accumulation of findings from Pfau and colleagues' research suggests that inoculation "is a viable approach for candidates to deflect the persuasiveness of political attack messages" (Pfau & Kenski, 1990, p. 160). Both of these studies used only a single inoculative message, administered during the final weeks of ardent campaigns, which makes the results even more remarkable. Pfau and colleagues' work suggests "considerable promise for inoculation" (Pfau, 1997, p. 147) in the context of political campaigns.

Smoking Prevention

Because inoculation is a particularly useful approach in contexts where existing attitudes are exposed to frequent challenge, it has received attention as a technique for preventing smoking initiation among adolescents. Most youths possess strong anti-smoking attitudes as a result of the efforts of parents, teachers, and older siblings. However, young adolescents are generally more likely to voice strong negative attitudes about smoking than are older adolescents (Schneider & Vanmastrigt, as cited in McAlister, Perry, & Maccoby, 1979). Therefore, Hamburg (1979) claimed that the crucial time for preventive smoking programs is the year of transition from elementary to secondary school because this transition produces "far-reaching physiological upheavals" in young adolescents, causing them to be more vulnerable to the onset of tobacco use (p. 1031). Hamburg argued that this particular time frame provides a "crucial opportunity for [preventive] intervention" *before* adolescents engage in "health-damaging patterns" (p. 1031).

During the critical transition from pre-adolescence to adolescence, parental influence on youths weakens and peer influence strengthens (Evans & Raines, 1982; Friedman, Lichtenstein, & Biglan, 1985; Goldberg & Garn, 1982; Gottlieb & Baker, 1986; McAlister et al., 1979). Furthermore, during this transition, adolescents are largely indifferent to the negative long-term health consequences of smoking. Adolescents tend to "think of themselves as invulnerable"; therefore, it is likely that they may begin smoking before they seriously consider the consequences (Gilpin & Pierce, 1998). These elements combined result in an indifference to the negative consequences of smoking (Killen, 1985; Pfau et al., 1992), which leads to an increased likelihood of smoking and a decreased likelihood of intolerance toward peer smoking (Pfau & Van Bockern, 1994). The average smoker begins to smoke at 14.5 years of age (O'Hara, 1993). In fact, around 50% of all adult smokers began smoking *prior to* high school (Landers & Orlandi, 1987; O'Hara, 1993).

Because the majority of smokers begin the habit during their teen years, and because the health consequences of early smoking initiation are grave, preventive strategies are essential. In 1994, the Centers for Disease Control (CDC) recommended that school-based smoking prevention programs begin during the last years of elementary school and continue through high school, with the greatest

intensity occurring during the sixth through eighth grades (CDC, 1998). Therefore, an important question to address is the following: What can be done to produce resistance in adolescents' anti-smoking attitudes? Obviously, the best strategy to use would "arrest attitude slippage among younger adolescents, rendering them less vulnerable to smoking onset" (Pfau, 1997, p. 148).

To date, "social inoculation" has been used extensively as a smoking prevention strategy. Social inoculation is a "melding of McGuire's inoculation and Bandura's social learning theories" (Wallack & Corbett, 1987). Social inoculation has proven to be effective in preventing (or delaying) the onset of smoking among adolescents (Botvin, Baker, Renick, Filazzola, & Botvin, 1984; Perry, 1987; Perry, Killen, & Slinkard, 1980). Unfortunately, the social inoculation approach uses only refutational preemption while neglecting threat. Omitting threat is problematic because it is the catalyst that motivates message recipients to protect their attitudes, rendering them resistant to challenges (McGuire, 1962).

Social inoculation uses a potpourri of strategies that include, but are not limited to, games, slide shows, role-playing, peer-led and/or teacher-led discussions, refusal skills training, video presentations, written rehearsal, and peer modeling (Flay, 1985). There are two main problems with using this broad array of approaches simultaneously. First, replication of the studies is costly and laborious. Second, none of the studies attempted to assess the effectiveness of each individual element, which also makes replication unfeasible. Flay (1985) argued that it is unclear which of social inoculation's elements are responsible for its success. Thus, the usefulness of social inoculation is called into question.

The practicality of McGuire's inoculation approach in producing smoking resistance was explored by Pfau and colleagues in a longitudinal field study involving students in transition from elementary school (sixth grade) to junior high school (seventh grade) in a South Dakota public school district. All students in this study were already randomly assigned to a health class. Pfau and colleagues further randomly assigned each of the 38 participating health classes to either treatment or control conditions. Inoculation videos, professionally prepared and ranging in length from 12 to 15 minutes, were shown to the 28 treatment groups in October. Furthermore, reinforcement videos were shown to 10 treatment groups in November. Consistent with the logic of inoculation as a resistance approach, those students indicating that they were current smokers (6.5% of all participants) were not included in the data analyses.

Pfau and colleagues' first-year results suggested that the inoculation videos were effective in helping students to maintain their existing anti-smoking attitudes, but only for low self-esteem students (Pfau et al., 1992). February measures indicated that the inoculation videos produced both less positive attitudes about smoking and a higher chance of behavioral intention to resist peer pressures to smoke. May measures, taken more than 33 weeks after administration of the inoculation videos and more than 25 weeks after reinforcement videos, suggested that inoculation resulted in less positive attitudes toward both smoking and smokers and reduced the likelihood of smoking (Pfau et al., 1992). Reinforcement videos did not produce additional attitude or behavior intention resistance.

The key finding of Pfau et al.'s (1992) research is that the success of inoculation was dependent on the youth's level of self-esteem. This finding helps to account for conflicting findings of past social inoculation research. In fact, many social inoculation attempts have been criticized for not taking into account important receiver characteristics such as gender and self-esteem. Researchers claim that these receiver characteristics most likely act as

a confound in the process of eliciting resistance (Best, Thomson, Santi, Smith, & Brown, 1988; Botvin, 1982; Flay, 1985). Furthermore, Pfau's research points to the usefulness of inoculation in smoking resistance programs because low self-esteem youths tend to be those most likely to initiate smoking (Best et al., 1988; Elder & Stern, 1986; Foon, 1986; Harken, 1987; Pfau et al., 1992; Pfau & Van Bockern, 1994).

This pattern of increased inoculation effectiveness for low self-esteem students persisted through September of the following year. However, this interaction effect vanished by the following May—84 weeks after viewing of the inoculation videos. By May 1992, the results indicated that inoculation videos made *all* inoculated students less positive toward smoking and smokers. However, all significant effects were restricted to attitudes and did not extend to behavioral intentions of smoking. Nonetheless, research suggests that "attitudes [are] indicative of future smoking behavior" (Harken, 1987, p. 381). This is especially true for adolescents (Allegrante, O'Rourke, & Tuncalp, 1977; McCaul, Glasgow, O'Neill, Freeborn, & Rump, 1982).

Pfau and colleagues' (Pfau & Van Bockern, 1994; Pfau et al., 1992) findings suggest that inoculation is a useful approach for smoking prevention. In addition, this strategy is much more parsimonious and economical than the potpourri of tactics used in social inoculation, making it a more viable option. The research summarized here suggests that inoculation should be used by both health educators and scholars interested in smoking prevention techniques.

To further examine the viability of inoculation as a smoking prevention tactic, Szabo's (2000) doctoral dissertation examined inoculation with fifth- and sixth-grade nonsmokers in both a metropolitan area and a rural setting. Her dissertation built on Pfau and colleagues' (Pfau & Van Bockern, 1994; Pfau et al., 1992) work while incorporating new elements motivated by recent research documenting an upsurge in smoking among pre-adolescents as well as contemporary research dealing with the nuances of inoculation.

First, working under the assumptions of Brehm's reactance theory, Szabo (2000) designed normative appeal and traditional health-based appeal messages to determine whether normative messages, which express peer disapproval of smoking, produce less threat to behavioral freedom than do health-based messages. Szabo presumed that traditional health-based messages may be partly responsible for the recent increase in adolescent smoking by triggering boomerang effects in some adolescents.

Szabo (2000) predicted that because normative and health-based inoculation appeals both include threat and refutational preemption, they would be able to render *most* pre-adolescents resistant to smoking. Nonetheless, she assumed that normative appeals would be *less* likely to motivate psychological reactance in *some* adolescents. To further understand affect in inoculation, Szabo included normative-anger and normative-cognitive messages.

Szabo's (2000) research provided further insight into the application of inoculation in smoking prevention. Her research suggested a fine line between anti-smoking messages that foster resistance and those that activate reactance. Contrary to her prediction that all inoculation treatments would foster resistance to smoking, Szabo's results suggest that inoculation's effectiveness was dependent on the subpopulation of interest. Inoculation was able to elicit resistance for only two of the four subpopulations. For rural sixth-graders, both the normative-anger and the health-based appeals conferred resistance. For urban fifth-graders, the normative-cognitive and health-based appeals fostered resistance.

Neither rural fifth-graders nor urban sixth-graders displayed enhanced resistance. To the contrary, they demonstrated highly reactant responses to all inoculation attempts. Furthermore, there was some evidence of reactance in all subpopulations. For instance, the health-based appeal produced reactance in rural fifth-graders, the cognitive message in rural sixth-graders, and the anger message in all urban participants. Szabo's (2000) study suggests that anti-smoking messages can produce both resistance and reactance in pre-adolecents, largely dependent on message strategy and subpopulation of interest. Finally, Szabo found evidence that receiver self-efficacy was significantly associated with smoking resistance for all students in all subpopulations. However, self-esteem had no real impact.

Adolescent Drinking Prevention

Because inoculation is an effective prevention strategy, it should be useful in assisting adolescents to maintain their attitudes opposing drinking. The social consequences of adolescent drinking are grave, as is evident in the significant proportion of crimes such as robbery, assault, and date rape that have been demonstrated to frequently involve alcohol (Gruber, DiClemente, Anderson, & Lodico, 1996). Therefore, it is important to attempt to render adolescents resistant to peer pressures to drink.

Resistance to influence has been promoted as a way to enhance abstinence, and researchers have argued that this method is more successful than attempting to persuade adolescents to cease drinking once they have begun (Hansen, Graham, Wokenstein, & Rohrbach, 1991; Kreutter, Gewirtz, Davenny, & Love, 1991; Webb, Baer, & McKelvey, 1995). While many studies have employed the social inoculation approach, only one study to date has employed McGuire's inoculation theory in the context of adolescent drinking.

Godbold and Pfau (2000) conducted an inoculation study employing sixth-graders who considered themselves to be nondrinkers. The students were randomly assigned to a condition, either informative or normative, and were shown an inoculative video. The informative appeals stressed arguments based on the consequences of drinking, whereas the normative appeals were grounded in social appeals (Kaplan, 1989). Two of the groups were shown an "informative" public service announcement (PSA) that focused on the effects of alcohol use such as lower grades and greater deviance, two groups were shown a "normative" PSA containing content concerning the negative climate of peer opinion about drinking, and two groups watched neutral PSAs on other topics. The alcohol PSAs were actual scenes from Alcoholics Anonymous videotapes, onto which was dubbed an audio track of the prepared script containing threat and refutational preemption.

Godbold and Pfau's (2000) attack messages either immediately followed inoculation or followed 2 weeks later. The attacks were actual beer commercials embedded in a series of television advertisements and made to look like a television break. All commercials featured young actors and music but no speaking. Measures of resistance gauged students' attitudes and behaviors about alcohol consumption and their perceptions of peer acceptance of drinking.

Godbold and Pfau (2000) predicted that both informative and normative inoculation approaches would be effective in conferring resistance to drinking initiation. However, they assumed that normative messages would work best because they have been shown to be better for judgmental tasks, while informative messages have been shown to work best with "correct judgment" tasks (Kaplan, 1989). Their results revealed that normative mes-

sages resulted in the lowest estimates of peer acceptance of drinking. However, normative inoculation messages were no better than informative messages in conferring resistance to the attacking commercials, and in fact both message strategies exerted limited influence on attitudes and behavioral intentions. The results also revealed that, contrary to prediction, the immediate attacks resulted in more resistant attitude and behavioral intentions than did the delayed attacks. For the most part, the results revealed weak effects for both inoculation strategies (informative and normative). Instead, the study suggested that the most important factor is adolescent perception of peer approval of drinking, which leads to threat and finally to resistance. Therefore, it seems that message designers working with adolescent audiences should employ normative messages to lower the estimates of peer acceptance and peer pressure to drink.

The failure of Godbold and Pfau's (2000) study to show strong inoculation effects may be explained by a number of problems inherent in the experimental design. The results indicated that the threat manipulation was not adequate. The inoculation messages were quite brief (less than 3 minutes), which might not be long enough to sufficiently threaten and motivate receivers.

Further Applications

A promising application of inoculation is in the public relations context. One recent investigation examined Mobil Oil Corporation's extensive issue advertising campaign (Burgoon, Pfau, & Birk, 1995). Corporations employ issue advocacy ads to communicate positions on issues (Sethi, 1979).

Advocacy advertising was traditionally viewed as an effort to influence targeted receivers' attitudes. However, studies that assessed Mobil's advocacy campaign produced equivocal results (Astor, 1976; Connor, 1975; Crable & Vibbert, 1982; Ross, 1976; Sethi, 1979). Researchers concluded that "little is known about the actual effects of advocacy advertising on audience members" (Reid, Soley, & Vanden Bergh, 1981, p. 310).

Burgoon and colleagues (1995) maintained that "issue/advocacy advertising has been viewed as a tool for corporate persuasion, but that perception may be inappropriate" (p. 487). They posited that advocacy ads are most likely to be read by those already supportive of the advocated position (Keim & Zeithaml, 1981; Woolward, 1982) and, therefore, that Mobil's issue advocacy campaign should be viewed as a strategy for "instilling resistance to potential slippage in the attitudes of supporters [of the company's position on an issue] rather than as a tool to convert opponents" (Burgoon et al., 1995, p. 487).

An extensive experimental test confirmed this assumption. Burgoon and colleagues (1995) found that Mobil's extensive issue advocacy advertising campaign functions to inoculate. When faced by counterattitudinal issue attacks, the company's "advertorials" function to inoculate readers against attitude slippage and to protect Mobil's overall credibility rating. The results also revealed that issue advocacy ads were more effective with political conservatives, who were even more committed to Mobil's position on issues, and when Mobil's position on an issue appeared to have no obvious self-benefit to the corporation.

Another potential application for inoculation in the public relations arena is as a proactive tactic in crisis communication. Indeed, experts advocate the use of proactive tactics because crises are inevitable and often uncontrollable. Coombs (1999) warned, "It is a mistake to believe that an organization can avoid or prevent all possible crises. Eventually, a crisis will befall an organization" (p. 126). Thus,

many crisis professionals and scholars suggest using proactive tactics to lessen the damage (Druckenmiller, 1993).

Proactive tactics include methods of establishing a base of goodwill that may assist in softening the damage a corporation often experiences when faced with a crisis. This proactive approach follows the reasoning that accumulating "image credits" from positive performance may "offset the reputational damage generated by the crisis" (Coombs, 1998, p. 182). However, evidence on the efficacy of this approach is only anecdotal. Indeed, "untested assumptions" are the norm in crisis communication (Coombs, 1999, p. 126).

Inoculation may be a promising alternative proactive approach in crisis communication. Inoculation treatments, in this context, would raise potential organizational vulnerabilities and then refute them by explaining actions the organization is taking to address these vulnerabilities. This proactive method may prove to be more effective in producing resistant attitudes than the more accepted approach of attempting to induce a positive image of the organization. It is also possible that inoculation in combination with image-enhancing tactics may provide the most protection to an organization in the face of a crisis, much as research suggests that a combination of supportive and inoculative messages protects attitudes more effectively than does either approach alone (McGuire, 1961a, 1962; Tannenbaum & Norris, 1965).

Wan's (2000) doctoral dissertation compared the efficacy of inoculation and image-enhancing preemptive approaches in crisis communication. Wan's investigation also examined the possibility that, absent a crisis, inoculation could undermine an organization's image because it raises an organization's vulnerabilities, which otherwise would not be exposed.

Wan's (2000) results indicated that for participants possessing initially positive attitudes toward the organization, all treatment approaches—same, different, image bolstering, and combination—effectively protected the image of the organization after exposure to the crisis scenario. However, no one approach proved to be superior. In fact, the bolstering approach produced slightly *more* resistance than inoculation for participants not exposed to the crisis scenario, suggesting some limitations to inoculation. Nonetheless, a lack of power rendered this finding tentative.

Further research on inoculation currently in progress is exploring its potential to soften the intimidating impact of majority opinion on minority attitudes. "Fear of isolation" is a core element in Noelle-Neumann's spiral of silence theory (see Noelle-Neumann, 1974, 1984). Spiral of silence posits that people's perceptions of majority opinion function to promote expression of opinions perceived to be in the majority and squelch expression of opinions perceived to be unfavorable (Noelle-Neumann, 1993).

Lin (2000) studied the potential of inoculation, administered to those holding what is perceived as the minority opinion, to militate fear of isolation, thereby facilitating people's willingness to express opinions. Lin posited that inoculation should facilitate opinion expression in interpersonal, group, and mediated settings.

Lin's (2000) study indicated that inoculation was able to enhance attitude strength. People receiving an inoculation treatment became increasingly confident in their attitudes, expressed greater willingness to verbalize their attitudes, and showed increased likelihood of resisting counterattitudinal attacks, in comparison to control group participants. Lin concluded that inoculation can shatter the spiral of silence and potentially foster public deliberation of important social issues. If inoculation can mitigate the fear of isolation, it should produce a different climate of opinion in which competing views are more likely to be expressed. The results of Lin's study carry important ramifications for participatory democracy.

DIRECTIONS FOR FUTURE RESEARCH

Theory

Unanswered questions about inoculation stem largely from its core theoretical elements. We are closer to knowing about the processes of threat, yet little is known about the workings of refutational preemption. For example, does refutational preemption prime attitudes, thereby making them more accessible for an individual when faced with a challenge? We cannot yet explain unaccounted for direct impacts of inoculation in resistance. Possibly, the concept of priming holds the key. Also, are refutational pretreatments using source derogations superior to those employing content-specific counterarguments? Stone (1969) found that source derogation was inferior to message inoculation, yet his is the only study to address this issue.

In addition, questions remain regarding optimal timing of inoculation treatments in relation to attacks and the role of booster treatments. Insko (1967) claimed that, for a period of time after encountering threat, a person continues to accumulate belief-bolstering information, thus producing increasing resistance to persuasion. Over time, however, as "induced motivation" falls, "the individual ceases to accumulate belief-bolstering material . . ., [dropping] off over time like the ordinary forgetting curve" (p. 316). Unfortunately, McGuire provided no suggestions about timing. In past studies, Pfau and colleagues have used various spacing for inocula- tion, booster, and attack sessions but have been unable to provide any further clarity on the issue.

Furthermore, the immediate and delayed impact of inoculation via threat in Pfau, Tusing, Koerner, et al. (1997), and via video in Pfau, Holbert, et al. (2000), remains unclear. In both of these studies, threat appeared to im- mediately render receivers' attitudes more resistant. Therefore, one must ask *how* threat elicited immediate resistance. What is the cog- nitive or affective process responsible? Fur- thermore, Pfau, Holbert, et al. (2000) re- vealed that print and video inoculation messages differ in the timing of their contribu- tions to resistance. This finding, combined with the finding of Pfau, Tusing, Koerner, et al. (1997), suggests that we need to further address the issue of timing of various compo- nents in the inoculation process.

Additional process directions for future inoculation research involve better under- standing of the role of affect, and of individual differences such as self-efficacy, in the resis- tance process. First, we need to test the assumption that affective-happiness messages are effective with low self-efficacy individuals because they serve to increase a person's self- efficacy (Pfau et al., 2001). As stated pre- viously, future research should assess self- efficacy across time rather than at only one point in time (Pfau et al., 2001). Second, be- cause self-efficacy was identified as a mod- erator in the process of resistance, the role of self-efficacy in resistance needs to be assessed further with various topics and involvement levels. Indeed, we should attempt to design inoculation messages targeting receivers based on self-efficacy levels. Finally, because the affect manipulations of Lee and Pfau (1997) were weak, additional research should at- tempt to determine effectiveness of affective messages in relation to cognitive attacks.

Applications

A number of potential applications of inoc- ulation are currently under study, including its use as a proactive strategy in crisis communi- cation, its potential to overcome fear of isola- tion and therefore foster more open demo- cratic participation, and its ability to foster resistance to smoking onset in adolescents but without simultaneously triggering psychologi- cal reactance. These topics were described in the previous section. In addition, there are other, yet unexplored applications.

In the context of health communication, Pfau, Dillard, and Keller (2000) proposed to study uses of inoculation to promote resis- tance to sexual activity in young adolescents. The researchers argued that inoculation is a viable tactic in this context because research indicates that young adolescents, during the transition from elementary to middle school, hold attitudes against sexual activity, yet these attitudes weaken during middle and high school (Zabin & Hayward, 1993). For the same reasons that inoculation has been effec- tive with adolescents in producing resistance to adolescent smoking, it should be effective in producing resistance to sexual activity.

The next field test of inoculation in the con- text of politics will probe questions such as whether it is possible to deliver inoculation treatments via telephone surveys. Further re- search on political applications should also address whether inoculation can bolster atti- tudes to the point of fostering political behav- iors, such as making people more likely to go to the polls, proselytize on behalf of candi- dates, and contribute money to campaigns.

Inoculation is appropriate for any context where strongly held attitudes are vulnerable to challenge. The inoculation approach should be a particularly viable tactic in contexts in- volving adolescents' risk-taking behavior, also referred to as "transition-marking behavior" (Jessor & Jessor, 1975, p. 49). Inoculation would be useful in areas such as drug use and gang involvement, where adolescents' pro-social attitudes, initially shaped by parents and teachers, are challenged by strong pressures from other adolescents during middle school years. Inoculation may assist young adolescents in resisting peer pressures to engage in these harmful activities.

CONCLUSION

Inoculation theory has been, and promises to be, a viable and serviceable approach to attitude resistance. Experimental research, coupled with more recent field experiments, demonstrates that inoculation provides resistance to attitude change in situations where challenges to attitudes are often inevitable. This chapter has explained the inoculation approach of resistance, reviewed early inoculation research, explored explanations of the processes triggered via inoculation, described contemporary applications of inoculation in a variety of contexts, provided a glimpse of as yet unresolved issues in inoculation research, and suggested further applications of inoculation.

REFERENCES

Adams, W. C., & Beatty, M. J. (1977). Dogmatism, need for social approval, and the resistance to persuasion. *Communication Monographs, 44,* 321-325.

Allegrante, J. P., O'Rourke, T. W., & Tuncalp, S. (1977). Multivariate analysis of select psychosocial variables in the development of subsequent youth smoking behavior. *Journal of Drug Education, 7,* 237-248.

Allen, M., Hale, J., Mongeau, P., Berkowitz-Stafford, S., Shanahan, W., Agee, P., Dillon, K., Jackson, R., & Ray, C. (1990). Testing model of message sidedness: Three replications. *Communication Monographs, 57,* 275-291.

Anatol, K. W. E., & Mandel, J. E. (1972). Strategies of resistance to persuasion: New subject matter for the teacher of speech communication. *Central States Speech Journal, 23,* 11-17.

Anderson, L. R., & McGuire, W. J. (1965). Prior reassurance of group consensus as factor in producing resistance to persuasion. *Sociometry, 28,* 44-56.

Armstrong, R. (1988). *The next hurrah: The communication revolution in American politics.* New York: William Morrow.

Astor, G. (1976, April). The gospel according to Mobil. *More,* pp. 12-15.

Atkin, C. K. (1984). Consumer and social effects of advertising. In B. Dervin & M. J. Voight (Eds.), *Progress in communication sciences* (Vol. 4, pp. 205-248). Norwood, NJ: Ablex.

Bandura, A. (1983). Self-efficacy determinants of anticipated fears and calamities. *Journal of Personality and Social Psychology, 45,* 464-469.

Benoit, W. L. (1991). Two tests of the mechanism of inoculation theory. *Southern Communication Journal, 56,* 219-229.

Best, J. A., Thomson, S. J., Santi, S. M., Smith, E. A., & Brown, K. S. (1988). Preventing cigarette smoking among school children. *Annual Review of Public Health, 9,* 161-201.

Bither, S. W., Dolich, I. J., & Nell, E. B. (1971). The application of attitude immunization techniques in marketing. *Journal of Marketing Research, 18,* 56-61.

Bless, H., Bohner, G., Schwarz, N., & Strack, F. (1990). Mood and persuasion: Cognitive response analysis. *Personality and Social Psychology Bulletin, 16,* 331-345.

Bohner, G., Crow, K., Erb, H., & Schwarz, N. (1991). Affect and persuasion: Mood effects on processing of message content and context cues and on subsequent behaviour. *European Journal of Social Psychology, 22,* 511-530.

Botvin, G. J. (1982). Broadening the focus of smoking prevention strategies. In T. J. Coates, A. C. Petersen, & C. Perry (Eds.), *Promoting adolescent health: A dialogue on research and practice* (pp. 137-147). New York: Academic Press.

Botvin, G. J., Baker, E., Renick, N. L., Filazzola, A. D., & Botvin, E. M. (1984). Cognitive-behavioral approach to substance abuse prevention. *Addictive Behavior, 9,* 137-147.

Brehm, J. W., & Cohen, A. R. (1962). *Explorations in cognitive dissonance.* New York: John Wiley.

Burgoon, M., Burgoon, J. K., Riess, M., Butler, J., Montgomery, C. L., Stinnett, W. D., Miller, M., Long, M., Vaughn, D., & Caine, B. (1976). Propensity of persuasive attacks and intensity of pretreatment messages as predictors of resistance to persuasion. *Journal of Psychology, 92,* 123-129.

Burgoon, M., & Chase, L. J. (1973). The effects of differential linguistic patterns in messages attempting to induce resistance to persuasion. *Speech Monographs, 40,* 1-7.

Burgoon, M., Cohen, M., Miller, M. D., & Montgomery, C. L. (1978). An empirical test of model of resistance to persuasion. *Human Communication Research, 5,* 27-39.

Burgoon, M., & King, L. B. (1974). The mediation of resistance to persuasion strategies by language variables and active-passive participation. *Human Communication Research, 1,* 30-41.

Burgoon, M., Pfau, M., & Birk, T. S. (1995). An inoculation theory explanation for the effects of corporate issue/advocacy advertising campaigns. *Communication Research, 22,* 485-505.

Centers for Disease Control. (1998, April 3). Tobacco use among high school students: United States 1997. *Morbidity and Mortality Weekly Report, pp.* 229-233.

Chaiken, S. (1980). Heuristic versus systematic information processing and the use of source versus message cues in persuasion. *Journal of Personality and Social Psychology, 39,* 752-766.

Chaiken, S., & Eagly, A. H. (1976). Communication modality as a determinant of message persuasiveness and message comprehensibility. *Journal of Personality and Social Psychology, 34,* 605-614.

Chaiken, S., & Eagly, A. H. (1983). Communication modality as a determinant of persuasion: The role of communicator salience. *Journal of Personality and Social Psychology, 45,* 241-256.

Chesebro, J. W. (1984). The media reality: Epistemological functions of media in cultural systems. *Critical Studies in Mass Communication, 1,* 111-130.

Connor, M. J. (1975, May 14). Arguing back: Mobil's advocacy ads lead growing trend, draw praise and criticism. *The Wall Street Journal,* pp. A1, A20.

Coombs, W. T. (1998). An analytic framework for crisis situations: Better responses from better understanding of the situation. *Journal of Public Relations Research, 10,* 177-191.

Coombs, W. T. (1999). Information and compassion in crisis responses: Test of their effects. *Journal of Public Relations Research, 11,* 125-142.

Crable, R. E., & Vibbert, S. L. (1982, November). *"Observations" of Prometheus-bound: Issues, identification, and the appeal to common sense.* Paper presented at the annual meeting of the Speech Communication Association, Louisville, KY.

Crane, E. (1962). Immunization—With and without use of counterarguments. *Journalism Quarterly, 39,* 445-450.

Cronen, V. E., & LeFleur, G. (1977). Inoculation against persuasive attacks: A test of alternative explanations. *Journal of Social Psychology, 102,* 255-265.

Dillard, J. P., Plotnick, C. A., Godbold, L. C., Freimuth, V. S., & Edgar, T. (1996, February). The multiple affective outcomes of AIDS PSAs: Fear appeals do more than scare people. *Communication Research, 23,* 44-72.

Droge, C. (1989). Shaping the route to attitude change: Central versus peripheral processing through comparative versus noncomparative advertising. *Journal of Marketing Research, 26,* 193-204.

Druckenmiller, B. (1993). Crises provide insights on image. *Business Marketing, 78,* 40.

Eagly, A. H., & Chaiken, S. (1993). *The psychology of attitudes.* Orlando, FL: Harcourt Brace Jovanovich.

Elder, J. P., & Stern, R. A. (1986). The ABCs of adolescent smoking prevention: An environment and skills model. *Health Education Quarterly, 13,* 181-191.

Evans, R. I., & Raines, B. E. (1982). Control and prevention of smoking in adolescents: Psychosocial perspective. In T. J. Coates, A. C. Petersen, & C. Perry (Eds.), *Promoting adolescent health: A dialogue on research and practice* (pp. 101-136). New York: Academic Press.

Farkas, B. G., & Anderson, N. H. (1976). Integration theory and inoculation theory as explanations for the "paper tiger" effect. *Journal of Social Psychology, 98,* 253-268.

Fazio, R. H. (1989). On the power and functionality of attitudes: The role of attitude accessibility. In A. R. Pratkanis, S. J. Breckler, & A. G. Greenwald (Eds.), *Attitude structure and function* (pp. 361-382). Hillsdale, NJ: Lawrence Erlbaum.

Flay, B. R. (1985). Prosaic approaches to smoking prevention: A review of findings. *Health Psychology, 4,* 449-488.

Foon, A. E. (1986). Smoking prevention programs for adolescents: The value of social psychological approaches. *International Journal of the Addictions, 21,* 1017-1029.

Freedman, J. L., & Sears, D. O. (1965). Warning, distraction, and resistance to influence. *Journal of Personality and Social Psychology, 1,* 262-266.

Friedman, L. S., Lichtenstein, E., & Biglan, A. (1985). Smoking onset among teens: An empirical analysis of initial situations. *Addictive Behaviors, 10,* 1-13.

Gardner, M., Mitchell, A., & Staelin, R. (1977). The effects of attacks and inoculations in public policy context. In B. A. Greenberg & D. N. Bellenger (Eds.), *Contemporary marketing thought: 1977 educators' proceedings* (pp. 292-297). Chicago: American Marketing Association.

Gilpin, E. A., & Pierce, J. P. (1998). *Smoking initiation* (Vol. 12, Lesson 5). [Online]. Available: http://chest-main.edoc.com/pccu/lesson5-12.html

Godbold, L. C., & Pfau, M. (2000). Conferring resistance to peer pressure among adolescents: Using inoculation theory to discourage alcohol use. *Communication Research, 27,* 411-437.

Goldberg, M. E., & Garn, G. J. (1982). Increasing the involvement of teenage cigarette smokers in antismoking campaigns. *Journal of Communication, 32,* 75-86.

Gottlieb, N., & Baker, J. (1986). The relative influence of health beliefs, parental and peer behaviors, and exercise program participation on smoking, alcohol use, and physical activity. *Social Science and Medicine, 22,* 915-927.

Graber, D. A. (1987). Television news with pictures? *Critical Studies in Mass Communication, 4,* 74-78.

Gruber, E., DiClemente, R. J., Anderson, M. M., & Lodico, M. (1996). Early drinking onset and its association with alcohol use and problem behavior in late adolescence. *Preventive Medicine, 25,* 293-300.

Hamburg, D. (1979). Disease prevention: The challenge of the future. *American Journal of Public Health, 69,* 1026-1033.

Hansen, W. B., Graham, J. W., Wokenstein, B. H., & Rohrbach, L. A. (1991). Program intensity as moderator of preventive program effectiveness: Results for fifth grade students in the adolescent alcohol prevention trial. *Journal of Studies on Alcohol, 52,* 568-579.

Harken, L. S. (1987). The prevention of adolescent smoking: A public health priority. *Evaluation & Health Professions, 10,* 373-393.

Hovland, C. I., Janis, I. L., & Kelly, H. H. (1953). *Communication and persuasion.* New Haven, CT: Yale University Press.

Hunt, H. K. (1973). Effects of corrective advertising. *Journal of Advertising Research, 13,* 15-22.

Insko, C. A. (1967). *Theories of attitude change.* Englewood Cliffs, NJ: Prentice Hall.

Izard, C. E. (1993). Four systems of emotion activation: Cognitive and noncognitive processes. *Psychological Review, 100,* 68-90.

Jackson, S., & Allen, M. (1987, May). *Meta-analysis of the effectiveness of one-sided and two-sided argumentation.* Paper presented at the annual meeting of the International Communication Association, Montreal.

Jamieson, K. H. (1992). *Dirty politics: Deceptions, distractions, and democracy.* New York: Oxford University Press.

Jessor, R., & Jessor, S. L. (1975). Adolescent development and the onset of drinking: A longitudinal study. *Journal of Studies on Alcohol, 36,* 27-51.

Johnson-Cartee, K. S., & Copeland, G. A. (1997). *Manipulation of the American voter: Political campaign commercials.* New York: Praeger.

Kamins, M. A., & Asseal, H. (1987). Two-sided versus one-sided appeals: A cognitive perspective on argumentation, source derogation, and the effect of disconfirming trial on belief change. *Journal of Marketing Research, 24,* 29-39.

Kaplan, M. F. (1989). Task, situational, and personal determinants of influence processes in group decision making. *Advances in Group Processes, 6,* 87-105.

Keim, G., & Zeithaml, V. (1981). Improving the return on advocacy advertising. *Financial Executive, 49,* 40-44.

Kendall, K. E. (1991, November). *Negative campaigning in the presidential primaries: 1912-1992.* Paper presented at the annual meeting of the Speech Communication Association, Atlanta, GA.

Kern, M. (1989). *Political advertising in the eighties.* New York: Praeger.

Kiesler, C. A., Collins, B. E., & Miller, N. (1969). *Attitude change.* New York: John Wiley.

Killen, J. D. (1985). Prevention of adolescent tobacco smoking: The social pressure resistance training approach. *Journal of Child Psychology and Psychiatry, 26,* 7-15.

Kreutter, K. J., Gewirtz, H., Davenny, J. E., & Love, C. (1991). Drug and alcohol prevention project for sixth graders: First year findings. *Adolescence, 26,* 287-293.

Landers, C., & Orlandi, M. A. (1987). Why do teenagers smoke and chew? *Education Horizons, 65,* 133-134.

Lau, R. R. (1982). Negativity in political perception. *Political Behavior, 4,* 353-377.

Lau, R. R. (1985). Two explanations for negativity effects in political behavior. *American Journal of Political Science, 29,* 119-138.

Lazarus, R. (1991). *Emotion and adaptation.* New York: Oxford University Press.

Lazarus, R. (1994). Appraisal: The long and short of it. In P. Ekman & R. J. Davidson (Eds.), *The nature of emotions: Fundamental questions* (pp. 208-215). New York: Oxford University Press.

Lee, W., & Pfau, M. (1997). *The effectiveness of cognitive and affective inoculation appeals in conferring resistance against cognitive and affective attacks.* Paper presented at the annual conference of the International Communication Association, Jerusalem, Israel.

Levy, R. (1987, February). Big resurgence in comparative ads. *Dun's Business Month, 129,* 56-58.

Lin, W-K. (2000). *Humans' internal- and external-oriented cognitions: Inoculation and the spiral of silence—A study of public opinion in democracy.*

Unpublished doctoral dissertation, University of Wisconsin–Madison.

Lumsdaine, A. A., & Janis, I. L. (1953). Resistance to "counterpropaganda" produced by one-sided and two-sided "propaganda" presentations. *Public Opinion Quarterly, 17,* 311-318.

McAlister, A. L., Perry, C., & Maccoby, N. (1979). Adolescent smoking: Onset and prevention. *Pediatrics, 63,* 650-658.

McCaul, K. D., Glasgow, R., O'Neill, H. K., Freeborn, V., & Rump, B. S. (1982). Predicting adolescent smoking. *Journal of School Health, 52,* 342-346.

McCroskey, J. C. (1970). The effects of evidence as an inhibitor of counter-persuasion. *Speech Monographs, 37,* 188-194.

McCroskey, J. C., Young, T. J., & Scott, M. D. (1972). The effects of message sidedness and evidence on inoculation against counterpersuasion in small group communication. *Speech Monographs, 34,* 205-212.

McGuire, W. J. (1961a). The effectiveness of supportive and refutational defenses in immunizing and restoring beliefs against persuasion. *Sociometry, 24,* 184-197.

McGuire, W. J. (1961b). Resistance to persuasion conferred by active and passive prior refutation of the same and alternative counterarguments. *Journal of Abnormal and Social Psychology, 63,* 326-332.

McGuire, W. J. (1962). Persistence of the resistance to persuasion induced by various types of prior belief defenses. *Journal of Abnormal and Social Psychology, 64,* 241-248.

McGuire, W. J. (1964). Inducing resistance to persuasion: Some contemporary approaches. In L. Berkowitz (Ed.), *Advances in experimental social psychology* (Vol. 1, pp. 191-229). New York: Academic Press.

McGuire, W. J. (1966). Persistence of the resistance to persuasion induced by various types of prior belief defenses. In C. W. Backman & P. F. Secord (Eds.), *Problems in social psychology* (pp. 128-135). New York: McGraw-Hill.

McGuire, W. J. (1970, February). A vaccine for brainwash. *Psychology Today, 3,* 36-39, 63-64.

McGuire, W. J., & Papageorgis, D. (1961). The relative efficacy of various types of prior belief-defense in producing immunity against persuasion. *Journal of Abnormal and Social Psychology,* 62, 327-337.

McGuire, W. J., & Papageorgis, D. (1962). Effectiveness of forewarning in developing resistance to persuasion. *Public Opinion Quarterly,* 26, 24-34.

Miller, G. R., & Burgoon, M. (1973). *New techniques of persuasion.* New York: Harper & Row.

Miller, M. D., & Burgoon, M. (1979). The relationship between violations of expectations and the induction of resistance to persuasion. *Human Communication Research, 5,* 301-313.

Noelle-Neumann, E. (1974). The spiral of silence: A theory of public opinion. *Journal of Communication, 24,* 43-51.

Noelle-Neumann, E. (1984). *The spiral of silence.* Chicago: University of Chicago Press.

Noelle-Neumann, E. (1993). *The spiral of silence: Public opinion—Our social skin* (2nd ed.). Chicago: University of Chicago Press.

O'Hara, J. (1993, August 23). *Children's future at risk from epidemic of tobacco use.* [Online]. Available: www.os.dhhs.gov/news/press/1996pres/

Paletz, D. L., & Guthrie, K. K. (1987). The three faces of Ronald Reagan. *Journal of Communication, 37,* 7-23.

Papageorgis, D., & McGuire, W. J. (1961). The generality of immunity to persuasion produced by pre-exposure to weakened counterarguments. *Journal of Abnormal and Social Psychology, 62,* 475-481.

Perry, C. L. (1987). Results of prevention programs with adolescents. *Drug and Alcohol Dependence, 20,* 13-19.

Perry, C. L., Killen, J., & Slinkard, L. A. (1980). Peer teaching and smoking prevention among junior high school students. *Adolescence, 40,* 275-281.

Petty, R. E., & Cacioppo, J. T. (1986). *Communication and persuasion: Central and peripheral routes to attitude change.* New York: Springer-Verlag.

Pfau, M. (1990). A channel approach to television influence. *Journal of Broadcasting and Electronic Media, 34,* 195-214.

Pfau, M. (1992). The potential of inoculation in promoting resistance to the effectiveness of comparative advertising messages. *Communication Quarterly, 40,* 26-44.

Pfau, M. (1994). Impact of product involvement, message format, and receiver sex on the efficacy of comparative advertising messages. *Communication Quarterly, 42,* 244-258.

Pfau, M. (1997). Inoculation model of resistance to influence. In G. A. Barnett & F. J. Boster (Eds.), *Progress in communication sciences: Advances in persuasion* (Vol. 13, pp. 133-171). Norwood, NJ: Ablex.

Pfau, M., & Burgoon, M. (1988). Inoculation in political campaign communication. *Human Communication Research, 15,* 91-111.

Pfau, M., Dillard, J. P., & Keller, M. L. (2000). *The potential of the inoculation pretreatment strategy to confer resistance to adolescent sexual involvement.* Unpublished manuscript, University of Wisconsin–Madison.

Pfau, M., Holbert, R. L., Zubric, S. J., Pasha, N. H., & Lin, W. (2000). Role and influence of communication modality in the process of resistance to persuasion. *Media Psychology, 2,* 1-33.

Pfau, M., & Kenski, H. C. (1990). *Attack politics.* New York: Praeger.

Pfau, M., Kenski, H. C., Nitz, M., & Sorenson, J. (1990). Efficacy of inoculation strategies in promoting resistance to political attack messages: Application to direct mail. *Communication Monographs, 57,* 25-43.

Pfau, M., Szabo, E. A., Anderson, J., Morrill, J., Zubric, J., & Wan, H. (2001). The role and impact of affect in the process of resistance to persuasion. *Human Communication Research, 27,* 216-252.

Pfau, M., Tusing, K. J., Koerner, A. F., Lee, W. P., Godbold, L. C., Penaloza, L. J., Yang, V. S., & Hong, Y. (1997). Enriching the inoculation construct: The role of critical components in the process of resistance. *Human Communication Research, 24,* 187-215.

Pfau, M., Tusing, K. J., Lee, W. P., Godbold, L. C., Koerner, A. F., Penaloza, L. J., Yang, V. S., & Hong, Y. (1997). Nuances in inoculation: The role of inoculation approach, receiver ego-involvement, and message processing disposition in resistance. *Communication Quarterly, 45,* 461-481.

Pfau, M., & Van Bockern, S. (1994). The persistence of inoculation in conferring resistance to smoking initiation among adolescents: The second year. *Human Communication Research, 20,* 413-430.

Pfau, M., Van Bockern, S., & Kang, J. G. (1992). Use of inoculation to promote resistance to smoking initiation among adolescents. *Communication Monographs, 59,* 213-230.

Reid, L. N., Soley, L. C., & Vanden Bergh, B. G. (1981). Does source affect response to direct advocacy print advertisements? *Journal of Business Research, 9,* 309-319.

Ross, I. (1976, September). Public relations isn't kid-glove stuff at Mobil. *Fortune,* pp. 106-111, 196-199, 201-202.

Sawyer, A. G. (1973). The effects of repetition of refutational and supportive advertising appeals. *Journal of Marketing Research, 10,* 23-33.

Schwarz, N., Bless, H., & Bohner, G. (1991). Mood and persuasion: Affective states influence the processing of persuasive communications. In M. P. Zanna (Ed.), *Advances in experimental social psychology* (Vol. 23, pp. 161-199). San Diego: Academic Press.

Sethi, S. P. (1979). Institutional/image advertising and idea/issue advertising as marketing tools: Some public policy issues. *Journal of Marketing, 43,* 68-78.

Shapiro, M. A., & Rieger, R. H. (1989, May). *Comparing positive and negative political advertising.* Paper presented at the annual meeting of the International Communication Association, San Francisco.

Stone, V. A. (1969). Individual differences and inoculation against persuasion. *Journalism Quarterly, 46,* 267-273.

Swinyard, W. R. (1981). The interaction between comparative advertising and copy claim variation. *Journal of Marketing Research, 28,* 175-186.

Szabo, E. A. (2000). *Inoculation, normative appeals, and emotion as strategies to promote resistance to adolescent smoking.* Unpublished doctoral dissertation, University of Wisconsin–Madison.

Szybillo, G. J., & Heslin, R. (1973). Resistance to persuasion: Inoculation theory in a marketing context. *Journal of Marketing Research, 10,* 396-403.

Tannenbaum, P. H., Macaulay, J. R., & Norris, E. L. (1966). Principle of congruity and reduction in persuasion. *Journal of Personality and Social Psychology, 2,* 223-238.

Tannenbaum, P. H., & Norris, E. L. (1965). Effects of combining congruity principle strategies for the reduction in persuasion. *Sociometry, 28,* 145-157.

Ullman, W. R., & Bodaken, E. M. (1975). Inducing resistance to persuasive attack: A test of two strategies of communication. *Western Journal of Speech Communication, 39,* 240-248.

U.S. Senate. (1956). *Communist interrogation, indoctrination, and exploitation of American military and political prisoners* (Committee on Government Operations, Permanent Subcommittee on Investigations, 84th Congress, 2nd session). Washington, DC: Government Printing Office.

Wallack, L., & Corbett, K. (1987). Alcohol, tobacco, and marijuana use among youth: An overview of epidemiological program and policy trends. *Health Education Quarterly, 14,* 223-249.

Wan, H-H. (2000). *Inoculation and priming in the context of crisis communication.* Unpublished doctoral dissertation, University of Wisconsin–Madison.

Webb, J. A., Baer, P. E., & McKelvey, R. S. (1995). Development of a risk profile for intentions to use alcohol among fifth and sixth graders. *Journal of the American Academy of Child and Adolescent Psychiatry, 34,* 772-778.

Woolward, I. (1982). How to make corporate advocacy ads more effective. *Marketing Communications, 17,* 60.

Zabin, L. S., & Hayward, S. C. (1993). *Adolescent sexual behavior and childbearing.* Newbury Park, CA: Sage.

14

The Theory of Reasoned Action

JEROLD L. HALE
BRIAN J. HOUSEHOLDER
KATHRYN L. GREENE

In his exploration of the parameters of persuasion, Miller (1980; see Chapter 1 in this volume) wrote that persuasion was an indirectly coercive process. His position was based on two arguments. First, he suggested that any coercion that accompanied persuasive attempts was a natural part of the social process. For example, by voting for Candidate X in an election, the voter is potentially deprived of any of the benefits of being represented by Candidate Y or Candidate Z. Miller also argued that when persuasion involved more direct coercion, it occurred only after a period of reasoned message exchange. In essence, Miller's position was that persuasion is a process of influencing behaviors that are voluntary and necessarily involve conscious decision making—in other words, volitional behaviors. Over the years, considerable attention has been paid in both academic research and applied communication campaigns to modifying volitional behaviors.

Born largely out of frustration with traditional attitude-behavior research, much of which found weak correlations between attitude measures and performance of volitional behaviors, Fishbein and Ajzen (1975, 1980) developed the theory of reasoned action (TRA). Their work, and the research that it has spawned, is the focus of this chapter. Before proceeding to an evaluation of that body of research, we present a brief explication of the theory and its components.

AN EXPLICATION OF THE THEORY OF REASONED ACTION

The aim of the TRA is to explain volitional behaviors. Its explanatory scope excludes a wide range of behaviors such as those that are spontaneous, impulsive, habitual, the result of cravings, or simply scripted or mindless (Bentler & Speckart, 1979; Langer, 1989).

Such behaviors are excluded because their performance might not be voluntary or because engaging in the behaviors might not involve a conscious decision on the part of the actor. The TRA also excludes from its scope those behaviors that may require special skills, unique opportunities or resources, or the cooperation of others to be performed (Liska, 1984). One may be prevented from performing a behavior because of a skill deficit, lack of opportunity, or lack of cooperation from others and not because of a voluntary decision not to engage in the behavior.

Behavioral Intentions, Attitudes, and Subjective Norms

The TRA posits that the strongest or most proximal predictor of volitional behavior is one's behavior intention. Behavioral intentions are thought to be the result of both an individual influence and a normative influence. The individual influence on intention is a person's attitude toward performing the volitional behavior. The normative influence on intention is what Fishbein and Ajzen referred to as one's subjective norm. In its simplest form, the TRA can be expressed as the following mathematical function:

$$BI = (A_B)W_1 + (SN)W_2,$$

where BI represents one's behavioral intention. The behavioral intention is a function of both A_B (one's attitude toward performing the behavior) and SN (one's subjective norm related to performing the behavior), and the Ws represent empirically derived weights.

An attitude, as it relates to the TRA, is an affective or valenced response *toward performing some behavior* and not toward some generalized attitude object. If the object of a communication campaign was to induce people to eat five helpings of fruits and vegetables

a day, then a target person's relevant attitude would be the degree to which he or she felt positively or negatively toward eating five helpings of fruits and vegetables a day. The attitude A_B is weighted (W_1) by the salience or importance of the attitude to the targeted person. A subjective norm is a person's belief about whether significant others feel that he or she should perform the target behavior (e.g., do significant others feel that the target person should eat five helpings of fruits and vegetables a day?). The influence of the subjective norm is also weighted (W_2) by the salience or relative importance of the normative influence to the target person.

Expressed in the form of a causal model as in Figure 14.1, the TRA posits that volitional behaviors are influenced directly by behavioral intentions and that behavioral intentions are the result of both attitudes toward performing the behavior and subjective norms related to the behavior. The TRA, when presented in the form of a causal model, is intuitively appealing because the components of the model represent target points for persuasive appeals. For example, if the object of a communication campaign was to induce young people to engage in safe sex behaviors, then at its most basic level, the TRA suggests that performance of the volitional behavior could be enhanced by targeting adolescent intentions, attitudes, or subjective norms. Persuasive messages could aim to influence the intention of an adolescent to abstain from sex or wear a condom, an adolescent's attitude toward abstaining or wearing a condom, an adolescent's beliefs regarding how significant others would feel about his abstinence or condom use, or some combination of these three components.

While the TRA appears to be uncomplicated on its face, the basic form of the theoretical components poses additional questions and issues that must be addressed.

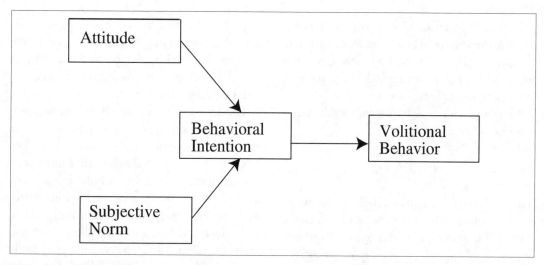

Figure 14.1. Causal Diagram of Basic Components of the Theory of Reasoned Action

Belief Strength and Belief Evaluation

One key component to the TRA is an attitude or valenced response toward engaging in some volitional behavior. While social scientists disagree about the origins of attitudes, Fishbein and Ajzen (1975) suggested that an attitude toward performing some behavior is a function of the beliefs that one holds regarding the behavior. This portion of the TRA is taken from Fishbein's (1967a, 1967b) Summative Model of Attitude. According to the Summative Model of Attitude, and subsequently the TRA, an attitude toward performing some behavior can be mathematically expressed in the following way:

$$A_B = \Sigma\, b_i\, e_i,$$

where A_B is one's attitude toward the behavior and that attitude is the sum of belief strength (b_i) and belief evaluation (e_i).

Beliefs generally link some attribute to a volitional behavior or an attitude. For example, the cognition "Wearing a condom will reduce my risk of HIV" represents a belief insofar as it links some attribute (safe sex) with a volitional behavior (decision to wear a con-

dom). Belief strength is the certainty with which the belief is held—in the preceding example, one's certainty or lack of certainty that wearing a condom will reduce the risk of HIV. Belief evaluation is the extent to which the attribute—in this example, safe sex—is judged to be positive or negative. One frequently cited reason for not insisting on condom use is that the insistence on condom use communicates a lack of trust in one's sexual partner.[1] For the belief "Insisting that my partner wear a condom will communicate that I do not trust him/her," both belief strength (likelihood that mistrust will be perceived) and belief evaluation (is mistrust positive or negative?) may be assessed. One's attitude toward a volitional behavior, then, is a function of the attributes one links to the behavior and whether those attributes are judged to be positive or negative.

Normative Beliefs and Motivation to Comply

A subjective norm is a function of a normative belief and motivation to comply with the normative belief. A normative belief is the perceived expectation of important others regarding the volitional behavior. Motivation to comply is real or imagined pressure one feels for his or her behavior to match the perceived expectation of others.

Subjective norm is expressed mathematically as follows:

$$SN = \sum b_j m_j,$$

where b_j is the normative belief or perceived expectation of salient others and m_j is one's motivation to comply with the perceived expectation of others. For example, recent research has shown that binge consumption of alcohol is increasing on college and university campuses. With regard to binge drinking, a college student might have a normative belief (e.g., "My friends think that binge drinking is a good thing to do") and a motivation to comply (e.g., "When it comes to drinking, I want to do what my friends think is a good thing"). Normative belief is a perception that is valenced and can be measured continuously. In the same way, one's motivation to comply with the perceived expectation of others can be weaker or stronger and can be measured continuously.

While Figure 14.1 represents the TRA in a very rudimentary form, once the determinants of an attitude toward some volitional behavior or the determinants of a subjective norm are considered, the process for explaining volitional behavior becomes much more complex. A more complete causal diagram of the process for explaining volitional behavior, according to the TRA, is shown in Figure 14.2.

Even in its more complex form, the TRA is intuitively and practically appealing because it identifies specific targets of influence that can more directly or indirectly influence the performance of volitional behaviors. Specifically, the source of a persuasive message may directly target the behavioral intentions of the message recipient. In a more indirect manner,

the source of the persuasive attempt may target the recipient's attitude toward the volitional behavior, the subjective norm, or any of the component parts that influence attitudes or subjective norms.

The TRA has been tested in numerous studies with a variety of volitional behaviors as the action component of the social influence attempt. Volitional behaviors that have been studied testing the TRA include, but are not limited to, reporting alien abductions (Patry & Pelletier, 2001), dieting (Sejwacz, Ajzen, & Fishbein, 1980), using condoms (Greene, Hale, & Rubin, 1997), consuming genetically engineered foods (Sparks, Shepherd, & Frewer, 1995), and limiting sun exposure (Hoffmann, 1999). The question, then, is whether the theory adequately predicted and explained volitional behaviors. In the portion of the chapter that follows, we summarize the results of research testing the TRA.

DATA BEARING ON THE THEORY OF REASONED ACTION

The Relationship Between Behavioral Intentions and Behaviors

Several primary studies have been conducted testing the relationship between behavioral intentions and volitional behaviors. As the body of research investigating the intention-behavior relationship has become more voluminous, several researchers have conducted meta-analyses to summarize the results of the primary studies. At least six meta-analyses of the relationship between behavioral intentions and volitional behaviors have been published. Table 14.1 summarizes the results of those meta-analyses related to the intention-behavior correlation. The mean uncorrected product-moment correlations (r) between intentions and behaviors in the six meta-analyses range from .44 to .53, and

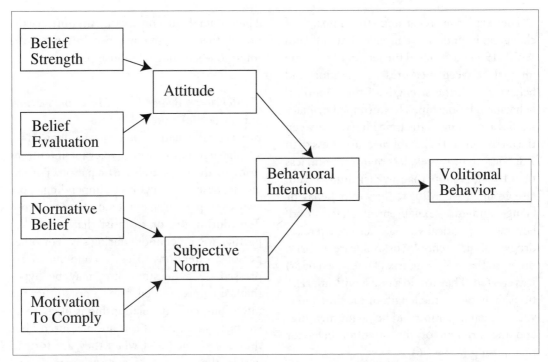

Figure 14.2. Causal Diagram of Complete Components of the Theory of Reasoned Action

mean r^2 values from them range from .19 to .38.

Social influence scholars disagree with regard to the implications of these effect sizes. For example, Marks (1996), commenting on the utility of the TRA to explain health-related behaviors, called the theory a failure, the behavioral intention construct one pursued for the sake of convenience, and a "notoriously poor predictor" (p. 8) of behavior. As Sutton (1998) noted, if the percentage of variance accounted for in volitional behaviors is judged against a standard of 100%, then Marks's appraisal is on point. However, if the percentage of variance accounted for in volitional behaviors is judged against typical levels of variance accounted for in social science research, then intentions predict volitional behaviors quite well (Conner & Armitage, 1998; Sutton, 1998).

It is likely that the intention-behavior relationship is attenuated in research testing the TRA. Several reasons for an attenuated intention-behavior relationship have been posited.[2] Some of the reasons for an attenuated intention-behavior relationship concern the nature of the behavioral intention construct, and others relate to the manner in which intentions and/or behaviors are measured.

Intentions Being Subject to Change. Sutton (1998) noted, as have Ajzen and Fishbein (1980), that intentions are subject to change. If, between the time an intention is measured and the time performance of the behavior is assessed, the intention changes, then the intention-behavior relationship will necessarily be attenuated. Ajzen and Fishbein (1980; see also Ajzen, 1985) recommended measuring intentions in close temporal proximity to the measure of behavioral performance to decrease the likelihood that intentions might change during the ensuing time interval.

The evidence regarding the impact of changing intentions is mixed. Randall and Wolff (1994) correlated the length of the time interval between measures of intention and behavior with the strength of the intention-behavior relationship. They grouped primary studies according to the time interval between the intention and behavior measures (less than 1 day, less than 1 week, less than 1 month, less than 1 year, or more than 1 year). Studies were also grouped according to the sort of behavior being studied (sexual/reproductive, food/beverage, political/voting, leisure/exercise, drug/alcohol, school/work/job/career, and other) so that a 5×7 matrix (Time × Behavior) was created. They found a nonsignificant relationship between the length of the time interval between intention and behavior measures and the strength of the intention-behavior relationship ($r = -.06$).

In 18 cells of the matrix created by Randall and Wolff (1994), there are one or fewer entries, so that time is confounded with behavior type. Even when the effect of time on the intention-behavior relationship is analyzed within behavior types, there are several empty cells in the design. A small number of estimates (k) makes the accuracy of a meta-analytic conclusion—in this case, the impact of time on the intention-behavior relationship—more suspect than a greater number of estimates (Hale & Dillard, 1991).

Sheeran and Oberall (1998) argued that a more accurate picture of the impact changing intentions would be garnered by assessing the effect of temporal contiguity on the intention-behavior relationship within the context of a single behavior as opposed to a context with several behaviors of the same type. They meta-analyzed data from studies solely of condom use and found that the time interval between intention and behavior measures was strongly and negatively correlated with the size of the intention-behavior relationship ($r = -.59$).

Their data lend convincing support to the notion that changing intentions attenuate the intention-behavior relationship.

Intentions Being Provisional in Nature. Sutton (1998) noted that intentions may be provisional in nature. Some participants in research may have formed relevant intentions prior to their research participation. For example, based on previous or impending experiences, a person may intend to wear a condom during sex or to insist that his or her partner wear a condom during sex. For other persons, intentions to use a condom, as expressed on a questionnaire, may be hypothetical or provisional. Sutton noted that the intention-behavior relationship is likely to be stronger when intentions are measured after they are formed and when they are formed within the context of a decision with real consequences.

Violation of the Principle of Compatibility. Intention-behavior relationships are most certainly attenuated because measures frequently violate the principle of compatibility. Fishbein and Ajzen (1975; see also Ajzen, 1988; Ajzen & Fishbein, 1977) suggested that predictive power would be heightened when measures of the predictor (behavioral intention) and the criterion (volitional behavior) matched with regard to the action, the target at which the action was directed, time, and context. Kim and Hunter (1993b) found that increased compatibility of the intention and behavior measures led to significantly stronger attitude-behavior relationships. For studies with low compatibility between the attitude measure and the behavior measure, the attitude-behavior relationship was $r = .28$. For studies with moderate compatibility between the attitude measure and the behavior measure, the attitude-behavior relationship was $r = .41$.

TABLE 14.1 Summary of Findings From Meta-Analyses of the Relationship Between Behavioral Intentions and Volitional Behaviors

Review	k	r	r^2
Ajzen (1991)	17	.45	.20
Godin & Kok (1996)	58	.46	.21
Hausenblaus et al. (1997)	39	.47	.22
Kim & Hunter (1993)	47	.46	.21
Randolf & Wolff (1994)	98	.45	.20
Sheeran & Oberall (1999)	28	.44	.19
Sheppard et al. (1988)	87	.53	.28

For studies with high compatibility between the attitude measure and the behavior measure, the attitude-behavior relationship was $r = .62$.[3] Moreover, of the four components identified by Fishbein and Ajzen (1975), Kim and Hunter (1993b) found that compatibility was most important for the action and target components and least important for the context and time components.

Restrictions in Range and Variance. Relationships between predictor and criterion variables are also made smaller by a restriction in the range of the values of either or both variables. When either the intention measure or the behavior measure allows for a small number of responses, the variance in one or both of the variables is restricted and the strength of the observed relationship is smaller that it would otherwise be. Of the 47 studies of the relationship between behavioral intentions and volitional behaviors meta-analyzed by Kim and Hunter (1993b), 5 of the studies dichotomized the behavioral intention measure and 16 studies dichotomized items in

the behavior measure. Recall from Table 14.1 that the uncorrected correlation between behavioral intentions and behaviors in that meta-analysis was .46. When the intention-behavior relationship was corrected for dichotomization, it increased to .54.

Measurement Error in Intention and Behavior Measures. Measurement error has a systematic effect on the relationship between any two variables: It attenuates the effect. Unreliability of intention or behavior measures would necessarily make the observed relationship between the two variables weaker than the true relationship between the same variables. There is a simple formula to correct a product-moment correlation for attenuation (see, e.g., Ferguson, 1976).

In a meta-analysis, the mean correlation between two variables can be corrected for measurement error by correcting the correlation for each individual study or estimate (k). When reliability information for measures is not reported in any given study, the reliability may be estimated if the number of items in a measurement scale is reported (see Hunter, Schmidt, & Jackson, 1982). Kim and Hunter (1993b) demonstrated the impact of measurement error on the relationship between behavioral intentions and volitional behaviors. With the uncorrected intention-behavior relationship of $r = .46$, the intention-behavior correlation, when corrected for measurement error and dichotomization, was $r = .82$.

From the available evidence, which is considerable, it is clear that behavioral intentions are related to the performance of volitional behaviors. Without taking into account any of the factors that might attenuate the relationship, the variance accounted for in volitional behaviors by behavioral intention compares favorably to effect sizes commonly observed in the social sciences. Several meta-analyses have carefully considered the impact of statistical errors and moderator variables on the intention-behavior relationship. When those factors are considered, the relationship between intentions and behaviors is significantly stronger.

The Relationship Between Attitudes and Behavioral Intentions

The TRA posits that behavioral intentions are influenced by attitudes toward the volitional behavior. The attitude-behavioral intention relationship has been investigated in a spate of primary studies. That body of research was quantitatively reviewed in the meta-analysis by Kim and Hunter (1993b), which consisted of 92 estimates (k) of the attitude-intention relationship, with a combined sample size of 16,785. The uncorrected mean correlation for the attitude-behavioral intention relationship was .65. Like the behavioral intention-behavior relationship, the relationship between attitude and behavioral intention is likely to be attenuated by factors such as

lack of compatibility between the measures, dichotomization of the measures, and error of measurement. Kim and Hunter (1993b) investigated the impact of scale compatibility on the attitude-intention relationship. They found that as compatibility of the measures increased, the attitude-intention relationship grew significantly stronger. For studies with low compatibility between the two measures, the attitude-intention correlation was .46. For studies with moderate compatibility between the two measures, the attitude-intention correlation was .62. For studies with a high degree of compatibility between the two measures, the correlation between attitudes and behavioral intentions was .69.

Kim and Hunter (1993b) also corrected the attitude intention correlation for the effects of dichotomization and measurement error. The uncorrected attitude-intention correlation was .65, but when the relationship was corrected for dichotomization and measurement error, the estimate of the strength of the relationship increased to .82.

Sheeran and Taylor (1999) meta-analyzed studies of the relationship between attitudes toward condom use on intentions to wear condoms. The effect sizes they reported were uncorrected for measurement error and dichotomization effects. The meta-analysis consisted of 32 estimates (k) and a sample size of 8,418. The attitude-behavioral intention correlation was .45.

Godin and Kok (1996) meta-analyzed studies of a variety of health-related behaviors. Their meta-analysis included $k = 56$ and reported a mean attitude-intention correlation of .46. There is limited overlap between the studies analyzed by Sheeran and Taylor (1999) and those analyzed by Godin and Kok (1996). The latter meta-analysis included 8 studies concerning HIV/AIDS and 48 studies of other health-related behaviors. Sheeran and Taylor (1999) analyzed studies of condom use (HIV/

TABLE 14.2 Summary of Findings From Meta-Analyses of the Relationahip Between Attitudes and Subjective Norms on Behavioral Intentions

Review	k	R	R^2
Ajzen (1991)	17	.71	.50
Godin & Kok (1996)	58	.64	.41
Randolf & Wolff (1994)	98	.45	.20
Sherran & Oberall (1999)	28	.44	.19
Sheppard et al. (1988)	87	.66	.44

AIDS) but also included several studies that were not part of the previous meta-analysis.

The Impact of Subjective Norms on Behavioral Intentions

In addition to an attitudinal influence on behavioral intentions, the TRA includes a normative influence on behavioral intentions. Subjective norms are a function of two components: perceptions of how significant others feel about performance of the volitional behavior and one's motivation to comply with the desires of significant others.

Sheeran and Taylor (1999) meta-analyzed studies of the impact of subjective norms on condom use. The meta-analysis consisted of 32 studies with a total sample size of 8,126. The mean correlation between subjective norms and behavioral intentions was .42. For any volitional behaviors, there may be more than one group of significant others. With condom use, for example, it is possible that the feelings of parents, adults outside the family, peers, and one's sexual partner might form a normative belief. Sheeran and Taylor (1999) found that the strongest normative influence

on intentions to wear condoms was the sexual partner norm ($r = .50$). The meta-analysis conducted by Godin and Kok (1996) also reported the subjective norm-intentions relationship. Where $k = 58$, the mean subjective norm-intentions relationship was $r = .34$.

Combined Effects of Attitudes and Subjective Norms on Behavioral Intentions

Several primary studies and meta-analyses have reported the joint effects of attitudes and subjective norms on behavioral intentions. The multiple correlation (R) values have ranged from a low of .63 to a high of .71, with multiple R^2 values ranging from a low of .40 to a high of .50. See Table 14.2 for a summary of meta-analytic results related to the joint effects of attitudes and subjective norms on behavioral intentions. The same arguments made in regard to the behavioral intentions-behaviors effect size may be made with regard to the ability of attitudes and subjective norms to predict behavioral intentions. Skeptics of the TRA may argue that, against an absolute standard of 100%, the percentage of variance in intentions explained by attitudes and subjective norms is quite small. Proponents of the TRA may quickly counter that, when compared to effect sizes that are typical in the social sciences, attitudes and subjective norms do well in predicting behavioral intentions.

The Relationship Between Beliefs and Attitudes

Several studies have tested the notion that attitudes are a result of belief strength and belief evaluation (e.g., Bagozzi, 1982; Davis & Runge, 1981; Fishbein, Ajzen, & Hinkle, 1980; Holbrook, 1977; Infante, 1971, 1973), and there is little doubt that beliefs influence attitudes. O'Keefe (1990) noted that the correlation between beliefs and attitudes has ranged from between .55 and .80 across a variety of attitude objects.

With regard to the role of beliefs in predicting attitude, two important issues should be considered: the role of belief salience in predicting attitude and the role of belief strength scores in predicting attitude (O'Keefe, 1990).

Including Belief Salience. According to the TRA, attitude is a function of belief strength and belief evaluation. Some scholars have argued that attitudes would be more accurately predicted if, in addition to assessing belief strength and belief evaluation, researchers also assessed the salience of beliefs. However, several studies (e.g., Anderson, 1970; Hackman & Anderson, 1968; Holbrook & Hulbert, 1975) have included a measure of the importance of beliefs and found that adding the additional component did not improve the prediction of attitudes. Holbrook and Hulbert (1975) suggested that measuring the importance of beliefs did not significantly improve the prediction of attitudes because more salient beliefs produce more extreme evalua-

tions. In that case, belief salience and belief evaluation would be confounded so that a measure of one component would indirectly include a measure of the other component. O'Keefe (1990) concluded that the prediction of attitudes is not likely to be improved by adding a belief importance or belief relevance component to the TRA.

Determining Whether Belief Strength Matters. According to the TRA, attitude is a function of both belief strength and belief evaluation. The evidence regarding the role of belief strength in predicting attitude is mixed. There are two common methods for assessing beliefs. One method entails providing individuals with a standardized list of beliefs that is generated by the researcher. An alternative method involves asking individuals to list unique sets of attributes related to a volitional behavior or attitude object. If the former technique is used, then each individual is provided with the same list of attributes and is asked to assess belief strength and belief evaluation based on those attributes. If the latter technique is used to assess beliefs, then each individual generates his or her own list of attributes from which belief strength and belief evaluation are assessed (O'Keefe, 1990).

The importance of measuring belief strength to predict attitude is influenced by the manner in which beliefs are assessed. Belief strength significantly improves the prediction of attitude when a standardized set of beliefs is used, but not when research participants generate unique individualized lists of beliefs (Cronen & Conville, 1975; Delia, Crockett, Press, & O'Keefe, 1975). By their very nature, individualized sets of beliefs include those attributes that the participant feels the volitional behavior or attitude object possesses. By contrast, standardized lists of beliefs may or may not include attributes that any given research participant feels are embodied by a volitional behavior or attitude object. One should not necessarily conclude that belief strength plays an insignificant role in explaining attitude. Belief strength may be an integral part of one's attitude, and the construct should be measured in research where a standardized belief list is used. The role of belief strength in explaining attitude may be equally important when individualized belief lists are generated, but the individualized lists are composed of attributes that are strongly associated with a volitional behavior or object. Of course, it may also be the case that belief strength does not play a true role in predicting attitude and that belief evaluation is the key to accurate predictions.

O'Keefe (1990) carried the argument regarding belief strength one step further. If variations in belief strength made a significant contribution in predicting attitudes, then individualized lists of beliefs would be a better predictor of attitudes than standardized belief lists. O'Keefe noted that neither procedure for assessing beliefs is significantly better than the other method at predicting attitudes.

Relationships Among Normative Belief, Motivation to Comply, and Subjective Norm

While the evidence concerning the impact of beliefs on attitudes is relatively straightforward, the same cannot be said for research concerning the normative belief and motivation to comply constructs. Correlations among normative belief, motivation to comply, and subjective norm are generally strong (see, e.g., Fishbein & Ajzen, 1981a; Fishbein, Jaccard, Davidson, Ajzen, & Loken, 1980; Hoogstraten, de Haan, & ter Horst, 1985; Riddle, 1980) and range from .50 to .70 (O'Keefe, 1990). Despite seemingly strong relationships between subjective norm and its

determinants, concerns have been raised about the normative component of the TRA. These concerns have led several scholars to question whether the TRA adequately captures the role of normative components in the persuasive process.

Research investigating the impact of normative belief and motivation to comply on subjective norm has reached inconsistent conclusions. Some research has found that normative belief predicts subjective norm better than does the joint function of normative belief and motivation to comply (Budd, North, & Spencer, 1984; Kantola, Syme, & Campbell, 1982; Miniard & Page, 1984). Other studies have found that intentions are more accurately predicted from attitude and normative belief than from attitude and subjective norm (Budd & Spencer, 1984; Chassin et al., 1981; de Vries & Ajzen, 1971; McCarty, 1981; Saltzer, 1981; Schlegel, Crawford, & Sanborn, 1977). So, while the relationship among normative belief, motivation to comply, and subjective norm is generally strong, there is research that calls into question the utility of the motivation to comply construct.

Concerns have also been raised about the specificity of measurement for the motivation to comply construct. Typical measures of motivation to comply ask about the respondent's general desire to comply with the wishes of a particular person or group. O'Keefe (1990) noted that "an act-specific referent" would enhance the ability of motivation to comply to predict subjective norm (p. 87). For example, if one were conducting research on alcohol consumption among college students, a general item assessing motivation to comply might read "It is very important for me to behave as my parents would like me to behave." Alternatively, an act-specific item assessing motivation to comply might read "When it comes to alcohol consumption, it is very important for me to do what my parents would like me to do."

CRITICISMS OF THE THEORY OF REASONED ACTION

Critics of the TRA have advanced several points of contention. In general, their criticisms cluster around three issues: the relationship between attitudes and normative beliefs, whether TRA components are sufficient predictors of intentions and behaviors, and the restricted range of meaning encompassed by the theory. We consider each of these issues in turn.

The Relationship Between Attitudes and Subjective Norms

The TRA posits that attitudes and subjective norms will have empirically separate and distinct influences on behavioral intentions. There is some compelling evidence that attitudes and subjective norms are positively correlated (e.g., Bearden & Crockett, 1981; Greene et al., 1997; Miniard & Cohen, 1981; Park, 2000; Ryan, 1982; Shepard & O'Keefe, 1984; Warshaw, 1980). The implication of that positive relationship is clear: Individuals with positive subjective norms toward a volitional behavior are likely to positive attitudes toward performing the behavior, and those with negative subjective norms are likely to have negative attitudes toward the behavior. Given strong evidence of the relationship between attitude similarity and interpersonal attraction, it is not surprising that attitudes of relevant peer group members are positively correlated with the respondent's attitude. In most studies where the relationship between attitudes and subjective norms is reported, or where it can be inferred, the correlations be-

tween the two components range between .50 and .70.

Miniard and Cohen (1981) argued that attitudes and subjective norms were correlated because the impact of one's behavior on others can be stated as either a behavioral belief or a normative belief. For example, a young person might have the belief "Reducing my consumption of alcohol will make my parents happy." That cognition is a behavioral belief insofar as it ties an attribute (parental happiness) to the performance of a volitional behavior (decreased alcohol consumption). The same general notion could be expressed as a normative belief. The same young person could have the cognition "My parents would like for me to consume less alcohol." In fact, Miniard and Cohen found that an experimental control that was designed to affect participants' attitudes also influenced their subjective norms. Conversely, an experimental control that was designed to influence participants' subjective norms also affected their attitudes. The blurred conceptual distinction between the sorts of beliefs that produce one's attitudes and those that produce one's subjective norms means that the two constructs are likely to be correlated.

One proposed solution to conceptual and statistical problems posed by the strong attitude-subjective norm relationship is to represent the preferences of others in terms of behavioral beliefs instead of normative beliefs. That solution would treat the normative component of the TRA as a determinant of attitudes (belief strength and belief evaluation), and indirectly of behavioral intentions, instead of including the normative component as a separate determinant of intentions (Eagly & Chaiken, 1993; Park, 2000; Smetana & Adler, 1980). Most TRA research reports a stronger relationship between attitudes and intentions than between subjective norms and intentions. The difference in the magnitude of the two relationships may reflect the indirect influence of norms, that is, as a determinant of attitudes and less directly of intentions.

However, using a threefold argument, Fishbein, Ajzen, and their colleagues have advocated treating the attitudinal and normative components of the TRA as distinct entities. First, there is evidence that some experimental controls have had the intended differential impacts on participants' attitudes and subjective norms. That is, controls designed to influence attitudes have done so without affecting subjective norms, and controls designed to affect subjective norms have done so without affecting attitudes (Ajzen & Fishbein, 1972; Fishbein & Ajzen, 1981b). Second, while attitudes and subjective norms may be highly correlated, Fishbein and Ajzen (1981b) noted that both components are strongly related to intentions and are more strongly related to intentions than to each other. Third, some studies indicate that attitudes and subjective norms correlate in different ways with behavioral intentions (Greene et al., 1997; Gur-Arie, Durand, & Bearden, 1979; Miller & Grush, 1986).

It would be theoretically useful to specify the conditions under which attitudes and subjective norms would or would not have distinct influences on intentions. The state of the current TRA literature makes such specification difficult.

TRA Components as Sufficient Predictors of Volitional Behavior

The TRA posits that attitudes and subjective norms are the only meaningful influences on behavioral intentions related to volitional behavior. According to Fishbein and Ajzen (1975, 1980), all other variables influence intentions and behaviors indirectly through antecedent components of the theory. Eagly and Chaiken (1993) discussed this notion as it relates to voting behavior. The TRA focuses on voting behavior, attitudes toward voting, and subjective norms regarding whether one votes. It does not explicitly include attitudes toward targets (political candidates), party identification, liberalism-conservatism, or some other variables that are routinely part of models of voting behavior. According to the TRA, attitudes toward targets and other potentially relevant variables affect behaviors only through the more proximal components of theory. For example, one's attitude toward Candidate X, or one's political liberalism or conservatism, is thought to influence one's attitude toward voting for Candidate X. Hence, Fishbein and Ajzen (1975, 1980) took the position that all variables that are not explicitly specified by the TRA are thought to be *external* variables that influence volitional behaviors indirectly through attitudes and subjective norms. Nevertheless, critics of the TRA have argued that attitudes and subjective norms are not sufficient predictors of behavioral intentions or indirectly of behaviors. Four variables have been identified as possible predictors of behavioral intentions: moral obligations, self-identity, affect, and prior behaviors. A discussion of each variable, and the supporting evidence for its impact on behavioral intentions, follows.

Moral Obligations and Intentions. Several studies have examined the impact of moral obligations on behavioral intentions (Ajzen & Fishbein, 1969, 1970; Prestholdt, Lane, & Mathews, 1987; Sparks et al., 1995; Warburton & Terry, 2000; Zuckerman & Reis, 1978). Moral obligations address what the individual believes is right or wrong with regard to a volitional behavior. Moral obligations are quite different from perceptions of how others believe one should behave and may be quite different from one's attitude toward the volitional behavior. Prestholdt et al. (1987) tested the impact of attitudes, subjective norms, and perceived moral obligations to predict voluntary job termination among nurses. They found that all three variables had a significant and direct impact on intentions to terminate employment. Conner and Armitage (1998) meta-analyzed studies of the relationship between moral obligation and intentions ($k = 11$) and reported a mean correlation of .50.

Self-Identity and Intentions. Self-identity has also been recognized as a potential predictor of intentions (Charng, Piliavin, & Callero, 1988; Sparks & Guthrie, 1998; Terry, Hogg, & White, 1999). For example, an environmental activist may participate in a roadside cleanup campaign because environmental action has become a key component of his or her self-concept. Similarly a parent might volunteer to participate in several activities at his or her child's school because doing so is central to how the parent defines himself or herself. In fact, several studies have demonstrated that self-identity variables add significantly to attitudes and subjective norms in predicting behaviors. Terry et al. (1999) conducted one such study. They tested the TRA, adding a measure of self-identity, to explain household recycling behaviors. They found that attitudes and subjective norms predicted intentions to recycle household waste. In addition to the effects of the two TRA components, Terry et al. found that self-identity was significantly related to behavioral intentions ($\beta = .18$). As household recycling was a stronger part of one's self-identity, one had stronger intentions to recycle. In this study, and in others, self-identity at least marginally improved the ability to predict behavioral intentions. Conner and Armitage (1998) meta-analyzed studies of the relationship between self-identity and behavioral intentions. The mean correlation between self-identity and behavioral intentions was .18.

Prior Behavior and Intentions. Whether one has previously performed the behavior in question has also been shown to influence behavioral intentions. The relationship between previous behaviors and behavioral intentions has been examined with regard to blood donation (Bagozzi, 1981; Charng et al., 1988), condom use (Baker, Morrison, Carter, & Verdon, 1996), voting behavior (Granberg & Holmberg, 1990), exercise behavior (Maddux, 1993; Yordy & Lent, 1993), learning behavior (Norwich & Duncan, 1990; Sideridis, Kaissidis, & Padeliadu, 1998), seat belt use (Thuen & Rise, 1994), and a variety of other behaviors. For example, Mullen, Hersey, and Iverson (1987) tested the TRA using consumption of unhealthy foods, smoking, and exercise as the volitional behaviors being predicted. They found that previous consumption, smoking, and exercise behaviors were significant predictors of behavioral intentions and behaviors, independent of components of the TRA.

Conner and Armitage (1998) conducted a meta-analysis related to the TRA and past behaviors. With $k = 16$, they reported that the product-moment correlation between previous behavior and behavioral intentions was .51. Previous behavior correlated more strongly with behavioral intentions than with attitudes or subjective norms. Only the previous behavior-future behavior relationship was stronger ($r = .68$) than the relationship between past behavior and intentions.

The precise role of previous behaviors in influencing behavioral intentions or future behaviors is subject to speculation of at least three sorts. First, it may be that past behavior has some causal effect on behavioral intentions (e.g., one may intend to wear a seat belt because he or she has done so in the past) (O'Keefe, 1990). Reasoning of this sort equates past behavior with habit, where the future performance of the behavior is automatic and occurs for no reason other than having been performed in the past (Tesser & Shaffer, 1990). Second, it is also possible that previous behavior reflects the influence of other components of the TRA. When an individual's past behavior includes seat belt use, the past behavior would presumably influence, or have been influenced by, his or her attitude toward wearing a seat belt. In the same way, past seat belt use may influence, or have been influenced by, a subjective norm regarding wearing a seat belt. In that sense, past behaviors may be residues of attitudes and subjective norms (Ajzen, 1991; Conner & Armitage, 1998). Third, either past or future behaviors may be influenced by variables such as perceived moral obligation and self-identity. If an individual participates in household recycling at Time 1 because his or her self-identity is strongly tied to stewardship of natural resources, then recycling of household items at Time 2 might be similarly influenced. In the same way, if an individual donates blood at Time 1 because he or she feels a moral obligation to do so, then a blood donation at Time 2 is also likely to be the result of a perceived moral obligation. Unfortunately, very few studies parse out the effects of these potential influences on behavior over time. Whether they reflect habitual responses or mediated effects, past behaviors exert the strongest impact on intentions and future behaviors of any variable not originally included in the TRA.

Affect and Intentions. As noted in an earlier chapter of this handbook, affect has profound effects on social influence. One way in which affect has an impact is via anticipated affective outcomes (Manstead & Parker, 1995; Triandis, 1977; van der Pligt & de Vries, 1998). Several recent studies have focused on the impact that anticipated regret has on behavior (e.g., Parker, Manstead, & Stradling, 1995; Richard, van der Pligt, & de Vries, 1996). In general, if an individual anticipates feelings of regret related to a behavior, then he

or she is less likely to perform the behavior. For example, if an individual anticipates feelings of regret over consuming alcohol, then he or she is less likely to intend to do so than a person who does not anticipate feelings of regret over the behavior.

There is some reason to doubt the robustness of the effect for anticipated negative outcomes. The effect for anticipated negative outcome has been found with regard to junk food consumption, drug use, and alcohol use (Richard et al., 1996). Other studies, including ones predicting safe driving behaviors (Parker et al., 1995), safe sex behaviors (Richard, van der Pligt, & de Vries, 1995), and consumer behaviors (Simonson, 1992), have failed to replicate the effect for anticipated negative affect. The impact of anticipated affect may depend on the perceived salience of the anticipated negative affect. Parker, Stradling, and Manstead (1996) tested four videotaped interventions designed to decrease intentions to violate the speed limit. Three of the interventions focused on altering attitudes, subjective norms, or perceived behavioral control related to driving behaviors. The content of the fourth intervention focused on anticipated regret for violating speed limits. The impact of anticipated negative affect increased as the salience of the negative affect increased.

Affect may also influence the TRA via one's mood state. In two studies, Armitage, Conner, and Norman (1999) investigated the impact of a mood induction, as opposed to anticipated affect, on intentions. In the first study, they examined the impact of mood and TRA components on intentions to use condoms. When a negative mood was induced, the attitude-intention relationship was strong and greater than when a positive mood was induced. The subjective norm-intention relationship was nonsignificant. When a positive mood was induced, there was a strong correlation between subjective norm and intention. That relationship was greater than the same relationship with a negative mood induction, and the attitude-intention relationship was nonsignificant.

In the second study, Armitage et al. (1999) examined dietary choices over a 1-week period, following either a positive or a negative mood induction. Intentions to consume healthy foods were significantly and positively related to dietary choices regardless of the mood induction. However, when a negative mood was induced, intentions to eat healthy foods were significantly predicted by attitudes and self-identity. When a positive mood was induced, only self-identity predicted intentions.

It is clear that anticipated negative affect, specifically anticipated regret, diminishes intentions to behave for some behaviors. Advocates extending or modifying the TRA would argue that anticipated affect is another variable that adds to the ability to predict intentions and behaviors beyond attitudes and subjective norms. Proponents of the TRA in its original form would most likely argue that anticipated negative affect is a residue of attitudes and subjective norms. It is easy to imagine how attitudes might influence, or be influenced by, anticipated negative affect. One can also imagine that subjective norms would influence anticipated negative affect (e.g., "I will regret disappointing my parents"). Induced mood states appear to moderate relationships between TRA components (i.e., to change the strength and/or direction of the relationships) but do not appear to enhance the ability to predict intentions or behaviors independently of TRA components.

Range of Meaning and the TRA

Miller and Nicholson (1976) suggested that useful theories were those that possessed "proper range of meaning." That is, theories ought to be of sufficient universality to encompass a broad scope of human activities. Theories should be sufficiently broad so that they neither confirm the obvious nor address socially trivial activities. Conversely, they should avoid being so general that they cannot be applied to behaviors that occur with regularity in everyday life. The range of meaning issue may be raised with regard to the TRA in two distinctive forms: one related to the inclusion of the behavioral intention construct and one criticizing its narrow application to volitional behaviors.

Range of Meaning and Behavioral Intentions. The range of meaning and behavioral intention criticism relates to whether the TRA merely confirms the obvious. To learn that people do what they say they intend to do should neither be surprising nor thought of as theoretically significant. This criticism suggests a tension among adequately describing, predicting, and explaining the cognitive processes that produce volitional behaviors and parsimony. Parsimony is logical simplicity, and the usual notion is that if two explanations for some phenomenon (e.g., volitional behavior) are equally valid, then the simplest or most parsimonious is thought to be preferable. Dubin (1978) made the point a bit differently when he argued that if parsimony is a desirable goal, then theories should include a minimal number of intervening or mediating variables.

The argument for parsimony concerns whether the behavioral intention construct is necessary to predict or explain volitional behaviors. A good deal of research has found that attitudes are strong predictors of behaviors. In studies that have path modeled social influence processes, results often show a direct effect for attitudes on behaviors and/or fail to find a significant intention-behavior relationship (e.g., Bagozzi & Warshaw, 1993; Bentler & Speckart, 1979, 1981). Eagly and Chaiken (1993) suggested that those results be viewed cautiously because either error of measurement or poor statistical power may account for small intention-behavior relations in those studies. However, the issue can be framed in a slightly different manner, that is, by asking what is gained by including the intention construct.

Proponents of the TRA would argue that, at the very least, by including behavioral intentions when modeling volitional behaviors, one gains a more accurate representation of the cognitive processes that produce the behaviors. Moreover, TRA proponents suggest that including the intention construct significantly improves the prediction of volitional behaviors.

Kim and Hunter (1993a) meta-analyzed the attitude-behavior literature. They found, after correcting for measurement error and dichotomization, a mean attitude-behavior relationship of $r = .79$. Moreover, when they grouped studies according to the compatibility of the attitude and behavior measures on the dimensions of action, target, context, and time (Fishbein & Ajzen, 1975), the mean attitude-behavior correlation was .86 when there was high compatibility between the intention and behavior measures.

A strong attitude-behavior correlation may tempt some to argue that behaviors are predicted well enough from attitudes without a mediating effect of behavioral intentions. However, a second meta-analysis (Kim & Hunter, 1993b) found a mean attitude-behavior relationship of $r = .87$ and a mean intention-behavior correlation of $r = .82$. If intention mediates the attitude-behavior relationship, then the attitude-intention relationship should be stronger than the attitude-behavior relationship because attitudes are more proximal to intentions in the causal chain than they are to behaviors. Indeed, the attitude-intention relationship ($r = .87$) is larger than the attitude-behavior relationship ($r = .79$). That the attitude-intention is stronger than the attitude-behavior relationship

supports the notion that intentions serve a mediating role between attitudes and behaviors. That finding also lends credence to Eagly and Chaiken's (1993) argument that the failure to find significant intention-behavior relationships in some studies is probably the result of measurement error, dichotomization of measurement, or low power in the statistical tests.

A convincing case can be made that including the behavioral intention construct when modeling volitional behaviors provides a more accurate description of the cognitive processes underlying those behaviors. Kim and Hunter (1993a, 1993b) also presented convincing evidence that including the intention construct improves the ability to predict behaviors beyond the contributions made by attitudes. With regard to the issue of parsimony, it is the case that omitting behavioral intentions would be more simplistic than including intentions in models of volitional behavior, but those models would predict behaviors significantly worse than the TRA.

Range of Meaning and Volitional Behaviors. The TRA has also been criticized for limiting its scope to volitional behaviors. As was noted earlier in this chapter, previous behaviors, or habits, are strong predictors of behavior (see, e.g., Tesser & Shaffer, 1990). Habitual behaviors are thought to be nonvolitional or outside of the individual's control.

Other research indicates that many behaviors are mindless or carried out without exerting cognitive effort in deciding how to behave. Langer and others (Bargh & Chartrand, 1999; Langer, 1978) have indicated that mindless behaviors are enacted using behavioral scripts. Scripts are cognitive schemata that contain expected sequences of behaviors used to achieve certain goals. Individuals may have scripts for routine or mundane behaviors (e.g., a grocery shopping script, a drive to work script) or for socially meaningful behaviors.

Recent research supports the idea that individuals have scripts for a wide variety of social behaviors including sexual one-night stands (Monahan, Miller, & Rothspan, 1997), sexual aggression (Krahe, 2000), negotiations (O'Connor & Adams, 1999), consumer behaviors (Rook, 1985), medical diagnoses (Charlin, Tardif, & Boshuizen, 2000), and interactions with disabled persons (Langer & Chanowitz, 1988). Differentiating habitual behavior and scripted behavior can be difficult, and indeed, Eagly and Chaiken (1993) suggested that scripts provide a model for cognitively representing habitual behaviors.

Regardless of the relationship of scripts to habits and vice versa, there is a wide range of socially meaningful behaviors that are either mindlessly performed or not under the control of the social actor. Going back to very early research on the attitude-behavior relationship, scholars questioned the value of explaining nonrepetitive behaviors. Tittle and Hill (1967) were critical of theories that had as their goal predicting or explaining singular responses to constructed circumstances unlikely to recur in everyday life. The range of meaning criticism of the TRA suggests that the boundary conditions of the theory exclude socially meaningful and repetitive behaviors in favor of a smaller set of less meaningful behaviors that are completely volitional in nature.

In addition to excluding behaviors that are habitual or scripted, the TRA excludes behavior that requires special skills, resources, opportunities, and/or the cooperation of others in order to be completed (Liska, 1984). Liska (1984) argued that limiting the TRA to behaviors that require no special skills, no unique opportunities, and/or no cooperation by others restricts the range of meaning of the theory to relatively simple behaviors such as voting, donating blood, and avoiding exposure to the sun. While those behaviors may be socially significant in their own right, Liska argued that the theory omitted a broader range of behaviors that were at least as socially salient.

Fishbein and Ajzen (1975) did speak to criticisms related to the need for resources, skills, and/or cooperation from others. They contended that the need for resources would not alter the basic form of the TRA but would change the relationship between behavioral intentions and attitudes. For example, if a consumer intended to buy a big-screen television but discovered that he or she lacked the money to do so, then it is likely that the consumer would change his or her purchasing intention at least temporarily.

The response that a resource deficit would change intentions is problematic for two reasons. First, lack of resources needed to engage in a behavior means that the behavior is not truly volitional. The consumer may desire to own a big-screen television, but without the financial resources to buy one, the purchasing decision is not truly voluntary. Second, the TRA specifies that intentions are the result of attitudes toward the behavior and subjective norms related to the behavior. It is quite conceivable that the consumer would continue to have a positive attitude toward purchasing a big-screen television and that his or her friends or family members would have positive feelings about such a purchase. The lack of resources, which is not explicitly included in the model, could predict intentions where attitudes and subjective norms would not do so. At the very least, omitting a resource variable from the model would introduce considerable error of prediction.

Fishbein and Ajzen (1975) made similar arguments related to behaviors that require the cooperation of others and those that require special skills. They argued that if cooperation from others is lacking, then an individual's intention toward performing a behavior will change. If special skills are required to complete some behavior, and if one is lacking in those skills, then the individual's intention to perform the behavior will be different from that if he or she possessed the requisite skills. These responses are no more satisfying for behaviors requiring cooperation or special skills than they are for behaviors requiring resources. The behaviors still will not be truly volitional in nature, and one's intentions to perform or not perform the behaviors will be influenced by factors other than those specified in the theory. Hence, the best response is that behaviors that require resources, cooperation of others, and/or special skills to perform are not truly volitional and fall outside the parameters of the TRA. However, that position fuels the range of meaning argument made by TRA critics.

THE THEORY OF PLANNED BEHAVIOR

In an effort to expand the range of behaviors encompassed by the TRA, Ajzen (1985) proposed the theory of planned behavior (TPB). Ajzen insisted that the TRA predicted and explained volitional behaviors quite well, but Ajzen presented the TPB to predict and explain behaviors that were not completely under the volitional control of the actor. The components of the TPB mirror those of the TRA, except that *perceived behavioral control* is added to the TPB. Perceived behavioral control is "one's perception of how easy or difficult it is to perform the behavior" (Eagly & Chaiken, 1993, p. 185).

Ajzen (1991) differentiated perceived behavioral control from related constructs such as locus of control (Rotter, 1966) and control as a general dispositional quality (Atkinson, 1964). The perceived behavioral control construct is most closely akin to Bandura's self-efficacy construct. Bandura (1982) described self-efficacy as "judgments of how well one can execute courses of action required to deal with prospective situations" (p. 122).

Bandura's (1982, 1991) research shows that self-efficacy influences the activities individuals choose, their preparation for the activities, and the amount of effort that is expended when completing the activities. In a similar vein, the TPB includes perceived behavioral control as a predictor of behavioral intentions and directly of behaviors.

Just as attitudes are a function of belief strength and belief evaluation, or subjective norms are a function of normative beliefs and motivation to comply, perceived behavioral control is posited to be a function of control beliefs and perceived power. Control beliefs are ones related to presence or absence of the resources and opportunities required for performance of the behavior. Perceived power is the ability of the control attribute to facilitate or inhibit the performance of the behavior. For example, a woman may reason that she has the knowledge or skill necessary to perform breast self-examination (a control belief) and that having that knowledge or skill will facilitate breast self-examination (perceived power). Perceived behavioral control can be expressed mathematically as follows:

$$PBC = \sum c_i \, p_i,$$

where c is a control belief (a perceived resource or opportunity) and p is perceived power or the perceived ability of the belief to facilitate or inhibit performance of the behavior. Figure 14.3 expresses the TPB in the form of a causal model.

DATA BEARING ON THE THEORY OF PLANNED BEHAVIOR

Much of discussion of data bearing on the TRA is relevant to the TPB. This discussion focuses on the perceived behavioral control and its component parts because those variables are unique to the TPB. This discussion

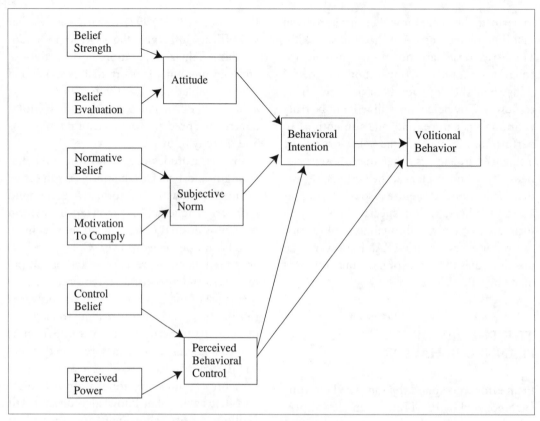

Figure 14.3. Causal Diagram of the Theory of Planned Behavior

also describes the effects of attitudes and subjective norms in combination with perceived behavioral control to predict intentions and the combined effects of behavioral intentions and perceived behavioral control to predict behaviors.

The Relationship Between Perceived Behavioral Control and Intentions

There have been a handful of meta-analyses of TPB studies. Two of the meta-analyses have been limited to studies of single classes of behaviors (i.e., studies of exercise-related behaviors) (Hausenblas, Carron, & Mack, 1997) and studies of condom use (Sheeran & Taylor, 1999). The meta-analysis conducted by Godin

and Kok (1996) was less restrictive and included studies of several classes of health-related behaviors (e.g., eating, exercise, oral hygiene, HIV/AIDS). Ajzen's (1991) meta-analysis was not class specific. The mean correlation between perceived behavioral control and intentions ranged from .35 to .53. A summary of the results of the three meta-analyses is shown in Table 14.3.

The Relationship Between Perceived Behavioral Control and Behaviors

Ajzen (1985, 1987) indicated that perceived behavioral control influenced behaviors directly in addition to the mediated effect via behavioral intentions. Of the TPB meta-analy-

TABLE 14.3 Summary of Findings From Metga-Analyses of the Theory of Planned Behavior

(a) Perceived Behavioral Control and Intentions			
Review	*k*	*r*	*r²*
Ajzen (1991)	17	.53	.28
Godin & Kok (1996)	58	.35	.12
Hausenblaus et al. (1997)	11	.43	.18
Attitudes, Subjective Norms, and Perceived Behavioral Control on Intentions			
Review	*K*	*R*	*R²*
Ajzen (1991)	17	.71	.50
Godin & Kok (1996)	58	.64	.41
Shereen & Taylor (1999)	24	.65	.42

ses cited previously, two analyzed the impact of perceived behavioral control on behaviors. In the meta-analysis of exercise behaviors, Hausenblas et al. (1997) reported a mean perceived control-behavior correlation of .45. Godin and Kok (1996) found a mean perceived behavioral control-behavior relationship of .39. Ajzen (1991) reported a mean perceived control-behavior correlation of .39. In these meta-analyses, perceived behavioral control had a statistically significant and substantial impact on behaviors.

Attitudes, Subjective Norms, Perceived Behavioral Control, and Intentions

The TPB can also be judged by the ability of the attitudes, subjective norms, and perceived behavioral control to predict intentions. Three meta-analyses related to the TPB reported the combined effects of the three predictors on intentions (Ajzen, 1991; Godin & Kok, 1996; Sheeran & Taylor, 1999). The results show that attitudes, subjective norms, and perceived behavioral control account for between 40% and 50% of the variance in behavioral intentions. The findings of the three meta-analyses are shown in Table 14.3.

Meta-analysts have argued that inclusion of the perceived behavioral control construct significantly improves the ability to predict intentions. For example, Hausenblas et al. (1997) posited that the "results of the present study clearly support a conclusion that TPB is superior to TRA for predicting and explaining exercise intentions and behaviors." Sheeran and Taylor (1999) found that perceived behavioral control accounted for an additional 5% of the variance in condom use intentions compared to the TRA.

Control Beliefs, Perceived Power, and Perceived Behavioral Control

Only a very few studies have measured perceived behavioral control as a function of control beliefs and perceived power (Ajzen, 1991). Most studies of the TPB measure have perceived behavioral control using a global measure without measuring the control belief and perceived power components of the global construct. Ajzen (1991) reported correlations ranging from .40 to .70 in the handful of studies that have assessed weighted control beliefs and a more global measure of perceived behavioral control.

CRITICISMS OF THE THEORY OF PLANNED BEHAVIOR

Eagly and Chaiken (1993) concluded that the TPB was quite successful "in those domains in which the TRA is less appropriate" (p. 189). However, they noted that several issues related to the TPB warranted closer examination. We consider three issues related to the TPB: the causal relationship between perceived behavioral control and intentions, the sufficiency of the TPB to predict and explain behaviors, and the role of "planning" in planned behavior.

The Causal Relationship Between Perceived Control and Intentions

The TPB posits a positive causal relationship between perceived behavioral control and intentions. The implication of that position is that individuals form intentions because they have control over the behaviors. That notion is a reasonable one for positively valenced behaviors. For example, losing weight may involve changing one's diet and engaging in increased exercise. If an individual is positively disposed toward losing weight and perceives that he or she has control over diet and exercise, then the perceived control may cause the individual to change his or her intentions to diet and exercise.

The idea that perceived behavioral control and intentions are causally related makes less sense for a behavior that is negatively valenced. For example, if a male is negatively disposed toward condom use, then even if he believes that condom use is completely under his control, the individual might not intend to use a condom during sex. Eagly and Chaiken (1993) noted that perceived behavioral control might interact with other variables (e.g., the desire to engage in a behavior or to attain a goal) to determine intentions, but interaction effects involving perceived behavioral control have not been investigated.

The TPB as a Sufficient Explanation for Behavior

Earlier in this chapter, we discussed four variables that significantly influence intentions and/or behaviors: moral obligation, self-identity, habit or prior behavior, and affect. Others (and we) were skeptical of Fishbein and Ajzen's (1975, 1980) claim that all other variables are residues of TRA components. If some combinations of moral obligations, self-identity, prior behaviors, and/or affect are significant predictors of intentions or behaviors, then their omission from the TPB is as serious as their omission from the TRA. While Fishbein and Ajzen argued that the TRA is a sufficient explanation of volitional behaviors, Ajzen (1991) discussed the possibility that moral obligation, affect, and past behaviors might also predict intentions and/or behaviors. He concluded that it is premature to draw conclusions about the sufficiency of the TPB, and he called for additional research to determine whether additional predictors should be added to the theory.

The Role of Planning in the TPB

Eagly and Chaiken (1993) also noted the irony of a theory of "planned" behavior that did not address the notion of plans. Dillard (1990) observed that "planning consists of producing one or more schemes for goal attainment, evaluating their overall effectiveness, and choosing among them" (p. 48). The TPB does not address the issue of how individuals formulate, evaluate, and/or act on plans. This omission would seem especially serious for behaviors that are less directly under the actor's control. If special skills, resources, and/or the cooperation of others were needed to perform a behavior, then formulating and evaluating plans about obtaining the requisite skills, resources, and/or cooperation would be particularly important.

CONCLUSION

The TRA is an attempt to explain volitional behaviors. Criticisms of the theory focus more on what the theory omits (e.g., additional predictors, nonvolitional behaviors) than on what it includes or the support for the hypothesized relationships. In an effort to expand the explanatory domain of the TRA, Ajzen (1985) formulated the TPB. He maintained that the TRA was a valid explanation for volitional behaviors but advocated the TPB, with its inclusion of perceived behavior control, to explain behaviors of a less volitional nature. The evidence supporting the TRA and the TPB is considerable. Together, the two theories provide a useful framework for explaining social influence outcomes that are thoughtful in nature.

Both the TRA and TPB identify natural targets of social influence attempts. When attempting to influence behaviors, one may construct persuasive messages that attempt to modify any of the components of the theories. Starting most proximally to behaviors, persuasive messages may target the message recipient's behavioral intentions. In the same vein, because intentions are a function of attitudes, subjective norms, and perceived behavioral control, persuasive messages whose content modified one or more of those components would also lead to changes in intentions and behaviors. Finally, the content of persuasive appeals can aim at the components that are least proximal to behaviors. Persuasive appeals may attempt to modify belief strength, belief evaluation, normative beliefs, motivation to comply, control beliefs, or perceived power. The theoretical and practical appeal of both the TRA and TPB is that the theories clearly direct researchers and practitioners toward proven strategies for successful influence.

NOTES

1. Research by Hocking, Turk, and Ellinger (1999) found that judgments of a partner who insists on condom use are quite positive.

2. Sutton (1998) presented nine reasons for attenuated relationships between intentions and behaviors. We chose to highlight four.

3. Kim and Hunter (1993b) reported that "virtually no studies have used time and context among their attitudinal and behavioral elements" (p. 341).

REFERENCES

Ajzen, I. (1985). From intentions to actions: A theory of planned behavior. In J. Kuhl & J. Beckmann (Eds.), *Action control: From cognition to behavior* (pp. 11-39). New York: Springer-Verlag.

Ajzen, I. (1987). Attitudes, traits, and actions: Dispositional predictions of behavior in personality and social psychology. In L. Berkowitz (Ed.),

Advances in experimental social psychology (Vol. 20, pp. 1-63). San Diego: Academic Press.

Ajzen, I. (1988). *Attitudes, personality, and behavior.* Chicago: Dorsey.

Ajzen, I. (1991). The theory of planned behavior. *Organizational Behavior and Human Decision Processes, 50,* 179-211.

Ajzen, I., & Fishbein, M. (1969). The prediction of behavioral intentions in a choice situation. *Journal of Experimental Social Psychology, 5,* 400-416.

Ajzen, I., & Fishbein, M. (1970). The prediction of behavior attitudinal and normative variables. *Journal of Experimental Social Psychology, 6,* 466-487.

Ajzen, I., & Fishbein, M. (1972). Attitudes and normative beliefs as factors influencing behavioral intentions. *Journal of Personal and Social Psychology, 21,* 1-9.

Ajzen, I., & Fishbein, M. (1977). Attitude-behavior relations: A theoretical analysis and review of empirical research. *Psychological Bulletin, 84,* 888-918.

Ajzen, I., & Fishbein, M. (1980). *Understanding attitudes and predicting social behavior.* Englewood Cliffs, NJ: Prentice Hall.

Anderson, L. R. (1970). Predictions of negative attitude from congruity, summation, and logarithm formulae for the evaluation of complex stimuli. *Journal of Social Psychology, 81,* 37-48.

Armitage, C. J., Conner, M., & Norman, P. (1999). Differential effects of mood on information processing: Evidence from the theories of reasoned action and planned behavior. *European Journal of Social Psychology, 29,* 419-433.

Atkinson, J. W. (1964). *An introduction to motivation.* Princeton, NJ: Van Nostrand.

Bagozzi, R. P. (1981). Attitudes, intentions, and behavior: A test of some key hypotheses. *Journal of Personality and Social Psychology, 41,* 607-627.

Bagozzi, R. P. (1982). A field investigation of causal relations among conditions, affects, intentions, and behaviors. *Journal of Marketing Research, 19,* 562-584.

Bagozzi, R. P., & Warshaw, P. R. (1992). An examination of the etiology of the attitude behavior relation for goal-directed behaviors. *Multivariate Behavioral Research, 27,* 601-634.

Baker, S. A., Morrison, D. M., Carter, W. B., & Verdon, M. S. (1996). Using the theory of reasoned action (TRA) to understand the decision to use condoms in an STD clinic population. *Health Education Quarterly, 23,* 528-542.

Bandura, A. (1982). Self-efficacy mechanism in human agency. *American Psychologist, 37,* 122-147.

Bandura, A. (1991). Social-cognitive theory of self-regulation. *Organizational Behavior and Human Decision Processes, 50,* 248-285.

Bargh, J. A., & Chartrand, T. L. (1999). The unbearable automaticity of being. *American Psychologist, 54,* 462-479.

Bearden, W. O., & Crockett, M. (1981). Self-monitoring, norms, and attitudes as influences on consumer complaining. *Journal of Business Research, 9,* 255-266.

Bentler, P. M., & Speckart, G. (1979). Models of attitude-behavior relations. *Psychological Review, 86,* 425-464.

Bentler, P. M., & Speckart, G. (1981). Attitudes cause behaviors: A structural equation analysis. *Journal of Personality and Social Psychology, 40,* 226-238.

Budd, R. J., North, D., & Spencer, C. (1984). Understanding seatbelt use: A test of Bentler and Speckart's extension of the "theory of reasoned action." *European Journal of Social Psychology, 14,* 69-78.

Budd, R. J., & Spencer, C. (1984). Latitude of rejection, centrality, and certainty: Variables affecting the relationship between attitudes, norms, and behavioral intentions. *British Journal of Social Psychology, 23,* 1-8.

Charlin, B., Tardif, J., & Boshuizen, H. P. A. (2000). Scripts and medical diagnostic knowledge: Theory and applications for clinical reasoning instruction and research. *Academic Medicine, 75,* 182-190.

Charng, H. W., Piliavin, J. A., & Callero, P. L. (1988). Role identity and reasoned action in the prediction of repeated behavior. *Social Psychology Quarterly, 51,* 303-317.

Chassin, L., Corty, E., Presson, C. C., Olshacsky, R. W., Bensenberg, M., & Sherman, S. J. (1981). Predicting adolescents' intentions to smoke cigarettes. *Journal of Health and Social Behavior, 22,* 445-455.

Conner, M., & Armitage, C. J. (1998). Extending the theory of planned behavior: A review and avenues for further research. *Journal of Applied Social Psychology, 28,* 1429-1464.

Cronen, V. E., & Conville, R. L. (1975). Fishbein's conception of belief strength: A theoretical, methodological, and experimental critique. *Speech Monographs, 42,* 143-150.

Davis, M. H., & Runge, T. E. (1981). Beliefs and attitudes in a gubernatorial primary: Some limitations on the Fishbein model. *Journal of Applied Social Psychology, 11,* 93-113.

Delia, J. G., Crockett, W. H., Press, A. N., & O'Keefe, D. J. (1975). The dependency of interpersonal evaluations on context-relevant beliefs about the other. *Speech Monographs, 42,* 10-19.

de Vries, D. L., & Ajzen, I. (1971). The relationship of attitudes and normative beliefs to cheating in college. *Journal of Social Psychology, 83,* 199-207.

Dillard, J. P. (1990). *Seeking compliance: The production of interpersonal influence messages.* Scottsdale, AZ: Gorsuch Scarisbrick.

Dubin, R. (1978). *Theory building* (2nd ed.). New York: Free Press.

Eagly, A. H., & Chaiken, S. (1993). *The psychology of attitudes.* Fort Worth, TX: Harcourt Brace Jovanovich.

Ferguson, G. A. (1976). *Statistical analysis in psychology and education.* New York: McGraw-Hill.

Fishbein, M. (1967a). Attitude and predicting behavior. In M. Fishbein (Ed.), *Readings in attitude theory and measurement* (pp. 477-492). New York: Wiley.

Fishbein, M. (1967b). A behavior theory approach to the relation between beliefs about an object and the attitude toward the object. In M. Fishbein (Ed.), *Readings in attitude theory and measurement* (pp. 389-400). New York: John Wiley.

Fishbein, M., & Ajzen, I. (1975). *Beliefs, attitude, intention, and behavior: An introduction to theory and research.* Reading, MA: Addison-Wesley.

Fishbein, M., & Ajzen, I. (1980). Predicting and understanding consumer behavior: Attitude-behavior correspondence. In I. Ajzen & M. Fishbein (Eds.), *Understanding attitudes and predicting social behavior* (pp. 148-172). Englewood Cliffs, NJ: Prentice Hall.

Fishbein, M., & Ajzen, I. (1981a). Attitudes and voting behavior: An application of the theory of reasoned action. In G. M. Stephenson & J. M. Davis (Eds.), *Progress in applied social psychology* (Vol. 1, pp. 253-313). New York: John Wiley.

Fishbein, M., & Ajzen, I. (1981b). On construct validity: A critique of Miniard and Cohen's paper. *Journal of Experimental Social Psychology, 17,* 340-350.

Fishbein, M., Ajzen, I., & Hinkle, R. (1980). Predicting and understanding voting in American elections: Effects of external variables. In I. Ajzen & M. Fishbein (Eds.), *Understanding attitudes and predicting social behavior* (pp. 173-195). Englewood Cliffs, NJ: Prentice Hall.

Fishbein, M., Jaccard, J. J., Davidson, A. R., Ajzen, I., & Loken, B. (1980). Predicting and understanding family planning behaviors: Beliefs, attitudes, and intentions. In I. Ajzen & M. Fishbein (Eds.), *Understanding attitudes and predicting social behavior* (pp. 130-147). Englewood Cliffs, NJ: Prentice Hall.

Godin, G., & Kok, G. (1996). The theory of planned behavior: A review of its applications to health-related behaviors. *American Journal of Health Promotion, 11,* 87-98.

Granberg, D., & Holmberg, S. (1990). The intention behavior relationship among U.S. and Swedish voters. *Social Psychology Quarterly, 53,* 44-54.

Greene, K., Hale, J. L., & Rubin, D. L. (1997). A test of the theory of reasoned action in the context of condom use and AIDS. *Communication Reports, 10,* 21-33.

Gur-Arie, O., Durand, R. M., & Bearden, W. O. (1979). Attitudinal and normative dimensions of opinion leaders and nonleaders. *Journal of Psychology, 101,* 305-312.

Hackman, J. R., & Anderson, L. R. (1968). The strength, relevance, and source of beliefs about an object in Fishbein's attitude theory. *Journal of Social Psychology, 76,* 55-67.

Hale, J. L., & Dillard, J. P. (1991). The uses of meta-analysis: Making knowledge claims and setting research agendas. *Communication Monographs, 58,* 463-471.

Hausenblas, H. A., Carron, A. V., & Mack, D. E. (1997). Application of the theories of reasoned action and planned behavior to exercise behavior: A meta-analysis. *Journal of Sports & Exercise Psychology, 19,* 36-51.

Hocking, J. E., Turk, J. E., & Ellinger, A. (1999). The effects of partner insistence of condom usage on perceptions of the partner, the relationship, and the experience. *Journal of Adolescence, 22,* 355-367.

Hoffmann, R. G. (1999). Effectiveness of a school-based program to enhance knowledge of sun exposure: Attitudes towards sun exposure and sunscreen use among children. *Children's Health Care, 28,* 69-86.

Holbrook, M. B. (1977). Comparing multi-attribute attitude models by optimal scaling. *Journal of Consumer Research, 4,* 165-171.

Holbrook, M. B., & Hulbert, J. M. (1975). Multi-attribute attitude models: A comparative analysis. In M. J. Schlinger (Ed.), *Advances in consumer research* (Vol. 2, pp. 375-388). Ann Arbor, MI: Association for Consumer Research.

Hoogstraten, J., de Haan, W., & ter Horst, G. (1985). Stimulating the demand for dental care: An application of Ajzen and Fishbein's theory of reasoned action. *European Journal of Social Psychology, 15,* 401-414.

Hunter, J. E., Schmidt, F. L., & Jackson, G. B. (1982). *Meta-analysis: Cumulating research findings across studies.* Beverly Hills, CA: Sage.

Infante, D. A. (1971). Predicting attitude from desirability and likelihood ratings of rhetorical propositions. *Speech Monographs, 38,* 321-326.

Infante, D. A. (1973). The perceived importance of cognitive structure components: An adaptation of Fishbein's theory. *Speech Monographs, 42,* 8-16.

Kantola, S. J., Syme, G. J., & Campbell, N. A. (1982). The role of individual differences and external variables in a test of the sufficiency of Fishbein's model to explain behavioral intentions to conserve water. *Journal of Applied Social Psychology, 12,* 70-83.

Kim, M. S., & Hunter, J. E. (1993a). Attitude-behavior relations: A meta-analysis of attitudinal relevance and topic. *Journal of Communication, 43,* 101-142.

Kim, M. S., & Hunter, J. E. (1993b). Relationships among attitudes, behavioral intentions, and behavior: A meta-analysis of past research, part 2. *Communication Research, 20,* 331-364.

Krahe, B. (2000). Sexual scripts and heterosexual aggression. In T. Eckes & H. M. Trautner (Eds.), *The developmental social psychology of gender* (pp. 273-292). Mahwah, NJ: Lawrence Erlbaum.

Langer, E. J. (1978). Rethinking the role of thought in social interaction. In J. H. Harvey, W. Ickes, & R. F. Kidd (Eds.), *New directions in attribution research* (Vol. 2, pp. 35-58). Hillsdale, NJ: Lawrence Erlbaum.

Langer, E. J. (1989). *Mindfulness reading.* Reading, MA: Merloyd Lawrence Books.

Langer, E. J., & Chanowitz, B. (1988). Mindfulness/mindlessness: A new perspective for the study of disability. In H. E. Yuker (Ed.), *Attitudes towards people with disabilities* (pp. 61-81). New York: Springer.

Liska, A. E. (1984). A critical examination of the causal structure of the Fishbein-Ajzen model. *Social Psychology Quarterly, 47,* 61-74.

Maddux, J. E. (1993). Social cognitive models of health and exercise behavior: An introduction and review of conceptual issues. *Journal of Applied Sports Psychology, 5,* 116-140.

Manstead, A. S. R., & Parker, D. (1995). Evaluating and extending the theory of planned behavior. In W. Stroebe & M. Hewstone (Eds.), *European review of social psychology* (Vol. 6, pp. 69-95). Chichester, UK: Wiley.

Marks, D. F. (1996). Health psychology in context. *Journal of Health Psychology, 1,* 7-21.

McCarty, D. (1981). Changing contraceptive usage intentions: A test of the Fishbein model of intention. *Journal of Applied Social Psychology, 11,* 192-211.

Miller, G. R. (1980). On being persuaded: Some basic distinctions. In M. E. Roloff & G. R. Miller (Eds.), *Persuasion: New directions in theory and research* (Sage Annual Reviews of Communication Research, Vol. 8, pp. 11-28). Beverly Hills, CA: Sage.

Miller, G. R., & Nicholson, H. E. (1976). *Communication inquiry: A perspective on a process.* Reading, MA: Addison-Wesley.

Miller, L. E., & Grush, J. E. (1986). Individual differences in attitudinal versus normative determination of behavior. *Journal of Experimental Social Psychology, 22,* 190-202.

Miniard, P. W., & Cohen, J. B. (1981). An examination of the Fishbein-Ajzen behavioral intentions model's concepts and measures. *Journal of Experimental Social Psychology, 17,* 309-399.

Miniard, P. W., & Page, T. J. (1984). Causal relationships in the Fishbein behavioral intention model. In T. C. Kinnear (Ed.), *Advances in consumer research* (Vol. 11, pp. 137-142). Provo, UT: Association for Consumer Research.

Monahan, J. L., Miller, L. C., & Rothspan, S. (1997). Power and intimacy: On the dynamics of risky sex. *Health Communication, 9,* 303-321.

Mullen, P. H., Hersey, J. C., & Iverson, D. C. (1987). Health behavior models compared. *Social Science and Medicine, 24,* 973-983.

Norwich, B., & Duncan, J. (1990). Attitudes, subjective norm, perceived preventative factors, intentions, and learning science: Testing a modified theory of reasoned action. *British Journal of Educational Psychology, 60,* 312-321.

O'Connor, K. M., & Adams, A. A. (1999). What novices think about negotiations: A content analysis of scripts. *Negotiation Journal, 15,* 135-147.

O'Keefe, D. J. (1990). *Persuasion: Theory and research.* Newbury Park, CA: Sage.

Park, S. H. (2000). Relationships among attitudes and subjective norms: Testing the theory of reasoned action across cultures. *Communication Studies, 51,* 162-175.

Parker, D., Manstead, A. R. S., & Stradling, S. G. (1995). Extending the theory of planned behavior: The role of personal norms. *British Journal of Social Psychology, 34,* 127-137.

Parker, D., Stradling, S. G., & Manstead, A. R. S. (1996). Modifying beliefs and attitudes to exceeding the speed limit: An intervention study based on the theory of planned behavior. *Journal of Applied Social Psychology, 26,* 1-19.

Patry, A. L., & Pelletier, L. G. (2001). Extraterrestrial beliefs and experiences: An application of the theory of reasoned action. *Journal of Social Psychology, 141,* 199-217.

Prestholdt, P. H., Lane, I. M., & Mathews, R. C. (1987). Nurse turnover as reasoned action: Development of a process model. *Journal of Applied Psychology, 72,* 221-227.

Randall, D. M., & Wolff, J. A. (1994). The time interval in the intention-behavior relationship: Meta-analysis. *British Journal of Social Psychology, 33,* 405-418.

Richard, R., van der Pligt, J., & de Vries, N. (1995). Anticipated affective reactions and prevention of AIDS. *British Journal of Social Psychology, 34,* 9-21.

Richard, R., van der Pligt, J., & de Vries, N. (1996). Anticipated affect and behavioral choice. *Basic and Applied Social Psychology, 18,* 111-129.

Riddle, P. K. (1980). Attitudes, beliefs, behavioral intentions, and behaviors of women and men towards regular jogging. *Research Quarterly for Exercise and Sports, 51,* 663-674.

Rook, D. W. (1985). The ritual dimension of consumer behavior. *Journal of Consumer Research, 12,* 251-264.

Rotter, J. B. (1966). Generalized expectancies from internal versus external control of reinforcement. *Psychological Monographs, 80* (whole No. 609).

Ryan, M. J. (1982). Behavioral intention formation: The interdependency of attitudinal and social influence variables. *Journal of Consumer Research, 9,* 262-278.

Saltzer, E. B. (1981). Cognitive moderators of the relationship between behavioral intentions and behavior. *Journal of Personality and Social Psychology, 41,* 260-271.

Schlegel, R. P., Crawford, C. A., & Sanborn, M. D. (1977). Correspondence and mediational properties of the Fishbein model: An application to adolescent alcohol use. *Journal of Experimental Social Psychology, 13,* 421-430.

Sejwacz, D., Ajzen, I., & Fishbein, M. (1980). Predicting and understanding weight loss: Intentions, behaviors, and outcomes. In I. Ajzen & M. Fishbein (Eds.), *Understanding attitudes and predicting social behavior* (pp. 101-112). Englewood Cliffs, NJ: Prentice Hall.

Sheeran, P., & Oberall, S. (1998). Do intentions predict condom use? Meta-analysis and examination of six moderator variables. *British Journal of Social Psychology, 37,* 231-250.

Sheeran, P., & Taylor, S. (1999). Predicting intentions to use condoms: A meta-analysis and comparison of the theories of reasoned action and planned behavior. *Journal of Applied Psychology, 29,* 1624-1675.

Shepard, G. J., & O'Keefe, D. J. (1984). Separability of attitudinal and normative influences on behavioral intentions in the Fishbein-Ajzen model. *Journal of Social Psychology, 122,* 287-288.

Sheppard, B. H., Hartwick, J., & Warshaw, P. R. (1988). The theory of reasoned action: A meta-analysis of past research with recommendations for modifications and future research. *Journal of Consumer Research, 15,* 325-343.

Sideridis, G. D., Kaissidis, A., & Padeliadu, S. (1998). Comparison of the theories of reasoned action and planned behavior. *British Journal of Educational Psychology, 68,* 563-580.

Simonson, I. (1992). The influence of anticipating regret and responsibility on purchase decisions. *Journal of Consumer Research, 19,* 105-118.

Smetana, J. G., & Adler, N. E. (1980). Fishbein's Value × Expectancy Model: An examination of assumptions. *Personality and Social Psychology Bulletin, 6,* 89-96.

Sparks, P., & Guthrie, C. A. (1998). Self-identity and the theory of planned behavior: A useful addition or an unhelpful artifice? *Journal of Applied Social Psychology, 28,* 1393-1410.

Sparks, P., Shepherd, R., & Frewer, L. J. (1995). Assessing and structuring attitudes toward the use of gene technology in food production: The role of perceived ethical obligation. *Basic and Applied Social Psychology, 16,* 267-285.

Sutton, S. (1998). Predicting and explaining intentions and behavior: How well are we doing? *Journal of Applied Social Psychology, 28,* 1317-1338.

Terry, D. J., Hogg, M. A., & White, K. M. (1999). The theory of planned behavior: Self-identity, social identity, and group norms. *British Journal of Social Psychology, 38,* 225-244.

Tesser, A., & Shaffer, D. R. (1990). Attitudes and attitude change. *Annual Review of Psychology, 41,* 479-523.

Thuen, F., & Rise, J. (1994). Young adolescents' intentions to use seat belts: The role of attitudinal and normative beliefs. *Health Education Research, 9,* 215-223.

Tittle, C. R., & Hill, R. J. (1967). Attitude measurement and prediction of behavior: An evaluation of conditions and measurement techniques. *Sociometry, 30,* 199-213.

Triandis, H. C. (1977). *Interpersonal behavior.* Pacific Grove, CA: Brooks/Cole.

van der Pligt, J., & de Vries, N. K. (1998). Expectancy-value models of health behaviors: The role of salience and anticipated affect. *Psychology and Health, 13,* 289-305.

Warburton, J., & Terry, D. J. (2000). Volunteer decision making by older people: A test of a revised theory of planned behavior. *Basic and Applied Social Psychology, 22,* 245-257.

Warshaw, P. R. (1980). A new model for predicting behavioral intentions: An alternative to Fishbein. *Journal of Marketing Research, 17,* 153-172.

Yordy, G. A., & Lent, R. W. (1993). Predicting aerobic exercise participation: Social cognitive, reasoned action, and planned behavior models. *Journal of Sports & Exercise Psychology, 15,* 363-374.

Zuckerman, M., & Reis, H. T. (1978). Comparison of three models for predicting altruistic behavior. *Journal of Personality and Social Psychology, 36,* 498-510.

PART III

AFFECT AND PERSUASION

15

Discrete Emotions and Persuasion

ROBIN L. NABI

Despite the pervasive use of emotional appeals in persuasive messages, this area of attitude change research is still relatively unexplored. To date, the study of emotion and persuasion has been largely defined by research on fear appeals (e.g., Leventhal, 1970; Witte, 1994). Although other approaches to affective influence have certainly been given their due, such as the effect of mood on social judgments (e.g., Forgas, 1991; Isen, 1987, 1993; Schwarz, Bless, & Bohner, 1991) and the role of emotional blends in advertising outcomes (e.g., Christ & Thorson, 1992; Holbrook & Batra, 1987), overlooked have been the persuasive effects of discrete emotions other than fear, such as anger, sadness, envy, and joy. Because of their unique adaptive functions, discrete emotions likely have particular implications for the process and direction of persuasive influence as well as appropriate application contexts, thus necessitating consideration of their persuasive impacts as separate phenomena, both from other approaches and from one another.

This chapter, then, has three objectives. First, it lays out the functional emotion perspective from which the notion of discrete emotions is derived. Second, it reviews the current state of our knowledge regarding the pervasive effects of several discrete negative emotions (fear, guilt, anger, sadness, disgust, and envy) and positive emotions (happiness/joy, pride, relief, hope, and compassion) in mediated contexts, interpreted from emotion's functional perspective. Finally, given our limited understanding of the persuasive role of most discrete emotions, the chapter concludes by considering the theoretical perspectives and questions that may effectively guide future research in this area.

EMOTION THEORY

Emotion Defined

Emotions are generally viewed as internal mental states representing evaluative reactions to events, agents, or objects that vary in intensity (Ortony, Clore, & Collins, 1988). They are generally short-lived, intense, and directed at some external stimuli. Different theorists define emotion by emphasizing different *physiological features,* such as neural processes (e.g., Izard, 1977; Tomkins, 1962) or facial expression (e.g., Ekman & Friesen, 1975), or more *psychological factors,* such as appraisal patterns (e.g., Scherer, 1984; Smith & Ellsworth, 1985), adaptive functions (e.g., Plutchik, 1980a), action tendencies (e.g., Arnold, 1960; Frijda, 1986), or motivations and/or goals (e.g., Lazarus, 1991; Roseman, 1984). However, general consensus suggests that emotion is a psychological construct consisting of five components: (a) cognitive appraisal or evaluation of a situation, (b) the physiological component of arousal, (c) motor expression, (d) a motivational component (including behavioral intentions or readiness), and (e) a subjective feeling state (Scherer, 1984; for reviews of emotion definitions, see Plutchik, 1980a, and Fiske & Taylor, 1991).

Functional Emotion Theories

Functional emotion theories are based largely on Darwin's (1872/1965) seminal work, in which he argued that behaviors in response to emotional feelings serve adaptive functions developed through evolutionary processes. Although all functional theories are based on this premise, they maintain great variation in the emotion features emphasized. Still, the fundamental principles of such theories can be summarized in four statements. First, emotions have *inherent adaptive functions.* Second, emotions are based on events that are *personally relevant.* Third, each emotion has a distinctive goal or motivation represented in its *state of action readiness or tendency to action* designed to arouse, sustain, and direct cognitive and/or physical ac-

tivity. Fourth, emotions are *organizers and motivators of behavior.* (See Arnold, 1960; Buck, 1985; Frijda, 1986, 1988; Izard, 1977; Lang, 1995; Lazarus, 1991; Leeper, 1948; Ortony et al., 1988; Plutchik, 1980a, 1980b; Roseman, 1984; Scherer, 1984; Tomkins, 1962.)

Based on these principles, the emotion process, as conceptualized by functional theorists, involves first perceiving an object or event in the environment and appraising its relevance for personal well-being. Particular patterns of appraisals then lead to certain states of action readiness, the awareness of which is the subjective emotional experience. These action tendencies are associated with physiological changes that together influence future perceptions, cognitions, and even behaviors in accordance with the goal set by the emotion's action tendency. It is these latter outcomes that support the relevance of emotion's functional approach to persuasion processes.

In accordance with this paradigm, several emotions—including fear, anger, sadness, disgust, guilt, and joy[1]—are commonly agreed to be discrete. That is, they have unique appraisal patterns, motivational functions, and behavioral associations. Although different theorists also recognize any of a number of other emotions as discrete, including envy, contempt, pride, love, relief, hope, compassion, surprise, interest, and anticipation (Ekman & Friesen, 1975; Frijda, 1986; Izard, 1977; Lazarus, 1991; Plutchik, 1980a; Tomkins, 1962, 1963). Lazarus's (1991) cognitive-motivational-relational theory, with its parsimonious approach to emotional appraisal and its inclusion of *core relational themes* that simply and reliably capture the essence of each emotion (see Table 15.1 and Smith & Lazarus, 1993), offers a particularly attractive paradigm through which to identify and study discrete emotions. Thus, with Lazarus as our guide, the following section introduces the reader to

TABLE 15.1 Core Relational Themes of Select Emotion According to Lazarus (1991)

Emotion	Core Relational Theme
Anger	"Demeaning offense against me and mine"
Fright	"Concrete and sudden danger of imminent physical harm"
Guilt/Shame	"Having transgressed a moral imperative"
Sadness	"Irrevocable loss"
Disgust	"Taking in or being too close to an indigestible object or idea"
Envy	"Wanting what someone else has"
Happiness/Joy	"Making reasonable progress toward the realization of our goals"

SOURCE: Adapted from Lazarus (1991).

a set of negative emotions (fear, guilt, anger, sadness, disgust, and envy) and positive emotions (happiness/joy, pride, compassion, relief, and hope), and the theoretical and empirical work relating each emotion to persuasive outcome.

DISCRETE EMOTIONS AND ATTITUDE CHANGE: THEORY AND RESEARCH

As noted earlier, fear is the only discrete emotion that has been studied thoroughly in the persuasion context with theoretical models developed to articulate the process through which its effects occur (Breckler, 1993). By comparison, guilt has received sporadic attention, whereas anger, disgust, sadness, envy, and nearly all of the positive emotions have been virtually ignored as intentionally evoked, message-relevant discrete emotions. The subsections that follow include brief descriptions of several discrete emotions from a functional perspective and summaries of the extant theoretical and/or empirical understanding of their persuasive impact, paying particular attention to how the findings comport with functional approach predictions. Given the often thin and disjointed nature of the study of each emotion, I conclude by attempting to summarize and integrate the disordered emotion-specific observations to suggest more general directions for future inquiry.

Negative Emotions

Fear. Fear is generally aroused when a situation is perceived as both threatening to one's physical or psychological self and out of one's control (e.g., Frijda, 1986; Lazarus, 1991; Scherer, 1984). Threatening situations can be either innate or learned, and individuals' thresholds for fear are determined by biological factors and sociocultural context as well as individual differences and experiences (Izard, 1977). Based on the desire for protection, fear's action tendency is to escape from the threatening agent, and if realized, avoidance behavior results (Frijda, 1986; Lazarus, 1991; Plutchik, 1980a; Roseman, Wiest, & Swartz, 1994).

The extensive fear appeal literature cannot be adequately addressed within the scope of this chapter (for detailed accounts, see Boster & Mongeau, 1984; Eagly & Chaiken, 1993; Leventhal, 1970; and other chapters in this volume). In sum, however, it suggests that, despite the evolution of fear appeal models from emphasis on affect (Hovland, Janis, & Kelley, 1953; Janis & Feshbach, 1953, 1954), to incorporation of and later emphasis on cognition (Leventhal, 1970; Rogers, 1975, 1983), and back to a focus on both emotion and cognition (Witte, 1992), no single fear appeal model appears to be well supported by empirical research (Boster & Mongeau, 1984; Eagly & Chaiken, 1993; Mongeau, 1998; Witte, 1994). However, meta-analyses of the empirical findings suggest that, in general, fear is positively correlated with both attitude and behavior change, although age and efficacy perceptions can moderate those relationships (Boster & Mongeau, 1984; Mongeau, 1998). Importantly, the totality of fear-related persuasion findings are compatible with the functional view of fear. That is, those experiencing fear desire protection. Subsequent message processing and acceptance are contingent on the level of fear experienced and perceived usefulness of the message-related information in offering the desired protection.

Recently, and also compatible with the functional perspective, fear appeal research has begun to explore the effects of fear on information processing depth and cognitive response (see Nabi, 1999). Although these studies do not reach consensus, in sum, they identify four variables that may interact to influence processing depth of a fear-inducing message: (a) type of fear (chronic vs. acute), (b) expectation of a message containing reassuring information, (c) type of behavior advocated (e.g., disease detection vs. health promotion), and (d) issue familiarity (Baron, Inman, Kao, & Logan, 1992; Baron, Logan, Lilly, Inman, & Brennan, 1994; Gleicher &

Petty, 1992; Hale, LeMieux, & Mongeau, 1995; Jepson & Chaiken, 1990; Millar & Millar, 1998; Nabi, 1998a). Further exploration into these moderators and how they relate to fear evocation and resolution will surely allow us to more accurately model the effects of fear on attitude change may be developed (see Nabi, 1999).

Guilt. Guilt arises from one's violation of an internalized moral, ethical, or religious code (Ausubel, 1955; Izard, 1977; Lazarus, 1991; Lindsay-Hartz, De Rivera, & Mascolo, 1995). Although causes of guilt vary widely across religions and cultures, guilt is usually experienced in the context of an interpersonal relationship and serves a relationship-enhancing function (Baumeister, Stillwell, & Heatherton, 1994; Tangney, Miller, Flicker, & Barlow, 1996). Characterized by a gnawing feeling that one has done something wrong, guilt's associated action tendency is to atone or make reparation for the harm done and perhaps to seek punishment for one's wrongdoing (Barrett, 1995; Izard, 1977; Lazarus, 1991; Lindsay-Hartz et al., 1995; Roseman et al., 1994).

Unlike fear appeals, there has been minimal theorizing regarding the effects of guilt on attitude change or information processing (for reviews of guilt and social influence, see O'Keefe, 2000, and other chapters in this volume). Although we have no working model of guilt appeals (but see Nabi, 1999), the literature suggests that guilt can enhance attainment of persuasive goals if evoked at moderate levels (Coulter & Pinto, 1995), even if unintentionally elicited (Dillard & Peck, 1998). However, messages designed to evoke high levels of guilt may instead arouse high levels of anger that may impede persuasive success (Coulter & Pinto, 1995; Pinto & Priest, 1991). Furthermore, guilt effects appear to be associated with and mediated by cognitions (Bozinoff & Ghingold, 1983), and comparable message manipulations may evoke different levels of guilt, depending on the context in which they are used (e.g., Coulter & Pinto, 1995, found greater guilt evocation for messages about dental floss vs. bread). These latter findings are consistent with the functional view of guilt as motivating deliberative efforts to determine ways to atone for wrongdoing, largely in situations where a relational violation has occurred. If guilt, in these circumstances, does encourage close message processing, then persuasive outcome is likely dependent on the nature of those cognitions (see Nabi, 1999). Future research on guilt, then, may wish to consider factors that may influence direction and depth of guilt-driven information processing and thus moderate guilt appeal success (e.g., cues to relational transgressions and efficacy perceptions of reparative information).

Anger. Although specific causes of anger are a function of personal experience, cultural conditioning, and social learning, anger is generally elicited in the face of obstacles interfering with goal-oriented behavior or demeaning offenses against oneself or one's loved ones (Averill, 1982; Hampton, 1978; Izard, 1977; Lazarus, 1991; Plutchik, 1980a). Anger is associated with highly focused attention and a desire to strike out at, attack, or in some way get back at the anger source (Arnold, 1960; Averill, 1982; Frijda, 1986; Izard, 1977; Lazarus, 1991; Roseman et al., 1994). Believed to mobilize and sustain high levels of energy, anger is often conducive to constructive problem solving, although the impulsiveness associated with extreme anger may be counterproductive (Averill, 1982).

Despite its prevalence in our daily lives and its association with many issues of political concern, the persuasive effect of anger has been virtually ignored in the literature. Two research efforts, however, combine to suggest that a positive relationship exists between anger and attitude change. Butler, Koopman, and Zimbardo (1995) found that anger aroused in response to the film *JFK* was associated with acceptance of conspiracy theories regarding President Kennedy's assassination. Similarly, Nabi (1998a) found that anger evoked in response to issues of juvenile crime and domestic terrorism correlated with acceptance of legislative initiatives proposed to address those issues. In the latter study, Nabi found that the cognitive processes underlying anger's persuasive effects differed depending on level of issue familiarity and expectation of the message content. Specifically, anger arousal prompted closer information processing for an unfamiliar topic and under conditions of uncertainty regarding message content (i.e., a quick and easy retributive solution was not readily identified).[2] These findings are consistent with the functional view of anger as promoting attention to determine an effective means of retribution.

Of note, whereas intentionally induced anger appears to correlate positively with persuasive outcome, unintentionally induced anger in response to supposed guilt and fear appeals has been shown to correlate *negatively* with attitudes (Dillard & Peck, 1998; Dillard, Plotnick, Godbold, Freimuth, & Edgar, 1996; Pinto & Priest, 1991). Here we might logically assume that the unintentionally elicited anger was directed against the message creators in light of what the receivers considered unjust attempts to manipulate their emotional responses, and thus persuasive influence was undermined. If so, we might further suppose that the direction of anger's persuasive effect and the process through which such effects occur are contingent on the target and context of anger arousal—a position consistent with the functional view of anger as motivating either impulsive or deliberative attacks against the anger source. This promises to be a useful direction for future research on anger and persuasion.

Sadness. Sadness is elicited by physical or psychological loss or separation, either real or imagined, or by failure to achieve a goal (Izard, 1977; Lazarus, 1991; Plutchik, 1980a; Tomkins, 1963). Those experiencing sadness feel isolated, wistful, and a sense of resignation, and their action tendency is really one of inaction or withdrawal into themselves to solicit comfort or dwell on that which was lost (Frijda, 1986; Izard, 1977; Lazarus, 1991; Roseman et al., 1994). Sadness motivates problem-solving activity by forcing people to focus inward for possible solutions and/or to passively invite help from others (Izard, 1977, 1993), which in turn strengthens social bonds and maintains social cohesion (Izard, 1977; Lazarus, 1991; Plutchik, 1980a; Tomkins, 1963). However, chronic sadness, or depression, may invite maladaptive outcomes.

Sadness as an intentionally evoked, message- and topic-relevant discrete emotion has been overlooked in the persuasion literature. As an *unintentionally evoked,* message-relevant emotion, sadness has evidenced a positive correlation with attitude change in the context of AIDS, illicit drugs, and juvenile crime (Dillard & Peck, 1998; Dillard et al., 1996; Nabi, 1998a) and appeared to motivate careful information processing of a juvenile crime message (Nabi, 1998a). This latter finding is consistent with both the functional view of sadness as motivating contemplative behavior and empirical findings that sad moods motivate more systematic information processing (Bless, Bohner, Schwarz, & Strack, 1990; Bless, Mackie, & Schwarz, 1992; Bohner, Chaiken, & Hunyadi, 1994; Bohner, Crow, Erb, & Schwarz, 1992; Schwarz, 1990; Schwarz & Bless, 1991). Of note, Nabi (1998a), found that conceptually similar fear evocation techniques resulted in heightened fear arousal for domestic terrorism but elevated sadness for juvenile crime. Reminiscent of Coulter and Pinto's (1995) guilt research,

this finding suggests that some topics lend themselves more readily to certain emotional evocations. Because we are just beginning to understand the persuasive effects of sadness as a discrete emotion, researchers may wish to investigate contexts in which sadness is likely to be induced (e.g., focus on circumstances of loss) as well as moderators to its effects on information processing as this line of research inevitably progresses.

Disgust. Aroused by objects or ideas that are either organically or psychologically spoiled (e.g., certain foods, body products, sexual behaviors, moral offenses [Rozin, Haidt, & McCauley, 1993]), disgust is understood to result from the closeness to or ingestion of a noxious object or idea (Lazarus, 1991). Those experiencing disgust feel nauseous or queasy and, consequently, are motivated to turn away from or defend against the object of disgust (Izard, 1977; Lazarus, 1991; Roseman et al., 1994; Rozin et al., 1993; Tomkins, 1963). Although it may have a strong reflexive nature, the disgust response is largely steeped in learned cultural practices (Lazarus, 1991), and like other emotions (e.g., fear, anger), it serves as a protection mechanism for the body, the soul, and the social order itself (Izard, 1993; Rozin et al., 1993).

Although some persuasion studies have included measures of disgust (e.g., Christ & Thorson, 1992; Krishnamurthy, 1986; Leventhal & Trembly, 1968), and past fear appeal studies have operationalized fear with disgust-evoking images (e.g., rotting teeth, diseased lungs), disgust's unique contribution to the process and outcome of attitude change has been largely untested. Recently, however, Nabi (1998b) found that message-induced disgust toward animal experimentation correlated negatively with attitude change when associated with the message's advocated position—a finding consistent with the functional emotion perspective that disgust evocation would lead to a rejection of its source. With so little known about the relationship between disgust and attitude change, future research might consider the emotion's target, the process of disgust's effects given its avoidant nature and protective function, and disgust's co-occurrence with other emotions, such as fear and anger, that might change the nature of the influence process.

Envy. Although envy and jealousy may be considered different emotions, with the former referring to wanting what someone else has and the latter referring to resenting another for loss or threat to another's affection or acquisition of a valued goal (Lazarus, 1991; Salovey & Rothman, 1991; Spielman, 1971), the two are often conflated in the English language (Smith, Kim, & Parrot, 1988). While recognizing their overlap, in this discussion I focus on the construct of envy. Envy is stimulated when we crave what another possesses; thus, its subjective feeling is one of yearning, and its action tendency mobilizes one to seek out what is coveted (Lazarus, 1991). Indirectly influenced by both social psychological and cultural factors (Salovey & Rothman, 1991), envy can promote positive outcomes if we are motivated to increase our own efforts to accomplish, but if we are thwarted from achievement, envy can lead to unhappiness, resentment, and ultimately rejection (Lazarus, 1991).

Surprisingly, one is hard-pressed to find a persuasion study with a focus on envy arousal. I say surprising because persuasive messages likely to evoke envy are prevalent, particularly in the form of product advertisements inviting social comparisons to beautiful, thin, wealthy, and/or happy people. Although Salovey and Rodin (1984) investigated envy as "social comparison jealousy," determining its poten-

tial consequences to include disparagement of the target of envy (see also Salovey, 1991), its relation to attitude change remains unexplored. By acknowledging that envy may be a significant motivator of consumer behavior, studying its effects on related attitudes becomes a prime area for future research. Important issues related to the process of envy's influence would likely include target or context appropriateness of envy arousal; information processing style, perhaps mediated by perceptions of goal attainment likelihood; and unintended consequences of envy arousal, including concomitant arousal of emotions that may compete against message goals (e.g., simultaneous anger elicitation could lead to source denigration) and promotion of unhealthy attitudes (e.g., poor body image and life dissatisfaction) and undesirable behaviors (e.g., those associated with bulimia and anorexia or with criminal activity).

Positive Emotions

Happiness/Joy. Although happiness is often conceptualized as a state of being akin to a mood, whereas joy is generally viewed as an emotional response to a specific occurrence, for the purposes of this chapter, the two are used synonymously to reflect the latter adaptational perspective. In this light, happiness can be seen as the state of gaining or making progress toward what one desires (Izard, 1977; Lazarus, 1991). Although personality and cultural factors, as well as our own perceptions and thought processes, can influence the circumstances and extent to which we experience happiness, some generally accepted joy elicitors include achievement, familiar objects, and the reduction of negative affect (Izard, 1977; Tomkins, 1962). An indicator that we are secure in our world and have positive expectations of the future, happiness generates feelings of confidence, expansiveness, and openness, and it promotes trusting and sharing behavior. Because people tend to be attracted to those who exude happiness, its adaptive function can be seen as promoting and maintaining strong social bonds (Izard, 1977; Tomkins, 1962).

Research on happiness and social influence has been based almost entirely on the conceptualization of happiness as a mood rather than as a discrete emotion. In sum, that research suggests that happy moods are associated with more simplified, heuristic, and creative processing, characterized by little attention to detail (for reviews, see Isen, 1987, 1993, and Schwarz et al., 1991; see also Mackie & Worth, 1991). However, assuming that at the heart of humor in advertising is the desire to put receivers in a happy state, that literature is certainly relevant to understanding the influence of happiness as a discrete emotion in persuasion.

Consistent with the functional view of happiness, particularly that it is associated with a preference for limited cognitive effort, the most recent review of humor in advertising suggests that humor's persuasive influence is most likely found in the context of new, low-involvement, and/or feeling-oriented products (Weinberger & Gulas, 1992). Whereas these findings imply that classical conditioning is the primary mechanism underlying humor's effects, Markiewicz (1974) and Sternthal and Craig (1973) offered an alternative view, arguing that humor can induce persuasion through its distracting influence. Regardless, both possibilities suggest a lack of in-depth information processing that would lead us to conclude that humor-generated persuasion is unlikely to be stable and long-lasting. Of note, humor attempts deemed by an audience to be offensive or inappropriate may be counterproductive to persuasive goals (Weinberger & Gulas, 1992). In light of these

issues, future research should investigate if and when humor/happiness results in stable and long-lasting persuasion and the effects that different types of humor might have in this pursuit.

Pride. Pride is characterized by an increase in perceived self-worth as a consequence of taking credit for an achievement—either one's own or that of someone with whom one identifies (Lazarus, 1991; Lewis, 1993). The notion of ascribing personal credit for achievement, rather than simply enjoying positive outcomes, is the key distinguishing characteristic between pride and happiness. Phenomenologically, pride is experienced as a feeling of expansiveness or swelling, and it promotes expressive behaviors, such as public announcement of an achievement. An inherently ego-focused yet social emotion, the acceptance of its expression, and even the likelihood of its being experienced are culturally determined. Although the expression of pride may enhance self-esteem, it may also evoke resentment in those less fortunate or less recognized.

Little studied in the social influence context, the one clearly identifiable study of pride and persuasion considered the role of culture in response to advertising, finding that members of a collectivist culture (China) responded more favorably to a pride-based appeal, whereas members of an individualist culture (the United States) responded more favorably to an empathy-based appeal (Aaker & Williams, 1998). The results, the authors believed, were mediated by the nature of collectivist versus individualist thoughts generated in response to message exposure. Although no clear connection between the functional perspective on pride and this study is apparent, one may imagine that pride might operate very similarly to happiness in limiting cognitive expenditure, although its self-focused nature might promote contemplation of the pride-inducing event. Investigating the process through which pride effects occur, determining whether or not it differs from that of happiness, and exploring the role of culture in the use and effect of emotional appeals generally are reasonable and interesting research topics to pursue in this context.

Relief. As Lazarus (1991) noted, relief has received little attention as a discrete positive emotion; however, its appraisal pattern and action tendency arguably qualify it as such. According to Lazarus, relief is unique as a positive emotion in that it occurs only after a goal-incongruent condition has been resolved. Thus, its eliciting condition may be considered the alleviation of emotional distress. Relief's subjective feeling is one of release of muscle tension, and its associated action tendency is one of inaction—a slumping of the body with the release of tension and cessation of vigilance.

Given its inevitable association with negative emotions, it is unsurprising that the one research program that has directly considered the persuasive effect of relief did so in the context of a negative affect—fear. Introducing the sequential-request, compliance-gaining strategy "fear-then-relief," Dolinski and Nawrat (1998) argued that anxiety followed by anxiety relief leads to greater compliance to an unrelated request than does fear alone because fear-then-relief promotes a temporary state of *mindlessness* or disorientation, leaving the individual momentarily vulnerable to requests. Although the compliance requests were unrelated to the cause of the fear or its relief, this research suggests that, in general, relief-based persuasion is likely a function of less careful information processing. This view is consistent with the functional emotion perspective, which suggests that relief is characterized by an interruption of attentive processing. An area ripe for research, potential topics include issues related to information processing depth, the window of opportunity associated with relief-based persuasion, and

whether the types of relief from different negative affects follow the same influence processes; the role of relief in fear appeals, particularly as related to perceptions of response efficacy; and how the promise or expectation of relief from existing negative circumstances (e.g., emotional or physical pain) can be used to motivate changes in attitudes and behaviors as compared to creating and alleviating the negative affect in a single message.

Hope. Lazarus (1991) acknowledged hope as a problematic emotion because it is, on its face, a positive emotion, although, like relief, it stems from negative circumstances. Hope represents a desire for a better situation than what currently exists, often when the odds are against a positive outcome (Lazarus, 1991). Hope is sustained in light of uncertain future expectations and is associated with a feeling of yearning. Although its action tendency is unclear, hope is associated with an approach response, eyes cast up as though visualizing the desired outcome. Whereas hope often helps to mitigate (but not alleviate) emotional distress, taken to the extreme, it may prevent one from striving to achieve more realistic goals.

Although the evocation of hope to influence attitudes and behaviors is not uncommon (e.g., in the context of quick weight loss programs, lottery and gambling opportunities, and political campaign messages), very little research directly addresses hope's persuasive effect. An exception is Roseman, Abelson, and Ewing (1986), who considered how those predisposed to experiencing hope, fear, pity, and anger responded to related appeals from political organizations. Consistent with the functional conceptualization of hope as a salve to negative circumstances, the authors found that hope appeals were successful only for those with self-reported predispositions to experiencing fear. Future research on hope would do well to consider the prevalence and context of such appeals, the direction and process of such effects (likely positive and unmediated by cognitions), individual affective predispositions to such appeals, the role of hope in negative affective appeals (e.g., fear appeals), and the potential unintended negative consequences of raising false hopes.

Compassion. Compassion is signified by an altruistic concern for another's suffering and the desire to relieve it (Lazarus, 1991). When experiencing compassion, one feels the desire to reach out and assist those in need; however, to become too close could lead to overwhelming feelings of distress. Compassion is generally viewed as a positive emotion, although it may arise in response to unpleasant circumstances, and those who demonstrate it genuinely are often admired because they provide important sources of social support.

Although pity (i.e., feeling sorry for one who is suffering) is often used synonymously with compassion, pity contains a nuance of condescension that distinguishes it from compassion (Lazarus, 1991). Similarly, some may lump compassion with empathy; however, the latter is perhaps better conceptualized as a capacity to vicariously experience any range of emotions rather than an emotion in itself (for more on empathy, see Hoffman, 1977). Because of the virtual equivalence of compassion and pity, research on both as they relate to persuasive outcome are reviewed, and studies examining empathy operationalized as compassion are also noted (e.g., Shelton & Rogers, 1981).

As it turns out, we know very little about the effect of compassion or pity on attitude change. Roseman et al. (1986) found that only those predisposed to feel pity tended to respond favorably to pity appeals on behalf of political organizations. Although researchers have generally assumed that promoting compassionate attitudes would have a positive effect on behavioral intentions and behavior

change (Shelton & Rogers, 1981; Warden & Koballa, 1995), others suggest that such efforts can backfire, with pity unintentionally reinforcing negative or outdated stereotypes (Sinson & Stainton, 1990). Such findings emphasize the danger of unintended outcomes when eliciting compassion, which in turn suggests the need to illuminate the message features and personality characteristics that may determine the extent and direction of compassion's influence. Although the functional approach to emotion implies that compassion may be associated with more in-depth processing, exploration into the conditions under which that may be true is surely needed.

THEORETICAL CONSIDERATIONS FOR THE FUTURE OF EMOTION AND PERSUASION RESEARCH

Any reader of the preceding review likely senses the unsettled and disjointed nature of the state of the study of discrete emotions and their persuasive influence. Although there are several interesting theoretical questions that seem applicable across each emotion (e.g., emotion's effects on information processing), there are a number of more specific, unresolved issues that seem to appear haphazardly, depending on the available research to date. Interestingly, a common observable theme is that the functional view of emotion fares rather well in explaining past research findings. Thus, its value as a guide in directing future persuasion research on discrete emotions is affirmed. This final section attempts to integrate the preceding reviews, first, by presenting general theoretical processes through which the effects of discrete emotions may be understood and, second, by identifying several, more specific issues regarding discrete emotions to be tackled. Where possible, ways in which the functional view of emotion can illuminate the still darkened corners of the otherwise well-traveled field of persuasion are noted.

Theoretical Processes of Emotion's Persuasive Effects

A central question only recently tackled in emotion and persuasion research involves the process through which emotions have their persuasive effect. Based on the functional emotion perspective, there are three processes we might consider, all of which revolve around depth or quality of information processing.[3]

First, emotions may serve as *heuristics*, or cognitive rules of thumb, guiding decisions with minimal information processing or thought (Cacioppo & Petty, 1989; Chaiken, 1980, 1987; Petty, Cacioppo, & Kasmer, 1988; Petty, Cacioppo, Sedikides, & Strathman, 1988; Petty, Gleicher, & Baker, 1991). Although theoretically each discrete emotion can serve this function, current evidence allows us to state with confidence only that positive emotions (e.g., happiness, relief) or extreme emotional arousal likely promotes heuristic decision making. Specifying the conditions under which each emotion might stimulate heuristic decision making and the extent, direction, and longevity of such effects is a challenge for future investigation.

Second, emotions can stimulate *careful information processing*. Researchers true to the cognitive response tradition of persuasion argue that under conditions of moderate or high elaboration, emotions influence the direction or depth of information processing, respectively (Cacioppo & Petty, 1989; Petty, Cacioppo, & Kasmer, 1988; Petty, Cacioppo, Sedikides, & Strathman, 1988; Petty et al., 1991). By slight contrast, the Cognitive-Functional Model (CFM) of negative emotions and persuasion (Nabi, 1999), developed from a functional emotion perspective, argues

that a key role of emotion resides in its influence over level of elaboration itself, characterized by selective information processing. According to the CFM, once a message-induced discrete emotion is experienced, depth and direction of information processing is determined by the type and intensity of the emotion experienced (i.e., motivated attention) in conjunction with the expectation of whether the message content will help to satisfy the emotion-induced goal. This approach suggests that under certain conditions, discrete emotions can themselves prompt careful information processing, which is likely to promote more enduring attitude change. Exploring the conditions under which emotions, particularly positive ones, might lead to attentive processing would most certainly be a worthy pursuit for persuasion scholars.

Third, emotions may promote *selective information processing*. Nabi (1998c) argued that emotions can be conceptualized as frames or perspectives infused into messages that promote the salience of selected pieces of information over others and thus encourage different problem definitions, causal interpretations, and/or treatment recommendations (Entman, 1993). More parsimonious than the CFM, the emotions-as-frames concept is consistent with the functional emotion approach, can account for different paths of emotion's persuasive influence, and is a more message-focused view of emotion than the previously presented perspectives. Early evidence suggests some validity to the idea, although future exploration would most certainly be welcome.

Specific Issues to Consider in the Study of Discrete Emotions and Persuasion

Apart from the broad theoretical issues related to the processes of emotions' persuasive influence, the preceding review either directly or indirectly raised several interesting issues that, if studied, would meaningfully advance our understanding of the roles that emotions play in the persuasion process. With an eye toward space limitations, I have selected five general areas of inquiry that I believe may prove to be theoretically and/or practically important to pursue during the coming years: (a) defining and constructing emotional appeals, (b) specifying moderators to the process of emotional influence, (c) identifying the role of discrete emotions in existing models of persuasion, (d) examining emotional flow within and across persuasive messages, and (e) considering the persuasive effects of emotion avoidance or emotion seeking versus emotional arousal.

Defining and Constructing Emotional Appeals. Although on the surface, issues surrounding the definition of fear appeals (or anger appeals or compassion appeals) may appear uninteresting, such inquiry is not only legitimate but in fact necessary. That is, do we define emotional appeals based on message characteristics or the emotional responses that the messages engender? If a message intended to evoke fear stimulates more anger instead, how do we classify that message? Ideally, a successful fear appeal, for example, should both contain characteristics designed to elicit fear in a target audience and evoke the desired affect. However, understanding the message characteristics—both concrete and abstract, both textual and visual—that reliably evoke particular emotions in particular audiences (and minimize unintended emotional arousal) for various topics and behaviors is essential to eliminating the conflation between the stimulus and the response and, hence, is an important topic for future research. By using functional emotion theory as a guide to message construction and mea-

suring a range of emotional responses after message exposure, we may systematize both message development and outcome classification and thus provide insight into the evocation and effects of discrete emotions. Exploring the factors that predispose receivers to respond more or less favorably to different message characteristics (e.g., personality traits, culture) would certainly enhance this intellectual pursuit.

Specifying Moderators to Emotions' Persuasive Effects. Earlier, I noted three broad approaches to studying the process of emotions' persuasive effects. Central to that research, although more specific, is the need to identify the relevant moderators to those processes. Evidence suggests that level of emotional arousal, target of emotional arousal, and expectation of reassurance against negative emotions (desire for enhancement is the likely equivalent for positive emotions) can influence information processing depth, and future research in these areas would be beneficial. However, at least one likely influential factor overlooked in the emotion literature is the role of prior knowledge in the predisposition to and effect of emotional arousal. Prior knowledge has already been shown to affect persuasive outcome by promoting more systematic processing (Wood & Kallgren, 1988; Wood, Kallgren, & Preisler, 1985), stronger resistance to attitude change (Wood, 1982), and greater attitude-behavior consistency (Kallgren & Wood, 1986). In the context of an emotional message, three potential outcomes of prior knowledge are worth exploring. First, information coupled with emotion may be more likely to be attended to, encoded, and more accessible to respondents, thus promoting stronger attitudes and stronger attitude-behavior relationships. Second, emotional evocation may make accessible already-held information that, in turn, may guide or bias information processing and thus likely alter persuasive effect. Third, prior knowledge about a topic may moderate emotional arousal itself. That is, it may be more or less difficult to evoke an emotion on a more familiar topic compared to a more novel one.

In addition to prior knowledge, other receiver factors that may moderate type and degree of emotional arousal include a host of personality variables, such as self-esteem, trait affectivity (e.g., trait anxiety, reactivity, empathy), extroversion, and psychoticism. Additional potential moderators may also be identified by considering the functional purpose of each emotion and its impact on receiver response. By exploring the receiver factors that influence and interact with emotional arousal, we will be better positioned to craft targeted and effective persuasive appeals.

Emotions and Established Models Relevant to Persuasion. Given that the majority of theories about attitudinal and behavioral response were developed during the age of rational imperialism without consideration for the role of discrete emotion, it would serve us well to reconsider established persuasion models in light of functional emotion theories and emotional arousal. Although other candidates likely exist, three theories that stand out as targets for reassessment include cognitive dissonance (Festinger, 1957), reactance (Brehm, 1966, 1968), and social comparison (Festinger, 1954).

At the risk of mild redundancy with Harmon-Jones (Chapter 6 in this volume), allow me to briefly point out that the aversive consequences perspective of cognitive dissonance suggests that guilt is central to that phenomenon. In essence, the forced compliance paradigm for testing cognitive dissonance induces a respondent to lie (e.g., to tell a future participant how interesting the study task is when in fact it is unequivocally boring) to deter-

mine whether behaviors inconsistent with currently held attitudes will bring attitudes in line with behaviors. From a cognitive appraisal perspective, those circumstances are indicative of guilt induction, and in fact some early studies of guilt and interpersonal compliance gaining used comparable manipulations for emotional arousal (e.g., Freedman, Wallington, & Bless, 1967). Certainly, not all cognitive dissonance involves guilt (see Harmon-Jones's chapter in this volume); however, it is intuitively obvious that guilt plays some role in the dissonance phenomenon. Yet minimal research exploring this relationship exists (see Stice, 1992).

As cognitive dissonance is related to guilt, reactance theory is linked to anger (see also Dillard & Meijnders's chapter in this volume [Chapter 16]). Reactance theory suggests that when people perceive their attitudinal freedoms to be restricted, they reassert those freedoms by clinging to their attitudes, perhaps even more strongly than before (Brehm, 1968). From an appraisal theory perspective, freedom restriction is a prime anger elicitor. Thus, it is entirely likely that the fundamental mechanism underlying reactance findings is anger arousal. In fact, the research on unintentional anger arousal discussed previously suggests that it is the sense of being manipulated by a persuasive message that underlies the negative relationship between anger and attitude change. Yet no published study to date looks specifically at anger in a reactance-arousing situation.

Finally, Festinger's (1954) social comparison theory suggests that individuals compare themselves to others for information relevant to self-evaluation. Elaborations of the theory suggest that comparisons can be made to those better off or worse off, either of which can positively or negatively influence self-concept. As mentioned previously, at least two studies have suggested that envy can be aroused in the process of social comparison (Salovey & Rodin, 1984; Tesser & Collins, 1988). However, Tesser (1991) argued not only that emotions other than envy can be evoked in this context but also, consistent with the functional emotion approach, that those emotions may, in turn, mediate behavior. For example, one could imagine how messages inviting upward social comparison (e.g., advertising with overly optimistic images of health, happiness, and beauty) could evoke hope to improve self-evaluation, envy of what others have, or anger or sadness if those goals seem out of reach. Conversely, messages inviting downward social comparison (e.g., pleas for donations) could evoke guilt for having what others do not, compassion for those suffering, or pride or relief for helping those in need. In each case, the emotion evoked is likely to moderate attitudinal and/or behavioral response (e.g., hope and envy could motivate purchase behavior, but anger might interfere). Comparable to the development of cognitive dissonance research, determining the situational factors that would ensure that the emotion evoked prompts the desired response (e.g., purchase behavior) rather than a maladaptive one (e.g., source denigration or minimization of the comparison person's assets) is critical to this line of investigation.

Emotional Flow. Implicit in much of the emotion and persuasion literature is the notion that either one emotion is driving persuasive effect or multiple emotions have influence but in no particular order. Yet, as we see in the fear-then-relief technique most directly but implicitly in compassion, hope, and even the desire for the alleviation of negative affect as noted in classic fear appeal work, persuasive messages might not only evoke multiple emotions but also do so in a particular order suggestive of success. Thus, I use the term *emotional flow* to indicate not only the movement from negative to positive emotion

(or visa versa) in reaction to an unfolding persuasive message but also the flow among negative or positive emotions (Kamp & MacInnis, 1995). By determining which patterns of emotions tend to work together and in what way, and by tying these emotional evocations back to message characteristics, we can develop a more sophisticated and complete view of the process of emotions' influence in persuasion. Relatedly, the notion of emotional flow can extend across messages throughout a campaign and thus prove useful to those engaged in ongoing persuasive efforts. That is, perhaps shifts in emotional appeals *across* messages over time can offer the type of issue reframing necessary to overcome resistance that might be incurred by (a) overexposure to a topic generally as well as to specific messages and (b) changes in an audience's topic-relevant knowledge base.

Emotion Avoidance and Emotion Seeking. We have spent much time and effort exploring how to arouse discrete emotions and to what effect. But perhaps just as important is how to use the desire to *avoid* experiencing unpleasant emotions or the desire to experience positive emotions to promote attitude and behavior change. This potential avenue for research recognizes our propensity to experience emotions in certain situations, based either on the issue or on the type of behavior suggested. For example, many of us experience a little guilt when watching stories about those less fortunate than ourselves. However, rather than emphasizing our guilt to encourage donation behavior, perhaps a successful approach would be to tacitly acknowledge the propensity to feel guilt and offer the solution (e.g., donate to the Red Cross) to help one not only avoid future guilt but also enhance self-esteem. This approach is not so different from traditional emotional appeals. However, rather than evoking emotions, it acknowledges and takes advantage of our emotional predispositions and thus may assist in minimizing reactance or defensive avoidance responses.

CONCLUSION

In this chapter, I have attempted to outline the state of the literature regarding discrete emotions and persuasion and, relying heavily on the functional perspective of emotion, to identify potentially fruitful directions for future research. A critical reader, however, may be left with a fundamentally important question: Why do discrete emotions matter? If disgust, fear, anger, and joy each can positively influence attitudes, why does it matter which one is evoked? In response, let me offer several possibilities. First, the ability to accurately capture the process through which effects occur is a fundamental goal of scholarly inquiry. Second, if attitudes are formed through processes driven by specific emotional evocation, it is possible that those attitudes may be vulnerable, or conversely resistant, to attacks based on other emotions (e.g., Edwards, 1990; Millar & Millar, 1990). Third, if some emotions are, as it has been argued, better suited for promoting certain types of behaviors than others, it would certainly matter if one emotion were evoked over another in those contexts. Finally, as campaigns mature and the effect of one type of appeal begins to fade, the introduction of another type of emotional appeal may help draw new attention to the issue at hand. Although the different emotions may have generally similar effects in that context, the emotional shift may result in increasing persuasive success rather than declining campaign interest.

With half a century of persuasion research behind us, we have seen an overwhelming focus on rational approaches to attitude change, making the recent growing interest in emotional appeals as welcome as it is overdue. Assuming that this interest persists into the new century, as well it should given the prevalence of emotional appeals in our personal, professional, and "consumer" lives, our field will be well poised to make great progress toward illuminating the influence of discrete emotions in the persuasion process.

NOTES

1. Not all emotion theorists believe in the concept of discrete emotions (Buck, 1985; Russell, 1980, 1983; Spencer, 1890; Watson & Tellegen, 1985; Weiner, 1985; Wundt, 1897/1902), and not all of those who endorse the concept agree as to which set of emotions should be considered primary or basic (e.g., Arnold, 1960; Ekman & Friesen, 1975; Izard, 1977; Lazarus, 1991; Oatley & Johnson-Laird, 1987; Panksepp, 1982; Plutchik, 1980a; Tomkins, 1962, 1963). For example, whereas some theorists do not consider guilt to be a primary emotion (e.g., Plutchik, 1980a) and others do not consider guilt to be an emotion at all (see Ortony, 1987), its status as a uniquely human emotion is recognized by many others.

2. Bodenhausen, Sheppard, and Kramer (1994) suggested that angry moods promote a heuristic processing strategy "regardless of whether the task requiring a response is related to the source of the anger or irrelevant to it" (p. 59). However, logical assessment of their arguments and data suggest that, in fact, anger likely promotes quickened but careful information processing, an outcome proposed and found by Nabi (1998a, 1999) under conditions of low issue familiarity.

3. Not included in these three processes is classical conditioning because, given its more automatic nature, its fit with the more deliberative nature of the functional view of emotion is questionable.

REFERENCES

Aaker, J. L., & Williams, P. (1998). Empathy versus pride: The influence of emotional appeals across cultures. *Journal of Consumer Research, 25,* 241-261.

Arnold, M. B. (1960). *Emotion and personality.* New York: Columbia University Press.

Ausubel, D. (1955). Relationships between shame and guilt in the socializing process. *Psychological Review, 62,* 378-390.

Averill, J. R. (1982). *Anger and aggression: An essay on emotion.* New York: Springer-Verlag.

Baron, R. S., Inman, M. B., Kao, C. F., & Logan, H. (1992). Negative emotion and superficial social processing. *Motivation and Emotion, 16,* 323-346.

Baron, R., Logan, H., Lilly, J., Inman, M., & Brennan, M. (1994). Negative emotion and message processing. *Journal of Experimental Social Psychology, 30,* 181-201.

Barrett, K. C. (1995). A functionalist approach to shame and guilt. In J. Tangney & K. Fischer (Eds.), *Self-conscious emotions: The psychology of shame, guilt, embarrassment, and pride* (pp. 25-63). New York: Guilford.

Baumeister, R. F., Stillwell, A. M., & Heatherton, T. F. (1994). Guilt: An interpersonal approach. *Psychological Bulletin, 115,* 243-267.

Bless, H., Bohner, G., Schwarz, N., & Strack, F. (1990). Mood and persuasion: A cognitive response analysis. *Personality and Social Psychology Bulletin, 16,* 331-345.

Bless, H., Mackie, D. M., & Schwarz, N. (1992). Mood effects on attitude judgments: Independent effects of mood before and after message elaboration. *Journal of Personality and Social Psychology, 63,* 585-595.

Bodenhausen, G. V., Sheppard, L., & Kramer, G. (1994). Negative affect and social judgment: The differential impact of anger and sadness. *European Journal of Social Psychology, 24,* 45-62.

Bohner, G., Chaiken, S., & Hunyadi, P. (1994). The role of mood and message ambiguity in the interplay of heuristic and systematic processing. *European Journal of Social Psychology, 24,* 207-221.

Bohner, G., Crow, K., Erb, H., & Schwarz, N. (1992). Affect and persuasion: Mood effects on the processing of message content and context cues and on subsequent behaviour. *European Journal of Social Psychology, 22,* 511-530.

Boster, F. J., & Mongeau, P. (1984). Fear-arousing persuasive messages. In R. N. Bostrom (Ed.), *Communication Yearbook 8* (pp. 330-375). Beverly Hills, CA: Sage.

Bozinoff, L., & Ghingold, M. (1983). Evaluating guilt arousing marketing communications. *Journal of Business Research, 11,* 243-255.

Breckler, S. J. (1993). Emotion and attitude change. In M. Lewis & J. M. Haviland (Eds.), *Handbook of emotions* (pp. 461-473). New York: Guilford.

Brehm, J. W. (1966). *A theory of psychological reactance.* New York: Academic Press.

Brehm, J. W. (1968). Attitude change from threat to attitudinal freedom. In A. G. Greenwald, T. C. Brock, & T. M. Ostrom (Eds.), *Psychological foundations of attitudes* (pp. 277-296). New York: Academic Press.

Buck, R. (1985). Prime theory: An integrated view of motivation and emotion. *Psychological Review, 92,* 389-413.

Butler, L. D., Koopman, C., & Zimbardo, P. (1995). The psychological impact of viewing the film *JFK*: Emotions, beliefs, and political behavioral intentions. *Political Psychology, 16,* 237-257.

Cacioppo, J. T., & Petty, R. E. (1989). The Elaboration Likelihood Model: The role of affect and affect-laden information processing in persuasion. In P. Cafferata & A. M. Tybout (Eds.), *Cognitive and affective responses to advertising* (pp. 69-90). Lexington, MA: Lexington Books.

Chaiken, S. (1980). Heuristic versus systematic information processing and the use of source versus message cues in persuasion. *Journal of Personality and Social Psychology, 39,* 752-766.

Chaiken, S. (1987). The Heuristic Model of persuasion. In M. P. Zanna, J. M. Olson, & C. P. Herman (Eds.), *Social influence: The Ontario Symposium* (Vol. 5, pp. 3-39). Hillsdale, NJ: Lawrence Erlbaum.

Christ, W., & Thorson, E. (1992). Attitudinal effects of commercials representing six categories of emotional response. In L. N. Reid (Ed.), *Proceedings of the 1992 Conference of the American Academy of Advertising* (pp. 189-198). Athens, GA: American Academy of Advertising.

Coulter, R. H., & Pinto, M. B. (1995). Guilt appeals in advertising: What are their effects? *Journal of Applied Psychology, 80,* 697-705.

Darwin, C. R. (1965). *The expression of the emotions in man and animals.* Chicago: University of Chicago Press. (Original work published 1872)

Dillard, J. P., & Peck, E. (1998, November). *Affect and persuasion: Emotional responses to public service announcements.* Paper presented at the meeting of the National Communication Association, New York.

Dillard, J. P., Plotnick, C. A., Godbold, L. C., Freimuth, V. S., & Edgar, T. (1996). The multiple affective outcomes of AIDS PSAs: Fear appeals do more than scare people. *Communication Research, 23,* 44-72.

Dolinski, D., & Nawrat, R. (1998). "Fear-then-relief" procedure for producing compliance: Beware when the danger is over. *Journal of Experimental Social Psychology, 34,* 27-50.

Eagly, A. H., & Chaiken, S. (1993). *The psychology of attitudes.* Fort Worth, TX: Harcourt Brace Jovanovich.

Edwards, K. (1990). The interplay of affect and cognition in attitude formation and change. *Journal of Personality and Social Psychology, 59,* 202-216.

Ekman, P., & Friesen, W. (1975). *Unmasking the face.* Englewood Cliffs, NJ: Prentice Hall.

Entman, R. M. (1993). Framing: Toward clarification of a fractured paradigm. *Journal of Communication, 43*(4), 51-58.

Festinger, L. (1954). A theory of social comparison processes. *Human Relations, 7,* 117-140.

Festinger, L. (1957). *A theory of cognitive dissonance.* Stanford, CA: Stanford University Press.

Fiske, S. T., & Taylor, S. E. (1991). *Social cognition.* New York: McGraw-Hill.

Forgas, J. P. (1991). *Emotion and social judgments.* New York: Pergamon.

Freedman, J. L., Wallington, S. A., & Bless, E. (1967). Compliance without pressure: The effect of guilt. *Journal of Personality and Social Psychology, 7,* 117-124.

Frijda, N. H. (1986). *The emotions.* New York: Cambridge University Press.

Frijda, N. H. (1988). The laws of emotion. *American Psychologist, 43,* 349-358.

Gleicher, F., & Petty, R. E. (1992). Expectations of reassurance influence the nature of fear-stimulated attitude change. *Journal of Experimental Social Psychology, 28,* 86-100.

Hale, J. L., LeMieux, R., & Mongeau, P. A. (1995). Cognitive processing of fear-arousing message content. *Communication Research, 22,* 459-474.

Hampton, P. (1978). The many faces of anger. *Psychology, 15,* 35-44.

Hoffman, M. L. (1977). Empathy, its development, and pro-social implications. In C. B. Keasey (Ed.), *Nebraska Symposium on Motivation* (Vol. 25, pp. 169-217). Lincoln: University of Nebraska Press.

Holbrook, M., & Batra, R. (1987). Assessing the role of emotions as mediators of consumer responses to advertising. *Journal of Consumer Research, 14,* 404-420.

Hovland, C. I., Janis, I. L., & Kelley, H. H. (1953). *Communication and persuasion.* New Haven, CT: Yale University Press.

Isen, A. M. (1987). Positive affect, cognitive processes, and social behavior. *Advances in Experimental Social Psychology, 20,* 203-253.

Isen, A. M. (1993). Positive affect and decision making. In M. Lewis & J. M. Haviland (Eds.), *Handbook of emotions* (pp. 261-277). New York: Guilford.

Izard, C. E. (1977). *Human emotions.* New York: Plenum.

Izard, C. E. (1993). Organizational and motivational functions of discrete emotions. In M. Lewis & J. M. Haviland (Eds.), *Handbook of emotions* (pp. 631-641). New York: Guilford.

Janis, I. L., & Feshbach, S. (1953). Effects of fear-arousing communications. *Journal of Abnormal and Social Psychology, 48,* 78-92.

Janis, I. L., & Feshbach, S. (1954). Personality differences associated with responsiveness to fear-arousing communications. *Journal of Personality, 23,* 154-166.

Jepson, C., & Chaiken, S. (1990). Chronic issue-specific fear inhibits systematic processing of persuasive communications. In M. Booth-Butterfield (Ed.), *Communication, cognition, and anxiety* (pp. 61-84). Newbury Park, CA: Sage.

Kallgren, C. A., & Wood, W. (1986). Access to attitude-relevant information in memory as a determinant of attitude-behavior consistency. *Journal of Experimental Social Psychology, 22,* 328-338.

Kamp, E., & MacInnis, D. J. (1995). Characteristics of portrayed emotions in commercials: When does what is shown in ads affect viewers? *Journal of Advertising Research, 35*(6), 19-28.

Krishnamurthy, T. (1986). The effect of fear communication on smoking behaviour through different modes of presentation. *Journal of Psychological Researches, 30,* 48-54.

Lang, P. (1995). The emotion probe: Studies of motivation and attention. *American Psychologist, 50,* 372-385.

Lazarus, R. S. (1991). *Emotion and adaptation.* New York: Oxford University Press.

Leeper, R. (1948). A motivational theory of emotion to replace "emotion as a disorganized response." *Psychological Review, 55,* 5-21.

Leventhal, H. (1970). Findings and theory in the study of fear communications. In L. Berkowitz (Ed.), *Advances in experimental social psychology* (Vol. 5, pp. 119-186). New York: Academic Press.

Leventhal, H., & Trembly, G. (1968). Negative emotions and persuasion. *Journal of Personality, 36,* 154-168.

Lewis, M. (1993). Self-conscious emotions: Embarrassment, pride, shame, and guilt. In M. Lewis & J. M. Haviland (Eds.), *Handbook of emotions* (pp. 563-573). New York: Guilford.

Lindsay-Hartz, J., De Rivera, J., & Mascolo, M. (1995). Differentiating guilt and shame and their effects on motivation. In J. Tangney & K. Fischer (Eds.), *Self-conscious emotions: The psychology of shame, guilt, embarrassment, and pride* (pp. 274-300). New York: Guilford.

Mackie, D. M., & Worth, L. T. (1991). Feeling good, but not thinking straight: The impact of positive mood on persuasion. In J. P. Forgas (Ed.), *Emotion and social judgments* (pp. 201-219). New York: Pergamon.

Markiewicz, D. (1974). Effects of humor on persuasion. *Sociometry, 37,* 407-422.

Millar, M. G., & Millar, K. U. (1990). Attitude change as a function of attitude type and argument type. *Journal of Personality and Social Psychology, 59,* 217-228.

Millar, M. G., & Millar, K. U. (1998). Processing messages about disease detection and health promotion behaviors: The effects of anxiety. *Health Communication, 10,* 211-226.

Mongeau, P. (1998). Another look at fear-arousing persuasive appeals. In M. Allen & R. W. Preiss (Eds.), *Persuasion: Advances through meta-analysis* (pp. 53-68). Cresskill, NJ: Hampton.

Nabi, R. L. (1998a, May). *Anger, fear, uncertainty, and attitudes: A test of the Cognitive-Functional Model.* Paper presented at the meeting of the International Communication Association, Jerusalem.

Nabi, R. L. (1998b). The effect of disgust-eliciting visuals on attitudes toward animal experimentation. *Communication Quarterly, 46,* 472-484.

Nabi, R. L. (1998c, November). *The framing effects of emotion: Can discrete emotions influence information recall and policy reference?* Paper presented at the meeting of the National Communication Association, New York.

Nabi, R. L. (1999). A Cognitive-Functional Model for the effects of discrete negative emotions on information processing, attitude change, and recall. *Communication Theory, 9,* 292-320.

Oatley, K., & Johnson-Laird, P. (1987). Towards a cognitive theory of emotion. *Cognition and Emotion, 1,* 29-50.

O'Keefe, D. J. (2000). Guilt and social influence. In M. E. Roloff (Ed.), *Communication Yearbook 23* (pp. 67-101). Thousand Oaks, CA: Sage.

Ortony, A. (1987). Is guilt an emotion? *Cognition and Emotion, 1,* 283-298.

Ortony, A., Clore, G. L., & Collins, A. (1988). *The cognitive structure of emotions.* New York: Cambridge University Press.

Panksepp, J. (1982). Toward a general psychobiological theory of emotions. *Behavioral and Brain Sciences, 5,* 407-467.

Petty, R. E., Cacioppo, J. T., & Kasmer, J. A. (1988). The role of affect in the Elaboration Likelihood Model of persuasion. In L. Donohew, H. E. Sypher, & E. T. Higgins (Eds.), *Communication, social cognition, and affect* (pp. 117-146). Hillsdale, NJ: Lawrence Erlbaum.

Petty, R. E., Cacioppo, J. T., Sedikides, C., & Strathman, A. J. (1988). Affect and persuasion: A contemporary perspective. *American Behavioral Scientist, 31,* 355-371.

Petty, R. E., Gleicher, F., & Baker, S. M. (1991). Multiple roles for affect in persuasion. In J. P. Forgas (Ed.), *Emotion and social judgments* (pp. 181-200). New York: Pergamon.

Pinto, M. B., & Priest, S. (1991). Guilt appeals in advertising: An exploratory study. *Psychological Reports, 69,* 375-385.

Plutchik, R. (1980a). *Emotion: A psychoevolutionary synthesis.* New York: Harper & Row.

Plutchik, R. (1980b). A general psychoevolutionary theory of emotion. In R. Plutchik & H. Kellerman (Eds.), *Emotion: Theory, research, and experience* (Vol. 1, pp. 3-34). New York: Academic Press.

Rogers, R. W. (1975). A protection motivation theory of fear appeals and attitude change. *Journal of Psychology, 91,* 93-114.

Rogers, R. W. (1983). Cognitive and physiological processes in fear appeals and attitude change: A revised theory of protection motivation. In J. T. Cacioppo & R. E. Petty (Eds.), *Social psychophysiology* (pp. 153-176). New York: Guilford.

Roseman, I. J. (1984). Cognitive determinants of emotions: A structural theory. In P. Shaver (Ed.), *Review of personality and social psychology: Emotion, relationships, and health* (Vol. 5, pp. 11-36). Beverly Hills, CA: Sage.

Roseman, I. J., Abelson, R. P., & Ewing, M. F. (1986). Emotion and political cognition: Emotion appeals in political communication. In R. R. Lau & D. O. Sears (Eds.), *Political cognition* (pp. 279-294). Hillsdale, NJ: Lawrence Erlbaum.

Roseman, I. J., Wiest, C., & Swartz, T. S. (1994). Phenomenology, behaviors, and goals differentiate discrete emotions. *Journal of Personality and Social Psychology, 67,* 206-221.

Rozin, P., Haidt, J., & McCauley, C. R. (1993). Disgust. In M. Lewis & J. M. Haviland (Eds.), *Handbook of emotions* (pp. 575-594). New York: Guilford.

Russell, J. A. (1980). A circumplex model of affect. *Journal of Personality and Social Psychology, 39,* 1161-1178.

Russell, J. A. (1983). Pancultural aspects of the human conceptual organization of emotions. *Journal of Personality and Social Psychology, 45,* 1281-1288.

Salovey, P. (1991). Social comparison processes in envy and jealousy. In J. Suls & T. A. Wills (Eds.), *Social comparison: Contemporary theory and research* (pp. 261-286). Hillsdale, NJ: Lawrence Erlbaum.

Salovey, P., & Rodin, J. (1984). Some antecedents and consequences of social-comparison jealousy. *Journal of Personality and Social Psychology, 47,* 780-792.

Salovey, P., & Rothman, A. J. (1991). Envy and jealousy: Self and society. In P. Salovey (Ed.), *The psychology of jealousy and envy* (pp. 271-286). New York: Guilford.

Scherer, K. R. (1984). On the nature and function of emotion: A component process approach. In K. R. Scherer & P. Ekman (Eds.), *Approaches to emotion* (pp. 293-318). Hillsdale, NJ: Lawrence Erlbaum.

Schwarz, N. (1990). Feelings as information: Informational and motivational functions of affective states. In E. T. Higgins & R. M. Sorrentino (Eds.), *Handbook of motivation and cognition: Foundations of social behavior* (Vol. 2, pp. 527-561). New York: Guilford.

Schwarz, N., & Bless, H. (1991). Happy and mindless, but sad and smart? The impact of affective states on analytic reasoning. In J. P. Forgas (Ed.), *Emotion and social judgments* (pp. 55-72). New York: Pergamon.

Schwarz, N., Bless, H., & Bohner, G. (1991). Mood and persuasion: Affective states influence the processing of persuasive communications. In M. P. Zanna (Ed.), *Advances in experimental social psychology* (Vol. 24, pp. 161-199). San Diego: Academic Press.

Shelton, M. L., & Rogers, R. W. (1981). Fear-arousing and empathy-arousing appeals to help: The pathos of persuasion. *Journal of Applied Social Psychology, 11,* 366-378.

Sinson, J. C., & Stainton, C. L. (1990). An investigation into attitudes (and attitude change) toward mental handicap. *British Journal of Mental Subnormality, 36,* 53-64.

Smith, C. A., & Ellsworth, P. C. (1985). Patterns of cognitive appraisal in emotion. *Journal of Personality and Social Psychology, 48,* 813-838.

Smith, R. H., Kim, S. H., & Parrot, W. G. (1988). Envy and jealousy: Semantic problems and experiential distinctions. *Personality and Social Psychology Bulletin, 14,* 401-409.

Smith, C. A., & Lazarus, R. S. (1993). Appraisal components, core relational themes, and the emotions. *Cognition and Emotion, 7,* 233-269.

Spencer, H. (1890). *The principles of psychology* (Vol. 1). New York: Appleton.

Spielman, P. M. (1971). Envy and jealousy: An attempt at clarification. *Psychoanalytic Quarterly, 40,* 59-82.

Sternthal, B., & Craig, C. S. (1973). Humor in advertising. *Journal of Marketing, 37,* 12-18.

Stice, E. (1992). The similarities between cognitive dissonance and guilt: Confession as a relief of dissonance. *Current Psychology: Research & Reviews, 11,* 69-77.

Tangney, J. P., Miller, R. S., Flicker, L., & Barlow, D. H. (1996). Are shame, guilt, and embarrassment distinct emotions? *Journal of Personality and Social Psychology, 70,* 1256-1269.

Tesser, A. (1991). Emotion in social comparison and reflection processes. In J. Suls & T. A. Wills (Eds.), *Social comparison: Contemporary theory and research* (pp. 115-145). Hillsdale, NJ: Lawrence Erlbaum.

Tesser, A., & Collins, J. (1988). Emotion in social reflection and comparison situations: Intuitive, systematic, and exploratory approaches. *Journal of Personality and Social Psychology, 55,* 695-709.

Tomkins, S. S. (1962). *Affect, imagery, consciousness,* Vol. 1: *The positive affects.* New York: Springer.

Tomkins, S. S. (1963). *Affect, imagery, consciousness,* Vol. 2: *The negative affects.* New York: Springer.

Warden, M. A., & Koballa, T. R. (1995). Using students salient beliefs to design an instructional intervention to promote AIDS compassion and understanding in the middle school. *AIDS Education and Prevention, 7,* 60-73.

Watson, D., & Tellegen, A. (1985). Toward a consensual structure of mood. *Psychological Bulletin, 98,* 219-235.

Weinberger, M. G., & Gulas, C. S. (1992). The impact of humor in advertising: A review. *Journal of Advertising, 21*(4), 35-59.

Weiner, B. (1985). An attributional theory of achievement motivation and emotion. *Psychological Review, 92,* 548-573.

Witte, K. (1992). Putting the fear back into fear appeals: The Extended Parallel Process Model. *Communication Monographs, 59,* 329-349.

Witte, K. (1994). Fear control and danger control: A test of the Extended Parallel Process Model (EPPM). *Communication Monographs, 61,* 113-134.

Wood, W. (1982). Retrieval of attitude-relevant information from memory: Effects on susceptibility to persuasion and on intrinsic motivation. *Journal of Personality and Social Psychology, 42,* 798-810.

Wood, W., & Kallgren, C. A. (1988). Communicator attributes and persuasion: Recipients' access to attitude-relevant information in memory. *Personality and Social Psychology Bulletin, 14,* 172-182.

Wood, W., Kallgren, C. A., & Preisler, R. M. (1985). Access to attitude-relevant information in memory as a determinant of persuasion: The role of message attributes. *Journal of Experimental Social Psychology, 21,* 73-85.

Wundt, W. (1902). *Outlines of psychology* (C. H. Judd, Trans.). New York: Engelmann. (Original work published 1897)

16

Persuasion and the Structure of Affect

JAMES PRICE DILLARD
ANNELOES MEIJNDERS

What is the role of affect in persuasion? When confronted with such a question, the 18th-century philosopher George Campbell offered this provocative reply:

> [The passions] are not the supplanters of reason, or even rivals in her sway; they are her handmaids, by whose ministry she is enabled to usher truth into the heart, and procure it there a favorable reception. As handmaids they are liable to be seduced by sophistry in the garb of reason, and sometimes are made ignorantly to lend their aid in the introduction of falsehood. But their service is not on this account to be dispensed with; there is even a necessity of employing it, founded on our nature. Our eyes and hands and feet will give us the same assistance in doing mischief as in doing good; but it would not therefore be better for the world, that all mankind were blind and lame. (Campbell, 1776/1988, p. 72)

Whereas it is common in Western cultures to conceive of logic and emotion as oppositional tendencies, Campbell's view is especially noteworthy. He claimed that not only do feelings serve reason, but they can do so in ways that "usher in the truth." Yet they may also entice opinion change based on specious logic. In his eyes, then, the relationship between affect and persuasion is a mercurial one that varies in outcome. In fact, as this chapter shows, his claim is borne out by contemporary empirical studies.

Perhaps the most striking aspect of the preceding quote is Campbell's contention that persuasion *cannot occur in the absence of passion*. Almost certainly, Campbell meant to say that persuasive messages must evoke passion if they are to succeed. That alone is a bold claim. Yet current views of affect suggest that an even broader interpretation is feasible. The notion that people are always in some state of affect (e.g., Fox, 1991) implies the possibility that affective states occurring prior to a suasory appeal might propel message recipients toward either veracity or beguilement. This possibility too is supported by the current research literature.

Campbell's thinking makes a case for the central role that affect plays in the process of persuasion. But before we can address the empirical research in a systematic fashion, it is useful to draw some distinctions regarding the affect-persuasion relationship.

The Source of Affect

First, we can ask about the origin of affect. One possibility is that it has nothing to do with the message whatsoever. Simonson and Lundy (1967) used the phrase *irrelevant fear* to describe an experiment in which fright was evoked just prior to the presentation of a message on an unrelated topic. That expression was later expanded to the more general *message-irrelevant affect* (Dillard & Wilson, 1993; Jorgensen, 1998). Although affect is expected to influence message processing in this research, the event that induces it, and indeed the affect itself, bears no logical relationship to the content of the message.

When affect is the product of the message itself we refer to it as *message-induced affect*. Some messages, such as appeals to fear and guilt, are designed to evoke particular affects so that those feelings serve as the basis for acceptance of the advocacy. However, many persuasive appeals attempt to elicit affect through means other than propositional content. Professionally produced advertisements often include eye-catching images and memorable melodies in addition to some propositional content. A clear conceptual line can be drawn between the affect stimulated by verbal content and that which arises from ancillary stylistic material. In addition, message-induced affect is not necessarily relevant; for example, humor often has little to do with the message topic. Primarily due to space constraints, we make very little of these nuances in the pages that follow.

The Structure of Affect

Conceptions of affect are nearly as diverse as emotional life itself. Yet for present purposes, we limit our focus to just three and distinguish among them by reference to their structural complexity. The simple *bipolar valence model* is the epitome of parsimony. Studies that adopt this approach treat affect as a phenomenon that varies along a dimension anchored by positive affect at one end and negative affect at the other. Slightly more complex are the *two-dimensional models* that may themselves take two forms. Some authors argue that pleasure and arousal are the terms that best characterize this affective space, whereas others advocate a bivariate model in which positive and negative affect constitute separate but interacting systems. What we call *discrete emotion models* are the most complex of the lot. From this perspective, affect is viewed as a set of distinct states such as anger, fear, and happiness, each of which may vary in intensity.

These three models are not an exhaustive classification scheme for the study of affect. Indeed, many alternatives exist (e.g., Ortony, Clore, & Collins, 1988; Plutchik, 1984; Shaver, Schwartz, Kirson, & O'Connor, 1987; for a review, see Guerrero, Andersen, & Trost, 1998). Their value arises from the fact that they allow us to partition research on persuasion and affect into groupings that share common assumptions and research focus. Accordingly, the bulk of this chapter is organized into three major sections that correspond to each of the models just described. We make frequent use of the message-relevant/message-irrelevant distinction to arrange the literature within sections.

BIPOLAR VALENCE MODEL

As its name so plainly suggests, the bipolar valence model assumes that the affect is best conceived as a single continuum described by antonymic pairs such as positive-negative, good-bad, and happy-sad (Thayer, 1989; Watson, Wiese, Vaidya, & Tellegen, 1999).[1] Recent articles build a strong case for bipolarity as a viable structure for the experience of affect when methodological artifacts are controlled (Green, Salovey, & Truax, 1999; Russell & Carroll, 1999). Importantly, the phrase *experience of affect* highlights the boundaries of the claim of bipolarity. Almost without exception, self-reports of subjective experience form the evidentiary base from which claims of bipolarity are issued. When questions are posed addressing the subjective structure of affect, this seems entirely appropriate. However, it merits mention that any number of mental and physical subsystems, themselves wholly distinct from one another, might interact to jointly produce "experience." When speaking of the structure of affect both here and elsewhere, we must be careful to distinguish the domain (i.e., subjective or physiological) in which that structure resides.

A great deal of persuasion research has asked how preexisting mood states might influence persuasion. As a group, these studies conceive of mood as structured in terms of a bipolar valence model. In addition, most of these studies, either implicitly or explicitly, conceptualize mood as a diffuse affective state that occupies the background of consciousness. There are several distinct theoretical approaches to this literature.

Theoretical Positions on the Effects of Mood on Persuasion

Much of the current interest in mood and persuasion can be traced to a study by Worth and Mackie (1987). That project is valuable not only for its place in the history of this area but also because its design is so typical of subsequent investigations. In Worth and Mackie's

study, positive mood participants won $1.00 in an allegedly random lottery, while neutral mood participants were simply asked whether or not they had participated in a lottery. All participants then read a message about acid rain containing either strong or weak arguments that was attributed to either an expert or nonexpert source. The results indicated that, relative to the neutral mood participants, those in the positive mood condition recalled fewer arguments, were less sensitive to the argument strength manipulation, and were more sensitive to the source cue manipulation. Overall, the evidence suggested that positive mood dampened systematic processing. From these and other findings (Mackie & Worth, 1989), the researchers concluded that positive moods consume *cognitive capacity*, thereby constraining participants' *ability* to engage in systematic message processing.

The notion that positive mood participants might have suffered *motivational* deficits provides the cornerstone to an alternative explanation. The *mood-as-information* hypothesis suggests that affective states may function as heuristics conveying to individuals whether there is a need to process the message carefully (Bless, Bohner, Schwarz, & Strack, 1990; for a revision of this position, see Bless & Schwarz, 1999). A positive mood signals that all is well, and by implication so is the advocacy of the suasory appeal. By contrast, a negative mood gives notice that something is amiss. The individual should, therefore, devote cognitive resources to an analysis of the environment, including the persuasive message.

The mood and persuasion research has depended heavily on the dual-process models of persuasion (i.e., the Elaboration Likelihood Model and the Heuristic-Systematic Model). Because both of these models suggest that biased message processing is likely under certain conditions, it is not surprising that this issue might arise in the context of mood research. In fact, earlier work on mood and cognition made it clear that individuals tended to produce cognitions that were evaluatively consistent with their mood states (Bower, 1981). This *mood congruity* position anticipates that cognitive responses to a persuasive appeal should mirror the valence of the individual's mood.

The *mood management* position provides another angle on this literature (Wegener & Petty, 1996). In this view, message recipients make careful decisions regarding message processing with an eye toward maintaining or improving their affective state. Persons in a positive mood are expected to be quite discriminating about the messages they choose to engage because there are so many ways in which their state of elation might be disrupted. They are likely to avoid (i.e., superficially process) depressing topics, loss-framed messages, and counterattitudinal claims. However, a positive mood might encourage systematic processing if the message recipient believes that close analysis would make him or her feel better. By contrast, a very sad mood should encourage systematic processing more generally. Affectively speaking, there is nothing left to lose and much to be gained.

A Meta-analysis of Mood and Persuasion Studies

Three major finding emerged from a meta-analysis of the mood and persuasion literature (Brentar, Dillard, & Smith, 1997). First, as positivity of mood increased, so did attitude change. Although this effect characterized the literature generally, it was qualified by the fact that the strength of the mood-persuasion relationship varied depending on features of the message. A stronger mood-attitude correlation was found for topics that were positive in tone, claims that were gain framed (as opposed to loss framed), and messages that were pro-attitudinal rather than counterattitudinal.

These moderator effects are most compatible with mood management theory.

Second, positive moods led to decreased depth of processing. That is, people in good moods tended to report fewer cognitive responses than did those in neutral or negative moods. This relationship was unaffected by any moderator. A legitimate question is whether the effect is due to motivation or to ability. Although the meta-analysis could not answer the question directly, the pattern of results slightly favored the motivational account over the cognitive capacity explanation.

Third, the more positive an individual's affective state, the greater the number of favorable cognitive responses. This biased processing result, which held across moderator variables, was predicted by mood congruency theory. Overall, these three findings point to the complexity of the mood-persuasion linkage. Although existing theoretical positions emphasize single processes, the data suggest that a more realistic portrayal would be one in which multiple processes occur simultaneously.

The Brentar et al. (1997) paper makes one final point pertinent to this chapter. Researchers in the mood and persuasion tradition have employed three different types of experimental designs. The most common approach is to induce positive and negative feelings. Other researchers contrasted positive affect with a no-induction control, whereas a third group considered three points on the bipolarity continuum: positive, neutral (control), and negative. Although meta-analytic tests for the effect of experimental design were conducted, no such effects were observed. Thus, for the mood and persuasion studies, there was no indication that the data required a more complex conception of affect than the bipolar valence model. At least in the context of these experimental studies of message-irrelevant affect, the bipolar valence model shows no incompatibility with the data.

Conclusions

Research in this tradition almost invariably induces mood through experimental induction (but see Mano, 1997). That is, some specific event, such as winning a lottery or recalling a bad experience, is the means by which affective state is manipulated. Typically, then, participants are told that they will take part in a second study unrelated to the first (in which affect was manipulated). At that time, they are presented with the persuasive messages and various outcome measures. These design features are significant in that they form an important scope condition. There is good reason to believe that the findings presented here hold only when individuals are unaware of the source of their affect. When individuals are prompted to consider the cause of their mood, the relationship between mood valence and persuasion disappears (Sinclair, Mark, & Clore, 1994). Thus, the mood and persuasion findings are circumscribed along two lines: They apply to circumstances in which (a) the affect is irrelevant to the message and (b) message recipients have no reason to de-bias the effects of mood.

TWO-DIMENSIONAL MODELS

Many studies have been conducted in which participants evaluate their chronic or acute affective state on a series of feeling-related words. These ratings are then submitted to some data reduction algorithm, typically factor analysis. Despite some dispute regarding the optimal number of factors needed to define affective space, the vast majority of investigations yield a two-factor solution. The question of how to interpret these two factors has generated a vigorous controversy that is briefly sketched in what follows.

Pleasure-Arousal Theory (and the Circumplex Model)

One camp contends that affect is structured in terms of pleasure and arousal (e.g., Reisenzein, 1994; Russell & Feldman Barrett, 1999). *Pleasure* is defined as the valence or hedonic tone of the affective experience, and values on this dimension run from pleasant to unpleasant. *Arousal,* which ranges from activation to deactivation, indexes the extent to which an individual experiences a sense of energy or mobilization. Together, pleasure and arousal are thought to define the "core" or elemental features of all affective experience (Russell & Feldman Barrett, 1999). At any given moment, core affect is a uniform composite of these two factors experienced as a point on the pleasant-unpleasant continuum.

Some pleasure-arousal theorists contend that there is value in viewing affective space as a circumplex organized around the pleasure-arousal continuum (e.g., Larsen & Diener, 1992; Reisenzein, 1994; Russell & Feldman Barrett, 1999) (see Figure 16.1). The statistical argument behind this claim is based on the observation that affect items form a rough circle around the two dimensions rather than forming the dense clusters suggestive of simple structure (Russell & Feldman Barrett, 1999). The conceptual allure of the circumplex is its ability to explain affective experience as blends of pleasure and arousal (Reisenzein, 1994). Depression, for instance, is a combination of unpleasantness and low arousal. Although generally true, this apparent advantage is troubled by the placement of fear and anger, two emotions that occupy the same space but are worlds apart subjectively and for which good evidence of physiological differentiation can be offered (e.g., Levenson, Ekman, & Friesen, 1990).

Message-Irrelevant Pleasure and Arousal. Although investigations of arousal are legion,

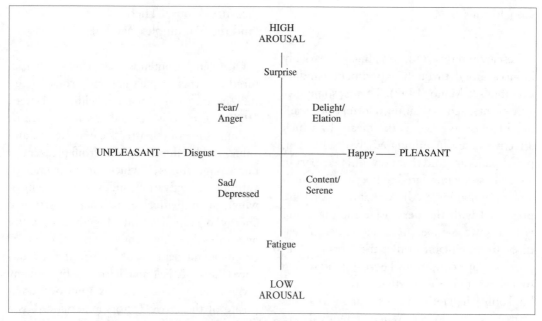

Figure 16.1. The Two-Factor Model Interpreted as Pleasure-Arousal
SOURCE: Adapted from Russell (1979).

studies of persuasion and arousal are fewer in number (Zanna, Deitweiler, & Olson, 1984), and studies of persuasion and *pleasure-arousal* are fewer still (but see Mano, 1997; Stout & Sego, 1994). With regard to arousal, researchers have argued that it constrains cognitive capacity, thereby limiting systematic processing and encouraging heuristic processing (Cox & Locander, 1986; Sonbonmatsu & Kardes, 1988). The findings conform to the claim that arousal can indeed reduce capacity. However, as arousal increases, individuals also become more selective in what they choose to process (Easterbrook, 1959; cf. Stiff, 1986). When faced with the reduced capacity resulting from arousal, message recipients may favor either central or peripheral cues depending on the information value of each. For example, if given the task of evaluating a brand, aroused consumers rely on the evidence presented in the message. If given the task of evaluating the advertisement, aroused message recipients tend to be influenced by the credibility of the message source (Pham, 1996). Other evidence consistent with this selectivity hypothesis can be found in studies of the relationship between message-relevant fear (Meijnders, 1998) and message-irrelevant fear/anxiety and persuasion (Baron, Logan, Lilly, Inman, & Brennan, 1994).

A Meta-analysis of Message-Induced Affect. The bipolar valence position, in addition to two alternatives, was tested in a meta-analysis of the persuasive effects of feelings evoked by advertisements. Brown, Homer, and Inman (1998) summarized the results of 55 studies that assessed the relationship between advertisement-evoked affect and attitude toward the advertisement (A_{ad}), attitude toward the brand (A_b), or both.

Brown et al. (1998) noted that the *bipolarity* position predicts that the relationship between positive affect and attitude (A_{ad} and A_b) should mirror the relationship between negative affect and attitude. This prediction was borne out. However, the data also revealed a correlation between positive and negative affect of −.26 corrected for measurement error. A coefficient of this size would appear to argue against bipolarity because a much larger negative correlation would be expected. However, this conclusion is suspect due to the means by which Brown et al. constructed the two variables of interest. Their method required that measured emotions be assigned to the categories *positive* and *negative*. A glance at the circumplex depicted in Figure 16.1 reveals the potential problem with this strategy: Many feelings that are broadly characterized as positive or negative are not located 180 degrees apart on the circumplex. The terms *delight* and *fear,* for instance, are not expected to be bipolar opposites, and therefore the expected magnitude of their negative correlation should be considerably smaller than −1.00. In short, because feelings were broadly classified prior to computing the positive-negative correlation, it is difficult to know exactly what to make of the −.26 correlation. It cannot be construed as strong evidence against bipolarity.

One alternative to bipolarity is *generalized asymmetry.* This position rests on research demonstrating that negative information is accorded greater weight in decision making than is positive information (Kellermann, 1984). In line with those findings, the generalized asymmetry position anticipates a main effect of feelings on A_{ad} and A_b such that negative feelings show a greater impact than positive feelings. The Brown et al. (1998) data showed the following: For A_{ad}, the corrected correlations were .55 and −.49 for positive and negative affect, respectively. The findings for A_b echoed that pattern, with corresponding coefficients of .37 and −.34. The relatively trivial differences in magnitude are inconsistent with the claim of generalized asymmetry.

A third possibility, *contingent asymmetry,* suggests that positive and negative affect are likely to manifest different effects depending on a variety of moderator variables. For example, the impact of positive and negative feelings on attitude may vary as a function of instructions to process systematically (vs. no instructions). When the effects of moderator variables were examined, the magnitude of the affect-attitude correlations were seen to vary as a function of two study features: (a) the use of a cover story and (b) experimental instructions to attend to the ads. In general, negative feelings showed a strong inverse relationship with A_{ad} and A_b in the absence of instructions or cover stories. The strength of that association was greatly diminished in studies that used either instructions or cover stories. By contrast, the positive affect-attitude correlation was unaffected by the cover story variable and slightly enhanced by experimental instructions to attend to the advertisements. All told, the data show that message-evoked positive affect and negative affect are contingently asymmetric in their associations with attitude.

It would appear that these latter findings run counter to the bipolar valence approach. Yet such an inference overlooks the important distinction between message-induced and message-irrelevant affect. Bipolarity seems suited to the study of irrelevant affect (as argued in the earlier section on the valence model). The Brown et al. (1998) meta-analysis indicates that feelings evoked by brief persuasive messages produce different effects on attitude as a function of the cognitive processes induced by cover stories or experimental instructions. Thus, it would not appear to be prudent to assume that affective processes operate identically in the domains defined by the relevant-irrelevant distinction. The Brown et al. findings resonate with a conception of affect in which positive and negative feelings result from two separate but interdependent psychophysiological systems. We turn next to a discussion of that perspective.

Dual-System Models

What would account for the existence of two separate systems, one devoted to the production of positive feelings and the other providing the basis for negative feelings? A common response given by advocates of the dual-system perspective is that these two systems are evolutionarily designed to enable successful interaction with the environment (Cacioppo & Berntson, 1994; Thayer, 1989; Watson et al., 1999). One system, *behavioral approach,* is sensitive to cues of reward, nonpunishment, and escape from punishment. Its function is to initiate goal-directed behavior, and activation of the approach system is thought to underlie the experience of positive feelings (Davidson, 1993; Gray, 1990). The *behavioral inhibition* system provides aversive motivation in response to cues associated with punishment, nonreward, and novelty. Its purpose is to inhibit actions that may lead to negative outcomes (Davidson, 1993; Gray, 1990). This system is believed to be responsible for the experience of negative affect.

Factor analytic evidence compatible with the dual-system position can be found in a sizable number of studies (Thayer, 1989; Watson & Tellegen, 1985). However, the degree to which these studies offer support to the dual-system model or its competitor, pleasure-arousal theory, is unclear. Rotating the positive-negative solution 45 degrees yields the pleasure-arousal solution discussed in the previous section. In fact, the debate over the preferred solution cannot be resolved by appeal to factor analytic data alone because any number of rotations are possible. Apart from the usual statistical criteria for interpretability, the only principled basis for preferring one rotation over another is to connect the factors to some theory and empirical phenomena external to the factored matrix.

In fact, there is support of this type in a great many places (e.g., Gray, 1971). Several studies show that changes in positive and negative affect display an intriguingly systematic correspondence to circadian rhythms (Thayer, 1989; Watson et al., 1999). Whereas negative affect is relatively independent of time of day (or time since rising), positive affect shows a curvilinear association that rises throughout the morning, remains high during most of the day, and then declines again in the evening.

There is also mounting psychophysiological evidence that positive and negative affect result from hemispherically lateralized brain systems (Fox, 1991). In general, relative right hemisphere activation has been linked to a propensity for negative affect arousal, whereas relative left hemisphere activation is associated with greater ease of activation of positive emotions (Davidson, 1993).

Elicitation and Effects of Positive and Negative Affect. Studies of the features of persuasive messages responsible for the evocation of positive and negative affect are surprisingly few. Those that do address the topic have produced rather equivocal results. Dalto, Ossoff, and Pollack (1994) reported a nonsignificant tendency for an image-oriented political address by then presidential candidate George Bush (the elder) to evoke greater positive affect than an issue-oriented message presented by the same speaker. Work in the area of organ donation found a nonsignificant trend such that the narrative form of an appeal generated more mentions of both positive and negative affect than the same advocacy cast in terms of statistical evidence (Kopfman, Smith, Ah Yun, & Hodges, 1998). To the extent that these trends are indicative of genuine relationships, both might be explained by the fact that these message forms (i.e., image and narrative) are themselves in part defined by the presence of emotionally evocative information.

LaTour and his colleagues have delivered a series of investigations in which Thayer's (1989) model of energetic (i.e., positive) and tense (i.e., negative) arousal takes center stage. One of their early efforts demonstrated that variations in female nudity in a perfume advertisement produced changes in both positive and negative affect (LaTour, Pitts, & Snook-Luther, 1990), often in combination with sex of participant. Across various studies, positive affect showed a consistent positive relationship with A_{ad}. The effects of negative affect were more unpredictable, showing an inverse relationship with persuasion in one study (LaTour et al., 1990), a direct relationship in another study (Henthorne, LaTour, & Nataraajan, 1993), and no reliable relationship in a third study (LaTour & Rotfeld, 1997). Consideration of the variability of these results suggests a conclusion quite in line with Brown et al.'s (1998) explication of contingent asymmetry as well as Campbell's (1776/1988) perspective with which we opened this chapter: Message-relevant affect is unlikely to produce any sort of invariant effect in the persuasive process.

Affect, Mental Imagery, and Radio Advertising. A series of studies into the role of mental imagery in radio advertising has yielded several conclusions relevant to our interests here (e.g., Bone & Ellen, 1992; Burns, Biswas, & Babin, 1993). Most significant among them is the detailing of a causal process that locates affect as a mediator between two features of mental imagery—vividness and quantity of images—and attitude toward the advertisement. Although there is some indication that imagery yields a variety of affective responses (Miller & Marks, 1992), the clearest evidence of mediation exists for positive feelings (Miller & Marks, 1997).

The research has explored various techniques for stimulating mental imagery, and there are sound theoretical reasons that some appear to be more effective than others (Miller & Marks, 1992, 1997). *Sound effects* are relatively powerful in their capacity to stimulate imagery and subsequent emotion because they directly stimulate memory structures containing auditory information that corresponds to the stimulus. *Vivid concrete language* is somewhat less impactful in that language activates semantic structures from which activation then spreads to the relevant perceptual structures. *Instructions to imagine* oneself in the advertisement show the weakest effect, presumably because individuals vary in their willingness and ability to adopt this general mind-set.

Affect Versus Cognition. As noted earlier, Western culture often portrays the relationship between affect and cognition as one of antagonism, a tendency that can be seen in studies that pit emotional messages against logical ones (e.g., Pallak, Murroni, & Koch, 1983; Preston, 1968). In fact, there is substantial evidence that these two processes generally go hand in hand. A classic case in point is Abelson, Kinder, Peters, and Fiske (1982), who used nationwide survey data to demonstrate that affective responses contribute to judgments of a political candidate above and beyond voter party affiliation, assessments of the candidate's character, or assessments of the candidate's stance on the issues. Positive and negative affect emerged as separate predictors in those same analyses, a finding that is perfectly compatible with the dual-system perspective. Similar results are reported in articles that also focus on judgments of political figures (e.g., Anderson & Granberg, 1991; Jones & Iacobucci, 1989) and of commercial advertising (e.g., Edell & Burke, 1987).

The dual-system model has also been fruitfully applied to other facets of the political process (Marcus, 1988). Marcus and Mackuen (1993) presented longitudinal data showing that changes in negative but not positive affect precede and predict *changes in knowledge* about presidential candidates. This is taken to indicate that anxiety about the campaign prompts learning. Interestingly, *changes in campaign involvement* correspond with changes in positive but not negative affect. By implication, enthusiasm prompts engagement (but see Hullett, 2000).

Conclusions

The pleasure-arousal conception of affect is attractive for its intuitive appeal, while the dual-system position seems preferable for its numerous theoretical and empirical connections to phenomena beyond the correlation matrix that yields two factors. Despite the ongoing controversy, one point is clear: Both positions have contributed to advances in persuasion research. However, the research findings examined in this section are not without limitations, one of the most evident being that most of the studies reviewed here used commercial advertisements as their persuasive stimuli. As a category of messages, advertisements tend to be overwhelmingly oriented to the production of positive affect. And the dependent variables of interest to persuasion researchers allied with the advertising discipline are generally A_{ad} and A_b. Although perfectly suited to the study of commercial advertising A_{ad} and A_b may have limited applicability to other realms of persuasion (Dillard & Peck, 2000). Consider that Brown's (1998) meta-analysis of advertising showed that negative affect diminished persuasion, while the fear/threat appeals literature shows that intensity of fear, a negative affect, is positively associated with persuasion (Meijnders, 1998; Mongeau, 1998). Guilt, another negative affect, also shows a direct relationship with persuasion (see O'Keefe's chapter in this volume [Chapter 17]). Next, we turn to a discussion of a theoretical position that anticipates nonuniform effects with the two broad categories of positive and negative affect.

DISCRETE EMOTION MODELS

A central premise of the discrete emotions perspective is that the primary function of emotion is to guide behavior. Over the course of the development of the species, the emotional system evolved because it enabled successful behavioral interaction with the environment (Darwin, 1872/1965; Tooby & Cosmides, 1990).

Although emotions share the property of variable intensity, they are also distinct from one another. Each one is represented by a unique pattern of changes in cognition (Roseman, Wiest, & Swartz, 1994), the autonomic nervous system (Levenson, 1988), neuroanatomical activity (Lane, Reiman, Ahern, Schwartz, & Davidson, 1997), facial expression, (Ekman, 1989) and action readiness (Frijda, 1987). These systemic changes are myriad but (usually) functionally coherent. Thus, this perspective suggests that affect is structured categorically. Discrete emotions are those feelings that manifest distinctive patterns of change across these various systems.

Particular emotions are evoked in response to recurring challenges to the well-being of the organism (Lazarus, 1991). There is a small and finite number of such challenges defined by a specific configuration of perceived environmental variables. The perception of this configuration elicits the particular emotion best suited to deal with it. In this vein, anger occurs in response to a thwarted goal, sadness occurs as a consequence of loss, fear follows from the perception of impending threat, and so on (Frijda, 1986; Roseman et al., 1994; Scherer, 1984).

Elicitation of Discrete Emotions. Whether behaving proactively or reactively, organisms must make sense of the environment. Whenever change is perceived, individuals appraise the state of the environment to ascertain the degree to which it harbors favorable or unfavorable implications for their own well-being. But this appraisal process is not simple. The environment is frequently multi-valenced, often ambiguous, and consistently dynamic. Of course, these same qualities can be seen in persuasive messages of all sorts. It is precisely these features that encourage multiple appraisals of any given message and that, in turn, should yield a corresponding multiplicity of emotional reactions. In fact, several studies report data that align well with this expectation. For example, in a study of emotional reactions to civic deliberation (i.e., persuasion in a group setting), 90% of the participants reported experiencing three or more of the emotions under study (i.e., hope, pride, contentment, anger, fear, and sadness) (Dillard & Backus, 1997).

Laboratory studies of commercial and noncommercial advertisements contribute to this same point. Dental floss advertisements, designed to make working mothers feel guilty about their children's dental health, yielded increases in anger and guilt as well as decreases in happiness (Coulter & Pinto, 1995; Pinto & Priest, 1991). In a study of AIDS-related public service announcements (PSAs), Dillard, Plotnick, Godbold, Freimuth, and Edgar (1996) reported that 30 of the 31 PSAs studied produced statistically significant changes in at least two emotions for the entire sample of participants. More than 75% of those same messages evoked changes in three or more emotions. Of particular interest was the fact that all 31 of the messages studied were structured as fear appeals; that is, they described a threat and a means of averting the threat. Despite their common design, only about two thirds of the messages actually induced fear (cf. Stout & Sego, 1994).

The findings reviewed in this section coalesce to make two important points. First, although message content and emotional outcome often show correspondence, persuasive messages cannot be classified as inherently emotional because they do not themselves elicit emotions. Rather, subjective appraisal of message content is the proximal cause of emotional experience. Whereas knowledge of message content and structure may offer useful guidelines for designing emotion-based appeals, content and structure alone do not guarantee that particular emotions will follow. A message and its emotional effects are not isomorphic.

Second, due to the complexity and ambiguity that are inherent in social interaction, persuasive messages are likely to elicit emotions other than those that might be anticipated on the basis of structure and content. These "collateral" emotions are noteworthy in that they may work in opposition to the advocacy of the messages (Coulter & Pinto, 1995; Dillard et al., 1996).

Discrete Effects of Emotion on Persuasion. The discrete emotions perspective contends that emotions alter an organism's mode of operation. That is, emotions mobilize and recruit resources from a variety of subsystems (e.g., the motivational, the cognitive), producing a complex set of changes that are nonetheless (usually) organized and unified in their function. If these patterns of change are distinct from one another (as the discrete approach would have us believe), then we should expect to see distinct effects on persuasion. Evidence consistent with that expectation is of three types:

1. Studies show variation in the sign and magnitude of the effects of *negative* emotions (e.g., fear, anger, sadness, guilt) on various persuasion outcomes (Dillard & Backus, 1997; Dillard & Peck, 2000; Dillard et al., 1996; Huang, 1997; Kinder, 1994; for parallel findings regarding persons with AIDS, see Diijker, Kok, & Koomen, 1996).

2. Studies show variation in the sign and magnitude of the effects of *positive* emotions (e.g., pride, happiness, contentment) on various persuasive outcomes (Batra & Ray, 1986; Dillard & Backus, 1997; Dillard & Peck, 2001; Kinder, 1994).

3. In one of the few efforts to directly compare the utility of different conceptions of affect, Huang (1997) examined the predictive power of a discrete emotions model, a general negative affect model, and a modal affect model (i.e., the most frequent affective response) on A. The discrete emotions model accounted for slightly more than twice as much variance as its closest competitor (i.e., the modal affect model). Dillard and Peck (2001) reported similar results.

In sum, there is evidence that emotions produced separable and unique effects on outcome measures that include the perceived persuasiveness of a message, A_{ad}, political involvement, and judgments of political figures. These data support the notion that fruitful study of emotions in persuasion requires a more nuanced approach than that offered by those more simple models of affective structure.

Affect and Cognition. Does the study of discrete emotions tell us something more about persuasion than the study of cognition alone? Yes. Studies that have assessed emotional responses in addition to cognitive responses consistently demonstrate the predictive power of emotions above and beyond that of cognition (Batra & Ray, 1986; Dillard & Peck, 2000, 2001; Dillard et al., 1996). Investigations that depend on other forms of cognitive judgment, such as prior attitude toward the candidate, also indicate that emotion reveals something more about the persuasive process than does cognition alone (Abelson et al., 1982; Kinder, 1994).

Theoretical Utility of a Discrete Emotions Perspective. The correspondence between theory and data is one criterion for evaluating a theory. Another point on which a theory's value is assessed is its capacity to recast old phenomena in novel ways. Although we believe that the discrete emotions perspective has much to offer persuasion theory in this regard, we develop only one example to illustrate the point (but see also see Dillard, 1994, and chapters in this volume by Harmon-Jones [Chapter 6], Nabi [Chapter 15], and O'Keefe [Chapter 17]).

Consider a conceptual framework with a long and distinguished career, that is, reactance theory (Brehm, 1966). Generally speaking, reactance is thought to be a state of (a) physiological arousal (b) with motivational properties that is (c) subjectively experienced as negative. As anyone who has experienced the conditions that lead to reactance arousal knows that this state feels like a member of the anger family of emotions (e.g., irritation, resentment, annoyance, vexation). Indeed, the appraisal pattern for anger is very similar to the determinants of reactance (cf. Brehm & Brehm, 1981; Roseman et al., 1994). These parallels are interesting, but they do not alone suggest any more than that reactance and anger might be viewed as two ways of examining the same phenomenon. It is when we reflect on other properties of reactance that the benefits of a discrete emotions perspective are seen more clearly.

Consider the following: "Formally, reactance has the status of an intervening, hypothetical variable. . . . We cannot measure reactance directly, but hypothesizing its existence allows us to predict a variety of behavioral effects" (Brehm & Brehm, 1981, p. 37). In fact, conceptualizing reactance as anger suggests that it can be measured through a variety of means, including inexpensive and subjectively valid self-reports. In addition, consider that reactance "exists only in the context of other forces motivating the person to give up the freedom and comply with the threat or elimination" (p. 37). What are those other forces? In most reactance studies, persuasive force derives from the arguments in the message. Yet a discrete emotions perspective directs us to consider a different set of variables, that is, other emotions. From an operational standpoint, the theory specifies a set of covariates that one would be prudent to include in the design of a study. Theoretically, reactance becomes one of several potential emotional influences on persuasion, thereby housing this classic theory in a broader and more contemporary framework.

Conclusions

The discrete emotions perspective is the least parsimonious of the three affect structures considered in this chapter. Although parsimony is to be valued, the studies reviewed here indicate that persuasive messages have the capacity to elicit multiple emotions and that those emotions can produce quite distinct effects on a variety of persuasive outcomes. Hence, complexity may be required to capture the reality of message-induced affect. What is largely absent from current theory is a clear understanding of the mechanisms by which emotions produce their many effects.

FUTURE DIRECTIONS FOR RESEARCH ON AFFECT AND PERSUASION

Resolving the Structure of Affect

The three positions on the structure of affect are frequently viewed as competing with one another. However, they might more profitably be seen as complementary (cf. Dillard, 1998). The bipolar valence position seems to accurately capture a good deal of the experience of affect. This seems particularly true when affect intensity is low, as in the case of mood. And the evidence suggests that the influence of mood on persuasion is limited to circumstances in which the individual is unreflective concerning the origin of his or her affective state. The bipolar valence model appears to be well-suited to the study of message-irrelevant affect.

Within the domain of two-dimensional models, argument abounds. And although a series of recent articles have clarified the issues on which the debate is founded (Cacioppo, Gardener, & Bernston, 1999; Green et al., 1999; Russell & Feldman Barrett, 1999; Watson et al., 1999), it is unlikely that consensus on the optimal rotation of the two-factor models will be reached in the immediate future. For present purposes, it may be sufficient to appeal to the distinction between experience and physiology. It is perfectly conceivable that affect is subjectively structured in terms of pleasure-arousal, while the physiological substrate responsible for experience consists of two distinct systems.

Persuasion research should not settle on either of the two-dimensional models when there is clear evidence of discriminable effects of specific emotions within the broad categories of positive and negative emotions. However, neither would it be prudent to ignore the claim that broad categories do structure various specific affects, at least at a fairly high level of abstraction. Perhaps the most fruitful approach would be to initiate persuasion research designed to explore the relationships among these various conceptions of affect. We speculate that the dual-system approach offers a sound framework for the study of emotional elicitation but that a discrete emotions perspective will prove more informative for examining the persuasive impact of affect.

Linking Message Features to Affective Responses

As noted in an earlier article, research on affect and persuasion has typically granted greater emphasis to the effects of emotion on persuasion than to the message features that generate those emotions (Dillard, 1994). Whereas the emotion-persuasion correlation has been of theoretical interest, the message-emotion correlation is characteristically treated as nothing more than a manipulation check. That should change. Essential to effecting such a change, but missing from the current literature, is a satisfactory means of classifying message features. One possibility is offered by appraisal theories of emotion (see Nabi's chapter in this volume [Chapter 15]). In essence, these theories suggest that certain types of message content are likely to produce particular emotional responses. There is certainly value in that, but thus far there has been little extension of the appraisal perspective to other message features such as style and structure (but see Deighton, Romer, & McQueen, 1989; Dillard, Kinney, & Cruz, 1996). A theory that provides linkages between affect and multiple message features is surely needed.

Whole-Message Studies Versus the Message Component Approach

Most research on persuasion and affect treats the message as if it were one indivisible unit. This tack may be warranted in many instances, but it is also evident that evaluating "the message" overlooks the fact that persuasive advocacies are constructed from a variety of components, including opening statements, arguments, backing, and conclusions. What would research look like that investigated the operation of message components instead of the message as a whole? One ready candidate for component analysis is research on threat appeals. Because these messages are generally structured in a problem-solution format (Hale & Dillard, 1995), it is surprising that more attention has not been given to the affective responses that might follow from the interplay between those message components. Drive theory, which framed early work on threat appeals, made the clear and specific claim that persuasion should result from the *reduction in fear* that occurs after exposure to the threat and as a function of the action (i.e., solution) component. A thorough test of this prediction would require evidence that fear was both (a) aroused (as assessed by a pre-threat vs. post-threat comparison) and (b) allayed (as assessed by a post-threat vs. post-action comparison). Curiously, we do not know of a single investigation in the half century of social scientific research on threat appeals that provides a complete test of this classic prediction.

Adopting a message component approach becomes more challenging when one considers suasory appeals that depart from standard methods of organization such as the problem-solution format. But methods developed for the study of conversational cognition (Waldron & Cegala, 1992) might be adapted to address this problem (see also Aaker, Stayman, & Hagerty, 1986). Asking message recipients to self-report their feelings while reading through a printed message would provide a much richer picture of affective impact of message components than does the usual post-message checklist. A similar end could be achieved via stimulated recall procedures in which participants view a commercial advertisement once and then review it, stopping the tape and describing their affective reactions as they occurred. Methods that put the participants in charge of these affective reporting points make no assumptions concerning the perceived structure of the advocacy. Moreover, it permits researchers to pose previously unconsidered questions concerning individuals' affective response styles. It is likely, however, that these "feel aloud" procedures have the potential to interfere with processes such as elaboration of message content and judgment formation. Experimental designs should be chosen that are capable of detecting reactive measurement if it exists.

CONCLUSION

Investigations of affect can be found in virtually every discipline that fall under that broad umbrella called persuasion. Consequently, we anticipate that our review is unlikely to satisfy anyone whose view of persuasion and affect is tied solely to one academic tradition. Indeed, our goal was a broader one. We sought to organize the wide-ranging literature by building on two distinctions: affect's structure and relevance to the appeal. Although it is difficult to judge the success of our efforts at this point, we hope that we have succeeded in convincing readers of George Campbell's important point: "To say that it is possible to persuade without speaking to the passions, is but at best a kind of specious nonsense" (p. 77).

NOTE

1. From this seemingly simple thesis flows a trio of distinct claims (Green, Salovey, & Truax, 1999). *Static bipolarity* references the idea that the zero-order correlation between antonyms is strongly negative when computed across persons. Dynamic bipolarity focuses on within-person change; when change in the affect system occurs, indexes of positive and negative feelings move in opposite directions with proportional magnitude. Finally, *causative bipolarity* suggests that pleasant and unpleasant feelings exert an influence on other processes, such as persuasion, that is opposite in sign and roughly equal in magnitude.

REFERENCES

Aaker, D. A., Stayman, D. M., & Hagerty, M. R. (1986). Warmth in advertising: Measurement, impact, and sequence effects. *Journal of Consumer Research, 12,* 365-381.

Abelson, R. P., Kinder, D. R., Peters, M. D., & Fiske, S. T. (1982). Affective and semantic components in political person perception. *Journal of Personality and Social Psychology, 42,* 619-630.

Anderson, E., & Granberg, D. (1991). Types of affective evaluators in recent U.S. presidential elections. *Polity, 24,* 147-155.

Baron, R. S., Logan, H., Lilly, J., Inman, M. L., & Brennan, M. (1994). Negative emotion and message processing. *Journal of Experimental Social Psychology, 30,* 181-201.

Batra, R., & Ray, M. L. (1986). Affective responses mediating acceptance of advertising. *Journal of Consumer Research, 13,* 234-249.

Bless, H., Bohner, G., Schwarz, N., & Strack, F. (1990). Mood and persuasion: A cognitive response analysis. *Personality and Social Psychology Bulletin, 16,* 331-345.

Bless, H., & Schwarz, N. (1999). Sufficient and necessary conditions in the dual-process models: The case of mood and information processing. In S. Chaiken & Y. Trope (Eds.), *Dual-process theories in social psychology* (pp. 423-440). New York: Guilford.

Bone, P. F., & Ellen, P. S. (1992). The generation and consequences of communication-evoked imagery. *Journal of Consumer Research, 19,* 93-104.

Bower, G. (1981). Mood and memory. *American Psychologist, 36,* 129-148.

Brehm, J. W. (1966). *A theory of psychological reactance.* New York: Academic Press.

Brehm, S. S., & Brehm, J. W. (1981). *Psychological reactance: A theory of freedom and control.* New York: Academic Press.

Brentar, J. E., Dillard, J. P., & Smith, B. A. (1997, May). *Message-irrelevant affect and persuasion: A meta-analysis.* Paper presented at the annual meeting of the International Communication Association, Montreal.

Brown, S. P., Homer, P. M., & Inman, J. J. (1998). A meta-analysis of relationships between ad-evoked feelings and advertising responses. *Journal of Marketing Research, 35,* 114-126.

Burns, A. C., Biswas, A., & Babin, L. A. (1993). The operation of visual imagery as a mediator of advertising effects. *Journal of Advertising, 22,* 71-85.

Cacioppo, J. T., & Berntson, G. G. (1994). Relationship between attitudes and evaluative space: A critical review, with emphasis on the separability of positive and negative substrates. *Psychological Bulletin, 115,* 401-423.

Cacioppo, J. T., Gardener, W. L., & Bernston, G. G. (1999). The affect system has parallel and integrative processing components: Form follows function. *Journal of Personality and Social Psychology, 76,* 839-855.

Campbell, G. (1988). *The philosophy of rhetoric* (L. Bitzer, Ed.). Carbondale: Southern Illinois University Press. (Original work published 1776)

Coulter, R. H., & Pinto, M. B. (1995). Guilt appeals in advertising: What are their effects? *Journal of Applied Psychology, 80,* 697-705.

Cox, D. S., & Locander, W. B. (1986). Product novelty: Does it moderate the relationship between ad attributes and brand attitudes? *Journal of Advertising, 16,* 39-44.

Dalto, C. A., Ossoff, E. P., & Pollack, R. D. (1994). Processes underlying reactions to a campaign speech: Cognition, affect, and voter concern. *Journal of Social Behavior and Personality, 9,* 701-713.

Darwin, C. (1965). *The expression of emotion in man and animals.* Chicago: University of Chicago Press. (Original work published 1872)

Davidson, R. J. (1993). Parsing affective space: Perspectives from neuropsychology and psychophysiology. *Neuropsychology, 7,* 464-475.

Deighton, J., Romer, D., & McQueen, J. (1989). Using drama to persuade. *Journal of Consumer Research, 16,* 335-343.

Diijker, A. J., Kok, G., & Koomen, W. (1996). Emotional reactions to people with AIDS. *Journal of Applied Social Psychology, 26,* 731-748.

Dillard, J. P. (1994). Rethinking the study of fear appeals: An emotional perspective. *Communication Theory, 4,* 295-323.

Dillard, J. P. (1998). The role of affect in communication, biology, and social relationships. In P. A. Andersen & L. K. Guerrero (Eds.), *Handbook of communication and emotion* (pp. xvii-xxxii). San Diego: Academic Press.

Dillard, J. P., & Backus, S. J. (1997, May). *An exploration into civic deliberation, emotional response, and political involvement.* Paper presented at the annual meeting of the National Communication Association, Montreal.

Dillard, J. P., Kinney, T. A., & Cruz, M. G. (1996). Influence, appraisals, and emotions in close relationships. *Communication Monographs, 63,* 105-130.

Dillard, J. P., & Peck, E. (2000). Affect and persuasion: Emotional responses to public service announcements. *Communication Research, 27,* 461-495.

Dillard, J. P., & Peck, E. (2001). Persuasion and the structure of affect: Dual systems and discrete emotions as complementary models. *Human Communication Research, 27,* 38-68.

Dillard, J. P., Plotnick, C. A., Godbold, L. C., Freimuth, V. S., & Edgar, T. (1996). The multiple affective consequences of AIDS PSAs: Fear appeals do more than scare people. *Communication Research, 23,* 44-72.

Dillard, J. P., & Wilson, B. J. (1993). Communication and affect: Thoughts, feelings, and issues for the future. *Communication Research, 20,* 637-646.

Easterbrook, J. A. (1959). The effects of emotion on cue utilization and the organization of behavior. *Psychological Bulletin, 66,* 183-201.

Edell, J. A., & Burke, M. C. (1986). The power of feelings in understanding advertising effects. *Journal of Consumer Research, 14,* 421-433.

Ekman, P. (1989). The argument and evidence about universals in facial expressions of emotion. In H. Wagner & A. S. R. Manstead (Eds.),

Handbook of social psychophysiology (pp. 143-164). Chichester, UK: Wiley.

Fox, N. A. (1991). If it's not left, it's right: Electroencephalograph asymmetry and the development of emotion. *American Psychologist, 46,* 863-872.

Frijda, N. H. (1986). *The emotions.* Cambridge, UK: Cambridge University Press.

Frijda, N. H. (1987). Emotion, cognitive structure, and action tendency. *Cognition and Emotion, 1,* 115-143.

Gray, J. A. (1971). *The psychology of fear and stress.* Cambridge, UK: Cambridge University Press.

Gray, J. A. (1990). Brain systems that mediate both emotion and cognition. *Cognition and Emotion, 4,* 269-288.

Green, D. P., Salovey, P., & Truax, K. M. (1999). Static, dynamic, and causative bipolarity of affect. *Journal of Personality and Social Psychology, 76,* 856-867.

Guerrero, L. K., Andersen, P. A., & Trost, M. R. (1998). Communication and emotion: Basic concepts and approaches. In P. A. Andersen & L. K. Guerrero (Eds.), *Handbook of communication and emotion* (pp. 5-29). San Diego: Academic Press.

Hale, J. L., & Dillard, J. P. (1995). Fear appeals in health promotion campaigns: Too much, too little, or just right? In E. Maibach & R. Parrott (Eds.), *Designing health messages: Approaches from communication theory and public health practice* (pp. 65-80). Thousand Oaks, CA: Sage.

Henthorne, T. L., LaTour, M. S., & Nataraajan, R. (1993). Fear appeals in print advertising: An analysis of arousal and ad response. *Journal of Advertising, 22,* 59-68.

Huang, M-H. (1997). Is negative affect in advertising general or specific? A comparison of three functional forms. *Psychology & Marketing, 14,* 223-240.

Hullett, C. R. (2000). *A critique and revision of Marcus and MacKuen's study of affect and political cognition.* Unpublished manuscript, Michigan State University.

Jones, L. E., & Iacobucci, D. (1989). The structure of affect and trait judgments of political figures. *Multivariate Behavioral Research, 24,* 457-476.

Jorgensen, P. F. (1998). Affect, persuasion, and communication processes. In P. A. Andersen & L. K. Guerrero (Eds.), *Handbook of communication and emotion* (pp. 404-423). San Diego: Academic Press.

Kellermann, K. (1984). The negativity effect and its implications for initial interaction. *Communication Monographs, 51,* 37-55.

Kinder, D. (1994). Reason and emotion in American political life. In R. C. Schank & E. Langer (Eds.), *Beliefs, reasoning, and decision-making* (pp. 272-314). Hillsdale, NJ: Lawrence Erlbaum.

Kopfman, J. E., Smith, S. W., Ah Yun, J. K., & Hodges, A. (1998). Affective and cognitive reactions to narrative versus statistical evidence organ donation messages. *Journal of Applied Communication Research, 26,* 279-300.

Lane, R. D., Reiman, E. M., Ahern, G. L., Schwartz, G. E., & Davidson, R. J. (1997). Neuroanatomical correlates of happiness, sadness, and disgust. *American Journal of Psychiatry, 154,* 926-933.

Larsen, R. J., & Diener, E. (1992). Promises and problems with the circumplex model of emotion. In M. S. Clark (Ed.), *Review of personality and social psychology: Emotion* (Vol. 13, pp. 25-50). Newbury Park, CA: Sage.

LaTour, M. S., Pitts, R. E., & Snook-Luther, D. C. (1990). Female nudity, arousal, and ad response: An experimental investigation. *Journal of Advertising, 19,* 51-62.

LaTour, M. S., & Rotfeld, H. J. (1997). There are threats and (maybe) fear-caused arousal: Theory and confusions of appeals to fear and fear arousal itself. *Journal of Advertising, 26,* 45-59.

Lazarus, R. S. (1991). *Emotion and adaptation.* New York: Oxford University Press.

Levenson, R. W. (1988). Emotion and the autonomic nervous system: A prospectus for research on autonomic specificity. In H. Wagner (Ed.), *Social psychophysiology and emotion: Theory and clinical applications* (pp. 17-42). Chichester, UK: Wiley.

Levenson, R. W., Ekman, P., & Friesen, W. V. (1990). Voluntary facial action generates emotion-specific autonomic nervous system activity. *Psychophysiology, 27,* 363-384.

Mackie, D. M., & Worth, L. T. (1989). Processing deficits and the mediation of positive affect in persuasion. *Journal of Personality and Social Psychology, 57,* 27-40.

Mano, H. (1997). Affect and persuasion: The influence of pleasantness and arousal on attitude formation and message elaboration. *Psychology & Marketing, 14,* 315-335.

Marcus, G. E. (1988). The structure of emotional response: 1984 presidential candidates. *American Political Science Review, 82,* 736-761.

Marcus, G. E., & Mackuen, M. B. (1993). Anxiety, enthusiasm, and the vote: The emotional underpinnings of learning and involvement during presidential campaigns. *American Political Science Review, 87,* 672-685.

Meijnders, A. L. (1998). *Climate change and changing attitudes: Effect of negative emotion on information processing.* Unpublished doctoral dissertation, Eindhoven University of Technology, Eindhoven, The Netherlands.

Miller, D. W., & Marks, L. J. (1992). Mental imagery and sound effects in radio commercials. *Journal of Advertising, 21,* 83-93.

Miller, D. W., & Marks, L. J. (1997). The effects of imagery-evoking radio advertising strategies on affective responses. *Psychology & Marketing, 14,* 337-360.

Mongeau, P. A. (1998). Another look at fear-arousing persuasive appeals. In M. Allen & R. W. Preiss (Eds.), *Persuasion: Advances through meta-analysis* (pp. 53-68). Cresskill, NJ: Hampton.

Ortony, A., Clore, G. L., & Collins, A. (1988). *The cognitive structure of emotions.* New York: Cambridge University Press.

Pallak, S. R., Murroni, E., & Koch, J. (1983). Communicator attractiveness and expertise, emotional versus rational appeals, and persuasion: A heuristic versus systematic processing interpretation. *Social Cognition, 2,* 122-141.

Pham, M. T. (1996). Cue representation and selection effects of arousal on persuasion. *Journal of Consumer Research, 22,* 373-387.

Pinto, M. B., & Priest, S. (1991). Guilt appeals in advertising: An exploratory study. *Psychological Reports, 69,* 375-385.

Plutchik, R. (1984). Emotions: A psychoevolutionary perspective. In K. R. Scherer & P. Ekman (Eds.), *Approaches to emotion* (pp. 197-219). Hillsdale, NJ: Lawrence Erlbaum.

Preston, I. L. (1968). Relationships among emotional, intellectual, and rational appeals in advertising. *Speech Monographs, 35,* 504-511.

Reisenzein, R. (1994). Pleasure-arousal theory and the intensity of emotions. *Journal of Personality and Social Psychology, 67,* 525-539.

Roseman, I. J., Wiest, C., & Swartz, T. S. (1994). Phenomenology, behaviors, and goals differentiate discrete emotions. *Journal of Personality and Social Psychology, 67,* 206-221.

Russell, J. A. (1979). Affective space is bipolar. *Journal of Personality and Social Psychology, 37,* 345-356.

Russell, J. A., & Carroll, J. M. (1999). On the bipolarity of positive and negative affect. *Psychological Bulletin, 125,* 3-30.

Russell, J. A., & Feldman Barrett, L. (1999). Core affect, prototypical emotional episodes, and other things called *emotion:* Dissecting the elephant. *Journal of Personality and Social Psychology, 76,* 805-819.

Scherer, K. R. (1984). On the nature and function of emotion: A component process approach. In K. R. Scherer & P. Ekman (Eds.), *Approaches to emotion* (pp. 293-317). Hillsdale, NJ: Lawrence Erlbaum.

Shaver, P., Schwartz, J., Kirson, D., & O'Connor, C. (1987). Emotion knowledge: Further exploration of a prototype approach. *Journal of Personality and Social Psychology, 52,* 1061-1086.

Simonson, N. R., & Lundy, R. M. (1967). The effectiveness of persuasive communication presented under conditions of irrelevant fear. *Journal of Communication, 16,* 32-37.

Sinclair, R. C., Mark, M. M., & Clore, G. L. (1994). Mood-related persuasion depends on (mis)attributions. *Social Cognition, 12,* 309-326.

Sonbonmatsu, D. M., & Kardes, F. R. (1988). The effects of physiological arousal on information processing and persuasion. *Journal of Consumer Research, 15,* 379-385.

Stiff, J. B. (1986). Cognitive processing of persuasive message cues: A meta-analytic review of the effects of supporting information on attitudes. *Communication Monographs, 53,* 75-89.

Stout, P. A., & Sego, T. (1994). Emotions elicited by threat appeals and their impact on persuasion. In K. W. King (Ed.), *Proceedings of the 1994 Con-*

ference of the American Academy of Advertising (pp. 8-16). Athens, GA: American Academy of Advertising.

Thayer, R. E. (1989). *The biopsychology of mood and arousal.* New York: Oxford University Press.

Tooby, J., & Cosmides, L. (1990). The past explains the present: Emotional adaptations and the structure of ancestral environments. *Ethology and Sociobiology, 11,* 375-424.

Waldron, V. R., & Cegala, D. J. (1992). Assessing conversational cognition: Levels of cognitive theory and associated methodological requirements. *Human Communication Research, 18,* 599-622.

Watson, D., & Tellegen, A. (1985). Toward a consensual structure of mood. *Psychological Bulletin, 98,* 219-235.

Watson, D., Wiese, D., Vaidya, J., & Tellegen, A. (1999). The two general activation systems of affect: Structural findings, evolutionary considerations, and psychobiological evidence. *Journal of Personality and Social Psychology, 76,* 820-838.

Wegener, D. T., & Petty, R. E. (1996). Effects of mood on persuasion processes: Enhancing, reducing, and biasing scrutiny of attitude-relevant information. In L. L. Martin & A. Tesser (Eds.), *Striving and feeling: Interactions among goals, affect, and self-regulation* (pp. 329-362). Mahwah, NJ: Lawrence Erlbaum.

Worth, L. T., & Mackie, D. M. (1987). Cognitive mediation of positive affect in persuasion. *Social Cognition, 5,* 76-94.

Zanna, M. P., Deitweiler, R. A., & Olson, J. M. (1984). Physiological mediation of attitude maintenance, formation, and change. In W. M. Waid (Ed.), *Sociophysiology* (pp. 163-195). New York: Springer-Verlag.

17

Guilt as a Mechanism of Persuasion

This chapter discusses the role of guilt as a mechanism of social influence. An introductory section offers a general sketch of the nature of guilt. The next two sections summarize extant research findings concerning guilt and anticipated guilt as mechanisms of persuasion, drawn from a variety of research venues. A concluding section fits together several puzzling research findings and identifies some promising foci for future research attention.

BACKGROUND

Guilt can be understood broadly as a negative emotional state aroused when an actor's conduct is at variance with an actor's own standards (Baumeister, Stillwell, & Heatherton, 1994; Miceli, 1992). A paradigmatic guilt-arousing circumstance is one in which a person has acted in some manner inconsistent with his or her own conception of proper conduct. For example, the sorts of situations that persons recall as especially associated with guilt feelings are ones that involve conduct such as ly-

ing, stealing, failing to perform duties, neglecting others, failing to maintain a diet or exercise plan, and cheating (Keltner & Buswell, 1996; Tangney, 1992). Thus, guilt involves some self-perceived shortfall with respect to one's own standards, where the focus of attention is some particular behavior.[1]

The reactions characteristically associated with guilt make it especially well-suited to exploitation for purposes of social influence. Among the beliefs and feelings distinctively associated with guilt (as opposed to other emotions) are reactions such as "thinking that you were in the wrong," "thinking that you shouldn't have done what you did," "feeling like undoing what you have done," "wanting to make up for what you've done wrong," and "wanting to be forgiven" (Roseman, Wiest, & Swartz, 1994, p. 215). When persons recall guilt experiences, they commonly describe themselves as wanting to make amends, feeling responsible, feeling as though they had violated some moral standard, and wishing they had acted differently (Tangney, Miller, Flicker, & Barlow, 1996).

329

Plainly, guilt (in contrast to, say, sadness) has a distinctive action-motivating character.

This action-motivating aspect of guilt presumably is connected to guilt's being based in a transgression of the actor's own standards. A person whose behavior violates some standard (norm or value) that he or she does not accept might acknowledge responsibility for the conduct but presumably will not experience guilt (Miceli, 1992, p. 99) and so might not feel quite the same motivation to make amends or take corrective action. But when the action is inconsistent with the self's own standards, then guilt (and its associated behavioral motivations) can be aroused.

AROUSING GUILT

Guilt can straightforwardly be put to the service of social influence by the influencing agent's arousing guilt in the target, which in turn motivates the target's performance of the desired action. There are two ways in which an influencing agent might attempt to arouse guilt in an influence target. One is for the influencer to draw the target's attention to some existing inconsistency between the target's standards and the target's previous conduct, and the other is for the influencer to induce the target to act in a way that creates such an inconsistency.

Drawing Attention to an Existing Inconsistency

An influencing agent can exploit some existing inconsistency between the target's previous behavior and the target's own standards simply by drawing the target's attention to the inconsistency; the target's resulting guilt feelings then provide a basis for shaping the target's future behavior. Three different areas of empirical research illuminate this sort of guilt-

based influence mechanism: studies of guilt arousal in interpersonal relationships, research concerning guilt appeals in persuasive messages, and studies of hypocrisy induction.

Guilt Arousal in Interpersonal Relationships. In everyday life, guilt arousal and attempted guilt arousal occur primarily in the context of close relationships (Baumeister, Reis, & Delespaul, 1995, Study 2; Baumeister, Stillwell, & Heatherton, 1995, Study 2; Jones, Kugler, & Adams, 1995; Vangelisti, Daly, & Rudnick, 1991). People seek to arouse guilt in others primarily for purposes of influence—as a means of inducing the target to undertake some action, refrain from some action, or stop some ongoing action (Vangelisti et al., 1991).

There are a variety of specific ways in which a person may attempt to arouse guilt, such as indicating that the target is not meeting some obligation that is part of the target's relationship with the influencer, pointing out that the target's behavior does not reflect the target's knowledge of appropriate conduct, and displaying some sacrifice being made on the influencer's part on behalf of the target (for a discussion of different techniques of guilt induction, see especially Vangelisti et al., 1991; see also Miceli, 1992, and Sommer & Baumeister, 1997). However, each of the different techniques "may generally be considered a variation on saying 'see how you are hurting me' " (Sommer & Baumeister, 1997, p. 43), and in the context of close relationships, hurting the other would plainly represent a transgression of the target's own standards. Drawing the target's attention to such conduct thus offers the prospect of guilt arousal and subsequent behavioral influence.

There has been little research directed at assessing the persuasive effectiveness of guilt induction in interpersonal relationships. Some self-report evidence suggests that targets of such guilt induction do perceive the aroused guilt to have had an impact on their subsequent behavior (Baumeister, Stillwell, & Heatherton, 1995, Study 1). However, targets of guilt induction also appear to resent this use of guilt (Baumeister, Stillwell, & Heatherton, 1995, Study 2; see also Rubin & Shaffer, 1987).

Guilt Appeals in Persuasive Messages. Guilt appeals in persuasive messages, such as advertisements, commonly have two parts. One presents material designed to evoke guilt, characteristically through drawing attention to some existing inconsistency between the receiver's standards and the receiver's actions, and the other describes the message's recommended viewpoint or action, which is meant to offer the prospect of guilt reduction. For example, a consumer advertisement might seek to make receivers feel guilt about the plight of the homeless and then ask for a charitable donation (which offers the prospect of reducing the guilt). Such guilt appeals can vary in any number of ways, but several studies of guilt appeal messages have examined the effects (on guilt arousal and persuasive outcomes) of variations in the explicitness of the guilt appeal (e.g., Coulter & Pinto, 1995; Pinto & Priest, 1991; Yinon, Bizman, Cohen, & Segev, 1976). The fundamental experimental contrast in this research thus is between relatively direct explicit guilt appeals and relatively less explicit ones.

A meta-analytic review of this research has found that more explicit guilt appeals do arouse significantly greater guilt than do less explicit appeals (expressed as a correlation, the mean observed effect corresponds to $r = .43$). However, more explicit guilt appeals are significantly less persuasive than their less explicit counterparts (mean $r = -.26$) (O'Keefe, 2000). This review also found no support for the supposition that moderately explicit appeals might yield both greater guilt and greater persuasion than would either more or less explicit appeals. In general, when guilt-based appeals (of any level of explicitness) successfully arouse relatively greater guilt, those appeals are unlikely to be persuasive.

The finding that appeals arousing greater guilt do not enjoy correspondingly greater persuasive success is rather striking. After all, guilt is characteristically associated with feelings of wanting to change one's actions, and hence appeals that arouse greater guilt might naturally be expected to effect greater change. A plausible explanation of the observed effect is that the more explicit guilt appeals might have evoked annoyance, resentment, anger, irritation, or similar reactions. As noted previously, studies of interpersonal guilt-based influence attempts have reported evidence of negative reactions such as anger and resentment (Baumeister, Stillwell, & Heatherton, 1995, Study 2; Rubin & Shaffer, 1987). And similar reactions have been reported in studies of guilt-based persuasive appeals (Coulter, Cotte, & Moore, 1997; Coulter & Pinto, 1995; Englis, 1990; Pinto & Priest, 1991). Thus, although explicit guilt appeals may create greater guilt, they may also arouse other negative feelings that interfere with persuasive success.

Hypocrisy Induction. The persuasive effects of drawing attention to inconsistencies between the target's conduct and the target's standards is also illustrated by research on hypocrisy induction. In these studies, hypocrisy condition participants are led to advocate some position they support but are reminded of their failure to act consistently with that view. The expectation is that participants will alter their behavior so as to become more consistent with their beliefs. For instance, in Aronson, Fried, and Stone's (1991) investigation, hypocrisy condition participants were asked to describe a situation in which they failed to use condoms; this served as a reminder of their past behavior. They then composed and delivered a short speech advocating condom use. Such participants subsequently avowed significantly greater intentions to increase their use of condoms than did participants in control conditions (for similar effects, see Dickerson, Thibodeau, Aronson, & Miller, 1992; Fried & Aronson, 1995; Stone, Aronson, Crain, Winslow, & Fried, 1994).

This research has usually been treated as exemplifying dissonance-based influence mechanisms. The hypocrisy induction is presumed to create dissonance through the "inconsistency between advocated personal standards and past inconsistent behaviors" (Fried & Aronson, 1995, p. 926). Plainly, however, such inconsistency is a paradigmatic guilt-inducing circumstance, and hence the observed effects of hypocrisy induction might reflect guilt arousal effects rather than dissonance arousal effects.[2] For present purposes, it is enough to notice that, viewed from a guilt-based perspective, hypocrisy induction research illustrates the persuasive power of drawing the attention of influence targets to existing inconsistencies between their conduct and their standards.

Summary. Arousing guilt by drawing the target's attention to existing inconsistencies between the target's conduct and the target's own standards is potentially a successful mechanism of influence but can also be counterproductive. In particular, interpersonal guilt induction and guilt-based persuasive appeals seem especially prone to evoke negative reactions that may undermine the success of influence attempts.

Creating an Inconsistency

Instead of drawing the target's attention to previous conduct that is inconsistent with the target's standards, an influencing agent might arouse guilt by inducing the target to act in a fashion inconsistent with the target's standards, thus creating the inconsistency that arouses guilt in the target. Two areas of research may illustrate this sort of guilt-based influence mechanism: research on the *transgression-compliance* hypothesis and studies of the *door-in-the-face* (DITF) influence strategy.

Transgression-Compliance. The natural action-motivating quality of guilt, and particularly the guilt-related impulse to alter one's actions and make up for what one has done, suggests that persons who commit transgressions (and so presumably experience guilt) will be more likely than persons who have not committed such transgressions to engage in helping behavior such as complying with a request. This transgression-compliance hypothesis has been studied very extensively (see, e.g., Boster et al., 1999; Carlsmith & Gross, 1969; Freedman, Wallington, & Bless, 1967; McMillen, Jackson, & Austin, 1974). A representative research design is that of Konoske, Staple, and Graf (1979), who had transgression condition participants apparently upset a graduate student's carefully arranged computer cards. Subsequently, participants were asked by a confederate to make telephone calls to prospective participants. Transgression condition participants volunteered to make significantly more calls than did participants in a nontransgression control condition. Notice that in this research paradigm, guilt is aroused not by the influencer's calling attention to some past transgression by the target but rather through the influencer's actually creating the target's transgression (or the appearance thereof).

A recent meta-analysis of this research concluded that transgressions have a powerful effect on subsequent guilt and compliance. Compared to persons in no-transgression control conditions, persons who have committed transgressions feel significantly greater guilt (the mean effect corresponds to $r = .45$) and are significantly more likely to comply (mean effect of $r = .28$) (O'Keefe, 2000). Moreover, the transgression-compliance effect is especially robust in the sense that it obtains under a variety of conditions. It occurs no matter whether the transgression is accidental (e.g., knocking over someone's computer cards) or purposeful (e.g., telling a lie), it occurs no matter whether the subsequent compliance involves a direct request (e.g., being asked to volunteer for an experiment) or simply an opportunity to help (e.g., encountering someone who has just spilled a stack of papers), it occurs irrespective of whether the request (or helping opportunity) is presented by the victim of the transgression or by someone else, and it occurs irrespective of whether compliance benefits the victim (O'Keefe, 2000). That is, under all of these conditions, there is a dependably positive effect of transgression on compliance, with no dependable difference in the size of the effects under these varying circumstances. These findings confirm the powerfulness of transgression-induced guilt as a motivator of compliance and testify to its vigor.

However, the negative feelings engendered by transgression can be neutralized prior to the compliance opportunity and thereby lose their compliance-motivating power. A number of transgression-compliance studies contain an experimental variation in which some event intervenes between transgression and compliance that offers the prospect of neutralizing or alleviating negative feelings (e.g., Cialdini, Darby, & Vincent, 1973; Dietrich & Berkowitz, 1997; McMillen, 1971). The intervening events vary across these studies (including things such as bolstering the participant's self-esteem, having the victim excuse the transgression, and having an opportunity to express one's feelings about one's conduct)

but share the property of potentially reducing or nullifying any negative feelings aroused by the transgression. A meta-analytic review has discovered that the observed general effect of transgression on compliance evaporates when such an event intervenes between transgression and compliance (O'Keefe, 2000).

The Door-in-the-Face Influence Strategy. In the DITF influence strategy, a relatively large initial request is made of a person, which the person declines. Then a smaller request is made, with the hope that the person's having declined the initial request will make the person more likely to comply with the second request. For example, in Cialdini et al.'s (1975, Experiment 1) classic investigation, unaccompanied individuals were approached on a campus sidewalk by a student who asked that each person spend 2 hours a week, for a minimum of 2 years, as an unpaid volunteer counselor at the County Juvenile Detention Center. This request was always refused. The second request was that the receiver serve as an unpaid volunteer chaperone, spending 2 hours one afternoon or evening taking a group of juveniles from the detention center to the zoo. When only the smaller request was presented, 17% agreed; however, in the DITF condition, 50% agreed. An extensive body of subsequent research has confirmed that the DITF strategy can indeed dependably yield such enhanced compliance, with a mean effect (expressed as r) of about .10 to .15 (for reviews, see Dillard, Hunter, & Burgoon, 1984; Fern, Monroe, & Avila, 1986; O'Keefe & Hale, 1998, 2001).

It does not seem to have been widely appreciated that the DITF format can be seen to parallel the format of transgression-compliance designs. In each situation, there is initially a transgression (e.g., harm is inflicted on another, a lie is told, a prosocial request is refused), and subsequently a compliance opportunity is presented (commonly in the form of a request). And in each situation, the occurrence of the transgression enhances compliance. Hence, just as transgression-compliance results naturally suggest a guilt-based explanation, so might DITF results, as proposed by O'Keefe and Figgé (1997). In their analysis, DITF success occurs because refusal of the initial request arouses guilt and acceptance of the second request reduces such guilt. That is, the influencer invites the target's transgression (through the refused initial request), thereby arousing guilt, and then proffers a guilt reduction mechanism (in the form of second-request compliance).

This guilt-based explanation appears consistent with the observed patterns of DITF effects. For example, DITF effects are stronger when the requests come from prosocial organizations (e.g., charities, environmental groups) as opposed to for-profit organizations (see Dillard et al., 1984; O'Keefe & Hale, 1998, 2001). From the perspective of a guilt-based analysis, this effect can be seen to reflect the greater guilt likely engendered by declining prosocial (as opposed to for-profit) requests (for more extensive discussion of factors moderating DITF effects, see O'Keefe & Hale, 1998, 2001). It remains to be seen whether more direct investigations of guilt's role in DITF processes will confirm the soundness of a guilt-based explanation (for some complexities, see O'Keefe & Figgé, 1999), but the parallels with transgression-compliance situations certainly are suggestive of similar underlying processes.

Summary. Guilt-based social influence mechanisms involving the influencing agent's creating an inconsistency between the target's standards and the target's conduct (i.e., creating a transgression) can be quite powerful means of influence.[3] Moreover, these influence mechanisms do not appear to have the same potential for evoking negative reactions (resentment or anger) as do guilt-based mechanisms based on pointing out the inconsistency.[4]

ANTICIPATED GUILT

Plainly, aroused guilt can be an important mechanism of influence. But there is another (as yet little studied) way in which guilt can figure in social influence, namely, through the behavioral effects of anticipated guilt feelings.

The general idea that anticipated feelings can shape behavioral choices has received support in various behavioral domains. Anticipated emotions have been found to play a role in shaping intentions and actions in studies of weight regulation (Bagozzi, Baumgartner, & Pieters, 1998), salesperson behavior (Brown, Cron, & Slocum, 1997), entertainment choices (Zillmann & Bryant, 1985, 1994), and drug and alcohol use (Richard, van der Pligt, & de Vries, 1996a). Intentions or behaviors concerning mammography participation (Lechner, de Vries, & Offermans, 1997), consumer purchases (Simonson, 1992), and safe sex practices (Bakker, Buunk, & Manstead, 1997; Richard, van der Pligt, & de Vries, 1996b) have been found to be related specifically to anticipated regret (for general discussions of research concerning anticipated regret, see van der Pligt & Richard, 1994; van der Pligt & de Vries, 1998). And although there is little direct evidence concerning guilt specifically, Birkimer, Johnston, and Berry (1993) did find that persons' estimates of how guilty they would feel if they were to engage in various health risk behaviors are related to avoidance of those behaviors; people avoid the actions that they expect would make them feel guilty.

Where anticipated guilt might influence conduct, a corresponding avenue for persuasion is available. An influencing agent might encourage the target's anticipated guilt feelings as a way of shaping the target's conduct.

There is some evidence that consumer advertisers are aware of this alternative guilt-based influence mechanism. In sampling 24 popular magazines, Huhmann and Brotherton (1997) found that guilt-based consumer advertising uses both advertisements that try to arouse guilt and advertisements that draw attention to anticipated guilt (using appeals that "offer consumers an opportunity to avoid a transgression" [p. 37]).

Not much is yet known about exactly what alternative means (e.g., message variations) might successfully arouse anticipated guilt, or about the nature of other elements (e.g., a recommended course of action) that might be needed to connect such anticipated guilt to desired influence outcomes, or about when or whether efforts at creating anticipated guilt might evoke the negative reactions sometimes associated with guilt arousal mechanisms. All of these are plainly useful foci for future research attention. But as one illustration of the unappreciated potential of anticipated guilt's role in social influence, consider its possible contribution to DITF effects. O'Keefe and Figgé's (1997) analysis proposed that second-request compliance in DITF settings is motivated by a desire to reduce the guilt created by first-request refusal (and so might be said to be motivated by the anticipation of guilt reduction); however, second-request compliance might instead (or also) be motivated by a desire to avoid additional guilt anticipated to arise from refusing the second request (for some relevant evidence, see O'Keefe & Figgé, 1999). In any case, the general point to be noticed is that anticipated guilt feelings may prove to be as useful a basis of social influence strategies as are actual guilt feelings.

PUZZLES AND CONJECTURES

A number of the research findings concerning guilt as a mechanism of influence are rather puzzling. As just one example, consider that transgression's compliance-enhancing effects are not influenced by whether the victim of the transgression benefits from the compliant act (O'Keefe, 2000). Given that one of the feelings characteristically associated with guilt is "wanting to make amends" (Tangney et al., 1996), one might expect that transgressions would be relatively more powerful motivators of compliance in circumstances where the victim benefits from compliance. This curious finding (and others) can perhaps be illuminated by reconsidering the nature of guilt.

Guilt Reconsidered

It is worth reanalyzing the close relationship between guilt and one's sense of self. Put briefly, I want to suggest that guilt motivates self-affirmation because guilt-inducing actions represent threats to self-integrity. This idea can be seen as derived from (or as fitting within) self-affirmation theory (Steele, 1988; Steele & Liu, 1983). Self-affirmation theory proposes that persons seek to maintain an image of the self as "adaptively and morally adequate"; hence, when faced with "information that threatens the perceived adequacy or integrity of the self," a person's self-affirmation processes are activated and continue until the self-image is restored (Steele, 1988, p. 262). This framework has been used to explain a number of diverse phenomena (e.g., how name-calling can enhance compliance [Steele, 1975]) and, in particular, has been offered as an alternative interpretation of much dissonance-based research (see, e.g., Steele & Spencer, 1992; Steele, Spencer, & Lynch, 1993).

Although self-affirmation theory appears to have given little explicit attention to guilt, it seems plain that the framework offers a promising way of understanding guilt. The general idea that guilt-inducing actions involve self-discrepancy is rather common (if sometimes implicit) and can be detected in a variety of theoretical discussions (e.g., Higgins, 1987; Kugler & Jones, 1992; Miceli, 1992). In fact, it is almost definitionally part of guilt that it involves conduct that is somehow discrepant from the actor's image of self (specifically, from the standards to which the actor holds his or her own conduct).[5]

This aspect of guilt is important for understanding the consequences of guilt arousal. Given that guilt-inducing actions challenge self-integrity, guilt should encourage a search for self-affirmation. Indeed, in the various research lines discussed previously, the observed sequelae to guilt induction all can be seen to represent means of self-affirmation. In transgression-compliance research formats and DITF situations, helping-related compliance plainly offers the prospect of reaffirming the self ("yes, I'm a good and helpful person"); in guilt appeals, the recommended course of action attempts to supply a means of self-affirmation ("yes, I'm a good parent"); in hypocrisy induction research formats, behavioral change reaffirms the self's values ("yes, I really do believe in safe sex practices"); and in interpersonal relationships, self-affirmation can be obtained through changing the behavior that is the basis of the influencer's complaint ("yes, I'm a good partner"). In short, then, the conjecture here is that guilt works as a mechanism of persuasion because it provokes self-affirmation processes.

Some Puzzles Illuminated

This way of approaching guilt promises to shed some light on various research findings concerning the role of guilt in social influence. These findings concern the moderators of transgression-compliance effects, negative reactions to guilt-based persuasive efforts, and the magnitude of the observed effects.

Moderators of Transgression-Compliance Effects. Consider again the seemingly curious finding that transgression enhances compliance independent of whether the person victimized by the transgression is helped by the act of compliance. This seems an unexpected result if one focuses on the guilt-related feelings of "wanting to make amends," "wanting to make up for what you've done wrong," and the like. But if, instead, people who are feeling guilty want first and foremost self-affirmation, then this finding is a little less puzzling. One way of achieving such self-affirmation might indeed be to "make amends"—to somehow try to "make it up to" the victimized party (and so do something that benefits the victim). But this is not the only way in which self-affirmation might be obtained. Any helping behavior (no matter whether the victim benefits from it) might provide such affirmation of the self's worth.

The same reasoning explains why the transgression-compliance effect is not influenced by whether the victim of the transgression makes the compliance request (O'Keefe, 2000). Again, affirmation of the self can be accomplished in various ways. Responding affirmatively to any helping request (whether from the victim or from someone else) can provide the desired self-affirmation. Indeed, there need not even be an explicit request for help; transgression leads to enhanced helping even when, instead of an explicit request, there is simply a behavioral opportunity to help (as when encountering someone who has just dropped a stack of papers [O'Keefe, 2000]). When a person who has committed a transgression is thereby more likely to spontaneously help in a circumstance where the victim neither presents the helping opportunity nor benefits from the helping, it is difficult to resist the conclusion that generalized self-affirmation processes are at work.

Finally, attention to self-affirmation processes also nicely accommodates the previously mentioned finding that the transgression-compliance effect can be eliminated by an intervening positive event (O'Keefe, 2000). This effect is another indication that guilt feelings, even if aroused by one's actions toward another, can be neutralized in ways other than compensatory action toward that other. Although people may genuinely want to make amends, the underlying function (of reactions to guilt feelings) appears to be self-repair. Hence, when self-repair is obtained in a way other than compliance or compensatory action (as through those intervening positive events), the person does not need to engage in compliance to obtain the self-affirming result.

In short, a number of otherwise curious findings concerning transgression's effects on compliance appear to be illuminated by recognizing the self-affirmation processes set in motion by guilt-inducing events. Guilt engages fundamentally self-directed, and not other-directed, processes. Some of the feelings characteristically associated with guilt do concern other-directed actions (e.g., wanting to make amends, wanting to undo what one has done), but these feelings arise because such actions provide a means of self-affirmation.[6]

Negative Reactions to Guilt-Based Persuasive Efforts. A variety of puzzles are connected with the negative reactions (e.g., anger, annoyance, resentment) sometimes associated with the use of guilt as an influence mechanism. It should be noticed that, as yet, there is little detailed evidence concerning the nature of the mechanisms underlying such reactions, the particular situations that might encourage such reactions, and so forth. This plainly provides an important area for future research. But the evidence in hand does offer two findings that need explanation. One is that the negative reactions occur at all, and the other is the apparent difference among various guilt arousal mechanisms in their propensity to evoke such reactions.

It seems that guilt arousal attempts have a distinctive capacity to evoke reactions such as resentment, anger, and annoyance. One might initially hypothesize that any attempted emotional manipulation will evoke similar reactions. However, there is no evidence to suggest that, say, empathy-based or altruism-based appeals are as prone to generate such effects (in fact, for precisely the opposite indication, see Rubin & Shaffer, 1987). Another more specific version of this hypothesis might be that attempted arousal of a negative emotion can induce such reactions. But even this seems insufficiently specific. For example, there is no indication that annoyance is routinely evoked by fear appeals in the way it seems to be by guilt appeals. And although the apparent resentment aroused in the target may have some similarities to reactance (Brehm & Brehm, 1981), a reactance-based account would need to indicate why specifically guilt arousal attempts would arouse reactance more commonly or forcefully than would influence attempts invoking some other basis of influence (e.g., fear, pity, empathy, self-interest). An additional complexity is introduced by the apparent differences among guilt arousal mechanisms in their propensity to arouse negative reactions. For instance, resentment and anger appear more likely to be evoked by relatively explicit guilt appeals in persuasive messages than by hypocrisy induction manipulations.

A focus on the connection between guilt and the self provides a useful basis for some conjectures concerning these findings. Because guilt involves self-discrepancies, an influencer who explicitly attempts to arouse guilt is, in a sense, questioning the target's self by pointing out the inconsistency between the target's conduct and the target's principles. That is, attempted guilt arousal involves a challenge to the target's self in ways that other influence mechanisms do not—and for precisely that reason has greater capacity to evoke resentment, anger, or annoyance. After all, I might (with some reason) think that others are not entitled to tell me what is discrepant from my self; only I get to decide that. It's one thing if I notice weaknesses in my self-integrity; it's something else if others deign to point them out to me.[7]

Thus, one ought to expect a difference between self-generated guilt (i.e., guilt arising from the target's having independently noticed the discrepancy between the target's conduct and the target's principles) and other-generated guilt (i.e., guilt arising from someone else's having pointed out the discrepancy to the target) with respect to accompanying anger or annoyance. When the target recognizes the inconsistency himself or herself without having it pointed out explicitly by the influencing agent (as in transgression-compliance formats, the DITF strategy, or hypocrisy induction manipulations), resentment or anger seem less likely to be evoked. However, when the influencing agent explicitly draws attention to the inconsistency (as in common interpersonal guilt induction methods or relatively explicit guilt-based persuasive appeals), such negative reactions are more likely.[8] That is, the more apparent the influencer's intention to arouse guilt, the more likely it is that the target will experience negative reactions such as resentment and anger. From this vantage point, it is unsurprising that studies of guilt-based persuasive appeals should have found that more explicit guilt appeals are less persuasive than less explicit ones (O'Keefe, 2000) given that presumably the more explicit efforts at arousing guilt will be more likely to produce negative reactions.

However, relationally significant others may have a special status as guilt inducers. Such others are in an especially good position to know what is discrepant from one's self and simultaneously may enjoy something of a privileged position with respect to pointing out discrepancies precisely because they are relationally significant. Hence, although influence targets report feelings of resentment from guilt-based interpersonal influence attempts, they also report changing their behavior in response to those attempts (Baumeister, Stillwell, & Heatherton, 1995). Indeed, one may sense something of a progression here: Consumer advertising that employs explicit guilt appeals arouses guilt but also resentment sufficient to undermine persuasion, guilt arousal by relationally significant others also creates both guilt and resentment but can still enjoy persuasive success, and nonobvious means of guilt arousal (as in the transgression-compliance or hypocrisy induction format) create guilt without much resentment and hence can have unalloyed persuasive impact.

This analysis of the negative reactions attendant to guilt induction attempts suggests a possible difference between the use of aroused guilt and the use of anticipated guilt in the service of social influence. The use of anticipated guilt as an influence mechanism may be less susceptible to reactions such as resentment and anger precisely because the use of anticipated guilt does not require claiming that the influence target has already committed a transgression.

To bring out the difference here, consider the very different stances (identities or roles) available to the influencing agent when attempting to arouse guilt or when attempting to employ anticipated guilt as a mechanism of influence. In the case of anticipated guilt, the influencing agent can act almost as a coach or helper: "I want to help you think through what you want, help you consider how you will feel if you do or don't do X, help you to see what actions will be consistent with your self, or help you see what you really want to do here by encouraging you to contemplate how you will feel." But in the case of guilt arousal, the influencer characteristically will have to adopt an oppositional accusatory stance: "You did this bad, self-inconsistent thing, and you should change or fix it." The resentment that might naturally be generated by an accusatory stance is perhaps less likely to be aroused when the influencer adopts a coaching role—and thus the use of anticipated guilt as an influence mechanism might not necessarily be subject to the same negative reactions sometimes aroused by the use of aroused guilt.

It plainly will be useful for future research to focus on the negative reactions to guilt induction attempts, especially as these appear to have the capacity to undermine the successful use of guilt as a mechanism of influence. Specification of exactly what negative reactions occur, identification of the specific features of guilt induction efforts that appear to evoke or minimize such reactions, information about the persuasion-relevant consequences of the negative reactions, and clarification of the underlying mechanisms will be welcomed.

Magnitude of Effects. There is one other aspect of these research findings worth noticing, namely, the relative size of compliance effects observed in standard transgression-compliance formats and in DITF implementations. As discussed previously, these two lines of research are conceptually parallel; there is initially a transgression of some sort (e.g., a lie is told, a prosocial request is refused), and subsequently a helping opportunity arises (typically in the form of a request). But transgression-compliance studies have produced a significantly larger mean effect size (mean $r = .28$, $k = 31$, 95% CI bounds of .22 and .34

[O'Keefe, 2000]) than have DITF studies (mean $r = .10$, $k = 88$, 95% CI bounds of .05 and .14 [O'Keefe & Hale, 1998]). Given the apparent parallelism between the two circumstances, the difference in effect size wants explanation.

One straightforward possibility is that the kinds of "transgressions" common in DITF research formats (i.e., refusal of rather large prosocial requests) do not represent as great a threat to self-integrity, and hence do not generate as much guilt, as do the transgressions common in transgression-compliance research (e.g., lying or damaging someone's equipment). Rationales may be ready at hand for why one might sensibly decline to volunteer to spend 2 hours a week for a minimum of 2 years working with disadvantaged youths, but not for why one broke someone's camera. Thus, the need for self-affirmation may typically be greater in transgression-compliance studies than in DITF studies, resulting in larger compliance effects.[9]

Research Priorities

A number of promising research questions have been mentioned in the preceding discussion. As a way of suggesting some priorities for research attention in this area—and a way of underscoring just how much remains to be learned about guilt as a social influence mechanism—these can usefully be collected under four broad research foci.

First, clarification is needed concerning how message variations produce differential guilt arousal. Although experimenters have proved capable of arousing different levels of guilt in message recipients, little attention has been given to careful description of the message features associated with such variation in effect. A complete understanding of the operation of guilt-based persuasive appeals will

require some account of how message variations are associated with guilt arousal variations. In the absence of such an account, we
may find ourselves able to specify the persuasive consequences of arousing guilt in receivers but unable to specify how to bring about
guilt.

Second, clarification is needed of the negative reactions that appear capable of undermining guilt-based influence. Just what are
the relevant negative reactions (e.g., anger,
resentment, both, something else entirely)?
What mechanisms (e.g., reactance, perhaps
arising from negative face threat) underlie
these evoked reactions? Exactly how and why
do these reactions undermine the success of
guilt-based influence? Are there identifiable
features of influence situations that affect the
likelihood of these negative reactions? For
example, is it in fact the case that the more
apparent the influencer's intention to arouse
guilt, the more likely it is that the target will
experience negative reactions?

Third, it will be useful to consider the possible roles of self-affirmation processes in guilt.
As one example, there may be distinguish-
able varieties of guilt-evoking threats to self-
integrity, with corresponding variation in
compliance effects. As another example,
the existence of alternative means of self-
affirmation may create challenges to the successful use of guilt as an influence mechanism;
a consumer advertisement that arouses guilt
might encourage self-affirmation efforts of
various sorts but not necessarily the specific
course of action sought by the advertisement.

Finally, the role of anticipated guilt in social
influence deserves greater research attention.
Studies of the behavioral effects of other anticipated emotions plainly suggest the usefulness
of such attention. But it is not known what
message variations might dependably influence the anticipation of guilt, nor is it known
whether anticipated guilt will provide the
magnitude of influence potential that aroused

guilt does, nor is it known whether (as speculated here) influence mechanisms based in
anticipated guilt are less likely to evoke the
negative reactions commonly attendant to
guilt arousal mechanisms.

CONCLUSION

Guilt is plainly a potentially powerful mechanism of persuasive influence, but many aspects of guilt-based social influence have received only slight research attention. In some
ways, the inattention to guilt is unsurprising
given that studies of communicative social
influence have commonly focused on "rational" or "logical" aspects of influence (e.g.,
Fishbein & Ajzen, 1975). But continuing
exploration of how aroused guilt and anticipated guilt operate as mechanisms of influence is surely justified. In particular, linking
research on guilt-based influence to more
general theoretical models of the self and its
management appears to yield promising lines
of inquiry. Placing guilt in the context of these
broader processes helps to explain a number
of findings concerning guilt-based influence
(e.g., why transgression's effects on compliance appear unaffected by what would seem
to be plausible moderators, why guilt-based
influence distinctively appears capable of
evoking negative reactions) and offers the
prospect of stitching together a number of
previously unconnected lines of research.

NOTES

1. Current conceptualizations of guilt thus differentiate it from shame (another negative affective
response to transgression or failure) by virtue of
different foci of attention. In shame, the focus is on
the self, whereas in guilt, it is on a specific behavior
(see especially Lewis, 1971; see also Niedenthal,
Tangney, & Gavanski, 1994; Tangney, 1992,

1995). Thus, paradigmatically, a person might be ashamed of who he or she is but feel guilty about what he or she did.

2. In fact, it might not be necessary to choose between a guilt-based and a dissonance-based interpretation of this research. For example, "guilt" might be a folk psychological term applied to certain species of dissonance; that is, guilt might be a special case of dissonance. For discussions of the relationship between dissonance and guilt, see Baumeister, Stillwell, and Heatherton (1995, pp. 190-191), O'Keefe (2000), and Stice (1992).

3. One might well wonder about the ethics of these transgression-inducing influence mechanisms. In the previously discussed influence mechanisms that involved drawing the target's attention to prior behavior that is inconsistent with the target's standards, the relevant transgression (the inconsistent behavior) has already occurred and the influencing agent is merely pointing it out. But in transgression-compliance implementations (and, arguably, the DITF strategy), the circumstance seems closer to entrapment; the influencing agent devises a situation in which a transgression (or apparent transgression) is encouraged or created and then exploits the resulting guilt feelings for purposes of social influence.

4. There is some evidence that DITF implementations with extremely large first requests impede the strategy's success, and there has been speculation that this might reflect negative reactions to the initial request (see Even-Chen, Yinon, & Bizman, 1978; Schwarzwald, Raz, & Zvibel, 1979; Wang, Brownstein, & Katzev, 1989). However, any such negative reactions might simply reflect irritation at receiving an unreasonably large request, not resentment at having one's guilt manipulated. That is, the negative reactions to very large initial DITF requests (if, in fact, there are such reactions) may be something quite different from the negative reactions engendered by, for example, explicit guilt-based persuasive appeals.

5. A clarification is in order here. There are many kinds of self-discrepancy and correspondingly various different challenges to self-integrity. Guilt-inducing actions are not the only ones or even necessarily the most important ones (for discussions, see Higgins, 1987; Tangney, Niedenthal, Covert, & Barlow, 1998). But plainly guilt-inducing actions do involve a self-discrepancy and hence seem appropriately considered from the vantage point of self-affirmation theory.

6. Because shame concerns the self generally whereas guilt concerns specific conduct, one might expect that shame would evoke general self-affirmation and guilt would evoke compensation for the particular guilt-inducing action. But, as just seen, the evidence in hand is consistent with guilt's being equally amenable to self-affirmation through compensatory actions and through other means.

7. Although the possible connection of reactance (Brehm & Brehm, 1981) and negative face threats (Brown & Levinson, 1987) appears not to have been much noticed previously, this circumstance makes plain their relationship: the imposition (negative face threat, i.e., threat to the want that one's actions be unimpeded by others) represented by attempted guilt arousal might naturally (through the motivational state of reactance) evoke efforts at restoring freedom (as by resisting the action being sought).

8. Hypocrisy induction research formats do not involve creating any inconsistency, but neither do they involve explicitly pointing out the inconsistency. Rather, the situation is one in which the target is led naturally to notice the inconsistency without the influencing agent's explicitly drawing attention to it.

9. This may also provide a basis for explaining why DITF effects are influenced by whether the same person makes both requests (O'Keefe & Hale, 1998, 2001) but transgression-compliance effects are uninfluenced by whether the victim makes the compliance request (O'Keefe, 2000). If first-request refusal in the DITF situation does not generate the same guilt as does lying, then the liar will be more desperate for self-affirmation than will the request refuser (and so the liar will leap at self-affirmation possibilities that are declined by the request refuser). That is, with a sufficiently large threat to self-integrity (as occurs, ex hypothesi, in transgression-compliance research settings), persons seize on any opportunity for self-affirmation. In the DITF circumstance, self-affirmation is really needed only when facing the prospect of refusing an additional request from the same person (or an additional request that has the same beneficiary).

REFERENCES

Aronson, E., Fried, C., & Stone, J. (1991). Overcoming denial and increasing the intention to use condoms through the induction of hypocrisy. *American Journal of Public Health, 81,* 1636-1638.

Bagozzi, R. P., Baumgartner, H., & Pieters, R. (1998). Goal-directed emotions. *Cognition & Emotion, 12,* 1-26.

Bakker, A. B., Buunk, B. P., & Manstead, A. S. R. (1997). The moderating role of self-efficacy beliefs in the relationship between anticipated regret and condom use. *Journal of Applied Social Psychology, 27,* 2001-2014.

Baumeister, R. F., Reis, H. T., & Delespaul, P. A. E. G. (1995). Subjective and experiential correlates of guilt in daily life. *Personality and Social Psychology Bulletin, 21,* 1256-1268.

Baumeister, R. F., Stillwell, A. M., & Heatherton, T. F. (1994). Guilt: An interpersonal approach. *Psychological Bulletin, 115,* 243-267.

Baumeister, R. F., Stillwell, A. M., & Heatherton, T. F. (1995). Personal narratives about guilt: Role in action control and interpersonal relationships. *Basic and Applied Social Psychology, 178,* 173-198.

Birkimer, J. C., Johnston, P. L., & Berry, M. M. (1993). Guilt and help from friends: Variables related to healthy behavior. *Journal of Social Psychology, 133,* 683-692.

Boster, F. J., Mitchell, M. M., Lapinski, M. K., Cooper, H., Orrego, V., & Reinke, R. (1999). The impact of guilt and type of compliance-gaining message on compliance. *Communication Monographs, 66,* 168-177.

Brehm, S. S., & Brehm, J. W. (1981). *Psychological reactance: A theory of freedom and control.* New York: Academic Press.

Brown, P., & Levinson, S. C. (1987). *Politeness: Some universals in language usage.* Cambridge, UK: Cambridge University Press.

Brown, S. P., Cron, W. L., & Slocum, J. W., Jr. (1997). Effects of goal-directed emotions on salesperson volitions, behavior, and performance: A longitudinal study. *Journal of Marketing, 61*(1), 39-50.

Carlsmith, J. M., & Gross, A. E. (1969). Some effects of guilt on compliance. *Journal of Personality and Social Psychology, 11,* 232-239.

Cialdini, R. B., Darby, B. L., & Vincent, J. E. (1973). Transgression and altruism: A case for hedonism. *Journal of Experimental Social Psychology, 9,* 502-516.

Cialdini, R. B., Vincent, J. E., Lewis, S. K., Catalan, J., Wheeler, D., & Darby, B. L. (1975). Reciprocal concessions procedure for inducing compliance: The door-in-the-face technique. *Journal of Personality and Social Psychology, 31,* 206-215.

Coulter, R. H., Cotte, J., & Moore, M. L. (1997). Guilt appeals in advertising: Are you feeling guilty? In D. T. LeClair & M. Hartline (Eds.), *1997 AMA Winter Educators' Conference: Marketing theory and applications* (pp. 109-115). Chicago: American Marketing Association.

Coulter, R. H., & Pinto, M. B. (1995). Guilt appeals in advertising: What are their effects? *Journal of Applied Psychology, 80,* 697-705.

Dickerson, C. A., Thibodeau, R., Aronson, E., & Miller, D. (1992). Using cognitive dissonance to encourage water conservation. *Journal of Applied Social Psychology, 22,* 841-854.

Dietrich, D. M., & Berkowitz, L. (1997). Alleviation of dissonance by engaging in prosocial behavior or receiving ego-enhancing feedback. *Journal of Social Behavior and Personality, 12,* 557-566.

Dillard, J. P., Hunter, J. E., & Burgoon, M. (1984). Sequential-request strategies: Meta-analysis of foot-in-the-door and door-in-the-face. *Human Communication Research, 10,* 461-488.

Englis, B. G. (1990). Consumer emotional reactions to television advertising and their effects on message recall. In S. J. Agres, J. A. Edell, & T. M. Dubitsky (Eds.), *Emotion in advertising: Theoretical and practical explorations* (pp. 231-253). New York: Quorum Books.

Even-Chen, M., Yinon, Y., & Bizman, A. (1978). The door-in-the-face technique: Effects of the size of the initial request. *European Journal of Social Psychology, 8,* 135-140.

Fern, E. F., Monroe, K. B., & Avila, R. A. (1986). Effectiveness of multiple request strategies: A synthesis of research results. *Journal of Marketing Research, 23,* 144-152.

Fishbein, M., & Ajzen, I. (1975). *Belief, attitude, intention, and behavior.* Reading, MA: Addison-Wesley.

Freedman, J. L., Wallington, S. A., & Bless, E. (1967). Compliance without pressure: The effect of guilt. *Journal of Personality and Social Psychology, 7,* 117-124.

Fried, C. B., & Aronson, E. (1995). Hypocrisy, misattribution, and dissonance reduction. *Personality and Social Psychology Bulletin, 21,* 925-933.

Higgins, E. T. (1987). Self-discrepancy: A theory relating self and affect. *Psychological Review, 94,* 319-340.

Huhmann, B. A., & Brotherton, T. P. (1997). A content analysis of guilt appeals in popular magazine advertisements. *Journal of Advertising, 26*(2), 35-45.

Jones, W. H., Kugler, K., & Adams, P. (1995). You always hurt the one you love: Guilt and transgressions against relationship partners. In J. P. Tangney & K. W. Fischer (Eds.), *Self-conscious emotions: The psychology of shame, guilt, embarrassment, and pride* (pp. 301-321). New York: Guilford.

Keltner, D., & Buswell, B. N. (1996). Evidence for the distinctness of embarrassment, shame, and guilt: A study of recalled antecedents and facial expressions of emotion. *Cognition & Emotion, 10,* 155-172.

Konoske, P., Staple, S., & Graf, R. G. (1979). Compliant reactions to guilt: Self-esteem or self-punishment. *Journal of Social Psychology, 108,* 207-211.

Kugler, K., & Jones, W. H. (1992). On conceptualizing and assessing guilt. *Journal of Personality and Social Psychology, 62,* 318-327.

Lechner, L., de Vries, H., & Offermans, N. (1997). Participation in a breast cancer screening program: Influence of past behavior and determinants on future screening participation. *Preventive Medicine, 26,* 473-482.

Lewis, H. B. (1971). *Shame and guilt in neurosis.* New York: International Universities Press.

McMillen, D. L. (1971). Transgression, self-image, and compliant behavior. *Journal of Personality and Social Psychology, 20,* 176-179.

McMillen, D. L., Jackson, J. A., & Austin, J. B. (1974). Effects of positive and negative requests on compliance following transgression. *Bulletin of the Psychonomic Society, 3,* 80-82.

Miceli, M. (1992). How to make someone feel guilty: Strategies of guilt inducement and their goals. *Journal for the Theory of Social Behavior, 22,* 81-104.

Niedenthal, P. M., Tangney, J. P., & Gavanski, I. (1994). "If only I weren't" versus "if only I hadn't": Distinguishing shame and guilt in counterfactual thinking. *Journal of Personality and Social Psychology, 67,* 585-595.

O'Keefe, D. J. (2000). Guilt and social influence. In M. E. Roloff (Ed.), *Communication Yearbook 23* (pp. 67-101). Thousand Oaks, CA: Sage.

O'Keefe, D. J., & Figgé, M. (1997). A guilt-based explanation of the door-in-the-face influence strategy. *Human Communication Research, 24,* 64-81.

O'Keefe, D. J., & Figgé, M. (1999). Guilt and expected guilt in the door-in-the-face technique. *Communication Monographs, 66,* 312-324.

O'Keefe, D. J., & Hale, S. L. (1998). The door-in-the-face influence strategy: A random-effects meta-analytic review. In M. E. Roloff (Ed.), *Communication Yearbook 21* (pp. 1-33). Thousand Oaks, CA: Sage.

O'Keefe, D. J., & Hale, S. L. (2001). An odds-ratio-based meta-analysis of research on the door-in-the-face influence strategy. *Communication Reports, 14,* 31-38.

Pinto, M. B., & Priest, S. (1991). Guilt appeals in advertising: An exploratory study. *Psychological Reports, 69,* 375-385.

Richard, R., van der Pligt, J., & de Vries, N. (1996a). Anticipated affect and behavioral choice. *Basic and Applied Social Psychology, 18,* 111-129.

Richard, R., van der Pligt, J., & de Vries, N. (1996b). Anticipated regret and time perspective: Changing sexual risk-taking behavior. *Journal of Behavioral Decision Making, 9,* 185-199.

Roseman, I. J., Wiest, C., & Swartz, T. S. (1994). Phenomenology, behaviors, and goals differentiate discrete emotions. *Journal of Personality and Social Psychology, 67,* 206-221.

Rubin, J., & Shaffer, W. F. (1987). Some interpersonal effects of imposing guilt versus eliciting altruism. *Counseling and Values, 31,* 190-193.

Schwarzwald, J., Raz, M., & Zvibel, M. (1979). The applicability of the door-in-the-face technique when established behavioral customs exist. *Journal of Applied Social Psychology, 9*, 576-586.

Simonson, I. (1992). The influence of anticipating regret and responsibility on purchase decisions. *Journal of Consumer Research, 19*, 105-118.

Sommer, K. L., & Baumeister, R. F. (1997). Making someone feel guilty: Causes, strategies, and consequences. In R. M. Kowalski (Ed.), *Aversive interpersonal behaviors* (pp. 31-55). New York: Plenum.

Steele, C. M. (1975). Name-calling and compliance. *Journal of Personality and Social Psychology, 31*, 361-369.

Steele, C. M. (1988). The psychology of self-affirmation: Sustaining the integrity of the self. In L. Berkowitz (Ed.), *Advances in experimental social psychology* (Vol. 21, pp. 261-302). New York: Academic Press.

Steele, C. M., & Liu, T. J. (1983). Dissonance processes as self-affirmation. *Journal of Personality and Social Psychology, 45*, 5-19.

Steele, C. M., & Spencer, S. J. (1992). The primacy of self-integrity. *Psychological Inquiry, 3*, 345-346.

Steele, C. M., Spencer, S. J., & Lynch, M. (1993). Self-image resilience and dissonance: The role of affirmational resources. *Journal of Personality and Social Psychology, 64*, 885-896.

Stice, E. (1992). The similarities between cognitive dissonance and guilt: Confession as a relief of dissonance. *Current Psychology: Research and Reviews, 11*, 69-77.

Stone, J., Aronson, E., Crain, A. L., Winslow, M. P., & Fried, C. B. (1994). Inducing hypocrisy as a means of encouraging young adults to use condoms. *Personality and Social Psychology Bulletin, 20*, 116-128.

Tangney, J. P. (1992). Situational determinants of shame and guilt in young adulthood. *Personality and Social Psychology Bulletin, 18*, 199-205.

Tangney, J. P. (1995). Shame and guilt in interpersonal relationships. In J. P. Tangney & K. W.

Fischer (Eds.), *Self-conscious emotions: The psychology of shame, guilt, embarrassment, and pride* (pp. 114-139). New York: Guilford.

Tangney, J. P., Miller, R. S., Flicker, L., & Barlow, D. H. (1996). Are shame, guilt, and embarrassment distinct emotions? *Journal of Personality and Social Psychology, 70*, 1256-1269.

Tangney, J. P., Niedenthal, P. M., Covert, M. V., & Barlow, D. H. (1998). Are shame and guilt related to distinct self-discrepancies? A test of Higgins's (1987) hypotheses. *Journal of Personality and Social Psychology, 75*, 256-268.

van der Pligt, J., & Richard, R. (1994). Changing adolescents' sexual behaviour: Perceived risk, self-efficacy, and anticipated regret. *Patient Education and Counseling, 23*, 187-196.

van der Pligt, J., & de Vries, N. K. (1998). Expectancy-value models of health behaviour: The role of salience and anticipated affect. *Psychology and Health, 13*, 289-305.

Vangelisti, A. L., Daly, J. A., & Rudnick, J. R. (1991). Making people feel guilty in conversations: Techniques and correlates. *Human Communication Research, 18*, 3-39.

Wang, T., Brownstein, R., & Katzev, R. (1989). Promoting charitable behaviour with compliance techniques. *Applied Psychology: An International Review, 38*, 165-183.

Yinon, Y., Bizman, A., Cohen, S., & Segev, A. (1976). Effects of guilt-arousal communications on volunteering to the civil guard: A field experiment. *Bulletin of the Psychonomic Society, 7*, 493-494.

Zillmann, D., & Bryant, J. (1985). Affect, mood, and emotion as determinants of selective exposure. In D. Zillmann & J. Bryant (Eds.), *Selective exposure to communication* (pp. 157-190). Hillsdale, NJ: Lawrence Erlbaum.

Zillmann, D., & Bryant, J. (1994). Entertainment as media effect. In J. Bryant & D. Zillmann (Eds.), *Media effects: Advances in theory and research* (pp. 437-461). Hillsdale, NJ: Lawrence Erlbaum.

18

Persuasive Effects of Product Warning Labels

MARK A. deTURCK

> If the present Congress errs too much in talking,
> how can it be otherwise that in a body to which people send 150 lawyers,
> whose trade it is to question everything, yield nothing and talk by the hour?
>
> — *Thomas Jefferson, 1821 (quoted in Jefferson, 1984)*

Thomas Jefferson's frustration over the inability of the Continental Congress to move forward is as poignant today as it was when he wrote his memoirs. An overwhelming number of members of Congress are attorneys by profession. While our current Congress debates the merits of tort reform, accidents attributable to consumer products inflict a physical, financial, and relational tragedy on the lives of millions of American consumers. Each year, approximately 22,000 deaths and 30 million injuries occur that are associated with consumer products and fall within the jurisdiction of the Consumer Product Safety Commission (CPSC). Unintentional injuries from consumer products are the leading cause of death for Americans under 35 years of age; more deaths occur in this age group from consumer products than from cancer, heart disease, or AIDS. Overall, accidents attributable to consumer products is the fifth leading cause of death in the nation. Accidents from consumer products cost the American public an incredible $400 billion annually.

These staggering figures are evinced in the epidemic of product liability litigation over the past few decades. Plaintiffs' attorneys (counsel representing the injured parties and/or families) frequently point an accusing finger at manufacturers' lack of diligence in communicating safety information to product users. Students of safety communication have responded to this accusation by initiating research programs to investigate the

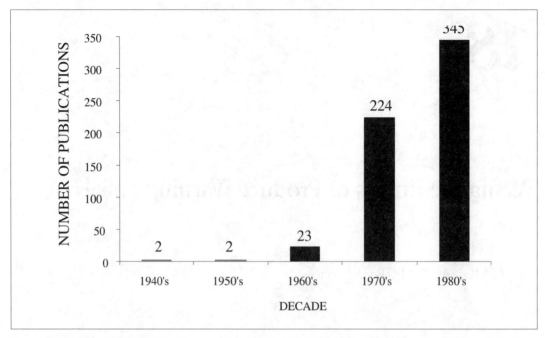

Figure 18.1. Number of Publications on Product Safety Information Based on Data From Miller, Lehto, and Frantz (1990)

factors that enhance or inhibit the persuasive effects of product safety information. The spiraling number of lawsuits stemming from consumers' claims that manufacturers' failure to warn, or inadequate safety communication, caused them (or family members) injury (or death) has prompted social scientists to devote an increasing amount of empirical energy to understanding the role of products' warning communication in consumers' safety behavior. This dramatic increase in the tide of research pages devoted to the effects of product safety communication (Figure 18.1) showed no signs of an ebb during the 1990s or early in the new century.

Because there are a number of published reviews of the product warning literature (deTurck, 1994; Lehto & Miller, 1986; Miller, Lehto, & Frantz, 1990; Wogalter, DeJoy, & Laughery, 1999), the intent of the current chapter is not to duplicate those ef-

forts. Rather, my aims are threefold: first, to discuss the purpose and structure of product warnings; second, to provide a model underlying consumers' processing of product safety information as a basis to review the research regarding the factors that enhance or inhibit the effectiveness of product safety messages and their utility; and third, to outline directions for future research endeavors. Toward these ends, the current chapter draws on literature on products' warnings, persuasion, health communication, consumer behavior, and social cognition.

PURPOSE AND STRUCTURE OF PRODUCT WARNING MESSAGES

Uncertainty refers to the gap in knowledge between what a consumer already knows with respect to using a product safely and what he or she needs to know so as to use the product safely. The purpose of product warnings is to reduce consumers' uncertainty with respect to how to use a product safely (deTurck, 1994). Thus, product safety messages serve as an informational bridge between consumers, on the one side, and manufacturers, wholesalers, retailers, and/or service vendors, on the other.

Unlike other messages in health communication, the structure of product warnings is often dictated by governmental agencies with regulatory power such as the Food and Drug Administration, the Occupational Safety and Health Organization, and the National Highway Traffic and Safety Administration. Many of the warnings that are approved by these regulating bodies are mandatory and afford manufacturers no discretion in their structure, content, and dissemination. The American National Standards Institute (ANSI) approved voluntary standards for manufacturers regarding the structure and general content for product warning messages (ANSI, 1991, 1997) that have received a substantial amount of research attention and legal application. ANSI Z535.4 suggests that a product warning message contain four categories of information: (a) signal word, (b) hazard statement, (c) hazard avoidance statement, and (d) consequences statement.

The *signal word* (e.g., DANGER, WARNING, CAUTION) serves as a quick reference guide to consumers with respect to the degree of hazard posed by a product or situation. The *hazard statement* refers to the specific facet of the product or situation that poses the risk of an injury to consumers (e.g., shallow water in an above-ground pool). The *hazard avoidance statement* communicates specific behavioral recommendations to consumers so as to avert the dangerous aspects of the product or situation (e.g., no diving in an above-ground pool). The *consequences statement* communicates

the adverse outcomes for consumers that may ensue if they fail to comply with the hazard avoidance statement.

Despite the suggestions of ANSI in Z535.4 that product safety messages should contain all four elements, research regarding the necessity of all four elements is inconclusive (Wogalter et al., 1987; Young, Wogalter, Laughery, Magurno, & Lovvoll, 1995). Young et al. (1995) asked research participants to construct the best warnings they could for a variety of hazards (shock, confined space, and slippery floor) using prepared information for each of the four warning elements. Their results indicated that only 30% of the warning messages contained all four message elements, most of the warnings (56%) contained only three components, and most of the remaining warnings (13%) contained only two elements.

PRODUCTS' WARNING MESSAGES AS FEAR APPEALS

Because products' warning messages communicate hazards, they function as a specific type of fear appeal. The persuasion and health communication literatures are replete with studies regarding the persuasive effects of fear-arousing messages (for reviews, see Boster & Mongeau, 1984; Dillard, 1994; Hale & Dillard, 1995; Mongeau, 1998; Sternthal & Craig, 1974; Witte, 1998). Building decades of research in the fear appeals tradition, the protection motivation theory (PMT) (Rogers, 1983) asserts that fear-arousing messages should possess four distinct content components: (a) severity of hazard, (b) likelihood of hazard, (c) response-efficacy, and (d) self-efficacy.

The *severity* of a hazard refers to the extent to which a product/context can harm an individual (e.g., death, paralysis) if he or she fails to comply with the safety recommendations,

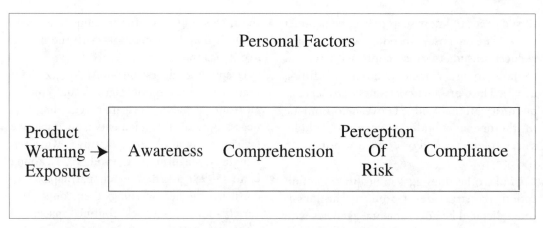

Figure 18.2. A Model of the Effects of Products' Warning Messages

whereas the *likelihood* of a hazard refers to the *probability* (e.g., low, moderate, high) that a negative consequence will be associated with a product/context if an individual fails to comply with the recommended safety precautions. *Self-efficacy* refers to a product user's ability to perform the recommended behavior(s), whereas *response-efficacy* refers to the utility of the recommended behavior(s) to prevent the noxious threat.

Although the four-part structure of a warning and the four components of PMT are not isomorphic, there is a degree of conceptual overlap that is worth noting. The signal word and consequences statement communicate the severity of the hazard, whereas specific linguistic choices in the consequences statement (e.g., *may* cause vs. *will* cause) indicate the likelihood that the negative consequences may occur. The hazard avoidance statement communicates varying degrees of response-efficacy depending on a product and the circumstances in which a product is used. Because of the apparent simplicity of recommended actions associated with warning labels, it is almost never the case that a warning label speaks to self-efficacy. Due to this overlap, it will be useful to consider all of these factors within a general model of product users' information processing.

A MODEL OF PRODUCT USERS' SAFETY INFORMATION PROCESSING

Several models depicting how product users process safety information have been advanced (deTurck, 1994; deTurck, Rachlin, & Young, 1994; Lehto & Miller, 1986; Wogalter et al., 1999). Figure 18.2 depicts the factors affecting consumers' processing of product safety information. It is apparent from this model that there is *not* a direct causal relationship between consumers' exposure to a product warning message and their safety behavior. If we were to assume a relatively high correlation (.60) between adjacent factors in the model (excluding for the moment personal and situational factors), from exposure to awareness, to comprehension, to perception of risk, to compliance, then the expected impact of Exposure on Compliance would be as follows: Exposure-Awareness (.60) × Awareness-Comprehension (.60) × Comprehension-Perception of Risk (.60) × Perception of Risk-Compliance (.60) or .13. Thus, the model, without taking into account the effects of personal and situational factors, predicts that the ultimate impact of exposing consumers to a product safety message on their safety behavior will be relatively small.

The constructs in the box (awareness, comprehension, perception of risk, and compliance) reflect the cognitive processing and behavior that occurs after consumers are exposed to a product warning message. Personal and situational factors are portrayed outside the box so as to reflect that they influence all aspects of product users' cognitive processing of safety information and safety behavior. Personal factors refer to individual differences among product users, such as age, gender, information processing objectives (goal when attending to safety information), familiarity with a product (frequency of using a product), and sensation seeking. Situational factors refer to physical and psychological contexts in which a product is used, such as role models (safety behavior of others present in the context), the cost of consensus (amount of energy needed to comply with the request), and outcome-relevant involvement. Both personal and situational factors that have been found to influence product users' cognitive processing of and compliance with warning messages.

Awareness

Research by Wogalter, Brelsford, Desaulniers, and Laughery (1991, Study I) found that both severity and likelihood of hazard were correlated with research participants' willingness to read products' warnings ($r = .89$ and $-.64$, respectively). Such findings parallel the results of meta-analytic summaries of the fear appeal literature (Witte & Allen, 2000). Other studies report similar findings; for example, an increase in severity of the hazard was associated with an increase in self-reported likelihood of reading warnings (Godfrey, Allender, Laughery, & Smith; 1983; Silver, Leonard, Ponski, & Wogalter; 1991; Young, Brelsford,

& Wogalter, 1990). However, reliance on participants' self-reports of their likelihood of reading warnings is likely an imperfect indicator of whether or not participants would actually read the warnings.

A number of studies have examined the impact of various presentation-oriented factors (e.g., pictograph, icon, color, border, raised border) on product users' awareness that a product warning was present in a product's label (Friedman, 1988; Laughery & Young, 1991; Young, 1991, 1997). Although Laughery and Young (1991) and Young (1991) reported results indicating that color, pictograph, and icon increased participants' awareness of the warnings, their methodology severely tempers the utility of their results. Each research participant was prompted to look at 96 alcohol beverage labels on a computer screen and to indicate when they saw a warning imbedded in the label by pressing a key. By prompting participants that they would be observing product labels and to search for a warning, it is difficult to generalize these results to naturalistic contexts in which consumers use products. Moreover, their results do not assess whether participants were aware of a warning message. Rather, their study measured research participants' response latency to notice whether a warning message was present on the label.

In a different empirical vein, studies examining consumers' awareness of warnings in field settings found that a minority of product users notice conspicuous warnings (deTurck & Goldhaber, 1991; Dorris & Purswell, 1977; Goldhaber & deTurck, 1988; Shinar & Drory, 1983). In deTurck and Goldhaber (1991), a NO DIVING sign (the sign had all four warning components plus a pictograph) was posted at one suburban middle and high school's natatorium for a month. Although students used the pool a couple of times a week as part of their physical education, only 41% of the middle school students correctly recalled seeing the conspicuous NO DIVING sign posted by the pool, whereas only 24% of the high school students correctly recalled noticing the NO DIVING sign. Similarly, students in home economics classes in suburban middle and high schools were exposed to an on-product warning message on an iron while it was used for a period of 2 weeks, but only 20% recalled seeing any information on the iron and only 40% recalled seeing a warning when prompted to consider specific hazard information (Goldhaber & deTurck, 1988). Dorris and Purswell (1977) found that none of their research participants was aware of a warning message on a hammer.

Consistent with the model presented previously, research evidence suggests that the effect of awareness on behavioral compliance is trivial (Friedmann, 1988; Gill, Barbera, & Precht, 1987; Otsubo, 1988). For example, in Friedmann (1988), although 88% of the research participants recalled seeing the warning on the product, only 46% reported reading the warning (most participants who reported reading the warning indicated that they read only a fraction of the warning) and only 27% of the participants complied.

Familiarity. Results obtained in several studies indicate that as consumers' familiarity—frequency of product use—with a product increases, they are less likely to notice the product's warning message (Godfrey et al., 1983; Godfrey & Laughery, 1984). This *familiarity effect* is likely to be due to consumers' lack of motivation to examine the product's label because they believe that they already know how to use the product safely.

Although consumers generally do not recall noticing a product warning message, it is possible that it still may exert some effect on their perceptions of risk posed by the product. Stated differently, product users might not have any conscious recollection of observing product safety information, but it may still

influence their judgments of the potential hazard associated with a product at a nonconscious level. To test this hypothesis, deTurck, Goldhaber, and Richetto (1992) exposed research participants to a safety information cue (signal word) at a conscious (500 milliseconds) versus nonconscious (33 milliseconds) rate prior to reading the government warning for alcoholic beverages. Research participants with moderate drinking habits rated the product to be more hazardous when the signal words were processed at a conscious level compared to the nonconscious conditions.

Information Processing Objectives. Research by deTurck and Goldhaber (1989a) examined the effect of information processing objectives (IPOs) on the amount of time product users devoted to reading a product's label. IPOs refer to a person's purpose or goal when attending to a corpus of information. IPOs play a significant role in human information processing (Wyer & Srull, 1986). Two IPOs that have received the lion's share of empirical attention are memory set and impression set. When using a memory-set IPO, people attempt to remember as much information as possible, whereas when using an impression-set objective, their goal is to form a unit evaluation (attitude) from the information.

One half of the participants in deTurck and Goldhaber (1989a) were instructed to try to remember as much information from the label as possible (memory-set IPO), whereas the other half of the participants were asked to form an impression of the product from the label (impression-set IPO). A research assistant assessed the length of time participants spent reading the labels of an oven cleaner and a prescription cough medicine. Participants in the memory-set condition paid attention to the labels longer for the oven cleaner (184 seconds) and the prescription cough medicine (211 seconds) than did participants in the impression-set condition (72 and 102 seconds, respectively).

Redundancy. Multiple warnings employing negative language also increase product users' awareness of safety information. Results obtained by deTurck, Goldhaber, and Richetto (1989) indicated that product users exposed to two warning messages (41%) were more aware of the presence of safety information than were product users exposed to a single warning message (29%). This effect was particularly pronounced when the warning employed negative language (51%) compared to positive language (31%). However, more recent evidence obtained by Chen and Gibson (1997) indicates that multiple warnings may serve to dilute the communicative effectiveness of the warnings—a dilution effect. Moreover, an increase in the amount of information may trigger information overload and, as a result, prompt consumers to ignore a warning (Scammon, 1977). It is likely that a single, strategically located warning message is sufficient to alert product users of potential hazards.

Comprehension

Comprehension refers to product users' understanding of the product safety information. Surprisingly, few studies have systematically studied the effects of various message-oriented factors or presentation-oriented factors on comprehension. For the most part, comprehension has been operationalized using recall measures. Several factors have been found to enhance product users' recall of safety information.

Severity of Hazard. Although a few studies have found that product users tend to recall more information from a product safety message when the warning communicates a moderate to high rather than a low degree of hazard (deTurck, Goldhaber, & Richetto, 1991a, 1991b; Young & deTurck, 1995), deTurck et al. (1994) found that participants recalled more information from the low- than the high-fear warning. Other studies have failed to obtain a reliable difference in recall between high- and low-fear conditions (deTurck, Chih, & Hsu, 1999, Studies II and III). The lack of consistency across studies may be due to the fact that the products and conditions for testing vary among the studies. Certain products are perceived to be more hazardous than others by product users, and therefore product users may be more receptive to a high- than a low-fear warning, depending on the product/context (Wogalter, Desaulniers, & Brelsford, 1987).

Information Processing Objectives. Consumers examining a product with a memory-set IPO recalled more information from the product's warning message than did their counterparts using an impression-set IPO (deTurck & Goldhaber, 1989a; deTurck, Goldhaber, & Richetto, 1995). Although these findings might seem to be intuitively obvious, they conflict with research in the social cognition literature in which participants tend to recall more information when using an impression-set rather than a memory-set objective (Hamilton, Katz, & Leirer, 1980). The difference between the two sets of results may be attributable to the different methodological paradigms and/or information content.

Icons. There is an increasing reliance on pictographs to communicate product safety information so as to enhance understanding in a multilingual marketplace. However, results are inconsistent as to the communicative value of pictographs (Booher, 1975; Friedmann, 1988; Ringseis & Caird, 1995; Young &

Wogalter, 1990). Pictographs may serve to distract product users away from textual information and/or to encourage product users to rely on pictographs because they require less cognitive effort. However, due to the lack of detail in pictographs they might not serve to reduce product users' uncertainty with respect to product safety to the same extent as does textual information.

Perception of Risk

Research in fear appeals demonstrates a clear relationship between the severity of hazard communicated in the message and the level of perceived fear (Mongeau, 1998). However, the relative effects of severity of hazard and likelihood of hazard on perceptions of hazard appear to vary depending on the context. Young, Wogalter, and Brelsford (1992) compared two lists of products/contexts that pose a hazard to consumers. The first list contained products/contexts from Slovic, Fischoff, and Lichtenstein's (1980) study on risk perceptions, and the second list was based on products/contexts analyzed in Wogalter et al.'s (1991) study on hazard perceptions. Separate regression analyses for each list indicated that likelihood of hazard accounted for 87% of the variance in perceptions of hazard for Slovic et al.'s (1980) list, whereas the severity of hazard accounted for 95% of the variance in perceptions of hazard for Wogalter et al.'s (1991) list.

The major difference between the two lists is that Wogalter et al.'s (1991) list of products/contexts contained very few items that would lead to catastrophic outcomes (e.g., battery alarm clock, baby powder, typewriter, vacuum cleaner), whereas Slovic et al.'s (1980) list contained a number of products/contexts that are more closely associated with devastating outcomes (e.g., commercial aviation, swimming, motor vehicles, firefighting). Young

et al. (1992) concluded that the severity of hazard is likely to be the most significant dimension underlying product users' perception of hazard for most consumer products. However, once the severity of threat reaches a certain threshold, the only remaining uncertainty for consumers is the likelihood of a hazard occurring.

Age and Gender. Age and gender are two factors that may jointly affect product users' perceptions of risk associated with a product. Results obtained by deTurck and Goldhaber (1991) indicated that high school males perceived less risk associated with diving into shallow water than did middle school males, especially when a NO DIVING sign was present. However, high school females perceived more risk associated with diving into shallow water than did their middle school counterparts. Differences in perceived hazard between males and females may stem from the fact that males perceive they are more capable (self-efficacy) of performing the recommended behaviors in some athletic contexts than do females (Vredenburgh & Cohen, 1993).

Relying on textual information to communicate product safety warnings to young children is especially difficult due to their inability to read. The use of pictorials in warnings is a useful communicative strategy for alerting young (preschool) children to hazardous products (Schneider, 1977). When a skull and crossbones or a Mr. Yuk pictorial appeared on the label, children were much less likely to open the container than when no pictorial was present. Interestingly, toddlers were more attracted to a container when it had a written warning than when no warning was present (Schneider, 1977).

Familiarity. One of the most consistent findings in the literature regarding product users' perception of risk associated with a product is their familiarity with the product. Numerous studies have found that consumers who are more familiar with a product tend to perceive it as less hazardous than do consumers with less experience with the product (deTurck & Goldhaber, 1989b, 1991; deTurck et al., 1992, 1995; Godfrey et al., 1983; Godfrey & Laughery, 1984; Goldhaber & deTurck, 1988; Karnes, Leonard, & Rachwal, 1986; Rethans & Hastek, 1981). Evidence supporting the familiarity effect is robust across a wide variety of products including, but not limited to, above- and in-ground pools, feminine hygiene, automobile tires, all-terrain vehicles, and alcoholic beverages. It is assumed that people who have frequently used a product know the risks associated with the product and, assuming they have not experienced an accident with the product, perceive that it is less likely they will experience an injury than do consumers who have used the product less frequently.

Compliance

Determining the effects of products' warning messages on compliance is often difficult due to the ethics of exposing research participants to the dangers associated with many products. Moreover, many products may require more than a single safety behavior. Whereas research participants may comply with some safety recommendations, they may fail to comply with others—partial compliance (Wogalter, Barlow, & Murphy, 1995; Young & deTurck, 1995). Thus, evaluating the effects of a product warning on compliance might not be as straightforward as with other dependent measures. Due to the significance attached to behavioral effects in the legal and scientific arenas, I review the research in this section in greater detail than in previous sections.

Cox, Wogalter, Stokes, and Murff's (1997) meta-analysis concluded that products' warning messages significantly affect product users' safety behavior. However, a number of shortcomings limit the utility of their conclusion. First, their meta-analysis included studies ($N = 15$) that only compared experimentally manipulated warning conditions to a no-warning control condition. However, for an overwhelming number of products and contexts, warning messages are mandated by government agencies and/or industry standards. Because a warning is required for so many types of products and contexts, and because consumers do not use products in a social vacuum, the conclusion that the presence of a warning is more effective than no warning is of indeterminate value.

Second, the mean compliance rate when a warning was present was .16 greater than in control conditions, with a range on compliance from −.22 to .60. The mean compliance rate is relatively small and is consistent with the argument raised earlier that the ultimate effect of warnings on behavioral compliance is small due to the fact that several variables, including personal and situational factors, moderate the effect of warnings on safety behavior. In addition, Cox et al.'s (1997) analysis indicated that the severity and likelihood of hazard did not affect compliance rates (in stark contrast to the fear appeals literature).

Third, the meta-analysis failed to examine the effects of moderating factors (e.g., message design, product, situation) other than comparing student-based samples to non-student-based samples on compliance. Because of the broad range of compliance rates, it is likely that a number of factors mediate the effects of warning messages on safety behavior. Given the fact that the presence of a warning actually decreased product users' compliance with safety recommendations in 19% of the experimental conditions and had no effect in another 14% of the experimental conditions (Cox et al., 1997), it is tenuous to conclude that a warning message is better than no warning. Although few studies have systematically varied message-oriented factors and personal or situational factors, research indicates that personal and situational factors exert more influence on consumers' safety behavior than do message-oriented factors.

Message Factors

Signal Word and Location. Wogalter, Fontenelle, and Laughery (1985, Study I) tested the effects of signal word (WARNING vs. NOTE) and location of warning (beginning of instructions vs. end of instructions) on research participants' likelihood of wearing protective gloves and a mask while mixing chemicals. In addition, Wogalter et al. observed the safety behavior for research participants who received no warning message (control condition).

Their results indicated that the signal word exerted no effect on safety behavior but that the presence and location of the warning significantly affected safety behavior. Whereas only 10% of the participants in the control condition wore the protective gear, 50% of the participants complied when the safety information appeared at the end of the instructions and 80% complied when the safety instructions were located at the beginning of the instructions. A second study by Wogalter et al. (1985) obtained results that were consistent with Study I with respect to the effect of location on compliance.

Redundancy. Wogalter et al. (1995) examined the effects of redundant warning messages on compliance. Research participants were instructed to perform three behaviors: (a) turn off the computer, (b) touch the metal connector on the back of the computer to

avoid static discharge, and (c) eject the transport disk from the drive. Compliance was measured by summing the number of behaviors research participants performed. In the two control conditions, research participants received the behavioral instructions either in the basic instruction manual or on a separate instruction sheet only (no manual). In the five experimental conditions, the behavioral instructions were communicated in the basic manual as well as on the supplemental instruction sheet located either (a) on the box, (b) as a cover page to the manual, (c) as a leaflet, (d) attached to the drive cable, or (e) attached to the front of the drive. Results indicated that more compliance behaviors were observed in the redundant conditions than in either of the two control conditions (one message only). Unfortunately, none of these behaviors could be considered a *safety* behavior. All three compliance indicators were designed to prevent property damage to the computer and were unrelated to personal injury to the computer operator.

Situational Factors

Role Modeling Effects. One of the most consistent findings to emerge in the products' warning literature is that the presence of other product users (role models) dramatically affects consumers' safety behavior. Product users' observations of others' safety behavior provide them with information regarding the efficacy of compliance for avoiding an injury. Observing others avoid an injury when using a product according to a warning's recommendations should enhance product users' perceptions of response-efficacy. Similarly, consumers' perceptions of response-efficacy should be enhanced when they observe others injured when using a product because they did not comply with a warning's recommendations. However, when consumers observe others escape injury when using a product, despite the fact that they did not comply with a warning's safety recommendations, it is likely that consumers' perceptions of response-efficacy would be diminished.

Results obtained by deTurck et al. (1994) indicated that product users' safety behavior was not influenced by the severity of hazard communicated in the warning message, but their safety behavior was influenced to a large extent by observing the safety behavior of another product user. Under the guise of a marketing study, research participants in the experimental conditions were paired with a confederate and asked to examine a product (oven cleaner) prior to testing the product. The warning recommended wearing protective rubber gloves when applying the oven cleaner. A pair of rubber safety gloves, paper towels, and a bucket of water were located next to a soiled hibachi.

The confederate was asked to test the product first on the dirty hibachi in one of three conditions. In the No Gloves/No Burn condition, the confederate applied the oven cleaner to the hibachi without wearing the rubber gloves and did not get any of the cleaner on him or her and experienced no chemical burn. In the Gloves condition, the confederate applied the oven cleaner to the hibachi after putting on the rubber gloves and experienced no chemical burn. In the No Gloves/Burn condition, the confederate applied the oven cleaner without wearing the gloves and got some of the cleaner on his or her hand and exclaimed, "Oh, I can feel that burns." The confederate immediately cleaned his or her hand with the towels and water. In all three conditions, the research participant was asked to test the product after the confederate was finished. Research participants in the control condition examined and tested the oven cleaner alone; no role model was present. Results indicated that 78% of the research participants in the control condition wore the

rubber gloves, compared to 36% in the No Gloves/No Burn condition, 98% in the Gloves condition, and 56% in the No Gloves/Burn condition.

In a series of three experiments, deTurck et al. (1999) extended the design of deTurck et al. (1994) to determine whether the role modeling effect is robust across role model likability, severity of burn, outcome-relevant involvement, and type of product. In the first study, they systematically varied the role model's likability, level of hazard communicated in the warning, and severity of chemical burn. Research participants were informed that they would be participating in a product marketing study with another person who was described as very friendly (or very unfriendly). While the research assistant was preparing the materials for the study, the confederate asked the naive participant a series of scripted questions. The confederate responded to the naive participant's answers in a very friendly (lauded answers) or very unfriendly (ridiculed answers) manner.

The research assistant instructed the confederate and research participant to examine the product (fictitious household cleaner) prior to testing the cleaner. The research assistant asked the participant to clean one of two particularly dirty smudges/stains (shoe polish) on the table. A pair of protective rubber gloves, roll of paper towels, and basin of water were conveniently located on the table. The confederate always tested the product first in one of four experimental conditions: (a) Gloves (confederate wore gloves with no chemical burn), (b) No Gloves/No Burn (confederate did not wear gloves and had no chemical burn), (c) No Gloves/Mild Burn (confederate did not wear gloves and experienced mild chemical burn as in preceding study), and (d) No Gloves/Painful Burn (confederate did not wear gloves and experienced a severe chemical burn, yelling, "Ow, that really burns"). Research participants in the

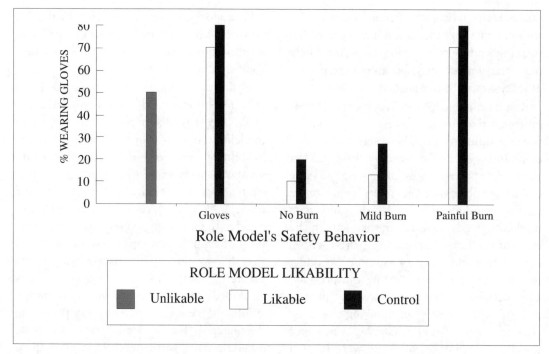

Figure 18.3. Effects of Role Model's Safety Behavior and Likability on Observers' Safety Compliance

SOURCE: Reprinted with permission from *Human Factors, 41,* 1999. Copyright 1999 by the Human Factors and Ergonomic Society. All rights reserved.

control condition examined and tested the product alone; no role model was present.

Results obtained by deTurck et al. (1999, Study I) indicated that although the role model's likability exerted no impact on naive participants' compliance, despite a successful manipulation, the role model's safety behavior exerted a substantial effect on naive observers' safety behavior (Figure 18.3). The results are generally consistent with the effects observed in deTurck et al. (1994). It is useful to note, however, that compliance in the control condition was 50%, compared to 78% in deTurck et al. (1994). Interestingly, only 80% of the naive participants wore the protective gloves after observing the confederate receive a severe chemical burn. Even if we allow that half of the noncompliant participants may have been suspicious of the confederate's painful condition, that still leaves 10% of the

group failing to comply despite the fact that they observed an extremely negative consequence for failing to comply.

A second study in deTurck et al. (1999) included the same role model conditions as in Study I and also varied the severity of hazard communicated in the household cleaner's warning message. Although no effect was obtained for the severity of hazard in the warning, a significant effect was obtained for the role model. The pattern of compliance (Figure 18.4) was similar to the results just reported; naive participants tended to imitate the safety behavior they observed from the role model. It is interesting to note that when naive participants tested the product alone (control condition), they were more likely to comply with the low- than the high-hazard warning.

A third study in deTurck et al. (1999) examined the effects of a role model's safety behav-

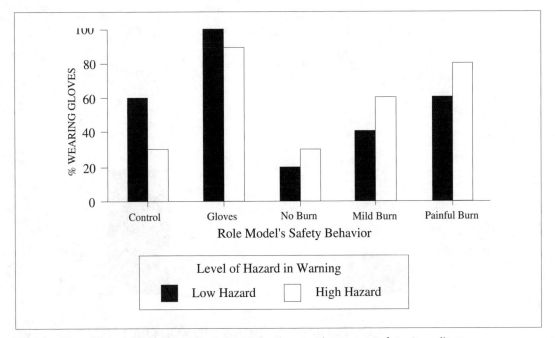

Figure 18.4. Effects of Role Model's Safety Behavior on Observers' Safety Compliance

ior, outcome-relevant involvement, and severity of hazard communicated in the product warning on naive observers' safety behavior. Research participants and a confederate were instructed that a pharmaceutical company was testing a new over-the-counter (OTC) analgesic. One half of the participants were instructed to examine the product's packaging for marketing purposes (low outcome-relevant involvement), whereas the other half of the participants were instructed to examine the product's packaging because they would be asked to try the product. One half of the containers' labels communicated a low-hazard warning (consuming alcoholic beverages with product may cause slight stomach discomfort), whereas the other half of the containers communicated a high-hazard warning (consuming alcoholic beverages with product may cause death). Despite naive participants' assignment to involvement conditions, all participants were instructed to take a normal

dosage (two caplets) of the pain reliever (actually a placebo).

After 20 minutes, participants completed a questionnaire. Another research assistant knocked on the door and informed the research assistant conducting the OTC analgesic study that the research participants for his or her study failed to show up and requested permission to use the research participants from the analgesic study in exchange for additional course credit. The confederate was instructed to agree to participate (all naive participants also agreed).

Research participants were led to another research site in a different building. On arriving at the new site, participants were informed that another marketing study was under way designed to determine consumers' preferences for a name for a new wine cooler product. Participants were asked to try an array of wine coolers on the table in front of them (actually fruit juice). Prior to participating, the confed-

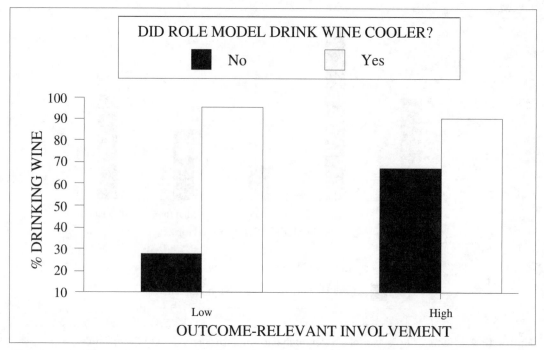

Figure 18.5. Effects of Role Model's Safety Behavior and Outcome-Relevant Involvement on Observers' Safety Compliance

SOURCE: Reprinted with permission from *Human Factors, 41,* 1999. Copyright 1999 by the Human Factors and Ergonomic Society. All rights reserved.

erate was instructed to politely decline tasting the wine coolers (comply with pain reliever's warning) without an explanation or to politely accept tasting the wine coolers (fail to comply with warning).

Results indicated that although the severity of hazard exerted no impact on participants' decision to drink the wine coolers, there was a joint effect for outcome-relevant involvement and the role model's safety behavior. The pattern of compliance indicates that when outcome-relevant involvement was low, participants were particularly likely to imitate the role model's unsafe behavior and drink the wine coolers (Figure 18.5). It is likely that when product users perceive little or no outcome-relevant involvement, they base their safety behavior on heuristic cues (Chaiken, 1987). Heuristic cues or situational information, such as role models' safety behavior,

exert a substantial influence on behavior when there is little motivation for product users to concentrate on cues in the warning message.

To the extent role models serve as an important cue guiding product users' safety behavior, product users should be less likely to imitate unsafe behavior when it results in an injury—negative consequences (Bandura, 1986). However, naive participants imitated the role models' unsafe behavior even though they observed the role models experience a negative consequence for their unsafe actions. This may be due to the proverbial "it can't happen to me" denial. Naive observers may assume that they can easily perform the desired behavior (cleaning) without experiencing a chemical burn. This still does not account for observers' willingness to drink the wine coolers despite a warning that they could die from it. Although some naive participants may have doubted that the pain reliever or wine coolers were genuine, the products were packaged using full-color labels from a professional vendor.

Cost of Compliance. Cost of compliance refers to the amount of effort product users must expend so as to comply with a warning's behavioral recommendations. Some product users may perceive that the behavioral requirements to comply with a warning message exceed their ability and/or motivation to comply (self-efficacy). To the extent that product users judge the cost of noncompliance to be less than the cost of injury (pain and suffering), they are likely to risk noncompliance.

A study by Wogalter, McKenna, and Allison (1988) examined the effects of cost of compliance (effort required to comply) on research participants' willingness to comply with safety recommendations. Participants were asked to mix a variety of chemicals; the warnings indicated that a safety mask and gloves should be worn while mixing the chemicals. The safety gear was located either right on the table by the chemicals (low cost) or across the room (high cost). Results indicated that research participants in the low-cost condition (73%) were significantly more likely than participants in the high-cost condition (17%) to wear the safety gear when it was close by.

An earlier study by Wogalter, Godfrey, et al. (1987) obtained results similar to those of Wogalter et al. (1988). In Wogalter, Godfrey, et al. (1987), when research participants were confronted with a broken door and advised to use a different door down the hall, they were significantly more likely to comply with the request when the alternative door was only 15 meters away (low cost, 94%) than when it was 60 meters away (high cost, 0%). Taken together, the results of Wogalter, Godfrey, et al. (1987) and Wogalter et al. (1988) indicate that when product users perceive the cost of compliance to exceed the risks for noncompli-

ance, they are much less likely to comply with a warning's recommendations.

Involvement. In addition to Study III in deTurck et al. (1999) reported earlier, Young and deTurck (1995) examined the effect of involvement on product users' compliance with safety recommendations. Research participants were informed that they would be testing a new cleaning product for computer monitors. Half of the research participants were instructed that they would be videotaped while testing the product to be used in an instructional tape being prepared (high involvement), whereas the remainder of the participants received no instructions that they would be videotaped (low involvement). One half of the cleaner labels communicated a low-hazard warning, whereas the other half communicated a high-hazard warning. Both the low- and high-hazard warnings instructed the users to turn off *and* unplug the computer prior to applying the cleaner.

Participants in the high-involvement condition (12%) were significantly more likely to turn off *and* unplug the computer than were participants in the low-involvement condition (0%). Measures of partial compliance (either turning off or unplugging the computer) revealed that participants in the high-involvement condition (58%) were significantly more likely to comply partially with the warning than were participants in the low-involvement condition (32%). Because unplugging the computer effectively eliminates any threat of shock or electrocution, the results on partial compliance may be more informative than the results on full compliance.

Personal Factors

Familiarity. Although there are no studies that have systematically varied levels of product users' familiarity with a product to determine its effect on compliance, there are a number of studies that provide indirect evidence. Wogalter et al. (1995) split research participants into low- and high-familiarity conditions based on their previous experience with computers. Their results indicated that research participants in the low-familiarity condition ($M = 2.52$) performed more of the three compliance behaviors than did participants in the high-familiarity condition ($M = 1.70$).

Results obtained by deTurck and Goldhaber (1991) found that swimmers with a history of diving into shallow water were significantly more likely to dive (self-report of intentions) into shallow water than were swimmers who never dove into the shallow end of the pool. This effect may be unique to swimmers. Students who are trained to perform shallow water dives (e.g., swim team members) might not only perceive that they are adept at shallow water dives but also feel compelled to make shallow water dives due to the demands of their sport.

Research that has examined the effects of product users' past accidents on their willingness to comply with safety instructions suggests that personal experience with negative consequences does not always induce greater diligence with hazardous products. According to Baltimore and Meyer (1969), households that experienced accidental poisonings were no more careful in storing poisons than were randomly selected households. Similarly, Bragg (1973) reported that many people previously involved in serious automobile accidents did not wear safety belts when they returned to the road after recovery.

Information Processing Objectives. Results obtained by deTurck and Goldhaber (1989a) indicated that IPOs moderated the effects of product users' compliance with a warning message. One half of the research participants were asked to examine a container of oven cleaner using either a memory-set IPO (try to remember as much information from the product label as possible), whereas the other half of the participants were asked to examine the oven cleaner label using an impression-set IPO (form an impression of the product as you examine its label). Research participants were asked to test the product (actually lemon yogurt) on a dirty hibachi. A pair of protective rubber gloves (recommended in label) was sitting on the table by the container of oven cleaner. Participants in the memory-set condition (63%) were more likely to wear the gloves prior to testing the cleaner than were participants in the impression-set condition (37%).

FUTURE RESEARCH DIRECTIONS

The effects of government-mandated warnings on product users' safety behavior is not particularly encouraging (McCarthy, Finnegan, Krumm-Scott, & McCarthy, 1984; McCarthy, Horst, Beyer, Robinson, & McCarthy, 1987). Indeed, the proliferation of mandated product warning messages may have contributed significantly to consumers' insouciant attitude toward safety behavior. The ubiquity of warning labels may be responsible for desensitizing consumers' awareness of and compliance with product safety information.

There is an urgent need in the warnings literature to conduct programmatic research based on theoretical models of persuasion, such as the Elaboration Likelihood Model (Petty & Cacioppo, 1986) and the Heuristic Model (Chaiken, 1987). Although these theories are acknowledged in reviews of warnings research (see Wogalter et al., 1999), the vast majority of published studies on the persuasive effects of warnings are relatively brief atheoretical research reports that tend to focus almost exclusively on message-oriented factors. The aforementioned models of persuasion would be extremely useful for researchers designing studies to determine the effectiveness/ineffectiveness of warning messages across a variety of products, product users, and contexts. Following is a brief road map to guide future research.

Additional research is necessary to determine the relationship between the severity of the hazard and product users' perception of risk and safety behavior. Although some warnings researchers have concluded that there is a correlation between severity of risk and consumers' perception of risk and safety behavior, the relationship is inconsistent (deTurck, Goldhaber, Richetto, & Young, 1992). The vast majority of warnings research testing the effects of severity have failed to conduct manipulation checks. In two of the studies reported earlier in which manipulation checks were performed (deTurck et al., 1999, Studies II and III), despite successful manipulations of severity of hazard, no effects were obtained for perception of risk and compliance.

Another reason for the disparity in effects of fear appeals between the persuasion and warnings literatures may be due to the fact that the persuasive messages in fear appeals research tend to be more graphic or explicit when communicating the severity of hazard. One strategy for increasing the perceived level of hazard might be to include more graphic representations of injuries in pictorials. Currently, warnings employ abstract drawings (icons) of potential injuries (e.g., a hand caught between moving machine parts). The effects of these pictographs on perceived risk and compliance are inconsistent (Booher, 1975; Friedmann, 1988; Ringseis & Caird, 1995; Young & Wogalter, 1990). It would be useful to design research that compares the relative effects of the abstract renderings approved by regulatory agencies and actual photographs of injuries.

It is apparent from the current review that there is a dearth of research designed to determine the role of response- and self-efficacy in the effectiveness of warnings. This may be attributable to the fact that behavioral compliance with warnings requires, for the most part, very simple discrete behaviors (e.g., wearing a bicycle helmet). By including specific information in a warning with respect to how many serious injuries are prevented by simple behaviors (e.g., wearing a bicycle helmet), product users may perceive greater response-efficacy and, as a result, be more likely to comply with a warnings' recommendations.

However, there are products (e.g., infant car seats) that require a relatively greater amount of behavioral complexity and/or effort for correct installation and use. It would be useful to compare the effects of warnings in which self-efficacy is systematically varied within warning messages. It would be particularly useful to determine whether visual demonstrations—role modeling effect—would enhance response-efficacy for difficult-to-use products compared to text-only on-product labels. This could be achieved in printed on-product labels by including photographs of the correct and incorrect use of a product (e.g., model wearing/not wearing safety goggles) or testing the effect of instructions to store safety equipment with a product (e.g., always hang helmet on bicycle handlebars) so as to minimize the effort required for compliance.

It would also be useful to study the effects of alternative media for providing warning messages. Consumers may have become inundated with on-product warning labels and, as a result, may devote less attention to this warning strategy than to alternative media for warnings. Moreover the effectiveness of an on-product warning label may be diminished by situational pressures or time constraints present when products are used. By targeting specific populations of product users using alternative media (e.g., newsletters) in situations where they are not so preoccupied with competing messages, manufacturers may be more effective at informing consumers of the hazards associated with a product/situation (Vetto, Dubois, & Vetto, 1996). Research should compare the effects of warnings embedded in a variety of different modalities (e.g., on-product labels, newsletters, audio/audiovisual messages). Research testing the effects of modality for warnings should also consider the effects of graphic detail for communicating the severity of hazard.

By examining alternative modalities for communicating warnings, researchers can also examine the effect of the source of the message on warning effectiveness. Currently, manufacturers of products or government agencies are the source of products' warnings. Research by Lirtzman and Shuv-Ami (1986) found that product testing labs were preferred over manufacturers and government agencies as sources of safety information. It would be useful to design several experiments comparing the effects of various sources (e.g., government agencies, manufacturers, celebrities, peers) across several modalities so as to determine the most effective source/medium combination for communicating product hazards across a variety of product classes.

Because familiarity exerts such a potent effect on all aspects of product users' processing of warning messages and safety behavior, the warnings and persuasion literatures would benefit from research designed to determine message strategies that overcome the debilitating effects of consumers' familiarity with products on their safety behavior. However, a necessary first step in this research program would be to determine whether familiarity is caused by frequency and/or duration of product use. It might be the case that a single exposure over a relatively extended period of time

(e.g., 8 hours) is sufficient to trigger the familiarity effect. Or perhaps repeated exposures for relatively short durations create a perception of familiarity among product users. Currently, warnings research on familiarity has divided research participants into groups of familiar/unfamiliar product users based on their frequency of exposure to a product in a naturally occurring context (e.g., frequency of using a swimming pool).

By comparing various message strategies across different frequencies and/or durations of product use, it may be possible to identify warning strategies that overcome the familiarity effect at different stages of familiarity. More specifically, simple instructions (e.g., "Even if you are familiar with this product, read the safety instructions") that are strategically located might be sufficient to override the familiarity effect. However, more strongly worded messages (language intensity) might be necessary as product users' familiarity increases (e.g., "You must read and follow all of the safety instructions no matter what your level of experience with this product is"). However, a warning that advocates levels of compliance that differs substantially from a consumer's perception of what is necessary might serve only to produce a "boomerang effect" among highly familiar users (Rhine & Severance, 1970). A boomerang effect refers to situations in which a persuasive message has the opposite than intended effect. In other words, rather than enhancing product users' compliance with safety instructions, a warning may serve to reduce consumers' compliance with the safety recommendations.

The persuasive impact of the role modeling effect may also prove to be a useful communication strategy for overcoming the familiarity effect. Various operationalizations of role models (e.g., pictorials, vocal messages, audiovisual portrayals) may effectively prompt product users to comply with warning messages' safety recommendations. Research designs that examine the effects of role models correctly demonstrating a product in a warning across several modalities (e.g., pictorial, vocal, and videotape) on product users who vary with respect to their product familiarity (frequency and/or duration of exposure) would shed some much needed light on how best to obtain compliance from consumers with a high level of product familiarity.

Another avenue of inquiry that would benefit the warnings and persuasion literature would be to design studies that systematically vary outcome-relevant involvement among participants serving as product users in laboratory settings. It is likely that the vast majority of research participants in laboratory studies perceive very little or no outcome-relevant involvement; participants do not believe that the safety information is all that important because the university would not allow them to be injured in a product testing study. It is vital that researchers yoke research participants' outcome-relevant involvement so as to enhance the mundane realism of product safety research in a laboratory context (Aronson & Carlsmith, 1968).

Finally, it would be useful to test the effectiveness of face-to-face warning interventions in educational, professional, and commercial settings. Face-to-face interventions allow for very targeted, specific, and detailed warning presentations and provide an opportunity for sources of warnings to determine whether their recommendations are received and understood—feedback. The opportunity to obtain feedback is lost in noninteractive methods for communicating warnings.

Although face-to-face communication can be labor intensive and cost prohibitive, it might prove to be very feasible and cost-effective in terms of reduced injuries due to accidents.

SUMMARY

Product warning messages have been the primary communication vehicle for alerting consumers about the hazards associated with using products. The goal of communicating product warnings is to provide product users with information they need to know so as to be able to use the products safely. Standards for the structure of products' warnings recommend four distinct types of information: signal word, hazard statement, hazard avoidance statement, and consequences statement. Research evaluating the effectiveness of the four facets of warnings has produced a mixed bag of results. Although some positive effects were obtained, it is uncertain whether all four elements are necessary to obtain behavioral compliance from product users.

A model of the effects of products' warnings on consumers' cognitive processing and compliance was proposed. The model suggests that personal and situational factors exert an influence on all facets of product users' safety information processing and behavioral compliance. Research examining the effects of products' warnings on consumers' awareness of warnings, comprehension of warnings, perception of risk, and compliance indicates that warnings exert a relatively small and inconsistent effect on these outcomes compared to situational factors (role models and cost of compliance) and personal factors (familiarity, age, gender, and IPOs).

REFERENCES

American National Standards Institute. (1991). *Product safety signs and labels: ANSI Z535.4.* Washington, DC: National Electrical and Manufacturing Association.

American National Standards Institute. (1997). *Product safety signs and labels: ANSI Z535.4.*

Washington, DC: National Electrical and Manufacturing Association.

Aronson, E., & Carlsmith, J. (1968). Experimentation in social psychology. In G. Lindzey & E. Aronson (Eds.), *Handbook of social psychology* (Vol. 2, pp. 1-79). Reading, MA: Addison-Wesley.

Baltimore, C., & Meyer, R. J. (1969). A study of storage, child behavioral traits, and mother's knowledge of toxicology in 52 poisoned families and 52 comparison families. *Pediatrics, 44,* 816-820.

Bandura, A. (1986). *Social foundation of thought and action: A social cognitive approach.* Englewood Cliffs, NJ: Prentice Hall.

Booher, H. R. (1975). Relative comprehensibility of pictorial information and printed words in proceduralized instructions. *Human Factors, 17,* 266-277.

Boster, F. J., & Mongeau, P. (1984). Fear-arousing persuasive messages. In R. N. Bostrom (Ed.), *Communication Yearbook 8* (pp. 330-375). Beverly Hills, CA: Sage.

Bragg, B. W. (1973). *A good idea but are they too much bother: An analysis of the relationship between attitudes toward seat belts and reported use.* Ottawa: Department of Transport, Road and Motor Vehicle Traffic Safety Branch.

Chaiken, S. (1987). The Heuristic Model of persuasion. In M. P. Zanna, J. M. Olson, & C. P. Herman (Eds.), *Social influence: The Ontario Symposium* (Vol. 5, pp. 2-39). Hillsdale, NJ: Lawrence Erlbaum.

Chen, J. Y. C., & Gibson, R. D. (1997). Perceived risk dilution with multiple warnings. In *Proceedings of the Human Factors Society 41st annual meeting* (pp. 831-835). Santa Monica, CA: Human Factors Society.

Cox, E. P., III, Wogalter, M. S., Stokes, S. L., & Murff, E. J. T. (1997). Do product warnings increase safe behavior? A meta-analysis. *Journal of Public Policy, 16,* 195-204.

deTurck, M. A. (1994). Developing product warnings: A communication theory perspective. *Product warnings, instructions, and user information, Section J.* Chicago: American Bar Association.

deTurck, M. A., Chih, I., & Hsu, Y. (1999). Three studies testing the effects of role models on product users' safety behavior. *Human Factors, 41,* 397-412.

deTurck, M. A., & Goldhaber, G. M. (1989a). Effectiveness of product warning labels: Effects of consumers' information processing objectives. *Journal of Consumer Affairs, 23,* 111-126.

deTurck, M. A., & Goldhaber, G. M. (1989b). Effectiveness of signal words in warnings: Effects of familiarity and gender. *Journal of Products Liability, 12,* 104-114.

deTurck, M. A., & Goldhaber, G. M. (1991). A developmental analysis of warning signs: The case of familiarity and gender. *Journal of Products Liability, 13,* 65-78.

deTurck, M. A., Goldhaber, G. M., & Richetto, G. M. (1989). Effectiveness of product warnings: Effects of language valence, redundancy, and color. *Journal of Products Liability, 17,* 187-195.

deTurck, M. A., Goldhaber, G. M., & Richetto, G. M. (1991a). Uncertainty reduction in product warnings: Effects of fear in signal word and hazard statement. *Journal of Products Liability, 13,* 339-346.

deTurck, M. A., Goldhaber, G. M., & Richetto, G. M. (1991b). Uncertainty reduction in product warnings: Effects of fear and color. *Journal of Products Liability, 13,* 329-338.

deTurck, M. A., Goldhaber, G. M., & Richetto, G. M. (1992). Familiarity and awareness: Effects of conscious and nonconscious safety information. *Journal of Products & Toxics Liability, 14,* 341-350.

deTurck, M. A., Goldhaber, G. M., & Richetto, G. M. (1995). Effectiveness of alcoholic beverage warning labels: Effects of consumer information processing objectives and color of signal word. *Journal of Products & Toxics Liability, 17,* 187-195.

deTurck, M. A., Goldhaber, G. M., Richetto, G. M., & Young, M. J. (1992). Effects of fear-arousing warning messages. *Journal of Products Liability, 14,* 217-223.

deTurck, M. A., Rachlin, R. A., & Young, M. J. (1994). Effects of a role model and fear in warning label on perceptions of safety and safety behavior. *Advances in Consumer Research, 21,* 208-212.

Dillard, J. P. (1994). Rethinking the study of fear appeals: An emotional perspective. *Communication Theory, 4*, 292-323.

Dorris, A. L., & Purswell, J. L. (1977). Warnings and human behavior: Implications for the design of product warnings. *Journal of Products Liability, 1*, 255-263.

Friedman, K. (1988). The effect of adding symbols to written warning labels on user behavior and recall. *Human Factors, 30*, 507-515.

Gill, R. T., Barbera, C., & Precht, T. (1987). A comparative evaluation of warning label designs. In *Proceedings of the Human Factors Society 31st annual meeting* (pp. 476-478). Santa Monica, CA: Human Factors Society.

Godfrey, S. S., Allender, L., Laughery, K. R., & Smith, V. L. (1983). Warning messages: Will the consumer bother to look? In *Proceedings of the Human Factors Society 27th annual meeting* (pp. 950-954). Santa Monica, CA: Human Factors Society.

Godfrey, S. S., & Laughery, K. R. (1984). The biasing effects of product familiarity on consumers' awareness of hazard. In *Proceedings of the Human Factors Society 28th annual meeting* (pp. 483-486). Santa Monica, CA: Human Factors Society.

Goldhaber, G. M., & deTurck, M. A. (1988). Effects of product warnings on adolescents in an education context. *Product Safety & Liability Reporter, 16*, 949-955.

Hale, J. L., & Dillard, J. P. (1995). Fear appeals in health promotion campaigns: Too much, too little, or just right? In E. Maibach & R. L. Parrott (Eds.), *Designing health messages: Approaches from communication theory and public health practice* (pp. 65-80). Thousand Oaks, CA: Sage.

Hamilton, D. L., Katz, L. B., & Leirer, V. O. (1980). Organizational processes in impression formation. In R. Hastie, T. M. Ostrom, E. B. Ebbesen, R. S. Wyer, D. Hamilton, & D. E. Carlston (Eds.), *Person memory: The cognitive basis of social perception* (pp. 121-153). Hillsdale, NJ: Lawrence Erlbaum.

Jefferson, T. (1984). *Jefferson: Autobiography, notes on the state of Virginia, public and private papers, addresses and letters.* New York: Library Classics of the United States.

Karnes, E. W., Leonard, S. D., & Rachwal, G. (1986). Effects of benign experiences on the per-ception of risk. In *Proceedings of the Human Factors Society 30th annual meeting* (pp. 121-125). Santa Monica, CA: Human Factors Society.

Laughery, K. R., & Young, S. L. (1991). Consumer product warnings: Design factors that influence noticeability. In *Proceedings of the 11th Congress International Ergonomics Association.* Santa Monica, CA: Human Factors Society.

Lehto, M. R., & Miller, J. M. (1986). *Warnings, Vol. 1: Fundamentals, design, and evaluation methodologies.* Ann Arbor, MI: Fuller Technical Publications.

Lirtzman, S. I., & Shuv-Ami, A. (1986). Credibility of sources of communication on product safety hazards. *Psychological Reports, 58*, 707-718.

McCarthy, R. L., Finnegan, J. P., Krumm-Scott, S., & McCarthy, G. (1984). Product information presentation, user behavior, and safety. In *Proceedings of the Human Factors Society 28th annual meeting* (pp. 81-84). Santa Monica, CA: Human Factors Society.

McCarthy, G. E., Horst, D. P., Beyer, R. R., Robinson, J. N., & McCarthy, R. L. (1987). Measured impact of a mandated warning on user behavior. In *Proceedings of the Human Factors Society 31st annual meeting* (pp. 479-483). Santa Monica, CA: Human Factors Society.

Miller, J. M., Lehto, M. R., & Frantz, J. P. (1990). *Instructions and warnings: The annotated bibliography.* Ann Arbor, MI: Fuller Technical Publications.

Mongeau, P. A. (1998). Another look at fear-arousing persuasive appeals. In M. Allen & R. W. Preiss (Eds.), *Persuasion: Advances through meta-analysis.* Cresskill, NJ: Hampton.

Otsubo, S. M. (1988). A behavioral study of warning labels for consumer products: Perceived danger and use of pictographs. In *Proceedings of the Human Factors Society 32nd annual meeting* (pp. 536-540). Santa Monica, CA: Human Factors Society.

Petty, R. E., & Cacioppo, J. T. (1986). The Elaboration Likelihood Model of persuasion. *Advances in Experimental Social Psychology, 19*, 123-205.

Rethans, A. J., & Hastek, M. (1981). Representation of product hazards in consumer memory. *Advances in Consumer Research, 9*, 487-491.

Rhine, R. J., & Severance, L. J. (1970). Ego-involvement, discrepancy, source credibility, and attitude change. *Journal of Personality and Social Psychology, 16,* 175-190.

Ringseis, E. L., & Caird, J. K. (1995). The comprehensibility and legibility of twenty pharmaceutical warning pictograms. In *Proceedings of the Human Factors 39th annual meeting* (pp. 974-978). Santa Monica, CA: Human Factors Society.

Rogers, R. W. (1983). Cognitive and psychological process in fear appeals and attitude change: A revised theory of protection motivation. In J. Cacioppo & R. Petty (Eds.), *Social psychophysiology: A sourcebook* (pp. 153-176). New York: Guilford.

Scammon, D. (1977). Information load and consumers. *Journal of Consumer Research, 4,* 148-155.

Schneider, K. C. (1977). Prevention of accidental poisoning through package and label design. *Journal of Consumer Research, 4,* 67-74.

Shinar, D., & Drory, A. (1983). Sign registration in daytime and nighttime driving. *Human Factors, 25,* 117-122.

Silver, N. C., Leonard, D. C., Ponski, K. A., & Wogalter, M. S. (1991). Warnings and purchase intentions for pest-control products. *Forensic Reports, 4,* 17-33.

Slovic, P., Fischoff , B., & Lichtenstein, S. (1980). Facts versus fears: Understanding perceived risk. In R. Schwing & W. A. Albers, Jr. (Eds.), *Societal risk assessment: How safe is safe enough?* (pp. 463-489). New York: Plenum.

Sternthal, B., & Craig, C. S. (1974). Fear appeals: Revisited and revised. *Journal of Consumer Research, 1,* 22-34.

Vetto, J. T., Dubois, P. M., & Vetto, I. P. (1996). The impact of distribution of a patient-education pamphlet in a multidisciplinary breast clinic. *Journal of Cancer Education, 11,* 148-152.

Vredenburgh, A. G., & Cohen, H. H. (1993). Compliance with warnings I: High risk recreational activities—Skiing and scuba. In *Proceedings of the Human Factors and Ergonomics Society 37th annual meeting* (pp. 945-949). Santa Monica, CA: Human Factors and Ergonomics Society.

Witte, K. (1998). Fear as motivator, fear as inhibitor: Using the Extended Parallel Process Model to explain fear appeal success and failure. In P. A. Andersen & L. K. Guerrero (Eds.), *Handbook of communication and emotion: Research, theory, applications, and contexts* (pp. 422-450). San Diego: Academic Press.

Witte, K., & Allen, M. (2000). A meta-analysis of fear appeals: Implications for effective public health campaigns. *Health Education and Behavior, 27,* 591-615.

Wogalter, M. S., Barlow, T., & Murphy, S. A. (1995). Compliance to owner's manual warnings: Influence of familiarity and the placement of a supplemental directive. *Ergonomics, 38,* 1081-1091.

Wogalter, M. S., Brelsford, J. W., Desaulniers, D. R., & Laughery, K. R. (1991). Consumer product warnings: The role of hazard perception. *Journal of Safety Research, 22,* 71-82.

Wogalter, M. S., DeJoy, D. M., & Laughery, K. R. (1999). *Warnings and risk communication.* Philadelphia: Taylor & Francis.

Wogalter, M. S., Desaulniers, D. R., & Brelsford, J. W. (1987). Consumer products: How are the hazards perceived? *Proceedings of the Human Factors Society 31st annual meeting* (pp. 615-619). Santa Monica, CA: Human Factors Society.

Wogalter, M. S., Fontenelle, G. A., & Laughrey, K. R. (1985). Behavioral effectiveness of warnings. In *Proceedings of the Human Factors Society 29th annual meeting* (pp. 664-668). Santa Monica, CA: Human Factors Society.

Wogalter, M. S., Godfrey, S. S., Fontenelle, G. A., Desaulniers, D. R., Rothstein, P. R., & Laughery, K. R. (1987). Effectiveness of warnings. In *Proceedings of the Human Factors Society 31st annual meeting* (pp. 599-612). Santa Monica, CA: Human Factors Society.

Wogalter, M. S., McKenna, N. A., & Allison, S. T. (1988). Warning compliance: Behavioral effects of cost and consensus. *Proceedings of the Human Factors 32nd annual meeting* (pp. 901-904). Santa Monica, CA: Human Factors Society.

Wyer, R. S., & Srull, T. K. (1986). Human cognition in its social context. *Psychological Review, 23,* 322-359.

Young, M. J., & deTurck, M. A. (1995, May). *Increasing compliance with safety instructions.* Paper presented at the meeting of the International Communication Association, Albuquerque, NM.

Young, S. L. (1991). Increasing the noticeability of warnings: Effects of pictorial, color, signal icon, and border. In *Proceedings of the Human Factors Society 35th annual meeting* (pp. 580-584). Santa Monica, CA: Human Factors Society.

Young, S. L. (1997). The role of pictorials in environmental safety signs. In *Proceedings of the Human Factors and Ergonomics Society 41st annual meeting* (pp. 797-800). Santa Monica, CA: Human Factors Society.

Young, S. L., Brelsford, J. W., & Wogalter, M. S. (1990). Judgments of hazard, risk, and danger: Do they differ? In *Proceedings of the Human Factors Society 34th annual meeting* (pp. 503-507). Santa Monica, CA: Human Factors Society.

Young, S. L., & Wogalter, M. S. (1990). Effects of conspicuous print and pictorial icons on comprehensive memory of instruction manual warnings. *Human Factors, 32,* 637-649.

Young, S. L., Wogalter, M. S., & Brelsford, J. W. (1992). Relative contribution of likelihood and severity of injury to risk perceptions. In *Proceedings of the Human Factors Society 36th annual meeting* (pp. 1014-1018). Santa Monica, CA: Human Factors Society.

Young, S. L., Wogalter, M. S., Laughery, K. R., Magurno, A., & Lovvoll, D. (1995). Relative order and space allocation of message components in hazard warning signs. *Proceedings of the Human Factors and Ergonomics Society 39th annual meeting* (pp. 969-973). Santa Monica, CA: Human Factors Society.

PART IV

MESSAGE FEATURES

19

Language and Persuasion

LAWRENCE A. HOSMAN

Persuasive messages contain various elements, but one of the most critical is language. This chapter reviews research that has examined the persuasive impact of various components of language. Because other chapters also focus on issues relating to language and persuasion, such as metaphor and message framing, they are not reviewed in this chapter.

NATURE OF LANGUAGE

Although many characterizations of language exist (e.g., Bradac, 1999), most agree that language has two general components: a structural component and a use component (Crystal, 1995). The structural component focuses on the hierarchical organization of language and consists of several parts, four of which are important for this chapter. These are phonology, syntax, lexicon, and texts or narratives.

Phonology deals with a language's sound system and how sounds are combined into meaningful units. *Syntax* addresses the rules underlying the construction of sentences. The *lexicon* originally referred to the vocabulary of a language. More recently, study of the lexicon has diversified (Crystal, 1995) and includes a language's words and meanings, idioms, abbreviations, euphemisms, and other meaningful units. *Texts* or *narratives* are "self-contained units of discourse" (p. 2), usually with some form of internal organization. Often, text is a frame of reference for the interpretation of a language's phonological, grammatical, and lexical elements.

The use component focuses on how speakers use language in communicative contexts. It includes several areas of study including regional variations in language use, ethnic and social variation in language use, and pragmatic variations in language use.

These general components and individual parts are interrelated, and the boundaries between them are fuzzy. For example, speakers can use lexical elements of a language in different ways and for different purposes. Not only are narratives an organized collection of sentences, but speakers can use them for particular purposes. Nonetheless, these various

371

language components will serve as the organizational basis for the research reviewed later in this chapter.

ASSUMPTIONS AND QUESTIONS UNDERLYING RESEARCH ON LANGUAGE AND PERSUASION

The central question that scholars of language and persuasion address is deceptively simple: What effects do variations in the phonological, syntactical, lexical, textual, and use elements of a message have on persuasion? Two aspects of the question are critical. First, what language variations are important? As Bradac, Bowers, and Courtright (1979) pointed out, variations in nearly all of the levels of language can be important. Later sections of this chapter review language variations that scholars have studied.

The second critical element is what aspects of the persuasion process these language variations affect. Most research assumes that language variations affect one of three elements of the persuasion process: judgments of the speaker, message comprehension or recall, or attitude toward the message. Numerous studies have focused on judgments of the speaker. The assumption is that language variation affects the impression formation process, and in a persuasion context an important impression affected is that of the speaker. Language variations may affect listeners' judgments of a speaker's source credibility, attractiveness, likability, and/or similarity. Other research has examined the impact of language variation on listeners' comprehension, recall, and/or understanding of a message. Finally, some research has investigated the effect of language variations on attitude toward the message. Research focusing on judgments of the speaker and message comprehension or recall implicitly assumes that effects in these two areas will ultimately affect attitude toward the message

and persuasion. That is, research assumes that if a particular language variation has a positive impact on speaker credibility, it will also have a positive impact on attitude toward the message. These assumed links among various elements are intuitively plausible but do not always exist. As discussed later in this chapter, researchers need to investigate these assumptions more explicitly.

LANGUAGE AND PERSUASION

Subsequent sections review research investigating the effects of language variations on the persuasion process. The research reviewed is limited to (a) research with a quantitative or empirical methodology and (b) research that focused on outcomes relevant to the persuasion process such as judgments of the speaker, message recall, and attitude toward the message.

Phonological Level

The phonological level deals with the sound system of a language. Although the study of phonology includes the formation of sounds or the combination of sounds, the research that is relevant to persuasion focuses on the perceptual outcomes of different sound combinations. Certain sound combinations may have different outcomes for the persuasion process than do others.

Little research has looked at the persuasive impact of this level of language, but two studies suggest its potential importance. Barry and Harper (1995) found that men's and women's first names could be distinguished by their phonetic attributes. Most important for the persuasion process is their claim that "phonetic attributes might contribute to the perception of a name as attractive or powerful" (p. 817). At least at the level of impression formation, a speaker's name might have persuasive implications.

Smith (1998) conducted a study in which he looked at the persuasive impact of political names. Using a category scheme that assigned weights to various phonetic features in a politician's name, such as the number of syllables or pattern of emphasis, he found that the model could predict 83% of the winners of presidential elections; 73% of the 1995 local elections in Spokane County, Washington; nearly 65% of the U.S. Senate elections in 1996; and 59% of the most competitive House elections in 1996. Although other factors undoubtedly influenced these election results, they clearly show that the phonetic properties of a politician's name may influence the electorate.

In short, the sound system of a language may have important consequences for persuasion. Because the research is not very extensive in this area, the nature and extent of these implications are not well-known.

Syntactic Level

The syntactic level of language deals with the rules governing the construction of sentences from the component parts of a language. More recently, scholars have studied the rules that govern the construction of larger chunks of discourse such as narratives or stories. The study of syntax shows that sentences can vary in their complexity. Some have a relatively simple structure such as "The cat chased the mouse." Other sentences are more complex, usually because a grammatical transformation has been applied. For example, if the passive sentence transformation were applied to the preceding sentence, it would become "The mouse was chased by the cat." Other sentences are more complex such as "The cat, focusing on its prey, chased the mouse." Sentences with more complex grammatical structures would be expected to be more difficult to understand or comprehend. This comprehension difficulty could affect the persuasion process negatively, presumably because comprehension of a message is an antecedent to persuasion or attitude change. This assumption is consistent with information processing models of persuasion (McGuire, 1969).

Jacoby, Nelson, and Hoyer (1982) looked at the effects of various syntactic constructions on the comprehension of corrective advertising. They found that positively worded statements (e.g., "Research has proven X") were more easily comprehended than negative ones (e.g., "Research has not proven X"). This result is consistent with other psycholinguistic research that has found that negative grammatical transformations are more complex than positive grammatical transformations because they either require a longer time to process (see Fodor, Bever, & Garrett, 1974) or tax the cognitive system more during processing (see Ratner & Gleason, 1993).

Motes, Hilton, and Fielden (1992) examined the effects of active and passive sentence structure on the perceived believability, clarity, appealingness, and attractiveness of print advertisements. They found that readers more favorably evaluated advertisements with active rather than passive sentence structure.

More recently, Lowrey (1998) conducted three studies examining the effect of syntactic complexity on advertising comprehension and attitudes toward the product. In one study, she found that simple syntax produced better recall than did complex syntax, but she also found that syntactic complexity was unrelated to attitude toward the product. A second study found that argument strength moderated the effects of syntactic complexity. With a complex syntactic structure, attitudes did not differ as a function of argument strength; however, with a simple syntactic structure, strong arguments were more persuasive than weak arguments. Cognitive response data also reflected this pattern. A third study showed that receiver involvement affects the motivation to process complex syntax. Only highly involved participants were willing to assess strong and weak claims when the syntax was complex.

Although the research literature is sparse, it suggests that the complexity with which persuasive materials are written affects their outcomes. Research has also begun to look at units larger than a sentence. Thorson and Snyder (1984) looked at the structure of television commercial scripts and their impact on the recall of these commercials. They used an "advertising language model" based on Kintsch and van Dijk's (1978) macropropositional model of discourse. This model provides several structural measures of advertising content. They found that several of these measures predicted commercial recall.

Adaval and Wyer (1998) studied the effect of narratives on the perceived attractiveness of vacation promotion literature. Two travel brochures described a vacation. One brochure described the vacation in a narrative form, while the other brochure described it in a list form. The authors also looked at the effect of undesirable information being contained in the two conditions. The results showed that participants evaluated vacations presented in a narrative form more positively than when the vacations were presented in a list form. This effect was enhanced when the brochure included undesirable information about the vacation site. That is, participants attended to negative information more when presented in a list form than when presented in a narrative form. The effects of a narrative information presentation were also enhanced when pictures accompanied the text.

The nature of a sentence's grammatical construction or of a narrative's construction has important persuasive consequences. Grammatically complex materials are more difficult to recall than grammatically simple materi-

als. This research has yet to address whether these differences have consequences for other aspects of the persuasion process such as speaker judgments and attitude change.

Lexical Level

Persuaders' choices about the words to use and the meaning of words in a persuasive message are critical. This section reviews research that has looked at the effect of lexical variation and semantic variation on the persuasion process.

Lexical Diversity. Lexical diversity refers to the vocabulary richness or vocabulary range that speakers exhibit and is assessed via a type-token ratio (TTR)—the number of different words in a message (types) divided by the total number of words (tokens). A low TTR means that a speaker's vocabulary is relatively redundant, while a high TTR means that it is relatively diverse. Lexical diversity affects listeners' judgments of speakers through a principle of "preference for complexity" (Bradac, Desmond, & Murdock, 1977). Simply stated, listeners prefer complexity because it is interesting, and lexical diversity should be preferred because it represents more complex lexical choice.

In a series of studies, Bradac and his associates (e.g., Bradac, Courtright, Schmidt, & Davies, 1976; Bradac, Davies, Courtright, Desmond, & Murdock, 1977; Bradac, Desmond, & Murdock, 1977) supported this principle, finding that lexical diversity is directly related to judgments of a speaker's competence and socioeconomic status and to perceptions of message effectiveness. Another study (Burroughs, 1991) found that these types of evaluations occurred when adults evaluated child speakers.

Subsequent studies (e.g., Bradac et al., 1976; Bradac & Wisegarver, 1984) found that ascribed speaker status interacted with diversity to affect a number of speaker judgments. A high-status speaker exhibiting high lexical diversity was perceived positively, while a high-status speaker exhibiting low lexical diversity was perceived negatively. In addition, some studies (Carpenter, 1990; Dulaney, 1982) have found that those who lie or are duplicitous exhibit higher lexical diversity than do those who do not lie. The explanation for this latter finding is that the process of lying requires speakers to plan their utterances more carefully, thus increasing the use of new words.

In sum, these studies show that the richness of a speaker's vocabulary is related to listeners' judgments about a speaker's credibility or status. No research has explored the relationship between lexical diversity and attitude change. The preference for complexity principle would suggest that high lexical diversity would have a positive effect on the persuasion process.

Language Imagery and Vividness. Another aspect of the lexicon studied by language and persuasion scholars is verbal imagery or the ability of words to elicit images in listeners. Some researchers call this the vividness effect. Some words or expressions seem to elicit more imagery than others. Typically, concrete words, use of detail, and/or emotional language should elicit more images or be more vivid than should abstract or unemotional language. Similarly, one would expect verbal imagery or vividness to have more of a positive impact on persuasion than would pallid language. Vivid language should be more memorable and accessible and should more favorably influence attitude change than should pallid language (Nisbett & Ross, 1980). These predictions are consistent with theories that focus on attitude accessibility (Fazio, 1989), theories such as information processing (McGuire, 1969) that include attention to the

message, and theories such as the Heuristic-Systematic Model (Eagly & Chaiken, 1993) that incorporate the availability of heuristics as part of the persuasion process.

Despite these expectations, research on the persuasive impact of language imagery is contradictory. Some early studies found that verbal imagery had a positive impact on persuasion. For example, Rossiter and Percy (1978) found that concrete words produced nearly twice as many favorable attitudes toward a product than did abstract words. An important literature review (Taylor & Thompson, 1982) concluded, however, that no conclusive evidence existed demonstrating that vividly presented information was more persuasive than nonvividly presented information.

Since Taylor and Thompson's (1982) review, the literature has been mixed with respect to the vividness effect. Some studies have continued to find a vividness effect (e.g., Burns, Biswas, & Babin, 1993; Rooks, 1986), while other studies have not (e.g., Collins, Taylor, Wood, & Thompson, 1988; Rooks, 1987).

Much recent research has attempted to account for these contradictory results. Some have argued that vividness effects will occur only under conditions of differential listener attention (Taylor & Thompson, 1982). That is, when listeners' attention is constrained, listeners attend to vivid information more than to pallid information, and this vivid information is more persuasive. When listeners' attention is not constrained, listeners attend to vivid and pallid information equally. Frey and Eagly (1993), however, did not support this account.

Others have argued for a resource-matching perspective (Keller & Block, 1997). This perspective contends that vivid or pallid information's impact depends on a match between the cognitive resources demanded by the information and the cognitive resources allocated by a listener. Other scholars have argued that the effect of vivid information depends on other receiver characteristics. Block and Keller (1997) found, for example, that vivid information in health communications was more persuasive when the receivers were high in self-efficacy.

Two problems surround this area of research. First, many different conceptualizations and operationalizations of vividness exist. Some scholars (e.g., Taylor & Thompson, 1982) consider vivid information to include concrete and specific language, pictures and videotapes, direct experience, and case histories. Other studies use only concrete language items (e.g., Keller & Block, 1997). Some investigators consider vivid information to be that communicated by face-to-face interaction as opposed to print (Herr, Kardes, & Kim, 1991). Other investigators include grammatical structures such as active voice and present tense (Burns et al., 1993) in their operationalizations of vividness. These various operationalizations make it difficult to compare results across studies.

Second, the concept of vividness overlaps with other ideas discussed in this chapter and others. For example, emotional language and concrete words could be related to the work on language intensity and equivocation. Abstract language may be equivocal and less effective persuasively than are specific or concrete words. Case histories are conceptually linked to narratives. Much of this research on vividness has continued independent of work in other related areas.

Language Intensity. Hamilton and Hunter (1998) noted that two major approaches exist to the definition of language intensity. The first views language intensity as a stylistic feature of messages. Intense language could include emotion-laden words, such as *horrible* and *excellent,* or specific graphic language, such as *astronomical* and *completely.* The second approach views intensity as reflecting the extremity of a source's position on an issue (e.g., Bowers, 1963). A speaker describing a government policy as *horrible* is using more intense language than a speaker who describes the policy as *disconcerting,* and this shows greater deviation from attitudinal neutrality on this issue.

Although Hamilton and Hunter (1998) noted that some conceptual overlap exists between the two approaches, they argued that the approaches should be considered discrete. That is, someone can use intense language and not express an attitudinally extreme position. Conversely, a speaker can express an attitudinally extreme position without using particularly emotional or specific language. This conceptual distinction is important because it has consequences for how language intensity affects the persuasion process.

Hamilton and Hunter (1998) summarized the language intensity research using meta-analytic techniques. Based on information processing theory (Hamilton, 1997; McGuire, 1969), they tested a causal model of language intensity's persuasive effects. The results supported two causal paths between intensity and attitude toward the source. The first path showed that language intensity (via perceived intensity) increased perceived speaker dynamism. In turn, speaker dynamism increased perceived message clarity. Speaker dynamism apparently increased receivers' interest in the message, causing receivers to focus more on the message and increasing its clarity.

Message clarity was positively related to perceived source competence, which in turn was positively related to perceived source trustworthiness. Finally, perceived source trustworthiness was positively related to attitude toward the source.

A second causal path existed between language intensity and perceived source competence. Specifically, language intensity was positively related to the perceived extremity of the source's position, which in turn was negatively related to perceived source competence. As in the other causal model, perceived source competence was linked to attitude toward the source through perceived source trustworthiness. Importantly, when language intensity suggested an extreme source position, it had negative effects on perceived source competence and, ultimately, on attitude toward the source.

As this second causal path suggests, the positive correlation between language intensity and attitude change may depend on the message's position—whether the persuasive message is attitudinally congruent with or discrepant from receivers' attitudes. The meta-analysis supported this. When a message was attitudinally congruent, language intensity had little persuasive impact. However, when a message was attitudinally discrepant, language intensity's effect was dependent on a receiver's ego involvement. With a receiver high in ego involvement, language intensity had a negative relationship with attitude toward the source. When the receiver was low in ego involvement, language intensity positively affected attitude toward the source. A field study of language intensity's effects in skin cancer prevention messages supported this meta-analysis (Buller, Borland, & Burgoon, 1998). This study found that high-intensity messages produced less attitude change in listeners not intending to increase their skin protection than in those intending to increase their skin protection, particularly when the message drew explicit conclusions for the listeners.

The relationship among language intensity, message discrepancy, and ego involvement was also dependent on the source's credibility. Language intensity had a negative impact on attitude change when a high-credibility speaker delivered a discrepant message to a receiver with high ego involvement. Language intensity positively affected attitude change when a high-credibility speaker delivered a discrepant message to a receiver with low ego involvement.

Another meta-analysis by Hamilton (1998) further explored the relationship between language intensity and source credibility. He found that argument quality enhanced the positive effects of language intensity on source competence, while opinionated language (i.e., receivers' positions on the issue are evaluated) enhanced the negative effect of language intensity on perceived source competence.

Equivocal Language. One choice communicators have to make is how clear or how vague to be in a persuasion context. Should politicians, for example, state their position on abortion clearly and unequivocally, or should they be vague and equivocal? Although some view equivocation negatively, Eisenberg (1984) discussed the valuable role that strategic ambiguity plays in organizations. Ambiguity, for example, helps to build consensus on abstract goals, such as a mission statement, while simultaneously allowing for individual interpretations of these goals.

Williams and his colleagues conducted some of the earliest empirical research in this area. In a series of three studies (Goss & Williams, 1973; Williams, 1980; Williams & Goss, 1975), he examined equivocation's impact on perceptions of source credibility, message recall, and agreement with the message. He defined equivocation in this research as vagueness. For example, a speaker would equivocate if the speaker said that he or she favored a change in abortion policies rather than specifically stating that he or she favored a ban on abortions. Williams found that equivocal, attitudinally incongruent messages led to higher ratings of speaker character, greater message acceptance, and greater recall of argument content than did unequivocal, attitudinally incongruent messages. These results suggested that receivers could easily reject clear, attitudinally incongruent messages but that receivers could not as easily reject vague, attitudinally incongruent messages. In this latter case, Williams argued that the vagueness allowed receivers to perceive the messages as congruent with their attitudes.

Bavelas, Black, Chovil, and Mullett (1990) developed a more extensive theory of equivocation. They argued that equivocal messages avoid one of four elements in a communicative situation: sender, content, receiver, or context. An equivocal message may avoid showing whether the message is a speaker's own opinion. A speaker using the expression "noted authorities say" is not clearly saying whether it is his or her opinion, and the message is therefore equivocal. A message may be equivocal because it does not have clear content. This is consistent with the operational definition used by Williams (1980). An equivocal message does not address a particular receiver in the setting. It may address someone as a category, as in "Conservatives really bother me," or not address any particular person. Finally, equivocation occurs if someone wants to avoid the immediate context. This occurs, for example, if someone does not offer a direct answer to a question. If a teenage girl asks a parent whether she can go 60 miles to a concert with a boyfriend, the parent might respond equivocally by saying "Is it hot in here?"

Fundamental to this theory of equivocation is the contention that equivocation is the result of avoidance-avoidance circumstances. Speakers equivocate because they must make some response, but each response has a negative consequence. For example, equivocation is likely to occur when a speaker must choose between telling a hurtful truth and telling a harmless lie (Bavelas et al., 1990). This may help to explain why politicians equivocate to such a large extent. Bavelas and her colleagues (1990) presented data supporting this contention.

Most of Bavelas's research has focused on the production of equivocal messages rather than on their persuasive consequences. Hamilton, however, has pursued the persuasive consequences of equivocal messages. In one study (Hamilton & Mineo, 1998), he found that equivocation, defined in the study as a lack of linguistic specificity, decreased perceived message clarity. This, in turn, made it more difficult for receivers to identify a speaker's position. This study also found that longer messages led to decreased linguistic specificity or greater equivocation. A second study (Hamilton, 1998) found that unequivocal or specific language enhanced source credibility, but only with high-quality arguments. Specific language apparently enhanced the perceived quality of the arguments and consequently enhanced the perceived credibility of the source. With low-quality arguments, unequivocal language accentuated the poor quality and negatively affected perceived source credibility.

Thus, the diversity of words used by persuaders, the images words create in listeners' minds, the intensity of their language choices, and the vagueness of their language choices affect judgments of speaker credibility and attitude change. As noted in this section, the vividness research suffers from inconsistent operationalizations of the concept. Some operationalizations of vividness are similar to those used in the equivocal language research. Conceptual overlaps between the work in language intensity and equivocal language also exist. Equivocal language also hides the degree to which a speaker's attitude deviates from neutrality. These are issues for future researchers to pursue.

LANGUAGE USE

Language use refers to the use of language in social contexts. Variables that fit in this area include pragmatics, power of speech style, and standard and nonstandard language varieties.

Pragmatic Implication

When a receiver listens and tries to understand language or messages, part of the process involves making inferences about the speaker's meaning. Harris and Monaco (1978) elaborated on the way in which this occurs and distinguished between logical implications and pragmatic implications. A logical implication occurs when a sentence necessarily implies some information. For example, the sentence "Bill hit Tom" logically implies that Tom was hit. Pragmatic implication is information that is neither directly stated nor logically implied. The statement "The hungry lion caught the gazelle" pragmatically implies that the lion killed the gazelle but does not logically imply it.

Several studies (e.g., Harris, 1977; Harris, Teske, & Ginns, 1975; Harris, Trusty, Bechtold, & Wasinger, 1989; Searleman & Carter, 1988) in both advertising and legal contexts have revealed that people are unable to distinguish between information that is directly asserted and information that is pragmatically implied. People were also more likely to remember as true pragmatically implied material than directly asserted information. These findings suggest that receivers add to the persuasive message via pragmatic inferences. These inferences may be warranted or unwarranted, but they would be related to processes critical to receivers' comprehension, understanding, and memory of persuasive messages.

Power of Speech Style

Erickson, Lind, Johnson, and O'Barr (1978) first distinguished between powerful

and powerless speech styles. Based on their examination of several trial transcripts, they observed that those high in status (judges, lawyers, and expert witnesses) spoke differently from those low in status (lay witnesses and defendants). Those low in status exhibited a relatively high frequency of language features such as hedges (e.g., "sort of," "kind of"), hesitations (e.g., "um," "er"), intensifiers (e.g., "certainly," "surely"), and polite forms (e.g., "please," "sir"), and Erickson et al. labeled this a powerless style. Those high in status spoke with relatively few of these language features, and this was called a powerful style. The authors subsequently conducted an experimental study comparing participants' evaluations of these styles and found that participants perceived a speaker exhibiting a powerful style as more credible, sociable, attractive, and certain than a speaker exhibiting a powerless style.

Since then, two lines of research have evolved. One approach continues to use the molar concepts of powerful and powerless speech styles. These studies (e.g., Bradac, Hemphill, & Tardy, 1981; Bradac & Mulac, 1984b; Gibbons, Busch, & Bradac, 1991; Grob, Meyers, & Schuh, 1997; Hahn & Clayton, 1996; Sparks, Areni, & Cox, 1998) have generally found that participants perceive speakers exhibiting a powerful style as more credible, attractive, sociable, and dynamic than speakers exhibiting a powerless style.

The other line of research has focused on the individual components contained in the styles and their implications for the impression formation process. This chapter earlier discussed one of these components—language intensity. Other studies (e.g., Bradac & Mulac, 1984a; Haleta, 1996; Hosman, 1989; Hosman & Siltanen, 1994) examining individual components have found that participants perceive speakers exhibiting hedges and hesitations as less credible, attractive, and dynamic than speakers not using them. Polite forms, however, constitute something of an anomaly. Bradac and Mulac (1984a) found that listeners perceive polite forms to be as powerful as a powerful style. Other researchers (e.g., Lakoff, 1975) have contended that polite forms are a powerless form of speech.

Two links exist between power of speech style and the persuasion process. The first is an indirect link among power of speech style, impression formation, and attitude change. Most of the research shows that a powerful speech style will enhance a speaker's perceived credibility, attractiveness, dynamism, and sociability, and to the extent these impressions will positively affect attitude change, a powerful style should be more persuasive.

The more direct link focuses on the direct impact of powerful and powerless speech styles on attitude change. This is an area of substantial controversy. One study (Gibbons et al., 1991) found that a powerful speech style did not produce more attitude change than did a powerless style. Two studies (Erickson et al., 1978; Hahn & Clayton, 1996) found that a powerful speech style resulted in a more favorable verdict than did a powerless style. A meta-analysis of studies prior to 1991 found that powerful speech styles produced positive effects on attitude change (Burrell & Koper, 1998). One recent study (Sparks et al., 1998) suggested that differences in the ability to find direct effects of power of speech style may be due to the modality of message presentation. The authors found that a powerful speech style was more persuasive than a powerless style when the message was presented via audiotape, but no significant differences between styles emerged when the messages were written.

Standard and Nonstandard Language Varieties

For years, scholars have studied the effects of regional and ethnic language variation on

the impression formation process (for reviews, see Bradac, 1990; Giles & Coupland, 1991). For example, Hopper and Williams (1973) investigated the impact of Standard American, Black, Mexican American, and Southern White speech characteristics on employment decisions. They found that participants evaluated Standard American speech more positively than they did the other three speech types.

Over the years, this research has shifted its characterization of these speech styles from one of regional and ethnic variation to one of standard and nonstandard language varieties. A standard variety is one linked with high socioeconomic status and power, while a nonstandard variety is one linked with low socioeconomic status and power. Nonstandard language varieties are usually associated with regional or ethnic minority dialects or accents.

In general, the research shows that listeners positively evaluate standard language varieties across several evaluative dimensions such as intelligence, competence, and social attractiveness. For example, de la Zerda and Hopper (1979) studied interviewers' reactions to Mexican American speech, finding that the degree of accentedness predicted evaluations of an interviewee's ambition, intelligence, and cooperativeness and predicted interviewers' likelihood of hiring the person. Furthermore, the greater the status of the position being interviewed for, the greater the importance language attitudes played in these evaluations. Atkins (1993) more recently confirmed this finding comparing Black English and Appalachian English speakers in an employment context. This pattern can be affected by the extent to which listeners identify with a language variety. If listeners perceive the language variety to be similar to their own, then they may be less likely to downgrade a nonstandard variety (Giles & Coupland, 1991).

Although this research suggests links between standard and nonstandard language varieties and persuasion, little research has directly addressed the issue. If listeners' perceptions of a speaker's competence, status, or attractiveness are related to the persuasion process, then one would expect standard language varieties to be more persuasive than nonstandard varieties. Two studies provide some evidence that standard and nonstandard language varieties may have effects that extend beyond speaker judgments. Koslow, Shamdasani, and Touchstone (1994) examined Hispanic consumers' reactions to print advertisements containing varying degrees of Spanish- and English-language use. They found that Spanish-language use enhanced Hispanic consumers' perceptions of an advertiser's sensitivity toward their culture and their attitude toward the advertisement. However, sole reliance on Spanish-language use decreased their attitude toward the advertisement, apparently reflecting Hispanic insecurities about language use. Rubin, Healy, Gardiner, Zath, and Moore (1997) examined reactions to a Standard American or South Asian accent in an AIDS prevention clinic. Participants judged a physician using a Standard American accent to be more interpersonally attractive and as possessing more general ability than a physician using a South Asian accent. Rubin et al. observed no significant differences between accents for recall of the AIDS message or intention to comply.

The use of language in persuasive contexts has important implications for the persuasion process. Most of this research, however, has focused on how stylistic or dialectical variations affect the impression formation process. Much more research needs to focus on their role in the attitude change process.

DIRECTIONS AND CHALLENGES FOR FUTURE RESEARCH

As the preceding literature review shows, research on language and persuasion has been conducted in many areas, with researchers working relatively independent of one another. Consequently, they have often not integrated findings in one area with relevant findings in other areas. Thus, theories or models that put research in a common framework or point to potentially fruitful areas of study need to guide the research. Two directions might help to accomplish this.

First, future research on the relationships between language variation and the impression formation process needs to be integrated within a more general model of the process. Most research has proceeded by merely investigating the impact of language variations on listener impressions related to the persuasion process such as perceived competence, attractiveness, and trustworthiness. A viable framework is a process model of language attitudes (Cargile, Giles, Ryan, & Bradac, 1994). Process models of language attitudes would encourage investigators to think more extensively about the link between language variation and impression formation. The Cargile et al. (1994) model emphasizes five features of the process by which listeners form attitudes about language variation: listener dynamics, interpersonal history, outcomes, the social situation, and perceived cultural factors.

Listener dynamics include several listener characteristics that may affect the process such as listeners' social group membership. Listeners' goals are relevant. The goals that listeners have for attending to a speaker or a persuasive message may influence the language features to which they attend. Listeners' moods may also be significant. A listener in a negative mood may be more receptive to messages that are syntactically easy to process than to messages that are syntactically difficult to process. A listener's expertise on an issue is potentially relevant as well. As Cargile et al. (1994) pointed out, if a listener has expertise on an issue, then he or she can invoke scripts or schemata to process information. This ability to invoke scripts or schemata frees cognitive resources, which allows the listener to process schema-inconsistent information more efficiently.

Researchers have neglected the area of listener dynamics. For example, they have not examined listener goals extensively. Fiske's work (Fiske, Morling, & Stevens, 1996) on power, social control, and anxiety suggests that listeners high in trait anxiety are motivated to regain control via impression formation processes when powerful people threaten their needs. Under certain conditions, they disregard negative information about a speaker and form an overly positive evaluation. They may also react differently to language variations in a message. For example, Hosman (1997) found that listeners with an external locus of control reacted more positively to a powerful speech style than did those with an internal locus of control. Similarly, little work has explored the impact of a listener's emotional state on his or her processing of various language forms. For instance, if a listener is in a negative mood, will this influence his or her processing of syntactically complex persuasive messages?

Listener dynamics also point toward a more sophisticated conceptualization of listener attitudes. Not only may listeners' attitudes toward language variations have a cognitive component, they also may have an emotional component and a behavioral component. Most current work on language and persuasion has focused on the cognitive component. That is, language variation causes listeners to believe that the speaker is trustworthy, competent, and/or suitable for employment. Little work has focused on the emotional and behavioral components.

A language attitude model also incorporates interpersonal history or how familiar a speaker and listener are with each other. Cargile et al. (1994) pointed out that when speakers and listeners are unfamiliar with each other, uncertainty reduction processes are more likely to occur, resulting in greater im-

pact of language variations. Similarly, expectancy violation processes are more likely to play a role when speakers and listeners are familiar with one another. For example, if a listener knows a speaker's status, then expectancy violations are more likely to affect the language attitude process.

The immediate social situation is also a factor important in the language attitude process. Many studies (e.g., Brown, Giles, & Thackerar, 1985; Johnson & Buttny, 1982; Street, Brady, & Lee, 1984) have found that listeners' attitudes toward a particular language variation vary from one context to another. For example, listeners may positively evaluate a fast rate of speech in informal contexts, but they may negatively evaluate it if technical or complex material is presented. The nature of the context may make some variations more salient than others. A courtroom context might make language variables that show uncertainty more salient than other language variables because judgments of witness uncertainty play a more pivotal role in the courtroom.

Finally, the cultural context also plays an important role in language attitudes. A particular aspect of the cultural context that is important is social norms. These social norms establish what the preferred or expected language behaviors are within a community. Holtgraves and Dulin (1994) found, for example, that African American and European American listeners evaluated bragging differently because the two cultures' norms about bragging differ.

This model begins to suggest additional interesting areas of research for language and persuasion. A potentially interesting research area is at the intersection of listener dynamics and cultural context. For example, do listeners from diverse cultures differ in their knowledge or expectations about what language variations are important in particular persuasion contexts? Friestad and Wright (1994) developed a persuasion knowledge model that emphasizes "the culturally supplied folk wisdom on persuasion" (p. 1) that people bring to persuasion contexts. We know very little about this knowledge and how it may vary between individuals from different cultures.

A second direction for researchers in language and persuasion is to conduct more theoretically grounded research (see Burgoon & Dillard, 1995). Much of the research on language and persuasion has been atheoretical in two senses. First, research has examined language variables without a well-developed explanation of why these variables should have particular effects. For example, although a powerful speech style clearly has positive effects across a variety of impression formation dimensions, it is unclear why it has such effects. At least two candidate explanations have been offered. One is that a powerful speech style indicates speaker self-control (e.g., behaving appropriately in a situation, exhibiting self-confidence). Research shows that receivers positively evaluate those who exhibit self-control (Stern & Manifold, 1977). The second explanation is that a powerful style suggests control over others. This control over others explanation has both a positive and a negative element. Control over others may be positive if it indicates effective behavior, but it may be negative if it suggests threatening or domineering behavior. Bradac and Street (1989-1990) argued that it is the positive perception that leads to the positive evaluation of a powerful style. Although a few studies have examined these explanations and found support for them (e.g., Hosman, 1997; Hosman & Siltanen, 1994), additional investigation is needed.

Second, and more important, most of the research has not integrated language variables into a coherent persuasion theory such as the Elaborated Likelihood Model of persuasion or the Heuristic-Systematic Model of persuasion. These process models highlight the different ways in which listeners process per-

suasive elements. Recent explications of dual-process models (e.g., Petty & Wegener, 1998) tend to ignore the role that language variables play in the process. However, such variables might be easily incorporated and studied within such models. In particular, investigators could examine these variables to see whether they operate as central, peripheral, or biasing cues. Most likely, they operate as peripheral or biasing cues, interacting with other elements of a message (e.g., argument quality) or other elements of the persuasion process (e.g., speaker credibility). For example, Hamilton's work on language intensity suggests that it interacts with argument quality. Other variables, such as syntactical complexity and narrative structure, could also affect the way messages high or low in argument quality are processed. Some variables may operate as biasing cues that affect the processing of some message elements more than others. For example, power of speech style may influence the processing of a low argument quality message more than that of a high argument quality message.

Examining language variables within these more comprehensive theoretical frameworks accomplishes two important goals. First, it moves language and persuasion research away from a focus on how language affects message comprehension or speaker judgments and toward an increased focus on how language affects attitude change. As mentioned earlier, too many researchers assume that messages positively affecting speaker credibility, for example, will also positively affect attitude change when in fact they need to investigate these linkages.

Second, because dual-process models emphasize cognitive responses to messages, they would encourage exploration of how listeners respond to language variables contained in persuasive messages. As Giles, Henwood, Coupland, Harriman, and Coupland (1992) pointed out, few studies have examined cognitive responses to language variables. For instance, we know little about how listeners cognitively respond to messages containing high-intensity language.

Studying the cognitive responses to these language variables will require more sophisticated content analytic schemes than are typically used in dual-processing research. Most of this research employs simple positive-negative coding schemes, sometimes dividing the categories into smaller units such as thoughts about the speaker. More sophisticated schemes, such as that used by Giles et al. (1992), allow for a more fine-grained understanding of cognitive responses to persuasive messages and the role they play as mediators in the persuasion process.

Other theories may also be valuable. For example, expectancy violation theory might enhance the study of language use variables (Burgoon, 1990). Put simply, this theory contends that listeners develop expectations about the language persuaders should use. When speakers violate these expectations by using language that is unexpected, listeners will evaluate them negatively. If, for example, listeners expect high-status speakers to speak with high lexical diversity and they do not, then listeners may perceive the speakers as having low source credibility. This theory has been successfully used to examine the impact of language intensity on attitude change and might be fruitfully used to explore other language variables.

Research examining the impact of language on persuasion also needs to focus on the relationships among language, cognitive responses, attention, comprehension, recall, and attitude change. As noted previously, research has investigated the effect of language variables on a limited number of outcomes. It seems reasonable to expect that some of these cognitive elements (e.g., cognitive responses) will mediate or moderate the effects of language variables on outcomes (e.g., attitude change). Examining such relationships will require the use of statistical techniques (e.g., path analysis, structural equation modeling) that allow for the exploration of interconnections among variables. Using such techniques, Hosman, Huebner, and Siltanen (1999) found that power of speech style did not have a direct effect on attitude change but had an indirect effect on attitude change via cognitive responses. Hamilton (1998) also fruitfully used such statistical techniques.

A challenge in this area is to increase the generalizability of research results. This is particularly important if practitioners are to be able to use results meaningfully. Usually, increasing the generalizability of research means extending the results to different groups of participants. Increasing a study's sample size and employing a sampling procedure that includes more diverse types of participants are methods to accomplish this. When researchers use language variables, however, generalization entails additional considerations. Here, generalization means to extend a study's results beyond the particular language sample used in the study. In a typical language and persuasion study, researchers construct a "template" message into which language variables of interest are inserted. Investigators might use a speech on a particular topic as a template message. They would then insert low- and high-language intensity forms into the template to create low- and high-intensity messages.

What investigators often forget is that these messages differ in more ways than simply the inclusion of high- and low-intensity language. The high- and low-intensity forms selected by the investigator might differ from the high- and low-intensity forms selected by another investigator. Furthermore, the template messages contain other language variables, and a template message written by one investigator might include different language variables from a template written by another investigator. These differences might interact in unknown ways with the language variables of interest. Thus, differences between low- and high-language intensity messages are limited to the template message into which researchers have inserted them.

Jackson and her colleagues (e.g., Brashers & Jackson, 1999; Jackson & Brashers, 1994a, 1994b; Jackson & Jacobs, 1983) have shown the implications of using single-message designs. Language effects can be extremely variable from one message to another. Brashers and Jackson (1999) discussed one study that looked at the impact of sexual content in advertising recall using 13 different topics. This study found that the impact of sexual content varied from "a standardized mean difference of –.49 to a standardized mean difference of .37" (pp. 469-470). Put simply, some messages had a positive impact on recall, while others had a negative impact. Not only do these findings have theoretical implications, but they also have practical implications. A practitioner developing messages designed to persuade an audience must be aware of how highly variable language effects can be and must consider this when constructing messages.

Jackson argued that not only should multiple message replications be used in studies, but the results should be analyzed appropriately. This means treating replications as random effects rather than fixed effects in the statistical analyses. Her work offers suggestions about how this can be done (e.g., Jackson & Brashers, 1994a, 1994b).

This is not to suggest that this challenge is without controversy (e.g., Burgoon, Hall, & Pfau, 1991; Hunter & Hamilton, 1998). Scholars must address issues such as the number of replications that should be used, the statistical power of such designs, the ease of writing multiple messages, the length of such replications and its effect on participant fatigue, and the impact on sample size. Never-

theless, researchers must be concerned with the continued excessive reliance on single messages in studies and the conclusions drawn from them.

CONCLUSION

More than 20 years ago, Miller and Burgoon (1978) lamented on the decline of research on language and persuasion. Since then, research has slowly increased as scholars in fields such as advertising, marketing, psychology, and communication investigate a variety of language variables. Some variables have been investigated extensively. We know, for example, the impact of lexical choices or standard and nonstandard language varieties on judgments of speaker credibility and attractiveness. We also have a better understanding of the factors that moderate and mediate the relationship between language intensity and attitude change.

At the same time, we still lack substantial knowledge about some important aspects of the relationship between language and persuasion. How do the various levels of language structure affect persuasion, and how do the various levels of language structure relate to each other in the persuasion process? For example, the syntactic complexity of a message may affect its recall or comprehension, but we are less able to draw conclusions about its impact on attitude toward the message. More generally, we have substantial knowledge about how some language variables affect attitude toward the speaker, but we have little (if any) information about how it affects the attitude toward the message. Alternatively, how do lexical diversity and syntactical complexity affect each other in a persuasive message?

The future of this area of research seems bright both theoretically and practically, but to achieve its potential, scholars must meet certain challenges. They should apply more systematic frameworks to organize their study of language variables. This chapter has suggested a process model of language attitudes as one possibility. A general model such as this not only helps to integrate research but also points to variables relatively unexamined such as the effect of listeners' moods on the processing of language variables.

Even using such frameworks, investigators must integrate more research into comprehensive theories of persuasion such as dual-process models. These theories will help investigators to focus on how language affects attitude change and how listeners respond cognitively to language variables.

Finally, researchers must increasingly worry about the generalizability of their results—generalizability that extends beyond the particular messages used in a study. Increasing the generalizability of results presents its own challenges, but being concerned with the issue is critical for practitioners to find the research valuable and useful.

REFERENCES

Adaval, R., & Wyer, R. S. (1998). The role of narratives in consumer information processing. *Journal of Consumer Psychology, 7,* 207-245.

Atkins, C. P. (1993). Do employment recruiters discriminate on the basis of nonstandard dialect? *Journal of Employment Counseling, 30,* 108-118.

Barry, H., III, & Harper, A. S. (1995). Increased choice of female phonetic attributes in first names. *Sex Roles, 32,* 809-819.

Bavelas, J. B., Black, A., Chovil, N., & Mullett, J. (1990). *Equivocal communication.* Newbury Park, CA: Sage.

Block, L. G., & Keller, P. A. (1997). Effects of self-efficacy and vividness on the persuasiveness of health communications. *Journal of Consumer Psychology, 6,* 31-54.

Bowers, J. W. (1963). Language intensity, social introversion, and attitude change. *Speech Monographs, 30,* 345-352.

Bradac, J. J. (1990). Language attitudes and impression formation. In H. Giles & W. P. Robinson (Eds.), *Handbook of language and social psychology* (pp. 387-412). Chichester, UK: Wiley.

Bradac, J. J. (1999). Language . . . and social interaction . . . : Nature abhors uniformity. *Research on Language and Social Interaction, 32,* 11-20.

Bradac, J. J., Bowers, J. W., & Courtright, J. A. (1979). Three language variables in communication research: Intensity, immediacy, and diversity. *Human Communication Research, 5,* 257-269.

Bradac, J. J., Courtright, J. A., Schmidt, G., & Davies, R. A. (1976). The effects of perceived status and linguistic diversity upon judgments of speaker attributes and message effectiveness. *Journal of Psychology, 93,* 213-220.

Bradac, J. J., Davies, R. A., Courtright, J. A., Desmond, R. J., & Murdock, J. I. (1977). Richness of vocabulary: An attributional analysis. *Psychological Reports, 41,* 1131-1134.

Bradac, J. J., Desmond, R. J., & Murdock, J. I. (1977). Diversity and density: Lexically determined evaluative and informational consequences of linguistic complexity. *Communication Monographs, 44,* 273-283.

Bradac, J. J., Hemphill, M. R., & Tardy, C. H. (1981). Language style on trial: Effects of "powerful" and "powerless" speech upon judgments of victims and villains. *Western Journal of Speech Communication, 45,* 327-341.

Bradac, J. J., & Mulac, A. (1984a). A molecular view of powerful and powerless speech styles: Attributional consequences of specific language features and communicator intentions. *Communication Monographs, 51,* 307-319.

Bradac, J. J., & Mulac, A. (1984b). Attributional consequences of powerful and powerless speech styles in a crisis-intervention context. *Journal of Language and Social Psychology, 3,* 1-19.

Bradac, J. J., & Street, R. L., Jr. (1989-1990). Powerful and powerless styles of talk: A theoretical analysis of language and impression formation. *Research on Language and Social Interaction, 23,* 195-242.

Bradac, J. J., & Wisegarver, R. (1984). Ascribed status, lexical diversity, and accent: Determinants of perceived status, solidarity, and control of speech style. *Journal of Language and Social Psychology, 3,* 239-255.

Brashers, D. E., & Jackson, S. (1999). Changing conceptions of "message effects": A 24-year overview. *Human Communication Research, 25,* 457-477.

Brown, B., Giles, H., & Thackerar, J. (1985). Speaker evaluations as a function of speech rate, accent, and context. *Language & Communication, 5,* 207-220.

Buller, D. B., Borland, R., & Burgoon, M. (1998). Impact of behavioral intention on effectiveness of message features: Evidence from the Family Sun Safety Project. *Human Communication Research, 24,* 433-453.

Burgoon, M. (1990). Language and social influence. In H. Giles & W. P. Robinson (Eds.), *Handbook of language and social psychology* (pp. 51-72). Chichester, UK: Wiley.

Burgoon, M., & Dillard, J. P. (1995). Communication and social influence: A prolegomenon. *Communication Research, 22,* 397-401.

Burgoon, M., Hall, J., & Pfau, M. (1991). A test of the "message-as-fixed-effect fallacy" argument: Empirical and theoretical implications of design choices. *Communication Quarterly, 39,* 18-34.

Burns, A. C., Biswas, A., & Babin, L. (1993). The operation of visual imagery as a mediator of advertising effects. *Journal of Advertising, 22,* 71-85.

Burrell, N. A., & Koper, R. J. (1998). The efficacy of powerful/powerless language on attitudes and source credibility. In M. Allen & R. W. Preiss (Eds.), *Persuasion: Advances through meta-analysis* (pp. 203-215). Cresskill, NJ: Hampton.

Burroughs, E. I. (1991). Lexical diversity in listeners' judgments of children. *Perceptual and Motor Skills, 73,* 19-22.

Cargile, A. C., Giles, H., Ryan, E. B., & Bradac, J. J. (1994). Language attitudes as a social process: A conceptual model and new directions. *Language & Communication, 14,* 211-236.

Carpenter, R. H. (1990). The statistical profile of language behavior with Machiavellian intent or while experiencing caution and avoiding self-incrimination. *Annals of the New York Academy of Sciences, 606,* 5-17.

Collins, R. L., Taylor, S. E., Wood, J. V., & Thompson, S. C. (1988). The vividness effect: Elusive or illusory? *Journal of Experimental Social Psychology, 24,* 1-18.

Crystal, D. (1995). *The Cambridge encyclopedia of the English language.* Cambridge, UK: Cambridge University Press.

de la Zerda, N., & Hopper, R. (1979). Employment interviewers' reactions to Mexican American speech. *Communication Monographs, 46,* 126-134.

Dulaney, E. F., Jr. (1982). Changes in language behavior as a function of veracity. *Human Communication Research, 9,* 75-82.

Eagly, A., & Chaiken, S. (1993). *The psychology of attitudes.* Fort Worth, TX: Harcourt Brace.

Eisenberg, E. M. (1984). Ambiguity as strategy in organizational communication. *Communication Monographs, 51,* 227-242.

Erickson, B., Lind, E. A., Johnson, B. C., & O'Barr, W. M. (1978). Speech style and impression-formation in a court setting: The effects of "powerful" and "powerless" speech. *Journal of Experimental Social Psychology, 14,* 266-279.

Fazio, R. H. (1989). On the power and functionality of attitudes: The role of attitude accessibility. In A. R. Pratkanis, S. J. Breckler, & A. G. Greenwald (Eds.), *Attitude structure and function* (pp. 153-179). Hillsdale, NJ: Lawrence Erlbaum.

Fiske, S. T., Morling, B., & Stevens, L. E. (1996). Controlling self and others: A theory of anxiety, mental control, and social control. *Personality and Social Psychology Bulletin, 22,* 115-123.

Fodor, J. A., Bever, T. G., & Garrett, M. F. (1974). *The psychology of language: An introduction to psycholinguistics and generative grammar.* New York: McGraw-Hill.

Frey, K. P., & Eagly, A. H. (1993). Vividness can undermine the persuasiveness of messages. *Journal of Personality and Social Psychology, 65,* 32-44.

Friestad, M., & Wright, P. (1994). The persuasion knowledge model: How people cope with persuasion attempts. *Journal of Consumer Research, 21,* 1-31.

Gibbons, P., Busch, J., & Bradac, J. J. (1991). Powerful versus powerless language: Consequences for persuasion, impression formation, and cognitive response. *Journal of Language and Social Psychology, 10,* 115-133.

Giles, H., & Coupland, N. (1991). *Language: Contexts and consequences.* Pacific Grove, CA: Brooks/Cole.

Giles, H., Henwood, K., Coupland, N., Harriman, J., & Coupland, J. (1992). Language attitudes and cognitive mediation. *Human Communication Research, 18,* 500-527.

Goss, B., & Williams, L. (1973). The effects of equivocation on perceived source credibility. *Central States Speech Journal, 24,* 162-167.

Grob, L. M., Meyers, R. A., & Schuh, R. (1997). Powerful/powerless language use in group interactions: Sex differences or similarities? *Communication Quarterly, 45,* 282-303.

Hahn, P. W., & Clayton, S. D. (1996). The effects of attorney presentation style, attorney gender, and juror gender on juror decisions. *Law and Human Behavior, 20,* 533-554.

Haleta, L. L. (1996). Student perceptions of teachers' use of language: The effects of powerful and powerless language on impression formation and uncertainty. *Communication Education, 45,* 16-28.

Hamilton, M. A. (1997). The phase-interfaced omnistructure underlying the processing of persuasive messages. In G. A. Barnett & F. J. Boster (Eds.), *Progress in communication sciences: Advances in persuasion* (Vol. 13, pp. 1-42). Greenwich, CT: Ablex.

Hamilton, M. A. (1998). Message variables that mediate and moderate the effect of equivocal language on source credibility. *Journal of Language and Social Psychology, 17,* 109-143.

Hamilton, M. A., & Hunter, J. E. (1998). The effect of language intensity on receiver evaluations of message, source, and topic. In M. Allen & R. W. Preiss (Eds.), *Persuasion: Advances through meta-analysis* (pp. 99-138). Cresskill, NJ: Hampton.

Hamilton, M. A., & Mineo, P. J. (1998). A framework for understanding equivocation. *Journal of Language and Social Psychology, 17,* 3-35.

Harris, R. J. (1977). Comprehension of pragmatic implications in advertising. *Journal of Applied Psychology, 62,* 603-608.

Harris, R. J., & Monaco, G. E. (1978). Psychology of pragmatic implication: Information processing between the lines. *Journal of Experimental Psychology: General, 107,* 1-22.

Harris, R. J., Teske, R. R., & Ginns, M. J. (1975). Memory for pragmatic implications from courtroom testimony. *Bulletin of the Psychonomic Society, 6,* 494-496.

Harris, R. J., Trusty, M. L., Bechtold, J. I., & Wasinger, L. (1989). Memory for implied versus directly stated advertising claims. *Psychology and Marketing, 6,* 87-96.

Herr, P. M., Kardes, F. R., & Kim, J. (1991). Effects of word-of-mouth and product-attribute information on persuasion: An accessibility-diagnosticity perspective. *Journal of Consumer Research, 17,* 454-462.

Holtgraves, T., & Dulin, J. (1994). The Muhammad Ali effect: Differences between African Americans and European Americans in their perceptions of a truthful bragger. *Language & Communication, 14,* 275-285.

Hopper, R., & Williams, F. (1973). Speech characteristics and employability. *Speech Monographs, 46,* 287-302.

Hosman, L. A. (1989). The evaluative consequences of hedges, hesitations, and intensifiers: Powerful and powerless speech styles. *Human Communication Research, 15,* 383-406.

Hosman, L. A. (1997). The relationship between locus of control and the evaluative consequences of powerful and powerless speech styles. *Journal of Language and Social Psychology, 16,* 70-78.

Hosman, L. A., Huebner, T. M., & Siltanen, S. A. (1999). *The impact of power of speech style, argument strength, and need for cognition on impression formation, cognitive responses, and persuasion.* Unpublished manuscript, University of Southern Mississippi.

Hosman, L. A., & Siltanen, S. A. (1994). The attributional and evaluative consequences of powerful and powerless speech styles: An examination of the "control over others" and "control of self" explanations. *Language & Communication, 14,* 287-298.

Hunter, J. E., & Hamilton, M. A. (1998). Meta-analysis of controlled message designs. In M. Allen & R. W. Preiss (Eds.), *Persuasion: Ad-*

vances through meta-analysis (pp. 29-52). Cresskill, NJ: Hampton.

Jackson, S., & Jacobs, S. (1983). Generalizing about messages: Suggestions for the design and analysis of experiments. *Human Communication Research, 9,* 169-181.

Jackson, S., & Brashers, D. E. (1994a). M > 1: Analysis of Treatment × Replication designs. *Human Communication Research, 20,* 356-389.

Jackson, S., & Brashers, D. E. (1994b). *Random factors in ANOVA.* Thousand Oaks, CA: Sage.

Jacoby, J., Nelson, M. C., & Hoyer, W. D. (1982). Corrective advertising and affirmative disclosure statements: Their potential for confusing and misleading the consumer. *Journal of Marketing, 46,* 61-72.

Johnson, F., & Buttny, R. (1982). White listeners' responses to "sounding Black" and "sounding White": The effects of message content on judgments about language. *Communication Monographs, 49,* 22-49.

Keller, P. A., & Block, L. G. (1997). Vividness effects: A resource-matching perspective. *Journal of Consumer Research, 24,* 295-304.

Kintsch, W., & van Dijk, T. A. (1978). Toward a model of text comprehension and production. *Psychological Review, 85,* 363-394.

Koslow, S., Shamdasani, P. N., & Touchstone, E. E. (1994). Exploring language effects in ethnic advertising: A sociolinguistic perspective. *Journal of Consumer Research, 20,* 575-585.

Lakoff, R. (1975). *Language and woman's place.* New York: Harper & Row.

Lowrey, T. M. (1998). The effects of syntactic complexity on advertising persuasiveness. *Journal of Consumer Psychology, 7,* 187-206.

McGuire, W. J. (1969). The nature of attitudes and attitude change. In G. Lindzey & E. Aronson (Eds.), *The handbook of social psychology* (2nd ed., Vol. 3, pp. 136-314). Reading, MA: Addison-Wesley.

Miller, G. R., & Burgoon, M. (1978). Persuasion research: Review and commentary. In B. D. Ruben (Ed.), *Communication yearbook* (Vol. 2, pp. 29-47). New Brunswick, NJ: Transaction Books.

Motes, W. H., Hilton, C. B., & Fielden, J. S. (1992). Language, sentence, and structural variations in print advertising. *Journal of Advertising Research, 32,* 63-77.

Nisbett, R., & Ross, L. (1980). *Human inference: Strategies and shortcomings of social judgment.* Englewood Cliffs, NJ: Prentice Hall.

Petty, R. E., & Wegener, D. T. (1998). Attitude change: Multiple roles for persuasion variables. In D. T. Gilbert, S. T. Fiske, & G. Lindzey (Eds.), *The handbook of social psychology* (4th ed., Vol. 1, pp. 323-390). New York: McGraw-Hill.

Ratner, N. B., & Gleason, J. B. (1993). An introduction to psycholinguistics: What do language users know? In J. B. Gleason & N. B. Ratner (Eds.), *Psycholinguistics* (pp. 1-40). Fort Worth, TX: Harcourt Brace.

Rooks, K. S. (1986). Encouraging preventive behavior for distant and proximal health threat: Effects of vivid versus abstract information. *Journal of Gerontology, 41,* 526-534.

Rooks, K. S. (1987). Effects of case history versus abstract information on health attitudes and behaviors. *Journal of Applied Psychology, 17,* 533-553.

Rossiter, J. R., & Percy, L. (1978). Visual imaging ability as a mediator of advertising response. In H. K. Hunt (Ed.), *Advances in consumer research* (Vol. 5, pp. 621-629). Ann Arbor, MI: Association for Consumer Research.

Rubin, D. L., Healy, P., Gardiner, T. C., Zath, R. C., & Moore, C. P. (1997). Nonnative physicians as message sources: Effects of accent and ethnicity on patients' responses to AIDS prevention counseling. *Health Communication, 9,* 351-368.

Searleman, A., & Carter, H. (1988). The effectiveness of different types of pragmatic implications found in commercials to mislead subjects. *Applied Cognitive Psychology, 2,* 265-272.

Smith, G. W. (1998). The political impact of name sounds. *Communication Monographs, 65,* 154-172.

Sparks, J. R., Areni, C. S., & Cox, K. C. (1998). An investigation of the effects of language style and communication modality on persuasion. *Communication Monographs, 65,* 108-125.

Stern, G. S., & Manifold, B. (1977). Internal locus of control as a value. *Journal of Research in Personality, 11,* 237-242.

Street, R. L., Jr., Brady, R., & Lee, R. (1984). Evaluative responses to communicators: The effects of sex and interaction context. *Western Journal of Speech Communication, 48,* 14-27.

Taylor, S. E., & Thompson, S. C. (1982). Stalking the elusive "vividness" effect. *Psychological Review, 89,* 155-181.

Thorson, E., & Snyder, R. (1984). Viewer recall of television commercials: Prediction from the propositional structure of commercial strips. *Journal of Marketing Research, 21,* 127-136.

Williams, M. L. (1980). The effect of deliberate vagueness on receiver recall and agreement. *Central States Speech Journal, 31,* 30-41.

Williams, M. L., & Goss, B. (1975). Equivocation: Character insurance. *Human Communication Research, 1,* 265-270.

20

Message Framing in the Prevention and Early Detection of Illness

PETER SALOVEY
TAMERA R. SCHNEIDER
ANNE MARIE APANOVITCH

The effectiveness of interventions designed to promote healthy behaviors often depends on the persuasiveness of a public service announcement (PSA), a brochure, a print advertisement, a government letter, an educational program, or a communication from a health professional. From a psychological vantage point, these communications represent persuasion opportunities in which to apply a technology derived from nearly a half century of research on attitude change. Psychological research on attitude change has focused primarily on one of three aspects of persuasive communication (Eagly & Chaiken, 1993; Hovland, Janis, & Kelley, 1953; McGuire, 1985). These are (a) the source of the persuasive message (e.g., the communicator's expertise, credibility, trustworthiness, attractive-

ness, and similarity to the recipient), (b) the recipient of the message (e.g., his or her knowledge about the attitude domain, experience with the attitude object, and demographic and dispositional characteristics expected to be associated with influenceability), and (c) aspects of the message itself.

Of these three areas of research activity, message variables have been studied the least systematically, although interesting findings have emerged (reviewed by Eagly & Chaiken, 1998; McGuire, 1985; Petty & Wegener, 1998). For example, anecdotes about particular people are more persuasive than the presentation of cold statistics (Hamill, Wilson, & Nisbett, 1980; Taylor & Thompson, 1982). Fear-arousing appeals are usually effective only when instructions about how to reduce

AUTHORS' NOTE: Preparation of this manuscript was facilitated by grants from the American Cancer Society (RPG-93-028-05-PBP), National Cancer Institute (R01-CA68427), and National Institute of Mental Health (P01-MH/DA56826) and by funding from the Ethel F. Donaghue Women's Health Investigator Program at Yale University.

the fear are included in the message (Janis, 1967; Leventhal, Singer, & Jones, 1965; Sutton, 1982). Messages encouraging personal responsibility can be more motivating than those that attribute responsibility to others (Rothman, Salovey, Turvey, & Fishkin, 1993). Forcefully delivered messages are more persuasive than subtle ones (Robinson & McArthur, 1982), and messages delivered quickly (even if by fast-talking salespeople) are surprisingly more effective than leisurely delivered messages (Miller, Maruyama, Beaber, & Valone, 1976).

An aspect of messages that has been studied quite systematically in the context of health and illness is framing. *Message framing* refers specifically to the emphasis in the message on the positive or negative consequences of adopting or failing to adopt a particular health-relevant behavior (Rothman & Salovey, 1997). *Gain-framed* messages usually present the benefits that are accrued through adopting the behavior (e.g., "Obtaining a mammogram allows tumors to be detected early; this maximizes your treatment options"). *Loss-framed* messages generally convey the costs of not adopting the requested behavior (e.g., "If you do not obtain a mammogram, tumors cannot be detected early; this minimizes your treatment options"). Although these two kinds of messages convey essentially the same information, one of these kinds of messages may be much more persuasive than the other.

PROSPECT THEORY AND THE FRAMING HYPOTHESIS

Prospect theory provides the context for understanding the psychological processes involved in the influence of framed persuasive messages on health behaviors. Prospect theory was proposed to understand decision making under conditions of uncertainty

(Kahneman & Tversky, 1979, 1982; Tversky & Kahneman, 1981). The framing postulate suggests that decision makers organize information in memory relevant to such decisions in terms of potential gains (i.e., benefits) or potential losses (i.e., costs) as compared to a current reference point (e.g., one's current level of health). Factually equivalent material can be presented differentially to individuals such that they encode it as either a gain or a loss from this reference point.

In an often-cited study, for example, Tversky and Kahneman (1981) presented individuals with a situation in which the outbreak of a disease is expected to kill 600 people. In one comparison, participants were presented with gain-framed information. They had to decide whether to endorse a program guaranteeing that 200 of the original 600 people would be *saved* or one claiming that there was a .33 probability that all 600 would be saved but also a .67 probability that no one would be saved. Note that although the "expected value" of the two programs was identical, the first option emphasized a *certain* outcome, but the second emphasized a *probabilistic* or *risky* outcome. Participants presented with these choices overwhelmingly selected the first option, the certain outcome, in which 200 people were guaranteed to be saved.

A second group of participants was presented with the same two options. However, this time, the potential losses were emphasized. In this comparison, participants had to choose between a first program in which 400 of the original 600 people would certainly *die* and one in which there was the same .33 probability that no one would die and a .67 probability that all would die. Once again, the expected value of these two options was identical. Furthermore, these two options differ from the two previous options only in that they make salient the potential costs or losses (i.e., deaths) as compared to the options that made salient potential benefits or gains (i.e., lives saved). In the loss salient situation, participants overwhelmingly chose the second option, in which there was a .67 probability that everyone would die. When losses are anticipated, people no longer prefer the option that is a sure bet. Rather, they choose the option that involves some uncertainty or risk.

The value function of prospect theory summarizes these decision strategies by noting that individuals are, in general, *risk seeking* in the domain of losses but *risk averse* in the domain of gains. The value function assumes that an S-shaped function relates outcomes to their subjective values and that the function is concave for gains and convex for losses and steeper in the loss domain. This function suggests that when behavioral choices involve some risk or uncertainty, individuals will be more likely to take these risks when information is framed in terms of the relative disadvantages (i.e., losses or costs) of the behavioral options. At the same time, conservative or risk-averse options are preferred when gains are made salient.

Loss-framed persuasive messages encourage people to consider the negative consequences of their choices. The associated subjective unpleasantness motivates a kind of loss aversion, and according to prospect theory, people are subsequently more likely to engage in a risky behavior (i.e., a behavior with an uncertain outcome) if there is a possibility of avoiding the loss. By contrast, exposure to gain-framed messages may cause people to feel less endangered, making them less likely to perform a behavior with uncertain outcomes. After processing gain-framed information, individuals may feel relatively satisfied with the outcomes of their choices and become risk averse; they do not want to do anything to jeopardize these gains.

Prior to our research program in this area, these principles had been applied to per-suading women to use monthly breast self-examination (BSE) (Meyerowitz & Chaiken, 1987). Women were asked to read one of two pamphlets describing BSE. The first emphasized the potential benefits of BSE, and the second emphasized the potential risks of not performing BSE. This latter, loss-framed pamphlet was more effective in promoting BSE than was the gain-framed pamphlet. The particular effectiveness of loss-framed messages in encouraging BSE makes sense in terms of prospect theory. BSE is perceived as a psychologically risky or uncertain behavior. It is not done to *prevent* cancer; rather, it is performed to *detect* cancer. Each time a woman performs BSE, she runs the risk of finding an abnormality.

Although Meyerowitz and Chaiken (1987) showed that loss-framed messages are especially effective in motivating women to perform BSE, the literature on framing and health promotion actually has yielded a more interesting pattern of results (reviewed by Rothman & Salovey, 1997; Wilson, Purdon, & Wallston, 1988). For example, while loss framing has been effective for promoting HIV screening (Kalichman & Coley, 1995) and mammography use (Banks et al., 1995; Schneider, Salovey, Apanovitch, et al., 2001), gain-framed messages have encouraged preferences for some surgical procedures (Levin, Schnittjer, & Thee, 1988, Experiment 2; Marteau, 1989; McNeil, Pauker, Sox, & Tversky, 1982; Wilson, Kaplan, & Schneiderman, 1987), the use of infant car restraints (Christophersen & Gyulay, 1981; Treiber, 1986), regular physical exercise (Robberson & Rogers, 1988), smoking cessation (Schneider, Salovey, Pallonen, et al., 2001), and using sunscreen to prevent skin cancer (Detweiler, Bedell, Salovey, Pronin, & Rothman, 1999; Rothman, Salovey, Antone, Keough, & Martin, 1993). Thus, it is not that either gain-framed messages or loss-framed messages are always more persuasive for all health behaviors; rather, it seems to depend on the type of behavior targeted for change.

Framing and the Prevention-Detection Distinction

Considering the type of behavior being promoted helps to clarify the influence of message framing on health behavior. In the research described previously, loss-framed messages were effective in promoting mammography, BSE, and HIV testing—all early detection (screening) behaviors. Conversely, gain-framed messages were effective in promoting infant car restraints, physical exercise, smoking cessation, and sunscreen—all prevention behaviors. The perceived uncertainty or risk (e.g., of finding an abnormality) associated with detection behaviors leads us to predict that loss-framed messages should be more persuasive in promoting them. However, prevention behaviors might not be perceived as risky at all; they are performed to deter the onset or occurrence of a health problem. Thus, choosing to perform prevention behaviors is a risk-averse option; it maintains good health. Because risk-averse options are preferred when people are considering benefits or gains, gain-framed messages may be more likely to facilitate performing prevention behaviors. We emphasize, in line with the framing postulate of prospect theory, that generally it is the *match* between a message frame (gain or loss) and the required health behavior (prevention or detection) that especially motivates behavior change (Rothman & Salovey, 1997).

These findings motivate the main hypothesis guiding our program of research:

> *Gain-framed messages are more persuasive when promoting prevention behaviors, but loss-framed messages are more persuasive when promoting early detection (screening) behaviors.*

Types of Framing

Another reason why investigators have not always reported consistent message framing effects in studies of persuasion concerns differences in the operationalization of framing (Fagley, 1993). There are two different ways in which gain and loss frames can be instantiated (Brendl, Higgins, & Lemm, 1995; Petty & Wegener, 1991). Gain-framed messages can focus on attaining a desirable outcome or on not attaining (avoiding) an undesirable outcome—both beneficial. For example, compare the message "If you decide to get HIV tested, you may feel the peace of mind that comes with knowing about your health" to "If you decide to get HIV tested, you may feel less anxious because you won't wonder whether you are ill." On the other hand, loss-framed messages can emphasize attaining an undesirable outcome or not attaining a desirable outcome—both costly. For example, compare "If you decide not to get HIV tested, you may feel more anxious because you may wonder whether you are ill" to "If you decide not to get tested, you won't feel the peace of mind that comes with knowing about your health."

In Figure 20.1, note that gain-framed messages can describe the benefits of attaining a desirable outcome (Cell A) or avoiding an undesirable one (Cell D). Loss-framed messages describe the risks of failing to attain a desirable outcome (Cell C) or attaining an undesirable one (Cell B). In our early experiments, comparisons between gain- and loss-framed messages focused primarily on Cells A and C. Other investigators have operationalized framing as the difference between Cells A and B. And little attention has been paid to messages of the form defined by Cell D. These differences in operationalizing framing may help to explain the findings in the literature on performing health behaviors described earlier (Rothman & Salovey, 1997). Loss-framed

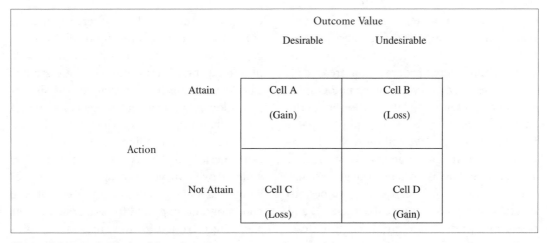

Figure 20.1. Four Kinds of Framing

messages that facilitated mammography and BSE involved comparing Cells A and C (Banks et al., 1995; Meyerowitz & Chaiken, 1987), but gain-framed messages that facilitated preferences for surgical procedures (Levin et al., 1988; Marteau, 1989; McNeil et al., 1982; Wilson et al., 1987) used a manipulation emphasizing either the positive or negative consequences of surgery (Cell A vs. Cell B). Attending to messages defined by all four cells allows us to explore whether the differential effects of framed messages are invariant across the desirability of the outcomes or whether outcome desirability moderates framing effects.

A DECADE OF EXPERIMENTS FROM FIELD AND LABORATORY SETTINGS

We have conducted research on the framing of persuasive messages to encourage prevention and early detection activities for more than 10 years. In this section, we summarize our findings to date. Experiments are not described chronologically but rather are grouped according to the behavior targeted for change and the hypotheses addressed.

Gain- and Loss-Framed Messages and Mammography

Experiment 1 was a framed mammography intervention conducted with women at a local telephone company, Experiment 2 tested this intervention with a very heterogeneous sample of women from community groups and churches, and Experiment 3 looked at both framing and targeting to ethnicity among African American, Latina, and White women recruited at community-based health clinics. All three of these experiments examined the effectiveness of gain- versus loss-framed messages in motivating women to obtain mammograms.

Experiment 1. Participants in Experiment 1 were 133 women over 40 years of age working at a telephone company, recruited because they had previously obtained fewer than 50% of the mammograms expected for someone their age. About 20% were minority group members. The protocol included random assignment to a videotaped educational program, a pre-intervention packet of measures, a post-intervention packet of measures, and follow-up for mammogram use 6 and 12 months after watching the videotape. We worked with the telephone company's television production team to create professional-looking videotaped educational programs on breast cancer and the value of screening mammography. One video presented all information about the value of screening mammography in gain-framed terms (e.g., "We will show that detecting breast cancer early can save your life. . . . The bottom line is—when you get regular mammograms, you are doing your best to detect breast cancer in its early stages"), and the second presented all information in loss-framed terms (e.g., "We will show that failing to detect breast cancer early can cost you your life. . . . The bottom line is—when you fail to get regular mammograms, you are not doing your best to detect breast cancer in its early stages"). The actual information conveyed about breast cancer and mammography was identical in both videos.

After viewing one of the 15-minute videos, women received a pamphlet about where to get a mammogram. Women were contacted by telephone 6 and 12 months later to determine whether they had obtained a mammogram since viewing the video. (Self-reports of mammography use are considered quite reliable [King, Rimer, Trock, Balshem, & Engstrom, 1990].) We predicted that information framed in terms of losses would be more persuasive than information framed in terms of gains because mammography is an early detection (screening) behavior. In fact, 12 months after the intervention, mammography use was 66.2% in the loss condition as compared to 51.5% in the gain condition (Banks et al., 1995).

Experiment 2. Because the regular use of mammography is lower among working-class women than among middle-class women, the same experimental conditions as in Experiment 1 were repeated with a low-income sample of women recruited from community so-

cial groups and churches. Differently framed videotapes and brochures, followed by a discussion session with a health educator, were presented at regular meetings of these groups. The 118 women in this sample had significantly lower family incomes, regardless of ethnicity, than those in Experiment 1. Of these women, 59% were White and 41% were African American or Latina. As in Experiment 1, women over 40 years of age who had previously obtained fewer than 50% of the mammograms expected for someone of their age were recruited for this study. The protocol for this experiment was much like that for Experiment 1.

Experiment 2 produced framing effects in the predicted direction—loss-framed videos worked better than gain-framed videos—but they were not quite statistically significant. Among African American and Latina women, 52% of those who viewed the loss-framed message subsequently obtained a mammogram in the following year, whereas only 43% of those who viewed a gain-framed message did likewise, as predicted. Among the White women, 78% who saw the loss-framed message obtained a mammogram as compared to 70% of those in the gain-framed condition (Salovey et al., 1994).

Experiment 3. We recently completed a much larger scale experiment in which African American, Latina, and White women viewed gain- or loss-framed videotapes (in English or Spanish) about mammography that also were either targeted to members of the women's ethnic group or were multicultural. The targeted messages included statistical information relevant to African American, Latina, or White women and models of similar ethnicities as well as familiar images of relevant places in the community. The multicultural messages presented information relevant to all women. The design of the experiment was a 2 (Framing) × 2 (Ethnic Targeting) factorial (when collapsed over ethnic group), and measures of attitudes and mammography-relevant behavior were administered prior to the video, immediately after the video, 6 months later, and 12 months later.

A total of 752 women were recruited into this experiment. Of these, 42% were African American, 25% Hispanic, 27% White, 1% Asian, and 2% American Indian or Alaskan Native. Six months after viewing the video, 43% of the women who saw a loss-framed version had obtained a mammogram, while 38% of those who saw a gain-framed version had done so. However, an interesting interaction between framing and targeting emerged in which the most persuasive messages in motivating mammography were those that were loss framed *and* multicultural. There was a large, significant, loss-framed advantage among the multicultural messages (50% for loss-framed videos and 36% for gain-framed videos). Among the targeted messages, the difference due to framing was not significant (36% vs. 41%). These findings were maintained after 12 months, although they were somewhat attenuated. There was a loss-framed advantage among the multicultural messages (61% for loss-framed videos vs. 55% for gain-framed videos), but for the targeted messages the differences due to framing were not significant (54% vs. 57%). In general, framing effects were stronger for Latina and White women than for African American women both 6 and 12 months following the presentation of the video (Schneider, Salovey, Apanovitch, et al., 2001).

Gain- and Loss-Framed Messages and Skin Cancer Prevention and Early Detection

Because Experiments 1 to 3 were focused on mammography, a screening behavior, we could not test whether gain-framed messages

might have persuaded women to engage in a preventive health behavior. Experiments 4 to 6 were designed to address this question. Experiment 7 primarily focused on skin cancer-related detection behaviors, and Experiment 8 tested whether the advantages of message framing could be demonstrated using very brief interventions conducted on a public beach.

Experiment 4. This experiment was designed to explore the part of our hypothesis that suggests that messages framed in terms of gains are more effective in promoting prevention behaviors. We can begin to assess this hypothesis by comparing the results of Experiment 4, in which the targeted behavior was sunscreen use (a prevention behavior), to the results of Experiments 1 to 3, in which the targeted behavior was mammography (a detection behavior). Recall that in Experiments 1 to 3, mammography use was facilitated by loss-framed messages. In Experiment 4, we predicted that sunscreen use would be facilitated by a gain-framed message.

A total of 146 young adults recruited from a college community were asked to read gain- or loss-framed pamphlets about skin cancer and its prevention. They then completed various psychological measures. At the end of the experiment, participants were given a pre-addressed and stamped postcard that they could mail to our laboratory to receive a free bottle of sunscreen. On the postcard, they were asked to choose the level of sun protection factor (SPF) they desired. Our hypothesis was that the participants exposed to gain-framed messages would be more likely to request sunscreen with an appropriate SPF (≥ 15), as encouraged by the pamphlets, than would those exposed to loss-framed messages.

The gain- and loss-framed pamphlets were designed to differ only in how the information was presented. Each pamphlet contained information concerning the incidence and etiology of skin cancer as well as how to prevent and detect the disease. The gain-framed pamphlet described the statistics, facts, and arguments by emphasizing benefits rather than risks and focusing on the positive aspects of being concerned about skin cancer (e.g., "Regular use of sunscreen products can protect you against the sun's harmful rays"). The loss-framed pamphlet described the same information but emphasized risks rather than benefits and especially focused on the risks of not performing cancer-related behaviors (e.g., "If you don't use sunscreen products regularly, you won't be protected against the sun's harmful rays").

Participants' knowledge about skin cancer was not affected differently by the two pamphlets. However, the loss-framed pamphlet resulted in higher estimates of one's perceived risk of contracting skin cancer and in more intense negative feelings after reading it. But it was the gain-framed pamphlet that was more likely to motivate cancer prevention behavior. Fully 71% of the participants who read the gain-framed pamphlet requested a sample of sunscreen with an SPF greater than or equal to 15, but only 46% of the participants who read the loss-framed pamphlet requested sunscreen with this recommended level of SPF. Although both women and men were more likely to request appropriate sunscreen if they had read the gain-framed pamphlet, this advantage for the gain-framed pamphlet was statistically significant for women but not for men. Women indicated that they were more invested (i.e., more highly involved) with the attitude object (i.e., skin cancer) than were men. Thus, exposure to a gain-framed message motivated a cancer prevention behavior, and this advantage was especially salient among more invested individuals for whom the disease was a more relevant concern (Rothman, Salovey, Antone, et al., 1993; but see Maheswaran & Meyers-Levy, 1990).

Experiment 5. This experiment was designed to explore further the role of involvement with the attitude object in determining the relative effectiveness of gain- versus loss-framed messages. In this experiment, we expected high-involvement participants to be more sensitive to framing than were low-involvement participants. A total of 525 young adults, recruited on campus and about equally divided by gender, read gain- or loss-framed pamphlets similar to those used in Experiment 4 about skin cancer and its prevention. We hypothesized that sex is associated with issue involvement, so we measured involvement more fully. In fact, as compared to men, women spent more time actively trying to tan, were indeed significantly more concerned about developing skin cancer, felt that skin cancer was a more serious health problem, and thought that developing a sunburn was more dangerous. Thus, in this experiment we allowed sex to serve as a proxy for involvement.

We asked participants to indicate their intention to perform skin cancer *prevention* behaviors, such as using sunscreen, and skin cancer *detection* behaviors, such as skin self-examinations and clinical skin examinations. Overall, as compared to men, women expressed greater intentions to perform detection behaviors related to skin cancer. However, this sex difference was qualified by a significant framing by participant sex interaction. As expected, women who read loss-framed information about skin cancer expressed greater intentions to perform skin cancer-related detection behaviors than did women who read gain-framed information. Conversely and unexpectedly, men who read gain-framed information about skin cancer expressed greater intentions to perform detection behaviors than did men who read loss-framed information. It appears that the loss frame/detection behavior principle holds more strongly for individuals invested in the attitude object (in this case, women) than for those who are less so (in this case, men) (Rothman, Salovey, Antone, et al., 1993).

Experiment 6. Given the more complex results of Experiment 5, Experiment 6 attempted to shore up support for the hypothesis that gain framing is most effective in promoting prevention behaviors and that loss framing is most effective in promoting detection behaviors relevant to skin cancer. This experiment promoted sunscreen use and attendance at a skin cancer screening clinic through differently framed videos modeled after the ones used in the mammography studies. A total of 453 young adults were assigned to view gain- and loss-framed videotapes that described the importance of sunscreen use and clinical skin examinations. The primary outcome variables were requests for sunscreen and intentions to attend a skin screening 1 month and 10 months after the intervention. As predicted, students who viewed the loss-framed messages expressed stronger intentions to obtain a clinical skin examination and to perform self-skin examinations (detection behaviors) than did those who viewed the gain-framed messages. Likewise, as predicted, students who viewed gain-framed messages requested higher levels of SPF sunscreen (a prevention behavior) than did those who viewed loss-framed messages. This interaction between framing and behavior type provides further support for the primary message framing hypothesis (Salovey, Pronin, Rothman, Zullo, & Leffell, 2001).

Experiment 7. This experiment involved the promotion of actual attendance at a skin cancer early detection screening program provided in a corporate health setting. We recruited individuals from workplaces and advertised a skin screening to be conducted later at the same site. Participants viewed either gain- or loss-framed videotapes promoting clinical skin examination. We recruited 256 assembly line workers from a manufacturing company, managers and scientists from a pharmaceutical laboratory, and retirees and their spouses from a diversified electronics company. The protocol included random assignment to a gain- or loss-framed videotaped educational program, pre- and post-video questionnaires, and follow-up for clinic attendance 1 and 6 months after the intervention.

In Experiment 7, the loss-framed program produced greater perceptions of personal risk for skin cancer, produced more personal concern about skin cancer, and was accompanied by less sanguine emotional reactions as compared to the gain-framed program. As predicted, at all three companies, intentions to obtain the clinical skin screening were higher among the viewers of the loss-framed messages. Viewing the gain-framed video elicited more agreement with pro-prevention attitude scales (Salovey & Pronin, 1995).

Experiment 8. In general, the experiments reviewed thus far suggest that gain-framed messages should be more effective in promoting cancer prevention behaviors but that loss-framed messages should be more effective in promoting cancer early detection behaviors. These studies have always manipulated framing in terms of desirable outcomes, emphasizing either their attainment (gain frame) or the failure to attain them (loss frame). However, framed messages can emphasize desirable or undesirable outcomes (Rothman & Salovey, 1997). Gain-framed messages can focus on the attainment of a desirable outcome or the avoidance of an undesirable outcome, both of which are beneficial. Loss-framed messages can emphasize the attainment of an undesirable outcome or the failure to attain a desirable outcome, both of which are costly. The primary hypothesis here was that the advantage for gain-framed messages in promoting prevention would be especially strong when such messages focus on desirable outcomes (e.g., "People who use sunscreen regularly have healthier looking skin when they grow older") but that loss-framed messages should be especially powerful when emphasizing the likelihood of experiencing undesirable outcomes (e.g., "People who don't use sunscreen regularly have unhealthy looking skin when they grow older").

Experiment 8 was a test of this hypothesis using a 2 × 2 randomized design in which two types of gain-framed messages (attaining desirable and avoiding undesirable) were contrasted with two types of loss-framed messages (attaining undesirable and avoiding desirable). With the permission of the State Parks Division of the Connecticut Environmental Protection Department, we recruited 217 individuals over 18 years of age sunbathing on a public beach. They randomly received one of the four brochures about skin cancer and sunscreen use. Of the participants in the two gain-framed conditions, 73% requested a bottle of sunscreen from our "supplier" at the beach, but only 53% of the loss-framed participants made a similar request, consistent with our basic gain prevention/loss detection hypothesis. As it turned out, both kinds of gain framing were equally effective; likewise, both types of loss framing were equally less effective—at least for sunscreen use (Detweiler et al., 1999).

Generalizing Framing Effects

Experiment 9: Regulatory Focus and Message Framing. Given the success of Experiment 8, in which sunscreen use by beachgoers was promoted better by gain-framed messages than by loss-framed messages, we conducted another beach experiment to pilot test whether psychological characteristics of individuals might make them more susceptible to certain framed messages. Higgins (1997, 1998; see also Crowe & Higgins, 1997; Shah, Higgins, & Friedman, 1998) has suggested that individuals tend to be guided by two general motives: safety (the avoidance of negative outcomes) and nurturance (the attainment of positive outcomes). He has found that individuals differ in the relative weights of these two motives in their lives, with some individuals working strenuously to feel safe and secure while others strive just as hard to feel accomplished and fulfilled. He has referred to this personality variable as *regulatory focus* and called this first group of people *prevention focused* and the second group *promotion focused*. Based on his laboratory work, we predicted that prevention-focused individuals might be more persuaded to use sunscreen by messages emphasizing negative consequences that could be avoided (e.g., melanoma) and that promotion-focused individuals might be more persuaded by messages emphasizing positive consequences that could be attained (e.g., living a full healthy life). As in Experiment 8, 437 individuals over 18 years of age were recruited on public beaches in Connecticut. They were given Harlow, Friedman, Higgins, Taylor, and Shah's (2001) measure of prevention versus promotion focus (the Regulatory Focus Questionnaire) and assigned to one of the same four message-framing conditions. We are currently analyzing these data, but it appears that prevention-focused individuals are more likely to be motivated to take action by any message that emphasizes undesirable outcomes and that promotion-focused individuals are more likely to be persuaded by messages that emphasize desirable outcomes. We are not certain, however, whether these trends are statistically significant.

Experiment 10: Regulatory Focus, Message Framing, and HIV Testing. This experiment investigated the effectiveness of differently framed messages designed to encourage low-income women to obtain an HIV test. We examined the influence of systematically different educational videos that were either gain or loss framed, emphasizing either the benefits of being screened for HIV or the costs of not being screened.

A total of 352 women completed a baseline interview that included the Regulatory Focus Questionnaire measuring promotion and prevention orientations. They were then randomly assigned to watch one of four framed videos aimed at persuading women to get an HIV test. HIV testing was assessed 9 months following baseline. Overall, 40% of the women who completed follow-up obtained an HIV test within 9 months. Promotion-focused women who viewed gain-framed messages were more likely to report getting an HIV test (50%) than were promotion-focused women who viewed a loss-framed message (23%). Among prevention-focused women, 42% who saw a gain-framed video and 36% who saw a loss-framed video obtained an HIV test, a difference that is not statistically reliable.

That gain-framed messages generally were more effective than the loss-framed messages in this domain, even though we consider HIV testing an early detection behavior, may at first seem puzzling. However, many of the women in this experiment indicated that the reason they would obtain an HIV test is to prevent the spread of HIV to partners rather than, necessarily, to detect illness in themselves. Recently, we completed a follow-up study to examine whether this difference in the way HIV testing is construed—as primarily serving a preventive rather than a detection function—accounts for our findings, and it seems likely that it does (Apanovitch, McCarthy, & Salovey, 2002). Meanwhile, it appears that differences in HIV testing decision making may also be a function of both the way a message is framed and the individual's regulatory focus. Stressing the benefits of HIV testing seems to increase testing behavior among

women who are more oriented toward seeking desirable outcomes in life rather than toward avoiding undesirable ones.

Experiment 11: Gain- and Loss-Framed Smoking Cessation Messages. In collaboration with the University of Rhode Island Cancer Center, we have conducted an experiment concerning smoking cessation among older adolescents. They viewed framed videotaped messages in which the textual elements were written in gain or loss terms and varied independently of the visual elements, which also were gain or loss framed. A total of 437 individuals participated in this experiment. If smoking cessation is viewed as a cancer prevention behavior, then consistent with the first hypothesis described earlier in this chapter, gain-framed messages should be more effective in encouraging this behavior. In fact, messages in which the text and visuals were gain framed were most effective. For smokers, any type of gain frame—visual or auditory—decreased temptations to smoke and actual number of cigarettes consumed (Schneider, Salovey, Pallonen, et al., 2001).

Experiment 12: The Same Behavior Framed in Gain or Loss Terms. We created four different professional-quality 15-minute videos about the value of pap testing. These videos placed pap testing in a preventive or early detection context and then framed this information in gain or loss terms. We expected gain-framed messages to be most effective in the prevention context and loss-framed messages to be most effective in the early detection context. We have recruited 512 women from community health clinics and randomly assigned them to view one of these four videos. Behavioral follow-ups are now being conducted, and we hope to be able to report on findings from this experiment quite soon. Recent findings from a laboratory analog experiment in which a mouthwash was described as either plaque preventing or plaque detecting lead us to suspect that we will obtain the predicted function by framing interaction (Rothman, Martino, Bedell, Detweiler, & Salovey, 1999).

MECHANISM

Behavioral decision theories, such as prospect theory, are rather silent with respect to the psychological mediation of framing effects. Most investigators working in this tradition have turned to shifts in the reference (inflection) point in the value function or changes in beliefs about the probability of pleasant and unpleasant outcomes as possible mechanisms. During recent years, we have focused on a more emotionally charged potential mediator of framing effects, anticipated affect, by which we mean the feelings a person simulates when considering performing (or being blocked from performing) the target behavior. We believe that framed messages motivate an individual to consider the affective consequences of initiating (or being prevented from initiating) a health behavior and that it is this anticipated affect that motivates salubrious action.

Our work on anticipated affect as the mediator of framing effects, however, is in its infancy. There are data that suggest that, at the very least, we may be on the right path. First, gain- and loss-framed messages can arouse different feelings; gain frames can lead to feelings of reassurance, but loss frames can generate anxiety (e.g., Rothman, Salovey, Antone, et al., 1993). Second, we conducted an experiment in which hypothetical prevention and early detection programs were described for addressing a fictitious disease called the "letrolisus virus." Participants were much more motivated to perform the prevention behavior after reading a gain-framed persua-

sive message and more likely to want to perform the detection behavior after reading a loss-framed message (Rothman et al., 1999; see also Detweiler et al., 1999). Moreover, the negative affect that participants expected to experience if not allowed to engage in these behaviors was greater after reading the more persuasive brochure. Finally, Wegener, Petty, and Klein (1994) showed that participants who have been induced to feel happy moods are more persuaded by gain-framed information, while those who have been induced to feel sad moods are more persuaded by loss-framed information. Although empirical support remains rather meager at present, we suggest that to understand framing, we will need a better handle on the emotions evoked by framed messages.

One additional issue that will need to be addressed by future researchers working on framing and health behavior is an elucidation of the meaning of our framing by behavior-type interactions. We are fairly certain that our "gain for prevention" and "loss for early detection" findings actually represent specific instances of more general principles. We have suggested that prevention and early detection behaviors differ in the uncertainty or risk involved in initiating them. But it is entirely possible that some other difference is what renders these behavior types as more or less influenced by gain versus loss framing. Even more fascinating is that some individuals (e.g., some of the women in our HIV testing experiment) appear to view testing as more of a prevention than a detection behavior. This finding suggests that a person's individualized construal of the function of a health behavior may be more important in predicting framing effects than is the "objective" function of that behavior (Apanovitch et al., 2002). Future work focused on persuading individuals to engage in healthy behaviors will need to address the interplay of objective and subjective functions of desired behaviors.

IMPLICATIONS

Interventions to encourage behaviors that can prevent or detect illness at an earlier, more treatable stage generally include the presentation of information in a didactic or persuasive context. Health communication experts can be given empirically based guidelines to optimize these messages. For example, the persuasiveness of information presented in terms of the benefits that might be associated with adopting a behavior versus the costs of not adopting it may depend on the type of health behavior one aims to encourage. The value function of prospect theory suggests hypotheses concerning the conditions under which such gain- or loss-framed messages are more or less effective.

Across a series of laboratory and field experiments concerning behaviors relevant to several illnesses, we have found that gain-framed messages generally are more persuasive when the target behavior serves to prevent illness but that loss-framed messages are more persuasive when the target behavior serves a screening or early detection function. These findings are consistent with the value function of prospect theory suggesting that gain-framed information motivates risk-averse certain choices but that loss-framed information motivates choices in which outcomes are uncertain, probabilistic, or risky. Moreover, we have also reported findings indicating that framing effects may be mediated by individual differences in the way people process health-relevant information. We have found interesting differences for people whose self-regulatory activities are organized around promotion versus prevention. Other individual differences in the way people respond to positive and negative information about themselves, such as monitoring versus blunting, may also be important in understanding framing (e.g., Miller et al., 1999).

Materials designed to influence health behavior—from billboard slogans to television PSAs—often are designed without much assistance from psychological theory. Yet the literatures concerning persuasion, social influence, and decision making may provide guidance for maximizing the effectiveness of these messages. Prevention behaviors may be better promoted by focusing on the positive consequences of adopting them. So, for example, warnings from the surgeon general on packages of cigarettes probably should focus on the benefits of cessation (e.g., increased stamina) rather than on the deleterious effects of continuing to light up (e.g., heart disease). Conversely, reminders to obtain annual mammogram screenings targeted to women over 40 years of age should make salient the negative consequences of ignoring this periodic event. Recent emotionally evocative PSAs shown on Connecticut television stations, for example, featured husbands and children who lost partners and mothers to breast cancer.

Influential health messages can be created by teams of psychologists with expertise in persuasion, health educators with an understanding of how such information is comprehended, and advertisers with a flair for the creative if they are based on principles of attitude change, motivation, and decision making. We look forward to the interdisciplinary development of an arsenal of health messages that really work.

REFERENCES

Apanovitch, A. M., McCarthy, D., & Salovey, P. (2002). *Using message framing to motivate HIV testing among low-income, ethnic minority women.* Unpublished manuscript, Yale University.

Banks, S. M., Salovey, P., Greener, S., Rothman, A. J., Moyer, A., Beauvais, J., & Epel, E. (1995).

The effects of message framing on mammography utilization. *Health Psychology, 14,* 178-184.

Brendl, C. M., Higgins, E. T., & Lemm, K. M. (1995). Sensitivity to varying gains and losses: The role of self-discrepancies and event framing. *Journal of Personality and Social Psychology, 69,* 1028-1051.

Christophersen, E. R., & Gyulay, J. E. (1981). Parental compliance with car seat usage: A positive approach with long term follow-up. *Journal of Pediatric Psychology, 6,* 301-312.

Crowe, E., & Higgins, E. T. (1997). Regulatory focus and strategic inclinations: Promotion and prevention in decision-making. *Organizational Behavior and Human Decision Processes, 69,* 117-132.

Detweiler, J. B., Bedell, B. T., Salovey, P., Pronin, E., & Rothman, A. J. (1999). Message framing and sunscreen use: Gain-framed messages motivate beach-goers. *Health Psychology, 18,* 189-196.

Eagly, A. E., & Chaiken, S. (1993). *The psychology of attitudes.* San Diego: Harcourt Brace.

Eagly, A. E., & Chaiken, S. (1998). Attitude structure and function. In D. T. Gilbert, S. T. Fiske, & G. Lindzey (Eds.), *The handbook of social psychology* (4th ed., pp. 269-322). New York: McGraw-Hill.

Fagley, N. S. (1993). A note concerning reflection effects versus framing effects. *Psychological Bulletin, 113,* 451-452.

Hamill, R., Wilson, T., & Nisbett, R. (1980). Insensitivity to sample bias: Generalizing from atypical cases. *Journal of Personality and Social Psychology, 39,* 578-589.

Harlow, R., Friedman, R., Higgins, E. T., Taylor, A., & Shah, J. (2001). *Promotion and prevention experiences as a personality variable.* Unpublished manuscript, Columbia University.

Higgins, E. T. (1997). Beyond pleasure and pain. *American Psychologist, 52,* 1280-1300.

Higgins, E. T. (1998). Promotion and prevention: Regulatory focus as a motivational principle. In M. P. Zanna (Ed.), *Advances in experimental social psychology* (Vol. 30, pp. 1-46). San Diego: Academic Press.

Hovland, C. I., Janis, I. L., & Kelley, H. H. (1953). *Communication and persuasion: Psychological studies of opinion change.* New Haven, CT: Yale University Press.

Janis, I. (1967). Effects of fear arousal on attitude change: Recent developments in theory and experimental research. In L. Berkowitz (Ed.), *Advances in experimental social psychology* (Vol. 3, pp. 166-224). New York: Academic Press.

Kahneman, D., & Tversky, A. (1979). Prospect theory: An analysis of decision under risk. *Econometrica, 47,* 263-291.

Kahneman, D., & Tversky, A. (1982). The psychology of preferences. *Scientific American, 247,* 160-173.

Kalichman, S. C., & Coley, B. (1995). Context framing to enhance HIV-antibody-testing messages targeted to African American women. *Health Psychology, 14,* 247-254.

King, E. S., Rimer, B. K., Trock, B., Balshem, A., & Engstrom, P. (1990). How valid are mammography self-reports? *American Journal of Public Health, 80,* 1386-1388.

Leventhal, H., Singer, R. P., & Jones, S. H. (1965). The effects of fear and specificity of recommendation. *Journal of Personality and Social Psychology, 2,* 20-29.

Levin, I. P., Schnittjer, S. K., & Thee, S. L. (1988). Information framing effects in social and personal decisions. *Journal of Experimental Social Psychology, 24,* 520-529.

Maheswaran, D., & Meyers-Levy, J. (1990). The influence of message framing and issue involvement. *Journal of Marketing Research, 27,* 361-367.

Marteau, T. M. (1989). Framing of information: Its influence upon decisions of doctors and patients. *British Journal of Social Psychology, 28,* 89-94.

McGuire, W. J. (1985). Attitudes and attitude change. In G. Lindzey & E. Aronson (Eds.), *Handbook of social psychology* (Vol. 2, pp. 233-346). New York: Random House.

McNeil, B. J., Pauker, S. G., Sox, H. C., & Tversky, A. (1982). On the elicitation of preferences for alternative therapies. *New England Journal of Medicine, 306,* 1259-1262.

Meyerowitz, B., & Chaiken, S. (1987). The effect of message framing on breast self-examination attitudes, intentions, and behavior. *Journal of Personality and Social Psychology, 52,* 500-510.

Miller, N. E., Maruyama, G., Beaber, R., & Valone, K. (1976). Speed of speech and persuasion. *Journal of Personality and Social Psychology, 34,* 615-624.

Miller, S. M., Buzaglo, J. S., Simms, S. L., Green, V., Bales, C., Mangan, C. E., & Selacek, T. V. (1999). Monitoring styles in women at risk for cervical cancer: Implications for the framing of health-relevant messages. *Annals of Behavioral Medicine, 21,* 27-34.

Petty, R. E., & Wegener, D. (1991). Thought systems, argument quality, and persuasion. In R. S. Wyer & T. K. Srull (Eds.), *Advances in social cognition* (Vol. 4, pp. 147-161). Hillsdale, NJ: Lawrence Erlbaum.

Petty, R. E., & Wegener, D. (1998). Attitude change. In D. T. Gilbert, S. T. Fiske, & G. Lindzey (Eds.), *The handbook of social psychology* (4th ed., pp. 323-390). New York: McGraw-Hill.

Robberson, M. R., & Rogers, R. W. (1988). Beyond fear appeals: Negative and positive persuasive appeals to health and self-esteem. *Journal of Applied Social Psychology, 13,* 277-287.

Robinson, J., & McArthur, L. Z. (1982). Impact of salient vocal qualities on causal attribution for a speaker's behavior. *Journal of Personality and Social Psychology, 43,* 236-247.

Rothman, A. J., Martino, S. C., Bedell, B., Detweiler, J., & Salovey, P. (1999). The systematic influence of gain- and loss-framed messages on interest in different types of health behavior. *Personality and Social Psychology Bulletin, 25,* 1357-1371.

Rothman, A. J., & Salovey, P. (1997). Shaping perceptions to motivate healthy behavior: The role of message framing. *Psychological Bulletin, 121,* 3-19.

Rothman, A. J., Salovey, P., Antone, C., Keough, K., & Martin, C. (1993). The influence of message framing on health behavior. *Journal of Experimental Social Psychology, 29,* 408-433.

Rothman, A. J., Salovey, P., Turvey, C., & Fishkin, S. A. (1993). Attributions of responsibility and persuasion: Increasing mammography utiliza-

tion among women over 40 with an internally oriented message. *Health Psychology, 12,* 39-47.

Salovey, P., Banks, S. M., Greener, S., Rothman, A. J., Moyer, A., Epel, E., & Beauvais, J. (1994, April). *The effects of message framing on mammography utilization.* Paper presented at the annual scientific sessions of the Society for Behavioral Medicine, Boston.

Salovey, P., & Pronin, E. (1995). Message framing and health promotion. In *Proceedings of the Conference on Telecommunications and Information Markets* (Vol. 1, pp. 342-348). Kingston: University of Rhode Island.

Salovey, P., Pronin, E., Rothman, A. J., Zullo, J., & Leffell, D. (2001). *Framing, involvement, and skin cancer prevention and early detection.* Unpublished manuscript, Yale University.

Schneider, T. R., Salovey, P., Apanovitch, A. M., Pizarro, J., McCarthy, D., Zullo, J., & Rothman, A. J. (2001). The effects of message framing and ethnic targeting on mammography use among low-income women. *Health Psychology, 20,* 256-266.

Schneider, T. R., Salovey, P., Pallonen, U., Mundorf, N., Smith, N. F., & Steward, W. (2001). Visual and auditory message framing effects on tobacco smoking. *Journal of Applied Social Psychology, 31,* 667-682.

Shah, J., Higgins, E. T., & Friedman, R. (1998). Performance incentives and means: How regulatory focus influences goal attainment. *Journal of Personality and Social Psychology, 74,* 285-293.

Sutton, S. R. (1982). Fear arousal and communication: A critical examination of theories and research. In J. Eiser (Ed.), *Social psychology and behavioral medicine* (pp. 303-337). Chichester, UK: Wiley.

Taylor, S. E., & Thompson, S. C. (1982). Stalking the elusive "vividness" effect. *Psychological Review, 89,* 155-181.

Treiber, F. A. (1986). A comparison of positive and negative consequences approaches upon car restraint usage. *Journal of Pediatric Psychology, 11,* 15-24.

Tversky, A., & Kahneman, D. (1981). The framing of decisions and the psychology of choice. *Science, 211,* 453-458.

Wegener, D. T., Petty, R. E., & Klein, D. J. (1994). Effects of mood on high elaboration attitude change: The mediating role of likelihood judgments. *European Journal of Social Psychology, 24,* 25-43.

Wilson, D. K., Kaplan, R. M., & Schneiderman, L. (1987). Framing of decisions and selections of alternatives in health care. *Social Behavior, 2,* 51-59.

Wilson, D. K., Purdon, S. E., & Wallston, K. A. (1988). Compliance to health recommendations: A theoretical overview of message framing. *Health Education Research: Theory and Practice, 3,* 161-171.

21

Figurative Language and Persuasion

PRADEEP SOPORY
JAMES PRICE DILLARD

P ublic discourse is rife with figurative comparisons designed to change people's minds. Metaphor is the typical trope of comparison in such messages, although use of other nonliteral comparisons such as similes, analogies, and personifications is also common. Despite this widespread use, do we know whether figurative comparisons in persuasive message are really effective? And if so, what is the process by which they achieve their impact? This chapter reviews possible answers to these two questions. After providing some background, we start by summarizing what is known about effect of metaphor on attitude and communicator credibility, sketch out relevant theories of metaphor comprehension, evaluate different views of metaphor and persuasion, and finally make suggestions for future research.

TERMINOLOGY AND SCOPE

A metaphor is customarily defined as a linguistic phrase of the form "A is B," such that a comparison is suggested between the two terms leading to a transfer of attributes associated with B to A. For example, "The global marketplace is a dictatorship" (from a flyer advertising a protest march) consists of two parts, A (global marketplace) and B (dictatorship), such that there is a comparison between A and B and properties associated with dictatorship are transferred to global marketplace. The two terms, A and B, are seen as representing different concepts or conceptual domains, and various theorists have used different terminology to describe the two parts. The more recent use is *target* and *base* (e.g., Gentner, 1983) for A and B, respectively.

Simile, analogy, and personification, albeit different in some surface respects, cognitively function similar to metaphor in that all three also involve comparison of concepts or systems of concepts.[1] Hence, their study is generally subsumed into that of metaphor. Accordingly, in this chapter, we use *metaphor* as a general term to refer to all tropes of comparison.

Usually the word *metaphor* is used to denote, as above, a particular language device or a characteristic of language, what Lakoff and Johnson (1980) called *linguistic metaphor*. In this sense, metaphor is a rhetorical property that is observed in spoken or written language. However, the term *metaphor* is also used in two other ways: as a cognitive process and as a cognitive structure. In the first instance, metaphor is a conceptual process by which one mental entity is understood via mapping to another mental entity. This is commonly referred to as metaphorical processing or reasoning. In the second instance, metaphor is a structure inherent in mental entities that come about as a consequence of a cognitive mapping process. Lakoff and Johnson (1980) referred to such metaphorically structured concepts as *conceptual metaphors*. This chapter employs the term *metaphor* in all three senses, and distinguishes among them wherever necessary.

Among linguistic metaphors, a distinction is usually made between novel and conventionalized (Lakoff & Johnson, 1980) or "dead" (Black, 1962) metaphors. Novel metaphors, sometimes inaccurately conflated with metaphor itself, are expressions whose equation of target with a base creates new information about the target. For example, the expression "This new legislation is no ordinary headache pill" provides novel information about the new legislation. Conventionalized metaphors (also called "frozen" metaphors) are figurative comparisons that were once novel but with repeated use have been completely absorbed into the conventions of everyday language (e.g., "the *arm* of a chair," "time just *flew* by"). Such metaphors are not immediately recognized as metaphors.

Natural language is so infused with conventionalized metaphors that it is hard to make any meaningful distinction between metaphorical and literal language. Similarly, most studies of metaphor comprehension conclude that the same cognitive machinery is most likely used for processing both figurative and literal language (Gibbs, 1994). However, a metaphor-literal distinction may be apparent in the process of language interpretation at a neurological level. In their review of the neurocognitive mechanisms underlying comprehension of metaphor and other figurative language, Burgess and Chiarello (1996) concluded that a right hemisphere advantage exists for figurative language over literal language. For example, studies using positron emission tomography to investigate brain functioning associated with language processing (e.g., Bottini et al., 1994) show that processing of novel metaphorical language may make a much heavier use of the right cerebral hemisphere, unlike literal language, which tends to use left and right brain neural assemblies equally. Thus, some type of a processing discrimination (as yet empirically unknown) may be reasonably made between metaphorical and literal language. Accordingly, it may be proper to study message (or language) effects on attitudes using a metaphor-literal distinction.

METAPHOR EFFECTS ON ATTITUDE AND COMMUNICATOR CREDIBILITY

Do metaphor-using messages exert a greater effect on attitude and communicator credibility than do literal messages? Sopory and Dillard (in press) provided an answer to this question in their meta-analytic review of the empirical literature on metaphor and persuasion. The main results of their meta-analysis are summarized briefly in what follows as nine propositions about the effects of metaphor.

Effect of Metaphor on Attitude

A total of 29 data-based studies with a metaphor versus literal experimental design and attitude as the dependent variable were used in the meta-analysis. These studies yielded 38 metaphor-literal comparison data points for the effect size (r) with approximately 4,000 participants. Also, a number of moderator variables of interest were identified in the studies based on their potential for influencing the persuasion process, including number of metaphors, extendedness of metaphors, position of metaphors, familiarity of target, novelty of metaphors, modality of presentation, and communicator credibility.

Proposition 1: Relative to their literal counterparts, metaphorical messages are more likely to produce greater attitude change. The results of the meta-analysis clearly revealed that metaphor-using messages do exhibit a small persuasive edge over literal-only messages for attitude change ($r = .07$). This relationship was positive across all moderator variable conditions except 2. In other words, the meta-analysis uncovered only 2 conditions (out of 14) in which the use of metaphor may be detrimental to the goal of generating agreement with the message advocacy. Thus, the positive effect of metaphor on attitude seems to be a reliable one.

The small effect size found here is not unlike the magnitude of effects obtained meta-analytically for other message variables in persuasion research. For example, a two-sided message containing refutation of counterarguments is superior to a one-sided message by roughly the same effect size of .07 (Allen, 1998). Similarly, Dillard (1998), after perusing effect sizes for nine different persuasion meta-analyses, observed that all were less than .30 and that their mean was only .18, which may be considered to be on the small side by Cohen's (1987) criteria. Hence, the effect of

metaphor on attitude is in the same order as other observed effects in persuasion research. Moreover, the effect of metaphor becomes more pronounced when particular moderator variables are taken into account, as the results that follow show.

Proposition 2: Use of 1 metaphor is associated with greater attitude change than is use of larger numbers. A metaphor-using persuasive message may contain any number of metaphors. In the message pool collated from the different studies, three ranges of metaphor use were identified: 1, 2 to 8, and 9 or more. The effect sizes from the meta-analysis showed that it was 1 metaphor that was associated with maximum attitude change ($r = .08$) as compared to the 2 to 8 ($r = .06$) and 9 or more ($r = .02$) ranges. Thus, less may be more when it comes to using figurative comparisons in a persuasive message, as there is a decreasing suasory effect with increasing number.

Proposition 3: Extended metaphors are associated with greater attitude change than are nonextended metaphors. Metaphors may be extended or nonextended. An extended metaphor uses one base to construct a number of different sub-metaphors with the same target. As seen on a flyer, for example, the base *dictatorship* may be used for the following metaphors, all with the target *global marketplace:* "The dictatorship of the global marketplace has set up a framework of rules that citizens have not voted for," ". . . in the name of the good of the citizenry, unaccountable despotic power given to corporations and elites . . .," and ". . . global marketplace . . . conspiring to chain dissenters in the dungeons of media non-access." A nonextended metaphor, by contrast, uses a given base only once to suggest a comparison with a target.

The effect sizes from the meta-analysis showed that extended metaphors ($r = .09$)

were associated with greater attitude change than were nonextended metaphors ($r = .05$). Thus, a message intending to use multiple metaphors to affect attitude may be better off using the same base repeatedly than using many distinct bases.

Proposition 4: Metaphors are associated with greater attitude change when positioned in the introduction of a message, rather than in the conclusion or the body of the message. A metaphor may be placed in the introduction, body (i.e., middle), or conclusion of a message. The effect sizes from the meta-analysis showed that metaphors were more persuasive when placed in the introduction ($r = .12$) than when placed in the body ($r = .07$) or the conclusion ($r = -.01$) of a message. Similarly, in the case of a message with multiple metaphors, a trope may first appear in the message in either the introduction, the body, or the conclusion of the message. Results for "first appearance in introduction" and for "first appearance in body or conclusion" also showed a similar pattern. Thus, using a metaphor to provide a title to a message or to frame a message at the beginning may be more persuasive than using it to summarize the message.

Proposition 5: Metaphors are associated with greater attitude change when there is high familiarity of the target than when there is low familiarity. The target and base of a metaphor may have varying degrees of familiarity for a message recipient. To facilitate transfer of information from base to target (as a metaphor does), the familiarity of the base is generally high. By contrast, the target term of a metaphor (typically the attitude object) may be familiar or unfamiliar to an audience of a particular message. For example, "Aid to Colombia is like . . ." is a low-knowledge target for North American undergraduate audiences, while "Seat belt use is like . . ." is most likely a

high-knowledge target. The effect sizes from the meta-analysis showed that metaphors were more persuasive when there was high familiarity of the target ($r = .07$) than when there was low familiarity ($r = .06$). Thus, having more, rather than less, familiarity with the target of a metaphor may foster enhanced persuasion.

Proposition 6: Metaphors are associated with greater attitude change when more novel than when less novel. Novelty of a metaphor for a given message recipient may be defined in terms of knowledge of the similarities between the two terms of a metaphor.[2] That is, novelty of an "A is B" equation depends on whether the similarities between A and B exist in the minds of a message recipient prior to encountering the metaphor. For example, the common saying, "She has a heart of gold," is of low novelty because the correspondences between the base and target already exist in the minds of people prior to the reception. On the other hand, the stanza from a classical Sanskrit poem, "Now the great cloud cat, darting out his lightning tongue, licks the creamy moonlight from the saucepan of the sky" (Ingalls, 1968, p. 104), will be of high novelty because (most likely) the similarities between *cloud* and *cat* do not exist for readers prior to comprehending this metaphor. It should be emphasized that the focus is on the familiarity of the similarities between the terms and not the familiarity of the target and base themselves per se. For example, people may be highly familiar with the terms *cloud* and *cat*, but the similarities between the two might not exist in their minds prior to encountering the metaphoric expression.

The effect sizes from the meta-analysis showed that novel metaphors ($r = .12$) were associated with more attitude change than were non-novel ones ($r = .01$). Thus, metaphors that create new similarities between entities, as their function has been traditionally described, may be more persuasive than ones that do not produce such new linkages.

Proposition 7: Metaphors in the audio modality are associated with greater attitude change than are metaphors in the written modality. People encounter persuasive messages through different media such as print, radio, and television. The effect sizes from the meta-analysis revealed that metaphors presented in the audio modality were more persuasive ($r = .09$) than those presented in the written modality ($r = .06$). Thus, metaphor-using messages may be more effective when listening, when one can process a message only once in a limited amount of time, than when reading, which allows for more processing time as well as multiple reviews of the message.

Proposition 8: Metaphor messages used by low-credibility communicators are associated with greater attitude change than those used by high-credibility communicators. Message recipients may perceive communicators as having low or high credibility prior to processing a message. The effect sizes from the meta-analysis showed that messages containing metaphors were associated with greater attitude change when the communicators had low credibility ($r = .12$) than when the communicators had high credibility ($r = .02$). Thus, message sources with low credibility may benefit more from using metaphors to affect attitudes than may message sources with high credibility.

Effect of Metaphor on Communicator Competence, Character, and Dynamism Judgments

Perceptions of credibility of a communicator can be determined at two points during message processing: pre-message, or before the audience members process a message (initial credibility), and post-message, or after the receivers process the message (terminal credibility). Metaphor's persuasive effects can also be assessed in terms of its impact on judgments of terminal credibility.

Many writers have asserted that communicators who use metaphorical language are judged more favorably than those who use literal language (e.g., Aristotle, 1952; Bowers & Osborn, 1966; McCroskey & Combs, 1969; Osborn & Ehninger, 1962). However, credibility is not a unitary construct (Berlo, Lemert, & Mertz, 1969; McCroskey & Young, 1981), and there are a number of subcomponents of credibility, with the three most common being competence, character, and dynamism.[3] For the credibility meta-analysis, 12 data-based studies with a metaphor versus literal experimental design and at least one of these three credibility aspects as the dependent variable were used. These studies yielded 20 metaphor-literal comparison data points for the effect size (r) with approximately 2,000 participants.

Proposition 9: Metaphors are more likely to be effective for enhancing terminal communicator credibility judgments for the dynamism aspect than for competence and character aspects. Of the three post-message credibility facets, the effect of metaphor was functionally nonexistent for character and competence aspects. For the *competence* aspect of credibility, the effect size r was $-.01$. Analysis of the moderator variable of initial (low and high) credibility showed the same null results. Similarly, there was no effect of metaphor on the *character* aspect of credibility ($r = -.02$). For both low and high initial credibility communicators, use of metaphors again did not affect character judgments. On the other hand, the r for *dynamism* was .06. Furthermore, the effect for both low- and high-credibility communicators was positive. Thus, of the three facets of terminal credibility, metaphor has its strongest effect on judgments of communicator dynamism.

THEORIES OF METAPHOR COMPREHENSION

Several answers have been proposed to the question of how metaphor may achieve its persuasive effects. To help explicate and evaluate these varied explanations, the theories dealing with metaphor comprehension need to be presented first. There are many views of how metaphor is understood. The four that have been used to theorize about metaphor and persuasion are summarized in what follows.[4]

The *literal primacy* view (Beardsley, 1962, 1976; MacCormac, 1985; Searle, 1979) sees metaphor as literally false or logically contradictory language, that is, a semantic anomaly. According to this view, there are three stages in the process of understanding a metaphorical expression: (a) deriving the literal meaning of the expression, (b) testing whether the literal meaning makes sense and consequently detecting an anomaly, and then (c) seeking an alternative meaning (i.e., the metaphorical meaning) because the literal meaning fails to make sense (for an elaborated discussion, see Gibbs, 1994). According to one variation of this view (e.g., MacCormac, 1985), when an interpreter confronts a semantic anomaly, cognitive tension is generated along with a desire to reduce it. By finding the nonliteral meaning of the literally false statement, the anomaly is resolved and the tension is dissipated.

While the literal primacy view treats metaphorical language as semantically deviant and exceptional, the next three positions reject the notion of metaphor as anomalous language. These theories assume that metaphoricity and literalness of language is a matter of degree

and that the same general psychological mechanism underlies processing of both forms of language.

Ortony's (1979, 1993; see also Ortony, Vondruska, Foss, & Jones, 1985) *salience imbalance* theory uses the notion of salience of attributes to explain how metaphors are comprehended. Salience is defined empirically as the relative importance of an attribute; that is, the first attribute that comes to mind is the most salient, and so on. The theory says that a metaphorical expression of the type "A is B" is understood by constructing the ground (i.e., the set of shared attributes) by selecting only those attributes that have low salience for the target and high salience for the base. For example, the metaphor "Encyclopedias are gold mines" is understood by choosing for the ground attributes such as *valuable nuggets* and *dig,* which have a high salience for gold mines and a low salience for encyclopedias. If the two terms are reversed (i.e., "Gold mines are encyclopedias"), then a different set of the shared attributes would be chosen; because the attributes that would be highly salient for encyclopedias would be different.

Gentner's (1982, 1983, 1989; see also Gentner & Clement, 1988) *structure mapping* theory, using an associative network model of memory, proposes that instead of comparing lists of attributes, the relations among the attributes are compared for similarities to interpret a metaphor. Gentner (1983) linked metaphor explicitly to analogy and defined a metaphor as "an assertion that a relational structure that normally applies in one domain can be applied in another domain" (p. 156). This view posits that metaphors convey a system of connected knowledge, not a mere collection of independent facts. In interpreting a metaphor, people attempt to obtain a match between target and base by seeking a relational mapping. For example, the metaphor "Encyclopedias are gold mines" is interpreted by noting the common relation *valuable nug-*

gets found by digging rather than the independent similar attributes *valuable nuggets* and *dig*.

The *conceptual structure* theory (Johnson, 1987; Lakoff, 1987, 1993; Lakoff & Turner, 1989; see also Albritton, McKoon, & Gerrig, 1995; Gibbs, 1994) considers metaphor as a thought process and defines it as "understanding and experiencing one kind of thing or experience in terms of another" (Lakoff & Johnson, 1980, p. 5). As a result of this metaphorical processing, long-term memory is organized as a system of metaphorical correspondences or mappings between different domains of experiences. These mappings are called conceptual metaphors. For example, the conceptual metaphor "Relationship is a journey" is a label for the mappings that exist in the long-term memory between the domains of *relationship* and *journey*. The conceptual system contains thousands of such correspondences among different domains that are used to produce and understand both conventional and novel metaphorical statements. For example, the expressions "Our relationship is *on the right track*," "We seem to be *stuck and going nowhere*," and "When did you *end* the relationship?" are conventional metaphors in which the domain of *relationship* is compared to the domain of *journey*. All of these expressions are understood via the conceptual metaphor "Relationship is a journey." Novel metaphorical expressions are understood by extending these preexisting conceptual metaphors through patterns of inferences authorized by them. For example, the novel metaphor "Hope their space shuttle doesn't blow up on launch" is understood by generalizing the existing mappings of "Relationship is a land journey" as a pattern of inferences to *space journeys*.

The preceding four theories of metaphor comprehension have been directly employed to derive different explanations of metaphor's persuasive impact. These metaphor and persuasion theories are examined next.

THEORIES OF METAPHOR AND PERSUASION

How does metaphor achieve its suasory outcomes? There are five general views of metaphor and persuasion available in the existing empirical literature that try to explain this process: pleasure/relief, communicator credibility, cognitive resources, stimulated elaboration, and superior organization. These views are evaluated next based on the results of the Sopory and Dillard (in press) meta-analysis and evidence from other relevant research.

Pleasure/Relief

The pleasure/relief view (e.g., Bowers & Osborn, 1966; Reinsch, 1971, 1974; Tudman, 1971) stems from the assumptions of the literal primacy view (e.g., Beardsley, 1962, 1967, 1976). There are two variants of this explanation, both arguing that a metaphorical expression is a semantic anomaly, recognition of which leads to negative tension that gets relieved when the metaphorical meaning is finally understood. In the persuasion literature, these three steps are called *perception of defect/error*, *conflict* (or *recoil*), and *resolution*. In the first variant, finding the metaphorical meaning, and thus the "unexpected similarities" between the target and base, is pleasurable. According to the second variant, finding the metaphorical meaning dissipates the negative tension, leading to relief. The reward of pleasure and relief leads to a reinforcement of the metaphorical meaning and the evaluation associated with it. By contrast, literal language does not pose any linguistic puzzle to resolve and consequently yields neither pleasure nor relief.

The data from the meta-analysis did not speak directly to the reinforcement principle of the pleasure/relief view. However, the assumptions of literal primacy theory that underlie this view are disputed by the results of the moderator analysis for modality of presentation. The literal primacy view suggests that the literal meaning of an expression is obligatorily understood before the metaphorical meaning is understood. As such, the comprehension of a metaphor should take longer than the comprehension of (equivalent) literal language. This should be an advantage for written modality by ensuring that cognizers have enough time to comprehend a message and, at the same time, depressing the likelihood of pleasure/relief in the audio modality. The results showed that audio modality was more persuasive, contradicting the prediction from the literal primacy view. In addition, Hoffman and Kemper (1987), after a review of reaction time studies, concluded that idioms, indirect requests, metaphors, and proverbs (i.e., different types of figurative language) did not take longer to be understood than did literal language. In fact, their review showed that some metaphors in the proper discourse context were processed faster than their literal counterparts in the same discourse context.

The assumption of the pleasure/relief view that metaphor represents defective language such that a prior step to understanding metaphorical meaning is identification of a defect is also untenable. Research shows that people draw metaphorical meanings out of metaphorical statements long before they judge such expressions anomalous in any way (McCabe, 1983). The perception of error and tension steps may perhaps be fruitfully resurrected in terms of expectancy violations of linguistic conventions (Nelson & Hitchon, 1999; see also Burgoon & Miller, 1985), but

the process of persuasion suggested in the pleasure/relief model remains based on an incorrect understanding of the nature of metaphor and the process of metaphor comprehension. Therefore, the pleasure/relief view of metaphor's persuasive advantage does not have any empirical support.

Communicator Credibility

The enhancement of communicator credibility view (e.g., Bowers & Osborn, 1966; McCroskey & Combs, 1969; Osborn & Ehninger, 1962; Reinsch, 1971) proposes that communicators who use metaphors are judged more credible than are those who use literal language. In turn, this enhanced source judgment leads to greater persuasion by making the attitude towards the message advocacy more positive. This higher credibility judgment may occur for two related reasons. First, as Aristotle (1952), in his *Poetics,* argued, "But the greatest thing by far is to be a master of metaphor. It is the one thing that cannot be learnt from others; and it is also a sign of genius" (p. 255). The assumption of this view is that metaphors are exceptional language and are like "ornaments" on the literal language that are used only by poets and writers, not by ordinary folks in everyday discourse. Thus, people who use metaphors are perceived as highly creative and are judged quite positively. The second reason (e.g., Bowers & Osborn, 1966; Osborn & Ehninger, 1962) is derived from metaphor's ability to point out previously unknown similarities between entities to a person. This newfound appreciation of commonalties is a source of interest and pleasure to the comprehender, who consequently is grateful to the message source, leading to enhanced judgment of communicator credibility. In contemporary terms, the key idea of the communicator credibility view is that the source judgment may act as a persuasion heuristic (Chaiken, Liberman, & Eagly, 1989).

The communicator credibility explanation was clearly not supported by the results of the meta-analysis, which showed that on the whole, people do not judge metaphor-using communicators more favorably than they do those who use literal language. Another line of research on effects of *rebuttal analogy* on receiver perceptions of communicators and message arguments corroborates this finding (Whaley, 1997, 1998; Whaley, Nicotera, & Samter, 1998). A rebuttal analogy serves two communicative functions: as a method of counterargumentation and as a method of social attack. Communicators who use such analogies are perceived as less polite, less ethical, and less competent, and their arguments are seen as less ethical and less effective than those of sources who use nonanalogy messages. Thus, the view that use of metaphor prompts a positive source heuristic to be engaged, leading to greater persuasion, is not the right explanation.

The assumption that metaphor is "exceptional language" is also not defensible. Metaphors are not mere ornaments on literal language used only by poets and writers; rather, they are common in everyday language. For example, Pollio, Barlow, Fine, and Pollio (1977), after examining various psychotherapeutic interviews, essays, and the Kennedy-Nixon presidential debates, estimated that 1.80 novel metaphors and 4.08 dead metaphors were used per minute of discourse. Another study looking at use of metaphors in news and public affairs programs found that one novel metaphor was used for every 25 words (Graesser, Mio, & Millis, 1989). Thus, use of metaphor does not seem to require any special genius, and as such, there is little reason to expect its use to enhance credibility, at least as related to expertise and character, of a communicator.

Cognitive Resources

Two views of metaphor and persuasion employ the assumption that understanding metaphors demands more cognitive resources than does understanding literal language. According to the *reduced counterarguments* view (Guthrie, 1972), the process of metaphor comprehension generates a great number of associations that result in "an overload in the receiver's mental circuitry" (p. 4). As a result, a high proportion of the cognitive resources of a comprehender are used up when encountering a metaphorical persuasive message, and consequently (assuming a counterattitudinal message) fewer resources are left to "derogate or exclude the message content or the source" (p. 4). The outcome is reduced counterargumentation and greater agreement with the message advocacy.

A more sophisticated version is the *resource matching* view (Jaffe, 1988). This perspective proposes that deriving meaning of a metaphorical expression requires elaboration to construct the ground (Ortony, 1979, 1993), which ensures better memory for (high-quality) message arguments and hence improved comprehension, leading to greater persuasion relative to a literal message. However, elaboration also requires greater mobilization of cognitive resources. If there is a match between the high cognitive resources required to understand the metaphorical message and the cognitive resources available to an interpreter, then maximum elaboration and thus maximum comprehension occurs; if there is a mismatch, then less comprehension occurs. Thus, if limited resources are available, then the message (whether pro- or counterattitudinal) is not adequately understood and persuasion is inhibited; similarly, the persuasive impact of a message is diluted when excess resources are available (e.g., for clichéd expressions) because irrelevant and idiosyncratic thoughts are generated. In this view, then, novel metaphorical messages have a persuasive advantage over literal messages only under resource-enhanced conditions, such as message repetition, where the knowledge generated by repetition ensures a match of resources to the requirements of a metaphorical message but leads to excess resources for a literal message.

Cognitive resource or effort was not indexed in any of the studies included in the meta-analysis, so the question of whether metaphors require more resources than do literal messages cannot be answered directly from its results. However, other findings run counter to the claims of the resource matching explanation. According to this view, metaphors should be persuasive only under resource-enhancing conditions such as message repetition. Contradicting this, all experiments in the meta-analysis presented messages only once, and the results do show that metaphors led to more attitude change than did literal language. Along the same lines, the greater amount of time spent processing a message in the written modality may be seen as enhancing cognitive resources facilitating resource matching. However, it was the audio modality, which allows only a single pass through a message, that was more persuasive. Similarly, evidence based on reaction time studies discussed earlier suggests that understanding metaphors does not demand greater cognitive resources than does understanding literal language. Furthermore, studies that have compared metaphor and literal processing using indexes of cognitive effort, such as eye movement tracking and gaze duration (Inhoff, Lima, & Carroll, 1984) and speech pauses (Pollio, Fabrizi, & Weedle, 1982), have also found that understanding metaphors requires no more effort than does understanding literal language when appropriate contextual information is provided. Therefore, given the outcomes of the meta-analysis and

other relevant research, these two cognitive resources views are not the ideal candidates for a theoretical explanation of metaphor's persuasive effects.

Stimulated Elaboration

The stimulated elaboration view is linked to two different metaphor processing theories. Hitchon (1991), using concepts of salience imbalance theory (Ortony, 1979, 1993), proposed that when the ground is assembled from the common attributes of target and base to comprehend a metaphor, the evaluation (valence) associated with the attributes is also part of the ground. In her view, formation of the ground requires elaboration of the ground-relevant attributes as well as their associated valence. Thus, elaboration leads to a greater number of valenced thoughts, which (when in the appropriate direction) lead to greater persuasion. By contrast, extracting the meaning of a literal expression does not require constructing a ground and hence elaboration of the message content.

Whaley (1991) used structure mapping theory (Gentner, 1982, 1989) to propose that understanding analogies stimulates thought through a focus on similar target-base relations (rather than attributes) and hence the evoking of a richer set of associations in semantic memory compared to literal language. This greater number of semantic connections produces greater elaboration of message content, which in turn leads to increased persuasion given suitable processing conditions. Whaley proposed that certain types of analogies (explanatory analogies [Gentner, 1982]) function as high-quality arguments, so their processing results in more elaboration than do literal messages. Then, if both motivation and ability are high and the message is compelling, the outcome is a greater number of thoughts agreeing with message advocacy and thus greater persuasion (Chaiken et al., 1989; Petty & Cacioppo, 1986).

The key variable in the stimulated elaboration account is the number of thoughts generated in response to a metaphorical language message as compared to a literal one. Studies investigating metaphor's persuasive effects that have measured this type of elaboration (Hitchon, 1991; Mitchell, Badzinski, & Pawlowski, 1994; Morgan, 1997; Sopory, 1999; Whaley, 1991) have not found that metaphorical language results in a greater number of cognitive responses than does literal language.

However, it may be the case that elaboration is influenced by other variables in tandem with type of language. This idea is developed as a more refined version of the stimulated elaboration hypothesis in the *motivational resonance* view (Ottati, Rhoads, & Graesser, 1999). Using the dual-process approach to persuasion (Chaiken et al., 1989; Petty & Cacioppo, 1986), this view proposes that metaphorical language creates greater interest in a message than does literal language, thereby increasing motivation to more systematically process the message. This motivation to elaborate the message content is moderated by argument strength/quality and prior interest toward the metaphor target. When the quality of message arguments is high and message recipients have a positive interest toward the metaphor target, such that the metaphor "resonates" with their prior preferences, maximum elaboration and hence greatest suasion occurs. Results of two studies (Ottati et al., 1999) largely confirmed this prediction as a condition for enhanced metaphor impact.

It may also be the case that linguistic metaphor does facilitate more thinking but that this thinking is not propositional (i.e., linguistic). For example, Coulson and Oakley (in press) used the theory of conceptual blending (Fauconnier, 1994; Fauconnier & Turner, 1998) to contend that comprehension of persuasive messages does require elaboration, but they conceived of elaboration in terms of mental simulation of the situation being described by the message content. Similarly, Paivio and Walsh (1993; see also Lakoff, 1993) pointed out that many linguistic metaphors may use more imagistic than linguistic processing. Along the same lines, Zaltman's metaphor elicitation technique (Zaltman & Coulter, 1995; Zaltman & Higie, 1993) also suggests that metaphorical thinking may engage substantial image-based processes. This research technique successfully assesses customers' metaphoric representations of products and consumer services using selection and arrangement of pictures and images, that is, via primarily nonlinguistic measures. Thus, the number of linguistic expressions might not be the only processual variable indexing elaboration as an explanation of metaphor's greater persuasive capacity.

Superior Organization

The superior organization view (Read, Cesa, Jones, & Collins, 1990), also derived from Gentner's (1982, 1989) structure mapping theory, proposes that a metaphor helps to better structure and organize the arguments of a persuasive message relative to literal language. A metaphor evokes a greater number of semantic associations, and the different arguments, when consistent with the metaphor, get connected together more coherently via the many available semantic pathways. In addition, the links to the metaphor "highlight" the arguments making them more salient. Consequently, this more coherent organization, and the resulting highlighting of the arguments, increases the persuasive power of metaphor-using messages. Literal-only messages lack this organizing function of metaphor and therefore are not as persuasive.

Results of the meta-analysis point to direct support for the superior organization view only. Metaphors were most persuasive when extended and when placed in the introduction position of a message. This suggests that persuasion occurred due to the organizing potential of metaphor as theme, which facilitated selection and integration of information from the message and prior knowledge. The results also showed that a single metaphor was more persuasive than greater numbers of metaphors. As the superior organization view implies, it is only a single metaphor that should provide the optimal opportunity for enhanced organization of the message information. Similarly, the persuasive superiority of metaphors with high knowledge of target over low-knowledge ones suggests that higher prior knowledge allowed recipients to better organize the target-base linkages. Therefore, the meta-analytic results favor superior organization's explanation of how metaphor may be more persuasive than literal language.

The *structural consistency* view (Sopory, 1999) adopts the superior organization view's insight but proposes a different account of how metaphor-using messages may lead to increased organization of information. Using the conceptual structure theory (Lakoff, 1987, 1993), this view claims that it is the emergent structural match between linguistic and conceptual metaphor during message processing that organizes the information. A unique property of this coherent information set is that it manifests high evaluative consistency of cognitive-affective-behavioral information available for attitude construction (i.e., high intra-attitudinal structural consistency), which in turn makes it more likely that receivers show enhanced attitude change in the desired direction with metaphorical messages than with literal ones. Results of two

studies (Sopory, 1999) provided moderate support for this view. Thus, metaphor may persuade not only by linking various arguments of a message into a coherent whole but also by organizing the attitude-relevant information into an evaluatively consistent package.

Other Metaphor and Persuasion Views

Research on effects of language intensity and message vividness on attitude has attempted to subsume metaphor under these two types of language variables. The metaphor and persuasion meta-analysis speaks directly to both views.

Metaphor as Intense Language. The empirical tradition of metaphor and persuasion originated with metaphor conceptualized as a form of intense language. *Language intensity* is defined as "the quality of language which indicates the degree to which the speaker's attitude toward a concept deviates from neutrality" (Bowers, 1963, p. 345; for an updated version, see Hamilton & Stewart, 1993). Based on the principle of reinforcement, Bowers (1963) proposed that such intense language messages should be more persuasive than nonintense ones and went on (Bowers, 1964) to distinguish four features of intense language: number of syllables, obscure words, qualifiers and intensifiers, and metaphors. Subsequent research (Bowers & Osborn, 1966; Reinsch, 1971; Siltanen, 1981) found that metaphors did behave as intense language and led to more persuasion than did literal language.

However, one of the key predictions of the language intensity view is that intense language either decreases the impact of or has no effect on attitude for low initial credibility sources (Hamilton & Hunter, 1998; see also, Burgoon, 1989). A meta-analytic model of language intensity effects on attitude (Hamilton & Hunter, 1998) largely confirmed this prediction. The results of the metaphor meta-analysis, by contrast, present an opposite pattern: Use of metaphor was more beneficial for communicators with low initial credibility than with high initial credibility. On the other hand, the finding of the language intensity meta-analysis that high-intensity language directly increases perceptions of communicator dynamism only, and not competence and trustworthiness, is in accord with the results of the metaphor meta-analysis, which showed a positive effect on the dynamism facet of credibility only. Overall, then, despite certain processing differences, intense and metaphorical language may bear some similarity in how they exert their suasory power.

Metaphor as Vivid Language. Metaphorical language has also been conceived of as a type of vivid language (Frey & Eagly, 1993; Mitchell et al., 1994). Nisbett and Ross (1980) defined vividness as information that is "(a) emotionally interesting, (b) concrete and imagery-provoking, and (c) proximate in a sensory, temporal, or spatial way" (p. 45). Vivid language has been operationalized in a variety of ways, and even then its effects on attitude have been generally hard to discover (Collins, Taylor, Wood, & Thompson, 1988; Taylor & Thompson, 1982). Frey and Eagly (1993) conceptualized vivid language to include "provocative metaphors" and found that vivid messages were not more persuasive than pallid ones, both when the participants' attentional focus on the message was high and when it was low. They interpreted the results in terms of vividness as a *distraction/interference,* especially for "complex messages . . . that contain a number of arguments that are logically related by virtue of their all being linked to a general position" (p. 41). The studies in the metaphor meta-analysis data set were characterized by high attentional focus, and many of

the messages were fairly complex. The results still showed that metaphorical messages were more persuasive than literal ones. Furthermore, there was little support for the view that metaphors consume cognitive resources (which can be as seen as similar to the interference explanation), but there was strong support for the claim that metaphors contribute to message organization and comprehension. Thus, metaphor may not function similar to vivid language as distraction because this explanation cannot account for the trope's persuasive effects.

FUTURE RESEARCH

There are a number of productive avenues for future research on metaphor and persuasion. New studies should build on past research to more clearly delineate conditions that enhance effectiveness of metaphors and the process(es) of these effects. Future investigations should also look at new lines of research regarding pictorial metaphor and the role of metaphor in development of attitudes.

Conditions of Metaphor Effectiveness

The metaphor and persuasion meta-analysis identified a number of variables that allow us to differentiate effective from ineffective conditions for metaphor use, and future research should continue their testing. Recent research points to six additional factors that may have bearing on metaphor's persuasive potential. *Literal-mindedness* (Morgan, 1997), an individual differences variable, is defined as the ability to understand figurative language. Metaphorical messages are more persuasive with people who are low on literal-mindedness because they find it easy to understand figurative language. The *metaphor extension hypothesis* (Mio, 1996) proposes that, in a debate-type situation, a metaphor is more effective when it builds on and extends the opponent's metaphor. A retort that uses a new metaphor or is literal is relatively ineffective as a persuasive tactic. Novel *synesthetic metaphors* may be particularly potent for persuasion (Nelson & Hitchon, 1995, 1999). Synesthesia is a neurological process whereby perceptions from one sensory modality are mapped onto perceptions from another modality, and utterances based on these cross-sensory mappings (e.g., auditory-visual as in "loud red") are called synesthetic metaphors (Cytowic, 1989; Marks, 1982). Message recipients' positive *prior involvement* (Johnson & Eagly, 1989) with the attitude objects may also contribute to the increased impact of metaphors (Ottati et al., 1999). Besides attitude, metaphor may be equally effective in successfully shaping other desired persuasion outcomes, such as *behavior change* (Mio, Thompson, & Givens, 1993) and *agreement with implications* of the metaphor (Bosman, 1987; Bosman & Hagendoorn, 1991). Future research should investigate all of these factors to develop a model of the conditions under which metaphor can have maximum persuasive effect.

Process of Metaphor Effects

Future research should concentrate on determining a more precise specification of the mechanism by which metaphor exerts its suasory effect. Of the different metaphor and persuasion theories, the superior organization view holds the greatest promise in this regard. New research can compare this view to other plausible explanations of the process and establish which one has the most accurate descriptive and predictive power.

Alternatively, future research can also attempt to integrate compatible metaphor and persuasion theories into a single framework.

For example, McGuire's (1972, 1985) view that the persuasion process requires at least two sequential information processing components, reception and yielding, can furnish such a framework. In this model, reception of a message consists of two substeps, attention and comprehension; to make a judgment about yielding to the message advocacy, the information available after the comprehension stage is used. It may be that the presence of a metaphor in a persuasive message, under proper processing conditions, affects the perception of communicator dynamism (communicator credibility view), leading to improved attention to the message arguments. After helping to focus attention onto the message content, the metaphor may next aid its comprehension by encouraging relevant thinking (stimulated elaboration view) and by organizing the available information (superior organization view). In turn, this more detailed and organized information may make it more likely that the message advocacy will be accepted. A comprehensive multiple-process framework of this sort may be better able to explain and systematically predict the persuasive effects of metaphorical language under different conditions.

Pictorial Metaphors

Pictures and images can also assert the "A is B" equation and thus be metaphorical in their meaning (Forceville, 1996; Indurkhya, 1992; Kennedy, 1982; Whittock, 1990). Although images are ubiquitous in and integral to advertising (Leiss, Kline, & Jhally, 1986; Messaris, 1997), there is a paucity of studies on the use of pictorial (or visual) metaphors in persuasive messages (for an exception, see Mcquarrie & Mick, 1999). One reason for this lack of research may be the difficulty in deciding whether pictorial metaphors function similarly to linguistic metaphors or not (Kaplan, 1992; Kennedy, Green, & Vervaeke, 1993), and whether visual rhetorical tropes in general can parallel those found in language so that they can be classified according to linguistic rhetorical tropes (for such an exercise, see Mcquarrie & Mick, 1996). These are, however, empirically resolvable questions that can be easily incorporated into any pictorial metaphor and persuasion investigations, although when doing so researchers should exercise appropriate caution to prevent overgeneralization from linguistic to visual metaphors.

Development of Attitudes

Abelson (1986; see also Abelson & Prentice, 1989) contended that a process of metaphorical mapping motivates the development of the attitudinal system. He considered attitudes to be evaluative beliefs and claimed, based on linguistic evidence (e.g., Lakoff & Johnson, 1980), that humans think about their beliefs in the same terms as they think about their possessions. He also provided developmental evidence showing that when children start understanding the concept of belief, they do so by thinking about their beliefs in the same way as they think about their possessions. That is, the belief system of children is developed and structured through a metaphorical mapping to the domain of their possessions. This metaphorical organization of the belief system can be tapped for persuasive ends by matching messages to the underlying and constitutive conceptual metaphor of "Beliefs are like possessions." Thus, research on how information from linguistic and conceptual metaphors combines to affect beliefs and attitudes may lead to identification of rewarding theoretical insights regarding how attitudes develop.

CONCLUSION

Figurative comparisons, and in particular metaphors, have a long history as a persuasion tool. However, there are two interrelated questions not yet fully answered regarding (a) their persuasive superiority over literal language and (b) the process by which this effect may arise. The summary of the empirical research on metaphor and persuasion presented in this chapter brings us closer to some probable answers to the two questions and contributes to more effective use of this trope to influence evaluations.

NOTES

1. A *simile* is usually regarded as an explicit comparison between two concepts, where the similarities are clearly defined. It is considered an overt nonliteral comparison and is identified by the use of *as* or *like* as in the statement "The global marketplace is *like* a dictatorship." An *analogy* is a kind of mapping or isomorphism between the relations and entities of two systems of concepts and explicitly states the comparison of relational similarities between its referents. For example, in the analogy "Old age is to life as autumn is to year," the relation between *old age* and *life* from the domain of *human life cycle* is mapped to the relation between *autumn* and *year* from the domain of *seasonal cycle*. A *personification* compares humans to inanimate entities and applies properties that are normally associated with humans to the nonhuman entity. An example is "Look at the face of the clock," where the human property of *face* is used for describing a machine.

2. Although metaphor novelty and *aptness* may be related, the two should not be conflated. Metaphor aptness may be defined as a global judgment of the appropriateness of a metaphor to its discourse and message context (for an alternative definition, see Tourangeau & Sternberg, 1981). This judgment may depend on the persuasive context (e.g., consumer advertising vs. politics), dis-

course type (e.g., headline or slogan vs. a long message), communicative goals (e.g., explanation of factual evidence vs. presentation of testimony and opinion), and logical fit with the message content.

3. The other major theories of metaphor interpretation are comparison (Miller, 1979), interaction (Black, 1962, 1979; Richards, 1936), domains interaction (Tourangeau & Sternberg, 1981, 1982), parallel constraint satisfaction (Holyoak, 1985; Holyoak & Thagard, 1989, 1995; Spellman & Holyoak, 1992), and class inclusion (Glucksberg & Keysar, 1990, 1993; Glucksberg, Keysar, & McGlone, 1992).

4. There also are other dimensions of credibility such as attractiveness and sociability. However, the studies in the database of the meta-analysis did not assess other credibility components in any consistent manner, so there was not enough of a pool of studies to conduct an analysis.

REFERENCES

Abelson, R. P. (1986). Beliefs are like possessions. *Journal for the Theory of Social Behavior, 16,* 223-250.

Abelson, R. P., & Prentice, D. A. (1989). Beliefs as possessions: A functional perspective. In A. R. Pratkanis, S. J. Breckler, & A. G. Greenwald (Eds.), *Attitude structure and function* (pp. 361-381). Hillsdale, NJ: Lawrence Erlbaum.

Albritton, D. W., McKoon, G., & Gerrig, R. J. (1995). Metaphor-based schemas and text representations: Making connections through conceptual metaphors. *Journal of Experimental Psychology: Learning, Memory, and Cognition, 21,* 612-625.

Allen, M. (1998). One- and two-sided messages. In M. Allen & R. W. Preiss (Eds.), *Persuasion: Advances through meta-analysis* (pp. 87-98). Cresskill, NJ: Hampton.

Aristotle. (1952). Poetics (I. Bywater, Trans.). In W. D. Ross (Ed.), *The works of Aristotle,* Vol. 11: *Rhetorica, de rhetorica ad Alexandrum, poetica.* Oxford, UK: Clarendon.

Beardsley, M. (1962). The metaphorical twist. *Philosophy and Phenomenological Research, 22,* 293-307.

Beardsley, M. (1967). Metaphor. In P. Edwards (Ed.), *The encyclopedia of philosophy* (pp. 284-289). New York: Macmillan.

Beardsley, M. (1976). Metaphor and falsity. *Journal of Aesthetics and Art Criticism, 35,* 218-222.

Berlo, D. K., Lemert, J. B., & Mertz, R. J. (1969). Dimensions for evaluating the acceptability of message sources. *Public Opinion Quarterly, 33,* 563-576.

Black, M. (1962). *Models and metaphors.* Ithaca, NY: Cornell University Press.

Black, M. (1979). More about metaphor. In A. Ortony (Ed.), *Metaphor and thought* (pp. 19-43). Cambridge, UK: Cambridge University Press.

Bosman, J. (1987). Persuasive effects of political metaphors. *Metaphor and Symbolic Activity, 2,* 97-113.

Bosman, J., & Hagendoorn, L. (1991). Effects of literal and metaphorical persuasive messages. *Metaphor and Symbolic Activity, 6,* 271-292.

Bottini, G., Corcoran, R., Sterzi, R., Paulesu, E., Schenone, P., Scarpa, P., Frackowiak, R. S. J., & Frith, C. D. (1994). The role of the right hemisphere in the interpretation of figurative aspects of language: A positron emission tomography activation study. *Brain, 117,* 1241-1253.

Bowers, J. W. (1963). Language intensity, social introversion, and attitude change. *Speech Monographs, 30,* 345-352.

Bowers, J. W. (1964). Some correlates of language intensity. *Quarterly Journal of Speech, 50,* 415-420.

Bowers, J. W., & Osborn, M. M. (1966). Attitudinal effects of selected types of concluding metaphors in persuasive speeches. *Speech Monographs, 33,* 147-155.

Burgess, C., & Chiarello, C. (1996). Neurocognitive mechanisms underlying metaphor comprehension and other figurative language. *Metaphor and Symbolic Activity, 11,* 67-84.

Burgoon, M. (1989). Messages and persuasive effects. In J. J. Bradac (Ed.), *Message effects in communication science* (pp. 129-164). Newbury Park, CA: Sage.

Burgoon, M., & Miller, G. R. (1985). An expectancy interpretation of language and persuasion. In H. Giles & R. N. St. Clair (Eds.), *Recent advances in language, communication, and social* psychology (pp. 199-229). Hillsdale, NJ: Lawrence Erlbaum.

Chaiken, S., Liberman, A., & Eagly, A. H. (1989). Heuristic and systematic processing within and beyond the persuasion context. In J. S. Uleman & J. A. Bargh (Eds.), *Unintended thought* (pp. 212-252). New York: Guilford.

Cohen, J. (1987). *Statistical power analysis for the behavioral sciences* (rev. ed.). Hillsdale, NJ: Lawrence Erlbaum.

Collins, R. L., Taylor, S. E., Wood, J. V., & Thompson, S. C. (1988). The vividness effect: Elusive or illusory? *Journal of Experimental Social Psychology, 24,* 1-18.

Coulson, S., & Oakley, T. (in press). Purple persuasion: Conceptual blending and deliberative rhetoric. In J. Luchenbroers (Ed.), *Cognitive linguistics: Investigations across languages, fields, and philosophical boundaries.* Amsterdam: John Benjamins.

Cytowic, R. E. (1989). *Synesthesia: A union of the senses.* New York: Springer-Verlag.

Dillard, J. P. (1998). Evaluating and using meta-analytic knowledge claims. In M. Allen & R. W. Preiss (Eds.), *Persuasion: Advances through meta-analysis* (pp. 257-270). Cresskill, NJ: Hampton.

Fauconnier, G. (1994). *Mental spaces.* Cambridge, UK: Cambridge University Press.

Fauconnier, G., & Turner, M. (1998). Conceptual integration networks. *Cognitive Science, 22,* 133-187.

Forceville, C. (1996). *Pictorial metaphor in advertising.* New York: Routledge.

Frey, K. P., & Eagly, A. H. (1993). Vividness can undermine the persuasiveness of messages. *Journal of Personality and Social Psychology, 65,* 32-44.

Gentner, D. (1982). Are scientific analogies metaphors? In D. Miall (Ed.), *Metaphor: Problems and perspectives* (pp. 106-132). Brighton, UK: Harvester.

Gentner, D. (1983). Structure-mapping: A theoretical framework for analogy. *Cognitive Science, 7,* 155-170.

Gentner, D. (1989). The mechanisms of analogical learning. In S. Vosniadou & A. Ortony (Eds.), *Similarity and analogical reasoning* (pp. 199-241). Cambridge, UK: Cambridge University Press.

Gentner, D., & Clement, C. (1988). Evidence for relational selectivity in the interpretation of analogy and metaphor. In G. Bower (Ed.), *The psychology of learning and motivation* (Vol. 22, pp. 307-358). San Diego: Academic Press.

Gibbs, R. W., Jr. (1994). *The poetics of mind: Figurative thought, language, and understanding.* Cambridge, UK: Cambridge University Press.

Glucksberg, S., & Keysar, B. (1990). Understanding metaphorical comparisons: Beyond similarity. *Psychological Review, 97,* 3-18.

Glucksberg, S., & Keysar, B. (1993). How metaphors work. In A. Ortony (Ed.), *Metaphor and thought* (2nd ed., pp. 401-424). New York: Cambridge University Press.

Glucksberg, S., Keysar, B., & McGlone, M. (1992). Metaphor understanding and accessing conceptual schema: Reply to Gibbs (1992). *Psychological Review, 99,* 578-581.

Graesser, A. C., Mio, J., & Millis, K. K. (1989). Metaphors in persuasive communication. In D. Meutsch & R. Viehoff (Eds.), *Comprehension of literary discourse: Results and problems of interdisciplinary approaches* (pp. 131-154). Berlin: Walter de Gruyter.

Guthrie, M. (1972). *Effects of credibility, metaphor, and intensity on comprehension, credibility, and attitude change.* Unpublished master's thesis, Illinois State University.

Hamilton, M. A., & Hunter, J. E. (1998). The effect of language intensity on receiver evaluations of message, source, and topic. In M. Allen & R. W. Preiss (Eds.), *Persuasion: Advances through meta-analysis* (pp. 99-138). Cresskill, NJ: Hampton.

Hamilton, M. A., & Stewart, B. L. (1993). Extending an information processing model of language intensity effects. *Communication Quarterly, 43,* 231-246.

Hitchon, J. C. (1991). To be or what to be: Metaphorical predication in advertising. (Doctoral dissertation, University of Wisconsin–Madison). *Dissertation Abstracts International, 52*(04A), 1438.

Hoffman, R., & Kemper, S. (1987). What could reaction time studies be telling us about metaphor comprehension? *Metaphor and Symbolic Activity, 2,* 149-186.

Holyoak, K. J. (1985). The pragmatics of analogical transfer. In G. H. Bower (Ed.), *The psychology of learning and motivation, 1,* 59-87.

Holyoak, K. J., & Thagard, P. (1989). Analogical mapping by constraint satisfaction. *Cognitive Science, 13,* 295-355.

Holyoak, K. J., & Thagard, P. (1995). *Mental leaps: Analogy in creative thought.* Cambridge, MA: MIT Press.

Indurkhya, B. (1992). *Metaphor and cognition.* Boston: Kluwer.

Ingalls, D. H. H. (Trans.). (1968). *Sanskrit poetry from Vidyakara's "Treasury."* Cambridge, MA: Harvard University Press.

Inhoff, A., Lima, S., & Carroll, P. (1984). Contextual effects on metaphor comprehension in reading. *Memory & Cognition, 12,* 558-567.

Jaffe, F. (1988). Metaphors and memory: A study in persuasion. (Doctoral dissertation, Northwestern University). *Dissertation Abstracts International, 49*(08A), 2311.

Johnson, B. T., & Eagly, A. H. (1989). Effects of involvement on persuasion: A meta-analysis. *Psychological Bulletin, 106,* 290-314.

Johnson, M. (1987). *The body in the mind: The bodily basis of meaning, imagination, and reason.* Chicago: University of Chicago Press.

Kaplan, S. J. (1992). A conceptual analysis of form and content in visual metaphors. *Communication, 13,* 197-209.

Kennedy, J. M. (1982). Metaphor in pictures. *Perception, 11,* 589-605.

Kennedy, J. M., Green, C. D., & Vervaeke, J. (1993). Metaphoric thought and devices in pictures. *Metaphor and Symbolic Activity, 8,* 243-255.

Lakoff, G. (1987). *Women, fire, and dangerous things.* Chicago: University of Chicago Press.

Lakoff, G. (1993). The contemporary theory of metaphor. In A. Ortony (Ed.), *Metaphor and thought* (2nd ed., pp. 202-251). New York: Cambridge University Press.

Lakoff, G., & Johnson, M. (1980). *Metaphors we live by.* Chicago: University of Chicago Press.

Lakoff, G., & Turner, M. (1989). *More than cool reason: A field guide to poetic metaphor.* Chicago: University of Chicago Press.

Leiss, W., Kline, S., & Jhally, S. (1986). *Social communication in advertising.* Toronto: Methuen.

MacCormac, E. (1985). *A cognitive theory of metaphor.* Cambridge, MA: MIT Press.

Marks, L. E. (1982). Synesthetic perception and poetic metaphor. *Journal of Experimental Psychology: Human Perception and Performance, 8,* 15-23.

McCabe, A. (1983). Conceptual similarity and the quality of metaphor in isolated sentences vs. extended contexts. *Journal of Psycholinguistic Research, 12,* 41-68.

McCroskey, J. C., & Combs, W. H. (1969). The effects and the use of analogy on attitude change and source credibility. *Journal of Communication, 19,* 333-339.

McCroskey, J. C., & Young, T. J. (1981). Ethos and credibility: The construct and its measurement after three decades. *Central States Speech Journal, 32,* 24-34.

McGuire, W. J. (1972). Attitude change: The information-processing paradigm. In C. G. McClintock (Ed.), *Experimental social psychology* (pp. 108-141). New York: Holt, Rinehart & Winston.

McGuire, W. J. (1985). Attitudes and attitude change. In G. Lindzey & E. Aronson (Eds.), *Handbook of social psychology* (3rd ed., Vol. 2, pp. 234-326). New York: Random House.

Mcquarrie, E. F., & Mick, D. G. (1996). Figures of rhetoric in advertising language. *Journal of Consumer Research, 22,* 424-438.

Mcquarrie, E. F., & Mick, D. G. (1999). Visual rhetoric in advertising: Text-interpretive, experimental, and reader-response analyses. *Journal of Consumer Research, 26,* 37-54.

Messaris, P. (1997). *Visual persuasion: The role of images in advertising.* Thousand Oaks, CA: Sage.

Miller, G. A. (1979). Images and models, similes and metaphors. In A. Ortony (Ed.), *Metaphor and thought* (pp. 202-250). Cambridge, UK: Cambridge University Press.

Mio, J. S. (1996). Metaphor, politics, and persuasion. In J. S. Mio & A. N. Katz (Eds.), *Metaphor: Implications and applications* (pp. 127-145). Mahwah, NJ: Lawrence Erlbaum.

Mio, J. S., Thompson, S. C., & Givens, G. H. (1993). The commons dilemma as metaphor: Memory, influence, and implications for environmental conservation. *Metaphor and Symbolic Activity, 8,* 23-42.

Mitchell, N. A., Badzinski, D. M., & Pawlowski, D. R. (1994). The use of metaphors as vivid stimuli to enhance comprehension and recall of print advertisements. In K. W. King (Ed.), *Proceedings of the 1994 conference of the American Academy of Advertising* (pp. 198-205). Athens, GA: American Academy of Advertising.

Morgan, S. E. (1997). Metaphorical messages and the literal-minded: Accounting for individual cognitive differences in the design of persuasive health messages. (Doctoral dissertation, University of Arizona). *Dissertation Abstracts International, 58*(04A), 1264.

Nelson, M. R., & Hitchon, J. C. (1995). Theory of synesthesia applied to persuasion in print advertising headlines. *Journalism and Mass Communication Quarterly, 72,* 346-360.

Nelson, M. R., & Hitchon, J. C. (1999). Loud tastes, colored fragrances, and scented sounds: How and when to mix the senses in persuasive communications. *Journalism and Mass Communication Quarterly, 76,* 354-372.

Nisbett, R. E., & Ross, L. (1980). *Human inference: Strategies and shortcomings of social judgment.* Englewood Cliffs, NJ: Prentice Hall.

Ortony, A. (1979). Beyond literal similarity. *Psychological Review, 87,* 161-180.

Ortony, A. (1993). The role of similarity in similes and metaphors. In A. Ortony (Ed.), *Metaphor and thought* (2nd ed., pp. 342-356). Cambridge, UK: Cambridge University Press.

Ortony, A., Vondruska, R., Foss, M., & Jones, L. (1985). Salience, similes, and the asymmetry of similarity. *Journal of Memory and Language, 24,* 569-594.

Osborn, M. M., & Ehninger, D. (1962). The metaphor in public address. *Speech Monographs, 29,* 223-234.

Ottati, V., Rhoads, S., & Graesser, A. C. (1999). *Journal of Personality and Social Psychology, 77,* 688-697.

Paivio, A., & Walsh, M. (1993). Psychological processes in metaphor comprehension and memory. In A. Ortony (Ed.), *Metaphor and thought* (2nd ed., pp. 307-328). New York: Cambridge University Press.

Petty, R. E., & Cacioppo, J. T. (1986). *Communication and persuasion: Central and peripheral routes to attitude change.* New York: Springer-Verlag.

Pollio, H., Barlow, J., Fine, H., & Pollio, M. (1977). *Psychology and the poetics of growth: Figurative language in psychology, psychotherapy, and education.* Hillsdale, NJ: Lawrence Erlbaum.

Pollio, H., Fabrizi, M., & Weedle, H. (1982). A note on pauses in spontaneous speech as a test of the derived process theory of metaphor. *Linguistics, 20,* 431-444.

Read, S. J., Cesa, I. L., Jones, D. K., & Collins, N. L. (1990). When is the federal budget like a baby? Metaphor in political rhetoric. *Metaphor and Symbolic Activity, 5,* 125-149.

Reinsch, N. L., Jr. (1971). An investigation of the effects of the metaphor and simile in persuasive discourse. *Speech Monographs, 38,* 142-145.

Reinsch, N. L., Jr. (1974). Figurative language and source credibility: A preliminary investigation and reconceptualization. *Human Communication Research, 1,* 75-80.

Richards, I. A. (1936). *The philosophy of rhetoric.* London: Oxford University Press.

Searle, J. R. (1979). Metaphor. In A. Ortony (Ed.), *Metaphor and thought* (pp. 92-123). Cambridge, U. K.: Cambridge University Press.

Siltanen, S. A. (1981). The persuasiveness of metaphor: A replication and extension. *Southern Speech Communication Journal, 47,* 67-83.

Sopory, P. (1999). *Metaphor and persuasion.* Unpublished doctoral dissertation, University of Wisconsin–Madison.

Sopory, P., & Dillard, J. P. (in press). The persuasive effects of metaphor: A meta-analysis. *Human Communication Research.*

Spellman, B. A., & Holyoak, K. J. (1992). If Saddam is Hitler, then who is George Bush? Analogical mapping between systems of social roles. *Journal of Personality and Social Psychology, 62,* 913-933.

Taylor, S. E., & Thompson, S. C. (1982). Stalking the elusive vividness effect. *Psychological Review, 89,* 155-181.

Tourangeau, R., & Sternberg, R. J. (1981). Aptness in metaphor. *Cognitive Psychology, 13,* 27-55.

Tourangeau, R., & Sternberg, R. J. (1982). Understanding and appreciating metaphors. *Cognition, 11,* 203-244.

Tudman, R. B. (1971). *An experimental study of the effects of thematic metaphor on readers' attitude toward message topic and message source.* Unpublished master's thesis, Central Missouri State College.

Whaley, B. B. (1991). Toward a comprehensive model of analogy in persuasion: A test of the persuasive roles of analogy. (Doctoral dissertation, Purdue University). *Dissertation Abstracts International, 53*(01A), 20.

Whaley, B. B. (1997). Perceptions of rebuttal analogy: Politeness and implications for persuasion. *Argumentation and Advocacy, 33,* 161-169.

Whaley, B. B. (1998). Evaluations of rebuttal analogy users: Ethical and competence considerations. *Argumentation, 12,* 351-365.

Whaley, B. B., Nicotera, A. M., & Samter, W. (1998). African-American women's perception of rebuttal analogy: Judgments concerning politeness, likability, and ethics. *Southern Communication Journal, 64,* 48-68.

Whittock, T. (1990). *Metaphor and film.* New York: Cambridge University Press.

Zaltman, G., & Coulter, R. H. (1995). Seeing the voice of the consumer: Metaphor-based advertising research. *Journal of Advertising Research, 4,* 35-51.

Zaltman, G., & Higie, R. A. (1993). *Seeing the voice of the customer: The Zaltman metaphor elicitation technique* (Report 93-114). Cambridge, MA: Marketing Science Institute.

22

Evidence

RODNEY A. REYNOLDS
J. LYNN REYNOLDS

It seems implausible that three decades ago the literature on the use of evidence in persuasive messages would foster the impression that "reactions to argument may have little or nothing to do with whether the argument includes fully documented or completely undocumented evidence, relevant or irrelevant evidence, weak or strong evidence, or any evidence at all" (Gregg, 1967, p. 180). The reasons for such conclusions, ironically, were later seen to be due to faulty theory and research data (see Kellermann, 1980; Reinard, 1988, 1998; Reynolds & Burgoon, 1983). We are now able to say with little reservation that when an advocate "quotes" information in support of an argument and the recipients of the message process the information as legitimate evidence, the advocate will be more persuasive than if the information was not presented or was not processed by receivers. In short, there are at least three conditions for the effective and persuasive use of evidence: The receivers must be aware that evidence is being presented, they must cognitively process the evidence, and they must evaluate the evidence as legitimate. Before returning to these conditions, a general survey of the research on evidence is in order.

WHAT WE KNOW
SO FAR ABOUT EVIDENCE

The General Persuasive
Effects of Evidence

There are a few recent affirmations for the persuasive effects of evidence. McLaughlin, Cody, and French (1990) showed that challenges in traffic court rarely win without supporting evidence. Allen and Burrell (1992) supported the claim that people assent to persuasive messages based on the quality of the justification provided. Indeed, Reinard (1998) offered meta-analytic results indicating that up to 26% of the variance in persuasion (which Reinard claimed is associated with up to 63% persuasive "success") could be attributed to the use of legitimate evidence quotations. Nevertheless, caution is in order given that between 20% and 30% of people appear to be willing to believe almost anything they are told. At least so claims the DiMassimo Brand Advertising research company (Rivenburg, 1999), which conducted a study in which it recruited 200 people to tell friends and neighbors relatively incredulous bits of information (e.g., Amazon.com is an Internet site for portly women, George W. Bush, Jr., is running for president as a Democrat, Kenneth Star is the president of Starbucks Coffee). The researchers found that 20% to 30% of the friends later indicated in a survey that they believed what they had been told.

Research that speaks of a clear effect for the use of data-like assertions and evidence can be seen in a number of studies. Hample (1978) pointed out that the conception of "no evidence" is faulty because arguments with no clear use of evidence will cause the receiver to inherently fill in the implied evidence. Nevertheless, studies that contain conditions with enthymematic arguments (i.e., with a premise implied or assumed) should offer comparisons to messages that clearly contain evidence. When Reinard (1988) chronicled the 18 major studies clearly supporting the effects of evidence, 15 had control groups with "no evidence (vague general statements)" (p. 11). Recall of the support for certain messages was found to combine with other communication or attitude variables to predict adoption of favorable attitudes toward the propositions (Burgoon, 1975). Hample (1977, 1978, 1979) tested models for the processing arguments and supportive data in messages and reported moderately high correlation coefficients (.50s to .60s) between predicted and obtained belief scores. In summary, the use of evidence produces more attitude change than the use of no evidence.

Evidence Enhances Credibility

The use of evidence enhances the credibility of the advocate. O'Keefe (1998) performed a meta-analysis on the credibility effects of evidence and noted consistently "positive mean effects for . . . credibility outcomes" (p. 71). Warren (1969) demonstrated that citing credible sources of evidence enhanced the rating of the speaker as fair and justified. Arnold and McCroskey (1967) and Anderson (1970) showed that unbiased and reluctant testimony resulted in higher ratings of credibility over biased testimonies. Whitehead (1971) reported that for speeches on taxation of religious organizations and federal regulation of medicine, giving evidence citations resulted in higher ratings of "professionalism" for the speaker than when the speaker offered the same material without citations, but only for participants who scored low on critical thinking ability. The Whitehead study is sometimes cited as supporting a main effect for evidence citations on speaker trustworthiness and objectivity, but the significance test actually failed to meet traditional probability levels.

CONDITIONS FOR THE EFFECTIVE USE OF EVIDENCE

There are some very obvious conditions underlying the effective use of evidence. First, there must be some awareness that "evidence" has indeed been presented. Second, the audience must be reasonably expected to process the message and the evidence. Finally, the audience must perceive the evidence to be legitimate.

Recipients Must Be Aware of the Evidence

Is it evidence to the audience? What do people regard as evidence? Typically, when we refer to evidence, we mean data (facts or opinions) presented as proof for an assertion. We hear or see evidence on a regular basis. The poster for a new movie offers quotes of supposedly reputable reviewers assuring us that the movie is worthwhile. Our lover offers an exceptional gift or sacrifice as proof of love. The traffic police officer carefully documents the calibration of the speed radar equipment to be used each day because that question of calibration will be the first one asked by the judge as the traffic cases come up in court. There are many different types and forms of evidence (see Reinard, 1991; Rothstein, Raeder, & Crump, 1997). In the vast majority of the research studies on evidence (for detailed reviews of the early research, see Reinard, 1988; Reynolds & Burgoon, 1983), the researchers operationalized evidence as testimonial quotes attributed (or not attributed) to a particular source (usually a person qualified to make the observation being made).

Does the audience recognize the evidence? The clever advocate will recognize that evidence must be recognized and accepted by the audience as evidence. Indeed, Hample (1977, 1978, 1979, 1980, 1981, 1985) claimed that most intelligent message receivers plug in their own understanding of the implied evidence behind a claim. On the other hand, when message receivers expect to hear some sort of evidence and they do not hear it, they are likely to remember the omission and even demand that the speaker fill in the missing data (even if the message recipients knew the data all along). In a study with Dutch high school students, van Eemeren, de Glopper, Grootendorst, and Oostdam (1994) found that research participants identified unexpressed major premises and nonsyllogistic premises more correctly than they did unexpressed minor premises. This was when no disambiguating contextual information was present.

Morley (1987; see also Morley & Walker, 1987) demonstrated that audience members respond more favorably when the arguments and the supportive data are novel (i.e., new), plausible, and important to the overall conclusion. The political communication "adwatch" literature (see Cappella & Jamieson, 1994; Kaid, Tedesco, & McKinnon, 1996; McKinnon & Kaid, 1999; Pfau & Louden, 1994) similarly indicates that without special visual and timing cues in the adwatch messages, audiences are likely to never notice that they are being given evidence critical of the claims being made in the original campaign ads. (Or, conversely, audiences such as juries may pay special attention to material they should ignore when their attention is drawn to it [Reinard & Reynolds, 1978]). Thus, to enhance persuasion, it is not merely enough to include evidence in a message; the audience must also perceive that evidence has indeed been deployed.

Do citations of the sources of evidence help? If receivers are going to become aware of evidence in a message, it is most likely to occur because of explicit features in the message that highlight that evidence is being presented. The citation of the sources of evidence should clue listeners in that evidence is being presented. A number of studies have examined the use of explicit citations of evidence sources within persuasive messages. O'Keefe's (1998) meta-analysis "indicates a significant persuasive advantage for messages providing information-source citations" (p. 67).

McCroskey and his associates (Luchok & McCroskey, 1978; McCroskey, 1967, 1969, 1970) presented data that citations of sources can increase attitude change and credibility for a less credible advocate but that the citation of sources does not necessarily aid a credible advocate. The effect can be explained as resulting from the receiver's preparation for believing the highly credible source and not needing additional justifications. Burgoon and Burgoon (1975) claimed, however, that "evidence seems to increase the persuasiveness of both high and low credible sources when a delayed measure of attitude change is obtained" (p. 153). O'Keefe (1998) questioned the existence of a credibility ceiling effect but admitted to lacking "sufficient quantitative information to permit useful meta-analytic treatment" (p. 70).

Luchok and McCroskey (1978) found that irrelevant evidence from an unqualified source will result in attitude change in the opposite direction from that advocated even when the speaker is highly credible. In addition, a moderate- to low-credible advocate is likely to get strong reverse attitude changes by citing an evidence source who is not qualified to comment on the topic. Indeed, a low- to moderate-credible advocate is most likely to obtain reverse attitude changes from an audience unless the advocate cites evidence from a qualified source. McCroskey (1970) also reported that in forums where alternative views are expressed, if a highly credible speaker does not include evidence citations following a speech with evidenced citations, the speaker tends to lose credibility. In summary, the use of irrelevant evidence from poorly qualified sources will produce counter to advocated attitude change regardless of the credibility of the advocate. The failure to use relevant evidence from qualified sources may produce counter to advocated attitude change for low- to moderately credible advocates. The failure to include evidence citations in a message following an evidenced message expressing opposing views will result in lowered credibility ratings for an advocate.

Some of the best and most specific data on the importance of evidence citations was provided by Bostrom and Tucker (1969) and by Fleshler, Ilardo, and Demoretcky (1974). Bostrom and Tucker (1969) found that speak-

ers who relied on simple assertions without clear supporting evidence were less persuasive than those who gave evidence to back the assertions, cited the sources of the evidence, and gave the qualifications of the sources. Similarly, Fleshler et al. (1974) found that when speakers employ specific documentation of evidence, the speakers got increased credibility ratings.

The direct effects of developed or underdeveloped arguments and evidence in a message obviously may vary with the particular receivers. Eagly and Warren (1976), for example, demonstrated that higher intelligence led to more critical assessments of messages that contained only "a short introduction stating the recommendation . . . and a short conclusion repeating the recommendation" around five paragraphs of material "irrelevant to the recommendation" (p. 230). The less intelligent, by contrast, offered only moderate assent to the recommendation even when the introduction and conclusion bounded five paragraphs of persuasive reasoning and evidence. Interestingly, the "arguments included" (p. 234) versions had only vague references to the source of the evidence. The lack of specific evidence citations may partially explain why Eagly and Warren's persuasive messages achieved only moderate levels of persuasion (e.g., an average of 2.95 on a scale of 1 to 7 with a high of 3.64).

The Evidence Must Be Cognitively Processed

There should be some reason to presume that the audience will be systematically (or elaboratively) processing the arguments in the message. While controversies about forms of processing may rage (see Allen & Reynolds, 1993; Eagly & Chaiken, 1993; Stiff, 1986), there is little disagreement among attitude change and persuasion scholars that the manner and extent of message processing matters (see Aune & Reynolds, 1994; Petty & Cacioppo, 1984). One of the more obvious instances when an audience might be assumed to engage in systematic message processing is when opposing advocates present competing evidence to the audience (Luchok & McCroskey, 1978; McCroskey, 1970).

Most of the studies on the persuasive effects of evidence take place within a one-to-many deliberative oratory scenario (see Miller & Burgoon, 1978) where the recipients are presumed to be engaged in policy or legal decision making. The vast majority of the participants in the studies have been college educated with, supposedly, some sensitivity to being diligent message processors. Nevertheless, it is unfortunate that we can only assume in most of these studies that the message recipients were engaged in message elaboration (see Reynolds, 1997).

Blasting the recipients with quotes of ungrounded statistics appears to be a sure way to distract them from systematically processing the evidence and the message (Harte, 1971; Kline, 1969; Nisbett, Borgida, Crandall, & Reed, 1976). Similarly, spinning a long but interesting yarn or offering a quick quip or an analogy may be so distracting or entertaining that at least some audience members may turn away (Whaley, 1997) or just be confused enough to become vulnerable to nearly any persuasive suggestion (Kassim, Reddy, & Tulloch, 1990). As an alternative to telling a long story, asking members of an audience, particularly females, to imagine their own versions of relevant scenarios can provoke particularly strong responses (Berger, 1998).

Statistical Versus Narrative Evidence. There is some inconsistency on the effects of statistical versus narrative (story) evidence. Some studies indicate that a meaningful story in support of an argument appears to be as persua-

sive as meaningful statistics for a moderately involved audience (Baesler, 1997; Baesler & Burgoon, 1994; Kazoleas, 1993). Other data seem to indicate that statistical data are more likely to result in persuasion than are pithy tales (Allen & Preiss, 1997), and the verdict is still out on how specific such quantification needs to be (O'Keefe, 1998). Furthermore, the effects of statistics versus "anecdotes" seem to vary with the initial position of the message recipients (Slater & Rouner, 1996) such that fellow supporters of the advocate prefer statistical evidence, while audience members who are opponents of the advocated position find anecdotal stories to be more persuasive. Kopfman, Smith, Ah Yun, and Hodges (1998) found "a main effect for evidence type such that statistical evidence messages produced greater results in terms of all the cognitive reactions, while narratives produced greater results for all of the affective reactions" (p. 279).

On balance, statistical evidence would seem to be the more persuasive form of evidence when compared to narrative evidence, but such effects will depend on the type and amount of cognitive processing of the evidence. Certainly, the initial attitudes of the audience members and the desired effects being sought are key to understanding the cognitive processing of different types of evidence. For now, the best conclusion may be that the effective advocate is best advised to use both statistical and narrative evidence (Allen et al., 2000).

Message strategies and tactics need to also be weighed within the broader context of the message reception environment. While specific message content is central to message processing (see Austin & Dong, 1994), the characteristics of the receivers are also key. In particular, Berger (1998) pointed out that "all messages are comprehended within the context of extant declarative and procedural knowledge" (p. 102).

Prior Knowledge and Evidence Processing. Prior knowledge of the topic may affect the potential processing of evidence. McCroskey (1969) found that only the participants without prior knowledge of the topic changed their attitudes when given evidence-laden messages. By contrast, a survey of the research on prior (working) knowledge and attitude change (Wood, Rhodes, & Biek, 1995) revealed that prior knowledge can facilitate or inhibit processing new information depending on the motivations or dispositions to process the information and the complexity of the material. Further advances in research on the effects of evidence will need to incorporate the theory and research on working knowledge and attitude change.

Harte (1976) investigated the effects of prior attitude, credibility of source (high or low), and evidence (maximum use or minimum use). Measurements were taken immediately after the experiment and again 3 weeks later. Findings showed that no attitude change took place in the immediate situation but that significant attitude change occurred in the maximal evidence/extreme attitude conditions after 3 weeks. There was no effect for credibility across the time periods. There was no significant attitude change for the neutral attitude condition.

The studies on prior knowledge and evidence so far suggest that evidence has an effect only on those who have some previous attitudes on (and presumably knowledge of) the persuasive topic. Furthermore, it appears that people with extreme attitudes naturally take longer to change their beliefs and attitudes after receiving persuasive messages than do people with initially moderate attitudes.

Information Processing Predispositions. Beyond simple prior knowledge, there are a host of recipients' factors that may influence the receipt of evidence data in messages. Berger (1998), for example, found that processing of quantitative data across adjacent messages may well vary with the personal involvement or stress levels of the recipients. Specifically, Berger found that men were better able to debias messages with prior information than were women, probably because men were less threatened by the subsequent information.

Both the content and the recipients have an impact on whether and how evidence is cognitively processed. Many questions remain to be explored about how much and which types of cognition are essential for evidence to aid persuasion.

The Evidence Must Be Judged as Legitimate

The sociocultural history of Western civilization has led us to learn the practice of expecting advocates to present arguments and evidence that can withstand counterargumentation (Kline & Oseroff-Varnell, 1993). On the other hand, the development of standards of evidence in legal and policy-making bodies can be traced to the suspicion that jurors and voters might not catch tainted testimony or data when left unchecked. There are, of course, lists of rules and "codes" for acceptable evidence that argumentation and law students learn to apply. But surprisingly little research has been done on what factors actually influence audiences to view evidence as legitimate.

Evaluation of Evidence and Arguments Mediating the Effects of Evidence. The study by Reynolds (1986/1987) supports a path structure where evidence evaluation leads to message evaluation, which leads to post-message belief in the message proposition. This same evidence evaluation to message evaluation to post-message belief path structure can be partially extrapolated from the data presented by Allen and Burrell (1992) and is also evident in the data presented by Slater and Rouner (1997). Similarly, Wood et al. (1995) claimed that "evaluation [of message content] mediates the link between knowledge and attitude change" (p. 301). In short, there is nearly perfect support in the literature and in the Reynolds (1986/1987) data for a casual path from evidence evaluation to message evaluation to post-message belief.

The implication for the mediating effects of evidence and message evaluation on persuasion is intensely important. Studies that look for direct effects of evidence manipulations on persuasion are probably missing two important steps in the chain of effects: (a) the perception that the evidence is high quality and (b) the overall evaluation of the quality of the message. Failing to incorporate the linkages among evidence evaluation, message evaluation, and persuasive effects will likely result in erroneous and misleading findings. There are a number of insights in the literature on the factors that influence assessments of evidence.

Finding Bias in the Evidence. One frame for evaluating whether evidence is legitimate is the potential bias in the evidence. Arnold and McCroskey (1967) demonstrated that reluctant testimony (i.e., statements at odds with the evidence source's own bias) is more persuasive than biased testimony and that audiences prefer speakers who present unbiased testimony. Similarly, Buckless and Peace (1993) showed that jurors respect external (and presumably objective) governmental standards to internal professional standards (i.e., industry standards) when making judgments about professional competence. Schul and Mayo (1999) demonstrated that once a source is seen as invalid on one bit of information, that source remains tainted even on valid bits of in-

formation. Schul and Mayo provided data showing that advocates should probably use multiple pieces of evidence from multiple sources.

In an interesting twist on how people think about evidence, Kline (1971a) investigated the way people categorized evidence. Kline's data showed that some participants sorted evidence along a content relevance dimension, while others created categories based more on the credibility of the sources of the evidence. Kline also had the participants select evidence for a persuasive message. Attitude pretests did not predict evidence selections, but after reading the evidence on the topic, the participants developed more positive attitudes toward the topic. Kline's follow-up study (1971b) showed that documented evidence (i.e., providing a source citation) was selected more often by high-dogmatic than by low-dogmatic individuals. Kline also showed that, in general, participants selected more undocumented than documented evidence. Bradac, Sandell, and Wenner (1979) followed up on Kline's (1971a) findings. Two Q-sort analysis studies revealed that the selections of evidence form two categories: those categorization schemes showing a preference for unknown but competent sources and those showing a preference for known and trusted sources.

Harte (1971) looked at respondents' ability to identify evidence and weaknesses in evidence. The results were primarily that evidence inconsistent with the arguments was more difficult to detect than either evidence from suspect sources or evidence that was irrelevant. O'Keefe (1998) noted that such comparisons of the linkages between evidence and argumentative strength, especially with comparisons to "shoddy arguments with information of dubious relevance or provenance" (p. 68), are seriously lacking in the research literature on evidence.

Handling of Anomalous Data. An interesting turn in the question of judgments of evidence is the handling of anomalous data (i.e., inconsistent with other known data and accepted theory). Chinn and Brewer (1993) contended that people can have one of seven responses to anomalous data: ignore it, reject it, exclude it, hold it in abeyance (waiting for further data), reinterpret it, make a minor repair to existing beliefs (i.e., assimilate the data in a way that makes it nonanomalous), or accept it. The research they reviewed that is relevant to the processing of anomalous data (which is primarily on science education) is potentially instructive for further research on the uses and effects of evidence in persuasion.

There is little direct data on what message recipients do when they hear an advocate present evidence that the recipients perceive to be anomalous with prior data. The resistance to persuasion literature (e.g., Burgoon, Cohen, Miller, & Montgomery, 1978; Pfau, 1992; Pfau, Van Bockern, & Kang, 1992; Zuwerink & Devine, 1996) could be applied if evidence and prior knowledge were to take a stronger position in that theory and research. The early resistance research (e.g., McGuire, 1961) in which the topics were truisms seemed to indicated a strong tendency to just accept anomalous data. Wood et al. (1995) noted that "knowledgeable subjects resist all but the most cogently argued persuasive appeals" (p. 302), but they also noted that "knowledge contributes to the biasing, defensive effects associated with strong attitudes when the attitude issue generates intense affects" (p. 304). Therefore, the application of the resistance to persuasion literature to the study of evidence as anomalous data may be worthwhile, but such attempts will encounter serious theoretic and operational difficulties.

Too Much Evidence to Be Legitimate? One consequence of employing evidence in a persuasive message may be only that the speaker is held in higher credibility than would otherwise be the case. Obviously, if a speaker already is seen as highly credible, then the inclusion of evidence can have only diminishing returns, if any, for enhancing the speaker's credibility or persuasiveness—assuming, that is, that the speaker's claims are unchallenged by the audience members or by an opposing advocate (McCroskey, 1970).

Lavasseur and Dean (1996) presented data that, on first glance, suggest that a speaker can use too much evidence and thus appear bookish or nerdy. But the speakers in their data were U.S. presidential candidates engaged in debates. These speakers probably had comparably less credibility to gain than to lose. Such speakers are also expected to have a facile command of the issues and data without having to belabor them. Thus, concern about too much evidence may need to be reserved for more unique circumstances. Students and practitioners should probably not start to worry about having too much evidence (or to use this "nerd effect" as an excuse for failing to provide evidence). The more everyday sort of speaker may want to include the best evidence possible because, even if a speaker does not have an obvious immediate opponent, most sophisticated audiences are quite capable of generating counterarguments against the claims of even the most highly regarded advocate.

WHAT WE NEED TO KNOW: FUTURE DIRECTIONS

There are a number of fruitful directions for future research on the use of evidence in persuasive discourse. The following ideas are grouped roughly in terms of how foundational they seem to be. Thus, the first suggestions would seem to be important first steps before researchers move on to the subsequent suggestions.

Evidence Belongs Within the Context of Presumption

Basic argumentation students learn that the presentation of evidence is inextricably linked to presumption (Whately, 1991) and the related concept of the burden of proof. In the courts of the United States, for example, there is a legal presumption that a defendant is innocent until the prosecutors have met the burden of proof by presenting a compelling case and, furthermore, that the compelling case has withstood the evidence, refutations, and arguments by the defense. Theoretically, in any context of discourse where evidence is presented, the presumption and the burden of proof underlying the event govern the strength and even the type of evidence that is to be presented.

There are a number of common presumptions in persuasive events. The presumption of innocence is based on the idea that the *status quo* will continue until there is just cause to make a change. With some groups and situations, however, the presumption is that change is actually preferred over maintaining the status quo, and greater evidence (the burden of proof) is required of the advocate who seeks to resist change. In policy disputes, some special interest groups (e.g., environmentalists, pro-choice or pro-life activists, victimized minorities) so narrowly define the issues that the range of relevant arguments and evidence is seriously constrained. Furthermore, some bureaucrats tend to be interested only in arguments and evidence that protect them and their institutions. There are many other presumptions advocates must adjust to in order to be persuasive.

Perhaps one of the reasons for some of the inconsistencies and confusions in the evidence research is the lack of effort at conceptualizing about the context of presumption in which the evidence manipulations are cast. For example, an audience of parents being told that they should support the legalization of drugs is more likely to rest on ethical absolutes about prohibitions than is an audience of drug rehabilitation counselors. Some basic exploratory work is needed on identifying the major presumptions advocates face and how those presumptions influence the selection and effects of evidence.

The Need to Measure the Perception of Evidence Quality

If the linkage among evidence evaluation, message evaluation, and persuasion is fundamental to the study of evidence and persuasion, then further work will be needed on the measurement of evaluations of evidence. An important aspect of this issue is that it is not merely enough to manipulate evidence (although further refinements are also needed there). Evidence, like credibility, rests in the perceptions of the message recipients.

A few studies have offered measures of argument and evidence evaluation. Allen and Burrell (1992) presented a four-item measure of argument quality and believability that included one item on the overall evidence in a message. Morley and Walker (1987) had participants rate the information in mock court testimony as to its importance (*very important* to *very unimportant*), novelty (*clearly did* to *clearly did not provide new information*), and plausibility (*very likely* to *very unlikely*). Wood, Kallgren, and Preisler (1985) used a thought-listing protocol and counted the number of thoughts critical of the message arguments. Reynolds (1986/1987) developed a measure of evidence evaluation with Likert-type scales. The stimulus statements were derived from discussions of the traditional tests of evidence employed in argumentation and debate (see McCroskey & Wheeless, 1976; Miller, 1966; Reinard, 1991). The strongest items in the scale are presented here:

> *The evidence* presented in the message:
>
> - was sufficient to prove the points being supported.
>
> - was irrelevant to the conclusions drawn in the message.
>
> - was not clear and understandable.
>
> - contained clear and understandable statistical information.
>
> - taken as a whole, supported the point being made.
>
> - came from experts on the topic.

Any effort at refining the measurement of evidence evaluation will need to start with untangling a number of interrelated concepts, manipulations, and measures. O'Keefe (1998), for example, pointed out that evidence researchers have not "sought to articulate palpably unsatisfactory support" (p. 69). When measures or manipulation checks are used, they often combine assessments of evidence with other characteristics or arguments or message construction. The "manipulation of a suite of message features does not necessarily enhance effect sizes" (p. 70) and certainly complicates untangling the separate effects. Correspondingly, Allen and Reynolds (1993) pointed out that the entire concept of "argument strength" from the Elaboration Likelihood Model literature continues to appear to be confounded (at least across research programs) with general affect, argument relevance, argument absurdity, and message/argument development (listings vs. coherent texts). One

obvious area where this conceptual measurement work can begin is with integrating theoretically and operationally Morley's (1987; Morley & Walker, 1987) concepts of important, novel, and plausible information.

Lingering Questions About Evidence in Public Advocacy

Even within the public communication context, there is a great deal of research yet to do on evidence and persuasion. There may be 60-plus years of research on the effects of evidence (see Reinard, 1988), but the significant advances have been sporadic at best. We need answers on the quantitative specificity of evidence. There need to be more concentrated and direct studies of the credibility ceiling effect claimed in earlier studies. The study of types of evidence needs to be expanded. And researchers need to further examine how the effects of evidence vary with different modes of cognitive processing.

Quantitative Specificity. O'Keefe (1998) noted that there are only four studies on the effects of quantitative specificity of evidence. Beyond modal terms such as *many* and *frequently* versus specific probabilities, advocates are also constantly confronted with balancing between detailed accounts of exacting scientific experiments and trying to ground the data in the experiences of the audience. Researchers may also want to consider whether the citation of studies with longitudinal data is more persuasive than the citation of similar findings from studies with controlled one-shot experiments. By extension, most of the research cited in public speech textbooks on the effects of visual displays of supporting materials rarely refers to studies employing a public advocacy context.

Credibility Ceiling Effects? While the vast majority of the published research articles supporting the effects of evidence (see, in particular, Reinard, 1988) generally conclude that there is a credibility ceiling effect beyond which evidence does not enhance persuasion, O'Keefe (1998) claimed that the actual research data paints less than clear support for the credibility ceiling. Unfortunately, most of the complicating data are so underreported that comparisons across studies are not justifiable. The picture is further complicated by vast inconsistencies across the studies in the manipulation and measurement of the initial credibility of the advocate. It is also not new to note that it is difficult to actually construct a low-credibility source induction, particularly when the audience is composed of American college students from the last half of the 20th century. Even the claim of long-term effects for evidence after the memory of advocate credibility fades is sparsely supported by a few studies. A stronger and systematic set of studies on the interplay of credibility and evidence use is needed.

The Further Study of Types of Evidence. The comparisons of statistical versus narrative forms of evidence notwithstanding, a weakness in the evidence research to date stems from the lack of satisfactory classification of types of evidence (Hample et al., 2000; Lavasseur & Dean, 1996). There are many different schemes for the classification of evidence (Reinard, 1991, p. 133). Some classifications focus on content (e.g., reports, exhibits, statistics, opinions, hearsay), some classifications address the connectedness of the datum to the claim being advanced (e.g., direct vs. circumstantial, factual vs. "desirable"), and still other classifications seem guided by the relationship of the evidence source, audience, or speaker to the evidence (e.g., common knowledge, unbiased or expert testimony, impromptu or reluctant testimony, artistic proofs or verbal evidence, personal anecdotes, negative evidence or failing to present evidence). Beyond the quantitative or storytelling research, what research there is on the effects of different types of evidence tends to merely suggest that evidence relevant to the arguments seems to be the most persuasive. (Reinard, 1991, p. 113, reviewed this research, most of which is in unpublished theses and dissertations.) Argumentation and persuasion scholars would be well-served by extended efforts at conceptualizing and testing different classifications of evidence types.

Multiple or Alternative Modes of Processing. Kopfman et al. (1998) presented direct evidence that different types of evidence influence different modes of processing and speculated about the joint effects of both types of evidence in the same message. Allen et al. (2000) demonstrated the superiority of multiple types of evidence in a single message. Similarly, O'Keefe (1998) noted that the research to date has not sufficiently allowed for the joint assessment of both heuristic and systematic modes of processing (Chaiken, 1987). Tangentially related is the call by Allen and Preiss (1997) to look at the effects of cultural variability on the impact of evidence because of "different expectations for forms of proof" (p. 129). For example, the higher avoidance of uncertainty and risks in some cultures would lead to the expectation of higher thresholds for evidentiary proof before assent is granted. Uncertainty avoidance would probably also lead to greater denial of the opportunity to persuade in the first place. Similar to Berger's (1998) suggestion that victimization led to unjustified acceptance of bad news about social problems, powerlessness or power distance could also have an impact on what evidence an audience is willing to process or is capable of processing.

Evidence in Interpersonal Communication

There is a great deal of research yet to be done on the use of evidence in interpersonal communication. O'Keefe (1977) distinguished between argument₁ (reasoning) and argument₂ (making an argument particularly in the interpersonal setting). Jackson and Jacobs (1981) have also argued that standards of argument between people tend to be set by the practices of the disputants (particularly dyads) over repeated episodes. Brockriede (1972) led us to the idea that "argument is for lovers" (meaning that only people who care for one another can manage to engage about differing views without falling into a mere quarrel). Several others have investigated argument from an interpersonal communication perspective (e.g., Alberts, 1989; Benoit & Benoit, 1990; Hample et al., 1999; Johnson & Roloff, 1998). Consistent with Miller and Burgoon's (1978) call to look more closely at the one-to-one or one-to-few contexts, explorations of argument and evidence in the interpersonal context are likely to reveal unique insights about evidence that the more traditional forensic and deliberative settings have not afforded us. When do we use evidence in interpersonal encounters? What evidence do we use? What are the effects of evidence in the interpersonal arena?

Presumption in Interpersonal Relationships. What presumptions influence how interpersonal dyads apportion responsibilities for the obligation of presenting evidence in the interpersonal setting is rarely, if ever, discussed in the interpersonal communication literature. If a neighbor, for example, suspects that the child of a close friend has lied to the friend, will the neighbor go to this friend and present evidence of the child's dissembling? Or is the neighbor more likely to ask probing questions that might draw out the friend into seeking

evidence of veracity from the child? In either case, what would count as prima facie (sufficient) evidence worthy of demanding a defense by the suspect child? Certainly, the court of family relations does not even approximate the presumptions or burdens that a formal legal body might have. Do people simply give presumption to relational partners on the basis of intimacy (Johnson & Roloff, 1998) until confronted with relational problems (Sprecher, 1986)? Or are better relationships characterized by loving arguments in which respectful partners are careful to present full reasoning and evidence (Benoit & Benoit, 1990) with a commitment to resolvability of conflicts (Johnson & Roloff, 1998) even if the arguments are performed in a way that is unique to the couple (van Eemeren & Grootendorst, 1991)?

Sproule (1976) pointed out that argumentative presumption can also be seen as showing deference to an opponent. Deference in argument and the acceptance of evidence is not yet a regular topic for research. A number of factors that could influence the showing of deference (granting presumption) to an adversary: the mood of either advocate, the credibility of the adversary, the topic under dispute, and the preference for a collective over an individual judgment.

Evidence Across Stages of Relationships. Interpersonal researchers could also take a longitudinal and evolutionary view of the process of argument and evidence use in relationships. In the course of a relationship, the substance of the arguments evolves, the couple's arguing style (particularly the use of evidence) evolves, and the amount of deference that occurs between the two evolves. Certainly, the status of the individuals within their shared and separate networks could strongly influence when and how demands for "proof" could be made.

Avtgis, West, and Anderson (1998) explored the cognitive, affective, and behavioral dimensions of Knapp's (1978) Relational Stages Model. Naturally, talking about everyday matters, "old news," and general information exchanges are scattered throughout the different stages. But during the "intensifying" stage, participants are more likely to probe for moral values and use moral principles in arguments than they would be during the initiating or experimenting stage.

During the initiating and experimenting stages, couples are probably more likely to play the game of argument more for testing and teasing than for serious conflict management. The inability to produce an efficient coherent argument may have devastating effects on the budding relationship.

During the differentiating stage of relational decay, the elaboration of premises probably often gets reduced to personal attacks. These arguments may be more likely to consist of hearsay and personal opinions and might not allow for much formally defined evidence. Newell and Stutman (1988) explored relationships and framed this type of argument as social confrontation.

Sillars (1998) discussed how "certain devious misunderstandings" may appear in particular arguments. In discussing the goals of argument in interpersonal relationships, Sillars stated that "evidence, in the form of past relationship events, might be selectively remembered, based on how the examples serve persuasive goals" (p. 88). In addition, Sillars mentioned "[how] 'metaperception' about the partner's opinions and intentions might be represented in simplified or distorted terms (as in the 'straw man' fallacy of argument), thereby, making it easier to refute or dismiss criticism" (p. 88).

According to Cupach and Metts (1986), conflicts during the terminating stage tend to look at the other partner's faults and the fact that issues have become unmanageable. Of the possible acts that might be expected in interpersonal conflict, statements of fact and attack-defend sequences would clearly be ones where we could expect the presentation of evidence (for a review of related research, see Messman & Canary, 1998).

It may well be that because satisfied couples use fewer negative statements and less negative reciprocation (Carrer & Gottman, 1999; Gottman, 1979; Gottman & Levenson, 1999), they may also see less need for the use of evidence in their deliberations. Conversely, it may just be that it is because they stay focused on the evidence that long-term satisfied couples are less likely to blow up and short-circuit their problem-solving efforts.

There certainly are sufficient entries into the interpersonal arena for argumentation and evidence scholars to pursue. When do lovers, friends, and family members grant or deny presumption? Are certain family members or friendship types best for presenting particular arguments and evidence? What are the burdens and standards we place on each other for presenting evidence? Are better relationships characterized by calm reasoning where there is an active refusal to leave the evidence as taken for granted?

The Study of Evidence Use and Effects Across Forums

Of all the studies by communication and persuasion scholars on the effects of evidence and arguments, only a few (most notably Luchok & McCroskey, 1978) are actually set up within the context of a forum of competing advocates. Perhaps it is the case that debate-like settings (even the artifice of political debates) foster greater uses of evidence. Could it be that the introduction of evidence actually seems odd and out of place in a rubber chicken circuit speech (especially to anyone outside of the speech, communication, and persuasion academic communities)? We also might undertake serious consideration of the influence that computer-mediated communication forums have on the use and effectiveness of evidence.

In most of the research on evidence, the message recipients are reading the message and only occasionally sitting alone in a booth listening to an audio recording. Could observable audience responses (Axsom, Yates, & Chaiken, 1987; Hocking, Margreiter, & Hylton, 1977) influence the reception of and yielding to evidentiary material? Certainly, it would be difficult to ignore evidence when others in the audience are giving nods of assent, defiant glares, or even occasional shouts of "Amen!" or "No way!" from the back of the room.

SUMMARY

Considering what we know about evidence, the conditions for the effective use of evidence, and what we need to know, there is a strong future for researchers interested in the study of evidence. The quality and quantity of research relevant to the study of the use and effects of evidence have advanced far beyond the early stages of doubt about the worthiness of the enterprise. Now there is an evolving research literature base on which evidence researchers can draw. There might not be a flood of studies over the next few decades, but there should be a continuing steady stream of theses, dissertations, and research articles. Perhaps some entire academic departments may wish to make evidence research a focal point in their collective efforts at development and advancement.

REFERENCES

Alberts, J. K. (1989). A descriptive taxonomy of couples' complaint interactions. *Southern Communication Journal, 54*, 125-143.

Allen, M., Bruflat, R., Fucilla, R., Kramer, M., McKellips, S., Ryan, D. J., & Spiegelhoff, M. (2000). Testing the persuasiveness of evidence: Combining narrative and statistical forms. *Communication Research Reports, 17*, 331-336.

Allen, M., & Burrell, N. (1992). Evaluating the believability of sequential arguments. *Argumentation and Advocacy, 28*, 135-144.

Allen, M., & Preiss, R. W. (1997). Comparing the persuasiveness of narrative and statistical evidence using meta-analysis. *Communication Research Reports, 14*, 125-131.

Allen, M. R., & Reynolds, R. A. (1993). Elaboration Likelihood Model: A methodological and conceptual assessment of definitions. *Communication Theory, 3*, 73-82.

Anderson, L. (1970). An experimental study of reluctant and biased authority based assertions. *Journal of the American Forensic Association, 7*, 79-84.

Arnold, W. E., & McCroskey, J. C. (1967). The credibility of reluctant testimony. *Central States Speech Journal, 18*, 97-103.

Aune, R. K., & Reynolds, R. A. (1994). The empirical development of the Normative Message Processing Scale. *Communication Monographs, 61*, 135-160.

Austin, E. W., & Dong, Q. (1994). Source vs. content effects on judgments of news believability. *Journalism Quarterly, 71*, 973-983.

Avtgis, T. A., West, D. V., & Anderson, T. L. (1998). Relationship stages: An inductive analysis identifying cognitive, affective, and behavioral dimensions of Knapp's Relational Stages Model. *Communication Research Reports, 15*, 280-287.

Axsom, D., Yates, S. M., & Chaiken, S. (1987). Audience response as a heuristic cue in persuasion. *Journal of Personality and Social Psychology, 53*, 30-40.

Baesler, E. J. (1997). Persuasive effects of story and statistical evidence. *Argumentation and Advocacy, 33*, 170-175.

Baesler, E. J., & Burgoon, J. K. (1994). The temporal effects of story and statistical evidence on belief change. *Communication Research, 21*, 582-602.

Benoit, P. J., & Benoit, W. L. (1990). To argue or not to argue: How real people get in and out of interpersonal arguments. In R. Tripp & J. Schuetz

(Eds.), *Perspectives on argumentation: Essays in honor of Wayne Brockriede* (pp. 55-72). Prospect Heights, IL: Waveland.

Berger, C. R. (1998). Processing quantitative data about risk and threat in news reports. *Journal of Communication, 48*, 87-106.

Bostrom, R. N., & Tucker, R. K. (1969). Evidence personality and attitude change. *Speech Monographs, 36*, 22-27.

Bradac, J. J., Sandell, K. L., & Wenner, L. A. (1979). The phenomenology of evidence: Information-source utility in decision making. *Communication Quarterly, 27*, 35-46.

Brockriede, W. (1972). Arguers as lovers. *Philosophy and Rhetoric, 5*, 1-11.

Buckless, F. A., & Peace, R. L. (1993). The influence of the source of professional standards on juror decision making. *Accounting Review, 66*, 164-175.

Burgoon, J. K. (1975). Conflicting information, attitude, and message variables as predictors of learning and persuasion. *Human Communication Research, 1*, 133-144.

Burgoon, M., & Burgoon, J. (1975). Message strategies in influence attempts. In G. Hanneman & W. McEwen (Eds.), *Communication and behavior* (pp. 149-165). Reading, MA: Addison-Wesley.

Burgoon, M., Cohen, M., Miller, M. D., & Montgomery, C. L. (1978). An empirical test of a model of resistance to persuasion. *Human Communication Research, 5*, 27-39.

Cappella, J. M., & Jamieson, K. H. (1994). Broadcast adwatch effects: A field experiment. *Communication Research, 21*, 342-365.

Carrer, S., & Gottman, J. M. (1999). Predicting divorce among newlyweds from the first three minutes of a marital conflict discussion. *Family Process, 38*, 293-300.

Chaiken, S. (1987). The Heuristic Model of persuasion. In M. P. Zanna, J. M. Olson, & C. P. Herman (Eds.), *Social influence: The Ontario Symposium* (Vol. 5, pp. 3-39). Hillsdale, NJ: Lawrence Erlbaum.

Chinn, C. A., & Brewer, W. F. (1993). The role of anomalous data in knowledge acquisition: A theoretical framework and implications for science instruction. *Review of Educational Research, 63*, 1-49.

Cupach, W. R., & Metts, S. (1986). Accounts of relational dissolution: A comparison of marital and non-marital relationships. *Communication Monographs, 53*, 311-334.

Eagly, A. H., & Chaiken, S. (1993). *The psychology of attitudes*. Fort Worth, TX: Harcourt Brace.

Eagly, A. H., & Warren, R. (1976). Intelligence, comprehension, and opinion change. *Journal of Personality, 44*, 226-242.

Fleshler, H., Ilardo, J., & Demoretcky, J. (1974). The influence of field dependence, speaker credibility set, and message documentation on evaluations of speaker and message credibility. *Southern Speech Communication Journal, 39*, 389-402.

Gottman, J. M. (1979). *Marital interaction: Experimental investigations*. New York: Academic Press.

Gottman, J. M., & Levenson, R. W. (1999). Rebound from marital conflict and divorce prediction. *Family Process, 38*, 287-292.

Gregg, R. B. (1967). The rhetoric of evidence. *Western Speech, 31*, 180-189.

Hample, D. (1977). Testing a model of value argument and evidence. *Communication Monographs, 44*, 106-120.

Hample, D. (1978). Predicting immediate belief change and adherence to argument claims. *Communication Monographs, 45*, 219-228.

Hample, D. (1979). Predicting belief and belief change using a cognitive theory of argument and evidence. *Communication Monographs, 46*, 142-151.

Hample, D. (1980). A cognitive view of argument. *Journal of the American Forensic Association, 17*, 151-158.

Hample, D. (1981). The cognitive context of argument. *Western Journal of Speech Communication, 45*, 145-158.

Hample, D. (1985). Refinements on the cognitive model of argument: Concreteness, involvement, and group scores. *Western Journal of Speech Communication, 49*, 267-285.

Hample, D., Baker, K., Luckie-Parks, A., Moore, R., Thorne, C., & Dorsey, C. (2000, November). *Toward a theory of evidence: An initial attempt to discover perceptual dimensions*. Paper presented at the convention of the National Communication Association, Seattle, WA.

Hample, D., Benoit, P. J., Houston, J., Purifoy, G., VanHyfte, V., & Wardwell, C. (1999). Naive theories of arguments: Avoiding interpersonal arguments or cutting them short. *Argumentation and Advocacy, 35,* 130-139.

Harte, T. B. (1971). Audience ability to apply tests of evidence. *Journal of the American Forensic Association, 8,* 109-115.

Harte, T. B. (1976). The effects of evidence in persuasive communication. *Central States Speech Journal, 27,* 42-46.

Hocking, J. E., Margreiter, D. G., & Hylton, C. (1977). Intra-audience effects: A field test. *Human Communication Research, 3,* 243-249.

Jackson, S., & Jacobs, S. (1981). The collaborative production of proposals in conversational arguments and persuasion: A study of disagreement regulations. *Journal of the American Forensic Association, 18,* 77-90.

Johnson, K. J., & Roloff, M. (1998). Serial arguing and relational quality: Determinants and consequences of perceived resolvability. *Communication Research, 25,* 327-343.

Kaid, L. L, Tedesco, J. C., & McKinnon, L. M. (1996). Presidential ads as nightly news: A content analysis of 1988 and 1992 televised adwatches. *Journal of Broadcasting & Electronic Media, 40,* 279-303.

Kassim, S. M., Reddy, M. E., & Tulloch, W. F. (1990). Juror interpretations of ambiguous evidence: The need for cognition, presentation order, and persuasion. *Law and Human Behavior, 14,* 43-55.

Kazoleas, D. C. (1993). A comparison of the persuasive effectiveness of qualitative versus quantitative evidence: A test of explanatory hypotheses. *Communication Quarterly, 41,* 40-50.

Kellermann, K. (1980). The concept of evidence: A critical review. *Journal of the American Forensic Association, 16,* 159-171.

Kline, J. A. (1969). Interaction of evidence and readers: Intelligence on the effects of short messages. *Quarterly Journal of Speech, 55,* 407-413.

Kline, J. A. (1971a). A Q-analysis of encoding behavior in the selection of evidence. *Communication Monographs, 38,* 190-197.

Kline, J. A. (1971b). Dogmatism of the speaker and selection of evidence. *Communication Monographs, 38,* 354-356.

Kline, S. L., & Oseroff-Varnell, D. (1993). The development of argument analysis skills in children. *Argumentation and Advocacy, 30,* 1-16.

Knapp, M. L. (1978). *Social intercourse: From greeting to goodbye.* Needham Heights, MA: Allyn & Bacon.

Kopfman, J. E., Smith, S. W., Ah Yun, J. K., & Hodges, A. (1998). Affective and cognitive reactions to narrative versus statistical evidence organ donation messages. *Journal of Applied Communication Research, 26,* 279-300.

Lavasseur, W., & Dean, K. W. (1996). The use of evidence in presidential debates: A study of evidence levels and types from 1960-1988. *Argumentation and Advocacy, 32,* 129-142.

Luchok, J., & McCroskey, J. C. (1978). The effect of quality of evidence on attitude and source credibility. *Southern Speech Communication Journal, 33,* 371-383.

McCroskey, J. C. (1967). The effects of evidence in persuasive communication. *Western Speech, 31,* 189-199.

McCroskey, J. C. (1969). A summary of experimental research on the effect of evidence in persuasive communication. *Quarterly Journal of Speech, 55,* 169-176.

McCroskey, J. C. (1970). The effects of evidence as an inhibitor of counter-persuasion. *Speech Monographs, 37,* 188-194.

McCroskey, J. C., & Wheeless, L. C. (1976). *Introduction to human communication.* Boston: Allyn & Bacon.

McGuire, W. J. (1961). The effectiveness of supportive and refutational defenses in immunizing and restoring beliefs against persuasion. *Sociometry, 24,* 184-197.

McKinnon, L. M., & Kaid, L. L. (1999). Exposing negative campaigning or enhancing advertising effects: An experimental study of adwatch effects on voters' evaluations of candidates and their ads. *Journal of Applied Communication Research, 27,* 217-236.

McLaughlin, M. L., Cody, M. J., & French, K. (1990). Account-giving and the attribution of responsibility: Impressions of traffic offenders. In M. J. Cody & M. L. McLaughlin (Eds.), *The psychology of tactical communication* (pp. 244-267). Bristol, PA: Multilingual Matters.

Messman, S. J., & Canary, D. J. (1998). Patterns of conflict in personal relationships. In B. H. Spitzberg & W. R. Cupach (Eds.), *The dark side of close relationships* (pp. 121-152). Mahwah, NJ: Lawrence Erlbaum.

Miller, G. R. (1966). Evidence and argument. In G. R. Miller & T. R. Nilsen (Eds.), *Perspectives on argumentation* (pp. 24-49). Glenview, IL: Scott, Foresman.

Miller, G. R., & Burgoon, M. (1978). Persuasion research: Review and commentary. In B. D. Ruben (Ed.), *Communication Yearbook 2* (pp. 29-47). New Brunswick, NJ: Transaction Books.

Morley, D. D. (1987). Subjective message constructs: A theory of persuasion. *Communication Monographs, 54,* 183-203.

Morley, D. D., & Walker, K. B. (1987). The role of importance, novelty, and plausibility in producing belief change. *Communication Monographs, 54,* 436-442.

Newell, S. E., & Stutman, R. K. (1988). The social confrontation episode. *Communication Monographs, 55,* 266-285.

Nisbett, R. E., Borgida, E., Crandall, R., & Reed, H. (1976). Popular induction: Information is not necessarily informative. In J. S. Carroll & J. W. Payne (Eds.), *Cognition and social behavior* (Vol. 2, pp. 227-236). Hillsdale, NJ: Lawrence Erlbaum.

O'Keefe, D. J. (1977). Two concepts of arguments. *Journal of the American Forensic Association, 13,* 121-128.

O'Keefe, D. J. (1998). Justification explicitness and persuasive effects: A meta-analytic review of the effects of varying support articulation in persuasive messages. *Argumentation and Advocacy, 35,* 61-75.

Petty, R. E., & Cacioppo, J. T. (1984). The effects of involvement or response to argument quantity and quality: Central and peripheral routes to persuasion. *Journal of Personality and Social Psychology, 46,* 69-81.

Pfau, M. (1992). The potential of inoculation in promoting resistance to the effectiveness of comparative advertising messages. *Communication Quarterly, 40,* 26-44.

Pfau, M., & Louden, A. (1994). Effectiveness of adwatch formats in deflecting political attack ads. *Communication Research, 21,* 325-341.

Pfau, M., Van Bockern, S., & Kang, J. G. (1992). Use of inoculation to promote resistance to smoking initiation among adolescents. *Communication Monographs, 59,* 213-230.

Reinard, J. C. (1988). The empirical study of persuasive effects of evidence: The status after fifty years of research. *Human Communication Research, 15,* 3-59.

Reinard, J. C. (1991). *Foundations of argument: Effective communication for critical thinking.* Dubuque, IA: William C. Brown.

Reinard, J. C. (1998). The persuasive effects of testimonial assertion evidence. In M. Allen & R. W. Preiss (Eds.), *Persuasion: Advances through meta-analysis* (pp. 69-85). Cresskill, NJ: Hampton.

Reinard, J. C., & Reynolds, R. A. (1978). The effects of inadmissible testimony objections and ruling on jury decisions. *Journal of the American Forensic Association, 15,* 91-108.

Reynolds, R. A. (1987). The effects of cognitive elaboration, valid arguments, evidence, and message style in persuasive discourse. (Doctoral dissertation, Michigan State University, 1986). *Dissertation Abstracts International, 47,* 4235A.

Reynolds, R. A. (1997). A validation test of a message elaboration measure. *Communication Research Reports, 14,* 269-278.

Reynolds, R. A., & Burgoon, M. (1983). Belief processing, reasoning, and evidence. In R. Bostrom (Ed.), *Communication Yearbook 7* (pp. 83-104). Beverly Hills, CA: Sage.

Rivenburg, R. (1999, August 9). Off-kilter: There's a sucker born every minute—and he probably lives next door. *Los Angeles Times, p. E5.*

Rothstein, P. F., Raeder, M. S., & Crump, D. (1997). *Evidence in a nutshell: State and federal rules* (3rd ed.). St. Paul, MN: West Publishing.

Schul, Y., & Mayo, R. (1999). Two sources are better than one: The effects of ignoring one message on using a different message from the same source. *Journal of Experimental Social Psychology, 35,* 327-345.

Sillars, A. L. (1998). (Mis)Understanding. In B. H. Spitzberg & W. R. Cupach (Eds.), *The dark side of close relationships* (pp. 73-102). Mahwah, NJ: Lawrence Erlbaum.

Slater, M. D., & Rouner, D. (1996). Value-affirma-tive and value-protective processing of alcohol education messages that include statistical evidence or anecdotes. *Communication Research, 23,* 210-235.

Slater, M. D., & Rouner, D. (1997). How message evaluation and source attributes may influence credibility assessment and belief change. *Journalism & Mass Communication Quarterly, 73,* 974-991.

Sprecher, S. (1986). The relation between inequity and emotions in close relationships. *Social Psychology Quarterly, 49,* 309-321.

Sproule, J. M. (1976). The psychological burden of proof: On the evolutionary development of Richard Whately's theory of presumption. *Communication Monographs, 43,* 115-129.

Stiff, J. B. (1986). Cognitive processing or persuasion message cues: A meta-analytic review of the effects of supporting information on attitudes. *Communication Monographs, 53,* 75-89.

van Eemeren, F. H., de Glopper, K., Grootendorst, R., & Oostdam, R. (1994). Identification of unexpressed premises and argumentation schemes by students in secondary school. *Argumentation and Advocacy, 31,* 151-162.

van Eemeren, F. H., & Grootendorst, R. (1991). Making the best of argumentative discourse. In F. H. van Eemeren, R. Grootendorst, J. A. Blair, & C. A. Willard (Eds.), *Proceedings of the Second International Conference on Argumentation*

(pp. 431-440). Amsterdam: International Centre for the Study of Argumentation.

Warren, I. D. (1969). The effect of credibility in sources of testimony on audience attitudes toward speaker and message. *Speech Monographs, 36,* 456-458.

Whaley, B. B. (1997). Perceptions of rebuttal analogy: Politeness and implication for persuasion. *Argumentation and Advocacy, 33,* 161-169.

Whately, R. (1991). *Elements of rhetoric* [facsimile reproduction with introductions by Charlotte Downey and Howard Coughlin]. Delmar, NY: Scholars' Facsimiles & Reprints.

Whitehead, J. L. (1971). Effects of authority based assertions on attitude change and credibility. *Speech Monographs, 38,* 311-315.

Wood, W., Kallgren, C. A., & Preisler, R. M. (1985). Access to attitude-relevant information in memory as a determinant of persuasion: The role of message attributes. *Journal of Experimental Social Psychology, 21,* 73-85.

Wood, W., Rhodes, N., & Biek, M. (1995). Working knowledge and attitude strength: An information-processing analysis. In R. E. Petty & J. A. Krosnick (Eds.), *Attitude strength: Antecedents and consequences* (pp. 283-313). Mahwah, NJ: Lawrence Erlbaum.

Zuwerink J. R., & Devine, P. G. (1996). Attitude importance and resistance to persuasion: It's not just the thought that counts. *Journal of Personality and Social Psychology, 70,* 931-944.

23

Nonverbal Influence

JUDEE K. BURGOON
NORAH E. DUNBAR
CHRIS SEGRIN

When asked, "How do you persuade others?," virtually everyone's first thoughts turn to the verbal messages he or she creates. And yet, if asked how others are persuaded, a person can, on a moment's reflection, generate an extensive list of nonverbal ways in which others are effectively moved to embrace or resist new attitudes and actions. Everything from the use of rewards and punishments to advertising's seductive use of imagery comes to mind. It is these latter forms of "hidden persuasion"—the often overlooked but nevertheless potent nonverbal means of influence—that are the subject of this chapter.

Due to space limitations, we limit our presentation to theories and research evidence pertaining to three classes of nonverbal appeals for influencing others: (a) appeals to attraction, similarity, intimacy, and trust; (b) dominance and power displays; and (c) expectancy

signaling and expectancy violations. The first category relies on establishing a favorable interpersonal relationship or fostering credibility and so could be related to a host of theories on interpersonal attraction, identification, relational communication, self-presentation, and image management. Here we consider Heider's balance theory, Duck's similarity theory, Byrne's attraction theory, Anderson's cognitive valence theory, and Giles's communication accommodation theory, although other theories of attraction and relational development, such as uncertainty reduction theory (Berger, 1987) and social penetration theory (Taylor & Altman, 1987), could also be applied to the understanding of nonverbal behavior and favorable interpersonal relations. The second category, that of dominance and power displays, is likewise broad enough to include not only matters of

AUTHORS' NOTE: This research was partially supported by funding from the U.S. Army Research Institute (Contract DASW01-98-K-009). The views, opinions, and findings in this report are those of the authors and should not be construed as official Department of the Army positions, policies, or decisions.

credibility and image management but also learning theory principles of rewards, threats, and punishments as well as ethological and organizational theories of power hierarchies. Here we center on social exchange theory, Lawler's bilateral deterrence theory, expectation states theory, and Rogers's relational control model. The final category encompasses a constellation of theories concerned with how interpersonal expectancies are formed and signaled and the effects of confirming or violating those expectations. Here we consider expectancy signaling models and expectancy violations theory.

Within each category, we identify what are thought to be the explanatory mechanisms that work directly or indirectly to effectuate persuasion and compliance. Because the matter of social skills tends to permeate or undergird much of the nonverbal influence literature, we include thoughts on the importance of nonverbal skill to communicator competence and successful influence and conclude with suggestions for directions that future research might profitably take.

APPEALS TO ATTRACTION AND SIMILARITY

Social scientists have for a long time been aware of the fact that physically attractive sources are more persuasive than their more ordinary-looking peers. Source attractiveness enhances persuasion independent of argument quality (Norman, 1976), expertise (Chaiken, 1979), and trustworthiness (Norman, 1976). Similarity between a source and target is also a strong determinant of attraction (Newcomb, 1961). Carl Hovland argued that one of the three main classes of stimuli that determine the success of persuasive attempts is "observable characteristics of the perceived source of the communication" (Hovland, Janis, & Kelly, 1953, p. 11). Of those observable characteris-

tics, ones that create perceptions of attractiveness and similarity are among the most powerful. Thus, nonverbal cues that promote or signify attraction and/or similarity have great potential to influence others.

Definitions

Attraction is a positive attitude or predisposition to respond to another in a positive way (Berscheid & Reis, 1998; Berscheid & Walster, 1978). These responses can entail positive appraisals of the target's qualities and attributes, positive emotions associated with that target, and positive behaviors enacted toward the target (Berscheid & Reis, 1998). Given the nature of these outcomes, it is clear that persuasion and compliance are also among the responses to which people are predisposed when attracted to another person. *Similarity* variously refers to sharing attitudes, background, values, knowledge, or communication styles in common. Because theories of attraction and similarity typically invoke each other, the two constructs are inevitably linked.

Theoretical Perspectives

A number of theories explain how and why attraction and similarity enhance persuasiveness. According to Heider's (1958) balance theory, people are motivated to hold consistent attitudes in their point of view toward other people and toward certain attitudinal objects. People tend to like others who exhibit signs of similarity because it is reinforcing to their own self-concept and helps them to predict and understand similar others. Thus, people should desire to hold an attitude toward a particular stimulus that is similar to that of a liked other or dissimilar to that of a disliked other. In the review that follows, we show that many nonverbal behaviors that are instrumental in creating a sense of liking can also enhance a source's persuasiveness. Balance theory offers one theoretical account of why this may be the case. If a source's nonverbal behaviors are immediate and likeable, we may be particularly motivated to hold attitudes similar to those that the source expresses.

Duck's (1994) similarity theory also explains how similarity and attraction may be influential in persuasive processes. Duck argued that the concept of similarity has four components that are the amalgamation of two dimensions: that which is evaluative versus nonevaluative and that which is undeclared versus declared. The evaluative/nonevaluative dimension references facts versus attitudes toward, and opinions about, those facts. The undeclared/declared dimension refers to background similarities of which two people are aware versus those of which they are unaware. Duck (1998) highlighted the role of nonverbal behavior in making similarities "declared" by stating, "We never see the internal states or attitudes of other persons directly, so we only infer them from . . . nonverbal and verbal behavior(s). . . . Because of this, the two people's readings of each other's nonverbal behavior will be critical to this inference process and highly significant in acquaintance" (p. 73). Nonverbal behaviors are essentially viewed as a fundamental means by which people infer similarity with another person. Recognition of this similarity, in turn, fuels attraction and enhances the ability to influence.

Byrne's (1971) similarity theory states a general "law of attraction" in that attraction toward an individual is thought to be a linear function of attitudinal similarity with that person. As Byrne (1961) pointed out, "Any time another person offers us validation by indicating that his percepts and concepts are congruent with ours, it constitutes a rewarding interaction and, hence, one element in forming a positive relationship" (p. 713). As already noted, attitudes toward those with whom we interact and ideas about which we interact are often conveyed nonverbally. According to Byrne's theory, awareness of these similarities is strongly associated with attraction toward a source. Nonverbal behaviors may convey a sense of attitudinal similarity between the source and target, reinforcing feelings of attraction and a predisposition to be persuaded. Additional theories that can explain the role of nonverbal behavior in creating attraction and possibly enhancing persuasiveness are the class of dyadic interaction theories such as cognitive valence theory (CVT) (Andersen, 1985, 1999), interaction adaptation theory (IAT) (Burgoon, Stern, & Dillman, 1995), and communication accommodation theory (CAT) (Giles, Coupland, & Coupland, 1991). The first two theories explain reactions to changes in nonverbal behavior during the course of an interaction. For example, CVT predicts that an increase in the nonverbal immediacy of a source, if noticed, creates some degree of arousal. This arousal then gets interpreted against a series of cognitive schemata related to factors such as cultural appropriateness, relational appropriateness, and personal predispositions. If the interaction has a generally positive tone, and if the evaluation of the change in behavior is positive, then the experienced arousal will be positively valenced, creating a good feeling about the source and the interaction. These positively valenced encounters are predicted to lead to positive relational outcomes such as positive affect, a reciprocal display of greater nonverbal immediacy, and increased relational closeness. One can predict a predisposition to agree or comply with the source as an additional positive relational outcome. CAT makes similar predictions. At its core is the assumption that people respond positively to others who adopt a nonverbal, particularly vocalic, style that is similar to their own. Listeners perceive nonverbal behavior that is similar to their own as more attractive and pleasant. As speakers adjust their behavioral style to one that is similar to targets, the targets are expected to respond positively despite being unaware of this accommodation on the part of the source. According to CAT, sources who adjust their behavioral style to be increasingly similar to targets should be perceived as more attractive and more persuasive.

Each of these theories focuses on the role of similarity and attractiveness in producing positive relational outcomes. Chaiken (1979, 1986) developed several explanations for their positive influence on persuasive outcomes. First, attractive people are thought to provide a sense of social reward. Receivers want to be with and be like attractive and similar others.

Second, source attractiveness triggers heuristic processing, whereby people mindlessly tend to agree with those who are seen as likeable. Perceived attractiveness is associated with a halo effect (Dion, Berscheid, & Walster, 1972) such that receivers ascribe a variety of other positive characteristics, including persuasiveness, to attractive sources. The belief that "what is beautiful is good" is a pervasive, if tacit, stereotype that is triggered by both physical beauty and attractive voices (Zuckerman, Hodgins, & Miyake, 1990). This may be one reason why attractive sources get more offers for help when in need (Benson, Karabenic, & Lerner, 1976), earn higher salaries (Hammermesh & Biddle, 1994), and are more able to change the attitudes of an audience (Chaiken, 1979) as compared to their less attractive peers. Because attractive people are generally likeable, the cognitive heuristics of many receivers predispose them to agree with messages from attractive sources.

Finally, some evidence suggests that attractive sources possess better social skills than do less attractive sources (Chaiken, 1979; Feingold, 1992). These heightened skills may allow attractive sources to be more effective and comfortable in persuasive contexts. This influence of social skills on persuasiveness presages the impact of another type of appeal—dominance—in that the portrait of the demeanor of socially skilled individuals corresponds closely with the profile of interpersonal dominance behaviors (Burgoon & Dunbar, 1998). Socially skilled individuals convey confidence, friendliness, dynamism, poise, and other favorable attributes through their communicative behavior, and these behaviors are seen as more dominant in interpersonal contexts (Burgoon & Dunbar, 2000). Thus, if dominant individuals appear more socially skilled, and socially skilled individuals are seen as more attractive, then dominant nonverbal behavior combines power and attraction, making it a doubly effective way to influence others.

Nonverbal Cues of Attractiveness, Attraction, and Similarity

There is good reason to suspect that the relationship between nonverbal behavior and persuasiveness is mediated by the sense of attraction and similarity that certain behaviors create. In many interactions, nonverbal behaviors simultaneously reflect a motivation to create a sense of intimacy and common ground as well as a motivation to exert control and influence over the receiver (Burgoon & Saine, 1978; Patterson, 1983). Research evidence shows that the same behaviors that often signal attraction and similarity between a source and receiver will also enhance the effectiveness of persuasive appeals, perhaps by virtue of promoting the receiver's sense of identification with the sender or creating a close interpersonal relationship on which the sender can draw. What follows is a sampling of that research evidence regarding which nonverbal behaviors make the sender appear more attractive, signal the sender's attraction for the receiver, or signify similarity between the sender and receiver. Among the cues reviewed, physical appearance, artifacts, gaze, and proximity may serve not only as behaviors that enhance attraction and similarity during an interaction but also as pre-interactional elements in that they may draw people together. In this manner, nonverbal cues may predispose people to interact and be susceptible to influence even before the first word is uttered.

Kinesics. Kinesics relates to all aspects of "body language"—movements of the head, face, eyes, limbs, and trunk—as a means of communication. Among the most powerful indicators of attraction are eye contact and mutual gaze. Gaze increases as a function of liking toward the target (Exline, 1963). Eye contact is both encoded (Rubin, 1970) and decoded (Kleinke, Bustos, Meeker, & Staneski, 1973) as a sign of attraction and relational positivity, and its absence is also a good indicator of relational distress (Noller, 1980).

Gaze has a very reliable effect of increasing compliance rates when compared to those who make requests while averting their gaze (Segrin, 1993). In persuasive contexts, the increased use of gaze has been associated with getting more rides while hitchhiking (Snyder, Grether, & Keller, 1974), having greater success in getting change from others to make a phone call (Brockner, Pressman, Cabitt, & Moran, 1982), getting targets to take pamphlets (Kleinke & Singer, 1979), and having success in requesting donations to a charity (Bull & Robinson, 1981). Given the powerful connection between gaze and attraction (Burgoon, Manusov, Mineo, & Hale, 1985), it is plausible to assume that in many of these cases, gazing confederates were seen as more attractive by targets than were those who averted eye contact.

Vocalics. There are a number of paralinguistic (vocal) variables that are associated with attraction between a source and target or that create such a sense of attraction. For example, those who speak at a relatively fast rate with short silent pauses are seen as having more favorable attributes than are those who speak at a slower rate (Siegman, 1987). Silent pauses, filled pauses, and speech hesitations all are negatively correlated with listeners' attraction toward speakers (Pope & Siegman, 1966). Some of these same behaviors, and those that are manipulated to create "warm" interviewer conditions (Siegman, 1987), are also those paralinguistic behaviors that appear to enhance speakers' persuasiveness.

A fast speech rate has been shown to be effective in gaining compliance, especially when recipients have good decoding skills (Buller & Aune, 1988; cf. Buller, Le Poire, Aune, & Eloy, 1992; Miller, Maruyama, Beaber, & Valone, 1976; Woodall & Burgoon, 1983). A requester's "tone of voice" may also have an impact on compliance. Buller and Burgoon (1986) employed interviewers who had either pleasant, neutral, or hostile voices. Participants classified as good decoders volunteered more hours of their time to requesters with a pleasant rather than neutral voice. On the other hand, participants classified as poor decoders volunteered more time to neutral speakers. Hall (1980) also found that good decoders of nonverbal communication were more sensitive to vocal cues of pleasantness and expressiveness and were more likely to be persuaded when these cues were intentionally manipulated. The association between perceived persuasiveness and greater vocal pleasantness, which is comprised of variables such as fluency and pitch variety, was also demonstrated by Burgoon, Birk, and Pfau (1990).

Proxemics and Haptics. Proxemics refers to messages entailing the use of distancing and space; haptics refers to nonverbal messages of touch. It is well-known that friends and intimate partners use less personal space in their interactions than do strangers (Aiello, 1987; Hayduk, 1983). People generally select closer interacting distances with others who are perceived to be attractive, friendly, and positively reinforcing (Byrne, Ervin, & Lamberth, 1970; Gifford, 1982). Likewise, touch functions to convey liking, affiliation, love, sexuality, and comfort toward receivers (Heslin & Alper, 1983; Jones, 1994). Touch plays such a potent role in communicating and establishing intimacy between the encoder and decoder that it is difficult to imagine a close, particularly romantic relationship entirely devoid of touch. It is therefore understandable that closer personal space and touch tend to be associated with increased persuasiveness.

Researchers have asked confederates to approach targets at either "close" (e.g., 1-2 feet) or "far" (e.g., 4-5 feet) distances while requesting behaviors such as volunteering to participate in a study (Baron, 1978; Baron & Bell, 1976), signing a petition (Buller, 1987), giving a confederate a nickel in exchange for five pennies (Ernest & Cooper, 1974), and completing a survey (Glick, DeMorest, & Hotze, 1988). Results generally indicate that compliance rates are inversely related to the distance between the source and target of the request (Segrin, 1993). It should be noted that sources who possess high reward value (e.g., wealthy, physically attractive, well-dressed) are better able to violate targets' personal space and still produce positive effects on targets' compliance (Burgoon & Aho, 1982).

The effectiveness of touch has been demonstrated in a number of field experiments where senders lightly touched, or did not touch, receivers while making requests. Such requests have included getting participants to return dimes that they took from a phone booth (Brockner et al., 1982; Kleinke, 1977), volunteer time for charity (Goldman, Kiyo-

hara, & Pfannensteil, 1984), take and mail in a card (Kurklen & Kassinove, 1991), help to score questionnaires (Patterson, Powell, & Lenihan, 1986), and sign petitions (Willis & Hamm, 1980). In all cases, behavioral compliance was increased by the use of light touch.

The use of touch has also been linked with positive attitude changes toward sources. Patients develop more positive attitudes toward nurses who touch them as compared to nurses who limit their interactions to just verbal behavior (Aguilera, 1967). Waiters and waitresses who touch restaurant patrons, product demonstrators who touch potential customers, and greeters who touch shoppers as they enter a store all are regarded more positively by receivers than are their counterparts who do not touch (Hornik, 1992). The effects of touch on attraction to the source might even operate outside of conscious awareness. Fisher, Rytting, and Heslin (1976) had library clerks touch, or not touch, patrons' palms when returning their library cards during book checkouts. Those who were touched later rated the library clerk more favorably than did those who were not touched, yet only 57% of the participants in the touch condition were even aware that they had been touched by the library clerk.

Physical Appearance and Artifacts. A final set of cues combines physical appearance with personal artifacts. Some evidence suggests that sources dressed similarly to their targets are more persuasive than those dressed differently. Hensley (1981) had well-dressed and casually dressed solicitors seek compliance at an airport, where targets are typically well-dressed, and at a bus stop, where targets are typically more casually dressed. As predicted, the well-dressed solicitor was more successful in the airport, and the casually dressed solicitor was more successful with those at the bus stop. This finding suggests that people may be inclined to comply with sources who are dressed similarly to the self, possibly through the mechanism of identification. For instance, all social groups—from street gangs, to work groups, to entire cultures—rely on clothing, insignias, ownership of certain brand-name products, and the like to symbolize their in-group status. In other cases, high-status clothing, attractive facial features, and conventional appearance have been shown to increase persuasiveness (Bickman, 1971, 1974; Brownlow & Zebrowitz, 1990; Pallak, 1983; Pallak, Murroni, & Koch, 1983). In these latter cases, attractive appearance may be persuasive in itself, or it may relate to violations of expectations (discussed in a later section).

APPEALS TO DOMINANCE, POWER, AND STATUS

Power, dominance, and status by their very nature imply influence. It necessarily follows that nonverbal indicators of these relational states may profoundly affect the ability to persuade another. These behaviors may exert direct influence independent of what is actually said. By defining the nature of the interpersonal relationship between two parties, they may also frame verbal messages in a way that enhances or diminishes the likelihood of their acceptance. For example, dominant individuals are judged as more credible than submissive individuals (Burgoon & Dunbar, 1998). It seems likely that dominant behaviors fit into a schema for successful communication, one that combines gestalt judgments of competence and credibility with particular communicative routines that qualify as dominant. Dominant interaction also may be effective because it shares key ingredients with socially skilled performances, enabling dominant individuals to influence and even deceive others (Riggio, Tucker, & Throckmorton, 1988).

Definitions

Power, dominance, and status have been defined in numerous, often synonymous, ways by a variety of theorists and researchers (see for example, Berger, 1994; Burgoon, Johnson, & Koch, 1998; Winter, 1973). To achieve conceptual clarity and to eliminate confusion, however, these concepts should be differentiated.

Most definitions of *power* contain a common theme of the ability to influence others, exercised through a variety of resources or power bases (Burgoon et al., 1998; Foa & Foa, 1974; French & Raven, 1959; Henley, 1995). Power is thus a perceptual variable that involves the potential for control or influence that may or may not be manifested behaviorally. Among the different power bases that have been delineated and have implications for nonverbal communication are the five identified by French and Raven (1959). These are *reward power* and *coercive power,* which represent a person's right to reward and punish respectively; *legitimate power,* which is power that comes from holding a high-status position that is sanctioned by society; *referent power,* which is the power that results when others admire and emulate a person; and *expert power,* which is derived from having expertise in a needed field. *Compliance* results when a target accepts influence in order to gain rewards or avoid punishments, *identification* results when a target wishes to be emulated or be identified with an influential other (i.e., from the exercise of referent power), and *internalization* results when messages are consistent with the target's value system, often due to reliance on expert or legitimate power (Berger, 1994; Kelman, 1958). Nonverbal cues that emphasize rewards or punishments, that underscore one's legitimate role or expertise, or that attempt to build identification by cementing interpersonal affinity are drawing on principles of power.

Whereas power may be latent, *dominance* is necessarily manifest. It refers to context- and relationship-dependent interactional patterns in which one actor's assertion of control is met by acquiescence from another (Burgoon et al., 1998; Rogers-Millar & Millar, 1979). Although dominance elsewhere may be viewed as a personality trait, in the context of communication, it is a dynamic state that reflects a combination of individual temperament and situational features that demand, release, or encourage dominant behavior (Aries, Gold, & Weigel, 1983; Burgoon & Dunbar, 2000). Unlike domineeringness, which refers to individual attempts to control the interaction, dominance refers to the acceptance of the control attempts by the interactional partner; that is, it is defined by the sequence of "one-up" and "one-down" acts between two parties (Rogers-Millar & Millar, 1979). Dominance is thus both behavioral and relational.

Status refers to one's position in a socially agreed-on hierarchy that is prevalent in all types of societies, including nonhuman ones (Lips, 1991). High status often fosters dominance and power because one is endowed with legitimate authority, but it does not guarantee the exercise of power or the display of dominant behavior (Burgoon, Buller, & Woodall, 1996). However, dominance is unlikely to be effective in a task group unless a member acts from a legitimated status position (Ridgeway, Diekema, & Johnson, 1995; Ridgeway, Johnson, & Diekema, 1994). Thus, status, dominance, and power are intertwined.

Theoretical Perspectives

Social exchange theories are one set of theories that emphasize the importance of power, status, and dominance. Social exchange theorists assume that individuals will act to maximize their interpersonal rewards and minimize their interpersonal costs (Blau, 1964;

Emerson, 1976; Homans, 1958; Thibaut & Kelley, 1959). A pivotal concept of this theory is dependence—the extent to which one's outcomes are contingent on exchange with another. Dependence is a function of both value and alternatives inasmuch as people are more dependent on those whose exchange relationships they value highly, especially when alternatives are few (Molm & Cook, 1995). Power, then, is achieved dyadically when one person values exchange with the other and has few alternatives (see, e.g., Emerson, 1962; Thibaut & Kelley, 1959). People often express this power-dependence relationship nonverbally by making themselves appear more attractive as exchange partners, by communicating their interest in building relationships, or by signaling that they are not interested in an exchange.

A second approach to the study of power in nonverbal influence is Lawler's (1986) bilateral deterrence theory. Lawler and Bacharach (1987) distinguished between *dependence power* (the control that is achieved by being less dependent on the other) and *punitive power* (the influence gained by a person perceived as likely to inflict harm). Because power in relationships is never zero sum, the total or absolute amount of power in a relationship can vary. *Total power* is the sum of each party's absolute power, and *relative power* is the power difference of each party's absolute power (Lawler, 1992). As Emerson (1962) and other theorists have noticed, power is rarely in the hands of one person; rather, it is shared as people become dependent on one another. This makes nonverbal communication so much more important because as power relationships are negotiated over time, much of this negotiation takes place without words. Thus, a handshake, a tone of voice, eye contact, and other nonverbal cues can have a profound effect on the power dynamic between two people.

A third theory that is especially relevant to the role of power, dominance, and status in nonverbal influence processes is *expectation states theory.* This theory, which focuses on influence and task performance in groups, revolves around expectations that establish a "power and prestige order" (Berger, Conner, & Fisek, 1974; Ridgeway & Berger, 1986; Ridgeway & Walker, 1995). Group members develop expectations about others' likely contributions to the task based on status characteristics, and these *performance expectations* confer an "expectation advantage or disadvantage," depending on whether the individual is expected to contribute favorably or unfavorably to successful task completion.

Status characteristics are any characteristic of actors around which evaluations of and beliefs about them come to be organized. Examples include age, sex, race, ethnicity, education, occupation, physical attractiveness, and intelligence (Berger, Rosenholtz, & Zelditch, 1980). Expectation states theory differentiates between specific and diffuse status characteristics. Specific status characteristics are socially valued skills, expertise, or social accomplishments that imply a specific and bounded range of competencies (e.g., computer skills, mathematical skills). Diffuse status characteristics, such as gender and race, are culturally associated with some specific skills but also carry general expectations for competence that are diffuse and unbounded in range (Ridgeway & Walker, 1995).

Many of these characteristics are signaled nonverbally through one's demeanor and appearance, making this theory especially relevant to nonverbal influence. Those who possess status-valued external characteristics "are more likely (1) to have chances to perform, (2) to initiate problem-solving performances, [and] (3) [to] have their performances positively evaluated, and [they] (4) are less likely to be influenced when there are disagreements" (Berger, Ridgeway, Fisek, & Norman, 1998, p. 381) than are those who lack such characteristics or who possess negatively valued characteristics. In this way, expectations translate into actual influence on group problem solving.

Related to performance expectations are *reward expectations,* which are expectations about whether the status characteristics are more or less likely to create benefits for individual perceivers or the group. There are three classes of reward structures: categorical, ability, and outcome (Ridgeway & Berger, 1986). *Categorical* structures are related to diffuse social status characteristics such as age, gender, and physical strength. These expectations are like the physical attractiveness stereotypes discussed earlier in their ability to engender attraction and confer credibility. A visible physical handicap or tattoo may be stigmatizing; a tall muscular stature and graying hair may, for a male, create a commanding impression. *Ability* structures are associated with the specific task to be performed. Speaking with an authoritative voice or using dramatic gestures may imply greater confidence and expertise (i.e., greater ability). *Outcome* structures are associated with actual accomplishments during the group task. Because the power and prestige order and reward expectations are interrelated, those with high-expectation advantages not only are more likely to take the initiative (e.g., talking first, establishing seating arrangements) and to be more participative but also are more likely to be accorded more deferential treatment by others. In this manner, they will have more of their recommendations acknowledged and accepted. They may also reinforce their advantage by exhibiting verbal and nonverbal status and potency cues, referred to as *task performance cues,* which further enable them to make more—and more influential—contributions to the group's communication and, in the process, to legitimate their power and prestige.

A fourth, closely related theoretical area is that concerning credibility. As noted previously, a person's demeanor and status charac-

teristics can confer credibility. Dominant behaviors, such as direct eye contact, brief casual
touching, voices with great energy and volume, short response latencies, and few disfluencies, are generally seen as more credible
because they connote confidence and poise
(Burgoon et al., 1996). Keating and Heltman
(1994), for instance, found that dominant
children and adults were better at encoding
deception than were submissive children, especially for males. They concluded that dominant individuals have a special capacity to per-
petrate convincing deception, that is, they are
likely to be viewed as credible even when
being deceptive.

In advancing a perspective on how nonverbal cues affect credibility and persuasion,
Burgoon et al. (1990) argued that distal cues
that can be objectively measured, such as a
speaker's vocal amplitude or frequency of
illustrator gestures, generate proximal percepts such as *warmth, pleasantness,* and *dominance* that represent subjective judgments
abstracted from the objective cues. It is these
proximal percepts that lead to perceptions of
credibility and persuasion. The authors found
that kinesic dominance cues (including distal
cues such as facial expressiveness and illustrator gestures) were especially important for
generating perceptions of competence, com-
posure, character, and sociability. Kinesic
dominance, along with vocal pleasantness,
kinesic and proxemic immediacy, and kinesic
relaxation, also affected the speaker's persuasiveness.

Dominance is clearly linked to both credibility and persuasiveness, but more research
is needed to explore more fully the relationships among persuasion, credibility, and
dominance. It is a long-standing assumption
in communication that higher credibility leads
to more compliance and attitude change
(Burgoon et al., 1996). Research such as that
by Burgoon et al. (1990) and Keating and
Heltman (1994) indicates that dominant com-

municators elicit perceptions of credibility
through their confident demeanor and dynamism. For example, they make direct eye contact, have rapid loud delivery, use facial
expressiveness, and use few adapters, all of
which serve to engender the perception of
credibility and to increase compliance.

A final theoretical perspective is reflected in
the program of research on relational control
by Rogers and her colleagues (e.g., Escudero,
Rogers, & Gutierrez, 1997; Millar & Rogers,
1987; Rogers, Castleton, & Lloyd, 1996;
Rogers & Farace, 1975; Rogers-Millar &
Millar, 1979). This perspective emphasizes
the interactional nature of dominance and
power. Examining pairs of messages in a dyad's conversation, they have found that in-
teractants continually define the degree of
dominance or submissiveness in their relationship based on who has the right to direct,
delimit, and define the action of the interpersonal system (Millar & Rogers, 1987; Rogers
& Farace, 1975). While the relational control
paradigm emphasizes verbalizations, Siegel,
Friedlander, and Heatherington (1992) expanded it to include nonverbal cues. They
found that certain nonverbal behaviors, such
as a head nod and a raised eyebrow, are commonly understood as discrete ways of either
gaining or relinquishing control of a social
relationship.

Nonverbal Expressions of
Power, Dominance, and Status

Nonverbal behavior is a major avenue for
the communication of power, dominance, and
status (Henley, 1995). The research on nonverbal communication demonstrates that status, power, and dominance are encoded and
decoded reliably by people in everyday interactions. This makes such behaviors a potentially universal means of achieving influence.

Kinesics. Eye contact is a complex way to communicate dominance and status. Staring is used to connote dominance, while averting gaze is likely to communicate submission. Dominant people break eye contact last. At the same time, high-status individuals are generally expected to make less frequent eye contact, especially while listening, and subordinates are required to make eye contact with their superiors as a function of attentive listening (Lips, 1991). This may seem like an apparent contradiction, but it becomes clearer in the context of "visual dominance"—defined as the ratio of the proportion of time spent looking while speaking to the proportion of time spent looking while listening. Higher status individuals display more visual dominance (i.e., more looking while speaking combined with less looking while listening) and are seen as more powerful by observers (Dovidio & Ellyson, 1982, 1985; Ellyson, Dovidio, Corson, & Vinicur, 1980).

Relaxation is also a marker of dominance and status. In mixed-status groups, individuals with higher rank typically exhibit postural relaxation (e.g., slumping in a chair, putting their feet up on the desk), but individuals with lower rank tend to show more postural restraint (Burgoon et al., 1996). This is probably due to the fact that, like soldiers standing at attention, low-status individuals must remain attentive and vigilant while the higher status individual is freer to relax and has less need to be watchful of others (Andersen & Bowman, 1999).

Various gestures have been associated with power, dominance, and status (although the amount of experimentally controlled research on the subject is limited). Some evidence suggests that pointing at another person, using expressive and expansive gestures, steepling the hands, and using gestures while directing others may be dominant gestures (Andersen & Bowman, 1999; Burgoon, 1994).

Vocalics. Dominance has been associated with vocal cues such as rapid speaking tempo, short response latencies, loudness, and a high proportion of speaking time (Burgoon, 1994). These vocal cues connote confidence and authority. Individuals expressing anger, a dominant type of expressive behavior, typically speak louder than do nondominant individuals (Kimble & Musgrove, 1988). Rogers and Jones (1975) found that the more dominant members of a dyad held the floor about twice as much of the time and interrupted their partners more than the less dominant partners. The person who speaks first in a group interaction typically speaks the most and is perceived as the highest in status (Lamb, 1981).

Silence can also be used to send messages about dominance and status. Subordinates must wait for their superiors to speak first and must wait to be acknowledged by their superiors. Failing to recognize another person can be a potent reminder of status differences, even when done unintentionally. Giving someone the "silent treatment" and using lengthy pauses while speaking are powerful reminders of status in relationships (Burgoon et al., 1996; Jaworski, 1993).

Proxemics and Haptics. Higher status individuals are afforded more personal space, control access to more desirable territory, and adopt body positions that occupy more space as compared to lower status individuals (Burgoon et al., 1996; Lips, 1991). In office environments, there are lines of power and prestige based on where one's office is located, how large it is, and how many windows it has (Hickson & Stacks, 1993). Some research has demonstrated that individuals with higher status (both experimentally controlled status and diffuse status) actually take up more space with their bodies and possessions than do those low in status (Leffler, Gillespie, & Conaty, 1982). This is consistent with Burgoon, Buller, Hale, and deTurck's (1984) finding that closer proximity conveys greater dominance because it means that a person with higher status is invading the space of a subordinate. Elevation also provides a symbolic hierarchical function and gives the dominant individual an advantage in both surveillance and protection (Burgoon, 1994). In a study using drawings of male and female figures, Schwartz, Tesser, and Powell (1982) found that dominance was associated with elevation, standing in front as opposed to behind, and standing as opposed to sitting.

In addition to using space, powerful individuals have the ability to deviate from conversational distancing norms. Studies have shown that both close and far interaction distances have been associated with high status and dominance. This is because dominant individuals are freer to deviate from normative distances than are submissive individuals because they must maintain deferential distances in conversations (Burgoon et al., 1996).

Nonreciprocal touch communicates power, status, and dominance (Henley, 1995). Status equals touch each other in similar ways and places on the body, but among status unequals, high-status individuals typically touch their subordinates more often, and those touches are not reciprocated by the subordinates (Burgoon et al., 1996). In addition to the frequency of touch, the type of touch as well as who initiates the touch determines whether or not it is perceived as powerful (Berger, 1994). Direct poking with a finger can be seen as a very dominant type of touch, especially when the response is a recoiling or cowing from the submissive partner. Hits, slaps, kicks, and other types of physical aggression are also considered haptic behavior and are clearly meant to convey power (Burgoon et al., 1996; Straus, 1979).

Physical Appearance and Artifacts. Physical appearance can have a potent effect on the credibility of a speaker, which in turn has a substantial impact on compliance gaining. Brownlow (1992) found that people with mature faces were considered more expert and more persuasive than people with "baby faces," but baby-faced individuals were seen as more honest and trustworthy, perhaps because their babyish facial features conveyed innocence. Rosenberg, Kahn, and Tran (1991) found that women who were dressed conservatively, appeared older, had almond- or triangular-shaped eyes, and wore their hair short were seen as more competent political candidates than were other women.

People surround themselves with status symbols or other artifacts to convey their power and prestige over others. Uniforms are often potent cues for manipulating behavior because they signify the ability to reward or punish due to their legitimate power and authority (Burgoon et al., 1996). Bickman (1971, 1974) found that people are willing to comply with the requests of a person wearing an unknown security uniform, even when the requests are outside that person's legitimate authority.

In addition to uniforms, other types of clothing can also be a nonverbal message of power and status. For example, both male and female models' intelligence was judged to be highest when the models were dressed formally (Behling & Williams, 1991). Many studies have shown that compliance gaining and helping behavior are affected by the attire of message sources (Bickman, 1971; Giles & Chavasse, 1975; Lambert, 1972; Lefkowitz, Blake, & Mouton, 1955). Segrin's (1993) meta-analysis of nonverbal communication and compliance gaining showed that sources wearing more formal and higher status clothing were more successful at gaining compliance from lower status targets. In the classroom, numerous studies have demonstrated that instructors who dress informally command limited respect and are viewed by students as not especially knowledgeable and less intelligent but also more friendly and fun than their formally dressed counterparts (Butler & Roesel, 1989; Davis, 1992; Workman, Johnson, & Hadeler, 1993). Credibility and persuasion ability are associated with formal attire because high-status and privileged members of society tend to wear formal forms of dress more often than do low-status members. Those wearing this high-status form of clothing are thus judged to be more attractive, persuasive, credible, and intelligent.

Chronemics. Time management can be a powerful status cue. In the fast-paced Western world where "time is money," we generally view people with higher status as having more valuable time. Doctors communicate their higher status by having others wait in a "waiting room," and interviewers communicate their hiring power by cutting the conversation short if they do not think the interview is going well or by prolonging the interview if it looks promising. In general, the longer people will wait for us, the more important we are, and the longer amount of time we spend with someone, the more important they are to us. Focusing on one task (monochronism) instead of doing many things at once (polychronism) also indicates that the task at hand must be an important one. The perception that time is valuable even extends to speakers with a fast speaking tempo, which is usually associated with perceptions of dominance, status, and increased compliance (Burgoon et al., 1996). Perhaps it is their attempt to maximize the use of their own time or our perception that people in a hurry are important that leads us to associate these people with credibility.

EXPECTANCY SIGNALING AND EXPECTANCY VIOLATIONS

A wide array of theories of human behavior and influence rely on the concept of expec-

tancies, whether labeled as such or embodied in kindred concepts such as scripts, schemata, frames, norms, anticipatory responses, advance organizers, or predictions. Here we consider two classes of theories that are especially relevant to communication expectancies and their capacity to influence others.

Definitions

Communicators enter interactions with expectations about others—expectations about their background, attitudes, beliefs, and likely communication behavior. *Expectations,* which are cognitions about the anticipated behavior of others, may range from the general (based on sociocultural and contextual roles, rules, norms, and practices) to the particular (adjusted for individuated knowledge or experience with a specific other) (Burgoon & Walther, 1990). Expectancy-related theories, then, draw on that which is typical, commonplace, or appropriate for a class of actors or acts but allow for expectations to take into account unique information about the specific actor.

Theoretical Perspectives

Two ways in which expectancies translate into nonverbal influence are by (a) signaling expectations to a target, who then meets those expectancies, producing a self-fulfilling prophecy, and (b) violating those expectancies in positive or negative ways that elicit corresponding positive or negative outcomes, including attitude and behavioral change or resistance. Theories related to *expectancy signaling* are variously referred to as theories of experimenter expectancy effects, self-fulfilling prophecies, or behavioral confirmation (see, e.g., Darley & Fazio, 1980; Jones, 1986; Jussim, 1990; Neuberg, 1996;

Rosenthal, 1976, 1985; Snyder, 1984; Snyder & Swann, 1978). These theories examine how actors' expectancies for a target person elicit the expected behavior from the target, leading to self-fulfilling prophecies and behavioral confirmation (i.e., confirming through the behavior what the actor had expected from them). For example, if teachers are led to believe that a class of students has high achievement potential, they are likely to behave in ways that actually elicit higher performance from their students, creating a self-fulfilling prophecy. Conversely, if they expect that the students are underachievers, they will manage to elicit poorer performance from these students. From a communication standpoint, issues of interest are what verbal and nonverbal behaviors by an actor exert this subtle, usually inadvertent influence on targets and the conditions under which targets confirm, disconfirm, or are responsive to these expectancies through their own behavior. Hundreds of studies have explored the issue of expectancy signaling, and there is substantial evidence—a sampling of which is included in what follows—that nonverbal cues are pivotal to achieving these behavioral confirmation effects.

Expectancy violations theory (Burgoon, 1978, 1983, 1992, 1993; Burgoon & Burgoon, 2001; Burgoon & Jones, 1976) posits that, contrary to popular belief, it is sometimes better to violate expectations than to conform to them. Like expectation states theory, some expectations are a function of characteristics of the individual actor (e.g., physical appearance, age, sex), some are a function of the *interpersonal relationship* between actor and perceiver (e.g., acquainted or not, equal or unequal, friendly or hostile), and some are a function of the *communication context* (e.g., formal or informal, task or social, public or private setting). These factors all combine to create expectations for how an actor will communicate nonverbally (or verbally). For example, an older, high-status male stranger may be expected to be somewhat distant, to initiate formal touch, to dress formally, and to speak with a deeper pitched, expressive, and articulate voice.

When expectations are violated, such as intruding on another's personal space or avoiding eye contact, the theory posits that this triggers an arousal or orientation response (Burgoon, Kelley, Newton, & Keeley-Dyreson, 1989; Le Poire & Burgoon, 1996) in which the violation galvanizes attention to itself and its source, deepens information processing, and instigates an appraisal and evaluation process that results in the violation being valenced as positive or negative. The appraisal process is a matter of determining the possible meanings of the violation. Does close distance, for instance, imply liking or threat? Approval seeking or intimidation? The evaluation process concerns the judgment of whether the act is desirable or undesirable. The combined interpretation and evaluation of the violation, taking into account who committed it, leads to the valencing of the violation. *Positive violations* are hypothesized to produce more favorable results (including more persuasion and compliance), and *negative violations* are hypothesized to produce less favorable results, than expectancy confirmations. According to this theory, then, an actor may be better advised to violate norms and expectations than to abide by them so long as the actor knows that the act will be valenced positively.

A key factor determining valencing of a violation is communicator *reward valence*. Reward valence is a summary term for all the characteristics of the actor that make the person, on balance, rewarding or unrewarding to interact with. Nonverbal features, such as the person's attractiveness and demeanor, may contribute to this reward quotient (just as they do in expectation states theory). When a violation occurs, the heightened activation is thought to make the characteristics of the actor—good or bad—more salient. These characteristics can directly influence interaction outcomes, such as an attractive or high-status actor being more persuasive. They can also affect the appraisal process by moderating whether favorable or unfavorable interpretations and evaluations are selected. As noted previously, with attractive sources, there is a halo effect such that their actions may be interpreted more charitably and judged as more desirable than those of unattractive sources. The same process applies to other reward characteristics. If, for example, an actor is held in high regard by virtue of having a charming communication style, he or she may be able to invade another's personal space and have that act not only interpreted as an expression of liking but also evaluated as welcome. Conversely, an actor who is unrewarding by virtue of being angry and abusive may have the same act of personal space violation judged as intimidation; even if it is interpreted as a show of liking, it might not be wanted by the recipient. In the former case, the act should qualify as a positive violation, thereby facilitating persuasion and compliance; in the latter case, it should constitute a negative violation that produces, at best, involuntary temporary compliance and not long-term behavioral or attitude change.

Although negative violations are generally thought not to be a prudent persuasive strategy, recent research has shown that the aversiveness of such violations may be due partly to the uncertainty that is provoked (Afifi & Burgoon, 2000). Moreover, even negative violations may confer some added benefit relative to confirmations, once the valence of the violation itself is accounted for, if paired with positive qualities of the communicator (Burgoon & Le Poire, 1993). In this case, the

uncertainty may actually permit holding onto initially positive views of the actor.

Nonverbal Cues That Signal or Violate Expectations

In reality, every nonverbal cue has the potential to activate expectancies or to violate them. Here we focus on findings from research that has expressly examined nonverbal cues that tacitly signal expectancies and elicit behavioral confirmation or that create violations and for which there are possible implications for influence processes.

Kinesics and Vocalics. A general theme in the expectancy signaling literature, and one that reappears in the expectancy violations literature, is that gestural, facial, and vocal expressivity have persuasive impact. For example, men who expect to interact with attractive women on the phone are more sociable, animated, and warm with them than when they expect to interact with unattractive women, and they elicit similar communication styles from the women (Snyder, Tanke, & Berscheid, 1977). The degree of positive or negative affect that is expressed through voice and body language also is persuasive. People expecting to interact with a hostile partner are themselves more hostile and elicit more hostility from their partner, thus confirming their expectations (Snyder & Swann, 1978). And judges may inadvertently cue juries to give more harsh sentences to defendants with prior felony convictions by instructing juries in a more negative and impatient voice (Blanck & Rosenthal, 1992).

Proxemics and Haptics. Nonverbal immediacy behaviors are ones that express psychological closeness. They include physical proximity, direct body orientation, forward lean, touch, and gaze. In the expectancy signaling model, these cues relate to the second factor of *affect* (i.e., creating a warmer and more supportive climate). Harris and Rosenthal (1985) conducted a meta-analysis of 135 experiments on communication of expectations. Their analysis showed that when communicators held high expectations for another's performance, they coupled increased immediacy with nonverbal cues of positive reinforcement. Specifically, they adopted closer distances, used more gaze, and smiled and nodded more. In turn, the presence of these behaviors (especially eye contact, proximity, and smiling) increased the probability of targets conforming to expectations by performing well.

In the program of research on expectancy violations, Burgoon and colleagues initially explored the impact of proxemic violations (Burgoon, 1978, 1991; Burgoon & Aho, 1982; Burgoon & Jones, 1976; Burgoon, Stacks, & Burch, 1982; Burgoon, Stacks, & Woodall, 1979). These experiments confirmed that both close and far distances can qualify as positive violations if committed by a high-reward communicator and that they enhance credibility and persuasiveness. Conversely, the same behaviors qualify as negative violations when committed by a low-reward communicator and have more adverse consequences than conforming to distancing norms (an intermediate conversational distance). For example, in one study, two confederates tried to persuade a third naive person. When the two confederates were both in the high-reward condition, the one who engaged in a proxemic violation was viewed as more credible and gained more acceptance of his or her advocated position as compared to the non-violating confederate. High-reward confederates were also more persuasive when violating norms in comparison to themselves when not

violating. However, committing a proxemic violation was a detrimental strategy for low-reward confederates. In those cases, the net effect was that a violation conferred greater credibility on the opponent—a contrast effect. Other research on proxemic violations (e.g., Baron, 1978; Baron & Bell, 1976; Buller, 1987; Konecni, Libuser, Morton, & Ebbesen, 1975) also fits an expectancy violations explanation in that invasions of personal space yielded more helping behavior when a violation could be justified or was seen as rewarding and less helping behavior when the violation was inexplicable or qualified as nonrewarding.

Subsequent violations research examined gaze (Burgoon, 1991; Burgoon, Coker, & Coker, 1986; Burgoon et al., 1985), touch (Burgoon, 1991; Burgoon & Walther, 1990, Burgoon, Walther, & Baesler, 1992), immediacy (Burgoon & Hale, 1988), and conversational involvement (Burgoon & Le Poire, 1993; Burgoon, Le Poire, & Rosenthal, 1995; Burgoon, Newton, Walther, & Baesler, 1989; Le Poire & Burgoon, 1994; Le Poire & Yoshimura, 1999), which combines immediacy with other nonverbal cues to create an overall level of engagement or disengagement in interaction. These investigations found that nearly constant gaze can be a positive violation but has different interpretations depending on whether it is displayed by a male or female; high conversational involvement is a positive violation, regardless of the reward level of the actor who commits it, but extreme immediacy may not be so; fleeting touch can be a positive violation if committed by a well-regarded person but is fraught with ambiguities that can make it a risky choice in low-reward, opposite-sex interactions; and gaze aversion and nonimmediacy tend to be negative violations, regardless of who commits them.

One investigation contrasted an expectancy signaling explanation with an expectancy violations explanation for the effects of high and low involvement during dyadic interaction (Burgoon, Le Poire, & Rosenthal, 1995). It confirmed that although targets reciprocate positive expectancies, they may engage in strategic compensatory responses when the expectancies are negative—responding, for example, to negative expectancies with higher levels of involvement and pleasantness compared to those without such expectancies. Thus, targets do not inevitably conform to what actors expect of them but instead may themselves employ communication to influence actor behavior.

Other research on immediacy has demonstrated that students develop more positive attitudes toward classes and learn more when teachers use an immediate rather than a nonimmediate teaching style (Andersen, 1986; Kleinfeld, 1974) and that job applicants are more likely to be chosen for a position when they use a highly immediate interviewing style (Imada & Hakel, 1977). Thus, immediacy is a potent factor in exercising influence and may do so by signaling positive expectations held by the actor for the target and/or serving as a positive violation of expectations for actor behavior.

Physical Appearance and Artifacts. Research showing that people who are well-groomed and dressed in more conventional or formal attire are more successful in getting others to sign petitions, make change, accept political literature, or pick them up when hitchhiking (e.g., Bickman, 1971; Darley & Cooper, 1972) implies that in the case of appearance, deviancy is a negative violation with negative impact on persuasion and compliance. One exception is when such deviant appearance is coupled with an unexpectedly well-argued cogent message or a message that is contrary to views stereotypically associated with that appearance (Cooper, Darley, & Henderson,

1974; McPeek & Edwards, 1975). For example, a "hippie-looking" speaker may be more effective than a conventional one in advocating tax reform or speaking against marijuana use. In these cases, the appearance sets up negative expectations that are positively violated by the verbal message, hence making the message more persuasive.

Chronemics. Rosenthal and colleagues (e.g., Babad, Bernieri, & Rosenthal, 1989; Rosenthal, 1976, 1985, 1993), in theorizing about how teachers (and others) signal their expectations to students (or other targets) and achieve self-fulfilling prophecies, have identified two major factors that communicate expectations about performance: effort and affect. The former is essentially a chronemics variable because it breaks down into more *input, feedback,* and *opportunities for output.* When actors have high expectations for another, they tend to give that person more, and more difficult, information; more time to respond to questions; and more feedback about the correctness of the person's responses to questions. Nonverbally, this translates into more undivided and focused attention to the person. It is manifested through more frequent and longer interactions and longer response latencies. These cues, in turn, were found to elicit more matching of the pre-interaction expectancies (Harris & Rosenthal, 1985). Such nonverbal cues, then, can shape another's responding toward the desired belief, attitude, or behavior.

CONCLUSIONS

It is clear that most of the behaviors that communicate a source's attraction toward a target and/or create perceptions of power and dominance are the same behaviors that increase persuasiveness and compliance-gaining effectiveness. The reason why behavioral signs of attractiveness and dominance might increase persuasiveness may stem from reciprocity of apparent attraction or from the connections among attraction, dominance, and social skills. When a source emits behaviors that are indicative of attraction, similarity, or dominance, it is likely that targets will respond positively to their requests. Cues of attraction and liking are easily expressed nonverbally while a persuasive appeal is being made verbally. Therefore, it is reasonable to assume that these accompanying nonverbal cues will facilitate persuasion, even though that "liking" may have been consciously fabricated by a source who is well-versed in the reciprocity of attraction. People also respect those in positions of power, assume that they are more credible and knowledgeable than those with lower status, and defer to their influence. It follows that nonverbal indicators of power and dominance, in addition to eliciting behavioral compliance in their own right, should enhance the persuasiveness of messages they accompany.

The inherent credibility attributed to attractive or dominant sources also may give them more leeway to violate expectancies, thus enhancing their persuasiveness even further if the violation is positively valenced. Nonverbal behaviors can provide subtle, but easily recognizable, cues that signal the norms and expectations of interaction partners. Socially skilled individuals, who are typically also viewed as attractive and dominant, are more capable of picking up on those cues and determining when to violate or conform to the expectancies. The ability to assess the situation and choose the appropriate behavior, whether it enhances senders' attractiveness, magnifies their similarities with the target, or demonstrates their power and/or status, is a key component of effective compliance gaining. The skillful use of expectancy violations, then, is

one additional means by which nonverbal influence can be achieved.

DIRECTIONS FOR FUTURE RESEARCH

The facile answer to the question of what directions future research should take is to include nonverbal facets in all influence research. But the injunction to incorporate nonverbal variables in communication research generally is an old one to which little heed has been paid in actual practice, despite the lip service paid to its merits. There are doubtless many reasons for the paucity of such integrative research, but one predominant one is the potential enormity of the task. Where does one begin? We offer here several possible directions that are both manageable and likely to yield payoffs in better understanding the nature of interpersonal influence.

First, it would be informative to return to a line of research that began during the 1960s and 1970s examining the impact of discrepancies between verbal and nonverbal channels (see, e.g., Archer & Akert, 1977; Argyle, Alkema, & Gilmour, 1971; Gitter, Black, & Fishman, 1975; Krauss, Apple, Morency, Wenzel, & Winton, 1981; Mehrabian & Wiener, 1967; Zahn, 1973). For example, those experiments might create combinations of friendly, neutral, and unfriendly vocal cues paired with friendly, neutral, or unfriendly verbal expressions to determine which had more influence on judged friendliness of the message. A primary objective of what became a rather voluminous body of research was to assess how people process mixed messages and whether they place greater reliance on nonverbal or verbal cues when interpreting such messages (see DePaulo & Rosenthal, 1979). Although this approach has since been discredited methodologically for its inability to yield valid claims about the relative potency of verbal versus nonverbal cues, the same research paradigm could be used to assess whether certain kinds of nonverbal cues moderate the impact of verbal messages. For example, an unpublished study that the senior author completed some years ago combined degrees of verbal intensity with degrees of vocal and facial intensity. If similar independent variables were used to test their impact on message persuasiveness, it would contribute to our understanding both of the extent to which nonverbal cues qualify interpretations of verbal messages and the kinds of nonverbal cues that have this moderating impact.

A related vein of research could profitably extend research on nonverbal expectancy violations to consider in more detail their impact on persuasion and compliance. Most of the language expectancy violations work has focused on influence-related outcomes, but most of the nonverbal expectancy violations work has focused on social judgments or interaction processes as outcomes. One of the rare exceptions, the study by Burgoon et al. (1982), produced some provocative findings about the ability of expectancy violations by one person to confer advantages or disadvantages on another group member of equal reward value who conformed to expectations. Not only could this kind of investigation be replicated using different nonverbal manipulations from the distance one used in that experiment, but also research could consider the sequential impact of first conforming to and then subsequently violating expectations or vice versa. The study of message sequencing in the persuasion literature has revealed some rather interesting reversals in message susceptibility over time. The possible benefits of using nonverbal behaviors to establish expectations that are subsequently violated by a verbal message is something about which Burgoon et al. (1996) speculated, based on limited evidence from studies of conventional and unconventional attire, but their speculations have not been subjected to extensive empirical testing. In light of research in the sales and marketing arena attests to the value of setting modest (rather than unduly high) expectations so that a delivered product or service then positively violates those expectations (Brandt, 1988; Cadotte, Woodruff, & Jenkins, 1987; Fisk & Young, 1985; Tse & Wilton, 1988; Woodruff, Cadotte, & Jenkins, 1983), it follows that nonverbal cues could be used to good effect to do the same thing. By leading receivers to have limited expectations about a communicator's abilities, competency, status, or the like, communicators might have greater opportunities to violate those expectations in a positive direction with a well-formulated and argued message. By the same token, it would be important to learn what kinds of nonverbal cues might "set up" communicators to create inadvertent negative violations. If expectations states theory is correct that influence in task groups partly flows from the expectations about a person's expertise and status that are established at the outset of any interactions, then it behooves us to investigate more deeply what nonverbal cues are responsible for establishing those expectations. In general, then, learning more about the juxtaposition of the verbal with the nonverbal from an expectancy confirmation or disconfirmation standpoint would seem to be a fruitful line of inquiry.

Just as cue combinations and their expectedness may attenuate or accentuate verbal influence, so may individual difference variables. Accordingly, the role of individual differences in nonverbal influence expressions warrants further exploration. The abilities to encode and decode nonverbal behaviors are part of individual difference variables such as social skills, nonverbal sensitivity, and communication competence (e.g., Riggio, 1986;

Rosenthal, Hall, Dimatteo, Rogers, & Archer, 1979; Wiemann, 1977). Here again, this is an issue that has received very little attention in the literature on nonverbal behavior and persuasion. Where such studies do exist, the results suggest that individual differences may account for a great deal of variance in persuasive outcomes. For example, people who are poor decoders of nonverbal communication do not appear to be strongly influenced by nonverbal vocal cues (Buller & Aune, 1988). On the other hand, appropriate use of vocal cues may enhance persuasive outcomes when aimed at audiences with good nonverbal decoding cues. There are also a number of personality traits such as Machiavellianism, self-monitoring, and extraversion with established associations to the use of certain nonverbal behaviors and/or persuasiveness. Such traits may prove to be important moderators of the association between nonverbal behavior and persuasive outcomes.

Yet another line of inquiry that would seem a necessity if we are to understand true interaction (i.e., interdependent actions between two or more people) is to expand research to interactions involving familiar others. Although a large body of literature has been amassed on the relationship between nonverbal behaviors and various social influence outcomes, that literature is focused almost exclusively on stranger interactions. It would be useful to extend the domain of inquiry into other relational contexts such as marriage, family, co-workers, and business transactions. A sufficient case already exists for the importance of nonverbal behaviors in these relational contexts (e.g., Gottman, Markman, & Notarius, 1977; Noller, 1984), and it would appear prudent to further explore how nonverbal patterns contribute to social influence processes in these relational contexts.

A final area that deserves future exploration is computer-mediated communication (CMC). With government, businesses, schools, and individuals relying increasingly on new technologies for communication such as e-mail, video-teleconferencing, virtual communication, and communication with intelligent computer agents, the need for more research into nonverbal cues is obvious. We need to learn more about the role of nonverbal cues when persuasive attempts are computer mediated or delivered via computer agents (Stoner, Burgoon, Bonito, Ramirez, & Dunbar, 1999). Although early researchers made the assumption that CMC filters out nonverbal cues (e.g., Culnan & Markus, 1987), these assumptions are being challenged, especially as we move beyond text-based interactions and into virtual reality, human-computer interactions, and beyond (Burgoon, Bengtsson, Bonito, Ramirez, & Dunbar, 1999; Stoner et al., 1999). Some researchers have already made strides in the examination of nonverbal messages in CMC. Spears and Lea (1992) argued in their social identity/deindividuation (SIDE) theory that when communicators lack visual information, they actually have increased social identification, relating to others on the basis of assumed similarities. Walther's (1996) principle of hyperpersonal communication draws on this possibility, suggesting that mediated communication affords us more opportunity for selective impression management and therefore a better chance to craft a more successful (persuasive) presentation by managing the nonverbal and verbal cues that are presented. Walther, Slovacek, and Tidwell (1999) argued that because some of the cognitive resources used in face-to-face (FtF) interaction are unnecessary in CMC, we may reallocate those resources to message construction as well as the monitoring and planning of our own responses. We need to test whether theories such as SIDE theory and the hyperpersonal framework are correct, that as cues are restricted, people place greater reliance on the few that are available so that nonverbal cues take on greater significance. These theories suggest that nonverbal communication will play a different role in mediated influence than in FtF interactions, and this changing role deserves more attention from future investigators.

A related line of research, still in its infancy, could investigate the effects of mediation on the perception of nonverbal cues to test whether mediated interaction is capable of achieving the same degree of mutuality and synchronicity that is present in FtF interaction. If one of the enabling features of interpersonal influence is interactional synchrony, can this be achieved in mediated environments or even amplified in environments such as virtual reality? Will attractiveness and similarity effects be magnified in CMC if the sources of messages are not visible and their attractiveness and similarity are assumed rather than observed? Will unscrupulous individuals be able to manipulate their potency and dominance to achieve greater influence if nonverbal cues are absent or highly constrained in mediated exchanges? Clearly, mediated interaction opens up a plethora of research opportunities and provides researchers with more questions that must be answered before nonverbal influence is truly understood in the 21st century.

REFERENCES

Afifi, W. A., & Burgoon, J. K. (2000). The impact of violations on uncertainty and consequences for attractiveness. *Human Communication Research, 26,* 203-233.

Aiello, J. R. (1987). Human spatial behavior. In D. Stokols & I. Altman (Eds.), *Handbook of environmental psychology* (Vol. 1, pp. 389-504). New York: John Wiley.

Aguilera, D. C. (1967). Relationship between physical contact and verbal interaction between nurses and patients. *Journal of Psychiatric Nursing, 5,* 5-21.

Andersen, J. F. (1986). Instructor nonverbal communication: Listening to our silent messages. In M. Civikly (Ed.), *Communicating in college classrooms: New directions for teaching and learning* (pp. 41-49). San Francisco: Jossey-Bass.

Andersen, P. A. (1985). Nonverbal immediacy in interpersonal communication. In A. W. Siegman & S. Feldstein (Eds.), *Multichannel integrations of nonverbal behavior* (pp. 1-36). Hillsdale, NJ: Lawrence Erlbaum.

Andersen, P. A. (1999). *Nonverbal communication: Forms and functions.* Mountain View, CA: Mayfield.

Andersen, P. A., & Bowman, L. L. (1999). Positions of power: Nonverbal influence in organizational communication. In L. K. Guerrero, J. A. DeVito, & M. L. Hecht (Eds.), *The nonverbal communication reader: Classic and contemporary readings* (pp. 317-334). Prospect Heights, IL: Waveland.

Archer, D., & Akert, R. M. (1977). Words and everything else: Verbal and nonverbal cues in social interpretation. *Journal of Personality and Social Psychology, 35,* 443-449.

Argyle, M., Alkema, F., & Gilmour, R. (1971). The communication of friendly and hostile attitudes by verbal and nonverbal signals. *European Journal of Social Psychology, 1,* 385-402.

Aries, E. J., Gold, C., & Weigel, R. H. (1983). Dispositional and situational influences on dominance behavior in small groups. *Journal of Personality and Social Psychology, 44,* 779-786.

Babad, E., Bernieri, F., & Rosenthal, R. (1989). Nonverbal communication and leakage in the behavior of biased and unbiased teachers. *Journal of Personality and Social Psychology, 56,* 89-94.

Baron, R. A. (1978). Invasions of personal space and helping: Mediating effects of invader's apparent need. *Journal of Experimental Social Psychology, 14,* 304-312.

Baron, R. A., & Bell, P. A. (1976). Physical distance and helping: Some unexpected benefits of "crowding in" on others. *Journal of Applied Social Psychology, 6,* 95-104.

Behling, D. U., & Williams, E. A. (1991). Influence of dress on perceptions of intelligence and expectations of scholastic achievement. *Clothing and Textiles Research Journal, 9*(4), 1-7.

Benson, P. L., Karabenic, S. A., & Lerner, R. M. (1976). Pretty please: The effects of physical attractiveness on race, sex, and receiving help. *Journal of Experimental Social Psychology, 12,* 409-415.

Berger, C. R. (1987). Communicating under uncertainty. In M. R. Roloff & G. R. Miller (Eds.), *Interpersonal processes: New directions in communication research* (pp. 39-62). Newbury Park, CA: Sage.

Berger, C. R. (1994). Power, dominance, and social interaction. In M. L. Knapp & G. R. Miller (Eds.), *Handbook of interpersonal communication* (2nd ed., pp. 450-507). Thousand Oaks, CA: Sage.

Berger, J., Conner, T. L., & Fisek, M. H. (1974). *Expectation states theory: A theoretical research program.* Cambridge, MA: Winthrop.

Berger, J., Ridgeway, C. L., Fisek, M. H., & Norman, R. Z. (1998). The legitimation and delegitimation of power and prestige orders. *American Sociological Review, 63,* 379-405.

Berger, J., Rosenholtz, S. J., & Zelditch, M., Jr. (1980). Status organizing processes. *Annual Review of Sociology, 6,* 479-508.

Berscheid, E., & Reis, H. T. (1998). Attraction and close relationships. In D. T. Gilbert, S. T. Fiske, & G. Lindzey (Eds.), *The handbook of social psychology* (4th ed., pp. 193-281). New York: Oxford University Press.

Berscheid, E., & Walster, E. H. (1978). *Interpersonal attraction* (2nd ed.). Reading, MA: Addison-Wesley.

Bickman, L. (1971). The effect of social status on the honesty of others. *Journal of Social Psychology, 85,* 87-92.

Bickman, L. (1974). The social power of a uniform. *Journal of Applied Social Psychology, 4,* 47-61.

Blanck, P. D., & Rosenthal, R. (1992). Nonverbal behavior in the courtroom. In R. S. Feldman (Ed.), *Applications of nonverbal behavioral theories and research* (pp. 89-115). Hillsdale, NJ: Lawrence Erlbaum.

Blau, P. M. (1964). *Exchange and power in social life.* New York: John Wiley.

Brandt, R. (1988). How service marketers can identify value-enhancing service elements. *Journal of Services Marketing, 2,* 35-41.

Brockner, J., Pressman, B., Cabitt, J., & Moran, P. (1982). Nonverbal intimacy, sex, and compliance: A field study. *Journal of Nonverbal Behavior, 6,* 253-258.

Brownlow, S. (1992). Seeing is believing: Facial appearance, credibility, and attitude change. *Journal of Nonverbal Behavior, 16,* 101-115.

Brownlow, S., & Zebrowitz, L. A. (1990). Facial appearance, gender, and credibility in television commercials. *Journal of Nonverbal Behavior, 14,* 51-60.

Bull, R., & Robinson, G. R. (1981). The influences of eye-gaze, style of dress, and locality on the amounts of money donated to a charity. *Human Relations, 34,* 895-905.

Buller, D. B. (1987). Communication apprehension and reactions to proxemic violations. *Journal of Nonverbal Behavior, 11,* 13-25.

Buller, D. B., & Aune, R. K. (1988). The effects of vocalics and nonverbal sensitivity on compliance. *Human Communication Research, 14,* 301-332.

Buller, D. B., & Burgoon, J. K. (1986). The effects of vocalics and nonverbal sensitivity on compliance. *Human Communication Research, 13,* 126-144.

Buller, D. B., LePoire, B. A., Aune, R. K., & Eloy, S. V. (1992). Social perceptions as mediators of the effect of speech rate similarity on compliance. *Human Communication Research, 19,* 286-311.

Burgoon, J. K. (1978). A communication model of personal space violations: Explication and an initial test. *Human Communication Research, 4,* 129-142.

Burgoon, J. K. (1983). Nonverbal violations of expectations. In J. M. Wiemann & R. P. Harrison (Eds.), *Nonverbal interaction* (pp. 77-112). Beverly Hills, CA: Sage.

Burgoon, J. K. (1991). Relational message interpretations of touch, conversational distance, and posture. *Journal of Nonverbal Behavior, 15,* 233-258.

Burgoon, J. K. (1992). Applying a comparative approach to nonverbal expectancy violations theory. In J. Blumler, K. E. Rosengren, & J. M. McLeod (Eds.), *Comparatively speaking: Communication and culture across space and time* (pp. 53-69). Newbury Park, CA: Sage.

Burgoon, J. K. (1993). Interpersonal expectations, expectancy violations, and emotional communication. *Journal of Language and Social Psychology, 12,* 13-21.

Burgoon, J. K. (1994). Nonverbal signals. In M. L. Knapp & G. R. Miller (Eds.), *Handbook of interpersonal communication* (2nd ed., pp. 229-285). Thousand Oaks, CA: Sage.

Burgoon, J. K., & Aho, L. (1982). Three field experiments on the effects of conversational distance. *Communication Monographs, 49,* 71-88.

Burgoon, J. K., Bengtsson, B., Bonito, J., Ramirez, A., Jr., & Dunbar, N. E. (1999, January). *Designing interfaces to maximize the quality of collaborative work.* Paper presented at the Hawaii International Conference on Computer and Systems Sciences, Maui, HI.

Burgoon, J. K., Birk, T., & Pfau, M. (1990). Nonverbal behaviors, persuasion, and credibility. *Human Communication Research, 17,* 140-169.

Burgoon, J. K., Buller, D. B., Hale, J. L., & deTurck, M. A. (1984). Relational messages associated with nonverbal behaviors. *Human Communication Research, 10,* 351-378.

Burgoon, J. K. Buller, D. B., & Woodall, W. G. (1996). *Nonverbal communication: The unspoken dialogue.* New York: McGraw-Hill.

Burgoon, J. K., & Burgoon, M. (2001). Expectancy theories. In W. P. Robinson and H. Giles (Eds.), *Handbook of language and social psychology* (2nd ed, pp. 79-101). Sussex, UK: Wiley.

Burgoon, J. K., Coker, D. A., & Coker, R. A. (1986). Communicative effects of gaze behavior: A test of two contrasting explanations. *Human Communication Research, 12,* 495-524.

Burgoon, J. K., & Dunbar, N. E. (1998, February). *Interpersonal dominance as a situationally, interactionally, and relationally contingent social skill.* Paper presented at the annual conference of the Western States Communication Association, Denver, CO.

Burgoon, J. K., & Dunbar, N. E. (2000). An interactionist perspective on dominance-submission: Interpersonal dominance as a dynamic, situationally contingent social skill. *Communication Monographs, 67,* 96-121.

Burgoon, J. K., & Hale, J. L. (1988). Nonverbal expectancy violations: Model elaboration and application to immediacy behaviors. *Communication Monographs, 55,* 58-79.

Burgoon, J. K., Johnson, M. L., & Koch, P. T. (1998). The nature and measurement of interpersonal dominance. *Communication Monographs, 64,* 308-335.

Burgoon, J. K., & Jones, S. B. (1976). Toward a theory of personal space expectations and their violations. *Human Communication Research, 2,* 131-146.

Burgoon, J. K., Kelley, D. L., Newton, D. A., & Keeley-Dyreson, M. P. (1989). The nature of arousal and nonverbal indices. *Human Communication Research, 16,* 217-255.

Burgoon, J. K., & Le Poire, B. A. (1993). Effects of communication expectancies, actual communication, and expectancy disconfirmation on evaluations of communicators and their communication behavior. *Human Communication Research, 20,* 75-107.

Burgoon, J. K., Le Poire, B. A., & Rosenthal, R. (1995). Effects of preinteraction expectancies and target communication on perceiver reciprocity and compensation in dyadic interaction. *Journal of Experimental Social Psychology, 31,* 287-321.

Burgoon, J. K., Manusov, V., Mineo, P., & Hale, J. L. (1985). Effects of eye gaze on hiring, credibility, attraction and relational message interpretation. *Journal of Nonverbal Behavior, 9,* 133-146.

Burgoon, J. K., Newton, D. A., Walther, J. B., & Baesler, E. J. (1989). Nonverbal expectancy violations and conversational involvement. *Journal of Nonverbal Involvement, 13,* 97-119.

Burgoon, J. K., & Saine, T. J. (1978). *The unspoken dialogue.* Boston: Houghton Mifflin.

Burgoon, J. K., Stacks, D. W., & Burch, S. A. (1982). The role of interpersonal rewards and violations of distancing expectations in achieving influence in small groups. *Communication, 11,* 114-128.

Burgoon, J. K., Stacks, D. W., & Woodall, W. G. (1979). A communicative model of violations of distancing expectations. *Western Journal of Speech Communication, 43,* 153-167.

Burgoon, J. K., Stern, L. A., & Dillman, L. (1995). *Dyadic adaptation: Dyadic interactional pattern.* New York: Cambridge University Press.

Burgoon, J. K., & Walther, J. B. (1990). Nonverbal expectancies and the consequences of violations. *Human Communication Research, 17,* 232-265.

Burgoon, J. K., Walther, J. B., & Baesler, E. J. (1992). Interpretations, evaluations, and consequences of interpersonal touch. *Human Communication Research, 19,* 237-263.

Butler, S., & Roesel, K. (1989). Research note: The influence of dress on students' perceptions of teacher characteristics. *Clothing and Textiles Research Journal, 7*(3), 57-59.

Byrne, D. (1961). Interpersonal attraction and attitude similarity. *Journal of Abnormal and Social Psychology, 62,* 713-715.

Byrne, D. (1971). *The attraction paradigm.* New York: Academic Press.

Byrne, D., Ervin, C. R., & Lamberth, J. (1970). Continuity between the experimental study of attraction and real-life computer dating. *Journal of Personality and Social Psychology, 16,* 157-165.

Cadotte, E. R., Woodruff, R. B., & Jenkins, R. L. (1987). Expectations and norms in models of consumer satisfaction. *Journal of Marketing Research, 24,* 305-314.

Chaiken, S. (1979). Communicator physical attractiveness and persuasion. *Journal of Personality and Social Psychology, 37,* 1387-1397.

Chaiken, S. (1986). Physical appearance of social influence. In C. P. Herman, M. P. Zanna, & E. T. Higgins (Eds.), *Physical appearance, stigma, and social behavior: The Ontario Symposium* (Vol. 3, pp. 143-177). Hillsdale, NJ: Lawrence Erlbaum.

Cooper, J., Darley, J. M., & Henderson, J. E. (1974). On the effectiveness of deviant- and conventional-appearing communicators: A field experiment. *Journal of Personality and Social Psychology, 55,* 937-949.

Culnan, M. J., & Markus, M. L. (1987). Information technologies. In F. M. Jablin, L. L. Putnam, K. H. Roberts, & L. W. Porter (Eds.), *Handbook of organizational communication: An interdisciplinary perspective* (pp. 420-443). Newbury Park, CA: Sage.

Darley, J. M., & Cooper, J. (1972). The "Clean for Gene" phenomenon: The effect of students' appearance on political campaigning. *Journal of Applied Social Psychology, 2,* 24-33.

Darley, J. M., & Fazio, R. H. (1980). Expectancy confirmation processes arising in the social interaction sequence. *American Psychologist, 35,* 867-881.

Davis, M. A. (1992). *Age and dress of professors: Influence on students' first impressions of teaching effectiveness.* Unpublished doctoral dissertation, Virginia Polytechnic Institute and State University, Blacksburg.

DePaulo, B. M., & Rosenthal, R. (1979). Ambivalence, discrepancy, and deception in nonverbal communication. In R. Rosenthal (Ed.), *Skill in nonverbal communication: Individual differences* (pp. 204-248). Cambridge, MA: Oelgeschlager, Gunn, & Hain.

Dion, K. K., Berscheid, E., & Walster, E. (1972). What is beautiful is good. *Journal of Personality and Social Psychology, 24,* 285-290.

Dovidio, J. F., & Ellyson, S. L. (1982). Decoding visual dominance: Attributions of power based on relative percentages of looking while speaking and looking while listening. *Social Psychology Quarterly, 45,* 106-113.

Dovidio, J. F., & Ellyson, S. L. (1985). Patterns of visual dominance behavior in humans. In S. L. Ellyson & J. F. Dovidio (Eds.), *Power, dominance, and nonverbal communication* (pp. 129-149). New York: Springer-Verlag.

Duck, S. (1994). *Meaningful relationships: Talking, sense, and relating.* Thousand Oaks, CA: Sage.

Duck, S. (1998). *Human relationships* (3rd ed.). Thousand Oaks, CA: Sage.

Ellyson, S. L., Dovidio, J. F., Corson, R. L., & Vinicur, D. L. (1980). Visual dominance behavior in female dyads: Situational and personality factors. *Social Psychology Quarterly, 43,* 328-336.

Emerson, R. M. (1962). Power-dependence relations. *American Sociological Review, 27,* 31-41.

Emerson, R. M. (1976). Social exchange theory. In A. Inkeles, J. Coleman, & N. Smelser (Eds.), *Annual review of sociology* (pp. 335-362). Palo Alto, CA: Annual Reviews.

Ernest, R. C., & Cooper, R. E. (1974). "Hey Mister, do you have any change?": Two real world studies of proxemic effects on compliance with a mundane request. *Personality and Social Psychology Bulletin, 1,* 158-159.

Escudero, V., Rogers, L. E., & Gutierrez, E. (1997). Patterns of relational control and nonverbal affect in clinic and nonclinic couples. *Journal of Social and Personal Relationships, 14,* 5-29.

Exline, R. V. (1963). Explorations in the process of person perception: Visual interaction in relation to competition, sex, and need for affiliation. *Journal of Personality, 31,* 1-20.

Feingold, A. (1992). Good-looking people are not what we think. *Psychological Bulletin, 111,* 304-341.

Fisher, J. D., Rytting, M., & Heslin, R. (1976). Hands touching hands: Affective and evaluative effects of an interpersonal touch. *Sociometry, 39,* 416-421.

Fisk, R. P., & Young, C. E. (1985). Disconfirmation of equity expectations: Effects of consumer satisfaction with services. In E. C. Hirschman & M. Holbrook (Eds.), *Advances in consumer research* (Vol. 12, pp. 340-345). Provo, UT: Association for Consumer Research.

Foa, E., & Foa, U. (1974). *Societal structures of the mind.* Springfield, IL: Charles C Thomas.

French, J. R. P., Jr., & Raven, B. (1959). The bases of social power. In D. Cartwright (Ed.), *Studies in social power* (pp. 150-167). Ann Arbor, MI: Institute for Social Research.

Gifford, R. (1982). Projected interpersonal distance and orientation choices: Personality, sex, and social situation. *Social Psychology Quarterly, 45,* 145-152.

Giles, H., & Chavasse, W. (1975). Communication length as a function of dress style and social status. *Perceptual and Motor Skills, 40,* 961-962.

Giles, H., Coupland, N., & Coupland, J. (1991). Accommodation theory: Communication, context, and consequence. In H. Giles, J. Coupland, & N. Coupland (Eds.), *Contexts of accommodation: Developments in applied sociolinguistics* (pp. 1-68). Cambridge, UK: Cambridge University Press.

Gitter, A. G., Black, H., & Fishman, J. E. (1975). Effects of race, sex, nonverbal communication, and verbal communication on perceptions of leadership. *Sociology and Social Research, 60,* 46-57.

Glick, P., DeMorest, J. A., & Hotze, C. A. (1988). Keeping your distance: Group membership, personal space, and requests for small favors. *Journal of Applied Social Psychology, 18,* 315-330.

Goldman, M., Kiyohara, O., & Pfannensteil, D. A. (1984). Interpersonal touch, social labeling, and the foot-in-the-door effect. *Journal of Social Psychology, 125,* 143-147.

Gottman, J., Markman, H., & Notarius, C. (1977). The topography of marital conflict: A sequential analysis of verbal and nonverbal behavior. *Journal of Marriage and the Family, 39,* 461-477.

Hall, J. A. (1980). Voice tone and persuasion. *Journal of Personality and Social Psychology, 38,* 924-934.

Hammermesh, D. S., & Biddle, J. E. (1994). Beauty and the labor market. *American Economic Review, 84,* 1174-1195.

Harris, M. J., & Rosenthal, R. (1985). Mediation of interpersonal expectancy effects: 31 meta-analyses. *Psychological Bulletin, 97,* 363-386.

Hayduk, L. A. (1983). Personal space: Where we now stand. *Psychological Bulletin, 94,* 293-335.

Heider, F. (1958). *The psychology of interpersonal relations.* New York: John Wiley.

Henley, N. M. (1995). Body politics revisited: What do we know today? In P. J. Kalbfleisch & M. J. Cody (Eds.), *Gender, power, and communication in human relationships* (pp. 27-61). Hillsdale, NJ: Lawrence Erlbaum.

Hensley, W. E. (1981). The effects of attire, location, and sex on aiding behavior: A similarity explanation. *Journal of Nonverbal Behavior, 6,* 3-11.

Heslin, R., & Alper, T. (1983). Touch: A bonding gesture. In J. M. Wiemann & R. P. Harrison (Eds.), *Nonverbal interaction* (pp. 47-75). Beverly Hills, CA: Sage.

Hickson, M. L., III, & Stacks, D. W. (1993). *Nonverbal communication: Studies and applications* (3rd ed.). Madison, WI: Brown & Benchmark.

Homans, G. C. (1958). Social behavior as exchange. *American Journal of Sociology, 62,* 597-606.

Hornik, J. (1992). Tactile stimulation and consumer response. *Journal of Consumer Research, 19,* 449-458.

Hovland, C., Janis, I. L., & Kelly, H. H. (1953). *Communication and persuasion.* New Haven, CT: Yale University Press.

Imada, A. S., & Hakel, M. D. (1977). Influence of nonverbal communication and rater proximity on impressions and decisions in simulated employment interviews. *Journal of Applied Psychology, 62*, 295-300.

Jaworski, A. (1993). *The power of silence: Social and pragmatic perspectives.* Newbury Park, CA: Sage.

Jones, E. E. (1986). Interpreting interpersonal behavior: The effects of expectancies. *Science, 234*, 41-46.

Jones, S. E. (1994). *The right touch.* Cresskill, NJ: Hampton.

Jussim, L. (1990). Social reality and social problems: The role of expectancies. *Journal of Social Issues, 46*, 9-34.

Keating, C. F., & Heltman, K. R. (1994). Dominance and deception in children and adults: Are leaders the best misleaders? *Personality and Social Psychology Bulletin, 20*, 312-321.

Kelman, H. C. (1958). Compliance, identification, and internalization: Three processes of attitude change. *Journal of Conflict Resolution, 2*, 51-60.

Kimble, C. E., & Musgrove, J. I. (1988). Dominance in arguing mixed-sex dyads: Visual dominance patterns, talking time, and speech loudness. *Journal of Research in Personality, 22*, 1-16.

Kleinfeld, J. S. (1974). Effects of nonverbal warmth on learning of Eskimo and White children. *Journal of Social Psychology, 92*, 3-90.

Kleinke, C. L. (1977). Compliance to requests made by gazing and touching experimenters in field settings. *Journal of Experimental Social Psychology, 13*, 218-223.

Kleinke, C. L., Bustos, A. A., Meeker, F. B., & Staneski, R. A. (1973). Effects of self-attributed and other-attributed gaze in interpersonal evaluations between males and females. *Journal of Experimental Social Psychology, 9*, 154-163.

Kleinke, C. L., & Singer, D. A. (1979). Influence of gaze on compliance with demanding and conciliatory requests in a field setting. *Personality and Social Psychology Bulletin, 5*, 386-390.

Konecni, V. J., Libuser, L. Morton, H., & Ebbesen, E. B. (1975). Effects of a violation of personal space on escape and helping responses. *Journal of Experimental Social Psychology, 11*, 288-299.

Krauss, R. M., Apple, W., Morency, N., Wenzel, C., & Winton, W. (1981). Verbal, vocal, and visible factors in judgements of another's affect. *Journal of Personality and Social Psychology, 40*, 312-319.

Kurklen, R., & Kassinove, H. (1991). Effects of profanity, touch, and subjects' religiosity on perceptions of a psychologist and behavioral compliance. *Journal of Social Psychology, 131*, 899-901.

Lamb, T. A. (1981). Nonverbal and paraverbal control in dyads and triads: Sex or power differences? *Social Psychology Quarterly, 44*, 49-53.

Lambert, S. (1972). Reactions to a stranger as a function of style of dress. *Perceptual and Motor Skills, 35*, 711-712.

Lawler, E. J. (1986). Bilateral deterrence and conflict spirals: A theoretical analysis. In E. J. Lawler (Ed.), *Advances in group processes* (Vol. 3, pp. 107-130). Greenwich, CT: JAI.

Lawler, E. J. (1992). Power processes in bargaining. *Sociological Quarterly, 33*(1), 17-34.

Lawler, E. J., & Bacharach, S. B. (1987). Comparison of dependence and punitive forms of power. *Social Forces, 66*, 446-462.

Leffler, A., Gillespie, D. L., & Conaty, J. C. (1982). The effects of status differentiation on nonverbal behavior. *Social Psychology Quarterly, 45*, 153-161.

Lefkowitz, M., Blake, R. R., & Mouton, J. S. (1955). Status factors in pedestrian violations of traffic signals. *Journal of Abnormal and Social Psychology, 51*, 704-706.

Le Poire, B. A., & Burgoon, J. K. (1994). Two contrasting explanations of involvement violations: Expectancy violations theory and discrepancy arousal theory. *Human Communication Research, 20*, 560-591.

Le Poire, B. A., & Burgoon, J. K. (1996). Usefulness of differentiating arousal responses within communication theories: Orienting response of defensive arousal within theories of expectancy violation. *Communication Monographs, 63*, 208-230.

Le Poire, B. A., & Yoshimura, S. M. (1999). The effects of expectancies and actual communication on nonverbal adaptation and communication outcomes: A test of interaction adaptation theory. *Communication Monographs, 66*, 1-30.

Lips, H. M. (1991). *Women, men, and power.* Mountain View, CA: Mayfield.

McPeek, R. W., & Edwards, J. D. (1975). Expectancy disconfirmation and attitude change. *Journal of Social Psychology, 96,* 193-208.

Mehrabian, A., & Wiener, M. (1967). Nonverbal concomitants of perceived and intended persuasiveness. *Journal of Personality and Social Psychology, 6,* 37-58.

Millar, F. E., & Rogers, L. E. (1987). Relational dimensions of interpersonal dynamics. In M. E. Roloff & G. E. Miller (Eds.), *Interpersonal processes: New directions in communication research* (pp. 117-139). Newbury Park, CA: Sage.

Miller, N., Maruyama, G., Beaber, R. J., & Valone, K. (1976). Speed of speech and persuasion. *Journal of Personality and Social Psychology, 34,* 615-624.

Molm, L. D., & Cook, K. S. (1995). Social exchange and exchange networks. In K. S. Cook, G. A. Fine, & J. S. House (Eds.), *Sociological perspectives on social psychology* (pp. 209-235). Boston: Allyn & Bacon.

Neuberg, S. L. (1996). Expectancy influences in social interaction. In P. M. Gollwitzer & J. A. Bargh (Eds.), *The psychology of action* (pp. 529-554). New York: Guilford.

Newcomb, T. M. (1961). *The acquaintance process.* New York: Holt, Rinehart & Winston.

Noller, P. (1980). Gaze in married couples. *Journal of Nonverbal Behavior, 5,* 115-129.

Noller, P. (1984). *Nonverbal communication and marital interaction.* Oxford, UK: Pergamon.

Norman, R. (1976). When what is said is important: A comparison of expert and attractive sources. *Journal of Experimental Social Psychology, 12,* 294-300.

Pallak, S. R. (1983). Salience of a communicator's physical attractiveness and persuasion: A heuristic versus systematic processing interpretation. *Social Cognition, 2,* 158-170.

Pallak, S. R., Murroni, E., & Koch, J. (1983). Communicator effectiveness and expertise, emotional versus rational appeals, and persuasion: A heuristic versus systematic processing interpretation. *Social Cognition, 2,* 122-141.

Patterson, M. L. (1983). *Nonverbal behavior: A functional perspective.* New York: Springer-Verlag.

Patterson, M. L., Powell, J. L., & Lenihan, M. G. (1986). Touch, compliance, and interpersonal affect. *Journal of Nonverbal Behavior, 10,* 41-50.

Pope, B., & Siegman, A. W. (1966). Ambiguity and verbal fluency in the TAT. *Journal of Consulting Psychology, 30,* 239-245.

Ridgeway, C. L., & Berger, J. (1986). Expectations, legitimation, and dominance behavior in task groups. *American Sociological Review, 62,* 218-235.

Ridgeway, C. L., Diekema, D., & Johnson, C. (1995). Legitimacy, compliance, and gender in peer groups. *Social Psychology Quarterly, 58,* 298-311.

Ridgeway, C. L., Johnson, C., & Diekema, D. (1994). External status, legitimacy, and compliance in male and female groups. *Social Forces, 72,* 1051-1077.

Ridgeway, C. L., & Walker, H. A. (1995). Status structures. In K. S. Cook, G. A. Fine, & J. S. House (Eds.), *Sociological perspectives on social psychology* (pp. 281-310). Boston: Allyn & Bacon.

Riggio, R. E. (1986). Assessment of basic social skills. *Journal of Personality and Social Psychology, 51,* 649-660.

Riggio, R. E., Tucker, J., & Throckmorton, B. (1988). Social skills and deception ability. *Personality and Social Psychology Bulletin, 13,* 568-577.

Rogers, L. E., Castleton, A., & Lloyd, S. A. (1996). Relational control and physical aggression in satisfying marital relationships. In D. D. Cahn & S. A. Lloyd (Eds.), *Family violence from a communication perspective* (pp. 218-239). Thousand Oaks, CA: Sage.

Rogers, L. E., & Farace, R. V. (1975). Analysis of relational communication in dyads: New measurement procedures. *Human Communication Research, 1,* 222-239.

Rogers, W. T., & Jones, S. E. (1975). Effects of dominance tendencies on floor holding and interruption behavior in dyadic interaction. *Human Communication Research, 1,* 113-122.

Rogers-Millar, E. L., & Millar, F. E. (1979). Domineeringness and dominance: A transactional view. *Human Communication Research, 5,* 238-246.

Rosenberg, S. W., Kahn, S., & Tran, T. (1991). Creating a political image: Shaping appearance and manipulating the vote. *Political Behavior, 13,* 345-367.

Rosenthal, R. (1976). *Experimenter expectancy effects in behavioral research* (enlarged ed.). New York: Irvington.

Rosenthal, R. (1985). Nonverbal cues in the mediation of interpersonal expectancy effects. In A. W. Siegman & S. Feldstein (Eds.), *Multichannel integrations of nonverbal behavior* (pp. 105-128). Hillsdale, NJ: Lawrence Erlbaum.

Rosenthal, R. (1993). Interpersonal expectations: Some antecedents and some consequences. In P. D. Blanck (Ed.), *Interpersonal expectations: Theory, research, and applications* (pp. 3-24). New York: Cambridge University Press.

Rosenthal, R., Hall, J. A., Dimatteo, M. R., Rogers, P. L., & Archer, D. (1979). *Sensitivity to nonverbal communication: The PONS test.* Baltimore, MD: Johns Hopkins University Press.

Rubin, Z. (1970). The measurement of romantic love. *Journal of Personality and Social Psychology, 16,* 265-273.

Schwartz, B., Tesser, A., & Powell, E. (1982). Dominance cues in nonverbal behavior. *Social Psychology Quarterly, 45,* 114-120.

Segrin, C. (1993). The effects of nonverbal behavior on outcomes of compliance gaining attempts. *Communication Studies, 44,* 169-187.

Siegel, S. M., Friedlander, M. L., & Heatherington, L. (1992). Nonverbal relational control in family communication. *Journal of Nonverbal Behavior, 16,* 117-139.

Siegman, A. W. (1987). The telltale voice: Nonverbal messages of verbal communication. In A. W. Siegman & S. Feldstein (Eds.), *Nonverbal behaviors and communication* (2nd ed., pp. 351-434). Hillsdale, NJ: Lawrence Erlbaum.

Snyder, M. (1984). When belief creates reality. In L. Berkowitz (Ed.), *Advances in experimental social psychology* (Vol. 18, pp. 247-305). New York: Academic Press.

Snyder, M., Grether, J., & Keller, K. (1974). Staring and compliance: A field experiment on hitchhiking. *Journal of Applied Social Psychology, 4,* 165-170.

Snyder, M., & Swann, W. B., Jr. (1978). Behavioral confirmation in social interaction: From social

perception to social reality. *Journal of Experimental Social Psychology, 14,* 148-162.

Snyder, M., Tanke, E. D., & Berscheid, E. (1977). Social perception and interpersonal behavior: On the self-fulfilling nature of social stereotypes. *Journal of Personality and Social Psychology, 35,* 656-666.

Spears, R., & Lea, M. (1992). Social influence and the influence of the "social" in computer-mediated communication. In M. Lea (Ed.), *Contexts of computer-mediated communication* (pp. 30-65). London: Harvester-Wheatsheaf.

Stoner, G. M., Burgoon, J. K., Bonito, J. A., Ramirez, A., Jr., & Dunbar, N. (1999, May). *Nonverbal cues in mediated communication.* Paper presented to the annual meeting of the International Communication Association, San Francisco.

Straus, M. A. (1979). Measuring intrafamily conflict and violence: The Conflict Tactics Scale. *Journal of Marriage and the Family, 41,* 75-88.

Taylor, D. A., & Altman, I. (1987). Communication in interpersonal relationships: Social penetration processes. In M. E. Roloff & G. R. Miller (Eds.), *Interpersonal processes: New directions in communication research* (pp. 257-277). Newbury Park, CA: Sage.

Thibaut, J. W., & Kelley, H. H. (1959). *The social psychology of groups.* New York: John Wiley.

Tse, D. K., & Wilton, P. C. (1988). Models of consumer satisfaction formation: An extension. *Journal of Marketing Research, 25,* 204-212.

Walther, J. B. (1996). Computer-mediated communication: Impersonal, interpersonal, and hyperpersonal interaction. *Communication Research, 23,* 3-43.

Walther, J. B., Slovacek, C. L., & Tidwell, L. C. (1999). *Is a picture worth a thousand words? Photographic image in long-term and short-term computer-mediated communication.* Paper presented to the annual meeting of the International Communication Association, San Francisco.

Wiemann, J. M. (1977). A model of communicative competence. *Human Communication Research, 3,* 195-213.

Willis, F. N., & Hamm, H. K. (1980). The use of interpersonal touch in securing compliance. *Journal of Nonverbal Behavior, 5,* 49-55.

Winter, D. G. (1973). *The power motive.* New York: Macmillan.

Woodall, W. G., & Burgoon, J. K. (1983). Talking fast and changing attitudes: A critique and clarification. *Journal of Nonverbal Behavior, 8,* 126-142.

Woodruff, R. B., Cadotte, E. R., & Jenkins, R. L. (1983). Modeling consumer satisfaction processes using experience-based norms. *Journal of Marketing Research, 20,* 296-304.

Workman, J. E., Johnson, K. K., & Hadeler, B. (1993). The influence of clothing on students'

interpretative and extended inferences about a teaching assistant. *College Student Journal, 27*(1), 119-128.

Zahn, G. L. (1973). Cognitive integration of verbal and vocal information in spoken sentences. *Journal of Experimental Social Psychology, 9,* 320-334.

Zuckerman, M., Hodgins, H., & Miyake, K. (1990). The vocal attractiveness stereotype: Replication and elaboration. *Journal of Nonverbal Behavior, 14,* 97-112.

PART V

CONTEXTS

24

Persuading in the Small Group Context

FRANKLIN J. BOSTER
MICHAEL G. CRUZ

From LeBon's (1896) fascination with mobs and Tarde's (1903) interest in imitation to studies of social impact (Latane, 1996) and legal decision making (Boster, Hunter, & Hale, 1991), the ways in which group members influence one another has occupied the attention of investigators from many and diverse disciplines. Contemporary scholarship considers as axiomatic the proposition that social influence occurs via several conceptually distinct processes. This chapter focuses on the manner in which one process of social influence, persuasion, operates in group settings. The chapter commences with a brief discussion of the focal terms *"persuasion"* and *"group."* The next several sections explore the various manifestations of persuasion within group settings, emphasizing the power of persuasion in producing group uniformity, and the conditions that contribute to its effectiveness or ineffectiveness. The chapter concludes with a sketch of some directions for future research.

A useful distinction made by Festinger (1953) facilitates the first goal of this chapter, namely, clarifying the use of the term *persuasion*. Festinger distinguished two forms of social influence or, as he put it, compliant behavior. He referred to *public conformity with private acceptance* as instances in which targets of social influence attempts behave in a manner both consistent with an influencing agent's message recommendations and consistent with their own attitudes. By contrast, *public conformity without private acceptance* refers to cases in which targets behave in a manner consistent with an influencing agent's message recommendations but inconsistent with their own attitudes.

Subsequently, Deutsch and Gerard (1955) made a similar, albeit not isomorphic, distinction employing the phrases *informational influence* and *normative influence* to refer to public conformity with private acceptance and public conformity without public acceptance, respectively. Yet later, Kelman (1961) used the terms *internalization* and *compliance* to refer to processes very similar to public conformity with and without private acceptance, respectively.

Within this intellectual tradition, the notion of internal (or private) acceptance of message recommendations distinguishes persuasion from other forms of social influence. And in this tradition, internal (or private) acceptance of message recommendations indicates a lack of discrepancy between either the valence or strength of an attitude advocated in a message and either the valence or strength of the attitude held internally by the target of the influence attempt. Consistent with this line of thought, in this chapter a *persuasion attempt* refers to an effort to change, reinforce, or shape the attitude of an other by the transmission of a message (cf. Bettinghaus, 1981), and the extent to which *persuasion* occurs then refers to the degree to which the persuasion attempt succeeds.

Despite the conceptual independence of Festinger's two forms of social influence, a substantial body of research indicates an empirical relationship between them. For instance, although theorists posit differing causal mechanisms, Festinger and Carlsmith's (1959) forced compliance experiment demonstrates that obtaining conformity may lead to the internalization of attitudes (cf. Bem, 1965, Romer, 1979). Because of this lack of empirical independence, investigators find it difficult to distinguish the two in natural settings, and consequently they seek tests for separating them. Kiesler and Kiesler (1969) provided two criteria to facilitate making this distinction: surveillance and resistance. The former alludes to the extent to which the target will continue to conform in the influencing agent's absence. When targets continue to conform, even in the influencing agent's absence, one infers that persuasion has occurred, but when conformity wanes in the influencing agent's absence, one rejects this conclusion

(see, e.g., Coch & French, 1948). The latter, more rigorous test alludes to the extent to which the target continues to conform when an outside party attempts to convince the target not to conform (see, e.g., Gerard, 1954). Substantial resistance results in the attribution that a substantial amount of persuasion has occurred, and a lack of resistance yields the opposite inference.

Ambiguity marks the manner in which scholars use the term *group* and makes difficult accomplishing the second goal of this section. One point of relative agreement revolves around the criterion of size. Certainly, groups have multiple members, although debate surfaces over whether or not dyads constitute groups. On the other hand, size provides little conceptual aid as an upper bound. Hence, although a size of two or three as a minimum provides a necessary condition to meet the classification of a group, what constitutes a sufficient condition provides a greater challenge. In a review of definitions of the term, Shaw (1981) characterized groups as collections of interdependent persons who interact frequently, have a collective identity, pursue common goals, have an organizational structure, and satisfy one another's needs. The greater the extent to which collections of persons have these attributes, the higher the probability that they constitute a group. Or considering *group* and *nongroup* as opposite anchors of a continuum rather than as a qualitative distinction, the greater the extent to which a set of persons possesses these qualities, the greater the extent to which that set of persons possesses the attribute of "groupness." In this chapter, the use of the term *group* employs Shaw's criteria.

MANIFESTATIONS OF PERSUASION IN GROUPS

To observers of small groups, scholars and nonscholars alike, the uniformity of beliefs, values, and attitudes among group members proves striking. At least two forces contribute to this commonly observed uniformity. First, human patterns of affiliation do not occur randomly. Rather, for various reasons, persons tend to affiliate with certain people to the exclusion of others. For instance, persons may join a group such as the Chamber of Commerce, the American Civil Liberties Union, or a local health spa because of a desire to pursue certain shared interests or shared goals. These common interests or goals tend to draw persons similar in beliefs, values, attitudes, and behavior, suggesting to scholars that birds of a feather flock together and implying that birds of differing feathers go their separate ways (Byrne, 1971; Newcomb, 1961; but see Rosenbaum, 1986; Sunnafrank, 1992).

Nevertheless, affiliation patterns alone cannot account for the magnitude of group uniformity. In addition, the experience of frequent message exchange with interdependent others results in mutual influence, and group members' similarity in outlook and behavior increases. Subsequently, these similarities frequently lead to the development of group norms, which provide an additional force promoting group member uniformity. Consequently, social influence processes, such as (but not restricted to) persuasion, serve to enhance group uniformity, both directly and indirectly.

Scholars face obstacles when attempting to assess the extent to which persuasion, as opposed to other forms of social influence, produces, sustains, and reinforces the uniformity of group member beliefs, values, attitudes, and behavior. In particular, studies performed in noncontrolled research settings pose formidable problems. Consider, for example, the challenges involved in parsing the roles of varying forms of social influence such as compliance, persuasion, identification, and legitimate power in processes commonly studied in noncontrolled settings, such as child

socialization (e.g., Harris, 1995, 1998) and organizational socialization (Jablin, 1984), or to naturally occurring events, such as the *Challenger* disaster (Gouran, Hirokawa, & Martz, 1986) and the Cuban Missile Crisis (Janis, 1982). No doubt, several forms of social influence contributed to these processes and events. In such cases, the complexity of the phenomenon, the lack of focus on distinguishing types of social influence, and the paucity of studies designed to measure the effect of the various forms of influence contribute to challenge those who seek to understand the impact of *persuasion* in small group settings. Consequently, few data can be found that address the issue directly.

The challenge measuring these effects renders the study of more difficult questions, such as comparisons of the relative effectiveness of the varying forms of influence and the relative effectiveness of varying kinds of messages in activating such processes, extremely difficult. Knowing about such matters has theoretical and practical import, yet to our knowledge they rarely receive scrutiny.

Yet some reasonable answers can be given to simpler questions. The remainder of this section poses three of these simpler questions. First, do group members persuade one another, and if so, then how, under what conditions, and to what extent? Second, do influencing agents have the ability to persuade members of groups to which they do not belong, and if so, then how, to what extent, and under what conditions? Third, do groups have the ability to persuade others who are not among their members, and if so, then how, to what extent, and under what conditions?

Persuasion Within Groups

Several lines of inquiry provide evidence that, within groups, members persuade one another effectively. Some of these research programs treat group decision making as a persuasion process. Research on the choice shift represents one of the best known of these programs.

The Choice Shift. A choice shift occurs when the extremity of a group's decision (i.e., its riskiness or cautiousness) exceeds the mean of the individual group members' pre-discussion decisions. Choice shift experiments often employ choice dilemma (CD) items. These items place group members in the context of choosing between two alternative courses of action. The cautious alternative provides a reasonably rewarding outcome that, if chosen, will occur with near certainty. The risky alternative, on the other hand, provides a lucrative outcome, but one much less likely to occur (for examples, see Wallach, Kogan, & Bem, 1962). Privately, respondents mark the probability necessary for the risky option to succeed before they would select it or advise another to do so. They then discuss the item until they reach consensus. Often, investigators again obtain private individual responses after discussion.

Social comparison theory (SCT) and the persuasive arguments theory (PAT) compete as explanations of the phenomenon. SCT describes the choice shift as a normative influence phenomenon (see Laughlin & Early, 1982), whereas (pertinent to this chapter) PAT describes it as a persuasion phenomenon. PAT postulates that a pool of arguments favoring the risky alternative exists, as does a separate pool favoring the cautious alternative. For CD items that produce a risky shift, the pool of risky arguments exceeds in number and persuasiveness the pool of cautious arguments, with the opposite state of affairs holding for CD items that produce a cautious shift. Not all group members know all arguments, but discussion results in argument sharing, so that during discussion members obtain a larger sample of the argument pools (i.e., they receive exposure to arguments novel to them). Because of the skewness in these argument pools, discussion results in the average group member learning of more reasons (and being persuaded by them) to accept the risky alternative for any CD item that yields a risky shift as well as more reasons to accept the cautious alternative for any CD item that yields a cautious shift. Notably, then, the novelty of arguments, as well as their soundness, contributes to their persuasiveness. Consequently, after discussion group members embrace more risky decision alternatives for CD items that produce a risky shift and accept more cautious decision alternatives for any CD items that produce a cautious shift (see also Boster, Fryrear, Mongeau, & Hunter, 1982; Boster, Mayer, Hunter, & Hale, 1980).

Isenberg's (1986) review concludes that available data conform to PAT predictions. The evidence from which Isenberg reached his conclusion comes from two kinds of studies. Some count the arguments generated during discussion and correlate the frequency of pro-risk versus pro-caution arguments with the direction and magnitude of the choice shift. Inquiries of this nature find that the greater the preponderance of risky arguments in discussion, the greater the risky shift, whereas the greater the preponderance of cautious arguments in discussion, the greater the cautious shift. This observed covariation might arise from other variables that drive both the number of arguments generated and the direction and magnitude of the choice shift, for example, compliance pressures emanating from a majority subgroup. Consequently, despite strong correlations, asserting confidently that the preponderance of arguments causes the direction and magnitude of the choice shift requires other forms of evidence.

One form that such evidence might take requires examining posttest judgments for the CD items. To the extent that persuasion occurs, one would expect individual posttest judgments to equal the group decision. Both Boster et al. (1980) and Boster et al. (1982)

reported data consistent with this expectation. Specifically, these correlations exceeded .80.

Isenberg's (1986) second type of evidence involves experiments in which investigators control the arguments respondents receive. These experiments tend to report that exposure to a set of predominately risky arguments produces a risky shift, whereas exposure to a set of predominately cautious arguments produces a cautious shift. And again, they reported ample effect sizes. Therefore, in sum, the available database indicates that a persuasion process accurately explains a substantial amount of the social influence that produces the choice shift.

Although these data provide evidence consistent with the proposition that group members persuade one another, and the effect sizes reported by Isenberg (1986) establish persuasion as a powerful form of social influence in these experiments, Isenberg's analysis also indicates that normative influence plays an important role in producing the choice shift, and although he speculated that these forms of social influence may produce independent effects on the choice shift, an experiment by Boster and Mayer (1984) challenged this notion.

Boster and Mayer (1984) varied argument strength and majority position as a method of assessing the effects of informational and normative influences, respectively. They found that the majority induction worked as designed, so that participants perceived the position of the majority of group members correctly. Despite extensive pretesting, however, the argument strength induction did not work as designed. Instead, the majority induction affected participants' judgments of argument quality. Specifically, when majority group members voiced arguments, participants perceived them as more compelling than the arguments voiced by minority group members. Boster and Mayer showed that a causal process in which differential argument qual-

ity, or perceptions of the quality of pro-risk arguments less the perception of the quality of pro-cautious arguments, mediates the effect of the majority induction on the choice shift fits these data (cf. Mongeau & Garlick, 1988).

Notably, the Boster and Mayer (1984) experiment employed experimental materials that allowed participants to make clear judgments on the CD items. However, when experimental materials, particularly the response scale employed for the CD items, vary in ambiguity, the experimental outcome may differ. Boster and Hale (1989) demonstrated just such an effect. Under conditions of low (but not high) ambiguity, PAT predicted choice shifts accurately. Under conditions of high (but not low) ambiguity, SCT predicted choice shifts accurately.

These outcomes, then, challenge Isenberg's (1986) suggestion of independent effects of normative and informational influence by demonstrating the substantial covariation between them in one instance and nonadditivity among them in another. As Asch (1948) demonstrated, the meaning of a persuasive message, and hence its persuasiveness, can depend on contextual features. The number of persons advocating a message or a position may provide such an important contextual cue (see Harkins & Petty, 1981a, 1981b).

Although an adequate explanation of the choice shift must include a discussion of the persuasion process, whether or not persuasion occurs in the manner posited by PAT remains a debated issue (Meyers & Seibold, 1990). For example, Hoffman's (1961) Group Valence Model (GVM) (see also Hoffman & Kleinman, 1994); McPhee, Poole, and Seibold's (1982) Distribution of Valence Model (DVM) (see also McPhee, 1994); and Boster's Linear Discrepancy Model (LDM) (Boster et al., 1980, 1982) provide other explanations.

Hoffman and Kleinman (1994) provided a clear statement of the GVM. They explained,

The purpose of discussion is finally to establish a group preference for a particular solution. During the discussion, members attempt to persuade each other about the positive and negative attributes of each alternative, thereby building sufficient positive valence in the group for one solution such that it will be adopted. The group valence model (GVM) assumes that individual valences for different solutions, reflecting although the members' personal feelings about them, are not important determinants of the likelihood that a solution will be adopted. Rather, it is the magnitude of the *group* valence for a solution that determines its adoption. (pp. 36-37)

So the GVM calculates, for each decision option that group members consider, the number of positive valence comments less the number of negative valence comments. The GVM predicts that groups choose the *decision option* with the largest difference score (i.e., with the highest valence).[1]

The McPhee et al. (1982; see also McPhee, 1994) DVM, on the other hand, concludes that individual group member valences drive group decision making. After discussion, investigators calculate the valence of *individual group member* comments. They then apply a decision criterion, such as a majority rule, to these data. The option with highest valence for the most group members serves as the group decision predicted by the model.[2]

Although these models derive from different views of the group decision-making process, they generally make similar predictions about group decision-making outcomes (e.g., Meyers & Brashers, 1998, pp. 276-277). Perhaps the clearest situation in which they make different predictions occurs when a minority subgroup makes numerous positive valence comments in favor of one decision alternative, say X, and a majority subgroup supports a different decision alternative, say Y, albeit less vociferously. The GVM predicts a group deci-

sion of X; the DVM predicts Y. Relatively few groups provide data of this sort that allow a critical test of these models. In a recent experiment, Meyers and Brashers (1998) found that, when discussing CD items, both models predicted the choice shift accurately, but that of five such groups, four produced decisions consistent with the DVM and one produced the decision predicted by the GVM.

Although the centrality of arguments, particularly their valences, characterizes these models, neither specifies the form of social influence that results in group decisions. At various points, proponents of each position acknowledge that compromise and negotiation, as well as persuasion, serve to promote group members reaching consensus. Neither does the GVM or the DVM specify the process by which group members persuade one another. The LDM, on the other hand, does so explicitly.

The development of the LDM (see Boster et al., 1980, 1982, 1991), a version of French's (1956) theory of communication discrepancy, begins by asserting that arguments advocate an attitudinal position. Because one may array attitudes on a continuum, so too may one array arguments on the same continuum. Consequently, it makes sense to speak of persons comparing their attitude to the attitude advocated in an argument. French's theory makes this comparison process central to attitude change and hence to the group decision-making process.

The LDM examines cases in which group members enter discussion with an initial attitude toward the topic. It then posits that when a group member advances an argument, the only messages deemed relevant to predicting the group's decision, that argument advocates the group member's attitude *at the time spoken*. Notice that at various points in the discussion, this attitude may differ from the attitude held by the group member initially because in the process of discussion other group members' messages may have changed it.

The LDM then claims that the process by which attitude change occurs involves group members listening to their fellow group members' arguments, comparing them to their own attitude, and adjusting their attitude to some degree in the direction of the attitude advocated in the message. As Boster et al. (1980) demonstrated in the context of group discussion, this model predicts that if group members speak with equal frequency, the position on which they reach consensus equals the mean of the individual group members' pre-discussion attitudes. But if group members speak with unequal frequency, the position on which they reach consensus equals a *weighted mean* of the individual group members' pre-discussion attitudes. Specifically, speaking frequency serves to weight the pre-discussion attitudes, such that the positions of those members who speak more frequently influence the group decision more heavily.

Data from two experiments demonstrate that the unequal speaking version of the LDM predicts the valence and magnitude of the choice shift accurately (Boster et al., 1980, 1982).[3] In the main, risky shifts occur because the group members with risky pre-discussion attitudes present more arguments than do group members with cautious pre-discussion attitudes. Cautious shifts occur because the group members with cautious pre-discussion attitudes present more arguments than do group members with risky pre-discussion attitudes. Presumably, as supposed by PAT, on CD items that consistently produce a risky shift, group members have more risky than cautious arguments available, with the opposite being the case for CD items that consistently produce a cautious shift. PAT may, however, be incorrect in positing that novel arguments play a pivotal role in changing attitudes (Meyers & Seibold, 1990). Perhaps, as suggested by the message repetition effect found in studies performed in passive communication contexts, repeated arguments may have equal or greater persuasive effectiveness.

In sum, Boster et al. (1980, 1982) adapted the LDM to explain the choice shift. This adaptation of the LDM began with the claim that the choice shift occurs as a result of a persuasion process to the exclusion of any other social influence process. The data yield little in the way of contradiction.

The Influence of Minorities. Minority group influence constitutes a second research program providing evidence of intragroup persuasion. Since Moscovici's initial investigation (Moscovici, Lage, & Naffrechoux, 1969), experiments that examine whether a small number of persons taking one position on an issue can influence a larger number of their fellow group members taking a different position on the same issue have abounded. Integrating their results, however, proves more difficult. Inconsistencies arise when comparing experimental results. The dual-process model, arguing that majorities employ normative influence pressures whereas minorities employ informational influence pressures (Moscovici, 1985), competes with single-process models (Latané & Wolf, 1981; Tanford & Penrod, 1984) and more general theories (e.g., Turner, 1991) as explanations of the phenomenon. Even the conclusions reached in review articles exhibit substantial disagreement (cf. Maas & Clark, 1984; Nemeth, 1986; Tanford & Penrod, 1984; Wood, Lundgren, Ouellette, Busceme, & Blackstone, 1994).

One reason for disagreement stems from these experiments being conducted differently. For instance, some tasks in this corpus require group members to make judgmental decisions (e.g., attitude toward abortion), whereas others require them to make intellective decisions (color perception). In some experiments, the measure of the dependent variable, influence, involves public declarations of opinion (i.e., that members announce their judgments in the presence of their fellow group members), whereas others obtain private measures (i.e., members check response options without their fellow group members having the ability to see the responses). And those studies that employ private measures may ask for judgments related directly or indirectly to the issue under discussion. Furthermore, in some experiments, group members interact face-to-face, whereas in others they do not (for a more thorough discussion of these differences, see Wood et al., 1994, p. 329).

Nevertheless, some empirical regularities emerge, and a discussion of several of the more salient of them follows. First, and most important, one must not overstate the extent of minority influence. In the main, majorities affect minorities to a greater extent than minorities affect majorities. On the other hand, minorities do have some influence on majorities, and Wood et al.'s (1994) very thorough review concluded that the evidence favors the dual-process model, although perhaps not as simple as the one Moscovici (1985) envisioned. Hence, some evidence consistent with the hypothesis that, at a minimum, minority group members persuade their majority counterpart exists.[4]

The extent to which minority group members persuade majority group members depends on numerous factors. For example, although the causal mechanism for the effect remains elusive, consistency appears as an important characteristic of successful minority influence (Wood et al., 1994, p. 338). So, for a set of persons holding a minority position to persuade a majority, they must assert a single deviant view and do so throughout discussion. Put negatively, if minority group members hold different positions that deviate from the group majority, then the minority members cannot influence the majority. For

example, contrast two groups making a personnel decision. In the first, the members of a six-person majority prefer candidate Clover, and the members of a two-person minority prefer candidate Varda. In the second, the members of a six-person majority prefer candidate Clover, one member of a two-person minority prefers candidate Varda, and the other member of the minority prefers candidate Hacia. In the first instance, if the minority members advocate Varda's candidacy and do so consistently, then they may influence those who prefer Clover. But in the second instance, if the two minority members advocate their preferred candidate, then the likelihood of the majority changing their attitudes diminishes.

Evidence suggests that minority size affects the extent of minority influence as well, although the effect depends on the measure of the dependent variable (Wood et al., 1994, p. 334). When employing public declarations or direct private attitude measures, as the size of the minority increases, their influence increases as well. But when using indirect private attitude measures, as the size of the minority increases, their influence decreases. Because the indirect private measure likely reflects a purer measure of persuasion in the absence of other social pressures, these data may indicate that larger minorities exert some normative influence, but less informational influence, than do smaller minorities. As with the consistency findings, these data want for a cogent theoretical explanation.

In addition, the discussion task affects the extent to which minorities can influence majorities. Specifically, minorities affect majorities to a greater extent when discussing intellective, rather than judgmental, matters (Wood et al., 1994, p. 333). Laughlin and Early (1982) characterized judgmental issues as having no demonstrably correct answers. Alternatively, one could describe them as problems with ambiguous solutions. On the other hand, intellective issues can be characterized as having demonstrably correct solutions, and one could describe them as problems with unambiguously correct answers. In a seminal series of experiments, Crutchfield (1955) demonstrated that increased ambiguity enhances the power of normative influence. To the extent that majority and minority influence forms a zero-sum game, intellective issues abate the majority's ability to exert normative pressures and create a context that makes minority influence possible.

Furthermore, for minorities, persuasion proves a more effective form of influence than do normative pressures. To the extent that the minority offers sound arguments, and one can reasonably assume that they generally do in these experiments, the likelihood of majority group members perceiving these arguments as sound increases with increasingly intellective issues. And to the extent that logical soundness translates into persuasive impact, one can expect to find greater minority influence on intellective tasks than on judgmental discussion tasks.

Finally, despite some attention from communication scholars (e.g., Garlick & Mongeau, 1992, 1993), in the main, communication processes pertinent to minority group influence remain unexamined. Recently, however, Limon (2000) advanced the sensible notion that presenting strong, rather than weak, arguments in support of their position enhances the extent to which minority group members persuade majority group members. In the experiment, confederates argued a minority position, and on a posttest attitude measure, majority members exhibited greater agreement with the minority position in the strong than in the weak argument condition.

In the main, then, to the extent that minorities influence majorities, they must persuade them. They enhance their persuasive effectiveness when advocating a single position consistently, being relatively small in number, and arguing intellective issues. A lack of theoretical agreement marks the area. And investigators have not examined pertinent communication processes in depth.

Outsiders Versus Insiders

Choice shift and minority influence experiments indicate that group members persuade one another to a considerable extent in the former instance and less so in the latter case. A set of experiments conducted by Lewin (1947) provided an inkling that group members may persuade one another *more* effectively than may outsiders. Lewin's research team attempted to modify women's attitudes toward food and nutrition products. In one rather dramatic demonstration, 32% of the members of decision groups indicated that they served the advocated foods—beef hearts, sweetbreads, and kidneys—whereas only 3% of those who listened to a lecture on the topic indicated that they served these rather unusual meats. And, building on Lewin's work, Pelz (1959) reported that group-induced change persisted longer than other methods of inducing change. Although one might prematurely attribute these outcomes to the effect of group discussion (i.e., the persuasive impact of messages that in-group members exchanged with one another), Lewin noted carefully several confounding factors that might have influenced the experimental outcome.

Despite the ambiguity in the interpretation of the data from Lewin's research program, these experiments raise the question of whether messages from one's fellow group members (i.e., in-group members) have greater, equal, or lesser suasory force as compared to messages from out-group members such as lecturers with expertise on the topic in question. A series of studies by Mackie and colleagues, as well as an experiment by Wilder, addresses this issue in a carefully controlled manner.

Mackie, Worth, and Asuncion (1990, Experiment 1) reported that messages delivered by in-group members had a more powerful persuasive impact than did messages from out-group members, but only when those messages contained strong arguments. In a second experiment, Mackie et al. replicated this effect for messages with content relevant to the in-group. For messages with irrelevant content, on the other hand, group members accepted the message recommendations of in-group sources to a greater extent than they accepted the message recommendations of out-group sources, regardless of the strength of the message. Mackie, Gastardo-Conaco, and Skelly (1992) extended these experiments by demonstrating that strong arguments produced more conformity with message recommendations than did weak arguments, but only when group members did *not* know the position favored by the in-group prior to hearing the arguments. These data suggest that, when receiving persuasive messages concerning a relevant topic on which the in-group position remains unknown, group members process messages from in-group sources systematically. But with less relevant topics, or when provided the in-group position, the sources' group membership serves as a heuristic cue, such that group members accept the recommendations of in-group sources to a greater extent than they do the recommendations of out-group sources.

Mackie and colleagues' experiments suggest that persuasion attempts by out-group sources have a low probability of producing substantial changes in group members' attitudes. Wilder (1990), on the other hand, investigated conditions under which out-group sources might persuade group members effectively. In two experiments, Wilder showed that group members accepted the recommendations of messages from in-group sources to a greater extent than they did messages from unknown sources and that they accepted the recommendations of messages from unknown sources to a greater extent than they accepted the recommendations of messages from out-group sources. In the third and fourth experiments, however, Wilder showed that messages from an *individuated* out-group source produced as much conformity to message recommendations as did messages from an in-group source. Wilder's individuation treatment consisted simply of providing some personal information (e.g., names, hometowns, major areas of study) about the student sources. Thus, Wilder's data indicate that group members may accept the message recommendations of out-group sources. Furthermore, they demonstrate one context in which this scenario unfolds, namely, when the out-group source provides personal individuating information.

In sum, the data from Mackie and colleagues' and Wilder's research programs suggest that in-group members generally persuade one another more effectively than do out-group members. Nevertheless, this generalization remains contingent on a number of factors. Conditions arise in which in-group members lack the ability to persuade one another (e.g., in-group members advance weak arguments on a highly relevant topic). Furthermore, conditions arise in which out-group members possess the ability to persuade those from other groups (e.g., when the investigator provides individuating information about the out-group source). Investigators frequently invoke information processing theories, such as the Heuristic-Systematic Model (Chaiken, 1980) and the Elaboration Likelihood Model (Petty, Cacioppo, & Goldman, 1981), to explain these effects. Without a well-conducted meta-analysis available to provide estimates of effect sizes, the strength of these effects remains a matter of speculation. Nevertheless, our calculations indicate that one could not dismiss the magnitude of these effects as trivial.

Groups Persuading
Out-Group Individuals

Employing sociological research methods in the service of testing psychological theory, Festinger, Riecken, and Schachter (1956) examined a group's reactions to the disconfirmation of a prophecy. They described their observations, and the theoretical interpretation of them, in the social scientific classic, *When Prophecy Fails.* This book tells the story of the merger of two groups, one led by a Mrs. Keech and the other by a Dr. Armstrong (both pseudonyms), and their highly publicized prediction that just before dawn on December 21 a flood would inundate North America from the Arctic Circle to the Gulf of Mexico.

Under a set of five conditions described, and amended, by Hardyck and Braden (1962, p. 137), dissonance theory predicts that group members will respond to the disconfirmation of the prophecy by seeking social support for their beliefs. Proselytizing provides one avenue for seeking social support. Consequently, Festinger et al. (1956) and Hardyck and Braden (1962) predicted increased proselytizing behavior as a response to dissonance when groups meet the initial five conditions.[5]

One could view proselytizing behavior as an attempt to persuade out-group members to join one's own group. Unfortunately, Festinger et al. (1956) did not inform us as to the success of these proselytizing attempts. They did, on the other hand, raise the question of the extent to which groups have success in persuading out-group individuals. And fortunately, a very different line of research hints at some answers.

Extending Hylton's (1971) study, Hocking, Margreiter, and Hylton (1977) performed an ingenious experiment in which they varied group feedback and observed the impact on audience members' attitudes. As part of a bogus classroom assignment, students went to a bar on one of two nights with instructions to observe and report on naturalistic communication behaviors. A group of 30 confederates (also undergraduate students) visited the same bar on each of these nights as well. On the first evening they responded with minimal interest to the band, and on the second evening they responded positively to the band. As Hocking et al. described this induction,

> The confederates also infiltrated the bar unobtrusively. On the first night they gave only minimal response to the band. They were instructed to look as if they did not enjoy the music. They did not applaud or dance. For the most part, they ignored the band and generally tried to respond as if they had a low evaluation of the quality of the music. On the second night they had been instructed to respond as positively as they could. Earlier that day, members of the band discussed with them typical positive responses in that bar. In the positive condition, confederates applauded enthusiastically, danced at times, shouted for an encore at the end, and generally tried to respond as if they had a high evaluation of the quality of the music. Care was taken to assure that all manipulated responses were within norms for appropriate behavior in this situation. (p. 244)

At the next class meeting, the students who had gone to the bar completed a questionnaire asking their evaluations of the band, how long they stayed at the bar, and the extent to which they would like to see the band again. The students who had attended when the confederates gave positive feedback evaluated the band more positively, stayed at the bar longer, and wanted to see the band again to a greater extent than did those who attended when the confederates provided negative feedback.

Reasonably, Hocking et al. (1977) attributed these persuasive outcomes to the messages (i.e., the nonverbal feedback) produced by the confederates.[6] The investigators did not, however, clarify the precise nature of the process that converted the confederates' feed-back into relatively positive or negative attitudes on the part of the student observers. Put differently, they failed to specify how persuasion occurred in this setting. Because student observers must make these judgments in the absence of objective criteria, the construction of these responses might involve social comparison processes. Specifically, in ambiguous contexts, the opinions of others, particularly relatively similar (albeit unknown) others, may serve to shape attitudinal judgments. But such speculation serves as a poor substitute for rigorous theory development and testing.

DIRECTIONS FOR THE FUTURE

The previous section introduced four lines of research involving persuasion in small group settings. Two of them, the choice shift and minority group influence, study persuasion processes that occur within groups. A third, the persuasive impact of an in-group versus an out-group source, examines the relative persuasive effectiveness of insiders and outsiders. The fourth, intra-audience effects, analyzes how groups influence out-group individuals. This concluding section characterizes each of these lines of research and suggests directions for extending them.

The Choice Shift. Numerous choice shift experiments have produced a spate of data, certainly sufficient for Isenberg (1986) to draw relatively firm conclusions in his review of this literature. And Isenberg concluded that at least the accumulation of many persuasive messages has a large impact. Moreover, theories abound in the choice shift corpus, although most scholars reject all but some version of PAT or some version of SCT. Remarkably, the phenomenon occurs consistently across experiments. Certain CD items

produce risky shifts, and they do so consistently; others produce cautious shifts, and they do so consistently, with investigators having produced only a few notable contingencies. Consequently, debate focuses primarily on the correct theoretical explanation of the phenomenon.

Certainly, this debate would profit from theoretical integration. PAT, the GVM, the DVM, and the LDM exhibit striking similarities. The first three, for instance, could profit from stating explicitly the operative persuasion process (or processes) that generates the choice shift. Nevertheless, Isenberg's (1986) review concluded that both informational and normative influences combine to produce the choice shift. Therefore, a more general theory incorporating both types of social influence likely would serve to explain the phenomenon more accurately and to move debate away from unproductive questions such as whether informational *or* normative influences explain the choice shift.

Developing such a theory would pose formidable challenges. Informational and normative influences could combine additively, nonadditively, sequentially, or in some other manner to produce the choice shift. Testing such a theory would pose an independent set of challenges. At a minimum, it would require that group dynamics and social influence scholars develop methods more effective at distinguishing the two types of influence. The analytic skills of the communication scientist could have particular utility in uncovering features of message exchanges that distinguish informational and normative influence attempts.

Despite these theoretical and methodological challenges, basic features of choice shift research require reexamination. Although one might use at least some of the results of these experiments to help explain certain natural events (e.g., see Janis, 1982, p. 300, n. 3), features of the typical choice shift experiment make this leap a particularly uncomfortable one. In general, in these experiments, student participants of relatively equal status discussed issues relatively low in outcome-relevant involvement and value-relevant involvement (see Johnson & Eagly, 1989). The groups had no history; they did not prepare prior to meeting. These characteristics deviated markedly from those present among persons involved in decisions such as those made during the Cuban Missile Crisis, the Bay of Pigs invasion, and the escalation of the Vietnam War. How these differences affect the dynamics of group decision making in general, and the manifestation of social influence processes in particular, remains unclear. Clarity can increase only when choice shift experiments begin to approximate more closely the conditions under which important decision-making groups do their work.

The Influence of Minorities. Like the choice shift, minority influence experiments abound, albeit with a greater diversity of experimental paradigms. But as the Wood et al. (1994) review indicates, numerous contingencies characterize these data. Investigators tend to find modest-sized effects, and they invoke several different theoretical explanations of their results. One could justifiably characterize this corpus as confusing, both empirically and theoretically. It resembles the status of social facilitation research prior to Zajonc's (1965) seminal drive theory synthesis in that new data would do little to clarify theoretical matters. Instead, only a theory capable of making sense of existing data would provide the impetus necessary for subsequent knowledge generation.

At a minimum, such a synthesizing explanation must account for the observation that, although both majorities and minorities can exert normative and information influence, majorities employ normative influence to a much greater extent than do minorities, and minorities employ informational influence as much as, or to a greater extent than, do majorities. As with the choice shift, the mechanisms that specify the effectiveness with which majorities and minorities employ these types of influence remain elusive. Whether or not they result from those same processes that produce the choice shift remains an interesting item to pursue.

As with the choice shift, both the external and ecological validities of some minority group influence experiments raise questions. Particularly, the experiments employing confederates lose some of the dynamic flavor of important features of minority influence. For instance, in natural settings, minorities might well know the majority position better than majority members know the minority position (e.g., Robinson & Keltner, 1996). Consequently, they may begin discussion better prepared to argue and counterargue, thus reaping at least an initial persuasive advantage. On the other hand, the majority, having larger numbers and thus a human resources edge, may cut into that persuasive advantage later in the discussion.

Similarly, initially majorities have more ability to exert normative influence pressures. But if minority members can sway or silence (see, e.g., Noelle-Neumann, 1993) a sufficient number of members initially in the majority, the direction of normative influence may change as well.

In addition, factors that mediate the effect of majority/minority status on changes in attitudes and behavior may themselves change during discussion. For example, the perception of minority members who advance strong arguments might modify majority members' perceptions of them. What was once seen as a wild-eyed radical might now be viewed, under certain conditions and after some discussion, as a more reasonable and committed, if perhaps somewhat misguided, person.

Coupled with changing source perceptions, the interpretation of, or the meaning one attributes to, the arguments advanced by one's fellow group members can change as well (see, e.g., Asch, 1948). For instance, majority members might interpret arguments, perceived initially as advocating an extreme position, as much less radical after obtaining a fuller understanding of the minority position. Robinson and Keltner's (1996) study illustrates this point well. Those aiming to modify the traditional English course syllabus, the Revisionists, generally suggest modifications much more modest than expected by the Traditionalists. In fact, the Revisionists recommend retaining a good portion of the Traditionalists' canon. Discussion between the factions opens the possibility that Traditionalists will view the Revisionists more favorably, judge their arguments as more reasonable, and perhaps accept some of their suggested recommendations for modification of the syllabus.

Examining changes in the suasory force of arguments, the extent and direction of normative pressures, source perceptions, and message interpretations require extending the design of the more typical types of majority/minority group influence experiments. As with the choice shift, it also requires developing reliable and valid methods of parsing normative and informational influence.

In-Group Versus Out-Group Sources. The lack of primary research limits the conclusions that scholars can draw about the effectiveness of in-group and out-group sources. The fact that investigators have located several factors that produce differences in the magnitude of the in-group/out-group source effect renders the need for additional primary research even more acute.

Ensuing primary research could profit by sharpening an important conceptual distinction, namely, that between an in-group and an out-group. The term *in-group* conjures images of primary affiliation aggregates, such as families and highly cohesive work groups, and the term *out-group* summons representations that lack this quality, notions arising largely from work in cross-cultural studies (Triandis, Botempo, Villareal, Asai, & Lucca, 1988). Persuasion and group dynamics scholars may invoke Turner's (1982) definition of an in-group as "two or more individuals who share a common identification" (p. 15), but what constitutes "common identification" varies widely and in important ways. In any case, Turner's definition broadens the concept considerably, perhaps so much so that it masks important distinctions.

Moreover, this conceptual distinction affects subsequent experimental inductions. For example, investigators usually induce the perception of an in-group or out-group source by varying the source's university affiliation (Mackie et al., 1990, 1992; Wilder, 1990, Experiments 2-4). This method of making the in-group/out-group distinction empirically differs substantially from the idea of members of a primary group attempting to persuade a fellow group member versus someone from outside of the primary group engaging in a persuasion attempt.

The Mackie et al. (1990, 1992) and Wilder (1990) studies take place in a passive communication context. In this context, the typical in-group/out-group induction may serve to vary a dimension of source credibility, albeit one less emphasized in contemporary persuasion research, namely, trustworthiness. If participants trust those with similar university affiliations more than those with dissimilar university affiliations, then they would likely reject the arguments of the out-group (untrustworthy) source. They might also consider the arguments of the in-group (trustworthy) source with a high-relevance topic and trust the in-group source's opinion with a low-relevance topic. An individuation induction might simply provide a means of increasing the source's, particularly the out-group source's, trustworthiness. If correct, this interpretation provides an interesting extension to existing cognitive responses theories.

Alternatively, one might seek to refocus this line of research to resemble more closely common notions of in-group and out-group. One potentially fruitful method of doing so requires changing the venue from a passive communication context to an interactive setting. For instance, in-group or out-group confederates could attempt to persuade group members (e.g., members of cohesive work groups such as those working on group projects in undergraduate communication courses) to accept a counterattitudinal proposition. Notably, this strategy reduces the problem to one of majority/minority group influence in which the in-group versus out-group status of the minority varies. Interestingly, such a strategy renders the problem more similar to the one posed originally by Lewin (1947).

Intra-audience Effects. The limited number of intra-audience effects experiments makes drawing any conclusions about this phenomenon hazardous. The Hylton (1971) and Hocking et al. (1977) experiments addressed an important issue and found reasonable-sized effects (in the .20 to .30 range by our estimates). Nevertheless, this topic has received insufficient attention. Do these results replicate with a less ambiguous issue? Do they replicate with an audience initially disposed to oppose the issue (one can assume with reasonable safety that Hocking et al.'s student participants liked the type of music played by the band)? Obtaining answers to these and numerous other basic questions can only come

from additional studies. Although theory may certainly advance in the absence of data, data may also stimulate theory. Progress in the study of intra-audience effects requires both.

NOTES

1. Hoffman (1979) included notions of adoption and rejection thresholds in his model. McPhee et al. (1982, pp. 262-264) criticized these ideas adroitly. Because the GVM has theoretical and empirical utility without them, no discussion of these concepts follows.

2. To be sure, when an individual group member has equal valences for two or more decision options, a problem arises (see Hoffman & Kleinman, 1994, p. 39). Meyers and Brashers (1998, pp. 270-271) provided multiple solutions to the problem.

3. For an extension of this model to another group persuasion context, jury decision making, see Boster et al. (1991).

4. This does *not* say that majority group members fail to ever persuade minority group members. Moscovici's (1985) claim might require softening. Perhaps majorities exceed minorities in the frequency and extent to which normative influence may be employed, and perhaps the opposite characterizes informational influence.

5. These conditions consist of (a) conviction, (b) commitment, (c) belief specificity, (d) undeniable disconfirmatory evidence, and (e) the presence of some social support. Hardyck and Braden (1962) suggested a modification of the fifth point to include some, but not too much, social support. They also raised the possibility that public ridicule contributes to the effect as a necessary condition.

6. One might criticize this conclusion on methodological grounds. For instance, as Hocking et al. (1977) noted, they employed intact groups, thus violating the assumption of independence of observations. And a no-feedback control condition would have provided valuable comparative information to justify or reject the conclusions that positive intra-audience feedback enhances conformity to message recommendations and negative intra-

audience feedback attenuates conformity to message recommendations.

REFERENCES

Asch, S. E. (1948). The doctrine of suggestion, prestige, and imitation in social psychology. *Psychological Review, 55,* 250-276.

Bem, D. J. (1965). An experimental analysis of self-persuasion. *Journal of Experimental Social Psychology, 1,* 199-218.

Bettinghaus, E. P. (1981). *Persuasive communication.* New York: Holt, Rinehart & Winston.

Boster, F. J., Fryrear, J. E., Mongeau, P. A., & Hunter, J. E. (1982). An unequal speaking linear discrepancy model: Implications for the polarity shift. In M. Burgoon (Ed.), *Communication Yearbook 6* (pp. 395-418). Beverly Hills, CA: Sage.

Boster, F. J., & Hale, J. L. (1989). Response scale ambiguity as a moderator of the choice shift. *Communication Research, 16,* 532-551.

Boster, F. J., Hunter, J. E., & Hale, J. L. (1991). An information-processing model of jury decision making. *Communication Research, 18,* 524-547.

Boster, F. J., & Mayer, M. E. (1984). Choice shifts: Argument qualities or social comparisons. In R. N. Bostrom (Ed.), *Communication Yearbook 8* (pp. 393-410). Beverly Hills, CA: Sage.

Boster, F. J., Mayer, M. E., Hunter, J. E., & Hale, J. L. (1980). Expanding the persuasive arguments explanation of the polarity shift: A linear discrepancy model. In D. Nimmo (Ed.), *Communication Yearbook 4* (pp. 165-176). New Brunswick, NJ: Transaction Books.

Byrne, D. (1971). *The attraction paradigm.* New York: Academic Press.

Chaiken, S. (1980). Heuristic versus systematic information processing and the use of source versus message cues in persuasion. *Journal of Personality and Social Psychology, 39,* 752-766.

Coch, L., & French, J. R. P., Jr. (1948). Overcoming resistance to change. *Human Relations, 1,* 512-532.

Crutchfield, R. S. (1955). Conformity and character. *American Psychologist, 10,* 191-198.

Deutsch, M., & Gerard, H. G. (1955). A study of normative and informational social influence upon individual judgment. *Journal of Abnormal and Social Psychology, 51,* 629-636.

Festinger, L. (1953). An analysis of compliant behavior. In M. Sherif & M. O. Wilson (Eds.), *Group relations at the crossroads* (pp. 232-256). New York: Harper.

Festinger, L., & Carlsmith, J. M. (1959). Cognitive consequences of forced compliance. *Journal of Abnormal and Social Psychology, 58,* 203-210.

Festinger, L., Riecken, H. W., & Schachter, S. (1956). *When prophecy fails.* New York: Harper & Row.

French, J. R. P., Jr. (1956). A formal theory of social power. *Psychological Review, 63,* 181-194.

Garlick, R., & Mongeau, P. A. (1992). Majority/minority size and the evaluations of persuasive arguments. *Communication Research Reports, 9,* 43-52.

Garlick, R., & Mongeau, P. A. (1993). Argument quality and group member status as determinants of attitudinal minority influence. *Western Journal of Communication, 57,* 289-308.

Gerard, H. B. (1954). The anchorage of opinions in face-to-face groups. *Human Relations, 7,* 313-325.

Gouran, D. S., Hirokawa, R. Y., & Martz, A. E. (1986). A critical analysis of factors related to decisional processes involved in the *Challenger* disaster. *Central States Speech Journal, 37,* 119-135.

Hardyck, J. A., & Braden, M. (1962). Prophecy fails again: A report of a failure to replicate. *Journal of Abnormal and Social Psychology, 65,* 136-141.

Harkins, S. G., & Petty, R. E. (1981a). Effects of source magnification of cognitive effort on attitudes: An information-processing view. *Journal of Personality and Social Psychology, 40,* 401-413.

Harkins, S. G., & Petty, R. E. (1981b). The multiple source effect in persuasion: The effects of distraction. *Personality and Social Psychology Bulletin, 7,* 627-635.

Harris, J. R. (1995). Where is the child's environment? A group socialization theory of development. *Psychological Review, 102,* 458-489.

Harris, J. R. (1998). *The nurture assumption*. New York: Free Press.

Hocking, J. E., Margreiter, D. G., & Hylton, C. (1977). Intra-audience effects: A field test. *Human Communication Research, 3*, 243-249.

Hoffman, L. R. (1961). Conditions for creative problem-solving. *Journal of Psychology, 52*, 429-444.

Hoffman, L. R. (1979). *The group problem solving process*. New York: Praeger.

Hoffman, L. R., & Kleinman, G. B. (1994). Individual and group in group problem solving: The valence model redressed. *Human Communication Research, 21*, 36-59.

Hylton, C. (1971). Intra-audience effects: Observable audience response. *Journal of Communication, 21*, 253-265.

Isenberg, D. J. (1986). Group polarization: A critical review and meta-analysis. *Journal of Personality and Social Psychology, 50*, 1141-1151.

Jablin, F. M. (1984). Assimilating new members into organizations. In R. Bostrom (Ed.), *Communication Yearbook 8* (pp. 594-626). Beverly Hills, CA: Sage.

Janis, I. L. (1982). *Groupthink*. Boston: Houghton Mifflin.

Johnson, B. T., & Eagly, A. H. (1989). The effects of involvement on persuasion: A meta-analysis. *Psychological Bulletin, 106*, 290-314.

Kelman, H. (1961). Processes of opinion change. *Public Opinion Quarterly, 25*, 57-78.

Kiesler, C. A., & Kiesler, S. B. (1969). *Conformity*. Reading, MA: Addison-Wesley.

Latane, B. (1996). Dynamic social impact: The creation of culture by communication. *Journal of Communication, 46*, 13-25.

Latane, B., & Wolf, S. (1981). The social impact of minorities and majorities. *Psychological Review, 88*, 438-453.

Laughlin, P. R., & Early, P. C. (1982). Social combination models, persuasive arguments theory, social comparison theory, and the choice shift. *Journal of Personality and Social Psychology, 42*, 273-280.

LeBon, G. (1896). *The crowd*. London: Unwin.

Lewin, K. (1947). Group decision and social change. In T. M. Newcomb & E. L. Hartley (Eds.), *Readings in social psychology* (pp. 330-344). New York: Holt.

Limon, S. M. (2000). *Minority influence: The role of consistency, number of minority members, and argument quality*. Unpublished dissertation, Michigan State University.

Maas, A., & Clark, R. D., III. (1984). Hidden impact of minorities: Fifteen years of minority influence research. *Psychological Bulletin, 95*, 428-450.

Mackie, D. M., Gastardo-Conaco, M. C., & Skelly, J. J. (1992). Knowledge of the advocated position and the processing of in-group and out-group persuasive messages. *Personality and Social Psychology Bulletin, 18*, 145-151.

Mackie, D. M., Worth, L. T., & Asuncion, A. G. (1990). Processing of persuasive in-group messages. *Journal of Personality and Social Psychology, 58*, 812-822.

McPhee, R. D. (1994). Response to Hoffman and Kleinman. *Human Communication Research, 21*, 60-63.

McPhee, R. D., Poole, M. S., & Seibold, D. R. (1982). The valence model unveiled: A critique and reformulation. In M. Burgoon (Ed.), *Communication Yearbook 5* (pp. 259-278). New Brunswick, NJ: Transaction Books.

Meyers, R. A., & Brashers, D. E. (1998). Argument in group decision making: Explicating a process model and investigating the argument-outcome link. *Communication Monographs, 65*, 261-281.

Meyers, R. A., & Seibold, D. R. (1990). Perspectives on group argument: A critical review of persuasive arguments theory and an alternative structurational view. In J. A. Anderson (Ed.), *Communication Yearbook 13* (pp. 268-302). Newbury Park, CA: Sage.

Mongeau, P. A., & Garlick, R. (1988). Social comparison and persuasive arguments as determinants of group polarization. *Communication Research Reports, 5*, 120-125.

Moscovici, S. (1985). Social influence and conformity. In G. Lindzey & E. Aronson (Eds.), *Handbook of social psychology* (3rd ed., Vol. 2, pp. 347-412). New York: Random House.

Moscovici, S., Lage, E., & Naffrechoux, M. (1969). Influence of a consistent minority on the responses of a majority in a color perception task. *Sociometry, 32*, 365-380.

Nemeth, C. (1986). Differential contributions of majority and minority influence. *Psychological Review, 93,* 23-32.

Newcomb, T. M. (1961). *The acquaintance process.* New York: Holt, Rinehart & Winston.

Noelle-Neumann, E. (1993). *The spiral of silence.* Chicago: University of Chicago Press.

Pelz, E. B. (1959). Some factors in group decision. In E. E. Maccoby, T. M. Newcomb, & E. L. Hartley (Eds.), *Readings in social psychology* (pp. 212-219). New York: Holt, Rinehart & Winston.

Petty, R. E., Cacioppo, J. T., & Goldman, R. (1981). Personal involvement as a determinant of argument-based persuasion. *Journal of Personality and Social Psychology, 41,* 847-855.

Robinson, R. J., & Keltner, D. (1996). Much ado about nothing? Revisionists and traditionalists choose an introductory English syllabus. *Psychological Science, 7,* 18-24.

Romer, D. (1979). Social comparison in the forced compliance situation. *Personality and Social Psychology Bulletin, 5,* 82-85.

Rosenbaum, M. E. (1986). The repulsion hypothesis: On the nondevelopment of relationships. *Journal of Personality and Social Psychology, 51,* 1156-1166.

Shaw, M. E. (1981). *Group dynamics.* New York: McGraw-Hill.

Sunnafrank, M. (1992). On debunking the attitude similarity myth. *Communication Monographs, 59,* 164-179.

Tanford, S. E., & Penrod, S. (1984). Social influence model: A formal integration of research on majority and minority influence processes. *Psychological Bulletin, 95,* 189-225.

Tarde, G. (1903). *The laws of imitation.* New York: Holt.

Triandis, H. C., Botempo, R., Villareal, M. J., Asai, M., & Lucca, N. (1988). Individualism and collectivism: Cross-cultural perspectives on self-ingroup relationships. *Journal of Personality and Social Psychology, 54,* 323-338.

Turner, J. C. (1982). Toward a cognitive redefinition of the social group. In H. Tajfel (Ed.), *Social identity and intergroup behavior* (pp. 15-40). Cambridge, UK: Cambridge University Press.

Turner, J. C. (1991). *Social influence.* Pacific Grove, CA: Brooks/Cole.

Wallach, M. A., Kogan, N., & Bem, D. J. (1962). Group influence on individual risk-taking. *Journal of Abnormal and Social Psychology, 65,* 75-86.

Wilder, D. A. (1990). Some determinants of the persuasive power of in-groups and out-groups: Organization of information and attribution of independence. *Journal of Personality and Social Psychology, 59,* 1202-1213.

Wood, W., Lundgren, S., Ouellette, J. A., Busceme, S., & Blackstone, T. (1994). Minority influence: A meta-analytic review of social influence processes. *Psychological Bulletin, 115,* 323-345.

Zajonc, R. B. (1965). Social facilitation. *Science, 149,* 269-274.

25

A Variable-Based Typology and a Review of Advertising-Related Persuasion Research During the 1990s

XINSHU ZHAO

Following an effort to summarize research on humor in advertising, Weinberger and Gulas (1992) concluded that "the broad question of humor's effectiveness is unanswerable" (p. 35) due to too many contingencies in terms of persuasion goals, message factors, the audience, the product advertised, and equivocal findings of the studies. The even broader question of what we know about the persuasive effects of advertising generally may be equally unanswerable, at least within the confines of a single chapter. This chapter, therefore, does not purport to summarize everything we know about the persuasive effects of advertising. Its more modest objective is to present a framework for the organization of advertising-related persuasion research. To illustrate the utility of the framework, selected research studies are reviewed.

THEORIES VERSUS VARIABLES

Many advertising researchers aim to build theories that predict and explain human behavior in a wide variety of persuasive situations. Those researchers often define areas of research in terms of the *theories* they test: spiral of silence, agenda setting, third-person effect, and framing. From this perspective, theory itself is the objective.

To theoretically oriented researchers, the history of advertising research is a history of one dominant theory following another

AUTHOR'S NOTE: This chapter would not have been completed without the extraordinary patience and encouragement of the editors, Michael Pfau and James Dillard, especially during the author's repeated injuries and surgeries. The influences of Esther Thorson, William Wells, and John Sweeney are everywhere in this chapter, as they are in other advertising-related work by the author. The assistance of Qimei Chen, Carrie James, and Hyunjoo Oh on an earlier draft is also greatly appreciated.

(Alwitt & Mitchell, 1983; Maloney, 1994). An admittedly oversimplified history of the field would be something like this: Hovland, Janis, and Kelley's (1953) source credibility theory during the 1950s, McGuire (1968) and others' learning theory during the 1960s, Krugman's (1965, 1966-1967) involvement theory during the 1970s, and Petty and Cacioppo's (1981) Elaboration Likelihood Model during the 1980s.

The regular emergence and replacement of one dominant theory with another seems to have stopped during the 1990s. During that decade, for the first time in nearly half a century, there was no single dominant theory in the field of advertising. Even before the mid-point of the decade, Maloney (1994) had anticipated that "advertising researchers in this century's closing decade may seem confused and floundering" (p. 48). Now, after the end of the decade, things do not seem any brighter. There is still no dominant theory or theories. The field seems no nearer to an answer for "how advertising works" than it was 10, 20, or 30 years ago.

This gloomy view ignores the other tradition of the field. Unlike many other areas of persuasion research, advertising has a parallel applied focus that is manifested in the existence of the advertising industry. From the beginning, the industry had a need for credible knowledge to guide practitioners' daily decision making. Pragmatically oriented advertising researchers were initially inspired to address questions such as "Should we run a 30-second or 60-second ad?" and "Should we use humor in this ad?" Such researchers often define their sub-areas of interests in terms of the *variables* they study including ad length research, celebrity effect research, and clutter research. One particular type of industry research, copy testing, attempts to predict advertising effectiveness in terms of a variety of variables, such as recall and ad liking, before the ads are released. While those re-searchers often evoke theories to predict or interpret results, the utility of theory lies in its implications for message design rather than for explanation.

A quick glance at issues of the *Journal of Advertising Research* shows that there have always been a substantial number of studies in this tradition. This literature has been largely ignored by previous academic syntheses of the field, as all of those syntheses were organized according to theories and psychological/ behavioral processes (e.g., Alwitt & Mitchell, 1983; Cafferata & Tybout, 1989; Clark, Brock, & Stewart, 1994). Implicitly, variables-oriented researchers rejected the assumption that answers to grand questions were possible. Instead, they attempted to make advertising questions more tractable by making them more narrow.

In that sense, the lack of a dominant theory is not an indication of floundering and confusion but instead a sign of progress. While fewer studies seek to produce the next dominant theory, new theories continue to be proposed, although they are often variable specific. The meaning transfer theory for celebrity effect (McCracken, 1989), the four-color theory for humor effect (Spotts, Weinberger, & Parsons, 1997), and the preceding-succeeding theory for clutter and serial effect (Zhao, 1997) are just a few examples. Many researchers have come to realize that theories, although useful, apply appropriately only within certain boundaries. Within such boundaries, published studies continue to use the theories, including source credibility theory, the Elaboration Likelihood Model, and every other theory in between. From a practical point of view, this signals the beginning of *real* successes for the theories; they are beginning to have an impact in the real world.

The focus on variables, especially independent variables, is an important distinction that separates much advertising research from other persuasion research. Furthermore, even

TABLE 25.1 A Typology of Advertising Studies

Independent Variables	Media				
	Outdoor	*Print*	*Radio*	*Television*	*Computer*
Directly manipulable Internal characteristics					
Directly manipulable External relations					
Indirectly manipulable					
Measured					

those advertising studies aimed at testing theories inevitably have variables. So a typology of advertising studies based on variables would not exclude those theory-oriented studies, while an organizing scheme based on theories would exclude many of the variable-oriented studies. Accordingly, this chapter proposes a typology of advertising effect studies according to the types of variables they investigate.

A TYPOLOGY OF ADVERTISING VARIABLES

From an advertiser's point of view, two factors may serve as starting points: the independent variable and the type of media in which the independent variables exert their effects. Although the type of media is itself a type of independent variable, it is granted special status here for reasons discussed in what follows.

Classifying the Independent Variables. Table 25.1 displays a four-category typology of independent variables based on their manipulability (in the leftmost column). From the perspective of a potential persuader, a most salient characteristic of an independent variable is the degree to which it can, in principle, be controlled. Previous writers have cast this distinction in terms of active versus attribute variables (Kerlinger, 1986) and, equivalently, manipulated versus measured variables. Manipulable variables include all those features of the advertising process that can be shaped by one or more message sources (e.g., ad placement, type of appeal), whereas measured variables are features of the product or audience that cannot be altered (e.g., age of the audience members).

As Table 25.1 shows, we propose some additional distinctions within these two broad categories. Manipulable variables are of two types. The phrase "manipulable *internal characteristics*" refers to features of the message or its implementation. Loosely speaking, these are variables most closely associated with the creative side of advertising. "Manipulable *external relations*" are relational, and they have two aspects. The first is the advertisement's relationship with other messages (e.g., news, entertainment, other ads) that surround the ad. Traditionally known as the media strategy variables, they are usually not directly controllable by an advertiser or advertising agency alone. The second aspect of *external characteristics* of advertising is its comparative relationship with other nonadvertising strategies. Advertisers have the choice of using advertising versus not using advertising at all or of using advertising versus using other strategies such as public relations (PR) news releases and coupon promotions. Advertisers may also choose the level of advertising budgets. Traditionally known as ad-related marketing variables, they are often decided by marketers/ producers in consultation with their advisers and business partners such as advertising agencies, PR agencies, retailers, and marketing research firms.

Some psychological and behavioral variables, such as attitude toward an advertised product and involvement in the product, are often treated as dependent variables in advertising research. However, message senders may hope to influence those variables in order to produce downstream changes in purchase intention or behavior. And these variables are only indirectly manipulable through more controllable variables such as creative and media strategies. In Table 25.1, they are labeled *indirectly manipulable variables*.

The final row of Table 25.1 pays homage to the fact that some aspects of the advertising process are functionally uncontrollable. These variables are characteristics of the products themselves or of the members of the target audience. Age, gender, and educational level are beyond the control of advertisers. Thus, this row represents *measured* variables.

Types of Media. Today, there are several different types of media from which advertisers can choose. One might argue that media type is another directly manipulable independent variable. That is true, but media are more than that. Different media evoke different sensory channels, evoke different levels of interactivity, and require different ways of managing

fundamental parameters such as time and space. Furthermore, particular independent variables are differentially relevant to different media. Image and color are important for print, television, and computer-related media but have no meaning for radio. Interactivity is fundamental for computer-related media but becomes a near constant for some other media. The clutter is a spatial concept for print media but a sequential concept for broadcast media. The juxtaposition of these five media (see Table 25.1) with the four types of independent variables yields a 4×5 matrix that is used to organize the remainder of this chapter.

EFFECTS OF DIRECTLY MANIPULABLE INTERNAL VARIABLES

Celebrity Endorsement in All Media. The analysis of 110 announcements of contracts of celebrity endorsements by various companies indicate that, on average, the announcements have led to higher stock prices for the companies. This suggests that the investors generally view the contracts as worthy investment in advertising (Agrawal & Kamakura, 1995).

Negative Strategy in Political Ads for Various Media. Based on a meta-analysis of 52 studies published between 1984 and 1998, Lau, Sigelman, Heldman, and Babbitt (1999) concluded that, contrary to the conventional wisdom, there is little evidence that negative ads produce more positive attitudes toward or win more votes for the sponsoring candidates relative to positive ads. There is also little indication that negative ads produce more negative attitudes toward or take more votes from the opposing candidates relative to positive ads. And people do not necessarily dislike the negative ads. The study also uncovered little support for the popular belief that negative ads discourage voters from participating in the political processes.

The effects of attacking strategy on voters' candidate preference depend on political involvement and attention to political news, according to Faber, Tims, and Schmitt (1993), whose study was not included in Lau et al.'s (1999) meta-analysis. Faber et al. (1993) found that, as a result of being exposed to negative ads, those who are highly involved are more likely to change their candidate preference (in either direction) than are those who are less involved. Nevertheless, after being exposed to negative ads, those who read more newspaper news are *less* likely to change their candidate preference than are less frequent readers.

Humor in Print and Broadcast Ads. Summarizing 20 years of research on the effects of humor, Weinberger and Gulas (1992) concluded that humor attracts attention but does not harm comprehension despite the belief that humor confuses the audience. Humor enhances ad liking, while it has little effect on source credibility, brand attitude, purchase intention, or purchase behavior. Research conducted subsequent to the Weinberger and Gulas review has suggested that humor does have a positive impact on ad attitude, brand attitude, and purchase intention (Zhang, 1996) and that people exposed to humorous television ads are more likely to consider the surrounding programs as entertaining (Perry, Jenzowsky, Hester, King, & Yi, 1997).

The effects of humor are moderated by many factors. Relevant humor is more effective than nonrelevant humor (Weinberger & Gulas, 1992). Humor is more effective when existing, feeling-oriented, low-involvement, and/or low-risk products are advertised (Weinberger & Gulas, 1992; Weinberger, Spotts, Campbell, & Parsons, 1995). The kind of audience also has an impact on humor's effectiveness (Weinberger & Gulas, 1992). In one study, participants with a positive prior

attitude toward a brand were positively affected by humor in terms of ad attitude, brand attitude, purchase intention, and purchase behavior, while participants with a negative prior attitude were negatively affected (Chattopadhyay & Basu, 1990). In an experiment using print ads, participants lower in need for cognition were more likely to be affected by humor in terms of developing a more positive ad attitude and brand attitude as well as higher purchase intention (Zhang, 1996). Humor in event promotions increased attendance to social events but helped little in attracting attendees to business events (Scott, Klein, & Bryant, 1990). Furthermore, it has been found that the effect of humor on brand attitude is mediated by ad attitude (Zhang, 1996) and by cognitive responses (Chattopadhyay & Basu, 1990).

Copy Vividness of Print Ads. More vivid copies tend to generate a more favorable attitude toward an advertised brand and make the audience more likely to choose the brand when the ads are shown together with other ads for competing brands *and* when the audience is engaged in issue-relevant thinking. The advantages of the vivid copies tend to disappear when, with other conditions unchanged, the ads are *not* shown together with other ads for competing brands (Heath, McCarthy, & Mothersbaugh, 1994).

Spokesperson in Print Ads. A company may choose a corporate official, such as the chief executive officer, or an outside noncommercial authority as the spokesperson in its ad. Straughan, Bleske, and Zhao's (1996) experiment shows that the audience is more likely to be interested in a message from a chief executive officer than in the identical message from an outside authority. The higher interest leads to more of the desired attitude change, which in turn leads to more of the desired behavioral change.

Message Appeal or Argument Strength in Print Ads. Stronger argument has a positive effect on ad attitude, brand attitude, and purchase intention. But the individuals in more need for cognition are more likely affected by argument strength in terms of developing a more positive ad attitude and brand attitude as well as higher purchase intention (Zhang, 1996).

Celebrity Endorsement in Print Ads. While Petty, Cacioppo, and Schumann (1983) showed that issue-relevant thinking can eliminate the positive effects of spokespersons' fame, competitive setting may also matter. In Heath et al.'s (1994) experiment, spokespersons' fame led to a more favorable attitude toward an advertised brand and made the audience more likely to choose the brand when the ads were shown together with other ads for competing brands, even when the audience was engaged in issue-relevant thinking. This positive celebrity effect disappeared when ads were not shown together with other ads for competing brands.

The audience's perception and attitude toward a celebrity and its attitude toward the ad become less and less favorable as the number of products endorsed by the celebrity increase (Tripp, Jensen, & Carlson, 1994). Furthermore, according to Till and Shimp (1998), the negative information about a celebrity resulted in a decline in attitude toward an endorsed brand, but only when the celebrity endorser was a fictitious figure. That general relationship was further moderated in varying degrees by three other variables: association set size, timing of the negative information, and strength of the link between brand and celebrity.

Attribute Versus Relation in Print Ads. An ad may focus on the attributes of a product or on the product's relation to people and its use. Malaviya, Kisielius, and Sternthal (1996) found that, when a commercial focused on attribute was placed together with ads for competing brands, the commercial tended to generate more favorable attitudes than did a commercial focused on relation. When the commercial was placed together with ads of noncompeting brands, however, the relation strategy produced more favorable attitudes than the attribute strategy.

Association Strategy in Print Ads. When an ad associates the advertised brand with another object, the result could be assimilation or contrast (Meyers-Levy & Sternthal, 1993). *Assimilation* refers to the phenomenon whereby consumers evaluate the advertised brand more like the associated object than they would if there had been no association between the brand and the object. An advertiser may take advantage of this phenomenon by associating its brand with an already positively evaluated object. *Contrast* refers to the opposite phenomenon whereby consumers evaluate the advertised brand more unlike the associated object than they would if there had been no association between the brand and the object. An advertiser may take advantage of this phenomenon by associating its brand with an already negatively evaluated object. Meyers-Levy and Sternthal's experiment shows that contrast occurs when (a) the consumers devote a substantial amount of cognitive resources to the processing of the ads and (b) there is little overlap between the advertised brand and the associated object. The absence of either of these two factors leads to assimilation.

Youth Appeal in Cigarette Print Ads. The youth appeal in Joe Camel ads appeared to encourage adolescents to pay more attention to the Camel ads than to other cigarette ads (Fox, Krugman, Fletcher, & Fischer, 1998).

Between-Information Interval Within Radio Ads. An ad often contains multiple pieces of information. Olsen (1997) investigated the effect of the between-information time interval together with two other factors: (a) whether the listeners' attention is focused on the ad or diverted and (b) whether there is background music or background silence. The results showed that as the between-information interval increased from 0 second to 1, 2, and 3 seconds, listeners' recall of the information also increased linearly in all but one situation. The only exception occurred when the listeners' attention was diverted *and* there was background silence *and* when the interval increased from 2 seconds to 3 seconds. In that situation, the recall decreased, and did so significantly, by about 50%.

Length of Television Commercials. A number of studies (Fabian, 1986; Mord & Gilson, 1985; Patzer, 1991) have suggested that 15-second ads are 50% to 90% as effective in creating learning and attitudinal change as are 30-second ads. Singh and Cole (1993) argued that the effect size of ad length depends on repetition and message content (i.e., emotional vs. informational). Indeed, their experiment showed that 30-second ads generated better brand memory and attitude than did 15-second ads when the appeal was emotional; when the appeal was informational, 15-second ads were generally as effective as 30-second ads. It was also found that the length effect on brand recall diminished as repetition increased. Pieters and Bijmolt (1997) analyzed data based on 2,677 television commercials of naturally varying lengths aired between 1975 and 1992 in The Netherlands, and they reported positive effects of

duration (length) on recall. Furthermore, because few interaction (moderating) effects with other independent variables were found, the researchers argued that perhaps the main effect of length should be the focus of the attention after all.

Emotional Appeals in Television Ads. In Hitchon and Thorson's (1995) experiment, higher emotional appeals produced more positive ad attitude than did lower emotional appeals. The effect of emotional appeals on brand recall depended on the audience's product involvement; the emotional appeals produced higher recall when the involvement was high, but emotion had little effect on recall when the involvement was low.

Music and Sound in Television Ads. Olsen (1995) compared three strategies: background music throughout an ad, background silence throughout the ad, and background silence only when key information is presented. The results show that the audience's recall of the key information was the highest when silence appeared only with key information. The effect was even stronger, however, when the key information was the last item in a series.

The Size and Type of Web Banner Ads. Web users clicked an animated banner ad more quickly and were more likely to recall the ad than to recall a nonanimated ad (Li & Bukovac, 1999). Web users were more likely to click a larger banner ad and clicked it more quickly.

EFFECTS OF DIRECTLY MANIPULABLE EXTERNAL VARIABLES

To Ad or Not to Ad (various media). Public service announcement (PSA) campaigns have traditionally relied on donated rather than paid media. In part due to the limitations that often come with the donations, the recent trend has been to switch to the paid schedule at the risk of losing future donations from the media. A three-market field experiment (Murry, Stam, & Lastovicka, 1996) found that the donated schedule was as effective and cost-efficient as the paid schedule in persuading the youths to avoid drinking and driving, thereby reducing the counts of incapacitating and fatal highway accidents. Given this knowledge, the researchers suggested that the public service campaign managers not abandon the donated media for the paid media.

Despite this recommendation, in 2000, the U.S. decennial population census used paid advertising for the first time in history in hopes of increasing participation. A study conducted by two researchers from the U.S. Bureau of the Census and U.S. Treasury Department (Bates & Buckley, 2000) found that exposure was significantly related to being knowledgeable about the census but was not significantly and directly related to the likelihood of completing the census forms. Furthermore, this lack of relationship was across the board with regard to factors such as race/ethnicity.

When a company wants to spread a message, it may choose to buy advertising space or to work with media reporters to generate news coverage. The message in an ad, however, is less likely to be believed by the audience than the identical message appearing in a news story, according to Straughan et al.'s (1996) experiment. This lower credibility leads to less of the desired attitude change, which in turn leads to less of the desired behavioral change.

Ad Budget for All Media. Based on a meta-analysis of 389 real-world split cable-television experiments, Lodish et al. (1995) reported that increasing the advertising budget, in rela-

tion to those of competitors, do *not* increase sales in general. Increasing the advertising budget, however, did seem to help increase the sales of the products/brands newly introduced to a market but not the sales of the established products/brands. Furthermore, prime-time gross rating points, which are nearly entirely dependent on budgets, have a highly significant and positive relation with sales (Lodish et al., 1995). Cobb-Walgren, Ruble, and Donthu (1995) reported that brands with higher advertising budgets yielded substantially higher levels of brand equity, which in turn led to significantly greater brand preferences and purchase intentions.

Clutter of Print Ads. Kent and Allen (1994) focused on a particular type of clutter (i.e., the other ads for directly competing brands). The study found that competitive clutter leads to less claim recall, but only when the advertised brands are unfamiliar.

Ha (1996) saw three dimensions in the concept of clutter in magazines—quantity, competitiveness, and intrusiveness—and manipulated each of them in her experiment. She also measured the participants' perceptions of the three dimensions as three mediating variables. In addition, she measured six dependent variables: the reading of, memory of, involvement in, and attitude toward the focal ad under test; the resistance toward competitive ads; and the attitude toward the focal brand. Of the several dozens of independent-dependent, independent-mediating, and mediating-dependent relations, half a dozen turned out to be statistically significant, among which a couple were surprises in terms of the direction of the effects. A higher quantity of ads led participants to perceive a higher quantity, a higher perceived quantity or a higher perceived competitiveness led to more negative attitudes toward the magazine that carried the ads, and a higher perceived intrusiveness was associated with less memory of the ads. Nevertheless, a higher perceived competitiveness was associated with *more* readers of the focal ad and *higher* involvement in the ad message.

Frequency (repetition) for Television Ads. Although the main effect of repetition was not Singh and Cole's (1993) central concern, their experimental results showed a general increase in brand recall and claim recall, as the frequency increased from 1 to 4 and then to 8. Singh, Mishra, Bendapudi, and Linville's (1994) experiment found that airing the same ad twice generated more recall than airing it once. In Hitchon and Thorson's (1995) experiment, the participants reported 17%, 21%, 53%, and 81% brand-name recall when commercial repetitions were 2, 4, 6, and 12, respectively. However, they also found that the attitudes toward the ad became more negative as the repetition increased.

An analysis of field data from three Super Bowl broadcasts found that every additional ad for a brand added 3.5 percentage points to brand recall, 6.5 percentage points to brand recognition, and one third of a percentage point to ad liking on a scale from 0 to 100 (Zhao, 1997).

Spacing of Television Ads. When multiple television ads are used for the same brand, how far apart should the ads be placed? The answer depends on whether the advertiser's objective requires immediate or delayed reaction from the audience. According to Singh et al.'s (1994) experiment, long lag (four other ads between the two focal ads) produced more day-after recall, while short lag (one ad in between) produced more short-delay recall.

Clutter of Television Ads. While an earlier experiment (Webb & Ray, 1979) reported a decreased brand recall as a result of the increased clutter of television ads, a later experi-

ment (Brown & Rothschild, 1993) found no such effect on brand recall or recognition. Brown and Rothschild (1993) speculated that the negative clutter effect might have diminished since the Webb and Ray (1979) study, which seemed to be consistent with Johnson and Cobb-Walgren's (1994) experiment that also failed to find a statistically significant clutter effect on recall or recognition.

Sizable negative effects of clutter on brand recall and recognition, however, were found in two quasi-experiments published later. One (Pieters & Bijmolt, 1997) was based on 39,000 consumers' reactions to 2,677 television commercials aired between 1975 and 1992 in The Netherlands, and the other (Zhao, 1997) was based on postgame interviews with more than 1,000 viewers of three Super Bowl broadcasts between 1992 and 1994. Extending clutter effect to attitudes, the ads in more crowded "pods" (commerical breaks) were less likely to be liked (Zhao, 1997).

Johnson and Cobb-Walgren (1994) found that the viewers with slower cognitive processing speed were more negatively affected by clutter in terms of recognition and recall of the brand name and ad message. It was also argued that the concept of television clutter should be divided into two parts: the ads *preceding* an advertisement and the ads *succeeding* the advertisement (Zhao, 1997). Indeed, while both have negative effects, the effects of preceding ads were found to be much larger.

Serial Position (presentation order) of Television Ads. Thorson, Reeves, Schleuder, Lang, and Rothschild (1985) and Thorson and Reeves (1986) reported that the commercials' presentation order had more significant effects than did content variables such as arguments, executional style, brand, and product. Later studies continued to confirm the primacy effect, showing that the first positions in a pod generate better memories (Burke & Srull, 1988;

Cameron, Schleuder, & Thorson, 1991; Pieters & Bijmolt, 1997; Stewart, Pechmann, Ratneswar, Stroud, & Bryant, 1985).

The situation with regard to the recency effect is more complicated. Controlled experiments continued to show the recency effect—that the last few positions generate better memories than do the middle positions—thereby further confirming the famous U-shaped curve that psychologists had demonstrated decades ago. Some researchers, however, argued that the recency effect might be a phenomenon limited to laboratory settings, where memory was tested immediately after the presentations of the ads, a setting that is quite different from most of the real-world advertising situations (Zhao, Shen, & Blake, 1995). They cited previous nonadvertising experiments (Craik, 1970; Glanzer & Cunitz, 1966) reporting that, when memory tests were delayed and distracting tasks were inserted in between, the advantage of the last positions disappeared and the U-shaped curve was replaced by a monotonically declining line. Indeed, in two advertising studies (Pieters & Bijmolt, 1997; Zhao, 1997) based on large-scale field data, it was the monotonically declining line—not the recency effect or U-shaped curve—that showed up for serial effects on memory.

Furthermore, serial position was redefined as a one-for-one exchange between the stronger negative effects of preceding ads and the weaker negative effects of succeeding ads. And it was argued that the monotonically declining curve and the lack of recency effects should be expected in field studies. A linear negative effect of serial position on ad liking was also found (Zhao, 1997).

Context of Television Ads. Context can be defined in many different ways. Cameron et al.'s (1991) experiment looked at the context in terms of the presence or absence of news teasers. The participants paid more attention to commercials following news teas-

ers. But the news teasers did not produce a detectable effect on visual or verbal recognition of the commercial contents. Perry, Jenzowsky, King, et al. (1997) looked at the context in terms of program content and found that humor in television programs had a negative effect on the recall of the advertised products.

Context of Web Ads. Stevenson, Bruner, and Kumar (2000) looked at Web page complexity in terms of number of items, colors, and animation, and they compared ads in a complex Web page to ads in a simpler page. The complexity had a negative impact on users' attitude toward the site, the ads in the site, and the advertised brand. It also reduced the users' intention to purchase the advertised brand. The complexity did not, however, seem to significantly reduce users' attention to the ad.

EFFECTS OF INDIRECTLY MANIPULABLE VARIABLES

Media Use Behavior (all media). People who watch many television channels or listen to many radio stations are most likely to avoid commercials (Speck & Elliott, 1997). African Americans who watch more television tend to have a more positive attitude toward advertising than do those who watch less television. The same relation between television watching and attitude toward advertising does not exist among Caucasians, according to Bush, Smith, and Martin (1999).

Attitude Toward Advertising in General (print and broadcast media). Consumers' positive attitude toward advertising in general is positively associated with involvement with specific advertisements (James & Kover, 1992). Those people who think advertising in general as interesting, useful, or believable are less likely to avoid ads, while those who view advertising as excessive, annoying, or a waste of time are more likely to avoid ads (Speck & Elliott, 1997).

Ad Attitude for Print and Broadcast Ads. Based on interviews of nearly 15,000 consumers after five matched pairs of commercials were aired, the Advertising Research Foundation's Copy Research Validity Project (Haley & Baldinger, 1991) found that liking of ads predicts product sales far better than do any of the other indicators often measured in copy testing. Biel and Bridgwater's (1990) smaller scale study showed a similarly stronger effect of ad liking than of any other independent variables.

While it had been known that more positive ad attitude leads to more positive brand attitude, Brown and Stayman (1992) showed that this effect is *both* direct and indirect. Ad attitude exerts this effect both directly and indirectly through the mediating variable of brand cognition.

Brand Equity for Various Media. Brand equity is a complex concept with multiple dimensions (Aaker, 1991; Aaker & Biel, 1993). Cobb-Walgren et al.'s (1995) definition of brand equity focuses on the consumer perception dimension, making it very close to brand attitude, hence something indirectly manipulable by advertisers. Their study found that higher brand equities generated significantly greater brand preferences and purchase intention.

Mood While Processing Television Advertising Messages. A positive mood assists an individual in remembering brand names better than does a neutral mood (Lee & Sternthal, 1999).

Within-Brand Versus Between-Brand Processing of Television Advertising Messages. A television ad viewer may focus on the characteristics of an advertised brand, a psychological phenomenon called *within-brand processing.* Or the viewer may be engaged in comparing the advertised brand to other competing brands, a process called *between-brand processing.* Kent and Machleit (1990) reported that between-brand processing leads to increased brand recall, while within-brand processing leads to better brand recognition.

Television Program-Related Psychological and Behavioral Variables. Individuals who pay more attention to television programs are more likely to watch television commercials (Krugman, Cameron, & White, 1995).

Murry, Lastovicka, and Singh (1992) reported that viewers' liking of programs positively influenced ad attitude and brand attitude, while program-induced affect (feelings or mood) had no effect on these same attitudes. Coulter (1998) also found a positive effect of program liking on ad attitude, but program liking was seen as a mediating variable that was directly affected by program cognition and program-induced affect, and program-induced affect was found to be directly affected by program cognition.

Furthermore, when the commercial is in the first position in a pod, higher liking of the program produced more positive ad attitude (Coulter, 1998) and more positive brand attitudes (Murry et al., 1992) as compared to commercials in other pod positions. Also, according to Coulter (1998), the effect of program liking on ad attitude is stronger when the ad and the program have congruent emotional contents.

Attitude Toward Web Sites. Chen and Wells (1999) first proposed this concept. In Stevenson et al.'s (2000) experiment, users with more positive attitudes toward a Web site were more likely to have a positive attitude toward an ad in the site, a positive attitude toward the brand advertised, and a stronger purchase intention regarding the brand.

EFFECTS OF MEASURED VARIABLES

Race (all media). African Americans watched more television and had more positive attitudes toward advertising than did their Caucasian counterparts (Bush et al., 1999).

Age (print and broadcast). As people get older, their cognitive processing speed declines, and consequently their brand and ad message memory (recall and recognition) decline significantly (Johnson & Cobb-Walgren, 1994). Older people are also more likely to avoid newspaper ads but less likely to avoid radio ads than are younger people (Speck & Elliott, 1997).

Gender (various media). Women have a more positive attitude toward advertising in general than do men (Bush et al., 1999). Men are more apt to change channels during television commercial breaks than are women (Krugman et al., 1995).

Male homosexuals (gays) tend to have more negative attitudes toward advertising than do female homosexuals (lesbians), while lesbians are less concerned with appropriate homosexual portrayals in advertising than are gays (Burnett, 2000).

Sexual Orientation (all media). Compared to other consumers, homosexual consumers read different newspapers and magazines, watch different television shows, listen to different radio programs, and are more likely to use catalogs and online resources (Burnett, 2000). They also tend to have a more negative attitude toward advertising.

Income (print and broadcast media). According to Speck and Elliott's (1997) survey, people with higher income are more likely to avoid ads in magazines, in newspapers, and on television.

Product Involvement (television ads). While advertisers may indirectly manipulate ad involvement, situation involvement, or even brand involvement, they may have little room to manipulate product involvement. Hitchon and Thorson (1995) reported that higher involvement with a product produced a more positive attitude toward an advertised brand, while product involvement produced no discernible effect on brand recall.

Family Communication Pattern (television ads). Researchers have identified two types of communication between parents and their children (McLeod & Chaffee, 1972). In concept-oriented communication, parents foster open two-sided communication, encouraging their children to discuss their ideas and develop an independent perspective. In socio-oriented communication, parents are concerned with maintaining control over their children's thoughts, behavior, and exposure to outside influences. A four-category typology was developed based on those two dimensions (Moschis, 1987): Laissez-faire parents are neither socio- nor concept oriented; protective parents have a high level of socio-oriented communication but a low level of concept-oriented communication; pluralistic parents are the opposite, having a high level of concept-oriented communication but a low level of socio-oriented communication; and consensual parents have high levels of communication of both types.

Rose, Bush, and Kahle's (1998) survey of mothers in the United States and Japan found that laissez-faire mothers had the most positive attitudes toward and the lowest mediation of their children's exposure to television advertising. Pluralistic and consensual mothers had the highest mediation of and most negative attitudes toward advertising. The responses of protective mothers were between those extremes.

Web User Mode. Web surfers are no more likely to click banner ads or remember the ads than are information seekers, according to Li and Bukovac's (1999) experiment.

MORE RELEVANT RESEARCH QUESTIONS

Most of the research questions in advertising research started with *whether*—whether negative strategy wins votes for the sponsoring candidate, whether a celebrity endorser helps to persuade consumers to buy the advertised brand, and so on. The expected answers are either yes or no. While those studies are all quantitative in terms of methodology, the questions are by nature qualitative or "dichotomous." More recent advertising studies were more likely to ask contingency questions involving moderating variables—whether the negative strategy is stronger when the voters are more involved, whether the celebrity effect is weaker when the product is more involving, and so on. Those questions probe in more details and require comparisons of magnitudes of the effects.

The next stage of development might be to ask more "quantitative" questions starting with *how much*—how much celebrity endorsers affect memory, attitude, or behavior; how much stronger or weaker the celebrity effects are than the effects of ad length, and so on. These would be entirely new types of questions that require entirely new types of answers, which may lead to entirely new types of theories. For practitioners and policy makers, "precision" answers to such "precision" ques-

tions should be more useful in the cost-benefit calculation of the daily decision making.

Two other recommendations might seem obvious due to the changes in the economic environment in general and in the advertising media in particular, but they merit mention nonetheless. First, there should be, and most likely will be, more studies on computer-related advertising. The trend is already quite clear in the most recent conferences and journals in the field. Second, there should be, but might not be, more studies on advertising effects in countries other than the United States, especially in the emerging economies. The financial cost and the cultural and language barriers make it difficult for U.S.- or Western Europe-based researchers to conduct research in those developing countries. The differences in research traditions and orientation make it difficult for the researchers based in those countries to produce the large amount of empirical research needed to participate in dialogue with the Western research community.

THE CRISES OF RELEVANCE

The preceding review and comments are based on the assumption that the prevailing methodologies can validly inform the goals of the advertising community. Unfortunately, the apparent mismatch between the goals and the methods of the advertising research troubled some observers during the 1990s, as it did during previous decades. As discussed previously, the research community has dual goals. One goal is applied—to create immediately useful knowledge that may help industry practitioners, public policy makers, and others make better decisions in their professions.

The second goal is theoretical—to advance the basic understanding of advertising processes, especially advertising's persuasive processes and effects, even if the knowledge might not have an immediate, clear, or specific application. For this second goal, it is also implied that ultimately it is the real-world processes and effects that should concern us, not some peculiar phenomena that occur only in laboratory settings with nonrepresentative ads on nonrepresentative subjects.

Accordingly, Sheth (1972) argued for "testing of theories *in naturalistic and realistic settings*" (pp. 565-566) as the appropriate methodology for the field. The advertising studies during the next few years failed to meet Sheth's standard. Jacoby (1976) complained that much of the consumer research, of which the advertising research is considered a subfield, "is not worth the paper it is printed on or the time it takes to read it" (p. 2). Preston (1985) reported a growing "detachment" of advertising research from the actual "marketing and advertising context" (p. 3) such that the selection of the major concepts and the manipulation of the major variables under study "digressed from actual advertising practice" (p. 5). Eight years after Preston's observations, Wells (1993, p. 489) saw the same thing, finding that the prevailing methodology in the field was moving "away from the real world," using students to represent consumers and laboratory to represent the environment (pp. 491-492). Resolution of this crisis of relevance requires that advertising researchers forsake traditional methodologies (Wells, 1993).

McQuarrie (1998) conducted a meta-analysis of more than 400 experimental studies of advertising published between 1965 and 1997. He measured those studies' methodological detachment from advertising goals in six respects: (a) forcing exposure rather than arranging for nonfocal attention to embedded advertisements, (b) failing to measure choices, (c) not incorporating competitive advertisements into the design to allow for interference, (d) taking immediate measurements instead of allowing for decay, (e) not arrang-

ing for repeated exposures, and (f) exclusively using fictitious or unfamiliar brands. McQuarrie's findings should be alarming. Advertising studies were relatively detached throughout the period between 1972 and 1998, and the detachment had grown even higher during the more recent years.

Most of the advertising researchers, however, did not appear to be alarmed by this finding or by the critiques offered by Jacoby (1976), Preston (1985), and Wells (1993). There has been no elaborated or systematic defense on behalf of the prevailing practice. The researchers did appear to be aware of the criticism, as some succinct statements scattered or buried in some articles' methodology or conclusion section might suggest. Those statements are usually along the lines that, because this is a *theory testing* or *basic research,* external validity is not that important. Here is an example from a highly respected researcher (Kamins, 1990):

> Although one could criticize the current research on the grounds of limited external validity (i.e., use of laboratory experiment and a student sample), the focus of the research was directed toward theory testing, therefore placing the value of internal validity as more important than external validity.

As discussed earlier, the advertising-related persuasion research is the child of a marriage between the advertising industry and experimental psychology, a marriage symbolized in the 1920 hiring of John B. Watson, then a leading experimental psychologist, by J. Walter Thompson, then America's largest advertising agency. From the very beginning, it appeared to be a marriage of convenience rather than of love. Watson ended up producing no research in advertising (Maloney, 1994). For a long time, consumer psychologists insisted on the traditions from experimental psychology in terms of both topic and methodology. In topic selection, they insisted on searching for universal theories. In methodology, they paid little attention to external validity, namely generalizability. Both mismatch the basic needs of the advertising industry (and public policy makers as another important patron), leading to a troubled marriage and an unhappy child.

As is the case with any troubled marriage, at least one party has to compromise or the marriage will not last. A divorce in this case would be easy. All it would take is for advertising practitioners and public policy makers to stop paying attention to advertising research. Many of them never paid attention to it anyway. Over the years, more and more advertising researchers are selecting their topics based on independent variables, a sign of compromise in one of the two major points in dispute. With regard to methodology, however, many of the researchers continue to ignore the criticism while doing what they always have done. Until more advertising researchers place more value on the generalizability and ultimate utility of the knowledge they create, the mismatches between the goals and the methods of the advertising research are likely to continue. So too are the crises of relevance and the troubles in the marriage.

REFERENCES

Aaker, D. A. (1991). *Managing brand equity*. New York: Free Press.

Aaker, D. A., & Biel, A. (1993). *Brand equity and advertising*. Hillsdale, NJ: Lawrence Erlbaum.

Agrawal, J., & Kamakura, W. A. (1995). The economic worth of celebrity endorsers: An event study analysis. *Journal of Marketing, 59*, 56-62.

Alwitt, L. F., & Mitchell, A. A. (Eds.). (1983). *Psychological processes and advertising effects*. Hillsdale, NJ: Lawrence Erlbaum.

Bates, N., & Buckley, S. K. (2000). Exposure to paid advertising and returning a census form. *Journal of Advertising Research, 40*, 65-73.

Biel, A., & Bridgwater, C. A. (1990). Attributes of likable television commercials. *Journal of Advertising Research, 30*, 38-44.

Brown, T. J., & Rothschild, M. L. (1993). Reassessing the impact of television advertising clutter. *Journal of Consumer Research, 20*, 138-146.

Brown, S. P., & Stayman, D. M. (1992). Antecedents and consequences of attitude toward the ad: A meta-analysis. *Journal of Consumer Research, 19*, 34-51.

Burke, R. R., & Srull, T. K. (1988). Competitive interference and consumer memory for advertising. *Journal of Consumer Research, 15*, 55-68.

Burnett, J. J. (2000). Gays: Feelings about advertising and media used. *Journal of Advertising Research, 40*, 75-84.

Bush, A. J., Smith, R., & Martin, C. (1999). The influence of consumer socialization variables on attitude toward advertising: A comparison of African-Americans and Caucasians. *Journal of Advertising, 28*, 13-25.

Cafferata, P., & Tybout, A. M. (Eds.). (1989). *Cognitive and affective responses to advertising*. Lexington, MA: Lexington Books.

Cameron, G. T., Schleuder, J., & Thorson, E. (1991). The role of news teasers in processing TV news and commercials. *Communication Research, 18*, 667-684.

Chattopadhyay, A., & Basu, K. (1990). Humor in advertising: The moderating role of prior brand evaluation. *Journal of Marketing Research, 27*, 466-476.

Chen, Q., & Wells, W. D. (1999). Attitude toward the site. *Journal of Consumer Research, 26*, 27-37.

Clark, E. M., Brock, T. C., & Stewart, D. W. (Eds.). (1994). *Attention, attitude, and affect in response to advertising*. Hillsdale, NJ: Lawrence Erlbaum.

Cobb-Walgren, C. J., Ruble, C. A., & Donthu, N. (1995). Brand equity, brand preference, and purchase intent. *Journal of Advertising, 24*, 25-40.

Coulter, K. S. (1998). The effects of affective responses to media context on advertising evaluation. *Journal of Advertising, 27*, 41-51.

Craik, F. I. M. (1970). The fate of primary items in free recall. *Journal of Verbal Learning and Verbal Behavior, 9*, 143-148.

Faber, R. J., Tims, R. A., & Schmitt, K. G. (1993). Negative political advertising and voting intent: The role of involvement and alternative information sources. *Journal of Advertising, 22,* 67-76.

Fabian, G. S. (1986). 15-Second commercials: The inevitable evolution. *Journal of Advertising Research, 26,* RC3-RC5.

Fox, R. J., Krugman, D. M., Fletcher, J. E., & Fischer, P. M. (1998). Adolescents' attention to beer and cigarette print ads and associated product warnings. *Journal of Advertising, 27,* 57-70.

Glanzer, M., & Cunitz, A. R. (1966). Two storage mechanisms in free recall. *Journal of Verbal Learning and Verbal Behavior, 5,* 351-360.

Ha, L. (1996). Advertising clutter in consumer magazines: Dimensions and effects. *Journal of Advertising Research, 36,* 76-84.

Haley, R. I., & Baldinger, L. (1991). The ARF copy research validity project. *Journal of Advertising Research, 31,* 11-31.

Heath, T. B., McCarthy, M. S., & Mothersbaugh, D. L. (1994). Spokesperson fame and vividness effects in the context of issue-relevant thinking: The moderating role of competitive setting. *Journal of Consumer Research, 20,* 520-534.

Hitchon, J. C., & Thorson, E. (1995). Effects of emotion and product involvement on the experience of repeated commercial viewing. *Journal of Broadcasting & Electronic Media, 39,* 376-389.

Hovland, C., Janis, I., & Kelley, H. (1953). *Communication and persuasion.* New Haven, CT: Yale University Press.

Jacoby, J. (1976). Consumer research: Telling it like it is. In B. B. Anderson (Ed.), *Advances in consumer research* (Vol. 3, pp. 1-11). Ann Arbor, MI: Association for Consumer Research.

James, W. L., & Kover, A. J. (1992). Observations: Do overall attitudes toward advertising affect involvement with specific ads? *Journal of Advertising Research, 32,* 78-83.

Johnson, R. L., & Cobb-Walgren, C. J. (1994). Aging and the problem of television clutter. *Journal of Advertising Research, 34,* 54-62.

Kamins, M. A. (1990). An investigation into the "match-up" hypothesis in celebrity advertising: When beauty may be only skin deep. *Journal of Advertising, 19,* 4-14.

Kent, R. J., & Allen, C. T. (1994). Competitive interference in consumer memory for advertising: The role of brand familiarity. *Journal of Marketing, 58,* 97-105.

Kent, R. J., & Machleit, K. A. (1990). The differential effects of within-brand and between-brand processing on the recall and recognition of television commercials. *Journal of Advertising, 19,* 4-14.

Kerlinger, F. N. (1986). *Foundations of behavioral research* (3rd ed.). Fort Worth, TX: Harcourt Brace Jovanovich.

Krugman, H. (1965). The impact of television advertising: Learning without involvement. *Public Opinion Quarterly, 29,* 349-356.

Krugman, H. (1966-1967). The measurement of advertising involvement. *Public Opinion Quarterly, 31,* 583-596.

Krugman, D. M., Cameron, G. T., & White, C. M. (1995). Visual attention to programming and commercials: The use of in-home observations. *Journal of Advertising, 24,* 1-12.

Lau, R. R., Sigelman, L., Heldman, C., & Babbitt, P. (1999). The effects of negative political advertisements: A meta-analytic assessment. *American Political Science Review, 93,* 851-875.

Lee, A. Y., & Sternthal, B. (1999). The effects of positive mood on memory. *Journal of Consumer Research, 26,* 115-127.

Li, H., & Bukovac, J. L. (1999). Cognitive impact of banner ad characteristics: An experimental study. *Journalism and Mass Communication Quarterly, 6,* 341-353.

Lodish, L. M., Abraham, M., Kalmenson, S., Livelsberger, J., Lubetkin, B., Richardson, B., & Stevens, M. E. (1995). How T.V. advertising works: A meta-analysis of 389 real world split cable T.V. advertising experiments. *Journal of Marketing Research, 32,* 125-139.

Malaviya, P., Kisielius, J., & Sternthal, B. (1996). The effect of type of elaboration on advertisement processing and judgment. *Journal of Marketing Research, 33,* 410-421.

Maloney, J. C. (1994). The first 90 years of advertising research. In E. M. Clark, T. C. Brock, & D. W. Stewart (Eds.), *Attention, attitude, and affect in response to advertising* (pp. 13-54). Hillsdale, NJ: Lawrence Erlbaum.

McCracken, G. (1989). Who is the celebrity endorser? Cultural foundations of the endorsement processes. *Journal of Consumer Research, 16,* 310-321.

McGuire, W. J. (1968). The nature of attitudes and attitude change. In G. Lindzey & E. Aronson (Eds.), *Handbook of social psychology* (2nd ed., Vol. 3, pp. 136-314). Reading, MA: Addison-Wesley.

McLeod, J. M., & Chaffee, S. H. (1972). The construction of social reality. In J. T. Tedeschi (Ed.), *The social influence process* (pp. 50-59). Chicago: Aldine-Atherton.

McQuarrie, E. F. (1998). Have laboratory experiments become detached from advertiser goals? A meta-analysis. *Journal of Advertising Research, 38,* 15-25.

Meyers-Levy, J., & Sternthal, B. (1993). A two-factor explanation of assimilation and contrast effects. *Journal of Marketing Research, 30,* 359-368.

Mord, M. S., & Gilson, E. (1985). Shorter units: Risk-responsibility-reward. *Journal of Advertising Research, 25,* 9-19.

Moschis, G. P. (1987). *Consumer satisfaction: A life-cycle perspective.* Lexington, MA: Lexington Books.

Murry, J. P., Jr., Lastovicka, J. L., & Singh, S. N. (1992). Feeling and liking responses to television programs: An examination of two explanations for media-context effects. *Journal of Consumer Research, 18,* 441-451.

Murry, J. P., Jr., Stam, A., & Lastovicka, J. L. (1996). Paid- versus donated-media strategies for public service announcement campaigns. *Public Opinion Quarterly, 60,* 1-29.

Olsen, G. D. (1995). Creating the contrast: The influence of silence and background music on recall and attribute importance. *Journal of Advertising, 24*(4), 29-44.

Olsen, G. D. (1997). The impact of interstimulus interval and background silence on recall. *Journal of Consumer Research, 23,* 295-304.

Patzer, G. L. (1991). Multiple dimensions of performance for 30-second and 15-second commercials. *Journal of Advertising Research, 31,* 18-25.

Perry, D. S., Jenzowsky, S. A., Hester, J. B., King, C. M., & Yi, H. (1997). The influence of commercial humor on program enjoyment and evaluation. *Journalism & Mass Communication Quarterly, 74,* 388-399.

Perry, S. D., Jenzowsky, S. A., King, C. M., Yi, H., Hester, J. B., & Gartenschlaeger, J. (1997). Using humorous programs as a vehicle for humorous commercials. *Journal of Communication, 47,* 20-39.

Petty, R. A., & Cacioppo, J. T. (1981). *Attitudes and persuasion: Classic and contemporary approaches.* Dubuque, IA: William C. Brown.

Petty, R. A., Cacioppo, J. T., & Schumann, D. (1983). Central and peripheral routes to advertising effectiveness. The moderating role of involvement. *Journal of Consumer Research, 10,* 135-146.

Pieters, R. M., & Bijmolt, T. H. A. (1997). Consumer memory for television advertising: A field study of duration, serial position, and competition effects. *Journal of Consumer Research, 23,* 362-372.

Preston, I. L. (1985). The developing detachment of advertising research from the study of advertiser goals. *Current Issues and Research in Advertising, 7,* 1-15.

Rose, G. M., Bush, V. D., & Kahle, L. (1998). The influence of family communication patterns on parental reactions toward advertising: A cross-national examination. *Journal of Advertising, 27,* 71-85.

Scott, C., Klein, D. M., & Bryant, J. (1990). Consumer response to humor in advertising: A series of field studies using behavioral observation. *Journal of Consumer Research, 16,* 498-501.

Sheth, J. N. (1972). The future of buyer behavior theory. In M. Venkatesan (Ed.), *Proceedings of the third annual conference of the Association for Consumer Research* (pp. 562-575). College Park, MD: Association for Consumer Research.

Singh, S. N., & Cole, C. A. (1993). The effects of length, content, and repetition on television commercial effectiveness. *Journal of Marketing Research, 30,* 91-104.

Singh, S. N., Mishra, S., Bendapudi, N., & Linville, D. (1994). Enhancing memory of television commercials through message spacing. *Journal of Marketing Research, 31,* 384-393.

Speck, P. S., & Elliott, M. T. (1997). Predictors of advertising avoidance in print and broadcast media. *Journal of Advertising, 26,* 61-76.

Spotts, H. E., Weinberger, M. G., & Parsons, A. L. (1997). Assessing the use and impact of humor on advertising effectiveness: A contingency approach. *Journal of Advertising, 26,* 17-32.

Stevenson, J. S., Bruner, G. C., II, & Kumar, A. (2000). Webpage background and viewer attitudes. *Journal of Advertising Research, 40,* 29-33.

Stewart, D. W., Pechmann, C., Ratneswar, S., Stroud, J., & Bryant, B. (1985). Methodological and theoretical foundations of advertising copytesting: A review. *Current Issues and Research in Advertising, 2,* 1-74.

Straughan, D., Bleske, G., & Zhao, X. (1996). Modeling format and source effects of an advocacy message. *Journalism and Mass Communication Quarterly, 73,* 135-146.

Thorson, E., & Reeves, B. (1986). Effects of overtime measures of viewer liking and activity during programs and commercials on memory for commercials. *Advances in Consumer Research, 13,* 549-553.

Thorson, E., Reeves, B., Schleuder, J., Lang, A., & Rothschild, M. (1985). Effects of program context on the processing of television commercials. In N. Stephens (Ed.), *Proceedings of the American Academy of Advertising* (pp. 58-63). Tempe: Arizona State University.

Till, B. D., & Shimp, T. A. (1998). Endorsers in advertising: The case of negative celebrity information. *Journal of Advertising, 27,* 67-82.

Tripp, C., Jensen, T. D., & Carlson, L. (1994). The effects of multiple product endorsements by celebrities on consumers' attitudes and intentions. *Journal of Consumer Research, 20,* 535-547.

Webb, P. H., & Ray, M. L. (1979). Effects of TV clutter. *Journal of Advertising Research, 19,* 7-12.

Weinberger, M. G., & Gulas, C. S. (1992). The impact of humor in advertising: A review. *Journal of Advertising, 21,* 35-59.

Weinberger, M. G., Spotts, H., Campbell, L., & Parsons, A. L. (1995). The use and effect of humor in different advertising media. *Journal of Advertising Research, 35,* 45-56.

Wells, W. D. (1993). Discovery oriented consumer research. *Journal of Consumer Research, 19,* 489-504.

Zhang, Y. (1996). Responses to humorous advertising: The moderating effect of need for cognition. *Journal of Advertising, 25,* 15-32.

Zhao, X. (1997). Clutter and serial order redefined and retested. *Journal of Advertising Research, 37,* 57-74.

Zhao, X., Shen, F., & Blake, K. (1995). Position of TV advertisements in a natural pod: A preliminary analysis of concepts, measurements, and effects. In C. Madden (Ed.), *Proceedings of the 1995 Conference of the American Academy of Advertising* (pp. 154-161). Waco, TX: Baylor University.

26

The Business of Influence

Principles That Lead to Success in Commercial Settings

KELTON V. L. RHOADS
ROBERT B. CIALDINI

In the advertising industry, there is a story about a frozen foods executive who was looking to hire an ad agency and, in the process, was interviewing one particular prospect.

"Do you have experience in selling frozen food?" the executive asked.

"Yes," said the ad agency representative.

"How about frozen vegetables?"

"Yes, several types."

"Spinach?"

"Yes," claimed the agency representative, "we successfully advertised spinach for another client several years ago."

Now leaning forward in his seat, his voice strained in anticipation, the executive asked, "Whole leaf or chopped?"

The story illustrates one of our central contentions: Although highly specialized knowledge in a narrow arena can be valuable, surely it would be more valuable to possess a broader expertise than that—expertise in the fundamental, cross-situational laws of human behavior. Even in just the commercial domain, knowing the laws that regulate human re-sponding would allow for the construction of effective appeals across a wide spectrum of circumstances—retail or wholesale, products or services, advertising or sales, whole leaf or chopped.

Influence settings, issues, modalities, and agents might change, but truly universal principles of influence should undergird successful persuasive attempts wherever they are applied. The question to be addressed in this chapter is whether such universal principles are known. While we certainly do not claim to have located or come to fully understand all of the universal principles of influence, we do believe that there is evidence pointing to the existence of at least six. We consider these six principles at length subsequently. However, before we do, it is important to consider a prior issue: How does one determine which are the most regular and powerful influences on the influence process?

One answer involves the systematic observation of the behaviors of commercial compliance professionals. Who are the commercial compliance professionals, and why should their actions be especially informative as to the identification of powerful influences on everyday compliance decisions? They can be defined as those individuals whose business or financial well-being is dependent on their ability to induce compliance with their requests, whether they are salespeople, fund-raisers, advertisers, political campaign managers, lobbyists, recruiters, negotiators, public relations specialists, or other influence agents. With this definition in place, one can begin to recognize why the regular and widespread practices of these professionals would be noteworthy indicators of the powerful influences on the compliance process: Because the livelihoods of commercial compliance professionals depend on the effectiveness of their procedures, those professionals who use procedures that work well to elicit compliance responses will survive and flourish. They will also pass on these successful procedures to succeeding generations—their trainees. However, those practitioners who use unsuccessful compliance procedures either will drop them or will quickly go out of business; in either case, the procedures themselves will not be passed on to newer generations.

The upshot of this process is that, over time and over the range of naturally occurring compliance contexts, the strongest and most adaptable procedures for generating compliance will rise, persist, and accumulate. Furthermore, these procedures should point a careful observer toward the major principles that people use to decide when to comply.

Employing this logic and the methodology of participant observation, one of us (Cialdini, 1993) engaged in an extended investigation of the influence techniques that are most frequently taught to and used by marketers, fundraisers, salespeople, and the like. What emerged was a list of six principles on which compliance professionals appeared to base most of their psychological influence attempts: reciprocity,

consistency, social validation, friendship/liking, authority, and scarcity. Subsequent research has documented the ability of these principles to mediate influence in diverse naturally occurring settings such as home Tupperware parties (Frenzen & Davis, 1990), telephone charity solicitations (Howard, 1995), bill collector-debtor interactions (Rafaeli & Sutton, 1991), corporate boardrooms (Belliveau, O'Reilly, & Wade, in press; Main, O'Reilly, & Wade, 1995), and retail clothing stores (Cody, Seiter, & Montagne-Miller, 1995). For example, the Cody et al. (1995) study found that each of these principles, when incorporated into the sales techniques of department store clerks, produced a significant increase in retail clothing purchases. The remainder of this chapter offers an account of the origins and workings of the principles as well as of the social scientific theory and evidence regarding how each principle functions to motivate compliance.

RECIPROCITY

Societies throughout the world abide by the norm of reciprocity, which obligates people to return assistance they may have received from others (Gouldner, 1960). One person can provide food, service, or information to another with confidence that the effort will not be lost but will be repaid in some fashion. Importantly, the norm safeguards those who are the first to give because the "rule of reciprocity" states that favors must be returned in kind.

The reciprocity norm frees people to initiate advantageous relationships where none existed previously. After all, the golden rule does not state, "When others do unto you, be sure you do unto them in return." Instead, it prescribes being the first to give: "Do unto others as you would have them do unto you." In fact, the sociologist Marcel Mauss, who studied gift giving around the world, stated that in every human society there are three obligations related to exchanges (Mauss, 1954). There is, of course, the obligation to repay. But there is also an obligation to give and an obligation to receive. By giving, receiving, and repaying, the rule of reciprocity allows societies to spin mutually supportive "webs of indebtedness" where everybody owes something to somebody else. These traded favors allow us to accomplish tasks that would be difficult to do alone (e.g., moving a heavy desk) and help us to manage uncertainty in our lives (e.g., "Drive me to work when my car won't start, and I'll do the same for you"). Those who violate the norm by taking more than they give are often the first to be cut from our circle of friends and are quickly avoided in business dealings. Anyone who violates the norm risks the relationship and all that it provides (Cotterell, Eisenberger, & Speicher, 1992; Meleshko & Alden, 1993).

Businesses frequently engage the rule of reciprocity in order to sell—offering "free gifts" for listening to a sales pitch, "free workouts" at health spas, "free inspections" in the home, and so on. Such techniques are often effective in getting people to buy products and services that they would not have purchased without the powerful social pressure produced by having accepted a gift (Gruner, 1996). Are small initial gifts effective in generating larger favors? Indeed they are (Howard, 1995). For example, research shows that waiters and waitresses can significantly increase the size of their tips by giving diners something as small as a single piece of candy (Lynn & McCall, 1998). Perhaps because of their primitive survival value, gifts of food seem especially obligating first favors (Eibl-Eibesfelt, 1975), which make them a favorite of compliance professionals the world over.

For people who are engaged in negotiations, concessions are often the focus of reciprocation. After receiving a concession (you

talk the dealer into selling you a car at a reduced cost), most people feel obligated to make a concession in return (you are willing to hand out the salesperson's business cards at work). A compliance tactic designed to engage this felt obligation is called the reciprocal concessions or door-in-the-face technique (Cialdini et al., 1975). Rather than starting with a small request and then advancing to the desired favor (as occurs in the foot-in-the-door tactic, which we discuss later in the "Consistency" section), someone using the door-in-the-face procedure goes in the opposite direction. Here the requester begins with a large request that, if rejected, temporarily places him or her in the unique position of being significantly more likely to hear "yes" on making a subsequent but smaller request. The reciprocal concessions tactic is a unique influence strategy because it actually empowers the requester through rejection. By retreating from a large first request to a smaller second one, the requester makes a concession to the target, who (through the rule of reciprocity) feels obligated to provide a return concession by agreeing to the smaller request.

Several years ago, a resourceful Boy Scout selling tickets to the circus used the technique on this chapter's second author. He asked if I wished to buy any tickets at $5 apiece, and I declined. "Well," he said, "if you don't want to buy any tickets, how about buying some of our big chocolate bars? They're only $1 each." I bought a couple and right away realized that something noteworthy had happened. I knew this to be the case because (a) I do not like chocolate bars, (b) I do like dollars, (c) I was standing there with two of his chocolate bars, and (d) he was walking away with two of my dollars (Cialdini, 1993, p. 34).

Although it cost $2, the episode with the Boy Scout did have a payoff. It led to a series of experiments exploring the door-in-the-face technique (Cialdini et al., 1975). In one study, researchers approached people walking along a sidewalk in Tempe, Arizona, and asked them if they would like to help the County Youth Counseling Program by chaperoning a group of juvenile delinquents on a day trip to the zoo. That request by itself was mostly ineffective; only 17% complied. However, the results changed when this request was preceded by a much larger one: "Would you be willing to spend 2 hours a week as a counselor for a juvenile delinquent for a minimum of 2 years?" After the participants said no to this initial huge request (as all of them did), the researchers retreated to the smaller one: "Oh, well, if you can't do that, would you be willing to chaperone a group of delinquents on a day trip to the zoo?" This approach proved to be much more effective; now fully 50% complied. Why? Because by presenting the zoo request as a concession—a retreat from the earlier request—the researchers had engaged the rule of reciprocity, which caused the participants to reciprocate with a concession of their own.

But is this tactic limited to charity-like organizations, or can it be successful for commercial entities as well? Some evidence indicates that it can be quite effective for business organizations. Mowen and Cialdini (1980) conducted an experiment in which people were asked to participate in an hour-long marketing survey for a California insurance company. After declining, these individuals were asked if they would just respond to one segment of the survey that would take "only" 15 minutes to complete. Compliance to this smaller request nearly doubled (44% vs. 25%) compared to that of control condition participants who received only the 15-minute request.

Those who comply in the face of concessions report that they feel more control over the outcome of a negotiation and are therefore more satisfied with it. In an experiment conducted at the University of California, Los Angeles (Benton, Kelley, & Liebling, 1972), a participant and a confederate were asked to negotiate the split of $15. The confederate would employ one of three strategies: (a) make the extreme demand of $10 for himself and $5 for the participant; (b) make a moderate demand of $8 for himself and $7 for the participant; or (c) start with the extreme demand of $10 and then, after being rejected by the participant, retreat to the more moderate demand of $8. The last strategy yielded the most money for the confederate and also caused there to be the fewest number of "bailouts," where the participant forfeited his share of the money in order to make certain the confederate did not get any of the money either. But what was particularly interesting about the confederate's strategy of retreating from a large to a small demand was how the participant felt about the negotiations. In the concession-compliance condition, participants reported that they felt they had "dictated" the terms of the agreement to a larger degree, reported more satisfaction with the outcome, and were more likely to agree to participating in similar negotiations in the future. This helps to explain the success of the reciprocal concessions tactic in stimulating future compliance: The targets of the tactic feel more responsible for, and more satisfied with, the outcome, making them more susceptible to similar subsequent requests.

Although the obligation to reciprocate what one has received exists in all human societies (Gouldner, 1960), it might not apply with the same strength in each. In its strictest form ("I am obligated to return to you precisely the kind of favor you gave me"), the rule of reciprocation involves a kind of economic exchange between two individuals (Clark & Mills, 1993). Thus, this strict form of the rule should be most powerful in a society such as the United States, where people are most likely to define themselves as free-standing individuals rather than as parts of groups (Schwartz, 2000). But in other cultures, where people see themselves as embedded in family, friendship, and organizational networks, other norms of obligation may predominate.

To test these ideas, Morris, Podolny, and Ariel (2001) gained access to a multinational bank, Citibank, with branches in 195 countries. Two features of Citibank's business operation lent themselves to a controlled investigation of the impact of cultural norms. First, the bank's policy was to minimize differences in the organization and structure of its branches around the world. That is, the services and products offered, the job categories and organizational charts, and even the physical aspects of the branch offices were highly similar in each location. Second, it was also bank policy to hire personnel nearly exclusively from the local countries. Of course, these employees could be expected to carry with them the norms of their respective nations. Thus, if differences were observed in patterns of obligation among employees in the various countries, they could be traced to different cultural norms rather than to differences in the organizational structure of the workplace.

The researchers selected four societies for examination: the United States, China, Spain, and Germany. They surveyed multiple Citibank branches within each society and measured employees' willingness to comply voluntarily with a request from a co-worker for assistance with a task. The main reason why employees felt obligated to comply differed among the four nations. Each of these reasons reflected a different normative approach to obligation.

- In the United States, employees took a market-based approach to the obligation to comply. They offered assistance on the basis of the norm for a reciprocal exchange of favors between two individuals. In deciding whether to comply, they asked the question, "What has this person done for me recently?" They felt obligated to comply if they owed the requester a favor.

- In China, employees took a family-based approach. They offered assistance on the basis of in-group/out-group norms that encourage loyalty only to those within one's small group. In addition, they felt especially loyal to those of high status within their small group. In deciding whether to comply, they asked the question, "Is this requester connected to someone in my unit, especially someone of high ranking?" If the answer was yes, they felt obligated to yield to the request.

- In Spain, employees took a friendship-based approach. They offered assistance on the basis of friendship norms that encourage loyalty to one's friends, regardless of the friend's position or status. They decided whether to comply by asking the question, "Is this requester connected to my friends?" If the answer was yes, they felt obligated to say yes.

- In Germany, employees took a system-based approach to obligation. They offered assistance on the basis of the existing norms and rules of the organization. Rather than feeling obligated to specific individuals or groups, they felt obligated to support the system that governed these individuals and groups. They decided whether to comply by asking the question, "According to official rules and categories, am I supposed to assist this requester?" If the answer was yes, the obligation to grant the request was high.

In sum, different norms of obligation to comply with requests predominate in different cultures. This is not to say, however, that the cultures are entirely different from one another in this regard. No doubt, obligations to prior benefactors, in-group members, friends, and legitimate systems exist in all four of the cultures studied by Morris et al. (2001). But as their findings make clear, the relative potency of these different norms of obligation varies from culture to culture. That is so because the social approval given to people who live up to these different norms varies accordingly in these cultures.

SCARCITY

Items and opportunities appear more attractive as they become less available (Lynn, 1991). This can hold true even when those items or opportunities cannot stand on their own merits. For example, undergraduates at Florida State University, like most college students, rated their cafeteria food as unsatisfactory. They changed their minds 9 days later, however, rating the cafeteria food as significantly more desirable than before. Why? The enhanced ratings could not be attributed to a new menu, new management, better cooks, or higher quality food. It was, in fact, a fire that led students to a new appreciation of their meals. Before rating their cafeteria food a second time, students learned that a portion of the cafeteria had burned and that they would not be able to obtain meals there for several weeks (West, 1975). The cafeteria food was regarded as more desirable the very moment that students realized it was unavailable.

The Desirable. The principle of scarcity appears to draw its power from two sources. First, items that are difficult to obtain are nearly always more desirable than those that require little effort (Lynn, 1992). As even Aristotle conceded, "What is rare is a greater good than what is plentiful." Thus, the scarcity of an item alone provides a frequently accurate cue as to that item's desirability (Cialdini, 1993; Ditto & Jemmott, 1989). This allows scarcity to be employed as a heuristic cue in decision making.

The scarcity heuristic is demonstrated by the results of a consumer preferences study conducted by researchers in North Carolina (Worchel, Lee, & Adewole, 1975). Participants in this study were given a jar of chocolate chip cookies to taste and rate. Some participants received 10 cookies in a jar; others received a jar that contained only 2 cookies.

Despite the fact that all of the cookies had come from the same Nabisco box in the back room, the people who got only 2 cookies rated them as more desirable to eat, more attractive, and able to bring a higher price at the store than did the people who received an abundant supply of the identical cookies. For these cookie-consuming critics, fewer meant better.

But how do we explain the behavior of those who desire the scarce and the rare along dimensions other than utility? What do we make of the popularity of the "limited edition," which might not vary from the standard model in any functional way? How can we explain the brief but rabid demand for Cabbage Patch Kids—ostensibly available in toy stores for $29 but known to sell at auctions for more than $900? How can we explain the fortunes of manufacturers who make *more profit* by making *less products,* whether those products are Beanie Babies or Harley-Davidson motorcycles? Why do people want what is rare, scarce, or dwindling in availability, even when that scarcity has been thoughtfully engineered?

The Forbidden. The second mechanism that fuels the principle of scarcity is our unrelenting desire to preserve our freedom of choice. Protecting freedom is the centerpiece of psychological reactance theory (Brehm, 1966; Brehm & Brehm, 1981). The theory was developed to explain the human response to diminishing personal control. According to the theory, whenever our freedoms are limited or threatened, the need to retain those freedoms makes us want them (as well as the goods and services associated with them) significantly more than previously. So, when increasing scarcity—or anything else—interferes with our prior access to some item, we will react against that interference by wanting and trying to possess the item more than before.

With scarcity operating powerfully on the worth assigned to things, it should not be surprising that compliance professionals have a variety of techniques designed to convert this power to compliance. Probably the most frequently used such technique is the "limited number" tactic in which the customer is informed that membership opportunities, products, or services exist in a limited supply that cannot be guaranteed to last for long.

Related to the limited number tactic is the "deadline" technique in which an official time limit is placed on the customer's opportunity to get what is being offered. Newspaper ads abound with admonitions to the customer regarding the folly of delay—"last three days," "limited time offer," "one week only sale," and so on. The purest form of a decision deadline—right now—occurs in a variant of the deadline technique in which customers are told that, unless they make an immediate purchase decision, they will have to buy the item at a higher price or they will not be able to purchase it at all. Cialdini (1993) reported this tactic's use in numerous compliance settings: A large child photography company urges parents to buy as many poses and copies as they can afford because "stocking limitations force us to burn the unsold pictures of your children within 24 hours." A prospective health club member or automobile buyer might learn that the deal offered by the salesperson is good for that one time; if the customer leaves the premises, the deal is off.

Competition for Scarce Resources. As powerful a motivator as reactance is, certain conditions can amplify its effect. To examine the amplifying power of competition on scarcity, let us revisit the cookie experiment mentioned previously. An additional condition in this study added competition to the mix. While some participants got 2 cookies and others got 10, a third condition was first given a jar of 10 cookies that was promptly replaced with a jar of 2 with the explanation, "I can't give you these 10 cookies after all. There's been such a demand for these cookies by the other participants in the study that I can only give you 2 of them." When these people rated the 2 remaining cookies, they evaluated them as more attractive than did any other participants in the entire experiment (Worchel, Lee, & Adewole, 1975). Although people value scarce resources more than abundant ones, this is especially true when they are in competition with others for those scarce resources.

Scarcity of Information. Other research has suggested that in addition to commodities, limited access to information makes the information more desirable—and more influential (Brock, 1968; Brock & Bannon, 1992). One test of Brock's thinking found good support in a business setting. Wholesale beef buyers who were told of an impending imported beef shortage purchased significantly more beef when they were informed that the shortage information came from certain "exclusive" contacts that the importer had (Knishinsky, 1982). Apparently, the fact that the scarcity news was itself scarce made it more valued and persuasive. Additional evidence—from the literature on censorship—suggests that restricting information can empower that information in unintended ways. Individuals typically respond to censorship by wanting to receive the banned information to a greater extent and by becoming more favorable to it than before the ban (e.g., Worchel, 1992; Worchel & Arnold, 1973). Especially interesting is the finding that people will come to believe in banned information more, even though they have not received it (Worchel, Arnold, & Baker, 1975). Even self-imposed bans on information can have powerful effects. Wegner, Lane, and Dimitri (1994) demonstrated that clandestine romantic relationships are more memorable than the nonsecret variety—and generate more attraction as well.

Loss Framing. People seem to be more motivated by the thought of losing something than by the thought of gaining something of equal value. For instance, college students experienced much stronger emotions when asked to imagine losses as opposed to gains in their romantic relationships or in their grade point averages (Ketelaar, 1995). Especially under conditions of risk and uncertainty, the threat of potential loss plays a powerful role in human decision making (De Dreu & McCusker, 1997; Tversky & Kahneman, 1981). This highlights the fact that humans consider gains and losses psychologically rather than logically. A decision maker will select the option with the highest subjective value, whether or not that option provides the highest objective gain. And more often than not, subjective value mandates no loss (Kahneman & Tversky, 1982). Investment counselors, for example, struggle against the "no loss" rule whenever they steer a client toward a potentially lucrative but risky investment.

Alexander Rothman and Peter Salovey have applied this insight to the medical arena, where individuals are frequently urged to undergo tests to detect existing illnesses (e.g., mammography procedures, HIV screenings, cancer self-examinations). Because such tests involve risks that diseases will be found and uncertainty regarding whether or not they can be cured, messages stressing potential losses are most effective (Rothman, Martino, Bedell, Detweiler, & Salovey, 1999; Rothman & Salovey, 1997). For example, pamphlets advising young women to check for breast cancer through self-examinations are significantly more successful if they state their case in terms of what stands to be lost rather than what stands to be gained (Meyerwitz & Chaiken, 1987). In a similar vein, physicians'

letters to smokers describing the number of years of life that would be lost if they did not quit were more effective than letters describing the number of years that would be gained if they did quit (Wilson, Kaplan, & Schneiderman, 1987; Wilson, Purdon, & Wallston, 1988).

AUTHORITY

Legitimate authorities are extremely influential sources (e.g., Aronson, Turner, & Carlsmith, 1963; Blass, 1991, 1999; Milgram, 1974). Whether authorities have acquired their positions through superior training, talent, or fortune, we have been raised from childhood to look to authorities for information and guidance. As children, we followed the directives of our parents and teachers—partly because of their greater wisdom and partly because they controlled our punishments and rewards. As adults, *who* the authority figures *are* have changed, but they continue to exist—as do the benefits associated with doing as they say. Consequently, it makes sense to comply with the wishes of recognized authorities. Following their advice often helps us to choose rapidly and correctly—so we sometimes continue to follow the directives of authority figures even when doing so makes no sense at all.

Examples of automatic but irrational compliance thrive in organizations with clearly defined hierarchies. One dramatic example comes from the airline industry, where insiders call the effect *captainitis* (Foushee, 1984). Accident investigators from the Federal Aviation Administration have noted that, on many occasions, an obvious error made by a flight captain will not be corrected by the other crew members. Despite clear evidence of the captain's mistake, crew members yield to the authority heuristic and fail to attend or respond to a captain's disastrous errors (Harper, Kidera, & Cullen, 1971). Further evidence suggests that when the captain maintains an authoritarian leadership style, crews are particularly susceptible to missing the captain's oversights (Kanki & Foushee, 1990). It comes as no surprise that individuals possessing strong authoritarian beliefs are especially likely to comply with the directives of an authority, as was demonstrated in the Milgram conformity experiments (Elms & Milgram, 1966) and in a variety of other settings (Ditto, Moore, Hilton, & Kalish, 1995; Miller, 1975; Miller, Collins, & Brief, 1995).

Symbols of Authority: Titles, Tailors, and Tone. Sometimes the smallest symbols of authority are sufficient to engage automatic deference (Bushman, 1984). One of the shortest but most effective of these symbols—the two letters "Dr."—have been shown to be surprisingly effective as a compliance-gaining device among trained hospital personnel. In one study, a group of physicians and nurses conducted an experiment that documented the degree of blind obedience accorded by hospital nurses to an individual whom they had never met but who claimed in a phone call to be a doctor (Hofling, Brotzman, Dalrymple, Graves, & Pierce, 1966). Although the phony phone-in physician violated no less than four hospital rules governing the administration of a particular drug, fully 95% of the nurses he contacted were willing to administer twice the maximum acceptable dose of it merely because that caller requested it. A follow-up study asked nurses to recall a time when they had obeyed a doctor's order that they considered inappropriate and potentially harmful to a patient. Those who admitted such incidents (46%) attributed their actions to their belief that the doctor was a legitimate and expert authority in the matter—the same two features of authority that appear to account for

obedience in the famous Milgram experiments (Krackow & Blass, 1995). Subsequent research has found that, by varying aspects of the situation (e.g., the nature of the request, the nurses' familiarity with the drug), it is possible to lower the level of obedience, but the amount of compliance remains dangerously high even under these conditions (Blass, 1999; Krackow & Blass, 1995; Rank & Jacobson, 1977).

Uniforms are another universally recognized symbol of authority that can bring about mindless compliance. In one study, a confederate wearing a security guard's uniform asked strangers to do things such as pick up a paper bag on the street, stand on the other side of a bus stop sign, and place money in an expired parking meter that was not theirs. When wearing the uniform rather than street clothes, the confederate could produce significantly more compliance with requests—even those that were irrelevant to a security guard's domain of authority (Bickman, 1974; Bushman, 1988). Another commonly encountered uniform—the well-tailored business suit—has also been shown to have dramatic effects on influence. Even without the aid of research, influence practitioners have long known the importance of the somber business suit in connoting authority. Dick Morris, the political operative to whom many credit President Clinton's reelection to a second term in office, insisted that Clinton adopt "a red tie and navy suit as standard" rather than Clinton's preferred light-colored suits and ties with intricate patterns (Morris, 1999). Morris intuited what social scientists had confirmed years earlier. An experiment revealed that three and a half times as many people were willing to follow a jaywalker into traffic when he wore a conservative business suit and tie as compared to a jaywalker attired more casually in a work shirt and trousers (Lefkowitz, Blake, & Mouton, 1955; see also Mullen, Cooper, & Driskell,

1990). Whether on the street or in the White House, the business suit connotes the type of authority that says "follow me."

The symbols of authority are not always as prominent and enduring as titles or as palpable as official-looking uniforms. Authority may also be communicated by the styles of speech one uses in conversation. Communication researchers have learned that people shift their voices and speech styles toward the styles of individuals in positions of power and authority (Giles & Coupland, 1991; Pittam, 1994). One study explored this phenomenon by analyzing interviews on the *Larry King Live* television show. When King interviewed guests with great social standing and prestige (e.g., George Bush, Bill Clinton), his voice style changed to match theirs. But when he interviewed guests of lower status and prestige (e.g., Dan Quayle, Spike Lee), King continued to communicate in his preferred style, and their voice styles shifted to match his (Gregory & Webster, 1996).

Credible Communicators. Although some authorities are in a position to force us to obey, it is more interesting to consider how effective they can be without the power to reward or punish. In these cases, authorities must rely on *expert power*—the power that comes from acknowledged competence in a particular field (French & Raven, 1959).

When circumstances disallow, or people are unmotivated to undertake, a thorough examination of a persuasive communication, people are especially likely to make a decision based on the credibility of the communicator (Chaiken & Maheswaran, 1994; Petty, Cacioppo, & Goldman, 1981). What are the characteristics of a credible communicator? During the 1st century A.D., the famous Roman orator Quintilian (1920) wrote, "For he who would have all men trust his judgment as to what is expedient and honorable, should possess and be regarded as possessing genuine

wisdom and excellence of character" (p. 13). After years of scientific research, Quintilian's two-part formula has been verified: A credible communicator is both expert and trustworthy (Perloff, 1993).

Expertise. The media's presentation of an expert's views on a topic has an immediate and dramatic result. A single expert opinion news story printed in *The New York Times* is associated with an average 2% shift in public opinion nationwide. When an expert's statement is aired on national television, public opinion shifts approaching 4% can be expected (Jorden, 1993; Page, Shapiro, & Dempsey, 1987). As agents of influence, looking for experts who will support our advocated positions is time and effort well spent. Research shows that offering the opinions of experts is particularly effective when the intended audience does not initially favor one's proposal (Aronson et al., 1963).

It is clear that people often employ heuristic thinking (e.g., "believe an expert") when forming opinions about simple topics in which they are uninvolved (Petty & Cacioppo, 1979). However, shortcut thinking appears on the other end of the scale as well. When issues are weighty and bewilderingly complex, people once again turn to those judgment strategies that have helped them to arrive at acceptable conclusions in the past. When faced with overwhelming complexity, even on topics of vital importance, people frequently prefer to detour around a great deal of thought by employing only a little (Chaiken, Liberman, & Eagly, 1989). It is instructive that even though people often do not take a fully considered approach to certain complicated, personally important topics, they wish that their advisers—their physicians, accountants, lawyers, and brokers—do precisely that for them (Kahn & Baron, 1995). When feeling overwhelmed by a complicated and consequential choice, most individuals still want a fully considered, point-by-point analysis of it—an analysis they might not be able to achieve except, ironically enough, through a shortcut—reliance on an expert. It is for this reason that a communicator's expertise becomes increasingly important as issues become increasingly complex.

Suppose that you are sitting on a jury deciding how much money to award a man who claims that he contracted cancer as a result of exposure to a particular chemical while on the job. His employer, a manufacturing firm, admits that the man was exposed to this chemical but disputes that it caused his cancer. One piece of evidence you hear is the testimony of an expert witness, Dr. Thomas Fallon, who states that scientific data show that the chemical does indeed lead to cancer in a variety of species, including humans. How swayed are you likely to be by this expert? According to a study done by Cooper, Bennett, and Sukel (1996), that would depend not just on how expert you think he is but also on how complex his testimony was.

In that study, mock jurors heard Dr. Fallon described either as highly expert or only moderately expert on the topic. Some of the jurors then heard him give his testimony in ordinary language—saying simply that the chemical causes liver cancer, several other diseases of the liver, and diseases of the immune system. Other jurors heard him give his testimony in complex, nearly incomprehensible language—saying that the chemical led to "tumor induction as well as hepatomegaly, hepatomegalocytosis, and lymphoid atrophy of the spleen and thymus." The most interesting finding of the study was that the highly expert witness was more successful in swaying the jury only when he spoke in complex, difficult-to-understand terms. Why? The study's authors stated that when Dr. Fallon used simple language, jurors could judge the case on the basis of the evidence itself. They did not need to use his expertise as a shortcut to accuracy.

However, when his testimony was too obscure to understand, they had to rely on his reputation as an expert to tell them what to think. These results suggest an interesting but discomforting irony: Acknowledged experts may be most persuasive when nonexperts cannot understand the details of what they are saying.

Trustworthiness. The reader may recall that expertise was only the first element in Quintilian's classic formula. Despite communicators' knowledge and experience, they will not be optimally persuasive simply by convincing an audience that they know what they are talking about. Research conducted around the world indicates that communicators must also convince the audience that they are *trustworthy* sources of that same information (McGuiness & Ward, 1980).

Whereas expertise refers to a communicator's knowledge and experience, trustworthiness refers to the communicator's honesty and lack of bias. Most of the time, we trust those who have an established track record or those whom we have known personally for a long period of time. How, then, can communicators appear to be honest and unbiased when delivering a persuasive message without the benefit of a previously existing relationship? One way they can do that is by conveying the impression that their message is not intended to change attitudes in order to serve the communicators' own interests but rather is intended to serve the audience members' interests by informing them accurately about the issues at hand (Campbell, 1995). Advertisements promising "straight talk" about a product illustrate one approach often taken to establish trustworthiness.

A second method of enhancing trustworthiness requires more finesse on the part of communicators. Rather than arguing only in their own favor, communicators can provide both sides of the argument—the pros and the cons—which gives the impression of honesty and impartiality. Researchers have long known that communicators who present two-sided arguments and who appear to be arguing against their own interests can gain the trust of their audiences and thereby become more influential (Eagly, Wood, & Chaiken, 1978; Smith & Hunt, 1978). This two-sided approach is especially effective when the audience initially disagrees with the communicator. It is less effective when "preaching to the choir" because giving both sides of an argument to those who are already inclined to accept the communicator's position simply provides the audience with novel ideas supporting the opposition (Hovland, Lumsdaine, & Sheffield, 1949).

Convert communicators— those who argue against their own previous ideas and behaviors—can efficiently make up for deficits in trustworthiness. Because humans universally strive to be, and to appear, consistent with their own beliefs and behaviors, we take notice when we observe a person arguing against his or her own previously held attitudes and actions. This is a particularly effective tactic when used by low-status communicators to whom we might not otherwise attend (Levine & Valle, 1975). Drug addicts, alcoholics, and former criminals may lack status and prestige but can nonetheless become extremely credible communicators when they tell us about their conversion from a previous lifestyle or ideology to an opposite set of beliefs and behaviors. Research has demonstrated that a reformed alcoholic is a significantly more persuasive communicator than a teetotaler on the subject of the importance of abstaining from alcohol (Perloff & Pettey, 1991). While convert communicators are better able to take strategic advantage of similarities between themselves and their audience, they are also able to demonstrate that they have overcome a past bias, which further serves to enhance their credibility.

Arguments against self-interest—in the guise of "straight talk," giving both sides of the argument, or in the mouths of convert communicators—are efficient and effective ways of enhancing communicator trustworthiness in the absence of previous relationships with the audience. While arguing against one's own position may appear counterproductive at first, savvy marketers have made frequent and effective use of this tactic. Attorneys are also taught to "steal the opponent's thunder" by mentioning a weakness in their own case before the opposing lawyer does, thereby establishing a perception of honesty in the eyes of jury members. Experiments have demonstrated that this tactic works. When jurors heard an attorney bring up a weakness in his own case first, jurors assigned him more honesty and were more favorable to his overall case in their final verdicts because of that perceived honesty (Williams, Bourgeois, & Croyle, 1993).

In sum, credible communicators possess both expertise and trustworthiness; but without trustworthiness, even experts will not be very persuasive. One way a communicator can acquire the trust of an audience is to appear to be honest by seeming to argue against self-interests by volunteering a weakness or drawback to the advocated position before delivering his or her strongest and best arguments. In this manner, those strong arguments have more impact because listeners will have lowered their cognitive defenses to a communicator who is now seen as more trustworthy.

COMMITMENT AND CONSISTENCY

Social scientists have long understood the fundamental role that the need for consistency plays in human behavior. Many theorists have viewed the desire to be consistent as a prime motivator of behavior (Festinger,

1957; Heider, 1958; Newcomb, 1953). Others have emphasized the additional desire to appear consistent (Baumeister, 1982; Tedeschi, 1981). But consistent with what? The evidence points clearly to existing commitments (Cialdini, 1993). Once an individual takes a stand, goes on record, or establishes a position, there is a tendency to respond in ways that are stubbornly consistent with it. Understanding this need for consistency with earlier commitments explains much about why people resist change. And, as we will see shortly, it also helps to explain how people can be induced to change.

Commitment in Resisting Change. Research by Pomeranz, Chaiken, and Tordesillas (1995) suggests that one reason why people resist changing an attitude is their commitment to it. When people are committed to an attitude, they are more certain the attitude is correct, they are more sure they will not change it, and their position on the issue is more extreme. As a result, they are typically unwilling to shift from it.

Being deeply committed to a particular attitude leads to resistance by causing people to dismiss contrary evidence. For example, in the Pomeranz et al. (1995) experiment, participants with committed attitudes toward capital punishment were shown a research study that opposed their position on the issue. They reacted by rejecting this information, dismissing the essay's arguments, and attacking the study's "flawed" methods.

Commitment in Causing Change. A great deal of research suggests that commitments can efficiently engage pressures to align oneself with salient positions. Depending on which internal element a particular commitment taps, those commitments can be followed by remarkable changes in a person's attitude and behavior. Once a commitment is

made, there is a marked tendency to behave in ways that are consistent with it (Deutsch & Gerard, 1955; Greenwald, Carnot, Beach, & Young, 1987; Howard, 1990; Sherman, 1980). Any of a variety of strategies may be used to generate the crucial instigating commitment. Let us look at several that differ primarily in the way they obtain the initial commitment.

Foot-in-the-Door. One such strategy is the foot-in-the-door technique (e.g., Freedman & Fraser, 1966; Schwartzwald, Bizman, & Raz, 1983). This term refers to the efforts of door-to-door salespeople to get "one foot in the door" as a prerequisite to gaining full entry. A solicitor using this procedure will first ask for a favor that is so small, it is virtually certain to be granted. The initial compliance is then followed by another request for a larger *related* favor. This tactic was first explored during the 1960s, and researchers have now amassed considerable evidence supporting the efficacy of the tactic (for reviews, see Burger, 2000; Dillard, Hunter, & Burgoon, 1984). A modern confirmation of the foot-in-the-door technique was conducted by Israeli researchers who went to a local apartment district, knocked on half of the doors, and asked residents to sign a petition favoring the establishment of a recreation center for the mentally handicapped. The cause was good, and the request was small, so nearly everyone agreed to sign. Residents in the other apartments did not receive a visit and, consequently, did not make a commitment to the mentally handicapped. Two weeks later, on National Collection Day for the Mentally Handicapped, all neighborhood residents were approached at home and asked to give money to this cause. Only about half (53%) of those who had not been previously asked to sign a petition made a contribution; nearly all (92%) of those who had signed 2 weeks earlier gave a donation (Schwartzwald et al., 1983).

Freedman and Fraser (1966) argued that the foot-in-the-door technique is successful because performance of the initially requested action causes a change in self-perception. They came to this conclusion when they observed a "halo effect" for the initial commitment that transferred to other remotely related behaviors. Considerable data support this interpretation, including a study showing that children are not influenced by the foot-in-the-door technique until they are around 6 or 7 years old, a time at which they begin to comprehend and appreciate stable personality traits. At the same time as children come to understand the meaning of a stable trait, the foot-in-the-door tactic becomes effective—especially among those children who prefer consistency in behavior (Eisenberg, Cialdini, McCreath, & Shell, 1987). Cialdini, Trost, and Newsom (1995) replicated this latter finding with adults; only those with a strong preference for consistency showed a foot-in-the-door effect. Gorassini and Olson (1995) provided data indicating that changes in self-perception are not sufficient to produce a foot-in-the-door effect. Although compliance with a small request led to greater self-perceptions of helpfulness, these shifts did not mediate willingness to comply with a related larger request. It may be that, for the foot-in-the-door effect to appear reliably, individuals must experience a self-perception change in response to initial compliance *and* must be inclined to behave consistently with that changed self-view. The inclination toward consistent responding may come about through dispositional factors, as in the Eisenberg et al. (1987) and Cialdini et al. (1995) studies, or through situational factors that make consistency salient.

Lowball. A similar strategy is employed by car dealers using the lowball technique, which proceeds by obtaining a commitment to an action and *then* increasing the costs of performing the action (Cialdini, Cacioppo, Bassett, &

Miller, 1978). Automobile salespeople have been known to use this technique regularly. They induce the customer to choose a particular car by offering it at an attractive low price. After the selection has been made—and, at times, after commitment to the car is enhanced by allowing the customer to take it home overnight or by arranging financing with the bank—the attractive price is removed before the final papers are signed. Perhaps a calculation error is "discovered" or the sales manager disallows the deal because "we'd be losing money at that price." By this time, however, many customers have experienced a strong desire to own that particular automobile. They often proceed with the purchase in the absence of the beneficial price that attracted them to the car in the first place.

This tactic has been shown to be surprisingly effective in the lab as well. For example, French cigarette smokers were asked to participate in a study in which they would fill out a short questionnaire. After committing to a date and time, they were then given information that made their commitment less attractive; they were told that the study required them to refrain from smoking for 18 hours before the experiment. Even though they were given the chance to back out after hearing of the nonsmoking requirement, an astounding 85% agreed to participate anyway—many more than the 12% who agreed to participate if informed of the nonsmoking requirement before they committed to a date and time (Joule, 1987).

Why do both consumers and laboratory participants forge ahead with a commitment after the reason they made the commitment in the first place has been removed? After making an active choice for something, people regard it more positively and are reluctant to relinquish it (Cioffi & Garner, 1996; Kahneman, Knetsch, & Thaler, 1991). This is especially the case when they have come to own the decision internally. Once people take "mental possession" of an important object or idea, it becomes part of their self-concept (Ball & Tasaki, 1992; Beggan & Allison, 1997).

Let us take a parting look at the low-balled automobile buyer and examine how commitment- and consistency-related phenomena worked together to make certain the automobile remained in the buyer's garage instead of back in the dealer's showroom. First, consistency pressures caused the buyer to view the features of the car more favorably. After having invested time, attention, and money, the car became increasingly attractive. Second, after taking the car home for a night to show neighbors and co-workers, the buyer's self-image shifted to include the new automobile. His previous car no longer fit that image. In this way, the automobile became embedded in the buyer's persona. Despite increased cost, many car consumers decide to buy anyway, saying to themselves, "It's worth a few hundred dollars extra to get the car I really like because it fits who I am." People tend to act in ways that make good psychological, if not good economic, sense.

Labeling Tactics. Another way to induce commitment to a course of action is to give a person a label that is consistent with the action we wish for the person to take. Some researchers call this tactic "altercasting" (Pratkanis, 2000; Weinstein & Deutschberger, 1963, 1964). For instance, when an adult told elementary school children that "You look to me like the kind of girl [or boy] who understands how important it is to write correctly," those children were more likely to work diligently on a penmanship task several days later in private (Cialdini, Eisenberg, Green, Rhoads, & Bator, 1998). Tybout and Yalch (1980) demonstrated how this same approach could be used to spur adults to vote. They interviewed 162 voters and, at random, told half of them that, according to their interview responses, they were "above average citizens likely to vote and participate in political events." The other half were told that they appeared to be average in these activities. Those given the above-average label appeared to internalize the feedback, reporting in a follow-up questionnaire that they saw themselves as better citizens. Tellingly, these same people were significantly more likely to vote more often in a local election held a week later.

Existing Commitments. So far, we have been discussing tactics that vary in the way they obtain an initial commitment. However, a vast amount of influence is accomplished not by obtaining new commitments but rather by tapping commitments that are already in place.

Drawing connections between ideas or products and preexisting commitments within the consumer is one of the most powerful, popular, and efficient techniques used by savvy marketing professionals. Rather than engaging in the laborious task of creating new commitments, clever marketers look for existing commitments within potential customers that are consistent with the products or services they are offering. If existing commitments can be made more salient to the customer, then the motivation to maintain consistency can direct behavior accordingly. For example, insurance agents are often taught to stress to new homeowners that the purchase of an expensive house reflects an enormous personal commitment to one's home and the well-being of one's family. Consequently, they argue that it would be consistent with such a commitment to home and family to purchase home and life insurance in amounts that befit the size of this commitment.

Ball-Rokeach, Rokeach, and Grube (1984) demonstrated long-term behavioral effects from a television program that focused viewers on their personal commitments to certain deep-seated values (e.g., freedom, equality), on the one hand, and their current beliefs and behaviors, on the other. Not only did uninterrupted viewers of this single program evidence enhanced commitment to these values, but they were significantly more likely to donate money to support causes consistent with the values 2 to 3 months after the program had aired. A similar effect occurred among Australian high-energy consumers after being shown the discrepancy between their current levels of consumption and their previous pro-conservation statements. They conserved significantly more energy than did control participants (Kantola, Syme, & Campbell, 1984). The tactic of pointing out the discrepancy ("hypocrisy") between an existing commitment and inconsistent current conduct has been employed successfully by Aronson and his colleagues to generate compliance with requests or recommendations for water conservation (Dickerson, Thibodeau, Aronson, & Miller, 1992), recycling action (Fried & Aronson, 1995), and condom use (Stone, Aronson, Crain, Winslow, & Fried, 1994).

The practice of recasting one's positions and aligning one's arguments with prevailing mores and popular values is a technique practiced by skillful influence professionals who mount media campaigns for political, commercial, public service, or propagandistic ends. Communicators are encouraged to frame issues so that "they are based on the most deeply ingrained core values" of the audience (Siegel & Doner, 1998, p. 242). Careful research into audience members' lifestyles, leisure activities, attitudes, preferred media channels, and sources of knowledge reveals the core attitudes, preferences, and values of targeted audience members to influence professionals, who then use that information to craft products and messages that are appealing, relevant, and (most important) *consistent* with the desires and commitments that already exist within the listening audience. From products to politics, successful persuaders know that it is much easier to promote a person, service, or product that can harness the "prevailing winds" of widely held attitudes and values than to create new attitudes, values, and demands within that same audience.

Because of a desire in people to maintain consistency and live up to their commitments, it is possible to influence a target person's actions by using any of several commitment-based tactics. Although these tactics differ in the way they engage commitment, they have in common the establishment of an early commitment, or the location of an existing commitment, that ties the target person's identity to the desired action. In the process of performing that action, the target person is able to enhance, confirm, and protect the self-concept.

However, not all types of commitments are equally effective. There is research evidence that demonstrates the particular types of commitments that lead to consistent future responding. A commitment is likely to be maximally effective in producing consistent future behavior to the extent that it is voluntary or uncoerced (Freedman, 1965; Lydon & Zanna, 1990), active or effortful (Aronson & Mills, 1959; Bem, 1967; Carducci, Deuser, Bauer, Large, & Ramaekers, 1989; Cioffi & Garner, 1996; Fazio, Sherman, & Herr, 1982), and public (Baumeister, 1982; Deutsch & Gerard, 1955; Kelly, 1998; Kelly & McKillop, 1996; Kiesler, Sproull, & Waters, 1996; Schlenker, 1980; Schlenker, Dlugolecki, & Doherty, 1994; Schlenker & Trudeau, 1990; Tice, 1992).

In sum, people can enhance, validate, and protect their identities by yielding to requests for action that fit with their self-concept. Several influence tactics (the foot-in-the-door, the lowball, the bait-and-switch, and labeling techniques) work by establishing an early commitment that links the target person's identity to a desired course of action. In addition, people have existing commitments in the form of personal values that spur them to comply with requests that are consistent with these values. These commitments are most effective when they are actively and publicly made, particularly when they are made with free choice. Therefore, influence practitioners can increase compliance by establishing connections between their requests and the values to which targets feel committed, especially when these values are prominent in consciousness.

SOCIAL VALIDATION

Fiske and Taylor (1991) identified us as "cognitive misers"—humans burdened with processing demands that far exceed our time frames and mental capacities. Because of this, we are forever seeking ways to arrive at correct solutions while avoiding a great deal of thought. Cognitive misers everywhere can rejoice in the next principle of influence—consensus. Through a cursory examination of what others (especially others *like us*) are doing, we can often obtain satisfactory outcomes. If all of your friends are raving about a new television show, restaurant, or personal digital assistant, you will probably like those things as well. We can use the actions of others ("social proof") as a means to locate and validate correct choices (Festinger, 1957).

Because the desire to choose correctly is powerful, and the time in which to choose is forever diminishing, the tendency to follow the crowd is both strong and widespread. Studies have shown that, based on evidence of what their peers are doing, bystanders decide whether to help an emergency victim (Darley & Latane, 1968), citizens decide whether to pay their taxes fully (Steenbergen, McGraw, & Scholtz, 1992), juveniles decide whether to commit crimes (Kahan, 1997), people decide whether to "cheat" sexually on their spouses (Buunk & Baker, 1995), and homeowners

decide whether to recycle their trash (Schultz, 1999).

In this last study (Schultz, 1999), residents of a Los Angeles suburb received information describing the recycling behavior of many of their neighbors who recycled regularly. This information produced an immediate increase in the amount of material the residents recycled. In addition, when observed up to a month later, the community was recycling more trash than ever. These improvements did not occur, however, for residents who received only a request to recycle.

Social proof accounts for an extensive array of human actions, from the ways we protect our environment to the ways we engage in exchange. Rutte, Wilke, and Messick (1987) manipulated conditions of scarcity or abundance in a common dilemma task by varying the amount of money that group members could harvest from a common pool. They artificially created the appearance that those who had harvested earlier in the trial either had taken more than their share (i.e., setting a norm of selfishness) or had taken less than their share (i.e., setting a norm of generosity). Their results supported the notion that the participants looked to the behavior of the group members who had gone before to decide how much money to take. Those who saw others acting in a selfish manner were selfish themselves, whereas those who saw others acting generously were more generous.

Whenever influence practitioners are able to identify a psychological principle that people use to reach their goals, those practitioners are sure to use it to advance their own goals. Sales and marketing professionals make a special point of informing us when a product is the "largest selling" or "fastest growing" in its market. Bartenders are known to "salt" their tip jars with dollar bills at the start of a shift to give the impression that previous customers tipped with folding money. Church ushers have been observed priming collection baskets for similar reasons and with similar effects on proceeds. Television sitcoms use canned laughter because it makes people laugh harder and longer (Smyth & Fuller, 1972). Television commercials depict crowds rushing into stores and hands depleting shelves of the advertised items. Consider the advice offered more than 350 years ago by the Spaniard Balthazar Gracian to those wishing to sell goods and services: "Their intrinsic worth is not enough, for not all turn the goods over or look deep. Most run where the crowd is—because the others run" (Gracian, 1649/1945, p. 142).

This tendency to run because others are running affects more than product sales. Indeed, it accounts for some of the most bizarre and befuddling forms of human behavior on record, including the ultimate choice of death over life. Research by Phillips and his colleagues (Phillips, 1974, 1989; Phillips & Carstensen, 1986) shows that suicides can have a decidedly copycat character. Thus, even in the extreme case of suicide, people feel that behaviors become more valid when others are performing them.

Although the tendency to follow the lead of our peers can lead to misguided behavior, most of the time it does not. Most of the time it sends us in the right directions—toward correct choices. Which are the factors that spur people to use the actions of others in the process of trying to choose correctly? Social scientists have uncovered several.

Uncertainty. When people do not trust their own judgments, they look to others for evidence of how to choose correctly (Wooten & Reed, 1998). This self-doubt may occur when a situation is ambiguous, as it was in a classic series of experiments by Sherif (1936). Sherif projected a dot of light on the wall of a darkened room and asked participants to indicate how much the light moved while they watched it. The light never actually moved at all; because of an optical illusion termed the *autokinetic effect,* it seemed to shift indeterminately about. The amount of that shift was, however, purely subjective. When in groups, participants announced estimates of light movement. It turned out that these estimates were strongly influenced by what other group members estimated; nearly everyone revised their estimates toward the group average over time. Sherif concluded that when there is no objectively correct response, people are likely to doubt themselves and, thus, are especially likely to assume that "the group must be right" (p. 111). Many studies have supported his conclusion (e.g., Bond & Smith, 1996; Tesser, Campbell, & Mickler, 1983). When uncertainty and ambiguity reign, people lose confidence in their ability to choose well. As a result, they rely more heavily on the gathered wisdom of others.

Despite initial uncertainty, once a group has agreed on a response, members often cling to it fervently (Jacobs & Campbell, 1961). In one study, group members who had undergone Sherif's autokinetic effect procedure returned many months later to be tested again, but this time without any other group members present. When placed in the darkened room once more, these individuals saw the light move a distance that was remarkably similar to the group answer formed a year earlier (Rohrer, Baron, Hoffman, & Swander, 1954).

Many Others. One researcher who puzzled over Sherif's (1936) findings was Solomon Asch. Asch wondered whether people would not be much more likely to resist social influence when the situation was *not* as ambiguous as it was in Sherif's experiment. In his well-known experiments, Asch (1956) asked college students to match the lengths of different lines. The task was not difficult. In the control condition, 95% of the participants got every one of 12 line matches right. Participants in the experimental condition, however, were faced with a social consensus that contradicted their own eyes. Before making their own judgments, they heard five other students (who were actually confederates of the experimenter) unanimously agree on an answer that was clearly wrong. Given the consensus of many others, only 25% of the participants were able to ignore the group's obvious errors and gave only correct answers. The other 75% went against the evidence of their senses and conformed to some extent. Although no one went along every single time, one individual conformed on 11 of the 12 choices. Asch's research demonstrated that people faced with the pressures of unanimous group consensus frequently conform to the crowd, doubting the clear evidence of their own senses in the process. Research on a variety of judgments and from a variety of cultures has continued to support Asch's conclusions (Baron, Vandello, & Brunsman, 1996; Bond & Smith, 1996). As powerful as the effect is, however, a single visible dissenter can break the spell (Allen & Levine, 1969; Morris & Miller, 1975).

Other research shows that the behavior of others shapes one's interpretation of and response to a situation, even without the social pressure brought to bear in Asch's experiments. For example, Milgram, Bickman, and Berkowitz (1969) were able to induce 84% of pedestrians passing a city street corner to gaze up into space at nothing by simply having a group of confederates model the behavior. According to Cialdini (1993), when we perceive sufficient social support for a particular behavior, we follow the lead of others because this heuristic of "social proof" saves us time and cognitive effort while still providing an outcome that has a high probability of being effective.

It is interesting to note that the classic conformity experiments yielded their effects from the most fleeting of groups. Milgram et al. (1969) were able to get hurried strangers to take a futile glance into the sky. Asch (1956)

obtained his results among students who were strangers convened for a short experiment. Think how much more potent the social pressure might be when those confident others are trusted members of one's inner circle—in groups ranging from the family and neighborhood to those of the workplace.

Similar Others. If people follow the lead of others to make good choices for themselves, then it stands to reason that most of the time they would want to follow the actions of individuals similar to themselves. We are all more likely to seek out and accept the advice of individuals like ourselves, who are similar in background, interests, and goals.

Heightened sensitivity to the responses of similar others appears in a wide variety of situations. For example, in one study, New Yorkers were strongly influenced to return a lost wallet after learning that a similar other had first tried to do so, but evidence that a dissimilar other—a foreigner—had tried to return the wallet had no effect on the New Yorkers' decisions (Hornstein, Fisch, & Holmes, 1968). In a different study, children watched a film depicting another child's positive visit to the dentist. Did watching this film reduce the children's dentist office anxieties? Yes, but that was so principally when the child in the movie was the same age as those viewing it (Melamed, Yurcheson, Fleece, Hutcherson, & Hawes, 1978).

Combining both consensus and similarity in the same procedure creates a highly effective fund-raising technique called the list procedure (Reingen, 1982). Researchers went door to door collecting money for charity, showing residents a list of others in the vicinity who had already given. The longer the list of neighbors (similar others) that residents saw, the more likely they were to give a donation.

In sum, the heuristic of social validation often provides an efficient shortcut to effective action. We are particularly likely to mimic the behaviors of others when we are uncertain of how to proceed, when many others are performing a certain behavior, and particularly when those others are like us.

LIKING

It is hardly surprising that people prefer to say yes to those they know and like. Consider, for example, the remarkable success of the Tupperware Corporation and its "home party" demonstration concept (Taylor, 1978). The demonstration party for Tupperware products is hosted by an individual, usually a woman, who invites to her home an array of friends, neighbors, and relatives, all of whom know that their hostess receives a percentage of the profits from every piece sold by the Tupperware representative who is also there. In this way, the Tupperware Corporation arranges for its customers to buy from and *for* a friend (a liked other) rather than from an unknown salesperson. One study (Frenzen & Davis, 1990) found that, in a home party setting, strength of social ties between a guest and the hostess accounted for twice as much variance (67%) in purchase likelihood as did preference for the product (33%). So favorable has been the effect on proceeds ($2.5 million in sales per day) that the Tupperware Corporation has wholly abandoned its early retail outlets, and according to company literature, a Tupperware party begins somewhere in the world every 2.7 seconds.

Indeed, not only has the Tupperware Corporation abandoned retail sales, but in another testament to the role of the liking/friendship rule, it has largely abandoned the U.S. market where the company is based. Why has Tupperware's success spread so rapidly to societies in Europe, Latin America, and Asia? In these countries, one's place in a network of friends and family is a more potent determinant of behavior than in the United States

(Markus & Kitayama, 1991; Triandis, 1995). As a result, now less than a quarter of Tupperware sales take place in North America.

But of course, most commercial transactions do not take place in home parties among already-liked others. Under these much more typical circumstances, practitioners who wish to commission the power of liking must resort to another strategy: They must first arrange for their influence targets to like them. How do they do it? The tactics that practitioners use to generate liking cluster around certain factors that also have been shown by controlled research to increase liking.

Physical Attractiveness. Although it is generally acknowledged that good-looking people have an advantage in social interaction, research findings indicate that we may have sorely underestimated the size and reach of that advantage. There appears to be a positive reaction to good physical appearance that generalizes to favorable trait perceptions such as a talent, kindness, honesty, and intelligence (for a review, see Eagly et al., 1991). As a consequence, attractive individuals are more persuasive in terms of both changing attitudes (Chaiken, 1979) and getting what they request (Benson, Karabenic, & Lerner, 1976).

For example, voters in a Canadian federal election gave physically attractive candidates several times as many votes as they gave unattractive ones—while insisting that their choices would never be influenced by something as superficial as appearance (Efran & Patterson, 1974, 1976). Voters can deny the impact of attractiveness on electability all they want, but evidence has continued to confirm its troubling presence (Budesheim & DePaola, 1994). Looks are influential in other domains as well. Good-looking fund-raisers for the American Heart Association generated nearly twice as many donations (42% vs. 23%) as did other requesters (Reingen & Kernan, 1993). Likewise, physically attractive salespeople are more effective at getting customers to part with their money (Reingen & Kernan, 1993).

A comparable effect has been found in hiring situations. In one study, good grooming of applicants in a simulated employment interview accounted for more favorable hiring decisions than did job qualifications—even though the interviewers claimed that appearance played a small role in their choices (Mack & Rainey, 1990). The advantage given to attractive workers extends past hiring day to payday. Economists examining U.S. and Canadian samples have found that attractive individuals get paid an average of 12% to 14%⁻ more than their unattractive co-workers (Hammermesh & Biddle, 1994).

Similarity. We like people who are similar to us (Byrne, 1971; Carli, Ganley, & Pierce-Otay, 1991; Hogg, Cooper-Shaw, & Holzworth, 1993) and grant them favorable treatment in charitable (Dovidio, 1984), negotiation (Kramer, Pommerenke, & Newton, 1993), and legal settings (Amato, 1979; Towson & Zanna, 1983). Thus, salespeople often search for (or fabricate) a similarity between themselves and their customers: "Well, no kidding, you're from Minneapolis? I went to school in Minnesota!" Fund-raisers do the same, with good results. In one study (Aune & Basil, 1994), donations to charity more than doubled when the requester claimed a shared group identity with the target person, such as "I'm a student, too." Instruction in generating more subtle forms of similarity occurs in many sales training programs. Trainees are urged to "mirror and match" the customer's body posture, mood, and verbal style, as similarities along each of these dimensions have been shown to lead to positive results (LaFrance, 1985; Locke & Horowitz, 1990; Woodside & Davenport, 1974).

Another similarity researcher was able to significantly increase the percentage of people who responded to a mailed survey by changing one small feature of the request: On a cover letter, he modified the name of the survey taker to be similar to that of the survey recipient. Thus, Robert Greer received the survey from a survey center official named "Bob Gregar," while Cynthia Johnston received hers from a survey center official named "Cindy Johanson." In two separate studies, adding this little bit of similarity to the exchange nearly doubled survey compliance (Garner, 1999). These seemingly minor commonalties can affect decisions that go well beyond whose insurance to purchase or whose survey to complete. They can affect the decision of whose life to save. When asked to rank-order a waiting list of patients suffering from kidney disorder as to their deservingness for the next available treatment, people chose those whose political party preference matched their own (Furnham, 1996).

Compliments. Praise and other forms of positive estimation also stimulate liking (e.g., Byrne & Rhamey, 1965). The simple information that someone appreciates us can be a highly effective device for producing return liking and willing compliance (Berscheid & Walster, 1978). For instance, one study demonstrating the rather remarkable impact of flattery on compliance occurred in the context of criminal interrogations, where the interrogator's job is to induce suspects to provide incriminating admissions. Sociologist Richard Leo, who watched 182 such interrogations, found that one of interrogators' most effective tactics for producing incriminating statements was to praise the suspect in some way (Leo, in press).

Additional evidence for the power of praise on liking comes from a study (Drachman, deCarufel, & Insko, 1978) in which men received personal comments from someone who needed a favor from them. Some of the men got only positive comments, some got only negative comments, and some got a mixture of positive and negative comments. There were three interesting findings. First, the evaluator who offered only praise was liked the best. Second, this was so even though the men fully realized that the flatterer stood to gain from their liking of him. Finally, unlike the other types of comments, pure praise did not have to be accurate to work. Compliments produced just as much liking for the flatterer when they were untrue as when they were true. It is for such reasons that direct salespeople are educated in the art of praise. A potential customer's home, clothes, car, taste, and the like all are frequent targets for compliments (Cialdini, 1993).

Cooperation. Cooperation is another factor that has been shown to enhance positive feelings and behavior (e.g., Aronson, Bridgeman, & Geffner, 1978; Bettencourt, Brewer, Croak, & Miller, 1992; Cook, 1990). Those who cooperate toward the achievement of a common goal are more favorable and helpful to each other as a consequence. That is why compliance professionals often strive to be perceived as cooperating partners with a target person (Rafaeli & Sutton, 1991). Automobile sales managers frequently set themselves as "villains" so that the salespeople can "do battle" on the customers' behalf. The cooperative, pulling together kind of relationship that is consequently produced between the salespeople and customers naturally leads to a desirable form of liking that promotes sales.

CONCLUSION

At the outset of this chapter, we suggested that an important question for anyone interested in understanding, resisting, or harnessing the compliance process is the following: "Which are the most powerful principles that motivate individuals to comply with another person's request?" We also suggested that one way to assess such power would be to examine the practices of commercial compliance professionals for their pervasiveness. That is, if compliance practitioners made widespread use of certain principles, this would be evidence for the natural power of these principles to affect everyday compliance. Six psychological principles emerged as the most popular in the repertoires of compliance professionals: reciprocity, scarcity, authority, commitment/consistency, social validation, and liking. Close examination of the principles revealed broad professional use that could be validated and explained by controlled experimental research. As with most research perspectives, additional work needs to be done. Nonetheless, there is considerable evidence at this juncture to indicate that these six principles engage central features of the human condition to motivate compliance.

However, just because effective compliance principles exist does not mean that they should be employed. Besides efficacy, there is another dimension that should be taken into account in deciding whether and how to engage a particular principle in the service of successful influence—the ethical acceptability of the principle's use in the situation. Indeed, the more powerful a principle is, the more significant the attendant issues of ethical practice should be. We believe that, in the case of the six compliance principles discussed in this chapter, there is special reason for a focus on ethics because they stand to be used increasingly by consumers in the future. That is so because these principles normally counsel consumers very well as to when to comply with a request. After all, it usually makes sense to say yes to a person we like or owe or recognize as an authority or to a person who is offering something rare or popular or to which we have already made a commitment. As such, these principles are often employed heuristically by consumers as shortcuts in their decision processes. Moreover, the pace and information overloaded character of modern life are causing people to rely increasingly on decision-making shortcuts (Cialdini, 1993; Kahn & Baron, 1995). It is for this reason that it seems so important to make consumers aware of their vulnerability to such principles as well as to make consumers and practitioners aware of the crucial distinction between the honest and dishonest uses of the principles (Cialdini, 1996; Cialdini, Sagarin, & Rice, 2001).

REFERENCES

Allen, V. L., & Levine, J. M. (1969). Consensus and conformity. *Journal of Experimental Social Psychology, 5,* 389-399.

Amato, P. R. (1979). Juror-defendant similarity and the assessment of guilt in politically motivated crimes. *Australian Journal of Psychology, 31,* 79-88.

Aronson, E., Bridgeman, D. L., & Geffner, R. (1978). The effects of a cooperative classroom structure on students' behavior and attitudes. In D. Bar-Tal & L. Saxe (Eds.), *Social psychology of education: Theory and research.* New York: Halstead.

Aronson, E., & Mills, J. (1959). The effect of severity of initiation on liking for a group. *Journal of Abnormal and Social Psychology, 59,* 177-181.

Aronson, E., Turner, J. A., & Carlsmith, J. M. (1963). Communicator credibility and communication discrepancy as a determinant of opinion change. *Journal of Abnormal and Social Psychology, 67,* 31-36.

Asch, S. E. (1956). Studies of independence and conformity: I. A minority of one against a unanimous majority. *Psychological Monographs, 70*(9).

Aune, R. K., & Basil, M. C. (1994). A relational obligations approach to the foot-in-the-mouth effect. *Journal of Applied Social Psychology, 24,* 546-556.

Ball, A. D., & Tasaki, L. H. (1992). The role and measurement of attachment in consumer behavior. *Journal of Consumer Psychology, 1,* 155-172.

Ball-Rokeach, S., Rokeach, M., & Grube, J. W. (1984). *The great American values test.* New York: Free Press.

Baron, R. S., Vandello, J., & Brunsman, B. (1996). The forgotten variable in conformity research: Impact of task importance on social influence. *Journal of Personality and Social Psychology, 71,* 915-927.

Baumeister, R. F. (1982). A self-presentational view of social phenomena. *Psychological Bulletin, 91,* 3-26.

Beggan, J. K., & Allison, S. T. (1997). More there than meets the eyes: Support for the mere-ownership effect. *Journal of Consumer Psychology, 6,* 285-297.

Belliveau, M. A., O'Reilly, C. A., & Wade, J. B. (in press). Social capital: The effects of social similarity and status on CEO compensation. *Academy of Management Journal.*

Bem, D. J. (1967). Self-perception: An alternative explanation of cognitive dissonance phenomena. *Psychological Review, 74,* 183-200.

Benson, P. L., Karabenic, S. A., & Lerner, R. M. (1976). Pretty pleases: The effects of physical attractiveness on race, sex, and receiving help. *Journal of Experimental Social Psychology, 12,* 409-415.

Benton, A. A., Kelley, H. H., & Liebling, B. (1972). Effects of extremity of offers and concession rate on the outcomes of bargaining. *Journal of Personality and Social Psychology, 24,* 73-83.

Berscheid, E., & Walster [Hatfield], E. (1978). *Interpersonal attraction.* Reading, MA: Addison-Wesley.

Bettencourt, B. A., Brewer, M. B., Croak, M. R., & Miller, N. (1992). Cooperation and the reduction of intergroup bias. *Journal of Experimental Social Psychology, 28,* 301-319.

Bickman, L. (1974). The social power of a uniform. *Journal of Applied Social Psychology, 4,* 47-61.

Blass, T. (1991). Understanding behavior in the obedience experiment: The role of personality, situations, and their interactions. *Journal of Personality and Social Psychology, 60,* 398-413.

Blass, T. (1999). The Milgram paradigm after 35 years: Some things we now know about obedience to authority. *Journal of Applied Social Psychology, 29,* 955-978.

Bond, M. H., & Smith, P. B. (1996). Culture and conformity: A meta-analysis of studies using Asch's (1952b, 1956) line judgment task. *Psychological Bulletin, 119,* 111-137.

Brehm, J. W. (1966). *A theory of psychological reactance.* New York: Academic Press.

Brehm, S. S., & Brehm, J. W. (1981). *Psychological reactance.* New York: Academic Press.

Brock, T. C. (1968). Implications of commodity theory for value change. In A. G. Greenwald, T. C. Brock, & T. M. Ostrom (Eds.), *Psychological foundations of attitudes* (pp. 243-275). New York: Academic Press.

Brock, T. C., & Bannon, L. A. (1992). Liberalization of commodity theory. *Basic and Applied Social Psychology, 13,* 135-143.

Budesheim, T. L., & DePaola, S. J. (1994). Beauty or the beast? The effects of appearance, personality, and issue information on evaluations of political candidates. *Personality and Social Psychology Bulletin, 20,* 339-348.

Burger, J. M. (2000). The foot-in-the-door compliance procedure: A multiple-process analysis and review. *Personality and Social Psychology Review, 3,* 303-325.

Bushman, B. J. (1988). The effects of apparel on compliance. *Personality and Social Psychology Bulletin, 14,* 459-467.

Bushman, B. J. (1984). Perceived symbols of authority and their influence on compliance. *Journal of Applied Social Psychology, 14,* 501-508.

Buunk, B. P., & Baker, A. B. (1995). Extradyadic sex: The role of descriptive and injunctive norms. *Journal of Sex Research, 32,* 313-318.

Byrne, D. (1971). *The attraction paradigm.* New York: Academic Press.

Byrne, D., & Rhamey, R. (1965). Magnitude of positive and negative reinforcements as a determinant of attraction. *Journal of Personality and Social Psychology, 2,* 884-889.

Campbell, M. C. (1995). When attention-getting advertising tactics elicit consumer inferences of manipulative intent. *Journal of Consumer Research, 4,* 225-254.

Carducci, B. J., Deuser, P. S., Bauer, A., Large, M., & Ramaekers, M. (1989). An application of the foot in the door technique to organ donation. *Journal of Business and Psychology, 4,* 245-249.

Carli, L. L., Ganley, R., & Pierce-Otay, A. (1991). Similarity and satisfaction in roommate relationships. *Personality and Social Psychology Bulletin, 17,* 419-426.

Chaiken, S. (1979). Communicator physical attractiveness and persuasion. *Journal of Personality and Social Psychology, 37,* 1387-1397.

Chaiken, S., Liberman, A., & Eagly, A. H. (1989). Heuristic and systematic processing within and beyond the persuasion context. In J. S. Uleman & J. A. Bargh (Eds.), *Unintended thought* (pp. 212- 252). New York: Guilford.

Chaiken, S., & Maheswaran, D. (1994). Heuristic processing can bias systematic processing. *Journal of Personality and Social Psychology, 66,* 460-473.

Cialdini, R. B. (1993). *Influence: Science and practice* (3rd ed.). New York: HarperCollins.

Cialdini, R. B. (1996). Social influence and the triple tumor structure of organizational dishonesty. In D. M. Messick & A. E. Tenbrunsel (Eds.), *Codes of conduct* (pp. 44-58). New York: Russell Sage.

Cialdini, R. B., Cacioppo, J. T., Bassett, R., & Miller, J. A. (1978). Low-ball procedure for producing compliance: Commitment then cost. *Journal of Personality and Social Psychology, 36,* 463-476.

Cialdini, R. B., Eisenberg, N., Green, B. L., Rhoads, K., & Bator, R. (1998). Undermining the undermining effect of reward on sustained interest. *Journal of Applied Social Psychology, 28,* 253-267.

Cialdini, R. B., Sagarin, B. J., & Rice, W. E. (2001). Training in ethical influence. In J. Darley, D. Messick, & T. Tyler (Eds.), *Social influences on ethical behavior in organizations* (pp. 137-153). Mahwah, NJ: Lawrence Erlbaum.

Cialdini, R. B., Trost, M. R., & Newsom, J. T. (1995). Preference for consistency. The development of a valid measure and the discovery of surprising behavioral implications. *Journal of Personality and Social Psychology, 69,* 318-328.

Cialdini, R. B., Vincent, J. E., Lewis, S. K., Catalan, J., Wheeler, D., & Darby, B. L. (1975). Reciprocal concessions procedure for inducing compliance: The door-in-the-face technique. *Journal of Personality and Social Psychology, 31,* 206-215.

Cioffi, D., & Garner, R. (1996). On doing the decision: The effects of active versus passive choice on commitment and self-perception. *Personality and Social Psychology Bulletin, 22,* 133-147.

Clark, M. S., & Mills, J. (1993). The difference between communal and exchange relationships: What it is and is not. *Personality and Social Psychology Bulletin, 19,* 684-691.

Cody, M. J., Seiter, J., & Montagne-Miller, Y. (1995). Men and women in the marketplace. In J. P. Kalbfleish & M. J. Cody (Eds.), *Gender, power, and communication in human relationships* (pp. 305-329). Hillsdale, NJ: Lawrence Erlbaum.

Cook, S. W. (1990). Toward a psychology of improving justice. *Journal of Social Issues, 46,* 147-161.

Cooper, J., Bennett, E. A., & Sukel, H. L. (1996). Complex scientific testimony: How do jurors make decisions? *Law and Human Behavior, 20,* 379-394.

Cotterell, N., Eisenberger, R., & Speicher, H. (1992). Inhibiting effects of reciprocation wariness on interpersonal relationships. *Journal of Personality and Social Psychology, 62,* 658-668.

Darley, J. M., & Latane, B. (1968). Bystander intervention in emergencies: Diffusion of responsibility. *Journal of Personality and Social Psychology, 8,* 377-383.

De Dreu, C. K. W., & McCusker, C. (1997). Gain-loss frames and cooperation in two-person social dilemmas: A transformational analysis. *Journal of Personality and Social Psychology, 72,* 1093-1106.

Deutsch, M., & Gerard, H. B. (1955). A study of normative and informational social influences upon individual judgment. *Journal of Abnormal and Social Psychology, 51,* 629-636.

Dickerson, C., Thibodeau, R., Aronson, E., & Miller, D. (1992). Using cognitive dissonance to encourage water conservation. *Journal of Applied Social Psychology, 22,* 841-854.

Dillard, J. P., Hunter, J. E., & Burgoon, M. (1984). Sequential-request persuasive strategies: Meta-analysis of foot-in-the-door and door-in-the-face. *Human Communication Research, 10,* 461-488.

Ditto, P. H., & Jemmott, J. B., III. (1989). From rarity to evaluative extremity. *Journal of Personality and Social Psychology, 57,* 16-26.

Ditto, P. H., Moore, K. A., Hilton, J. L., & Kalish, J. R. (1995). Beliefs about physicians: Their role in health care utilization, satisfactions, and compliance. *Basic and Applied Social Psychology, 17,* 23-48.

Dovidio, J. F. (1984). Helping behavior and altruism: An empirical and conceptual overview. In L. Berkowitz (Ed.), *Advances in experimental social psychology* (Vol. 17, pp. 361-427). New York: Academic Press.

Drachman, D., deCarufel, A., & Insko, C. A. (1978). The extra credit effect in interpersonal attraction. *Journal of Experimental Social Psychology, 14,* 458-465.

Eagly, A. H., Wood, W., & Chaiken, S. (1978). Causal inferences about communicators and their effect on opinion change. *Journal of Personality and Social Psychology, 36,* 424-435.

Efran, M. G., & Patterson, E. W. J. (1974). Voters vote beautiful: The effects of physical appearance on a national election. *Canadian Journal of Behavioral Science, 6,* 352-356.

Efran, M. G., & Patterson, E. W. J. (1976). *The politics of appearance.* Unpublished manuscript, University of Toronto.

Eibl-Eibesfelt, I. (1975). *Ethology: The study of behavior.* New York: Holt, Rinehart & Winston.

Eisenberg, N. E., Cialdini, R. B., McCreath, H., & Shell, R. (1987). Consistency-based compliance: When and why do children become vulnerable? *Journal of Personality and Social Psychology, 52,* 1174-1181.

Elms, A. C., & Milgram, S. (1966). Personality characteristics associated with obedience and defiance toward authoritative command. *Journal of Experimental Research in Personality, 1,* 282-289.

Fazio, R. H., Sherman, S. J., & Herr, P. M. (1982). The feature-positive effect in the self-perception process. *Journal of Personality and Social Psychology, 42,* 404-411.

Festinger, L. (1957). *A theory of cognitive dissonance.* Stanford, CA: Stanford University Press.

Fiske, S. T., & Taylor, S. E. (1991). *Social cognition* (2nd ed.). New York: McGraw-Hill.

Foushee, M. C. (1984). Dyads at 35,000 feet: Factors affecting group processes and aircraft performance. *American Psychologist, 39,* 885-893.

Freedman, J. L. (1965). Long-term behavioral effects of cognitive dissonance. *Journal of Experimental Social Psychology, 1,* 145-155.

Freedman, J. L., & Fraser, S. C. (1966). Compliance without pressure: The foot-in-the-door technique. *Journal of Personality and Social Psychology, 4,* 195-203.

French, J. R. P., Jr., & Raven, B. (1959). The bases of social power. In D. Cartwright (Ed.), *Studies in social power* (pp. 150-167). Ann Arbor, MI: Institute for Social Research.

Frenzen, J. R., & Davis, H. L. (1990). Purchasing behavior in embedded markets. *Journal of Consumer Research, 17,* 1-12.

Fried, C. B., & Aronson, E. (1995). Hypocrisy, misattribution, and dissonance reduction. *Personality and Social Psychology Bulletin, 21,* 925-933.

Furnham, A. (1996). Factors relating to the allocation of medical resources. *Journal of Social Behavior and Personality, 11,* 615-624.

Garner, R. L. (1999). *What's in a name: Persuasion perhaps?* Unpublished manuscript, Sam Houston State University.

Giles, H., & Coupland, N. (1991). *Language: Contexts and consequences.* Pacific Grove, CA: Brooks/Cole.

Gorassini, D. R., & Olson, J. M. (1995). Does self-perception change explain the foot-in-the-door effect? *Journal of Personality and Social Psychology, 69,* 91-105.

Gouldner, A. W. (1960). The norm of reciprocity: A preliminary statement. *American Sociological Review, 25,* 161-178.

Gracian, B. (1945). *The art of worldly wisdom.* New York: Charles C Thomas. (Original work published 1649)

Greenwald, A. F., Carnot, C. G., Beach, R., & Young, B. (1987). Increasing voting behavior by asking people if they expect to vote. *Journal of Applied Psychology, 72,* 315-318.

Gregory, S. W., & Webster, S. (1996). A nonverbal signal in voices of interview partners effectively predicts communication accommodation and social status perceptions. *Journal of Personality and Social Psychology, 70,* 1231-1240.

Gruner, S. J. (1996, November). Reward good consumers. *Inc., p.* 84.

Harper, C. R., Kidera, C. J., & Cullen, J. F. (1971). Study of simulated airplane pilot incapacitation. *Aerospace Medicine, 42,* 946-948.

Heider, F. (1958). *The psychology of interpersonal relations.* New York: John Wiley.

Hofling, C. K., Brotzman, E., Dalrymple, S., Graves, N., & Pierce, C. M. (1966). An experimental study of nurse-physician relationships. *Journal of Nervous and Mental Disease, 143,* 171-180.

Hogg, M. A., Cooper-Shaw, L., & Holzworth, D. W. (1993). Group prototypicality and depersonalized attraction in small interactive groups. *Personality and Social Psychology Bulletin, 19,* 452-565.

Hornstein, H. A., Fisch, E., & Holmes, M. (1968). Influence of a model's feeling about his behavior and his relevance as a comparison other on observers' helping behavior. *Journal of Personality and Social Psychology, 10,* 222-226.

Hovland, C. I., Lumsdaine, A. A., & Sheffield, F. D. (1949). *Studies in social psychology during World War II* (Vol. 3). Princeton, NJ: Princeton University Press.

Howard, D. J. (1990). The influence of verbal responses to common greetings on compliance behavior: The foot-in-the-mouth effect. *Journal of Applied Social Psychology, 20,* 1185-1196.

Howard, D. J. (1995). "Chaining" the use of influence strategies for producing compliance behavior. *Journal of Social Behavior and Personality, 10,* 169-185.

Jacobs, R. C., & Campbell, D. T. (1961). The perpetuation of an arbitrary tradition through several generations of a laboratory microculture. *Journal of Abnormal and Social Psychology, 62,* 649-658.

Jorden, D. L. (1993). Newspaper effects on policy preferences. *Public Opinion Quarterly, 57,* 191-204.

Joule, R. V. (1987). Tobacco deprivation: The foot-in-the-door technique versus the low-ball technique. *European Journal of Social Psychology, 17,* 361-365.

Kahan, D. M. (1997). Social influence, social meaning, and deterrence. *Virginia Law Review, 83,* 349-395.

Kahn, B. E., & Baron, J. (1995). An exploratory study of choice rules favored for high-stakes decisions. *Journal of Consumer Psychology, 4,* 305-328.

Kahneman, D., & Tversky, A. (1982). The psychology of preferences. *Scientific American, 246,* 160-173.

Kahneman, D., Knetsch, J. L., & Thaler, R. H. (1991). The endowment effect, loss aversion, and status quo bias. *Journal of Economic Perspectives, 5,* 193-206.

Kanki, B. J., & Foushee, H. C. (1990). Crew factors in the aerospace workplace. In S. Oskamp & S. Spacapan (Eds.), *People's reactions to technology.* Newbury Park, CA: Sage.

Kantola, S. J., Syme, G. J., & Campbell, N. A. (1984). Cognitive dissonance and energy conservation. *Journal of Applied Psychology, 69,* 416-421.

Kelly, A. E. (1998). Clients' secret keeping in outpatient therapy. *Journal of Counseling Psychology, 45,* 50-57.

Kelly, A. E., & McKillop, K. J. (1996). Consequences of revealing personal secrets. *Psychological Bulletin, 120,* 450-465.

Ketelaar, T. (1995). *Emotions as mental representations of gains and losses: Translating prospect theory into positive and negative affect.* Paper presented at the meeting of the American Psychological Society, New York.

Kiesler, S., Sproull, L., & Waters, K. (1996). A prisoner's dilemma experiment on cooperation with people and human-like computers. *Journal of Personality and Social Psychology, 70,* 47-65.

Knishinsky, A. (1982). *The effects of scarcity of material and exclusivity of information on industrial buyer perceived risk in provoking a purchase decision.* Doctoral dissertation, Arizona State University.

Krackow, A., & Blass, T. (1995). When nurses obey or defy inappropriate physician orders: Attributional differences. *Journal of Social Behavior and Personality, 10,* 585-594.

Kramer, R. M., Pommerenke, P., & Newton, E. (1993). The social context of negotiation: Effects of social identity and interpersonal accountability on negotiator decision making. *Journal of Conflict Resolution, 37,* 633-654.

LaFrance, M. (1985). Postural mirroring and intergroup relations. *Personality and Social Psychology Bulletin, 11,* 207-217.

Lefkowitz, M., Blake, R. R., & Mouton, J. S. (1955). Status factors in pedestrian violation of traffic signals. *Journal of Abnormal and Social Psychology, 51,* 704-706.

Leo, R. A. (in press). *Police interrogation in America: A study of violence, civility, and social change.*

Levine, J. M., & Valle, R. S. (1975). The convert as a credible communicator. *Social Behavior and Personality, 3,* 81-90.

Locke, K. S., & Horowitz, L. M. (1990). Satisfaction in interpersonal interactions as a function of similarity in level of dysphoria. *Journal of Personality and Social Psychology, 58,* 823-831.

Lydon, J. E., & Zanna, M. P. (1990). Commitment in the face of adversity: A value-affirmation approach. *Journal of Personality and Social Psychology, 58,* 1040-1047.

Lynn, M. (1991). Scarcity effects on value. *Psychology and Marketing, 8,* 43-57.

Lynn, M. (1992). Scarcity's enhancement of desirability. *Basic and Applied Social Psychology, 13,* 67-78.

Lynn, M., & McCall, M. (1998). *Beyond gratitude and gratuity.* Unpublished manuscript, Cornell University.

Mack, D., & Rainey, D. (1990). Female applicants grooming and personnel selection. *Journal of Social Behavior and Personality, 5,* 399-407.

Main, B. M., O'Reilly, C. A., & Wade, J. B. (1995). The CEO, the board of directors, and executive compensation. *Industrial and Corporate Change, 4,* 293-332.

Markus, H., & Kitayama, S. (1991). Culture and the self: Implications for cognition, emotion, and motivation. *Psychological Bulletin, 98,* 224-253.

Mauss, M. (1954). *The gift* (I. G. Cunnison, Trans.). London: Cohen & West.

McGuiness, E., & Ward, C. D. (1980). Better liked than right: Trustworthiness and expertise as factors in credibility. *Personality and Social Psychology Bulletin, 6,* 467-472.

Melamed, B. F., Yurcheson, E., Fleece, L., Hutcherson, S., & Hawes, R. (1978). Effects of film modeling on the reduction of anxiety-related behaviors in individuals varying in levels of previous experience in the stress situation. *Journal of Consulting and Clinical Psychology, 46,* 1357-1374.

Meleshko, K. G. A., & Alden, L. E. (1993). Anxiety and self-disclosure: Toward a motivational model. *Journal of Personality and Social Psychology, 64,* 1000-1009.

Meyerwitz, B. E., & Chaiken, S. (1987). The effect of message framing on breast self-examination attitudes, intentions, and behavior. *Journal of Personality and Social Psychology, 52,* 500-510.

Milgram, S. (1974). *Obedience to authority: An experimental view.* New York: Harper & Row.

Milgram, S., Bickman, L., & Berkowitz, L. (1969). Note on the drawing power of crowds of different size. *Journal of Personality and Social Psychology, 13,* 79-82.

Miller, A. G., Collins, B. E., & Brief, D. E. (Eds.). (1995). Perspectives on obedience to authority: The legacy of the Milgram experiments [special issue]. *Journal of Social Issues, 51*(3).

Miller, F. D. (1975). *An experimental study of obedience to authorities of varying legitimacy.* Unpublished doctoral dissertation. Harvard University.

Morris, D. (1999). *Behind the Oval Office: Getting reelected against all odds.* New York: St. Martin's.

Morris, M. W., Podolny, J. M., & Ariel, S. (2001). Cultural norms and obligations: Cross-national differences in patterns of interpersonal norms and felt obligations toward co-workers. In W. Wosinska, R. B. Cialdini, D. W. Barrett, & J. Reykowski (Eds.), *The practice of social influence in multiple cultures* (pp. 97-124). Mahwah, NJ: Lawrence Erlbaum.

Morris, W. N., & Miller, R. S. (1975). The effects of consensus-breaking and consensus-preempting partners on reduction of conformity. *Journal of Experimental Social Psychology, 11,* 215-223.

Mowen, J. C., & Cialdini, R. B. (1980). On implementing the door-in-the-face compliance technique in a business context. *Journal of Marketing Research, 17,* 253-258.

Mullen, B., Cooper, C., & Driskell, J. E. (1990). Jaywalking as a function of model behavior. *Personality and Social Psychology Bulletin, 16,* 320-330.

Newcomb, T. (1953). An approach to the study of communicative acts. *Psychological Review, 60,* 393-404.

Page, B. I., Shapiro, R. Y., & Dempsey, G. (1987). What moves public opinion? *American Political Science Review, 81,* 23-43.

Perloff, R. M. (1993). *The dynamics of persuasion.* Hillsdale, NJ: Lawrence Erlbaum.

Perloff, R. M., & Pettey, G. (1991). Designing an AIDS information campaign to reach intravenous drug users and sex partners. *Public Health Reports, 106,* 460-463.

Petty, R. E., & Cacioppo, J. A. (1979). Issue involvement can increase or decrease persuasion by enhancing message-relevant cognitive responses. *Journal of Personality and Social Psychology, 37,* 1915-1926.

Petty, R. E., Cacioppo, J. A., & Goldman, R. (1981). Personal involvement as a determinant of argument-based persuasion. *Journal of Personality and Social Psychology, 41,* 847-855.

Phillips, D. P. (1974). The influence of suggestion on suicide: Substantive and theoretical implications of the Werther effect. *American Sociological Review, 39,* 340-354.

Phillips, D. P. (1989). Recent advances in suicidology: The study of imitative suicide. In R. F. W. Diekstra, R. Maris, S. Platt, A. Schmidtke, & G. Sonneck (Eds.), *Suicide and its prevention: The role of attitude and imitation* (pp. 299-312). Leiden, Netherlands: E. J. Brill.

Phillips, D. P., & Carstensen, M. S. (1986). Clustering of teenage suicides after television news stories about suicide. *New England Journal of Medicine, 315,* 685-689.

Pittam, J. (1994). *Voice in social interaction: An interdisciplinary approach.* Thousand Oaks, CA: Sage.

Pomeranz, E. M., Chaiken, S., & Tordesillas, R. S. (1995). Attitude strength and resistance processes. *Journal of Personality and Social Psychology, 69,* 408-419.

Pratkanis, A. R. (2000). Altercasting as an influence tactic. In D. J. Terry & M. A. Hogg (Eds.), *Attitudes, behavior, and social context* (pp. 201-226). Mahwah, NJ: Lawrence Erlbaum.

Quintilian. (1920). *Institutio oratoria* (H. E. Butler, Trans., Vol. 3). Cambridge, MA: Harvard University Press, Loeb Classical Library.

Rafaeli, A., & Sutton, R. I. (1991). Emotional contrast strategies as means of social influence. *Academy of Management Journal, 34,* 749-775.

Rank, S. G., & Jacobson, C. K. (1977). Hospital nurses' compliance with medication overdose orders: A failure to replicate. *Journal of Health and Social Behavior, 18,* 188-193.

Reingen, P. H. (1982). Test of a list procedure for inducing compliance with a request to donate money. *Journal of Applied Psychology, 67,* 110-118.

Reingen, P. H., & Kernan, J. B. (1993). Social perception and interpersonal influence: Some consequences of the physical attractiveness stereotype in a personal selling setting. *Journal of Consumer Psychology, 2,* 25-38.

Rohrer, J. H., Baron, S. H., Hoffman, E. L., & Swander, D. V. (1954). The stability of autokinetic judgments. *Journal of Abnormal and Social Psychology, 49,* 595-597.

Rothman, A. J., Martino, S. C., Bedell, B. T., Detweiler, J. B., & Salovey, P. (1999). The systematic influence of gain- and loss-framed messages on interest in and use of different types of health behavior. *Personality and Social Psychology Bulletin, 25,* 1355-1369.

Rothman, A. J., & Salovey, P. (1997). Shaping perceptions to motivate healthy behavior: The role of message framing. *Psychological Bulletin, 121,* 3-19.

Rutte, C. G., Wilke, H. A. M., & Messick, D. M. (1987). Scarcity or abundance caused by people or the environment as determinants of behavior in the resource dilemma. *Journal of Experimental Social Psychology, 23,* 208-216.

Schlenker, B. R. (1980). *Impression management: The self-concept, social identity, and interpersonal relationships.* Pacific Grove, CA: Brooks/Cole.

Schlenker, B. R., Dlugolecki, D. W., & Doherty, K. (1994). The impact of self-presentations on self-appraisals and behavior: The power of public commitment. *Personality and Social Psychology Bulletin, 20,* 20-33.

Schlenker, B. R., & Trudeau, J. V. (1990). The impact of self-presentations on private self-beliefs. *Journal of Personality and Social Psychology, 58,* 22-32.

Schultz, P. W. (1999). Changing behavior with normative feedback interventions: A field experiment on curbside recycling. *Basic and Applied Social Psychology, 21,* 25-36.

Schwartz, B. (2000). Self-determination: The tyranny of freedom. *American Psychologist, 55,* 79-88.

Schwartzwald, J., Bizman, A., & Raz, M. (1983). The foot-in-the-door paradigm: Effects of second request size on donation probability and donor generosity. *Personality and Social Psychology Bulletin, 9,* 443-450.

Sherif, M. (1936). *The psychology of social norms.* New York: Harper.

Sherman, S. J. (1980). On the self-erasing nature of errors of prediction. *Journal of Personality and Social Psychology, 39,* 211-221.

Siegel, M., & Doner, L. (1998). *Marketing public health: Strategies to promote social change.* Gaithersburg, MD: Aspen.

Smith, R. E., & Hunt, S. D. (1978). Attributional processes in promotional situations. *Journal of Consumer Research, 5,* 149-158.

Smyth, M. H., & Fuller, R. G. C. (1972). Effects of group laughter on responses to humorous materials. *Psychological Reports, 30,* 132-134.

Steenbergen, M. R., McGraw, K. M., & Scholtz, J. T. (1992). Adaptation to the 1986 Tax Reform Act. In J. Slemrod (Ed.), *Why people pay taxes* (pp. 21-45). Ann Arbor: University of Michigan Press.

Stone, J., Aronson, E., Crain, A. L., Winslow, M. P., & Fried, C. B. (1994). Inducing hypocrisy as a means for encouraging young adults to use condoms. *Personality and Social Psychology Bulletin, 20,* 116-128.

Taylor, R. (1978). Marilyn's friends and Rita's customers: A study of party selling as play and as work. *Sociological Review, 26,* 573-611.

Tedeschi, J. T. (Ed.). (1981). *Impression management theory and social psychological research.* New York: Academic Press.

Tesser, A., Campbell, J., & Mickler, S. (1983). The role of social pressure, attention to the stimulus, and self-doubt in conformity. *European Journal of Social Psychology, 13,* 217-233.

Tice, D. M. (1992). Self-concept change and self-presentation. *Journal of Personality and Social Psychology, 63,* 435-451.

Towson, S. M. J., & Zanna, M. P. (1983). Retaliation against sexual assault. *Psychology of Women Quarterly, 8,* 89-99.

Triandis, H. C. (1995). *Individualism and collectivism.* Boulder, CO: Westview.

Tversky, A., & Kahneman, D. (1981). The framing of decisions and the psychology of choice. *Science, 211,* 453-458.

Tybout, A. M., & Yalch, R. F. (1980). The effect of experience: A matter of salience? *Journal of Consumer Research, 6,* 406-413.

Wegner, D. M., Lane, J. D., & Dimitri, S. (1994). The allure of secret relationships. *Journal of Personality and Social Psychology, 66,* 287-300.

Weinstein, E. A., & Deutschberger, P. (1963). Some dimensions of altercasting. *Sociometry, 26,* 454-466.

Weinstein, E. A., & Deutschberger, P. (1964). Task, bargains, and identities in social interaction. *Social Forces, 42,* 451-456.

West, S. G. (1975). Increasing the attractiveness of college cafeteria food. *Journal of Applied Psychology, 10,* 656-658.

Williams, K. D., Bourgeois, M., & Croyle, R. T. (1993). The effects of stealing thunder in criminal and civil trials. *Law and Human Behavior, 17,* 597-609.

Wilson, D. K., Kaplan, R. M., & Schneiderman, L. J. (1987). Framing of decisions and selection of alternatives in health care. *Social Behaviour, 2,* 51-59.

Wilson, D. K., Purdon, S. E., & Wallston, K. A. (1988). Compliance to health recommendations: A theoretical overview of message framing. *Health Education Research, 3,* 161-171.

Woodside, A. G., & Davenport, J. W. (1974). Effects of salesman similarity and expertise on consumer purchasing behavior. *Journal of Marketing Research, 11,* 198-202.

Wooten, D. B., & Reed, A. (1998). Informational influence and the ambiguity of product experience: Order effects on the weighting of evidence. *Journal of Consumer Research, 7,* 79-99.

Worchel, S. (1992). Beyond a commodity theory analysis of censorship: When abundance and personalism enhance scarcity effects. *Basic and Applied Social Psychology, 13,* 79-93.

Worchel, S., & Arnold, S. E. (1973). The effects of censorship and the attractiveness of the censor on attitude change. *Journal of Experimental Social Psychology, 9,* 365-377.

Worchel, S., Arnold, S. E., & Baker, M. (1975). The effect of censorship on attitude change: The influence of censor and communicator characteristics. *Journal of Applied Social Psychology, 5,* 222-239.

Worchel, S., Lee, J., & Adewole, A. (1975). Effects of supply and demand on ratings of object value. *Journal of Personality and Social Psychology, 32,* 906-914.

27

Persuasion in the Legal Setting

JOHN C. REINARD

The study of persuasion in the courts has been a major part of communication studies. Aristotle (1941) identified the forensic exchange as a major division of oratory (1358^b6) and explained the close link:

> Since rhetoric exists to affect the giving of decisions—the hearers decide between one political speaker and another, and a legal verdict *is* a decision—the orator must not only try to make the argument of his speech demonstrative and worthy of belief; he must also make his own character look right and put his hearers, who are to decide, into the right frame of mind. (1377^b21-1377^b24)

With the founding of European universities during the Middle Ages, the study of rhetoric (expanded to include law) was at the center of the core curriculum. With a few breaks in the link along the way, this close tie has endured as a standard part of both communication studies and the practice of law. Today, the study of communication and the law has grown from a cottage industry to a major part of the communication field. Each professional organization

in the field has an interest group, division, or commission dedicated to legal communication. The American Society of Trial Consultants, which claims many members from psychology and communication studies, has more than 340 members. There is little doubt that legal persuasion is a major part of the field. This chapter reviews elements of persuasion in the legal setting and considers theories, basic literature on sources, courtroom messages, jurors as audiences, and the status of the research area.[1] The emphasis is on social science work in the subject, although much intriguing work has been completed using other methods of inquiry.

THEORETIC ORIENTATIONS IN LEGAL PERSUASION

Work in legal persuasion frequently has been driven by practical needs of lawyers. Although this link has kept such studies grounded, it often has placed theory development in a secondary role. Even so, two different strains have dominated theoretic work: the application of existing theories and orientations and the development of conceptualizations specific to the law.[2]

Application of Existing Theory

Although recognizing communication constraints created by legal procedures, Mills (1976) argued for approaching much legal communication as an extension of rhetorical theory, small group communication, and argumentation studies. There can be no doubt that many rhetorical principles apply to courtroom settings. Especially in areas where research specific to legal settings had not been completed, scholars often relied on research in general communication. For instance, Rieke and Stutman's (1990) excellent textbook covered the use of humor (pp. 69-70) by reviewing non-courtroom research exclusively. Fewer than 20% of the sources cited in their chapter on "Credibility" were specific studies of courtroom behavior. The National Jury Project's (1986) sourcebook similarly could not rely exclusively on court-specific research; for example, all citations about jury nonverbal communication were from general communication sources (pp. 11-25 to 11-33). Although directly applying communication to the legal setting has intuitive appeal, it also is the case that special constraints in the legal setting limit the reasonable bounds of such applications.

Because legal advocacy is persuasive argument, Rieke and Sillars (1997) argued that legal case reasoning is frequently analogic and syllogistic: "[major premise:] This is the relevant law. . . . [minor premise:] The facts of the present case are embraced within those contemplated in the law. . . . [conclusion:] This case should be decided according to the law stated in the major premise" (pp. 95-96). Because the legal setting also is a forum for persuasion, some scholars attempted to apply theories of attitude change. Varying degrees of success were found by applying the Linear Discrepancy Model (Boster, Hunter, & Hale, 1991) and the Elaboration Likelihood Model (Floyd, 1998/1999; Wursten, 1986/1987).[3] This approach to legal persuasion has had the advantages of exploring boundaries of existing theories and identifying predictive relationships.

Other attempts were made to describe the flow of courtroom persuasion. One promising direction viewed legal persuasion as a game in which the players used strategies to manage payoffs (Kalai, 1993). Yet other approaches to predicting jury decision making that have been tested and generally found wanting have included multinomial decision making involving decision criteria used by juries, Bayesian probability models of defendant propensities to commit charged crimes, models of jury size and accuracy, juror and deliberation error catching, and simple computer simulation assuming differing degrees of juror resistance to persuasion (Penrod & Hastie, 1979).

Conceptualizations Specific to the Legal Persuasion

Thinking in legal influence has been dominated by psychologists who have focused attention on two major views of the trial: the story model and varieties of the information acquisition model. In essence, the story model describes the courtroom as an arena in which competing stories vie for the favor of jurors (Hastie, Penrod, & Pennington, 1983, pp. 22-23; Pennington & Hastie, 1986, 1990, 1992). In particular, the story model treats juror decision making as a three-stage cognitive process. During the first stage, jurors attempt to comprehend and organize evidence to create rational versions of the events giving rise to the trial. Jurors frame their explanations of reasonable cause and effect and intentional behavior patterns based on their "general knowledge" of the ways people act. During the second phase, the "verdict-category-establishment" stage, jurors attempt to identify a different verdict alternative and to choose a decision rule that would be required to arrive at a verdict. During the third phase, jurors select the verdict category that seems to be the best match with the plausible stories. Pennington and Hastie (1993) explained that story acceptance depended on the degree to which it covered all of the information presented to jurors, maintained a sense of coherence, appeared to be unique among competing explanations, and established its "goodness-of-fit" with the evidence. The story model seems compatible with other theories of narrative communication. For instance, Bennett and his associates (Bennett, 1978, 1979; Bennett & Feldman, 1981) considered storytelling not just as a way to share information but also as a way for jurors to make sense out of the trial evidence.

Research on the story model has been mixed. Some work observed that jurors often describe trial evidence in story terms (Pennington & Hastie, 1986). Experimental studies that drafted cases as stories found that these adaptations promoted desired verdicts (Pennington & Hastie, 1992; for similar support, see Kuhn, Weinstock, & Flaton, 1994). Hastie and Pennington (2000) observed that the believability of the crime story predicted verdicts even more than did the quality of the evidence. Yet other studies did not support the story model when exploring the predicted role of juror reliance on social problem solving (Becker, 1998/1999). Others found that opening and closing statements were not made increasingly persuasive by organizing them as stories (McCullough, 1991), even after controlling for the type of organization

used in the opposition's opening and closing statements (Spiecker, 1998/1999). Conceptually, the story model has had its limitations. First, given that some trials deal with more vivid stories than do others, it may be that the model is least useful when non-narrative materials are presented. Second, the model might not be testable given that it is most difficult to identify any predictions that are recognized as clearly contrary to the theory. Nearly any form of trial outcome could be enlisted to support the story model's view of what makes persuasive and unpersuasive narratives. These limitations have not been an impediment to trial consultants. One consulting team used the story model to identify coherent "guilty" and "not guilty" stories that could be understandable and potentially persuasive to jurors (Olsen-Fulero, Fulero, & Wulff, 1989).

A strong alternative to the story model has been the information acquisition model. This approach views jurors as recipients of information who make decisions based on the amount and nature of information with which they are presented. Calling this approach the "meter model," Lopes (1993) observed that jurors often keep track of subjective values they place on the merit of evidence for each side in a trial. Although finding much to admire in this view, Lopes suggested acceptance of both the meter and story models. Using an averaging model of information integration, Ostrom, Werner, and Saks (1978) noted that mock jurors initially presumed a defendant to be not guilty, but by the end of the trial, the amount and degree of incrimination in the evidence was averaged with the presumption of innocence to reach a decision. Although many researchers were implicitly guided by this approach, they did not always explain their work as such an application. Furthermore, this category of theorizing has not always promoted consistent predictions of jury behavior. Some might consider it an invitation to incoherent collections of research rather than a body of theoretically valuable materials.

SOURCES OF PERSUASIVE COMMUNICATION IN LEGAL SETTINGS

Many excellent books (Gibson, 1991; Matlon, 1988; Rieke & Stutman, 1990), articles, chapters, and papers (Boyll, 1991; Devine, Clayton, Dunford, Seying, & Pryce, 2001; Elwork, Sales, & Suggs, 1981; Erlanger, 1970; Linz & Penrod, 1984; Nietzel, Mc-Carthy, & Kern, 1999; Wright & Hosman, 1980) have summarized varying portions of the literature on communication and the law. Unlike those assessing general issues in legal communication, this review examines social science research dealing with persuasion exclusively. Thus, there are major areas of study that this review excludes.[4] This review of sources considers influences of lawyers, plaintiffs, defendants, victims, and judges.

Lawyers as Sources

Although the aphorism that jurors try the attorneys rather than the clients overstates the matter, there is little doubt that attorney conduct and characteristics affect jury decisions. The credible attorney appears to possess the factors of character, competence, extroversion (Hirsch, Reinard, & Reynolds, 1976), supplemented with a vital factor identified as "likeability" (Rickun, 1977). How attorneys acquire and use such credibility, however, remains an area for serious attention.

Research is very mixed on the impact of the type of lawyer representing defendants. For instance, some inquiry has suggested that privately retained attorneys have a better record than do public defenders. Lizotte (1978) observed that court-appointed attorneys are defeated more often than private attorneys. One study reported that private attorneys lost 48% of cases as compared to 59% for public defenders (Wilbanks, 1985, as described in Wilbanks, 1987, p. 92). Reiman (1995) reported statistical claims that private attorneys were successful as often as 56% of the time, unlike public defenders who secured acquittals or dismissals of charges only 11.4% of the time (p. 117). Another study found that private attorneys have a superior record of representing minority group defendants (Wheeler & Wheeler, 1980, esp. pp. 319-323). Some work has indicated that private attorneys secure longer sentences for their clients (Wilbanks, 1985), but a review of California cases found no differences (Truitt, 1997). Other research has suggested that any advantages private attorneys have in reducing rates of conviction may have disappeared during recent years. A review of criminal cases in U.S. district courts and the 75 largest counties in the United States revealed that conviction rates for defendants with private attorneys were nearly identical to conviction rates for those secured by public defenders or other court-assigned attorneys (Harlow, 2000). Overall rates of guilty verdicts (90% in federal courts in 1998 and 75% in county courts in 1996) remained high for defendants, even though convicted defendants who had private attorneys were more likely to receive prison sentences than were those with court-appointed lawyers. Although research has not directly linked attorney effort to actual verdicts, it seems that attorneys were motivated to enhance their performance when they thought that their cases were likely to go against their clients (Lind, Thibaut, & Walker, 1973).

Attorneys' personal characteristics may predict jury decisions. Some research suggests that male attorneys have greater trial success than do female lawyers (Hahn & Clayton, 1996). Yet male attorneys' physical attractiveness did not influence verdicts (Taylor, 1993).

Furthermore, male (but not female) jurors rated the defendant as guilty least often when the prosecutor was female (Pfeifer, 1988). In rape trials, if the defendant is represented by a female attorney, the rate of acquittal increased from 49% to 71% in one study (Villemur & Hyde, 1983) and from 47.5% to 68.8% in another (Yanchar, 1982/1983). Apparently, when a woman was willing to defend a man accused of rape, jurors inferred that the case against the defendant was not particularly influential. Attorney race may affect juror decision making in combination with jury authoritarianism. Among highly authoritarian jurors, Anglos' verdicts were most influenced by Anglo defense attorneys, and African American jurors were most persuaded by African American attorneys (Boliver, 1999).

Plaintiffs as Sources

A sense of how deserving and desirable a plaintiff is seems to affect jury assessments. In fact, although social desirability of both plaintiffs and defendants predicted verdicts, only plaintiff desirability predicted size of monetary awards granted (Egbert, Moore, Wuensch, & Castellow, 1992). Jurors in civil cases tended to decide in favor of attractive litigants (Snyder, 1971; Stephen & Tully, 1977). But this preference for attractive plaintiffs seemed to depend on whether people processed information in a rational mode (dedicating energy to the information they heard) or an experiential mode (responding to information on an emotional level). Attractive plaintiffs were favored only by individuals in the rational mode (Lieberman, 1998).

Defendants as Sources

Defendant characteristics that have been the object of research attention include the defendant's race, attractiveness, and various personal characteristics. Each of these elements is reviewed in this section.

Race. The defendant's race may affect case outcome, but not under every circumstance. Concerns that ethnic minorities are overrepresented in the prison system (e.g., Clayton, 1983; Radelet, 1981) may complicate the matter. Although studies through the early 1960s showed that African American defendants were found guilty most often and were given the longest sentences (Bullock, 1961; Garfinkle, 1949; Johnson, 1941), research since that time has not always found such a pattern. Indeed, Anglos received longer sentences than did Latinos in Texas noncapital felony trials (Daudistel, Hosch, Holmes, & Graves, 1999), and Anglos on trial in Los Angeles were convicted more often than were African Americans (Petersilia, 1983). In a controversial summary statement, Wilbanks (1987) asserted, "The overwhelming consensus of recent studies (obviously, conviction rates may have been higher for blacks in earlier periods) has been that blacks are less likely to be convicted than whites" (p. 98). A battle of literature reviews has raged on the subject. Reviewing 20 articles, Hagan (1974) found that defendant race effects explained between 0.4% and 8.0% of the variance on sentences. But studies controlling for the defendant's prior criminal record and the type of crime did not produce significant effects. Kleck's (1981) review of 57 empirical studies revealed that in the South the death penalty was imposed in ways that reflected racial discrimination. Otherwise, he stated that discrimination was not widespread in the legal system, a position for which he was attacked, sometimes personally (see Austin, 1984; Dehais, 1983). A review completed by the Panel on Sentencing Research of the National Academy of Sciences examined 60 studies (Blumstein, Cohen, Martin, & Tonry, 1983) and opined that racial discrimination effects in sentencing were not general but "may play a more important role in some regions, jurisdictions, crime types, or the decisions of individual participants" (Vol. 1, p. 92). On the other hand, some (Hagan & Bumiller, 1983, esp. pp. 31-32) have noted the existence of studies completed after the mid-1960s that controlled for major intervening variables and still reported racial bias. For instance, Hall and Simkus (1975) found that 76% of Native Americans convicted of crimes were sentenced to jail time as compared to 59% of Anglos. One study observed a general tendency toward bias by Anglo mock jurors in a rape case resulting in light sentences for Anglo defendants, especially when jurors were given no pre-deliberation instructions or were presented with strong jury nullification instructions (Hill & Pfeifer, 1992). Other researchers completing controlled work have found evidence of conviction proneness toward African American defendants (Lands, 1986/1987; Townsend, 1996; but see Rector, Bagby, & Nicholson, 1993) and of increasingly severe decisions during the death penalty phase of a trial (Lynch, 1997).

But given that ethnic minorities often are poor and tend to be represented by public defenders, it is difficult to accept the notion that racial prejudice is largely inoperative. The controlled research suggests that prejudice is most likely to be found against ethnic minority defendants when cases were tried in the South (particularly in death penalty cases) or in rural areas (Austin, 1981); when jurors in cases involving African American defendants were identified as highly prejudiced (Dovidio, Smith, Donnella, & Gaertner, 1997); when jurors in forcible rape cases were of a different race from the defendant (Feild, 1979; Ugwuegbu, 1976) and when student jurors viewed themselves as dissimilar to the defendant in basic values and background (Reynolds, 1977); when female jurors in an acquaintance rape trial learned that the victim

was not a member of their own race (Hymes, Leinart, Rowe, & Rogers, 1993); and when student jurors tried the defendant of a crime that fit a racial stereotype, including an African American accused of burglary or a violent crime (Bodenhausen & Wyer, 1985; Gordon, 1990; Gordon, Bindrim, McNicholas, & Walden, 1988; Rickman, 1988/1989). Elements that seem to inhibit this effect against ethnic minority defendants included when the jury was composed of middle or upper class student jurors (Nemeth & Sosis, 1973) and when the defendant in an insanity defense had low socioeconomic status (Towers, McGinley, & Pasewark, 1992). In an effort to explore reasons for some of these differing results, Sommers and Ellsworth (2000) suggested that Anglo jurors are motivated to appear unprejudiced. Thus, in cases where race seemed salient, Anglo student jurors would be expected to become vigilant and avoid prejudicial decision making against African American defendants. Contrariwise, when racial issues were not salient to cases, increased guilty verdicts against African American defendants might be enhanced. By manipulating trial summaries presented to student jurors to illustrate different levels of race salience, the researchers found support for their expectations. On the other hand, African American student jurors showed leniency toward African American defendants regardless of the race salience levels. Membership in a racial minority seemed to benefit defendants when an African American defendant pleaded not guilty by reason of insanity (Poulson, 1990); when prosecution evidence in child molestation cases was strong, and mock jurors who believed they would be in the racial minority on the jury were of the same race as the defendant (Kerr, Hymes, Anderson, & Weathers, 1995); and when student jurors tried an African American defendant on a charge that defied a racial stereotype, such as embezzlement or white-collar crime, a crime for which Anglos were most often convicted (Bodenhausen & Wyer, 1985; Gordon, 1990; Gordon et al., 1988; Rickman, 1988/1989).

Defendant Attractiveness. In criminal cases, as in civil cases, jurors tend to favor the attractive source (Calhoun, Selby, Cann, & Keller, 1978; Darby & Jeffers, 1988; Kulka & Kessler, 1978; Landy & Aronson, 1969; Leventhal & Krate, 1977; McFatter, 1978; Reynolds & Sanders, 1975; Seligman, Brickman, & Koulack, 1977; Solomon & Schopler, 1978; Tieger, 1981; Wyatt, 1982/1983). Looking at defendant character rather than attraction directly, Barnett and Feild (1978) found that the character of the defendant had a significant effect in a case involving rape but played only a minor role in juror sentencing in a burglary case. Yet some interactions of attractiveness with other variables seem to exist. Although attractiveness predicted sentences and even amounts judges set for bail (Downs & Lyons, 1991), it did not always predict verdicts (Erian, Lin, Patel, Neal, & Geiselman, 1998). This information was intriguing for the courtroom persuader because, in one study (Sigall & Landy, 1972), a participant was made to seem attractive simply by describing him as "loving and warm" instead of "cold and unapproachable." Similar labeling also was found to be effective for participants in a traffic collision case (Kaplan & Kemmerick, 1974). Yet the type of crime with which a defendant was charged made a difference. When the charge was swindling, where attractiveness might facilitate committing the crime, an attractive defendant was more likely to be convicted than was a nonattractive source (Sigall & Ostrove, 1975). Similar results were found when comparing attractive and unattractive men and women charged with either burglary or swindling (Wuensch, Chia, Castellow, Chuang, & Cheng, 1993). Effects seemed to be most pronounced when jurors were high in authoritarianism (Mitchell

& Byrne, 1973) or when student jurors had low socioeconomic status (Nemeth & Sosis, 1973). The impact of defendant attractiveness was reduced by actual jury deliberations (Izzett & Leginski, 1974). Even though deliberations shifted decisions toward acquittal for attractive defendants, they did not affect decisions for unattractive defendants (MacCoun, 1990).

Victim attractiveness also affected decisions. With strong prosecution evidence, unattractive defendants were given the harshest sentences for harming attractive victims (Erian et al., 1998; see also Feild, 1979). Interestingly enough, the effects of defendant attractiveness did not wizen when the trial was long instead of short (Kramer & Kerr, 1989). Related to attractiveness is defendant appearance. One study found that jurors were most receptive to defendants who were neither dressed in prison clothes nor attended by armed guards (Dane & Wrightsman, 1982; Fontaine & Kiger, 1978).

Personal Characteristics of Defendants. Matters such as defendant socioeconomic status and perceived similarity and sympathy with jurors have been examined in the research. The defendant's socioeconomic status can influence perceptions of the case. In one inquiry, research controlling the degree of premeditation of murders and race of defendants, low socioeconomic status defendants received the longest sentences (Osborne & Rappaport, 1985). When physicians from high-status specialties were charged with murder, convictions were greatest. Yet when they were charged with fraud, the highest status specialties received the lowest rate of convictions (Rosoff, 1987).

Defendant status does not always affect verdicts (Adler, 1973; Gleason & Harris, 1976; Gordon & Jacobs, 1969). Yet once high-status figures were found guilty in murder cases, both community and student samples recommended the harshest punishments for these same defendants (Bray, Struckman-Johnson, Osborne, McFarlane, & Scott, 1978). Yet in other types of trials, low-status defendants received the longest sentences (Landy & Aronson, 1969; Reed, 1965). Related to status is juror knowledge of defendants' "deep pockets" in civil cases. In one study, jurors who learned of the defendant's insurance increased the plaintiff awards from $33,000 to $36,000, and when the jurors were told to disregard it, the awards jumped to $46,000 (Broeder, 1959). Similar support was found in a dog bite injury suit (Reinard, 1993). This effect was most pronounced when the defendant was a corporation rather than an individual (MacCoun, 1996). In follow-up work, Anderson and MacCoun (1999) noted that jurors who were not permitted to award punitive damages inflated "pain and suffering" compensation.

Sympathetic defendants and those similar to the jury tended to have advantages in different kinds of cases. In civil cases, jury sympathy for the plaintiff was a strong indicator of decisions (Darden, DeConinck, Babin, & Griffin, 1991). In product liability suits, this sympathy led jurors to favor plaintiffs out of a general desire to promote a healthy social fabric for society rather than simply out of a commitment to follow the law. In criminal cases, defendants who are viewed as dissimilar to jurors tended to be found guilty less often than were others (Dane & Wrightsman, 1982). This effect even outweighed racial biases that may have been operating against minority group defendants in highly charged rape cases (Reynolds, 1977). Jurors also were most likely to convict defendants whose attitudes were perceived as dissimilar to their own (Griffitt & Jackson, 1973; Shepherd & Sloan, 1979). Defendant sex affected jurors in a criminal case. College students who read case summaries gave men shorter sentences than they gave women for purse snatching (Angira, 1991). In

another study contrasting shoplifting and assault cases, female defendants received fewer guilty verdicts from student jurors than did male defendants, although sentence recommendations were not different for the two types of defendants (Dravin, 1982/1983). Empathy with the defendant was tested in a patricide trial in which a child defendant claimed self-defense due to sexual abuse by the victim (Haegerich & Bottoms, 2000). When student jurors were asked to take the perspective of the defendant and to consider how they would feel under the circumstances of the trial, jurors were most likely to decide not guilty. When a landlord defendant treated tenants coldly and as objects, the plaintiff awards increased (Holt et al., 1997). On the other hand, when criminal defendants already had suffered greatly, the severity of jury decisions was reduced (Shaffer, Plummer, & Hammock, 1986), especially when the defendants' suffering was linked to the crime with which they were charged (Austin, Walster, & Utne, 1976).

Victim Characteristics

Who the victim is makes a difference in jury decision making, particularly in regard to race and the victim's conduct before commission of the crime. A literature review on the subject (Kleck, 1981) observed that when the victim was African American, punishment was less severe than when the victim was Anglo, particularly in death penalty cases. Furthermore, the victim's age did not appear to produce significant effects on verdicts (Nunez, McCoy, Clark, & Shaw, 1999).

The victim's conduct makes a difference in jury decisions, sometimes in surprising ways. If the victim were called to testify in a rape trial, mock jurors were most likely to return guilty verdicts when the victim avoided eye contact with the defendant (Weir

& Wrightsman, 1990). In rape cases, defense attorneys sometimes attempt to place the victim's past sexual conduct on trial despite great limits on this strategy. When student jurors read case summaries with medical reports and testimony including information about the victim's past sexual history, the victim's past reckless conduct did, in fact, reduce guilt ratings and sentence recommendations (Pugh, 1983). Convictions increased if jurors learned that rape victims attempted to resist the attacks (Krulewitz & Nash, 1979; Scroggs, 1976) and if the rapes resulted in pregnancies (Scroggs, 1976). Yet if the defendants were acquaintances rather than strangers, rates of acquittal increased (Calhoun, Selby, & Warring, 1976; Smith, Keating, Hester, & Mitchell, 1976).

Some research investigated the "just world" hypothesis, which holds that if one believes the world is a fair and just place, people pretty much get what they deserve. Thus, jurors may reason that respectable people must have particularly deserved the bad treatment they received given that they were victimized (Lerner, 1965). Some work has supported this notion, including a study completed in both the United States and the United Kingdom where the defendant was most likely to be acquitted if the victim took reasonable precautions to avoid the crime (Kerr, Bull, MacCoun, & Rathborn, 1985). Jones and Aronson (1973) found that respectable victims (women identified as married or as virgins) were blamed more for their victimage in rape cases than were divorced women. Yet the just world hypothesis has not always been supported. Despite their other findings, for instance, Jones and Aronson observed that the longest sentences were recommended when the victims were respectable. Others observed that conviction rates decreased when rape victims were disreputable, variously described as prostitutes (Feldman-Summers & Lindner, 1976) or topless/bottomless dancers, whereas convictions increased when the victims were described as social workers or Roman Catholic nuns (Smith et al., 1976). In compatible work, mock jurors' empathy for rape victims increased rates of guilty verdicts (Weir & Wrightsman, 1990). Similarly, Kerr and Kurtz (1977) presented student jurors with case summaries and found that the defendants were given the longest sentences when the victims were made to suffer. Contrary to the just world hypothesis, the victim's status was not denigrated when the respondents believed in a just world.

Judges as Sources

Judges often influence the jury through nonverbal cues. In one case that was the object of misconduct charges, the judge listening to a witness alternately shook his head, rolled his eyes heavenward, and turned around in his chair and stared at the wall for 45 minutes (*State v. Jenkins,* 1994). Even without such extreme cues, judges actively communicate their sentiments through cues such as smiles, nods, and frowns (Blanck, Rosenthal, & Cordell, 1985). The ways a judge looked at defendants and witnesses were eventually reflected in the jury verdicts among judges in municipal and magistrate courts (Dorch & Fontaine, 1978). There was a moderate correlation (.48) between the amount of a judge's gaze at the defendant and the severity of the fine the defendant received.

MESSAGES IN THE COURTROOM

Persuasive messages include many elements at trial. This section examines the influence of charges and burden of proof, pretrial publicity, persuasion during jury selection, opening statements, closing statements, defense strategy, case evidence, direct examination, cross-examination, and judge instructions.

Charges, Requested Civil Remedies, and Burden of Proof

The charge or complaint itself is a proposition that may sensitize some jurors. For instance, mock jurors hearing a murder trial were more likely to return a guilty verdict than those who heard a burglary trial (Paris, 1985). In criminal trials, there is a general pattern that as the severity of the charges and penalties increases, juries become less and less willing to convict, even if the defendants are viewed as guilty (Grofman, 1985). Indeed, increasing the number of options to return reduced charges seems to enhance the chances that jurors will convict on one (Larntz, 1975). Jurors given the option of returning "guilty but mentally ill" rendered that verdict two thirds of the time instead of using the options of "guilty" and "not guilty by reason of insanity" (Poulson, 1990). The sequence in which instructions about different possible verdicts is given has been investigated. In two experiments, when verdict options were introduced in order ranging from the most to the least severe, mock jurors rendered harsher verdicts than when the possible verdicts were arranged from least severe to most severe (Greenberg, Williams, & O'Brien, 1986). To convict on a case involving severe penalties, jurors seemed to demand increased amounts of evidence (Thomas & Hogue, 1976), and they usually reduced their overall rates of conviction (Kerr, 1978). Sometimes trials involve multiple counts of crimes alleged against defendants. Experiments (Tanford, 1985; Tanford & Penrod, 1984) using both actual jurors and student jurors and controlling for similarity of the charges, evidence, and judges' instructions found that defendants charged with three crimes were most likely to be convicted.

Jurors also showed great confusion in keeping track of which evidence related to which charges despite the efforts of judges to provide clear instructions.

Verdicts are affected by the burden of proof shouldered by prosecutors and plaintiffs. The standard of proof required for a decision against the defendant may be proof "beyond a reasonable doubt," "by a preponderance of the evidence," or "clear and convincing evidence." As the standard of proof increases, rates of guilty verdicts decline (see Kagehiro, 1990). Yet when the judge defined "beyond a reasonable doubt" as one's being firmly convinced of guilt, rates of guilty verdicts for murder increased (Koch & Devine, 1999). In civil cases, jurors who took notes during the trial made objectively sound decisions on compensatory awards when the evidence modestly or strongly favored the plaintiff (ForsterLee & Horowitz, 1997).

Formal presumptions on the interpretation of evidence are meaningful elements of jurors' decision making when jurors are made aware of them. Three types of presumptions (conclusive, mandatory, and permissive) were presented to student jurors as part of criminal trials in which the defendant blameworthiness was manipulated (Schmolesky, Cutler, & Penrod, 1988). The conclusive presumption used to suggest defendant guilt increased the numbers of guilty verdicts, although other presumptions did not. Even so, when ratings of defendant culpability were high, jurors were willing to discount presumptions that tended to benefit the defendant.

In civil cases, the higher the damages plaintiffs request, the more money they seem to receive. Of course, judging whether this pattern is causal required experimental work holding the trial evidence constant. Such work with mock jurors supported these expectations (Hastie, Schkade, & Payne, 1999; Raitz, Greene, Goodman, & Loftus, 1990) across types of personal injury cases, regardless of victim sex and race (Malouff & Schutte, 1989).

Pretrial Publicity

The impact of pretrial publicity remains a concern among constitutional scholars as well as persuasion researchers. The American Bar Association reported that pretrial publicity descriptions of 27% of criminal suspects were "problematic" (Imrich, Mullin, & Linz, 1995). Not surprisingly, most research indicates that pretrial publicity influences jurors (Constantini & King, 1980-1981; Ogloff & Vidmar, 1994; Padawer-Singer & Barton, 1975; Tans and Chaffee, 1966; Tarrence, 1991/1992; Wright & Ross, 1997; for a meta-analysis, see Steblay, Besirevic, Fulero, & Jimenez-Lorente, 1999), especially when it involves eyewitness identifications (Devenport, Studebaker, & Penrod, 1999), and character evidence (Otto, Penrod, & Dexter, 1994), regardless of whether the trial is short or long (Kramer & Kerr, 1989). Although most pretrial publicity was inimical to defendants (Imrich et al., 1995; Riley, 1973; Tankard, Middleton, & Rimmer, 1979), sometimes it benefited defendants, as when the pretrial publicity reports also included the suggestion that there were racist intentions behind spreading the publicity (Fein, Morgan, Norton, & Sommers, 1997), the publicity involved stories of mistaken identification of an innocent man (Greene & Loftus, 1984), or the publicity involved trials similar to the defendant's (Greene & Wade, 1988). Yet another study found no effects from pro-defendant pretrial publicity (Riedel, 1993).

Naturally, pretrial publicity affects jurors differently. Mock jurors with high ego levels tended to become less confident in their verdicts (Freundlich, 1984/1985). Among jurors with strong pretrial beliefs in the defendant's guilt, ceiling effects prevented identifying fur-

ther effects from prejudicial pretrial publicity (Finkelstein, 1994/1995). One study (Hoiberg & Stires, 1973a) found that lowly intelligent women presented with strongly biased pretrial publicity of a heinous rape were most influenced by it, although men and highly intelligent women were not. Even among men, the publicity sometimes can backfire. Men presented with pretrial publicity portraying perpetrators of acquaintance rape as predators responded with increased pro-defendant judgments in an acquaintance rape case (Mullin, 1997; Mullin, Imrich, & Linz, 1996).

Attorneys and judges seem assured that intensive *voir dire* examinations to select jurors protect against pretrial publicity bias (Hans & Vidmar, 1986, pp. 63-78). Attorneys rarely present change of venue motions, and 88% of judges have never ruled on one (Siebert, Wilcox, & Hough, 1970, pp. 4-6). Research does not suggest that active *voir dire* actually reduces pretrial publicity effects (Dexter, Cutler, & Moran, 1992; Kerr, Kramer, Carroll, & Alfini, 1991; Kerr, Niedermeier, & Kaplan, 1999; Sue, Smith, & Pedroza, 1975; but see Padawer-Singer, Singer, & Singer, 1974). Methodologically, using student jurors tended to inhibit pretrial publicity effects (Steblay et al., 1999), as did publicity related to some types of crimes. Dismissed and retained jurors did not seem to report different verdicts when the pretrial publicity involved emotional or factual material (Kerr et al., 1991; Sue et al., 1975). Another method of control, a continuance or delay for a couple of days, appeared to help partially overcome the effects of pretrial publicity bias (Kramer, Kerr, & Carroll, 1990). Even when a judge admonished jurors to disregard any pretrial publicity, student jurors, especially women, still were influenced by the damaging publicity (Sue, Smith, & Gilbert, 1974).

Despite the results based on experimental and laboratory studies, Bruschke and Loges (1999) launched a broadside attack against such study results. Taking the view that laboratory research on the subject is unrealistic, these authors argued for the use of survey methods. Examining the opportunity of jurors to be exposed to publicity (as tracked by the Lexis/Nexis database of print media), verdicts, and sentences in 134 federal murder trials, they found no significant association between publicity and conviction rates. Indeed, the low-publicity condition was associated with the highest conviction rates. Another study (Bruschke & Loges, 2001) of newspaper publicity related to federal murder and robbery trials in Atlanta, Detroit, and Los Angeles found no publicity effects on verdicts, and after an interaction effect was examined, sentence recommendations were inversely related to the amount of publicity. Hence, when the actual amount of pretrial publicity is experimentally controlled, influences on juror decisions exist. When estimates of juror opportunity to be exposed to print news are used (excluding television news as a source), the damaging effects of publicity seem limited at best.

Voir Dire Messages

Voir dire, or the questioning of potential jurors to select a jury, may be a persuasive process in which attorneys build rapport, obtain commitments, preview the case (Rieke & Stutman, 1990, pp. 70-71), introduce the client in a favorable light, begin arguing the case, guide the jury in its methods of deliberating (Crump, 1980), and familiarize the jury with relevant factual and legal concepts (Mauet, 1980, p. 31). In practice, statements and questions from judges and attorneys accounted for approximately 60% of the sentences uttered during the voir dire "questioning" of potential jurors (Johnson & Haney, 1994). Defense attorneys used voir dire more aggressively than did prosecutors (Johnson & Haney,

1994), and attorney-led questioning stimulated more candid self-disclosure than did judge questioning (Jones, 1987). Ironically, in California, where great restrictions have been placed on attorney questioning, judges were pleased with their own abilities to conduct voir dire examinations, although they believed that attorneys took too much time with juror questioning (Smith, 1994/1995). Dismissed jurors tended to score low in positive self-disclosure (Wigley, 1986/1987; but see Wigley, 1995); high in verbal aggressiveness, dominance, and contentiousness (Wigley, 1999); and high in communication apprehension with friends (Wigley, 1986/1987). When voir dire questions were completed individually rather than en masse, attorneys raised increased numbers of objections to jurors for cause (Nietzel & Dillehay, 1982). Yet this aggressive questioning still often failed to exclude jurors who were opposed to basic foundations of the U.S. legal system (Johnson & Haney, 1994).

In addition to securing information to identify favorable or unfavorable jurors, questioning strategies frequently included building the case, introducing a theme, and "humanizing" the defendant (Waddell, 1988/1989). At the very least, voir dire processes taught jurors the importance of setting aside their ordinary decision-making processes and deciding cases based on the law (Balch, Giffiths, Hall, & Winfree, 1976). Moreover, jurors exposed to extensive voir dire examination perceived the defendant as less culpable than did other jurors (Dexter et al., 1992; Moran, Cutler, & Loftus, 1990). Indeed, lawyers were least effective in securing desired verdicts when they avoided the use of voir dire questions strategically designed to influence jurors (Arsenault & Reinard, 1997). Such strategic questions functioned by altering perceptions of the defendant's character that, in turn, affected verdicts (Reinard, Arsenault, & Geck, 1998). Another study found that strategic questions asking jurors to overlook the defendant's undesirable past reduced verdicts of guilt, whereas the absence of any strategic *voir dire* questions negatively affected defendant credibility ratings (Reinard & Arsenault, 2000). Extending this work into contrasts of strategic questions attempting to promote a sense of juror rapport or empathy with the defense, Reinard, Khalid, and Liso (2001) found that verdicts for the defense were enhanced by the use of questions that requested jurors to reciprocate positively to the defense expressions of trust in them.

Opening Statements

Attorneys' opening statements are supposed to provide a case preview rather than extended argument. But because trials are forums for argument, and distinguishing argumentative from nonargumentative statements can be difficult in practice, one should not be surprised that opening statements have powerful argumentative functions (see Perrin, 1999, esp. pp. 110-132), even though such strategies as fanciful name calling (*People v. Johnston*, 1994), directly refuting the opposition's case (e.g., *State v. Bell*, 1972), and interpreting upcoming evidence (Strong, 1992, pp. 17-19) have been ruled argumentative. Indeed, an examination of 19 opening statements found that all were subject to some objection from the opposition, the plurality of which involved "various types of circumstantial evidence—using a theme, drawing inferences for the jury, characterizing a person or event in some argumentative way, or discussing the mental condition of a person" (Perrin, 1999, p. 140). Opening statements also were believed to be influential given that the jurors tended to make decisions early in the trial process (Freundlich, 1984/1985; Pyszczynski & Wrightsman, 1981; Stone, 1969; but see Weld & Danzig, 1940).[5] Pettus (1990) learned that

"critical moments" jurors identified as decision points were during first sight of the defendant, opening statements, and presentation of the prosecution arguments. Across varying circumstances, opening statements have not been found as influential as closing arguments (Walker, Thibaut, & Andreoli, 1972; Wilson & Miller, 1968; Zdep & Wilson, 1968). The influence of the prosecution's opening statement was reduced when the defense argument that followed was strong (Wallace & Wilson, 1969). One might suppose that attorneys prepare opening statements carefully. Yet a review of 50 trials revealed that juries thought defense opening statements were less well prepared than prosecutors' statements, even though, of course, defense attorneys did not perceive any inferiority in themselves (Linz, Penrod, & McDonald, 1986). The first opening statement juries hear seems to be particularly important in a couple of ways. First, the first opening statement serves a strong agenda-setting function. The first opening statement appears to "prime the pump" such that jurors' assessments of witnesses and evidence tend to follow its organization (Bayly, 1988/1989). Second, the length of the first opening statement appears to affect reactions to others that follow. The defense enhanced the likelihood of securing not guilty verdicts if it responded to prosecutors' brief opening statements with extensive ones (Pyszczynski & Wrightsman, 1981). Curiously, guilty verdicts were increased when the defense made lengthy opening statements in response to lengthy prosecution opening statements. Similarly, the decision to delay an opening statement until halfway though a trial can damage the chances of a defendant's securing the desired verdict (Wells, Wrightsman, & Miene, 1985). Jurors relied most on the message to which they were first exposed (a primacy effect) when jury deliberations were delayed a week following their hearing both messages (Miller & Campbell, 1959). When there was a 1-week delay before hearing the second message, the message heard last was most influential (a recency effect). Other work did not support the primacy effect, although the recency effect was observed (Insko, 1964; Wilson & Miller, 1968).

Opening statement structure has been examined. It appeared to make no difference whether the opening statement used a "story" format or a legal comparison-expository structure (McCullough, 1991), regardless of whether the attorney represented the plaintiff or the defendant (Spiecker, 1998/1999). If the defense attorney's opening statement promised evidence exonerating the defendant and then failed to introduce such proof, the prosecution's reminder to the jury (in this case, presentation of an alibi witness) reduced the defense attorney's influence on the verdict (Pyszczynski, Greenberg, Mack, & Wrightsman, 1981). Yet if the prosecution failed to remind jurors of the broken promise, the defense opening statement increased the likelihood of an acquittal. In fact, if a potential witness were absent, the mere mention of that fact by the judge or by the attorney affected jury decision making against the side that was expected to produce the witness (Johnstone, 1993/1994).

The effectiveness of attorney delivery during the opening statement was not influenced by whether the attorneys were male or female (Barge, Schlueter, & Pritchard, 1989). The initial manner of delivery seemed to determine perceptions of the appropriateness of disfluencies in the rest of the message. A lawyer's great vocal variation stimulated increased perceptions of dynamism, but it also tended to promote perceptions that the attorney was not as trustworthy or friendly as others. Contrariwise, other work found that increased fluency and gestures during the opening statement were unrelated to source credibility but vocal variety reduced ratings of character and competence, while increas-

ing volume and variety in speaking rate enhanced perceptions of friendliness (Rockwell & Hubbard, 1999).

Closing Statements

Much lore and a little research have been dedicated to the closing statement. Jurors reported believing that the closing argument was vital, some rating it as second only to the presentation of evidence (Matlon, Davis, Catchings, Derr, & Waldron, 1985). Furthermore, 75% of lawyers believed that the closing arguments could have decisive effects in close cases (Walter-Goldberg, 1985). Disturbingly, in death penalty cases, improper statements made by prosecuting attorneys in the closing statements increased the rates at which jurors voted for the death penalty (Platania, 1995/1996). Significant relationships existed among actual jurors' favoring the prosecutor's closing argument and juror recall, belief, and interestingness. Yet no relationship was found among these elements and juror verdicts. Some studies noted a general recency effect favoring the influence of closing arguments over opening statements (Insko, 1964; Miller & Campbell, 1959; Walker et al., 1972; Weld & Danzig, 1940; Wilson & Miller, 1968; Zdep & Wilson, 1968). But in a critique of these primacy-recency studies, Benoit and French (1983, p. 389) warned that many of these studies included conditions for control purposes that were incompatible with actual courtroom practice.

The message structure may make a difference. A test of the story model revealed that the legal comparison-expository format for the closing statement was superior to the use of narrative structure (McCullough, 1991). Structurally, when a one-sided closing argument was followed by a two-sided closing argument, the two-sided closing argument was most persuasive (Insko, 1962). In this context, a two-sided presentation does not just mention the opposition but actually responds to it. Student jurors who heard a two-sided summation followed by a one-sided summation favored the first attorney. When jurors were familiar with the case issues, a two-sided presentation was most influential generally, although unfamiliar jurors were most influenced by one-sided case summations (Dipboye, 1977).

Defense Case Strategies

Defendants may deny charges, or they may present "affirmative defenses" that offer outside explanations as excuses. When simply denying the charges, exonerating and incriminating facts about the defendant were most influential on intensifying jurors' verdict dispositions when the attorney presented the information in a heterogeneous, rather than a homogeneous, order (Kaplan & Miller, 1977). Affirmative defenses seem difficult to argue. For instance, when defendants gave affirmative defenses for retracting confessions, they were more likely to be convicted of murder than when pleas included appeals to the Fifth Amendment or denial of the charges by reference to an alibi (Fischer & Fehr, 1985). Even so, an affirmative defense including testimony to prove mitigating circumstances was effective in reducing mock jurors' recommended sentence (Suggs & Berman, 1979). When defendants invoked the Fifth Amendment by itself, simulated jurors increased rates of guilty verdicts (Shaffer, Case, & Brannen, 1979). In one experiment, mock jurors placed approximately the same proof obligations on both sides in a murder case, regardless of the defense strategy (simple denial or self-defense) and despite the judge's instruction about the location of the burden of proof (Posey, 1995/1996). In a medical malpractice lawsuit, damage awards were cut in half when the plaintiff was shown to be partially negligent (Zickafoose & Bornstein, 1999).

Insanity Defenses. Arguing the insanity defense is particularly challenging (see Simon, 1967; Winslade & Ross, 1983) and appears to succeed slightly less than 1% of the time (Cirincione, Steadman, & McGreevy, 1995; McGinley & Pasewark, 1989) and only when defendants suffer from the most severe disorders (Boardman, 1995/1996; Lymburner & Roesch, 1999). Insanity pleas were most successful when a mentally ill defendant was accused of a property crime (Kidd & Sieveking, 1974) as well as when jurors were assured that the defendant accused of a non-murder charge would be in a mental hospital for an extended period (Carroll, 1981/1982). There are many reasons insanity defenses are risky. In the first place, the insanity defense is often misperceived and unpopular with the public (Borum & Fulero, 1999). In the second place, defining "insanity" has proven to be quite nettlesome, and lawyers and psychiatrists sometimes bewilder each other (Gutheil, 1999). Because *insanity* is not a medical term describing a particular malady, complicated rules such as the McNaughton, the Durham, the Brawner, Michigan's Guilty But Mentally Ill statute, and the American Law Institute's Model Penal Code have formed various notions of insanity. When jurors have been tested on their understanding of the various rules on which they have been instructed, comprehension has averaged between 40% (Arens, Granfield, & Susman, 1965) and slightly more than 50% accuracy (Elwork et al., 1981; Ogloff, 1993). Moreover, student jurors exposed to trial excerpts were unable to identify the defendant's mental state when a crime was committed despite hearing depositions on the matter (Whittemore & Ogloff, 1995). Although an early literature review (Casper, 1964) claimed that jurors tended to make their decisions based more on the nature of the crime than on the psychiatric evidence, surveys of a large county's records in Oregon (Steadman, Keitner, Braff, & Arvanites, 1983) and 128 cases in Virginia (Jones, 1995/1996) found a close association between pretrial psychiatric evaluations and verdicts (see also supportive studies by Jeffrey, 1986/1987; Slutsky, 1975/1977). Women who successfully argued insanity differed from others in their past criminal records and in the nature of psychiatric testimony about them at trial (Morris, 1992/1993). Overall, jury assessments appeared to be highly consistent with pretrial psychiatric evaluations, evincing a correlation of .68 (Jones, 1995/1996). Moreover, in a murder trial, path analysis found that mock jurors' evaluations of the evidence were stronger influences than their initial attitudes (Poulson, Brondino, Brown, & Braithwaite, 1998). Expert testimony and juror reasoning were significant predictors of verdicts (Hernandez, 1985/ 1986), especially when the jurors had low issue involvement (Wursten, 1986/1987). Similar work has found that student jurors presented with conflicting testimony from expert witnesses in a murder case viewed a medical doctor as more credible than a psychologist (Belon, 1991). Furthermore, an unbiased expert's testimony (indicated by revealing that the expert often gives legal testimony for both sides) stimulated more verdicts in the direction of the testimony than did the biased expert.

Claims of insanity were most persuasive when student jurors were presented with evidence that the crimes were committed in a strange (Pickel, 1998) or "bizarre" manner (Boardman, 1995/1996) without a "reasonable" (Pickel, 1998) or "criminal" (Boardman, 1995/1996) motive. Whereas those found not guilty of homicide by reason of insanity usually killed family members or parents, those found guilty usually had killed their spouses or lovers, often while under the influence of drugs or alcohol (Nestor & Haycock, 1997). Women who had killed their children and subsequently were successful in pleading not guilty by reason of insanity tended to attempt suicide after the killings and did not kill the children because they were unwanted or because the acts were revenge against wayward husbands (Holden, Stephenson-Burland, & Lemmen, 1996). Initially, it was found that defendants were most likely to use the insanity defense successfully if they were uneducated, diagnosed as schizophrenic, not drug users, and not young (Pasewark, Jeffrey, & Bieber, 1987). Some research reported that African American defendants, especially males who were diagnosed as schizophrenics (Linhorst, Hunsucker, & Parker, 1998), were most likely to win their insanity defenses (Poulson, 1990). Yet other work found no significant race effects when socioeconomic status was controlled (Towers et al., 1992). Survey work has not settled these matters. A 7-year survey in Knox County, Tennessee, revealed that violent young White men were most successful in their insanity defenses (Windham, 1990/ 1992). Bogenberger (1989/1990) found that defendants who were successful in their insanity defenses had prior diagnoses of psychosis or insanity, were unemployed, and were not young. When mock jurors in another study heard an insanity defense in a case involving either serious or trivial matters, the jurors were most willing to attribute reduced responsibility to lowly intelligent defendants, especially when the crimes were not serious (McGraw & Foley, 2000). Sometimes an insanity defense is not introduced until the penalty phase of a capital case. In one study, mock jurors heard any of four defense strategies (White, 1987). Although a defense based on mental illness was least effective, a conceptual argument against the death penalty per se was most persuasive.

Some jurors are more receptive to the insanity defense than are others. Among participants drawn from actual juror venires, images of insanity and individuals for whom jurors were willing to consider such a defense defied simple identification. But the match between jurors' images of insane defendants and the actual defense portrayals was important in deciding the cases (Skeem, 1999). Those jurors most willing to accept insanity defenses were young and highly educated, without strong moralistic attitudes (Casper, 1964), and with high levels of emotional empathy for others (Poulson, Wuensch, Brown, & Braithwaite, 1997). Least willing to accept insanity defenses were jurors with highly authoritarian personalities, those with negative attitudes toward the insanity defense and sources of expert testimony (Tezza, 1995/1996), and believers in capital punishment (Poulson et al., 1997). Believers in the death penalty discounted insanity pleas based on nonorganic mental deficiencies such as schizophrenia, but they did not differ from other jurors in accepting insanity based on organic disorders such as mental retardation and psychomotor epilepsy (Ellsworth, Bukaty, Cowan, & Thompson, 1984).

Some states have adopted variations of the insanity plea. The "diminished capacity" defense involves claiming that the defendant lacked the ability to premeditate the crime, in which case the defendant is convicted of a lesser offense than the one charged. In a multi-year survey, women pleading diminished responsibility were more successful than were men (Mitchell, 1997). In another variation, some states permit declaring a defendant "guilty but mentally ill," in which case the defendant is sentenced to prison following treatment for the mental illness. When jurors were given this alternative, they tended to use it two thirds of the time (Poulson, 1990; see also Bourdouris, 2000). Without this option, even jurors who believed the defendant was insane voted guilty a disproportionate amount of the time (Poulson, Wuensch, & Brondino,

1998). A literature review noted that the guilty but mentally ill verdict option increased confusion among jurors (Palmer & Hazelrigg, 2000) and often was used when innocent defendants were tried by jurors with low levels of control (Seymour, 1986) or as a way to signal reduced blame toward the defendant (Roberts, Sargent, & Chan, 1993). Although the option has tended to be used most for White males who were seriously mentally disturbed (Callahan, McGreevy, Cirincione, & Steadman, 1992), defendants who pleaded straight insanity and were found "guilty but mentally ill" were given more severe sentences than those who were found guilty.

Responding to such a defense can be tricky. Prosecutors usually attempt to show that the defendant premeditated and carefully planned the crime, thus suggesting that the crime was not an impulsive and irrational decision. Yet student jurors used such data to judge the wrongfulness of the conduct but not the defendant's capacity to control his or her actions (Roberts & Golding, 1991).

Recovered Memory Cases. In some cases, counselors and hypnotists have encouraged children and adult witnesses—often believed to be victims of sexual abuse—to testify about "events" they had "forgotten" or "repressed." Although this controversial approach has been attacked as little more than the power of suggestion, in a criminal case "repressed" testimony was only slightly less influential on convictions (58%) than was "nonrepressed" testimony (67%) (Key, Warren, & Ross, 1996). Whether jurors believed in such evidence depended on the perceived strength of evidence, their belief in the repression of memory, and the kinds of mass media news stories they had heard about the credibility of recovered memories (Rosen, 1996/1997). In child abuse cases featuring "repressed memory" evidence, victims who were either 3 or 13 years old at the time were not as believable as 8-year-old victims (Key et al., 1996). In defense against repressed memory cases, presenting counterexperts to testify about false recovered memories blunted the impact of the prosecution evidence (Rotzien, 1997/ 1998). Recovered memory cases—with their full retinue of expert witnesses—were most influential with female jurors, especially in cases involving female victims (Griffith, Libkuman, Kazen, & Shafir, 1999), and in civil cases with female, highly religious, and highly authoritarian jurors (Schutte, 1994). In different work, many jurors were found to doubt the credibility of hypnosis, as indicated by a sample of actual jurors who judged hypnosis-induced memories as less reliable than immediate recall but more reliable than 1 week's delayed recall (Greene, 1986).

The Entrapment Defense. One way to respond to criminal charges is by claiming that defendants were induced to engage in illegal behavior by law enforcement officials. Because such a strategy admits the illegal behavior itself, it requires subtle argument, and jurors have had difficulty understanding judges' instructions on the defense (Borgida & Park, 1988). As a result, juries have relied predominately on evidence of the defendants' past criminal conduct to reach verdicts. Lewis (1997) found that jurors in a drug case carefully tracked information about the number of times that the defendant refused enticements from law enforcement officers. If the defendant initially turned down suggestions from law enforcement officials, the jury grew increasingly receptive to the entrapment defense.

The Battered Woman Defense. The defense has been made that a "battered woman" is justified in homicide as a form of self-defense brought about by her chronic beating by an abusive spouse. Research is mixed on whether expert testimony has great (Kasian, Spanos,

Terrance, & Peebles, 1993) or limited influence on jurors' decisions (Mechanic, 1996/1997; Schuller & Hastings, 1996). In one study, jurors were most influenced by an expert witness who also was female (Schuller & Cripps, 1998). In another study, jurors were exposed to a wife accused of killing her abusive husband as he attacked her (Terrance, Matheson, & Spanos, 2000). Jurors using the "objective standard" to assess defendant fear were less convinced of the defendant's innocence than were those using the "subjective standard."

Case Evidence

Survey research has shown that case evidence is the most potent single influence on verdicts (Bayly, 1988/1989; Bridgeman & Marlowe, 1979; Cassidy, 1993/1994; Pettus, 1990; Poulson, Braithwaite, Brondino, & Wuensch, 1997; Weld & Danzig, 1940). In observations of trials and interviews with 331 jurors in sexual assault cases, matters other than evidence influenced jurors most often when the prosecution had weak cases with little hard evidence (Reskin & Visher, 1986; see also Feild, 1979). In follow-up work, juror decisions were dominated by case evidence, particularly physical evidence, although sentiments toward victims and defendants sometimes played a secondary role (Visher, 1987). Experimental work has revealed that case evidence influenced jurors more than did sentiments toward victims (Cather, Greene, & Durham, 1996) and defendants (Clary & Shaffer, 1985). Evidence of a confession, for instance, affected verdicts of student jurors more than did eyewitness identification or character testimony (Kassin & Neumann, 1997). Although student jurors were able to reject confessions that were the result of threats of punishment against the defendants, they were strongly influenced when confessions were either freely given or the products of offers of leniency (Kassin & Wrightsman, 1980). On the other hand, character evidence suggesting that defendants were not the sorts of people who would be likely to commit the alleged crimes did not affect mock jurors' verdicts unless the prosecution cases included little relevant evidence (Smith, Stasson, & Hawkes, 1998-1999). In criminal cases, verdicts seemed to balance initial bias toward the defendants with the perceived guilt appearance of the evidence (Kaplan & Miller, 1978). As the importance of one factor increased, the influence of the other factor declined. As jurors' positive attitudes toward defendants increased, evidence played a less and less important role in predicting convictions (Kaplan & Kemmerick, 1974; Perry, 1976).

What makes evidence strong or weak remains an open issue. One explanation was offered by Pettus (1990), who summarized some of her interview data: "The clear and well told story is considered effective evidence, whereas the unclear, nonsensical story is considered ineffective evidence" (p. 92). The tone set by key witnesses can make a difference. When testimony against a defendant in a murder case was introduced in an opinionated manner, judgments of guilt increased. But when the testimony was presented in an unopinionated way, student jurors were likely to find the defendant guilty of the lesser charge of manslaughter (Ludwig & Fontaine, 1978). Beyond verdicts alone, jurors' overall interpretations were affected by the placement of judges' instructions to jurors (Elwork, Sales, & Alfini, 1977). When the judge explained the burden of proof before the presentation of evidence, conviction rates declined (Kerr et al., 1976). Furthermore, when an active judge commented on testimony from a doubtful eyewitness by issuing limiting instructions, summarizing relevant testimony, and explaining the role of eyewitness testimony, the jury disregarded the troubled

material during its deliberations (Katzev & Wishart, 1985).

Witness Evidence. Research on the presentation of evidence by witnesses involves the study of testimony from defendants, children, eyewitnesses, and experts. In addition, the impact of inadmissible evidence has been investigated.

Defendant testimony may be presented in a manner that affects juries. In one of the few controlled experiments on the subject, three stereotypical signals of lying (fidgeting, avoiding eye contact, and disfluencies) were used in a deposition by an African American defendant accused of breaking and entering (Pryor & Buchanan, 1984). Not surprisingly, student jurors rated the defendant as least guilty when the signs of nervousness were minimized. Other work found reduced defendant believability when the deposition was presented in a case involving a minor crime but not a major crime (Feldman & Chesley, 1984). A defendant's decision not to testify is not supposed to affect jurors, but it does. In experimental work, jurors over 60 years old thought that the defendant's failure to testify indicated an attempt to hide guilt (Zeiglar, 1978). Yet fewer than 15% of jurors under 30 years old held such a view. Highly dogmatic jurors were particularly harsh on such defendants (Shaffer & Case, 1982). Field studies show a mixed record. Defendants who took the stand in Indiana were most likely to be convicted (Myers, 1979), whereas defendants who testified in Utah were least likely to be convicted (Werner, Strube, Cole, & Kagehiro, 1985).

Children called as witnesses are most persuasive when they appear confident, intelligent, and ready to provide details (Goodman, Goldings, & Haith, 1984). The literature suggests that juries tend to stereotype children as essentially honest but easily manipulated by parents or lawyers, sometimes unable to distinguish reality from imagination, and generally unsophisticated thinkers (Goodman et al., 1984). Nevertheless, when a child's testimony is uncorroborated or attacked successfully during cross-examination, its persuasiveness can be largely eliminated. In sexual abuse cases, otherwise dramatic influences of child witnesses appear to be ameliorated somewhat by the use of defense expert witnesses who can place the testimony in context (Kovera & Borgida, 1996). On the other hand, corroborating expert testimony enhanced the impact of the children's testimony (Kovera, Gresham, Borgida, Gray, & Regan, 1997), especially when the expert did not present material about child sexual abuse accommodation syndrome (Kovera, Levy, Borgida, & Penrod, 1994). Survey work with actual jury venires revealed that decisions were strongly influenced by the confidence of the mental health professionals who assessed the credibility of children's reports (Corder & Whiteside, 1988).

The child's age makes a difference. When a 6- or 12-year-old child testified in a sexual abuse case or in a personal injury lawsuit, expert corroboration of the testimony enhanced persuasiveness (Nightingale, 1993). This corroboration had no influence when the witness was 9 years old. When the witness was 14 years old, the child's influence was not particularly enhanced by expert corroboration. Yet others (Crowley, O'Callaghan, & Ball, 1994) found no relationship between children's ages and influence, although expert testimony alone was persuasive. Female student jurors were most likely to rate a child's testimony as credible and to vote guilty in child abuse cases. It seemed to make no difference whether the child's testimony was presented live or on videotape (Hagen, 1990/1991).

Eyewitness testimony can be quite influential with jurors (Lindsay, 1994), with as many as 83% of mock jurors unduly influenced by such evidence (Brigham & Bouthwell, 1983). Yet the fallibility of eyewitness testimony is well established and need not be reviewed here. Lindsay, Lim, Marando, and Cully (1986) exposed mock jurors to various numbers of eyewitnesses testifying for the prosecution and defense in a purse-snatching case. Although unopposed witnesses were most effective, internally inconsistent testimony (including alibi testimony) also was persuasive for the defense. Whether the eyewitness identified or failed to identify the suspect made a difference. Student jurors were exposed to two types of nonidentification information (eyewitness testimony and fingerprint evidence) in situations where there were one or two eyewitnesses or contradictory evidence (McAllister & Bregman, 1986). Regardless of the evidence type, identifications influenced decisions more than did nonidentifications (i.e., statements that a person was not at a location). In other inquiry, when eyewitness evidence and fingerprint evidence were contrasted, positive examples of each were most influential on verdicts, and the absence of interactions indicated that the effects were independent of each other (Bregman & McAllister, 1987). Similarly, when an alibi eyewitness claimed that the defendant either was or was not at another location when a crime was committed, mock jurors tended to discount nonidentification information if it failed to meet their expectations (McAllister & Bregman, 1989). The confidence of eyewitnesses seemed directly related to their influence (Cutler, Penrod, & Dexter, 1990; Cutler, Penrod, & Stuve, 1988; Fox & Walters, 1986; Lindsay, Wells, & O'Connor, 1989; Penrod & Cutler, 1995; Sporer, Penrod, Read, & Cutler, 1995). Even though confidence can be manipulated by lawyers' preparation of witnesses (Luus & Wells, 1994), jurors seem to be relatively unaffected by elements such as cross-examination and judges' instructions regarding the fallibility of eyewitness testimony. In another study (Wells, Lindsay, & Ferguson,

1979), even though juror perceptions of witness confidence were unrelated to witness accuracy, these perceptions predicted nearly 50% of the variance in jurors' willingness to believe witnesses. As it turned out, witnesses often expressed their confidence not through nonverbal cues but simply by making assertions such as "I am 100% sure" of an identification. Even when the levels of evidence incrimination (corroboration with physical evidence) and perceived confidence of the eyewitness were experimentally manipulated, both factors produced significant and independent effects on mock jury verdicts (Moore & Gump, 1995). The type of information to which the witness testified made a difference. In three experiments, Whitley and Greenberg (1986) found that mock jurors assessed eyewitness accuracy in identifying and describing the criminal suspect based on perceptions of witness expertise. On the other hand, eyewitness confidence affected witness persuasiveness when the issue involved the description of the crime. For instance, eyewitnesses to an auto-pedestrian incident were most influential when increasing the details of their testimony (Bell & Loftus, 1988). Disturbingly, when accurate eyewitnesses had a difficult time recalling trivial elements of the identifications, jurors became less confident of them as sources of information (Wells & Leippe, 1981).

To reduce the influence of faulty eyewitness testimony, three techniques have been explored. First, psychologists have been called to offer advice to jurors, although courts have been reluctant to embrace such an approach (see Raimo, 1987). One study (Wells, Lindsay, & Tousignant, 1980) found that having a psychologist testify that eyewitness confidence had nothing to do with identification accuracy increased doubt in the eyewitness testimony. Including testimony from a psychologist explaining the fallibility of eyewitness testimony

reduced conviction rates from 47% to 35% in an assault case and from 68% to 43% in a murder case (Loftus, 1980). Such results have been supported with adult jurors (Hosch, Beck, & McIntyre, 1980), but not always (Warner, 1987/1988). To reduce rates of guilty verdicts, the information did not even have to be presented by a psychologist (Cutler, Dexter, & Penrod, 1989; Paris, 1985; but see Fox & Walters, 1986). Sometimes judges' cautionary instructions about eyewitness testimony affected jury decisions (Ramirez, Zemba, & Geiselman, 1996). Using a court-appointed expert did not seem to make a difference. Yet when expert testimony exposed problems with identifying the suspect from a police lineup, no significant juror skepticism about lineup testimony occurred (Devenport, 1996/1997; Devenport, Cutler, & Penrod, 1998). Moreover, psychologists' comments were not influential when unrelated to the specific testimony under consideration (Maas, Brigham, & West, 1985). Second, some have suggested that active *voir dire* could be a safeguard, but research did not indicate that juror overestimation of eyewitness credibility was reduced by this method (Narby & Cutler, 1994). One would be surprised if *voir dire* inhibited eyewitness influence given that community members were somewhat likely to confuse the influence of stress, fear, and witness confidence with the credibility of such testimony (Rahaim & Brodsky, 1982). Third, a view has been argued that eyewitness fallibility can be revealed by active cross-examination. Student jurors exposed to experienced and inexperienced lawyers engaging in cross-examination continued to rate the testimony of accurate and inaccurate eyewitnesses as equally credible (Lindsay et al., 1989). Lawyers' abilities made no difference. In other words, when an eyewitness was discredited, the eyewitness was still more persuasive on verdicts than when no eyewitness testified at all (Whitley,

1987). Without the direct contradiction of an eyewitness by another eyewitness, the original testimony remained very influential (Leippe, 1985).

Expert witnesses tended to be influential, especially when the testimony was presented early in the trial and when it was specifically linked to the case under consideration (Brekke & Borgida, 1988). In contrasts of expert witness varieties (e.g., physicians, psychiatrists, psychologists, chemists, document examiners, polygraph examiners, police, eyewitnesses, firearms experts, accountants, appraisers), members of the professions were most persuasive with actual jurors, although other experts could be influential when the relevance of their testimony could be established (Saks & Wissler, 1984). Jurors were strongly influenced by testimony from psychiatrists (McMahon, 1974). In somewhat related inquiry, judges and lawyers considered forensic evidence on mental health to be most useful when it dealt with clinical diagnoses and analyses of whether legal thresholds had been met (Redding, Floyd, & Hawk, 2001). In another study, jurors were persuaded by expert presentation of data about groups of people most likely to commit rape (Brekke & Borgida, 1988). In a civil case, expert economic testimony of the plaintiff's loss of wages and benefits seemed influential to juries (Greene, Downey, & Goodman-Delahunty, 1999), whereas juries tended to discount the lawyer's recommendations about "pain and suffering" awards. Expert psychologists' race and sex did not affect credibility or perceived effectiveness in the eyes of student jurors (Miyatake, 1998/1999). Other research (Dravin, 1982/1983) found that although female expert witnesses were perceived as most credible by student jurors in shoplifting and assault cases, no significant influence was seen on actual jury verdicts. In medical malpractice cases, although one study found that the most persuasive expert was an African American

woman (Memon & Shuman, 1998), another study found that male experts were perceived as more authoritative than female experts (Monroe, 1993/1994).

Not all expert testimony is influential. Although expert testimony about repressed memory was persuasive to mock jurors who heard only the testimony favoring the recovered memory notion (Reince, 1991), such expert testimony was not persuasive to male jurors or to those who were unsympathetic to the recovered memory concept (Rotzien, 1997/1998). In a rape case, when expert witnesses dueled over whether the victim had rape trauma or had made up her charge of rape as a result of borderline personality disorder, the introduction of expert witnesses by the prosecution backfired and the acquittal rate increased (Burnstein, 1995/1996).

Inadmissible evidence sometimes is presented to jurors. Although few claim that jurors can "unlisten" to what they have heard, the most common remedy is for judges to instruct jurors to disregard the questionable material.[6] Yet such instructions are not always effective. In the first place, few jurors seem able to remember the instructions to disregard the testimony (Hoffman & Brodely, 1952). In the second place, jurors seem able to disregard only mundane information (Hirsch et al., 1976; Konopka et al., 1974; Miller & Fontes, 1978; Poole, Lefebvre, Miller, & Fontes, 1975; Reynolds, 1977). Retracted confessions (Kassin & Wrightsman, 1981), evidence of a past criminal record (Greene & Dodge, 1995; Hans & Doob, 1976; Pickel, 1995; but see Cornish & Sealy, 1973), and emotional materials remained influential and were amplified by judges' instructions (Edwards & Bryan, 1997). Similar effects also were found on perceptions of witness credibility (Horn, 1976). Whereas some work using mock jurors observed that anti-defendant information was not ignored (Lenehan & O'Neill, 1981), another study found that pro-acquittal inadmissible testimony also was not ignored (although pro-conviction evidence sometimes was) (Thompson, Fong, & Rosenhan, 1981). Disturbingly, the little research on the subject indicates that judges are not superior to juries in ignoring biasing or inadmissible material (Landsman & Rakos, 1994; Wells, 1992).

If there is a pattern to the matter, it seems that jurors use inadmissible materials along with other case arguments and evidence when they believe such information is true and relevant (Mosmann, 1998). Hearsay evidence introduced to mock jurors during expert testimony was readily dismissed, and the judge's instructions further reduced the perception that the witness's conclusions were supported (Schuller & Paglia, 1999). Moreover, jurors were most likely to reject inadmissible materials when the judge gave detailed explanations why coerced confessions were both unreliable and unjust (Kassin & Wrightsman, 1981); when wiretap evidence in a murder trial was explained to be unreliable (as opposed to reasoning that it violated due process protections) (Kassin & Sommers, 1997); in the unlikely event that the admonition preceded the inadmissible material (Kassin & Wrightsman, 1979); when jurors were given reason to be suspicious about the motives of the advocates and witnesses who introduced the inadmissible evidence (Fein, McCloskey, & Tomlinson, 1997); when an official source (Reinard, 1989), especially a police officer (Reinard, 1981) or a county government fingerprint expert (Reinard, 1985), introduced the inadmissible materials; when the jurors had negative attitudes toward the criminal justice system and the police (Casper & Benedict, 1993); when inadmissible testimony involved a "mild" violation of due process guarantees (Fleming, Wegener, & Petty, 1999); and when jurors in some cases deliberated before rendering decisions (Kerwin & Shaffer, 1994; Weld & Danzig, 1940; but see Reinard, 1985, 1986a). Some jurors seemed more willing

than others to reject inadmissible materials. Sommers and Kassin (2001) found that when student jurors reading a trial summary were high in need for cognition, they not only were willing to discount inadmissible materials identified as unreliable but also tended to "overcorrect" by assessing defendant guilt lower than did others. In related but different work using adult jurors, Sutton (1979) found that inadmissible evidence about the character of the accused was curvilinearly related to guilt ratings and that testimony alleging the low moral character of the defendant in a rape case was most easily discounted.

It seems that inadmissible testimony is more damaging to some types of defendants than to others. In an effort to include fairly emotional information, Reynolds (1977) presented simulated jurors with a rape trial involving an Anglo victim. He found that when controlling for homophily and race of the defendant, inadmissible testimony damaging to the defendant predicted 22% of the variance in jury verdicts. Wolf and Montgomery (1977) presented mock jurors with a criminal trial about a barroom brawl in which the defendant was alleged to have stabbed the victim with a broken glass. In the experiment, the questionable evidence was ruled either admissible, inadmissible, or inadmissible accompanied by the judge's instruction to disregard the evidence. The researchers reported that biasing effects were eliminated when the judge ruled the material inadmissible, whereas the testimony was amplified when the judge ordered jurors to disregard it. Reinard and Reynolds (1978) found that raising an objection to inadmissible testimony in a criminal trial amplified it despite the judge's ruling.. When the objection was overruled, the bias was greatest. The seeming contradiction about the impact of judges' instructions was explained by Loh (1985), who drew a distinction among limited admission of criminal background, limited admissions, and total exclusion of such materials. Careful reading of the research revealed the following:

> Conviction rates were highest under unlimited admission, lowest under complete exclusion, and in-between under limited admission. . . . Instructions on limitation are effective (in the sense of reducing guilty verdicts) when compared to the admission of the evidence without any instructions. They obviously are not effective or are less effective, however, when compared to the exclusion of the evidence. (p. 27)

In civil cases (Cox & Tanford, 1989), inadmissible testimony by itself was most persuasive when favoring the defendant instead of the victim or others in the trial. Adult jurors presented with inadmissible evidence were unable to disregard inadmissible evidence when objections to it were sustained unless the judge also gave a specific instruction on the matter (Schaffer, 1984/1985). Evidence of insurance coverage by the defendant led to increased awards in cases involving auto collisions (Broeder, 1959) and attacks by a homeowner's escaped pet dog (Reinard, 1993). In each instance, the judge's instructions seemed to amplify the illicit impact of such evidence.

How inadmissible testimony produces its effects has been investigated. Developing a causal model of the impact of inadmissible testimony, Reinard (1989) found that the sentence recommendations were a function of the verdict and the character perceptions of the defendant. The nature of the inadmissible testimony, the type of witness introducing it (official or nonofficial source), and the perceived character of the defendant influenced verdicts.

Manner of Evidence Presentation. Not surprisingly, sensational materials possessed by prosecutors may influence decisions if judges permit their introduction. Sensational crime scene photos seemed to influence jury deci-

sions (Russo, 1992), although to produce such an effect, grisly video recordings had to be relevant to the case (Kassin & Garfield, 1991). Juries easily discounted recreations, as in the case of video reenactments in a wrongful death civil case (Fishfader, Howells, Katz, & Teresi, 1996). Attorneys in one sample expressed their opinions that jurors were suspicious of animated presentations of information if they were overly realistic because such materials created an impression that the attorneys were attempting to manipulate the facts (Cusick, 1994/1995). Yet the use of prototypes or models of crime scenes seemed to enhance persuasion (Filkins, 1996/1997).

Jurors often have a difficult time in dealing with scientific and statistical information, resulting in confusion and reduced influence of such evidence. In one study involving DNA evidence, jurors (particularly women) separated or combined probabilities incorrectly and gave such probabilistic evidence less influence than it should have received (Schklar & Diamond, 1999). Juries sometimes do not know what to do with statistics. For instance, Thompson and Schumann (1987) examined a case in which blood typing evidence showed that only 1 person in 100 shared the actual perpetrator's blood type. Fully 60% of the jurors decided for the defendant when the defense responded by arguing that such numbers meant that in the city of 100,000 people, 1,000 people had the same blood type. Using tortured statistical sophistry, the defense attorney opined that because the defendant was only 1 of the 1,000 people in the city with the culprit's blood type, that fact meant that there was only 1 chance in 1,000 that the defendant committed the crime. The problem of dealing with statistical evidence has been vexing, and proper interpretation of statistics presented by expert witnesses remains at an unsatisfactory level (see Fienberg, 1989, esp. pp. 149-189).

The language and manner of trial participants can influence jurors. Non-Latino jurors tended to judge defendants who testified through translators as more likely to be guilty than English-speaking defendants (Stephan & Stephan, 1986). Similar results were found for Thai defendants speaking through translators. Dialects also introduced similar effects. Members of a jury pool in Hawaii who listened to direct examination of witnesses, including speakers of Hawai'i Creole English, rated speakers of Standard English as most credible (Takakawa, 1999). The phrasings of defendants also affected jurors. A defendant who loudly denied the charges and intemperately protested against them was likely to be perceived as more guilty than a defendant who testified with a tone of moderation (Yandell, 1979). In a case involving a husband's assisted suicide of a terminally ill wife, an emotional explanation of how the defendant helped in the suicide amplified the sympathy or hostility that the jurors had toward the means of suicide (disconnecting a respirator or shooting through the wife's skull) (Pfeifer, Brigham, & Robinson, 1996). Yet a study of 13 trials showed no changes in credibility or believability when the witness made repeated use of disclaimers in reaction to assertions from the questioning attorneys (Stutman, 1986b).

Occasionally, witnesses appear in some form of disguise or identity masking, such as when government agents or organized crime informants present evidence. One study attempted to check the effect of electronic masking of videotaped testimony (Towell, Kemp, & Pike, 1996). None of the methods (placing a gray circle over the witness's face, using pixelation masking, using negation of the witness's face, repeating out of synchrony video images of the courtroom, or placing a static image of a witness's face before jurors as the audio portion of the testimony was played to them) affected witness credibility ratings, but all methods except the negation and out of synchrony conditions impaired jurors' ability to remember the testimony.

Another area of interest has been the use of powerful and powerless speech. Powerless speech consists of language that reduces dominance in an exchange such as unnecessary intensifiers, tag questions, hedges, and indirect language. Attorneys seemed to emphasize powerful speech styles. Parkinson (1981) found that successful prosecutors were verbally assertive, took command of the courtroom, spoke at length, asked large numbers of questions, usually employed direct language in the indicative case, and referred directly to witnesses. On the other hand, unsuccessful prosecutors tended to use many expressions of politeness, excessively correct grammatical speech, and increased numbers of conditional statements. Successful defense attorneys tended to use large amounts of abstract and ambiguous language, increased legal jargon, reduced numbers of adverbs, and reduced numbers of words expressing affects. Losing defense attorneys tended to use language with much demonstrative pronoun use and increased grammatically correct speech. Whether these elements were contributors to success or artifacts remained unknown. Powerful speech styles by witnesses for the plaintiff stimulated increased awards (Erickson, Lind, Johnson, & O'Barr, 1978) and made witness testimony increasingly believable (Stutman, 1986b) and credible (Chapman, 1993/1994). In particular, dysfluent witnesses, witnesses with poor grammar, and witnesses who used lower class language styles were viewed as less credible than those whose speech approximated Standard English (Conley, O'Barr, & Lind, 1978). A combination of powerful verbal and nonverbal cues also affected perceptions of witness credibility (Lisko, 1992/1993; see also Lind & O'Barr, 1979; Scherer, 1979). A meta-analysis of powerless speech research in both courtroom and non-courtroom settings found an average correlation effect size of .23 with persuasion, corresponding to 5.3% of the variance explained (Burrell & Koper, 1998). Yet not all research has supported this effect on awards (Bradac, Hemphill, & Tardy, 1981). Manipulating the use of hedges and intensifiers, Wright and Hosman (1987) exposed participants to testimony from male and female witnesses in a traffic collision case. Although verdicts were not measured, women who used the hedges gained in credibility. Similar results were found in other courtroom applications (Hosman & Wright, 1987).

Direct Examination and Cross-Examination

Direct examination is the chance for one side to introduce evidence to support essential claims. One might imagine that the opposition would have its own plan for undermining this set of claims through cross-examination. But in a study of rape trials, whatever the direct examination covered tended to be reviewed in the same order in all subsequent questioning (Sanford, 1987). The agenda-setting function of the direct examination is quite strong. Although attorneys might wish to read a physician's deposition into the record, controlled experimentation in an industrial accident case revealed that direct testimony was most influential on the awards granted (Jacoubovitch, Bermant, Crockett, McKinley, & Sanstad, 1977). Court-appointed experts in a rape trial were not more influential than witnesses called by attorneys and subjected to detailed cross-examination (Brekke, Enko, Clavet, & Seelau, 1991). Based on observations of actual trials, Antieau (1998/1999) found that attorneys using indirect language in direct examination enhanced jurors' favorable impressions of witnesses. The phrasing of questions made a significant difference in the answers secured and, as a consequence, the potential influence produced. In one study, simply asking a car crash eyewitness, "About how fast were the cars going when they *smashed into* each other?" increased mock jurors' perceptions of the speed of the cars more than when the collision was described as cars that "hit" or "contacted" each other (Loftus & Palmer, 1974). Similar work involving car crashes revealed that using unmarked adverbs (e.g., "How fast was the car going?") during witness questioning induced witnesses to report that the car was moving faster and that more damage was done than when the attorney asked questions with very specific phrasing (Lipscomb, McAllister, & Bregman, 1985). Jurors also seemed to pay attention to the practical implications of witness answers. If the witness made a statement with indirect language (e.g., "After I heard the shot, I went to the telephone"), jurors completed the implication in their own minds (e.g., inferring that the witness made a phone call, probably to the police) (Harris, Teske, & Ginns, 1978). Nonverbal elements sometimes can make a difference. One writer has suggested that nonverbal cues are potentially influential but that only those who are sensitive to such cues, typically women, are likely to be influenced by them (LeVan, 1984). Another legal scholar (Dombroff, 1988, p. 340) asserted that a lawyer's tone of voice may be the most significant factor causing objections to be raised to questions asked during examinations.

Cross-examination can be very influential, sometimes even reversing juror decisions (Spanos, Dubreuil, & Gwynn, 1991-1992). In the case of eyewitnesses, defense attorney cross-examination that exposed inconsistencies in testimony reduced rates of conviction among mock jurors (Berman & Cutler, 1996). These effects were great even when the inconsistencies dealt with peripheral rather than central case facts (Berman, Narby, & Cutler, 1995). Even among highly credible witnesses, exposing inconsistencies in testimony resulted in discounting the evidence (Devine & Ostrom,

1985). The phrasing of cross-examination questions can influence jurors. A lawyer's asking for very brief responses to specific questions stimulated the impression that witnesses were not as competent, intelligent, or assertive as those whose answers were not so constricted by the cross-examiner (Conley et al., 1978). Cross-examining attorneys often use leading questions that suggest desired answers. In one study of 42 cross-examination sessions, student jurors exposed to extensive use of leading questions during cross-examination were more likely to believe accurate than inaccurate witnesses, whereas nonleading questions were most likely to stimulate belief in inaccurate witnesses (Wells et al., 1979). Even so, the use of leading questions and questions designed to increase control over the witness resulted in decreased amounts of the witness's testimony (Stutman, 1986a). Among the "dirty tricks" of cross-examination is posing a question that presumes information not in evidence and asking the witness to react to it. When mock jurors heard an expert witness presented with a presumptive question casting aspersions on a rape victim's character, the target's credibility was unaffected (Kassin, Williams, & Sanders, 1990). But the expert witness's credibility was reduced, even when the content of the question had been denied or when the question produced an objection and jurors were instructed to ignore it.

Apparently, invasions of witness space during direct examination and cross-examination are not particularly effective. Field observations revealed that attorneys tended to shorten the distance between themselves and witnesses more during cross-examination than during direct examination (Brodsky, Hooper, Tipper & Yates, 1999). But the impact on juries seemed to be a negative one. The authors suggested that proxemics in interpersonal settings simply are not the same as the structural proxemics in the courtroom setting.

Judge's Instructions

Judges are considered the captains of the court. Although lawyers' lore probably exaggerates this effect, there is little doubt that judges' comments affect jurors. Jurors have been found to return verdicts designed to please the judge (O'Mara, 1972). In one experiment with jury-eligible adults, even when admonished to disregard the judge's behavior and form their own opinions, jurors returned verdicts in accordance with the judge's bent (Hart, 1995). Even elements of judges' nonverbal activity during trials affected jury attention as well as perceptions of witness credibility and attractiveness (Badzinski & Pettus, 1994).

The judge's instructions are designed to influence jurors to promote the cause of justice, but they have often featured jargon, passive voice, and odd syntax (Buchanan, Pryor, Taylor, & Strawn, 1978). Indeed, 45% of judges' instructions were misunderstood (Charrow & Charrow, 1979). Even in capital cases, where courts have paid great attention to refining instructions, jurors tend not to understand them, and closing arguments by attorneys have seemed impotent to overcome the defect (Haney & Lynch, 1997).

In trials involving technical evidence, judges sometimes introduce instructions before presentation of such evidence. Jurors given instructions before hearing the evidence were able to make clear compensation distinctions among four plaintiffs involved in the case (ForsterLee, Horowitz, & Bourgeois, 1993).

Jury attitudes toward the law have affected the impact of judges' instructions (Pryor, Taylor, Buchanan, & Strawn, 1980). Because juries are charged with attempting to advance the cause of justice, some hold that juries have the right to ignore (nullify) a law that they believe is unfairly applied. A controversy involves what happens if the judge informs jurors of the opportunity to nullify. Some work found that judges who introduced the nullification option actually influenced jurors to return reduced numbers of guilty verdicts (Davis, 1998; Pfeifer et al., 1996). Other research did not find this effect (Niedermeier, Horowitz, & Kerr, 1999). Willingness to entertain the nullification option depended on juror attitudes toward the law, perceived physical attractiveness of the defendant, and schemata about the crimes involved (Clark, 2000).

JURORS AS AUDIENCES

Because few researchers have been allowed in jury rooms, most evidence on jury deliberations derives from simulations or interview studies. Nevertheless juror elements affect their decision making on the evidence and their dispositions toward various judgments.

Decision Making on the Evidence

Common folk wisdom and some research (MacCoun & Kerr, 1988; McCoy, 1997/ 1998; Reinard & Arsenault, 2000) hold that jurors rarely change their verdicts as a result of deliberations. This thinking is based on the simple observation that most juries start with a majority sentiment. Because the odds favor jurors in the minority changing their minds, any statistics would naturally indicate that most juror decisions were unchanged as a result of deliberations. But of course, there is more to this story. Jurors in the majority generally were effective in influencing others (Marcus, Lyons, & Guyton, 2000), a fact that gave the appearance of polarizing the direction of mock jury verdicts. This pattern was observed when evidence was presented in a heterogeneous order (Kaplan & Miller, 1977;

see also MacCoun & Kerr, 1988) and when jurors were not sound reasoners (Weinstock, 1999). This influence appeared as jurors articulated their own arguments and as the influence of witnesses and trial participant credibility decreased (Sonaike, 1977).

Yet deliberating jurors may be restricted in their discussion of issues. Interviews with jurors in Oregon and California revealed that the capital sentencing instructions limited the realm of legitimate discussion and discouraged jurors from considering the moral aspects of their decision making (Haney, Sontag, & Costanzo, 1994). To trace the flow of persuasive communication among jurors, efforts have been made to identify persuasive functions. Kaplan (1983) explained that deliberating jurors might influence each other with messages that serve either of two functions. First, informational influence takes the form of information sharing and direct persuasive argumentation. Second, normative influence consists of pressures to conform to the group. According to this model, informational influence occurs as a result of responding to the mass of information. Whereas informational influence is directed at changing subjective or private beliefs, normative influence is focused on changing public beliefs. Although one might speculate to the contrary based on small group communication research, verdicts were unrelated to how much a juror talked, the juror's sex, or the juror's initial confidence in his or her opinion (McCoy, 1997/1998).

Juror Dispositions

A tradition of lawyers' lore has produced contradictory advice about juror dispositions and has often substituted opinions for answers to empirical questions (see Fulero & Penrod, 1990a, 1990b). Although jury selection—and nearly all of work called scientific or systematic jury selection—is rooted in juror demography,[7] survey research has not always supported the notion that such matters influence either procedural or outcome variables (Bridgeman & Marlowe, 1979). In their development of the Juror Bias Scale, Kassin and Wrightsman (1983) found that conviction proneness was predictable from an interrelated set of factors, including authoritarianism, acceptance of a relaxed view of the "reasonable doubt" standard, conservative political views, belief in a just world view of reality, and adoption of an internal locus of control. In fact, when one looks at the nature of the jury variables, most research has shown that these elements accounted for very small proportions of effects. Moreover, when scholars have looked at the power of systematic jury selection to identify receptive juries, support has ranged from partial (Brand, 1985/1986) to supportive of the "survey approach" (Frederick, 1984). Controlled experimental studies contrasting various techniques, however, found that "scientific jury selection" was not particularly effective in selecting favorable juries (Baker, 1984/1985; McGowen, 1981). Even so, research interest has remained in investigating jury characteristics such as juror sex, social and economic status, age, race/ethnicity, prior experience, personalities, and death qualification.

Juror Sex. The influence of juror sex has produced a mixed record. Some work found that men were more conviction prone than women (Angira, 1991; Elkins & Philips, 1999; Simon, 1967; Steffensmeier, 1977), some studies found that women were more conviction prone and recommended more severe sentences than men (Austin et al., 1976; Griffitt & Jackson, 1973; Scroggs, 1976), and some studies found no differences on verdicts and recommended sentences (McCoy, 1997/1998; Nemeth, Endicott, & Wachtler, 1976)

unless the prosecution evidence proved to be weak (Rosen, 1996/1997). Student jurors were least likely to find a defendant of their own sex guilty (Stephan, 1974). In civil cases, women generally seemed most plaintiff prone (McCullough, 1991).

In rape cases, women were both more likely to return guilty verdicts and to recommend severe sentences than were men (Beauvais, 1982/1983; Calhoun et al., 1978; Feldman-Summers & Lindner, 1976; Lyons & Regina, 1986; Miller & Hewitt, 1978; Rumsey & Rumsey, 1977; Spanos et al., 1991-1992; Yanchar, 1982/1983; but see Jones & Aronson, 1973; Scroggs, 1976; Smith et al., 1976; Kahn et al., 1977), especially when defendants and victims were from different races (Hymes et al., 1993). Not only were men less likely to find rape defendants guilty in the presence of strong evidence (McNamara, Vattano, & Viney, 1993), but men were increasingly likely to believe that the rape victims were partially to blame for the rapes (Calhoun et al., 1978) and that the victims may have been careless or behaved provocatively (Smith et al., 1976). Women were more likely than men to accept evidence of a recovered memory used against a defendant (ForsterLee, Horowitz, Ho, ForsterLee, & McGovern, 1999; Griffith et al., 1999; Key et al., 1996; Rotzien, 1997/1998). In non-rape cases, females were more likely than men to accept an affirmative defense such as insanity or self-defense (Posey, 1995/1996).

Men and women differed in a variety of other dispositions. In cases involving the insanity defense, women were more likely than men to accept such a defense, especially when the defendant was female (Towers, 1996/1997). Women also were more likely than men to favor the plaintiff in a sexual harassment case (Gowan & Zimmerman, 1996), to recommend increased damage awards in a medical malpractice suit (Bensko,

1995/1996), to find a child witness credible in a child abuse case (Crowley et al., 1994), and to render guilty verdicts in child abuse cases (Hosch, Chanez, Bothwell, & Munoz, 1991). Men tended to be more influenced by expert testimony than did women (Kovera, McAuliff, & Hebert, 1999). In general, women were more likely to conform to the views of the majority of the jury than were men (Prager, 1995/1996).

Juror Social and Economic Status. Upper class jurors tended to be more conviction prone than lower class jurors (Rose & Prell, 1955), especially as the disparities between the juror and defendant socioeconomic status grew (Adler, 1973). In civil cases, the situation is not so clear. In wrongful death suits, although juror sex, age, marital status, and occupation were unrelated to damages awarded, juror beliefs and attitudes about monetary damages influenced verdicts (Goodman, Loftus, & Greene, 1990). Juror income also was only weakly related to amounts awarded (Hastie, Schkade, & Payne, 1998). The political background of the jurors also seemed to make a difference, with political conservatives awarding reduced damages in a malpractice suit (Bensko, 1995/1996). Highly educated jurors tended to return more guilty verdicts than did others (Reed, 1965). When the jurors and the defendant had the same religious affiliation, decisions tended to be more lenient than when their religions were different (Kerr et al., 1995).

Juror Age. Although sometimes it is believed to play a major role in predicting decisions, age does not seem to produce consistent effects. Some work indicated that young jurors had an increased tendency to acquit the defendant (Stephen & Tully, 1977), but others found no significant effects (Goodman et al., 1990). During deliberations, age groups did not differ in their rates of changing their verdicts (Prager, 1995/1996).

Juror Race/Ethnicity. A common attorney belief is that African American jurors are acquittal prone (Turner, Lovell, Young, & Denny, 1986). Although highly authoritarian jurors had a preference for defense attorneys of their own race (Boliver, 1999), when defendant socioeconomic status was controlled, neither the defendant's race nor the jurors' race affected verdicts or sentence recommendations (Towers et al., 1992). When African Americans were on the jury, no negative biases against African American defendants were significant (Tinsley, 1991/1992). In a child neglect case, Anglos and Latinos did not differ in their judgments (Hosch et al., 1991). In civil cases, ethnicity was slightly related to amounts awarded, with Anglos awarding slightly less than did members of ethnic groups (Hastie et al., 1998). In product liability cases, minority members and poorly educated jurors from the community most often found for the plaintiff (Bornstein & Rajki, 1994).

Juror Prior Experience. Jurors who previously served on juries may have distinct views of what jury service involves (Durand, Bearden, & Gustafson, 1978), but the influence of this experience on verdicts remains inconclusive. In one study of 143 criminal trials in Kentucky, jurors with experience in either civil or criminal trials rendered more severe verdicts in criminal cases than did first-time jurors (Himelein, Nietzel, & Dillehay, 1991). Another analysis of 206 criminal cases revealed a similar effect for small juries composed of a majority of experienced jurors (Werner et al., 1985), as did a review of 175 criminal trials throughout a year (Dillehay & Nietzel, 1985). To test whether this effect could be verified experimentally, students either were or were not given experience as mock jurors and subsequently were put on mock juries (Kassin & Juhnke, 1983). No significant differences were found between verdicts of experienced and inexperienced jurors.

Juror Personality Characteristics. Although one's degree of general or social intelligence was unrelated to verdicts (Becker, 1998/1999), defense-prone jurors tended to be high in autonomy and most likely to advocate acquittal when given instructions on nullification (Laird, 1997/1998), high in attributional complexity (similar to cognitive complexity) (Pope & Meyer, 1999), and low in alienation (Claghorn, Hays, Webb, & Lewis, 1991). Locus of control research is mixed. Some studies in criminal venues showed that jurors whose internal locus of control was high were least likely to convict (Kurdys, 1983/1984), especially when the jurors shared similar attitudes with the defendant (Kauffman & Ryckman, 1979). Yet other research has found no effect on verdicts regarding locus of control (Villemur & Hyde, 1983). In civil cases, jurors with a high internal locus of control viewed plaintiffs as contributing increasing amounts of liability, and, hence, they reduced awards (Rowland, 1991; Sosis, 1974). Jurors who scored high in boredom proneness were more critical in their verdicts of a male defendant in a civil case than were others (Salmons, 1995/1996). When a child abuse case was presented to student jurors, those jurors who scored high on the "hostility-guilt" scale did not differ from others in verdicts, although they tended to recommend shorter sentences than did others (Ackerman, McMahon, & Fehr, 1984).

Authoritarian personalities tend to be resistant to influence unless the source is an authority figure. Although a meta-analysis found that authoritarianism predicted guilty verdicts (Narby, Cutler, & Moran, 1993), many studies did not show this effect (Shay, 1987/1988; Weir & Wrightsman, 1990).

Many times the authoritarianism appeared to produce its effects as part of an interaction with other variables. In a case involving an insanity defense, highly authoritarian jurors tended to render high rates of guilty verdicts (Tezza, 1996). Yet jurors with high emotional empathy tended to render more not guilty by reason of insanity verdicts than did others. Other studies found that high authoritarians tended to oppose insanity defenses (Cutler, Moran, & Narby, 1992) and were willing to consider the prosecution's expert testimony on repressed memory evidence in a civil case (Schutte, 1994). Highly authoritarian mock jurors who were presented with a defendant who possessed dissimilar attitudes to their own recommended harsh verdicts and sentences (Mitchell & Byrne, 1973). When the defendants were from races or socioeconomic groups different from those of the jurors, high authoritarians gave the harshest verdicts and sentences to those who were similar to them (McGowen & King, 1982). In one study, mock jurors who scored high in authoritarianism were most malleable and willing to change their views of the verdicts during jury deliberations, but authoritarians were not more prone than others to return guilty verdicts (Lamberth, Krieger, & Shay, 1982). In another study, highly authoritarian mock jurors hearing a murder trial most often rendered guilty verdicts and recommended increasingly severe sentences. But these jurors showed increased verdict changes during deliberations (Bray & Noble, 1978). Yet other studies found that high authoritarians were willing to change their minds during deliberations (Berg & Vidmar, 1975). The seeming contradictory results for authoritarians were explained by noting that individuals with this character trait were prone to comply with those whom they believed to be in positions of authority. Thus, the conviction proneness would be most pronounced for those defendants of low status and least pronounced for those of high status.

When a defendant simply used the defense that the action was taken in an effort to obey a superior authority, highly authoritarian jurors tended to respond more favorably than did lowly authoritarian jurors (Hamilton, 1978). Akin to high authoritarians, juries composed of dogmatic personalities tended to return more severe decisions than did others (Shaffer et al., 1986). Highly dogmatic jurors presented with a homosexual defendant in a murder case viewed the defendant's case less favorably than when the defendant was straight (Shaffer & Case, 1982). Actual jurors in criminal cases who were highly dogmatic tended to identify with victims or with authority figures on either side, and this bias was reflected in their verdicts (Wyman, 1984/1985).

Death-Qualified Jurors. "Death-qualified" jurors are those identified as willing to apply the death penalty. Interestingly, jurors who were death qualified showed increasingly harsh judgments in non-capital trials as well. Such jurors were more conviction prone than were other jurors (Bronson, 1970; Cowan, Thomson, & Ellsworth, 1987; Filkins, Smith, & Tindale, 1998; Haney, 1984; Jurow, 1971; Moran & Comfort, 1986; but see Russell, 1991). Some research found that death-qualified women were most likely to convict the defendant (Seguin & Horowitz, 1984). A meta-analysis revealed that belief in the death penalty was positively related to a juror's returning a verdict of guilty (Allen, Mabry, & McKelton, 1998). As is the case with most jury variables, the effect size was small, accounting for an average of only 3% of the variance.

AN INTERIM STATUS OF LEGAL PERSUASION RESEARCH

Social science inquiry in legal persuasion has grown to a stage where general claims of research paucity no longer can be made. Partic-

ularly in the areas of the impact of trial participants, types of evidence/testimony, and jury dispositions, considerable progress has been made over the years. Somewhat curiously, however, research on the impact of *voir dire* as persuasion, on the persuasiveness of general argument strategies, and on organization of materials remains in its infancy. It is with some irony that one observes that persuasion in the legal setting has involved more inquiry into non-message factors than into central message elements. For scholars of legal communication, the priority on the influence of message cues would seem particularly invited.

Because many studies of legal persuasion have reflected variable by variable inquiry, advances in the study of persuasion in the law have suffered from the failure to guide much research by relevant theories or conceptualizations. To be sure, the story model has focused much research, but the failure to provide consistent support for this theory may be taken as a general sign that the search for theoretic alternatives still is required. Some have thought of enlisting the contributions of other theories designed for the general study of persuasion, and there is little question that such an approach may be of some benefit. Yet it also must be recognized that the legal setting is a genre of communication (the forensic setting) that also is typified by distinct forms of language, lines of argument, and case construction forms. Thus, it would make sense for legal persuasion theorists to search for new analogies to guide research or, at least, to adapt existing theories to the unique influences of the legal setting. Such projects require movement beyond simple appropriation of influence theories to the full development of new applications.

Despite the contributions of research in legal persuasion, considerable criticism—often from practitioners—has been directed at the entire domain of study. The primary charges involve issues of research using mock jurors and the realism of laboratory research in legal persuasion. Each of these issues invites comment.

Much research on legal persuasion has enlisted mock juries in simulated trials. One might ask whether results drawn from such samples are generalizable to actual jurors. McGaffey (1983) put the question briskly: "Many of our early experiments were limited to college sophomores. Now we are trying to see if real people react differently" (p. 251). Surely, there is some merit in this reservation, especially among research projects studying jury characteristics and demographics. Of course, despite witticisms and doubts to the contrary, students *are* people, and they also are called to serve on juries. But most jurors are not students, and a reasonable concern for generalizability should be a concern of serious researchers and practitioners alike. There are two approaches to this matter. First, one may dismiss all research using simulated jurors. This step would leave a tidy collection of survey research on actual jurors to guide drawing some conclusions. Such work is identified in this chapter for those wishing to take this perspective. In the areas where survey research has not been completed, attorneys might rely on their own opinions or on those of consultants. With no real test of such opinions, however, it would be difficult to draw any general conclusions with confidence. For all the limits one might place on simulated jury research, it would be difficult to prove that sampling mock jurors is a priori inferior to reliance on opinions alone. It might be mentioned that occasionally claims are made that consultants have completed research to answer many relevant questions but that they cannot reveal such work due to proprietary contracts. But it is difficult to assess such assertions or the quality of the research. Indeed, as one skeptical scholar explained, "If you ask the trial consultant[s] for their data, with all due respect, they

don't really have it" (Simon, 1983, p. 287). On such a matter, the "jury" may still be out. Second, researchers might examine the limits of laboratory results by the use of corroborative surveys to test boundaries of relationships found with mock jurors. This approach would reveal an interesting pattern. There appear to be few studies to show the generalizability of student jurors' findings on impact of organismic variables (e.g., personality, age, socioeconomic status). Nevertheless, when defendant source and message variables are examined (e.g., inadmissible testimony, compliance with the judge's instructions), relationships found among student jurors tend to be found among adult juries as well. Researchers have long found that community and student jurors looking at defendant characteristics seemed to deliver the same verdicts and sentences (Bray et al., 1978). When the impact of message variables is assessed, student jurors do not seem to report results different from adult juror samples (Bray et al., 1978; Feild & Barnett, 1978; Nunez et al., 1999; Reinard, 1985; Tanford, 1985; see also a review by Bornstein, 1999) or from those of actual jury venires (Cutler et al., 1989; Cutler, 1990; Zickafoose & Bornstein, 1999). Regarding source and victim variables, on the other hand, noteworthy differences have been found between student and adult populations. In one study, adult and student jurors differed in the perceived persuasiveness of an expert witness in a battered woman defense case (Schuller & Hastings, 1996). Also involving a battered wife incident, student jurors were found to hold fewer stereotypes about battered women than were adult jurors from voter registration lists (Aubrey & Ewing, 1989). Another study revealed that adult and student jurors differed in attribution assessments of an assault victim who was portrayed as either a male or a female (Howard & Leber, 1988). Student jurors' attributions of the source sex variable were more influential than those of adult jurors. Attributions of adult jurors were more influenced by testimony information than was the case with student jurors. Additional research seems invited to identify where results with student jurors can and cannot be replicated with adult jurors. Hence, of the two options to the sampling issue, the second choice seems to make the most temperate use of available information.

The realism of mock trials has been criticized. Although experimental exposure to trial reenactments (often abbreviated for the practical purposes of data collection) may be required for control purposes, realism concerns may limit the external validity of research findings. This criticism is particularly troublesome in experiments where either of two limitations exists. First, when jurors are presented with trial summaries rather than reenactments, the trial communication effects might not find broad application. One group of researchers found that mock jurors returned verdicts that were different from that returned by the actual jury from which the trial manipulation was taken (Bermant, McGuire, McKinley, & Salo, 1974). It seems that researchers must commit themselves to the use of trial reenactments in some medium. Some practitioners doubt that any manipulations employing trials abbreviated in any manner can be realistic enough to justify drawing conclusions. Yet the research suggests that salient variables might not decay as rapidly as critics fear. Contrary to a popular expectation, for instance, a study found that as the length of the trial increased, the influence of trial variables, such as defendant attractiveness, did not seem to be reduced in impact (Kramer & Kerr, 1989). Of course, the presence of uncontrolled variables in field settings might ameliorate the influence of nearly any factor under the right circumstances, but in controlled research such effects could be identified and studied. Moreover, such claims about the richness of uncontrolled variables also place limits on conclusions drawn by practitioners and consultants. A second problem in some research is the failure to include juror deliberations. In their summary of simulation research in legal communication, Miller and his associates concluded that trial simulations were useful provided that jury deliberations were included and that due attention was paid to the types of jurors and the realism of the trial (Miller, Fones, Boster, & Sunnafrank, 1983). Other research has found that jury deliberations sometimes can overcome biasing effects created by defendant attractiveness (Izzett & Leginski, 1974) and some forms of inadmissible testimony (Kerwin & Shaffer, 1994; Weld & Danzig, 1940). Sound research in legal persuasion appears to require that designs include deliberations as a distinctive element in developing juror reactions. Some critics have doubted that research even is possible. For instance, this claim was made at a national conference on legal advocacy: "Whatever model is used, the researcher will never be able to find out what really goes on during the deliberative process of even one *real* jury because seclusion and secrecy are themselves significant factors in the jury process; if we observed or bugged the jury room, we would change the process" (McDermid, 1983, p. 284). If taken literally, this concern might lead one to conclude that no social science research should ever be done in legal persuasion and rarely in any applied area of the social sciences. Furthermore, such a position may be an example of using the ideal in research to exclude the adequate. Of course, this concern for an empirical study's external validity is not new to social science researchers in any field. Empirical researchers in any field constantly address such issues. But it should be remembered that external invalidity—even if found—does not mean that the results of a study are unsound. The relationships found in laboratory research are real relationships among variables, and the data do not go away because of attacks on their breadth of application. Instead, external invalidity limits the situations in which the results may be applied. Thus, concerns for external validity should be accompanied by alternative explanations of applications for the data by practitioners and critics before they are casually dismissed. In passing, it might be mentioned that some social scientists take the position that because they are strictly researchers of behavior, it is not their job to solve problems in the legal setting and so questions of such applications are not their concern. Even so, it remains the case that most legal persuasion researchers were drawn to the field out of a legitimate sense that relevant research in legal persuasion holds the exciting potential to enrich understanding of both processes of persuasion and processes of justice. The concern for external validity gives rise to a third opportunity. The concern for realism among consultants, lawyers, and researchers might be taken as an invitation for consultants and lawyers to sponsor research with funds sufficient to support development of increasingly realistic materials with professional actors and professional video production. Because research in this area is typically unsupported financially, compromises to realism might be eliminated if those who wish to benefit from the research help to support its completion. In reality, much—if not most—experimental research has relied on trial recordings presented to jurors. One might wonder whether the absence of a live trial adversely affects realism. Yet the use of videotaped trials does not seem to alter jury verdicts either in civil suits (Miller & Fontes, 1978) or in perceptions of children's testimony (Davies, 1999).

Research and theorizing in legal persuasion remains a dynamic process. Even so, it seems that the research to date has emphasized that major trends are visible in the areas of the influence of trial participants, evidence types, and jury variables. For legal persuasion researchers, however, a gap remains in the development of relevant theory and inquiry into the message variables of research. Such a condition may be taken both as a suggestion for the direction of future work and as a limitation on claims of accomplishment thus far.

NOTES

1. It should be mentioned that this chapter is limited to trial-related persuasion, although of course lawyers often have to persuade their clients during interviews. Furthermore, negotiation and alternative dispute resolution issues are excluded from this discussion largely for practical reasons of space limitations. Similarly, parole board decisions, juvenile justice hearings, and family court hearings are excluded.

2. In his review of the theoretic foundations of communication in the practice of law, Gibson (1991, pp. 31-35) identified the following areas of relevant communication theory: storytelling, temporal density, dramatism, legal action stages, argumentation, linguistics, psychometrics, and language. Although each of these approaches has played a part in communication studies, especially enriching the scope of rhetorical-critical studies in the field, social science inquiry dealing with influence in the legal setting has been dominated by the conceptual discussions listed here.

3. Despite predictions from the Elaboration Likelihood Model, argument and evidence quality—associated with the central route to persuasion—were most influential among those jurors with a low need for cognition.

4. In this review, a number of studies are excluded such as the following: studies that do not deal with actual trials or at least summaries of them (e.g., Efron's [1974] study of attraction among college students in an academic discipline setting; Kassin, Reddy, & Tulloch's [1990] study of evidence order), studies on detection of deception, studies on the role of polygraph evidence, studies of mistaken eyewitness identification (e.g., Cutler & Penrod, 1995), studies of reactions to police reports (e.g., Dean, Holliday, Mack, & Thomas, 2000), studies of the Wells (1992) effect on cogni-

tion, studies on the legal systems of nations other than the United States (e.g., Wall & Schuller, 2000; Clark, 1994), studies of courts in which lawyer-advocates do not operate (e.g., small claims court, [Hollihan, Riley, & Freadhoff, 1986]), studies involving jurors under 18 years of age (e.g., Hoiberg & Stires, 1973b), and studies of comprehension of judges' instructions (e.g., Morier, Borgida, & Park, 1996).

5. A popular figure has been the assertion that 80% of jurors make up their minds during the opening statement (see Perrin, 1999, p. 124). Apparently, this often cited statistic was based on a misreading of the American Jury Project of Kalven and Zeisel (1966, esp. p. 488). These authors found that in nearly 90% of the cases, the jurors' initial opinions on entering the jury rooms did not change. In addition, because more than 80% of the criminal cases were decided in favor of the prosecution, there was opportunity for the statistic to take on a life of its own as it was retold as trial lore. In 1988, Zeisel responded to users of the misrepresented statistic and encouraged them to use caution (Zeisel, 1988).

6. Some studies claimed to investigate inadmissible testimony but really did not. For instance, Carretta and Moreland (1983); Johnson (1994); Simon (1967); Sue, Smith, and Caldwell (1973); and Werner, Kagehiro, and Strube (1982) presented participants with newspaper-style summaries of trials in which inadmissible testimony was included. Participants did not actually hear trials in which the evidence was or was not presented.

7. Not all consultants' advice or systematic jury selection is based on juror background alone. Some emphasize the use of nonverbal cues. Vaughan (1986a, 1986b) advised selecting jurors based on the shapes of various body parts. Starr (1979) adapted general nonverbal work to suggest assessing juror dispositions by (among other things) body type, manner of walking to the jury box, and the distance prospective jurors stood from each other during breaks. Such approaches have been controversial. Although they praised scientific jury selection as a form of "community or courtroom research involving systematic attention to the problem of bias," Rieke and Stutman (1990, p. 78) also accused many commercial research firms of passing off "canards of nonverbal behavior

as proprietary wisdom" (p. 79) and compared many jury consultants with astrologers relying on "stereotypical signs, ranging from particular nonverbal behaviors to the dress or cosmetics worn by prospective jurors" (p. 79). Making unqualified translations from one area of research to another is troubling at best (Reinard, 1986b), and Rieke and Stutman (1990) declared, "Evidence for generalizing from juror idiosyncrasies does not exist, and claims based on this evidence are generally without foundation" (p. 79).

REFERENCES

Ackerman, A. M., McMahon, P. M., & Fehr, L. A. (1984). Mock trial jury decisions as a function of adolescent juror guilt and hostility. *Journal of Genetic Psychology, 144,* 195-201.

Adler, F. (1973). Socioeconomic factors influencing jury verdicts. *New York University Review of Law and Social Change, 3,* 1-10.

Allen, M., Mabry, E., & McKelton, D. M. (1998). Impact of juror attitudes about the death penalty on juror evaluations of guilt and punishment: A meta-analysis. *Law and Human Behavior, 22,* 715-731.

Anderson, M. C., & MacCoun, R. J. (1999). Goal conflict in juror assessments of compensatory and punitive damages. *Law and Human Behavior, 23,* 313-330.

Angira, K. K. (1991). Effect of sex of transgressor on the juridic judgement of male and female simulated jurors. *Psycho-Lingua, 21,* 79-84.

Antieau, L. D. (1999). Indirectness in the courtroom: A question of politeness or control? (Master's thesis, Eastern Michigan University, 1998). *Masters Abstracts International, 37,* 0430.

Arens, R., Granfield, D. D., & Susman, J. (1965). Jurors, jury charges, and insanity. *Catholic University Law Review, 14,* 1-29.

Aristotle. (1941). *Rhetorica.* In W. R. Roberts (Trans.), *The works of Aristotle* (Vol. 11). Oxford, UK: Clarendon.

Arsenault, D. J., & Reinard, J. C. (1997, April). *The effect of attorney-directed question types in* voir dire *upon jury deliberation, defendant culpability, and attorney sociability.* Paper presented at the meeting of the Western Psychological Association, Seattle, WA.

Aubrey, M., & Ewing, C. P. (1989). Student and voter subjects: Differences in attitudes toward battered women. *Journal of Interpersonal Violence, 4,* 289-297

Austin, R. L. (1984). The court and sentencing of Black offenders. In D. Georges-Abeyie (Ed.), *The criminal justice system and Blacks* (pp. 167-193). New York: Clark Boardman.

Austin, T. L. (1981). The influence of court location on type of criminal sentencing: The rural-urban factor. *Journal of Criminal Justice, 9,* 305-316.

Austin, W., Walster, E., & Utne, M. K. (1976). Equity and the law: The effect of a harmdoers "suffering in the act" on liking and assigned punishment. In L. Berkowitz & E. Walster (Eds.), *Advances in experimental social psychology* (Vol. 9, pp. 163-190). New York: Academic Press.

Badzinski, D. M., & Pettus, A. B. (1994). Nonverbal involvement and sex: Effects on jury decision making. *Journal of Applied Communication, 22,* 309-321.

Baker, E. (1985). Conviction proneness as a predictor of sworn juror decisions. (Doctoral dissertation, City University of New York, 1984). *Dissertation Abstracts International, 45,* 2354B-2355B.

Balch, R. W., Giffiths, C. T., Hall, E. L., & Winfree, L. T. (1976). The socialization of jurors: The *voir dire* as a rite of passage. *Journal of Criminal Justice, 4,* 271-273.

Barge, J. K., Schlueter, D. W., & Pritchard, A. (1989). The effects of nonverbal communication and gender on impression formation in opening statements. *Southern Communication Journal, 54,* 330-349.

Barnett, N. J., & Feild, H. S. (1978). Character of the defendant and length of sentence in rape and burglary crimes. *Journal of Social Psychology, 104,* 271-277.

Bayly, M. J. (1989). The impact of opening statement presentation order and trial information content on jurors' evaluations of the trial and defendant. (Doctoral dissertation, University of Kansas, 1988). *Dissertation Abstracts International, 50,* 2203B.

Beauvais, C. G. (1983). Perceptions of rape victims in mock trials. (Master's thesis, California State University, Fullerton, 1982). *Masters Abstracts International, 21,* 0100.

Becker, S. A. (1999). Individual differences in juror reasoning: General intelligence, social intelligence, and the story model. (Doctoral dissertation, Fairleigh Dickinson University, 1998). *Dissertation Abstracts International, 59,* 4533B.

Bell, B. E., & Loftus, E. F. (1988). Degree of detail of eyewitness testimony and mock juror judgments. *Journal of Applied Social Psychology, 18,* 1171-1192.

Belon, H. P. (1991). Combat in the courtroom: The battle of the experts, reputation bias, and perceived credibility. (Doctoral dissertation, University of Arizona). *Dissertation Abstracts International, 52,* 1775B.

Bennett, W. L. (1978). Storytelling in criminal trials. *Quarterly Journal of Speech, 64,* 1-22.

Bennett, W. L. (1979). Rhetorical transformation of evidence in criminal trials: Creating grounds for legal judgment. *Quarterly Journal of Speech, 65,* 311-322.

Bennett, W. L., & Feldman, M. S. (1981). *Reconstructing reality in the courtroom.* New Brunswick, NJ: Rutgers University Press.

Benoit, W. L., & French, J. S. (1983). Review of research on opening statements and closing arguments. In R. Matlon & R. Crawford (Eds.), *Communication strategies in the practice of lawyering* (pp. 384-400). Annandale, VA: Speech Communication Association.

Bensko, N. L. (1996). The effect of extra-legal influences on juror decision making. (Doctoral dissertation, Colorado State University, 1995). *Dissertation Abstracts International, 57,* 731B.

Berg, K., & Vidmar, N. (1975). Authoritarianism and recall of evidence about criminal behavior. *Journal of Research in Personality, 9,* 147-157.

Berman, G. L., & Cutler, B. L. (1996). Effects of inconsistencies in eyewitness testimony on mock-juror decision making. *Journal of Applied Psychology, 81,* 170-177.

Berman, G. L., Narby, D. J., & Cutler, B. L. (1995). Effects of inconsistent eyewitness statements on mock-jurors' evaluations of the eyewitness, perceptions of defendant culpability, and verdicts. *Law and Human Behavior, 19,* 79-88.

Bermant, G., McGuire, M., McKinley, W., & Salo, C. (1974). The logic of simulation in jury research. *Criminal Justice and Behavior, 1,* 224-233.

Blanck, P. D., Rosenthal, R., & Cordell, L. H. (1985). The appearance of justice: Judges' verbal and nonverbal behavior in criminal jury trials. *Stanford Law Review, 38,* 89-164.

Blumstein, A., Cohen, J., Martin, S. E., & Tonry, M. H. (Eds.). (1983). *Research on sentencing: The search for reform* (2 vols.). Washington, DC: National Academy Press.

Boardman, A. F. (1996). A comparative investigation of insanity acquittees and unsuccessful insanity evaluatees. (Doctoral dissertation, Kent State University, 1995). *Dissertation Abstracts International, 56,* 7038B.

Bodenhausen, G. V., & Wyer, R. S. (1985). Effects of stereotypes on decision making and information processing strategies. *Journal of Personality and Social Psychology, 48,* 267-282.

Bogenberger, R. P. (1990). The NGRI plea in Hawaii, 1970-1976: A discriminant analysis of variables associated with a successful plea. (Doctoral dissertation, University of Wyoming, 1989). *Dissertation Abstracts International, 50,* 5297B.

Boliver, S. E. (1999). The effects of attorney race and use of racially relevant arguments on juror decision-making. (Doctoral dissertation, California School of Professional Psychology). *Dissertation Abstracts International, 60,* 1911B.

Borgida, E., & Park, R. (1988). The entrapment defense: Juror comprehension and decision making. *Law and Human Behavior, 12,* 19-40.

Bornstein, B. H. (1999). The ecological validity of jury simulations: Is the jury still out? *Law and Human Behavior, 23,* 75-91.

Bornstein, B. H., & Rajki, M. (1994). Extra-legal factors and product liability: The influence of mock jurors' demographic characteristics and intuitions about the cause of an injury. *Behavioral Sciences and the Law, 12,* 127-147.

Borum, R., & Fulero, S. M. (1999). "Empirical research on the insanity defense and attempted reforms: Evidence toward informed policy": Erratum. *Law and Human Behavior, 23,* 375-394.

Boster, F. J., Hunter, J. E., & Hale, J. L. (1991). An information-processing model of jury decision making. *Communication Research, 18,* 524-547.

Bourdouris, J. (1993). A case study in trial consulting. *American Journal of Forensic Psychology, 11,* 3-15.

Bourdouris, J. (2000). The insanity defense in Polk County, Iowa. *American Journal of Forensic Psychology, 18,* 41-79.

Boyll, J. R. (1991). Psychological, cognitive, personality, and interpersonal factors in jury verdicts. *Law and Psychology Review, 15,* 163-184.

Bradac, J. J., Hemphill, M. R., & Tardy, C. H. (1981). Language style on trial: Effects of "powerful" and "powerless" speech upon judgments of victims and villains. *Western Journal of Speech Communication, 45,* 327-341.

Brand, A. H. (1986). Predicting juror bias and its effects on group deliberation, verdict, and recall of trial information. (Doctoral dissertation, University of Florida, 1985). *Dissertation Abstracts International, 47,* 1712B.

Bray, R. M., & Noble, A. M. (1978). Authoritarianism and decisions of mock juries: Evidence of jury bias and group polarization. *Journal of Personality and Social Psychology, 36,* 1424-1430.

Bray, R. M., Struckman-Johnson, C., Osborne, M. D., McFarlane, J. B., & Scott, J. (1978). The effects of defendant status on the decisions of student and community juries. *Social Psychology, 41,* 256-260.

Bregman, N. J., & McAllister, H. A. (1987). Perceived innocence or guilt: Role of eyewitness identification and fingerprints. *Southern Psychologist, 3,* 49-52.

Brekke, N., & Borgida, E. (1988). Expert psychological testimony in rape trials: A social-cognitive analysis. *Journal of Personality and Social Psychology, 55,* 372-386.

Brekke, N. J., Enko, P. J., Clavet, G., & Seelau, E. (1991). Of juries and court-appointed experts: The impact of nonadversarial versus adversarial expert testimony. *Law and Human Behavior, 15,* 451-475.

Bridgeman, D. L., & Marlowe, D. (1979). Jury decision making: An empirical study based on actual felony trials. *Journal of Applied Psychology, 64,* 91-98.

Brigham, J. C., & Bouthwell, R. K. (1983). The ability of prospective jurors to estimate the accuracy of eyewitness identifications. *Law and Human Behavior, 7,* 19-30.

Brodsky, S. L., Hooper, N. E., Tipper, D. G., & Yates, S. B. (1999). Attorney invasion of witness space. *Law and Society Review, 23,* 49-68.

Broeder, D. (1959). The University of Chicago Jury Project. *Nebraska Review, 38,* 744-760.

Bronson, E. J. (1970). On the conviction proneness and representativeness of the death-qualified jury: An empirical study of Colorado venire men. *Colorado Law Review, 42,* 1-32.

Bruschke, J., & Loges, W. E. (1999). Relationship between pretrial publicity and trial outcomes. *Journal of Communication, 49*(4), 104-120.

Bruschke, J., & Loges, W. E. (2001, February). *The effect of pretrial newspaper coverage on federal murder and robbery cases.* Paper presented at the meeting of the Western States Communication Association, Couer D'Alene, ID.

Buchanan, R. W., Pryor, A., Taylor, K. P., & Strawn, D. (1978). Legal communication: An investigation of juror comprehension of pattern instructions. *Communication Quarterly, 26,* 31-35.

Bullock, H. A. (1961). Significance of the racial factor in the length of prison sentences. *Journal of Criminal Law, Criminology, and Police Science, 52,* 411-417.

Burnstein, V. J. (1996). Effects of a defense psychological expert witness in acquaintance rape trials. (Doctoral dissertation, University of Texas, 1995). *Dissertation Abstracts International, 56,* 5830B.

Burrell, N. A., & Koper, R. J. (1998). The efficacy of powerful/powerless language on attitudes and source credibility. In M. Allen & R. W. Preiss (Eds.), *Persuasion: Advances through meta-analysis* (pp. 203-215). Cresskill, NJ: Hampton.

Calhoun, L. G., Selby, J. W., Cann, A., & Keller, G. T. (1978). The effects of victim physical attractiveness and sex of respondent on social reactions to victims of rape. *British Journal of Social and Clinical Psychology, 17,* 191-192.

Calhoun, L. G., Selby, J. W., & Warring, L. J. (1976). Social perception of the victim's causal role in rape. *Human Relations, 29,* 517-526.

Callahan, L. A., McGreevy, M. A., Cirincione, C., & Steadman, H. J. (1992). Measuring the effects of the guilty but mentally ill (GBMI) verdict: Georgia's 1982 GBMI reform. *Law and Human Behavior, 16,* 447-462.

Carretta, T. R., & Moreland, R. L. (1983). The direct and indirect effects of inadmissible evidence. *Journal of Applied Social Psychology, 13,* 291-309.

Carroll, K. R. (1982). Factors affecting juror response to the insanity defense. (Doctoral dissertation, University of South Carolina, 1981). *Dissertation Abstracts International, 42,* 3029B-3030B.

Casper, E. W. (1964). Jurors view mental illness: A review of the literature. *Pennsylvania Psychiatric Quarterly, 4,* 63-67.

Casper, J. D., & Benedict, K. M. (1993). The influence of outcome information and attitudes on juror decision making in search and seizure cases. In R. Hastie (Ed.), *Inside the juror: The psychology of juror decision making* (pp. 65-83). New York: Cambridge University Press.

Cassidy, J. J. (1994). Juror decision-making: Evidence and personality factors. (Doctoral dissertation, Hahnemann University Graduate School, 1993). *Dissertation Abstracts International, 54,* 4431B.

Cather, C., Greene, E., & Durham, R. (1996). Plaintiff injury and defendant reprehensibility: Implications for compensatory and punitive damage awards. *Law and Human Behavior, 20,* 189-205.

Chapman, V. V. (1994). The effects of language style on the credibility of legal testimony. (Doctoral dissertation, Indiana University, 1993). *Dissertation Abstracts International, 54,* 3263A.

Charrow, R. P., & Charrow, V. R. (1979). Making legal language understandable: A psycholinguistic study of jury instructions. *Columbia Law Review, 79,* 208-218.

Cirincione, C., Steadman, H. J., & McGreevy, M. A. (1995). Rates of insanity acquittals and the factors associated with successful insanity pleas. *Bulletin of the American Academy of Psychiatry and the Law, 23,* 399-409.

Claghorn, J., Hays, J. R., Webb, L., & Lewis, N. (1991). Juror personality characteristics and the insanity defense. *Forensic Reports, 4,* 61-65.

Clark, J. (2000). The social psychology of jury nullification. *Law and Psychology Review, 24,* 39-57.

Clark, R. D., III. (1994). The role of censorship in minority influence. *European Journal of Social Psychology, 24,* 331-338.

Clary, E. G., & Shaffer, D. R. (1985). Another look at the impact of juror sentiments toward defendants on juridic decisions. *Journal of Social Psychology, 125,* 637-651.

Clayton, O. (1983). A reconsideration of the effect of race in criminal sentencing. *Criminal Justice Review, 8,* 15-20.

Conley, J. M., O'Barr, W. M., & Lind, E. A. (1978). The power of language: Presentation style in the courtroom. *Duke Law Journal, 6,* 1375-1399.

Constantini, E., & King, J. (1980-1981). The partial juror: Correlates and causes of prejudgment. *Law and Society Review, 15,* 9-40.

Corder, B. F., & Whiteside, R. (1988). A survey of jurors' perception of issues related to child sexual abuse. *American Journal of Forensic Psychology, 6,* 37-43.

Cornish, W. R., & Sealy, A. P. (1973). Juries and rules of evidence. *Criminal Law Review, 17,* 208-218.

Cowan, C., Thomson, W., & Ellsworth, P. (1987). The effects of death qualification of jurors' predisposition to convict and other the quality of deliberation. *Law and Human Behavior, 8,* 53-80.

Cox, M., & Tanford, S. (1989). Effects of evidence and instructions in civil trials: An experimental investigation of rules of admissibility. *Social Behavior, 4,* 31-55.

Crowley, M. J., O'Callaghan, M. G., & Ball, P. J. (1994). The juridical impact of psychological expert testimony in a simulated child sexual abuse trial. *Law and Human Behavior, 18,* 89-105.

Crump, D. (1980). Attorneys' goals and tactics in *voir dire* examination. *Texas Bar Journal, 43,* 244-246.

Cusick, J. G. (1995). The improvement of animated presentations in the courtroom: A study of what trial attorneys believe would increase the value of this presentation technology. (Doctoral dissertation, Purdue University, 1994). *Dissertation Abstracts International, 56,* 0520A.

Cutler, B. L., Dexter, H. R., & Penrod, S. D. (1989). Expert testimony and jury decision making: An empirical analysis. *Behavioral Sciences and the Law, 7,* 215-225.

Cutler, B. L., Moran, G. P., & Narby, D. J. (1992). Jury selection in insanity defense cases. *Journal of Research in Personality, 26,* 165-182.

Cutler, B. L., & Penrod, S. D. (1995). *Mistaken identification: The eyewitness, psychology, and the law.* New York: Cambridge University Press.

Cutler, B. L., Penrod, S. D., & Dexter, H. R. (1990). Juror sensitivity to eyewitness identification evidence. *Law and Human Behavior, 14,* 185-191.

Cutler, B. L., Penrod, S. D., & Stuve, T. E. (1988). Juror decision making in eyewitness identification cases. *Law and Human Behavior, 12,* 41-55.

Dane, F. C., & Wrightsman, L. S. (1982). Effects of defendants' and victims' characteristics on jurors' verdicts. In N. L. Kerr & R. M. Bray (Eds.), *The psychology of the courtroom* (pp. 83-115). New York: Academic Press.

Darby, B. W., & Jeffers, D. (1988). The effects of defendant and juror attractiveness on simulated courtroom trial decisions. *Social Behavior and Personality, 16,* 39-50.

Darden, W. R., DeConinck, J. B., Babin, B. J., & Griffin, M. (1991). The role of consumer sympathy in product liability suits: An experimental investigation of loose coupling. *Journal of Business Research, 22,* 65-89.

Daudistel, H. C., Hosch, H. M., Holmes, M. D., & Graves, J. B. (1999). Effects of defendant ethnicity on juries' dispositions of felony cases. *Journal of Applied Social Psychology, 29,* 317-336.

Davies, G. (1999). The impact of television on the presentation and reception of children's testimony. *International Journal of Law and Psychiatry, 22,* 241-256.

Davis, J. P. (1998). When jurors ignore the law and the evidence to do justice (nullification). (Doctoral dissertation, University of Washington). *Dissertation Abstracts International, 59,* 1411B.

Dean, K., Holliday, W., Mack, D., & Thomas, K. (2000). An examination of happiness, racism, and demographics on judgments of guilt. *Journal of Applied Social Psychology, 30,* 816-832.

Dehais, R. J. (1983, November). *Racial disproportionality in prison and racial discrimination in the criminal justice process: Assessing the empirical evidence.* Paper presented at the meeting of the American Society of Criminology, Denver, CO.

Devenport, J. L. (1997). Does expert psychological testimony improve juror sensitivity to lineup suggestiveness? (Doctoral dissertation, Florida International University, 1996). *Dissertation Abstracts International, 57,* 5387B.

Devenport, J. L., Cutler, B. L., & Penrod, S. D. (1998, March). *The impact of opposing expert testimony in cases involving eyewitness identification evidence.* Paper presented at the biannual meeting of the American Psychology-Law Society, Redondo Beach, CA.

Devenport, J. L., Studebaker, C. A., & Penrod, S. D. (1999). Perspectives on jury decision making: Cases with pretrial publicity and cases based on eyewitness identifications. In F. T. Durso, R. Nickerson, S. Dumais, R. Schvaneveldt, M. Chi, & S. Lindsay (Eds.), *Handbook of applied cognition* (pp. 819-845). New York: John Wiley.

Devine, D. J., Clayton, L. D., Dunford, B. B., Seying, R., & Pryce, J. (2001). Jury decision making: 45 years of empirical research on deliberating groups. *Psychology, Public Policy, and Law, 7,* 622-727.

Devine, P. G., & Ostrom, T. M. (1985). Cognitive mediation of inconsistency discounting. *Journal of Personality and Social Psychology, 49,* 5-21.

Dexter, H. R., Cutler, B. L., & Moran, G. (1992). A test of *voir dire* as a remedy for the prejudicial effects of pretrial publicity. *Journal of Applied Social Psychology, 22,* 819-832.

Dillehay, R. C., & Nietzel, M. T. (1985). Juror experience and jury verdicts. *Law and Human Behavior, 9,* 179-191.

Dipboye, R. L. (1977). The effectiveness of one-sided and two-sided appeals as a function of familiarization and context. *Journal of Social Psychology, 102,* 125-131.

Dombroff, M. A. (1988). *Dombroff on unfair tactics* (2nd ed.). New York: Wiley Law Publications.

Dorch, E., & Fontaine, G. (1978). Rate of judges' gaze at different types of witnesses. *Perceptual and Motor Skills, 46,* 1103-1106.

Dovidio, J. F., Smith, J. K., Donnella, A. G., & Gaertner, S. L. (1997). Racial attitudes and the death penalty. *Journal of Applied Social Psychology, 27,* 1468-1487.

Downs, A. C., & Lyons, P. M. (1991). Natural observations of the links between attractiveness and initial legal judgments. *Personality and Social Psychology Bulletin, 17,* 541-547.

Dravin, L. P. (1983). Effect of sex of defendant, sex of expert witness, and type of crime on judicial decisions: A mock jury study. (Doctoral dissertation, Texas Tech University, 1982). *Dissertation Abstracts International, 43,* 2740B.

Durand, R. M., Bearden, W. O., & Gustafson, A. W. (1978). Previous jury service as a moderating influence on jurors' beliefs and attitudes. *Psychological Reports, 42,* 567-572.

Edwards, K., & Bryan, T. S. (1997). Judgmental biases produced by instructions to disregard: The (paradoxical) case of emotional information. *Personality and Social Psychology Bulletin, 23,* 849-864.

Efron, M. B. (1974). The effects of physical appearance on the judgment of guilt interpersonal attraction and severity of recommended punishment in a simulated jury task. *Journal of Research in Personality, 8,* 45-54.

Egbert, J. M., Moore, C. H., Wuensch, K. L., & Castellow, W. A. (1992). The effect of litigant social desirability on judgements regarding a sexual harassment case. *Journal of Social Behavior and Personality, 7,* 569-579.

Elkins, T. J., & Philips, J. S. (1999). Evaluating sex discrimination claims: The mediating role of attributions. *Journal of Applied Psychology, 84,* 186-199.

Ellsworth, P. C., Bukaty, R. M., Cowan, C. L., & Thompson, W. C. (1984). The death-qualified jury and the defense of insanity. *Law and Human Behavior, 8,* 81-93

Elwork, A., Sales, B. D., & Alfini, J. J. (1977). Juridic decisions: In ignorance of the law or in light of it? *Law and Human Behavior, 1,* 163-169.

Elwork, A., Sales, B. D., & Suggs, D. (1981). The trial: A research review. In B. D. Sales (Ed.), *The trial process* (pp. 1-68). New York: Plenum.

Erian, M., Lin, C., Patel, N., Neal, A., & Geiselman, R. E. (1998). Juror verdicts as a function of victim and defendant attractiveness in sexual assault cases. *American Journal of Forensic Psychology, 16,* 25-40.

Erickson, B., Lind, E. A., Johnson, B. C., & O'Barr, W. M. (1978). Speech style and impression formation in a court setting: The effects of "powerful" and "powerless" speech. *Journal of Experimental Social Psychology, 14,* 266-279.

Erlanger, H. S. (1970). Jury research in America: Its past and future. *Law and Society Review, 4,* 345-370.

Feild, H. S. (1979). Rape trials and jurors' decisions: A psycholegal analysis of the effects of victim, defendant, and case characteristics. *Law and Human Behavior, 3,* 261-284.

Feild, H. S., & Barnett, N. J. (1978). Simulated jury trials: Students vs. real people as jurors. *Journal of Social Psychology, 104,* 271-277.

Fein, S., McCloskey, A. L., & Tomlinson, T. M. (1997). Can the jury disregard that information? The use of suspicion to reduce the prejudicial effects of pretrial publicity and inadmissible testimony. *Personality and Social Psychology Bulletin, 23,* 1215-1226.

Fein, S., Morgan, S. J., Norton, M. I., & Sommers, S. R. (1997). Hype and suspicion: The effects of pretrial publicity, race, and suspicion of jurors' verdicts. *Journal of Social Issues, 53,* 487-502.

Feldman, R. S., & Chesley, R. B. (1984). Who is lying, who is not: An attributional analysis of the effects of nonverbal behavior on judgements of defendant believability. *Behavioral Sciences and the Law, 2,* 451-461.

Feldman-Summers, S., & Lindner, K. (1976). Perception of victims and defendants in criminal assault cases. *Criminal Justice and Behavior, 3,* 135-149.

Fienberg, S. E. (Ed.). (1989). *The evolving role of statistical assessments as evidence in the courts.* New York: Springer-Verlag.

Filkins, J. W. (1997). The interactive effects of crime prototype and criminal stereotype on juridical decisions. (Doctoral dissertation, Loyola University of Chicago, 1996). *Dissertation Abstracts International, 57,* 4780B.

Filkins, J. W., Smith, C. M., & Tindale, R. S. (1998). An evaluation of the biasing effects of death qualification: A meta-analytic/computer simulation approach. In R. S. Tindale, J. Edwards, & J. Myers (Eds.), *Theory and research on small groups: Social psychological applications to social issues* (Vol. 4, pp. 153-175). New York: Plenum.

Finkelstein, D. B. (1995). The consequences of exposure to pretrial publicity: Effects on pretrial beliefs and effects on juror verdicts. (Doctoral dissertation, University of California, San Diego, 1994). *Dissertation Abstracts International, 55,* 3062B.

Fischer, S. M., & Fehr, L. A. (1985). The effect of defendant's plea on mock juror decisions. *Journal of Social Psychology, 125,* 531-533.

Fishfader, V. L., Howells, G. N., Katz, R. C., & Teresi, P. S. (1996). Evidential and extralegal factors in juror decisions: Presentation mode, retention, and level of emotionality. *Law and Human Behavior, 20,* 565-572.

Fleming, M. A., Wegener, D. T., & Petty, R. E. (1999). Procedural and legal motivations to correct for perceived judicial biases. *Journal of Experimental Social Psychology, 35,* 186-203.

Floyd, K. D. (1999). The effects of need for cognition, argument quality, and attitudes on rape juror verdicts: An Elaboration Likelihood Model perspective. (Doctoral dissertation, Virginia Commonwealth University, 1998). *Dissertation Abstracts International, 60,* 0410B.

Fontaine, G., & Kiger, R. (1978). The effects of defendant dress and supervision on judgments of simulated jurors. *Law and Human Behavior, 2,* 63-75.

ForsterLee, L., & Horowitz, I. A. (1997). Enhancing juror competence in a complex trial. *Applied Cognitive Psychology, 11,* 305-319.

ForsterLee, L., Horowitz, I. A., & Bourgeois, M. J. (1993). Juror competence in civil trials: Effects of preinstruction and evidence technicality. *Journal of Applied Psychology, 78,* 14-21.

ForsterLee, R., Horowitz, I. A., Ho, R., ForsterLee, L., & McGovern, A. (1999). Community members' perceptions of evidence: The effects of gender in a recovered memory civil trial. *Journal of Applied Psychology, 84,* 484-495.

Fox, S. G., & Walters, H. A. (1986). The impact of general versus specific expert testimony and eyewitness confidence upon mock juror judgment. *Law and Human Behavior, 10,* 215-228.

Frederick, J. T. (1984). Social science involvement in *voir dire:* Preliminary data on the effectiveness of "scientific jury selection." *Behavioral Sciences and the Law, 2,* 375-394.

Freundlich, K. F. (1985). Effects of pretrial publicity and ego level on verdict and jury deliberation styles. (Doctoral dissertation, University of Florida, 1984). *Dissertation Abstracts International, 45,* 3055B-3056B.

Fulero, S. M., & Penrod, S. D. (1990a). Attorney jury selection folklore: What do they think and how can psychology help? *Forensic Reports, 3,* 233-254.

Fulero, S. M., & Penrod, S. D. (1990b). The myths and realities of attorney jury selection folklore and scientific jury selection: What works? *Ohio Northern University Law Review, 17,* 229-253.

Garfinkle, H. (1949). Research note on inter- and intra-racial homicides. *Social Forces, 27,* 369-381.

Gibson, D. C. (1991). *The role of communication in the practice of law.* Lanham, MD: University Press of America.

Gleason, J. M., & Harris, V. A. (1976). Group discussion and defendant's socio-economic status as determinants of judgments by simulated jurors. *Journal of Applied Social Psychology, 6,* 186-191.

Goodman, G. S., Goldings, J. M., & Haith, M. M. (1984). Jurors' reactions to child witnesses. *Journal of Social Issues, 40,* 139-156.

Goodman, J., Loftus, E. F., & Greene, E. (1990). Matters of money: *Voir dire* in civil cases. *Forensic Reports, 3,* 303-329.

Gordon, R. A. (1990). Attributions for blue-collar and white-collar crime: The effects of subject and defendant race on simulated juror decisions. *Journal of Applied Social Psychology, 20,* 971-983.

Gordon, R. A., Bindrim, T. A., McNicholas, M. L., & Walden, T. L. (1988). Perceptions of blue-collar and white-collar crime: The effect of defendant race on simulated juror decisions. *Journal of Social Psychology, 128,* 191-197.

Gordon, R. I., & Jacobs, P. D. (1969). Forensic psychology: Perception of guilt and income. *Perceptual and Motor Skills, 28,* 143-146.

Gowan, M. A., & Zimmerman, R. A. (1996). Impact of ethnicity, gender, and previous experience on juror judgments in sexual harassment cases. *Journal of Applied Social Psychology, 26,* 596-617.

Greenberg, J., Williams, K. D., & O'Brien, M. K. (1986). Considering the harshest verdict first: Biasing effects on mock juror verdicts. *Personality and Social Psychology Bulletin, 12,* 41-50.

Greene, E. (1986). Forensic hypnosis to lift amnesia: The jury is still out. *Behavioral Sciences and the Law, 4,* 65-72.

Greene, E., & Dodge, M. (1995). The influence of prior record evidence on juror decision making. *Law and Human Behavior, 19,* 67-78.

Greene, E., Downey, C., & Goodman-Delahunty, J. (1999). Juror decisions about damages in employment discrimination cases. *Behavioral Sciences and the Law, 17,* 107-121.

Greene, E., & Loftus, E. F. (1984). What's new in the news? The influence of well-publicized news events on psychological research and courtroom trials. *Basic and Applied Social Psychology, 5,* 211-221.

Greene, E., & Wade, R. (1988). Of private talk and public print: General pre-trial publicity and juror decision-making. *Applied Cognitive Psychology, 2,* 123-135.

Griffith, J. D., Libkuman, T. M., Kazen, J., & Shafir, Z. (1999). Repressed memories in the courtroom: Trial characteristics affecting mock jurors' decision making. *American Journal of Forensic Psychology, 17*(2), 5-24.

Griffitt, W., & Jackson, T. (1973). Simulated jury decisions: The influence of jury-defendant attitude similarity-dissimilarity. *Social Behavior and Personality, 1,* 1-7.

Grofman, B. (1985). The effect of restricted and unrestricted verdict options on juror choice. *Social Science Research, 14,* 195-204.

Gutheil, T. G. (1999). A confusion of tongues: Competence, insanity, psychiatry, and the law. *Psychiatric Services, 50,* 767-773.

Haegerich, T., & Bottoms, B. L. (2000). Empathy and jurors' decisions in patricide trials involving child sexual assault allegations. *Law and Human Behavior, 24,* 421-448.

Hagan, J. (1974). Extra-legal attributes and criminal sentencing: An assessment of a sociological viewpoint. *Law and Society Review, 8,* 357-383.

Hagan, J., & Bumiller, K. (1983). Making sense of sentencing: A review and critique of sentencing research. In A. Blumstein, J. Cohen, S. E. Martin, & M. H. Tonry (Eds.), *Research on sentencing: The search for reform* (Vol. 2, pp. 1-54). Washington, DC: National Academy Press.

Hagen, S. K. (1991). The child witness: The effects of videotaped versus live testimony on juror perceptions of guilt. (Doctoral dissertation, University of North Dakota, 1990). *Dissertation Abstracts International, 52,* 1060B-1061B.

Hahn, P. W., & Clayton, S. D. (1996). The effects of attorney presentation style, attorney gender, and juror gender on juror decisions. *Law and Human Behavior, 20,* 533-554.

Hall, E., & Simkus, A. (1975). Inequality in the types of sentences received by Native Americans and Whites. *Criminology, 13,* 199-232.

Hamilton, V. L. (1978). Obedience and responsibility: A jury simulation. *Journal of Personality and Social Psychology, 36,* 126-146.

Haney, C. (1984). On the selection of capital juries: The biasing effects of the death-qualification process. *Law and Human Behavior, 8,* 121-132.

Haney, C., & Lynch, M. (1997). Clarifying life and death matters: An analysis of instructional comprehension and penalty phase closing arguments. *Law and Human Behavior, 21,* 575-595.

Haney, C., Sontag, L., & Costanzo, S. (1994). Deciding to take a life: Capital juries, sentencing instructions, and the jurisprudence of death. *Journal of Social Issues, 50,* 149-176.

Hans, V. P., & Doob, A. N. (1976). Section 12 of the Canada Evidence Act and the deliberations of simulated jurors. *Criminal Law Quarterly, 18,* 235-253.

Hans, V. P., & Vidmar, N. (1986). *Judging the jury.* New York: Plenum.

Harlow, C. W. (2000, November). *Defense counsel in criminal cases* (NCJ 179023). Rockville, MD: U.S. Department of Justice, Bureau of Justice Statistics.

Harris, R. J., Teske, R. R., & Ginns, M. J. (1978). Memory for pragmatic implications from courtroom testimony. *Bulletin of the Psychonomic Society, 6,* 494-496.

Hart, A. J. (1995). Naturally occurring expectation effects. *Journal of Personality and Social Psychology, 68,* 109-115.

Hastie, R., & Pennington, N. (2000). Explanation-based decision making. In T. Connolly & H. R. Arkes (Eds.), *Judgment and decision making: An interdisciplinary reader* (2nd ed., pp. 212-228). New York: Cambridge University Press.

Hastie, R., Penrod, S. D., & Pennington, N. (1983). *Inside the jury.* Cambridge, MA: Harvard University Press.

Hastie, R., Schkade, D. A., & Payne, J. W. (1998). A study of juror and jury judgments in civil cases: Deciding liability for punitive damages. *Law and Human Behavior, 22,* 287-314.

Hastie, R., Schkade, D. A., & Payne, J. W. (1999). Juror judgments in civil cases: Effects of plaintiff's requests and plaintiff's identity on punitive damage awards. *Law and Human Behavior, 23,* 445-470.

Hernandez, M. G. (1986). The influence of psychiatric testimony, criteria for insanity, and juror legal reasoning level on verdict choice and satisfaction with verdict choice. (Doctoral dissertation, University of Texas at Austin, 1985). *Dissertation Abstracts International, 12,* 4385B.

Hill, E. L., & Pfeifer, J. E. (1992). Nullification instructions and juror guilt ratings: An examination of modern racism. *Contemporary Social Psychology, 16,* 6-10.

Himelein, M. J., Nietzel, M. T., & Dillehay, R. C. (1991). Effects of prior juror experience on jury sentencing. *Behavioral Sciences and the Law, 9,* 97-106.

Hirsch, R. O., Reinard, J. C., & Reynolds, R. A. (1976, May). *The influence of objection to mundane and sensational testimony on attorney credibility.* Paper presented at the meeting of the Rocky Mountain Psychological Association, Phoenix, AZ.

Hoffman, H. M., & Brodley, J. (1952). Jurors on trial. *Missouri Law Review, 17,* 235-251.

Hoiberg, B. C., & Stires, L. K. (1973a). The effect of several types of pretrial publicity on the guilt attributions of simulated jurors. *Journal of Applied Social Psychology, 3,* 267-275.

Hoiberg, B. C., & Stires, L. K. (1973b). Effects of pre-trial publicity and juror traits on the guilt attributions of simulated jurors. In *Proceedings of the annual convention of the American Psychological Association* (Vol. 8, pp. 269-270). Washington, DC: American Psychological Association.

Holden, C. E., Stephenson-Burland, A., & Lemmen, C. A. (1996). Insanity and filicide:

Women who murder their children. In E. P. Benedek (Ed.), *Emerging issues in forensic psychiatry: From the clinic to the courthouse* (New Directions for Mental Health Services, No. 69, pp. 25-34). San Francisco: Jossey-Bass.

Hollihan, T. A., Riley, P. A., & Freadhoff, K. (1986). Arguing for justice: An analysis of arguing in small claims court. *Journal of the American Forensic Association, 22,* 187-195.

Holt, R. W., O'Connor, J. A., Smith, J. L., Gessner, T. L., Clifton, T. C., & Mumford, M. D. (1997). Influences of destructive personality information on decision making. *Journal of Applied Social Psychology, 27,* 781-799.

Horn, E. R. (1976). The effects of a prior conviction and kind of conflicting evidence on the attribution of credibility to a witness by a juror. (Doctoral dissertation, University of Kentucky). *Dissertation Abstracts International, 37,* 2570B.

Hosch, H. M., Beck, E. L., & McIntyre, P. (1980). Influence of expert testimony regarding eyewitness accuracy on jury decisions. *Law and Human Behavior, 4,* 287-296.

Hosch, H. M., Chanez, G. J., Bothwell, R. K., & Munoz, H. (1991). A comparison of Anglo-American and Mexican-American jurors' judgments of mothers who fail to protect their children from abuse. *Journal of Applied Social Psychology, 21,* 1681-1698.

Hosman, L. A., & Wright, J. W., II. (1987). The effects of hedges and hesitations on impression formation in a simulation courtroom context. *Western Journal of Speech Communication, 51,* 173-188.

Howard, J. A., & Leber, B. D. (1988). Socializing attribution: Generalization to "real" social environments. *Journal of Applied Social Psychology, 18,* 664-687.

Hymes, R. W., Leinart, M., Rowe, S., & Rogers, W. (1993). Acquaintance rape: The effect of race of defendant and race of victim on White juror decisions. *Journal of Social Psychology, 133,* 627-634.

Imrich, D. J., Mullin, C., & Linz, D. (1995). Measuring the extent of prejudicial pretrial publicity in major American newspapers: A content analysis. *Journal of Communication, 45*(3), 94-117.

Insko, C. A. (1962). One-sided versus two-sided communication and countercommunications.

Journal of Abnormal and Social Psychology, 65, 203-206.

Insko, C. A. (1964). Primacy versus recency in persuasion as a function of the timing of arguments and measures. *Journal of Abnormal and Social Psychology, 69,* 381-391.

Izzett, R. R., & Leginski, W. (1974). Group discussion and the influence of defendant characteristics in a simulated jury setting. *Journal of Social Psychology, 93,* 271-279.

Jacoubovitch, M. D., Bermant, G., Crockett, G. T., McKinley, W., & Sanstad, A. (1977). Juror responses to direct and mediated presentations of expert testimony. *Journal of Applied Social Psychology, 7,* 227-238.

Jeffrey, R. W. (1987). Characteristics of persons pleading and adjudicated insane in Colorado. (Doctoral dissertation, University of Wyoming, 1986). *Dissertation Abstracts International, 47,* 3112B.

Johnson, C., & Haney, C. (1994). Felony *voir dire:* An exploratory study of its content and effect. *Law and Human Behavior, 18,* 487-506.

Johnson, G. B. (1941). The Negro and crime. *Annals of the American Academy of Political and Social Sciences, 271,* 93-104.

Johnson, J. D. (1994). The effect of rape type and information admissibility on perceptions of rape victims. *Sex Roles, 30,* 781-792.

Johnstone, R. (1994). The empty chair doctrine revisited: An examination of the relative influences of attorneys and judges. (Master's thesis, San Jose State University, 1993). *Masters Abstracts International, 32,* 0734.

Jones, A. J. (1996). The insanity defense in Virginia: The relationship between pre-trial evaluation of criminal responsibility and legal outcome. (Doctoral dissertation, George Mason University, 1995). *Dissertation Abstracts International, 56,* 4584B.

Jones, C., & Aronson, M. (1973). Attribution of fault to a rape victim as a function of respectability of the victim. *Journal of Personality and Social Psychology, 26,* 415-419.

Jones, S. E. (1987). Judge- versus attorney-conducted *voir dire:* An empirical investigation of juror candor. *Law and Human Behavior, 11,* 131-146.

Jurow, G. L. (1971). New data on the effects of a death-qualified jury on the guilt determination process. *Harvard Law Review, 84,* 567-611.

Kagehiro, D. K. (1990). Defining the standard of proof in jury instructions. *Psychological Science, 1,* 194-200.

Kahn, A., Deutsch, L. A., Hagan, R., Hill, M., McGaughey, T., Ryen, A. H., & Wilson, D. W. (1977). Attribution of fault to a rape victim as a function of respectability of the victim: A failure to replicate or extend. *Representative Research in Social Psychology, 8,* 98-107.

Kalai, E. (1993). A rational game theory framework for the analysis of legal and criminal decision making. In R. Hastie (Ed.), *Inside the juror: The psychology of juror decision making* (Cambridge Series on Judgment and Decision Making, pp. 235-241). New York: Cambridge University Press.

Kalven, H., & Zeisel, H. (1966). *The American jury.* Boston: Little, Brown.

Kaplan, M. F. (1983). A model of information integration in jury deliberation. *Academic Psychology Bulletin, 5,* 91-96.

Kaplan, M. F., & Kemmerick, G. D. (1974). Juror judgment as information integration: Combining evidential and nonevidential information. *Journal of Personality and Social Psychology, 30,* 493-499.

Kaplan, M. F., & Miller, C. E. (1977). Judgments and group discussion: Effect of presentation and memory factors on polarization. *Social Psychology Quarterly, 40,* 337-343.

Kaplan, M. F., & Miller, L. E. (1978). Reducing the effects of juror bias. *Journal of Personality and Social Psychology, 36,* 1443-1455.

Kasian, M., Spanos, N. P., Terrance, C. A., & Peebles, S. (1993). Battered women who kill: Jury simulation and legal defenses. *Law and Human Behavior, 17,* 289-312.

Kassin, S. M., & Garfield, D. A. (1991). Blood and guts: General and trial-specific effects of videotaped crime scenes on mock jurors. *Journal of Applied Social Psychology, 21,* 1459-1472.

Kassin, S. M., & Juhnke, R. G. (1983). Juror experience and decision making. *Journal of Personality and Social Psychology, 44,* 1182-1191.

Kassin, S. M., & Neumann, K. (1997). On the power of confession evidence: An experimental test of the fundamental difference hypothesis. *Law and Human Behavior, 21,* 469-484.

Kassin, S. M., Reddy, M. E., & Tulloch, W. F. (1990). Juror interpretations of ambiguous evidence: The need for cognition, presentation order, and persuasion. *Law and Human Behavior, 14,* 43-55.

Kassin, S. M., & Sommers, S. R. (1997). Inadmissible testimony, instructions to disregard, and the jury: Substantive versus procedural considerations. *Personality and Social Psychology Bulletin, 23,* 1046-1054.

Kassin, S. M., Williams, L. N., & Sanders, C. L. (1990). Dirty tricks of cross-examination: The influence of conjectural evidence on the jury. *Law and Human Behavior, 14,* 373-384.

Kassin, S. M., & Wrightsman, L. S. (1979). On the requirement of proof: The timing of judicial instruction and mock juror verdicts. *Journal of Personality and Social Psychology, 37,* 1877-1887.

Kassin, S. M., & Wrightsman, L. S. (1980). Prior confessions and mock juror verdicts. *Journal of Applied Social Psychology, 10,* 133-146.

Kassin, S. M., & Wrightsman, L. S. (1981). Coerced confessions, judicial instructions, and mock juror verdicts. *Journal of Applied Social Psychology, 11,* 489-506.

Kassin, S. M., & Wrightsman, L. S. (1983). The construction and validation of a Juror Bias Scale. *Journal of Research in Personality, 17,* 423-442.

Katzev, R. D., & Wishart, S. S. (1985). The impact of judicial commentary concerning eyewitness identifications on jury decision making. *Journal of Criminal Law and Criminology, 76,* 733-745.

Kauffman, R. A., & Ryckman, R. M. (1979). Effects of locus of control, outcome severity, and attitudinal similarity of defendant on attributions of criminal responsibility. *Personality and Social Psychology Bulletin, 5,* 340-343.

Kerr, N. L. (1978). Severity of prescribed penalty and mock jurors' verdicts. *Journal of Personality and Social Psychology, 36,* 1431-1442.

Kerr, N. L., Atkin, R. S., Stasser, G., Meek, D., Holt, R. W., & Davis, J. H. (1976). Guilt beyond a reasonable doubt: Effects of concept definition and assigned decisional rule on the judgments of mock jurors. *Journal of Personality and Social Psychology, 34,* 282-294.

Kerr, N. L., Bull, R. H., MacCoun, R. J., & Rathborn, H. (1985). Effects of victim attractiveness, care, and disfigurement on the judgements of American and British mock jurors. *British Journal of Social Psychology, 24,* 47-58.

Kerr, N. L., Hymes, R. W., Anderson, A. B., & Weathers, J. E. (1995). Defendant-juror similarity and mock juror judgments. *Law and Human Behavior, 19,* 545-567.

Kerr, N. L., Kramer, G. R., Carroll, J. S., & Alfini, J. J. (1991). On the effectiveness of *voir dire* in criminal cases with prejudicial pretrial publicity: An empirical study. *American University Law Review, 40,* 665-701.

Kerr, N. L., & Kurtz, S. T. (1977). Effects of a victim's suffering and respectability on mock juror judgments: Further evidence on the just world theory. *Representative Research in Social Psychology, 8,* 42-56.

Kerr, N. L., Niedermeier, K. E., & Kaplan, M. F. (1999). Bias in jurors vs. bias in juries: New evidence from the SDS perspective. *Organizational Behavior and Human Decision Processes, 80,* 70-86.

Kerwin, J., & Shaffer, D. R. (1994). Mock jurors versus mock juries: The roles of deliberations in reactions to inadmissible testimony. *Personality and Social Psychology Bulletin, 20,* 153-162.

Key, H. G., Warren, A. R., & Ross, D. F. (1996). Perceptions of repressed memories: A reappraisal. *Law and Human Behavior, 20,* 555-563.

Kidd, R. F., & Sieveking, N. A. (1974). Effects of labeling and of theoretical explanations of deviancy on juror attitudes: An exploratory investigation. *Journal of Community Psychology, 2,* 187-191.

Kleck, G. (1981). Racial discrimination in criminal sentencing: A critical evaluation of the evidence with additional evidence on the death penalty. *American Sociological Review, 46,* 783-805.

Koch, C. M., & Devine, D. J. (1999). Effects of reasonable doubt definition and inclusion of a lesser charge on jury verdicts. *Law and Human Behavior, 23,* 653-674.

Konopka, A., Miller, G. R., Siebert, F. S., Bender, D., Florence, B. T., Nicholson, H., Boster, F., Hocking, J., & Nesterenko, A. (1974, December). *Effects of videotaped testimony on information processing and decision-making in jury trials.* Paper presented at the meeting of the Speech Communication Association, Chicago.

Kovera, M. B., & Borgida, E. (1996). Children on the witness stand: The use of expert testimony and other procedural innovations in U.S. child sexual abuse trials. In B. L. Bottoms & G. S. Goodman (Eds.), *International perspectives on child abuse and children's testimony: Psychological research and law* (pp. 201-220). Thousand Oaks, CA: Sage.

Kovera, M. B., Gresham, A. W., Borgida, E., Gray, E., & Regan, P. C. (1997). Does expert psychological testimony inform or influence juror decision making? A social cognitive analysis. *Journal of Applied Psychology, 82,* 178-191.

Kovera, M. B., Levy, R. J., Borgida, E., & Penrod, S. D. (1994). Expert testimony in child sexual abuse cases: Effects of expert evidence type and cross-examination. *Law and Human Behavior, 18,* 653-674.

Kovera, M. B., McAuliff, B. D., & Hebert, K. S. (1999). Reasoning about scientific evidence: Effects of juror gender and evidence quality on juror decisions in a hostile work environment case. *Journal of Applied Psychology, 84,* 362-375.

Kramer, G. P., & Kerr, N. L. (1989). Laboratory simulation and bias in the study of juror behavior: A methodological note. *Law and Human Behavior, 13,* 89-99.

Kramer, G. P., Kerr, N. L., & Carroll, J. S. (1990). Pretrial publicity, judicial remedies, and jury bias. *Law and Human Behavior, 14,* 409-438.

Krulewitz, J. E., & Nash, J. E. (1979). Effects of rape victim resistance, assault outcome, and sex of observer on attributions about rape. *Journal of Personality, 47,* 557-574.

Kuhn, D., Weinstock, M., & Flaton, R. (1994). How well do jurors reason? Competence dimensions of individual variation in a juror reasoning task. *Psychological Science, 5,* 289-296.

Kulka, R. A., & Kessler, J. D. (1978). Is justice really blind? The influence of litigant physical attractiveness on juridical judgment. *Journal of Applied Social Psychology, 8,* 366-381.

Kurdys, D. B. (1984). Bias and locus of control expectancy in jurors. (Doctoral dissertation, California School of Professional Psychology, Berkeley/Alameda, 1983). *Dissertation Abstracts International, 44,* 2248B.

Laird, P. G. (1998). Predicting juror decisions: The impact of judicial admonition and moral reasoning. (Doctoral dissertation, Simon Fraser University, 1997). *Dissertation Abstracts International, 58,* 6836B.

Lamberth, J., Krieger, E., & Shay, S. (1982). Juror decision making: A case of attitude change mediated by authoritarianism. *Journal of Research in Personality, 16,* 419-434.

Lands, N. E. (1987). Race and jury verdict predictions: When is race a factor in conviction proneness? (Doctoral dissertation, University of Miami, 1986). *Dissertation Abstracts International, 47,* 3961B.

Landsman, S., & Rakos, R. F. (1994). A preliminary inquiry into the effect of potentially biasing information on judges and jurors in civil litigation. *Behavioral Sciences and the Law, 12,* 113-126.

Landy, D., & Aronson, E. (1969). The influence of the character of the criminal and his victim on the decision of simulated jurors. *Journal of Experimental Social Psychology, 5,* 141-152.

Larntz, K. (1975). Reanalysis of Vidmar's data on the effects of decision alternatives on verdicts of simulated jurors. *Journal of Personality and Social Psychology, 31,* 123-125.

Leippe, M. R. (1985). The influence of eyewitness nonidentification on mock jurors. *Journal of Applied Social Psychology, 15,* 656-672.

Lenehan, G. E., & O'Neill, P. (1981). Reactance and conflict as determinants of judgment in a mock jury experiment. *Journal of Applied Social Psychology, 11,* 231-239.

Lerner, M. J. (1965). Evaluation of performance as a function of performers' reward and attractiveness. *Journal of Personality and Social Psychology, 1,* 355-360.

LeVan, E. A. (1984). Nonverbal communication in the courtroom: Attorney beware. *Law and Psychology Review, 8,* 83-104.

Leventhal, G., & Krate, R. (1977). Physical attractiveness and severity of sentencing. *Psychological Reports, 40,* 315-318.

Lewis, E. W. (1997). A social psychological investigation of legal entrapment. (Doctoral dissertation, University of Nevada, Reno, 1996). *Dissertation Abstracts International, 58,* 458B.

Lieberman, J. D. (1998). Cognitive-experiential self-theory and juror decision making. (Doctoral dissertation, University of Arizona, 1997). *Dissertation Abstracts International, 58,* 4525B.

Lind, E. A., & O'Barr, W. (1979). The social significance of speech in the courtroom. In H. Giles & R. N. St. Claire (Eds.), *Language and social psychology* (pp. 65-87). Oxford, UK: Basil Blackwell.

Lind, E. A., Thibaut, J., & Walker, L. (1973). Discovery and presentation of evidence in adversary and nonadversary proceedings. *Michigan Law Review, 71,* 1129-1144.

Lindsay, R. C. L. (1994). Expectations of eyewitness performance: Jurors' verdicts do not follow from their beliefs. In D. F. Ross, J. D. Read, & M. P. Toglia (Eds.), *Adult eyewitness testimony: Current trends and developments* (pp. 362-384). New York: Cambridge University Press.

Lindsay, R. C., Lim, R., Marando, L., & Cully, D. (1986). Mock-juror evaluations of eyewitness testimony: A test of metamemory hypotheses. *Journal of Applied Social Psychology, 16,* 447-459.

Lindsay, R. C., Wells, G. L., & O'Connor, F. J. (1989). Mock-juror belief of accurate and inaccurate eyewitnesses: A replication and extension. *Law and Human Behavior, 13,* 333-339.

Linhorst, D. M., Hunsucker, L., & Parker, L. D. (1998). An examination of gender and racial differences among Missouri insanity acquittees. *Journal of the American Academy of Psychiatry and the Law, 26,* 411-424.

Linz, D. G., & Penrod, S. (1984). Increasing attorney persuasiveness in the courtroom. *Law and Psychology Review, 8,* 1-47.

Linz, D., Penrod, S., & McDonald, E. (1986). Attorney communication and impression making in the courtroom: Views from off the bench. *Law and Behavior, 10,* 281-302.

Lipscomb, T. J., McAllister, H. A., & Bregman, N. J. (1985). Bias in eyewitness accounts: The effects of question format, delay interval, and stimulus presentation. *Journal of Psychology, 119,* 207-212.

Lisko, K. O. (1993). Juror perceptions of witness credibility as a function of linguistic and nonverbal power. (Doctoral dissertation, University of

Kansas, 1992). *Dissertation Abstracts International, 54,* 371A.

Lizotte, A. J. (1978). Extra-legal factors in Chicago's criminal courts: Testing the conflict model of social justice. *Social Problems, 25,* 564-580.

Loftus, E. F. (1980). The impact of expert psychological testimony on the unreliability of eyewitness identification. *Journal of Applied Psychology, 65,* 9-15.

Loftus, E. F., & Palmer, J. P. (1974). Reconstruction of automobile destruction: An example of the interaction between language and memory. *Journal of Verbal Learning and Behavior, 13,* 585-589.

Loh, W. D. (1985). The evidence and trial procedure: The law, social policy, and psychological research. In S. M. Kassin & L. S. Wrightsman (Eds.), *The psychology of evidence in legal procedure* (pp. 13-39). Beverly Hills, CA: Sage.

Lopes, L. (1993). Two conceptions of the juror. In R. Hastie (Ed.), *Inside the juror: The psychology of juror decision making* (Cambridge Series on Judgment and Decision Making, pp. 255-262). New York, Cambridge University Press.

Ludwig, K., & Fontaine, G. (1978). Effect of witnesses' expertness and manner of delivery of testimony on verdicts on simulated jurors. *Psychological Reports, 42,* 955-961.

Luus, C. A. E., & Wells, G. L. (1994). The malleability of eyewitness confidence: Co-witness and perseverance effects. *Journal of Applied Psychology, 79,* 714-723.

Lymburner, J. A., & Roesch, R. (1999). The insanity defense: Five years of research (1993-1997). *International Journal of Law and Psychiatry, 22,* 213-240.

Lynch, M. P. (1997). Defendent/victim [sic] race, juror comprehension, and capital sentencing: An experimental approach. (Doctoral dissertation, University of California, Santa Cruz). *Dissertation Abstracts International, 58,* 3369B.

Lyons, A. W., & Regina, J. (1986). Mock jurors' behavior as a function of sex and exposure to an educational videotape about jury duty. *Psychological Reports, 58,* 599-604.

Maas, A., Brigham, J. C., & West, S. G. (1985). Testifying on eyewitness reliability: Expert advice is not always persuasive. *Journal of Applied Social Psychology, 15,* 207-229.

MacCoun, R. J. (1990). The emergence of extra-legal bias during jury deliberation. *Criminal Justice and Behavior, 17,* 303-314.

MacCoun, R. J. (1996). Differential treatment of corporate defendants by juries: An examination of the "deep pockets" hypothesis. *Law and Society Review, 30,* 121-161.

MacCoun, R. J., & Kerr, N. L. (1988). Asymmetric influence in model jury deliberation: Jurors' bias for leniency. *Journal of Personality and Social Psychology, 54,* 21-33.

Malouff, J., & Schutte, N. S. (1989). Shaping juror attitudes: Effects of requesting different damage amounts in personal injury trials. *Journal of Social Psychology, 129,* 491-497

Marcus, D. K., Lyons, P. M., Jr., & Guyton, M. R. (2000). Studying perceptions of juror influence in vivo: A social relations analysis. *Law and Human Behavior, 24,* 173-186.

Matlon, R. J. (1988). *Communication in the legal process.* New York: Holt, Rinehart & Winston.

Matlon, R. J., Davis, J. W., Catchings, B. W., Derr, W. R., & Waldron, V. R. (1985, November). *Factors affecting jury decision-making.* Paper presented at the meeting of the Speech Communication Association, Denver, CO.

Mauet, T. A. (1980). *Fundamentals of trial techniques.* Boston: Little, Brown.

McAllister, H. A., & Bregman, N. J. (1986). Juror underutilization of eyewitness nonidentifications: Theoretical and practical implications. *Journal of Applied Psychology, 71,* 168-170.

McAllister, H. A., & Bregman, N. J. (1989). Juror underutilization of eyewitness nonidentifications: A test of the disconfirmed expectancy explanation. *Journal of Applied Social Psychology, 19,* 20-29.

McCoy, M. L. (1998). Jurors' reasoning skills and verdict decisions: The effect of jury deliberations. (Doctoral dissertation, University of Wyoming, 1997). *Dissertation Abstracts International, 59,* 0436B.

McCullough, G. W. (1991). Juror decisions as a function of text format of opening statements and closing arguments. (Doctoral dissertation, University of Kansas). *Dissertation Abstracts International, 52,* 3768A.

McDermid, N. G. (1983). Jury selection and jury behavior [response]. In R. Matlon & R. Crawford (Eds.), *Communication strategies in the practice of lawyering* (pp. 278-285). Annandale, VA: Speech Communication Association.

McFatter, R. M. (1978). Sentencing strategies and justice: Effects of punishment philosophy on sentencing decisions. *Journal of Personality and Social Psychology, 36,* 1490-5000.

McGaffey, R. (1983). Communication strategies and research needs in selecting juries. In R. Matlon & R. Crawford (Eds.), *Communication strategies in the practice of lawyering* (pp. 250-273). Annandale, VA: Speech Communication Association.

McGinley, H., & Pasewark, R. A. (1989). National survey of the frequency and success of the insanity plea and alternate pleas. *Journal of Psychiatry and Law, 17,* 205-221.

McGowen, K. R. (1981). Systematic jury selection: What's the verdict? (Doctoral dissertation, Auburn University). *Dissertation Abstracts International, 42,* 2540B.

McGowen, R., & King, G. D. (1982). Effects of authoritarian, anti-authoritarian, and egalitarian legal attitudes on mock juror and jury decisions. *Psychological Reports, 51,* 1067-1074.

McGraw, S. L., & Foley, L. A. (2000). Perceptions of insanity based on occupation of defendant and seriousness of crime. *Psychological Reports, 86,* 163-174.

McMahon, E. A. (1974). A study of the relationship of psychiatric testimony and juror variables to the decision process. (Doctoral dissertation, University of Florida). *Dissertation Abstracts International, 35,* 3025B.

McNamara, K., Vattano, F., & Viney, W. (1993). Verdict, sentencing, and certainty as a function of sex of juror and amount of evidence in a simulated rape trial. *Psychological Reports, 72,* 575-583.

Mechanic, M. B. (1997). Battered woman syndrome: Juror common understanding and expert testimony. (Doctoral dissertation, University of Illinois at Urbana-Champaign, 1996). *Dissertation Abstracts International, 57,* 5335B.

Memon, A., & Shuman, D. W. (1998). Juror perception of experts in civil disputes: The role of race and gender. *Law and Psychology Review, 22,* 179-197.

Miller, G. R., & Fontes, N. (1978). *Reel versus real: Final report.* East Lansing, MI: Michigan State University, Department of Communication.

Miller, G. R., Fontes, N. E., Boster, F. J., & Sunnafrank, M. J. (1983). Methodological issues in legal communication research: What can trial simulations tell us? *Communication Monographs, 50,* 33-46.

Miller, M., & Hewitt, J. (1978). Conviction of a defendant as a function of juror-victim racial similarity. *Journal of Social Psychology, 105,* 159-160.

Miller, N., & Campbell, D. T. (1959). Recency and primacy in persuasion as a function of the time of speeches and measurements. *Journal of Abnormal and Social Psychology, 59,* 1-9.

Mills, G. E. (1976). Legal argumentation: Research and teaching. *Western Speech Communication, 40,* 83-90.

Mitchell, B. (1997). Diminished responsibility manslaughter. *Journal of Forensic Psychiatry, 8,* 101-117.

Mitchell, H. E., & Byrne, D. (1973). The defendant's dilemma: Effects of jurors' attitudes and authoritarianism on judicial decisions. *Journal of Personality and Social Psychology, 25,* 123-129.

Miyatake, R. K. (1999). White racial identity attitudes as predictors of preference and credibility of African-American, Asian-American, and White female and male psychologists. (Doctoral dissertation, University of Maine, 1998). *Dissertation Abstracts International, 59,* 6074B.

Monroe, T. L. (1994). The credibility of male versus female expert witnesses. (Doctoral dissertation, California School of Professional Psychology, Los Angeles, 1993). *Dissertation Abstracts International, 54,* 4968B.

Moore, P. J., & Gump, B. B. (1995). Information integration in juror decision making. *Journal of Applied Social Psychology, 25,* 2158-2179.

Moran, G., & Comfort, J. C. (1986). Neither "tentative" nor "fragmentary": Verdict preference of impaneled felony jurors as a function of attitude toward capital punishment. *Journal of Applied Psychology, 71,* 146-155.

Moran, G., Cutler, B. L., & Loftus, E. F. (1990). Jury selection in major controlled substance trials: The need for extended *voir dire*. *Forensic Reports, 3,* 331-348.

Morier, D., Borgida, E., & Park, R. C. (1996). Improving juror comprehension of judicial instructions on the entrapment defense. *Journal of Applied Social Psychology, 26,* 1838-1866.

Morris, A. V. (1993). Insanity defense: Gender differences. (Doctoral dissertation, University of Wyoming, 1992). *Dissertation Abstracts International, 54,* 504B.

Mosmann, A. L. (1998). Nothing but the truth: Mock jurors' use of stricken evidence in decision-making. (Doctoral dissertation, University of Michigan). *Dissertation Abstracts International, 59,* 893B.

Mullin, C. R. (1997). The impact of acquaintance rape scripts and case-specific pretrial publicity on juror decision-making. (Doctoral dissertation, University of California, Santa Barbara, 1996). *Dissertation Abstracts International, 57,* 3733.

Mullin, C., Imrich, D. J., & Linz, D. (1996). The impact of acquaintance rape stories and case-specific pretrial publicity on juror decision making. *Communication Research, 23,* 100-135.

Myers, M. A. (1979). Rule departures and making law: Juries and their verdicts. *Law and Society Review, 13,* 781-797.

Narby, D. J., & Cutler, B. L. (1994). Effectiveness of *voir dire* as a safeguard in eyewitness cases. *Journal of Applied Psychology, 79,* 724-729.

Narby, D. J., Cutler, B. L., & Moran, G. (1993). A meta-analysis of the association between authoritarianism and jurors' perceptions of defendant culpability. *Journal of Applied Psychology, 78,* 34-42

National Jury Project. (1986). *Jurywork: Systematic techniques* (2nd ed., E. Krauss & B. Bonora, Eds.). New York: Clark Boardman.

Nemeth, C., Endicott, J., & Wachtler, J. (1976). From the 50's to the 70's: Women in jury deliberations. *Sociometry, 39,* 293-304.

Nemeth, C., & Sosis, R. H. (1973). A simulated jury study: Characteristics of the defendant and the jurors. *Journal of Social Psychology, 90,* 221-229.

Nestor, P. G., & Haycock, J. (1997). Not guilty by reason of insanity of murder: Clinical and neuropsychological characteristics. *Journal of the American Academy of Psychiatry and the Law, 25,* 161-171.

Niedermeier, K. E., Horowitz, I. A., & Kerr, N. L. (1999). Informing jurors of their nullification power: A route to a just verdict or judicial chaos? *Law and Human Behavior, 23,* 331-351.

Nietzel, M. T., & Dillehay, R. C. (1982). The effects of variations in *voir dire* procedures in capital murder trials. *Law and Human Behavior, 6,* 1-13.

Nietzel, M. T., McCarthy, D. M., & Kern, M. J. (1999). Juries: The current state of the empirical literature. In R. Roesch & S. D. Hart (Eds.), *Psychology and law: The state of the discipline* (Perspectives in Law and Psychology, Vol. 10, pp. 23-52). New York: Kluwer Academic/Plenum.

Nightingale, N. N. (1993). Juror reactions to child victim witnesses: Factors affecting trial outcome. *Law and Human Behavior, 17,* 679-694.

Nunez, N., McCoy, M. L., Clark, H. L., & Shaw, L. A. (1999). The testimony of elderly victim/witnesses and their impact on juror decisions: The importance of examining multiple stereotypes. *Law and Human Behavior, 23,* 413-423.

Ogloff, J. R. P. (1993). Jury decision making and the insanity defense. In N. J. Castellan, Jr. (Ed.), *Individual and group decision making: Current issues* (pp. 167-201). Hillsdale, NJ: Lawrence Erlbaum.

Ogloff, J. R. P., & Vidmar, N. (1994). The impact of pretrial publicity on jurors: A study to compare the relative effects of television and print media in a child sex abuse case. *Law and Human Behavior, 5,* 507-525.

Olsen-Fulero, L., Fulero, S., & Wulff, K. (1989, August). *Who did what to whom? Modeling rape jurors' cognitive processes.* Paper presented at the meeting of the American Psychological Association, New Orleans, LA.

O'Mara, J. J. (1972). The courts, standard jury charges: Findings of a pilot project. *Pennsylvania Law Review, 120,* 166-175.

Osborne, Y. H., & Rappaport, N. B. (1985). Sentencing severity with mock jurors: Predictive validity of three variable categories. *Behavioral Sciences and the Law, 3,* 467-473.

Ostrom, T. M., Werner, C., & Saks, M. J. (1978). An integration theory analysis of jurors' presumptions of guilt or innocence. *Journal of Personality and Social Psychology, 36,* 436-450.

Otto, A. L., Penrod, S. D., & Dexter, H. R. (1994). The biasing impact of pretrial publicity on juror judgments. *Law and Human Behavior, 18,* 453-469.

Padawer-Singer, A. M., & Barton, A. H. (1975). The impact of pretrial publicity on jurors' verdicts. In R. J. Simon (Ed.), *The jury system in America: A critical overview* (pp. 123-139). Beverly Hills, CA: Sage.

Padawer-Singer, A. M., Singer, A., & Singer, R. (1974). *Voir dire* by two lawyers: An essential safeguard. *Judicature, 57,* 386-391.

Palmer, C. A., & Hazelrigg, M. (2000). The guilty but mentally ill verdict: A review and conceptual analysis of intent and impact. *Journal of the American Academy of Psychiatry and the Law, 28,* 47-54

Paris, D. A. (1985). The effect of type of crime, age of eyewitness, and juror informedness on mock jury decisional outcome. (Doctoral dissertation, University of Montana). *Dissertation Abstracts International, 46,* 967B.

Parkinson, M. G. (1981). Verbal behavior and courtroom success. *Communication Education, 30,* 22-32.

Pasewark, R. A., Jeffrey, R., & Bieber, S. (1987). Differentiating successful and unsuccessful insanity plea defendants in Colorado. *Journal of Psychiatry and Law, 15,* 55-71.

Pennington, N., & Hastie, R. (1986). Evidence evaluation in complex decision making. *Journal of Personality and Social Psychology, 51,* 242-258.

Pennington, N., & Hastie, R. (1990). Practical implications of psychological research on juror and jury decision making. *Personality and Social Psychology Bulletin, 16,* 90-105.

Pennington, N., & Hastie, R. (1992). Explaining the evidence: Tests of the story model for juror decision making. *Journal of Personality and Social Psychology, 62,* 189-206.

Pennington, N., & Hastie, R. (1993). Reasoning in explanation-based decision making. *Cognition, 49,* 123-163.

Penrod, S., & Cutler, B. (1995). Witness confidence and witness accuracy: Assessing their forensic relation. *Psychology, Public Policy, and Law, 1,* 817-845.

Penrod, S., & Hastie, R. (1979). Models of jury decision making: A critical review. *Psychological Bulletin, 86,* 462-492.

People v. Johnston, 641 N.E. 2d 898, 905, Ill. App. Ct. (1994).

Perrin, L. T. (1999). From O. J. to McVeigh: The use of argument in the opening statement. *Emory Law Journal, 48,* 107-167.

Perry, R. W. (1976). The effects of apparent guilt and prior attitudes on the verdicts of student juries. *European Journal of Social Psychology, 6,* 115-118.

Petersilia, J. (1983). *Racial disparities in the criminal justice system.* Santa Monica, CA: RAND.

Pettus, A. B. (1990). The verdict is in: A study of jury decision making factors, moment of personal decision, and jury deliberations—From the jurors' point of view. *Communication Quarterly, 38,* 83-97.

Pfeifer, J. E. (1988). Courtroom prejudice: An application of symbolic sexism. *Contemporary Social Psychology, 13,* 1-8.

Pfeifer, J. E., Brigham, J. C., & Robinson, T. (1996). Euthanasia on trial: Examining public attitudes toward non-physician-assisted death. *Journal of Social Issues, 52,* 119-129.

Pickel, K. L. (1995). Inducing jurors to disregard inadmissible evidence: A legal explanation does not help. *Law and Human Behavior, 19,* 407-424.

Pickel, K. L. (1998). The effects of motive information and crime unusualness on jurors' judgments in insanity cases. *Law and Human Behavior, 22,* 571-584.

Platania, J. (1996). Prosecutorial misconduct promotes wrongful death sentences. (Doctoral dissertation, Florida International University, 1995). *Dissertation Abstracts International, 56,* 5226B.

Poole, S., Lefebvre, D. J., Miller, G. R., & Fontes, N. (1975, April). *The effects of inadmissible testimony and order of presentation on juror informa-*

tion processing. Paper presented at the meeting of the International Communication Association, Chicago.

Pope, J., & Meyer, R. (1999). An attributional analysis of jurors' judgements in a criminal case: A preliminary investigation. *Social Behavior and Personality, 27*, 563-574.

Posey, A. J. (1996). Blame assignment in affirmative defense cases: Who has the burden of proof? (Doctoral dissertation, University of Kansas, 1995). *Dissertation Abstracts International, 56*, 7098B.

Poulson, R. L. (1990). Mock juror attribution of criminal responsibility: Effects of race and the guilty but mentally ill (GBMI) verdict option. *Journal of Applied Social Psychology, 20*, 1596-1611.

Poulson, R. L., Braithwaite, R. L., Brondino, M. J., & Wuensch, K. L. (1997). Mock jurors' insanity defense verdict selections: The role of evidence, attitudes, and verdict options. *Journal of Social Behavior and Personality, 12*, 743-758.

Poulson, R. L., Brondino, M. J., Brown, H., & Braithwaite, R. L. (1998). Relations among mock jurors' attitudes, trial evidence, and their selections of an insanity defense verdict: A path analytic approach. *Psychological Reports, 82*, 3-16.

Poulson, R. L., Wuensch, K. L., & Brondino, M. J. (1998). Factors that discriminate among mock jurors' verdict selections: Impact of the guilty but mentally ill verdict option. *Criminal Justice and Behavior, 25*, 366-381.

Poulson, R. L., Wuensch, K. L., Brown, M. B., & Braithwaite, R. L. (1997). Mock jurors' evaluations of insanity defense verdict selection: The role of death penalty attitudes. *Journal of Social Behavior and Personality, 12*, 1065-1078.

Prager, I. R. (1996). Age differences and conformity in juror decision-making. (Doctoral dissertation, Florida International University, 1995). *Dissertation Abstracts International, 56*, 7068B.

Pryor, B., & Buchanan, R. W. (1984). The effects of a defendant's demeanor on juror perceptions of credibility and guilt. *Journal of Communication, 34*(3), 92-99.

Pryor, B., Taylor, K. P., Buchanan, R. W., & Strawn, D. U. (1980). An affective-cognitive consistency explanation for comprehension of standard jury instructions. *Communication Monographs, 47*, 68-76.

Pugh, M. D. (1983). Contributory fault and rape convictions: Log-linear models for blaming the victim. *Social Psychology Quarterly, 46*, 233-242.

Pyszczynski, T. A., Greenberg, J., Mack, D., & Wrightsman, L. S. (1981). Opening statements in a jury trial: The effect of promising more than the evidence can show. *Journal of Applied Social Psychology, 11*, 434-444.

Pyszczynski, T. A., & Wrightsman, L. S. (1981). The effects of opening statements on mock jurors' verdicts in a simulated criminal trial. *Journal of Applied Social Psychology, 11*, 301-313.

Radelet, M. L. (1981). Racial characteristics and the imposition of the death penalty. *American Sociological Review, 46*, 918-927.

Rahaim, G. L., & Brodsky, S. L. (1982). Empirical evidence versus common sense: Juror and lawyer knowledge of eyewitness accuracy. *Law and Psychology Review, 7*, 1-11.

Raimo, A. M. (1987). Psychological challenges to eyewitness testimony. *American Journal of Forensic Psychology, 5*, 23-36.

Raitz, A., Greene, E., Goodman, J., & Loftus, E. F. (1990). Determining damages: The influence of expert testimony on jurors' decision making. *Law and Human Behavior, 14*, 385-395.

Ramirez, G., Zemba, D., & Geiselman, R. E. (1996). Judges' cautionary instructions on eyewitness testimony. *Journal of Forensic Psychology, 14*, 31-66.

Rector, N. A., Bagby, R. M., & Nicholson, R. (1993). The effect of prejudice and judicial ambiguity on defendant guilt ratings. *Journal of Social Psychology, 133*, 651-659.

Redding, R. E., Floyd, M. Y., & Hawk, G. L. (2001). What judges and lawyers think about the testimony of mental health experts: A survey of the courts and bar. *Behavioral Sciences and the Law, 19*, 583-594.

Reed, J. P. (1965). Jury deliberations, voting, and verdict trends. *Southwestern Social Science Quarterly, 45*, 361-370.

Reiman, J. (1995). *The rich get richer and the poor get prison: Ideology, crimes, and criminal justice.* Boston: Allyn & Bacon.

Reinard, J. C. (1981, February). *Effects of inadmissible evidence from law enforcement officers on jury decisions.* Paper presented at the meeting of the Western Speech Communication Association, San Jose, CA.

Reinard, J. C. (1985, February). *The effects of witness inadmissible testimony on jury decisions: A comparison of four sources.* Paper presented at the meeting of the Western Speech Communication Association, Fresno, CA.

Reinard, J. C. (1986a, February). *Effects of inadmissible testimony on jury verdicts: Phase three in a program of legal communication.* Paper presented at the meeting of the Western States Communication Association, Tucson, AZ.

Reinard, J. C. (1986b, February). *Nonverbal communication research in legal settings: Considerations of limits and effects.* Paper presented at the meeting of the Western States Communication Association, Tucson, AZ.

Reinard, J. C. (1989, February). *Explaining inadmissible testimony effects on jurors: Crucial experimental tests of a model of the influence of inadmissible material.* Paper presented at the meeting of the Western Speech Communication Association, Spokane, WA.

Reinard, J. C. (1993, February). *A model of the effects of inadmissible testimony on civil case decisions.* Paper presented at the meeting of the Western States Communication Association, Albuquerque, NM.

Reinard, J. C., Arsenault, D. J. (2000). The impact of forms of strategic and non-strategic *voir dire* questions on jury verdicts. *Communication Monographs, 67,* 159-177.

Reinard, J. C., Arsenault, D. J., & Geck, S. (1998, February). *Models of the influence of strategic* voir dire *questions on jury decision making.* Paper presented at the meeting of the Western States Communication Association, Denver, CO.

Reinard, J. C., Khalid, O., & Liso, J. (2001, February). *Persuading the jury through* voir dire *questioning designed to establish rapport and empathy.* Paper presented at the meeting of the Western States Communication Association, Coeur d'Alene, ID.

Reinard, J. C., & Reynolds, R. A. (1978). The effects of inadmissible testimony objections and rulings on jury decisions. *Journal of the American Forensic Association, 15,* 91-109.

Reince, D. A. (1991). The effects of expert witness testimony on decisions of a mock judicial panel: Expert's credentials, delivery style, and authoritarianism of the juror. (Doctoral dissertation, University of South Carolina). *Dissertation Abstracts International, 52,* 2311B.

Reskin, B. F., & Visher, C. A. (1986). The impacts of evidence and extralegal factors in jurors' decisions. *Law and Society Review, 20,* 423-438.

Reynolds, D., & Sanders, M. (1975). Effects of defendant attractiveness, age, and injury on severity of sentence given by simulated jurors. *Journal of Social Psychology, 92,* 149-150.

Reynolds, R. A. (1977, November). *The impact of defendant race, defendant characteristics, and inadmissible testimony upon results of a simulated jury trial.* Paper presented as the meeting of the Western Speech Communication Association, Phoenix, AZ.

Rickman, L. E. (1989). Juror and defendant characteristics, "crime-stereotype," and jurors' guilty verdicts. (Doctoral dissertation, Howard University, 1988). *Dissertation Abstracts International, 50,* 2672B.

Rickun, R. (1977). *Credibility in the courtroom.* Master's thesis, University of Wisconsin–Milwaukee.

Riedel, R. G. (1993). Effects of pretrial publicity on male and female jurors and judges in a mock rape trial case. *Psychological Reports, 73,* 819-832.

Rieke, R. D., & Sillars, M. O. (1997). *Argumentation and critical decision making* (4th ed.). New York: Longman.

Rieke, R. D., & Stutman, R. K. (1990). *Communication in legal advocacy.* Columbia: University of South Carolina Press.

Riley, S. G. (1973). Pretrial publicity: A field study. *Journalism Quarterly, 50,* 17-23.

Roberts, C. F., & Golding, S. L. (1991). The social construction of criminal responsibility and insanity. *Law and Human Behavior, 15,* 349-376.

Roberts, C. F., Sargent, E. L., & Chan, A. S. (1993). Verdict selection processes in insanity cases: Juror construals and the effects of guilty but mentally ill instructions. *Law and Human Behavior, 17,* 261-275.

Rockwell, P., & Hubbard, A. E. (1999). The effect of attorney's nonverbal communication on perceived credibility. *Journal of Credibility Assessment and Witness Psychology, 2,* 1-13.

Rose, A., & Prell, A. (1955). Does the punishment fit the crime? A study in social valuation. *American Journal of Sociology, 61,* 247-251.

Rosen, A. P. (1997). Factors affecting juror decision-making in repressed-memory cases. (Doctoral dissertation, Allegheny University of Health Science, 1996). *Dissertation Abstracts International, 58,* 0447B.

Rosoff, S. M. (1987). Physicians as criminal defendants: Specialty, status, and sanctions. (Doctoral dissertation, University of California, Irvine). *Dissertation Abstracts International, 48,* 2166B.

Rotzien, A. L. (1998). A mock jury study of expert witness testimony in an adult survivor of sexual abuse case. (Doctoral dissertation, Texas A&M University, 1997). *Dissertation Abstracts International, 58,* 3969B.

Rowland, J. A. (1991). Locus-of-control and juror attributions of comparative negligence. (Doctoral dissertation, University of Kansas). *Dissertation Abstracts International, 52,* 4147A.

Rumsey, M. G., & Rumsey, J. M. (1977). A case of rape: Sentence judgments of males and females. *Psychological Reports, 41,* 459-465.

Russell, G. D. (1991). Support for the death penalty, death certification, and systematic bias: A test of Supreme Court assumptions. (Doctoral dissertation, University of Georgia). *Dissertation Abstracts International, 52,* 4460A.

Russo, M. J. (1992). The effects of emotionally charged evidence on juror verdicts: Photographic evidence. (Doctoral dissertation, Ohio State University). *Dissertation Abstracts International, 53,* 3211B.

Saks, M. J., & Wissler, R. L. (1984). Legal and psychological bases of expert testimony: Surveys of the law and of jurors. *Behavioral Sciences and the Law, 2,* 435-449

Salmons, S. D. (1996). A new approach to *voir dire:* Selecting jurors based upon boredom proneness rather than demographics. (Doctoral dissertation, DePaul University, 1995). *Dissertation Abstracts International, 56,* 4644B.

Sanford, S. (1987). The nature of discourse in the courtroom: The complete rape trial. (Doctoral dissertation, Indiana University). *Dissertation Abstracts International, 48,* 2460A.

Schaffer, S. J. (1985). Can jurors disregard inadmissible evidence? (Doctoral dissertation, American University, 1984). *Dissertation Abstracts International, 45,* 1595B.

Scherer, K. R. (1979). Voice and speech correlates of perceived social influence in simulated juries. In H. Giles & R. N. St. Claire (Eds.), *Language and social psychology* (pp. 88-120). Oxford, UK: Basil Blackwell.

Schklar, J., & Diamond, S. S. (1999). Juror reactions to DNA evidence: Errors and expectancies. *Law and Human Behavior, 23,* 159-184.

Schmolesky, J. M., Cutler, B. L., & Penrod, S. D. (1988). Presumption instructions and juror decision making. *Forensic Reports, 1,* 165-192.

Schuller, R. A., & Cripps, J. (1998). Expert evidence pertaining to battered women: The impact of gender of expert and timing of testimony. *Law and Human Behavior, 22,* 17-31.

Schuller, R. A., & Hastings, P. A. (1996). Trials of battered women who kill: The impact of alternative forms of expert evidence. *Law and Human Behavior, 20,* 167-187.

Schuller, R. A., & Paglia, A. (1999). An empirical study: Juror sensitivity to variations in hearsay conveyed via expert evidence. *Law and Psychology Review, 23,* 131-152.

Schutte, J. W. (1994). Repressed memory lawsuits: Potential verdict predictors. *Behavioral Sciences and the Law, 12,* 409-416.

Scroggs, J. R. (1976). Penalties for rape as a function of victim provocativeness, damage, and resistance. *Journal of Applied Social Psychology, 6,* 335-346.

Seguin, D. G., & Horowitz, I. A. (1984). The effects of "death *qualification*" on juror and jury decision making: An analysis from three perspectives. *Law and Psychology Review, 8,* 49-81.

Seligman, C., Brickman, J., & Koulack, D. (1977). Rape and physical attractiveness: Assigning responsibility to victims. *Journal of Personality, 45,* 554-563.

Seymour, H. L. (1986). Perceived control, crime severity and the not guilty by reason of insanity verdict. (Doctoral dissertation, Purdue University). *Dissertation Abstracts International, 47,* 2633B-2634B.

Shaffer, D. R., & Case, T. (1982). On the decision to testify in one's own behalf: The effects of withheld evidence, defendant's sexual preferences, and juror dogmatism on juridic decisions. *Journal of Personality and Social Psychology, 42,* 335-346.

Shaffer, D. R., Case, T., & Brannen, L. (1979). Effects of withheld evidence on juridic decisions: Amount of evidence withheld and its relevance to the case. *Representative Research in Social Psychology, 10,* 2-15.

Shaffer, D. R., Plummer, D., & Hammock, G. (1986). Hath he suffered enough? Effects of jury dogmatism, defendant similarity, and defendant's pretrial suffering on juridic decisions. *Journal of Personality and Social Psychology, 50,* 1059-1067.

Shay, S. (1988). Effects of defendant character and juror authoritarianism on the decision making process. (Doctoral dissertation, Temple University, 1987). *Dissertation Abstracts International, 49,* 259B.

Shepherd, D. H., & Sloan, L. R. (1979). Similarity of legal attitudes, defendant social class, and crime intentionality as determinants of legal decisions. *Personality and Social Psychology Bulletin, 5,* 245-248.

Siebert, F., Wilcox, W., & Hough, G., III (C. R. Bush, Ed.). (1970). *Free press and fair trial: Some dimensions of the problem.* Athens: University of Georgia Press.

Sigall, H., & Landy, D. (1972). Effects of the defendant's character and suffering on juridic judgment: A replication and clarification. *Journal of Social Psychology, 88,* 149-150.

Sigall, H., & Ostrove, N. (1975). Beautiful but dangerous: Effects of offender attractiveness and nature of the crime on juridic judgment. *Journal of Personality and Social Psychology, 31,* 410-414.

Simon, R. J. (1967). *The jury in the defense of insanity.* Boston: Little, Brown.

Simon, R. J. (1983). Responses to jury selection and jury behavior program. In R. Matlon & R. Crawford (Eds.), *Communication strategies in the practice of lawyering* (pp. 286-289). Annandale, VA: Speech Communication Association.

Skeem, J. L. (1999). Understanding juror decision making and bias in insanity defense cases: The role of lay conceptions and case-relevant attitudes. (Doctoral dissertation, University of Utah). *Dissertation Abstracts International, 60,* 5240B.

Slutsky, G. N. (1977). Jurors' evaluation and utilization of expert psychiatric testimony. (Doctoral dissertation, University of Florida, 1975). *Dissertation Abstracts International, 37,* 3633B.

Smith, H. D., Stasson, M. F., & Hawkes, W. G. (1998-1999). Dilution in legal decision making: Effect of non-diagnostic information in relation to amount of diagnostic evidence. *Current Psychology, 17,* 333-345.

Smith, M. (1995). Evaluation of the effects of Proposition 115 on *voir dire* practices in the criminal justice system. (Master's thesis, California State University, Fullerton, 1994). *Masters Abstracts International, 33,* 769.

Smith, R. E., Keating, J. P., Hester, R. K., & Mitchell, H. E. (1976). Role and justice considerations in the attribution of responsibility to a rape victim. *Journal of Research in Personality, 10,* 346-357.

Snyder, E. C. (1971). Sex role differential and juror decisions. *Sociology and Asocial Research, 55,* 442-448.

Solomon, M. R., & Schopler, J. (1978). The relationship of physical attractiveness and punitiveness: Is the linearity assumption out of line? *Personality and Social Psychology Bulletin, 4,* 483-486.

Sommers, S. R., & Ellsworth, P. C. (2000). Race in the courtroom: Perceptions of guilt and dispositional attributions. *Personality and Social Psychology Bulletin, 26,* 1367-1379.

Sommers, S. R., & Kassin, S. M. (2001). On the many impacts of inadmissible testimony: Selective compliance, need for cognition, and the overcorrection bias. *Personality and Social Psychology Bulletin, 27,* 1368-1377.

Sonaike, S. A. (1977). The impact of deliberation on juror perceptions of trial participants' credibility and of verdicts and awards in simulated trial situations. (Doctoral dissertation, Michigan State University). *Dissertation Abstracts International, 38,* 1473B-1474B.

Sosis, R. H. (1974). Internal-external control and the perception of responsibility of another for an accident. *Journal of Personality and Social Psychology, 30,* 393-399.

Spanos, N. P., Dubreuil, S. C., & Gwynn, M. I. (1991-1992). The effects of expert testimony concerning rape on the verdicts and beliefs of mock jurors. *Imagination, Cognition, and Personality, 11,* 37-51.

Spiecker, S. C. (1999). The influence of opening statement/closing argument organizational strategy on juror reasoning and decision-making. (Doctoral dissertation, University of Kansas, 1998). *Dissertation Abstracts International, 59,* 1399A.

Sporer, S., Penrod, S., Read, D., & Cutler, B. L. (1995). Choosing, confidence, and accuracy: A meta-analysis of the confidence-accuracy relation in eyewitness identification studies. *Psychological Bulletin, 118,* 315-327.

Starr, V. H. (1979). *The effective use of nonverbal communication in jury selection* [audiocassette]. Washington, DC: Association of Trial Lawyers of America.

State v. Bell, 268 So. 2d 610, 615, La. (1972).

State v. Jenkins, 445 S.E. 2d 622, 625, N.C. Ct. App. (1994).

Steadman, J. J., Keitner, L. Braff, J., & Arvanites, T. M. (1983). Factors associated with a successful insanity plea. *American Journal of Psychiatry, 140,* 401-405.

Steblay, N. M., Besirevic, J., Fulero, S. M., & Jimenez-Lorente, B. (1999). The effects of pretrial publicity on juror verdicts: A meta-analytic review. *Law and Human Behavior, 23,* 219-235.

Steffensmeier, D. J. (1977). The effects of judge's and defendant's sex on the sentencing of offenders. *Psychology, 14,* 3-9.

Stephan, C. W. (1974). Sex prejudice in jury simulation. *Journal of Psychology, 88,* 305-312.

Stephan, C. W., & Stephan, W. G. (1986). *Habla Ingles?* The effects of language translation on simulated juror decisions. *Journal of Applied Social Psychology, 16,* 577-589.

Stephen, C., & Tully, J. C. (1977). The influence of physical attractiveness of a plaintiff on the decisions of simulated jurors. *Journal of Social Psychology, 101,* 149-150.

Stone, V. E. (1969). A primacy effect in decision-making by jurors. *Journal of Communication, 19*(3), 239-247.

Strong, J. W. (Ed.). (1992). *McCormick on evidence* (4th ed.). New York: John Wiley.

Stutman, R. K. (1986a, February). *Testimony control and witness narration during courtroom examination.* Paper presented at the meeting of the Western Speech Communication Association, Tucson, AZ.

Stutman, R. K. (1986b). Witness disclaiming during examination. *Journal of the American Forensic Association, 23,* 96-101.

Sue, S., Smith, R., & Caldwell, C. (1973). Effects of inadmissible evidence on the decisions of simulated jurors: A moral dilemma. *Journal of Applied Social Psychology, 3,* 345-353.

Sue, S., Smith, R., & Gilbert, R. (1974). Biasing effects of pretrial publicity on judicial decisions. *Journal of Criminal Justice, 2,* 163-171.

Sue, S., Smith, R. E., & Pedroza, G. (1975). Authoritarianism, pretrial publicity, and awareness of bias in simulated jurors. *Psychological Reports, 37,* 1299-1302.

Suggs, D., & Berman, J. J. (1979). Factors affecting testimony about mitigating circumstances and the fixing of punishment. *Law and Human Behavior, 3,* 251-260.

Sutton, G. (1979, November). *Effects of inadmissible evidence on jury deliberations.* Paper presented at the meeting of the Speech Communication Association, San Antonio, TX.

Takakawa, N. N. (1999). A study of jurors' attitudes toward testimony in Hawai'i Creole English. (Master's thesis, University of Hawaii). *Masters Abstracts International, 37,* 1612.

Tanford, S. (1985). Decision-making processes in joined criminal trials. *Criminal Justice and Behavior, 12,* 367-385.

Tanford, S., & Penrod, S. (1984). Social inference processes in juror judgments of multiple-offense trials. *Journal of Personality and Social Psychology, 47,* 749-765.

Tankard, J. W., Middleton, K., & Rimmer, T. (1979). Compliance with American Bar Association fair trial-free press guidelines. *Journalism Quarterly, 56,* 464-468.

Tans, M. D., & Chaffee, S. H. (1966). Pretrial publicity and juror prejudice. *Journalism Quarterly, 43,* 647-654.

Tarrence, J. R. P. (1992). Juror decision making and attributions of criminal responsibility. (Doctoral dissertation, University of Louisville, 1991). *Dissertation Abstracts International, 53,* 1111B.

Taylor, E. S. (1993). The physical attributes of male attorneys and their effect of the outcome of the jury (jury verdicts). (Doctoral dissertation, California School of Professional Psychology, Los Angeles). *Dissertation Abstracts International, 54,* 4968B.

Terrance, C. A., Matheson, K., & Spanos, N. P. (2000). Effects of judicial instructions and case characteristics in a mock jury trial of battered women who kill. *Law and Human Behavior, 24,* 207-229.

Tezza, C. (1996). Predicting verdicts in cases of insanity. (Doctoral dissertation, University of South Carolina, 1995). *Dissertation Abstracts International, 56,* 4595B.

Thomas, E. A., & Hogue, A. (1976). Apparent weight of evidence, decision criteria, and confidence ratings in juror decision making. *Psychological Review, 83,* 442-465.

Thompson, W., Fong, G., & Rosenhan, D. (1981). Inadmissible evidence and juror verdicts. *Journal of Personality and Social Psychology, 40,* 453-463.

Thompson, W. C., & Schumann, E. L. (1987). Interpretation of statistical evidence in criminal trials. *Law and Human Behavior, 11,* 167-187.

Tieger, T. (1981). Self-rated likelihood of raping and the social perception of rape. *Journal of Research in Personality, 15,* 147-158.

Tinsley, K. M. (1992). Influence of race of juror on jury decision-making. (Doctoral dissertation, University of Virginia, 1991). *Dissertation Abstracts International, 53,* 3213B.

Towell, N. A., Kemp, R. I., & Pike, G. E. (1996). The effects of witness identity masking on memory and person perception. *Psychology, Crime, and Law, 2,* 333-346.

Towers, T. M. (1997). Gender and the not guilty by reason of insanity plea. (Doctoral dissertation, University of Wyoming, 1996). *Dissertation Abstracts International, 58,* 430B.

Towers, T., McGinley, H., & Pasewark, R. A. (1992). Insanity defense: Ethnicity of defendants and mock jurors. *Journal of Psychiatry and Law, 20,* 243-256.

Townsend, T. N. (1996). Is justice color blind? The effect of race on perceptions of crime severity. (Doctoral dissertation, Temple University). *Dissertation Abstracts International, 57,* 4095B.

Truitt, L. (1997). Analysis of racial disparity in felony criminal court sentencing. (Doctoral dissertation, University of California, Irvine). *Dissertation Abstracts International, 58,* 2400A.

Turner, B. M., Lovell, R. D., Young, J. C., & Denny, W. F. (1986). Race and peremptory challenges during coir dire: Do prosecution and defense agree? *Journal of Criminal Justice, 14,* 61-69.

Ugwuegbu, D. C. (1976). Black jurors' personality trait attribution to a rape case defendant. *Social Behavior and Personality, 4,* 193-201.

Vaughan, B. L. (1986a). *Courtroom psychology and jury selection.* Sacramento, CA: Interstate College of Personology.

Vaughan, B. L. (1986b, February). *Jury selection and nonverbal cues.* Paper presented at the meeting of the Western States Communication Association, Tucson, AZ.

Villemur, N. K., & Hyde, J. S. (1983). Effects of sex of defense attorney, sex of juror, and age and attractiveness of the victim on mock juror decision making in a rape case. *Sex Roles, 9,* 879-889.

Visher, C. A. (1987). Juror decision making: The importance of evidence. *Law and Human Behavior, 11,* 1-17.

Waddell, J. R. M. (1989). An analysis of rhetorical and psychological strategies in a trial format. (Specialist in Education thesis, University of Northern Colorado, 1988). *Masters Abstracts International, 28,* 344.

Walker, L., Thibaut, J., & Andreoli, V. (1972). Order of presentation at trial. *Yale Law Journal, 82,* 219-233.

Wall, A. M., & Schuller, R. A. (2000). Sexual assault and defendant/victim intoxication: Juror perceptions of guilt. *Journal of Applied Social Psychology, 30,* 253-274.

Wallace, W., & Wilson, W. (1969). Reliable recency effects. *Psychological Reports, 25,* 311-317.

Walter-Goldberg, B. (1985). The jury summation as speech genre: An ethnographic study of what it means to those who use it (language/lawyer). (Doctoral dissertation, University of Pennsylvania). *Dissertation Abstracts International, 46,* 3710A.

Warner, T. D. (1988). The effects of judge's instructions and expert testimony on jurors' reactions to an eyewitness. (Doctoral dissertation, University of Kansas, 1987). *Dissertation Abstracts International, 49,* 1997B.

Weinstock, M. P. (1999). Epistemological understanding and argumentative competence as foundations of juror reasoning skill. (Doctoral dissertation, Columbia University). *Dissertation Abstracts International, 60,* 393B.

Weir, J. A., & Wrightsman, L. S. (1990). The determinants of mock jurors' verdicts in a rape case. *Journal of Applied Social Psychology, 20,* 901-919.

Weld, H. P., & Danzig, E. R. (1940). A study of the way in which a verdict is reached by a jury. *American Journal of Psychology, 53,* 518-536.

Wells, G. L. (1992). Naked statistical evidence of liability: Is subjective probability enough? *Journal of Personality and Social Psychology, 62,* 739-752.

Wells, G. L., & Leippe, M. R. (1981). How do triers of fact infer the accuracy of eyewitness identifications? Memory for peripheral detail can be misleading. *Journal of Applied Psychology, 66,* 682-687.

Wells, G. L., Lindsay, R. C., & Ferguson, T. J. (1979). Accuracy, confidence, and juror perceptions in eyewitness identification. *Journal of Applied Psychology, 64,* 440-448.

Wells, G. L., Lindsay, R. C., & Tousignant, J. P. (1980). Effects of expert psychological advice on human performance in judging the validity of eyewitness testimony. *Law and Human Behavior, 4,* 275-285.

Wells, G. L., Wrightsman, L. S., & Miene, P. K. (1985). The timing of the defense opening statement: Don't wait until the evidence is in. *Journal of Applied Social Psychology, 15,* 758-772.

Werner, C. M., Strube, M. J., Cole, A. M., & Kagehiro, D. K. (1985). The impact of case characteristics and prior jury experience on jury verdicts. *Journal of Applied Social Psychology, 15,* 409-427.

Wheeler, G. R., & Wheeler, C. L. (1980). Reflection on legal representation of the economically disadvantaged: Beyond assembly line justice—

Type of counsel, pretrial detention, and outcomes in Houston. *Crime & Delinquency, 26,* 319-332.

White, L. T. (1987). Juror decision making in the capital penalty trial: An analysis of crimes and defense strategies. *Law and Human Behavior, 11,* 113-130.

Whitley, B. E., Jr. (1987). The effects of discredited eyewitness testimony: A meta-analysis. *Journal of Social Psychology, 127,* 209-214.

Whitley, B. E., & Greenberg, M. S. (1986). The role of eyewitness confidence in juror perceptions of credibility. *Journal of Applied Social Psychology, 16,* 387-409.

Whittemore, K. E., & Ogloff, J. R. P. (1995). Factors that influence jury decision making: Disposition instructions and mental state at the time of the trial. *Law and Human Behavior, 19,* 283-303.

Wigley, C. J., III. (1987). Communication variables as predictors of decisions in the *voir dire* process. (Doctoral dissertation, Kent State University, 1986). *Dissertation Abstracts International, 48,* 514A.

Wigley, C. J., III. (1995). Disclosiveness, willingness to communicate, and communication apprehension as predictors of jury selection in felony trials. *Communication Quarterly, 43,* 342-352.

Wigley, C. J., III. (1999). Verbal aggressiveness and communicator style characteristics of summoned jurors as predictors of jury actual selection. *Communication Monographs, 66,* 266-275.

Wilbanks, W. (1985). *Does type of counsel make a difference?* Unpublished manuscript, Florida International University.

Wilbanks, W. (1987). *The myth of a racist criminal justice system.* Pacific Grove, CA: Brooks/Cole.

Wilson, W., & Miller, H. (1968). Repetition, order of presentation, and timing of arguments and measures as determinants of opinion change. *Journal of Personality and Social Psychology, 9,* 185-194.

Windham, D. L. (1992). The insanity defense in Knox County, Tennessee, 1978-1984: A case study. (Doctoral dissertation, University of Tennessee, 1990). *Dissertation Abstracts International, 53,* 1620B.

Winslade, W. J., & Ross, J. W. (1983). *The insanity plea.* New York: Scribner.

Wolf, S., & Montgomery, D. A. (1977). Effects of inadmissible evidence and level of judicial admonishment to disregard on the judgments of mock jurors. *Journal of Applied Social Psychology, 7,* 205-219.

Wright, J. W., & Hosman, L. A. (1980). Communication and trial advocacy: A review and critique of the literature. In *Proceedings of the Florida Institute for the Study of the Trial* (pp. 30-43). Orlando: Florida Institute for the Study of the Trial.

Wright, J. W., II, & Hosman, L. A. (1983). Language style and sex bias in the courtroom: The effects of male and female use of hedges and intensifiers on impression formation. *Southern Speech Communication Journal, 48,* 137-152.

Wright, J. W., II, & Ross, S. D. (1997). Trial by media? Media reliance, knowledge of crime, and perception of criminal defendants. *Communication Law and Policy, 2,* 397-416.

Wuensch, K. L., Chia, R. C., Castellow, W. A., Chuang, C. J., & Cheng, B. S. (1993). Effects of physical attractiveness, sex, and type of crime on mock juror decisions: A replication with Chinese students. *Journal of Cross-Cultural Psychology, 24,* 414-427.

Wursten, A. (1987). The psychologist and psychiatrist in court: Perceived expertness and influence. (Doctoral dissertation, University of Arizona, 1986). *Dissertation Abstracts International, 47,* 4319B.

Wyatt, R. L. (1983). The effects of the defendant's characteristics, authoritarianism, and group discussion on simulated juror's [sic] decisions. (Doctoral dissertation, Ohio University, 1982). *Dissertation Abstracts International, 43,* 2748B.

Wyman, R. G. (1985). Dogmatism as an important consideration in the conduct of *voir dire.* (Doctoral dissertation, U.S. International University, 1984). *Dissertation Abstracts International, 46,* 0320B.

Yanchar, N. V. (1983). Subject-juror decision-making in rape cases: Effects of status of the complainant and gender of the defense attorney, the prosecuting attorney, and the subject-juror. (Doctoral dissertation, Bowling Green State University, 1982). *Dissertation Abstracts International, 43,* 2364B.

Yandell, B. (1979). Those who protest too much are seen as guilty. *Personality and Social Psychology Bulletin, 5,* 44-47.

Zdep, S., & Wilson, W. (1968). Recency effects in opinion formation. *Psychological Reports, 23,* 199-204.

Zeiglar, D. H. (1978). Young adults as a recognizable group in jury selection. *Michigan Law Review, 76,* 1045-1110.

Zeisel, H. (1988, Summer). A jury hoax: The superpower of the opening statement. *The Litigator,* pp. 17-18.

Zickafoose, D. J., & Bornstein, B. H. (1999). Double discounting: The effects of comparative negligence on mock juror decision making. *Law and Human Behavior, 23,* 577-596.

PART VI

PERSUASION CAMPAIGNS

28

Political Campaign Persuasion and Its Discontents

Perspectives From the Past and
Research Prescriptions for the Future

RICHARD M. PERLOFF

Political philosophers hold widely divergent views about the role that persuasion should play in a democratic society. Some theorists favor "no-holds-barred" persuasive debates, believing that uninhibited public discussion is the best mechanism for ferreting out truth and the most effective way to generate innovative policy (Holmes, 1995; Mill, 1859/1951). Other scholars, observing that angry political discourse is destroying the civic fabric of the nation (Tannen, 1998), urge that persuasive communicators help Americans to recover their "civic voice" (Sandel, 1996, p. 324) by creating messages that build communities and affirm civic obligations (Etzioni, 1998). Still other philosophers yearn for a more deliberative democracy in which political persuasion engages the public in morally constructive policy debates (Gutmann & Thompson, 1996). But for all their differences, scholars who prescribe and researchers who describe have no difficulty in agreeing that persuasion plays a pivotal role in democratic politics.

Could anyone with just the briefest exposure to contemporary events doubt that this is true? What, if not persuasion, was involved in former President Bill Clinton's attempt to convince members of the public that he deserved their trust after acknowledging he lied about his sexual relationship with Monica Lewinksy? What, if not persuasion, was at issue when liberals sought to frame the debate around privacy (Lewis, 1998; Patterson, 1998) and conservatives emphasized the president's reprehensible moral conduct (Bennett, 1998; Hedges, 1998)? What better word than *persuasion* to describe the first post-presidential election marketing campaign in the nation's history, waged for 36 days in 2000 by Al Gore and George W. Bush in the state of Florida? And, of course, what term other than *persuasion* could possibly describe the ardent efforts of the Bush administration to secure domestic and world support for the U.S. war on terrorism (Becker, 2001)?

These events are only the most recent examples of how persuasion plays out in politics. In a nation, America, that has historically prized persuasion over coercion (Paisley, 1981), there is no end to the list of persuaders who have plied their oratorial skills to shape public sentiments. From the eloquent persuasion of the Revolutionary Generation (Wood, 1992) to Andrew Jackson (whose talents were commemorated in a book aptly called *The Jacksonian Persuasion* (Meyers, 1957), to Abraham Lincoln (who pointed explicitly to the role public opinion plays in policy making), to Franklin D. Roosevelt, to Lyndon Johnson, to Ronald Reagan, there is no question that national leaders with a talent for persuasive communication have moved political mountains. So too have countless activists and reformers working at the grassroots level. Unfortunately, persuasive communication has been used effectively by those with more nefarious motives, including well-heeled special interest groups that donate millions to presidential campaigns and the many charismatic, but hate-mongering, political persuaders who have captivated vulnerable followings throughout American history.

If we want to understand political campaign persuasion, we must appreciate that it is a two-headed beast that is part politics and part persuasion. That means one cannot understand the area by blandly applying social psychological theories to political contexts, operating on the assumption that politics is no different from the dozens of other situations in which persuasion occurs. As scholars have observed (e.g., Mutz, Sniderman, & Brody, 1996; Newman, 1994), persuasion in political campaigns differs markedly from persuasion in other arenas. Politics involves a set of philosophical assumptions about the relationship between citizens and leaders, assumptions that

theoretically transform individuals from message recipients to participants in a democratic deliberation about policies and people. Politics also calls on storied—and sometimes tainted—images of the United States of America that people (and candidates) carry around in their heads and that influence public and elite persuasive discourse. These historical memories (or reconstructed memories) exert a more profound impact in the political context than in other arenas in which persuasion occurs (e.g., commercial advertising). Thus, symbols that elicit hate and love and are integrally connected with the self play a more important role in political persuasion than in most other arenas (e.g., Sears, Van Laar, Carrillo, & Kosterman, 1997).

Political persuasion also involves the interposition of institutions between people and persuaders. Elected representatives and an alarming number of interest groups shape persuasive communications through polls and other technologies, powerfully mediating message impact. Not only are there complex relationships among elites, media, and citizens, but campaign effects manifest themselves on the macrosocial level as well, exemplified by the profound impact that media-instigated changes in the presidential nomination system have had on electoral politics.

At the same time, it is important to recognize the role that micro-level attempts at changing attitudes play in politics (Mutz et al., 1996). On the elite level, leaders try to change the beliefs and priorities of their colleagues in government, and at the mass level, political leaders employ a host of media-oriented strategies to mold public opinion. Perceptions of campaign persuasion and individual-level effects of persuasive messages play a critical role in politics and bridge the micro- and macrosocial levels of analysis (McLeod, Kosicki, & McLeod, 1994).

In keeping with the orientation of this handbook, I discuss individual-level influences of campaign persuasion while recognizing that such impacts occur in a larger political and cultural context (Swanson & Mancini, 1996). This chapter focuses on American presidential campaigns, necessarily mirroring the state of the field. A comprehensive approach to campaign persuasion requires that we understand historical changes and continuities; thus, the first section of this chapter reviews the political psychology of presidential campaigns over the past two centuries. In addition, because campaigns are rooted in a set of normative assumptions, I call on political philosophy throughout the chapter to shed light on campaign contexts and also to suggest directions for future research.

HISTORICAL FOUNDATIONS

After the persuasive communication that launched the American Revolution (Wood, 1992) and played an instrumental role in deliberations over the Constitution (Schudson, 1997) had become the stuff of myth, persuasion became inextricably intertwined with political campaigns in ways that have both benefited and hurt the republic. In post-Revolutionary America, educated White male elites dominated politics. Influenced by republican ideals that emphasized public virtue and the subordination of individual interests to the common good, the idealistic activists of the Revolutionary Generation believed that campaigns were unnecessary (Morone, 1990; Troy, 1996). In the republican view, candidates need not do anything special to get elected; "they simply had to allow those who knew them to recognize their virtue" (Troy, 1996, p. 8). During the elite era, presidential candidates did not campaign; indeed, they did little in public to suggest they harbored an interest in holding office.

Yet campaigns were hardly docile. Thomas Jefferson and Alexander Hamilton organized competing newspapers, and their supporters engaged in no-holds-barred persuasive argumentation to promote the Republican and Federalist causes. Not content to rely exclusively on ideology, partisans of both sides resorted to personal attacks. In 1800, Republican editors smeared John Adams, charging that he was a monarchist, an egotist, and a traitor (Troy, 1996, p. 13). Federalist supporters called Jefferson an atheist and a swindler and accused him of raping a slave (the now-famous Sally Hemings). The discourse of the era was coarse and uncivil; some of it would make mincemeat of today's partisan slurs. And yet there was a silver lining in this cloud of partisan warfare, for it led inexorably to the formation of political parties, which allowed people to express their Hobbesian political strivings in more socially acceptable institutionalized ways.

Party politics became mass entertainment in 1840, the year of the nation's first popular presidential election campaign. During this unabashedly image-based campaign, the Whigs promoted candidate William Henry Harrison as the down-to-earth quintessential "log-cabin-hard-cider candidate" (Boller, 1996), although in truth he was the son of a governor and resided comfortably on a bucolic farm in Ohio. Whig party leaders organized rallies that attracted thousands and featured speeches, songs, and Tippecanoe badges (in honor of Harrison's now-controversial routing of the Shawnee Indians at Tippecanoe, Indiana), as well as plenty of hard cider. Nowadays, the attempt to link Harrison with popular values might be deconstructed by invoking psychological concepts such as higher order conditioning and associative network representations. The use of log cabin imagery and the euphony of Harrison's name (Smith, 1998) would be viewed as peripheral cues (Petty & Cacioppo, 1986) that facilitated persuasion among the low involved.

Gradually, it became more accepted for candidates to campaign, although their rhetoric rarely rose to the heights of that of Abraham Lincoln and Stephen Douglas (Zarefsky, 1990). After the Civil War, parties became the centerpiece of public political life. White men—rich and poor, blue bloods and immigrants—exuberantly marched in torchlight parades, carrying flags and cheering wildly as speakers sung their party's praises and lambasted the opposition (McGerr, 1986). For White men living during the late 18th century, politics was a major leisure time activity—an attitude that fulfilled instrumental and symbolic functions (Katz, 1960; see also Shavitt & Nelson's chapter in this volume [Chapter 8]). Persuasion seemed to chiefly involve accessing (Fazio, 1989) party loyalty. Unfortunately, for the millions of women and Blacks who could not vote, political persuasion was a strange spectator sport played in smoke-filled rooms and grimy city streets.

Popular spectacular campaigns began to decline during the 1890s, a casualty of Progressive reforms, the increasing division of economic classes, the emergence of new leisure time pursuits, and the application of a business model to politics (Perloff, 1999). Beginning in 1896, party managers such as Mark Hanna introduced merchandising techniques to presidential politics, borrowing the sloganeering and advertising strategies that were becoming increasingly popular in American business. Party leaders used speeches to make salient voter loyalty to political parties and worked the wards to mobilize voters in the fall campaign. Throughout the 19th and 20th centuries, party served as a cognitive schema, profoundly influencing voters' interpretations of political messages (Lazarsfeld, Berelson, & Gaudet, 1944).

By 1968, with party loyalty beginning to decline, television serving as the nation's information conduit, and a new political entrepreneur—the consultant—taking party lead-

ers' place, campaigns began to shift from a party to a marketing model (McGinniss, 1969; Newman, 1994). This model, with its emphasis on strategic marketing, voter segmentation, and candidate positioning, dominates politics today (Kotler & Kotler, 1999).

Viewing presidential campaigns from the lofty precipice of history, one glimpses continuities and changes. Campaigns always have been colorful, dirty, and divisive. Personal attacks run rampant, and only occasionally has eloquent rhetoric filled the air. From the beginning, campaigns have been dominated by elites. Patrician elites dominated campaigns throughout the early 19th century; bosses, partisan editors, and political managers ran the shows from the mid-19th to the late 20th century; today, marketing experts dominate electoral campaigns. Campaigns have always centered on persuasion. Candidates—the great ones and the mediocre—have seized on the dominant media of their eras (print, stump speeches, parades, and electronic media) to convince people to cast votes in their behalf.

Campaigns have changed over the years. Structural impediments to voting have been lifted, candidates campaign to attract the people's votes, and the public has more access to presidential communication than ever before. Campaigns are candidate centered rather than party oriented, longer when one considers the months-long primary season, and far more dynamic (i.e., susceptible to media-generated gaffes such as Gerald Ford's 1976 debate comment about Eastern Europe).[1] Campaigns no longer take place in old-fashioned public spaces such as streets and railroad stations; rather, they take place in mediated public settings where television advertising, debates, and increasingly Internet Web sites play crucial roles. Politicians and journalists occupy prominent roles in these spaces (Reese, Grant, & Danielan, 1994) and are highly visible during national elections, whereas citizens are left out, consigned to the private spaces of their living rooms, increasingly alienated from national politics, dominated as it is by lobbyists, lawyers, consultants, and other members of what Abramson (1998) called "the influence industry."

WHAT WE KNOW ABOUT NATIONAL CAMPAIGN PERSUASION

Overview

Graduate students know the mantra. The early history of research in our field understated campaign effects for a host of reasons, ranging from inadequate methodology to inattention to subtle cognitive effects (Becker, McCombs, & McLeod, 1975; Chaffee & Hochheimer, 1985). Contemporary researchers have a different view—a function of a host of social factors, including the ubiquity of television, the decline of political institutions (e.g., political parties) and concomitant emergence of marketing as a major force in politics, the volatility of voter behavior during an age of rapid cultural change, and the development of methodologies that can pinpoint campaign effects.

While macroeconomic and micropsychological factors set limits on presidential campaign effects (Holbrook, 1996), we now recognize that campaigns have numerous cognitive effects on voters and influence candidates, the media, and the larger political system in myriad ways. There remain questions about the nature of these effects and the extent to which campaigns affirm or undermine democratic values (Dye & Zeigler, 1996). Furthermore, during a postmodern era, the term *campaign* is open to question. Is a campaign an exercise in elite manipulation (Margolis & Mauser, 1989) or an entity built by interactions of candidates, media, and citizens (Just et al., 1996)?

Is the campaign an objective entity or a construction, with different constructions crafted by different actors in the process? Campaigns are all of these. We cannot understand campaigns without recognizing that people see them in different ways, yet campaigns do have a practical edge. They are, as Rogers and Storey (1987) noted, intended to "generate specific outcomes or effects in a relatively large number of individuals, usually within a specified period of time and through an organized set of communication activities" (p. 821).

The next section of the chapter synthesizes research in different areas of campaign persuasion. My focus, in light of the orientation of the preponderance of research, is persuasion as it occurs in presidential elections and national issue campaigns. Political advertising, debates, talk radio, and news are separated for purposes of discussion, although in reality they frequently overlap. From campaign managers' perspective, advertising, debates, and news are not isolated modalities but rather part of an overall marketing mix. Voters amalgamate information from different sources, frequently forgetting what contributed most to their impressions. Nonetheless, contexts provide a useful heuristic for viewing campaign effects, and persuasion theories offer insights about mediating processes (see Figure 28.1).

Political Advertising

Political ads provide candidates for public office with a method of communicating with voters that is unmediated by the gargantuan, ubiquitous press. In contrast to news and debates, political advertising is under the control of the party or candidate (Kaid & Holtz-Bacha, 1995). Political commercials exemplify the best and worst of liberal democracy. They are unadulterated persuasive messages operating in a competitive political market-

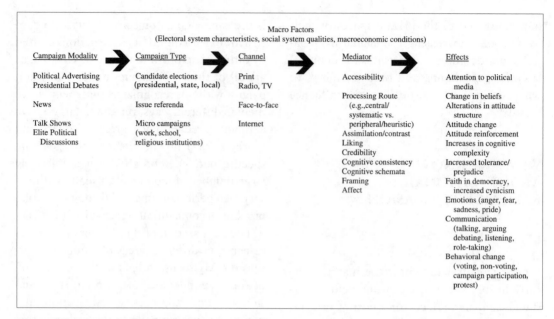

Figure 28.1. Model of Campaign Persuasion Effects

place; advertising is based on the laudable libertarian assumption that voters are capable of sorting out truth from falsehood and that candidates have the right to persuade their brethren to cast votes in their behalf (Held, 1996; Siebert, Peterson, & Schramm, 1956). On the other hand, political spots trouble critics of liberalism, such as communitarian philosophers (Etzioni, 1998), who believe that negative ads pollute "the civic life on which democracy depends" (Sandel, 1996, p. 351). They also tend to unnerve deliberative democrats (e.g., Gutmann, 1993; Gutmann & Thompson, 1996), who yearn for enlightened and principled political debates, and move the more Marxist of deliberative democratic philosophers to lament that in a system awash with political money, all citizens are not equal in their ability to use paid media to gain access to the electorate.

While empirical research cannot settle normative disputes, it can clarify them. Thus, it is useful to examine studies of advertising content and effects, both to understand the nature of contemporary political ads and to shed light on the degree to which advertising serves democracy.

Political ads are the centerpiece of contemporary electoral campaigns and are believed by consultants to influence the agendas for news, debates, and interpersonal discussion. The impact of advertising varies across democratic societies, with cultural, economic, and electoral system factors determining the role that advertising plays in particular Western democracies (Kaid & Holtz-Bacha, 1995).

Over the preceding three decades, numerous studies have explored the content of televised political spots, with the majority of U.S. content analyses focusing on presidential campaign ads. Research has explored (a) the valence of ads (spots are increasingly negative), (b) the appeals used by challengers and incumbents (challengers are more apt to advocate change), and (c) the use of image versus issue appeals (both are employed and are hard to disentangle (Kaid, 1994; Kaid & Holtz-Bacha, 1995; Kaid & Tedesco, 1999).

A time-honored finding that at first blush seems to fly in the face of deliberative democrats' lamentations about lack of thoughtful political discourse is that televised political spots contain a great deal of issue information. A content analysis of televised presidential campaign ads from 1960 to 1988 found that 67% of positive ads and 79% of negative ads contained substantive issue information (Kaid & Johnston, 1991; see also Kaid & Holtz-Bacha, 1995). There is thriving debate about the degree to which candidates can reasonably discuss issues in ads; one side says candidates can communicate a great deal in 30 seconds, and the other side claims that issue appeals are superficial or sidestep genuine concerns of the electorate.

Political spots are ultimately amalgamations of many persuasion strategies, including direct rational appeals (Falbo, 1977) that convey candidates' issue positions, credibility-building spots, evidence-filled appeals such as Ross Perot's infomercials, and an array of "soft sell" ads that play on emotions (Kern, 1989; Schwartz, 1973). Some of the most memorable televised political ads fall into the latter category; appeals such as "Daisy," "Morning in America," and "Revolving Door" strived to access affect.

When it comes to emotional appeals, it is difficult to make meaningful judgments about advertising content in isolation from viewers' perceptions of the spots. Some of the best political spots invite viewers to do a good deal of cognitive work and inference making; the ads are effective because they contain code words (e.g., quotas) that voters connect to the candidate or access feelings that viewers associate with the praised or attacked candidate (Fazio, 1989; Roth, 1987).

Impact. Commonly assumed to exert massive effects on the electorate, political spots (notably negative ones) have been teasingly called the Darth Vader of modern politics

and "the electronic equivalent of the plague" (Perloff, 1998; West, 1993, p. 51). Because anyone who saw *Star Wars* knows that Darth Vader is more foreboding than a 30-second spot, and scholars who study bubonic plagues (e.g., Ziegler, 1969) would find the comparison with ads strange to say the least, it is likely that there are numerous third-person perceptions going on here—tendencies to assume that political ads exert a stronger (and more negative) impact on the average voter than on the self. Yet ads do have effects, although as is typical with political communications, it is difficult to confidently judge the strength and duration of impact, due partly to shortcomings in the research itself, such as the frequent use of contrived advertising messages (Ansolabehere & Iyengar, 1996).

Normatively, advertisements are expected to inform voters about the main issues in the campaign and help them to make reasoned decisions. Research shows that political advertising enhances knowledge about candidate issue positions (Just, Crigler, & Wallach, 1990; Patterson & McClure, 1976) and can promote issue-based evaluations of candidates (Brians & Wattenberg, 1996; Ansolabehere & Iyengar, 1995), although perhaps not as well as does news (Zhao & Chaffee, 1995). Thus, despite—or perhaps because of—their brevity, campaign ads help voters to take better account of issues when making judgments about the candidates (Ansolabehere & Iyengar, 1995), although typically this involves activating or readjusting already existing schemata rather than ruminating about policy issues in any detailed way.

Critics charge that ads are manipulative and "persuade voters to support a candidate or cause that they would reject if the issues were more clearly or comprehensively presented" (Ansolabehere & Iyengar, 1995, p. 7). While scholars have argued that negative ads such as "Willie Horton" lead viewers to make false inferences about the targeted candidate's record (Jamieson, 1992), this claim has not been tested empirically. Theory suggests that such ads may exert the greatest impact on low-involved voters (Perloff, 1984), but evidence supporting this proposition is sparse and involvement has proven to be a more complex construct than is commonly assumed (e.g., Miller & Krosnick, 1996). Moreover, there is abundant evidence that, in the main, ads do not manipulate so much as they add fodder to partisan beliefs. Advertising rarely converts people from one political party to another; instead, ads strengthen partisans' commitment to their party and can push low-interest Democrats or Republicans into voting for the party's nominee (Ansolabehere & Iyengar, 1995).

The preceding discussion has centered on presidential elections, the focus of political communication research. Political advertising also influences attitudes in lower level races where voters are less cognitively engaged and perhaps more susceptible to the types of peripheral appeals commonly found in ads such as mere exposure (Grush, McKeough, & Ahlering, 1978) and the euphony of the candidate's name (O'Sullivan, Chen, Mohapatra, Sigelman, & Lewis, 1988).

Negative Ads. Unquestionably the most controversial aspect of modern political advertising, negative advertising has been on the upswing during recent years (Johnson-Cartee & Copeland, 1991; Kaid, 1994), although it may abate temporarily in the wake of a post-September 11 patriotic norm of consensus. Negative advertising is multidimensional, consisting of direct attack, direct comparison, and implied comparison and varying in thematic design and style (Johnson-Cartee & Copeland, 1991).

Negative ads are frequently more memorable than positive ads. Research participants remember negative spots better than they do positive ones, and they recognize negative ads more quickly and accurately than they do pos-

itive ads (Newhagen & Reeves, 1991; Shapiro & Rieger, 1992). There are a variety of reasons for this, including the psychological tendency to place more weight on negative than on positive information, the stronger impact of negative information on already-existing impressions, and the better production value of many negative spots (Kellermann, 1984).

There is abundant evidence that negative ads influence candidate attitudes. They can shape agendas and prime voters (Schleuder, McCombs, & Wanta, 1991; West, 1993, 1997), as well as lower targeted candidate evaluations (Budesheim, Houston, & DePaola, 1996; Faber, Tims, & Schmitt, 1993; Garramone, 1985; Kaid & Boydston, 1987; Pinkleton, 1997, 1998; Roddy & Garramone, 1988). Regrettably, researchers have not probed the mechanisms that mediate negative ad effects on candidate attitudes, although reduced liking, decreased credibility, and accessing negative associations would seem to be reasonable contenders (Cialdini, 1993; Fazio, 1989; Perloff, 1993).

Fraught with risks, negative advertising also can backlash against the sponsor (Garramone, 1985; Merritt, 1984; Pinkleton, 1998; Roddy & Garramone, 1988). Negative image ads produce greater backlash than do negative issue ads (Roddy & Garramone, 1988), particularly when the source makes unjustified character attacks (Budesheim et al., 1996) and when the opposing candidate, rather than an independent group (e.g., political action committee), sponsors the ad (Garramone, 1985). It is possible that these studies overstate backlash effects given that the attacks were delivered by fictitious or unknown candidates who have less credibility than do actual candidates, whose names and reputations can bolster the perceived quality of the messages (Pfau, Holbert, Szabo, & Kaminski, 1999). As a general rule, negative issue and character attacks perceived as fair can reduce support for the critiqued candidate; those that are viewed as taking unfair advantage of a characterological weakness in the opponent are less likely to succeed.

Political advertising does not operate in a vacuum; instead, it operates in a dynamic media environment where news plays an important part. Stung by criticism that they were soft on George Bush's misleading ads in 1988, the news media devised ad watches, in which a misleading advertising claim is repeated and then corrected. Ad watches are a mixed bag. They can boomerang, strengthening the influence of the misleading commercial by making negative information about the targeted candidate more accessible in memory or by framing issues using criteria employed by the candidate (Ansolabehere & Iyengar, 1995; Pfau & Louden, 1994). On the other hand, ad watches can succeed in reducing viewers' beliefs that the targeted ad is fair (Cappella & Jamieson, 1994); they may be more likely to work if televisual technology is used to make it clear that viewers are not watching an ordinary political commercial and if experts are employed to debunk the misleading information (Ansolabehere & Iyengar, 1995; Jamieson, 1992).

Unquestionably, the most disturbing aspect of negative ads is that, at least in theory, they set up a spiral of cynicism that drives people away from politics (Cappella & Jamieson, 1997). This seems increasingly plausible in light of the increasing number of negative spots and the fact that consultants counsel candidates not to respond to opponents' attacks with silence but instead to respond with a battery of persuasive counterpunches, including denial, refutation, obfuscation (Johnson-Cartee & Copeland, 1991), and inoculation—actually a preemptive attack that has the most empirical support behind it (Pfau & Kenski, 1990).

Communitarian fears that negative advertising increases citizens' alienation from politics receive little vindication from empirical research. While experiments conducted by Ansolabehere and Iyengar (1995) showed that negative campaign messages reduce confidence in government and lower intentions to vote, survey research offers a resoundingly different conclusion. West (1997) examined the relationship between ad negativity and turnout in presidential elections from 1952 to 1996, controlling for voter mistrust of government. When mistrust was controlled, there was no significant relationship between negativity of political ads and turnout. This suggests that voter distrust of politics is more likely to have roots in low political efficacy than in exposure to negative ads.

In a survey of presidential campaign advertising effects from 1960 to 1992, using National Election Studies data, Finkel and Geer (1998) found that campaigns with more negative advertising did not reduce voter turnout rates or demobilize Independent voters. On the contrary, these campaigns were associated with higher levels of concern about the electoral outcome. In a similar fashion, Pfau (1999) provided experimental evidence that viewer exposure to negative candidate-sponsored advertising in congressional races stimulated interest in the campaigns and elicited greater knowledge of candidates. It remains possible that negative advertising reduces political efficacy, as Ansolabehere and Iyengar (1995) suggested, but this is overridden by a countervailing effect—the tendency of negative ads to stimulate interest, arguably because the emotional content intensifies voters' support for their preferred candidates or produces dissonance that sets in motion selective exposure or possibly attitude change processes (Finkel & Geer, 1998). While this remains speculative, the most reasonable conclusion at present is that claims that negative advertising demobilizes the electorate are interesting but unproven. To be sure, the notion that negative campaigning produces a spiral of cynicism strikes a responsive chord in many of us. Yet we must, as social scientists, "guard against accepting too quickly a politically appealing hypothesis" (p. 592), for more convincing evidence is needed before researchers can credibly call on policy makers to make changes in electoral policies.

Political advertising remains "a problematic art," as Diamond and Bates (1992) observed. Empirical studies show that advertising promotes liberal ideals by instructing voters about candidates' positions and helping people to select candidates who best represent their interests (Ansolabehere & Iyengar, 1995). Ads do not manipulate voters in the sense that they cause most people to vote against their interests. Filtering ads through preexisting attitudes, viewers take political ads with a grain of salt; they dislike many of them, but under some conditions, they readjust their cognitions or alter vote intentions. Attack ads have stimulated considerable debate; although troubling to communitarian critics, they are defended by libertarians who point out that negative spots are frequently more substantive and informative than their positive counterparts. Yet even liberal defenders worry that deliberately ambiguous issue advocacy spots and increasingly affective negative ads, while not deterring turnout, discourage the type of thoughtful reflection on which democracy depends.

Presidential Debates

With debates, it is best to begin with semantics. Using the classical definition of debate as a benchmark for evaluating contemporary presidential debates, there is no question that we have not yet witnessed an authentic debate. None of the presidential encounters from 1960 through 1996 focused on "a stated proposition to gain an audience decision" (Auer, 1962, p. 146). Instead, campaign debates are best viewed as "the joint appearance by two or more opposing candidates, who expound on their positions, with explicit and equitable provisions for refutation without interruption" (Martel, 1983, p. 3).

Debates have been regular features of presidential campaigns since those between Gerald Ford and Jimmy Carter in 1976. Formats have become more variegated, expanding from the reporter-dominated press conference format to town hall meeting debates and a single-moderator format (Kraus, 1988; Meyer & Carlin, 1994). News media play an important role in framing debate outcomes and influencing voter interpretations.

As quintessential exemplars of persuasion, debates are fraught with rhetorical strategies, persuasive appeals, and verbal argumentation. Rhetoric scholars have cataloged these, pointing out ways in which debaters articulate a vision (typically in the opening statement), strive to identify themselves with the main aspirations of the electorate, draw sharp contrasts between their positions and those of their opponents, use evidence to bolster arguments, and bring to bear an array of paralinguistic appeals (e.g., metaphors, pauses, sound bites) and nonverbal communication devices (e.g., smiles, eye contact, physical movement) to score points with the electorate (e.g., Bitzer & Rueter, 1980; Friedenberg, 1994; Hellweg, Pfau, & Brydon, 1992; Hodgkinson & Leland, 1999; Perloff, 1998). Candidates have used these techniques not only to inform but also to obfuscate and mislead, for example, vague discussion of how to change social security in 1996, factual distortions by both candidates in 1976, and John F. Kennedy's deliberate exaggeration of U.S. vulnerability to Soviet attack in 1960 (see Bitzer & Rueter, 1980; Matthews, 1996).

This brings us to the question of debate effects. Like political advertising research, studies of presidential debate effects fail to offer precise knowledge of when debates are most impactful and why. Moreover, debate studies have been spotty; we know more about certain electoral debates (e.g., 1960, 1976, 1992) than about others. Nonetheless, because of the relatively large number of panel studies, empirical research provides us with useful clues about debate effects.

Recalling Gertrude Stein's remark that the answer depends on the nature of the query, one can look at debate impact from the perspectives of the candidates, the media, and the voters. From candidates' perspective, debates are first and foremost about influencing image assessments and pushing the voters toward casting votes in the candidates' behalf. Holbrook (1996) conducted both aggregate and panel studies of 1984 to 1992 presidential debates and reported significant debate effects on candidate opinions and post-debate vote intentions. Other research also reports debate effects on image assessments (Katz & Feldman, 1962; Lemert, Elliott, Bernstein, Rosenberg, & Nestvold, 1991), with effects stronger on those with more "cognitive room for influence," that is, voters with weak initial attitudes (Sears & Chaffee, 1979) and low levels of political knowledge (Lanoue, 1992). Some of the variance in post-debate evaluations is attributable to news media pronouncements of who won. Post-debate news analysis influences viewer evaluations of the candidates in the direction advocated by the network commentators (Lemert et al, 1991; Lemert, Elliott, Rosenberg, & Bernstein, 1996). In at least one case, the "Eastern European gaffe" debate of 1976, news media verdict effects were particularly significant, arguably altering the dynamics of the campaign (Patterson, 1980).

The best inference from the literature is that most voters during most debates engage in what Chaiken, Liberman, and Eagly (1989) referred to as biased systematic processing. Prior attitudes influence interpretation of what candidates say, so much so that voters typically judge that their preferred candidate

won the debate (Holbrook, 1996). Debates persuade, but their effects fall mostly under the domain of response reinforcement rather than response change (Miller, 1980), largely because during this stage of the campaign attitudes serve as selective screens for voters, many of whom have already made up their minds for whom to cast their votes. Thus, presidential debates are most apt to strengthen attitudes, confer resistance to persuasion, enhance consistency among disparate attitude elements (Sears & Chaffee, 1979), and promote attitude-behavior consistency (Fazio & Williams, 1986); in close elections, these effects may be politically consequential. Under specific conditions, presidential debates probably shape attitudes as well as reinforce them. When uncertainty prevails, as it does during primaries, in elections featuring two nonincumbents, and on the individual level among mid- and late-campaign deciders (Chaffee & Choe, 1980), presidential debates are likely to have significant effects in bonding attitude elements and shifting public perceptions, although the strength of these effects remains in doubt (Hellweg et al., 1992).

But even if debates had no political impact (and such a conclusion seems unwarranted based on research), they would still be important from a democratic theory perspective. They are the quintessential deliberative democratic format, and in an ideal world they should promote learning, deliberation, and more thoughtful consideration of campaign issues. Viewers learn from presidential and vice presidential debates, if by learning we mean increasing information about candidate issue positions (e.g., Chaffee, Zhao, & Leshner, 1994; Miller & MacKuen, 1979). Yet questions remain about how long the information gain persists past the debate and how much of the cognitive learning resulted from voters' acquiring new knowledge from the debate as opposed to the debate stimulating voters to turn to other sources to learn about the issues (Miller & MacKuen, 1979).

Critics—and there are many—lament that because of television exigencies, rigid debate formats, and candidate ambition, debates fail to provide an enriching give-and-take on issues of the day. While 1970s-style debates increased voters' confidence that government is responsive to its citizens (Sears & Chaffee, 1979), this may no longer be the case during an age when voters increasingly believe that candidates skirt the issues (Lemert, 1991) and candidates validate this belief by shamelessly playing to the camera. Philosophically, debates affirm one of liberal democracy's greatest values: "choice through rational dialogue" (Hinck, 1993, p. 7). They also may meet communitarian standards by civilizing bitterly fought presidential campaigns. But the scripted answers, use of formats that discourage classical debate, and declining audience attention raise questions as to whether debates can survive during the 21st century without making substantive changes.

Opinion Leaders, Talk Radio, and News

Other persuasion modalities also influence voters during campaigns. Candidate speeches can influence attitudes, particularly when they employ optimistic appeals (Zullow & Seligman, 1989), are delivered during conventions (Holbrook, 1996), and employ political accounts appropriately (McGraw & Hubbard, 1996). At the same time, voters can be influenced by interpersonal discussion (Huckfeldt & Sprague, 1995). Discussion typically occurs among people who agree on politics, but not always (Huckfeldt & Sprague, 1987). Respected others still guide opinions (Weimann, 1994), and opinion leader effects can be observed in mass media as well as interpersonal settings. One can glimpse mediated opinion

leadership effects in newspaper editorial endorsements (Robinson, 1976) and talk radio, a modality that frequently functions more as interpersonal than as mass communication (Beniger, 1987).

Radio talk show hosts, such as the inimitable Rush Limbaugh, are credible sources to millions of listeners; they influence attitudes through a variety of cognitive and affective mediators. In addition, given that well-known hosts and listeners tend to share a conservative Republican worldview (Herbst, 1995), shows may set in motion attitude-strengthening opinion processes, such as "looking glass" projections of public opinion and selective exposure that serve to increase accessibility of agreement between the self and others (Fields & Schuman, 1976; Marks & Miller, 1987). Survey research indicates that political talk radio exerts a highly significant impact on candidate attitudes during primary campaigns (Pfau et al., 1997); under these and related conditions, radio talk is apt to strengthen and prime political attitudes (Owen, 1997), in some cases stimulating political interest (Bucy, D'Angelo, & Newhagen, 1999) and occasionally leading listeners to translate opinions into politically consequential behavior, as in the health care reform campaign and "Nannygate" (Page & Tannenbaum, 1996). The downside is that talk radio can depict the most negative aspects of political institutions, contributing to reduced confidence in these institutions, particularly when political knowledge is lacking (Pfau et al., 1998).

News falls into a gray area of persuasion; it is not ipso facto persuasive communication because journalists do not intend or consciously attempt to alter voters' political attitudes in a manner that would benefit news organizations. Yet news, reflecting candidate, journalist, and public agendas, unquestionably influences political beliefs, as the voluminous literature on agenda setting, priming, and framing indicates (e.g., Cappella & Jamieson,

1997; Iyengar, 1991; Iyengar & Kinder, 1987; Weaver, Graber, McCombs, & Eyal, 1981). Experiments demonstrate that strategically framed news can activate strategy-oriented interpretations of a campaign as well as increase cynicism (Cappella & Jamieson, 1997; Rhee, 1997). However, the popular view that horse race news persuades citizens to distrust politicians is modest at best, undermined as it is by the fact that factors unexamined in the studies (e.g., negative campaigning) may lead to the same effects as well as by the paradox that if voters have been goaded into viewing campaigns through strategy-oriented lenses, then why do they persist in telling researchers such as Patterson (1993) that they judge candidates primarily in terms of the issues?

These problems notwithstanding, there is considerable evidence that news changes political attitudes and beliefs, particularly those that pertain to the larger collective of political life that people do not experience directly. In a thorough review of the literature on impersonal influence, Mutz (1998) concluded that media under some conditions can strongly influence the degree to which people politicize their personal concerns, which in turn can affect their propensity to hold leaders accountable for national problems they may or may not have caused.

Issue Campaigns

In our media-centered democracy, elites recognize that public opinion plays a key role in influencing policy. Political leaders now circumvent established institutional channels, opting instead to mount media campaigns to win press and public support that they hope will influence elite decision makers. Reagan's mobilization of public opinion—or perceived public opinion (Schudson, 1995)—in the 1981 budget battle, George Bush's and

George W. Bush's strategic use of communication to win support for the Gulf War (Manheim, 1994) and war on terrorism, billion-dollar campaigns for and against health care reform and the North American Free Trade Agreement (NAFTA) (Johnson & Broder, 1996), and the Clinton administration's public relations blitz to forestall impeachment (Kurtz, 1998) illustrate this trend aptly. These, as well as the array of campaigns to win support of state initiatives and constitutional amendments, make heavy use of issue advertising (Kaid, Tedesco, & Spiker, 1996).

The 1993 health care reform campaign was the most far-reaching of the issue campaigns and generated the most academic research. In the wake of the death of health reform in 1994, scholars described flaws in Clinton's crisis rhetoric (Holloway, 1996) as well as the ways in which proponents and opponents used marketing techniques to bombard the airwaves with pro and con ads such as "Harry and Louise." While advertising perhaps fulfilled a libertarian ideal of giving the public access to different arguments, it fell short of contemporary deliberative democratic standards by offering little in the way of dialogue or constructive debate. Content analyses show that ads on both sides were more unfair than fair, centered more on attack than advocacy, and were filled with inaccurate claims (Jamieson & Cappella, 1995; Kaid et al., 1996). Available evidence suggests that the campaign influenced public opinion. Clinton helped to increase the salience of health care in people's minds (Kaid et al., 1996). Over time, health insurance industry counterattacks made inroads as support for Clinton's plan dropped dramatically over the course of 1993-1994, particularly among the moderately politically aware (Cobb & Kuklinksi, 1997; Koch, 1998). There was also confusion about substantive issues in the debate, which was not surprising given strategy-dominated news coverage, the

Byzantine complexity of the Clinton plan, and deficiencies in the ads noted previously.

Normative Implications

Some 2,000 years after Plato mused about appearances and reality in the parable of the cave, we still ponder the degree to which politics serves a higher purpose. The same questions that occupied Plato still bedevil us today. Do simple but misleading persuasive messages manipulate people (particularly those most vulnerable and least informed), exploiting their inclination to rely on cognitive heuristics? Do people process messages systematically enough to see through deceptive peripheral cues? Are judgmental heuristics reasonable ways to reduce informational complexity or short-circuited strategies that lead to undemocratic outcomes such as that which occurred with Lyndon LaRouche candidates in 1986 (O'Sullivan et al., 1988)? The consensus is that, in most cases in contemporary America, citizens are capable of thinking quite reasonably about politics, rationally interpreting persuasive messages, and using heuristics to efficiently monitor public affairs (Mondak, 1993).

Yet democracy's contradictions are nowhere more apparent than in campaigns. Liberal democratic theory provides the philosophical foundation for the egalitarian notion that anyone can run for office and even get elected, as the hitherto-unknown ex-wrestler Jessie Ventura discovered in the Minnesota gubernatorial race in 1998. Yet liberalism also encourages candidates to take liberties to win, for example, to make simplistic misleading appeals (Cobb & Kuklinski, 1997) and sponsor verbally aggressive ads. Liberalism laudably encourages the news media to serve as a check on candidate excesses. Yet the market mechanism pushes the media to charge large sums of money for political ads, thereby man-

dating that candidates will turn to special interests to raise the money. Classical liberalism enshrines citizen liberties. People may actively partake in or totally ignore campaigns, but in refraining from demanding that voters act as citizens as well as ballot punchers, liberalism ensures that participation in national campaigns will be limited to the very few.

SUMMARY AND RESEARCH DIRECTIONS

Research tells us that it is more effective to give the good news before the bad (McGuire, 1985). Accordingly, I will do just that in assessing research in political persuasion. To paraphrase Reagan, we are better off now than we were six decades ago, when campaign research began in Erie County, Ohio. Scholars have accumulated considerable valuable knowledge regarding the content and persuasive effects of political campaigns. Research has pointed to the limits of campaign communications, documented a host of subtle cognitive effects, and demonstrated complex contextual influences of media and interpersonal communication. While no middle-range theories have evolved, frameworks for understanding political campaigns have emerged from research that has cut across disciplines.

The prevailing view today—troubling to communitarians—is that campaigns are battles fought with the tools of persuasion. This said, there are divergent views on what the battle is for (e.g., a fight to shape public opinion, an attempt to win over key elites, an effort to convince people that a particular candidate's election will not portend catastrophe) (see Diamond & Cobb, 1996). A host of social psychological processes seem to mediate campaign persuasion effects, including central/peripheral processing, reliance on heuristics, accessibility, and assimilation and contrast.

Current wisdom suggests that while media campaigns are constrained by macro conditions and micropsychological factors (e.g., preexisting attitudes [but see Zaller, 1992]), they can influence how voters make sense of campaigns and can readjust meanings of issues, candidates, and social groups in the minds of voters (Biocca, 1991) as well as among journalists. The effects are less often dramatic than subtle. Persuasive political media seem to exert a stronger impact the more consonant they are with voters' schema, the more accessible they are in memory, and the more they jibe comfortably with existing attitudes and cognitions.

Although much is known about political campaign effects, gaps in knowledge remain. We do not know the precise impact of persuasive modalities such as advertising and debates, lack knowledge about the conditions under which campaign persuasion is most effective, and are in the dark about the processes by which communications achieve some of their effects during electoral campaigns. Knowledge deficiencies stem from the difficulty of scientifically studying complex stimuli such as campaign communications, problems in parceling out one influence from another, excessive use of linear models to study effects that are not always linear, unreliability of survey measures, and "inadequate variation in the media inputs to mass opinion for ready detection of media effects, even if such effects are massively present" (Zaller, 1996, p. 19).

The field of campaign research has, like the journalists we study, missed a number of big stories. Fixated on the view that top-down ideology determines political orientations (Shoemaker & Reese, 1996), we neglected to explore the role of communications at grassroots levels, evident in populist anger at government during the 1980s and 1990s (Tolchin, 1996). Enamored by cognitive models, we have played insufficient attention to

the role of affect and visual symbols (e.g., the impact of televised pictures of police beating Blacks during the 1950s, Reagan's nonverbal communication skills during the 1980s). Obsessed by the presidency, we have ignored the impact of media in lower level elections and the plethora of issue campaigns, arenas in which communications are apt to have stronger effects given that attitudes are more malleable. Socialized during an era of logical positivist inquiry and trained in programs emphasizing methodology at the expense of philosophy, scholars have until recently neglected to consider how research consumed by narrow questions of effects can reinforce the status quo; we have (sometimes very skillfully) examined the impact of media institutions while neglecting to empirically explore ways in which communication can build a stronger democracy.

Directions for Research During the New Century

There are numerous directions for research on persuasive political campaigns. In this last section of the chapter, I offer suggestions, moving from conventional to less traditional and from descriptive to prescriptive.

1. *We need more in-depth knowledge of campaign processes and effects.* Scholars need to elaborate on the conditions under which campaign messages are most likely to influence voters. Urgently needed are meta-analyses of research on political advertising and presidential debates; such meta-summaries can clarify what we know, articulate gaps in knowledge, and shed light on operational definitions (see, e.g., Allen & Preiss, 1998).

To the extent that we value precise scientific knowledge, we need to conduct more theory-driven studies that hone in on conditions and processes, employing panel studies and field experiments that employ realistic stimulus materials. For example, political advertising research should explore how advertising interacts with macro variables (e.g., economic conditions), campaign phase, time of decision, and candidate gender, with the latter being a factor that will assume increasing importance as more women enter the campaign fray and influence the nature of political communication (Bystrom & Miller, 1999; Chang & Hitchon, 1997). Research should also examine the dynamic, causally complex ways in which political ads influence people over the course of campaigns, characterized as they are by one candidate's negative spots, the opponent's response, the first candidate's counterpunch, and news coverage that highlights argumentative aspects of the exchanges. Linear models that assume additive effects should be supplemented by nonlinear ones that take into account cross-cutting influences of today's nonrational campaigns.

Psychologically oriented researchers should consider how we can translate knowledge of attitude processes into hypotheses about campaign effects. Clearly, models that view attitudes as organized around values or as latitudes (Diamond & Cobb, 1996) will articulate different theories of political persuasion effects than will those that see attitudes as constructed "on the spot" (Zaller, 1992) or updated "online" (Lodge, 1995).

Research also needs to go beyond examining effects of familiar modalities such as advertising and debates and to test theory-driven hypotheses about opinion polls and push polls, particularly as they relate to the Internet. We are witnessing increasing numbers of Web site polls, many of which are unscientific and susceptible to exploitation by advocacy groups. The attitude-changing impact of other new modalities, such as political Web sites, also warrants investigation (e.g., Tedesco, Miller, & Spiker, 1999). Candidate Web sites are frequently warm and fuzzy, suggesting that peripheral cues may be influential, although perhaps not so much as popular observers believe inasmuch as many of those who frequent political cyberspace are the highly engaged who favor deeper arguments (Johnson, 1999). Even so, the Internet offers up new possibilities for political persuasion, such as interactive Web sites in which voters can communicate with the sites and receive information tailor-made for them, Web site national town meetings that promise to shape political agendas (Morris, 1999), and multiple opportunities for children to develop citizenship skills. Theorists will want to consider how to adapt contemporary information processing models to a medium in which audiences play an increasingly active role in message generation and selection. They will also want to apply persuasion theories to political advocacy sites in which advertising and information will be seamlessly merged (Alexander & Tate, 1999), making it possible for political advertisers to mislead the least motivated and cognitively able of Internet consumers.

2. *Scholars should programmatically examine communication and political affect.* During an era when people are angry (Tolchin, 1996), outraged (Bennett, 1998), or (alternatively) proudly patriotic (Lanzetta, Sullivan, Masters, & McHugo, 1985), we need to better understand the role that affect plays in campaign persuasion. Contemporary models of affect and persuasion (e.g., Glaser & Salovey, 1998; Jorgensen, 1998; Schwarz, Bless, & Bohner, 1991) suggest a host of studies of the impact that political anger, sadness, fear, and happiness exert on message processing.

Schwarz et al. (1991) note that mood states can influence motivation to process persuasive messages, as well as cognitive capacity. They argue that when in a negative state, people are more apt to systematically process messages "to avoid erroneous decisions in a situation that is already characterized as problematic" (Schwarz et al., 1991, p. 166). By contrast, when people are in a good mood, they may be less inclined to cognitively elaborate on a communication, preferring to steer clear of activities that might disrupt their positive affective state. This has interesting implications for politics. In 1992, when the electorate was angry, people seemed to pay more attention than usual to campaign communications such as Clinton's ads about the economy and Perot's infomercials (Perloff, 1998). Six years later, during the throes of the Clinton sex scandal, some critics (e.g., Bennett, 1998) argued that Americans refrained from systematically processing the scandal because they were in a good mood induced by the economy. Although anecdotal evidence suggests that Americans did process scandal information systematically, the affect hypothesis remains interesting. It would be intriguing to determine whether Americans would have processed the Clinton impeachment differently had they been in a rotten political mood rather than a good one. It also would be useful to examine whether their pleasant affective state increased the accessibility of positive political information and whether a similar positive political mood worked to Reagan's advantage in 1984.

It can also be argued that negative moods bias systematic processing (Chaiken et al., 1989). People may be so swept up in their fury at "the system" that they may ignore more reasonable temperate appeals in favor of simplistic, misleading neo-populist appeals. Tolchin (1996) suggested that just this occurred in 1994, when the Republicans swept to election by sensing and manipulating public anger against government. A host of questions present themselves. How do argument quality and involvement interact with mood to influence political processing? How do political sadness, fear, anger, and anxiety—all negative affective states—differ in their implications

for political processing? Do political speeches that vary in optimism-pessimism (Zullow & Seligman, 1989), use of accounts (McGraw & Hubbard, 1996), and candidates' nonverbal displays (Lanzetta et al., 1985) have different effects when voters are angry than when they are sad or euphoric? Do incumbents benefit more by arousing pride, and challengers benefit more by eliciting hope, as Kinder (1994) suggested. What happens when people's mood matches the affective tone of the persuaders (e.g., angry voters attending to angry talk show or chat room hosts)? Can communications that encourage deliberation (e.g., electronic town meetings) reduce anger by increasing connectiveness among people? When is it functional for political communicators to raise ire, and when is it disadvantageous?

3. *Research needs to extensively examine campaigns other than the presidency.* From reading our literature, you would assume that the only campaigns in America are for the presidency. Using appropriate theories, researchers should systematically examine voter processing and message effects in campaigns for Congress, the statehouse, and local office, with the latter offering particularly intriguing opportunities to study political involvement (as when candidate yard signs function as peripheral cues engendering heuristics such as "He must have something on the ball if so many people put signs in their yards").

We know embarrassingly little about communication effects in national issue campaigns, such as NAFTA, and in the plethora of state referenda that run the gamut from legalizing medical use of marijuana to eliminating bilingual education. At the same time, the proliferation of marketing and easy access to a new campaign medium, the Internet, will lead to a dramatic upsurge in the number of grassroots campaigns. In these campaigns, information will be critical and opinions will be malleable—just the sorts of situations in which mass media should be consequential.

Scholars must adopt a broad view of politics, recognizing with Schudson (1998) that people "exercise citizenship in many other locations" and "do politics" in all sorts of locales (p. 299). Researchers need to study these micropolitical persuasion situations, for example, those that occur in neighborhoods (e.g., a fight to change zoning laws to prevent fast-food chains from moving in), the schools (e.g., a Parent-Teacher Association [PTA] campaign against adoption of a left-liberal history textbook), workplaces (e.g., an American Association of University Professors [AAUP] push to unionize faculty), and places of worship (e.g., a clash in a synagogue over hiring an openly gay rabbi). In sum, we need to stop focusing exclusively on presidential communication and instead look at a host of other campaigns that occur in this country and abroad.

4. *Research should pay greater attention to how elites use and are used by persuasive political media.* Our scholarship has focused nearly exclusively on campaign effects on the mass public, thereby ignoring the impact of communication on elites. We need to know how politicians, consultants, lobbyists, and journalists are influenced by news stories, talk radio, and polls (Perloff, 1996); the types of third-person perceptions they make about media influence; and the ways in which their interpretations influence decision making. For example, what kinds of heuristics do politicians invoke to interpret interest group-stimulated mass mailings such as those that besieged moderate Republicans during the Clinton impeachment? At the same time, elite influence should be included in models of political persuasion so that we can better understand how elites build mass consensus (e.g., through the moderating role of political

awareness, as Zaller [1992] suggested), and when the mass public influences elites.

5. *Scholars should examine the interface between culture and campaign effects.* As diverse races and ethnic groups populate the America of the 21st century, it becomes increasingly important to consider how candidate and issue campaigns play out differently among people of different ethnic backgrounds. As candidates take into account the values and highly specialized media habits of new and emerging ethnic minorities, researchers should consider how minorities and cultural majorities make sense of campaigns, what they find salient, and how campaign messages influence them (e.g., Morris, Roberts, & Baker, 1999). We can expect to witness an extraordinary use of political symbols (Sears et al., 1997), designed in some cases to incite violence; there will be increasing numbers of clashes via mass media and the Internet among different cultural groups, more efforts by journalists and activists of different stripes to label politically and historically ambiguous events in varied ideological ways, and attempts to bridge differences through condensational symbols. No less than the definition of America is at stake, and researchers will want to make sense of the battle. Our efforts at sense making will be aided by applying cross-cultural theories, social scientific operationalizations of semiotic approaches (Berger, 1998), and flexible methods that shed empirical light on subjective readings of politics (e.g., Carter & Stamm, 1994).

6. *Research must be increasingly guided by normative theories that spell out how persuasion should occur in a democracy.* Campaign research implicitly reflects a normative perspective; the favored view, until recently, has been liberal theory. Rather than shying away from normative approaches because they are

"value laden," we should realize that campaign research can enhance democratic as well as empirical goals by hewing closely to a political philosophy that advocates a particular role for persuasion in a democratic society. Teasing out empirical implications of normative theory is not easy. There are numerous treatises on philosophies such as liberalism and deliberative democracy, concepts (e.g., civil society) are elastic and subject to multiple interpretations, and few theories explicate the role persuasion ought to play in political campaigns. However, implications can be derived, which in turn generate research and democracy-strengthening ideas (Barber, 1998a).

Serious scholarship is needed that integrates normative and empirical theory (Marcus & Hanson, 1993). Needless to say, multiple normative approaches—as diverse as the opinions of researchers—should guide scholarship. Let me offer a few general prescriptions.

Liberal theory suggests that persuasion should promote greater attention to political issues and ensure more diversity of points of view (Sunstein, 1993). Liberalism asserts that the clash of competing ideas should lead to more innovative thinking and tolerance. Given liberalism's dominance, some of these ideas—but not all—have been implicitly tested. One can envision an experiment in which some participants could be exposed to a raucous debate of issues, while others could hear a kinder gentler debate of the sort preferred by communitarians. Liberalism would predict greater enthusiasm for democracy, more innovative political thinking, and greater political tolerance from the first message; communitarianism would forecast increases in cynicism and political withdrawal. Research might also look at whether liberal democracy has been able to accommodate changes in persuasion techniques. Are voters fooled by misleading television ads (Jamieson, 1992)? Do viewers infer that issue advocacy ads convey the message "Don't vote for Candidate X" even if

such words are never explicitly mentioned in the ad (West, 1997)? Given its increasing prominence in campaigns and disturbing implications for democratic decision making, issue advocacy advertising deserves special attention from researchers.

The grand tradition of liberalism urges tolerance for individual differences. As political minority candidates become more commonplace—and such candidates run the gamut from Hispanics to gay men—researchers will want to explore the types of messages that encourage acceptance of minority campaigns. For example, an experiment by Golebiowska (1996) suggests that candidates from negatively stereotyped groups should devise messages emphasizing their individuality.

Communitarianism emphasizes that campaigns should build a thriving, vigorous civil society. Communitarian thinkers urge that public space be transformed so that it fulfills civic needs (Barber, 1998b). Formatively oriented persuasion scholars might explore how civic space—in malls, in subdivisions, or on the Internet—could best be used to promote humane political persuasion. What sorts of national civic discussions (facilitated by the Internet and freighted with persuasive arguments) reinvigorate citizens, what types polarize people, and what kinds of civic forums are too monotonous to endure? How also can civic forums be designed to encourage people to speak their minds? (The latter is a value cherished by libertarians as well as communitarians.) Lastly, how can forums on the Internet or in interpersonal settings be designed to encourage mutual respect and participation in the community?

A third political philosophy, deliberative democracy, puts a premium on morally constructive debate and critical reasoning that emerges through dialogue. It suggests that we expand our dependent variables beyond "the usual suspects" of recall, attitude change, and voting. A research question derived from deliberative democracy is whether current modalities, such as presidential debates and ads (as well as new media forms), increase complexity of thinking, multidimensionality of reasoning, and critical reading of others' arguments. Deliberative democrats would also want to uncover the types of campaign persuasion that enhance listening and honest review of one's political attitudes. Research should investigate whether listening, whereby people "modulate their own voices so that the voices of others can be heard" (Barber, 1998b, p. 118), is encouraged by certain forums (e.g., town hall meeting debates, Internet discussion groups) and discouraged by others (e.g., talk radio). (The latter may provide a trade-off, enhancing the libertarian value of speaking up but minimizing the deliberative democratic/communitarian value of listening.) Persuasion can be a good thing if it causes us to deliberate more intensely on our own values, rethink our prejudices, and absorb others' points of view. A question for the new century is whether campaign persuasion will accomplish this goal or cause us to retreat more rapidly into our own cognitive cocoons.

An interesting avenue for research on these topics is an old friend recently reinvigorated by the Internet: interpersonal communication. According to proponents of deliberative democracy (e.g., Schudson, 1997), political talk advances democracy when it is based on debate and rule-governed discourse. A libertarian approach is less restrained and contends that discussion, proceeding without formal arguments and rules, can increase political participation. Wyatt, Katz, and Kim (2000) made this argument and obtained this result in a penetrating study.

Pitting traditional liberal theory against deliberative democracy is intriguing. It requires that we look at how people talk about politics—the arguments they use or do not use (Wyatt et al., 2000), the nature of their arguments (the coin of our realm), what people say

to each other when they talk about politics (defining the term rather broadly), when political discussion leads to participation and when it promotes polarization, and the type of political talk that occurs in virtual communities, with the latter offering up interesting possibilities for the construction of "fictitious" and authentic political identities (Holmes, 1997).

The implications of liberalism, deliberative democracy, and communitarianism for persuasive talk on the Internet are particularly intriguing. As a starting point, it would be interesting to explicate the conditions that each political philosophy stipulates must be present if the Internet is to strengthen democratic discourse. Classical liberalism would harbor the most Panglossian scenario, endlessly upbeat about the future during a digital age. Liberals would emphasize that the Internet's interactive capability allows citizens to actively use communications to shape public debate and to vigorously participate in all manner of opinionated discussions, national referenda, and electronic town meetings. Classical liberalism would put forth the fewest conditions necessary for democracy-strengthening effects, stating only that if there are equal opportunities to express diverse views, the Internet will be good for democracy.

Communitarians would fear a "Pandora scenario" in which the Internet is "dominated by profit mongering and private interests" (and multinational ones at that) rather than by a robust concern for the civic good (Barber, 1998a, pp. 252, 262). Prizing constructive discussion rather than arguments, communitarian thinkers would stress that Internet political talkers rarely cross ideological lines and infrequently work for the good of the commons or toward constructing a healthier political *community* (Whillock, 1999). According to Barber, a communitarian (but a deliberative democrat as well), the Internet can strengthen democracy only if technology is deployed in the service of democratic goals, rather than vice versa, and (more to the point of this chapter) only if civic-minded rhetoric is rewarded.

Deliberative democracy proponents, emphasizing the need for constructive debate, would argue that the Internet can enhance democracy provided that its political dialogues give all participants an equal opportunity to express divergent views and that "Netiquette" rules stipulating how discussion should proceed are firmly in place. Research could empirically examine these issues, testing hypotheses, recognizing that a variety of outcomes congenial (or not so congenial) to proponents of a given philosophy could simultaneously occur and that researchers from different philosophical bents would operationalize democracy-enhancing effects differently.

CONCLUSION

No one knows the shape that politics or communication will take during the decades to come. If the past is any guide, all prognosticators will be wrong. The urge to guess is strong; at the very least, one can assume that marketing on both the micro and macro levels will play a critical role in 21st-century campaigns, elites will continue to mold policy, ethics will play second fiddle to Realpolitik, technology—in concert with economics—will alter political communications, and people will find creative ways to build agendas in a contradictory and flawed system. Campaigns will continue, but their meanings will change dramatically during the years to come. Communication research has a vital role to play. Our work should extend science and embellish democracy.

NOTE

1. During the second debate of 1976, in response to a question about the relationship be-

tween the United States and the Soviet Union, Ford blundered, "There is no Soviet domination of Eastern Europe, and there never will be under a Ford administration."

REFERENCES

Abramson, J. (1998, September 29). The business of persuasion thrives in nation's capital. *The New York Times*, pp. A1, A22.

Alexander, J. E., & Tate, M. A. (1999). *Web wisdom: How to evaluate and create information quality on the Web*. Mahwah, NJ: Lawrence Erlbaum.

Allen, M., & Preiss, R. W. (1998). *Persuasion: Advances through meta-analysis*. Cresskill, NJ: Hampton.

Ansolabehere, S., & Iyengar, S. (1995). *Going negative: How political advertisements shrink and polarize the electorate*. New York: Free Press.

Ansolabehere, S., & Iyengar, S. (1996). The craft of political advertising: A progress report. In D. C. Mutz, P. M. Sniderman, & R. A. Brody (Eds.), *Political persuasion and attitude change* (pp. 101-122). Ann Arbor: University of Michigan Press.

Auer, J. J. (1962). The counterfeit debates. In S. Kraus (Ed.), *The great debates: Kennedy vs. Nixon, 1960* (pp. 142-150). Bloomington: Indiana University Press.

Barber, B. R. (1998a). *A passion for democracy: American essays*. Princeton, NJ: Princeton University Press.

Barber, B. R. (1998b). *A place for us: How to make society civil and democracy strong*. New York: Hill & Wang.

Becker, E. (2001, November 11). In the war on terrorism, a battle to shape opinion. *The New York Times, pp.* A1, B4-B5.

Becker, L. B., McCombs, M. E., & McLeod, J. M. (1975). The development of political cognitions. In S. H. Chaffee (Ed.), *Political communication: Strategies for research* (pp. 21-63). Beverly Hills, CA: Sage.

Beniger, J. R. (1987). Personalization of mass media and the growth of pseudo-community. *Communication Research, 14,* 352-371.

Bennett, W. J. (1998). *The death of outrage: Bill Clinton and the assault on American ideals*. New York: Free Press.

Berger, A. A. (1998). *Media analysis techniques* (2nd ed.). Thousand Oaks, CA: Sage.

Biocca, F. (1991). Viewers' mental models of political messages: Toward a theory of the semantic processing of television. In F. Biocca (Ed.), *Television and political advertising, Vol. 1: Psychological processes* (pp. 27-89). Hillsdale, NJ: Lawrence Erlbaum.

Bitzer, L., & Rueter, T. (1980). *Carter vs. Ford: The counterfeit debates of 1976*. Madison: University of Wisconsin Press.

Boller, P. F., Jr. (1996). *Presidential campaigns* (rev. ed.). New York: Oxford University Press.

Brians, C. L., & Wattenberg, M. P. (1996). Campaign issue knowledge and salience: Comparing reception from TV commercials, TV news, and newspapers. *American Journal of Political Science, 40*, 172-193.

Bucy, E. P., D'Angelo, P., & Newhagen, J. E. (1999). The engaged electorate: New media use as political participation. In L. L. Kaid & D. G. Bystrom (Eds.), *The electronic election: Perspectives on the 1996 campaign communication* (pp. 335-347). Mahwah, NJ: Lawrence Erlbaum.

Budesheim, T. L., Houston, D. A., & DePaola, S. J. (1996). Persuasiveness of in-group and out-group political messages: The case of negative political campaigning. *Journal of Personality and Social Psychology, 70*, 523-534.

Bystrom, D. G., & Miller, J. L. (1999). Gendered communication styles and strategies in Campaign 1996: The videostyles of women and men candidates. In L. L. Kaid & D. G. Bystrom (Eds.), *The electronic election: Perspectives on the 1996 campaign communication* (pp. 293-302). Mahwah, NJ: Lawrence Erlbaum.

Cappella, J. N., & Jamieson, K. H. (1994). Broadcast adwatch effects: A field experiment. *Communication Research, 21*, 342-365.

Cappella, J. N., & Jamieson, K. H. (1997). *Spiral of cynicism: The press and the public good*. New York: Oxford University Press.

Carter, R. F., & Stamm, K. R. (1994). The 1992 presidential campaign and debates: A cognitive view. *Communication Research, 21*, 380-395.

Chaffee, S. H., & Choe, S. Y. (1980). Time of decision and media use during the Ford-Carter campaign. *Public Opinion Quarterly, 44*, 53-69.

Chaffee, S. H., & Hochheimer, J. L. (1985). The beginnings of political communication research in the United States: Origins of the "limited effects" model. In M. Gurevitch & M. R. Levy (Eds.), *Mass communication review yearbook* (Vol. 5, pp. 75-104). Beverly Hills, CA: Sage.

Chaffee, S. H., Zhao, X., & Leshner, G. (1994). Political knowledge and the campaign media of 1992. *Communication Research, 21*, 305-324.

Chaiken, S., Liberman, A., & Eagly, A. H. (1989). Heuristic and systematic information processing within and beyond the persuasion context. In J. S. Uleman & J. A. Bargh (Eds.), *Unintended thought* (pp. 212-252). New York: Guilford.

Chang, C., & Hitchon, J. (1997). Mass media impact on voter response to women candidates: Theoretical development. *Communication Theory, 7*, 29-52.

Cialdini, R. B. (1993). *Influence: Science and practice* (3rd ed.). New York: HarperCollins.

Cobb, M. D., & Kuklinski, J. H. (1997). Changing minds: Political arguments and political persuasion. *American Journal of Political Science, 41*, 88-121.

Diamond, E., & Bates, S. (1992). *The spot: The rise of political advertising on television* (3rd ed.). Cambridge, MA: MIT Press.

Diamond, G. A., & Cobb, M. D. (1996). The candidate as catastrophe: Latitude theory and the problems of political persuasion. In D. C. Mutz, P. M. Sniderman, & R. A. Brody (Eds.), *Political persuasion and attitude change* (pp. 225-247). Ann Arbor: University of Michigan Press.

Dye, T. R., & Zeigler, H. (1996). *The irony of democracy: An uncommon introduction to American politics* (10th ed.). Belmont, CA: Wadsworth.

Etzioni, A. (Ed.). (1998). *The essential communitarian reader*. Lanham, MD: Rowman & Littlefield.

Faber, R. J., Tims, A. R., & Schmitt, K. G. (1993). Negative political advertising and voting intent: The role of involvement and alternative information sources. *Journal of Advertising, 22*, 67-76.

Falbo, T. (1977). Multidimensional scaling of power strategies. *Journal of Personality and Social Psychology, 35*, 537-547.

Fazio, R. H. (1989). On the power and functionality of attitudes: The role of attitude accessibility. In A. R. Pratkanis, S. J. Breckler, & A. G. Greenwald (Eds.), *Attitude structure and function* (pp. 153-179). Hillsdale, NJ: Lawrence Erlbaum.

Fazio, R. H., & Williams, C. J. (1986). Attitude accessibility as a moderator of the attitude-perception and attitude-behavior relations: An investigation of the 1984 presidential election. *Journal of Personality and Social Psychology, 51*, 505-514.

Fields, J., & Schuman, H. (1976). Public beliefs about the beliefs of the public. *Public Opinion Quarterly, 40*, 427-448.

Finkel, S. E., & Geer, J. G. (1998). A spot check: Casting doubt on the demobilizing effect of attack advertising. *American Journal of Political Science, 42*, 573-595.

Friedenberg, R. V. (Ed.). (1994). *Rhetorical studies of national political debates, 1960-1992* (2nd ed.). Westport, CT: Praeger.

Garramone, G. M. (1985). Effects of negative political advertising: The roles of sponsor and rebuttal. *Journal of Broadcasting & Electronic Media, 29*, 147-159.

Glaser, J., & Salovey, P. (1998). Affect in electoral politics. *Personality and Social Psychology Review, 2*, 156-172.

Golebiowska, E. A. (1996). The "pictures in our heads" and individual-targeted tolerance. *Journal of Politics, 58*, 1010-1034.

Grush, J. E., McKeough, K. L., & Ahlering, R. F. (1978). Extrapolating laboratory exposure research to actual political elections. *Journal of Personality and Social Psychology, 36*, 257-270.

Gutmann, A. (1993). The disharmony of democracy. In J. W. Chapman & I. Shapiro (Eds.), *Democratic community: Nomos XXXV* (pp. 126-160). New York: New York University Press.

Gutmann, A., & Thompson, D. (1996). *Democracy and disagreement*. Cambridge, MA: Belknap.

Hedges, H. R. (1998, September 15). Is sexual harassment "only about sex"? *The Wall Street Journal*, p. A22.

Held, D. (1996). *Models of democracy* (2nd ed.). Stanford, CA: Stanford University Press.

Hellweg, S. A., Pfau, M., & Brydon, S. R. (1992). *Televised presidential debates: Advocacy in contemporary America*. New York: Praeger.

Herbst, S. (1995). On electronic public space: Talk shows in theoretical perspective. *Political Communication, 12*, 263-274.

Hinck, E. A. (1993). *Enacting the presidency: Political argument, presidential debates, and presidential character*. Westport, CT: Praeger.

Hodgkinson, G., & Leland, C. M. (1999). Metaphors in the 1996 presidential debates: An analysis of themes. In L. L. Kaid & D. G. Bystrom (Eds.), *The electronic election: Perspectives on the 1996 campaign communication* (pp. 149-161). Mahwah, NJ: Lawrence Erlbaum.

Holbrook, T. M. (1996). *Do campaigns matter?* Thousand Oaks, CA: Sage.

Holloway, R. L. (1996). The Clintons and the health care crisis: Opportunity lost, promise unfulfilled. In R. E. Denton, Jr., & R. L. Holloway (Eds.), *The Clinton presidency: Images, issues, and communication strategies* (pp. 159-187). Westport, CT: Praeger.

Holmes, D. (Ed.). (1997). *Virtual politics: Identity and community in cyberspace*. Thousand Oaks, CA: Sage.

Holmes, S. (1995). *Passions and constraint: On the theory of liberal democracy*. Chicago: University of Chicago Press.

Huckfeldt, R., & Sprague, J. (1987). Networks in context: The social flow of political information. *American Political Science Review, 81*, 1197-1216.

Huckfeldt, R., & Sprague, J. (1995). *Citizens, politics, and social communication: Information and influence in an election campaign*. New York: Cambridge University Press.

Iyengar, S. (1991). *Is anyone responsible? How television frames political issues*. Chicago: University of Chicago Press.

Iyengar, S., & Kinder, D. R. (1987). *News that matters*. Chicago: University of Chicago Press.

Jamieson, K. H. (1992). *Dirty politics: Deception, distraction, and democracy*. New York: Oxford University Press.

Jamieson, K. H., & Cappella, J. N. (1995). *Media in the middle: Fairness and accuracy in the 1994 health care reform debate*. Report, Annenberg Public Policy Center, University of Pennsylvania.

Johnson, D. W. (1999). The cyberspace election in your future. In B. Newman (Ed.), *Handbook of political marketing*. Thousand Oaks, CA: Sage.

Johnson, H., & Broder, D. S. (1996). *The system: The American way of politics at the breaking point*. Boston: Little, Brown.

Johnson-Cartee, K. S., & Copeland, G. A. (1991). *Negative political advertising: Coming of age*. Hillsdale, NJ: Lawrence Erlbaum.

Jorgensen, P. F. (1998). Affect, persuasion, and communication processes. In P. F. Andersen (Ed.), *Handbook of communication and emotion: Research, theory, applications, and contexts* (pp. 403-421). Orlando, FL: Academic Press.

Just, M. R., Crigler, A. N., Alger, D. E., Cook, T. E., Kern, M., & West, D. M. (1996). *Crosstalk: Citizens, candidates, and the media in a presidential campaign*. Chicago: University of Chicago Press.

Just, M. R., Crigler, A. N., & Wallach, L. (1990). Thirty seconds or thirty minutes: What voters learn from spot advertisements and candidate debates. *Journal of Communication, 40*(3), 120-133.

Kaid, L. L. (1994). Political advertising in the 1992 campaign. In R. E. Denton, Jr. (Ed.), *The 1992 presidential campaign: A communication perspective* (pp. 111-127). Westport, CT: Praeger.

Kaid, L. L., & Boydston, J. (1987). An experimental study of the effectiveness of negative political advertisements. *Communication Quarterly, 35*, 193-201.

Kaid, L. L., & Holtz-Bacha, C. (1995). Political advertising across cultures: Comparing content, styles, and effects. In L. L. Kaid & C. Holtz-Bacha (Eds.), *Political advertising in Western democracies: Parties and candidates on television* (pp. 206-227). Thousand Oaks, CA: Sage.

Kaid, L. L., & Johnston, A. (1991). Negative versus positive television advertising in U.S. presidential campaigns, 1960-1988. *Journal of Communication, 41*(3), 53-64.

Kaid, L. L., & Tedesco, J. C. (1999). Presidential candidate presentation: Videostyle in the 1996 presidential spots. In L. L. Kaid & D. G. Bystrom (Eds.), *The electronic election: Perspectives on the 1996 campaign communication* (pp. 209-221). Mahwah, NJ: Lawrence Erlbaum.

Kaid, L. L., Tedesco, J. C., & Spiker, J. A. (1996). Media conflicts over Clinton policies: Political advertising and the battle for public opinion. In R. E. Denton, Jr., & R. L. Holloway (Eds.), *The Clinton presidency: Images, issues, and communication strategies* (pp. 103-121). Westport, CT: Praeger.

Katz, D. (1960). The functional approach to the study of attitudes. *Public Opinion Quarterly, 24*, 163-204.

Katz, E., & Feldman, J. J. (1962). The debates in the light of research: A survey of surveys. In S. Kraus (Ed.), *The great debates: Background, perspective, effects* (pp. 173-223). Bloomington: Indiana University Press.

Kellermann, K. (1984). The negativity effect and its implications for initial interaction. *Communication Monographs, 51*, 37-55.

Kern, M. (1989). *30-second politics: Political advertising in the eighties*. New York: Praeger.

Kinder, D. R. (1994). Reason and emotion in American political life. In R. C. Schank & E. Langer (Eds.), *Beliefs, reasoning, and decision making: Psycho-logic in honor of Bob Abelson* (pp. 277-314). Hillsdale, NJ: Lawrence Erlbaum.

Koch, J. W. (1998). Political rhetoric and political persuasion: The changing structure of citizens' preferences on health insurance during policy debate. *Public Opinion Quarterly, 62*, 209-229.

Kotler, P., & Kotler, N. (1999). Political marketing: Generating effective candidates, campaigns, and causes. In B. Newman (Ed.), *Handbook of political marketing* (pp. 3-18). Thousand Oaks, CA: Sage.

Kraus, S. (1988). *Televised presidential debates and public policy*. Hillsdale, NJ: Lawrence Erlbaum.

Kurtz, H. (1998). *Spin cycle: Inside the Clinton propaganda machine*. New York: Free Press.

Lanoue, D. J. (1992). One that made a difference: Cognitive consistency, political knowledge, and the 1980 presidential debate. *Public Opinion Quarterly, 56*, 168-184.

Lanzetta, J. T., Sullivan, D. G., Masters, R. D., & McHugo, G. J. (1985). Emotional and cognitive responses to televised images of political leaders. In S. Kraus & R. M. Perloff (Eds.), *Mass media and political thought: An information-*

processing approach (pp. 85-116). Beverly Hills, CA: Sage.

Lazarsfeld, P. F., Berelson, B., & Gaudet, H. (1944). *The people's choice: How the voter makes up his mind in a presidential campaign.* New York: Columbia University Press.

Lemert, J. B., Elliott, W. R., Bernstein, J. M., Rosenberg, W. L., & Nestvold, K. J. (1991). *News verdicts, the debates, and presidential campaigns.* New York: Praeger.

Lemert, J. B., Elliott, W. R., Rosenberg, W. L., & Bernstein, J. M. (1996). *The politics of disenchantment: Bush, Clinton, Perot, and the press.* Cresskill, NJ: Hampton.

Lewis, A. (1998, September 15). Muddying the waters. *The New York Times, p. A31.*

Lodge, M. (1995). Toward a procedural model of candidate evaluation. In M. Lodge & K. M. McGraw (Eds.), *Political judgment: Structure and process* (pp. 111-139). Ann Arbor: University of Michigan Press.

Manheim, J. B. (1994). *Strategic public diplomacy and American foreign policy: The evolution of influence.* New York: Oxford University Press.

Marcus, G. E., & Hanson, R. L. (Eds.). (1993). *Reconsidering the democratic public.* University Park: Pennsylvania State University Press.

Margolis, M., & Mauser, G. A. (Eds.). (1989). *Manipulating public opinion: Essays on public opinion as a dependent variable.* Pacific Grove, CA: Brooks/Cole.

Marks, G., & Miller, N. (1987). Ten years of research on the false-consensus effect: An empirical and theoretical review. *Psychological Bulletin, 102,* 72-90.

Martel, M. (1983). *Political campaign debates: Images, strategies, and tactics.* New York: Longman.

Matthews, C. (1996). *Kennedy and Nixon: The rivalry that shaped postwar America.* New York: Simon & Schuster.

McGerr, M. E. (1986). *The decline of popular politics: The American North, 1865-1928.* New York: Oxford University Press.

McGinniss, J. (1969). *The selling of the president.* New York: Trident.

McGraw, K. M., & Hubbard, C. (1996). Some of the people some of the time: Individual differences in acceptance of political accounts. In D. C. Mutz, P. M. Sniderman, & R. A. Brody

(Eds.), *Political persuasion and attitude change* (pp. 145-170). Ann Arbor: University of Michigan Press.

McGuire, W. J. (1985). Attitudes and attitude change. In G. Lindzey & E. Aronson (Eds.), *Handbook of social psychology* (3rd ed., Vol. 2, pp. 233-346). New York: Random House.

McLeod, J. M., Kosicki, G. M., & McLeod, D. M. (1994). The expanding boundaries of political communication effects. In J. Bryant & D. Zillmann (Eds.), *Media effects: Advances in theory and research* (pp. 123-162). Hillsdale, NJ: Lawrence Erlbaum.

Merritt, S. (1984). Negative political advertising: Some empirical findings. *Journal of Advertising, 13,* 27-38.

Meyer, J., & Carlin, D. B. (1994). The impact of formats on voter reaction. In D. B. Carlin & M. S. McKinney (Eds.), *The 1992 presidential debates in focus* (pp. 69-83). Westport, CT: Praeger.

Meyers, M. (1957). *The Jacksonian persuasion: Politics and beliefs.* Stanford, CA: Stanford University Press.

Mill, J. S. (1951). *On liberty. In three essays.* Oxford, UK: Oxford University Press. (Original work published 1859)

Miller, A. H., & MacKuen, M. (1979). Informing the electorate: A national study. In S. Kraus (Ed.), *The great debates: Carter vs. Ford, 1976* (pp. 269-297). Bloomington: Indiana University Press.

Miller, G. R. (1980). On being persuaded: Some basic distinctions. In M. E. Roloff & G. R. Miller (Eds.), *Persuasion: New directions in theory and research* (pp. 11-28). Beverly Hills, CA: Sage.

Miller, J. M., & Krosnick, J. A. (1996). News media impact on the ingredients of presidential evaluations: A program of research on the priming hypothesis. In D. C. Mutz, P. M. Sniderman, & R. A. Brody (Eds.), *Political persuasion and attitude change* (pp. 79-100). Ann Arbor: University of Michigan Press.

Mondak, J. J. (1993). Public opinion and heuristic processing of source cues. *Political Behavior, 15,* 167-192.

Morone, J. A. (1990). *The democratic wish: Popular participation and the limits of American government.* New York: Basic Books.

Morris, D. (1999). *The new prince: Machiavelli up-dated for the twenty-first century.* Los Angeles: Renaissance Books.

Morris, J. D., Roberts, M. S., & Baker, G. F. (1999). Emotional responses of African American voters to ad messages. In L. L. Kaid & D. G. Bystrom (Eds.), *The electronic election: Perspectives on the 1996 campaign communication* (pp. 257-274). Mahwah, NJ: Lawrence Erlbaum.

Mutz, D. C. (1998). *Impersonal influence: How perceptions of mass collectives affect political attitudes.* New York: Cambridge University Press.

Mutz, D. C., Sniderman, P. M., & Brody, R. A. (1996). Political persuasion: The birth of a field of study. In D. C. Mutz, P. M. Sniderman, & R. A. Brody (Eds.), *Political persuasion and attitude change* (pp. 1-14). Ann Arbor: University of Michigan Press.

Newhagen, J. E., & Reeves, B. (1991). Emotion and memory responses for negative political advertising: A study of television commercials used in the 1988 presidential election. In F. Biocca (Ed.), *Television and political advertising, Vol. 1: Psychological processes* (pp. 197-220). Hillsdale, NJ: Lawrence Erlbaum.

Newman, B. I. (1994). *The marketing of the president: Political marketing as campaign strategy.* Thousand Oaks, CA: Sage.

O'Sullivan, C. S., Chen, A., Mohapatra, S., Sigelman, L., & Lewis, E. (1988). Voting in ignorance: The politics of smooth-sounding names. *Journal of Applied Social Psychology, 18,* 1094-1106.

Owen, D. (1997). Talk radio and evaluations of President Clinton. *Political Communication, 14,* 333-353.

Page, B. I., & Tannenbaum, J. (1996). Populistic deliberation and talk radio. *Journal of Communication, 46*(2), 33-54.

Paisley, W. J. (1981). Public communication campaigns: The American experience. In R. E. Rice & W. J. Paisley (Eds.), *Public communication campaigns* (pp. 15-40). Beverly Hills, CA: Sage.

Patterson, O. (1998, September 15). What is freedom without privacy? The *New York Times,* p. A31.

Patterson, T. E. (1980). *The mass media election: How Americans choose their president.* New York: Praeger.

Patterson, T. E. (1993). *Out of order.* New York: Knopf.

Patterson, T. E., & McClure, R. D. (1976). *The unseeing eye: The myth of television power in national elections.* New York: G. P. Putnam.

Perloff, R. M. (1984). Political involvement: A critique and a process-oriented reformulation. *Critical Studies in Mass Communication, 1,* 146-160.

Perloff, R. M. (1993). *The dynamics of persuasion.* Hillsdale, NJ: Lawrence Erlbaum.

Perloff, R. M. (1996). Perceptions and conceptions of political media impact: The third-person effect and beyond. In A. N. Crigler (Ed.), *The psychology of political communication* (pp. 177-197). Ann Arbor: University of Michigan Press.

Perloff, R. M. (1998). *Political communication: Politics, press, and public in America.* Mahwah, NJ: Lawrence Erlbaum.

Perloff, R. M. (1999). Elite, popular, and merchandised politics: Historical origins of presidential campaign marketing. In B. I. Newman (Ed.), *Handbook of political marketing* (pp. 19-40). Thousand Oaks, CA: Sage.

Petty, R. E., & Cacioppo, J. T. (1986). The elaboration likelihood model of persuasion. In L. Berkowitz (Ed.), *Advances in experimental social psychology* (Vol. 19, pp. 123-205). San Diego: Academic Press.

Pfau, M., Holbert, R. L., Szabo, E. A., & Kaminski, K. (1999, August). *Impact of soft-money-sponsored issue advocacy advertising versus candidate-sponsored positive and negative advertising: Influences on candidate preferences and democratic processes.* Paper presented at the meeting of the Association for Education in Journalism and Mass Communication, New Orleans, LA.

Pfau, M., Kendall, K. E., Reichert, T, Hellweg, S. A., Lee, W., Tusing, K. J., & Prosise, T. O. (1997). Influence of communication during the distant phase of the 1996 Republican presidential primary campaign. *Journal of Communication, 47*(4), 6-26.

Pfau, M., & Kenski, H. C. (1990). *Attack politics.* New York: Praeger.

Pfau, M., & Louden, A. (1994). Effectiveness of adwatch formats in deflecting political attack ads. *Communication Research, 21,* 325-341.

Pfau, M., Moy, P., Holbert, R. L., Szabo, E. A., Lin, W-K., & Zhang, W. (1998). The influence of political talk radio on confidence in democratic institutions. *Journalism & Mass Communication Quarterly, 75,* 730-745.

Pinkleton, B. E. (1997). The effects of negative comparative political advertising on candidate evaluations and advertising evaluations: An exploration. *Journal of Advertising, 26,* 19-29.

Pinkleton, B. E. (1998). Effects of print comparative political advertising on political decision making and participation. *Journal of Communication, 48,* 24-36.

Reese, S. D., Grant, A., & Danielan, L. H. (1994). The structure of news sources on television: A network analysis of "CBS News," "Nightline," "MacNeil/Lehrer," and "This Week With David Brinkley." *Journal of Communication, 44*(2), 84-107.

Rhee, J. W. (1997). Strategy and issue frames in election campaign coverage: A social cognitive account of framing effects. *Journal of Communication, 47*(3), 26-48.

Robinson, J. P. (1976). The press as king-maker. *Journalism Quarterly, 51,* 587-594, 606.

Roddy, B. L., & Garramone, G. M. (1988). Appeals and strategies of negative political advertising. *Journal of Broadcasting & Electronic Media, 32,* 415-427.

Rogers, E. M., & Storey, J. D. (1987). Communication campaigns. In C. R. Berger & S. H. Chaffee (Eds.), *Handbook of communication science* (pp. 817-846). Newbury Park, CA: Sage.

Roth, M. S. (1987). *Psycho-analysis as history: Negation and freedom in Freud.* Ithaca, NY: Cornell University Press.

Sandel, M. J. (1996). *Democracy's discontent: America in search of a public philosophy.* Cambridge, MA: Belknap.

Schleuder, J., McCombs, M., & Wanta, W. (1991). Inside the agenda-setting process: How political advertising and TV news prime viewers to think about issues and candidates. In F. Biocca (Ed.), *Television and political advertising,* Vol. 1: *Psychological processes* (pp. 265-309). Hillsdale, NJ: Lawrence Erlbaum.

Schudson, M. (1995). *The power of news.* Cambridge, MA: Harvard University Press.

Schudson, M. (1997). Why conversation is not the soul of democracy. *Critical Studies in Mass Communication, 14,* 297-309.

Schudson, M. (1998). *The good citizen: A history of American civic life.* New York: Free Press.

Schwartz, T. (1973). *The responsive chord.* Garden City, NY: Anchor.

Schwarz, N., Bless, H., & Bohner, G. (1991). Mood and persuasion: Affective states influence the processing of persuasive communications. In M. P. Zanna (Ed.), *Advances in experimental social psychology* (Vol. 24, pp. 161-199). San Diego: Academic Press.

Sears, D. O., & Chaffee, S. H. (1979). Uses and effects of the 1976 debates: An overview of empirical studies. In S. Kraus (Ed.), *The great debates: Carter vs. Ford, 1976* (pp. 223-261). Bloomington: Indiana University Press.

Sears, D. O., Van Laar, C., Carrillo, M., & Kosterman, R. (1997). Is it really racism? The origins of White Americans' opposition to race-targeted policies. *Public Opinion Quarterly, 61,* 16-53.

Shapiro, M. A., & Rieger, R. H. (1992). Comparing positive and negative political advertising on radio. *Journalism Quarterly, 69,* 135-145.

Shoemaker, P. J., & Reese, S. D. (1996). *Mediating the message: Theories of influences on mass media content* (2nd ed.). White Plains, NY: Longman.

Siebert, F. S., Peterson, T., & Schramm, W. (1956). *Four theories of the press.* Urbana: University of Illinois Press.

Smith, G. W. (1998). The political impact of name sounds. *Communication Monographs, 65,* 154-172.

Sunstein, C. R. (1993). *Democracy and the problem of free speech.* New York: Free Press.

Swanson, D. L., & Mancini, P. (Eds.). (1996). *Politics, media, and modern democracy: An international study of innovations in electoral campaigning and their consequences.* Westport, CT: Praeger.

Tannen, D. (1998). *The argument culture: Moving from debate to dialogue.* New York: Random House.

Tedesco, J. C., Miller, J. L., & Spiker, J. A. (1999). Presidential campaigning on the information superhighway: An exploration of content and form. In L. L. Kaid & D. G. Bystrom (Eds.), *The electronic election: Perspectives on the 1996 campaign communication* (pp. 51-63). Mahwah, NJ: Lawrence Erlbaum.

Tolchin, S. J. (1996). *The angry American: How voter rage is changing the nation*. Boulder, CO: Westview.

Troy, G. (1996). *See how they ran: The changing role of the presidential candidate* (rev. ed.). Cambridge, MA: Harvard University Press.

Weaver, D. H., Graber, D. A., McCombs, M. E., & Eyal, C. H. (1981). *Media agenda-setting in a presidential election: Issues, images, and interest*. New York: Praeger.

Weimann, G. (1994). *The influentials: People who influence people*. Albany: State University of New York Press.

West, D. M. (1993). *Air wars: Television advertising in election campaigns, 1952-1992*. Washington, DC: Congressional Quarterly Press.

West, D. M. (1997). *Air wars: Television advertising in election campaigns, 1952-1996* (2nd ed.). Washington, DC: Congressional Quarterly Press.

Whillock, R. K. (1999). Giant sucking sounds: Politics as illusion. In D. Slayden & R. K. Whillock (Eds.), *Soundbite culture: The death of discourse in a wired world* (pp. 5-28). Thousand Oaks, CA: Sage.

Wood, G. S. (1992). *The radicalism of the American Revolution*. New York: Knopf.

Wyatt, R. O., Katz, E., & Kim, J. (2000). Bridging the spheres: Political and personal conversation in public and private spaces. *Journal of Commmunication, 50*(1), 71-92.

Zaller, J. R. (1992). *The nature and origins of mass opinion*. New York: Cambridge University Press.

Zaller, J. (1996). The myth of massive media impact revived: New support for a discredited idea. In D. C. Mutz, P. M. Sniderman, & R. A. Brody (Eds.), *Political persuasion and attitude change* (pp. 17-78). Ann Arbor: University of Michigan Press

Zarefsky, D. (1990). *Lincoln, Douglas, and slavery: In the crucible of public debate*. Chicago: University of Chicago Press.

Zhao, X., & Chaffee, S. H. (1995). Campaign advertisements versus television news as sources of political issue information. *Public Opinion Quarterly, 59*, 41-65.

Ziegler, P. (1969). *The black death*. London: Collins.

Zullow, H. M., & Seligman, M. E. P. (1989). Pessimistic rumination predicts defeat of presidential candidates, 1900 to 1984. *Psychological Inquiry, 1*, 52-61.

29

Enlarging the Role of Environment as a Social Influence Construct in Health Campaigns

ROXANNE PARROTT
NICHOLE EGBERT
JOHN ANDERTON
ENID SEFCOVIC

Few would disagree with the statement that "good health is a desirable state of being, while bad health is to be avoided." Such is the underlying premise of strategic health communication activities, which include efforts to understand and influence health policy, health campaigns, provider-patient interaction, and social support (for a discussion, see Sharf, 1993). The primary goals of health communication strategic activities are to control and prevent disease and illness. Health campaigns aim to achieve these ends via the promotion of (a) screening, which should save lives and money by detecting disease at early stages, and (b) healthy behaviors, which could avoid disease and illness altogether. "It should never be forgotten that the great victories against typhoid fever, cholera, infantile diarrhea, malaria, smallpox, diphtheria, whooping cough, tetanus, and poliomyelitis were won by the application of preventive medicine" (Terris,

1968, p. 11). Yet in 1993, more than 5,000 children in the United States got pertussis, also known as whooping cough (Centers for Disease Control and Prevention [CDC], 1993), suggesting that much remains to be done in the area of health promotion and prevention via strategies that include health campaigns. Similar data exist for disease control, as the underuse of detection methods such as mammography is a prevalent concern among health professionals (Salazar & de Moor, 1995).

Comprising the focus of this chapter, health campaigns have been a mainstay of persuasive communication activities for several decades, with a number of these endeavors constituting exemplars of this form of social influence. These include the Stanford Three Community and Five City projects (Farquhar et al., 1990; Flora, Maccoby, & Farquhar, 1989), the Minnesota Heart Health Program (Carlaw,

Mittelmark, Bracht, & Luepker, 1984; Finnegan, Bracht, & Viswanath, 1989), and the North Karelia project (Puska, 1985), with the first two occurring in the United States and the third taking place in eastern Finland. The first and third projects, which developed "almost concurrently," formed "mutually beneficial scientific exchanges" (Puska et al., 1985, p. 150). We review the lessons learned about social influence in health campaigns based on these and other endeavors designed to benefit individuals' health and well-being, summarizing the previous work of communication scholars' contributions (e.g., Backer & Rogers, 1993; Backer, Rogers, & Sopory, 1992), adding the findings about health campaigns from research published in two journals devoted to the topic of health communication (the *Journal of Health Communication* and *Health Communication*) and highlighting health campaign research exemplars discussed in related fields' publication outlets.

HEALTH CAMPAIGNS DEFINED

Health campaigns are characterized by features common to all persuasive communication campaigns, including planning, implementation, and evaluation (Pfau & Parrott, 1993). It seems simple enough: Translate the findings from basic science into workable prescriptions for daily living, and communicate these to the public. Two challenges unique to health campaigners must be addressed in their pursuit of these ends. First, health campaigners are unlikely to be health experts or health professionals, so translating the research into prescriptive practices requires assistance. To accomplish this, health campaigners forge relationships with health experts, often in the form of expert advisory panels, which may include physicians, medical researchers, and others who have devoted their careers

to understanding the etiology of a particular disease or illness. These team efforts—combining health experts with communication campaigners—have been found to lead to an increase in the content validity of recommendations to be promoted during health interventions (Veneziano & Hooper, 1997).

A second challenge facing health campaigners is the need to understand how a particular audience defines "good health." For some audiences, good health is the ability to work. Farmers, for example, have high levels of satisfaction with their occupation and life in general (Wozniak, Draughn, & Knaub, 1993). Health messages promoting behaviors that appear likely to interfere with a farmer's work will fall on deaf ears. Others, however, may define health in terms of the ability to live a pain-free existence while living with a chronic disease or illness. Persons living with arthritis, cancer, or HIV all have different perspectives to bring to their definitions of good health and interpretations of health information. Still others may be housebound or living with pain, but their health is "good" because it grants them the opportunity to witness the birth of another generation. Understanding how primary audience members define health gives health campaigners insights into their motivations to perform a health practice. To gain this understanding and begin the process of developing expert advisory panels, health campaigners undertake systematic formative evaluation, a vital component of all campaigns (Atkin & Freimuth, 1989) and a characteristic of effective health campaigns (Backer et al., 1992).

FORMATIVE EVALUATION AND HEALTH CAMPAIGNS

Many, if not most, of the great achievements in public health have involved major emphasis on the environment. (Puska et al., 1985, p. 157)

Formative evaluation for health campaigns often relies on the framework of a particular planning model, which integrates diverse theories into a single perspective to guide the focus of activities. Mainstays in the health arena include the Health Belief Model (Becker, 1974) and the Precede/Proceed Model (Green & Kreuter, 1991). The latter emphasizes individual predisposing variables such as knowledge, attitudes, feelings, values, and perceptions, but it acknowledges that these work in concert with enabling characteristics such as the availability and affordability of resources, together with personal skills, which may be reinforced by the attitudes and actions of others in one's social network. This model draws on much of the research that has been conducted using social cognitive theory (Bandura, 1986) and highlights elements from organizational theory as well, a little-acknowledged backdrop for health campaigners' activities (Backer & Rogers, 1993). Use of the Precede/Proceed Model to conduct community assessment, a formative evaluation process that identifies both the strengths and the weaknesses associated with a community, emphasizes the larger social-structural environment in which behavior occurs, a practice common to effective campaigns (Backer et al., 1992; Rice & Foote, 1989). Baseline population surveys, community leadership studies, census information, and interviews are but a few of the approaches used to conduct community assessment, suggesting the time-consuming and creative energies that must be devoted to formative research to achieve the intended outcomes (Finnegan et al., 1989).

Social Environment

Campaigns are inherently social events, depending on the impact that human communication has on the behavior of other humans; health campaigns are imminently social, as the meaning of health is socially constructed. Identifying the social processes that contribute to the particular definition of health within a group, and striving to assess whether personal and social responsibility are compatible with social values (see Guttman, 1997), vitally contribute to the health campaigner's ability to influence an audience. The social environment consists of the health knowledge, attitudes, and practices of a primary audience's families, friends, co-workers, and others in the social network as they relate to a designated campaign topic. The social environment contributes significantly to one's own health knowledge, attitudes, and practices, creating some lifestyles and inhibiting the initiation or maintenance of others (Becker, 1986). The social environment, particularly friends and peers, has been found to be the most important social influence in predicting smoking behavior (Botvin, Epstein, Schinke, & Diaz, 1994). A review of the literature associated with alcohol use and abuse emphasizes the importance of the social environment on alcohol use as well, leading to the recommendation for interventionists to focus on relational barriers to alcohol prevention, especially with regard to drinking and driving (Seibold & Thomas, 1994).

The social environment affords one explanation for the knowledge-behavior gap (Hornik, 1989) and demonstrates that closing the gap is difficult when cultural values are not considered (Alcalay & Bell, 1996). Formative evaluation of the social environment contributed to the recognition that the high prevalence of obesity among African American women relates to cultural eating and exercise patterns, a realization that led the "Sisters Together, Move More Eat Better" project to recommend changes that adapted to the culture rather than invalidating it, successfully encouraging improved nutrition and increased physical exercise among young Black women in three inner-city communities (Rudd, Goldberg, & Dietz, 1999). The Stanford Five City (Flora et al., 1989), Minnesota Heart Health (Carlaw et al., 1984), and North Karelia (Puska et al., 1985) projects' formative evaluation efforts focused significant resources on the social environment, which contributed to understanding about who had direct interpersonal influence on the primary target audiences and the conclusion that more successful campaigns direct health messages at people linked to targeted individuals, especially those with direct interpersonal influence such as peers and parents (Backer et al., 1992).

During Georgia's "Got Youth Covered" campaign development, field observation of coaches' and parents' sun protection behaviors, interviews of coaches and parents about sun protection awareness and behaviors, and surveys of coaches and parents about sun protection and efforts to promote it to youths revealed that coaches and parents were more often modeling tanning behaviors than sun protection and had little understanding about the risk posed by overexposure to the sun for youths (Parrott, Duggan, et al., 1999). Coaches and parents were also found to be willing to reform their behavior in the interest of youths' health and well-being but in need of a little "coaching" about how best to go about the process of influence (Parrott & Duggan, et al., 1999). Formative evaluation of the social environment revealed that both knowledge deficits and social norms functioned as relational barriers to the performance of a health practice, informing message design as well as source and channel selection. Health campaigners' efforts to understand a primary audience's social environment comprise a critical component of systematic formative evaluation. The most efficacious formative evaluation efforts include an examination of the structural environment as well.

Structural Environment

Campaigns coexist with a structural environment that has been identified as a critical focus for formative evaluation in the health campaign planning stage for some years now. The structural environment may support or fail to support access to information and tangible resources needed to perform a recommended health practice, together with those that can make the practice easier, thereby facilitating performance. To assess the structural environment, health campaigners specify what information and tangible resources are needed or could facilitate adoption of a recommended practice to avoid or adapt to a health risk. Once identified, health campaigners assess whether these are available in the audience's realm of day-to-day experience. For example, if parents are expected to obtain immunizations for their children, they require both information about why this practice is necessary and access to clinics that are geographically nearby and that maintain hours of operation allowing working parents to visit during times when they are not working. This suggests that if health campaigners tackled the underuse of immunization in this country, an analysis of the structural environment might lead campaigners to coordinate with direct service delivery components so that parents could follow through on recommended behaviors. Such coordination is a feature associated with more effective health campaigns (Backer et al., 1992) and is a practice closely aligned with attending to the structural environment. The success of these endeavors may well depend on interorganizational collaboration and relationships between those involved in the campaign and those responsible for decision making within the organization (Backer & Rogers, 1993).

One strategy increasingly employed by health campaigners to respond to the structural environment is social marketing, with

Backer & Rogers (1993) identifying its use with effective health campaigns. Social marketing, which focuses on using the right mix of product, price, promotion, and place, often guides the use of mass media in public health from practical and theoretical perspectives (Winett & Wallack, 1996), as health campaign messages often advise individuals to obtain and use particular products to maintain well-being. These items range from sunscreen (to reduce the chances of skin cancer) to low-fat foods (to reduce the risk of heart disease). The Georgia Harvesting Healthy Habits campaign, for example, formatively evaluated whether sunscreen was available in places where farmers were likely to shop, such as feed and seed stores, and finding that it was not, the campaigners widened the secondary audiences to be influenced in the campaign to include sunscreen distributors in the project area (Parrott, Steiner, & Goldenhar, 1996) as well as feed and seed store owners (to carry and promote the product) (Parrott, Lewis, Jones, Steiner, & Goldenhar, 1998). The needs assessment phase of project SALSA, a community-based health promotion project in San Ysidro, California, included a food vendor survey of owners and managers of grocery stores that revealed the presence of no stores involved in nutrition promotion efforts and vendors' belief that customers were not interested in nutrition (Peplinski et al., 1989). These findings expanded the realm of secondary audiences for the project SALSA endeavors to include food vendors, using grocery stores as a site of nutrition promotion (Delapa et al., 1990).

The structural environment has been used to provide an explanation for knowledge-behavior gaps (for a discussion, see Hornik, 1989) and also affords one framework for understanding knowledge gaps. The knowledge gap hypothesis asserts that as mass media information is infused into a social system, some parts of the population with higher socioeconomic status acquire information at a faster rate than do lower status segments, actually widening the knowledge differences between segments (Tichenor, Donohue, & Olien, 1970). The hypothesis has not received consistent support, as motivation to gain information is one variable that reduces gap effects (Ettema, Brown, & Luepker, 1983; Kwak, 1999). The hypothesis is an important consideration in situations where health campaigners are targeting generally uninvolved or unmotivated audiences. The knowledge gap hypothesis has been offered as an explanation for the findings of one study in which people with high levels of education had fewer knowledge gaps regarding knowledge about ways in which HIV/AIDS is transmitted and misconceptions about how the disease is spread (Salmon, Wooten, Gentry, Cole, & Kroger, 1996). The acquisition of knowledge among persons of higher education levels may have been due, in part, to greater availability of information in places where these people spent time. Both the availability and affordability of information and tangible resources to support a recommended health practice are necessary, although not sufficient, for individuals to follow through with most health campaign prescriptions. Through the assessment of the structural environment, health campaigners may broaden the scope of audiences to be addressed or narrow the focus of prescriptions to be promoted to the primary audience. As a result, the campaigners will avoid promoting behaviors that the structural environment cannot support as well as claiming failure in the wake of misdirected campaign efforts.

Finally, finding too little structural support in the environment may create awareness for health campaigners of the need for efforts to change policy. Many health campaigners begin their formative analysis with some ideas about goals and objectives, but as Brown and Einsiedel (1990) reported, while the authors expected to find a need to increase awareness of dangers of HIV virus and knowledge about how the virus is spread, they found a need to change existing laws so that clean needles could be distributed. As Salmon (1992) observed, sometimes to achieve equality of access to information, power strategies such as policy makers' passing laws are needed, as illustrated by the National Childhood Vaccine Injury Act of 1986, which mandates that information about the benefits and side effects of vaccines be distributed before shots are given. In sum, health campaigners' efforts to evaluate the social and structural dimensions of environment should focus the campaign's goals, although the audiences to be addressed may broaden in direct response to findings associated with the primary audience and the health campaign topic. Each audience may be in a different stage of change (Prochaska, DiClemente, & Norcross, 1992; Prochaska et al., 1994) with regard to the health topic, and each audience requires the identification of a specific goal or goals, as is the case in all persuasive communication campaigns (Backer et al., 1992; Pfau & Parrott, 1993; Rice & Atkin, 1989; Salmon, 1989b). With specific audiences and goals in mind, principles based on previous successful use of social influence theories in health campaigns afford insights about the process of audience segmentation, designing health messages, and the selection of sources and channels by which to disseminate the messages.

PRESCRIPTIONS FOR HEALTH CAMPAIGN PRACTICE

A multiplicity of messages, sources, channels, and even audiences are likely to comprise health campaigns. Numerous theories often guide the assessment and goal-setting steps in the questions asked, the data to be collected (indicating what to evaluate and what variables are likely to be influential), and the selection of priorities within campaign objectives. These include the use of theories reviewed in Part I of this volume and others, such as problematic integration theory (Babrow, 1992), an underused perspective that may explain individuals' reactions to the uncertainty created by health information. Most of these perspectives are of the type that Salmon (1992) described as theory "for" campaigns, treating campaigns as independent variables in which the messages, sources, channels, and audiences can be varied for the purpose of changing knowledge, attitudes and practices. A review of health campaign undertakings and prior summaries of the practices associated with more effective campaigns suggests a number of dictums in association with audience segmentation, message design, and channel and source selection. The goal of all of these efforts is "to make the campaign's prescribed actions real to the individual" (Dervin, 1989, p. 68), whether the "individual" is a member of the primary audience's social network, an organizational member within some associated part of the structural environment, a policy maker, or a member of the primary audience. Most evaluation relating these principles to practice has been published in association with primary health campaign audiences. When they are available, we review published findings associated with a prescribed practice and a secondary audience, noting the limits in this regard as both a cautionary note and a direction for future research.

Audience Segmentation

A fundamental principle of all persuasion is to begin with audience analysis, and health campaigns are no different. The purpose of audience segmentation is to identify which members of an audience "share similar antecedent qualities—knowledge, concerns, motivations—

that determine the health behavior in question and that permit tailoring of messages or interventions to those members" who will be reached through similar channels and affected by similar sources (Slater, 1995, p. 197). The approaches to be used in achieving understanding about how to segment an audience are varied, ranging from reliance on demographic characteristics (which have often proven to be too encompassing) to dependence on underlying motivations or constraints (Slater, 1995). Reference to individual motivation requires the campaigner to match a motive to a health practice. For example, an audience's level of altruism was predicted to relate to willingness to be an organ donor, a generally altruistic act, and research demonstrated that college students who were more altruistic responded with a greater willingness to be organ donors when messages appealed to their altruism; less altruistic students responded less favorably (Kopfman & Smith, 1996).

In addition to cognitive and motivational considerations, individual affective traits and states may guide campaigners' segmentation decisions. A research program examining the variable of sensation seeking, "a biologically based characteristic," relating to one's need or preference for novel, complex, and ambiguous stimuli (Palmgreen et al., 1991, p. 218) is based on the argument that one way to segment mass audiences is through the use of sensation seeking as a trait that determines responses to messages (Donohew, Helm, Lawrence, & Shatzer, 1990). Sensation seeking has been found to be one trait related to unsafe sexual behavior, with high versus low sensation seekers responding in predictably different ways to appeals associated with their health and health behavior (Sheer & Cline, 1995; Witte & Morrison, 1995). Sensation seeking also predicts marijuana use and responses to messages designed to inhibit use (Stephenson et al., 1999), contributing to the validity of the statement that segmenting target audiences based on this variable increases effectiveness.

Regardless of the decisions made concerning audience segmentation in association with motivational and affective characteristics of an audience, health campaigners should segment audiences based on literacy levels and physical characteristics such as visual and hearing acuity and health status. The use of appropriate reading levels has a positive impact on closing knowledge gaps (Krishman, 1996). Yet too often, health messages are still constructed beyond the average adult's reading capacity (Slaten, Parrott, & Steiner, 1999). The use of appropriate reading levels is by no means a guarantee of sufficient audience segmentation to promote health behavior, however, as vaccine information statements are written at a fifth- to seventh-grade level and are available in 13 languages (Institute of Medicine, 1997), yet the noncompliance with this child health care routine remains a concern. Beyond audience segmentation principles to guide the development of messages for a health campaign, a number of message design considerations have been found to increase health campaigns' effectiveness.

Message Design

Theories "for" campaigns (Salmon, 1992) are probably most often associated with efforts to design the messages, with considerable time and effort having been expended on the identification of strategies to increase the success associated with health campaign messages (e.g., Maibach & Parrott, 1995). Freimuth (1995) said that too often, however, we simply do not know the message content of a particular intervention because space limitations preclude including it in a published report. More knowledge based in theory or practice likely exists in the experience of campaigners than is accessible through an analysis of campaign literature, but a number of pre-scriptions for practice emerge, including recommendations to (a) repeat a single message, (b) emphasize positive outcomes associated with behavior change rather than negative consequences of failure to change, (c) specify ways to reduce anxiety created by fear appeals (Backer et al., 1992), (d) emphasize specific procedures and knowledge rather than more general information (Parrott, Monahan, Ainsworth, & Steiner, 1998), (e) advise audiences to discuss the campaign with others (Hafstad & Aaro, 1997), and (f) use participatory messages and message strategies (Maibach, Flora, & Nass, 1991).

The first principle, to repeat a single message, tells us nothing about what content to include in the health message but instead emphasizes the importance of having a core or focal message for a campaign that will likely exist in a message environment cluttered with competing and conflicting information. For example, the core message in the Georgia "Got Youth Covered" campaign was "Make It Your GOAL to BLOCK the Sun!" (Parrott & Duggan, 1999), a memorable prescription for soccer-playing youths around which all other campaign messages revolved. Repeating a core message has been found to lead to more effective health campaigns than does the use of multiple messages (Backer et al., 1992), contributing to Dervin's (1989) assertion to "buy as much redundancy as you can afford" (p. 68). There are limits to this recommendation, of course, as research in marketing (e.g., Tyebjee, 1979) and persuasion (e.g., Cacioppo & Petty, 1979) is consistent in finding that a moderate number of message repetitions increases awareness and learning, with the benefits associated with repetition peaking at about three and leading to frustration and hostility with five or more.

Emphasizing positive outcomes associated with behavior change rather than negative consequences of failure to change relies on a gain frame as compared to a loss frame (Rothman & Salovey, 1997). This second recommendation associated with health message design has also been supported with consistency in effective health campaigns (Backer et al., 1992). Emphasizing the positive outcomes of quitting rather than the negative outcomes of continuing, for example, was found to have a greater impact on undergraduates' smoking behavior (Babrow, 1991). Similar results were obtained with adults and smoking, regardless of level of education, although less educated adults believed less strongly in positive health consequences from quitting (Sengupta, 1996). In an extension of efforts to design messages that emphasize positive outcomes, low-income women were found to be more positively disposed toward messages promoting mammograms when the messages were life affirming and logical than when the messages referred to pain or other fearful matters (Marshall, Smith, & McKeon, 1995).

The third recommendation, to specify ways to reduce anxiety created by fear appeals (Backer et al., 1992), is a primary focus within the Extended Parallel Process Model (Witte, 1994), which advances the need for an individual to feel personally able to address a health threat in order to engage in an adaptive response. Too often, health messages intended to arouse fear fail to include message components to address self-efficacy. One analysis of 31 artifacts to promote immunization that were obtained from 27 national childhood health organizations, for example, demonstrated that response efficacy and susceptibility were often present but that self-efficacy and seriousness were not (Smith, 1997). Fear appeals are often effective in making a health topic real to the target audience (Hale & Dillard, 1995), but as some research has demonstrated, health messages designed to arouse fear also arouse other emotions, including surprise and sadness as well as puzzlement and anger, with the former two fostering acceptance of persuasive messages and the latter two discouraging message acceptance (Dillard, Plotnick, Godbold, Freimuth, & Edgar, 1996). This suggests the need for careful piloting of health messages to assess emotional effects before widely disseminating the content.

The fourth principle associated with effective health message design, emphasizing specific procedures and knowledge rather than more general information, has received support with regard to a variety of health topics. Sometimes, a relational barrier to a health practice may be associated with a lack of specific knowledge, and training may reduce the barrier. For example, hair stylists, when trained to give a personalized message promoting mammography to clients, significantly affected clients' intention to get mammograms, knowledge about risk for breast cancer, response efficacy perceptions, and feelings of self-control (Howze, Broyden, & Impara, 1992). Detailed knowledge about specific procedures is necessary to perform a health practice and is too often lacking, as illustrated by the finding that knowledge about different contraceptive methods was low, ranging from one fourth to just under one half correct responses (Valente, Paredes, & Poppe, 1998). The most effective public service announcements (PSAs) about AIDS presented information in a simple and straightforward manner, while complex and emotional messages drew negative responses (Baggaley, 1988; Perse, Nathanson, & McLeod, 1996). There has, however, been too much emphasis on information and too little on specific recommendations, as illustrated by one content analysis of PSAs from 33 countries (Johnson, Flora, & Rimal, 1997) and an analysis of AIDS work site programs that concluded that materials were too complex to be successful, suggesting the need to redesign messages around this principle (Backer & Rogers, 1998). The outcomes of using concrete plans of action, as compared to abstract messages, include the

findings that such specific messages contributed to (a) personalizing AIDS risk (Waldron, Caughlin, & Jackson, 1995), (b) increasing compliance with immunization (McDivitt, Zimicki, & Hornik, 1997), and (c) learning to differentiate accurate from inaccurate information about eating smart (Chew, Palmer, & Kim, 1998).

Telling audiences to discuss the campaign with others, a fifth practice to be incorporated into health campaign message design activities, extends the recommendation to give specific information, going beyond the domain of health procedures to the realm of interpersonal relationships. Discussing the campaign with others has been found to be associated with a reduction in and postponement of smoking among adolescents (Hafstad & Aaro, 1997). The principle may be associated with making a public commitment to behave in a particular fashion, with such commitment contributing to the likelihood that one will adapt one's behavior to reduce a health risk (Parrott, Monahan, et al., 1998). Three nutrition communication programs in Africa successfully integrated African folk communication norms, including talking with others about nutrition, to develop efficacious nutrition interventions in Sub-Saharan Africa (Pratt, Silva-Barbeau, & Pratt, 1997).

The sixth recommendation for health message designers to incorporate into campaign planning, intervention, and evaluation is the use of participatory messages and message strategies, which may increase feelings of self-efficacy and also make one feel committed to a practice. To engage through participation is more effective than diffusion alone (Krishnatray & Melkote, 1998). Message strategies applying this practice might include verbal and pictorial modeling, which is participatory in a vicarious sense (Anderson & McMillion, 1995). Other media might also be used so long as the message includes role models demonstrating an activity and providing detailed

illustrations of how to perform a recommended practice, which combines elements of
the fourth prescription (Witte, Cameron,
Lapinski, & Nzyuko, 1998). This message
strategy has also proven to be effective with
regard to a secondary health campaign audience, community leaders, as they have been
found to be more involved with contributing
to positive health changes in a primary audience when they are asked to actively participate than when they are just included as supporters of change (Myrick, 1998).

The Stanford Five City project, which had a
significant impact on individual self-efficacy
through minimal contact, used a number of
the preceding practices. The project repeated
a single message using varied outlets, including newsletters, self-help behavior change
kits, and reinforcement/complementary messages on television and radio programs. These
messages were designed to promote self-
efficacy through modeling, which encouraged
participation and discussion with others
(Maibach et al., 1991). The successful use of
modeling depends partly, of course, on the
selection of an appropriate role model, with
the message source comprising an important
consideration for all health campaign message
development.

Message Source

As with the specific verbal content to be
used in health campaign messages, the specific
source used to deliver the content is a critical
consideration. Three principles for practice
emerge from an analysis of previous effective
health campaigns, with one overarching prescription: Identify credible spokespersons.
These credible spokespersons may include any
or all of the following, based on previous successful health campaigns: (a) the use of celebrities to attract attention, (b) inclusion of key
power figures and government bodies (Backer

& Rogers, 1993; Backer et al., 1992), and (c)
careful selection of role models given that they
may become negative models, as well as positive models, through personal actions (Parrott
& Duggan, 1999). Celebrities may be very
influential as role models—more than the use
of logic or common sense—as was illustrated
with basketball star Magic Johnson, whose
personal experience with and concern about
AIDS contributed to success in message outcomes (Brown & Basil, 1995). Similarly, AIDS
work site programs developed by the CDC's
Business Responds to AIDS programs were
found to be most effective when they focused
around a champion or the occurrence of a
tragic event (Backer & Rogers, 1998).

The second practice, the use of a powerful
or government spokesperson, may evoke a
different response set in an audience, one
associated with legitimacy of the campaign
topic as compared to the identification factor
that celebrities may arouse. The Drug Abuse
Resistance Education (DARE) program used
uniformed police officers to teach the curriculum, one of the unique aspects considered
to be noteworthy and effective (Clayton,
Cattarello, & Walden, 1991). The decision to
use a source whose position of power or authority suggests that he or she will increase an
audience's positive response to a message because of the position must be considered in
light of the target audience's perceptions of
the credibility of the source. Not all audiences
would be expected, for example, to judge uniformed police officers to be credible sources because of either personal or group experience.

Whether using celebrities, individuals in
positions of power, or other sources, health
campaigners must address the very real possibility that the sources may model inappropriate rather than appropriate behaviors, a third
prescription for practice associated with
health campaigners' decision making regarding message sources. Soccer coaches in the
Georgia "Got Youth Covered" program, for

example, more often modeled tanning behaviors than sun protection (Parrott, Duggan, et al., 1999). When identifying such inconsistencies in behavior prior to a campaign, opportunities to obtain buy-in from particular sources exist, as was the case with youths' soccer coaches (Parrott & Duggan, 1999). The highly successful A Su Salud campaign used role models who were actual members of the target audience and who demonstrated personal health decisions to exhibit the behaviors the campaign promoted with regard to tobacco use (Ramirez & McAlister, 1988).

One outcome associated with a secondary health campaign audience has been found to relate to source selection and the overarching principle that should direct this activity. Health campaigners, who may use PSAs as one method for delivering health messages to an audience, recognize that many campaign PSAs never get past gatekeepers to reach a target audience. One of the reasons why a PSA *does* get selected to air, however, is the use of a credible spokesperson, which increases the chances of getting past the media gatekeepers (Hammond, Freimuth, & Morrison, 1987). No message will be effective if it never airs or if it appears in time slots when an intended audience is unlikely to be exposed to it. While both selecting the content of the health message and selecting the specific source to deliver the message are vital and time-consuming tasks, and initial decisions should be pilot-tested before widespread dissemination, deciding which modes of delivery to use in disseminating the campaign message is no less important.

Message Channel

Several principles for practice with regard to channel selection during health campaigns have been identified from previous theory-driven efforts. More effective campaigns (a) use more than one type of media, recognizing, for example, that PSAs alone do not bring behavior change; (b) combine mass media with other activities, using a systems approach to involve community, small groups, and individuals (Backer et al., 1992); (c) recognize that people use print medium or seek experts with specific health concerns, although other media may generate interest in health matters (Hofstetter, Shultze, & Mulvihill, 1992); and (d) realize that channel selection involves trade-offs among different effects (Schooler, Chaffee, Flora, & Roser, 1998).

With regard to the first prescription, as observed under the discussion about message design, redundancy is important—to a point, with the use of different media to repeat the same message affording one way to sustain and even extend interest in the message. The first and second practices were evident in a 1993-1994 campaign in Zimbabwe designed to motivate men to participate in family planning and use modern contraception. Radio and television, in addition to print materials, were used in combination with community events that focused on football games, demonstrating an increase in couples' discussion of family planning, a desire by men to be involved in family planning, and an increase in actual contraceptive use; men exposed to three or more campaign elements were 1.6 times more likely to use a modern contraceptive method (Kim & Marangwanda, 1997). An intervention in North Karelia to attain smoking cessation exemplified the second practice as well, including worksite activities, contests, lay opinion leaders, and health organizations as channels to disseminate the focal messages (Korhonen, Uutela, Korhonen, & Puska, 1998).

The third and fourth recommendations draw campaigners' attention to the reality that some media are better at capturing an audience's attention, while others will be selected for intentional efforts to gain health information, and that different media have different impacts on health outcomes. One study found that television news and information programs were rated highest for learning about preventing illness and maintaining good health, followed by health professionals, family, and friends; then magazines and newspapers; and finally print educational materials (O'Keefe, Boyd, & Brown, 1998). Older, better educated, and motivated persons learned more from newspapers and magazines, while younger and less educated persons got more health information from television (O'Keefe et al., 1998). Interactive media and interpersonal sources were used to complement more traditional channels, encouraging diffusion of information through an overlap of channels and sources (O'Keefe et al., 1998). Immediacy to the topic has been observed to affect channel selection and outcomes significantly in a seat belt campaign, with radio messages being the only medium that related to reported seat belt use (Gantz, Fitzmaurice, & Yoo, 1990). Findings from the Stanford Five City project revealed that reaching a specific type of target audience has been found to be greatest with booklets and then television programs, while reach is highest for tip sheets (Schooler et al., 1998). Impact, which was the amount of knowledge gained during the 5-year campaign, was greatest for a weekly health feature newspaper column written for the project, followed by booklets and television PSAs, then tip sheets, and finally television programs (Schooler et al., 1998). These findings support research that affirms that mass media communicate simple messages well, leading to behavior change (Alcalay, 1983).

Health campaigners may use two additional influence strategies involving the decision to use media as a channel for disseminating health messages. Media advocacy is a systematic approach to increasing community members' skills in taking advantage of the strengths of media, including reach and frequency (Winett & Wallack, 1996). Health campaigners may develop a program to train members of a community, or (more likely) some subgroup of the primary audience responsible for acting as liaisons or representatives of a primary audience, to become their own advocates by teaching them how to access the media, shape stories, and even advance policy solutions over time (Wallack, 1993). Agricultural extension agents, for example, are already advocates for farmers, so gaining skills in media advocacy should broaden their capacity to function efficaciously in their job, making them a good potential secondary audience for training in media advocacy.

Health campaigners may also use entertainment-education, or "edutainment," as an approach to reach a mass audience with a health message via the media. These intentional efforts to have positive health messages and examples embedded in media portrayals are a response to research that demonstrates that media often portray health behaviors that may have negative health effects when modeled by viewers. One study, for example, found that of 210 servings of food served during nine episodes each of *The Cosby Show, Family Ties,* and *Growing Pains,* children ate more nutritiously than did adults, and snacks comprised nearly half of all food consumed (Larson, 1991).

Edutainment depends on successful efforts to influence scriptwriters, directors, and producers of a television series to incorporate a health issue into the story line. An increasing number of lobbyists expend time and money to gain attention for their causes on television through edutainment (Montgomery, 1988). This strategy recognizes that politics, values, and ethics enter into decision making about the inclusion of specific health content in entertainment shows and the adoption of edutainment as a strategy. Organizational representatives from the CDC and the American Cancer Society, therefore, are more likely to lobby Hollywood successfully to gain access to an entertainment setting as a channel to use in delivering health messages. These organizations may become involved, however, as a result of health campaigners' efforts to involve them through strategies that may include organizational membership on campaign steering committees or expert advisory panels, explaining why this strategy often requires health campaigners to think in terms of secondary audiences to influence with regard to the primary audience.

When successful, edutainment can lead to the inclusion of story lines associated with health issues such as breast cancer, as illustrated by the television show *Thirty-something*, which portrayed a character's bout with the disease, providing the opportunity to both destigmatize individuals with cancer and portray ways to deal with breast cancer (Sharf & Freimuth, 1993). Audiences form parasocial relationships with characters who serve as reference points making involvement likely and lessons more easily integrated (Sharf, Freimuth, Greenspon, & Plotnick, 1996).

In sum, the findings from basic research conducted in communication afford health campaigners the opportunity to apply the findings to field settings, with the results contributing to the availability of a number of tried-and-true tools in campaigners' toolboxes for use in conducting efficacious health campaigns. With careful application and understanding, the successful practices associated with previous campaigns' message design and dissemination efforts may be used, leading to the strongest likelihood of bridging basic and applied communication sciences for the benefit of humanity, a claim that no other social influencer may make with such validity. As with any set of tools, however, no matter how exacting they may be, in the absence of good materials to work with and skilled practitioners to apply the tools, their availability will have little impact. Moreover,

the need exists for attention to issues related to social influence that are specific to health campaigns.

FUTURE DIRECTIONS FOR HEALTH CAMPAIGN RESEARCH

With every theory-driven study conducted in the social influence arena, an opportunity exists to posit relationships between the findings and the conduct of health campaigns. On occasion, a reciprocal relationship exists in which the conduct of health campaigns contributes to social influence theory or understanding about the relationships between and among variables associated with social influence. There are numerous opportunities to examine both macro and micro issues relating to social influence and health campaigns during the years to come. We examine a few of these in what follows.

1. *Health campaigners should expand the boundaries of formative research to the ecological environment, addressing the intersection between risk communication and health communication in health campaigns.* As Shelton (1991) observed, "Everyone has the right to an environment adequate for general health and well-being" (p. 125), a direct reference to the ecological environment. The ecological environment consists, quite literally, of the actual physical conditions—including the weather, terrain, air quality, and water quality—in which the primary audience lives. Health campaigners should systematically evaluate the relationship of these matters to intended promotion efforts as part of formative evaluation activities, as the ecological environment is a pre-condition for well-being (Bandi, 1993).

While the ecological environment is not directly discussed in prior campaign literature, campaigns coexist with both structural and ecological environments. The ecological environment contributes to exercise, eating, and drinking practices, to name but a few topics commonly associated with health campaigns that are affected by the geography and climate in which a campaign takes place. During formative evaluation for the Georgia Harvesting Healthy Habits project, the ecological environment proved to be a barrier to south Georgia farmers' use of sunscreen, as the farmers revealed that heat and humidity make pesticides stick to their skin when they use sunscreen, creating more irritation than that caused by the sun (Parrott et al., 1996). This finding led to formal efforts with agricultural extension service staff and farmers to sample sufficient numbers of sunscreens to determine which ones were less likely to leave sticky residue on the skin, leading to messages promoting the use of particular products as solutions to a specific problem recognized in relation to the ecological environment.

Emphasizing the social environment to the neglect of the ecological environment has been found to contribute to inappropriate foci for health campaign topics:

> Because various ethnic groups live in different regions of the country or in different areas of one region, patterns of cancer risk that are actually attributed to different environmental factors may be considered "racial" patterns and mistakenly attributed to cultural or inherent biological factors. (Kumanyika, 1995, p. 299)

The need to incorporate this aspect of environment into health campaign planning may bring into focus risk communication, where the public is informed about a health risk associated with an environmental hazard such as radon gas in homes. Health communication and risk communication may conflict, making both less effective, as risk communication messages designed to inform the public about an environmental hazard's impact on health could contribute to knowledge that makes

undertaking some practices recommended in health communication messages less likely. For example, an increasing number of Americans find themselves with less than desirable drinking water in their homes, a fact that may be revealed to them in risk communication messages. Because these people have knowledge about their water quality, health communication messages recommending that they drink eight glasses of water a day may be less palatable, either because of perceived harm associated with consumption of tap water or because of cost associated with the use of bottled water for drinking. Many Americans also live in or near cities where the poor air quality leads to frequent "smog alerts" or public announcements to stay indoors—an example of risk communication. Health communication messages recommending exercise, such as a daily walk or run outdoors, need to be tailored with these ecological environments in mind.

Failure to communicate environmental risks is not a viable solution to possible conflicts between risk and health communication messages; the Universal Declaration of Human Rights asserts that when governments withhold information that results in deaths from environmental factors, it violates guarantees to life and information (Cuomo, 1993). Health campaigners should stay informed about the political debate surrounding the ecological environment, which considers issues such as whether the environment should be free from contamination, safe from nuclear weapons and other threats to human survival, or undisturbed—preserving the aesthetic national heritage (Shelton, 1991). This debate has important implications for health campaigners as we progress in the 21st century, and information about the ecological environment continues to clash with prescriptions for health in varied arenas. The rhetoric associated with Gore (1993) and his book on the subject of ecology suggests that Americans will be exposed to more discussion and debate related to the ecological environment in the future. Some politicians will take seriously the view that participation in decisions about the ecological environment necessitates widespread dissemination of information, with such participation balancing competing interests, gaining support for public policies, aiding enforcement efforts, and promoting free exchange of information between public and government agencies (Bandi, 1993).

Guarantees of human rights are generally restraints on government action, however, not proscription for government action, as providing a decent standard of living for all citizens is beyond the means of most governments to provide (Rubin, 1986). "Protecting humans from environmental harms, and broader protection of the environment's ecosystems, ultimately require[s] more than expression of fundamental rights" (Strasser, 1993, p. 426). It requires legal rules that are enforced, economic incentives, and production-consumption decisions that are broad based (Shelton, 1991), leading to yet another dimension of environment as a social influence construct to consider as part of planning, implementing, and evaluating health campaigns during the 21st century.

2. *We need more knowledge about how health campaigners influence health policy and vice versa.* The health policy environment consists of (a) statements of national standards relating to a health condition, (b) domestic and international laws to observe the standard, (c) federal administrative goals and institutions to support the domestic laws, and (d) state and local rules and actions to facilitate or inhibit the attainment of federal administrative goals and institutions (Parrott, Kahl, & Maibach, 1995, p. 272). A health campaigner's evaluation of the policy environment with regard to a health topic will promote the ability to (a) determine the likelihood of obtaining financial support to undertake a campaign in the first place, thus predicting which health campaigns will be conducted, directed at which audiences, and for what purposes; (b) describe the general perspective that will be deemed to be acceptable in message design and source selection and, to a lesser extent, the channel selection; and (c) identify the availability of support to enhance the structural environment. A careful analysis of the health policy environment will enable a health campaigner to narrow goals and objectives in appropriate ways to increase the likelihood of success in obtaining support for a campaign before and after its inception, contributing to the likelihood of long-term institutional change to support a health practice (Backer & Rogers, 1993).

Backer et al. (1992) stated that the role of the government in health campaigns is to act as funders and provide appropriate leadership on controversial issues. While this statement seems somewhat obvious, its significance should be considered systematically. Health campaigns are large and expensive undertakings, and although they are not financially costly in comparison to some possible other choices for dealing with human health issues (for a discussion, see Salmon, 1992), health campaigns are not events that occur without funding. The fact that the government often acts as the funding agent behind a health campaign is important. It points to the likelihood of some organizational culture conflict due to differences between the organizational cultures of government and private organizations, and it points to the dependence of the timing of a health campaign on the government (Backer & Rogers, 1993). From a social influence perspective, it suggests that the government is a gatekeeper, an idea expressed by McGrath (1995) with regard to the planning and strategizing stage of health campaigns as well as the feedback and program refinement stage (p. 203).

Consider the example of the "5 a Day" campaign, which promotes consumption of fruits and vegetables as a strategy to prevent cancer. This program evolved as a result of the National Cancer Institute's award of a grant to develop capacity for cancer prevention and detection to California's Department of Health Services (Foerster, Kizer, & DiSogra, 1995). California formed the Nutrition and Cancer Prevention Program (NCCP) to address dietary concerns associated with cancer prevention, and the NCCP staff reviewed scientific literature to establish a behavioral goal for the health campaign, identifying several reasons for choosing five servings a day (Foerster et al., 1995). Then,

> Legislation was drafted to establish 5 a Day as a state health goal, and the logo and slogan were developed and registered with state and federal trademark agencies as protected service marks. . . . Legal registration was necessary to protect the integrity of the campaign by preventing use of its identifiers in ways other than those approved by the department, assuring coherence and consistency of the message in materials developed by many diverse partners, and reserving participation for organizations willing to work in partnership toward a common social goal. (p. 126)

Five servings became national policy in 1990 (Foerster et al., 1995), exemplifying the tight link between health policy and health campaigns.

Perhaps even more significant for health campaigners is the role of the health policy environment and the government as a gatekeeper on decisions about what messages will be used. In many areas associated with health, a model of behavior adaptation (see Parrott, Monahan, et al., 1998) may be more appropriate than a more usual approach of behavior avoidance. Communication from an adaptation perspective acknowledges that people are engaging in behavior that threatens their

health and promotes specific procedures to adopt as a method of reducing the probability of harm associated with the behavior. Behavior avoidance messages, on the other hand, promote staying out of situations that encourage a particular behavior and/or gaining control over cognitive, affective, and social drives to behave in ways that lead to negative outcomes. With regard to matters such as the prevention of skin cancer, promoting behavior adaptation rather than behavior avoidance raises few hackles. When it comes to drug use in this nation, however, the policy is "zero tolerance" and "abstinence," although programs that include messages of responsible use may be more efficacious (Resnicow & Botvin, 1993). An analysis of the health policy environment may forewarn health campaigners that such messages are unlikely to be approved and/or may foretell the need to become involved in efforts to influence government as a vital social influence strategy in health campaigns. One strategy for health campaigners to consider is membership on the scientific review panels of the National Institutes of Health and the CDC. Only through such involvement will we lend our discipline's expertise and knowledge to decision making at levels that determine the nation's priorities for both the undertaking of specific health campaigns and the design of messages associated with those projects.

3. *Health campaigners should apply more of the existing knowledge base associated with behavioral inoculation in the design of messages to confer resistance to persuasion, evaluating subsequent outcomes.* A great deal has been accomplished in the application and use of social influence theory and research to guide the design of messages for health campaigns, but too little attention has been given to the use of theory and research to address the media message environment in terms of countermessages, including commercial mes-

sages about health that promote unhealthy behaviors. The media message environment consists of information about a health topic to which a primary audience has exposure beyond specific "change" messages associated with the campaign. Such messages include content in both paid and unpaid modalities, as news media seek interesting stories for their outlets and profiteers strive for commercial success. The media message environment coexists with the health campaign, often determining which messages an audience will attend to and believe:

> The mass media, well aware that we are now a society obsessed with health matters, often increase our difficulties by attributing an unjustified degree of certainty to new health-related findings, portraying limited, incremental advances in research as major developments or breakthroughs, exaggerating the risks posed by putative health hazards, and so forth. (Becker, 1986, p. 17)

While health campaigners should not attempt to address all messages in the environment, they should address those that a primary audience is more likely to be exposed to and that offer conflicting, especially if credible, advice associated with the health topic. Immunization is just one arena demonstrating the effects of failure to address countermessages in an information environment. Immunization is one of the most cost-effective health interventions available. Yet only 77% of the 2-year-old population of the United States is fully immunized, despite a goal of 90% by the year 2000 (CDC, 1994). Many variables account for low vaccination rates, including missed opportunities by health care providers to vaccinate—an issue related to the social environment, systemic barriers in the structural environment, and resistance to vaccination due to potential rare side effects or homeopathic approaches to health in the mes-

sage environment (Lannon et al., 1995). Health campaigners must reckon with the reality that inadvertent adverse health outcomes may arise as a result of their efforts to promote particular practices in lieu of others (for a discussion, see Stone, 1987). Parents report that they talk to one another and their pediatricians about vaccine horror stories that, in turn, have attracted local or national media attention (McCormick, Bartholomew, Lewis, Brown, & Hanson, 1997). These accounts, offered by parents, may appear to be very credible to other parents, who are highly unlikely to observe children suffering from the maladies that vaccines are designed to prevent. The use of inoculation theory (McGuire, 1964) should be systematically extended to health campaigns "whenever supportive prevailing attitudes are subject to serious challenges" (Pfau, 1995, p. 102). Efforts to confer resistance to parents complying with immunization recommendations and adults attempting to follow low-fat diets and to exercise regularly, for example, may benefit from the systematic application of inoculation principles.

Planning for an inoculation component of a health campaign requires advance analysis of the media message environment and awareness of the importance of promoting the ability to counterargue. Beyond the media messages included in news stories, the commercial media messages an audience receives affect its members' health beliefs and behavior. Numerous content analyses of commercial ad content demonstrate that health information is frequently included as marketers strive to sell products that will promote health and well-being (for a discussion, see Parrott & Condit, 1996, pp. 414-425). One area in which the negative effects of commercial messages on health behavior has been demonstrated is with adolescents and cigarette smoking. One study found that the more time adolescents spent looking at cigarette ads in magazines, the more likely they were to be smokers, according to several measures of smoking behavior, including the number of cigarettes smoked the previous day, the previous week, and the previous month. Adolescents who looked at cigarette ads more often also intended to smoke more in the future (Botvin, Goldberg, Botvin, & Dusenbury, 1993). Pfau (1995) summarized a program of social influence research that applied inoculation theory to adolescent smoking, finding that the message strategy is appropriate in conferring resistance in this situation. Drawing on this research, health campaigners could design an anti-smoking campaign targeting adolescents who do not smoke and perhaps counter the persuasive effects of commercial advertising in this regard.

4. *Communication researchers should critically assess audience responses to conflicting health advice and information, and health campaigners should use the research findings.* Individuals working in the area of public health, including health campaigners, do not have to be involved with the task for very long before they will hear complaints about conflicting advice associated with health messages. This sometimes occurs with regard to when one should begin to perform a practice associated with early detection, as with mammography. Conflicting messages also occur between prescriptions for practice associated with the reduction of one type of illness or disease as compared to recommendations associated with another illness or disease. Americans may associate such conflict, for example, with messages designed to promote low-fat diets to reduce heart disease versus messages designed to reduce the incidence of bone disease, including osteoporosis, that inform the audience that fat promotes the absorption and retention of calcium. Similar confusion may exist regarding the consumption of alcohol or caffeine, with some advice promoting moderate consumption to benefit one's heart with

regard to the former and one's mind with regard to the latter; other messages proclaim that avoidance of both substances is the path to the best health outcomes. Little wonder, then, that health experts and others working in the area of health promotion, as well as well-meaning friends and families passing along sage health advice, hear the response, "We all gotta die of something—I may as well enjoy myself along the way."

Considerable energy has been expended toward understanding burnout as a syndrome that occurs among workers, especially in the helping professions, many of which are in health contexts (for a discussion, see Maslach, 1982). Overload has been found to be a consistent variable predicting burnout, with overload being comprised of too much information and too many demands in association with the information (p. 38). An overload of health information, particularly conflicting health information, may contribute to individuals' reactance and learned helplessness. Frustration and hostility characterize reactance as a response to individual perceptions of limits on their freedom or control in a situation (Brehm, 1966). Wortman and Brehm (1975) combined the concepts of reactance and learned helplessness in a model that suggests that conflicting health information or information overload may contribute to individuals' perceptions that, regardless of what they do, they will be unable to control their future health. Mikulincer (1988) examined the role of one's internal versus external attribution for failure, finding that internal attributors, as compared to external attributors, demonstrated *both* greater frustration and hostility *and* better performance in subsequent tasks following *one* failure; *four* failures, however, led to feelings of incompetence and a decrease in performance as compared to external attributors. This suggests that the perception that avoidance of bad health is within one's sphere of control, combined with an initial failure, may lead one to try harder; repeated failure, however, is likely to be associated with resignation and the hostility and frustration associated with reactance, perhaps affecting other health domains as well. This might be a hypothesis worth examining, particularly in situations where individuals have attempted to lose weight, quit smoking, or reduce dependence on drugs or alcohol—all behaviors associated with high relapse rates and likely spillover effects.

5. Communication researchers, especially health campaigners, should strive to expand society's commitment to training in media literacy. One strategy with particular salience for reducing the impact of a media message environment filled with conflicting information is training in media literacy, which educates individuals about the persuasive intent of media content so that they recognize the inherent strengths and weaknesses associated with messages. Health campaigners should examine the value of media literacy training and in what settings and for which audiences this strategy could be efficacious and cost-effective. The outcomes associated with media literacy training include the ability to decode, evaluate, and analyze print and electronic media, gaining an understanding that "media are constructed and construct reality; media have commercial implications; media have ideological and political implications; [and] form and content are related in each medium" (Christ & Potter, 1998, pp. 7-8). Persons with media literacy skills, for example, were more likely to recognize that top national newspapers sensationalized the results of a study published in the *New England Journal of Medicine*, even reporting the opposite of the medical journal's recommendations and omitting important information relating the use of aspi-

rin to prevention of heart attack (Molitor, 1993).

Media literacy training was also found to be effective in increasing 225 Minnesota third-graders' understanding of television's persuasive intent, decreasing their desire to be like the characters, decreasing expectations of positive consequences from drinking alcohol, and decreasing the likelihood of choosing an alcohol-related product (Austin & Johnson, 1997). Media literacy training may be effective as an inoculation strategy, reducing the necessity for constant attention to maintenance among converts in a health arena by providing a broad blanket of protection and resistance. Until media literacy training is integrated into public education, however, training might not be economically feasible for primary audiences. Health campaigners should examine whether a media literacy seminar for a secondary audience, such as a group found to be influential within the social environment, may reduce the potential negative impact of the mass media environment on campaign outcomes.

6. Health campaigners need to identify creative ways to assess the environment of a primary campaign audience. With the emphasis that should be given by health campaigners to environment as a multifaceted social influence construct in the design and evaluation of health campaigns, approaches to assess the environment become a critical linchpin in campaign success. The diversity of the American population and the inability of campaign staff to represent such diversity create the need for novel methods to approach evaluating the environment and involving communities in their own health promotion. As Freimuth (1995) asserted, "New formative research techniques are needed that create a dialogue among the participants" (p. 100). One efficacious approach to assessing the environment used in the Georgia Harvesting Healthy Habits and Georgia "Got Youth Covered" campaigns was a strategy called "photovoice," a method whereby members of a primary audience, secondary audiences, and even project staff create and discuss photographs of the primary audience's environment (Wang, 1997; Wang, Yi, Tao, & Carovano, 1998). Using cameras, members of a community document their lives, making photovoice an extension of documentary photography. The power of the visual image includes its ability to invoke critical reflection about what is seen as members of the community discuss the pictures one-on-one with interviewers or in focus groups.

Through the use of photovoice, the Georgia Harvesting Healthy Habits campaign identified a sun protection hat that some farmers and farmworkers themselves had created through the use of a bandanna and a baseball cap. With input from the expert advisory panel, the campaign staff devised a similar hat with a somewhat broader brim and produced such hats as an incentive for completing a survey. They also avoided giving a message to farmworkers about hanging laundry in the sun to dissipate residuals of pesticide in and on the fabric, a practice recommended because the sun breaks down the pesticides. Photographs revealed, however, that farmworkers' housing, including clotheslines, is often just yards away from the fields where they harvest crops. Any pesticides that are sprayed on the fields would be likely to carry over to any clothing hung on those nearby clotheslines. The use of photovoice helped the project to avoid promoting a message in an environment not suited to support the message. A gap in understanding about the reach of pesticides applied to crops was identified in a similar fashion; farmworkers reported during face-to-face interviews that they did not eat fruits and vegetables they harvested without washing them first due to the pesticides on them, but we ob-

served in photographs that they ate wild fruit growing on the fences lining the fields, suggesting that they did not recognize the reach of aerial pesticide application (Parrott, Wilson, Buttram, Jones, & Steiner, 1999). In each of these scenarios, this more novel method of evaluating the environment produced results that none of the other approaches used revealed (see Parrott, Duggan, et al., 1999; Parrott, Wilson, et al., 1999).

As part of efforts to be more creative in formative research, campaigners should identify strategies to initiate and maintain expert advisory panels and steering committees to consult with health campaigners. In addition to identifying and using novel approaches to assess the environment, expert advisory panels and community steering committees are invaluable assets to health campaigners, providing input regarding the validity of assumptions and conclusions. Building and sustaining relationships with these groups is a time-consuming process about which little has been said in campaign literature. Stedronsky (1998) placed primary importance on convening a panel of experts to "provide campaign leadership and guide the development of messages" (p. 758). Thus, their value goes beyond the formative research period, as they contribute to the validity of message design. More knowledge about these relationships is needed.

7. *Health campaigners should examine the role of receiver affect, including initial states and traits, as related to cognitive, affective, and behavioral outcomes in health campaigns.* As stated previously, many of the findings from social influence research in the future will have the potential to affect health campaigns through the design of messages and the selection of sources and channels to deliver the messages. Of particular relevance for health campaigns, audience segmentation research needs to critically examine the role of

receiver affect as it relates to health campaigns. As observed earlier in this chapter, some research has demonstrated that health messages designed to arouse fear also arouse other emotions, including surprise and sadness as well as puzzlement and anger, with the former fostering message acceptance and the latter discouraging message acceptance (Dillard et al., 1996). The arousal of different emotions in response to health messages is an area where health campaigns might contribute to the extant social influence knowledge base.

Affective traits or states of receivers prior to receipt of campaign messages, such as depression, anger, and happiness, may predict responses to health messages, with theory examined in Part I of this volume suggesting avenues for future research in this regard in association with health campaigns. At present, the knowledge base is insufficient to advance specific guidelines for the design of campaign messages based on receivers' emotions or moods. Research has demonstrated, however, that individuals who are sad report feeling more aches, pains, and discomfort than do individuals who are happy. Sad individuals also feel less confident about their ability to carry out behavior to alleviate illness than do happy individuals (Salovey & Birnbaum, 1989). This suggests that mood may well moderate the effects of health messages. As Wartella and Middlestadt (1991) stated, "Presumably, when forming a judgment at the time of encoding, the mood at that time will influence the judgment, whereas if one forms a judgment later, on retrieval, the mood at that time is the relevant one" (p. 212).

Audience member traits, such as empathy, may also relate to responses to health campaign messages. Empathy has been found to be directly related to support message sophistication (Burleson, 1983; Tamborini, Salomonson, & Bahk, 1993) and altruistic motivation to engage in helping behavior such as being a hospice volunteer (Wilkinson & Wilkinson, 1986). Recall the earlier reference to the finding that more altruistic audience members responded with a greater willingness to be organ donors when messages appealed to their altruism; less altruistic students responded less favorably (Kopfman & Smith, 1996). Empathy may be the variable that explains conflicting findings associated with health campaign efforts to appeal to an audience's altruism in reference to performing particular health practices. Additional research considering this trait and others associated with audience members' emotions may afford opportunities to expand the knowledge base of health campaign prescriptions. By these efforts, health campaigners may avoid the much decried tendency "to locate the responsibility for the cause and the cure of health problems in the individual" (Becker, 1986, p. 18).

CONCLUSION

A distinguishing hallmark of social influence in health campaigns is the significance of environment, a multifaceted construct with wide-ranging implications for explaining the results of previous endeavors and guiding the future direction of health campaigns. While both the social and structural environments vitally contribute to individuals' health knowledge, attitudes, and practices, planning models often incorporate, and previous successful health campaigns demonstrate, that environment as a social influence construct in health campaigns includes ecological, policy, and message components as well. Systematic consideration of each of these during health campaign planning, implementation, and evaluation increases the likelihood that health campaigners will effectively bridge the gap between basic and applied sciences associated with health and avoid raising the specter of paternalism sometimes associated with campaign endeavors (Salmon, 1989a). Much discussion over the last decade of the 20th century faulted campaigners' social engineering philosophy for the failure of health campaigners to gain an understanding not only of how but also of why an intended audience defines "good health" the way it does (for a discussion, see Dervin, 1989). Such "sense making" relies on what Salmon (1992) labeled theories "of" campaigns that examine them as dependent variables, noting their obvious reliance on "social, political, and ideological forces peculiar to a social system at a given point in time" (p. 347). Our discussion of environment as a social influence construct in health campaigns subsumes these arenas.

In the final analysis, in no other arena does the opportunity to benefit people based on the application of social influence theory and practice appear to be so rich. Yet in no other arena does the opportunity to harm people based on the application of social influence theory and practice appear to be so likely. To design messages that advise people to act in their own best health interests in an environment where such action conflicts with family and/or cultural values threatens the very core of their identity if they follow through, and so of course many will not. To design messages that promote health behaviors that the structural environment lacks the necessary resources to support frustrates people and may lessen the likelihood that they will even listen to such messages in the future. To design messages that promote behaviors that conflict with the ecological environment in which an audience lives only makes the campaigner appear to be naive, and again such prescriptions will fall on deaf ears. To design messages that the policy environment will not support reduces the chances of the messages ever being disseminated in the first place. To design messages that ignore competing and conflicting information in the media message environ-ment creates doubt and indecision. All of these considerations, therefore, comprise the health campaigner's tasks and responsibilities.

REFERENCES

Alcalay, R. (1983). The impact of mass communication campaigns in the health field. *Social Science & Medicine, 17,* 87-93.

Alcalay, R., & Bell, R. A. (1996). Ethnicity and health knowledge gaps: Impact of the California "Wellness Guide" on poor African American, Hispanic, and non-Hispanic White women. *Health Communication, 8,* 303-329.

Anderson, R. B., & McMillion, P. Y. (1995). Effects of similar and diversified modeling on African American women's efficacy expectations and intentions to perform breast self-examination. *Health Communication, 7,* 327-343.

Atkin, C. K., & Freimuth, V. (1989). Formative evaluation research in campaign design. In R. E. Rice & C. K. Atkin (Eds.), *Public communication campaigns* (2nd ed., pp. 131-150). Newbury Park, CA: Sage.

Austin, E. W., & Johnson, K. K. (1997). Effects of general and alcohol-specific media literacy training on children's decision making about alcohol. *Journal of Health Communication, 2,* 17-42.

Babrow, A. S. (1992). Communication and problematic integration: Understanding diverging probability and value, ambiguity, ambivalence, and impossibility. *Communication Theory, 2,* 95-130.

Babrow, A. S. (1991). Tensions between health beliefs and desires: Implications for a health communication campaign to promote a smoking-cessation program. *Health Communication, 3,* 93-112.

Backer, T. E., & Rogers, E. M. (1993). *Organizational aspects of health communication campaigns: What works?* Newbury Park, CA: Sage.

Backer, T. E., & Rogers, E. M. (1998). Diffusion of innovations theory and work-site AIDS programs. *Journal of Health Communication, 3,* 17-28.

Backer, T. E., Rogers, E. M., & Sopory, P. (1992). *Designing health communication campaigns: What works.* Newbury Park, CA: Sage.

Baggaley, J. P. (1988). Perceived effectiveness of international AIDS campaigns. *Health Education Research: Theory and Practice, 3,* 7-17.

Bandi, G. (1993). A right to environment in theory and practice: The Hungarian experience. *Connecticut Journal of International Law, 9,* 439-465.

Bandura, A. (1986). *Social foundation of thought and action: A social cognitive approach.* Englewood Cliffs, NJ: Prentice Hall.

Becker, M. H. (1974). The Health Belief Model and personal health behavior. *Health Education Monographs, 2,* 324-473.

Becker, M. H. (1986). The tyranny of health promotion. *Public Health Review, 14,* 15-25.

Botvin, G. J., Epstein, J. A., Schinke, S. P., & Diaz, T. (1994). Predictors of cigarette smoking among inner-city minority youth. *Journal of Developmental and Behavioral Pediatrics, 15,* 67-73.

Botvin, G. J., Goldberg, C. J., Botvin, E. M., & Dusenbury, L. (1993). Smoking behavior of adolescents exposed to cigarette advertising. *Public Health Reports, 108,* 217-224.

Brehm, J. (1966). *A theory of psychological reactance.* New York: Academic Press.

Brown, J. D., & Einsiedel, E. F. (1990). Public health campaigns: Mass media strategies. In E. B. Ray & L. Donohew (Eds.), *Communication and health: Systems and applications* (pp. 153-170). Hillsdale, NJ: Lawrence Erlbaum.

Brown, W. J., & Basil, M. D. (1995). Media celebrities and public health: Responses to "Magic" Johnson's HIV risk and high-risk behaviors. *Health Communication, 7,* 345-370.

Burleson, B. R. (1983). Social cognition, empathic motivation, and adults' comforting strategies. *Human Communication Research, 10,* 295-304.

Cacioppo, J. T., & Petty, R. E. (1979). Attitudes and cognitive response: An electro-physiological approach. *Journal of Personality and Social Psychology, 37,* 2181-2199.

Carlaw, R., Mittlelmark, M., Bracht, N. F., & Luepker, R. V. (1984). Organization for a community cardiovascular disease health program: Minnesota Heart Health Program. *Health Education Quarterly, 11,* 243-252.

Centers for Disease Control and Prevention. (1993). Resurgence of pertussis: United States, 1993. *Morbidity and Mortality Weekly Report, 42,* 952-953, 959-960.

Centers for Disease Control and Prevention. (1994, January 28). General recommendations on immunization: Recommendations of the advisory committee on immunization practices. *Morbidity and Mortality Weekly Report, pp.* 1-38.

Chew, F., Palmer, S., & Kim, S. (1998). Testing the influence of the Health Belief Model and a television program on nutrition behavior. *Health Communication, 10,* 227-245.

Christ, W. G., & Potter, W. J. (1998). Media literacy, media education, and the academy. *Journal of Communication, 48,* 5-15.

Clayton, R. R., Cattarello, A., & Walden, K. P. (1991). Sensation seeking as a potential mediating variable for school-based prevention intervention: A two-year follow-up of DARE. *Health Communication, 3,* 229-239.

Cuomo, K. K. (1993). Human rights and the environment: Common ground. *Yale Journal of International Law, 18,* 227-233.

Delapa, R. M., Mayer, J. A., Candelaria, J., Hammond, N., Peplinski, S., deMoor, C., Talavera, G., & Elder, J. (1990). Food purchase patterns in a Latino community: Project SALSA. *Journal of Nutrition Education, 22,* 133-136.

Dervin, B. (1989). Audience as listener and learner, teacher and confidante: The sense-making approach. In R. E. Rice & C. K. Atkin (Eds.), *Public communication campaigns* (2nd ed., pp. 67-86). Newbury Park, CA: Sage.

Dillard, J. P., Plotnick, C. A., Godbold, L. C., Freimuth, V. S., & Edgar, T. (1996). The multiple affective outcomes of AIDS PSAs: Fear appeals do more than scare people. *Communication Research, 23,* 44-72.

Donohew, L., Helm, D. M., Lawrence, P., & Shatzer, M. J. (1990). Sensation seeking, marijuana use, and responses to prevention messages. In R. R. Watson (Ed.), *Drug and alcohol abuse prevention* (pp. 73-93). Clifton, NJ: Humana Press.

Ettema, J. S., Brown, J. W., & Luepker, R. V. (1983). Knowledge gap effects in a health information campaign. *Public Opinion Quarterly, 47,* 516-527.

Farquhar, J. W., Fortmann, S. P., Flora, J. A., Taylor, B., Haskell, W. L., Williams, P. T., Maccoby, N., & Wood, P. D. (1990). Effects of community-wide education on cardiovascular disease risk factors: The Stanford Five City project. *Journal of the American Medical Association, 264,* 359-365.

Finnegan, J. R., Bracht, N., & Viswanath, K. (1989). Community power and leadership analysis in lifestyle campaigns. In C. T. Salmon (Ed.), *Information campaigns: Balancing social values and social change* (pp. 54-84). Newbury Park, CA: Sage.

Flora, J. A., Maccoby, N., & Farquhar, J. W. (1989). Communication campaigns to prevent cardiovascular disease: The Stanford community studies. In R. Rice & C. Atkin (Eds.), *Public communication campaigns* (2nd ed., pp. 233-252). Newbury Park, CA: Sage.

Foerster, S. B., Kizer, K. W., & DiSogra, L. K. (1995). California's "5 a Day—For Better Health!" campaign: An innovative population-based effort to effect large-scale dietary change. *American Journal of Preventive Medicine, 11,* 124-131.

Freimuth, V. S. (1995). Mass media strategies and channels: A review of the use of media in breast and cervical cancer screening programs. *Wellness Perspectives: Research, Theory, and Practice, 11,* 79-106.

Gantz, W., Fitzmaurice, M., & Yoo, E. (1990). Seat belt campaigns and buckling up: Do media make a difference? *Health Communication, 2,* 1-12.

Gore, A. (1993). *Earth in the balance: Ecology and the human spirit.* New York: Plume.

Green, L. W., & Kreuter, M. W. (1991). *Health promotion planning: An educational and environmental approach.* Palo Alto, CA: Mayfield.

Guttman, N. (1997). Ethical dilemmas in health campaigns. *Health Communication, 9,* 155-190.

Hafstad, A., & Aaro, L. E. (1997). Activating interpersonal influence through provocative appeals: Evaluation of a mass media-based antismoking campaign targeting adolescents. *Health Communication, 9,* 253-272.

Hale, J. L., & Dillard, J. P. (1995). Fear appeals in health promotion campaigns: Too much, too little, or just right? In E. Maibach & R. L. Parrott (Eds.), *Designing health messages: Approaches from communication theory and public health practice* (pp. 65-80). Thousand Oaks, CA: Sage.

Hammond, S. L., Freimuth, V. S., & Morrison, W. (1987). The gatekeeping funnel: Tracking a major PSA campaign from distribution through gatekeepers to target audience. *Health Education Quarterly, 14,* 153-166.

Hofstetter, C. R., Shultze, W. A., & Mulvihill, M. M. (1992). Communications media, public health, and public affairs: Exposure in a multimedia community. *Health Communication, 4,* 259-271.

Hornik, R. (1989). The knowledge-behavior gap in public information campaigns: A development communication view. In C. T. Salmon (Ed.), *Information campaigns: Balancing social values and social change* (pp. 113-138). Newbury Park, CA: Sage.

Howze, E. H., Broyden, R. R., & Impara, J. C. (1992). Using informal caregivers to communicate with women about mammography. *Health Communication, 4,* 227-244.

Institute of Medicine. (1997). *Risk communication and vaccination: Workshop summary.* Washington, DC: National Academy Press.

Johnson, D., Flora, J. A., & Rimal, R. N. (1997). HIV/AIDS public service announcements around the world: A descriptive analysis. *Journal of Health Communication, 2,* 223-234.

Kim, Y. M., & Marangwanda, C. (1997). Stimulating men's support for long-term contraception: A campaign in Zimbabwe. *Journal of Health Communication, 2,* 271-297.

Kopfman, J. E., & Smith, S. W. (1996). Understanding the audiences of a health communication campaign: A discriminant analysis of potential organ donors based on intent to donate. *Journal of Applied Communication Research, 24,* 33-49.

Korhonen, T., Uutela, A., Korhonen, J. J., & Puska, P. (1998). Impact of mass media and interpersonal health communication on smoking cessation attempts: A study in North Karelia, 1989-

1996. *Journal of Health Communication, 3,* 105-118.

Krishman, S. P. (1996). Health education and family planning clinics: Strategies for improving information about contraception and sexually transmitted diseases for low-income women. *Health Communication, 8,* 353-366.

Krishnatray, P. K., & Melkote, S. R. (1998). Public communication campaigns in the destigmatization of leprosy: A comparative analysis of diffusion and participatory approaches. A case study in Gwalior, India. *Journal of Health Communication, 3,* 327-344.

Kumanyika, S. (1995). Nutrition and health campaign for all women. *Journal of the American Dietetic Association, 95,* 299-300.

Kwak, N. (1999). Revisiting the knowledge gap hypothesis: Education, motivation, and media use. *Communication Research, 26,* 385-413.

Lannon, C., Brack, V., Stuart, J., Caplow, M., McNeil, A., Bordley, W. C., & Margolis, P. (1995). What mothers say about why poor children fall behind on immunizations: A summary of focus groups in North Carolina. *Archives of Pediatrics & Adolescent Medicine, 149,* 1070-1075.

Larson, M. S. (1991). Health-related messages embedded in prime-time television entertainment. *Health Communication, 3,* 175-184.

Maibach, E., Flora, J. A., & Nass, C. (1991). Changes in self-efficacy and health behavior in response to a minimal contact community health campaign. *Health Communication, 3,* 1-16.

Maibach, E., & Parrott, R. (Eds.). (1995). *Designing health messages: Public health practice and communication theory.* Thousand Oaks, CA: Sage.

Marshall, A. A., Smith, S. W., & McKeon, J. K. (1995). Persuading low-income women to engage in mammography screening: Source, message, and channel preferences. *Health Communication, 7,* 283-299.

Maslach, C. (1982). *Burnout: The cost of caring.* Englewood Cliffs, NJ: Prentice Hall.

McCormick, L. K., Bartholomew, L. K., Lewis, M. J., Brown, M. W., & Hanson, I. C. (1997). Parental perceptions of barriers to childhood immunization: Results of focus groups conducted in an urban population. *Health Educa-*

tion and Research: Theory and Practice, 12, 355-362.

McDivitt, J. A., Zimicki, S., & Hornik, R. C. (1997). Explaining the impact of a communication campaign to change vaccination knowledge and coverage in the Philippines. *Health Communication, 9,* 95-118.

McGrath, J. (1995). The gatekeeping process: The right combinations to unlock the gates. In E. Maibach & R. L. Parrott (Eds.), *Designing health messages: Approaches from communication theory and public health practice* (pp. 199-216). Thousand Oaks, CA: Sage.

McGuire, W. J. (1964). Inducing resistance to persuasion. Some contemporary approaches. In L. Berkowitz (Ed.), *Advances in experimental social psychology* (Vol. 5, pp. 191-229). New York: Academic Press.

Mikulincer, M. (1988). Reactance and helplessness following exposure to unsolvable problems: The effects of attributional style. *Journal of Personality and Social Psychology, 54,* 679-686.

Molitor, F. (1993). Accuracy in science news reporting by newspapers: The case of aspirin for the prevention of heart attacks. *Health Communication, 5,* 209-224.

Montgomery, K. (1988). *Target prime time.* New York: Oxford University Press.

Myrick, R. (1998). In search of cultural sensitivity and inclusiveness: Communication strategies used in rural HIV prevention campaigns designed for African Americans. *Health Communication, 10,* 65-85.

O'Keefe, G. J., Boyd, H. H., & Brown, M. R. (1998). Who learns preventive health care information from where: Cross-channel and repertoire comparisons. *Health Communication, 10,* 25-36.

Palmgreen, P., Donohew, L., Lorch, E. P., Rogus, M., Helm, D., & Grant, N. (1991). Sensation seeking, message sensation value, and drug use as mediators of PSA effectiveness. *Health Communication, 3,* 217-227.

Parrott, R., & Condit, C. M. (1996). *Evaluating women's health messages: A resource book.* Thousand Oaks, CA: Sage.

Parrott, R., & Duggan, A. (1999). Using coaches as role models of sun protection for youth: Georgia's "Got Youth Covered" project. *Journal of Applied Communication, 27,* 1-13.

Parrott, R., Duggan, A., Cremo, J., Eckles, A., Jones, K., & Steiner, C. (1999). Communicating youths' sun exposure risk to soccer coaches and parents: A pilot study in Georgia. *Health Education & Behavior, 26,* 385-395.

Parrott, R., Kahl, M., & Maibach, E. (1995). Enabling health: Policy and administrative practices at a crossroads. In E. Maibach & R. L. Parrott (Eds.), *Designing health messages: Approaches from communication theory and public health practice* (pp. 270-283). Thousand Oaks, CA: Sage.

Parrott, R., Lewis, D., Jones, K., Steiner, C., & Goldenhar, L. (1998). Identifying feed and seed stores as a site to promote skin cancer control: A social marketing approach to agricultural health communication. *Journal of Agricultural Safety and Health, 4,* 149-158.

Parrott, R., Monahan, J., Ainsworth, S., & Steiner, C. (1998). Communicating to farmers about skin cancer: The behavior adaptation model. *Human Communication Research, 24,* 386-409.

Parrott, R., Steiner, C., & Goldenhar, L. (1996). Georgia's Harvesting Healthy Habits: Formative evaluation. *Journal of Rural Health, 12,* 291-300.

Parrott, R., Wilson, K., Buttram, C., Jones, K., & Steiner, C. (1999). Migrant farmworkers' access to pesticide protection and information: Cultivando buenos habitos campaign development. *Journal of Health Communication, 4,* 49-64.

Peplinski, S. K., Hammond, N. R., Candelaria, J. I., Talavera, G., Mayer, J. A., Hofstetter, C. R., & Elder, J. P. (1989). Assessing nutritional health needs in a United States border community. *Border Health [Salud Fronteriza], 5,* 2-8.

Perse, E. M., Nathanson, A. I., & McLeod, D. M. (1996). Effects of spokesperson sex, public service announcement appeal, and involvement on evaluations of safe-sex PSAs. *Health Communication, 8,* 171-189.

Pfau, M. (1995). Designing messages for behavioral inoculation. In E. Maibach & R. L. Parrott (Eds.), *Designing health messages: Approaches from communication theory and public health practice* (pp. 99-113). Thousand Oaks, CA: Sage.

Pfau, M., & Parrott, R. (1993). *Persuasive communication campaigns.* Needham Heights, MA: Allyn & Bacon.

Pratt, C. B., Silva-Barbeau, I., & Pratt, C. A. (1997). Toward a symmetrical and an integrated framework of norms for nutrition communication in Sub-Saharan Africa. *Journal of Health Communication, 2,* 43-58.

Prochaska, J. O., DiClemente, C. C., & Norcross, J. C. (1992). In search of how people change: Applications to addictive behaviors. *American Psychologist, 47,* 1102-1114.

Prochaska, J. O., Velicer, W. F., Rosssi, J. S., Goldstein, M. G., Marcus, B. H., Rakowski, W., Flore, C., Harlow, L., Redding, C. A., Rosenbloom, E., & Rossi, S. R. (1994). Stages of change and decisional balance for 12 problem behaviors. *Health Psychology, 13,* 39-46.

Puska, P., Nissinen, A., Tuomilehto, J., Salonen, J. T., Koskela, K., McAlister, A., Kottke, T. E., Maccoby, N., & Farquhar, J. W. (1985). The community-based strategy to prevent coronary heart disease: Conclusions from the ten years of the North Karelia project. *Annual Review of Public Health, 6,* 147-193.

Ramirez, A. G., & McAlister, A. L. (1988). Mass media campaign: A Su Salud. *Preventive Medicine, 17,* 608-621.

Resnicow, K., & Botvin, G. (1993). School-based substance use prevention programs: Why do effects decay? *Preventive Medicine, 22,* 484-490.

Rice, R. E., & Atkin, C. K. (Eds.). (1989). *Public communication campaigns* (2nd ed.). Newbury Park, CA: Sage.

Rice, R. E., & Foote, D. (1989). A systems-based evaluation planning model for health communication campaigns in developing countries. In R. E. Rice & C. K. Atkin (Eds.), *Public communication campaigns* (2nd ed., pp. 151-174). Newbury Park, CA: Sage.

Rothman, A. J., & Salovey, P. (1997). Shaping perceptions to motivate healthy behavior: The role of framing. *Psychological Bulletin, 121,* 3-19.

Rubin, S. J. (1986). Economic and social human rights and the new international economic order (NIEO). *American University Journal of International Law, 1,* 67-96.

Rudd, R. E., Goldberg, J., & Dietz, W. (1999). A five-stage model for sustaining a community campaign. *Journal of Health Communication, 4,* 37-48.

Salazar, M. K., & de Moor, C. (1995). An evaluation of mammography beliefs using a decision model. *Health Education Quarterly, 22,* 110-126.

Salmon, C. T. (1989). Campaigns for social "improvement": An overview of values, rationales, and impacts. In C. T. Salmon (Ed.), *Information campaigns: Balancing social values and social change* (pp. 19-53). Newbury Park, CA: Sage.

Salmon, C. T. (1989). *Information campaigns: Balancing social values and social change.* Newbury Park, CA: Sage.

Salmon, C. T. (1992). Bridging theory "of" and theory "for" communication campaigns: An essay on ideology and public policy. In S. A. Deetz (Ed.), *Communication Yearbook 15* (pp. 346-358). Newbury Park, CA: Sage.

Salmon, C. T., Wooten, K., Gentry, E., Cole, G. E., & Kroger, F. (1996). Knowledge gaps: Results from the first decade of the epidemic and implications for future public information efforts. *Journal of Health Communication, 1,* 141-155.

Salovey, P., & Birnbaum, E. (1989). Influence of mood on health-relevant cognition. *Journal of Personality and Social Psychology, 57,* 539-551.

Schooler, C., Chaffee, S. H., Flora, J. A., & Roser, C. (1998). Health campaign channels: Tradeoffs among reach, specificity, and impact. *Human Communication Research, 24,* 410-432.

Seibold, D. R., & Thomas, R. W. (1994). Rethinking the role of interpersonal influence processes in alcohol intervention situations. *Journal of Applied Communication Research, 22,* 177-197.

Sengupta, S. (1996). Understanding less educated smokers' intention to quit smoking: Strategies for antismoking communication aimed at less educated smokers. *Health Communication, 8,* 55-72.

Sharf, B. (1993). Reading the vital signs: Research in health care communication. *Communication Monographs, 60,* 35-41.

Sharf, B. F., & Freimuth, V. S. (1993). The construction of illness on entertainment television: Coping with cancer on *Thirty-something. Health Communication, 5,* 141-160.

Sharf, B. F., Freimuth, V. S., Greenspon, P., & Plotnick, C. (1996). Confronting cancer on *Thirty-something:* Audience response to health content on entertainment television. *Journal of Health Communication, 1,* 157-172.

Sheer, V. C., & Cline, R. J. (1995). Individual differences in sensation-seeking and sexual behavior: Implications for communication intervention for HIV/AIDS prevention among college students. *Health Communication, 7,* 205-223.

Shelton, D. (1991). Human rights, environmental rights, and the right to environment. *Stanford Journal of International Law, 28,* 103-138.

Slaten, D., Parrott, R., & Steiner, C. (1999). Readability of skin cancer prevention brochures targeting parents of young children. *Journal of the American Academy of Dermatology, 40,* 997-998.

Slater, M. D. (1995). Choosing audience segmentation strategies and methods for health communication. In E. Maibach & R. L. Parrott (Eds.), *Designing health messages: Approaches from communication theory and public health practice* (pp. 186-198). Thousand Oaks, CA: Sage.

Smith, S. L. (1997). The effective use of fear appeals in persuasive immunization: An analysis of national immunization intervention messages. *Journal of Applied Communication Research, 25,* 264-292.

Stedronsky, F. M. (1998). Child nutrition and health campaign: A member update. *Journal of the American Dietetic Association, 98,* 758-759.

Stephenson, M. T., Palmgreen, P., Hoyle, R. H., Donohew, L., Lorch, E. P., & Colon, S. E. (1999). Short-term effects of an anti-marijuana media campaign targeting high sensation seeking adolescents. *Journal of Applied Communication Research, 27,* 175-195.

Stone, D. A. (1987). The resistible rise of preventive medicine. In L. D. Brown (Ed.), *Health policy in transition: A decade of health politics, policy, and law.* Durham, NC: Duke University Press.

Strasser, K. A. (1993). Pollution control in an era of economic redevelopment: An overview. *Connecticut Journal of International Law, 9,* 425-437.

Tamborini, R., Salomonson, K., & Bahk, C. (1993). The relationship of empathy to comforting behavior following film exposure. *Communication Research, 20,* 723-738.

Terris, M. (1968). A social policy for health. *American Journal of Public Health, 58,* 5-12.

Tichenor, P. J., Donohue, G. A., & Olien, C. N. (1970). Mass media and differential growth in knowledge. *Public Opinion Quarterly, 34,* 158-170.

Tyebjee, T. T. (1979). Refinement of the involvement concept: An advertising planning point of view. In J. C. Maloney & B. Silverman (Eds.), *Attitude research plays for high stakes* (pp. 94-111). Chicago: American Marketing Association.

Valente, T. W., Paredes, P., & Poppe, P. R. (1998). Matching the message to the process: The relative ordering of knowledge, attitudes, and practices in behavior change research. *Human Communication Research, 24,* 366-385.

Veneziano, L., & Hooper, J. (1997). A method for quantifying content validity of health-related questionnaires. *American Journal of Health Behavior, 21,* 67-70.

Waldron, V. R., Caughlin, J., & Jackson, D. (1995). Talking specifics: Facilitating effects of planning on AIDS talk in peer dyads. *Health Communication, 7,* 249-266.

Wallack, L. M. (1993). *Media advocacy and public health: Power for prevention.* Newbury Park, CA: Sage.

Wang, C. (1997). Photovoice: Concept, methodology, and use for participatory needs assessment. *Health Education & Behavior, 24,* 369-387.

Wang, C. C., Yi, W. K., Tao, Z. W., & Carovano, K. (1998). Photovoice as a participatory health promotion strategy. *Health Promotion International, 13,* 75-86.

Wartella, E., & Middlestadt, S. (1991). The evolution of models of mass communication persuasion. *Health Communication, 3,* 205-215.

Wilkinson, H. J., & Wilkinson, J. W. (1986). Evaluation of a hospice volunteer training program. *Omega, 17,* 263-275.

Winett, L. B., & Wallack, L. (1996). Advancing public health goals through the mass media. *Journal of Health Communication, 1,* 173-196.

Witte, K. (1994). Fear control and danger control: A test of the Extended Parallel Process Model (EPPM). *Communication Monographs, 61,* 113-133.

Witte, K., Cameron, K. A., Lapinski, M. K., & Nzyuko, S. (1998). A theoretically based evaluation of HIV/AIDS prevention campaigns along the trans-African highway in Kenya. *Journal of Health Communication, 3,* 345-363.

Witte, K., & Morrison, K. (1995). Using scare tactics to promote safer sex among juvenile detention and high school youth. *Journal of Applied Communication Research, 23,* 128-142.

Wortman, C. B., & Brehm, J. W. (1975). Responses to uncontrollable outcomes: An integration of reactance theory and the learned helplessness model. In L. Berkowitz (Ed.), *Advances in experimental social psychology* (Vol. 8, pp. 278-336). New York: Academic Press.

Wozniak, P. J., Draughn, P. S., & Knaub, P. K. (1993). Domains of subjective well-being in farm men and women. *Journal of Family and Economic Issues, 14*(2), 97-114.

30

Overcoming the Challenges of Environmental Public Information and Action Programs

GARRETT J. O'KEEFE
ROBIN L. SHEPARD

Environmentally related information campaigns and action programs provide a unique challenge to communication strategists and a fertile ground for examining theories of social and political change at the community as well as interpersonal and individual levels of analysis. Environmental programs aimed at public awareness, understanding, attitudes, and behaviors have a relatively short history. We analyze the key issues facing such campaigns at present and recommend research strategies for addressing them. Among the campaign content areas reviewed are water quality and conservation, air quality, soil conservation, pesticide use, energy, the greenhouse effect, global warming, recycling, and sustainable agriculture.

We begin by noting departures of environmental issue programs from the other types of programs noted in this volume. The need for formative research—both quantitative and qualitative—on appropriate publics is emphasized, with optimal methods described for carrying out such inquiry regarding environmental problems. Current studies of public attitudes and behaviors toward environmental issues are analyzed, including public perceptions of environmental risks and the cost and effectiveness of various remedies in light of those risks.

The application of research findings to development of strategies for reaching these publics is then highlighted, with variations noted for the types of environmental problems being dealt with (e.g., water quality protection vs. conservation).

The ethics of and values associated with information campaigns in general, and with environmental campaigns in particular, are considered, as are private sector environmental programs. More traditional models of campaigns based on more hierarchical "social marketing" models are considered and contrasted with what may be more effective, locally derived participatory models of campaign planning, design, and production involving stronger community inputs. Conclusions include recommendations based on these contrasts. We conclude with a model for implementing an environmental action program that takes into account social as well as physical environment factors, both of which we believe are critical to effective environmental interventions. An agriculturally based environmental action study is offered as but one example of how the model can be applied.

CHALLENGES TO ENVIRONMENTAL PROGRAMS

Chechile (1991) noted several of the more perplexing factors in environmental decision making, including issue complexity, scientific conflict, and the need for interdisciplinary approaches.

Environmental Issue Complexity

The complexity of most environmental issues, and the solutions to them, can at times seem insurmountable to lay citizens and policy makers alike. The interconnectedness of elements in ecological systems renders most environmental problems more vexing than even those found in public health, politics, or global economics. In terms of information or persuasion programs, this requires detailed, often scientific information prepared for lay audiences who might not have the background to grasp the complex interactions of the factors involved. Problematic issues such as global warming, species endangerment, air and water pollution, and energy conservation involve not only a gamut of biological, physical, and social science knowledge but at times

equally compelling conflicts among political, economic, technological, cultural, and religious value frameworks and institutions.

As Orr (1992) noted in his seminal work, *Ecological Literacy,* ecology is at once an "old science," as a search for efficient resource management, and a "new science," as much concerned with a broader search for pattern and meaning, including issues of values and ethics:

> The study of environmental problems is an exercise in despair unless it is regarded as only a preface to the study, design, and implementation of solutions. The concept of sustainability implies a radical change in the institutions and patterns that we have come to accept as normal. It begins with ecology as the basis for the redesign of technology, cities, farms, and educational institutions and with a change in metaphors from mechanical to organic, industrial to biological. As part of the change, we need alternative measures of well-being. (p. 94)

No small undertaking, to be sure—and one that, if taken seriously, involves small- and large-scale informational, educational, and persuasive efforts on a multitude of fronts.

Conflicting Evidence on Problems and Solutions

Conflicting scientific evidence is often readily available concerning environmental problems themselves and their remedies. The novelty and interactive nature of many environmental issues lend to greater scientific incertitude than is found in many other endeavors. As Chechile (1991) emphasized, environmental problems require *multidisciplinary* approaches to problems; physicists, botanists, biochemists, wildlife ecologists, geologists, and social scientists often must interact to have a chance of successfully attacking our more severe environmental concerns. Given that conflicts over approaches and interpretations are common within any research field, the cacophony heightens as more and more cooperative efforts are required. This is in part because of disagreement among many of the scientific findings themselves; differing results can occur depending on geographic location, type of measurement, or basic errors in methodology. Moreover, even similar results can be interpreted differently based on varying theoretical perspectives, vested interests in the issue, or the context in and purposes for which the research was carried out. And as Sexton, Marcus, Easter, and Burkhardt (1999) indicated, the context and process for framing the problem, doing the research, and making decisions based on the research can differ markedly depending on whether the key players are in government, commercial business, or public community sectors of society.

Public understanding of science, and confidence in it, is often diminished by such conflict (Friedman, Dunwoody, & Rogers, 1999; Nelkin, 1995), lessening the chances for convincing arguments advocating change in attitudes and behaviors to be heard or understood by the public—or by policy makers, for that matter.

Delay in Visible Consequences

The dynamics of ecological interventions often call for immediate action, the consequences of which might not be apparent for years or decades to come. This makes it difficult to reinforce citizen actions in environmental remediation of, for example, air and water quality, and this can reduce motivation for continued action. As Rogers (1995) postulated, this reinforcement of behavioral change, as specified in the adoption of innovations and other persuasion-based models, can

be a critical ingredient; people want to see that their efforts are indeed making a difference. Magnifying the problem, Swap (1991) applied the psychological risk strategies demonstrated by Kahneman and Tversky (1984) to this environmental dilemma: People are more likely to risk uncertain large future losses than to immediately accept smaller certain ones. On the other hand, when faced with a choice between a smaller certain gain and a larger uncertain one, they tend to choose the former. Thus, from the point of view of persuasive strategizing, it may be more effective to emphasize whatever immediate gains can be had, no matter how meager, than to stress a doomsday approach that may occur somewhere down the road. Saving a few dollars a month by conserving energy, for example, may have more citizen appeal than forecasting ahead to blackouts and potential calamity (Aronson & Gonzales, 1990; Dennis & Soderstrom, 1988). Fortunately, many of the remedies for cleaner air and water mandated during the 1970s are now producing evidence of their validity, especially in the Northeast and Upper Midwest. Moreover, particularly in the case of conservation of untrammeled lands, the desire of many citizens to serve as stewards of those so that their descendants can share in their pleasures can be a strong motivating force.

The Risk Factor

Substantial social, economic, and political risks are often involved in changing behaviors on behalf of environmental protection or remediation. While this is not always the case, major decisions involving industrial cleanup or remodeling, land use disputes, transportation (e.g., automotive use), and (probably above all) agricultural practices carry potentially great costs to those being asked to carry them out, and in many cases they carry considerable risk of profit loss or even closure. These risks can be borne by people from 40-acre farmers being asked to change decades-old tillage or fertilizer practices, to corporate czars being ordered to cut air emissions, to legislators being lobbied into lose-lose votes on land use policies that divide their constituencies. Mandated curbside recycling or changing home gardening practices may pose little such risk, but more environmentally impactful actions often do. The considerable recent literature on risk behavior and communication (Chess, Salomone, Hance, & Saville, 1995; Dunwoody & Neuwirth, 1991; Griffin, Dunwoody, & Zabala, 1998; Peters, Covello, & McCallum, 1997; Rimal, Fogg, & Flora, 1995; Trumbo, 1998) has enlightened not only public reaction to environmental (as well as health and other) threats but also citizens' willingness to take appropriate actions.

The Need for Critical Public Mass for Action

Change among significant numbers of members of a community over time is required for effective environmental action in most cases. This is clear from low public cost examples such as recycling and energy conservation; to expensive and often risky farm, ranch, and timberland management practices; to industrial smokestack air pollutants. The analogy from public health would be that of an inoculation program to ward off a virulent contagious epidemic. Simply having a small portion of the at-risk population take part will not do the trick. Rather, some critical mass has to be reached for effectiveness. The situation is not unlike that captured in Hardin's (1968) now-classic treatise, *Tragedy of the Commons,* in which a probabilistic model is offered involving how many sheep farmers are willing to forgo further breeding that would

lead to overgrazing of common lands, pitting their own immediate profits against the greater good of their fellow herders and their community.

Similarly, just a handful of neighbors engaged in recycling will have virtually no impact on resource consumption or landfill needs and will very likely make the recycling effort unprofitable to manufacturers. What is needed is that critical mass to make the system work within the community, state, or nation. And in some cases, the populations involved have to be selective. Agriculturally, for example, it makes little difference whether ranchers or farmers, either away from stream flowage or far downstream, curtail manure use if the producers upstream do not. In terms of intervention programs, this suggests that both community and population-wide campaigns are needed, often with carefully targeted messages for various subgroups, and coupled with as much attention to social norms or peer pressure as can be mustered.

Environmental Knowledge Versus Attitudes Versus Behaviors

We come to the sticky situation of a lack of congruence among environmental knowledge, attitudes, and in particular behaviors. While low correlations among these three variables are sometimes found in regard to nonenvironmental issues, rarely are they as disparate as in the case of ecological support. If we begin with attitudinal data—and in some cases values data—we learn that the vast majority of studies during the 1990s indicated that typically on the order of 75% of U.S. adults are *concerned* or *very concerned,* or express similar sentiments, about the environment either locally, nationally, or globally (Arcury, 1990; Dunlap & Scarce, 1991; Natural Resources Conservation Service, 1995;

Nowak, O'Keefe, Bennett, Anderson, & Trumbo, 1997; O'Keefe & Shepard, 1998; Swenson & Wells, 1997; Trumbo & O'Keefe, 1999; Vining & Ebreo, 1990; Zimmerman, 1996). These same studies reflect a willingness to act or at least to support public policy for environmental protections. These attitude levels are on a par with those during the large-scale environmental awakenings of the late 1960s and early 1970s, including the first "Earth Day" and similar programs, which were followed by something of a downswing in positive attitudes during the later 1970s and into the 1980s (Dunlap & Scarce, 1991; Van Liere & Dunlap, 1980).

Yet when reasonable comparisons are made between attitudes and indicators of public knowledge about environmental issues per se and potential resolutions to them, the correspondence is usually low; more positive attitudinal support does not mean greater knowledge, and vice versa (Arcury, 1990; Nowak et al., 1997; O'Keefe & Shepard, 1998), even concerning high news agenda topics such as global warming, water quality, and pesticides. Much of this can be attributed to the controversies among scientists and policy makers on certain issues (Friedman et al., 1999), but well-tested and indeed commonsensical statements are too often disagreed with or not responded to. And correlations between environmental attitudes and actions—or willingness to act—are even more disparate (Nowak et al., 1997; O'Keefe & Shepard, 1998; Trumbo & O'Keefe, 1999). Perhaps the highest consistent correlations on specific attitudes and behaviors in a national sample have been reported by Swenson and Wells (1997), based on substantial 1992 and 1993 probability samples, but those correlation coefficients were no higher than .27 and .25, respectively. A host of other demographic, psychological, and lifestyle predictors entered into a regression equation produced a total R^2 of less than .25, or explaining less than 25% of the total variance in the environmental behavior scores. This was one of the more comprehensive studies on this complex issue.

Pickett, Kangun, and Grove (1993) rightfully noted that the more vague or diffuse the issue, the lower the consensus among knowledge, attitude, and behavior scores, and they argued that this could well be the case for the environmental topic. However, comparisons in specific areas such as recycling, purchasing decisions, agricultural water protection, and household water and energy conservation have not proven this to be the case. Some interesting consistencies do occur, however. One is that there is usually somewhat greater congruence among these variables among the more highly educated and younger population sectors. These are also apt to score higher on all indexes.

There may well be an underlying psychological involvement factor here; as Chaffee and Roser (1986) found, greater involvement is associated with greater congruence. Another factor that bears mentioning is a decided *proximity* effect. With respect to farm water quality issues, Nowak et al. (1997) and O'Keefe and Shepard (1998) consistently found that citizens rate more distal sites as having more severe water pollution problems, with the nation scoring highest in water pollution, then their own state, then their own community, and then their own land. The progression is usually nearly linear and highly significant. The Natural Resources Conservation Service (1995) received a similar pattern of responses in asking about the condition of the environment in general. We are exploring this relationship more closely. For example, do heavier news users see pollution as more of a problem for other locales as a result of news coverage of highly problematic but remote ecological events? In any case, existing data suggest that for many, environmental protection may be seen as more of a problem for others rather than in their own backyards.

The Role of
Citizen Involvement

Many environmental interventions are indeed initiated and stimulated by citizen involvement, especially when dangers are seen close to home. This reverse "NIMBY" ("Not in my backyard!") effect has been seen repeatedly in toxic waste scandals such as the Love Canal incidents in New York State during the 1970s, and it carried over into the environmental justice movement of the 1990s, borne out of concern that economically disadvantaged locales are disproportionately chosen for landfills and other potentially hazardous sitings (Bullard, 1994). Similarly, the multiplicity of local, regional, national, and international organizations supporting environmental change is staggering, with major groups such as the Sierra Club, the Nature Conservancy, the Wilderness Society, and Greenpeace wielding considerable memberships, funding, and political clout (Dowie, 1995; Gottleib, 1993). While this should be seen as a distinct advantage for environmental protection movements, and overall it likely is, it can have the downside of at times sounding too shrill a note, perhaps adding to public confusion over "the facts" or science of ecological issues.

The "Biosocial" Challenge

Backes (1995) argued that communicating about the environment should take into account reciprocal relationships between society and the environment that generally go under the rubric of biosocial theory. That is,

human social systems are invariably linked with what we normally consider ecological biophysical systems, yet communication research on environmental issues sticks quite closely with the social systems side of the interchange:

Research using the perspective provided by biosocial theory examines two subsystems and their linkages. One subsystem is the ecosubsystem, which is characterized by biophysical processes. The other subsystem is the social system, which is characterized by cultural processes. The systems are linked, not by geography or by mechanical or biological laws, but by human perceptions of and behavior toward the ecosystem. Individuals and groups in society intentionally or unintentionally affect their physical environments, which respond to those actions in some manner, and this response, when perceived by individuals and organizations, encourages them to continue or change their actions. Biosocial theory predicts that effects may be expected not only in the direction of mass communication-human perceptions/behavior-ecosystem, but also in the reverse direction. (pp. 149-150)

Backes (1995) gave the example of communication campaigns that may well work to change ecological variables in one way (reduced logging and forest fires), but with those changes causing other ones in the environment (less animal forage), leading to a consequence of increased deer and wolf habitation of human-populated areas. A similar argument was raised by Cronon (1995) in his critique of viewpoints that take humans and their activities out of nature and calls for a new environmental ethic that admits an appropriate, responsible human interchange with nature. The challenge, of course, is to determine that role and the means of effective communication to pursue it.

Delayed Policy Making

Chechile (1991) also suggested that all-too-rapid technological development can create ecological disputes worldwide that traditional diplomatic processes are too slow or cumbersome to react to in a timely way (e.g., global warming). We add that from a public communication program perspective within the United States alone, the panoply of municipal, county, state, and federal agencies involved in environmental decision making—and carrying out intervention programs of various and sometimes conflicting kinds—can form another barrier to citizen knowledge and action. At the federal level alone, we have the Environmental Protection Agency, the Department of the Interior, the Department of Agriculture, and the Department of Health and Human Services, to name but the major players, all with some forms of environmental advocacy programs. Cooperation often exists and succeeds, but sometimes it does not, even given the best of intentions.

Walker (1994) criticized the lack of cohesive framework for interagency dealings with critical problems such as drinking water safety and pesticide use. He also charged the federal government with putting too much emphasis on policy formulation and with not providing enough enforcement or funding for policy *implementation*. One of Walker's recommendations was more cohesive congressional oversight of the agencies involved, with more consistent budgeting to ensure policy effectiveness. In a 5-year study of an agricultural water quality demonstration program within one such agency that involved four subunits of it, as well as state and county cooperators, it is fair to say that confusion over roles, funding, and mandates lessened the potential impact of the program (Anderson, O'Keefe, & Nowak, 1997). On the other hand, lessons were learned to likely improve such joint efforts in the future. And we fully agree with Chechile and others that multidisciplinary, as well as multiagency, cooperation is critical to successful communication with and action by the public. Sexton (1999) argued for integrated environmental decision-making strategies among governments, business, and communities, fostered by adopting sustainability as a unifying principle to build greater trust, respect, and fairness in policies. (In a later section, we detail one path to such improved cooperation.)

Ethical Considerations

The ethics of persuasive (or informational/educational) communication programs has been challenged for decades. As one early health communication critic (Chapin, 1915) put it in his chairman's address published in the *American Journal of Public Health,*

> Clear, forceful, and catchy writing is worse than useless if it fails to teach the truth and the truth only. So far as it departs from this, our health literature approaches that of the fake medicine factory—and perhaps does more harm. The space writer is the curse of our day and generation, and especially in our business. (p. 502)

Salmon (1989) and others have more recently noted other ethical concerns in communication programs and campaigns, many with strong ramifications for environmental efforts. Salmon particularly questioned the setting of the issue agenda in campaigns—who decides which issues will come to the fore, the financing of them (public or private), and how far such messages should go in taking a "paternalistic" view of the public, something of a "big brother" approach, as opposed to setting out the facts as we have them and letting citizens decide for themselves. As indicated previously, the precise definition of the problem and solutions to it can be problematic, particularly when they may conflict with other important behaviors or social imperatives and may be based on still controversial science. "Tokenism" is another risk pointed out by Salmon, that is, using the campaign to show that "something" is being done rather than putting more resources into the problem itself or the underlying causes of it.

Similarly, Pollay (1989) suggested three domains of ethical problems in campaigns with ramifications for environmental ones. First, is the information correct to begin with, and can the recommendations be used with confidence? Second, does the program get overenthusiastic in attempting to manipulate citizens through exaggeration, outright falsehoods, overly emotional appeals (particularly fear arousal), or other deceptions? Third, have potentially unintended consequences been explored, such as causing more problems than the original one being attacked and drawing attention from possibly more serious issues?

The institutional problems of such programs were addressed more directly by Rakow (1989) in her argument that many such programs are unequal power interchanges between citizens and government, with the institutions holding by far the superior information and technique structure, which may be shared only selectively with the public. Is the public getting the information it needs and wants, or is it getting more of what the institutions believe the public should have? A related concern has been addressed in the health communication arena by Guttman (1997), who called for study of the values embedded in such programs, particularly concerning decisions about what issues are highlighted and what solutions are proposed. Witte (1994) proposed seeking out of the highest "common good" standards for such decisions. Environmental programs certainly should have no less of a concern with this matter.

Thus, we have a long and perplexing list of issues that daunt the effective design of environmental information and action programs. Again, not all of these are exclusive to ecological issues, but the mix, we argue, is quite unparalleled. Environmental policy decisions typically depend on sophisticated and often conflicting scientific premises, transcending several fields of inquiry. Solutions offered may pose public expense, effort, and risk with payoffs far in the future. Substantial numbers of citizens are needed for effective action. Sentiment toward environmental protection is strong but is usually only weakly related to taking action. Governmental, commercial, and community sector organizations may conflict within and among one another on problem-solving processes and solutions. We now turn to what previous and current work has taught us about how we might begin to deal with at least some of them.

APPROACHES TO OVERCOMING ENVIRONMENTAL PROGRAM CHALLENGES

Given the central persuasion theme of this handbook, we do not deal with two other common approaches to environmental intervention: regulation and economic rewards or penalties. Nowak (1987) and Nowak and Korsching (1998), among others, have contrasted the advantages and disadvantages of these solutions as compared to more persuasion-based and volitional approaches.

Each method has its place, depending on the types of ecological degradation of concern, the citizens or institutions involved, and the apparent solutions to the problems. In the case of large-scale industrial pollution of air or water, for example, as in many manufacturing processes, governmental regulation and/or economic sanctions may be highly appropriate and effective. Similar regulatory action in dealing with toxic waste, land resource protection (e.g., grazing, mining, timber), endangered species, and the like may also be the most effective option. In many cases, a combination of regulatory and economic measures may be coupled with psychological appeals for even greater effect.

This is most likely to occur in situations involving "non-point" pollution, that is, instances where the offender is not a single source or group but that involve large numbers of enterprises—typically each under individual control—cumulatively adding to pollution. In many cases, the contribution of any one source is small or even inconsequential, but the combination of sources makes for a serious problem. Agricultural producers are a classic example here, but included in this category can be many forms of energy use, including automobiles, recycling behavior, product consumption patterns, water conservation, recreational practices (e.g., hiking, biking, boating, camping), home pesticide use, and lawn and gardening practices. The behaviors involved can range from expensive to cheap, from effortful to trivial. A classic successful example often raised in this regard is that of littering. Up until about the 1960s, roadsides and other public places were often quite littered with bits of paper and other trash simply tossed from passersby. However, a combination of laws carrying moderate fines (and in some cases the threat of jail), extensive public awareness campaigns, and more and more social norms against such practices severely curtailed them.

Nowak and Korsching (1998) pointed to a continuing debate among policy makers, especially with respect to agricultural practices, over how far to go in promoting programs and campaigns calling for voluntary restraints on polluting behaviors versus increased regulation, economic sanctions, and/or (in many cases) assistance in implementing new practices and technologies. While there are no universally applicable answers, citizen compliance in cases of non-point pollution is clearly enhanced when citizens know why they are asked to change behaviors, whether regulation or economic motives are involved or not.

As in most programs or campaigns aimed at behavioral change, the term *persuasion* has lost some currency, particularly where governmental agencies are concerned. Most now go under nomenclature such as awareness programs and information or education campaigns. We largely adopt those terms here, although in most cases we are talking about persuasive strategies discussed in previous chapters, often based in some way on one or more "knowledge-attitude-behavior" change paradigms.

Behavior Analysis

Swap (1991) presented a cogent analysis of Hardin's "commons" model as applied to promoting conservation, including psychological "behavior analysis" approaches and more overtly persuasive ones. Behavioristically, he advocated the learning theory approach of quickly rewarding appropriate short-term behaviors that foster conservation and bringing the negative longer term consequences to bear more rapidly. One such behavioristic approach involves municipalities simply making separate recycling receptacles mandatory, easy to use, and delivered without charge to every household, with stiff fines for non-use on pickup days (Geller, 1989).

Positive motivational techniques can be pitted against coercive motivational techniques (De Young, 1993). In the former case, positive inducements are offered such as monetary rewards for buying back used cans or bottles, contests, utility rate savings for conservation, and social recognition or support. Coercive techniques are more apt to involve not direct punishment but rather financial disincentives such as higher tax rates for greater consumption and negative peer or social norm pressure for not cooperating. As we discuss later, the jury is still out on nearly all of these techniques in terms of their longer term effectiveness in maintaining change.

A related but more complex example is the attempt by agricultural agents to provide immediate on-site, hands-on technical assistance in teaching farmers accurate use of more sustainable practices and technologies. A common delivery tool for such instruction is the demonstration project, which has picked up currency in energy conservation and other sectors as well (Hancock, 1992; Macey & Brown, 1990). A basic principle here is that actually trying out a technique (much in the sense of Rogers's [1995] "trial" stage of adoption), perhaps simultaneous with or even before substantial knowledge of it or attitude change, may facilitate both of the former steps and have a better chance of leading directly to adoption of or change in behavior.

Environmental Information and Education Programs

Our own experiences (Nowak et al., 1997; O'Keefe & Shepard, 1998), as well as the environmentally based research of others (Keown, 1998; McMullin & Nielsen, 1991; Waddell, 1995; White, 1998), have led us to the following general program/campaign principles, some of which are applicable to most persuasive settings but most of which are more peculiar to environmental ones.

Emphasizing Community Interaction. One should build on existing public networks and levels of knowledge, interest, and involvement in the problem. One should look for general trends in community consensus about problems and solution options but should

seek out and recognize differences among the various stakeholders. This approach obviously calls for extensive formative research before the program is planned or designed. If at all possible, local participants should be invited into even this early formative research stage. Moreover, all too often the citizens involved are those selected for their positions of responsibility, knowledge, or prestige. As Glicken (1999) argued, increasingly members of the broader public are demanding a role in environmental and other decisions that will affect their lives.

If sample surveys, focus groups, expert informant interviews, and other such techniques are to be used, then local input, discussion, and negotiation can make such techniques more effective by posing questions in terms that will be more understandable to the publics involved and in interpreting responses in ways more appropriate to the publics involved. Information from these tools should be shared with local participants and stakeholders rather than used as "top-down" strategizing mechanisms to attempt to sway public opinion and action one way or the other from the planners' perspective (for additional perspectives on such methodological issues, see Hale, 1993; Kathlene & Martin, 1991; U.S. Department of Agriculture, 1998; Wellman & Fahmy, 1985). Rather, the context should be a cooperative one with stakeholders, looking for agreement on problem perceptions and on a range of possible solutions, from "probable" to "wholly unacceptable." Much can also be learned from the more internationally applied Rural Rapid Appraisal tools used to involve local citizens directly in agricultural, environmental, and health changes by working with them through the whole process—in a sense moving from their "participation" in the project to "ownership" of it (Freudenberger, 1995). Such formative research can, of course, provide baseline data useful for midcourse corrections in programs as they develop and are further scrutinized and for summative evaluation efforts determining the extent of success of the programs.

Finnegan and Sexton (1999) argued, in particular, for following models of analysis that have been successful in the public health sector, beginning with the defining of geographic, social, cultural, and political outlines of a community and following this with more intensive analysis examining, in particular, the power and leadership patterns within a community. While such patterns may differ for environmental interventions as compared to health-related ones, the basic premises and processes are the same.

The Need for Theory. Well-developed psychological models of persuasion developed earlier in this volume can provide a wellspring of rationales, strategies, and optimal techniques for understanding and dealing with various cognitive, attitudinal, and behavioral situations. Moreover, they can provide a structural framework for program development. This does not mean that they need to be applied in a "top-down," "me expert, you subject" manner. Rather, they can readily become educational tools to be shared in developing informational and educational programs aimed at and used by various constituencies. This has been demonstrated repeatedly in the public health arena, both nationally and internationally (Backer, Rogers, & Sapory, 1992; Bracht, Kingsbury, & Rissel, 1999; Finnegan & Viswanath, 1999; Israel, Checkoway, Schulz, & Zimmerman, 1994; Middlestadt, Schechter, Peyton, & Tjugum, 1997; Rogers, 1995).

Working *with* citizen groups to plan, strategize, and implement programs around their own informational, social, and environmental needs and capabilities may be far more effective than "targeting" publics to act in ways that planners alone may believe are relevant.

McKee (1994) and Middlestadt (1997) presented process outlines adapting the traditional social marketing approach to such a participatory process based on work on health and related social development programs. Granted, the technical skills of scientists and program planners are critical to the process, but decades of public reluctance to follow the "ideal" scenarios often proposed for environmental protections should teach us that compromise solutions are better than none.

Community-based campaigns in many ways resemble more traditional social marketing efforts directed at individuals in that the programs require formative assessment of audiences or publics, defined mass media and interpersonal strategies, and well-orchestrated message and dissemination activities. However, Finnegan and Sexton (1999) concluded that community-based programs, as used in both health and environmental programming, also try to take into account a greater aggregate of outcomes on a more complex scale. Not only may disparate populations within a community be targeted for varied outcomes, but attempts may be made to change public policy or to modify community resources aimed at the problem as well as social norms concerning it. Moreover, given their scale, the programs rely on multiple activities across the community aimed not only at individuals but also at business, educational, political, and other institutions as appropriate. And the time scale is definitely long range as opposed to the more typical, one-shot, information education approach, often resulting in at least marginal changes in community structure and norms with respect to the issue(s) of concern.

The levels of program involvement and participation now called for in international development, environmental or otherwise, can also find application in U.S. settings (Monroe, 1999; Servaes, 1996; Thompson & Winner,

1999; White, 1994). These again often call for a wider range of social, cultural, and political changes.

Evaluative Criteria and Processes. While often quite difficult in a new arena of programming, every effort should be made to develop at the outset clear and empirically measurable program goals and objectives. Formative, process, and summative evaluation can provide baselines, progress checkpoints, and indicators of success or failure. This is likely the central failing of most environmental information and education programs—and indeed of most communication campaigns. Without such criteria, we often continue to fly along blindly, assuming that a 10% gain in knowledge in one study is the Holy Grail because it was "statistically significant" while having no point of comparison to related programs.

Similarly, as we have already noted, such evaluation should include programming assessments as well (Anderson et al., 1997; Patton, 1997). Careful qualitative evaluation of program management, strategizing, networking, internal and external communication audits, and the like can provide a mine of information that, when related to program outcomes, can go far in explaining degrees of effectiveness and in which areas. And following from our previous recommendations, various stakeholders in the community can and should play key roles in the evaluation process (Patton, 1997; Whitmore, 1998).

An additional evaluative component that comes to the forefront in environmental programs is, of course, environmental impact. While this is often beyond the ken of communication researchers, the more sophisticated studies attempt to eventually determine what impact the behavioral and communicative interventions had on actual environmental quality (Nowak & Korsching, 1998; Nowak et al., 1997). This is clearly a mission for phys-

ical and/or biological scientists and may be years in the undertaking.

Systemic and Social Norm Factors. Hornik (1997) identified several factors that he found to be related to the success of public health education and communication programs that fit well for environmental programs. These include (a) support of the recommended behaviors by the health (or other appropriate environmental policy agency) system, (b) reaching much of the targeted audience repeatedly with appropriate messages, (c) an expectation that the change will occur through slow social norm changes rather than through effects of direct message exposure on individuals, and (d) desired new behaviors that fit easily with current behavioral patterns. Unfortunately, proper orchestration of these factors can require large-scale undertakings, with a great coordination among several levels of actors. Even agreement on the recommended behaviors by the policy agencies involved can be problematic, and reaching targeted diverse publics with varied messages that carry the same theme toward the same societal goal can take considerable mastery of combining interpersonal, organizational, and mass media skills—no easy task.

Keeping It Going. A key problem in many environmental action programs is keeping the appropriate behaviors in motion once the major program or campaign stimuli have subsided. Rogers (1995) pointed to the need for continued reinforcement and self-evaluation by individuals to ensure that a new behavior is still worthwhile or, worse, is not causing unforeseen negative consequences. De Young (1993) deftly categorized several behavioral change techniques according to their reliability in consistently instigating behavior change, the speed of their effectiveness, their particular appropriateness across of range of environmentally relevant behaviors, and (perhaps most important) their durability over time. Persuasive techniques such as active prompting (e.g., by advertising) and material incentives ("bribery" to some) appear to be useful only in the short term, while the (admittedly little) evidence for social pressure and material disincentives seem to provide more hope. Public commitments to changes of one form or another seem the most promising.

What is obviously going on here is a psychological range of internalization of attitudes or values, probably not unlike Kelman's (1971) trajectory of social influence ranging from compliance, to identification, to internalization. Only when internalization of an attitude and congruent behavior is accomplished within one's value system is long-term durable change likely to take hold. This is not unlike the failure one might expect from dependence on more heuristic message strategies discussed in earlier chapters of this volume in campaigns dealing with potentially involving issues as opposed to more elaborate, logical spelling out of the practices desired and the reasons underlying those.

Tied to this is another problem raised by De Young and others of the generalizability of appropriate behaviors across the nearly befuddling range of environmental issues. Apart from the likely small segment of "true" environmentalists who have the internalized ecological ethic (or "literacy," as Orr [1992] put it), we are probably talking about one-shot programs aimed at fairly limited issues, although not unimportant ones. It takes a fair amount of cognitive work to see the interrelationships among most of these issues, let alone nearly all of them. Major's (1993) suggestion for further research on "environmental publics" and the concerns that both separate and link various groupings might at least lay out the citizen landscape of what levels of involvement are tied to what groupings of issues. The same goes for her proposition that information and education may be more important stimulants to environmental change than are more persuasive attitudinal efforts. Again, Orr's call for a more holistic environmental educational effort, beginning in the schools, appears to hold validity here as well.

THE COMMERCIAL SECTOR AND ENVIRONMENTAL ACTION

The environmental concerns of the public have not been lost on the corporate world of product manufacturers and service providers. Contemporary advertising and marketing, for example, are rife with tie-ins of products and services to environmentally friendly themes—sports utility vehicles (SUVs) and nation park protection, saving on energy consumption, and a seeming contest as to which manufacturers can promote the most recyclable "earth-friendly" containers, to name a very few.

A cynic can easily view many, if not most, of these campaigns as trying to sell more products and increasing consumption by simply tying a "green ribbon" around the products. Many have complained, for example, that gas-guzzling SUVs, if used to their full four-wheel-drive capabilities, are indeed a formidable threat to sensitive wilderness soils and flora. Indeed, books such as Coddington's (1993) *Environmental Marketing* seem to stress corporate image building as much as, or more than, genuine ecological concern and substance in the design and manufacture of products. The focus appears more on identifying target audiences and markets among which environmental concerns are highest and designing campaigns to attract their business.

However, this is not always the case, and even where it may be, an optimist might argue that at least such campaigns may draw more public attention to or concern with environmental issues. In fact, there is some recent evidence that many corporations are becoming "greener" in product design per se, whether out of genuine ecological concerns, a bottom-line belief that greener is indeed cheaper, fear of public backlash or governmental regulation, or some combination of these. Many businesses have heeded Hawken's (1993) call for action by the corporate world as the planet's "dominant institution." Hawken's oft-quoted triangle of issues that business faces environmentally—"what it takes" (in resources), "what it makes" (and the consequences of those), and "what it wastes" (in manufacturing and/or in detritus)—provides a compelling model of how corporations can and do control elements of the ecosystem, for better or worse.

Carrying the banner a step further, Fuller (1999) offered more specific advice on how companies can design holistic marketing efforts that involve the full cycle of product and service design, manufacture or delivery, and consumption. He staked out a middle ground for sustainable commerce as not a sales gimmick or sheer altruism but simply good business. He defined *sustainable marketing* as

> the process of planning, implementing, and controlling the development, pricing, promotion, and distribution of products in a manner that satisfies the following three criteria: (1) customer needs are met, (2) organizational goals are attained, and (3) the process is compatible with ecosystems. (p. 4)

Fuller (1999) compared sustainable marketing systems with sustainable ecosystems in that both consume resources and create wastes, but in the former benefits must be provided to consumers in a way that maintains the natural balance of the ecosystem. This is no small task, but Fuller provided a framework with implications for marketing communication processes as well. Simply stated, the process begins by traditional marketing audits,

but adding an ecological component to them—what is the current ecosystem status the product (or service) is entering, what are the positive or negative ramifications of the product on that system, and so forth. These audit data are then incorporated into designing, manufacturing, and marketing the product.

Similarly, the channeling of products from manufacturer to consumer factors in ecological considerations such as using energy (e.g., in transportation), educating retailers (and direct consumers) as to ecologically efficient sale and use habits, and using already environmentally conscious retailers as primary outlets for goods, reinforcing their capacities and building their ability to serve as models for other retailers.

Most interesting for our purposes, the traditional marketing communication process is rendered more sustainable by (a) making it more interactive (vs. hierarchical), (b) making it more educational (vs. persuasive) regarding environmental issues appropriate to the product, and (c) building the environmental credibility of the products and their makers. Here, Fuller (1999) turned to the kinds of message appeals used by the "green for gold" merchants and their more responsible cohorts alike: (a) cultural pressure (it is "in" to be green), (b) environmentalism's considerable emotional capital, (c) the fact that ecological products are more rational and can be cheaper in the short or long run, (d) the fact that ecological products are healthier, (e) the corporate commitment of the manufacturer to a better world, (f) testimonials from prominent environmentalists or groups, and (g) comparative benefits of more ecologically sound products over less sound ones.

Schrum, Lowery, and McCarty (1996) warned, however, that despite the attitudinal and value-driven support for environmentally sound products and services, and despite polls indicating willingness to pay a premium for them, the bottom-line sales records for such items has been largely disappointing. It is not clear why.

SEGMENTING PUBLICS AND ENVIRONMENTAL COMMUNICATION PRINCIPLES: A CASE STUDY

We now present an applied model for assessing needs, segmenting publics, and selecting targeted programs. This program has been under development during recent years aimed at agricultural watershed protection, but we believe it has ramifications for numerous other resource-based conservation and sustainability efforts. Moreover, the program is highly regarded as an innovative, cooperative, evaluation-based effort that incorporates many (but not all) of the recommendations noted previously, and components of it are under study by numerous environmental agencies, from local to international.

The Watershed Context

Watershed program strategies often begin with the selection of a small geographic area defined by scope and scale. The people living in this target area are then offered various technical and financial assistance, often through broad-based information and education campaigns. Although most educators would subscribe to audience segmenting, rarely is it done beyond superficial levels such as education and income.

Nationally, more than $40 billion is spent annually to protect and restore the quality of our rivers, streams, estuaries, and lakes due to non-point source pollution (Wayland, 1993). U.S. Environmental Protection Agency (EPA, 1993) reports indicate that 76% of the impaired acres of lake water, 65% of impaired

stream miles, and 45% of impaired estuary square miles had been affected by non-point source pollution. Moreover, between 50% and 70% of these surface waters had been adversely affected by agricultural non-point source pollution due to soil erosion from cropland, from overgrazing, and from pesticide and fertilizer application (Council for Agricultural Science and Technology, 1992).

Agricultural policy is often implemented along political jurisdictions or boundaries such as states, counties, and townships. However, when agricultural policy incorporates environmental goals such as reducing non-point source pollution, these political jurisdictions may be further divided into geographic regions based on hydrologic units or watersheds. These largely represent the most detailed level of distinction by which agencies segment groups of farmers.

Traditionally, these agencies assume that everyone in the target area is the same and offer the same types of remedial assistance to anyone in that area. This approach largely ignores variation in institutional and infrastructure factors, characteristics of the land and water, prevailing agronomic behaviors, structure of the farm firms, and personal characteristics of the farm operator and others (Brown, 1981). Yet it is variation in these same factors that is often considered most salient when attempting to explain the adoption of agricultural best management practices (Lockeretz, 1990; Nowak & Korsching, 1983; Rogers, 1995).

In addition, agencies may respond to a situation by redefining the problem in terms of their own capabilities, further complicating the use of targeting principles in water quality programs (Rolling, Ashcroft, & Wa Chege, 1976). Regardless of the nature or causes of a specific problem, agencies often create their unique definition of the problem based on prevailing forms of available professional expertise and resources (Clarke & McCool, 1985).

The concept of targeting is nothing new to most water quality agencies. Likewise, the use of formative research techniques to assess characteristics of targeted groups is fairly common. However, what has been lacking is a model that uses strategic assessments to measure the land user characteristics related to the adoption of remedial practices and then divides or segments the audience members based on their needs and existing behaviors (Winett, 1986).

Logically, there is little reason to think that "superficial" targeting can address agricultural non-point source pollution problems effectively. Even if an agency can begin to address audience variation and complexity, such differences are rarely used to identify or segment distinct groups within the larger population. Furthermore, there are few examples from which public agencies might extrapolate ways of identifying and segmenting audience groups based on actual needs.

One way for a public agency to improve its effectiveness of program delivery is through marketing strategies. These strategies are often tailored to customer perceptions, needs, and wants. However, it can be overwhelming for a public agency to design message strategies that take into account the complexity of audience needs and preferred media for message delivery and then to deploy them in the context of a watershed-focused program.

Because of the complexity of audience needs and limitations in financial and human resources, nonprofit organizations and agencies often produce one message for distribution to every eligible person (Kotler & Andreasen, 1987). Yet the themes or content of these messages often lack a theoretical or empirical base. That is, they are designed on the basis of what program managers think farmers need to hear. These messages often end up being built around generalized themes associated with stewardship, desirability of quality water, or remedial program characteristics (Shepard, 1999). A more effective alternative to such generalized approaches involves narrowly defining target audiences, determining the content and quantity of information each audience needs through formative assessment (O'Keefe & Reid, 1990), and then considering those needs in the context of the biophysical landscape in which they occur (Brown, 1981).

Consumer marketing, economics, and mass communication research all have propounded message processing theories, but there are few applied examples available that are pertinent to public nonprofit organizations charged with protecting water quality. Furthermore, there is even less research on linking common market segmentation principles with the target principles applied by most environmental programs focusing on a watershed's biophysical condition or location.

The development of an applied model for incorporating communication and marketing principles with geographic influences on farm management should be an important contribution to watershed management and protection programs aimed at rural and agricultural problems. What is needed is a conceptual model that considers the biophysical features of a watershed along with landowner (farm operator) characteristics related to the adoption of remedial practices. Such a model would make it possible, first, to determine who needs what help most and, after that, to design an overall program based on meeting specific needs of target audiences. This audience segmentation within a targeted area (watershed) should allow the agencies concerned to marshal the appropriate policy tools based on the needs and capabilities of each segment.

Using assessment data and landscape/ geographic data to segment audiences brings the dimension of local policy flexibility to targeted watersheds. Such flexibility provides an alternative to the traditional assumptions that water quality programming can be accomplished through "technical fixes" or that farmers will voluntarily make long-term changes in their operation if the agency provides enough cost-sharing assistance.

Segmentation of rural farm audiences can follow several approaches. Many water quality projects follow fate transport processes or known areas of degradation in the watershed, a process that relies on the biophysical indicators of watershed quality (e.g., habitat, sedimentation, biological dissolved oxygen). Other methods require water quality projects to follow vulnerability indexes (e.g., scarce or endangered species/habitats, remedial and restoration areas). Still other ways of segmenting watershed audiences focus on socioeconomic or political boundaries (e.g., county boundaries/ lines, jurisdictions, agency clients).

To illustrate a more objective approach to audience segmentation in a rural-focused watershed program incorporating landscape/ geographic data and characteristics of the target audience, data from five areas are considered (a) landscape and topography (hydrology), (b) soil texture and attenuation potential for excess nutrients, (c) farm firm characteristics, (d) farm management behaviors, and (e) communication linkages and network characteristics.

Landscape and Topography. Data are collected on the landscape and topography of the geographic setting in which the problem occurs. Landscape and topography influence the location and severity of water quality problems through fate and transport processes and by defining potential agricultural activities. Variations in landscape and topography influence field sizes and cropping patterns.

Soil Texture and Attenuation Potential. Soil texture refers to the composition of the soil particles. Soil texture is generally described by proportion of sand, silt, and clay. Texture is one indicator of the soil's capability to react to variation in climate conditions, tillage practices, and application of agrichemicals (National Research Council, 1993). Its attenuation potential refers to a soil's ability to absorb or hold nutrients such as phosphorus rather then letting them pass directly to ground or surface waters (Madison, 1986). When soils are of a finer texture, such as clay, there is greater potential for nutrients to bind with those particles; if the particles do not erode or move, then the nutrient stays with them. Course-textured soils, such as sand, allow water to pass through more freely and thus have a higher potential for leaching nutrients. Furthermore, soil texture is an important consideration in most crop fertility recommendations. For the purpose of segmenting audiences in a watershed, soil groupings called "soil associations" are likely general enough to distinguish crop fertility influences without becoming too detailed and attempting to extend program delivery resources on a field-by-field level.

Farm Firm Characteristics. Farm firm characteristics pertain to the economic characteristics of the farm as a business (Pampel & van Es, 1977; Rogers, 1995). These characteristics often include farm size in terms of acres operated, ownership or tenure, legal structure, and the farmer's short-term planning horizon cropping patterns as well as investment in land and equipment. Understanding the distribution of farm firm characteristics within a watershed provides an indication of what types of practices would be considered appropriate. It also provides some understanding of the reason why farmers may be unwilling or unable to adopt promoted practices (Nowak, 1993).

Farm Management Behaviors. Many factors influence the adoption of new agricultural technologies (National Research Council, 1993). Only certain of these factors can be manipulated or changed as part of a water quality program. These include beliefs surrounding the causes, severity, and location of the problem (Lockeretz, 1990; Nowak & Korsching, 1983); current knowledge of remedial practices and access to educational assistance (Brown, 1981; Nowak & Korsching, 1983; Rogers, 1995); managerial capacity (Nowak & Korsching, 1983; Pampel & van Es, 1977); and the farmer's institutional connections and interpretations placed on past experiences with resource management agencies (Lockeretz, 1990). These factors provide a basis for further segmentation of the overall target audiences based on what their current behaviors are (management strategies) concerning water quality protection practices. Messages can be designed to change existing beliefs and knowledge that may be acting as barriers to adopting remedial practices.

Communication Linkages and Network Characteristics. Finally, audience segmentation requires an understanding of how various messages are communicated and received by the individual target audiences. This goes beyond determining what needs to be communicated and to whom; it also considers the sources of information and the communication channels that are familiar and most often used by those who need assistance the most. Different subgroups that distinguish sources in terms of credibility, trustworthiness, and prior access can be identified. Communication research suggests that farmers who do not adopt or who adopt late relative to other farmers do so for a variety of reasons. These in-

clude failure to promote appropriate techniques, distribution of technical information that farmers feel is not relevant to their situations (Grunig, Nelson, Richburg, & White, 1988), and delivery of information in a way that is not compatible with the target audience's current information-seeking behaviors (Hornik, 1988).

Segmenting audiences and targeting the watershed's programming approaches respect the heterogeneity of individuals in the overall watershed. While much past communication research has described various methods of focusing on or targeting audience groups, much of this research still treats audiences, and particularly audiences such as farmers, as homogeneous. The process of integrating the landscape/geographic characteristics with audience behaviors requires an accurate assessment of audience needs. This needs assessment considers characteristics of the farm as an agricultural enterprise, what types of management practices the farmer is or is not engaging in that may contribute to water quality protection, and farmer preferences for specific types of information and assistance that watershed program staff can provide.

An Example of How the Process Works

The Tomorrow/Waupaca River watershed is located in central Wisconsin. The Wisconsin Department of Natural Resources and the Wisconsin Department of Agriculture, Trade, and Consumer Protection designated this 330 square miles a Wisconsin priority watershed in 1995 because of degraded water quality, the impact of sedimentation on the aquatic habitat, and concern over nitrate levels in local groundwater supplies. The watershed's rural agricultural characteristics include croplands, pasture lands, irrigated lands, and Christmas tree farms. Even with such agricultural diversity, dairy farming is the major agricultural activity, making animal manure management and the use of commercial nutrients a major concern. Finally, two specific areas of the watershed contain areas of shallow sand- and gravel-based aquifers that supply drinking water to approximately 10,000 residents.

Local watershed staff identified all producers in the watershed who operated at least 40 acres of land and who had at least 15 head of cattle. A questionnaire was designed to record (a) characteristics of the farm firm, (b) the farmer's current level of nitrogen application in the production of corn and the use of specific farm management practices such as soil testing, and (c) information preferences in how the farmer receives information about farm management. The survey was conducted with 175 producers or 76% of the identified farmer population in the watershed. The assessment reviewed differences in the production practices that producers used within the watershed. Watershed program staff targeted two specific regions based on similar characteristics of topography, soils, farm firm, farm management, and communication preferences. The result was an 8-year watershed protection plan that featured specific behavior change objectives for each of the targeted areas of the watershed. These objectives were established through interaction among project staff and local citizens.

If a project were to follow the traditional ways of programming, the overall use of averages or statistical means would be relied on for general characteristics about this watershed. But instead, the variation in farmer behavior becomes more important. For example, the average nitrogen application in corn production for the Tomorrow/Waupaca River watershed was 195 pounds per acre, with an average recommendation of 120 pounds per acre. However, following the target strategy outline discussed previously, it was found that specific geographic areas of the water-

shed ranged from 143 to 256 pounds per acre. If the targeting strategy is followed just on nitrogen application alone, those areas of higher nitrogen application would merit more attention than would areas of lower nitrogen application.

When following the suggested strategy of incorporating landscape/geographic data with behavioral information about the land user in the watershed, a clearer picture of program targeting becomes evident. On the first level of segmentation, the Tomorrow/Waupaca River watershed is unique in its landscape/ geography. Here the watershed is separated into seven distinct drainage areas or sub-watersheds. The second level of segmentation considers soil texture and the ability of the soil to attenuate potential contaminants or reduce their leaching into the groundwater. The Waupaca and Waupaca/Weyauwega sub-watersheds are distinctive areas of coarse-textured or sandy soils, which are the most susceptible to leaching and groundwater contamination. Other sub-watersheds within the overall watershed have coarse- to medium-textured soils that are somewhat less porous and thus less susceptible to leaching of material through the soil profile.

The next step in segmenting the Tomorrow/ Waupaca River watershed is to consider the characteristics of the farm firm in the respective sub-watersheds and within the unique areas identified by soil texture/association. Because soil association identified two distinctive regions (Waupaca and Waupaca-Weyauwega), farm characteristics are compared to other regions of the overall watershed. In this case, the sub-watersheds differ only slightly in that the farms on the more sandy soils have more acres in cash grain production than do the farms in the other five regions.

The fourth level of the segmentation strategy aims at the greatest differences among the sub-watersheds. When consideration is given

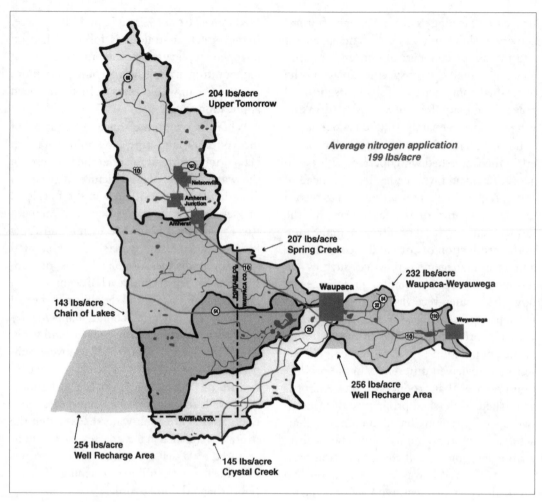

Figure 30.1. Nitrogen Application in a Central Wisconsin Watershed (average nitrogen application by sub-watershed)

to nitrogen application rates, those farms in the Waupaca and Waupaca/Weyauwega sub-watersheds are the highest (see Figure 30.1). After considering soil type (Level 2 segmenting) and nitrogen application rates, a much more appropriate targeting criterion emerges based on local needs. For example, the soils with the greatest potential for leaching are also the soils where the highest application of nitrogen is occurring. Consequently, these two areas (Waupaca and Waupaca-Weyauwega) should receive specific program attention. In a watershed such as the Tomorrow/Waupaca

River watershed, it is unrealistic to assume that efforts from local soil and water conservation professionals can reach all farmers equally; nor should they receive the same amount of attention. This segmentation example suggests that farmers in the Waupaca and Waupaca/Weyauwega sub-watersheds are in greater need of assistance. Therefore, if the program is to be both efficient and effective, it should focus the limited amount of staff time and program resources on those farmers.

Once these two sub-watersheds were identified, the final step in the segmentation model was to apply the principles of communication theory in developing an information and education program to reach those who need it most. Once again, if traditional program targeting had been followed, then a broad-based communication campaign would have been designed, probably relying only on mass information delivery channels such as the mass media or farm publication, as suggested by general information-seeking research.

In this case, Waupaca and Waupaca/Weyauwega farmers were specifically asked where they would turn for information about manure management and interpreting nitrogen application rates. The farmers indicated they would prefer multiple information delivery channels. In the Waupaca sub-watershed, 50% of the respondents selected the Extension Service as the most important source of information about manure management, while 50% selected farm supply representatives. In the Waupaca/Weyauwega sub-watershed, 29% selected the Extension Service, 29% selected farm supply representatives, and 29% indicated other farmers are their preferred source of information. The other sub-watersheds of the Tomorrow/Waupaca River watershed were more likely to select either the Extension Service or the farm supply representatives as their most important source of information about manure management. While this finding by itself is not that significant, when combined with the other elements of the segmentation process (most notably soil texture/association and actual farm management behavior), these information preferences guide project staff in choosing the most effective information channels for targeting those farmers most in need.

Final Points

Segmenting audiences and targeting program elements based on landscape/geographic and behavioral characteristics of the water-

shed can establish priorities for limited program resources (e.g., staff time, landowner contacts). For example, to encourage the adoption of specific agricultural management practices, watershed staff use on-farm demonstrations, local field days, and direct farmer contact. By first considering the geographic information about topography and soils and then considering the farm firm characteristics and information preferences of farmers in those targeted areas, an educational assistance campaign can focus valuable staff time through door-to-door visits and on-farm demonstrations specific to the areas in greatest need. A program following this strategy could easily confine such approaches to the sub-geographic areas of the watershed for a few years and then move to other areas of the watershed over time. This offers specific information for program staff to systematically choose spatial locations of the watershed for unique assistance efforts and to justify those decisions based on both audience needs and their characteristics by providing a more direct assessment and identification of those who need education assistance the most. This approach affords watershed staff and program planners a better understanding both of the problem they are addressing and of the land user behaviors that contribute to that problem. Educational campaigns designed to encourage farm management change should include multiple messages and multiple delivery channels to reflect the diversity within the target audience. The most effective campaign would focus on multiple personal information sources but not exclusively on a single personal information source, and they should include a strategy to guide education activities. This strategy should assess audience needs and communication preferences, designate audience groups based on common sets of behaviors or needs, and then strategically target agency programs toward segments of the audience. Prior research in

Wisconsin (Shepard, 1999) has shown that this approach is unique and in sharp contrast to more common models that segment audiences on landscape/geography or audience characteristics alone.

CONCLUSIONS

The preceding case example illustrates at once both the complexities of environmental information, education, and action programs and those of the potential for strategies to accomplish protective and remedial ecological objectives more effectively. Agriculture and water quality is but one instance where critical environmental safeguards are needed, but it is one of the most pervasive in the world and one often overlooked by more visible pollution issues. Agriculture and related large-scale land practices (e.g., ranching, timber) can be considered as *the* focus of perhaps most of our major environmental problems at this time. Regulation and other forms of policy enforcement may be at least somewhat effective tools for much industrial pollution control, but non-point pollution emanating from multiply owned and independent smaller units— whether agricultural or not—is where communication programs are required to lead to adequate safeguards.

In sum, environmental communication programs face unique and multiple hurdles. They must deal with complex issues straddling many fields of inquiry in the physical, biological, and social sciences. Ecological interconnectedness simply requires no less. A seemingly positive solution to Situation A might have disastrous consequences for Situations B and C. Values and ethics also play key roles here, along with the usual interplay of social and cultural norms, politics, and economics. A given is that people can and will interact with and influence their environment and will, in turn, be influenced by it.

We are also faced with little scientific knowledge in some areas and perhaps too much in others—too much in the sense of conflicting data, hypotheses, and theories. These can and do work against public support of what may be viable solutions, especially when the media provide their journalistic role of communicating these contradictions and uncertainties. We are also often asking citizens to take actions that may at times be expensive, effortful, and risky and that may not bear fruit in terms of environmental change for years or decades to come. Psychologically, this is not always an easy sell to the public at large.

Yet a grassroots movement of locally concerned individuals and groups can at times be at the forefront of taking action. But in most cases, a critical mass of active individuals is required for significant environmental solutions to be implemented. The difficulty in bringing this about is often exacerbated by distinct gaps among what people know about environmental issues, what they think about and are willing to do about them, and what they actually do about them.

Unfortunately, our policy-making systems are not always geared up for decisive action at the most appropriate times. Internationally, nationally, and locally, agencies at times are forced by their nature to move too slowly and/ or in conflict with other agencies, sometimes within the same overall institution. Funding and enforcement for program implementation can be delayed by bureaucratic processes of policy formulation. The private sector also has a distinctive role in the development and marketing of environmentally appropriate products and services. As in any communication program effort, ethical considerations must play a major role. Which issues should be promoted with which solutions, how accurate the information is, and how manipulative of public sentiments campaigns risk becoming are major considerations that cannot escape the influences of individual and institutional values in their design and implementation.

So how do we find our way through this thicket of barriers to actively engage citizens in thwarting threats to our biosphere and to our own survival as a species? For some issues, greater regulation, economic incentives or disincentives, and behavioral motivation techniques will doubtlessly help. For others, more emphasis on information and education, sometimes combined with the preceding, are critical.

However, hierarchical "top-down" models of asking, or telling, members of the public what is good or bad for them, and expecting them to comply, are too often ineffective. Rather, public engagement in the process has proven itself to be a more effective path, as in other areas of public communication programming. Citizen interaction, networking, and sharing of information with appropriate agencies concerned with environmental problem solving and decision making are called for, often with public participation in the evaluation, strategizing, and implementation of the programs themselves.

The need to take advantage of the wealth of research and theory from previous communication program efforts is likewise crucial. These tend to be less developed in the environmental field per se, but applied research from public health and safety areas, and the abundance of psychological, sociological, and communication-based theory on cognitive, attitudinal, and behavioral change, is there for the taking and for the testing. Again, as has been demonstrated, these theories and models can be worked in with the participatory approaches called for earlier. It is often overlooked that basing a program on one clear theoretical perspective can also provide organization and focus.

Along with this comes setting clear and empirically testable criteria for the relative success of such programs and following through

with formative, in-process, and summative evaluation. Past attempts have been quite scattershot, across the full range of communication program efforts. Environmental programs also need to demonstrate that the remediations called for actually led to some ecological benefit, as is similarly the case in areas such as health and public safety.

Finally, simple one-shot or one-topic programs will not do the trick here. We need unified educational efforts that will tie together the often bewildering mix of environmental issues at hand. And the actions taken need to be over the long term—as in over lifetimes.

REFERENCES

Anderson, S. S., O'Keefe, G. J., & Nowak, P. (1997, November). *The value of integrating qualitative data with quantitative evaluations: Implications for data analysis and explanatory power.* Paper presented at the annual meeting of the American Evaluation Association, San Diego.

Arcury, T. A. (1990). Environmental attitude and environmental knowledge. *Human Organization, 49,* 300-304.

Aronson, E., & Gonzales, M. H. (1990). Alternative social influence processes applied to energy conservation. In J. Edwards, R. S. Tindale, L. Heath, & E. J. Posavac (Eds.), *Social influence processes and prevention* (pp. 301-326). New York: Plenum.

Backer, T. E., Rogers, E. M., & Sapory, P. (1992). *Designing health communication campaigns: What works?* Newbury Park, CA: Sage.

Backes, D. (1995). The biosocial perspective and environmental communication research. *Journal of Communication, 45,* 147-163.

Bracht, N., Kingsbury, L., & Rissel, C. (1999). A five-stage community organization model for health promotion: Empowerment and partnership strategies. In N. Bracht (Ed.), *Health promotion at the community level,* Vol. 2: *New advances* (pp. 83-104). Thousand Oaks, CA: Sage.

Brown, L. (1981). *Innovation diffusion: A new perspective.* New York: Methuen.

Bullard, R .D. (Ed.). (1994). *Unequal protection: Environmental justice and communities of color.* Boston: South End Press.

Chaffee, S. H., & Roser, C. (1986). Involvement and the consistency of knowledge, attitudes, and behaviors. *Communication Research, 13,* 373-399.

Chapin, C. Y. (1915). Truth in publicity. *American Journal of Public Health, 5,* 493-502.

Chechile, R. A. (1991). Introduction to environmental decision making. In R. A. Chechile & S. Carlisle (Eds.), *Environmental decision making.* New York: Van Nostrand & Reinhold.

Chess, C., Salomone, K. L., Hance, B. J., & Saville, A. (1995). Results of a national symposium on risk communication: Next steps for government agencies. *Risk Analysis, 15,* 115-125.

Clarke, J. N., & McCool, D. (1985). *Staking out the terrain.* Albany: State University of New York Press.

Coddington, W. (1993). *Environmental marketing.* New York: McGraw-Hill.

Council for Agricultural Science and Technology. (1992). *Water quality: Agriculture's role* (Task Force Report No. 120). Ames, IA: Author.

Cronon, D. (Ed.). (1995). *Uncommon ground.* New York: Norton.

Dennis, M. L., & Soderstrom, E. J. (1988). Application of social psychological and evaluation research: Lessons from energy information programs. *Evaluation and Program Planning, 11,* 77-84.

De Young, R. (1993). Changing behavior and making it stick: The conceptualization and management of conservation behavior. *Environment and Behavior, 25,* 485-505.

Dowie, M. (1995). *Losing ground: American environmentalism at the close of the twentieth century.* Cambridge, MA: MIT Press.

Dunlap, R. E., & Scarce, R. (1991). The polls—poll trends: Environmental problems and protection. *Public Opinion Quarterly, 55,* 651-672.

Dunwoody, S., & Neuwirth, K. (1991). Coming to terms with the impact of communication on scientific and technological risk judgments. In L. Wilkins & P. Patterson (Eds.), *Risky business: Communicating issues of science, risk, and public policy* (pp. 11-30). New York: Greenwood.

Finnegan, J. R., & Sexton, K. (1999). Community-based environmental decisions: Analyzing power and leadership. In K. Sexton, A. A. Marcus, K. W. Easter, & T. D. Burkhardt (Eds.), *Better environmental decisions* (pp. 331-352). Washington, DC: Island Press.

Finnegan, J. R., & Viswanath, K. (1999). Mass media and health promotion: Lessons learned, with implications for public health campaigns. In N. Bracht (Ed.), *Health promotion at the community level,* Vol. 2: *New advances* (pp. 119-126). Thousand Oaks, CA: Sage.

Freudenberger, K. S. (1995). *Tree and land tenure: Using rapid rural appraisal to study natural resource management.* Rome: Food and Agriculture Organization of the United Nations.

Friedman, S. M., Dunwoody, S., & Rogers, C. L. (1999). *Communicating uncertainty: Media coverage of new and controversial science.* Mahwah, NJ: Lawrence Erlbaum.

Fuller, D. A. (1999). *Sustainable marketing: Managerial-Ecological issues.* Thousand Oaks, CA: Sage.

Geller, E. S. (1989). Applied behavior analysis and social marketing: An integration for environmental preservation. *Journal of Social Issues, 45,* 17-36.

Glicken, J. (1999). Effective public involvement in public decisions. *Science Communication, 20,* 298-327.

Gottleib, R. (1993). *Forcing the spring: The transformation of the American environmental movement.* Washington, DC: Island Press.

Griffin, R. J., Dunwoody, S., & Zabala, F. (1998). Public reliance on risk communication channels in the wake of a cryptosporidium outbreak. *Risk Analysis, 18,* 367-375.

Grunig, J. E., Nelson, C. L., Richburg, S. J., & White, T. (1988). Communication by agricultural publics: Internal and external orientations. *Journalism Quarterly, 65,* 26-38.

Guttman, N. (1997). Beyond strategic research: A value-centered approach to health communication interventions. *Communication Theory, 7,* 95-124.

Hale, E. O. (1993). Successful public involvement. *Journal of Environmental Health, 12,* 17-19.

Hancock, J. (1992). *Extension education: Conducting effective agricultural demonstrations.*

Lexington: University of Kentucky, Cooperative Extension Service.

Hardin, G. (1968). Tragedy of the commons. *Science, 63*, 1243-1248.

Hawken, P. (1993). *The ecology of commerce: A declaration of sustainability.* New York: Harper-Collins.

Hornik, R. C. (1988). *Development communication: Information, agriculture, and nutrition in the Third World.* New York: Longman.

Hornik, R. (1997). Public health education and communication as policy instruments for bringing about changes in behavior. In M. E. Goldberg, M. Fishbein, & S. E. Middlestadt (Eds.), *Social marketing: Theoretical and practical perspectives* (pp. 45-60). Mahwah, NJ: Lawrence Erlbaum.

Israel, B. A., Checkoway, B., Schulz, A., & Zimmerman, M. (1994). Health education and community empowerment: Conceptualizing and measuring perceptions of individual, organizational, and community control. *Health Education Quarterly, 21*, 149-170.

Kahneman, D., & Tversky, A. (1984). Choices, values, and frames. *American Psychologist, 39*, 341-350.

Kathlene, L., & Martin, J. A. (1991). Enhancing citizen participation: Panel designs, perspectives, and policy formation. *Journal of Policy Analysis and Management, 10*, 46-63.

Kelman, H. C. (1971). Processes of social change. In W. Schramm & D. F. Roberts (Eds.), *The process and effects of mass communications: Revised edition* (pp. 399-425). Urbana: University of Illinois Press.

Keown, L. D. (1998). Using collaborative leadership to manage conservation issues and conflicts. *Conservation Voices, 1*, 23-26.

Kotler, P., & Andreasen, A. R. (1987). *Strategic marketing for nonprofit corporations.* Englewood Cliffs, NJ: Prentice Hall.

Lockeretz, W. (1990). What have we learned about who conserves soil? *Journal of Soil and Water Conservation, 45*, 517-524.

Macey, S. M., & Brown, M. A. (1990). Demonstrations as a policy instrument with energy technology examples. *Knowledge: Creation, Diffusion, Utilization, 11*, 219-236.

Madison, F., Kelling, K. A., Peterson, J., Daniel, T. C., Jackson, G., & Massie, L. (1986). *Managing manure and ground waste: Guidelines for applying manure to pasture and cropland in Wisconsin* (Extension Publication A3394). Madison: University of Wisconsin.

Major, A. M. (1993). Environmental concern and situational communication theory: Implications for communicating with environmental publics. *Journal of Public Relations Research, 5*, 251-268.

McKee, N. (1994). A community-based learning approach: Beyond social marketing. In S. A. White, K. S. Nair, & J. Ashcroft (Eds.), *Participatory communication: Working for change and development* (pp. 15-32). Thousand Oaks, CA: Sage.

McMullin, S. L., & Nielsen, L. A. (1991). Resolution of natural resource allocation conflicts through effective public involvement. *Policy Studies Journal, 19*, 553-559.

Middlestadt, S. E., Schechter, C., Peyton, J., & Tjugum, B. (1997). Community involvement in health planning from practicing social marketing in a context of community control, participation, and ownership. In M. E. Goldberg, M. Fishbein, & S. E. Middlestadt (Eds.), *Social marketing: Theoretical and practical perspectives* (pp. 291-312). Mahwah, NJ: Lawrence Erlbaum.

Monroe, M. C. (1999). *What works: A guide to environmental education and communication projects for practitioners and donors.* Gabriola Island, British Columbia: New Society.

National Research Council. (1993). *Soil and water quality: An agenda for agriculture.* Washington, DC: National Academy Press.

Natural Resources Conservation Service. (1995). *National survey of attitudes towards agricultural natural resource conservation.* West Lafayette, IN: Conservation Technology Information Center.

Nelkin, D. (1995). *Selling science: How the press covers science and technology.* New York: Freeman.

Nowak, P. J. (1987). The adoption of agricultural conservation technologies: Economic and diffusion explanations. *Rural Sociology, 52*, 208-220.

Nowak, P. J. (1993). Why farmers adopt production technology. *Journal of Soil and Water Conservation, 47,* 14-16.

Nowak, P. J., & Korsching, P. F. (1983). Social and institutional factors affecting the adoption and maintenance of agricultural BMPs. In F. W. Schaller & G. W. Bailey (Eds.), *Agricultural management and water quality* (pp. 349-373). Ames: Iowa State University Press.

Nowak, P. J., & Korsching, P. F. (1998). The human dimension of soil and water conservation: A historical and methodological perspective. In F. J. Pierce & W. W. Frye (Eds.), *Advances in soil and water conservation* (pp. 159-184). Chelsea, MI: Sleeping Bear Press.

Nowak, P. J., O'Keefe, G. J., Bennett, C., Anderson, S., & Trumbo, C. (1997). *Communication and adoption of the USDA Water Quality Demonstration Projects.* Washington, DC: U.S. Department of Agriculture.

O'Keefe, G. J., & Reid, K. (1990). The uses and effects of public service advertising. In L. A. Grunig & J. E. Grunig (Eds.), *Public relations research annual* (Vol. 2, pp. 67-96). Hillsdale, NJ: Lawrence Erlbaum.

O'Keefe, G. J., & Shepard, R. (1998). Assessing public attitudes prior to watershed program planning: A comparison of rural, agricultural, and urban populations. In *Proceedings of the National Conference on Watershed Management* (pp. 331-338). Denver, CO: Water Environment Federation.

Orr, D. (1992). *Ecological literacy.* Albany: State University of New York Press.

Pampel, F., & van Es, J. C. (1977). Environmental quality and issues of adoption research. *Rural Sociology, 42,* 57-71.

Patton, M. Q. (1997). *Utilization-focused evaluation: The new century text.* Thousand Oaks, CA: Sage.

Peters, R. G., Covello, V. T., & McCallum, D. B. (1997). The determinants of trust and credibility in environmental risk communication: An empirical study. *Risk Analysis, 17,* 43-54.

Pickett, G. M., Kangun, N., & Grove, S. J. (1993). Is there a generally conserving consumer? A public policy concern. *Journal of Public Policy and Marketing, 12,* 234-243.

Pollay, R. W. (1989). Campaigns, change, and culture: On the polluting potential of persuasion. In C. T. Salmon (Ed.), *Information campaigns: Balancing social values and social change* (pp. 185-198). Newbury Park, CA: Sage.

Rakow, L. F. (1989). Information and power: Toward a critical theory of information campaigns. In C. T. Salmon (Ed.), *Information campaigns: Balancing social values and social change* (pp. 164-184). Newbury Park, CA: Sage.

Rimal, R. N., Fogg, B. J., & Flora, J. A. (1995). Moving toward a framework for the study of risk communication: Theoretical and ethical considerations. In *Communication Yearbook 18* (pp. 320-342). Austin, TX: International Communication Association.

Rogers, E. M. (1995). *The diffusion of innovations* (4th ed.). New York: Free Press.

Rolling, N. G., Ashcroft, J., & Wa Chege, F. (1976). The diffusion of innovations and the issue of equity in rural development. *Communication and Development, 10,* 64-78.

Salmon, C. T. (1989). Campaigns for social improvements: An overview of values, rationales, and impacts. In C. T. Salmon (Ed.), *Information campaigns: Balancing social values and social change* (pp. 19-53). Newbury Park, CA: Sage.

Schrum, L. J., Lowery, T. M., & McCarty, J. A. (1996). Using marketing and advertising principles to encourage pro-environmental behaviors. In R. P. Hill (Ed.), *Marketing and consumer research in the public interest* (pp. 197-216). Thousand Oaks, CA: Sage.

Servaes, J. (1996). Introduction: Participatory communication and research in development settings. In J. Servaes (Ed.), *Participatory communication for social change* (pp. 13-28). Thousand Oaks, CA: Sage.

Sexton, K., Marcus, A. A., Easter, K. W., & Burkhardt, T. D. (1999). Introduction: Integrating government, business, and community perspectives. In K. Sexton, A. A. Marcus, K. W. Easter, & T. D. Burkhardt (Eds.), *Better environmental decisions* (pp. 1-14). Washington, DC: Island Press.

Shepard, R. (1999, May). *Taking aim in water quality education: Designing audience-specific programs.* Paper presented at the Sixth National Watershed Conference, Austin, TX.

Swap, W. (1991). Psychological factors in environmental decision making: Social dilemmas. In R. A. Chechile & S. Carlisle (Eds.), *Environmental decision making*. New York: Van Nostrand & Reinhold.

Swenson, M. R., & Wells, W. D. (1997). Useful correlates of pro-environmental behaviors. In M. E. Goldberg, M. Fishbein, & S. E. Middlestadt (Eds.), *Social marketing: Theoretical and practical perspectives* (pp. 91-110). Mahwah, NJ: Lawrence Erlbaum.

Thompson, B., & Winner, C. (1999). Durability of community intervention programs: Definitions, empirical studies, and strategic planning. In N. Bracht (Ed.), *Health promotion at the community level*, Vol. 2: *New advances* (pp. 137-154). Thousand Oaks, CA: Sage.

Trumbo, C. T. (1998). Communication channels and risk information. *Science Communication, 20,* 190-202.

Trumbo, C. T., & O'Keefe, G. J. (1999, May). *Attitudinal communities for water conservation*. Paper presented at the Sixth National Watershed Conference, Austin, TX.

U.S. Department of Agriculture. (1998). *A content summary for developing your skills to implement locally led conservation*. Grand Rapids, MI: Social Sciences Institute, Natural Resources Conservation Service.

U.S. Environmental Protection Agency. (1993). *Managing nonpoint source pollution* (Office of Water Publication WH-553). Washington, DC: Author.

Van Liere, K. D., & Dunlap, R. E. (1980). The social bases of environmental concern: A review of hypotheses, explanations, and empirical evidence. *Public Opinion Quarterly, 44,* 181-197.

Vining, J., &. Ebreo, A. (1990). What makes a recycler? A comparison of recyclers and non-recyclers. *Environment and Behavior, 22,* 55-73.

Waddell, C. (1995). Defining sustainable development: A case study in environmental communication. *Technical Communication Quarterly, 4,* 201-218.

Walker, B. (1994). Impediments to the implementation of environmental policy. *Journal of Public Health Policy, 15,* 186-204.

Wayland, R. (1993). What progress in improving water quality? *Journal of Soil and Water Conservation, 48,* 262-266.

Wellman, J. D., & Fahmy, P. A. (1985). Resolving resource conflict: The role of survey research in public involvement programs. *Environmental Impact Assessment Review, 5,* 363-372.

White, K. B. (1998, May). Towards a successful public outreach and stakeholder involvement process. In *Proceedings of the National Conference on Watershed Management* (pp. 317-324). Denver, CO: Water Environment Federation.

White, S. A. (1994). The concept of participation: Transforming rhetoric to reality. In S. A. White, K. S. Nair, & J. Ashcroft (Eds.), *Participatory communication: Working for change and development* (pp. 15-32). Thousand Oaks, CA: Sage.

Whitmore, E. (1998). *Understanding and practicing participatory evaluation*. San Francisco: Jossey-Bass.

Winett, R. A. (1986). *Information and behavior: Systems of influence*. Hillsdale, NJ: Lawrence Erlbaum.

Witte, K. (1994). The manipulative nature of health communication research. *American Behavioral Scientist, 38,* 285-293.

Zimmerman, L. K. (1996). Knowledge, affect, and the environment: 15 years of research (1979-1993). *Journal of Environmental Education, 27,* 41-44.

PART VII

MEDIA

31

The Impact of News and Entertainment Media on Perceptions of Social Reality

WILLIAM P. EVELAND, JR.

Often the role of the mass media in persuasion is perceived to be limited to the impact of overtly persuasive communications such as newspaper editorials, television advertisements, and public service announcements (PSAs). However, other media content may have a more subtle, but more pervasive, impact on the beliefs of the public, regardless of whether or not this was the intention of the message producer. That is, public beliefs are often shaped by subtle but repetitive messages contained in news and entertainment media content that are not overtly persuasive. These beliefs may eventually translate into opinions and even socially relevant behaviors. It is this typically unintentional persuasive impact of news and entertainment media on public beliefs—specifically perceptions of social reality—that is the focus of this chapter.

INTRODUCTION TO THE STUDY OF SOCIAL REALITY PERCEPTIONS

A common focus of social science research is the public's perceptions of their neighbors, community, state, nation, or world. The public's perceptions of the climate of public opinion on policy issues and elections and the public's beliefs about the rate of crime, social norms, stereotypes, the impact of the mass media on public attitudes and behaviors, and many other social reality perceptions have been studied in fields such as public opinion, sociology, psychology, and communication.

Social reality perceptions are best defined as "individuals' conceptions of the world" (Hawkins & Pingree, 1982, p. 224). Because there are so many perceptions that individuals

AUTHOR'S NOTE: The author thanks Amy Nathanson and Michael Pfau for their comments on earlier drafts of this chapter.

have about the world, so many potential causes of these perceptions, and so many levels of analysis at which to examine them, research on social reality perceptions has spanned a number of related fields (Shrum & O'Guinn, 1993). Often this research has taken complementary directions despite a relative lack of cross-citations. For example, one common finding of the research on social reality perceptions is simply put as follows: They are often wrong—very wrong—and this can have important implications for both individuals and society as a whole. Unfortunately, social reality perception research has tended to be somewhat compartmentalized because different fields both use different terminology to describe public misperceptions of social reality and offer different explanations for these misperceptions.

Generally speaking, the notion that the public misperceives the opinions and behaviors of others may be labeled "pluralistic ignorance," although some scholars using this term define it more narrowly as specific types of misperceptions. Research on pluralistic ignorance as defined here has been conducted in psychology, sociology, and public opinion under the rubric of the false consensus effect (Ross, Greene, & House, 1977), the false idiosyncrasy effect (Sherman, Presson, & Chassin, 1984), social projection or the "looking glass perception" (Fields & Schuman, 1976), and disowning projection (Fields & Schuman, 1976).

Research conducted in communication has also examined perceptions of media content and effects, including the third-person effect (Davison, 1983), the hostile media phenomenon (Perloff, 1989; Vallone, Ross, & Lepper, 1985), and the persuasive press inference (Gunther, 1998). Noelle-Neumann's (1993) spiral of silence model is a broader and more well-defined theory that incorporates research on perceptions of public opinion as well as their causes and implications. Another

more fully specified theory originating in the field of communication, cultivation theory (Gerbner, Gross, Morgan, & Signorielli, 1994), is concerned with misperceptions of social reality in the form of beliefs about the characteristics of individuals and society. These communication-related theories also deal with pluralistic ignorance in one way or another, but for the sake of clarity I do not use the term *pluralistic ignorance* to describe theories in communication.

These theories—or at least hypotheses—about perceptions of social reality generally focus on misperceptions of different facts such as public opinion, media effects, and social indicators. Persuasion research can benefit from better understanding how perceptions of social reality are shaped by a number of factors, including the use of entertainment and news media, and from a review of the potential influence of social reality perceptions on attitudes and behaviors. The organization of this chapter is as follows: (a) a discussion of the concept of pluralistic ignorance, which may be defined as misperceptions of social reality, (b) models of social reality perceptions in communication, (c) integration of perspectives on misperceptions of social reality, (d) integration with persuasion theories, and (e) applications to communication campaigns.

PLURALISTIC IGNORANCE: CONTEXTS AND CAUSES

Before discussing theories specifically focusing on the role of mass media in the development of perceptions of social reality, it is useful to review evidence pertaining to the general accuracy of public perceptions of social reality. While theories focusing on mass media provide evidence of inaccurate perceptions of social reality, the greatest number of studies demonstrating inaccuracy come from the fields of public opinion, psychology, and sociology.

Research on perceptions of public opinion has consistently found that people are inaccurate in their judgments of the climate of opinion (for a rare opposing view, see Nisbett & Kunda, 1985). This inaccuracy has been demonstrated at both the aggregate and individual levels. Among other labels, researchers have termed this general inaccuracy about the distribution of opinions pluralistic ignorance.

Pluralistic ignorance is a term that was introduced by Floyd Allport (e.g., Katz & Allport, 1931) to refer to a situation in which members of the majority believe that they are actually in the minority. Research on this topic was continued by one of Allport's students, Richard Schank, in a study of a small community in New York (Schank, 1932). Since the early days of pluralistic ignorance research, the original definition has been contested, becoming for some authors more restrictive and for other authors less so. Breed and Ktsanes (1961) argued that simple inaccuracy in estimates of public opinion is evidence of pluralistic ignorance. Similarly, Merton (1968) expanded the definition to include "the unfounded assumption that one's own attitudes and expectations are unshared and the unfounded assumption that they are uniformly shared" (p. 431). Despite the advantages of these more inclusive definitions, some theorists have continued to argue for a more narrow conceptualization. For instance, Miller and McFarland (1987) argued that the term should apply only to "those illusions of uniqueness that emerge in the face of evidence of behavioral similarity" (p. 298, note 1). However, I concur with O'Gorman that pluralistic ignorance is "an erroneous cognitive belief shared by two or more people regarding the ideas, sentiments, and actions of other individuals" (O'Gorman, 1975, p. 314, note 3) or, more briefly, "false social knowledge of other people" (O'Gorman, 1988, p. 145).

This expanded definition of pluralistic ignorance subsumes several other concepts that have been studied in the area of perceptions of others' opinions. For example, the "false consensus effect" has been defined as occurring when people "see their own behavioral choices and judgments as *relatively* common and appropriate to existing circumstances while viewing alternative responses as uncommon, deviant, or inappropriate" (Ross et al., 1977, p. 280, emphasis added). Mullen (1983) argued that the false consensus effect should be distinguished from the overestimation of consensus in general. He noted that the false consensus effect is demonstrated when a person sees his or her position on an issue as more common than someone who holds an alternative position would see it. Thus, for the false consensus effect, the misperception is *relative to others* and would be measured as a correlation between own opinion and perception of the opinion of others. Alternatively, the overestimation of consensus is when people holding a given opinion perceive more support for this opinion than there is *in reality*. This misperception is "absolute" in the sense that it is objectively false. Overestimate of consensus is tested as the aggregate difference (paired samples *t* test) between own opinions and perceived opinions, with a significant difference in the correct direction considered supportive evidence.

Still other terms have been used to describe similar misperceptions. Fields and Schuman (1976) noted that people tend to presume that others hold the same opinions as they do themselves, which they termed "looking glass perceptions" or social projection. Researchers have tested for the presence of looking glass perceptions in several different ways. One of these tests is analogous to the test for a false consensus effect: a correlation between perceptions of others' opinions and perceptions of one's own opinion. Thus, from this perspective, false consensus effects and looking glass perceptions are equivalent (Eveland, McLeod, & Signorielli, 1995), although some still distinguish them (e.g., Glynn, Ostman & McDonald, 1995) and use different methods to test for them.

Finally, Fields and Schuman (1976) described what they termed "disowning projection" as providing the socially desirable response when asked for one's own opinion but then projecting one's true opinion onto the majority. In this way, one can validate one's unpopular opinion by saying that it is held by most others while avoiding possible scorn from the interviewer for expressing a deviant opinion. While Fields and Schuman concluded that there was no evidence for this effect in their data, Glynn et al. (1989) suggested that it could account for some of her findings. In fact, this hypothesis could explain situations where the majority believes it is in the minority and the minority believes it is in the majority on sensitive social issues. Note, again, that this is specifically what Schank (1932) found and called pluralistic ignorance.

Because I have followed others and broadened the term *pluralistic ignorance* to include all errors in perception of public opinion, I follow Sherman et al. (1984) and specifically label the majority perceiving itself as a minority the "false idiosyncrasy" effect (although others [Korte, 1972] have called this the "silent majority" effect). Also in regard to terminology, I use the terms *false consensus effect, projection,* and *looking glass perceptions* interchangeably but distinguish them from the concept of *overestimation of consensus,* as Mullen (1983) suggested. Despite the fact that many of the theories in communication may also be subsumed under the label of *pluralistic ignorance* as defined here, for clarity I refer to them separately by name in this chapter. A hierarchy of terms pertaining to pluralistic ignorance is presented in Figure 31.1.

Now that definitions have been clarified, it is possible to review some of the empirical findings in the pluralistic ignorance literature. After the work of Allport and his students Katz and Schank, pluralistic ignorance research seemed to enter a long period of hibernation (O'Gorman, 1986). The next explicit study appearing in the literature was in 1961, when Breed and Ktsanes reported their findings on attitudes and perceptions of segregation in Louisiana. They found that people perceived more segregationist attitudes than actually existed but that, at least in one of two tests, the more educated respondents were less likely to hold incorrect perceptions. They noted that pluralistic ignorance is nearly always in a conservative direction because "the error will tend to favor the older existing beliefs in the system rather than the direction of change" (Breed & Ktsanes, 1961, p. 383).

Apparent contradictory evidence for this "conservative bias" explanation was reported more than a decade later in the next study of pluralistic ignorance, when Korte (1972) revealed that students at Vassar consistently overestimated how radical the student body was in two different surveys over the course of 2 years. He labeled this phenomenon a "radical bias." Glynn (1989) found both a conservative and a liberal bias and thus coined the term "ideological bias."

Most other research appearing under the label of pluralistic ignorance during the mid-1970s focused on racial attitudes. O'Gorman (1975, 1979, 1976) and Fields and Schuman (1976) found consistent evidence of pluralistic ignorance in terms of false idiosyncrasy errors, overestimates of consensus, and projection effects. To date, research appearing under the label of pluralistic ignorance has expanded beyond its original home in social psychology and public opinion, appearing in areas as diverse as criminology (e.g., Kauffman, 1981; McGarrell & Sandys, 1996; Toch &

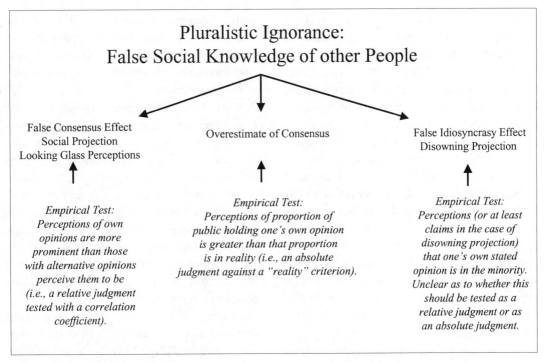

Pluralistic Ignorance:
False Social Knowledge of other People

False Consensus Effect
Social Projection
Looking Glass Perceptions

Overestimate of Consensus

False Idiosyncrasy Effect
Disowning Projection

Empirical Test:
Perceptions of own
opinions are more
prominent than those
with alternative opinions
perceive them to be
(i.e., a relative judgment
tested with a correlation
coefficient).

Empirical Test:
Perceptions of proportion of
public holding one's own opinion
is greater than that proportion
is in reality (i.e., an absolute
judgment against a "reality" criterion).

Empirical Test:
Perceptions (or at least
claims in the case of
disowning projection)
that one's own stated
opinion is in the minority.
Unclear as to whether this
should be tested as a
relative judgment or as
an absolute judgment.

Figure 31.1. Pluralistic Ignorance: False Social Knowledge of Other People

Klofas, 1984), education (e.g., Long & Willower, 1980), sex research (e.g., Cohen & Shotland, 1996), and gerontology (e.g., O'Gorman, 1980) while retaining its presence in the broad fields of public opinion (e.g., O'Gorman, 1988; Shamir, 1993, 1998) and social psychology (e.g., Miller & McFarland, 1987; Miller & Prentice, 1994; Schroeder & Prentice, 1998).

It was not until the mid-1970s that social psychologists coined the term *false consensus effect* (Ross et al., 1977). Since the introduction of this term, the phenomenon has been studied extensively. Throughout the 1980s, researchers replicated and extended the findings of Ross et al. (1977) and attempted to provide theoretical explanations for the effect (Marks & Miller, 1987). In their meta-analysis, Mullen and his associates (1985) found 115 tests of the false consensus effect in the literature at that time and determined that the effect

was quite robust. Research on the false consensus effect and overestimation of consensus has remained relatively separate from research appearing under the label of pluralistic ignorance, despite their obvious similarities. In part, this is the result of differing definitions of what constitutes an important misperception and different methods used to test hypotheses.

Generally speaking, pluralistic ignorance researchers have two distinct issues to address (Eveland et al., 1995). First, *why* are perceptions of public opinion inaccurate? Second, what are the *implications* of this inaccuracy? Neither of these questions has been a substantial focus of the lines of research described in this section. This is likely in part because, as Glynn et al. (1995) noted, the research has stemmed from evidence of an empirical generality and not a complete theory, thus leading research in this area to focus on "product" over "process." Nonetheless, recently there has been some progress made toward developing explanations for pluralistic ignorance and its potential social relevance.

Prentice and Miller (1993) argued that there are at least four possible causes of pluralistic ignorance. *Impression management* (sometimes termed the "self-serving bias") is a motivational explanation suggesting that people hope to see themselves as unique or common, depending on the context. For instance, when one is successful, one is motivated (for self-impression reasons) to consider oneself as unique or "better than the rest." On the other hand, when one fails, one is motivated to see oneself as typical; as the saying goes, misery loves company. In terms of perceptions of the opinions of others, it has been argued that people rarely want to see themselves as part of the minority.

The second explanation for pluralistic ignorance is *cognitive errors*. This explanation, which has its roots in the work on accessibility biases and selective attention (e.g., Tversky & Kahneman, 1974), suggests that people derive their estimates of public opinion based on the biased pieces of information that are accessible in their memory. Thus, (a) because people tend to associate with others who are similar to themselves, (b) because consistent information is often more likely to be attended to and recalled than is inconsistent information, and (c) because one's own opinions are more accessible than others' opinions, cognitive errors based on this biased accessibility are believed to be the source of misperceptions of public opinion.

The *differential interpretation* explanation suggests that individuals publicly misrepresent their opinions, expressing more support for what they believe to be the normative position on an issue than is accurate. This is a conscious decision. However, when they use the public statements of others to assess public opinion, they do not take into account the possibility that others are also being disingen-

uous. This inability to interpret others' public statements for what they are—essentially exercises in politically correctness—despite doing the same oneself leads to a state of pluralistic ignorance.

Finally, the *differential encoding* explanation is similar to the differential interpretation explanation except it does not assume that individuals intentionally misrepresent their own opinions publicly. For example, if a given individual is opposed to the community norm, then the individual will assume that his or her behaviors and statements will make this clear to others. However, this is not always the case. For example, Prentice and Miller (1993) noted, "Students may fail to recognize how pro-norm their public behavior actually is, mistakenly believing that their private discomfort with alcohol practices is clear from their words and deeds" (p. 253). By the same token, these same individuals will assume that others' behaviors and statements are indicative of their respective beliefs. Once again, this is not necessarily true. Thus, when one bases his or her judgment of the opinions of others on their statements and behaviors, the judgment could be in error.

The most common of these four explanations in the social psychological literature are the impression management explanation (Gilovich, 1990; Hollander, 1994; Sherman et al., 1984) and the cognitive errors explanation (e.g., Marks & Miller, 1987; Mullen, 1983; Mullen et al., 1985). The impression management explanation and the cognitive error explanation both have been proposed as causes of biased attribution generally. However, as with the attribution literature, it is nearly impossible to distinguish these two explanations for pluralistic ignorance empirically because neither explanation is developed enough to provide for a critical test (Tetlock & Levi, 1982). Despite this problem, some researchers (e.g., Mullen, 1983) have made flawed assumptions (e.g., that impression management is necessarily conscious and intentional) and then concluded that the evidence indicates that this explanation is implausible. Perhaps the best effort to sort out the possible explanations in the pluralistic ignorance literature comes from Sherman et al. (1984). They found evidence in support of both the cognitive error explanation (effects of information on perceptions of others' opinions, controlling for own success or failure) and the impression management explanation (greater false consensus effects when the self fails than when the self succeeds, controlling for information effects) in the same experiment. This suggests that both processes may occur simultaneously.

MODELS OF SOCIAL REALITY MISPERCEPTIONS IN COMMUNICATION

In this section of the chapter, I review theories dealing specifically with communication and social reality perceptions. I describe the context of each theory, relevant evidence for and against the theory, and potential causal mechanisms that could account for the effects.

Research in communication pertaining to misperceptions of social reality can be classified into two general types. The first type of misperception studied is a misperception of media content or impact. Beliefs about what the content of media is (e.g., media bias), or beliefs about the effects that this content may have on individuals or society, are studied by researchers in the areas of third-person perceptions and the hostile media phenomenon. The second type of misperception is of the state of public opinion, or of social reality more generally, with a focus on some form of communication as a key contributing factor to the misperception. Research of this type is conducted under the rubric of the spiral of silence, the persuasive press inference, and cultivation. Thus, these two types of research

can be distinguished given that the first examines perceptions of mass media content or impact as a dependent measure, while the second considers mass and/or interpersonal communication as an independent variable accounting for misperceptions of social reality.

Misperceptions of Media Impact and Content

Third-Person Effect. The third-person effect hypothesis, as formulated by Davison (1983), has both a perceptual and a behavioral component. The first component of the hypothesis (the "third-person perception") predicts a biased perception such that, in the aggregate, people will perceive greater media impact from persuasive messages on others than on themselves. The second (behavioral) component builds on the perceptual component, predicting that these biased perceptions will result in action designed to mitigate the perceived negative impact on others. Perloff's (1996) review of the third-person effect literature concluded that the perceptual component was strongly supported but that the behavioral component had not received similar support. Recent evidence, however, suggests that there is at least some support for the behavioral component as well (e.g., Gunther, 1995; McLeod, Eveland, & Nathanson, 1997; Rojas, Shah, & Faber, 1996).

To demonstrate that the perceptual component of the third-person effect is actually a *mis*perception, it is necessary to determine what an accurate perception would be. This can be done in two ways. Most third-person perception research compares the aggregate perceptions of media effects on self to aggregate perceptions of media effects on others via paired sample *t* tests. While a significant difference provides evidence for a third-person perception, it is not necessarily evidence of an individual-level misperception given that self-reports of media effects on oneself, unlike statements of one's own opinion on an issue, are not necessarily accurate. Therefore, an aggregate measure of perceived effects on self is not necessarily the appropriate baseline to determine whether aggregate perceptions of media impact on others are inaccurate in the absolute sense.

Some researchers, however, have actually been able to provide estimates of the real effect of the media content on the sample, which is an appropriate baseline for a determination of accuracy of perceptions of others. In one of the first empirical studies of the third-person perception, Cohen, Mutz, Price, and Gunther (1988) found that people tended to underestimate the effects of libelous newspaper articles on themselves and generally overestimated the effects on others. Further research by Gunther (1991) demonstrated an overestimation of effects on others as compared to actual opinion change from elite and tabloid newspapers, while perceptions of effects on self were not significantly different from the actual effects. Similar conclusions about the accuracy of perceptions of media impact on others judged against some objective measure of effects have been provided by more recent studies as well (e.g., Gunther & Thorson, 1992; Perloff, Neuendorf, Giles, Change, & Jeffres, 1992; Price, Tewksbury, & Huang, 1998).

A brief examination of the attribution literature makes it clear why researchers have tapped attribution theory as a possible explanation for third-person perceptions, just as it has been tapped by pluralistic ignorance researchers. Most of the literature on biases in attribution could be applied to third-person perceptions; the trick, apparently, is choosing which type of bias, if any, should be seen as the basis of third-person perceptions. Researchers have not yet come to a firm conclusion on this point.

Rucinski and Salmon (1990) argued that the fundamental attribution error (FAE) runs counter to third-person perceptions because it concerns the attribution of dispositional factors to others and the attribution of situational (in this case media) factors to self. However, the exception based on effectance motivation makes this internal versus external distinction more appropriate. Effectance motivation suggests that people make attributions to maintain a belief that they have control over the world around them, as evidenced in terms such as "unrealistic optimism" (Weinstein, 1980), "just world beliefs" (Lerner, 1980), and the "illusion of control" (Langer, 1975). Therefore, although normally actors attribute the responses of self to situational factors (the FAE), the effectance motivation essentially reverses the FAE. In this case, actors would not want to see themselves as easily swayed by the media messages (and hence unable to control the world outside), so instead they infer a dispositional ability to resist persuasive media messages. But they maintain the belief that others will respond to this situational factor (the media message). This is consistent with research in social psychology that has found that sometimes actors do avoid situational attributions of their own actions (e.g., Miller & Norman, 1975).

Gunther (1991) interpreted the FAE link somewhat differently. He argued that the actor sees himself or herself as responding to situational cues (e.g., the intent to persuade, the possible harmful effects of the media message) in order to avoid negative effects. However, the actor perceives others to be unresponsive to these situational cues. When it comes to possible positive media influence (e.g., PSAs), Gunther stated that effectance motivation takes over and the actor perceives himself or herself as being likely to be influenced by a positive message due to an internal disposition.

Gunther and Mundy (1993) relied more heavily on the notion of effectance motivation, specifically the notion of "unrealistic optimism." They argued that the tendency to believe that bad things (e.g., negative media effects) will not happen to the self, but can happen to others, is a suitable explanation for third-person perceptions. They see this unrealistic optimism as a means of ego enhancement. A similar motivational explanation of biased optimism and ego defensiveness has been promoted by Perloff (1989) and Hoorens and Ruiter (1996), although Perloff (1996) also acknowledged that an information processing (or "cognitive error") account for the third-person perception may also be appropriate.

Eveland, Nathanson, Detenber, and McLeod (1999) provided yet another explanation for third-person perceptions that draws on attribution theory. Their explanation is derived from the more general underlying notion of attribution theory that suggests that individuals have an innate need to provide explanations for things they observe in the world around them and that these explanations are likely to be rather naive. They suggested that individuals hold a schema for media effects that is consistent with the so-called "magic bullet" theory such that perceptions of the media exposure of others are directly linked to perceptions of media effects on those others. However, the evidence (McLeod, Detenber, & Eveland, 2001) suggests that the process of estimation of media effects on oneself is more complex than that on others and takes into account different factors.

The key implication of third-person perceptions is dealt with in the behavioral component of the third-person effect hypothesis. Davison (1983) initially noted that the social relevance of the third-person perception was that individuals would take some action based on the belief that others were influenced by some media message. Initially, there was little

evidence for this component of the hypothesis. However, the mid- to late 1990s produced a wealth of data suggesting that, if nothing else, perceptions of media impact in the form of perceived effects on self (e.g., Gunther & Hwa, 1996; McLeod et al., 1999; Rojas et al., 1996), perceived effects on others (e.g., McLeod et al., 1999; Rojas et al., 1996; Salwen, 1998), or specifically the third-person perception (e.g., Gunther, 1995; Gunther & Hwa, 1996; McLeod et al., 1997; Rojas et al., 1996; Salwen, 1998; Shah, Faber, & Youn, 1999) can lead to support for censorship of the corresponding media content. Thus, it is still unclear exactly which component of perceptions of media impact is the central force behind support for censorship. If third-person perceptions (in the aggregate a misperception) are the cause, then we can be confident that support for censorship is at least in part based on a misperception. However, given that it is not completely clear whether perceived effects on self or perceived effects on others are accurate or not, we cannot say that evidence of a correlation between support for censorship and perceived effects on self or perceived effects on others is definitively the result of a misperception.

Hostile Media Phenomenon. Political observers have noted that claims of media bias by politicians as well as academics have come from both the left and right sides of the political fence. Indeed, often both liberals and conservatives will claim to observe bias against their position in the same media coverage. The hostile media phenomenon describes the situation in which partisans on both sides misperceive what is probably relatively neutral news content as biased against their own position.

The seminal study of the hostile media phenomenon was undertaken by psychologists at Stanford University during the early 1980s (Vallone et al., 1985). They conducted a pilot study just before the 1980 presidential election and found that a majority (66%) of the respondents did not perceive media bias in the election. However, among those who perceived bias, it was nearly always in a hostile direction. Nearly 90% of those perceiving bias perceived it to be taking place against their favored candidate. This trend was slightly stronger for Reagan supporters (96%) than for Carter (83%) or Anderson (88%) supporters. Gunther's (1992) survey findings also indicated that Republicans believed that both television news and newspaper coverage of Democrats was too positive, whereas Democrats thought that both television news and newspaper coverage of Republicans was too positive. A more recent summary of poll findings from the 1996 presidential campaign again demonstrated that both Republicans and Democrats perceived bias in the news but that the bias they perceived was in different directions (Dautrich & Dineen, 1996).

Vallone and his colleagues (1985) also found that news coverage of the Beirut massacre in 1982 was perceived differently by pro-Israeli and pro-Arab partisans. Pro-Israeli partisans believed that the coverage was biased across seven different items. Pro-Arab partisans, on the other hand, believed that the direction of bias was in favor of Israel (and against the Arabs). These means were significantly different in each case. In addition, on four of these tests, a "neutral" group was significantly different from *both* of the partisan groups in perceptions of media bias (falling between them). Later research has, in part, replicated these findings in similar contexts (Giner-Sorolla & Chaiken, 1994; Perloff, 1989).

When partisans on different sides of an issue have strongly divergent perceptions of bias in the exact same news coverage, at least one of the groups must be inaccurate. Thus, the hostile media phenomenon indicates that perceptions of the slant of news may be inac-

curate. It may be assumed that the neutral groups—those without an ax to grind—have the most accurate perceptions. However, even this is difficult to ascertain because neutral groups, as well as partisan groups, have preconceived notions that may contribute to misperceptions of the nature of media coverage.

Vallone et al. (1985) described two possible mechanisms that might produce the hostile media phenomenon. Both explanations assume that, in reality, the media content is relatively unbiased. The first explanation is based on the notion of biased assimilation (see also Kressel, 1987). It suggests that, based on past experience and observation, partisans believe that the bulk of information and factual evidence supports their own position. When presented with news content that is effectively neutral (showing equal parts favorable and unfavorable information), this appears to be inconsistent with what partisans believe to be the broader population of information available on the topic. Thus, partisans will perceive bias because the content of the media is not consistent with their perceptions of the actual broader information environment.

The second explanation suggests that partisans on different sides of an issue may actually perceive different things when viewing, for instance, the same television newscast. Each will selectively recall hostile information better than information that is consistent with their own viewpoint. Thus, when making decisions about the fairness of a media report, partisans from different camps will effectively be making their assessments based on the different parts of the report they are best able to recall. Each will conclude that the content was biased against their position because each is better able to remember the information from the report that was hostile to their opinion.

There was evidence that each of these processes played some role in the findings of Vallone et al. (1985). Partisans did in fact have different perceptions of the content, suggesting support for the second explanation just provided. However, even after controlling for these perceptual differences, partisans still differed in their beliefs about media bias. Through a subtractive logic (i.e., if the second explanation did not account for the difference completely, then the first explanation must also be valid), the authors concluded that both mechanisms played a role in the hostile media phenomenon.

Misperceptions Produced by Media Content

Spiral of Silence. The spiral of silence, introduced to American researchers during the early 1970s, is a cross-level model of opinion dynamics that has received considerable research attention, if not support, in the United States. My discussion of the spiral of silence hypothesis draws heavily from the English-language writings of Noelle-Neumann (1974, 1977, 1979, 1985, 1989, 1991, 1993, 1995).

The spiral of silence hypothesis consists of several different stages and includes several important variables. First, the theory assumes that (a) most people fear social isolation and believe that to express minority opinions on "moral" issues is to risk social isolation; (b) people have a "quasi-statistical sense" that allows them to determine, if not the actual distribution of public opinion, then at least the relative trends in public opinion (sometimes called "future trend"); and (c) these perceptions come from evidence in the environment, most importantly mass and interpersonal communication.

Thus, the public opinion process, according to the spiral of silence, works like this. To avoid the negative feelings of social isolation, people scan their environment in order to sense the climate of opinion. They make use of their perceptions of the climate of opinion to determine what opinions *can* be expressed in

public and what opinions *must* be expressed in public. When their private opinions cannot be expressed in public due to a fear of isolation, they remain silent. As others go through this same process, there is a change in the climate of opinion; the interpersonal environment appears to be even more one-sided as members of the perceived minority fail to speak out in favor of their position. This produces changes in perceptions of the climate of opinion, which reinforces minority members' unwillingness to speak out. The process continues until one position becomes dominant. In addition to changes in the climate of opinion, this process can change private opinions for those who are undecided or weakly committed to their viewpoint.

The role of the mass media in the spiral of silence is to serve as an indicator of the climate of opinion. Noelle-Neumann has identified the *New York Times,* the *Washington Post,* and possibly the major television news networks in the United States as the "trend-setting" mass media because they tend to set the agenda for other news media outlets such as local newspapers. People sense public opinion via the trend-setting mass media, which Noelle-Neumann has claimed are consonant (all the same), ubiquitous (omnipresent), and cumulative (effects accumulate with repetition) and therefore not susceptible to selective exposure, attention, or recall.

According to the spiral of silence, the mass media serve as agents of social control. They convey information—although not necessarily accurate information—about the norms of society and thus opinions that may be expressed without fear of isolation. These clues may be portrayed in several different ways, including but not limited to camera angles (Noelle-Neumann, 1993), general statements about public opinion by reporters, invocation of social norms as boundaries of mainstream public opinion, actions in relation to community laws, "man-on-the-street" interviews

(McLeod & Hertog, 1992), and reports of opinion polls (Salmon & Kline, 1985).

The literature has provided some evidence for the role of news media use in perceptions of public opinion. Glynn (1987) found that those who were frequent users of mass media tended to perceive that they were dissimilar from their neighbors, whereas those who were high in interpersonal communication tended to perceive that they were similar to their neighbors. Similarly, Salmon and Neuwirth (1990) found that media message discrimination (remembering information about the relevant issue appearing in the news media) was negatively associated with perceiving one's own opinion as being in the majority of community opinion. That is, the more a person remembered about news media coverage of the issue (abortion in this case), the more likely the person was to believe he or she was in the minority. Eveland and his associates (1995) also found that during the Persian Gulf War, television news viewing and, to a lesser extent, radio news use were related to the perception that most people supported the war. This perception was consistent with news media coverage of public opinion about the war during this time, which portrayed consonant support for the war.

On the one hand, evidence that media use can lead to misperceptions of public opinion can be interpreted as support for Noelle-Neumann's hypothesis that media portrayals of public opinion are biased. On the other hand, it reveals that people are not necessarily capable of using their quasi-statistical sense to develop *accurate* perceptions of the distribution of opinion in society. Noelle-Neumann has sidestepped this criticism of her theory by arguing that people are not necessarily able to accurately perceive the climate of opinion at any one time but that they are capable of sensing changes in the climate such that they can identify which side is gaining or losing favor. This question has rarely been examined in the literature, however, because most studies continue to be cross-sectional despite early pleas for more sophisticated designs (Glynn & McLeod, 1983). Consistent with Noelle-Neumann's claims, however, Shamir (1995) found that perceptions of the future trend did track along with aggregate opinions over several years. But the perceptions of majority opinion followed aggregate opinion only when an election made the current state of opinion abundantly clear.

While Shamir's (1995) evidence appears to support Noelle-Neumann's theory, the study also suggested that these accurate future trend perceptions did not derive from media coverage of opinions or from interpersonal discussion as Noelle-Neumann has claimed. Instead, perceptions of future trends came from media reports of objective events that would presumably influence public opinion. This is consistent with Gunther's (1998) persuasive press inference hypothesis (to be discussed in the next section). Perceptions of the current climate (which were inaccurate in the aggregate), on the other hand, were derived by extrapolation from "known distributions of opinion" such as party membership and ideological distributions. Thus, these findings shed some doubt on Noelle-Neumann's version of the spiral of silence.

However, it should be noted that known distributions of opinion must come from somewhere. The reason why these opinion distributions are "known," I would submit, is that they are covered in the news media via polls and other means. Therefore, while the distributions may be "known" (i.e., in the mind) at the time they are used to estimate other opinion distributions, they are known only because they were at some point learned via the news media reports of public opinion polls, the party controlling the government, election results, and so on.

As already noted, the spiral of silence suggests that a quasi-statistical sense allows individuals to use information in the environment—primarily news media and interpersonal communication—to shape perceptions of the climate of opinion. Based on the spiral of silence, *mis*perceptions of the state of public opinion could be caused by several sources. One of the key explanations has been labeled the "dual climate of opinion" (Noelle-Neumann, 1993). This explanation centers on situations in which the climate of opinion generated through interpersonal expression of opinions is inconsistent with the climate of opinion portrayed in the trend-setting mass media. For example, if media coverage portrayed public opposition to the impeachment of President Bill Clinton during the fall of 1998, but those in support of impeachment appeared to be the majority based on public expressions of opinion, then a dual climate of opinion would exist. In this situation, some might misperceive the climate of opinion to be that portrayed by the mass media. In effect, this explanation for misperceptions of the state of opinion is simple: media bias (or at least inaccurate media coverage).

Alternatively, because those who perceive themselves to be in the minority are less willing to publicly express their opinions, opinions held by these individuals will become less prominent in public conversations. As this happens, it leads to an incongruity between the expressed climate of opinion and the sum of individual personal opinions. Social observers will infer that a given viewpoint is in the minority because few individuals are expressing this view publicly, but in fact this unexpressed view may be the privately held view of the majority. President Richard Nixon claimed just this when he spoke of a "silent majority" that supported the conservative cause.

Research on the influence of perceptions of being in the minority (whether or not this is a misperception) and willingness to speak out publicly from the spiral of silence perspective has produced mixed results in the United States (for a meta-analysis, see Glynn, Hayes, & Shanahan, 1997). Despite this, there has been enough positive evidence to suggest that something like the spiral of silence does indeed occur. In fact, one of the most vocal American critics of the spiral of silence, Chuck Salmon, acknowledged, "The essence of the model—that individuals' perceptions of their environment do have some bearing on their communication and behavior . . . is incontestable" (Salmon & Moh, 1992, p. 159).

In addition to affecting willingness to speak out, perceptions of public opinion can eventually influence private opinions, at least among those who initially hold weak opinions. Some evidence has provided support for this notion. For instance, pluralistic ignorance researchers have demonstrated that perceptions of being in the minority can, over time, produce conformity (Prentice & Miller, 1993; Schroeder & Prentice, 1998). Public opinion research (e.g., Eveland et al., 1995; Glynn & McLeod, 1984, 1985) has also provided some evidence for this component of the spiral of silence hypothesis.

Persuasive Press Inference. The persuasive press inference (Gunther, 1998) is the most recent of a long line of research on perceptions of media impact, and it draws heavily on research examining the third-person perception and hostile media phenomenon. The persuasive press inference is the inference that individuals make about the power and reach of news media. In essence, the claim is that individuals observe news content and come to some conclusion about the valence of this content relative to a particular topic.

For example, news of the murder of more than a dozen people in Columbine, Colorado, by two students using semi-automatic weapons and bombs may be evaluated as providing an argument in favor of more strict gun control laws. Some evidence indicates that the hostile media phenomenon would play a role in the development of perceptions of the direction of media coverage (Gunther & Christen, 1999b). Therefore, those opposed to gun control would likely perceive the content to be even more slanted in favor of gun control. In general, viewers would assume that the coverage to which they are personally exposed is representative of the population of news media coverage. They would also make assessments about the extent of potential impact from this content. Finally, using an existing perceived opinion baseline, they would update their perceptions of public opinion to include perceived effects of the media coverage in the direction of the slant that they perceive. The research to date in both experimental and survey contexts (Gunther, 1998; Gunther & Christen, 1999a, 1999b) generally supports the persuasive press inference. This support holds, in most cases, even after controlling for the effects of opinion projection on estimates of overall public opinion.

The persuasive press inference suggests that misperceptions of public opinion may be due to misperceptions of mass media impact on public opinion. Specifically, Gunther (1998) argued that people will overestimate the impact of news media coverage on public opinion and that, therefore, estimates of public opinion will be inaccurate. The underlying mechanisms that cause misperceptions of the impact of mass media, however, are not clearly defined from this admittedly new perspective, although the theory draws on the existing research on third-person perceptions (Gunther & Christen, 1999b).

Cultivation. The cultural indicators approach to the study of mass media effects provides a well-rounded theoretical perspective from which to examine more general perceptions of social reality. This section, where not referenced, draws heavily from the writings of the key members of the cultural indicators group that originated at the University of

Pennsylvania, including George Gerbner, Michael Morgan, Larry Gross, and Nancy Signorielli (e.g., Gerbner, Gross, Morgan, & Signorielli, 1980, 1994; Morgan & Shanahan, 1997; Signorielli & Morgan, 1990, 1996).

The cultural indicators approach has three main components. *Media message analysis* is the component of the cultural indicators approach that examines the content of television. Other media forms—newspapers, radio, magazines, and the like—are outside the domain of cultivation theory as described by its originators. The most prominent finding of the media message analysis is that television is full of violence and mayhem. Research has also consistently demonstrated that the characters and situations shown on television are different from those in the real world. For example, television characters are more likely to be male, White, and young as compared to other segments of the U.S. population. This disparity between the television world and the real world is a linchpin of the theory.

Institutional process analysis is the component of the cultural indicators approach that focuses on how the media messages that exist are chosen. Specifically, this component attempts to answer the question, "Why are the media messages we have the way they are?" Researchers have pointed to the roles of the profit motive in commercial television as well as the culture and ownership structure of the television industry as potential answers to this question.

Cultivation analysis seeks to connect the content of television to the public's perceptions of social reality. Because media message analysis indicates that the content of television is not an accurate portrayal of the real world, people who use the television world to shape their perceptions of the real world will come away with a serious misunderstanding. Cultivation analysis suggests that this is exactly what happens. Specifically, the most prominent claim of cultivation researchers is that the violent world of television has created a "mean world syndrome" in which heavy viewers believe that crime and violence are much more prevalent than they are in reality and that most people cannot be trusted.

In addition to perceptions of a mean and dangerous world, other misperceptions of social reality have been linked to television viewing. Cultivation researchers have examined the role of television in forming stereotypes of social groups and behaviors, including perceptions of social out-groups and minorities (Gandy & Baron, 1998; Kiecolt & Sayles, 1988), perceptions of professionals such as lawyers and doctors (Pfau, Mullen, Deidrich, & Garrow, 1995; Pfau, Mullen, & Garrow, 1995), and perceptions of sex roles and marriage among young people (Morgan & Rothschild, 1983; Rosenwasser, Lingenfelter, & Harrington, 1989; Signorielli, 1991; Signorielli & Lears, 1992). Generally speaking, television use tends to produce stereotypical perceptions of these groups and behaviors.

Beginning during the early 1980s, researchers began to directly challenge the findings of the original cultivation researchers, sometimes reanalyzing the same data but producing conflicting results (e.g., Hirsch, 1980, 1981a, 1981b; Hughes, 1980; for a more recent critique, see Potter, 1994). These researchers demonstrated that simultaneous controls for demographic characteristics substantially reduced or eliminated relationships between television viewing and perceptions of social reality. They criticized the underpinnings of the theory, including the assumptions that television viewing is nonselective and television viewing's effects on social reality perceptions are linear. Many researchers have also clearly demonstrated that exposure to different genres of television, including television news, has different effects (e.g., Hawkins & Pingree, 1981; McLeod et al., 1995; O'Keefe, 1984; O'Keefe & Reid-Nash, 1987; Potter & Chang, 1990; Rubin, Perse, & Taylor, 1988).

This suggests that overall television viewing is unlikely to be the true culprit. The early criticisms and their corresponding rebuttals in major communication journals—sometimes known as the "cultivation battles"—led the original researchers to make several revisions to the theory. However, they remained steadfast in most of their major claims and assumptions.

The two major changes to cultivation theory were labeled "mainstreaming" and "resonance." These revised versions of cultivation were designed to account for nonsignificant and contradictory findings by specifying the potential for cultivation effects to vary across social categories. Both mainstreaming and resonance thus suggest interactions between background characteristics or personal experience and the effects of television viewing, but the forms of these interactions differ.

Mainstreaming suggests that television can move heavy viewers toward a mainstream view or perception by having different effects on viewers with different background characteristics—a prediction of a "convergent" interaction (see Figure 31.2). In so doing, for instance, heavy television viewers from the South and Northeast would become more similar in their views on morality despite the fact that light television viewers from both regions were very different in their views on morality. Another means of testing this hypothesis suggested by some authors (e.g., Morgan, 1986) is to compare the variance in the criterion measure for heavy and light television viewers. The hypothesis would be supported statistically if the variance were significantly less among heavy television viewers than among light television viewers, using Levene's test for homogeneity of variance as the statistical criterion (McLeod et al., 1995). Some researchers have found evidence consistent with mainstreaming effects (e.g., Shanahan, Morgan, & Stenbjerre, 1997), but a lack of theoretical specification about when main-

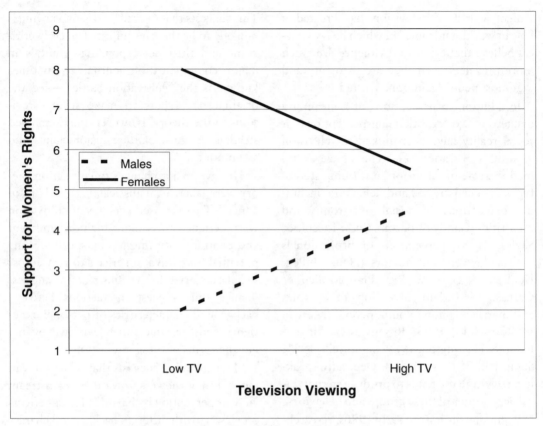

Figure 31.2. Hypothetical Example of a Mainstreaming Effect

streaming effects should be expected (as opposed to overall cultivation effects), a lack of
use of appropriate statistics to test this hypothesis (see Eveland, 1997; McLeod et al.,
1995), and confusion about what the mainstreaming hypothesis really means make generalizations about support difficult.

The resonance hypothesis also predicts an
interaction between background characteristics and television viewing such that effects
of television are greater when its content is
consistent with the real-life situation of the
viewer. Thus, unlike mainstreaming (which
predicts a convergent interaction), resonance predicts a "contributory" interaction
(McLeod & Reeves, 1980). That is, the impact
of television viewing would be greater among
groups of individuals for whom the television

messages "resonate," thus leading perceptions of these groups to be even more different from other heavy viewers than light viewers are from other light viewers (see Figure
31.3). Once again, while some studies have
found evidence for resonance (Gerbner et al.,
1980), there is a serious lack of a priori specification of what situations warrant resonance
versus mainstreaming versus overall cultivation predictions. When predictions are vague,
both finding significant differences across subgroups and not finding significant differences
across subgroups can be interpreted as consistent with the theory. This has led some
researchers to argue that the mainstreaming
and resonance hypotheses, as formulated by
Gerbner et al. (1980), make cultivation unfalsifiable (Hirsch, 1981b).

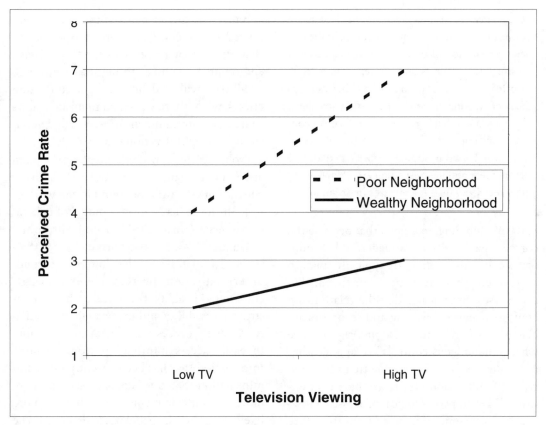

Figure 31.3. Hypothetical Example of a Resonance Effect

The surface explanation for misperceptions as demonstrated by cultivation research would point to the results of the media message analysis component of the cultural indicators program. These content analyses, primarily conducted by the original cultivation researchers (e.g., Signorielli, 1981, 1986, 1990), have consistently demonstrated that television misrepresents social reality along a number of dimensions. Television programs suggest that crime is more likely to be violent than it is in reality (e.g., Oliver, 1994). Television also misrepresents the distribution of people along various demographic characteristics such as gender, ethnicity, age, and marital status (Signorielli, 1981). Thus, the underlying claim of the cultivation hypothesis is that these (mis)representations of reality on tele-

vision are learned by viewers (particularly heavy viewers) and used in judgments about the real social world. If television provided an accurate description of the real world, then cultivation would change from an antisocial effect leading to misperceptions to a prosocial effect of simple learning about the world.

Despite scores of empirical studies of cultivation (for a qualitative and quantitative review, see Morgan & Shanahan, 1997), early researchers made few attempts to address the cognitive processes through which cultivation effects occur. One prominent exception was the program of research by Hawkins and Pingree (e.g., Hawkins & Pingree, 1982, 1990). A key distinction advanced by these authors is that there are two types of cultivation perceptions: first order and second order.

First-order (also called *demographic*) beliefs are estimates of the frequency or probabilities or characterization of events, and one can clearly distinguish a "television" answer from a "real-world" answer. . . . Second-order beliefs, such as fear of walking alone or mistrusting strangers, have no quantifiable referent in television content, but one can argue that the prevalence of violence between strangers *implies* that one should fear and mistrust strangers. (Hawkins & Pingree, 1990, p. 49, emphases in original)

Hawkins and Pingree argued that because the correlations between first-order and second-order cultivation beliefs are typically small to nonexistent (but see Potter, 1991), and because research indicates that the relationship between television viewing and second-order beliefs is often reduced to nonsignificance when simultaneous controls are applied (but see Potter, 1991), it is possible that these two types of cultivation effects are based on entirely different psychological processes. However, despite some basic suggestions for future research to determine the processes involved in these cultivation perceptions, Hawkins and Pingree were unable to offer solid empirical evidence for any particular psychological process.

Following Hawkins and Pingree (1982, 1990), researchers have recently made more explicit efforts to understand the underlying processes that drive the cultivation effect (e.g., Mares, 1996; Shapiro, 1991; Tapper, 1995). For example, Shapiro (1991) argued for a model of retrieval, weighting, and balancing of specific events from episodic memory as the cognitive process behind social reality perceptions. As part of the weighting and balancing process, individuals were thought to make use of factors such as the source of the memory (e.g., direct experience, television, newspapers). In a related vein, Mares (1996) argued that source confusions—the tendency for individuals to think that events from entertainment actually came from the news—were related to the cultivation effect. Specifically, she argued that those who tend to mistake entertainment sources to be news sources in recall tests will evidence stronger cultivation effects, while those who tend to mistake news sources as entertainment sources will demonstrate weaker cultivation effects.

Probably the most empirically successful attempt to explain the mechanisms behind the cultivation effect can be found in the work of L. J. Shrum in his "heuristic model of cultivation effects" (Shrum, 1997, 1998). Shrum and O'Guinn (1993; see also Shrum, 1995, 1996) suggested that first-order (but not second-order) cultivation effects may be explained by combining insights from research on construct accessibility and the availability heuristic. Construct accessibility refers to the ability to easily access information from memory. Information that has been recently used, and information that is frequently used, both are more accessible in memory and thus are more likely to be used in making judgments. The availability heuristic suggests that because individuals are cognitive misers, they normally do not make thorough searches of memory when faced with the need to make decisions. Instead, they use cognitive shortcuts that often achieve acceptable results with significantly less effort. The availability heuristic states that information that is found to be easily accessible (i.e., information that comes easily to mind) is believed to be common and typical.

Given this, Shrum and O'Guinn (1993) provided the following account of cultivation. When asked to make a judgment about the frequency of some event, such as the relative amount of violence, individuals use the availability heuristic. The information that is most accessible is the information that has been recently and frequently activated. Given the high rate of violence on television, heavy television viewers will have instances of violence easily accessible. Thus, television viewing should contribute to higher (and generally inaccurate) estimates of the rate of violence in society. The limited research evidence for this model so far generally supports these assertions (Shrum, 1996; Shrum & O'Guinn, 1993).

As Hawkins and Pingree (1990) correctly noted, "First-order beliefs are trivial if there is no further connection to other beliefs or behavior" (p. 45). What they meant is that if there is little relationship between perceptions of the demographics of the real world and things such as fear, interpersonal mistrust, racism, and so forth, then why should we care about the impact of television viewing on perceptions of social reality? Unfortunately, there appears to be only a weak relationship between first-order and second-order cultivation beliefs (Hawkins & Pingree, 1982, 1990; but see Potter, 1991), so the socially relevant impact of first-order cultivation beliefs is unclear.

However, the admittedly limited direct impact of television on second-order cultivation beliefs does have important implications. Gerbner, Gross, Signorielli, Morgan, and Jackson-Beeck (1979) argued that the images of violence on television cultivate perceptions of fear of crime. What is most important about this, they argued, is that those who hold these mean world perceptions "may grow up demanding protection and even welcoming repression in the name of security" (p. 196). There is in fact some recent evidence that this claim is true (McLeod et al., 1996). McLeod and his students demonstrated that fear of crime is a significant and strong predictor of support for punitive measures to reduce crime (e.g., the death penalty, "three strikes" laws), whereas it is unrelated to support for preventive measures such as spending money to create jobs and requiring rehabilitation for prisoners. These relationships (and lack thereof) held up at several levels of control, including controlling demographics, political ideology,

modes of thought (similar to authoritarianism), media use, and information processing. However, it should be noted that in this study it was not television generally, but instead exposure and attention to crime news in newspapers and on television, that was hypothesized and found to be driving fear of crime. The impact of time spent watching television more broadly was not examined.

INTEGRATION OF PERSPECTIVES ON MISPERCEPTIONS OF SOCIAL REALITY

It should be evident to the reader after this review of each of the preceding areas of research on perceptions of social reality that many connections among these areas exist. Scholars studying perceptions of social reality should attempt to integrate these different programs of research by searching for areas of agreement and disagreement among theories and perspectives that all focus in some way on misperceptions of the world around us, explanations for these observed misperceptions, or socially relevant implications of these misperceptions. Where agreement across threads of research is found, integration of research programs can take place and contribute to theoretical parsimony and cross-disciplinary collaboration. Where disagreement exists, competing hypotheses may be developed and tested, leading to a further reduction in the number of theories and potentially a greater understanding of misperceptions of social reality.

Some scholars have already been working to integrate at least two or three of these areas and should be congratulated for doing so (e.g., Edelstein, 1988; Glynn et al., 1995; Gunther, 1998; Mutz, 1998). As another step toward facilitating this integration, Tables 31.1, 31.2, and 31.3 lay out some initial di-

TABLE 31.1 Relevant Perceptions About Social Reality

Content of Mass Media	Effects of Mass Media	Characteristics of Others and Society
Hostile media phenomenon	Third-person perceptions	Pluralistic ignorance
	Persuasive press inference	Cultivation
		Spiral of silence
		Persuasive press inference

mensions on which these perspectives share foci, explanations, and implications.

The most obvious connection that can be made between these areas of research on social reality perceptions is on the basis of their common foci (see Table 31.1). Pluralistic ignorance research, the persuasive press inference, the spiral of silence, and cultivation all deal, at least in part, with how individuals misperceive characteristics of others and of society. However, the spiral of silence and the persuasive press inference are more closely related to pluralistic ignorance research than to cultivation because they generally focus on perceptions of the opinions of others. Research on the third-person perception (and to some extent the persuasive press inference) is concerned with misperceptions of the impact of mass media messages on the public. The persuasive press inference in some ways provides an explanation for why the third-person perception can lead to pluralistic ignorance, that is, by updating perceptions of public opinion when media impact is perceived. Finally, the hostile media phenomenon is focused on the content, instead of the effects, of mass media; therefore, it is probably not well-connected to pluralistic ignorance but can provide some help in understanding the third-person perception and the persuasive press inference. Given all of these (and potentially other) connections, it only makes sense that interested researchers work to integrate findings from each of the traditions both within and outside of communication.

Table 31.2 reveals that, as might be expected, there is some disagreement about the causes of misperceptions across the areas reviewed in this chapter. Many of these differences are, in part, the result of research originating in different fields. Theories originating in communication, such as cultivation, the persuasive press inference, and the spiral of silence, tend to rely on the media and interpersonal communication as at least part of the explanation for misperceptions of public opinion. Specifically, these theories suggest that when the content of communication does not mirror reality, it can produce misperceptions of reality. By the same token, if communication were an accurate representation of the true world (i.e., if we all told the truth and if both news and entertainment content in the media portrayed the world as it is), then communication could lead to accurate perceptions of reality. However, particularly for mass communication—even news media—portraying the world accurately is unlikely to happen because most people want to experience a world that is different from the one they experience every day. News, for instance, does not tell us what is normal about our world but instead stresses that which is atypical such as natural disasters, terrorist attacks, and mass murders.

TABLE 31.2 Explanations for Misperceptions of Social Reality

Inaccurate Media Portrayals	Inaccurate Interpersonal Portrayals	Motivational or Cognitive Biases
Cultivation	Spiral of silence	Third-person perceptions
Spiral of silence	Pluralistic ignorance	Cultivation
Persuasive press inference		Hostile media phenomenon
		Pluralistic Ignorance
		Persuasive press inference

Theories going through their infancy in psychology tend to focus on psychological processes such as motivational or cognitive biases in perception. In the case of motivational explanations, it is suggested that individuals have either a conscious or an unconscious desire to see themselves as better than others. Perceptions are thus shaded by this need. Cognitive error explanations rely on research demonstrating that individuals use heuristics to simplify decision-making and inference processes. These heuristics sometimes lead to errors, including errors in perceptions of social reality.

Despite differences, there has been a trend toward cross-disciplinary similarities in explanations during recent years. For example, much of the current theorizing about cultivation focuses on cognitive processes, specifically biases introduced by heuristics (e.g., Shrum, 1995). Similarly, explanations for the third-person perception have drawn heavily from the attribution literature that is the basis of much of pluralistic ignorance (e.g., Eveland et al., 1999; Gunther, 1991). Third-person perception researchers have also struggled with the same problem of distinguishing motivational from cognitive error explanations that has plagued theoretical advancement of research on pluralistic ignorance. Nevertheless, it appears that, more often than not, motivational biases are suggested as explanations for third-person perceptions.

The diffusion of theoretical explanations across disciplinary lines tends to be unidirectional in the case of communication. That is, while communication researchers have begun to borrow theory related to social reality perceptions from the level fields of psychology and sociology, there has been relatively little movement of theory from communication to researchers studying pluralistic ignorance outside of communication. One exception is that scholars studying pluralistic ignorance have acknowledged the potential role of interpersonal communication (both verbal and nonverbal) in contributing to misperceptions of the opinions of others (e.g., Korte, 1972; Prentice & Miller, 1993). Specifically, of the four explanations for pluralistic ignorance provided by Prentice and Miller (1993) and described in an earlier section—impression management, cognitive errors, differential interpretation, and differential encoding—at least three involve either interpersonal or mass communication, in conjunction with psychological processes, as central components. In fact, the differential interpretation explanation is wholly consistent with the interpersonal component of the spiral of silence, albeit much less fully developed than Noelle-Neumann's theory.

TABLE 31.3 Effects of Misperceptions

Communication	Attitudes	Behaviors
Spiral of silence	Cultivation	Cultivation
Third-person perception	Spiral of silence	Pluralistic ignorance

While implications are often suggested but rarely examined empirically in this literature (exceptions are the spiral of silence and the third-person effect), it is also instructive to compare the claims for the ultimate social relevance of misperceptions of social reality (see Table 31.3). As might be expected, communication theories of social reality perceptions have, in part, focused on the impact on further communication. The spiral of silence suggests self-censorship of opinions deemed to be in the minority, whereas third-person effect researchers have demonstrated support for societal-level censorship in response to third-person perceptions. Researchers have also posited that misperceptions of public opinion can potentially change opinions on that same topic (e.g., the spiral of silence, pluralistic ignorance) or more general attitudes such as beliefs about the need for social control (e.g., cultivation). Finally, some theories describe a more ambiguous impact on behaviors due to misperceptions of public opinion.

INTEGRATION WITH THEORIES OF PERSUASION

We know that the empirical link between perceptions or beliefs and attitudes and behaviors is often limited by a number of factors. Despite this, research on social reality perceptions across a number of fields has repeatedly demonstrated that one's perceptions of the world are at least a partial determinant of attitudes and behaviors (e.g., Glynn et al., 1997; Hetherington, 1996; McLeod et al., 1996, 1997; Perkins & Wechsler, 1996; Prentice & Miller, 1993). This is consistent with a number of theories of persuasion that may be instrumental in any theorizing about perceptions of social reality.

By now, the reader with a background in persuasion has probably noted a number of theories of persuasion that would suggest how perceptions of social reality as described in this chapter would be used in an individual's construction of attitudes and behaviors. Many theories of persuasion suggest some form of a link between perceptions and opinions and behaviors or are in some other way concerned with perceptions of social reality. For illustrative purposes, I discuss how the research reviewed in this chapter may be integrated with several theories of persuasion both to advance social reality perception research and to extend persuasion research.

Balance and Coorientation Theories

Balance theory (Heider, 1958; Monsour, Harvey, & Betty, 1997) and coorientation theory (McLeod & Chaffee, 1973; Newcomb, 1953) both deal with the interrelationships among an individual, his or her perceptions of other individuals (or groups), and evaluations of objects. Balance theory is more closely related to persuasion, while coorientation theory is more closely related to communication. However, both theories are centrally focused on the role of perceptions of others as an important component of how individuals respond to objects in their social environment. As such, both theories can draw important insights from research on perceptions of social reality.

Briefly, balance theory postulates that an individual (*p*) has an evaluation of both an object (*x*) and another individual (*o*). The individual also perceives the relationship between the object and the other person. These three evaluations may be in balance or out of balance. If the triad is out of balance (e.g., the individual likes both the object and the other but perceives that the other does not like the object), there is a motivation to bring the system into balance. This can be done by changing any one of the three relationships. Change can occur if the individual (a) decides that he or she does not like the object (to bring the individual's attitude in line with a liked other), (b) decides that he or she does not like the other (to bring the individual's attitude about the other in line with his or her attitude about the object disliked by the other), or (c) he or she may change the perception that the other dislikes the object. Thus, balance theory can be used to explain both how perceptions of the opinions of others can potentially lead to attitude change and how perceptions of the attitudes of others may be inaccurate due to a motivation to maintain balance.

From the perspective of coorientation theory, McLeod and Chaffee (1973) argued that interpersonal communication can lead to accuracy in perceptions of others. This, they claimed, "seems an ideal criterion for communication in that it is (theoretically, at least) achievable through communication alone" (p. 487). However, they acknowledged that this is not always the case (communication often is used to decrease accuracy), nor should it be given that accuracy is not always the most productive condition for social relationships.

Mass communication could, theoretically, also increase accuracy in perceptions of others, especially if the other is a social group as opposed to an individual. Indeed, researchers have tested the coorientation model in the context of social groups (e.g., Grunig & Stamm, 1973). However, mass communication is more likely to decrease accuracy through its role in the development of pluralistic ignorance as described previously. This was first noted decades ago (Tichenor & Wackman, 1973), but little connection has been made since then between coorientation (or balance theory) and research on social reality perceptions in mass communication. Despite this lack of follow-up, progress in social reality perception research could do much to inform persuasion research from the balance theory perspective, and social reality perception research could benefit from a review of the literature from balance theory and coorientation.

Theory of Reasoned Action

One classic persuasion theory that is dependent on perceptions of social reality is the theory of reasoned action (Fishbein & Ajzen, 1975; Sutton, 1998). The theory of reasoned action predicts that behaviors are most proximally determined by behavioral intentions. Behavioral intentions, in turn, are determined by attitudes toward the behavior and "subjective norms." A subjective norm has two components: normative beliefs and the motivation to comply. The normative belief is a perception of what opinions or behaviors are considered acceptable or favored (or unacceptable or disfavored) by important others along with a "motivation to comply."

Research on the construction of social reality could make a substantial contribution to the theory of reasoned action by providing a solid basis of research for the development of normative beliefs and the potential impact of motivations to comply on behavioral intentions. Therefore, those interested in persuasion might consider integrating research described in this chapter pertaining to the development of perceptions of social reality with the theory of reasoned action. Specifically, ideas of how perceptions of public opinion are shaped based on research in pluralistic ignorance, the spiral of silence, and the persuasive press inference would fit nicely into the theory of reasoned action to demonstrate one potential avenue for attitude change and behavior modification.

In addition, the spiral of silence's concept of fear of isolation appears to be closely related to the theory of reasoned action's notion of motivation to comply. Specifically, the spiral of silence suggests that individuals have an innate fear of social isolation and that they engage—or choose not to engage—in communication behaviors based on this fear of isolation. Thus, fear of isolation provides at least one motivation to comply, although there are likely others as well. However, this connection between the spiral of silence and the theory of reasoned action again indicates that research on social reality perceptions may be able to contribute both theoretical advances and a substantial base of research toward a theory of persuasion.

Cognitive Response Theory

Cognitive response theory (Greenwald, 1968; Petty & Cacioppo, 1981) claims that attitude change in response to persuasive messages takes place through an internal process of argument and counterargument generation. That is, when exposed to a persuasive communication, individuals will be persuaded not by the message itself but rather by the arguments they are able to generate in favor of

and opposition to the position advocated in the message. Thus, it is the individual's cognitive response to the message, and not the message itself, that is the ultimate source of persuasion.

Advancing the cognitive response model, Mutz (1992, 1998) argued that when individuals are presented with information about the state of public opinion from poll information (in our case, this could simply be perceptions of public opinion), they sometimes go through a process of cognitive response that results in attitude change. Faced with a belief (potentially created through media poll reports or other depictions of public opinion as described by the spiral of silence) that a majority of the public supports a certain policy proposal, individuals produce arguments to explain and understand this position. They also develop counterarguments about why the majority position might be wrong. In the end, as with the cognitive response model more generally, it is the arguments generated in response to the communication, and not the communication itself, that determines whether a change in attitude or behavior will take place. By focusing on the role of perceptions of social reality in the form of public opinion, Mutz's extension of the cognitive response model provides an important linkage between persuasion research and both pluralistic ignorance research in psychology and the spiral of silence model.

Credibility and Social Reality Perceptions

A key construct that can influence the persuasive potential of a message is the perception of the credibility of the source of the message (Hovland, Janis, & Kelley, 1953; Slater & Rouner, 1996). In his study of perceptions of news media bias, Gunther (1992) argued that credibility perceptions may be determined more by the characteristics of the individual than by the characteristics of the source itself. For example, he found that the best predictor of perceptions of biased media coverage of social groups was membership in those social groups, which is consistent with the hostile media phenomenon. Given the centrality of the credibility construct in persuasion, and given that media credibility perceptions are susceptible to bias through the hostile media phenomenon, there is a need for integration of these strains of research. Specifically, persuasion researchers concerned about the credibility of different media sources should be sure to take into account the fact that those who are highly involved, such as members of certain social groups, may perceive the content to be biased even when the source appears to be objectively credible.

There is an additional linkage between credibility research and social reality perceptions. The "sleeper effect" described in early research on source credibility and persuasion (Hovland et al., 1953; Pratkanis, Leippe, Greenwald, & Baumgardner, 1988) may also be at play in media influence on perceptions of social reality. When a message from a source lacking credibility has a greater persuasive effect after a delay than immediately after exposure, this is labeled a sleeper effect. One explanation for sleeper effects is that, over time, the message and source are dissociated. When this occurs, the individual is unable to discount the message based on the source and thus is more likely to accept the message.

Cultivation researchers have used this basic groundwork to explain the impact of televised entertainment content on perceptions of social reality. Mares (1996) argued that the impact of television entertainment programming on social reality perceptions is greater among those individuals who regularly misremember the source of information to be

from a newscast instead of an entertainment show. Basically, Mares was interested in tapping an individual difference in susceptibility to a sleeper effect. Her reasoning, consistent with the sleeper effect, was that those individuals who can accurately link the source of a message with its content are less likely to be influenced by entertainment media because they are able to discount the source. However, over time, some individuals are more likely to misremember the source such that information garnered from entertainment television is thought to originate from the more credible news genre. This confusion of source, and thus source credibility, leads to a greater impact on perceptions of social reality. Mares found support for this interpretation of the cultivation effect.

APPLICATIONS TO COMMUNICATION CAMPAIGNS

Miller and McFarland (1987) provided a concise statement of the general fear expressed by many researchers about the social consequences of misperceptions of social reality: "Pluralistic ignorance can lead a group to act in a manner that is inconsistent with the inclinations of its members" (p. 304). One avenue that campaigners may pursue is to attempt to alter perceptions of social reality to more closely match reality. As I have already described, research indicates that perceptions of social reality may be influenced by exposure to both entertainment media and news media. Furthermore, many different types of perceptions—including perceptions of public opinion, of the behavior of others, and of social conditions—are susceptible to influence.

Much of the research on perceptions of social reality described in this chapter places the finger of blame on the media for inaccurate perceptions of social reality. It has also taken a relatively deterministic perspective regarding the content of the media. That is, the existing research takes media content as a starting point to determine its effects. However, a campaigner would likely examine media content from another perspective: How might media content be influenced to produce a more desirable outcome?

One means of exerting influence over media content is through public pressure on networks (Weinraub, 1999). Protests may be held, or a broad-based boycott may be attempted. Similarly, social action campaigners may privately lobby television producers to adjust their content for some socially desirable purpose and then publicly reward the producers when they respond appropriately (Montgomery, 1989). Unfortunately, the truly successful application of these types of influence is likely to be relatively rare in the United States because the creative forces behind television content are typically reticent to give in to attempts at control over their creative product. However, campaigners may have greater influence on noncommercial stations such as PBS or in contexts where television is viewed more as a public commodity such as in developing or socialist countries.

Influence over news media content, on the other hand, is a major focus and goal of public relations practitioners and political consultants. The impact of public relations on news content takes place through the framing of press releases, press conferences, and on-air interviews. Presidential administrations attempt to influence which issues are considered important to the public by maintaining a consistent theme among all members of the administration, sometimes called the "line of the day" (Maltese, 1992).

Provided that they are able to exert some influence over media content, there are a number of ways in which campaigners could use the persuasive power of entertainment and news media to influence public beliefs about social reality. In what follows, I describe three areas in which campaigners might wish to apply the research on communication and social reality perceptions to real-world issues. These issues are health and development campaigns, changing racial and sexual stereotypes, and political campaigns.

Health and Development Campaigns

Social reality perceptions play a significant role in a number of health-related concerns. For instance, a number of social scientists (e.g., Marks, Graham, & Hansen, 1992; Perkins & Wechsler, 1996; Prentice & Miller, 1993; Schroeder & Prentice, 1998) have demonstrated that perceptions of social reality in the form of perceived norms have important implications for the use of alcohol by adolescents and college students. Research has consistently demonstrated that "one of the most consistent predictors of an adolescent's alcohol use is perceived alcohol use by his or her peers" (Schroeder & Prentice, 1998, p. 2151). Importantly, longitudinal research (Marks et al., 1992) has demonstrated that the social conformity effect (changing one's own behaviors to fit perceptions of others) is stronger than the social projection effect (changing one's perceptions of others to fit one's own behavior). The link between perceived norms and behavior has been replicated for other health-related behaviors, including sexual experiences and smoking among young adults (e.g., Botvin, Botvin, Baker, Dusenbury, & Goldberg, 1992; Cohen & Shotland, 1996).

Any health campaign designed to reduce alcohol use, smoking, or risky sexual behaviors by adolescents and college students would be well-served by attempting to alter perceptions of the social norm regarding the behavior. As Montgomery (1989) detailed, there is a substantial history of groups attempting to influence American television content for public health purposes. For example, characters on entertainment television programs can regularly engage in safe sex as opposed to unprotected sex or can abstain from sexual activity altogether.

One example of how change might occur in public perceptions of social norms regarding health behaviors can be drawn from the 1990s teen soap opera *Beverly Hills 90210.* For several years of this series, the character "Donna" abstained from sexual intercourse while her high school and college peers were sexually active. For a truly significant impact, more than a single character would probably be necessary to influence perceptions of the number of individuals who remain virgins through late high school or early college.

Another context in which television content could be influenced would be in automotive safety. For example, based on outside pressures, characters on several popular television series during the 1980s, including *The A-Team,* began to visibly buckle their seat belts each time they entered their cars (Geller, 1989). This change in behavior could have led viewers to perceive a change in public norms regarding the use of safety belts and to adjust their own behaviors accordingly. Similarly, if instances of drinking and driving are followed by accidents and other negative consequences, such as the drunk driving accident of the character "Bailey" on *Party of Five,* regular viewers may become likely to associate these events occurring together frequently. A related approach would be to portray more occurrences of the use of designated drivers in situations where a lead character is drinking before driving.

News media content can also be influenced to more accurately portray the frequency of healthy and unhealthy behaviors. Surveys can

be publicized that report the frequency of, for instance, unprotected sex or the number of sexual partners by a given age. These figures can be contrasted with the nature of sex portrayals on television. Given the common misperception of drinking norms on college campuses, college newspapers might consider reporting statistics on the actual occurrence of binge drinking on campus to help correct students' erroneous perceptions.

A final approach to influencing social reality perceptions on health issues is to institute a form of media literacy training. In general, this type of training is aimed at children with the goal of helping them to better understand the content of the media and to increase skepticism of many of the images and inferences in media content. There is some evidence that this type of literacy training is successful in limiting the influence of television viewing on perceptions of alcohol norms (Austin & Johnson, 1997).

In Third World countries, development messages have been included in soap operas to introduce or change social norms about a number of issues (e.g., Kottak, 1990; Singhal & Rogers, 1989). For example, if campaigners hope to reduce the infant mortality rate in a developing country, they might develop a drama or soap opera focusing on people with whom the target audience could easily identify. Characters in the soap opera would explicitly and frequently engage in the appropriate behaviors (e.g., use the proper medicine when babies had diarrhea) and be positively rewarded for doing so. Those who did not do so would receive negative social feedback or experience negative consequences. Over time, these portrayals could cultivate the perception that the health behaviors are normative and thus should be followed as standard practice because they must be appropriate and effective. If nothing else, individuals may simply engage in these behaviors to avoid social isolation. This same logic could be applied to the use of new agricultural methods or other innovative practices.

Racial and Sexual Stereotypes

In addition to changing behaviors, media content can be developed to produce counter-stereotypical beliefs and engender tolerance toward minority groups. Television news organizations can change their patterns of displaying minority criminal suspects in handcuffs. Newspapers can refrain from mentioning the race of suspects, especially because race is rarely a relevant factor in crime news stories. Entertainment shows can portray minority characters in prominent, powerful, and pro-social roles (e.g., as doctors and lawyers) and can limit the frequency with which they portray minorities stereotypically.

There is evidence that change in the typical demographics of television is possible. A number of minority groups expressed outrage at the small number of minority characters being presented in major roles in prime-time television during the Fall 1999 season. A "brownout," in which minorities would boycott network television to demonstrate their displeasure as well as their importance, was threatened. In response, producers promised to add more minority characters (Weinraub, 1999).

Changes in media content to reflect greater diversity of jobs and activities among women can help to reduce stereotypical beliefs of young children regarding sex roles. For example, one episode of the *Freestyle* program on PBS (LaRose, 1989) showed a young female character engaging in counterstereotypical behavior (playing football) as part of a campaign to reduce sex role stereotyping among children. More generally, female characters on television can be shown to be just as important—

and capable of the same feats—as male characters instead of being portrayed as simply victims, "prizes," or bystanders. When these nontraditional gender roles are presented on television, there is some evidence that they may lead to a reduction in children's stereotypical perceptions about gender roles (e.g., Corder-Bolz, 1980; Rosenwasser et al., 1989).

Political Campaigns

The impact of perceptions of public opinion on voter attitudes and behavior, especially during primary campaigns, is an important area of research in political science (e.g., Bartels, 1988; Ceci & Kain, 1982; Joslyn, 1997; Mehrabian, 1998; Mutz, 1998; Nadeau, Niemi, & Amato, 1994; West, 1991) and a potential avenue for persuasive impact. The persuasive press inference suggests that individuals will infer public opinion from the slant of news media coverage. And political communication research has often found either that voters tend to side with the perceived winner (bandwagon effects) or that they give renewed effort for a candidate perceived to be losing ground (underdog effects). In addition, the spiral of silence (Noelle-Neumann, 1993) suggests that perceiving public opinion to be incongruent with one's own opinion can further shape public opinion indirectly by leading members of the minority to refrain from expressing their opinions publicly. Equally important is the potential impact of perceived public support for presidents in their dealings with legislators and other politicians. As Kernell (1986) noted, "A president with a strong reputation does better in his dealings largely because others expect fewer concessions from him. . . . Saddled with a weak reputation, conversely, a president must work harder, because others expect him to bargain less effectively" (p. 146). Reputation, of course, is enhanced by the perception that the politician has strong public support.

Combining these theories and findings has important implications that have not been lost on political campaign managers. By attempting to alter perceptions of candidate support via "spin" that is then conveyed in news media coverage, candidates can potentially increase their standings in the polls as well as their chances of receiving monetary contributions and volunteer efforts (Henshel & Johnston, 1987). Although candidates can provide bogus poll findings to the news media, poll findings are not the only means of influencing news media coverage. "Perhaps more than the polling results, it is the interpretation of the results that informs and persuades" (DeRosa & Tedesco, 1999, p. 67). Therefore, candidate representatives do their best to portray their candidates as being successful and influencing public opinion by, for instance, criticizing polls when their candidates are trailing (DeRosa & Tedesco, 1999), trumpeting the poll findings when their candidates are leading, and claiming that their candidates "won" debates (Lemert, Wanta, & Lee, 1999). Significantly, debate verdicts have been repeatedly shown to have a significant impact on perceptions of which candidates won the debates as well as candidate image, above and beyond the impact of debate exposure itself (Lemert, 1996; Lemert, Elliott, Bernstein, Rosenberg, & Nestvold, 1991). Unfortunately for campaign workers, however, their ability to influence debate verdicts has been reduced during recent years because they are less likely to be invited on debate specials and newscasts (Lemert et al., 1999).

CONCLUSIONS

It has often been said that "perception is reality." Our perceptions of the world and people around us, and not their "real" referents, are what drive our opinions, underlying attitudes, and everyday behavior. As such, perceptions should be, and are, important variables in many theories of persuasion.

Many forms of mass media are designed to shape our perceptions of the world. Television advertisements tell us that we will be ostracized if we smell bad, so we should buy Right Guard deodorant. We are led to believe that we can be a hip member of the Gen-X culture if we just "do the Dew" by drinking Mountain Dew. Many advertisements encourage us to join the majority by using a particular product. However, these are not the only messages that can have a persuasive impact on our beliefs about the world and people around us. Entertainment television, although not typically an intentionally persuasive form of content, has been demonstrated to have at least some impact on our perceptions of social reality. News media content, while generally not intended by its producers to persuade us, is intended to inform us about the world around us. When the information we derive from the news media is accurate, this is considered a prosocial learning outcome. However, often individuals use news media content to infer facts about the world, and often these inferences are inaccurate. So, while the intention to persuade is not commonly associated with news and entertainment media, they often have a persuasive impact nonetheless.

The study of misperceptions of social reality has a long history in a number of related fields. However, for most of this history, the research on social reality perceptions has proceeded without important integration across theoretical perspectives or disciplinary boundaries. It is my hope that this review of the research will assist researchers in studying persuasion to integrate and advance both persuasion theory and the study of how entertainment and news media, in conjunction with motivational and cognitive processes, can influence our perceptions—and, more important, our misperceptions—of social reality.

REFERENCES

Austin, E. W., & Johnson, K. K. (1997). Immediate and delayed effects of media literacy training on third graders' decision making for alcohol. *Health Communication, 9,* 323-349.

Bartels, L. M. (1988). *Presidential primaries and the dynamics of public choice.* Princeton, NJ: Princeton University Press.

Botvin, G. J., Botvin, E. M., Baker, E., Dusenbury, L., & Goldberg, C. J. (1992). The false consensus effect: Predicting adolescents' tobacco use from normative expectations. *Psychological Reports, 70,* 171-178.

Breed, W., & Ktsanes, T. (1961). Pluralistic ignorance and the process of opinion formation. *Public Opinion Quarterly, 25,* 382-392.

Ceci, S. J., & Kain, E. L. (1982). Jumping on the bandwagon with the underdog: The impact of attitude polls on polling behavior. *Public Opinion Quarterly, 46,* 228-242.

Cohen, J., Mutz, D., Price, V., & Gunther, A. (1988). Perceived impact of defamation: An experiment on third-person effects. *Public Opinion Quarterly, 52,* 161-173.

Cohen, L. L., & Shotland, R. L. (1996). Timing of first sexual intercourse in a relationship: Expectations, experiences, and perceptions of others. *Journal of Sex Research, 33,* 291-299.

Corder-Bolz, C. R. (1980). Mediation: The role of significant others. *Journal of Communication, 30*(3), 106-118.

Dautrich, K., & Dineen, J. N. (1996, October-November). Media bias: What journalists and the public say about it. *The Public Perspective,* pp. 7-14.

Davison, W. P. (1983). The third-person effect in communication. *Public Opinion Quarterly, 47,* 1-15.

DeRosa, K. L., & Tedesco, J. C. (1999). Surveying the spin: Interpretation of the 1996 presidential polls. In L. L. Kaid & D. G. Bystrom (Eds.), *The electronic election: Perspectives on the 1996 campaign communication* (pp. 65-79). Mahwah, NJ: Lawrence Erlbaum.

Edelstein, A. S. (1988). Communication perspectives in public opinion: Traditions and innovations. In J. A. Anderson (Ed.), *Communication Yearbook 11* (pp. 502-533). Newbury Park, CA: Sage.

Eveland, W. P., Jr. (1997). Interactions and nonlinearity in mass communication: Connecting theory and methodology. *Journalism and Mass Communication Quarterly, 74,* 400-416.

Eveland, W. P., Jr., McLeod, D. M., & Signorielli, N. (1995). Actual and perceived U.S. public opinion: The spiral of silence during the Persian Gulf War. *International Journal of Public Opinion Research, 7,* 91-109.

Eveland, W. P., Jr., Nathanson, A. I., Detenber, B. H., & McLeod, D. M. (1999). Rethinking the social distance corollary: Perceived likelihood of exposure and the third-person perception. *Communication Research, 26,* 275-302.

Fields, J. M., & Schuman, H. (1976). Public beliefs about the beliefs of the public. *Public Opinion Quarterly, 40,* 427-448.

Fishbein, M., & Ajzen, I. (1975). *Belief, attitude, intention, and behavior: An introduction to theory and research.* Reading, MA: Addison-Wesley.

Gandy, O. H., Jr., & Baron, J. (1998). Inequality: It's all in the way you look at it. *Communication Research, 25,* 505-527.

Geller, E. S. (1989). Using television to promote safety belt use. In R. E. Rice & C. K. Atkin (Eds.), *Public communication campaigns* (2nd ed., pp. 201-203). Newbury Park, CA: Sage.

Gerbner, G., Gross, L., Morgan, M., & Signorielli, N. (1980). The "mainstreaming" of America: Violence Profile No. 11. *Journal of Communication, 30*(3), 10-29.

Gerbner, G., Gross, L., Morgan, M., & Signorielli, N. (1994). Growing up with television: The cultivation perspective. In J. Bryant & D. Zillmann (Eds.), *Media effects: Advances in theory and research* (pp. 17-41). Hillsdale, NJ: Lawrence Erlbaum.

Gerbner, G., Gross, L., Signorielli, N., Morgan, M., & Jackson-Beeck, M. (1979). The demonstration of power: Violence Profile No. 10. *Journal of Communication, 29*(3), 177-196.

Gilovich, T. (1990). Differential construal and the false consensus effect. *Journal of Personality and Social Psychology, 59*, 623-634.

Giner-Sorolla, R., & Chaiken, S. (1994). The causes of hostile media judgments. *Journal of Experimental Social Psychology, 30,* 165-180.

Glynn, C. J. (1987). The communication of public opinion. *Journalism Quarterly, 64,* 688-697.

Glynn, C. J. (1989). Perceptions of others' opinions as a component of public opinion. *Social Science Research, 18,* 53-69.

Glynn, C. J., Hayes, A. F., & Shanahan, J. (1997). Perceived support for one's opinions and willingness to speak out: A meta-analysis of survey studies on the "spiral of silence." *Public Opinion Quarterly, 61,* 452-463.

Glynn, C. J., & McLeod, J. M. (1983). Public opinion, communication processes, and voting decisions. In M. Burgoon (Ed.), *Communication Yearbook 6* (pp. 759-774). Beverly Hills, CA: Sage.

Glynn, C. J., & McLeod, J. M. (1984). Public opinion du jour: An examination of the spiral of silence. *Public Opinion Quarterly, 48,* 731-740.

Glynn, C. J., & McLeod, J. M. (1985). Implications of the spiral of silence theory for communication and public opinion research. In D. Nimmo & K. Sanders (Eds.), *Political communication yearbook, 1984* (pp. 43-65). Carbondale: Southern Illinois University Press.

Glynn, C. J., Ostman, R. E., & McDonald, D. G. (1995). Opinions, perception, and social reality. In T. L. Glasser & C. T. Salmon (Eds.), *Public opinion and the communication of consent* (pp. 249-277). New York: Guilford.

Greenwald, A. G. (1968). Cognitive learning, cognitive response to persuasion, and attitude change. In A. G. Greenwald, T. C. Brock, & T. M. Ostrom (Eds.), *Psychological foundations of attitudes* (pp. 361-388). New York: Academic Press.

Grunig, J. E., & Stamm, K. R. (1973). Communication and coorientation of collectives. *American Behavioral Scientist, 16,* 567-591.

Gunther, A. (1991). What we think others think: Cause and consequence in the third-person effect. *Communication Research, 18,* 355-372.

Gunther, A. C. (1992). Biased press or biased public? Attitudes toward media coverage of social groups. *Public Opinion Quarterly, 56,* 147-167.

Gunther, A. (1995). Overrating the X-rating: The third-person perception and support for censorship of pornography. *Journal of Communication, 45*(1), 27-38.

Gunther, A. C. (1998). The persuasive press inference: Effects of mass media on perceived public opinion. *Communication Research, 25,* 486-504.

Gunther, A. C., & Christen, C. T. (1999a). Effects of news slant and base rate information on perceived public opinion. *Journalism and Mass Communication Quarterly, 76,* 277-292.

Gunther, A. C., & Christen, C. T. (1999b, May). *Projection or persuasive press? Effects of personal opinion and perceived news coverage on estimates of public opinion.* Paper presented at the annual meeting of the International Communication Association, San Francisco.

Gunther, A. C., & Hwa, A. P. (1996). Public perceptions of television influence and opinions about censorship in Singapore. *International Journal of Public Opinion Research, 8,* 248-265.

Gunther, A. C., & Mundy, P. (1993). Biased optimism and the third-person effect. *Journalism Quarterly, 70,* 58-67.

Gunther, A. C., & Thorson, E. (1992). Perceived persuasive effects of product commercials and public service announcements: Third-person effects in new domains. *Communication Research, 19,* 574-596.

Hawkins, R. P., & Pingree, S. (1981). Uniform messages and habitual viewing: Unnecessary assumptions in social reality effects. *Human Communication Research, 7,* 291-301.

Hawkins, R. P., & Pingree, S. (1982). Television's influence on social reality. In D. Pearl, L. Bouthilet, & J. Lazar (Eds.), *Television and behavior: Ten years of scientific progress and implications for the eighties* (DHHS Publication No. [ADM] 82-1196, Vol. 2, pp. 224-247). Washington, DC: Government Printing Office.

Hawkins, R. P., & Pingree, S. (1990). Divergent psychological processes in constructing social reality from mass media content. In N. Signorielli & M. Morgan (Eds.), *Cultivation* analysis: New directions in media effects research (pp. 35-50). Newbury Park, CA: Sage.

Heider, F. (1958). The psychology of interpersonal relations. New York: John Wiley.

Henshel, R. L., & Johnston, W. (1987). The emergence of bandwagon effects: A theory. Sociological Quarterly, 28, 493-511.

Hetherington, M. J. (1996). The media's role in forming voters' national economic evaluations in 1992. American Journal of Political Science, 40, 372-395.

Hirsch, P. M. (1980). The "scary world" of the nonviewer and other anomalies: A reanalysis of Gerbner's findings on cultivation analysis, Part I. Communication Research, 7, 403-456.

Hirsch, P. M. (1981a). Distinguishing good speculation from bad theory: Rejoinder to Gerbner Communication Research, 8, 73-95.

Hirsch, P. M. (1981b). On not learning from one's own mistakes: A reanalysis of Gerbner's findings on cultivation analysis, Part II. Communication Research, 8, 3-37.

Hollander, B. A. (1994, August). Question order effects on estimates of consensus. Paper presented at the annual meeting of the Association for Education in Journalism and Mass Communication, Atlanta, GA.

Hoorens, V., & Ruiter, S. (1996). The optimal impact phenomenon: Beyond the third person effect. European Journal of Social Psychology, 26, 599-610.

Hovland, C. I., Janis, I. L., & Kelley, H. H. (1953). Communication and persuasion: Psychological studies of opinion change. New Haven, CT: Yale University Press.

Hughes, M. (1980). The fruits of cultivation analysis: A reexamination of some effects of television watching. Public Opinion Quarterly, 44, 287-302.

Joslyn, M. R. (1997). The public nature of personal opinion: The impact of collective sentiment on individual appraisal. Political Behavior, 19, 337-363.

Katz, D., & Allport, F. H. (1931). Student attitudes. Syracuse, NY: Craftsman Press.

Kauffman, K. (1981). Prison officers' attitudes and perceptions of attitudes: A case of pluralistic ignorance. Journal of Research in Crime and Delinquency, 18, 272-294.

Kernell, S. (1986). Going public: New strategies of presidential leadership. Washington, DC: Congressional Quarterly Press.

Kiecolt, K. J., & Sayles, M. (1988). Television and the cultivation of attitudes toward subordinate groups. Sociological Spectrum, 8, 19-33.

Korte, C. (1972). Pluralistic ignorance about student radicalism. Sociometry, 35, 576-587.

Kottak, C. P. (1990). Prime time society: An anthropological analysis of television and culture. Belmont, CA: Wadsworth.

Kressel, N. J. (1987). Biased judgments of media bias: A case study of the Arab-Israeli dispute. Political Psychology, 8, 211-227.

Langer, E. J. (1975). The illusion of control. Journal of Personality and Social Psychology, 32, 311-328.

LaRose, R. (1989). Freestyle, revisited. In R. E. Rice & C. K. Atkin (Eds.), Public communication campaigns (2nd ed., pp. 207-209). Newbury Park, CA: Sage.

Lemert, J. B. (1996). News verdicts and their effects. In J. B. Lemert, W. R. Elliott, W. L. Rosenberg, & J. M. Bernstein (Eds.), The politics of disenchantment: Bush, Clinton, Perot, and the press (pp. 175-198). Cresskill, NJ: Hampton.

Lemert, J. B., Elliott, W. R., Bernstein, J. M., Rosenberg, W. L., & Nestvold, K. J. (1991). News verdicts, the debates, and presidential campaigns. New York: Praeger.

Lemert, J. B., Wanta, W., & Lee, T. T. (1999). Winning by staying ahead: 1996 debate performance verdicts. In L. L. Kaid & D. G. Bystrom (Eds.), The electronic election: Perspectives on the 1996 campaign communication (pp. 179-189). Mahwah, NJ: Lawrence Erlbaum.

Lerner, M. J. (1980). The belief in a just world: A fundamental delusion. New York: Plenum.

Long, J. N., & Willower, D. J. (1980). Pupil control, pluralistic ignorance, and teachers' ratings of their principals' leadership. Educational Research Quarterly, 5, 33-39.

Maltese, J. A. (1992). Spin control: The White House Office of Communications and the management of presidential news. Chapel Hill: University of North Carolina Press.

Mares, M. L. (1996). The role of source confusions in television's cultivation of social reality judgments. *Human Communication Research, 23,* 278-297.

Marks, G., Graham, J. W., & Hansen, W. B. (1992). Social projection and social conformity in adolescent alcohol use: A longitudinal analysis. *Personality and Social Psychology Bulletin, 18,* 96-101.

Marks, G., & Miller, N. (1987). Ten years of research on the false-consensus effect: An empirical and theoretical review. *Psychological Bulletin, 102,* 72-90.

McGarrell, E. F., & Sandys, M. (1996). The misperception of public opinion toward capital punishment: Examining the spuriousness explanation of death penalty support. *American Behavioral Scientist, 39,* 500-513.

McLeod, D. M., Detenber, B. H., & Eveland, W. P., Jr. (2001). Behind the third-person effect: Differentiating perceptual processes for self and others. *Journal of Communication, 51*(4), 678-695.

McLeod, D. M., Eveland, W. P., Jr., & Nathanson, A. I. (1997). Support for censorship of violent and misogynic rap lyrics: An analysis of the third-person effect. *Communication Research, 24,* 153-174.

McLeod, D. M., & Hertog, J. K. (1992). The manufacture of "public opinion" by reporters: Informal cues for public perceptions of protest groups. *Discourse & Society, 3,* 259-275.

McLeod, J. M., & Chaffee, S. H. (1973). Interpersonal approaches to communication research. *American Behavioral Scientist, 16,* 469-499.

McLeod, J. M., Daily, K., Eveland, W., Guo, Z., Culver, K., Kurpius, D., Moy, P., Horowitz, E., & Zhong, M. (1995, August). *The synthetic crisis: Media influences on perceptions of crime.* Paper presented at the annual meeting of the Association for Education in Journalism and Mass Communication, Washington, DC.

McLeod, J. M., Eveland, W. P., Jr., Moy, P., Scheufele, D., Yang, S., Horowitz, E. M., Guo, Z., & Zhong, M. (1996, August). *Is what we see what they get? Probing the processes of media effects on support for crime policy proposals.* Paper presented at the annual meeting of the Association for Education in Journalism and Mass Communication, Anaheim, CA.

McLeod, J. M., & Reeves, B. (1980). On the nature of mass media effects. In S. B. Withey & R. P. Abeles (Eds.), *Television and social behavior: Beyond violence and children* (pp. 17-54). Hillsdale, NJ: Lawrence Erlbaum.

Mehrabian, A. (1998). Effects of poll reports on voter preferences. *Journal of Applied Social Psychology, 28,* 2119-2130.

Merton, R. K. (1968). *Social theory and social structure.* New York: Free Press.

Miller, D. T., & McFarland, C. (1987). Pluralistic ignorance: When similarity is interpreted as dissimilarity. *Journal of Personality and Social Psychology, 53,* 298-305.

Miller, D. T., & Norman, S. A. (1975). Actor-observer differences in perceptions of effective control. *Journal of Personality and Social Psychology, 31,* 503-515.

Miller, D. T., & Prentice, D. A. (1994). Collective errors and errors about the collective. *Personality and Social Psychology Bulletin, 20,* 541-550.

Monsour, M., Harvey, V., & Betty, S. (1997). A balance theory explanation of challenges confronting cross-sex friendships. *Sex Roles, 37,* 825-845.

Montgomery, K. C. (1989). *Target—Prime time: Advocacy groups in the struggle over entertainment television.* New York: Oxford University Press.

Morgan, M. (1986). Television and the erosion of regional diversity. *Journal of Broadcasting & Electronic Media, 30,* 123-139.

Morgan, M., & Rothschild, N. (1983). Impact of the new television technology: Cable TV, peers, and sex-role cultivation in the electronic environment. *Youth & Society, 15,* 33-50.

Morgan, M., & Shanahan, J. (1997). Two decades of cultivation research: An appraisal and meta-analysis. In B. R. Burleson (Ed.), *Communication Yearbook 20* (pp. 1-45). Thousand Oaks, CA: Sage.

Mullen, B. (1983). Egocentric bias in estimates of consensus. *Journal of Social Psychology, 121,* 31-38.

Mullen, B., Atkins, J., Champion, D., Edwards, C., Hardy, D., Story, J., & Vanderklok, M. (1985). The false consensus effect: A meta-analysis of 115 hypothesis tests. *Journal of Experimental Social Psychology, 21,* 262-283.

Mutz, D. C. (1992). Impersonal influence: Effects of representations of public opinion on political attitudes. *Political Behavior, 14*(2), 89-122.

Mutz, D. C. (1998). *Impersonal influence: How perceptions of mass collectives affect political attitudes.* New York: Cambridge University Press.

Nadeau, R., Niemi, R. G., & Amato, T. (1994). Expectations and preferences in British general elections. *American Political Science Review, 88,* 371-383.

Newcomb, T. (1953). An approach to the study of communicative acts. *Psychological Review, 60,* 393-404.

Nisbett, R. E., & Kunda, Z. (1985). Perception of social distributions. *Journal of Personality and Social Psychology, 48,* 297-311.

Noelle-Neumann, E. (1974). The spiral of silence: A theory of public opinion. *Journal of Communication, 24,* 43-51.

Noelle-Neumann, E. (1977). Turbulences in the climate of opinion: Methodological applications of the spiral of silence theory. *Public Opinion Quarterly, 41,* 143-158.

Noelle-Neumann, E. (1979). Public opinion and the classical tradition: A re-evaluation. *Public Opinion Quarterly, 43,* 143-156.

Noelle-Neumann, E. (1985). The spiral of silence: A response. In D. Nimmo & K. Sanders (Eds.), *Political communication yearbook, 1984* (pp. 43-65). Carbondale: Southern Illinois University Press.

Noelle-Neumann, E. (1989). Advances in spiral of silence research. *KEIO Communication Review, 10,* 3-29.

Noelle-Neumann, E. (1991). The theory of public opinion: The concept of the spiral of silence. In J. A. Anderson (Ed.), *Communication Yearbook 14* (pp. 256-287). Newbury Park, CA: Sage.

Noelle-Neumann, E. (1993). *The spiral of silence: Public opinion—Our social skin* (2nd ed.). Chicago: University of Chicago Press.

Noelle-Neumann, E. (1995). Public opinion and rationality. In C. T. Salmon & T. Glasser (Eds.), *Public opinion and the communication of consent* (pp. 33-54). New York: Guilford.

O'Gorman, H. J. (1975). Pluralistic ignorance and White estimates of White support for racial segregation. *Public Opinion Quarterly, 39,* 313-330.

O'Gorman, H. J., with Garry, S. L. (1976). Pluralistic ignorance: A replication and extension. *Public Opinion Quarterly, 40,* 449-458.

O'Gorman, H. J. (1979). White and Black perceptions of racial values. *Public Opinion Quarterly, 43,* 48-59.

O'Gorman, H. J. (1980). False consciousness of kind: Pluralistic ignorance among the aged. *Research in Aging, 2,* 105-128.

O'Gorman, H. J. (1986). The discovery of pluralistic ignorance: An ironic lesson. *Journal of the History of the Behavioral Sciences, 22,* 333-347.

O'Gorman, H. J. (1988). Pluralistic ignorance and reference groups: The case of ingroup ignorance. In H. J. O'Gorman (Ed.), *Surveying social life* (pp. 145-173). Middleton, CT: Wesleyan University Press.

O'Keefe, G. J. (1984). Public views on crime: Television exposure and media credibility. In R. N. Bostrom (Ed.), *Communication Yearbook 8* (pp. 514-535). Beverly Hills, CA: Sage.

O'Keefe, G. J., & Reid-Nash, K. (1987). Crime news and real-world blues: The effects of the media on social reality. *Communication Research, 14,* 147-163.

Oliver, M. B. (1994). Portrayals of crime, race, and aggression in "reality-based" police shows: A content analysis. *Journal of Broadcasting & Electronic Media, 38,* 179-192.

Perkins, H. W., & Wechsler, H. (1996). Variation in perceived college drinking norms and its impact on alcohol abuse: A nationwide study. *Journal of Drug Issues, 26,* 961-974.

Perloff, R. M. (1989). Ego-involvement and the third person effect of televised news coverage. *Communication Research, 16,* 236-262.

Perloff, R. M. (1996). Perceptions and conceptions of political media impact: The third-person effect and beyond. In A. N. Crigler (Ed.), *The psychology of political communication* (pp. 177-197). Ann Arbor: University of Michigan Press.

Perloff, R. M., Neuendorf, K., Giles, D., Change, T. K., & Jeffres, L. W. (1992). Perceptions of "Amerika." *Mass Communication Review, 19*(3), 42-48.

Petty, R. E., & Cacioppo, J. T. (1981). *Attitudes and persuasion: Classic and contemporary approaches.* Dubuque, IA: William C. Brown.

Pfau, M., Mullen, L. J., Deidrich, T., & Garrow, K. (1995). Television viewing and public perceptions of attorneys. *Human Communication Research, 21,* 307-330.

Pfau, M., Mullen, L. J., & Garrow, K. (1995). The influence of television viewing on public perceptions of physicians. *Journal of Broadcasting & Electronic Media, 39,* 441-458.

Potter, W. J. (1991). The relationships between first- and second-order measures of cultivation. *Human Communication Research, 18,* 92-113.

Potter, W. J. (1994). Cultivation theory and research: A methodological critique. *Journalism Monographs, 147,* 1-34.

Potter, W. J., & Chang, I. C. (1990). Television exposure measures and the cultivation hypothesis. *Journal of Broadcasting & Electronic Media, 34,* 313-333.

Pratkanis, A. R., Leippe, M. R., Greenwald, A. G., & Baumgardner, M. H. (1988). In search of reliable persuasion effects: III. The sleeper effect is dead—Long live the sleeper effect. *Journal of Personality and Social Psychology, 54,* 203-218.

Prentice, D. A., & Miller, D. T. (1993). Pluralistic ignorance and alcohol use on campus: Some consequences of misperceiving the social norm. *Journal of Personality and Social Psychology, 64,* 243-256.

Price, V., Tewksbury, D., & Huang, L. N. (1998). Third-person effects on publication of a holocaust-denial advertisement. *Journal of Communication, 48*(2), 3-26.

Rojas, H., Shah, D. V., & Faber, R. J. (1996). For the good of others: Censorship and the third-person effect. *International Journal of Public Opinion Research, 8,* 163-186.

Rosenwasser, S. M., Lingenfelter, M., & Harrington, A. F. (1989). Nontraditional gender role portrayals on television and children's gender role perceptions. *Journal of Applied Developmental Psychology, 10,* 97-105.

Ross, L., Greene, D., & House, P. (1977). The "false consensus effect": An egocentric bias in social perception and attribution processes. *Journal of Experimental Social Psychology, 13,* 279-301.

Rubin, A. M., Perse, E. M., & Taylor, D. S. (1988). A methodological examination of cultivation. *Communication Research, 15,* 107-134.

Rucinski, D., & Salmon, C. T. (1990). The "other" as the vulnerable voter: A study of the third-person effect in the 1988 U.S. presidential campaign. *International Journal of Public Opinion Research, 2,* 345-368.

Salmon, C. T., & Kline, F. G. (1985). The spiral of silence ten years later: An examination and evaluation. In D. Nimmo & K. Sanders (Eds.), *Political communication yearbook, 1984* (pp. 3-30). Carbondale: Southern Illinois University Press.

Salmon, C. T., & Moh, C. (1992). The spiral of silence: Linking individual and society through communication. In J. D. Kennamer (Ed.), *Public opinion, the press, and public policy* (pp. 145-161). Westport, CT: Praeger.

Salmon, C. T., & Neuwirth, K. (1990). Perceptions of opinion "climates" and willingness to discuss the issue of abortion. *Journalism Quarterly, 67,* 567-577.

Salwen, M. B. (1998). Perceptions of media influence and support for censorship: The third-person effect in the 1996 presidential election. *Communication Research, 25,* 259-285.

Schank, R. L. (1932). A study of a community and its groups and institutions conceived of as behaviors of individuals. *Psychological Monographs, 43*(2), 1-133.

Schroeder, C. M., & Prentice, D. A. (1998). Exposing pluralistic ignorance to reduce alcohol use among college students. *Journal of Applied Social Psychology, 28,* 2150-2180.

Shah, D. V., Faber, R. J., & Youn, S. (1999). Susceptibility and severity: Perceptual dimensions underlying the third-person effect. *Communication Research, 26,* 240-267.

Shamir, J. (1993). Pluralistic ignorance revisited: Perceptions of opinion distributions in Israel. *International Journal of Public Opinion Research, 5,* 22-39.

Shamir, J. (1995). Information cues and indicators of the climate of opinion: The spiral of silence theory in the Intifada. *Communication Research, 22,* 24-53.

Shamir, J. (1998). Motivation and accuracy in estimating opinion distributions: A survey experiment. *International Journal of Public Opinion Research, 10,* 91-108.

Shanahan, J., Morgan, M., & Stenbjerre, M. (1997). Green or brown? Television and the cultivation of environmental concern. *Journal of Broadcasting & Electronic Media, 41,* 305-323.

Shapiro, M. A. (1991). Memory and decision processes in the construction of social reality. *Communication Research, 18,* 3-24.

Sherman, S. J., Presson, C. C., & Chassin, L. (1984). Mechanisms underlying the false consensus effect: The special role of threats to the self. *Personality and Social Psychology Bulletin, 10,* 127-138.

Shrum, L. J. (1995). Assessing the social influence of television: A social cognition perspective on cultivation effects. *Communication Research, 22,* 402-429.

Shrum, L. J. (1996). Psychological processes underlying cultivation effects: Further tests of construct accessibility. *Human Communication Research, 22,* 482-509.

Shrum, L. J. (1997). The role of source confusion in cultivation effects may depend on processing strategy: A comment on Mares (1996). *Human Communication Research, 24,* 349-358.

Shrum, L. J. (1998). Development of a cognitive process model to explain the effects of heavy television viewing on social judgment. *Advances in Consumer Research, 25,* 289-294.

Shrum, L. J., & O'Guinn, T. C. (1993). Processes and effects in the construction of social reality: Construct accessibility as an explanatory variable. *Communication Research, 20,* 436-471.

Signorielli, N. (1981). Content analysis: More than just counting minorities. In *In search of diversity: Symposium on minority audience and programming research* (pp. 97-108). Washington, DC: Corporation for Public Broadcasting, Office of Communication Research.

Signorielli, N. (1986). Selective television viewing: A limited possibility. *Journal of Communication, 36*(3), 64-76.

Signorielli, N. (1990). Television's mean and dangerous world: A continuation of the cultural indicators perspective. In N. Signorielli & M. Morgan (Eds.), *Cultivation analysis: New directions in media effects research* (pp. 85-106). Newbury Park, CA: Sage.

Signorielli, N. (1991). Adolescents and ambivalence toward marriage: A cultivation analysis. *Youth & Society, 23,* 121-149.

Signorielli, N., & Lears, M. (1992). Children, television, and conceptions about chores: Attitudes and behaviors. *Sex Roles, 27,* 157-170.

Signorielli, N., & Morgan, M. (1990). *Cultivation analysis: New directions in media effects research.* Newbury Park, CA: Sage.

Signorielli, N., & Morgan, M. (1996). Cultivation analysis: Research and practice. In M. Salwen & D. Stacks (Eds.), *An integrated approach to communication theory and research* (pp. 111-126). Mahwah, NJ: Lawrence Erlbaum.

Singhal, A., & Rogers, E. M. (1989). Prosocial television for development in India. In R. E. Rice & C. K. Atkin (Eds.), *Public communication campaigns* (2nd ed., pp. 331-350). Newbury Park, CA: Sage.

Slater, M. D., & Rouner, D. (1996). How message evaluation and source attributes may influence credibility assessment and belief change. *Journalism and Mass Communication Quarterly, 73,* 974-991.

Sutton, S. (1998). Predicting and explaining intentions and behavior: How well are we doing? *Journal of Applied Social Psychology, 28,* 1317-1338.

Tapper, J. (1995). The ecology of cultivation: A conceptual model for cultivation research. *Communication Theory, 5,* 36-57.

Tetlock, P. E., & Levi, A. (1982). Attribution bias: On the inconclusiveness of the cognition-motivation debate. *Journal of Experimental Social Psychology, 18,* 68-88.

Tichenor, P. J., & Wackman, D. B. (1973). Mass media and community public opinion. *American Behavioral Scientist, 16,* 593-606.

Toch, H., & Klofas, J. (1984). Pluralistic ignorance, revisited. In G. M. Stephenson & J. H. Davis (Eds.), *Progress in applied social psychology* (Vol. 2, pp. 129-159). New York: John Wiley.

Tversky, A., & Kahneman, D. (1974). Judgment under uncertainty: Heuristics and biases. *Science, 185,* 1124-1131.

Vallone, R. P., Ross, L., & Lepper, M. R. (1985). The hostile media phenomenon: Biased perception and perceptions of media bias in coverage of the Beirut massacre. *Journal of Personality and Social Psychology, 49,* 577-585.

Weinraub, B. (1999, September 20). Outrage over White casts spurs TV to add ethnicity. *Santa Barbara News Press, pp.* A1, A10.

Weinstein, N. D. (1980). Unrealistic optimism about future life events. *Journal of Personality and Social Psychology, 39,* 806-820.

West, D. M. (1991). Polling effects in election campaigns. *Political Behavior, 13,* 151-163.

32

The Role of Meaning Construction in the Process of Persuasion for Viewers of Television Images

JOHN E. NEWHAGEN

> The Jesuit dean asks Stephen if the fire in the fireplace, while pleasing
> to the eye, is therefore beautiful. He answers, "In so far as it is
> apprehended by the sight, which I suppose means here esthetic intellection.
> In hell, however, it is an evil."
>
> —*A Portrait of the Artist as a Young Man (Joyce, 1966, p. 186)*

The sun does not persuade me of its warmth, nor does the wind on my brow persuade me of the coming storm; their meaning is apparent and extant. However, if persuasion is defined to be the intentional effort at influencing another's mental state through communication (O'Keefe, 1990), then nearly everything outside of direct sensory experience qualifies (O'Keefe, 1990). Critical theory supports this notion when it challenges the idea that there can be a fixed or intrinsic relationship between words and the world (Gergen, 1994). From this view, *any* information communicated to me in messages based on some symbol system is, at a fundamental level, an effort to persuade, and only information from the "here and now" of direct sensory experience is real (Worth & Gross, 1974). Worth and Gross (1974) made the distinction between direct sensory experience and the symbolic representation of information as well. They recognized that a television message is not the same as "being there," but they made a curious exception by stating that an image from a fixed television camera would be as veridical as sensory experience. They recognized that cuts, pans, and other production techniques add meaning, but they missed the point that *any* television message is no more than luminescent images radiating from the phosphorus coating on the picture tube and is in no sense real. Media critic Jean Baudrillard said the question of whether or not television is "as good as real" is not really interesting (Baudrillard, 1983). Television is, in a psychological sense, better than real—or what he called "hyperreal."

At first blush, the application of cognitive psychology to the study of television, which has come to be known as the "information processing perspective," might seem a strange bedfellow for the postmodernist view. However, the power of the information processing perspective is that it shows the psychological mechanisms that convince us that television images are the same as those from the "here and now" and therefore worthy of belief. The dynamics of evolution mandate that our cognitive systems operate quickly and accurately to ensure our survival. One way in which this end is accomplished is by using outputs of early stages of sensory processing, and organisms need not question perceptions because they are, for the most part, faithful representations of reality (Gilbert, 1991). However, information embedded in symbols, such as natural language, comes under more effortful and time-consuming cognitive scrutiny. Bem's (1970) discussion of beliefs echoes this notion: "Our faith in the validity of our sensory experience is the most important primitive belief of all" (p. 5). He called a belief based on direct sensory perception "zero order," where all higher order beliefs involve the processing of verbal information.

Working from this view, the persuasive portion of a television message is frequently conceptualized to reside solely in verbal content. For instance, a political spot may be deemed "negative" if it features a verbal attack on the opponent (Kern, 1989). Petty and Cacioppo (1981) supported this notion when they conceptualized an attitude as a meta-assessment resulting in a "general and enduring positive or negative feeling" about a belief. Implicit in this conceptualization of an attitude is the assumption that assessment involves the processing of natural language, a complex and high-order cognitive activity. However, focusing solely on the narrative overlooks television's single most distinguishing feature—its ability to generate a real-time stream of images—and failing to study images for their persuasive effects would be to overlook McLuhan's (1964/1994) mantra that "the medium *is* the message." However, the assessment of hedonic valence, whether positive or negative, takes place in primitive areas of the brain within only a few milliseconds after an object comes into the visual field. Thus, distinctions separating attitude from belief, or even high-order from zero-order beliefs, might not play out in terms of the way in which we actually processes information and construct meaning from it. On the other hand, Newhagen and Reeves (1992) conceptualized the negativity of a political television spot in terms of the ability of images to elicit negative emotion in the viewer, regardless of narrative content. That work represents an example of research that has looked at the effects of television from an information processing perspective. While that stream of research spans back 15 years, it is just now being recognized for its value in the study of communication processes such as persuasion (see Newhagen, 1999a).

The information processing paradigm plays off an important paradox; while television viewing is frequently conceptualized as passive or lazy, the viewer has to make sense out of a complex stream of sounds and images in real time. The viewer does so by employing a set of psychological heuristics, or shortcuts, that may have profound effects on the construction of meaning and in persuasion. This stream of research can roughly be divided into three categories: the study of emotion-laden images (e.g., images of human death and suffering), the study of formal production features (e.g., cuts, pans, shot pacing), and interface characteristics (e.g., screen size). An important feature of this body of research is that it looks primarily at the effects of the nonverbal component of the television message, especially its images. In some cases, this research uses concepts familiar to the social psychological field such as attitude and belief. But in most cases, it does not, embracing instead concepts more familiar to cognitive psychology such as memory and attention.

At first glance, this perspective may appear to have reduced the viewing experience to a level below where meaning construction takes place. Some might argue that studying television frame by frame, at 33-millisecond intervals, is not interesting because it does not help to explain processes such as persuasion. One response to that critique is that a great deal of belief and attitude formation takes place very rapidly and below conscious awareness. Biocca (1991) pointed out that "an eon of processing" goes on in the course of a 30-second political spot. A second response would be to point out that the operational *unit* of measure in such work ought not be confused with the theoretical *level* of analysis. While responses to stimuli may sometimes be measured in millisecond units, the effects are still inferred at the level of the individual viewer, the standard for most work on persuasion. Cappella (1991) pointed out that a science should not be equated with its methods; rather, a science should be equated with the kinds of knowledge claims it establishes. While the information processing approach does deal with concepts such as emotion as heuristic processes, going on very rapidly and largely below the conscious awareness, it still

regards meaning as something that resides at the level of the individual viewer. Furthermore, it might be argued that attention and memory, concepts central to the information processing perspective, are not key to the study of persuasion. But cognitive models place attention and memory right at the heart of the process of meaning creation (Biocca, 1991). Biocca (1991) pointed out that meaning does not exist within the television message itself; rather, it is constructed by the psychological processes of attention and memory inside the viewer's head. Meaning is the activation of a set of semantic links associated in memory triggered by the use of signs. Persuasive television messages, such as political spots, do not contain meaning; they evoke it. Because of the centrality of these concepts to persuasion, it ought not be surprising that Krugman's (1977) seminal work on the preattentive processing of television was first published in an advertising journal. In that article, he described a viewer with limited cognitive resources confronting a constantly changing stream of sound and image. Krugman's work really gave psychological substance to Packard's (1980) idea of the "hidden persuaders" in contemporary media.

This chapter looks at how both the theory and method of studying the effects of television from an information processing perspective can be useful to the study of persuasion by first looking at the theoretical contribution it has to make, especially in the areas of attention and memory. It then turns to a discussion of how emotion-evoking content, production techniques, and the television interface itself affect the meaning construction process. Finally, it looks at how the information processing paradigm can be brought to bear on the task of building a more general theory of narrative structure, which includes both verbal and nonverbal information, to deal with the issue of persuasion in converging media technologies.

THE THEORETICAL CONTRIBUTION OF THE INFORMATION PROCESSING APPROACH

Social psychology has made an important contribution to our study of persuasion since Carl Hovland and his Yale University group created the field during the 1940s (Rogers, 1994). Petty and Cacioppo (1981) detailed progress since then in areas such as message learning, judgmental, attributional, and motivational approaches. Many of those perspectives continue to be active in some form today. But however useful persuasion research has been during the past 60 years, it has a shortcoming: It tends to "black box" the actual mental processes on which its theories are grounded. That fact ought not be surprising given that, during this same era, behavioral psychology generally black boxed internal mental processes in favor of an emphasis on an operant approach, concerned only with inputs and outputs or responses to stimuli. But the urge to peer inside the black box has always been strong, and Cappella and Street (1988) went so far as to say that many early social psychological models were simplistic "closet" cognitive theories (Thorson, 1989). Thorson (1989) pointed out that much of the research into the persuasive effects of television advertising simply ignores modeling concepts about cognitive processing, even though they are central to hypothesized outcomes. As an example she used cognitive consistency theory, which models how a message is represented and how message features are integrated with existing attitudes or belief systems.

However, experimental psychology moved away from behaviorism and toward cognitive processing models (Greenwald, 1992). This shift in theoretical framework resulted in enormous strides in the understanding of psychological processes such as vision (Marr, 1968), memory (Schacter, 1989), and attention (Allport, 1989)—processes thought to be so complex as to be insoluble problems just a generation before. More recently, cognitive psychology has become so ambitious as to model the process of consciousness itself (Nelson, 1996).

Adapting cognitive models to communication ought not be a great leap because understanding how individuals process messages should be central to any comprehensive theory for the field (Geiger & Newhagen, 1994). As self-evident as this statement may seem, communication research has been slow in adopting an information processing approach to the conceptualization of mass media effects. The approach presents a unique characterization of individuals and of media messages. Conceptually, it emphasizes the way in which people make sense of, attend to, remember, and are persuaded by television messages. Television messages, in turn, are defined to have psychological dimensions and attributes that are likely to influence these processes. These attributes include how a message is constructed and presented in addition to the more traditional notions of content and program genre. Persuasion research has looked at the component processes within the black box as intermediate stages between message reception and the traditional outcomes of learning, attitudes, and behaviors. Instead, an information processing perspective views these component processes as both important outcomes and predictors in their own right. In short, the perennial black box of persuasion can be better illuminated by examining the information processing that goes on within it.

OUTCOMES: ATTENTION AND MEMORY FOR TELEVISION

The centrality of memory and attention as outcomes in the study of persuasion might not be obvious. It could be argued that the use of memory as a dependent variable in the study of television advertising, for instance, is more a matter of convenience than of choice. The advertiser's prepotent objective is to persuade the viewer to purchase its product or service. Experience has shown, however, that the purchasing decision is influenced by any number of different factors both within media and elsewhere. The same can be said for messages to promote a public health program or a candidate running for office. The truth is that memory and attention are the best and most reliable measures of the effects of a single exposure to a televised appeal. This, however, overlooks the importance of both memory and attention to the process of persuasion.

Attention for Television

Cognitive models of attention and memory have lent themselves well to communication research because of their centrality to any theory of media effects and because the very idea of mere exposure suggests that a message must first be attended to and then remembered. The work from this perspective places two important constraints on assumptions about media exposure. These are that (a) the message stream is extremely complex and (b) the message receiver has limited cognitive resources to make sense out of it. These two constraints impose the paradox of the passive viewer making sense of a complex message stream and compels the viewer to employ psychological heuristics that run in the background of consciousness to husband cognitive resources. Thus, a viewer may be processing information in a television message without being consciously aware of attending to it—what Krugman (1977) called "pre-attentive processing." Early persuasion models did not always make that important distinction. For example, Roberts and Maccoby's (1973) idea

of counterarguing seems to model viewers as consciously attending to persuasive appeals and rehearsing defenses to them by talking to themselves. What the theory does not consider is the idea that the entire counterarguing process could be going on at a more subtle pre-attentive level. Fink (1988) called processing at this level "mere exposure."

A third constraint critical to this perspective is that processing goes on in parallel and is distributed throughout the brain, modeled by connectionists as a vast multilayered network of information nodes (McClelland & Rumelhart, 1987). One of the important implications of the parallel distributed process model is that it allows for the television viewer to allocate attentional resources to more than one thing at a time. This capacity helps to further explain the "lazy viewer, complex message" paradox because being able to attend to more than one message feature at a time increases processing efficiency. This position challenges persuasion theories that model attention as a linear serial process such as "issue versus image" studies in political television advertising (Garramone, 1984) that pit attention to information embedded in the narrative against information embedded in the image stream (see, e.g., Garramone, 1984). While that distinction might prove meaningful to the researcher, it might not have much meaning for the way in which viewers process such ads if they have the capacity to deal with both information streams simultaneously.

Memory for Television

Is memory an interesting process in the study of persuasion? Here, the advantage of unpacking memory's black box is the ability to look at discrete stages of remembering—including encoding, storage, and retrieval—and apply them to issues surrounding persuasion. Take, for example, Festinger's (1957) classic discussion of cognitive dissonance. Festinger detailed a number of ways in which people may deal with information dissonant to their own worldview, including ignoring it and adjusting existing attitudes to accommodate it. However compelling his theory is even today, it still begs the question of just where and how the processes he described take place. From an information processing perspective, ignoring would constitute filtering and would probably take place during encoding, while attitude adjustment would likely take place during recall.

Information processing models memories as associative schematic networks (Anderson & Bower, 1973). Those models have only been reinforced by the connectionist view, which specifies how those schemata are arranged in layers and suggests a number of algorithms they may use to "learn" (Hinton & Anderson, 1981). The structure of memory is a function of the strength of the connections between the nodes; when one node becomes active, the activity spreads throughout the network according to the differential strengths of the connections within it. This can be demonstrated simply by a little free association. Activate a node by saying the name "Winston Churchill," and then see what happens. If "cigar," "England," and "World War II" come to mind, then those nodes have strong connections with the cue.

An information processing view of meaning construction can even accommodate critical theorists such as Jacques Derrida and Roland Barthes, who have contended that all meaning is context dependent (see Landow, 1992). From this view, *any* memory is what Bem (1970) called a belief, and attitudes are the output of the meta-assessments of them. Even the most straightforward newspaper report has to be seen as an attempt to persuade the reader that some event happened in the manner rendered by the author (Newhagen & Levy, 1998). Roeh (1989) pointed out that idea to journalists when he reminded them that they are storytellers in the fullest sense.

The insight to be gained from peering into the black box can again be seen in the transition of agenda-setting theory (McCombs & Shaw, 1972) to issue framing (Iyengar & Kinder, 1987). Agenda setting goes so far as to claim that media tell news consumers what to think about, but it stops short of saying how that process takes place (McCombs & Shaw, 1972). Issue framing expands on agenda setting to the degree that it models the actual process of viewer cognition and suggests that the context in which an issue is presented can affect the way in which the news is remembered (Iyengar & Kinder, 1987).

Chaiken's (1980) work modeling heuristic information processing of message source cues versus systematic processing of message content represents one of the earliest applications of schema theory to persuasion (Cacioppo & Petty, 1985). Cacioppo and Petty's (1985) Elaboration Likelihood Model (ELM) of persuasion extends that idea to what they called the central and peripheral routes to persuasion. The central route has to do with information in the narrative portion of a persuasive appeal, and the peripheral route has to do with nonverbal information such as the expertise or attractiveness of the message giver. Their model depicts two information steams: one in the foreground and the other in the field of the message receiver's cognition. Under some circumstances, peripheral cues, such as positive or negative cues not associated with the intrinsic appeal, can affect acceptance. The authors' research did not, however, come to terms with the issue of just what causes the switch between central and peripheral cues. While Petty, Cacioppo, and Kasmer (1988) expanded their discussion of the ELM to include emotion, it is in this area that information processing theory really picks up where social psychology leaves off in the study of persuasion.

THE ROLE OF EMOTION

Emotion plays a role in advertising, politics, health communication, and virtually any other form of persuasive communication. The Jeffersonian democratic tradition, with its foundations stretching back as far as Milton, elevates reason to be "good" in that logic drives decision, while persuasion is "bad" because it is driven by emotion. However, information processing theory challenges the value of the emotion-reason dichotomy on two grounds. First, information-evoking emotion can also be "good," especially if the cognitive system is under stress. Second, a growing body of research shows that electronic media users simultaneously process a complex stream of *both* rational and emotional information (Geiger & Newhagen, 1994). There is even evidence coming from neuropsychology that emotion may play a key role in integrating reason, acting as the bedrock on which consciousness itself is formed (Watt, 1998).

From the functionalist perspective on which information processing theory resides, emotion represents an internal alarm system to warn of problems that demand attention and immediate real-time resolutions. Emotion is, perhaps, the psychological heuristic key to human survival. Remember that information processing models place a limited resource organism in a potentially dangerous, complex, and volatile information ecology. To the degree that reason is a serial process and is resource demanding, it might not be able to generate adaptive behavioral decisions in time to face imminent threat. On the other hand, limited or fragmentary information is sufficient to activate emotional "action states" that provoke approach-avoidance behaviors appropriate to survival (Frijda, 1988). In this sense, emotion is as good as, or even better than, reason in solving some problems.

Of course, emotion evolved prior to the invention of mass media and was intended to guard against "real" threats such as the appearance of a predator. The astonishing thing, which most of us take for granted, is that television viewers respond to emotion-evoking images on the screen of a cathode ray tube just as they do to the same stimuli in real life (Reeves & Nass, 1996). Doubters of this proposition ought to pause and consider the impact of the images of commercial jetliners smashing into the sides of the World Trade Center buildings. For instance, viewer approach-avoidance ratings of images that elicit discrete negative emotion in television news mirror responses to the same stimuli in real life (Newhagen, 1998b). Newhagen's (1998b) study showed that images of anger elicit approach responses to the screen, while images of fear and disgust elicit avoidance responses. Work looking at emotion in terms of its intensity and valence has generated similar results (Lang, Newhagen, & Reeves, 1996; Lang, Pinkleton, & Newhagen, 1994).

Emotion-evoking stimuli on television have the potential to be "bad" to the degree that they evoke emotions in the viewer not appropriate to his or her real-life surroundings. Gerbner, Gross, Morgan, and Signorielli (1980) is perhaps the best-known example of such a theory, where excessive depictions of violence on television can "persuade" viewers that the world is a more dangerous place than it really is (Newhagen & Reeves, 1992).

While information processing tends to stress memory and attention as outcomes, more attention is being given to variables more commonly associated with persuasion. For instance, Bucy and Newhagen (1999) examined how television viewers assess how appropriate a public figure's emotional response is to a news event. Research participants first viewed a news story and then an image of President Clinton. Both the emotion of the images in the news story and of Clinton's response were varied for both their valence and their intensity. Viewers reported that they found Clinton's responses to be inappropriate if the emotional valence of his reaction did not match that of the news story. Furthermore, they generally found *any* highly intense response from Clinton to be inappropriate, regardless of the preceding news story. In concrete terms, this suggests that politicians will be the most persuasive when they project themselves as being moderately aroused. Newhagen (1994) integrated both memory and counterarguing as dependent variables into his study of the censorship disclaimers in Persian Gulf War news. Television networks included a short 5-second disclaimer in the lower left-hand corner of the screen when a story was censored. The study first examined whether the disclaimers were even noticed by viewers and hypothesized that if the disclaimers were being processed as "noise" in the image rather than for their narrative content, they would negatively affect memory for the images in the story. Second, it was hypothesized that if the disclaimers were being processed for their verbal content, viewers would counterargue against the story's theme. Results show that viewers did indeed process the disclaimers, listing more negative thoughts about stories with disclaimers than for stories without disclaimers, even though they could not remember seeing the disclaimers. The inclusion of the information processing perspective in the study helped to demonstrate that the messages were being processed into memory below conscious awareness, a result that would not have been obvious if the study had been conducted using only counterarguing as a measure.

The information processing perspective did not bring the study of emotion to persuasion; affect has long been central to the topic. Looking inside the black box has, however, given considerable insight into our understanding of the role that emotion plays in persuasion. Information processing explicates the idea of emotion as a discrete state within the viewer rather than as a feature of the message. A political ad is only "negative" or "positive" in that it has certain qualities that elicit emotion in the viewer. Viewer emotion is then conceptualized as a psychological state that can have profound effects on the meaning of persuasive appeals.

The Role of Formal Production Features

Looking at how production features can contribute to meaning construction addresses McLuhan's (1964/1994) point that the medium is the message most directly. This is because production features, such as cuts, pans, and shot angles, have to do with the way in which a television's images are assembled rather than with the content of the images themselves. Those techniques are used to construct narrative meaning in a television message in the same way as paragraphs and chapters are used in a text. As obvious as that might seem on its surface, it is less apparent to the viewer when it comes time to make veracity or credibility assessments. This is due, in large part, to the fact that the maxim "seeing is believing" has substantial psychological credulity. Evolution has equipped us to act quickly, and as noted earlier, one way in which this end is accomplished is by using outputs of early stages of processing to guide urgent action; we need not question perception because, for the most part, it is a faithful representation of reality (Gilbert, 1991). In the real world, that makes sense, and the maxim "I couldn't believe my own eyes" gives credence to the idea that we can and should believe direct sensory experience.

But it makes much less sense when the images are mediated, and advances in digital technology make it increasingly easy for the message producers to manipulate content both within and between images, making the impossible possible and the unbelievable believable. Opinion polls asking respondents to rate the credibility of news sources during the past 40 years bear this idea out, with television consistently rated as more credible than newspapers (Newhagen & Nass, 1989).

Structurally, television viewers could not be more mistaken when they say they actually *saw* an event take place on television. A television news story about the terrorist attacks on the World Trade Center, for instance, is as much a narrative reconstruction of an event as is a textual account in a newspaper. Note that newspaper readers would report that they *read* about the event and not that they *saw* it, even if the story were accompanied by still photographs.

Reeves, Thorson, & Rothschild, (1985) pioneered work in this field by showing how scene changes affected alpha brain waves and caused the viewer to orient to the screen. The fact that such a technique can trigger this response is of considerable importance because it is so basic to the human psychology of attention. Orienting is a response to the idea that it is imperative to turn toward any dramatic change in the information ecology, be it a loud sound or a sudden flash (Lang, 1990). Geiger and Reeves (1992) extended that work by showing that the cuts cause viewer arousal, measured by heart rate, to increase (Geiger & Reeves, 1993). Geiger and Reeves (1993) found that viewers oriented after a cut if the new material was semantically related to the previous material. On the other hand, they found that the length of time spent viewing an initial message influences attention to an unexpected cut such as an abrupt shift to a commercial. The longer the interval of initial viewing, the longer it takes the viewer to orient to the new material. Subjectively, viewers reported that a dynamic presentation (i.e., one with a lot of cuts) is more pleasing than a static

one (Geiger & Reeves, 1992). However, that is true only up to the point where the presentation becomes so complex as to be difficult to view. The actual time required to orient to material after a cut is about 1 second. Those who argue that such an epoch is too short to be important to the processes of persuasion should reflect on the fact that political spots, packed with cuts, last only 15 or 30 seconds.

The Role of the Interface

While the term has more currency in the study of computers than in that of other technologies, all media can be described in terms of a discrete interface. In this broad sense, a media interface is the place where information is physically embodied; for newspapers it is paper and ink, and for television it is the screen. Laurel (1991) used the theater stage as a metaphor for a computer interface, but the idea works equally well for television. From the perspective of the viewer, if the presentation "works," then the interface is "all there is." This view isolates the viewing experience from the technology behind and the "noise" around the interface. Similar to the theatrical notion of *suspension of belief,* the more immersive a presentation is, the more persuasive it will be.

Important interface features include screen size and resolution and sound reproduction. In the real world, an object's size matters because if it is big and/or close, it could be dangerous. Reeves and Nass (1996) proposed the credo that "big is good" and pointed out that the tallest candidate for president has won every election but two since the 1860s. Detenber and Reeves (1996) found presentations on big screens to be arousing, better remembered, and better liked than images on small screens. They also found that horizontal screens, such as those employed by high-definition television, were liked better than conventional square screens. Lombard, Reich, Grabe, and Bolmarcich Ditton (1999) found that screen size affects viewers' sense of presence for the television presentation. Viewers reported presentations on large screens to be more enjoyable and had a greater sense of physical movement, excitement, involvement, and participation than did viewers of the same images on small screens.

Audio and video fidelity also play a part, as Reeves, Detenber, and Steuer (1993) found that enhancing the audio fidelity of a television presentation increased attention and liking. Perhaps the most counterintuitive finding in this area is that image resolution does not seem to make a difference to memory, attention, or liking for television images (Lang, 1995). Research participants could not even tell the difference between very high- and low-quality images (Reeves et al., 1993).

THE METHODOLOGICAL CONTRIBUTION OF INFORMATION PROCESSING THEORY

A full discussion of information processing has to include the methodological contribution it has made to the study of television. On its surface, the biggest difference between research in this area and much of mass media effects research is that the method of choice in the former is the laboratory experiment rather than the survey or field experiment. Much of the criticism of effects research can be viewed as a critique of the limitations of the survey. However, the difference between information processing research and traditional media effects research has more to do with measurement technique than with method. Media effects research, including persuasion studies, usually have relied on some form of self-report, which is limited in that the respondent must have access to the information

demanded by the task and then be able to articulate it verbally. As has been shown time and time again by research done from an information processing perspective, many—if not most—of the key psychological processes of interest go on below conscious awareness and very rapidly, thus excluding self-report as a viable data retrieval strategy (for example, see Newhagen & Newhagen, 2000). Instead, research in the area has borrowed heavily from the implicit measures used in cognitive psychology (for a discussion of an application to psychology, see Bower & Clapper, 1989; for a discussion of an application to communication research, see Lang, 1994). Reeves, Thorson, and Schleuder's (1985) discussion of "online" measures of attention used an electroencephalogram (EEG) to monitor alpha brain waves as a measure of attention to television. At the time the research was done, the actual apparatus employed was both expensive and cumbersome. While the apparatus for physiological measurement remains relatively high, advances in personal computing have reduced both complexity and cost substantially. For example, personal computers have been used with considerable success in monitoring heart rate as a measure of attention, where subtle differences between systolic and diastolic blood pressure predict emotional readiness (see Lang & Thorson, 1992).

Perhaps the most cost-effective techniques in this category are latency to response and response to secondary task measures. Both can be implemented using a standard personal computer, a game paddle, and a nominal amount of peripheral equipment such as a television time code reader-generator (for an implementation, see Newhagen, 1993). The latency to respond measure of memory works on the assumption that the stronger a memory, the more rapidly an individual will be able to recall it, while the secondary task measure assumes that the more attention an individual pays to a presentation, the slower he or she will be at responding to a tone or other secondary task. Davidson (1992) pointed out that many of the facial manifestations of emotion last only 1 to 2 seconds and recommended that the ideal measure of their effects be in units shorter than 1 second. Typically, the measures employed from this perspective yield results with millisecond accuracy.

BACK TO THE FUTURE: THE ROLE OF NARRATIVE IN PERSUASION

The past few years have seen the rise of the Internet as a communication media in its own right. Among the most prominent technological advances that accompanied its development is the ability to digitize *all* information— be it images, sounds, or text—and integrate it into one convergent message stream (Negroponte, 1995). Having said that, if one takes the keyboard away from a personal computer, it looks a lot like a television receiver. This is good news to the degree that the literature reviewed here concerning the study of television from an information processing perspective should map straight onto the study of the Internet. (It is interesting to note that image resolution, the one big difference between computer and television displays, does not appear to make much difference in memory, attention, or liking.) However, the bad news is that conceptual problems with the persuasion literature on television may also bleed across into the study of the Internet. That could be expected because it is not unusual for theory to lag behind the actual implementation of news technologies (Newhagen, 1998a).

The curious thing about the Internet is that while the computer looks physically similar to the television in many respects, the computer tends to be a text-dominant medium (Bolter,

1991). One might argue that the importance of text to the Internet just has to do with the fact that, early in its development, the technology did not exist to do images well. However, even though advances in graphical user interfaces (GUIs) have made the Internet browsers easier to use, text seems to persist, especially when information becomes very dense. It would be ironic if information processing theory turned attention to the study of images and other nonverbal information on the Internet just as the narrative returns to prominence. To avoid this is important to be sure that as media technologies converge, the conceptual agenda for persuasion research converges as well, generating a general theoretical framework that can span across both technological platforms and message structure.

Convergence and Persuasion

The tension between image and text brings persuasion research back to a fundamental problem that has plagued it from the outset: Conceptually, where does content reside? Nabi (1999) described the problem in terms of the dichotomy between emotional and rational appeals and sought a model that will accommodate both. Her cognitive functional model states that the emotional component of a message will be subject to heuristic processing, while the rational portion is subject to what she calls information processing. Furthermore, the model accommodates the idea that the two are interactive and that both information streams are processed simultaneously. But the model still falls short because, like much traditional persuasion research, Nabi reified both emotion and reason as being message attributes rather than psychological constructs. The task is to identify message attributes that constitute "content" in the sense that they can affect the meaning that the viewer or user constructs from them.

What do "rational" and "emotional" mean? If a rational appeal is defined to include deliberate and conscious thought, then we may be disappointed to discover that very little in life fits that bill. Jaynes (1990) pointed out that much of what we consider high-order mental activity, including problem solving, does not necessarily require conscious awareness. Furthermore, deliberate conscious thought is inefficient to the degree that it is linear, serial, logic bound, and generally effortful, which means trouble for the user if the media system exerts any real-time pressure as both television and the Internet do. Much of persuasion literature describing "rational" appeals make two important assumption: that the message receiver is consciously aware of it and that the "content" of the message resides in a verbal narrative. In the same vein, "emotional" appeals are messages that contain nonverbal "content" that produces emotion in the message receiver, which in turn may affect the way in which the message is processed. In either case, it is important to be clear that the message itself does not in any sense contain emotion or reason. There can be emotion-eliciting messages or thought-provoking appeals, but the processes of emotion and reason reside within the viewer or user. Adopting this perspective moves the rational-emotional dichotomy away from the message to the message processor. Here, a distinction between verbal and nonverbal information streams may better describe the messages and the reason or emotion they generate within the message processor.

What is the modality problem? Another important distinction, also frequently convoluted in the discussion of persuasion, is sensory modality. In media effects research, this problem is made manifest in redundancy studies, where memory is generally better if information in the visual stream is redundant to information in the audio stream (Lang, 1995).

Here, the problem is that the modality of the technological platform's interface is convoluted with the representational structure of the information encoded within it. That is, information contained in the audio track is assumed to contain natural language, while the video track contains nonverbal images (David, 1998). Communication research is not the only place where this problem crops up; it is central to psychology as well. Paivio (1986) based his theory of dual processing on the idea that aural information is processed by different mental systems than is visual information. However, on closer examination, what Paivio (1986) was talking about was speech, or verbal information coded into the aural stream, and images, or nonverbal information coded into the visual stream. Thus, there appears to be at least three orthogonal dimensions having to do with modality and/or message representation convoluted in the study of persuasive appeals: verbal-nonverbal, visual-sound, and rational-emotional.

What and where is content? The issue becomes one of clarifying what we really mean by the idea of message content. First, messages do not think and feel; viewers and users think and feel. Second, the role of conscious awareness in thinking is overstated and might not even be a factor in the processing of the majority of persuasive appeals. Third, television and Internet message producers create "content," which is *always* intended to be persuasive, to the degree that they embed meaning in symbols. Television and the Internet are especially persuasive to the degree that they can fool the message receiver's psychological apparatus into processing mediated information as if it were the result of direct sensory experience. Simply stated message content is either representational or extant. This scheme allows for issues of processing style and sensory modality to be integrated into a broader discussion of narrative content.

		Sensory Modality	
		Vision	Sound
Representational System	Verbal	I Text on Screen	II Spoken Words
	Non-Verbal	III Emotion-laden images Production Techniques	IV Emotion-laden sounds Production Techniques

Figure 32.1. Representational System, Sensory Modality, and Narrative Form

The Role of the Narrative in the Creation of Content

The implicit assumption that the direct route to persuasion resides in the verbal portion of television appeals is the correct assumption that the narrative is the most effective way to tell a story and that stories are effective vehicles for persuasion. Aristotle (1941) described the narrative as having a beginning, a middle, and an end. The classic dramatic curve extends the idea to include an introduction, rising action, a climax, and denouement. Convergent technologies suggest theories of narration in much broader terms, as the very architecture of semiotic meaning (Taborsky, 1998). From this view, all knowledge is organized into inclusive metanarrative codes, ranging from the heuristics of emotion to the processes of logical reason. Narrative structure is the technology of content creation and can be conceptualized as programming. At a biological level, the program is DNA; at a psychological level, the programs are heuristic; and at a societal level, the programs are norms and customs. This view allows for the consideration of a system of simultaneous meaning creation across a broad range of mental processes.

Figure 32.1 shows how unpacking the distinction between sensory modality and representational systems yields the narrative architectures, or programs, used in meaning creation of Internet and television messages.

I. *Verbal Symbols Encoded in the Visual Stream: Narrative as Text on Screen.* Television is notoriously bad at doing this, and when it is attempted, text tends to be large, bold, and simple. One example would be the censorship disclaimers placed in the bottom left-hand corner of news during the Persian Gulf War such as "censored by Iraq." The surprising thing about this particular example is that the viewers in an experiment actually did process the disclaimers for their verbal meaning despite not remembering the appearance of the disclaimers on the screen (Newhagen, 1994). More complex examples of text on television, such as the boiler plate at the end of some automobile leasing ads, is ludicrously difficult to read and surely appears only at the behest of someone's legal department. Rarely, if ever, will a textual narrative appear on a television screen. The narratives that once introduced feature films seem not to have made the cut on television.

The Internet, however, may prove to be an able vehicle for narration, largely because high-quality screen resolution makes text more readable than does television. Landow (1992) saw the nonlinear text, or hypertext, as a revolution in narrative form. He proposed that the Internet has the capacity to liberate text in the sense suggested by critical theory.

Hypertext also embodies the potential for interactivity between message senders and receivers. Widely regarded as the single most distinguishing feature of the Internet, the implications of an interactive media system pose perhaps the richest area for research persuasion. The heritage of persuasion research, spanning back to World War I, has nearly always worked from the assumption that the message receiver was passive (see Lippmann, 1922), an idea that will now have to be reconsidered in the context of an active user engaged with an interactive medium. To date, most research in the area has focused on content analysis tests for the presence or absence of interactivity in discrete Internet genres such as e-mail, bulletin boards, and chat groups. Massey and Levy (1999), for instance, looked at the interactivity of Asian online newspapers. A larger challenge will be to assess how interactivity effects persuasion. For instance, Newhagen (1999b) found that for both newspapers and television, perceived credibility predicted information usefulness. However, for online news, interactivity displaced credibility as the best predictor of information usefulness.

II. *Verbal Symbols Encoded in the Aural Stream: Narrative as the Spoken Word.* This is perhaps the most studied cell for television, where the verbal narrative is assumed to hold the persuasive appeal. This is the ELM's "central route" to processing, while emotional cues (Cell III) represent the "peripheral route"(Cacioppo & Petty, 1985).

The spoken word is just now coming to the Internet, held back primarily by the constraint of information bandwidth. Currently, the only spoken words an Internet user is likely to hear are glib announcements such as America Online's greeting, "You've got mail." A good case can be made that, all other things being equal, the written narrative is superior to the spoken narrative because it allows more deliberation and separation from the physical presence of the message source. It will be interesting to see to what degree the spoken narrative is employed as bandwidth increases.

III. *Nonverbal Images and Production Features: Emotion-Laden Images as Narrative.* This cell has come under the most scrutiny in the information processing approach to television viewing and can be thought of as the study of either within-image or between-image content. Within-image content focuses on the study of the effects of emotion-laden images, while between-image content studies the use of production features such as cuts and pans. The main insight to be gained from this strain of research is that television has the capacity to represent images in such a way as to be processed by the viewer as if they were real. While progress has been made in the areas of memory and attention, which are central to persuasion, images have not been studied for their persuasive character per se. They are more frequently studied in terms of how they might color the processing of a verbal appeal. This is especially evident in research into person perception (see, e.g., Bassili, 1989; Fiske, 1980). One route to bringing the information processing perspective to bear on persuasion would be to conceptualize the psychological heuristics that come into play as "grammars." Doing so would help to explain why nonverbal images are so powerful in the sense that the viewer is employing psychological programs, or meta-narratives, intended for use in real life.

Policy makers and academics frequently call for the inclusion of "visual literacy" courses in the curricula of schools and universities. However, by their nature, nothing short of turning away from the television set will alter the effects of these heuristic programs.

The idea of a nonverbal "grammar" is more intuitive when thinking about how production techniques can be used to construct a nonverbal narrative. Cuts, pans, fades, and other techniques give viewers cues about relationships in time and space. The study of production features looks at how the basic narrative units are assembled. The cut has been the most carefully examined technique used to shift between scenes, perhaps because it represents the most radical shift in image content. Some work has been done in this area. For instance, Lopez (1994) applied standard narrative structure (i.e., introduction, rising action, climax, and resolution) to images in television news stories while holding the verbal narrative constant. She discovered that information was more memorable for stories organized as traditional narrative than for stories using the journalistic "inverted pyramid."

Much of the work in this area should map directly onto research for the Internet, but the added dimension of interactivity should play an important role here as it does in Cell I. It is not hard to imagine an interface that allows the user, either above or below conscious attention, to essentially do his or her own video editing in real time. Murray (1997) described several attempts to do just that, including the highly successful computer game *Myst*.

IV. *Nonverbal Sound and Production Features: Music as Narrative.* There has not been a great deal of research into emotion-laden sound on television, which seems odd given Reeves and Nass's (1996) findings about the importance of sound fidelity on television.

Sound can be as compelling as images in its ability to orient viewers to the screen. The heritage of poor audio reproduction in television receivers may have influenced disinterest in this cell, but that now may change as digitization and more emphasis on reproduction in receivers have vastly increased the presence of audio in television.

Emotion-laden sounds include human, animal, and ecological noises that may be processed as extant and real, just as is the case for compelling images (Newhagen, 1995). Newhagen (1995) looked at the effects of novel sound on memory and attention in a study of television advertisements for a popular battery. The ads featured the unexpected drum beat followed by the intrusion of a pink bunny in what appeared to be appeals for standard household products. By varying the presence or absence of both the image of the bunny and the drum beat accompanying its appearance, the study found that the sound of the drum increased attention to the ads, but the image of the bunny did not. On the other hand, the image of the bunny enhanced memory for the ads, while the sound of the drum did not. This effect may be an artifact of the fact that the human visual and auditory systems evolved separately (Yost, 1992). Thus, a great deal of auditory and visual processing goes on independently and does not integrate into larger meaning schemata until very late stages of cognition.

Another special aspect of sound in this category is music, which clearly has its own rules of grammar and is intended to evoke emotion or mood. Sound engineers employ their own set of production techniques, such as the segue, to achieve their narrative. As subtly persuasive as music can be in enhancing a video production, we might have to be reminded occasionally that real life is not accompanied by a sound track.

Again, results for television research should map well into this cell for the Internet. However, it is not clear how sound can be linked to a highly volatile, user-driven video stream. While the Internet is increasingly being used as a carrier for sound, with the implementation of online radio and the Internet juke box, these applications appear to be convergent with what radio already does but with more user control.

The persuasive effect of simple sounds, such as the "ta-dah" rendered by Windows when it opens, to create mood ought not be overlooked. Sound may play an important part in the way individuals perceive the computer as a social actor, as documented by Reeves and Nass (1996).

Wag the Dog. The 1997 release of *Wag the Dog* gave movie goers a glimpse, however paranoid, of just how far the art of persuasion has come. It features a "spin doctor" working for the presidential reelection campaign who must create a situation that will distract the public from the president's scandalous affairs (Samudrala, 2000). The spin doctor, with the help of movie producer Stanley Motss, manages to convince the public, using the production techniques discussed in this chapter, that America is at war with Albania. The headlines that result from this manipulation soon take precedent over the president's alleged tryst with a young girl. The timing of the movie, by chance or otherwise, coincided with extensive real-world press coverage of President Clinton's sex scandal with White House intern Monica Lewinsky. Protesters in the Middle East were seen brandishing placards inscribed with the movie's title after Clinton authorized missile strikes against suspected guerrilla bases in Afghanistan at the height of the scandal.

The striking thing about the film is its plausibility. The fake news events depicted in the film were created in the fullest sense by employing narrative in each of the cells described in this chapter, including both written and spoken verbal appeals and the use of both image and sound. However fanciful the film might seem, it nevertheless invites the reconsideration of just what persuasion is and how it is accomplished. This chapter has suggested that an information processing perspective might facilitate a view that would renew the "strong effects" agenda that has been so elusive to demonstrate but has lurked behind the study of persuasion for nearly a century.

REFERENCES

Allport, A. (1989). Visual attention. In M. Posner (Ed.), *Foundations of cognitive science* (pp. 631-682). Cambridge, MA: MIT Press.

Anderson, J. R., & Bower, G. H. (1973). *Human associative memory.* Washington, DC: Winston.

Aristotle. (1941). *Poetics.* New York: Random House.

Bassili, J. N. (1989). *On-line cognition in person perception.* Hillsdale, NJ: Lawrence Erlbaum.

Baudrillard, J. (1983). *Simulations.* New York: Semiotext(e).

Bem, D. (1970). *Beliefs, attitudes, and human affairs.* Pacific Grove, CA: Brooks/Cole.

Biocca, F. (1991). Looking for units of meaning in political ads. In F. Biocca (Ed.), *Television and political advertising,* Vol. 2: *Signs, codes, and images* (pp. 17-25). Hillsdale, NJ: Lawrence Erlbaum.

Bolter, J. D. (1991). *Writing space: The computer, hypertext, and the history of writing.* Hillsdale, NJ: Lawrence Erlbaum.

Bower, G., & Clapper, J. (1989). Experimental methods in cognitive science. In M. Posner (Ed.), *Foundations of cognitive science* (pp. 245-300). Cambridge, MA: MIT Press.

Bucy, E. P., & Newhagen, J. E. (1999). The emotional appropriateness heuristic: Viewer assessments of televised presidential reactions to compelling news events. *Journal of Communication,* 49(4), 59-79.

Cacioppo, J., & Petty, R. (1985). Central and peripheral routes to persuasion: The role of message repetition. In L. Alwitt & A. Mitchell

(Eds.), *Psychological processes and advertising effects.* Hillsdale, NJ: Lawrence Erlbaum.

Cappella, J. N. (1991). The biological origins of automated patterns of human interaction. *Communication Theory, 1*(1), 4-35.

Cappella, J. N., & Street, R. (1988). Message effects: Theory and research on mental models of messages. In J. Bradac (Ed.), *Message effects in communication science* (pp. 24-51). Newbury Park, CA: Sage.

Chaiken, S. (1980). Heuristic versus systematic information processing and the use of source versus message cues in persuasion. *Journal of Personality and Social Psychology, 39,* 752-766.

David, P. (1998). News concreteness and visual-verbal association: Do news pictures narrow the real gap between concrete and abstract news? *Human Communication Research, 25,* 180-201.

Davidson, R. (1992). Emotion and affective style: Hemispheric substrates. *Psychological Science, 3,* 39-43.

Detenber, B., & Reeves, B. (1996). A bio-information theory of emotion: Motion and image size effects on viewers. *Journal of Communication, 46*(3), 66-84.

Festinger, L. (1957). *A theory of cognitive dissonance.* Stanford, CA: Stanford University Press.

Fink, E. (1988, May). *Brain asymmetry and the mere exposure effect: The processing of affect without cognition.* Paper presented at the meeting of the International Communication Association, New Orleans, LA.

Fiske, S. (1980). Attention and weight in person perception: The impact of negative and extreme behavior. *Journal of Personality and Social Psychology, 38,* 889-906.

Frijda, N. (1988). The laws of emotion. *American Psychologist, 43,* 349-358.

Garramone, G. (1984). Candidate image formation. In L. L. Kaid, D. Nimmo, & K. R. Sanders (Eds.), *New perspectives on political advertising* (pp. 235-247). Carbondale: Southern Illinois University Press.

Geiger, S., & Newhagen, J. E. (1994). Revealing the black box: Information processing and media effects. In M. R. Levy & M. Gurevitch (Eds.), *Defining media studies* (pp. 284-292). New York: Oxford University Press.

Geiger, S., & Reeves, B. (1992). Evaluation and memory for political candidates in televised commercials. In F. Biocca (Ed.), *Television and political advertising: Psychological processes* (pp. 125-144). Hillsdale, NJ: Lawrence Erlbaum.

Geiger, S., & Reeves, B. (1993). We interrupt this program . . . : Attention for television sequences. *Human Communication Research, 19,* 368-387.

Gerbner, G., Gross, L., Morgan, M., & Signorielli, N. (1980). The mainstreaming of America: Violence Profile No. 11. *Journal of Communication, 30*(3), 10-29.

Gergen, K. J. (1994). Exploring the postmodern: Perils or potentials? *American Psychologist, 49,* 412-416.

Gilbert, D. (1991). How mental systems believe. *American Psychologist, 46,* 107-119.

Greenwald, A. G. (1992). New Look 3: Unconscious cognition reclaimed. *American Psychologist, 47,* 766-779.

Hinton, G. E., & Anderson, J. A. (1981). *Parallel models of associative memory.* Hillsdale, NJ: Lawrence Erlbaum.

Iyengar, S., & Kinder, D. (1987). *News that matters.* Chicago: University of Chicago Press.

Jaynes, J. (1990). *The origin of consciousness in the breakdown of the bicameral mind.* Boston: Houghton Mifflin.

Joyce, J. (1966). *A portrait of the artist as a young man.* New York: Viking.

Kern, M. (1989). *30-second politics: Political advertising in the eighties.* New York: Praeger.

Krugman, H. (1977). Memory without recall: Exposure without perception. *Journal of Advertising Research, 17*(4), 7-12.

Landow, G. P. (1992). *Hypertext: The convergence of contemporary critical theory and technology.* Baltimore, MD: Johns Hopkins University Press.

Lang, A. (1990). Involuntary attention and physiological arousal evoked by structural features and emotional content in TV commercials. *Communication Research, 17,* 275-299.

Lang, A. (1994). *Measuring psychological responses to media messages.* Hillsdale, NJ: Lawrence Erlbaum.

Lang, A. (1995). Defining audio/video redundancy from a limited capacity information processing perspective. *Communication Research, 22*, 86-115.

Lang, A., Newhagen, J. E., & Reeves, B. (1996). Negative video as structure: Emotion, attention, capacity, and memory. *Journal of Broadcasting & Electronic Media, 40*, 460-477.

Lang, A., Pinkleton, B. E., & Newhagen, J. (1994, August). *Categorical and dimensional theories of emotion: How they predict memory for television messages.* Paper presented to the Theory and Methodology division of the Association for Education in Journalism and Mass Communication, Atlanta, GA.

Lang, A., & Thorson, E. (1992). The effects of television videographics and lecture familiarity on adult cardiac orienting responses and memory. *Communication Research, 19*, 346-369.

Laurel, B. (1991). *Computers as theatre.* Reading, MA: Addison-Wesley.

Lippmann, W. (1922). *Public opinion.* New York: Free Press.

Lombard, M., Reich, R. D., Grabe, M. E., & Bolmarcich Ditton, T. (1999). Presence and television: The role of screen size. *Human Communication Research, 26*, 75-98.

Lopez, C. G. (1994). *Effects of dramatic structure on attention, memory, and comprehension for television news.* Unpublished master's thesis, University of Maryland.

Marr, D. (1968). *Vision.* San Francisco: Freeman.

Massey, B. L., & Levy, M. R. (1999). Interactivity, online journalism, and English-language Web newspapers in Asia. *Journalism and Mass Communication Quarterly, 76*, 138-151.

McClelland, J., & Rumelhart, D. (1987). A distributed model of human learning and memory. In J. McClelland & D. Rumelhart (Ed.), *Parallel distributed processing: Explorations in the microstructure of cognition* (pp. 170-215). Cambridge, MA: MIT Press.

McCombs, M., & Shaw, D. (1972). The agenda-setting function of mass media. *Public Opinion Quarterly, 36*, 176-187.

McLuhan, M. (1994). *Understanding media: The extensions of man.* Cambridge, MA: MIT Press. (Original work published 1964)

Murray, J. H. (1997). *Hamlet on the holodeck: The future of narrative in cyberspace.* New York: Free Press.

Nabi, R. L. (1999). A cognitive-functional model for the effects of discrete negative emotions on information processing, attitude change, and recall. *Communication Theory, 9*, 292-320.

Negroponte, N. (1995). *Being digital.* New York: Vintage.

Nelson, T. (1996). Consciousness and metacognition. *American Psychologist, 51*, 102-116.

Newhagen, J. E. (1993, May). *SLIMY: A demonstration of the pSychoLogical Instrumentation for Memory and Yes/no responses.* Paper presented to the Information Systems division of the International Communication Association, Washington, DC.

Newhagen, J. E. (1994). Effects of televised government censorship on memory and thought elaboration during the Gulf War. *Journal of Broadcasting & Electronic Media, 38*, 339-351.

Newhagen, J. E. (1995, May). *Effects of verbal and nonverbal aural redundancy on memory and attention for television.* Paper presented to the Information Systems division of the International Communication Association, Albuquerque, NM.

Newhagen, J. E. (1998a). Hitting the agenda reset button: Matching research with development. *Convergence, 4*(4), 112-119.

Newhagen, J. E. (1998b). TV images that induce anger, fear, and disgust: Effects on approach-avoidance responses and memory. *Journal of Broadcasting & Electronic Media, 42*, 265-276.

Newhagen, J. E. (1999a). Information processing: A more inclusive paradigm for the study of mass media effects. *Human Communication Research, 26*, 99-103.

Newhagen, J. E. (1999b). The role of feedback in assessing the news on mass media and the Internet. In A. Kent (Ed.), *Encyclopedia of library and information science* (Vol. 65, pp. 209-215). New York: Marcel Dekker.

Newhagen, J. E., & Levy, M. R. (1998). The future of journalism in a distributed communication architecture. In D. L. Borden & H. Kerric (Eds.), *The electronic grapevine: Rumor, reputation, and reporting in the new on-line environment* (pp. 9-21). Mahwah, NJ: Lawrence Erlbaum.

Newhagen, J. E., & Nass, C. (1989). Differential criteria for evaluating credibility of newspapers and TV news. *Journalism Quarterly, 66,* 277-284.

Newhagen, J. E., & Newhagen, A. M. (2000, June). *Comparing self-report to latency to respond as measures of political attitudes on the Internet.* Paper presented at the meeting of the International Communication Association, Acapulco, Mexico.

Newhagen, J., & Reeves, B. (1992). This evening's bad news: Effects of compelling negative television news images on memory. *Journal of Communication, 42*(2), 25-41.

O'Keefe, D. J. (1990). *Persuasion: Theory and research.* Newbury Park, CA: Sage.

Packard, V. (1980). *The hidden persuaders.* New York: Pocket Books.

Paivio, A. (1986). *Mental representations: A dual coding approach.* New York: Oxford University Press.

Petty, R. E., & Cacioppo, J. T. (1981). *Attitudes and persuasion: Classic and contemporary approaches.* Dubuque, IA: William C. Brown.

Petty, R., Cacioppo, J., & Kasmer, J. (1988). The role of affect in the Elaboration Likelihood Model of persuasion. In L. Donohew, H. Sypher, & E. T. Higgins (Eds.), *Communication, social cognition, and affect* (pp. 117-146). Hillsdale, NJ: Lawrence Erlbaum.

Reeves, B., Detenber, B., & Steuer, J. (1993, May). *New televisions: The effects of big pictures and big sound on viewer responses to the screen.* Paper presented to the Information Systems division of the International Communication Association, Chicago.

Reeves, B., & Nass, C. (1996). *The media equation: How people treat computers, television, and new media like real people and places.* Cambridge, UK: Cambridge University Press.

Reeves, B., Thorson, E., Rothschild, M., McDonald, D., Hirsch, J., & Goldstein, B. (1985). Attention to television: Intrastimulus effects of movement and scene changes on alpha variation over time. *International Journal of Neuroscience, 27,* 241-255.

Reeves, B., Thorson, E., & Schleuder, J. (1985). Attention to television: Psychological theories and chronometric measures. In J. Bryant & D. Zillman (Eds.), *Perspectives in mass communication research.* Hillsdale, NJ: Lawrence Erlbaum.

Roberts, D., & Maccoby, N. (1973). Information processing and persuasion: Counter arguing behavior. In P. Clarke (Ed.), *New models for communication research.* Beverly Hills, CA: Sage.

Roeh, I. (1989). Journalism as storytelling, coverage as narrative. *American Behavioral Scientist, 33,* 162-168.

Rogers, E. M. (1994). *A history of communication study: A biographical approach.* New York: Free Press.

Samudrala, R. (2000). *Wag the Dog: Full review with images.* [Online]. Retrieved January 15, 2000, from www.movieeye.com/reviews/wagthedog.html

Schacter, D. L. (1989). Memory. In M. Posner (Ed.), *Foundations of cognitive science* (pp. 683-726). Cambridge, MA: MIT Press.

Taborsky, E. (1998). *Architectonics of semiosis.* New York: St. Martin's.

Thorson, E. (1989). Television commercials as mass media messages. In J. Bradac (Ed.), *Message effects in communication science* (pp. 195-230). Newbury Park, CA: Sage.

Watt, D. F. (1998). *Emotion and consciousness: Implications of affective neuroscience for extended reticular thalamic activating system theories of consciousness.* [Online]. Available: www.phil.vt.edu/assc/esem.html

Worth, S., & Gross, L. (1974). Symbolic strategies. *Journal of Communication, 24*(4), 27-39.

Yost, W. (1992). Auditory perception and sound source determination. *Current Directions in Psychological Science, 1*(1), 179-184.

33

The Embodied Meaning of Media Forms

R. LANCE HOLBERT

From its inception, most social scientific persuasion research has dealt with the influence of content on attitude formation and change (e.g., Janis & Feshbach, 1953; Johnson & Eagly, 1989; Petty & Cacioppo, 1986; Sherif & Hovland, 1961). Indeed, a tendency to privilege content over form is endemic to all areas of the communication sciences (McLuhan, 1964). This chapter seeks to establish a theoretical foundation that allows for a systematic empirical analysis of a particular type of media form effect, one that stems from the inherent physical constraints of media technologies. Once this theoretical groundwork is presented, focus is given to future areas of research in the context of persuasion.

The definition of form effect used in this chapter stems directly from Meyrowitz (1997). He defined the central question of medium theory, a line of theorizing devoted to form effects, as the following: "How do the particular characteristics of a medium make it physically, psychologically, and socially different

from other media and from face-to-face interaction, regardless of the particular messages that are communicated through it?" (p. 61). Thus, a form effect is the result of inherent physical, psychological, and social constraints established by a particular media technology, not the messages that are disseminated via that technology.

The theoretical approach outlined in this chapter is born from a marriage of a physiological perspective for the study of media form influence outlined by McLuhan (1964) and some of the recent theoretical work on embodied cognition (e.g., Barsalou, 1999; Glenberg, 1997). The focus of this approach is on the unique environments created by various media technologies, with particular attention being paid to how we physically engage with these environments at the sensory level (e.g., use of the ear to engage radio, use of the eye to engage television). This chapter posits that before individuals begin to engage and process the content being

AUTHOR'S NOTE: The author gives thanks to James Chesebro and Arthur Glenberg for their insightful comments regarding media form influence and embodied cognition, respectively.

provided through media, they must first inter-act with the environment created by these technologies. It is the unique physical environ-ment created by each form that constrains the possible meanings that can be extracted from media content, and this manner of a media form effect may have an important set of implications for several areas of persuasion re-search (e.g., involvement, attitude accessibil-ity, affect).

PRIOR STUDIES OF FORM

There are several lines of research that have focused on various aspects of form influence. Some of these areas are more closely aligned than others with an embodied approach. However, the approach outlined in this chap-ter builds on portions of each of the areas summarized in what follows. It is important that each approach be outlined in brief to better establish where an embodied approach to form fits in relative to these more well-established lines of research.

The most widely recognized form-based theoretical construct is medium theory (e.g., Meyrowitz, 1994). However, Meyrowitz (1985) pointed out that most work in medium theory tends to provide more of a perspective than actual social scientific theory. Indeed, medium theory can best be defined as a meta-concept. This term describes conceptual con-glomerates, each of which refers to a domain of phenomena rather than to "a specific set of concepts and their connections" (Pan & McLeod, 1991, p. 141). If communication scientists are going to be able to better under-stand the role of form, then they are going to have to construct a more well-structured theo-retical approach that will allow for an analysis of the underlying processes of the effects described by Meyrowitz and other medium theorists. To achieve an empirically testable theory of the type of form influence described

by medium theorists, the first step that needs to be taken is to turn away from the macro-level theorizing that has dominated this study of form (e.g., Eisenstein, 1979; Havelock, 1963, 1982; Ong, 1977, 1982) and return to a micro-level perspective.[1] An embodied ap-proach to form seeks to return to a focus on the individual.

In terms of more empirically minded lines of research, there has been a series of studies that have focused on a micro-level analysis of form influence. A line of research defined as a limited capacity approach centers on a study of human physical reactions to media forms, with the bulk of this work centering on the study of one medium: television (e.g., Lang, Dhillon, & Dong, 1995; Lang, Newhagen, & Reeves, 1996; Thorson & Lang, 1992). This theoretical framework suggests that viewers of television have a limited capacity to process information and that television messages can "overload this processing system fairly easily and as a result the information contained in the television message is lost" (Lang, 1995, p. 88).[2] All of the previously mentioned re-search points to the fact that channel factors are at play in how a message is processed and, as a result, have an influence on how effective a message can be in terms of attitude change.

However, it is important to note that the type of form effect outlined by Lang and col-leagues is not the same type of form influence outlined by medium theorists. Medium theory deals with a comparative analysis of influence in order to detect the unique impact of each medium. By contrast, each study conducted by Lang and colleagues focuses on a single medium and deals with a set of structural fea-tures (e.g., edits, cuts, zooms) that are alter-able by the creator of a message. The form effects given attention in medium theory fall beyond the scope of human manipulation and are the lone result of the constraints created by our media technologies. This chapter defines the form effects of medium theory as primary and those studied by Lang as secondary. This differentiation parallels that which is pointed to by Meyrowitz (1998).

Another important area of research is the work of Salomon (1979), who argued that each medium of communication creates its own unique symbol system. The inherent characteristics of a medium allow for the creation of unique symbols, and this has an impact on the cognitive skills that are employed by individuals to extract meaning from the messages. However, Salomon revealed his frustration with the information processing school of psychology, an approach that, broadly defined, was employed by Lang and others. Salomon concluded that Fodor's (1975) mentalese is not a theoretical grounding that serves well to explain the type of form influence he found in his research. Finally, in reference to his own approach to how individuals gain meaning from medium-based symbols, Salomon (1979) stated the following: "Although the conception of internalized language [an information processing/cognitivist approach] may still be vague, we have no plausible alternatives to replace it with" (p. 125). An embodied approach to the study of form may be just such an alternative.

Finally, several empirical analyses have been conducted to study the relative strength of various media forms in inducing a broad range of effects (Burns & Beier, 1973; Cantril & Allport, 1935; Cohen, 1976; McGinnies, 1965; Neuman, Just, & Crigler, 1992; Pfau, 1990; Wiegman, 1989; Wilke, 1934; Wilson, 1973; Worchel, Andreoli, & Eason, 1975). At best, the findings concerning the influence of form in these studies are inconclusive.

Some studies show that one medium of communication is more influential under certain conditions (e.g., print is superior to radio [McGinnies, 1965]), but others find that under other conditions the opposite is true (e.g., radio is superior to print [Cantril & Allport, 1935; Wilke, 1934]). Still other studies have

shown little in the way of main effects in terms of media form influence on behavior or attitude change (Neuman, 1992; Worchel et al., 1975), yet some have found that there is significant influence of form (Burns & Beier, 1973). Much of the difficulty in trying to amass any coherent understanding of the impact of form based on these studies is that there is no clear or consistent theoretical construct employed by these researchers. Many of the questions posed by these studies are haphazard at best, and as a result, the findings remain muddied and unstable across time. This chapter is a first step in trying to remedy this unfortunate situation.

In terms of persuasion, there are two studies that are of particular interest. A study by Chaiken and Eagly (1976) revealed that media forms interact with important components of the persuasion process such as comprehension. Print messages were found to be more persuasive for material deemed difficult, and television and radio messages were found to be more persuasive for material defined as easy. In addition, a study by Pfau (1990), building on the theoretical work of Meyrowitz (1985), found that relational (source) cues were dominant for the medium of television as compared to print's primary source of influence being its content. What is most important to recognize from these studies is that media form effects have been found in the context of persuasion.

SYNTHESIS OF PAST RESEARCH

In summation, in the context of the study of form, we have a theoretical base that addresses the issue of primary form effects, but it is a framework that does not deal effectively with the individual (physiological and psychological) levels of analysis. In addition, this approach currently does not lend itself well to empirical analysis (cf. Pfau, 1990). Conversely, we have a series of empirical studies encompassing several different research agendas that show that media form effects do exist at the lower levels of analysis. Although many of these studies focus on the levels of analysis that are of interest to this chapter, the overwhelming majority of these studies deal with secondary form effects. In the end, what is needed is a theoretical base that will allow for the study of primary media form influence at the micro levels of analysis. This chapter seeks to outline the makings of this sort of a theory. By combining the theoretical work of McLuhan (1964) with the work on embodied cognition, more specifically Glenberg (1997), a framework can be created that will allow for a systematic analysis of primary form effects at the individual level.[3] In the end, this new theoretical approach is seen as an extension of much of the work of Salomon (1979) and Olson (1988), but with an interest on the study of both the inherent constraints of a medium and several individual difference variables that can affect the role of form influence.

MCLUHAN'S PHYSIOLOGICAL PERSPECTIVE

McLuhan's physiological perspective has met with much criticism (e.g., O'Neill, 1981), and even medium theorists such as Meyrowitz (1985) have stated that McLuhan was not at all specific as to how the media have an impact in this manner. However, it is important to note that the early work of McLuhan (1962, 1964) was focused at the physiological level of analysis, and with the notable exception of Carey (1967), few have recognized this nuance within McLuhan's work. When McLuhan (1964) first claimed that *the medium is the message,* he was stating that "the effects of technology do not occur at the level of opinion or concepts but alter the sense ratios or patterns of perception steadily and without resistance" (p. 33). He went on to

state, "As an extension and expediter of the sense life, any medium at once affects the entire field of the senses" (p. 54). It is important to note that when McLuhan talked about involvement with a medium, he was focusing on how we are physiologically connected to our forms of communication.

For McLuhan, form embodied meaning (Carey, 1981). As McLeod and Chaffee (1972) correctly pointed out, McLuhan's approach to media is centered around the role of constraints. Each media form inherits a set of constraints within which it is able to present a view of the world. It is within these constraints that meaning of the world is constructed by a particular technology (akin to the formation of a media epistemology [Chesebro, 1984]). McLuhan (1989) was naturally drawn to the work of Gibson (1979) and his ecological approach to perception. Gibson introduced the concept of affordances, and this concept is an important component of the theoretical framework outlined in this chapter. The underlying premise in all of McLuhan's work is that each medium creates its own unique sensorial environment and that our interactions with these environments have a profound impact on our behavior at all subsequent levels of analysis. This perspective fits well with Gibson, who stated that we must first assess the environment before we can extract any meaning from a given situation. The environment created by each media form stems directly from the inherent constraints of a given technology, whether it is the printed word or an image on a television screen.

THEORY OF EMBODIED COGNITION

The primary theoretical void that led Glenberg (1997) to ask what memory is for is defined as the symbol grounding problem of past theories of memory, most notably the information processing/cognitivist approach.[4] Glenberg's theory of embodiment centers around the fact that "the meaning of an object, event, or sentence is what that person can do with the object, event, or sentence" (p. 3). Glenberg stressed that context is extremely important and that memory ultimately serves perception. The implications of Glenberg's theory of memory for the study of media form influence are important and could be the key that unlocks the door to how changes in sensorial environments created by media can have an effect on individuals.

To better understand the connections between Glenberg and McLuhan, there are three concepts from Glenberg's work that must be presented in some detail. The first two concepts (meshing and affordances) are explicit in Glenberg's work, and a third (sensori-motor schemata) has been referred to by several commentators of Glenberg's theory as having a great deal of relevance (e.g., Jacobs & Ziegler, 1997).

Meshing

The concept of meshing establishes a basis for how we take an object from the outside world (the world that exists outside of our heads) and assign utility to it. In particular, what is being meshed are the "embodied conceptualization of projectable properties of the environment" and "the embodied experiences that provide nonprojectable properties" (Glenberg, 1997, p. 4). Therefore, the properties an object presents to us are twofold: (a) a set of physical characteristics and (b) a set of characteristics based on our past experiences with that object. The combination of these characteristics represents the embodied meaning of the object. In terms of the study of media, we can associate a distinct set of projectable properties that stem from the inherent physical constraints of a media form. It is these projectable properties that are constructed by media forms, and this important part in the meshing equation can possibly lead to a subsequent media form effect on comprehension, memory, and attitude formation and change.

Two mechanisms, clamping and suppression, play important roles in the process of meshing. The process of clamping allows all forms of experience to remain reality oriented, and suppression is the mechanism whereby an individual is able to make predictions about how the world functions. In terms of the study of media effects, each media form represents a different type of clamping of projectable properties, and each variation in clamping results in a different mode of suppression. Glenberg (1997) argued that language (print or oral) represents a very loose form of suppression relative to the suppression employed for extracting meaning from real-world experiences, and this is largely due to the variance in constraints created by each type of interaction. Language offers few constraints, but a real-world environment offers many. Applying an extension of Glenberg's argument to the study of media form, it can be posited that each media technology, having a unique set of constraints, requires an individual to employ a distinct mode of suppression. In short, it is from a medium's constraints that a unique form of processing takes place allowing for meaning to be created within the mind of an individual.

Affordances

Much like McLuhan, Glenberg (1997) employed the concept of Gibson's affordances and assigned to them an important role in the meshing process. According to Gibson (1979), what is most important are the physical characteristics of the environment with which we have to engage in order to survive. Gibson dealt solely with the sense of sight, but the characteristics of the physical world in which we interact create constraints for our other senses as well.

In terms of media, the claim being made here is that the distinct sensorial environment of each media form creates a unique set of affordances. As an example, the affordances I am granted by the words "hammer pounding nail" are distinct from the affordances I extract from seeing the moving image of a hammer pounding a nail. Furthermore, these affordances are distinct from those I would gain from actually seeing a hammer being used in this fashion right in front of me or the affordances of physically using a hammer to pound a nail. In short, the unique sensorial environments that stem from the inherent constraints of each medium create a unique set of affordances.

Sensori-Motor Schemata

In reaction to several commentators having connected his theory of embodiment to the work of Piaget (e.g., Carlson, 1997; Jacobs & Ziegler, 1997; Velichkovsky, 1997), Glenberg (1997) stated that the connection may be even closer than one would initially think. In particular, Glenberg highlighted that Piaget was one of the first to stress the importance of linking thought with the projectable properties of our physical world.

Piaget (1959) described sensori-motor schemata as consisting "of a stable pattern of movements together with a perceptual component geared to the recognition of appropriate signals" (p. 372). A particular sensori-motor schema is formed out of a set base of perceptual formulations and is engaged when specific intensive and extensive properties of the environment are joined. Intensive properties are the "relations governing the properties of the various objects, and extensive properties are the series of objects and situations to

which it can be applied" (p. 372). It is the combination of these two elements that engages a particular sensori-motor schema.

It is most important to recognize the strength of the sensori-motor schemata in determining the formation of all subsequent content-based schemata. Piaget (1959) stated, "The origin of all classification and seriation is to be found in sensori-motor schema" given that sensori-motor schemata are the first true schemata formed by humans (p. 372).[5] Piaget stated that all information must pass through these schemata before linking itself to some content-based schematic structure. It is also important to note that Piaget (1952) stressed that these sensori-motor schemata are constantly modified via a process he defined as accommodation. This is a process by which sensori-motor schemata are strengthened to better extract from the environment the information that is of the greatest utility to the receiver; the sensori-motor schemata form from a solid foundation, but they are constantly being improved through use.[6] Piaget's process of accommodation can be thought of as a physiological quality of a unique learning process. The sensori-motor schema outlined by Piaget can be thought of as integral to functioning as efficiently and effectively as possible in our physical environment. So, how do sensori-motor schemata relate to media form effects? The answer to this question might be found in the study of medium-specific sensori-motor schemata.

MEDIUM-SPECIFIC SENSORI-MOTOR SCHEMATA

Piaget (1952) stated that a specific sensori-motor schema is used when (a) properties of various objects are similar to those encountered in the past and (b) the situation in which they are applied is similar to that of the past. The foundation of McLuhan's *the medium is the message* is that each form of communication retains a unique set of physical properties and a unique situation within which a user of that medium is engaged. As an example, a television screen (which McLuhan [1964] defined as a mosaic) creates a picture based on the properties of the pixel. The unique physical characteristic of the television pixel creates for the user of that form of communication a physiological connection to his or her stimulus environment that is unlike any other connection being made with another form of communication. A specific set of stimulus modules are employed by the user to access the information being presented through a particular form of communication, and the balance regarding the relative strength and weakness of how much each sense module is used also varies across media forms. This is the primary form effect envisioned by McLuhan.

The culmination of this marriage of Glenberg's theory of embodiment and McLuhan's physiological perspective to the study of media form influence is the creation of what can be defined as medium-specific sensori-motor schemata. This chapter presents an argument that individuals develop a set of form-based schemata in accordance with those forms of communication that have been employed at some point in the past. The medium-specific sensori-motor schemata we maintain vary across individuals in terms of strength, but each medium-specific schema retains some degree of similarity across individuals given that the structure of these medium-specific schemata are constrained by the unique physiological characteristics of a particular medium that exists outside of our heads. As an example, my television sensori-motor schema might not be of the same strength as my neighbor's television sensori-motor schema, based on our relative levels of use of that medium, but my schema will maintain many of the same properties as my neighbor's schema because the physiological engagement we maintain with our television sets is the same due to the unique characteristics of the medium.

ADVANCING THE WORK OF SALOMON

As stated earlier, an embodied approach to form is seen as an extension of the work of Salomon and Olson. If we attempt to deal with the symbol grounding problem implied in Salomon's (1979) indifference toward the work of Fodor by offering embodiment as a remedy, then there is a heightened role for form compared to what was offered by Salomon. Salomon (1990) stated that the effects he was looking at "is a case of effects not of a technology but with it" (p. 29). This is an important distinction that differentiates the assumptions that exist with an embodied approach to form relative to the work of Salomon in this area. By dealing with only the cognitive skills and not the symbol grounding problem, Salomon turned his attention to the work of the individual at the expense of understanding the true role of form. If we begin to study media form influence from an embodiment perspective, then there is a return to an increased role for form in shaping human cognition (very much in line with McLuhan's perspective of sensorial change). It is not that form has a universal impact on all individuals in terms of making them think in one way, but that a media form constricts the ways in which individuals construct meaning from a mediated experience. Thus, this chapter is not making a clear case for *the medium is the message* as outlined by McLuhan. In short, if we deal with the symbol grounding problem by introducing embodiment, then there is a heightened role for form in the process of a human's ability to obtain meaning. However, it is important to be clear that the embodied approach to media, although being close to

McLuhan's, is not technological determinism in the strict sense given that there is still an important role for the individual in this process.

THE EMBODIED APPROACH TO MEDIA FORMS IN THE CONTEXT OF PERSUASION

Reassessment of Previous Lines of Persuasion Research

Not only is an embodied approach to media form influence an extension of much of the work conducted by Salomon and Olson, but it can also be connected to the work of other communication scholars interested in the impact of media technologies. More specifically, the work of Chesebro and Bertelsen (1996) parallels many of the ideas being presented in this chapter. There are three points raised by Chesebro and Bertelsen in the first half of their approach to the study of media influence that are important for an embodied approach to the study of form. Each of these points highlights the fact that form may have an important set of effects on several fronts that are of interest to the study of persuasion, many of which have been focused on from a strictly content-based approach: attention, information processing, knowledge, values, and (ultimately) attitude formation and change. Chesebro and Bertelsen highlighted the following points.

Form generates a different kind of knowledge than does content. There should be some connection between our respective media forms and different ways of processing information. Ultimately, these unique modes of processing may have an impact on how knowledge is obtained and constructed within an individual. There are physical limitations inherent to each medium and to human sensorial perception; it is at the crossroads of these limitations that the conditions are formed from which knowledge about the world becomes embodied (via meshing).

As a result, Chesebro and Bertelsen (1996) concluded that "the medium employed to present information determines how experiences are utilized and incorporated into the human being as mental skills or abilities" (pp. 21-22). This approach conforms well with Glenberg (1997) and Gibson (1979), both of whom stated that an important component to any process of obtaining meaning is an understanding of the environment (i.e., projectable properties) from which information is obtained. However, it is also important to recognize that the creation of meaning is not a one-way street from media to individual. Instead, the theory of embodied cognition also states that it is the psychological baggage an individual brings to a mediated experience that also has an impact on how knowledge is constructed. Thus, it is with the interaction of these two influences that embodied meaning is constructed from a mediated experience.

In the study of persuasion, the role of knowledge has long been seen as playing an important role in attitude-based cognitions (e.g., Tesser, 1976; Tesser & Conlee, 1975). However, research in this area assumes that all knowledge (schematic) structures are based on content (e.g., Cacioppo, Petty, & Sidera, 1982; Wood, 1982) and not that other form-based schematic structures may have an impact on attitude formation and change. As outlined earlier, Piaget (1954) stressed that sensori-motor schemata are employed prior to content-based schemata, and if this is the case, then these form-based schemata should play an important role in the context of persuasion.

Each form of communication equates with a unique view of reality. Chesebro and Bertelsen (1996) stressed that the distinct view of reality created by a media form may stem, in large part, from the different cognitive processes that individuals have to employ when engaging different media forms. Krugman (1971) analyzed actual physiological involvement with various media forms via measurement of brain wave activity. In line with Krugman, McLuhan (1978) discussed the shifting in use of different hemispheres of the brain caused by different media forms, with print being a left hemisphere medium and television being a right hemisphere medium. The study of brain hemispheres has been the focus of much past research, especially in the area of affect (e.g., Lang & Friestad, 1993; Reeves, Lang, Thorson, & Rothschild, 1989). Krugman was not focusing on which hemisphere was being used for which medium, but he did conclude that the cognitive responses to media forms are unique.

There have been several advancements in the study of brain activity regarding the use of variations in sensorial input systems (e.g., Cohen, Semple, Gross, King, & Nordahl, 1992), and an important next step in this process may be to study which parts of the brain actually fire when interacting with various media forms. However, it will be important to make sure that the study of brain activity at this level of analysis is still driven by theory to allow for a more comprehensive understanding of what these different firings mean (e.g., Sarter, Bernstein, & Cacioppo, 1996). If different areas of the brain fire, then there is an unequivocal form effect. However, the important empirical question is not whether there is a physiological effect but rather what impact this variation in processing has on subsequent variables deemed important to persuasion (e.g., knowledge, memory, involvement with media content).

Once again, in terms of the study of persuasion, one of the most basic areas of study is how information is being processed by the individual (e.g., Chaiken & Maheswaran, 1994; Petty & Priester, 1994). This chapter proposes that the inherent physical constraints of a media form will affect what type of information processing is enacted during a mediated experience. It is not just the message being provided that spurs processing but, on a more base level, the media form as well. This also may have an important impact on attitude formation and change.

Habitual use of specific media systems privileges certain values. If it is taken as given that different media forms bring with them different ways of knowing (Chesebro, 1984), then shifts in media dominance will have profound effects on how we look at the world. The bulk of work in medium theory focuses on societal-wide shifts in media dominance, from oral to print (Ong, 1977, 1982), from print to electronic (Meyrowitz, 1985), and from analog to digital (Stephens, 1998). The point raised here is that the way we look at the world may be influenced by the media forms we use most often.

The study of values and worldviews is a well-established line of research—and one that has been the focus of attention in the study of attitude formation and change (e.g., Ball-Rokeach, Rokeach, & Grube, 1984; Feather, 1984, 1985). Inglehart (1977) pointed to media as being important components in his materialist/postmaterialist value shift, but he was unable to elaborate on exactly how they may have an impact. However, Inglehart, as with most scholars, stressed the role of media content without taking into account the role of form. Holbert (1998) introduced the notion that this value shift may be more the result of a shift in media form dominance than the result of any changes in content. It might not be just media content that affects these value structures; form might affect them as well. This would imply that media forms will have an indirect influence on attitude formation and change through their impact on value formation.

New Avenues of Research

In addition to these three areas of persuasion research (knowledge, information processing, and values) that need to be re-addressed in order to better understand the relative impact of content and form, there are several new lines of research that stem from an embodied approach. These areas are form-based involvement, form-induced affect, and form-based attitude accessibility.

Form-Based Involvement. Involvement with media content has been shown to have a tremendous impact on attitude formation and change (e.g., Petty & Cacioppo, 1979). This type of issue involvement occurs at a psychological level of analysis where an individual perceives whether the topic being discussed in the message is of any importance to his or her life. By contrast, the study of involvement being focused on in this chapter resides in a physiological level of analysis. In particular, focus is being given to how an individual becomes sensorially involved with a particular media form. As McLuhan (1964) summarized, what is of importance to this type of involvement is (a) which sensorial input systems are being employed and (b) what is the balance of senses being used relative to one another during a mediated experience. In terms of embodiment, the physical environment created by a medium form constrains what meaning can be extracted from the content provided through the medium. Just as involvement with content is important to attitude formation and change, so too may involvement with our media technologies.

Form-Induced Affect. Dillard and Wilson (1993) outlined two specific types of affect that can affect the processing of persuasive messages: message-induced affect and message-irrelevant affect. The former is an emotional response to a particular piece of media content, and the latter is the emotional baggage an individual brings to a mediated experience. The approach to media form effects outlined in this chapter offers an advancement in the study of induced affect by putting forth the possibility that it is not just content that can spark a particular emotional reaction but form as well.

Several studies have pointed to the connection between use of specific brain hemispheres and emotional responses to media messages (e.g., Lang & Friestad, 1993; Reeves et al., 1989). It has been theorized by McLuhan (1978) and found by Krugman (1971) that different media forms lead to different modes of brain activity. If, as Reeves et al. (1989) found, positive messages can be associated with the right hemisphere and negative messages can be associated with the left hemisphere, then any condition that influences use of a particular hemisphere will affect the relative strength of an emotional response to a particular piece of media content. The theoretical base forged in this chapter would point to media form having exactly this type of an impact.

Form-Based Attitude Accessibility. A final avenue for future research based on an embodied approach to form concerns attitude accessibility. A number of previous studies have shown attitude accessibility to have an impact on a number of different areas of concern to the process of persuasion (e.g., Fazio, Chen, McDonel, & Sherman, 1982; Fazio, Powell, & Herr, 1983). In particular, past work in this area has shown that previous experiences with an attitude object have an impact on an individual's attitudes toward that object (Fazio,

Sanbonmatsu, Powell, & Kardes, 1986). The theory of form influence presented in this chapter provides an argument that an important component of past experience with an attitude object may be the medium through which the object has been engaged. If media forms have an influence on how subsequent content-based cognitive structures are constructed, then an individual's attitude toward a given object may be influenced by the manner in which the individual has previously come into contact with that object. In short, attitudes may be linked to specific mediated experiences. If this is the case, then particular media forms may be better able to access a given attitude based on what form affected the construction of that attitude.

Of particular interest to this area of study are (a) those media forms that have been used in the past relative to gaining information about an attitude object and (b) the media form being used in an experimental condition to measure attitude accessibility. If attitudes are linked to mediated experiences, then media form is one condition that can influence how and/or when a particular attitude is activated. If an attitude can be defined as an association between an object and an evaluation of that object, then the strength of this association may be based on a particular mediated experience. If an individual can associate an object with a particularly strong media experience, then the best medium through which to access an attitude concerning that object will be through the same medium. Just as with form-based involvement and form-induced affect, this is an important area for future study in the area of persuasion research.

CONCLUSION

The theoretical approach to the study of media effects outlined in this chapter, defined as the embodied meaning of media forms, provides a base from which to systematically analyze the type of form effects outlined by McLuhan and other medium theorists. This approach is seen as most closely associated with previous work on media form influence performed by Salomon (1979) and Olson (1988), but with an increased emphasis given to the role of form relative to the individual. Meyrowitz (1985) correctly pointed out that McLuhan offered few specifics regarding how changes in sensory balances induced by the use of various media forms can alter an individual's behavior. This chapter is a first step in attempting to provide some of the details that may result in some answers as to how media forms may have an influence in this manner. As a result, this theoretical approach initiates a shift in levels of analysis in medium theory away from broader macro-level change and toward a more micro-level orientation. However, this does not mean that there should not be every attempt made to create cross-level linkages within these studies of primary form influence (e.g., Pan & McLeod, 1991). The theoretical advances made by past studies of medium theory are important, and the theoretical work advanced in this chapter will not achieve its full potency if it does not seek to generate theoretical links with the macro-level work of Meyrowitz and others.

As noted previously, this theoretical approach has broad implications for the study of persuasion. Six areas are highlighted: three calling for a reassessment of a predominantly content-based approach to attitude formation and change and three representing new avenues for future research in this area. This is by no means an exhaustive list, but it is representative of a number of possible media effects. It is my hope that not only will this theoretical foundation prove fruitful for future research, but it will also spark a discussion that will lead to new theoretical advances in the area of media form effects research.

NOTES

1. Meyrowitz (1997) claimed, "The most interesting—and most controversial—medium theory deals with the macro level" (p. 61). However, different generations of medium theorists have focused on different levels of analysis, and this has created difficulty in trying to establish a unified empirical approach to this area of media studies (Meyrowitz, 1994). Earlier theorists of the role of form influence gave focus to the lower levels of analysis (e.g., McLuhan, 1964; see also McLuhan & McLuhan, 1988), and this chapter seeks to return to a more micro-level study of media form effects while remaining true to the tradition established by medium theory.

2. The theoretical base for much of the work conducted by Lang and colleagues is grounded in an information processing approach to the study of the mind. This approach does not conform with the embodied approach employed in this chapter (for a lengthy discussion of distinctions between the two approaches, see Barsalou, 1999). Although Lang did not employ the same theory of cognition as that which is presented in this chapter, her work is important in that it reveals that form effects are evident.

3. Glenberg's research focuses specifically on memory, but several other works deal with other facets of the embodiment approach (see also Barsalou, 1993, 1999; Barsalou & Prinz, 1998; Clark, 1997; Gibbs, 1997; MacWhinney, 1998; Newton, 1996).

4. Other psychologists and philosophers have raised this same argument, with the most well-known being Searle's (1980) Chinese room argument (see also Harnard, 1990).

5. Although Piaget's theory states that sensorimotor schemata are important early on in life, he also concluded that they fade in terms of influence as a human grows into adulthood. The work of Glenberg (1997) implies that these form-based schemata play a larger role in later life than Piaget

outlined, and the theory presented in this chapter assumes this to be the case as well.

6. However, what is important to recognize here is that the flexibility and the strength of these form-based schematic formations are restricted by the inherent physical constraints of each media form.

REFERENCES

Ball-Rokeach, S. J., Rokeach, M., & Grube, J. W. (1984). *The great American values test: Influencing behavior and beliefs through television.* New York: Free Press.

Barsalou, L. W. (1993). Flexibility, structure, and linguistic vagary in concepts: Manifestations of a compositional system of perceptual systems. In A. C. Collins, S. E. Gathercole, & M. A. Conway (Eds.), *Theories of memories* (pp. 29-101). Hillsdale, NJ: Lawrence Erlbaum.

Barsalou, L. W. (1999). Perceptual symbol systems. *Behavioral and Brain Sciences, 22,* 577-609.

Barsalou, L. W., & Prinz, J. J. (1998). Mundane creativity in perceptual symbol systems. In T. B. Ward, S. M. Smith, & J. Vaid (Eds.), *Creative thought* (pp. 267-308). Washington, DC: American Psychological Association.

Burns, K. L., & Beier, E. (1973). Significance of vocal and visual channels in the decoding of emotional meaning. *Journal of Communication, 23,* 118-130.

Cacioppo, J. T., Petty, R. E., & Sidera, J. (1982). The effects of a salient self-schema on the evaluation of proattitudinal editorials: Top-down versus bottom-up message processing. *Journal of Experimental Social Psychology, 18,* 324-338.

Cantril, H., & Allport, G. (1935). *The psychology of radio.* New York: Harper.

Carey, J. W. (1967). Harold Adams Innis and Marshall McLuhan. *The Antioch Review, 27,* 5-39.

Carey, J. W. (1981). McLuhan and Mumford: The roots of modern media analysis. *Journal of Communication, 31*(3), 162-178.

Carlson, R. (1997). Meshing Glenberg with Piaget, Gibson, and the ecological self. *Behavioral and Brain Sciences, 20,* 21.

Chaiken, S., & Eagly, A. (1976). Communication modality as a determinant of message persuasiveness and message comprehensibility. *Journal of Personality and Social Psychology, 34*, 605-614.

Chaiken, S., & Maheswaran, D. (1994). Heuristic processing can bias systematic processing: Effects of source credibility, argument ambiguity, and task importance on attitude judgment. *Journal of Personality and Social Psychology, 66*, 460-473.

Chesebro, J. W. (1984). The media reality: Epistemological functions of media in cultural systems. *Critical Studies in Mass Communication, 1*, 111-130.

Chesebro, J. W., & Bertelsen, D. A. (1996). *Analyzing media*. New York: Guilford.

Clark, A. (1997). *Being there*. Cambridge, MA: MIT Press.

Cohen, A. (1976). Radio vs. TV: The effect of the medium. *Journal of Communication, 26*, 29-35.

Cohen, R. M., Semple, W. E., Gross, M., King, A. C., & Nordahl, T. E. (1992). Metabolic brain pattern of sustained auditory discrimination. *Experimental Brain Research, 92*, 165-172.

Dillard, J. P., & Wilson, B. J. (1993). Communication and affect: Thoughts, feelings, and issues for the future. *Communication Research, 20*, 637-646.

Eisenstein, E. (1979). *The printing press as an agent of change*. New York: Cambridge University Press.

Fazio, R. H., Chen, J., McDonel, E. C., & Sherman, S. J. (1982). Attitude accessibility, attitude-behavior consistency, and the strength of object-evaluation association. *Journal of Experimental Social Psychology, 18*, 339-357.

Fazio, R. H., Powell, M. C., & Herr, P. M. (1983). Toward a process model of the attitude-behavior relation: Accessing one's attitude upon mere observation of the attitude object. *Journal of Personality and Social Psychology, 44*, 723-735.

Fazio, R. H., Sanbonmatsu, D. M., Powell, M. C., & Kardes, F. R. (1986). On the automatic activation of attitudes. *Journal of Personality and Social Psychology, 50*, 229-238.

Feather, N. T. (1984). Protestant ethic, conservatism, and values. *Journal of Personality and Social Psychology, 46*, 1132-1141.

Feather, N. T. (1985). Attitudes, values, and attributions: Explanations of unemployment. *Journal of Personality and Social Psychology, 46*, 876-889.

Fodor, J. (1975). *The language of thought*. New York: Crowell.

Gibbs, R. W. (1997). How language reflects the embodied nature of creative cognition. In T. B. Ward, S. M. Smith, & J. Vaid (Eds.), *Creative thought* (pp. 351-374). Washington, DC: American Psychological Association.

Gibson, J. J. (1979). *The ecological approach to visual perception*. Boston: Houghton Mifflin.

Glenberg, A. M. (1997). What memory is for. *Behavioral and Brain Sciences, 20*, 1-55.

Harnard, S. (1990). The symbol grounding problem. *Physica D, 42*, 335-346.

Havelock, E. (1963). *Preface to Plato*. Cambridge, MA: Harvard University Press.

Havelock, E. (1982). *The literate revolution in Greece and its cultural consequences*. Princeton, NJ: Princeton University Press.

Holbert, R. L. (1998, April). *The role of the mass media in Inglehart's materialist-postmaterialist value shift*. Paper presented at the annual meeting of the Midwest Political Science Association, Chicago.

Inglehart, R. (1977). *The silent revolution: Changing values and political styles among Western publics*. Princeton, NJ: Princeton University Press.

Jacobs, A., & Ziegler, J. (1997). Has Glenberg forgotten his nurse? *Behavioral and Brain Sciences, 20*, 26-27.

Janis, I. L., & Feshbach, S. (1953). Effects of fear-arousing communications. *Journal of Abnormal and Social Psychology, 48*, 78-92.

Johnson, B. T., & Eagly, A. H. (1989). Effects of involvement on persuasion: A meta-analysis. *Psychological Review, 106*, 290-314.

Krugman, H. E. (1971). Brain wave measures of media involvement. *Journal of Advertising Research, 11*, 3-9.

Lang, A. (1995). Defining audio/video redundancy from a limited-capacity information processing perspective. *Communication Research, 22*, 86-115.

Lang, A., Dhillon, K., & Dong, Q. (1995). The effects of emotional arousal and valence on television viewers' cognitive capacity and memory. *Journal of Broadcasting & Electronic Media, 39,* 313-327.

Lang, A., & Friestad, M. (1993). Emotion, hemispheric specialization, and visual and verbal memory for television messages. *Communication Research, 20,* 647-670.

Lang, A., Newhagen, J., & Reeves, B. (1996). Negative video as structure: Emotion, attention, memory. *Journal of Broadcasting & Electronic Media, 40,* 460-477.

MacWhinney, B. (1998). *The emergence of language.* Mahwah, NJ: Lawrence Erlbaum.

McGinnies, E. (1965). A cross-cultural comparison of printed communication versus spoken communication in persuasion. *Journal of Psychology, 60,* 1-8.

McLeod, J. M., & Chaffee, S. (1972). The construction of social reality. In J. Tedeschi (Ed.), *The social influence process* (pp. 50-99). Chicago: Aldine.

McLuhan, M. (1962). *The Gutenberg galaxy.* Toronto: University of Toronto Press.

McLuhan, M. (1964). *Understanding media: The extensions of man.* New York: Mentor.

McLuhan, M. (1978). The brain and the media: The "Western" hemisphere. *Journal of Communication, 28,* 54-60.

McLuhan, M. (1989). The role of new media in social change. In G. Sanderson & F. MacDonald (Eds.), *McLuhan: The man and his message* (pp. 34-40). Golden, CO: Fulcrum.

McLuhan, M., & McLuhan, E. (1988). *The laws of media.* Toronto: University of Toronto Press.

Meyrowitz, J. (1985). *No sense of place.* New York: Oxford University Press.

Meyrowitz, J. (1994). Medium theory. In D. Crowley & D. Mitchell (Eds.), *Communication theory today* (pp. 50-77). Stanford, CA: Stanford University Press.

Meyrowitz, J. (1997). Shifting worlds of strangers: Medium theory and changes in "them" versus "us." *Sociological Inquiry, 67,* 59-71.

Meyrowitz, J. (1998). Multiple media literacies. *Journal of Communication, 48*(1), 96-108.

Neuman, W. R., Just, M. R., & Crigler, A. N. (1992). *Common knowledge: News and the construction of political meaning.* Chicago: University of Chicago Press.

Newton, N. (1996). *Foundations of understanding.* Philadelphia: Benjamins.

Olson, D. R. (1988). Mind and media: The epistemic functions of literacy. *Journal of Communication, 38,* 27-36.

O'Neill, J. (1981, May). McLuhan's loss of Innis-sense. *Canadian Forum, pp.* 13-15.

Ong, W. J. (1977). *Interfaces of the word.* Ithaca, NY: Cornell University Press.

Ong, W. J. (1982). *Orality and literacy: The technologizing of the word.* New York: Methuen.

Pan, Z., & McLeod, J. (1991). Multilevel analysis in mass communication research. *Communication Research, 18,* 140-173.

Petty, R. E., & Cacioppo, J. T. (1979). Issue-involvement can increase or decrease persuasion by enhancing message-relevant cognitive responses. *Journal of Personality and Social Psychology, 37,* 1915-1926.

Petty, R. E., & Cacioppo, J. T. (1986). The Elaboration Likelihood Model of persuasion. *Advances in Experimental Social Psychology, 22,* 123-205.

Petty, R. E., & Priester, J. R. (1994). Mass media attitude change: Implications of the Elaboration Likelihood Model of persuasion. In J. Bryant & D. Zillmann (Eds.), *Media effects* (pp. 91-122). Hillsdale, NJ: Lawrence Erlbaum.

Pfau, M. (1990). A channel approach to television influence. *Journal of Broadcasting & Electronic Media, 34,* 195-214.

Piaget, J. (1952). *The origins of intelligence in the child.* New York: International Universities Press.

Piaget, J. (1954). *The construction of reality in the child.* New York: Basic Books.

Piaget, J. (1959). The early growth of logic in the child: Classification and seriation. In H. Gruber & J. J. Voneche (Eds.), *The essential Piaget* (pp. 359-393). New York: Basic Books.

Reeves, B., Lang, A., Thorson, E., & Rothschild, M. (1989). Hemispheric specialization and emotional television scenes. *Human Communication Research, 15,* 493-508.

Salomon, G. (1979). *Interaction of media, cognition, and learning.* San Francisco: Jossey-Boss.

Salomon, G. (1990). Cognitive effects with and of computer technology. *Communication Research, 17,* 26-44.

Sarter, M., Bernstein, G., & Cacioppo, J. (1996). Brain imaging and cognitive neuroscience:

Toward strong inference in attributing function to structure. *American Psychologist, 51,* 13-21.

Searle, J. R. (1980). Minds, brains, and programs. *Behavioral and Brain Sciences, 3,* 417-424.

Sherif, M., & Hovland, C.W. (1961). *Social judgment: Assimilation and contrast effects in communication and attitude change.* New Haven, CT: Yale University Press.

Stephens, M. (1998). Which communications revolution is it, anyway? *Journalism and Mass Communication Quarterly, 75,* 9-13.

Tesser, A. (1976). Thought and reality constraints as determinants of attitude polarization. *Journal of Research in Personality, 10,* 183-194.

Tesser, A., & Conlee, M. C. (1975). Some effect of time and thought on attitude polarization. *Journal of Personality and Social Psychology, 13,* 340-356.

Thorson, E., & Lang, A. (1992). The effects of television videographics and lecture familiarity on adult cardiac orienting responses and memory. *Communication Research, 19,* 346-369.

Velichkovsky, B. (1997). The "mesh" approach to human memory: How much cognitive psychology has to be thrown away? *Behavioral and Brain Sciences, 20,* 39.

Wiegman, O. (1989). Communication modality and attitude change in a realistic experiment. *Journal of Applied Social Psychology, 19,* 828-840.

Wilke. W. H. (1934). An experimental comparison of the speech, the radio, and the printed page as propaganda devices. *Archive of Psychology, 169.*

Wilson. C. E. (1973). The effect of medium on loss of information. *Journalism Quarterly, 60,* 111-115.

Wood, W. (1982). Retrieval of attitude-relevant information from memory: Effects on susceptibility to persuasion and on intrinsic motivation. *Journal of Personality and Social Psychology, 42,* 798-810.

Worchel, S., Andreoli, V., & Eason, J. (1975). Is the medium the message? A study of the effects of media, communicator, and message characteristics on attitude change. *Journal of Applied Social Psychology, 5,* 157-172.

34

Interactive Technology and Persuasion

B.J. FOGG
ELISSA LEE
JONATHAN MARSHALL

Since the advent of modern computing in 1946, the uses of computing technology have expanded far beyond their initial role of performing complex calculations (Denning & Metcalfe, 1997). Today, computers are not just for scientists; they are an integral part of workplaces and homes. The diffusion of computers has led to new uses for interactive technology, including one that computing pioneers of the 1940s never imagined: using computers to change people's attitudes and behavior—in a word, *persuasion*.

Recent research and new computing products illustrate interactive technology's potential for motivating and influencing people (see, e.g., Dijkstra, Liebrand, & Timminga, 1998; Fogg, 2002; King & Tester, 1999; Lieberman, 1992; Schumann & Thorson, 1999). However, scholarly research on how computer technologies persuade is only beginning to gain momentum (Crawford, 1999). Often referred to as "captology" (Anthes, 1999; Berdichevsky & Neunschwander, 1999; Caruso, 1997,

1998; Fogg, 1998; Khaslavsky & Shedroff, 1999), the study of computers as persuasive technologies is a relatively recent endeavor, yet interest in this area is likely to increase, expanding our theoretical understanding about how computers can persuade as well as showing the many possibilities for using computing systems to motivate and influence people.

Research on persuasive technologies is an interdisciplinary pursuit. Because computing technologies are so versatile and diverse, no single theory or academic perspective adequately captures the persuasive possibilities of interactive technologies. As a result, theories and methods from psychology, communication, design, human-computer interaction, and other disciplines inform the study of persuasive technologies. Captology not only crosses academic boundaries but also brings together academic researchers and industry innovators, creating understanding that is at once theoretical and practical.

In this chapter, we present research and perspectives about computers designed to change people's attitudes and behaviors. We first offer definitions and examples and then present a framework that illustrates various ways in which technology can motivate and influence people. We next review the existing work on computer credibility. We conclude the chapter by outlining future directions for increasing understanding of computers as persuasive technologies.

PERSUASIVE TECHNOLOGY: A DEFINITION AND TWO EXAMPLES

A "persuasive technology" is any type of computing system, device, or application that was designed to change a person's attitudes or behavior in a predetermined way (Berdichevsky & Neunschwander, 1999; Fogg, 1998; King & Tester, 1999). One illuminating example is a product named "Baby Think It Over." A U.S. company (www.btio.com) designed this computerized doll to simulate the time and energy required to care for a baby, with the purpose of persuading teens to avoid becoming parents prematurely. Used as part of many school programs in the United States, the Baby Think It Over infant simulator looks, weighs, and cries something like a real baby. The computer embedded inside the doll triggers a crying sound at random intervals; to stop the crying sound, the teen caregiver must pay immediate attention to the doll. If the caregiver fails to respond appropriately, the computer embedded inside the doll records the neglect. After a few days of caring for the simulated infant, the teenager generally reports less interest in becoming a parent in the near future (see www.btio.com/btiostud.htm), which—along with reduced teen pregnancy rates—is the intended outcome of the device.

Another example of a persuasive technology is a CD-ROM titled "5 a Day Adventures" (www.dole5aday.com). Created by Dole Foods, this computer application was designed to persuade kids to eat more fruits and vegetables. Using 5 a Day Adventures, children enter a virtual world with characters such as "Bobby Banana" and "Pamela Pineapple," who teach kids about nutrition and coach them to make healthy food choices.

Not all computing technologies are persuasive; in fact, only a small subset of today's computing technologies fit into this category. A computer qualifies as a persuasive technology when the people who create the product do so with an intent to change attitudes or behaviors in a predetermined way (Berdichevsky & Neunschwander, 1999; Fogg, 1998, 2002). This point about intentionality may seem subtle, but it is not trivial. Intentionality determines whether behavior or attitude change is a *side effect* or a *planned effect* of a technology. While acknowledging unintended side effects, captology focuses on the planned persuasive effects of using computer technologies.

APPLICATIONS OF PERSUASIVE TECHNOLOGY SYSTEMS

Using computing technology to change attitudes and behaviors has applications in various domains. Areas that have shown considerable promise include health interventions (Binik, Westbury, & Servan-Schreiber, 1989; Bosworth, Gustafson, & Hawkins, 1994; Lieberman, 1992, 1997; Marshall & Maguire, 1971; Parise, Kiesler, Sproull, & Waters, 1999; Reardon, 1987; Schneider, Walter, & O'Donnell, 1990; Street, Gold, & Manning, 1997), business applications such as buying and branding (Anthes, 1999; Davis, 1999; Demaree, 1987; Feldstein & Kruse, 1998; Gopal, 1997; Henke, 1999; Karson,

1998; Lohse & Spiller, 1998; Nowak, Shamp, Hollander, & Camerson, 1999; Risden, 1998; Rowley, 1995; Schlosser & Kanifer, 1999), and education and training (Hennessy & O'Shea, 1993; Lester, 1997; Sampson, 1992; Stoney & Wild, 1998). Less developed application areas for persuasive technologies include ecology, personal management and improvement, occupational productivity, social activism and politics, and safety (Fogg, 1998; King & Tester, 1999).

Although the applications for persuasive technologies are diverse, the computing products for these applications share predictable similarities. The framework we present in the next section provides one way to identify the similarity and differences among persuasive technologies. In a larger sense, the framework provides a way to organize research and understanding in this domain.

A FRAMEWORK FOR PERSUASIVE TECHNOLOGY: THE FUNCTIONAL TRIAD

Computers play many roles, some of which go unseen and unnoticed. From a user's perspective, computers function in three basic ways: as tools, as media, and as social actors. During the past two decades, researchers and designers have discussed variants of these functions, usually as metaphors for computer use (e.g., Kay, 1984; Verplank, Fulton, Black, & Moggridge, 1993). However, these three categories are more than metaphors; they are basic ways in which people view or respond to computing technologies.

Described in more detail elsewhere (Fogg, 1999, 2002), the Functional Triad is a framework that makes explicit these three computer functions: tools, media, and social actors. First, as this framework suggests, computer applications or systems function as tools, pro-

viding users with new abilities or powers. Using computers as tools, people can do things they could not do before or can do things more easily.

The Functional Triad also suggests that computers function as media, a role that grew dramatically during the 1990s as computers became increasingly powerful in displaying graphics and in exchanging information over a network such as the World Wide Web. As a medium, a computer can convey either symbolic content (e.g., text, data graphs, icons) or sensory content (e.g., real-time video, virtual worlds, simulation).

Finally, computers also function as social actors. Empirical research demonstrates that people form social relationships with technologies (Reeves & Nass, 1996). Although the precise causal factors for these social responses have yet to be outlined in detail, one could reasonably hypothesize that users respond socially when computers do at least one of the following: (a) adopt animate characteristics (e.g., physical features, emotions, voice communication), (b) play animate roles (e.g., coach, pet, assistant, opponent), or (c) follow social rules or dynamics (e.g., greetings, apologies, turn taking).

The Functional Triad is not a theory; it is a framework for analysis and design. In all but the most extreme cases, a single interactive technology is a mix of these three functions, combining them to create an overall user experience. In captology, the Functional Triad is useful because it helps to show how computer technologies can employ different techniques for changing attitudes and behaviors. For example, computers as tools persuade differently from computers as social actors. The strategies and theories that apply to each function differ. This chapter next describes aspects of persuasive technology, organizing the content according to the three elements in the Functional Triad.

Computers as Persuasive Tools

In general, computers as persuasive tools induce attitude and behavior changes by increasing a person's abilities or making something easier to do (Tombari, Fitzpatrick, & Childress, 1985). Although one could propose numerous possibilities for persuasion in this manner, here we suggest four general ways in which computers persuade as tools: by (a) increasing self-efficacy, (b) providing tailored information, (c) triggering decision making, and (d) simplifying or guiding people through a process.

Computers That Increase Self-Efficacy. Computers can increase self-efficacy (Lieberman, 1992), an important contributor to attitude and behavior change processes. Self-efficacy describes individuals' beliefs in their ability to take successful action in specific domains (Bandura, 1997; Bandura, Georgas, & Manthouli, 1996). When people perceive high self-efficacy in a given domain, they are more likely to take action. And because self-efficacy is a perceived quality, even if individuals merely believe that their actions are more effective and productive (perhaps because they are using a specific computing technology), they are more likely to perform a particular behavior (Bandura, 1997; Bandura et al., 1996). As a result, functioning as tools, computing technologies can make individuals feel more efficient, productive, in control, and generally effective (DeCharms, 1968; Kernal, 2000; Pancer, George, & Gebotys, 1992). For example, a heart rate monitor may help people to feel more effective in meeting their exercise goals when it provides ongoing information on heart rate and calories burned. Without the heart rate monitor, people could still take their pulse and calculate calories, but the computer device—whether it be worn or part of the exercise machinery—makes these tasks easier. The ease of tracking heart rate

and calories burned likely increases self-efficacy in fitness behavior, making it more likely individuals will continue to exercise (Brehm, 1997; Strecher, DeVellis, Becker, & Rosenstock, 1986; Thompson, 1992).

Computers That Provide Tailored Information. Next, computers act as tools when they tailor information, offering people content that is pertinent to their needs and contexts. Compared to general information, tailored information increases the potential for attitude and behavior change (Beniger, 1987; Dijkstra et al., 1998; Jimison, Street, & Gold, 1997; Nowak et al., 1999; Strecher et al., 1999; Strecher et al., 1994).

One notable example of a tailoring technology is the Chemical Scorecard Web site (www.scorecard.org), which generates information according to an individual's geographical location in order to achieve a persuasive outcome. After people enter their zip code in this Web site, the Web technology reports on chemical hazards in their neighborhood, identifies companies that create those hazards, and describes the potential health risks. Although no published studies document the persuasive effects of this particular technology, outside research and analysis suggests that making information relevant to individuals increases their attention and arousal, which can ultimately lead to increased attitude and behavior change (Beniger, 1987; MacInnis & Jaworski, 1989; MacInnis, Moorman, & Jaworski, 1991; Strecher et al., 1999).

Computers That Trigger Decision Making. Technology can also influence people by triggering or cueing a decision-making process. For example, today's Web browsers launch a new window to alert people before they send information over insecure network connections. The message window serves as a signal to consumers to rethink their planned actions.

A similar example exists in a very different context. Cities concerned with automobile speeding in neighborhoods can use a stand-alone radar trailer that senses the velocity of an oncoming automobile and displays that speed on a large screen. This technology is designed to trigger a decision-making process regarding driving speed.

Interactive technologies that provide cues at strategic places and times fit well within the cognitive and affective response systems that humans already possess. Research has shown the effect of cues in attitude formation (Petty & Cacioppo, 1986) as well as how people use cues to assess their environment and their own feelings quickly (Petty, Cacioppo, Sedikides, & Strathman, 1988; Petty, Schumann, Richman, & Strathman, 1993).

Computers That Simplify or Guide People Through a Process. By facilitating or simplifying a process for users, technology can minimize barriers that may impede a target behavior. For example, in the context of Web commerce, technology can simplify a multistep process down to a click of the mouse. Typically, to purchase something online, a consumer needs to select an item, place it in a virtual shopping cart, proceed to checkout, enter personal and billing information, and verify an order confirmation. Amazon.com and other e-commerce companies have simplified this process by storing customer information so that consumers need not reenter information for every transaction. By lowering the time commitment and reducing the steps needed to accomplish a goal, these companies have reduced the barriers for purchasing products from their sites. The principle used by Web and other computer technology (Todd & Benbasat, 1994) is similar to the dynamic that Ross and Nisbett (1991) discussed on facilitating behaviors through modifying the situation.

In addition to reducing barriers for a target behavior, computers can lead people through

processes to help them change attitudes and behaviors (Muehlenhard, Baldwin, Bourg, & Piper, 1988; Tombari et al., 1985). For example, a computer nutritionist can guide individuals through a month of healthy eating by providing recipes for each day and grocery lists for each week. In general, by following a computer-led process, users (a) are exposed to information they might not have seen otherwise and (b) are engaged in activities they might not have done otherwise (Fogg, 2002).

Computers as Persuasive Media

The next area of the Functional Triad deals with computers as persuasive media. Although *media* can mean many things, here we focus on the power of computer simulations. In this role, computer technology provides people with experiences, either firsthand or vicarious. By providing simulated experiences, computers can change people's attitudes and behaviors. Outside the world of computing, experiences have a powerful impact on people's attitudes, behaviors, and thoughts (Reed, 1996). Experiences offered via interactive technology have similar effects (Bullinger, Roessler, & Mueller-Spahn, 1998; Fogg, 2002). In what follows, we describe three types of persuasive computer simulations.

Computers That Simulate Cause and Effect. One type of computer simulation allows users to vary the inputs and observe the effects (Hennessy & O'Shea, 1993)—what we call "cause-and-effect simulators." The key to effective cause-and-effect simulators is their ability to demonstrate the consequence of actions immediately and credibly (Alessi, 1991; Balci, 1986, 1998; Crosbie & Hay, 1978; de Jong, 1991; Hennessy & O'Shea, 1993; Zietsman & Hewson, 1986). These computer simulations give people firsthand insight into how inputs (e.g., putting money into a savings account) affect an output (e.g., accrued retirement savings). By allowing people to explore causes and effects of situations, these computer simulations can shape attitudes and behaviors.

Computers That Simulate Environments. A second type of computer simulation is the "environment simulator." These simulators are designed to provide users with new surroundings, usually through images and sound. In these simulated environments, users have experiences that can lead to attitude and behavior change (Bullinger et al., 1998), including experiences that are designed as games or explorations (Lieberman, 1992; Schlosser & Kanifer, 1999; Schneider et al., 1990; Woodward, Carnine, & Davis, 1986).

The efficacy of this approach is demonstrated by research on the Tectrix Virtual Reality Bike (an exercise bike that includes a computer and monitor that shows a simulated world). Porcari, Zedaker, and Maldari (1998) found that people using an exercise device with computer simulation of a passing landscape exercised harder than those who used an exercise device without simulation. Both groups, however, felt that they had exerted themselves a similar amount. This outcome caused by simulating an outdoor experience mirrors findings from other research; people exercise harder when outside than when inside a gym (Ceci & Hassmen, 1991).

Environmental simulators can also change attitudes. Using a virtual reality environment in which the people saw and felt a simulated spider, Carlin, Hoffman, and Weghorst (1997) were able to decrease the fear of spiders in the participants. In this research, participants wore a head-mounted display that immersed them into a virtual room, and they were able to control both the number of spiders and their proximity. In this case study, Carlin and colleagues found that the virtual reality treat-ment reduced the fear of spiders in the real world. Other similar therapies have been used for fear of flying (Klein, 1999; Wiederhold, Davis, Wiederhold, & Riva, 1998), agoraphobia (Ghosh & Marks, 1987), claustrophobia (Bullinger et al., 1998), and fear of heights (Bullinger et al., 1998), among others (Kirby, 1996).

Computers That Simulate Objects. The third type of computer simulations are "object simulators." These are computerized devices that simulate an object (as opposed to an environment). The "Baby Think It Over" infant simulator described at the beginning of this chapter is one such device. Another example is a specially equipped car, created by Chrysler Corporation, designed to help teens experience the effect of alcohol on their driving. Used as part of high school programs, teen drivers first navigate the special car under normal conditions. Then the operator activates an onboard computer system that simulates how an inebriated person would drive—sluggish brakes, inaccurate steering, and so on. This computer-enhanced care provides teens with an experience designed to change attitudes and behaviors about drinking and driving. Although the sponsors of this car do not measure the impact of this intervention, the anecdotal evidence is compelling (Machrone, 1998).

Computers as Persuasive Social Actors

The final corner of the Functional Triad focuses on computers as persuasive social actors, a view of computers that has only recently become widely recognized. Past empirical research has shown that individuals form social relationships with technology even when the stimulus is rather impoverished (Fogg, 1997; Marshall & Maguire, 1971; Moon & Nass, 1996; Muller, 1974; Nass, Fogg, & Moon, 1996; Nass, Moon, Fogg,

Reeves, & Dryer, 1995; Nass & Steuer, 1993; Nass, Moon, Morkes, Eun-Young, & Fogg, 1997; Parise et al., 1999; Quintanar, Crowell, & Pryor, 1982; Reeves & Nass, 1996). For example, individuals share reciprocal relationships with computers (Fogg & Nass, 1997a; Parise et al., 1999), can be flattered by computers (Fogg & Nass, 1997b), and are polite to computers (Nass, Moon, & Carney, 1999).

Laboratory experiments have demonstrated how computers can be persuasive social actors (Fogg, 1997; Fogg & Nass, 1997a, 1997b; Nass, Fogg, & Moon, 1996). In particular, computers as social actors can persuade people to change their attitudes and behaviors by (a) providing social support, (b) modeling attitudes or behaviors, and (c) leveraging social rules and dynamics.

Computers That Provide Social Support. Computers can provide a form of social support in order to persuade, a dynamic that has long been observed in human-human interactions (Jones, 1990). While the potential for effective social support from computer technology has yet to be fully explored, a small set of empirical studies provide evidence for this phenomenon (Fogg, 1997; Fogg & Nass, 1997b; Nass, Fogg, & Moon, 1996; Reeves & Nass, 1996). For example, computing technology can influence individuals by providing praise or criticism, thus manipulating levels of social support (Fogg & Nass, 1997b; Muehlenhard et al., 1988).

Outside of the research context, various technology products use the power of praise to influence users. For example, the Dole 5 a Day Adventures CD-ROM, discussed earlier, uses a cast of more than 30 on-screen characters to provide social support to users who perform various activities. Characters such as Bobby Banana and Pamela Pineapple praise individuals for checking labels on virtual frozen foods, for following guidelines from the food pyramid, and for creating a nutritious virtual salad.

Computers That Model Attitudes and Behaviors. In addition to providing social support, computer systems can persuade by modeling target attitudes and behaviors. In the natural world, people learn directly through firsthand experience and indirectly through observation (Bandura, 1997). When a behavior is modeled by an attractive individual or is shown to result in positive consequences, people are more likely to enact that behavior (Bandura, 1997). Lieberman's (1997) research on a computer game designed to model health maintenance behaviors shows the positive effects that an on-screen cartoon model had on those who played the game. In a similar way, the product "Alcohol 101" (www.centurycouncil.org/underage/education/a101.cfm) uses navigable on-screen video clips of human actors dealing with problematic situations that arise during college drinking parties. The initial studies on the Alcohol 101 intervention show positive outcomes (Reis, 1998). In the future, computer-based characters, whether artistically rendered or video images, are increasingly likely to serve as important models for attitudes and behaviors.

Computers That Leverage Social Rules and Dynamics. Computers have also been shown to be effective persuasive social actors when they leverage social rules and dynamics (Fogg, 1997; Friedman & Grudin, 1998; Marshall & Maguire, 1971; Parise et al., 1999). These rules include turn taking, politeness norms, and sources of praise (Reeves & Nass, 1996). The rule of reciprocity—that we must return favors to others—is among the most powerful social rules (Gouldner, 1960) and is one that has been shown to also have force when people interact with computers. Fogg and Nass (1997a) showed that people performed more work and better work for a computer that assisted them on a previous task. In essence, users reciprocated help to a computer. On the retaliation side, the inverse of reciprocity, the research showed that people performed lower quality work for a computer that had served them poorly in a previous task. In a related vein, Moon (1998) found that individuals followed rules of impression management when interacting with a computer. Specifically, when individuals believed that the computer interviewing them was in the same room, they provided more honest answers than did individuals who interacted with a computer believed to be a few miles away. In addition, participants were more persuaded by the "proximate" computer.

The preceding paragraphs outline some of the early demonstrations of computers as social actors that motivate and influence people in predetermined ways, often paralleling research from long-standing human-human research.

Functional Triad Summary

The Functional Triad is a useful framework for the study of computers as persuasive technologies. It makes explicit how a technology can change attitudes and behaviors—either by increasing a person's capability, by providing users with an experience, or by leveraging the power of social relationships. Each of these paths suggests related persuasion strategies, dynamics, and theories. One element that is common to all three functions is the role of credibility. Credible tools, credible media, and credible social actors all will lead to increased power to persuade. In the next section, we discuss the elements of computer credibility.

COMPUTERS AND CREDIBILITY

One key issue in captology is computer credibility, a topic that suggests questions such as "Do people find computers to be credible sources?" "What aspects of computers boost credibility?" and "How do computers gain and lose credibility?" Understanding the elements of computer credibility promotes a deeper understanding of how computers can change attitudes and behaviors, as credibility is a key element in many persuasion processes (Gahm, 1986; Lerch, Prietula, & Kulik, 1997).

In this section, we address two aspects of computer credibility. First, we discuss computer credibility in general—what computer credibility is and what the existing literature says about this topic. Next, we look specifically at computer credibility as it relates to the World Wide Web, an area of increasing importance as more computing information and experiences become Web based (Caruso, 1999).

What Is Credibility?

Credibility has been a topic of social science research since the 1930s (for reviews, see Petty & Cacioppo, 1981; Self, 1996). Virtually all credibility researchers have described credibility as a perceived quality made up of multiple dimensions (e.g., Buller & Burgoon, 1996; Gatignon & Robertson, 1991; Petty & Cacioppo, 1981; Self, 1996; Stiff, 1994). This description has two key components germane to computer credibility. First, credibility is a perceived quality; it does not reside in an object, a person, or a piece of information. Therefore, in discussing the credibility of a computer product, one is always discussing the *perception* of credibility for the computer product.

Next, researchers generally agree that credibility perceptions result from evaluating multiple dimensions simultaneously. Although the literature varies on exactly how many dimensions contribute to the credibility construct, the majority of researchers identify trustworthiness and expertise as the two key components of credibility (Self, 1996). Trustworthiness, a key element in the credibility calculus, is described by terms such as *well-intentioned, truthful,* and *unbiased.* The trustworthiness dimension of credibility captures the perceived goodness or morality of the source. Expertise, the other dimension of credibility, is described by terms such as *knowledgeable, experienced,* and *competent.* The expertise dimension of credibility captures the perceived knowledge and skill of the source.

Extending research on credibility to the domain of computers, it has been proposed that *highly credible computer products will be perceived to have high levels of both trustworthiness and expertise* (Fogg & Tseng, 1999). In evaluating credibility, a computer user will make an assessment of the computer product's trustworthiness and expertise to arrive at an overall credibility assessment.

Overview of Computer Credibility Research

The research relating to computer credibility is often obscured by semantic issues (Fogg & Tseng, 1999). A number of studies do not use the term *credibility* but instead use phrases such as "trust in the information," "believe the output," and "trust in the advice" (see, e.g., Kantowitz, Hanowski, & Kantowitz, 1997; Muir, 1994; Muir & Moray, 1996). These phrases are essentially synonymous with credibility; they refer to the same psychological construct.

In some situations, computer credibility is not an issue for those who use computers. Sometimes, the computer system is invisible to users (e.g., a fuel injection system), or users do not question the device's competence or bias (e.g., a pocket calculator). But in many situations, computer credibility matters a great deal (Sampson et al., 1992). Tseng and Fogg (1999) proposed that computer credibility matters when computing products do one of eight things: act as knowledge sources, instruct or tutor users, act as decision aids, report measurements, run simulations, render virtual environments, report on work performed, or report about their own state.

Although computer credibility is relevant to computer users in these eight areas, a relatively small body of research addresses perceptions of credibility in human-computer interactions. In what follows, we draw on the work of Fogg and Tseng (1999) to describe how previous research on computer credibility clusters into six domains.

Cluster 1: The Credible Computer Myth

One cluster of research investigates the notion that people automatically assume computers are credible. In framing these studies, the authors state that people perceive computers as "magical" (Bauhs & Cooke, 1994; Hennessy & O'Shea, 1993) with an " 'aura' of objectivity" (Andrews & Gutkin, 1991), as having a "scientific mystique" (Andrews & Gutkin, 1991), as "awesome thinking machines" (Pancer et al., 1992), as "infallible" (Kerber, 1983), as having "superior wisdom" (Sheridan, Vamos, & Aida, 1983), and as "faultless" (Sheridan et al., 1983). In sum, researchers have long suggested that people generally are in "awe" of computers (Honaker, Hector, & Harrell, 1986) and that people "assign more credibility" to computers than to humans (Andrews & Gutkin, 1991). In addition, anecdotal experience suggests that—at least during one period in history—computers were perceived by the general public as virtually infallible (Pancer et al., 1992; Sheridan et al., 1983).

But what does the empirical research show? Most studies that directly examine assumptions about computer credibility conclude that computers are *not* perceived as more credible than human experts (Andrews & Gutkin, 1991; Honaker et al., 1986; Matarazzo, 1986; Northcraft & Earley, 1989; Pancer et al., 1992). In some cases, computers may be perceived as *less* credible (Lerch & Prietula, 1989; Rieh & Belkin, 1998; Waern & Ramberg, 1996). Although anecdotal evidence suggests that people perceive computers as more credible than humans in some situations, little solid empirical evidence supports this notion (for exceptions, see Dijkstra et al., 1998; Ingle, 1975). Future research is needed to reconcile anecdotal experience with the majority of research findings, which have largely failed to document that people assume computers to be highly credible.

Cluster 2: Dynamics of Computer Credibility

Another cluster of research examines the dynamics of computer credibility—how it is gained, how it is lost, and how it can be regained. Some studies demonstrate what is highly intuitive: Computers gain credibility when they provide information that users find accurate or correct (Amoroso, Taylor, Watson, & Weiss, 1994; Hanowski, Kantowitz, & Kantowitz, 1994; Kantowitz et al., 1997; Muir & Moray, 1996); conversely, computers lose credibility when they provide information that users find erroneous (Kantowitz et al., 1997; Lee, 1991; Muir & Moray,

1996). Although these conclusions seem obvious, we find this research valuable because it represents the first empirical evidence for these ideas. Other findings on the dynamics of credibility are less obvious, which we summarize in the following paragraphs.

Effects of Computer Errors. A few studies have investigated the effects of computer errors on perceptions of computer credibility. Although researchers acknowledge that a single error may severely damage computer credibility in certain situations (Kantowitz et al., 1997), no study has clearly documented this effect. In fact, in some research, error rates as high as 30% did not cause users to dismiss an on-board automobile navigation system (Fox, 1998; Hanowski et al., 1994; Kantowitz et al., 1997). In other situations, an error rate of this size would likely not be acceptable.

Impact of Small Errors. Another research area has been the effects of large and small errors on credibility. Virtually all researchers agree that computer errors damage credibility—at least to some extent. One study demonstrated that large errors hurt credibility perceptions more than did small errors, but not in proportion to the gravity of the error (Lee, 1991; Lee & Moray, 1992). Another study showed no difference between the effects of large and small mistakes on credibility (Kantowitz et al., 1997). Findings from these studies and other work (Muir & Moray, 1996) suggest that small computer errors have disproportionately large effects on perceptions of credibility.

Regaining Credibility. Researchers have also examined how computer products can regain credibility (Lee & Moray, 1992). Two paths are documented in the literature. First, the computer product may regain credibility by providing good information over a period of time (Hanowski et al., 1994; Kantowitz et al., 1997). Or, the computer product may regain some credibility by continuing to make the identical error; users then learn to anticipate and compensate for the persistent mistake (Muir & Moray, 1996). In either case, regaining credibility is difficult, especially from a practical standpoint. Once users perceive that a computer product lacks credibility, they are likely to stop using it, which provides no opportunity for the product to regain credibility (Muir & Moray, 1996).

Cluster 3: Situational Factors That Affect Credibility

The credibility of a computer product does not always depend on the computer product itself. Context of computer use can affect credibility. The existing research shows that three related situations increase computer credibility. First, in unfamiliar situations, people give more credence to a computer product that orients them (Muir, 1987). Next, computer products have more credibility after people have failed to solve a problem on their own (Waern & Hagglund, 1992). Finally, computer products seem more credible when people have a strong need for information (Hanowski et al., 1994; Kantowitz, 1997). Indeed, other situations are likely to affect the perception of computer credibility such as situations with varying levels of risk, situations with forced choices, and situations with different levels of cognitive load. However, research is lacking on these points.

Cluster 4: User Variables That Affect Credibility

Although individual differences among users likely affect perceptions of computer credibility in many ways, the extant research allows us to draw two general conclusions. First, users who are familiar with the content will evaluate the computer product more stringently (Honaker et al., 1986; Kantowitz et al., 1997; Lerch & Prietula, 1989). Conversely, those who are not familiar with the subject matter are more likely to view the computer product as more credible (Waern & Hagglund, 1992; Waern & Ramberg, 1996). These findings match credibility research outside of human-computer interaction (Gatignon & Robertson, 1991; Self, 1996; Zajonc, 1980).

Next, researchers have investigated how user acceptance of computer advice changes when users understand how the computer arrives at its conclusions. One study showed that knowing more about the computer actually reduced users' perception of computer credibility (Bauhs & Cooke, 1994). However, other researchers have shown the opposite to be the case; users were more inclined to view a computer as credible when they understood how it worked (Lee, 1991; Lerch & Prietula, 1989; Miller & Larson, 1992; Muir, 1987).

Cluster 5: Visual Design and Credibility

Another line of research has investigated the effects of interface design on computer credibility (Friedman & Grudin, 1998; Kim & Moon, 1997). These experiments have shown that—at least in laboratory settings—certain interface design features, such as cool (as opposed to warm) color tones and balanced layout, can enhance users' perceptions of interface trustworthiness. Although these design implications may differ according to users, cultures, and target applications, this research sets an important precedent in studying the effects of interface design elements on perceptions of trustworthiness and credibility.

Cluster 6: Human Credibility Markers in Human-Computer Interaction

An additional research strategy has been investigating how credibility findings from human-human interactions apply to human-computer interactions. Various researchers have taken this approach (Burgoon et al., 2000; Fogg, 1997; Kim & Moon, 1997; Muir, 1987; Quintanar et al., 1982; Reeves & Nass, 1996), as discussed earlier in the section on computers as persuasive social actors. A handful of such studies have measured credibility as an outcome to various experimental manipulations. In what follows, we describe two lines of research as they relate to the credibility of technology devices.

Affiliation Effects. In most situations, people find members of their "in-groups" (e.g., those from the same company or the same team) to be more credible than people who belong to "out-groups" (Mackie, Worth, & Asuncion, 1990). Researchers demonstrated that this dynamic also held true when people interacted with a computer they believed to be a member of their in-group (Fogg, 1997; Nass, Fogg, & Moon, 1996). Specifically, users reported the in-group computer's information to be of higher quality, and they were more likely to follow the computer's advice.

Labeling Effects. Titles that denote expertise (e.g., *Dr., Professor*) make people seem more credible (Cialdini, 1993). Applying this phenomenon to the world of technology, researchers labeled a technology as a "specialist." This study showed that people perceived the device labeled as a specialist to be more credible than the device labeled as a generalist (Nass, Reeves, & Leshner, 1996; Reeves & Nass, 1996).

In addition to the preceding lines of research, other human-human credibility dynamics are likely to apply to human-computer interaction. Outlined elsewhere (Fogg, 1997), the possibilities include the following principles to increase computer credibility: *physical attractiveness* (Byrne, 1971; Chaiken, 1979) or making the computing device or interface attractive, *association* (Cialdini, 1993) or associating the computer with desirable things or people, *authority* (Gatignon & Robertson, 1991; Zimbardo & Leippe, 1991) or establishing the computer as an authority figure, *source diversification* (Gatignon & Robertson, 1991; Harkins & Petty, 1981) or using a variety of computers to offer the same information, *nonverbal cues* (Larson, 1995) or endowing computer agents with nonverbal markers of credibility, *familiarity* (Gatignon & Robertson, 1991; Self, 1996; Zajonc, 1980) or increasing the familiarity of computer products, and *social status* (Cialdini, 1993) or increasing the status of a computer product.

Research has yet to specifically show how the preceding principles—which are powerful credibility enhancers in human-human interactions—might be implemented in computing systems (Fogg, 1998).

We now turn our attention to credibility perceptions of the World Wide Web, an increasingly important aspect of computers as persuasive technologies.

Credibility and the World Wide Web

The nearly nonexistent barriers to publishing material on the World Wide Web has made the Internet a repository for all types of information, including misinformation. As a result, credibility has become a major concern for those seeking or posting information on the Web (Caruso, 1999; Johnson & Kaye, 1998;

Kilgore, 1998; McDonald, 1999; Nielsen, 1997). During the second half of 1990, librarians, designers, and researchers have addressed these problems in different ways. The existing literature on Web credibility can therefore be divided into three categories: (a) evaluation guidelines, (b) design guidelines, and (c) research findings on credibility evaluations.

Evaluation Guidelines on Web Credibility. The first category of Web credibility literature is clearly the most plentiful: guidelines on how to evaluate sources. Often discussed under the label of "information quality," this aspect of Web credibility has been embraced by librarians and others. They see themselves as having key skills to evaluate Web sources and to train others to do so (Tillman, 2000). As a result, many excellent guides exist to help students and researchers evaluate the information they find online (e.g., Caywood, 1999; Grassian, 1998; Rosenfeld, 1994; Smith, 1997; Stoker & Cooke, 1995; Tate & Alexander, 1996; Tillman, 2000; Wilkinson, 1997). The creators of these guidelines often have adapted evaluation strategies for other media and applied them to the Web, which includes examining elements such as purpose, authority, scope, audience, cost, and format (Katz, 1992).

Design Guidelines on Web Credibility. The second category of Web credibility literature takes a different approach. While the information is still prescriptive in nature, the aim is to help designers create Web sites that convey maximum credibility to users. In essence, these are design guidelines. For example, in his online column (www.useit.com), Nielsen has addressed the issue of designing for Web credibility (e.g., Nielsen, 1997; Nielsen, 1999a, 1999b). Other designers and researchers have also suggested approaches to make

Web sites more credible or trustworthy (Cheskin Research & Studio Archetype, 1999; Johnson, 1999). There is no universal consensus on how to design for credibility, but most sources discuss the importance of elements such as attractive layouts, intuitive navigation systems, and clear presentation of material (Dormann, 1997).

Research on How People Assess Web Credibility. The third category of Web credibility literature is also the least common: research studies that examine how people evaluate the credibility of Web sites (Cheskin Research & Studio Archetype, 1999; Critchfield, 1998; Eighmey, 1997; Fogg et al., 2000; Rieh & Belkin, 1998). In one small study, notable because so few exist, Critchfield (1998) tentatively concluded that users' "perception of the credibility of a resource was influenced by an aesthetically pleasing, usable Web site design." With similar intent, Morkes and Nielsen (1997) conducted a study examining how writing style on the Web affected user responses, including credibility impressions. Although not statistically based, this work concluded that objective writing (as opposed to promotional writing) enhances credibility.

A larger study by Cheskin Research and Studio Archetype (1999), two commercial firms in the Silicon Valley area of California, examined "e-commerce trust"—a related, but not identical, construct to Web credibility. This study consisted of 138 participants and found six important elements that gave people confidence to transact business with Web sites: (a) brand ("the company's reputation"), (b) navigation ("ease of finding what the user seeks"), (c) fulfillment ("the process users experience from when they begin a purchase until they receive a shipment"), (d) presentation ("how the site communicates meaningful information"), (e) technology ("ways in which the site functions technically"), and (f) seals of approval ("symbols that represent companies that assure the safety of Web sites").

Building on research described previously, Fogg and colleagues (2000) collaborated with industry partners to conduct an online study focusing on perceptions of Web credibility (www.webcredibility.org). This study consisted of more than 1,400 participants and examined 51 elements relating to credibility evaluations. The data suggest five major conclusions: (a) Web sites gain credibility when they convey a real-world presence (e.g., listing a physical address or a phone number); (b) even small errors (e.g., typos, broken links) hurt credibility substantially; (c) ease of navigation leads to enhanced perceptions of credibility; (d) Web ads that distract or confuse reduce credibility, while other ads can enhance credibility; and (e) technical problems weaken credibility.

Taken together, these research studies suggest similar findings, but further research is needed to understand deeply what leads people to believe—or not believe—what they find on the Web. Further insight into Web credibility will contribute significantly to the study of computers as persuasive technologies.

KEY QUESTIONS AND FUTURE DIRECTIONS

This chapter has provided definitions and a framework for better understanding computers as persuasive technologies. Although knowledge about the theory, design, and analysis of persuasive technology continues to increase, many key questions in captology remain unanswered. They include the following:

- What are the *best applications* of persuasive technologies?
- What are the *potentials* of persuasive technologies?

- What are the *limits* of persuasive technologies?
- What are the *effects* and *side effects* of using persuasive technologies?
- What are the *ethical implications* of persuasive technologies? (Berdichevsky & Neunschwander, 1999; Friedman & Grudin, 1998)

Although the extant literature that focuses directly on computers as persuasive technologies is relatively small, the future possibilities are large. To help move work forward in this area—both in research and in design—in what follows, we suggest future directions for captology in terms of who, what, how, and why.

Who Is Best Positioned to Research Captology?

The study of computers as persuasive technologies is an interdisciplinary endeavor by definition. As a result, captology does not fit neatly into a single academic department. Those who research computers and persuasion are likely to be individuals or teams with interdisciplinary interests, combining social science approaches with technology and design insights.

Interdisciplinary Academics. Some academic departments are better suited for captology research than are others. For example, departments of communications have a history of using social science methods to study the impact of new technologies. This is likely to be a good fit. Many psychology researchers have relevant skills for research in captology. However, traditional psychology departments have been slow to study new technologies, and they may fail to reward people who make this an area of research. Fortunately, some institutions have interdisciplinary programs, such as symbolic systems and human-computer interaction, that bring together areas germane to persuasive technologies.

Industry Researchers. Industry researchers are in a good position to study persuasive technologies. Because the ability to influence is a core competency of—and presents a strategic advantage to—many companies, captology has been a good fit with industry researchers. The major disadvantage of industrial research in this area is that, for the most part, the research findings are not publicly shared. This approach, then, makes little contribution to a wider understanding of persuasive technologies.

Industry and Academic Partnerships. A third approach, which seems to be the most promising, is collaborative research among academics and industry players. Each party can bring what it does well to the endeavor. If academics are slow to partner with industry in this research, it is likely that academics will be left behind in understanding persuasive technologies. The persuasive devices and Web sites launched during the past few years have been well ahead of most academic understanding in this area. Academics would do well to partner with industry in order to move quickly, staying abreast of new developments.

What Should We Focus on in Captology?

Because captology is relatively uncharted territory, many paths will offer new insights and understanding. However, not all paths have equal potential or value. In what follows, we describe directions we deem most profitable, organized into the categories of dependent variables and independent variables.

Dependent Variables

Although most of the psychology literature on persuasion is based on measuring attitude formation and change, people involved in captology would do well to focus on behavior change as the principal dependent variable for persuasive technologies. Behavior change is a more compelling metric than attitude change for at least three reasons: (a) behavior change is thought to be more difficult to achieve than attitude change (Larson, 1995; Zimbardo & Leippe, 1991), (b) behavior change is more useful to people concerned with real-world outcomes (Graeff, Elder, & Booth, 1993; Street et al., 1997), and (c) researchers can measure behavior change without relying on self-reports.

Our bias for behavioral measures is not intended to discourage research with attitudinal measures or other types of data collection. We simply propose that a focus on behavior change in captology will give clear evidence of how computers can motivate and influence people.

In addition, we advocate studying the planned effects of technology, not the side effects. Although the side effects of technology use is an important area of inquiry, this is not central to the study of persuasive technologies. The core of captology deals with planned effects—the attitude or behavior changes that were anticipated and intended. By researching these planned effects, we will be better able to build a body of knowledge about technologies designed to influence and motivate.

Independent Variables

What variables are most profitable to manipulate in the study of persuasive technologies? A wealth of possible research directions awaits captology researchers. In what follows, we propose some paths we view as most

important to increasing our shared understanding of persuasive technology.

Technology Forms. From our vantage point,
many persuasive technologies of the future
will be specialized, distributed, or embedded
computing systems—what some call "pervasive" or "ubiquitous" computing (Weiser,
1991). Ubiquitous computing systems, which
might not look anything like today's desktop
computers, hold special implications for the
study of persuasive technologies. Because persuasive situations occur most frequently in
the context of normal life activities—not
when people are seated at their desktop
computers—we advocate researching the impact of different technology forms on persuasion. This line of research examines, in part,
the differential persuasive outcomes of using
an identical computing application in different formats, for example, a handheld device
versus a wearable computer versus a desktop
machine. With computing technology moving
toward portable and wearable devices, it is important to understand how these new forms
change the persuasive potentials of interactive
technology.

Same Strategy, Different Manifestations.
Another profitable path for those studying
persuasive technologies is to focus on a single
persuasion strategy and vary how a computing
device can implement that strategy. For example, positive feedback (e.g., praise) is a persuasion strategy that computers can manifest in
various ways—a text message, a human voice,
a musical passage, and so on. By keeping the
strategy constant and varying the manifestations, researchers can learn about the impact
of each manifestation type. Over time, we
then may be able to draw general conclusions
about the persuasive impact of different manifestations (e.g., how a voice from a computer
persuades vs. how text messages from a computer persuade).

Same Manifestation, Different Strategies. A
complementary approach to the preceding
approach is to hold the manifestation constant
in research while varying the persuasion strategy the computer uses. For example, the computer could always use voice but could vary
the persuasive strategy used (e.g., compare
praise, criticism, threats, and promises). By
keeping the manifestation of the strategy constant and varying the strategies, researchers
can, over time, theorize and generalize how
persuasive strategies function in a computing
system.

Avoiding Cross-Media Comparisons. An ongoing issue is the comparative effectiveness
of persuasive media types, for example, print
versus video versus interactive technologies.
These cross-media comparisons have limited
usefulness (for a longer discussion, see Kuomi,
1994). It is rare that a cross-media comparison
study has been able to generalize its conclusions beyond the specific stimuli used in the
particular study (for an exception, see Kernal,
2000). Although a researcher can clearly determine that Computer Program X is more
persuasive than Video Y or Pamphlet Z, these
results hold only for Artifacts X, Y, and Z—
not for comparing computers, videos, and
pamphlets in general. Too many variables are
at play in cross-media studies; as a result, no
useful theoretical understanding comes from
this type of research (Nass & Mason, 1990).

How Should We Study
Persuasive Technologies?

Like most research endeavors, the study of
computers as persuasive technologies lends
itself to various research methodologies.

Quantitative Research. Studying persuasive
technologies from a quantitative point of
view, such as experiments and surveys, can

produce conclusions supported by statistical evidence. Many studies discussed in this chapter are quantitative in nature, but we acknowledge that other approaches add significant value in researching persuasive technologies.

Qualitative Research. Studying persuasive technology products from a qualitative standpoint can offer insights not available through quantitative means. Participant-observer research, content analyses, heuristic analyses, and focus groups can be helpful. There are at least three reasonable outcomes to this type of research: generating rich insight into a particular persuasive technology (e.g., the strengths and weaknesses of a product), generating insight into a particular user group for a persuasive technology (e.g., a target group's biases and reactions to the product), and creating hypotheses for future research and design efforts. All of these outcomes are valuable contributions.

Literature Reviews. In addition to the methods just discussed, our understanding of persuasive technologies can be enhanced by careful reviews of literature from diverse fields. For example, Aristotle certainly did not have computers in mind when he wrote about the art of persuasion, but his work on rhetoric can broaden and deepen our understanding of how computers can motivate and influence people. In general, we can speed our understanding of persuasive technologies by gleaning the relevant work from other fields. The field of psychology—both cognitive and social—has a tradition of examining different types of persuasion and influence. The theories and methods from psychology transfer well to captology. In addition, the field of communication has a history of examining the persuasive effects of media and other types of message sources. Specifically, the applied domain of public information campaigns has a set of theories and practices that

can provide insight into the study of persuasive technologies.

Why Should We Research Persuasive Technologies?

In addition to the who, what, and how of future research on persuasive technologies, we also outline the "whys" or motives for engaging in this work.

Commercial Application. The commercial possibilities for persuasive technologies will continue to generate research for the foreseeable future. As corporations learn to create interactive technologies that influence individuals, they will most likely profit financially or gain a market advantage. The commercial applications are unlikely motivators for academics who study persuasive technologies.

Theoretical Understanding. One compelling reason to study captology, from an academic's perspective, is to increase knowledge about the theory and application of persuasive technology. As with other academic pursuits, the process of research and the insights gained can be intrinsically rewarding. The theoretical understanding not only can form a foundation for subsequent research in persuasive technologies but also can enhance research in other areas.

Prosocial Interventions. Another motive for researching persuasive technology is the potential for positive outcomes. Because many social problem can be minimized by changing attitudes and behaviors, persuasive technologies have a place in prosocial interventions. Many examples exist, addressing social issues that range from environmental issues to HIV transmission.

IMPACT OF PERSUASIVE TECHNOLOGIES

As computing technology becomes ubiquitous, we will see more examples—both good and bad—of computers designed to change attitudes and behaviors. We will see computers playing new roles in motivating health behaviors, promoting safety, promoting eco-friendly behavior, and selling products or services. To be sure, persuasive technologies will emerge in areas we cannot yet predict.

To some people, this forecast may sound like bad news—a world full of inescapable computer technology constantly prodding and provoking us. While it could happen, this "dystopian" scenario seems unlikely. We propose that in many cases, people will choose the technologies they want to influence them—just as people can choose a personal trainer at the gym or a tutor for their children. And even though certain types of persuasive technologies will be imposed on people—by corporations and government institutions—people will learn to recognize and respond appropriately to these persuasive appeals. In the extreme cases, we—as an association of persuasion scholars—will need to help create public policy to influence the design and uses of computers as persuasive technologies. However, to effectively shape the landscape of persuasive technologies, we need to educate ourselves and others about the potentials and pitfalls of this domain. In this way, we can leverage the power of persuasive technologies to improve our lives, our communities, and our society.

REFERENCES

Alessi, S. M. (1991). Fidelity in the design of instructional simulations. *Journal of Computer-Based Instruction, 15,* 40-47.

Amoroso, E., Taylor, C., Watson, J., & Weiss, J. (1994). A process-oriented methodology for assessing and improving software trustworthiness. In *Proceedings of the 2nd ACM Conference on Computer and Communications Security* (p. 39-50). New York: ACM Press.

Andrews, L. W., & Gutkin, T. B. (1991). The effects of human versus computer authorship on consumers' perceptions of psychological reports. *Computers in Human Behavior, 7,* 311-317.

Anthes, G. H. (1999, June 28). Persuasive technologies. *Computerworld,* pp. 76-77.

Balci, O. (1986). *Credibility assessment of simulation results: The state of the art.* Blacksburg: Virginia Polytechnic Institute and State University, Systems Research Center.

Balci, O. (1998, December). *Verification, validation, and accreditation.* Paper presented at the Winter Simulation Conference, Washington, DC.

Bandura, A. (1997). *Self-efficacy: The exercise of control.* New York: Freeman.

Bandura, A., Georgas, J., & Manthouli, M. (1996). Reflections on human agency. In J. Georgas, M. Manthouli, (Eds.), *Contemporary psychology in Europe: Theory, research, and applications* (pp. 194-210). Seattle, WA: Hogrefe & Huber.

Bauhs, J. A., & Cooke, N. J. (1994). Is knowing more really better? Effects of system development information in human-expert system interactions. In *Proceedings of the Conference on Human Factors and Computing Systems* (pp. 99-100). New York: ACM Press.

Beniger, J. R. (1987). Personalization of mass media and the growth of pseudo-community. *Communication Research, 14,* 352-371.

Berdichevsky, D., & Neunschwander, E. (1999). Towards an ethics of persuasive technology. *Communications of the ACM, 42*(5), 51-58.

Binik, Y. M., Westbury, C. F., & Servan-Schreiber, D. (1989). Interaction with a "sex-expert" system enhances attitudes towards computerized sex therapy. *Behaviour Research and Therapy, 27,* 303-306.

Bosworth, K., Gustafson, D. H., & Hawkins, R. P. (1994). The BARN system: Use and impact of adolescent health promotion via computer. *Computers in Human Behavior, 10,* 467-482.

Brehm, B. (1997, December). Self-confidence and exercise success. *Fitness Management,* pp. 22-23.

Buller, D. B., & Burgoon, J. K. (1996). Interpersonal deception theory. *Communication Theory, 6*, 203-242.

Bullinger, A. H., Roessler, A., & Mueller-Spahn, F. (1998). From toy to tool: The development of immersive virtual reality environments for psychotherapy of specific phobias. In G. Riva (Ed.), *Virtual reality in clinical psychology and neuroscience* (pp. 103-111). Amsterdam: IOS Press.

Burgoon, J. K., Bonito, J. A., Bengtsson, B., Cederberg, C., Lundeberg, M., & Allspach, L. (2000). Interactivity in human-computer interaction: A study of credibility, understanding, and influence. *Computers in Human Behavior, 16*, 553-574.

Byrne, D. E. (1971). *The attraction paradigm.* New York: Academic Press.

Carlin, A. S., Hoffman, H. G., & Weghorst, S. (1997). Virtual reality and tactile augmentation in the treatment of spider phobia: A case report. *Behaviour Research and Therapy, 35*, 153-158.

Caruso, D. (1997, December 29). Digital commerce: Knowing when you're being seduced by powerful persuasive techniques. *The New York Times.*

Caruso, D. (1998, June). Avoiding extinction. *I.D. Magazine, pp.* 39-40.

Caruso, D. (1999, November 22). Digital commerce: Self-indulgence in the Internet industry. *The New York Times.*

Caywood, C. (1999). *Library selection criteria for WWW resources.* [Online]. Available: www6.pilot.infi.net/:carolyn/criteria.html

Ceci, R., & Hassmen, P. (1991). Self-monitored exercise at three different PE intensities in treadmill vs. field running. *Medicine and Science in Sports and Exercise, 23*, 732-738.

Chaiken, S. (1979). Communicator physical attractiveness and persuasion. *Journal of Personality and Social Psychology, 37*, 1387-1397.

Cheskin Research & Studio Archetype. (1999). *eCommerce Trust Study.* [Online]. Available: www.studioarchetype.com/cheskin

Cialdini, R. B. (1993). *Influence: Science and practice* (3rd ed.). New York: HarperCollins.

Crawford, D. (1999). Forum. *Communications of the ACM, 42*(5), 11-13.

Critchfield, R. (1998). *Credibility and Web site design.* [Online]. Available: www.warner.edu/critchfield/hci/critchfield.html

Crosbie, R. E., & Hay, J. L. (1978). The credibility of computerised models. In R. E. Crosbie & J. L. Hay (Eds.), *Toward real-time simulation: Languages, models, and systems* (pp. 35-44). La Jolla, CA: Society of Computer Simulation.

Davis, J. F. (1999). Effectiveness of Internet advertising by leading national advertisers. In D. W. Schumann & E. Thorson (Eds.), *Advertising and the World Wide Web: Advertising and consumer psychology* (pp. 81-97). Mahwah, NJ: Lawrence Erlbaum.

de Jong, T. (1991). Learning and instruction with computer simulations. *Education & Computing, 6*, 217-229.

DeCharms, R. (1968). *Personal causation: The internal affective determinants of behavior.* New York: Academic Press.

Demaree, S. W. (1987). Interactive technology: The greatest sales tool ever invented? *Magazine of Bank Administration, 63*(1), 16, 18.

Denning, P., & Metcalfe, R. (1997). *Beyond calculation: The next fifty years of computing.* New York: Springer-Verlag.

Dijkstra, J. J., Liebrand, W. B. G., & Timminga, E. (1998). Persuasiveness of expert systems. *Behavior and Information Technology, 17*(3), 155-163.

Dormann, C. (1997). Persuasive interface: Designing for the WWW. In *1997 IEEE International Professional Communication Conference: Crossroads in communication.* New York: IEEE Computer Society.

Eighmey, J. (1997). Profiling user responses to commercial Web sites. *Journal of Advertising Research, 37*(3), 59-66.

Feldstein, M., & Kruse, K. (1998). The power of multimedia games. *Training & Development, 52*(2), 62-63.

Fogg, B. J. (1997). *Charismatic computers: Creating more likable and persuasive interactive technologies by leveraging principles from social psychology.* Doctoral dissertation, Stanford University.

Fogg, B. J. (1998). Persuasive computers: Perspectives and research directions. In *Proceedings of the Conference on Human Factors in Computing Systems* (pp. 225-232). New York: ACM Press.

Fogg, B. J. (1999). Persuasive technologies. *Communications of the ACM, 42*(5), 26-29.

Fogg, B. J. (2002). *Persuasive technologies: Using computer power to change attitudes and behaviors.* San Francisco: Morgan Kaufmann.

Fogg, B. J., & Nass, C. (1997a). How users reciprocate to computers: An experiment that demonstrates behavior change. In *Proceedings of the Conference on Human Factors in Computing Systems.* New York: ACM Press.

Fogg, B. J., & Nass, C. (1997b). Silicon sycophants: The effects of computers that flatter. *International Journal of Human-Computer Studies, 46,* 551-561.

Fogg, B. J., Swani, P., Treinen, M., Marshall, J., Laraki, O., Osipovich, A., Varma, C., Fang, N., Paul, J., Rangnekar, A., & Shon, J. (2000). What makes Web sites credible? A report on a large quantitative study. In *Proceedings of the Conference on Human Factors in Computing Systems* (pp. 61-68). New York: ACM Press.

Fogg, B. J., & Tseng, H. (1999). The elements of computer credibility. In *Proceedings of the Conference on Human Factors and Computing Systems* (pp. 80-87). New York: ACM Press.

Fox, J. E. H. (1998). *The effects of information accuracy on user trust and compliance.* Doctoral dissertation, George Mason University.

Friedman, B., & Grudin, J. (1998). Trust and accountability: Preserving human values in interactional experience. In *Proceedings of the Conference on Human Factors in Computing Systems* (p. 213). New York: ACM Press.

Gahm, G. A. (1986). *The effects of computers, source salience, and credibility on persuasion.* Doctoral dissertation, State University of New York at Stony Brook.

Gatignon, H., & Robertson, T. S. (1991). *Innovative decision processes.* Englewood Cliffs, NJ: Prentice Hall.

Ghosh, A., & Marks, I. M. (1987). Self-treatment of agoraphobia by exposure. *Behavior Therapy, 18,* 3-16.

Gopal, Y. (1997). *Selling in cyberspace: An investigation of modality effects on cognitive processing of persuasive communication on the Internet.* Doctoral dissertation, University of Georgia.

Gouldner, A. W. (1960). The norm of reciprocity: A preliminary statement. *American Sociological Review, 25,* 161-178.

Graeff, J., Elder, J., & Booth, E. (1993). *Communication for health and behavior change.* San Francisco: Jossey-Bass.

Grassian, E. (1998). *Thinking critically about World Wide Web resources.* [Online]. Available: www.library.ucla.edu/libraries/college/instruct/web/critical.htm

Hanowski, R. J., Kantowitz, S. C., & Kantowitz, B. H. (1994). Driver acceptance of unreliable route guidance information. In *Proceedings of the Human Factors and Ergonomics Society 38th annual meeting* (pp. 1062-1066). Santa Monica, CA: Human Factors and Ergonomics Society.

Harkins, S. G., & Petty, R. E. (1981). Effects of source magnification of cognitive effort on attitudes: An information-processing view. *Journal of Personality and Social Psychology, 40,* 401-413.

Henke, L. L. (1999). Children, advertising, and the Internet: An exploratory study. In D. Schumann & E. Thorson (Eds.), *Advertising and the World Wide Web: Advertising and consumer psychology* (pp. 73-80). Mahwah, NJ: Lawrence Erlbaum.

Hennessy, S., & O'Shea, T. (1993). Learner perceptions of realism and magic in computer simulations. *British Journal of Educational Technology, 24*(2), 125-138.

Honaker, L. M., Hector, V. S., & Harrell, T. H. (1986). Perceived validity of computer versus clinician-generated MMPI reports. *Computers in Human Behavior, 2,* 77-83.

Ingle, H. T. (1975). *Children's perceptions of the computer as an expert source of information* (Technical Report No. 44). Stanford, CA: Center for Research and Development in Teaching.

Jimison, H. B., Street, R. L., Jr., & Gold, W. R. (1997). *Patient-specific interfaces to health and decision-making information.* Mahwah, NJ: Lawrence Erlbaum.

Johnson, J. (1999). Inspiring trust online. *Info-Links.* [Online]. Available: www.info-links.com/art7.html

Johnson, T. J., & Kaye, B. K. (1998). Cruising is believing? Comparing Internet and traditional sources on media credibility measures. *Journalism and Mass Communication Quarterly, 75,* 325-340.

Jones, E. E. (1990). *Interpersonal perception.* New York: Freeman.

Kantowitz, B. H., Hanowski, R. J., & Kantowitz, S. C. (1997). Driver acceptance of unreliable traffic information in familiar and unfamiliar settings. *Human Factors, 39*(2), 164-176.

Karson, E. J. (1998). *Internet advertising: New media, new models?* Doctoral dissertation, Florida Atlantic University.

Katz, W. (1992). *Introduction to reference work.* New York: McGraw-Hill.

Kay, A. (1984). Computer software. *Scientific American, 251,* 53-59.

Kerber, K. W. (1983). Attitudes towards specific uses of the computer: Quantitative, decision-making, and record-keeping applications. *Behavior and Information Technology, 2,* 197-209.

Kernal, H. K. (2000, July). *Effects of design characteristics on evaluation of a home control system: A comparison of two research methodologies.* Paper presented at the annual meeting of the Special Interest Group on Computer Graphics and Interactive Techniques, New Orleans, LA.

Khaslavsky, J., & Shedroff, N. (1999). Understanding the seductive experience. *Communications of the ACM, 42*(5), 45-49.

Kilgore, R. (1998, November 30). Publishers must set rules to preserve credibility. *Advertising Age, p.* 31.

Kim, J., & Moon, J. Y. (1997). Designing towards emotional usability in customer interfaces: Trustworthiness of cyber-banking system interfaces. *Interacting With Computers, 10,* 1-29.

King, P., & Tester, J. (1999). The landscape of persuasive technologies. *Communications of the ACM, 42*(5), 31-38.

Kirby, K. C. (1996). Computer-assisted treatment of phobias. *Psychiatric Services, 4*(2), 139-140, 142.

Klein, R. A. (1999). Treating fear of flying with virtual reality exposure therapy. In L. VandeCreek, T. L. Jackson, (Eds.), *Innovations in clinical practice: A source handbook* (Vol. 17, pp. 449-465). Sarasota, FL: Professional Resource Press/ Professional Resource Exchange.

Kuomi, J. (1994). Media comparison and deployment: A practitioner's view. *British Journal of Educational Technology, 25*(1), 41-57.

Larson, C. (1995). *Persuasion: Reception and responsibility* (7th ed.). Belmont, CA: Wadsworth.

Lee, J. (1991). The dynamics of trust in a supervisory control simulation. In *Proceedings of the Human Factors Society 35th annual meeting* (pp. 1228-1232). Santa Monica, CA: Human Factors Society.

Lee, J., & Moray, N. (1992). Trust, control strategies, and allocation of function in human-machine systems. *Ergonomics, 35,* 1243-1270.

Lerch, F. J., & Prietula, M. J. (1989). How do we trust machine advice? Designing and using human-computer interfaces and knowledge based systems. In G. Salvendy & M. J. Smith (Eds.), *Designing and using human-computer interface and knowledge-based systems* (pp. 411-419). Amsterdam: Elsevier.

Lerch, F. J., Prietula, M. J., & Kulik, C. T. (1997). The Turing effect: The nature of trust in expert system advice. In P. J. Feltovich, K. M. Ford, & R. R. Hoffman (Eds.), *Expertise in context: Human and machine* (pp. 417-448). Cambridge, MA: MIT Press.

Lester, J. C., Converse, S. A., Kahler, S. E., Barlow, S. T., Stone, B. A., & Bhogal, R. S. (1997). The persona effect: Affective impact of animated pedagogical agents. In *Proceedings of the Conference on Human Factors in Computing Systems* (pp. 359-366). New York: ACM Press.

Lieberman, D. (1992). The computer's potential role in health education. *Health Communication, 4,* 211-225.

Lieberman, D. (1997). Interactive video games for health promotion. In R. L. Street, W. R. Gold, & T. Manning (Eds.), *Health promotion and interactive technology* (pp. 103-120). Mahwah, NJ: Lawrence Erlbaum.

Lohse, G. L., & Spiller, P. (1998). Quantifying the effect of user interface design features on cyberstore traffic and sales. In *Proceedings of the Conference on Human Factors in Computing Systems* (pp. 211-218). New York: ACM Press.

Machrone, B. (1998, July 1). Driving drunk. *PC Magazine.* [Online]. Available: www.zdnet.com/ pcmag/insites/machrone/bm980625.htm

MacInnis, D. J., & Jaworski, B. J. (1989). Information processing from advertisements: Toward an integrative framework. *Journal of Marketing, 53*(4), 1-23.

MacInnis, D. J., Moorman, C., & Jaworski, B. J. (1991). Enhancing and measuring consumers' motivation, opportunity, and ability to process brand information from ads. *Journal of Marketing, 55*(4), 32-53.

Mackie, D. M., Worth, L. T., & Asuncion, A. G. (1990). Processing of persuasive in-group messages. *Journal of Personality and Social Psychology, 58,* 812-822.

Marshall, C., & Maguire, T. O. (1971). The computer as social pressure to produce conformity in a simple perceptual task. *AV Communication Review, 19*(1), 19-28.

Matarazzo, J. D. (1986). Response to Fowler and Butcher on Matarazzo. *American Psychologist, 41,* 96.

McDonald, M. (1999). Cyberhate: Extending persuasive techniques of low credibility sources to the World Wide Web. In D. W. Schumann & E. Thorson (Eds.), *Advertising and the World Wide Web: Advertising and consumer psychology* (pp. 149-157). Mahwah, NJ: Lawrence Erlbaum.

Miller, C. A., & Larson, R. (1992). An explanatory and "argumentative" interface for a model-based diagnostic system. In *Symposium on User Interface Software and Technology* (pp. 43-52). New York: ACM Press.

Moon, Y. (1998). The effects of distance in local versus remote human-computer interaction. In *Proceedings of the Conference on Human Factors in Computing Systems* (pp. 103-108). New York: ACM Press.

Moon, Y., & Nass, C. (1996). How "real" are computer personalities? Psychological responses to personality types in human-computer interaction. *Communication Research, 23,* 651-674.

Morkes, J., & Nielsen, J. (1997). *Concise, scannable, and objective: How to write for the Web.* [Online]. Available: www.useit.com/papers/webwriting/writing.html

Muehlenhard, C. L., Baldwin, L. E., Bourg, W. J., & Piper, A. M. (1988). Helping women "break the ice": A computer program to help shy women start and maintain conversations with men. *Journal of Computer-Based Instruction, 15*(1), 7-13.

Muir, B. M. (1987). Trust between humans and machines, and the design of decision aids. *International Journal of Man-Machine Studies, 27,* 527-539.

Muir, B. M. (1994). Trust in automation: I. Theoretical issues in the study of trust and human intervention in automated systems. *Ergonomics, 37,* 1905-1922.

Muir, B. M., & Moray, N. (1996). Trust in automation: II. Experimental studies of trust and human intervention in a process control simulation. *Ergonomics, 39,* 429-460.

Muller, R. L. (1974). *Conforming to the computer: Social influence in computer-human interaction.* Doctoral dissertation, Syracuse University.

Nass, C., Fogg, B. J., & Moon, Y. (1996). Can computers be teammates? *International Journal of Human-Computer Studies, 45,* 669-678.

Nass, C. I., & Mason, L. (1990). On the study of technology and task: A variable-based approach. In J. F. C. Steineld (Ed.), *Organizations and communication technology* (pp. 46-67). Newbury Park, CA: Sage.

Nass, C., Moon, Y., & Carney, P. (1999). Are people polite to computers? Responses to computer-based interviewing systems. *Journal of Applied Social Psychology, 29,* 1093-1110.

Nass, C., Moon, Y., Fogg, B. J., Reeves, B., & Dryer, D. C. (1995). Can computer personalities be human personalities? *International Journal of Human-Computer Studies, 43,* 223-239.

Nass, C., Reeves, B., & Leshner, G. (1996). Technology and roles: A tale of two TVs. *Journal of Communication, 46*(2), 121-128.

Nass, C., & Steuer, J. (1993). Voices, boxes, and sources of messages: Computers and social actors. *Human Communication Research, 19,* 504-527.

Nass, C. I., Moon, Y., Morkes, J., Eun-Young, K., & Fogg, B. J. (1997). Computers are social actors: A review of current research. In B. Friedman (Ed.), *Human values and the design of computer technology* (pp. 137-162). Stanford, CA: Center for the Study of Language and Information.

Nielsen, J. (1997). *How users read on the Web.* [Online]. Available: www.useit.com/alertbox/9710a.html

Nielsen, J. (1999a). *Reputation managers are happening.* [Online]. Available: www.useit.com/alertbox/990905.html

Nielsen, J. (1999b). *Trust or bust: Communicating trustworthiness in Web design.* [Online]. Available: www.useit.com/alertbox/990307.html

Northcraft, G. B., & Earley, P. C. (1989). Technology, credibility, and feedback use. *Organizational Behavior and Human Decision Processes, 44*(1), 83-96.

Nowak, G. J., Shamp, S., Hollander, B., & Cameron, G. T. (1999). Interactive media: A means for more meaningful advertising? In D. W. Schumann & E. Thorson (Eds.), *Advertising and the World Wide Web: Advertising and consumer psychology* (pp. 99-117). Mahwah, NJ: Lawrence Erlbaum.

Pancer, S. M., George, M., & Gebotys, R. J. (1992). Understanding and predicting attitudes toward computers. *Computers in Human Behavior, 8*, 211-222.

Parise, S., Kiesler, S., Sproull, L., & Waters, K. (1999). Cooperating with life-like interface agents. *Computers in Human Behavior, 15*, 123-142.

Petty, R. E., & Cacioppo, J. T. (1981). *Attitudes and persuasion: Classic and contemporary approaches.* Dubuque, IA: William C. Brown.

Petty, R. E., & Cacioppo, J. T. (1986). *Communication and persuasion: Central and peripheral routes to attitude change.* New York: Springer-Verlag.

Petty, R. E., Cacioppo, J. T., Sedikides, C., & Strathman, A. J. (1988). Affect and persuasion: A contemporary perspective. *American Behavioral Scientist, 31*, 355-371.

Petty, R. E., Schumann, D. W., Richman, S. A., & Strathman, A. J. (1993). Positive mood and persuasion: Different roles for affect under high- and low-elaboration conditions. *Journal of Personality and Social Psychology, 64*, 5-20.

Porcari, J. P., Zedaker, M. S., & Maldari, M. S. (1998). Virtual motivation. *Fitness Management, 14*(13), 48-51.

Quintanar, L., Crowell, C., & Pryor, J. (1982). Human-computer interaction: A preliminary social psychological analysis. *Behavior Research Methods and Instrumentation, 14*, 210-220.

Reardon, K. K. (1987). The role of persuasion in health promotion and disease prevention: Review and commentary. In J. A. Anderson (Ed.), *Communication Yearbook 11* (pp. 277-297). Newbury Park, CA: Sage.

Reed, E. (1996). *The necessity of experience.* New Haven, CT: Yale University Press.

Reeves, B., & Nass, C. I. (1996). *The media equation: How people treat computers, television, and new media like real people and places.* New York: Cambridge University Press.

Reis, J. (1998). *Research results: National data analysis.* [Online]. Available: www.centurycouncil.org/alcohol101/dem_nat.cfm

Rieh, S. Y., & Belkin, N. J. (1998). Understanding judgment of information quality and cognitive authority in the WWW. *Journal of the American Society for Information Science, 35*, 279-289.

Risden, K., Czerwinski, M., Worley, S., Hamilton, L., Kubiniec, J., Hoffman, H., Mickel, N., & Loftus, E. (1998). Interactive advertising: Patterns of use and effectiveness. In *Proceedings of the Conference on Human Factors in Computing Systems* (pp. 219-224). New York: ACM Press.

Rosenfeld, L. (1994). Guides, clearinghouses, and value-added repackaging: Some thoughts on how librarians can improve the Internet. *Reference Services Review, 22*(4), 11-16.

Ross, L., & Nisbett, R. E. (1991). *The person and the situation: Perspectives of social psychology.* New York: McGraw-Hill.

Rowley, J. (1995). Multimedia kiosks in retailing. *International Journal of Retail and Distribution Management, 23*(5), 32-40.

Sampson, J. P., Peterson, G., Reardon, R., Lenz, J., Shahnasarian, M., & Ryan-Jones, R. (1992). The social influence of two computer-assisted career guidance systems. *Career Development Quarterly, 41*(1), 75-83.

Schlosser, A. E., & Kanifer, A. (1999). Current advertising on the Internet: The benefits and usage of mixed-media advertising strategies. In D. W. Schumann & E. Thorson (Eds.), *Advertising and the World Wide Web* (pp. 41-62). Mahwah, NJ: Lawrence Erlbaum.

Schneider, S. J., Walter, R., & O'Donnell, R. (1990). Computerized communication as a medium for behavioral smoking cessation treatment: Controlled evaluation. *Computers in Human Behavior, 6*, 141-151.

Self, C. S. (1996). Credibility. In M. B. Salwen & D. W. Stacks (Eds.), *An integrated approach to communication theory and research* (pp. 421-441). Mahwah, NJ: Lawrence Erlbaum.

Sheridan, T. B., Vamos, T., & Aida, S. (1983). Adapting automation to man, culture, and society. *Automatica, 19*, 605-612.

Schumann, D. W., & Thorson, E. (1999). Thoughts regarding the present and future of Web advertising. In D. W. Schumann & E. Thorson (Eds.),

Advertising and the World Wide Web (pp. 309-314). Mahwah, NJ: Lawrence Erlbaum.

Smith, A. G. (1997). Testing the surf: Criteria for evaluating Internet information resources. *Public-Access Computer Systems Review, 8*(3). [Online]. Available: http://info.lib.uh.edu/pr/v8/n3/smit8n3.html

Stiff, J. B. (1994). *Persuasive communication.* New York: Guilford.

Stoker, D., & Cooke, A. (1995). Evaluation of networked information sources. In A. H. Helal & J. W. Weiss (Eds.), *Information superhighway: The role of librarians, information scientists, and intermediaries—Proceedings of the 17th International Essen Symposium* (pp. 287-312). Essen, Germany: Universitatsbibliothek Essen.

Stoney, S., & Wild, M. (1998). Motivation and interface design: Maximising learning opportunities. *Journal of Computer-Assisted Learning, 14*(1) 40-50.

Strecher, V. J. (1999). Computer-tailored smoking cessation materials: A review and discussion. *Patient Education & Counseling, 36*(2), 107-117.

Strecher, V. J., DeVellis, B. M., Becker, M. H., & Rosenstock, I. M. (1986). The role of self-efficacy in achieving health behavior change. *Health Education Quarterly, 13*(1), 73-92.

Strecher, V. J., Kreuter, M., Den Boer, D-J., Kobrin, S., Hospers, H. J., & Skinner, C. S. (1994). The effects of computer-tailored smoking cessation messages in family practice settings. *Journal of Family Practice, 39,* 262-270.

Street, R., Gold, W., & Manning, T. (1997). *Health promotion and interactive technology.* Mahwah, NJ: Lawrence Erlbaum.

Tate, M., & Alexander, J. (1996). Teaching critical evaluation skills for World Wide Web resources. *Computers in Libraries, 16*(10), 49-56.

Thompson, C. A. (1992). *Exercise adherence and performance: Effects on self-efficacy and outcome expectations.* Doctoral dissertation, Illinois Institute of Technology.

Tillman, H. (2000). *Evaluating quality on the Net.* [Online]. Available: www.tiac.net/users/hope/findqual.html

Todd, P. A., & Benbasat, I. (1994). The influence of decision aids on choice strategies under condi-tions of high cognitive load. *IEEE Transactions on Systems, Man, & Cybernetics, 24,* 537-547.

Tombari, M. L., Fitzpatrick, S. J., & Childress, W. (1985). Using computers as contingency managers in self-monitoring interventions: A case study. *Computers in Human Behavior, 1*(1), 75-82.

Tseng, S., & Fogg, B. J. (1999). Credibility and computing technology. *Communications of the ACM, 42*(5), 39-44.

Verplank, B., Fulton, J., Black, A., & Moggridge, B. (1993). *Observation and invention: Uses of scenarios in interaction design.* Handout for tutorial at INTERCHI '93, Amsterdam.

Waern, Y., & Hagglund, S. (1992). Communication knowledge for knowledge communication. *International Journal of Man-Machine Studies, 37,* 215-239.

Waern, Y., & Ramberg, R. (1996). People's perception of human and computer advice. *Computers in Human Behavior, 12,* 17-27.

Weiser, M. (1991). The computer for the 21st century. *Scientific American, 265,* 94-104.

Wiederhold, B. K., Davis, R., Wiederhold, M. D., & Riva, G. (1998). The effects of immersiveness on physiology. *Studies in Health Technology and Informatics, 58,* 52-60.

Wilkinson, G. (1997). Evaluating the quality of *Internet information sources.* [Online]. Available: http://itech1.coe.uga.edu/faculty/gwilkinson/webeval. html

Woodward, J. P., Carnine, D., & Davis, L. G. (1986). Health ways: A computer simulation for problem solving in personal health management. *Family and Community Health, 9*(2), 60-63.

Zajonc, R. B. (1980). Feeling and thinking: Preferences need no inferences. *American Psychologist, 35,* 151-175.

Zietsman, A. I., & Hewson, P. W. (1986). Effect of instruction using microcomputer simulations and conceptual change strategies on science learning. *Journal of Research in Science Teaching, 23*(1), 27-39.

Zimbardo, P. G., & Leippe, M. R. (1991). *The psychology of attitude change and social influence.* New York: McGraw-Hill.

Summary

Final Thoughts About Persuasion

MICHAEL PFAU
JAMES PRICE DILLARD

In much the same way as the empirical study of persuasion took off during the middle of the 20th century, so too did the study of other forms of human communication. Delia (1987) traced the "initial coalescence of the field [of communication] as a distinct domain" to the 1940s (p. 20). Historically, the trajectories for the study of human communication in general, and for persuasion in particular, have closely paralleled each other. However, it was persuasion that led the way. Miller and Burgoon (1978) maintained that this was still true in 1978—that the study of persuasion continued to contribute to an understanding of all communication. "Many of the most interesting, significant issues of the field are inextricably bound up in persuasive communication" (p. 45). As a result, "continued interest in this problem area [persuasion] is essential to our eventual understanding of human communication" (p. 29). Other scholars echo this position. Roloff and Miller (1980) observed, "Persuasion seems to underlie many of the other areas of communication" (p. 8). Miller and Levine (1996) maintained, "Implicitly or explicitly, persuasion underlies much of mass and human communication theory and research" (p. 261).

FOCUS ON FUNCTIONAL QUESTIONS ABOUT INFLUENCE

What excites us as scholars of persuasion is that much of the scholarship in this area addresses core *functional questions about influence,* and the answers to these questions carry both theoretical and practical import. Functional questions embody theoretical content about communication processes. Most of the chapters in this volume address such questions—basic issues about how the human mind organizes and processes information, various theoretical explanations for how influence occurs, the role and impact of affect in persuasion, how message strategies exert influence, and the role that communication media play in persuasion. Because these chapters address functional questions about influence, the findings that are described carry important theoretical implications and, consequently, are of interest to scholars who seek the advancement of knowledge about persuasion for its own sake. And because such functional knowledge claims cross contexts, the findings are of interest to a broad array of scholars as well as practitioners.

Initially, the study of persuasion was confined to limited contexts, mainly those of public speaking and media in politics. Today, the study of persuasion features many contexts, as the sections of this volume on contexts (Section V) and campaigns (Section VI) illustrate. Specific chapters address uses of persuasion in interpersonal communication, small group communication, business (marketing and public relations), advertising, the legal setting, politics, and social action (health and environmental) campaigns. Burgoon and Miller (1990) attributed the resurgence of academic interest in persuasion during the 1980s to the growing appreciation of its applied potential. Academic interest in persuasion continues to be strong because, as Miller (1987) observed, the study of persuasion "stimulates perennial interest because of its potential social significance" (p. 447). In addition, the chapters in this volume attest to the overall breadth and depth of scholarship on persuasion.

However, despite enthusiasm for applications of persuasion, we maintain that *the process of influence* is the heart and soul of the study of persuasion. Most authors who contributed chapters in the dual areas of context and campaigns expressed much the same sentiment. We share the hopes expressed by Burgoon and Miller (1990) that "interest in applied problems will help researchers uncover . . . cross-situational universals of communication" (p. 154). However, we recognize that many of the academics drawn to applied persuasion domain, as embodied in subfields such as advertising, public relations, health communication, and political communication, are focused narrowly on their specific niche and uninterested in "cross-situational

universals." We urge all scholars with interests in applied influence to follow the model of the authors of this volume and make functional questions about persuasion the engine that drives their scholarship. This approach ensures that their research findings have theoretical implications that cross contexts and, therefore, are of interest to the maximum possible audience.

FUTURE DIRECTIONS IN PERSUASION SCHOLARSHIP

Prior to the final three sections on contextual factors (Section V), persuasive campaigns (Section VI), and media forms/channels (Section VII), all chapters in this book are organized around theoretical content. They summarize the status of knowledge in their respective domains, explore recent nuances, and discuss theory and research needs. The latter content, found toward the end of each chapter, is particularly important because it sketches an outline of where persuasion scholarship is likely headed.

So, where does the study of persuasion go from here? What functional questions remain unresolved? We asked the respective chapter authors to sketch future research needs, identifying programs of research in their areas for the coming decade. Some of the suggestions for future research are specific to the niches that the chapters address. Recommendations offered for future research should inform scholarship in the respective areas for the next decade and beyond. We review these more idiosyncratic suggestions first.

Some of the chapters in this volume reintroduce and add to the base of knowledge of long-established theories of persuasion. These theories received considerable attention by scholars during the first decade or so following their introduction, then turned largely dormant as scholars shifted their attention elsewhere, but have experienced a regeneration in interest during recent years. Harmon-Jones (Chapter 6), for example, addresses cognitive dissonance theory, calling for further research concerning the role and impact of motivational mechanisms and individual differences in the process of dissonance and dealing with the impact of cognitive process in reducing dissonance levels. Shavitt and Nelson (Chapter 8) update the role of attitude functions in influence and suggest future study about the role of choice and competition in informing the links between attitude functions, absolute judgments, and selections among alternatives and also concerning cultural differences. Szabo and Pfau (Chapter 13) examine recent work on the process of resistance and call for additional work to explain the additional increment of resistance that is independent of the threat and counterarguing mechanisms and further research to pinpoint the optimal timing of treatments and reinforcements. Burgoon, Alvaro, Grandpre, and Voloudakis (Chapter 12) revisit psychological reactance, recommending research on its use in mediated (as opposed to face-to-face) contexts and on applications involving adolescents.

Other chapters address established theories that continue to hold the attention of persuasion scholars. For example, Roskos-Ewoldsen, Arpan-Ralstin, and St. Pierre (Chapter 3) focus on attitude accessibility and persuasion. They call for future research applying attitude accessibility to two-sided arguments and to inoculation and the treatment of accessibility as an independent variable, examining its impact on persuasion. Kosicki (Chapter 4) focuses on priming, suggesting future research identifying mechanisms of priming, message and media impacts on priming, and efforts to disentangle priming and negativity effects. Burgoon, Denning, and Roberts (Chapter 7) describe the workings of language expectancy theory and detail research that underlies its

propositional logic. They call for future research that provides a clearer sense of expectation (predictive vs. mainly prescriptive), on the universality of expectations (which requires studies set in other cultures), that is longitudinal in nature and conducted in field settings, and that applies this theory to sequential interpersonal contexts.

Booth-Butterfield and Welbourne (Chapter 9) address the logic and data supporting the Elaboration Likelihood Model (ELM), while Slater (Chapter 10) posits an Extended ELM. Booth-Butterfield and Welbourne provide refutation of criticisms of the ELM and offer recommendations for further work providing clearer conceptualization and more precise measurement of what they term the "fuzzy notion" of argument quality and for studies that manipulate argument quality and cue strength and probe their relationship to determine the "parameters of persuasion." Slater employs the Extended ELM to examine the influence of low-involvement processes—what he characterizes as "nonovertly" and "implicitly" persuasive messages often found in entertainment contexts. He calls for more exploratory research about processing contexts and models and for the identification of mediating and contingency variables unique to different types and genres of messages. Todorov, Chaiken, and Henderson (Chapter 11) provide a detailed account of the propositional logic and status of extant research on the Heuristic-Systematic Model (HSM). They recommend disentangling processing mode and persuasion variables, urging "*direct* evidence for the qualitatively different nature of systematic and heuristic processing," which they suspect requires online measures that are independent of informational cues. They also recommend research to confirm the bias hypothesis of the HSM and to determine the relative accuracy of systematic and heuristic judgments.

Nabi (Chapter 15) and Dillard and Meijnders (Chapter 16) examine the role and impact of affect in persuasion. Both chapters call for further clarity concerning different conceptualizations of affect, especially the interrelationships among specific emotions or what Nabi calls "emotional flow" (the patterns of emotion working together). Both of these chapters also urge future study of the trait and message features that elicit particular emotional responses. In addition, Nabi recommends research to understand how to use the desire to experience—or to avoid—specific emotions in order to produce attitude and behavior change.

Finally, two chapters focus on relatively new theories of persuasion. Fink, Kaplowitz, and Hubbard (Chapter 2) introduce an intriguing perspective called belief oscillation. They describe the theory and summarize research that informs their predictions, and they call for future research on the process of oscillation and the factors that are responsible for it. Salovey, Schneider, and Apanovitch (Chapter 20) use prospect theory to explain the way in which people frame information in memory in terms of potential gains or losses relative to a current reference point. In the case of prevention and early detection of illness, which is the concentration of Chapter 20, the current reference point is an individual's current health. The authors suggest future research on emotions evoked by framed messages and on framing and behavior-type interactions.

Other chapters explore message strategies in influence such as the role of guilt, product warning labels, the structure and use of language, negative appeals, metaphor, and evidence in persuasion. Still other chapters focus on the role and impact of communication form and channel in persuasion such as media form, television images, interactive technologies, and nonverbal influence. These chapters provide excellent recommendations for future research, but for the most part, these calls are unique to the authors' particular message and communication form/channel areas.

Possibilities for More Integrated Macro Theorizing

In other instances, authors identify in their suggestions for future research what turn out to be common themes that cross niches. These themes call attention to the current and future state of knowledge about persuasion.

One of the broader themes that emerges from the suggestions for future research offered by a number of authors is the need for more integrated macro theorizing within the realm of social influence. This call, of course, is not new to persuasion, nor is it unique to persuasion. Berger and Burgoon (1998) recently lamented the myriad of "micro theories of persuasion, which, so far, seem to have defied all efforts to conceptually integrate them" (p. xi). Nonetheless, they urged continued efforts based on new assumptions about communication and the availability of new and more sophisticated methodological tools. They called for integrated theorizing that places communication at center stage. "What is needed is a new and more inclusive conceptualization of the role played by communication in exercise of social influence" (p. xi).

This volume suggests some directions for integration and/or synthesis. Both Nabi (Chapter 15) and Dillard and Meijnders (Chapter 16) urge a synthesis of different conceptualizations of affect, including examination of interrelationships across emotions. In addition, Nabi argues for the need to reconceptualize existing theories of persuasion in light of the wealth of relatively recent findings on affect. Hosman (Chapter 19) advocates a synthesis of extant knowledge about language variables in persuasion. Burgoon, Denning, and Roberts (Chapter 7), who also are advocates for more emphasis on message-based considerations in persuasion, argue that language expectancy theory is a robust tool to understand influence and recommend the integration of a number of theories, some of which deal with language and others that address other concerns—that rely explicitly or implicitly on the concept of expectation.

Newhagen (Chapter 32) advocates macro theorizing across technological platforms (e.g., television screens, computer screens) and message structures. Burgoon, Dunbar, and Segrin (Chapter 23) urge integrative theorizing and research on nonverbal influence, delineating a number of promising directions.

Boster and Cruz (Chapter 24) and Eveland (Chapter 31), in separate chapters, call for systematic integration of theories in their respective areas. Boster and Cruz recommend an integration of a number of micro explanations for choice shift in the group context and synthesis of explanations for majority/minority influence in small groups. They generally urge more general theorizing across the small group literature. Eveland suggests an integration of theories and research programs in the area of social reality perception. Specifically, he argues that persuasion theories might assist in sorting out the myriad of micro perspectives that are used to explain narrow slices of television's influence in its news and programming venues.

Possibilities for Cross-Fertilization in Theory and Research

Another theme that emerges from the suggestions for future research is the possibility for cross-fertilization in theory and research. Authors often suggest research possibilities that involve theories and/or specific concepts drawn from different content domains. Furthermore, these possibilities appear to be concentrated in a few limited niches, thus intimating which conceptual areas are likely to

receive the most interest and attention during the coming decade.

One important conceptual domain is attitude accessibility. Roskos-Ewoldsen and colleagues (Chapter 3) make a case for the centrality of accessibility to persuasion. They observe that accessibility dictates how messages are processed and the likely impact of these messages. Citing Dillard, they conclude that "increasing attitude accessibility is probably more important than changing someone's evaluative response to an object."

The potential of the accessibility construct in persuasion is evidenced by the number of authors writing in altogether unique content areas who include it in the recommendations for future research in their respective niches. Roskos-Ewoldsen and colleagues (Chapter 3) set the stage in their chapter in calling for research on the impact of elaborative message processing on accessibility and study of the relationship involving affect and accessibility. Kosicki (Chapter 4) recommends further theorizing and research on priming and accessibility. Despite the obvious interconnections among these explanatories, there has been surprising little cross-fertilization. Domke, Shah, and Wackman (1998) explored the relationship of priming and accessibility, although their foray into this area is in its infancy. They identified two mechanisms for priming: *accessibility,* which they perceive to be short-term and involving the temporary activation of a memory node, and *spreading activation,* which presupposes the presence of more elaborate schemata, where activation spreads across interconnected nodes, achieving a more lasting effect. We believe that there are many other interconnections involving priming and accessibility, and we suspect that this will be a fruitful area for future theory and research.

Finally, Szabo and Pfau (Chapter 13) and Holbert (Chapter 33) call for research on accessibility in their respective contributions.

Szabo and Pfau argue that recent inoculation research has confirmed the role of threat and counterarguing in the process of resistance, but they note that it has also revealed the presence of a direct path from inoculation treatment to resistance that operates independent of inoculation theory's causal mechanisms. They speculate that accessibility may hold the key to explaining this path—that treatments may make a person's current attitudes more accessible and, therefore, that attitude accessibility may contribute to resistance above and beyond the impact of threat and counterarguing. Holbert calls for research on form-induced accessibility, maintaining that media form, quite independent of its content, may facilitate accessibility of some schemata, thus triggering influence.

It is also clear, however, that continuing forays into the way the mind organizes and processes information will require a leap forward in measurement. Permutations of the thought-listing approach are not capable of carrying researchers any further. As Todorov and colleagues (Chapter 11) warn, the thought-listing approach assumes cognitive effort on the part of respondents that cannot account for automatic or implicit processes. They argue that future research on processing requires the use of online measures, which are administered at the point of processing and, therefore, function largely "independent of informational cues." The response latency technique, which is employed by Fazio, Roskos-Ewoldsen, and others who research attitude accessibility, is one alternative assessment tool (see Roskos-Ewoldsen & Fazio, 1992).

Another important conceptual domain involves affect. The role and influence of affect in persuasion has not received as much attention as is warranted (Ottati & Wyer, 1993). Jorgensen (1998) characterized the underemphasis on affect in persuasion research as "lamentable" (p. 404). However, this is changing. Today, there is growing appreciation of

the integral role that emotion plays in influence (Arnold, 1985; Dillard & Wilson, 1993; Jorgensen, 1998), and based on the number of contributors to this volume who raised the possibility of potential linkages between their respective conceptual domains and affect in their calls for future research, affect is likely to be a significant source of cross-fertilization in research during the next decade.

Roskos-Ewoldsen and colleagues (Chapter 3) call for research on the use of emotional appeals and attitude accessibility, whereas Kosicki (Chapter 4) recommends an exploration of the linkages involving priming and negative affect. Salovey and colleagues (Chapter 20) suggest research on the emotions evoked by framed messages, and Holbert (Chapter 33) urges study of affect induced through specific media forms independent of media content. Szabo and Pfau (Chapter 13) synopsize their initial probe of the role and impact of affect in the process of resistance (see also Pfau et al., 2001) and identify additional issues involving affect and resistance that need to be explored.

Finally, two of the chapters in the section on persuasive campaigns (Section VI) suggest future research involving affect. Perloff (Chapter 28) identifies affect and visual form as two underemphasized potential sources of political influence, and Parrott, Egbert, Anderton, and Sefcovic (Chapter 29) urge researchers to focus their attention on the role and influence of affect in health campaigns.

The authors of the two chapters that address persuasion and business, Rhoads and Cialdini (who co-authored the chapter on the uses of persuasion in a business context [Chapter 26]) and Zhao (who authored the chapter on persuasion in advertising [Chapter 25]), do not include affect in their recommendations for future research. The reason is that affect is not viewed as novel in these contexts. Both scholars and practitioners in the advertising and marketing contexts have long recognized the importance of affect in consumer behavior (Peterson, Hoyer, & Wilson, 1986).

The final conceptual domain that holds considerable promise for future research involves message features. Burgoon, Alvaro, Grandpre, and Voloudakis (Chapter 12) criticize scholarship in persuasion for a nearly total preoccupation with message processing, which has resulted in "a nearly total lack of attention to message features, structure, and content." Based on authors' recommendations for future research that crosses content niches, we conclude that there is much untapped potential here. In a linkage involving affect and message design, both Nabi (Chapter 15) and Dillard and Meijnders (Chapter 16) indicate a need to systematically isolate the message features that elicit specific emotional responses. In a related vein, O'Keefe (Chapter 17) posits the need to learn how message variables trigger guilt. Finally, Reinard (Chapter 27), writing on persuasion in the legal setting, calls for research addressing how message factors elicit influence.

Applied Research Agenda

Thus far, we have limited discussion of the directions for future research mainly to conceptual chapters that address functional questions about the process of influence. However, such issues can also be found in an applied influence setting, and we have identified a number of conceptual research directions that are posited by authors whose chapters are organized under contexts (Section V), persuasive campaigns (Section VI), and media forms/ channels (Section VII).

There is no question that interest and scholarship in applied influence are alive and well. We hope, as Burgoon and Miller (1990) forecasted, that scholars' current enthusiasm for applied persuasion will provide theoretical payoffs on top the obvious tangible rewards

(e.g., research grants, consulting opportunities).

Authors of the more applied chapters often call for more conceptual work. Rhoads and Cialdini (Chapter 26) suggest a continuing search for additional universal principles of influence and integrative efforts to learn the relative power of the known principles of influence. O'Keefe and Shepard (Chapter 30) call for the need for theorizing about environmental campaigns, whereas Zhao (Chapter 25) stresses the need to integrate theory and research in advertising. Zhao maintains that much research in this domain is theoretical but without pragmatic utility, whereas even more research is pragmatic but completely atheoretical. Reinard (Chapter 27) stresses the need for more theoretical and conceptual work in legal influence, describing current research in this area as "interim status." Finally, Perloff (Chapter 28) calls for more emphasis on normative theory in political communication research—"theories that spell out how persuasion should occur in a democracy."

Both Parrott and colleagues (Chapter 29) and O'Keefe and Shepard (Chapter 30) call attention to the problem of conflicting research findings in the health and environmental contexts. In both domains, members of the lay public often are overwhelmed by the quantity, intricacy, and seeming inconsistency of research findings. This problem is compounded by ineffective and sometimes harmful news media reporting of research findings that is often mired in the idiosyncratic findings of individual studies.

CONCLUSION

We began work on this handbook motivated by a desire to provide a contemporary synthesis of extant knowledge and with the hope of influencing the research agenda in persuasion through the first decade of the 21st century.

Having now read through each of the chapters in this book and surveyed the field, we are convinced that persuasion research is both robust and vibrant. On the basis of the research agendas provided by the contributors to this volume, we anticipate continuing growth in our knowledge of one of the most fundamental processes of social existence—persuasion.

REFERENCES

Arnold, V. D. (1985). The importance of pathos in persuasive appeals. *Bulletin of the Association for Business Communication, 48*(4), 26-27.

Berger, C. R., & Burgoon, M. (Eds.). (1998). *Communication and social influence processes.* East Lansing: Michigan State University Press.

Burgoon, M., & Miller, G. R. (1990). Paths. *Communication Monographs, 57,* 152-160.

Delia, J. G. (1987). Communication research: A history. In C. R. Berger & C. H. Chaffee (Eds.), *Handbook of communication science* (pp. 20-98). Newbury Park, CA: Sage.

Dillard, J. P., & Wilson, B. J. (1993). Communication and affect: Thoughts, feelings, and issues for the future. *Communication Research, 20,* 637-646.

Domke, D., Shah, D. V., & Wackman, D. B. (1998). Media priming effects: Accessibility, association, and activation. *International Journal of Public Opinion Research, 10,* 51-74.

Jorgensen, P. F. (1998). Affect, persuasion, and communication processes. In P. A. Andersen & L. K. Guerrero (Eds.), *Handbook of communication and emotion: Research, theory, applications, and contexts* (pp. 403-422). San Diego: Academic Press.

Miller, G. R. (1987). Persuasion. In C. R. Berger & C. H. Chaffee (Eds.), *Handbook of communication science* (pp. 446-483). Newbury Park, CA: Sage.

Miller, G. R., & Burgoon, M. (1978). Persuasion research: Review and commentary. In B. D. Rubin (Ed.), *Communication Yearbook 2* (pp. 29-47). New Brunswick, NJ: Transaction Books.

Miller, M. D., & Levine, T. R. (1996). Persuasion. In M. B. Salwen & D. W. Stacks (Eds.), *An integrated approach to communication theory and research* (pp. 261-276). Mahwah, NJ: Lawrence Erlbaum.

Ottati, V. C., & Wyer, R. S., Jr. (1993). Affect and political judgment. In S. Iyengar & W. J. McGuire (Eds.), *Explorations in political psychology* (pp. 296-315). Durham, NC: Duke University Press.

Peterson, R. A., Hoyer, W. D., & Wilson, W. R. (1986). Reflections on the role of affect in consumer behavior. In R. A. Peterson, W. D. Hoyer, & W. R. Wilson (Eds.), *The role of affect in consumer behavior: Emerging theories and applications* (pp. 141-159). Lexington, MA: Lexington Books.

Pfau, M., Szabo, E. A., Anderson, J., Morrill, J., Zubric, J., & Wan, H-H. (2001). The role and impact of affect in the process of resistance to persuasion. *Human Communication Research, 27,* 216-252.

Roloff, M. E., & Miller, G. R. (1980). Foreword. In M. E. Roloff & G. R. Miller (Eds.), *Persuasion: New directions in theory and research* (pp. 7-10). Beverly Hills, CA: Sage.

Roskos-Ewoldsen, D. R., & Fazio, R. H. (1992). The orienting value of attitudes: Attitude accessibility as a determinant of an object's attraction of visual attention. *Journal of Personality and Social Psychology, 63,* 198-211.

Author Index

Subject Index

About the Editors

James Price Dillard (Ph.D., Michigan State University, 1983) is Professor of Communication Arts at the University of Wisconsin–Madison. His research interests revolve around interpersonal influence, emotion, and persuasion, with an emphasis on the communication of risk. He has authored or co-authored more than 50 articles and chapters, primarily on persuasion and interpersonal influence, that have appeared in books and leading journals. The majority of his published works appear in *Human Communication Research, Communication Monographs,* and *Communication Research.* He is the editor of the volume *Seeking Compliance: The Production of Interpersonal Influence Messages* and was the first recipient of the John E. Hunter Award for Meta-analysis. He currently sits on seven editorial boards and recently served as chair of the Interpersonal Division of the International Communication Association.

Michael Pfau (Ph.D., University of Arizona, 1987) is Professor and Chair of the Department of Communication at the University of Oklahoma. His research interests concern resistance to influence and mass media influence, particularly in a political context. His works on resistance have appeared in *Communication Monographs, Human Communication Research,* and other journals, and his research on mass media influence has appeared in *Journal of Broadcasting & Electronic Media, Journal of Communication,* and other venues. He has co-authored six books, most recently *With Malice Toward All? The Media and Public Confidence in Democratic Institutions* (with Patricia Moy). His articles have won the National Communication Association's Golden Anniversary Monograph Award and the Southern Communication Association's Rose B. Johnson Award.

About the Contributors

Mike Allen (Ph.D., Michigan State University, 1987) is Professor in the Department of Communication at the University of Wisconsin–Milwaukee. His more than 100 published works deal with issues of social influence in public, social, and organizational settings. His works have appeared in journals such as *Law and Human Behavior, Journal of Personal and Social Relationships, Human Communication Research,* and *Journal of Communication.*

Eusebio Alvaro (Ph.D., M.P.H.) is Director of the Health Communication Research Office in the Arizona Cancer Center at the University of Arizona. He is concerned with the testing and application of social science theory in the context of health promotion and disease prevention to further understanding of social influence processes and have a positive impact in an area of social import. His specific research efforts have addressed resistance to persuasion and defensive processing of persuasive messages in projects including the prevention of HIV/AIDS, the prevention of marijuana and inhalant use, workplace wellness, and the prevention and cessation of tobacco use.

John Anderton (M.P.A., Georgia State University, 1992; A.B.D., University of Georgia [dissertation in progress], 2000) is Acting Associate Director for Communications of the National Center for HIV, STD, and TB Prevention

at the Centers for Disease Control and Prevention.

Anne Marie Apanovitch (Ph.D., Kent State University, 1996) completed her undergraduate education at Saint Olaf College in Minnesota and then her doctoral work in social psychology at Kent State University. At the time this chapter was written, she served as Associate Research Scientist in the Department of Psychology at Yale University, where she coordinated HIV/AIDS prevention research in the Health, Emotion, and Behavior Laboratory. She is now Senior Analyst at Bayer Corporation in Connecticut. She has conducted research on sexual violence toward women as well as persuasion in the context of HIV/AIDS prevention and early detection.

Laura Arpan-Ralstin (Ph.D., University of Alabama, 1999) is Assistant Professor in the Department of Communication at Florida State University. Her research interests include attitude formation and persuasion, international communication, and crisis communication.

Steve Booth-Butterfield (Ed.D., West Virginia University, 1988) is affiliated with the Health Communication Research Branch of the National Institute for Occupational Safety and Health at the Centers for Disease Control and Prevention. His research interests include persuasion, mass media effects, and communication interventions for behavior change. His works have been published with or presented at meetings of a variety of communication, psychology, public health, and medical associations.

Franklin J. Boster (Ph.D., Michigan State University, 1978) is Professor in the Department of Communication at Michigan State University. His research interests are in the areas of social influence processes and group dynamics.

Judee K. Burgoon is Professor of Communication, Professor of Family Studies and Human Development, and Director of Human Communication Research for the Center for the Management of Information at the University of Arizona. She has authored or co-authored seven books and monographs and nearly 200 articles, chapters, and reviews related to nonverbal and relational communication, interpersonal relationship management, dyadic interaction patterns, deception, computer-mediated communication, research methods, and public opinion toward the media. Among her research-related honors are the NCA's Golden Anniversary Monographs Award, the Charles H. Woolbert Research Award for Scholarship of Lasting Impact, election as a fellow of the International Communication Association, and election into the Society for Experimental Social Psychology. A recent published survey identified her as the most prolific female scholar in the field of communication in the 20th century. In 1999, she was awarded the NCA's Distinguished Scholar Award, its highest award for a lifetime of scholarly achievement.

Michael Burgoon (Ph.D., Michigan State University, 1970) is Professor of Medicine, Public Health, and Family and Community Medicine at the University of Arizona College of Medicine. He has done some work in the area of social influence.

Nancy Burrell (Ph.D., Michigan State University, 1987) is Associate Professor in the Department of Communication at the University of Wisconsin–Milwaukee. Her research centers on managing conflict in family, workplace, and educational contexts as well as on the use of language in a variety of settings. She has edited a book and has published in *Management Communication Quarterly, Communication Monographs,* and *Argumentation and Advocacy.*

Shelly Chaiken (Ph.D., University of Massachusetts at Amherst) is Professor of Psychology at New York University. She co-authored *The Psychology of Attitudes* (with Alice H. Eagly) and is the author of numerous theoretical, review, and empirical articles on attitude structure, formation, and change. Her works have appeared in *Journal of Personality and Social Psychology* and *Personality and Social Psychology Bulletin.* She co-edited *Dual-Process Theories in Social Psychology* (with Yaacov Trope).

Robert B. Cialdini is Regents Professor of Psychology at Arizona State University, where he has also been named Distinguished Graduate Research Professor. He received undergraduate, graduate, and postgraduate education in psychology at the University of Wisconsin, the University of North Carolina, and Columbia University, respectively. He has held visiting scholar appointments at Ohio State University; the University of California, San Diego; the University of California, Santa Cruz; the Annenberg School of Communications; and both the Department of Psychology and Graduate School of Business at Stanford University. His book *Influence,* which was the result of a

3-year program of study of the reasons why people comply with requests in everyday settings, has appeared in numerous editions and 10 languages.

Michael G. Cruz (Ph.D., Michigan State University, 1994) is Senior Analyst with Gartner G2, where he is responsible for forecasts of Internet and technology adoption.

Vickie Pauls Denning (B.A., University of Kansas) was Project Coordinator in the Health Communication Research Office of the Arizona Cancer Center and a graduate student in the Department of Communication at the University of Arizona, Tucson, at the time of this research.

Mark A. deTurck (Ph.D., Michigan State University, 1984) is a Director with Decision Quest in Atlanta, Georgia. His applied and theoretical interests revolve around the study of risk communication, with an emphasis on warning labels.

Norah E. Dunbar (Ph.D., University of Arizona, 2000) is Associate Professor of Communication Studies at California State University, Long Beach. Her main research interests are in interpersonal relationships, particularly issues of power and dominance, deception, and conflict management.

Nichole Egbert (Ph.D., University of Georgia, 2000) is Assistant Professor in the School of Communication Studies at Kent State University. Her research interests focus predominantly on the effects of social support and social influence on health behavior. Her work has appeared in journals such as the *Archives of Family Medicine* and *Journal of Health Communication*. In 2001, she received the Outstanding Dissertation Award from the Health Communication divisions of the International Communication Association and the National Communication Association.

William P. Eveland, Jr. (Ph.D., University of Wisconsin–Madison, 1997) is Assistant Professor in the School of Journalism and Communication at Ohio State University. His research focuses on the roles of motivation and information processing in the influence of traditional media and the World Wide Web on users' knowledge, perceptions, and opinions. His research has appeared in various outlets, including *Communication Research, Journal of Communication, Political Communication, International Journal of Public Opinion Research,* and *Media Psychology.*

Edward L. Fink is Professor and Chair in the Department of Communication at the University of Maryland. His research involves creating and testing mathematical models of attitude and belief change. He has investigated the effects of message discrepancy and message disconfirmation on message effectiveness. He has examined how a message can induce several minutes of oscillation before it reaches a new attitude equilibrium. He currently is engaged in research on the effect of threats and persuasive attempts on the perception of both a message's sender and its target. In 1988, he was named a University Distinguished Scholar-Teacher. He co-authored *The Measurement of Communication Processes* (1980) and has published more than 40 articles and chapters in the communication, sociology, psychology, criminology, and health education literatures, and several of his articles have been awarded "top" paper status. From 1991 to 1996, he served as Associate Editor of the *Journal of Communication,* and from 1998 to 2000, he was editor of *Human Communication Research.*

B. J. Fogg (Ph.D., Stanford University, 1997) leads research and design at Stanford's Persuasive Technology Lab, a group that generates insight into computing products designed to change attitudes and behaviors. An experimental psychologist, he teaches courses in persuasive technology for the Department of Computer Science. He is also on the consulting faculty for Stanford's School of Education, where he teaches in the Learning, Design, and Technology Program. In addition to his academic endeavors, he works in high-tech industry, most recently as the senior director of research and innovation at Casio U.S. Research and Development Center. In previous industry positions, he led innovation efforts at HP Labs, Interval Research, and Sun Microsystems. He holds several patents, mostly relating to user interface design.

Joseph Grandpre (Ph.D., University of Arizona, 1999) is Research Specialist, Principle, with the Arizona Cancer Center and Director of Field Research for the Health Communication Research Office in the Arizona Cancer Center at the University of Arizona. He received a master of public health degree in 1998 from the University of Arizona before receiving his Ph.D. in communication. He has worked for the Health Communication Research Office as project coordinator on one state grant concerning adolescent tobacco use and on one federally funded grant pertaining to drug use among adolescents. His research interests include adolescent reactance, health campaigns, and genetic testing.

Kathryn L. Greene (Ph.D., University of Georgia, 1992) is Associate Professor in the Department of Communication at Rutgers University. She has written in the area of health communication, where her research foci explore the role of communication in health decision making. One series of studies examines the design of messages targeting adolescent risk decision making. Other studies examine decisions to disclose stigmatized health infor-

mation (e.g., HIV) and the role of disclosure in relational development and maintenance.

Jerold L. Hale (Ph.D., Michigan State University, 1984) is Professor and Head of the Department of Speech Communication at the University of Georgia. His research interests include the study of relational messages and rule violations as well as the study of persuasive message strategies such as fear-arousing persuasive messages, two-sided messages, and sequential persuasive requests.

Eddie Harmon-Jones (Ph.D., University of Arizona, 1995) is Assistant Professor of Psychology at the University of Wisconsin–Madison. His research interests are focused on motivation and emotion and on how these processes relate to attitude formation and change. Most of his publications have appeared in *Journal of Personality and Social Psychology* and *Personality and Social Psychology Bulletin*. He recently edited *Cognitive Dissonance: Progress on a Pivotal Theory in Social Psychology*.

Marlone D. Henderson is a doctoral student in the Department of Psychology at New York University. His research interests are in the areas of motivation and volition, specifically motivational influences on information processing.

R. Lance Holbert (Ph.D., University of Wisconsin–Madison, 2000) is Assistant Professor of Communication at the University of Missouri–Columbia. His research interests include media form influence, persuasion, and political communication. Some of his published works appear in *Communication Monographs, Journalism and Mass Communication Quarterly,* and *Communication Research*.

Lawrence A. Hosman (Ph.D., University of Iowa, 1978) is Professor of Speech Communication at the University of Southern Mississippi. His research interests focus on language and persuasion, with particular interest in how power is communicated via messages. His research has been published in *Communication Monographs, Human Communication Research,* and *Journal of Language and Social Psychology.* He is a past president of the Southern States Communication Association and a recipient of the National Communication Association's Golden Anniversary Monograph Award.

Brian J. Householder (M.A., Wake Forest University, 2000) is a doctoral student in the Department of Speech Communication at the University of Georgia. His research interests focus on communication in personal relationships and a broad interest in communication and social influence processes, including persuasive message strategies, the impact of individual difference variables on persuasive outcomes, and influence strategies in forensics.

Susan McGreevy Hubbard (Ph.D., University of Maryland, 1996) is a Visiting Assistant Professor of Communication at the University of Maryland. Her primary research interests are persuasion and attitude change, health communication, and communication theory. She is currently working on a national evaluation project for the Center for Substance Abuse Treatment, investigating the dissemination and adoption of "best practice" guidelines in substance abuse treatment.

Stan A. Kaplowitz (Ph.D., University of Michigan, 1971) is Professor of Sociology at Michigan State University. Most of his research interests involve various aspects of attitudes, persuasion, and communication, including perception of power, doctor-patient communication, racial attitudes, and attitudes toward a student riot. Several of his articles have been awarded "top paper" status. He is currently engaged in a study to determine which survey

questions are useful predictors of lead poisoning. He has published many articles in communication journals as well as several in *Social Psychology Quarterly, Public Opinion Quarterly,* and various sociology research annuals.

Gerald M. Kosicki (Ph.D., University of Wisconsin–Madison, 1987) is Director of the Center for Survey Research, an interdisciplinary center housed in the College of Social and Behavioral Sciences at Ohio State University. He is also Associate Professor in the School of Journalism and Communication at Ohio State. His works on framing, priming, and agenda setting have appeared in journals such as *Communication Research, Journal of Communication, Political Communication,* and *Political Behavior.*

Elissa Lee (Ph.D., Stanford University, 2001) is Head of Human Research at Casio U.S. Research and Development Center. Her primary research area is narrative and persuasion. Her most recent work focuses on the persuasive effects of storytelling in online hate Web sites.

Jonathan Marshall is a doctoral candidate in counseling psychology at Stanford University and a psychology intern in the Department of Psychiatry at Kaiser Permanente in Milpitas, California. He currently studies persuasive techniques used in different technologies, the treatment of long-term depression using hypnosis and meditation, and the importance of spirituality as a moderator of outcome in treating mental illness. His recent work has been published in the *Journal of Child Sexual Abuse* and *Journal of Psychology* as well as in the proceedings of the Human-Computer Interaction conference for the Association of Computing Machinery.

Anneloes L. Meijnders (Ph.D., Eindhoven University of Technology, 1998) is Assistant

Professor in the Department of Human-Technology Interaction at Eindhoven University of Technology in The Netherlands. Her research interests are in the area of environmental attitudes and behavior, with an emphasis on the role of emotions in public acceptance of technology.

Gerald R. Miller (Ph.D., University of Iowa, 1961) was University Distinguished Professor and Chair of the Department of Communication at Michigan State University. He was the founding editor of *Human Communication Research* and an editor of *Communication Monographs*. He served as president of the International Communication Association. His books include *Videotape on Trial* (with Norm Fontes), which won the Golden Book Award; *Handbook of Interpersonal Communication* (co-edited with Mark Knapp); *Interpersonal Processes: New Directions in Communication Research* (co-edited with Michael Roloff); *Persuasion: New Directions in Theory and Research* (co-edited with Michael Roloff); and *New Techniques of Persuasion* (with Michael Burgoon). He was the recipient of the B. Aubrey Fisher Mentoring Award and a fellow of the American Psychological Association, the American Psychological Society, the International Communication Association, and the National Communication Association.

Robin L. Nabi (Ph.D., University of Pennsylvania, 1998) is Assistant Professor of Communication at the University of Arizona. Her research interests include the role of emotion in social influence and mass media effects. Her works have appeared in *Communication Theory, Communication Research,* and *Cognition & Emotion.*

Michelle R. Nelson (Ph.D., University of Illinois at Urbana-Champaign, 1997) is Assistant Professor in the School of Journalism and Mass Communication at the University of Wisconsin–Madison. Her research examines persuasion processes in strategic communications and cross-cultural consumer behavior. She has published in *Journalism & Mass Communication Quarterly, Journal of Advertising, Journal of Economic Psychology,* and *Advances in Consumer Research,* and she has contributed other book chapters.

John E. Newhagen (Ph.D., Stanford University, 1990) is Assistant Professor in the Philip Merrill College of Journalism, University of Maryland, College Park. His research has focused on the effects of emotion-laden television images on viewer emotion and memory. He has extended his research to include new technology such as the Internet. He is currently looking at the role of emotion in social desirability biasing on Web-based surveys and has recently written about the effects of new media on journalism. He worked as a journalist in Central America and the Caribbean during the 1970s and 1980s, covering civil strive and guerrilla insurrections in the area. He was bureau manager for United Press International in San Salvador, El Salvador (1981-1983); regional correspondent for Central America, Mexico, and the Caribbean for United Press International, Mexico City (1983-1984); and international news editor for United Press International in Washington, D.C. (1984-1985).

Daniel J. O'Keefe (Ph.D., University of Illinois at Urbana-Champaign, 1976) is Professor of Speech Communication at the University of Illinois at Urbana-Champaign. His work focuses on research synthesis in persuasion. He has received the National Communication Association's Charles Woolbert Research Award and its Golden Anniversary Monograph Award, the International Communication Association's Division 1 John E. Hunter Meta-analysis Award, the American Forensic Association's Outstanding Monograph Award, and the International Society for the Study of Argumentation's Distinguished Scholar Award. He is the author of *Persuasion: Theory and Research*.

Garrett J. O'Keefe (Ph.D., University of Wisconsin–Madison, 1970) is Professor and Chair in the Department of Journalism and Technical Communication at Colorado State University. His main research interests focus on uses and influences of public information programs, most recently those dealing with environmental issues and public health and safety. He has published in journals such as *Human Communication Research, Communication Research, Public Opinion Quarterly, Journal of Communication,* and *Journalism and Mass Communication Quarterly*. He is the co-author of three books dealing with persuasive campaigns and public opinion.

Roxanne Parrott (Ph.D., University of Arizona, 1990) is Professor of Communication at Pennsylvania State University. Her research interests emphasize social influence and message design in health contexts, including formal health care organizations and community-based and health policy settings. Results of her federally funded research have been published in outlets such as *Human Communication Research, Journal of Applied Communication Research, Social Science and Medicine, Health Education and Behavior,* and *Journal of the American Academy of Dermatology*. She is the co-editor of *Designing Health Messages: Approaches From Communication Theory and Public Health Practice* (1995), *Evaluating Women's Health Messages: A Resource Book* (1996), and *Health Communication Handbook* (in press).

Richard M. Perloff (PhD, University of Wisconsin-Madison, 1978) is Professor of Communication at Cleveland State University. His research interests concern the psychology of persuasive communication and political

communication effects. He co-edited a book on political information-processing and has written three books on persuasion topics, including *Political Communication: Politics, Press, and Public in America*, and *The Dynamics of Persuasion*. The latter was recognized as an Outstanding Book of 1993 by *Choice*. A leading scholar of the third-person effect, he has published articles on this topic in *Communication Research* and *International Journal of Public Opinion Research*, as well as a book chapter in *Media Effects: Advances in Theory and Research (2nd ed.)*. Perloff received a Distinguished Faculty Research Award at Cleveland State University and has served on the editorial board of the *Journal of Communication*.

John C. Reinard (Ph.D., University of Southern California, 1975) is Professor of Speech Communication at California State University, Fullerton. His research has focused on persuasion, communication and the law, and argumentation. He is the author of *Introduction to Communication Research* (now in its third edition) and *Foundations of Argument: Effective Communication for Critical Thinking*. In addition to other edited volumes including his work, his research on persuasion and legal communication has appeared in *Communication Monographs, Human Communication Research,* and *Argumentation and Advocacy*.

J. Lynn Reynolds (Ph.D., Regent University, 1998) is Assistant Professor of Communication at Pepperdine University. Her research interests include the influence of media on social and intercultural change. Her most recent work includes a chapter, "Ecumenical Promise Keepers: Oxymoron or Fidelity?," in *The Promise Keepers: Essays on Masculinity and Christianity*. She was named Seaver Fellow of Communication by the Pepperdine University Board of Visitors for the 2000-2001 school year.

Rodney A. Reynolds (Ph.D., Michigan State University, 1986) is Professor of Communication at Pepperdine University. The emphasis of his research is on the effects of message processing in social influence events. He has published in a number of academic outlets, including *Human Communication Research, Communication Monographs,* and *Communication Yearbook.*

Kelton v. L. Rhoads (Ph.D., Arizona State University) is a Psychological Consultant specializing in influence and virtual teams. He has provided training and consulting for industry, governmental agencies, political candidates, credit and banking firms, nonprofit philanthropic organizations, educational agencies, public relations firms, and a number of medical and dental entities, helping them to apply psychological principles to real-world situations. He has published in a variety of scholarly journals, has given radio interviews, and has received print and television advertising awards. He has taught statistics, psychology, and English at the university level, and he currently serves as Adjunct Professor at the University of Southern California's Annenberg School for Communication.

Laura Roberts was a student in the Department of Communication and a graduate research associate in the Health Communication Research Office of the Arizona Cancer Center at the University of Arizona, Tucson, at the time of this research.

David R. Roskos-Ewoldsen (Ph.D., Indiana University) is Reese Phifer Professor of Communication Studies at the University of Alabama. His research focuses on attitude change and persuasion and mental models of the media. He has published in *Human Communication Research, Communication Yearbook, Journal of Personality and Social Psychology, Journal of Experimental Social Psychology,*

and *Journal of Experimental Psychology: Applied.* He is the founding co-editor of *Media Psychology.*

Peter Salovey (Ph.D., Yale University, 1986) is Chris Argyris Professor of Psychology and Professor of Epidemiology and Public Health, and Chairman of the Department of Psychology, at Yale University. He is also Director of the Health, Emotion, and Behavior Laboratory and Deputy Director of the Yale Center for Interdisciplinary Research on AIDS. He is the co-author (with V. J. D'Andrea) of *Peer Counseling* (1983) and *Peer Counseling: Skills, Ethics, and Perspectives* (1996), and he co-edited *Reasoning, Inference, and Judgment in Clinical Psychology* (1988) (with Dennis C. Turk). Some of his more recent books include *The Psychology of Jealousy and Envy* (1991), *The Remembered Self: Emotions and Memory in Personality* (1993, with Jefferson A. Singer), *Psychology* (1993, with Zick Rubin and Letitia Anne Peplau), *Emotional Development and Emotional Intelligence: Educational Implications* (1997, with David Sluyter), and *At Play in the Fields of Consciousness* (1999, with Jefferson A. Singer). He edits the Guilford Press series on Emotions and Social Behavior. He completed a 6-year term as Associate Editor of *Psychological Bulletin* and was named the first Editor of the *Review of General Psychology*, and he serves as Associate Editor of *Emotion.*

Tamera R. Schneider (Ph.D., State University of New York at Stony Brook, 1997) is Assistant Professor of Psychology at Wright State University. At the time this chapter was written, she served as Associate Research Scientist in the Department of Psychology at Yale University, where she coordinated cancer prevention research in the Health, Emotion, and Behavior Laboratory. She has conducted research on persuasion and cancer early detection, especially screening mammography. She has also established a line of research in psychophysiology, especially focused on stress and cardiovascular reactivity.

Enid Sefcovic is Assistant Professor of Journalism, Media Studies, and Rhetoric at Florida Atlantic University. Her contribution to the chapter (for which Roxanne Parrott is the lead researcher) in this volume is part of her ongoing research interest in the significations of rights/human rights as a social justice concept.

Chris Segrin, Ph.D., is Associate Professor of Communication at the University of Arizona, where he also holds adjunct appointments in the Department of Psychology and in the Department of Family Studies. His research focuses on the role of interpersonal relationships and social skills in psychosocial problems such as depression, loneliness, and anxiety.

Sharon Shavitt (Ph.D., Ohio State University, 1985) is Professor of Business Administration at the University of Illinois at Urbana-Champaign. Her interests focus on consumer attitudes and social cognition, cross-cultural consumer psychology, and survey methodology. She has published in *Journal of Personality and Social Psychology, Journal of Experimental Social Psychology, Personality and Social Psychology Bulletin, Journal of Consumer Psychology, Journal of Advertising,* and other outlets. She is co-editor (with Timothy Brock) of *Persuasion: Psychological Insights and Perspectives* (1994).

Robin L. Shepard (Ph.D., University of Wisconsin–Madison, 1993) is Assistant Professor of Life Science Communication at the University of Wisconsin–Madison. His research focuses on the communication of new agricultural practices to farmers. He is the author of *Wisconsin's Best Breweries and Brewpubs.*

Michael D. Slater (Ph.D., Stanford University, 1988) is Professor of Journalism and Technical Communication at Colorado State University, with a joint appointment in the Department of Psychology. Current and recent research includes serving as the primary investigator of National Institutes of Health–funded studies of media- and community-based substance abuse prevention efforts, alcohol-related risk perceptions and media coverage, responses to alcohol advertisements, and effects of televised alcohol warnings. He has also conducted investigations of persuasion processes (particularly as they apply to influencing health-related attitudes). He has published more than 50 articles, book chapters, and reports on these and related topics. He also serves as the chair of the Health Communication division of the International Communication Association.

Pradeep Sopory (Ph.D., University of Wisconsin–Madison, 1999) is Assistant Professor of Communication at the University of Memphis. His research interests are persuasion, communication campaigns, and media influence, with a focus on metaphor and figurative language. He is the co-author of a book on health campaigns and has published his research in *Communication Research* and *Human Communication Research.*

James St. Pierre (Ph.D., University of Alabama, 2001) is Assistant Professor in the Department of Communication at the University of Louisiana. His research interests include persuasion and humor.

Erin Alison Szabo (Ph.D., University of Wisconsin–Madison, 2000) is Assistant Professor of Communication at St. John's University/College of St. Benedict. Her research interests include resistance and reactance to influence and mass media influence, with a particular emphasis on adolescent risk behaviors.

Alexander Todorov is a doctoral candidate in the Department of Psychology of New York University. His research interests are in the areas of communication, social judgments, and decision making. He has published in *Public Opinion Quarterly, American Journal of Public Health, Applied Cognitive Psychology,* and *European Journal of Social Psychology.*

Michael Voulodakis (M.A., M.P.H.) is a doctoral candidate in the Department of Communication and a senior research specialist in the Southwest Border Rural Health Research Center at the University of Arizona College of Public Health. He has worked as a research associate at the Arizona Cancer Center in the Behavioral Science and Epidemiological Units, the Department of Management Information Systems, and the Department of Communication. He has also taught undergraduates at the University of Arizona. His current research interests surround the methodological and design components of epidemiological studies, specifically participant recruitment and retention.

Jennifer Welbourne (Ph.D., Ohio State University, 1999) is Social Psychologist in the Health Communication Research Branch of the National Institute for Occupational Safety and Health at the Centers for Disease Control and Prevention. Her research interests include persuasion processes in health communication and person perception. Her work has been published in *Social Cognition, Journal of Experimental Social Psychology,* and *Personality and Social Psychology Bulletin.*

Xinshu Zhao (Ph.D., University of Wisconsin–Madison, 1989), one of the many students of Steven H. Chaffee, is Associate Director of the Center for Research in Journalism and Mass Communication at the University of North Carolina at Chapel Hill and a Research Fellow in the Center for Research in Information and Communication at Fudan University, Shanghai, China. His research has appeared in English-language journals such as *American Behavioral Scientist, Communication Research, Comparative Education Review, Harvard International Journal of Press/Politics, Journal of Advertising Research, Journalism and Mass Communication Quarterly,* and *Public Opinion Quarterly* as well as Chinese journals such as *Journalism and Communication, Journalism Practice, Journalistic University,* and *Twenty First Century.*